Short Story Criticism

Guide to Gale Literary Criticism Series

When you need to review criticism of literary works, these are the Gale series to use:

If the author's death date is:	You should turn to:
After Dec. 31, 1959 (or author is still living)	***CONTEMPORARY LITERARY CRITICISM*** for example: Jorge Luis Borges, Anthony Burgess, William Faulkner, Mary Gordon, Ernest Hemingway, Iris Murdoch
1900 through 1959	***TWENTIETH-CENTURY LITERARY CRITICISM*** for example: Willa Cather, F. Scott Fitzgerald, Henry James, Mark Twain, Virginia Woolf
1800 through 1899	***NINETEENTH-CENTURY LITERATURE CRITICISM*** for example: Fedor Dostoevski, Nathaniel Hawthorne, George Sand, William Wordsworth
1400 through 1799	***LITERATURE CRITICISM FROM 1400 TO 1800 (excluding Shakespeare)*** for example: Anne Bradstreet, Daniel Defoe, Alexander Pope, Francois Rabelais, Jonathan Swift, Phillis Wheatley
	SHAKESPEAREAN CRITICISM Shakespeare's plays and poetry
Antiquity through 1399	***CLASSICAL AND MEDIEVAL LITERATURE CRITICISM*** for example: Dante, Homer, Plato, Sophocles, Vergil, the Beowulf Poet

---

Gale also publishes related criticism series:

CHILDREN'S LITERATURE REVIEW

This ongoing series covers authors of all eras. Presents criticism on authors and author/illustrators who write for the preschool through high school audience.

CONTEMPORARY ISSUES CRITICISM

This two-volume set presents criticism on contemporary authors writing on current issues. Topics covered include the social sciences, philosophy, economics, natural science, law, and related areas.

SHORT STORY CRITICISM

This series covers the major short fiction writers of all nationalities and periods of literary history.

0895-9439

Short Story Criticism

Excerpts from Criticism of the Works of Short Fiction Writers

Laurie Lanzen Harris
Sheila Fitzgerald
Editors

Gale Research Company
Book Tower
Detroit, Michigan 48226

STAFF

Library of Congress Catalog Card Number
ISBN 0-8103-2550-0
ISSN 0895 9439

Computerized photocomposition by Typographics, Incorporated,
Kansas City, Missouri

Printed in the United States

Contents

Preface

Short Story Criticism (SSC) presents significant passages from criticism of the greatest short story writers of all time and provides supplementary materials—biographical and bibliographical—to guide the interested student to a greater understanding of the authors of short fiction. The series was developed in response to librarians serving high school, college, and public library patrons who had noted an increasing number of requests for critical material on short story writers. Although the major short story writers are covered in four of Gale's Literary Criticism Series, *Contemporary Literary Criticism (CLC), Twentieth-Century Literary Criticism (TCLC), Nineteenth-Century Literature Criticism (NCLC),* and *Literature Criticism from 1400 to 1800 (LC),* these librarians perceived a need for a series devoted solely to writers of the genre. A survey conducted in September 1986 provided the editors with fuller information on the library patrons' needs, and, with these criteria in mind, the scope of *SSC* was defined.

The Scope of the Work

SSC is designed to serve as an introduction for the student of the short story to the major writers in the genre and to the major commentators on those writers. The major short story writers of all eras and nationalities will be covered in the series, from Edgar Allan Poe and Guy de Maupassant, whom many critics consider the creators of the modern short story, to such contemporary practitioners as John Cheever and Eudora Welty. Since these authors have inspired a vast amount of relevant critical material, *SSC* is necessarily selective, and the editors have chosen the most important published criticism to aid students in their study of short story writers.

Each author entry is intended to provide a comprehensive overview of major criticism on an author. Fifteen to twenty authors will be included in each volume (compared with approximately forty-five authors in a *CLC* volume of similar size) so that more attention may be given to an author. Each author entry represents a historical survey of the critical response to that author's work: some early criticism is presented to indicate initial reaction, later criticism is selected to represent any rise or decline in the author's reputation, and current analyses provide students with a modern view. The length of an author entry is intended to reflect the amount of critical attention the author has received from critics writing in English, and from foreign critics in translation. Critical articles and books that have not been translated into English are excluded. Every attempt has been made to identify and include excerpts from the seminal essays on each author's work. In order to provide these important critical pieces, the editors will sometimes reprint essays that have appeared in previous volumes of the Literary Criticism Series. However, such duplication is limited to twenty to twenty-five percent of the author entry.

The Organization of the Book

The author entry consists of the following elements: author heading, biographical and critical introduction, a list of principal works, excerpts of criticism (each followed by a bibliographical citation), and an additional bibliography for further reading.

- The *author heading* consists of the author's full name, followed by birth and death dates. The unbracketed portion of the name denotes the form under which the author most commonly wrote. If the author wrote consistently under a pseudonym, the pseudonym will be listed in the author heading and the real name given in parentheses on the first line of the biographical and critical introduction. Also located at the beginning of the introduction to the author entry are any name variations under which the author wrote, including transliterated forms for authors whose languages use nonroman alphabets. Uncertainty as to a birth or death date is indicated by a question mark.

- *The biographical and critical introduction* contains background information designed to introduce the reader to an author and to the critical debates surrounding his or her work. Parenthetical material following the introductions provides references to biographical and critical reference series published by Gale, including *CLC, TCLC, NCLC,* and *LC, Children's Literature Review, Contemporary Authors, Dictionary of Literary Biography,* and *Something about the Author.*

• *SSC* entries include *portraits of the author*. Many entries also contain illustrations of materials pertinent to an author's career, including holographs of manuscript pages, title pages, dust jackets, letters, or representations of important people, places, and events in an author's life.

• The list of *principal works* is chronological by date of first publication and lists the most important works by the author. The first section comprises the short story collections, novellas, and novella collections. The second section gives information on other major works by the author. For foreign authors where there are both foreign language collections and English translations, the editors have provided original foreign language publication information and have selected what are considered the best and most complete English language editions of the short fiction.

• *Criticism* is arranged chronologically in each author entry to provide a useful perspective on changes in critical evaluation over the years. All short story, novella, and collection titles by the author featured in the entry are printed in boldface type to enable the user to ascertain without difficulty the works discussed. Also for purposes of easier identification, the critic's name and the publication date of the essay are given at the beginning of each piece of criticism. Unsigned criticism is preceded by the title of the journal in which it appeared. When an anonymous essay is later attributed to a critic, the critic's name appears in brackets at the beginning of the excerpt and the bibliographical citation.

• Critical essays are prefaced with *explanatory notes* as an additional aid to students using *SSC*. The explanatory notes provide several types of useful information, including: the reputation of a critic, the importance of a work of criticism, the specific type of criticism (biographical, psychoanalytic, structuralist, etc.) and a synopsis of the criticism.

• A complete *bibliographical citation*, designed to facilitate location of the original essay or book by the interested reader, follows each piece of criticism.

• The *additional bibliography* appearing at the end of each author entry suggests further reading on the author. In some cases it includes essays for which the editors could not obtain reprint rights.

An *appendix* lists the sources from which material in each volume has been reprinted. It does not, however, list every book or periodical consulted in the preparation of the volume.

Cumulative Indexes

Each volume of *SSC* includes a cumulative index to authors listing all the authors who have appeared in *SSC, CLC, TCLC, NCLC,* and *LC,* as well as cross-references to the Gale series *Children's Literature Review, Authors in the News, Contemporary Authors, Contemporary Authors Autobiography Series, Dictionary of Literary Biography, Something about the Author, Something about the Author Autobiography Series,* and *Yesterday's Authors of Books for Children.* Users will welcome this cumulated author index as a useful tool for locating an author within the Literary Criticism Series.

Each volume of *SSC* also includes a cumulative title index. This index lists all short story, novella, and collection titles contained in the series in alphabetical order. Titles of short story collections, novellas, and novella collections are printed in italics, while all individual short stories are printed in roman type with quotation marks. Titles are followed by the corresponding volume and page numbers where they may be located. In cases where the same title is used by different authors, the author's surname is given in parentheses after the title, e.g., *Collected Short Stories* (Welty), *Collected Short Stories* (Faulkner). For foreign titles, a cross-reference is given to the translated English title in the index.

Acknowledgments

No work of this scope can be accomplished without the cooperation of many people. The editors especially wish to thank the copyright holders of the excerpted essays included in this volume, the permissions managers of many book and magazine publishing companies for assisting us in securing reprint rights, and the photographers and other individuals who provided portraits of the authors. We are grateful to the staffs of the Detroit Public Library, the Wayne State University Library, the University of Michigan Library, and the

University of Detroit Library for making their resources available to us. We also wish to thank Anthony Bogucki for his assistance with copyright research. The editors would like to extend special thanks to the survey respondents, whose comments were so important in shaping the series.

Suggestions Are Welcome

The editors welcome the comments and suggestions of readers to expand the coverage and enhance the usefulness of the series.

Authors to Be Featured in *SSC*, Volumes 2 and 3

Margaret Atwood (Canadian short story writer, novelist, poet, and critic, born 1939).—- Atwood is recognized as a preeminent woman of letters, both in her own country and the United States. Her short story collections *Dancing Girls* and *Bluebeard's Egg* express the overrriding concern with feminine identity and cultural alienation that informs all her writings.

Donald Barthelme (American short story writer and novelist, born 1931).—-A well-known writer of experimental fiction, Barthelme explores in his sometimes surrealist short stories the possibilities and restrictions of language and its uses.

Truman Capote (American short story writer, novelist, essayist, and nonfiction writer, 1924-1984).—-While his short fiction ranges from the grotesque to the experimental, Capote is perhaps best known for poignant stories such as "A Christmas Memory" and "The Thanksgiving Visitor" that draw on his own southern childhood. His final book, *Music for Chameleons,* features provocative short pieces that, like his novel *In Cold Blood,* mingle fact and fiction to create an innovative new form.

Willa Cather (American short story writer, novelist, essayist, journalist, and poet, 1873-1947).—-Revered as a supreme stylist, Cather radiantly evoked her Nebraska upbringing in novels such as *My Antonia* and in many short stories. Detailing the settings and manners of pioneering immigrant people of the prairie, she conveyed the universal themes of endurance and triumph, both physical and spiritual.

Anton Chekhov (Russian short story writer, novelist, and dramatist, 1860-1904).—-Chekhov is acknowledged as a master of the modern short story, particularly for the emotional balance and stylistic control evident in his best tales, including "Duel" and "A Dull Story."

Colette (French short story writer, novelist, and journalist, 1873-1954).—-Colette is praised for her warm, subjective style and lyricism. In her stories as in her novels she explores the theme of woman's desire for personal autonomy in conflict with the demands of romance and passion.

Thomas Hardy (English novelist, poet, and short story writer, 1840-1928). The author of such acclaimed novels as *Jude the Obscure* and *Tess of the d'Urbervilles,* Hardy further explored the lives of English rural characters in several volumes of short fiction. In tales such as "The Three Strangers" and "The Withered Arm," he views often grotesque situations with masterful irony.

Nathaniel Hawthorne (American short story writer and novelist, 1804-1864).—-Best-known for his novel *The Scarlet Letter,* Hawthorne is also a noted master of the short story, particularly the allegorical romance. Tales such as "Young Goodman Brown" and "The Minister's Black Veil" illuminate with concision and power the themes of pride, guilt, sin, and retribution that he probed in all his writings.

Dorothy Parker (American short story writer, poet, critic, and journalist, 1893-1967).—-A prominent humorist of the 1920s and 30s, Parker wrote two volumes of short stories, including the well-known "Big Blond," that reflect her wit and sardonic humor.

J. D. Salinger (American short story writer and novelist, born 1919).—-Salinger is recognized by critics and readers alike as one of the most popular and influential contemporary writers. In his *Nine Stories* and four novellas of the Glass family, including *Franny and Zooey,* he speaks with humor and immediacy to succeeding generations of young readers.

P. G. Wodehouse (English-born American short story writer, novelist, lyricist, dramatist, and critic, 1881- 1975).—-An acclaimed humorist, Wodehouse is noted for his meticulous style and gift for farcical plots. His most noted characters, Bertie Wooster and his valet, Jeeves, are often placed with the finest duos of world literature, and they feature in many of Wodehouse's entertaining short stories.

Richard Wright (Black American short story writer, novelist, and essayist, 1908-1960).—-Wright became the preeminent spokesman for black Americans in the 1930s and 40s. Along with his best-known novel, *Native Son,* such short stories as "Long Black Song" and "Fire and Cloud" chronicle the black American's struggle for self- knowledge and freedom in a bigoted world.

Additional Authors to Appear in Future Volumes

Agnon, Shmuel Yosef 1888-1970
Aiken, Conrad 1889-1973
Aldiss, Brian 1925-
Aleichem, Sholom 1859-1916
Andersen, Hans Christian 1805-1875
Asimov, Isaac 1920-
Babel, Isaac 1894-1941?
Baldwin, James 1924-
Balzac, Honore de 1799-1850
Barnes, Djuna 1892-1982
Barth, John 1930-
Beattie, Ann 1947-
Beerbohm, Max 1872-1956
Bellow, Saul 1915-
Benet, Stephen Vincent 1898-1943
Bierce, Ambrose 1842-1914?
Boccaccio, Giovanni 1313?-1375
Boll, Heinrich 1917-1985
Borges, Jorge Luis 1899-1986
Bowen, Elizabeth 1899-1973
Bowles, Paul 1910-
Boyle, Kay 1903-
Buck, Pearl S. 1892-1973
Bunin, Ivan 1870-1953
Caldwell, Erskine 1903-
Calisher, Hortense 1911-
Calvino, Italo 1923-1985
Carter, Angela 1940-
Carver, Raymond 1938-
Cassill, R. V. 1919-
Cervantes 1547-1616
Chandler, Raymond 1888-1959
Chaucer, Geoffrey 1345-1400
Chopin, Kate 1851-1904
Clarke, Arthur C. 1917-
Conrad, Joseph 1857-1924
Cortazar, Julio 1914-1984
Coover, Robert 1932-
Crane, Stephen 1871-1900
Dahl, Roald 1916-
Dante Alighieri 1265-1321
de la Mare, Walter 1873-1956
Dick, Philip K. 1928-1982
Dinesen, Isak (ps. of Karen Blixen) 1885-1962
Disch, Thomas M. 1940-
Doyle, Arthur Conan 1859-1930
Elkin, Stanley 1930-
Ellison, Harlan 1934-
Fast, Howard 1914-
Fitzgerald, F. Scott 1896-1940
Flaubert, Gustave 1821-1880
Forster, E .M. 1879-1970
France, Anatole (ps. of Anatole-Francois Thibault) 1844-1924
Friedman, Bruce J. 1930-
Gaines, Ernest J. 1933-
Gallant, Mavis 1922-
Galsworthy, John 1867-1933
Garcia-Marquez, Gabriel Garcia 1928-
Garland, Hamlin 1860-1940
Gass, William H. 1924-
Gide, Andre 1869-1951
Gilchrist, Ellen 1935-
Gogol, Nikolai 1809-1852
Golding, William 1911-
Gordimer, Nadine 1923-
Gordon,Caroline 1845-1981
Grau, Shirley Ann 1929-
Greene, Graham 1904-
Grimm, Jakob Ludwig 1785-1863
Grimm, Wilhelm Karl 1786-1859
Hammett, Dashiell 1894-1961
Harris, Joel Chandler 1848-1908
Harte, Bret 1836-1902
Heinlein, Robert A. 1907-
Henry, O. (ps. of William Sidney Porter) 1862-1910
Hesse, Herman 1877-1962
Hoffmann, E. T. A. 1776-1822
Homer 8th Century B.C.
Hughes, Langston 1902-1967
Irving, Washington 1783-1859
Jackson, Shirley 1919-1965
James, Henry 1843-1916
Jewett, Sarah Orne 1844-1909
Jhabvala, Ruth Prawer 1927-
Joyce, James 1882-1941
Juvenal A.D. 60?-130?
Kafka, Franz 1883-1924
King, Stephen 1947-
Kipling, Rudyard 1865-1936
Knowles, John 1926-1979
Lardner, Ring 1885-1933
Laurence, Margaret 1926-1987
Lavin, Mary 1912-
LeFanu Joseph Sheridan 1814-1873
LeGuin, Ursula K. 1929-
Lessing, Doris 1919-
London, Jack 1876-1916
Lovecraft, H. P. 1890-1937
Machado de Assis, Joaquim Maria 1839-1908
Malamud, Bernard 1914-1986
Mann, Thomas 1914-1986
Mansfield, Katherine 1888-1923
Mason, Bobbie Ann 1940-
Masters, Edgar Lee 1869?-1950
McCullers, Carson 1917-1967
Maugham, W. Somerset 1874-1965
Merimee, Prosper 1803-1870
Mishima, Yukio 1925-1970
Munro, Alice 1931-
Oates, Joyce Carol 1938-
O'Brien, Edna 1936-
O'Connor, Frank (ps. of Michael Francis O'Donovan) 1903-1966
O'Faolain, Sean 1900-
O'Flaherty, Liam 1896-1984
Olsen, Tillie 1913-
Ozick, Cynthia 1928-
Paley, Grace 1922-
Pasternak, Boris 1890-1960
Pavese, Cesare 1908-1950
Perelman, S. J. 1904-1976
Porter, Katherine Anne 1890-1980
Pritchett, V. S. 1900-
Robbe-Grillet, Alain 1922-
Roth, Philip 1933-
Saki (ps. of H. H. Munro) 1870-1916
Saroyan,William 1908-1981
Schwartz, Delmore 1913-1966
Scott, Sir Walter 1771-1832
Singer, Isaac Bashevis 1904-
Solzhenitsyn, Alexander 1918-
Spark, Muriel 1918-
Stafford, Jean 1915-1979
Stead, Christina 1902-1983
Stein, Gertrude 1874-1946
Steinbeck, John 1902-1983
Stevenson, Robert Louis 1850-1894
Sturgeon, Theodore 1918-1985
Tagore, Rabindranath 1861-1941
Taylor, Peter 1917-
Thackeray, William Makepeace 1811-1863
Tolstoy, Leo 1828-1910
Turgenev, Ivan 1818-1883
Twain, Mark (ps. of Samuel Langhorne Clemens) 1835-1910
Updike, John 1932-
Virgil 70-19 B.C.
Vonnegut, Kurt, Jr. 1922-
Walker, Alice 1944-
Warren, Robert Penn 1905-
Wells, H. G. 1866-1946
West, Nathanael 1904-1940
Wharton, Edith 1862-1937
White, E. B. 1899-1986
Zola, Emile 1840-1902

Sherwood (Berton) Anderson

1876-1941

American short story writer, novelist, autobiographer, essayist, poet, editor, and dramatist.

Anderson was one of the most original and influential twentieth-century American writers. The author of brooding, introspective works, he was among the first American authors to explore the unconscious in his fiction. His self-acknowledged "hunger to see beneath the surface of lives" was best expressed in the collection of bittersweet short stories that form *Winesburg, Ohio,* a work today considered an American classic. This, his most important book, exhibits the author's characteristically simple, unornamented prose style and his personal vision, which combines a sense of wonder for the beauty of life with despair over its tragic aspects. The style and outlook of *Winesburg, Ohio* and of Anderson's three other short story collections—*The Triumph of the Egg, Horses and Men,* and *Death in the Woods, and Other Stories*—were instrumental in shaping the writings of Ernest Hemingway, William Faulkner, Thomas Wolfe, John Steinbeck, and many other American authors.

The Granger Collection, New York

Born in Ohio to an out-of-work harnessmaker and a washerwoman, Anderson was raised in the small town of Clyde, which later served as the model for Winesburg. There, as he grew older, he came to hate the self-sacrificing drudgery to which his mother was reduced and the irresponsibility of his alcoholic father. But the boy first learned the art of telling stories from his father, who was an adept and entertaining yarn-spinner. Attending school infrequently, Sherwood took a number of temporary jobs to help his impoverished family, working as a newsboy, a housepainter, a field worker, and a "swipe," or stablehand. These experiences, along with the awkward sexual initiation described in his *Memoirs* (1941), later provided thematic and incidental material for his fiction. After a stint in the U.S. Army during the Spanish-American War, he married, became an advertising copywriter in Chicago, and then went on to manage his own paint factory, the Anderson Manufacturing Company, in Elyria, Ohio. But his commercial success did not satisfy his awakening artistic aspirations, and he spent his spare time—and a fair amount of company time—writing fiction.

Scholars have noted that the year 1912 marked a watershed in Anderson's artistic and professional life. In November of that year, overworked and beset by various worries, Anderson suffered a mental breakdown; as best as can be determined from the conflicting accounts in his writings, he suddenly walked out of his office in the midst of dictating a letter, and was discovered four days later many miles away, babbling incoherently and amnestic. Shortly afterward, his marriage and business failed, and he returned to Chicago to resume work in advertising. There he met such writers of the Chicago Renaissance as Floyd Dell, Carl Sandburg, Theodore Dreiser, Ben Hecht, and Burton Rascoe, who read his early fiction and encouraged him. Although Anderson's first published short story, "The Rabbit Pen," appeared in William Dean Howells's *Harper's* magazine, most of his early stories were printed in the *Masses, Little Review, Seven Arts,* and other "little" magazines. After publishing two novels and a book of verse to moderate critical acclaim, Anderson attained recognition as an important new voice in American literature with the appearance of *Winesburg, Ohio* in 1919. Some critics denounced the book as morbid, depressing, and overly concerned with sex; others, however, praised it for its honesty and depth, comparing Anderson's accomplishment with that of Anton Chekhov and Fedor Dostoevski in its concern with the buried life of the soul. Commentators noted that Anderson achieved a fusion of simply stated fiction and brooding psychological analysis—"half tale and half psychological anatomizing" was H. L. Mencken's description—which reveal the essential loneliness and beauty of ordinary people living out their lives during the twilight days of agrarian America in a fading Ohio town.

Anderson's style was shaped during the 1920s by the works of Gertrude Stein, particularly her *Three Lives,* while his personal philosophy reflected that of D. H. Lawrence. In such stories as "'Unused'" and "The New Englander" he attempted to write with the simple, repetitive verbiage and rhythms of Stein and to develop Lawrence's beliefs concerning the psychologically crippling effects of sexual repression. Exploring the psychological undercurrents of life in industrialized America, Anderson wrote some of his strongest works in the 1920s, although he was compelled to continue working in advertising until 1922. That year he received the *Dial* magazine's first annual Dial Award for his accomplishment in *The Triumph of the Egg,* and the cash award enabled Anderson to leave advertising and to devote himself full-time to writing.

In 1927, with the earnings from his novel *Dark Laughter*—the only commercially successful work of his lifetime—Anderson settled in the town of Marion, Virginia, where he bought two weekly newspapers that he wrote for and edited. He spent much of the rest of his life in rural southwestern Virginia among the small-town people with whom he had always felt a warm kinship, occasionally publishing collections of his newspaper columns and essays on American life. His final collection of fiction, *Death in the Woods,* appeared in 1933 during the Great Depression and sold poorly. He wrote little during the last few years of his life, declaring that writing was a dead art in America and that the future for artistic achievement lay in motion pictures. While on a cruise to South America in 1941, Anderson died of peritonitis after accidentally swallowing part of a wooden toothpick at a shipboard banquet. He is buried just outside Marion, with his chosen epitaph inscribed upon his gravestone: "Life, not death, is the great adventure."

Critics agree that Anderson's short stories best convey his vision of life, which is often despairing but tempered by his folksy, poignant tone and sense of wonder. In addition to "Hands," "The Untold Lie," and "Sophistication" from *Winesburg, Ohio,* commentators place the stories "The Egg," "Death in the Woods," "I'm a Fool," "The Man Who Became a Woman," and "I Want to Know Why" among his best tales and among the best works of American short fiction. Utilizing as they do Anderson's innovative form, these stories capture the essence of lives divided by insensitivity, convention, circumstance, and personal weakness, which are joined but briefly by love, sympathy, and shared moments of spiritual epiphany. "In Anderson, when all is said and done," wrote Henry Miller, "it is the strong human quality which draws one to him and leads one to prefer him sometimes to those who are undeniably superior to him as artists."

Scholars of Anderson's work have found the author to be a much more complex writer than his simple stories suggest. He was long called a leader in "the revolt from the village" in American literature, an often-quoted appellation given him by Carl Van Doren in a 1921 essay. But while Anderson examined the troubled, darker aspects of provincial life, he saw the small town as an essential and admirable part of America, and he attacked Sinclair Lewis and Mencken for their incessant satirical gibes at village vulgarity. Hostile reviewers of his works called him "Sherwood Lawrence" and tended to portray him as a writer obsessed with sex, though the next generation of American writers made his treatment of sexual relations seem tame by comparison. And some critics and readers who had early enjoyed Anderson's books found them in later years stylistically and thematically adolescent and repetitive: reviewing *Death in the Woods* for the *New Republic* in 1933, T. S. Matthews spoke for many critics when he wrote that he was "so used to Anderson now, to his puzzled confidences, his groping repetitions, his occasional stumblings into real inspiration that perhaps we tend to underrate him as an American phenomenon. Or perhaps we no longer overrate him"—a thesis later developed, independently, by Lionel Trilling in one of the most important negative assessments of Anderson. Anderson's many critical admirers and defenders include Waldo Frank and Paul Rosenfeld who, while describing Anderson in a 1922 essay, coined for his friend the widely quoted sobriquet "a phallic Chekhov." Dreiser spoke for many of Anderson's readers when in 1941 he wrote: "Anderson, his life and his writings, epitomize for me the pilgrimage of a poet and dreamer across this limited stage called Life, whose reactions to the mystery of our beings and doings here . . . involved tenderness, love and beauty, delight in the strangeness of our will-less reactions as well as pity, sympathy and love for all things both great and small."

Anderson's simple, impressionistic style and his frequent acknowledgement that he was puzzled by life's basic questions have often led critics to dismiss him as a primitive minor talent who was of more value as a literary catalyst than as an artist in his own right. But the continued popularity of his books has prompted such noted scholars as Walter B. Rideout, Welford Dunaway Taylor, David D. Anderson, and Ray Lewis White to examine his work more closely, and Anderson is again recognized as an important American author. Perhaps Faulkner best summed up Anderson's current status when he said, "He was the father of my generation of American writers and the tradition of American writing which our successors will carry on. He has never received his proper evaluation."

(See also *Twentieth-Century Literary Criticism,* Vols. 1, 10, and 24; *Contemporary Authors,* Vol. 104; *Dictionary of Literary Biography,* Vols. 4 and 9; and *Dictionary of Literary Biography Documentary Series,* Vol. 1.)

PRINCIPAL WORKS

SHORT FICTION

Winesburg, Ohio: A Group of Tales of Ohio Small Town Life 1919
The Triumph of the Egg: A Book of Tales of Impressions from American Life in Tales and Poems 1921
Horses and Men: Tales, Long and Short, from Our American Life 1923
Death in the Woods, and Other Stories 1933
The Sherwood Anderson Reader 1947
Short Stories 1962

OTHER MAJOR WORKS

Windy McPherson's Son (novel) 1916
Marching Men (novel) 1917
Mid-American Chants (poetry) 1918
Poor White (novel) 1920
Many Marriages (novel) 1923
A Story Teller's Story: The Tale of an American Writer's Journey through His Own Imaginative World and through the World of Facts, with Many of His Experiences and Impressions among Other Writers (autobiography) 1924
Dark Laughter (novel) 1925
Tar: A Midwest Childhood (autobiography) 1926
A New Testament (poetry) 1927
Beyond Desire (novel) 1932
Kit Brandon (novel) 1936

BURTON RASCOE (essay date 1919)

[Rascoe, an American literary critic who wrote for several influential periodicals during the early and mid-twentieth century, was

one of the Chicago writers who encouraged Anderson in his early literary efforts. In the following excerpt from a review originally published in June 1919 in the Chicago Daily Tribune, *Rascoe favorably assesses* Winesburg, Ohio, *comparing Anderson's vision with that of Chekhov, Dostoevski, and Edgar Lee Masters.*]

Comparison of Sherwood Anderson's new book, ***Winesburg, Ohio***, and *The Spoon River Anthology* is rather inevitable, possibly so inevitable that it may be questioned whether the analogy is entirely legitimate. The prevailing tone of Mr. Anderson's prose tales and of Mr. Masters' mephitic monologues is gray; both books are concerned with life in small midwestern communities a couple of decades or so ago; and in each there is a very justifiable recognition of the motivating force of sex in the life of all sentient creatures, among whom is not included, of course, the hurt and vegetative organism of an eastern paper who referred to love as portrayed by Mr. Anderson as "obscene acts."

But to press the likeness further would, I think, lead into the difficulties encountered in the linking of any two quite dissimilar things. The temperaments of the two men are widely at variance and their literary method is no less so. Mr. Masters says, in short, "Here are human beings for you! What imbeciles, groveling, hopeless vermin they are!" Mr. Anderson says in effect, "Here are the human beings of whom I am one. Even our errors, our grossest weaknesses have about them something of tragic beauty. Are we not worthy of your sympathy no less than of your disgust? Isn't it possible that you, too, are one of us—a human being for whom unhappiness means frustrated desire, to whom life is a perturbing mystery, in whom there is a spiritual impulse to be 'good' which is plagued and balked by a natural urgency at times to be otherwise?" Into the soul of Mr. Masters the iron has sank; he is bitter, reproachful, and removed. In Mr. Anderson there is fraternal pity and a lonely tender feeling of participation in human destiny.

Of course, both Mr. Masters and Mr. Anderson are right. . . . They are right for life itself is a point of view; and one's enjoyment of life and literature is dependent upon the catholicity of one's tastes, one's capacity for partaking of it and benefiting from points of view differing from one's own.

Than with *The Spoon River Anthology*, it seems to me that a comparison of ***Winesburg, Ohio*** with the Russians, Chekhov and Dostoevski, is a more suitable one. Unquestionably, Mr. Anderson's book will offend a great number of readers, many of whom are quite willing to admit that Chekhov and Dostoevski, being Russian, are great and significant writers. These people, too, it is likely, are among the numerous derogators of our native literature who frequently ask why America does not produce writers of the caliber to be found abroad. The answer is that for the most part America does, and in far greater numbers than the reading public is entitled to; for the closer an American approximates the literary excellence of Europe, the more shameless is the nation's neglect of him.

Mr. Anderson's unified series of stories in ***Winesburg, Ohio***, possess actually for Americans not only a higher literary value than any one volume of Chekhov, but in interpretation and relation of a phase of our national life of far greater importance to us than the stories of Russian life in Chekhov's day can ever be. If I was asked to name half a dozen contemporary indigenous products of American literature for translation abroad, I should name Mr. Anderson's book as one of them. The Russian life that we read about in translations from Chekhov was a thing of the past even before war; it relates to conditions vastly changed even before the fall of czarism. The American life Europeans would read about in a translation of these Winesburg stories obtains in a certain degree in every small town throughout the United States at the present time.

Mr. Anderson has in this book eclipsed the exellence he achieved in his novel, *Windy McPherson's Son*. Its form is something of an innovation; he has, with much the continuity of a novel, written a series of complete short stories in which the same characters recur at different times. As a result we have the fluid illusion of life, together with the heightened drama of it, the relation of character in crucial flashes instead of by arduous development, the selection of incident without the detail that is part of the method of the novel, a group portrait of a community in an interwoven series of stories.

It is to Mr. Anderson's artistic credit, too, that he frequently suggests rather than depicts; that he respects the imaginative faculty of his reader by refusing to be explicit wherever overtones of emotion are already involved by the reader; that he is selective, indefinite and provocative instead of inclusive, precise, and explanatory. He, one of the most personal and subjective of writers, has in these stories achieved a fine effect of impersonality.

His personal ethics or beliefs obtrude, I think, but once, and that is the one unconvincing and manufactured story in the book—the story of the preacher who at night peeped through the window of his study into the bedroom of the pretty school teacher and afterwards delivered impassioned sermons on human frailty and temptation.

These stories are practically all concerned chiefly wth the sex life of the inhabitants of the Ohio village—of the doctor, the bartender, the school teacher, the young reporter, the hired girl, the bumpkin lad, the village "sport," the woman hater—of every one in this drab community, where there was little incentive to sublimated desire, and where emotion was all the more intense for being defeated and repressed at every turn.

There the rigid old Puritan ethic, to which this community owes at once so much of good and evil, was an ineradicable and saving instinct and yet an instinct constantly at war with the instinct for mating; the conflict itself produces drama of an intensely poignant kind, romance of effective and realistic beauty. The awakening of sex in the idealistic youth; the harassing desire for love and companionship that obsessed the lonely school teacher, the simple surrender of the ignorant young girl; all these constantly recurrent incidents of life are told with sympathy, skill, and sincerity.

Mr. Anderson is frequently crude in his employment of English, he has not a sense of word values; but he has an intense vision of life; he is a cautious and interpretive observer; and he has recorded here a bit of life which could rank him with the most important contemporary writers in this country. He may not be, as some one called him, the American Dostoevski, but he is the American Sherwood Anderson. (pp. 599-602)

Burton Rascoe, in a review of "Winesburg, Ohio," in The Road to Winesburg: A Mosaic of the Imaginative Life of Sherwood Anderson *by William A. Sutton, The Scarecrow Press, Inc., 1972, pp. 599-602.*

H. L. MENCKEN (essay date 1919)

[*Mencken was one of the most influential social and literary critics in the United States from the start of World War I until the early years of the Great Depression. As coeditor of the* Smart Set *magazine, he published several of Anderson's stories in the magazine. But he rejected some of the Winesburg tales, explaining, according to Anderson, that they "wouldn't go. They were not stories, etc, etc." Still, upon the publication in 1919 of* Winesburg, Ohio, *Mencken wrote two glowing reviews of the work. In the following excerpt from his review in* Smart Set *in August 1919, he praises* Winesburg *as a unique accomplishment in American literature. (Please see Additional Bibliography for another review of* Winesburg, Ohio *by Mencken.)*]

[***Winesburg, Ohio*** is] a collection of short stories of a new order, including at least half a dozen of a very striking quality. This Anderson is a man of whom a great deal will be heard hereafter. Along with Willa Sibert Cather, James Branch Cabell and a few others, he belongs to a small group that has somehow emancipated itself from the prevailing imitativeness and banality of the national letters and is moving steadily toward work that will do honor to the country. His first novel, *Windy McPherson's Son,* printed in 1916, had plenty of faults, but there were so many compensating merits that it stood out clearly above the general run of the fiction of its year. Then came *Marching Men,* another defective but extremely interesting novel, and then a book of dithyrambs, *Mid-American Chants*. But these things, for all their brilliant moments, did not adequately represent Anderson. The national vice of ethical purpose corrupted them; they were burdened with *Tendenz*. Now, in ***Winesburg, Ohio,*** he throws off that handicap. What remains is pure representation—and it is representation so vivid, so full of insight, so shiningly life-like and glowing, that the book is lifted into a category all its own. Nothing quite like it has ever been done in America. It is a book that, at one stroke, turns depression into enthusiasm.

In form, it is a collection of short stories, with common characters welding them into a continued picture of life in a small inland town. But what short stories! Compare them to the popular trade goods of the Gouverneur Morrises and Julian Streets, or even to the more pretentious work of the Alice Browns and Katharine Fullerton Geroulds. It is the difference between music by a Chaminade and a music by a Brahms. Into his brief pages Anderson not only gets brilliant images of men and women who walk in all the colors of reality; he also gets a profound sense of the obscure, inner drama of their lives. Consider, for example, the four-part story called **"Godliness."** It is fiction for half a page, but after that it seems indubitable fact—fact that is searching and ferret-like—fact infinitely stealthy and persuasive—the sort of fact that suddenly changes a stolid, inscrutable Captain MacWhirr into a moving symbol of man in his struggle with the fates. And then turn to **"Respectability,"** and to **"The Strength of God,"** and to **"Adventure,"** and to **"The Teacher."** Here one gets all the joy that goes with the discovery of something quite new under the sun—a new order of short story, half tale and half psychological anatomizing, and vastly better than all the kinds that have gone before. Here is the goal that *The Spoon River Anthology* aimed at, and missed by half a mile. Allow everything to the imperfection of the form and everything to the author's occasional failure to rise to it: what remains is a truly extraordinary book, by a man of such palpably unusual talent that it seems almost an impertinence to welcome him. (pp. 272-73)

H. L. Mencken, "Sherwood Anderson: Something New under the Sun," in his H. L. Mencken's "Smart Set" Criticism, *edited by William H. Nolte, Cornell University Press, 1968, pp. 272-73.*

WALLACE SMITH (essay date 1919)

[*Smith was an American journalist, novelist, and short story writer. A native of Chicago, he was well known in that city as a newspaperman and artist by 1919, when he reviewed* Winesburg, Ohio *in September for the* Chicago Daily News. *In the following excerpt from that article, Smith sarcastically attacks Anderson's work, censuring among other things the critically acclaimed "Russian" element in the stories.*]

Have a look at Sherwood Anderson's ***Winesburg, Ohio***. Here's a fine rainy afternoon of gossip set down in the pat phrases of the sewing circle and the party whirl. Here's a record of what the members of the ladies aid society always wanted to know about the real reason for Mrs. Applegate's visits to the doctor's office and what led to the engagement of the girl around the corner who paints and powders.

And little else.

Sherwood Anderson's friends claim for this ***Winesburg, Ohio*** the force of what questionable translations from the Russians are supposed to be: typical literature of the country where it is always house cleaning time. Not so! In ***Winesburg, Ohio*** Anderson falls short of being a Maumee Tchekoff by at least three murders, two criminal assaults and a suicide.

Other friends ballyhoo that from this source will come "the great American novel." Nonsense! If such stuff makes the great American novel we have that precious volume already in the latest report of the psychopathic hospital, and the history of the world has for its author Dr. P. von Kraft-Ebing.

Anderson has nosed out from the Winesburg population the subjects most intriguing to the psychophysical, the juggler of weird neuroses. He describes their least pleasant symptoms in the terms of Little Red Riding Hood.

In fact so labored is his simplicity that at the beginning one gets the picture of a patient, plump uncle telling his nieces and nephews long fireside stories. But no uncle would attempt these Winesburg gossipings as bedtime tales for juveniles—not even in this day when the "adults only" sign lures our youngsters to a broader if not a higher education.

The collection of small town sketches calls to mind the deplorable Jukes family, still the favorite of the barking statistician to prove the hereditary horrors made possible by the mating of a thoroughly undesirable male to even a less desirable female. All this revealed in a style marred by hefty platitude—for instance, the sententious declaration that railroads, newspapers and other developments have made quite a difference in this country since the civil war. Another instance, the observation that after all country folks and city folks think and speak a great deal alike.

It is marred, too, by tricks having the feel of laziness. He falls back from the work of establishing characters with a futile wish for the pen of a poet or the assertion that it really would take an entire novel to do justice to the subject in hand.

Despite these faults of delivery and craftsmanship there are splendid bits in the book—the simple report of youth in his first "romance" for one; the cruel irony of the two tales, **"The Strength of God"** and **"The Teacher"** for another. Larded with the whiskey platitudes are encouraging slices of writing streaks here and there, which one hopes indicate what Anderson really can do when he rolls back his sleeves and dashes off the American novel his friends are megaphoning.

But always it goes back to the same monotonous level. Always it returns to a decadent exposure of strange neurotics and the search for the wen and the wart on the face of humanity. The only young woman in the village left by Anderson and the

Winesburg males is the daughter of the town banker. Not a surprising fact to one acquainted with the chastity of such young ladies through the pages of Horatio Alger and Oliver Optic.

It is palpable that in drafting such a criticism as this one bends over invitingly to a Chaplin kick from those who will look upon it as raving puritanism.

But this is not written in shocked indignation. One who has scanned the report of the Chicago vice commission—1911—the volume was the gift of a bishop—one who is familiar with the analysis of Dr. William A. Hammond; one who has witnessed a private exhibition of the censor's movie cutouts—such a one will not shrink from ***Winesburg, Ohio,*** except perchance in ennui.

And as an evidence of friendliness and good wishes for future Andersonia, it is suggested that Anderson devote himself next time to some Illinois town. A traveling insurance man once informed me that the insanity rate on the Illinois prairies is higher than in any other state in the union. (pp. 604-06)

Wallace Smith, in a review of "Civilian Communique," in The Road to Winesburg: A Mosaic of the Imaginative Life of Sherwood Anderson *by William A. Sutton, The Scarecrow Press, Inc., 1972, pp. 604-06.*

CARL VAN DOREN (essay date 1921)

[*Van Doren is considered one of the most perceptive American literary critics of the first half of the twentieth century. He coined the expression "the revolt from the village" to describe the works of Anderson, Lewis, Masters, and other American authors he perceived as thematically united in their contempt for the American small town and its image as a haven of innocent goodness. "The Revolt from the Village" was in fact originally the subtitle of an article, one of a series, published by Van Doren in the* Nation *in October 1921. In the following excerpt from that essay, he compares* Winesburg, Ohio *with* The Spoon River Anthology *and praises Anderson and Masters as iconoclasts of the village myth.*]

The newest style in American fiction dates from the appearance, in 1915, of *Spoon River Anthology,* though it required five years for the influence of that book to pass thoroughly over from poetry to prose. For nearly half a century native literature had been faithful to the cult of the village, celebrating its delicate merits with sentimental affection and with unwearied interest digging into odd corners of the country for persons and incidents illustrative of the essential goodness and heroism which, so the doctrine ran, lie beneath unexciting surfaces. (p. 146)

The village seemed too cosy a microcosm to be disturbed. There it lay in the mind's eye, neat, compact, organized, traditional: the white church with tapering spire, the sober schoolhouse, the smithy of the ringing anvil, the corner grocery, the cluster of friendly houses; the venerable parson, the wise physician, the canny squire, the grasping landlord softened or outwitted in the end; the village belle, gossip, atheist, idiot; jovial fathers, gentle mothers, merry children; cool parlors, shining kitchens, spacious barns, lavish gardens, fragrant summer dawns, and comfortable winter evenings. These were elements not to be discarded lightly, even by those who perceived that time was discarding many of them as the industrial revolution went on planting ugly factories alongside the prettiest brooks, bringing in droves of aliens who used unfamiliar tongues and customs, and fouling the atmosphere with smoke and gasoline. (p. 147)

Spoon River Anthology has called forth a smaller number of deliberate imitations than might have been expected, and even they have utilized its method with a difference. Sherwood Anderson, for example, in ***Winesburg, Ohio*** speaks in accents and rhythms obstinately his own, though his book is, in effect, the *Anthology* "transprosed." (p. 153)

[Touching] scandal with beauty as his predecessor touched it with irony, Mr. Anderson constantly transmutes it. The young man who here sets out to make his fortune has not greatly hated Winesburg, and the imminence of his departure throws a vaguely golden mist over the village, which is seen in considerable measure through his generous if inexperienced eyes. A newspaper reporter, he directs his principal curiosity towards items of life outside the commonplace and thus offers Mr. Anderson the occasion to explore the moral and spiritual hinterlands of men and women who outwardly walk paths strict enough.

If the life of the tribe is unadventurous, he seems to say, there is still the individual, who, perhaps all the more because of the rigid decorums forced upon him, may adventure with secret desires through pathless space. Only, the pressure of too many inhibitions can distort human spirits into grotesque forms. The inhabitants of Winesburg tend toward the grotesque, now this organ of the soul enlarged beyond all symmetry, now that wasted away in a desperate disuse. They see visions which in some wider world might become wholesome realities or might be dispelled by the light but which in Winesburg must lurk about till they master and madden with the strength which the darkness gives them. Religion, deprived in Winesburg of poetry, fritters its time away over Pharisaic ordinances or evaporates in cloudy dreams; sex, deprived of spontaneity, settles into fleshly habit or tortures its victim with the malice of a thwarted devil; heroism of deed or thought either withers into melancholy inaction or else protects itself with a sullen or ridiculous bravado.

Yet even among such pitiful surroundings Mr. Anderson walks tenderly. He honors youth, he feels beauty, he understands virtue, he trusts wisdom, when he comes upon them. He broods over his creatures with affection, though he makes no luxury of illusions. Much as he has detached himself from the cult of the village, he still cherishes the memories of some specific Winesburg. Much as he has detached himself from the hazy national optimism of an elder style in American thinking, he still cherishes a confidence in particular persons. ***Winesburg, Ohio*** springs from the more intimate regions of his mind and is consequently more humane and less doctrinaire than his earlier novels. It has a similar superiority over the book he wrote for 1920, *Poor White*. . . . (pp. 155-56)

Perhaps he tried in *Poor White* to manipulate a larger bulk than he is yet ready for. Perhaps because he was aware of that he has worked on his latest book, ***The Triumph of the Egg,*** with a variety of brief themes and has excelled even ***Winesburg, Ohio*** in both poetry and truth. (p. 157)

Carl Van Doren, "New Style: The Revolt from the Village," in his Contemporary American Novelists: 1900-1920, *The Macmillan Company, 1922, pp. 146-76.*

HEYWOOD BROUN (essay date 1921)

[*Broun was a highly respected American sportswriter, critic, essayist, and fiction writer who gained a wide audience through the syndicated daily newspaper column he wrote from 1912 until his death in 1939. In the following excerpt, he offers an admiring, if tongue-in-cheek, review of* The Triumph of the Egg.]

More than any other writer in America, Sherwood Anderson brings emotion into his work. He is tipsy with life and sometimes this condition makes him eloquent and sometimes incoherent. He cannot stay on the ground, but must dig so deep that it is hard to follow him or leap up and grow a little misty in the fog. We wish he were a little calmer or, at any rate, more articulate.

If a man gets hold of a piece of truth he ought to share it with many. Throwing pearls before swine is among the most snobbish pursuits in the world. We do not think that Anderson has a right to the full extent of his present obscurity. After all, the thing which is agitating him is something which touches most of us, whether we realize it or not. The fact that Anderson does understand imposes upon him the responsibility of revelation.

We think we catch a glint of what he means in the story called **"Seeds,"** the second in his latest collection, ***The Triumph of the Egg***. . . . "She needed a lover," explains one of the men in the story, "and at the same time a lover was not what she needed. The need of a lover was, after all, a quite secondary thing. She needed to be loved, to be long and quietly and patiently loved. To be sure, she is a grotesque, but then all the people in the world are grotesques. We all need to be loved. . . ."

Practically every character who appears in the pages of ***The Triumph of the Egg*** is suffering from an idealization of sex. Somehow or other sex and civilization do not get along together very well. There is no use in trying to find out at this late date whose fault it is. Neither factor in the misunderstanding can be abolished, but Anderson is not discouraged by that into silence. He seeks to bring understanding not through argument and logic but through emotion.

Anderson is definitely and unfailingly committed to the subjective method. Indeed his latest book might well be retitled and changed from ***The Triumph of the Egg*** into *The Triumph of the Ego*.

We wish Anderson were a less literary person. In the full gallop of emotional expression he will suddenly stoop to pick up some tricky device of writing as if he were a circus cowboy doing stunts with a handkerchief. We feel that he is potentially America's foremost figure in the field of fiction. He has not only emotion but understanding, and such a person has no business to be so frequently bothered with the thought, "How shall I phrase it?" An author ought to pause long enough to be sure he is right and then go ahead and damn the torpedoes.

The first story in ***The Triumph of the Egg,*** which is called **"I Want to Know Why,"** is the finest short story of the year to the best of our knowledge and belief. Here for the first time in the writing career of Sherwood Anderson simplicity predominates. A rather subtle emotion is made clear and understandable. It is the story of a boy who watches the saddling of the great racehorse Sunstreak in the paddock at Saratoga. He knows what is going on in the heart of Sunstreak, and as he sees the shining eyes of Jerry Tillford, the trainer, he realizes that Tillford knows too. . . .

It is quite evident that Sherwood Anderson has read his Mark Twain to good purpose. The downfall of Jerry, whose eyes could shine for a great race horse or a cheap woman, gives the boy "the fantods." He is the first victim of this ailment whom we have come across since the days of Huckleberry Finn.

Incidentally, **"I Want to Know Why"** presents a new system of how to win money at the race track which is much better than any of the others which we have heard. "It brings a lump up into my throat when a horse runs," says the narrator of the story. "I don't mean all horses, but some. I can pick them nearly every time. It's in my blood like in the blood of race track niggers and trainers. Even when they just go slop-jogging along with a little nigger on their backs I can tell a winner. If my throat hurts and it's hard for me to swallow, that's him."

But we too have had a strikingly similar feeling about some certain horse at the race track only to discover that it was not inspiration but merely tonsillitis. . . .

To readers we recommend ***The Triumph of the Egg,*** by Sherwood Anderson, with the postscript that most of it is difficult and some of it almost incoherent. But a little of it is great.

Heywood Broun, "It Seems to Me," in The World, *New York, December 6, 1921, p. 11.*

GERTRUDE STEIN (letter date 1922)

[*An American autobiographer, novelist, poet, and critic, Stein was an outstanding cultural force both as a daring experimentalist and as a patron of avant-garde artists and writers. She met Anderson in 1921 when he visited Paris, beginning a close friendship that lasted until his death twenty years later. In the following brief excerpt, she favorably appraises* The Triumph of the Egg.]

Thanks so much for your book [***The Triumph of the Egg***]. I like **"The Egg."** The good part of your work is that it is direct. Most of the realistic work of America is translated one does not quite know from what or where but it is a translation. Perhaps it's Zola and they don't know it. Perhaps it isn't. Anyway you have brains valuable brains that translate into style conception. You are not among the muck of them who crying give them liberty or give me death when you give them liberty give you death. But anyhow it's alright and I am looking forward very genuinely to the new novel. (p. 12)

Gertrude Stein, in a letter to Sherwood Anderson in January, 1922, in Sherwood Anderson/Gertrude Stein: Correspondence and Personal Essays, *edited by Ray Lewis White, The University of North Carolina Press, 1972, pp. 11-13.*

PAUL ROSENFELD (essay date 1922)

[*Rosenfeld, a respected music and literary critic, was the editor of* The Sherwood Anderson Reader *(1947) and a longtime friend of Anderson; it was he who dubbed Anderson a "phallic Chekhov." In the following excerpt from an essay originally published in 1922 in the* Dial, *Rosenfeld discusses Anderson's simple, earthy language and his role as a voice of the forgotten and the inarticulate.*]

They pass us every day, a gray and driven throng, the common words that are the medium of Sherwood Anderson. . . . They lie in the range of those who ride dully into country towns over dusty roadways, or work about their barns or in their fields or inside farm cottages. But the walls of the city thoroughfares do not impinge on us, or on the men who talk, or on the hacks who write. The earth and board sides and fences and plantations remain in a sullen murk. And the words that signify the things and their simple qualities remain in millions of voices dreary dead. (p. 175)

But out of these fallen creatures, Sherwood Anderson has made the pure poetry of his tales. He has taken the words surely, has set them firmly end to end, and underneath his hand there has come to be a surface as clean and fragrant as that of joyously made things in a fresh young country. The vocabulary of the simplest folk; words of a primer, a copy-book quotidianness, form a surface as hard as that of pungent fresh-planed boards of pine and oak. Into the ordered prose of Anderson the delicacy and sweetness of the growing corn, the grittiness and firmness of black earth sifted by the fingers, the broad-breasted power of great laboring horses, has wavered again. The writing pleases the eye. It pleases the nostrils. It is moist and adhesive to the touch, like milk.

No rare and precious and technical incrustations have stiffened it. . . . The language remains homely, sober, and spare. The simplest constructions abound. Few adjectives arrest the course of the sentence. At intervals, the succession of simple periods is broken by a compound sprawling its loose length. Qualifying clauses are unusual. Very occasionally, some of the plain massive silver and gold of the King James version shines when Biblical poetry is echoed in the balancing of phrases, in the full unhurried repetition of words in slightly varied order. But the words themselves are no longer those that daily sweep by us in dun and opaque stream. They no longer go bent and grimy in a fog. Contours are distinct as those of objects bathed in cool morning light. The words comport themselves with dignity. They are placed so quietly, so plumbly, so solidly, in order; they are arrayed so nakedly, so four-squarely; stand so completely for what they are; ring so fully, that one perceives them bearing themselves as erectly and proudly as simple healthy folk can bear themselves. (pp. 176-77)

It is the vague uncertain elusive music of folk in America that comes through this medium of words. Body of feeling in a groping struggling shoot of the Ohio countryside marshals the phrases, compels them into patterns, and makes the words pregnant with their real and transcendental meanings. In this writer, brother to all the dumb chaotic folk produced by two centuries of the pioneersman's life, the desire of the race is full a-cry. (p. 178)

Wherever he goes, in Chicago, out on the sandy foggy plain without the monster town, in the tiresome burgs where he sells the ideas of the advertising man, the state of life in him, the echo of the inner columnar movement of his being, is audible above the roar. It is ever near the surface, ready to spurt. The most ordinary objects glimpsed from an office-window high in the loop; the most ordinary sad bits of life seen in the endless avenues, a tree in a backyard, a layer of smoke, a man picking butts out of the gutter, can start it making gestures. A cake of cowdung rolled into balls by beetles, a flock of circling crows, milk turned sour by hot weather, give Anderson the clue of a thin gray string and set him winding through his drab and his wild days to find the truth of some cardinal experience and fill himself. The premature decay of buildings in America, the doleful agedness of things that have never served well and have grown old without becoming beautiful, the brutality of the Chicago skyline, open to him through a furtive chink some truth of his own starved powerful life, his own buried Mississippi Valley, his own unused empire. Or, the health that is left in the fecund soil of the continent, in the great watered spread of land, the nourishing life of forests and plantations, is powerful to make known to him in mad drunken bursts his own toughness and cleanness and healthiness. . . . Horses trampling through the grain are to him certitude eternal of the ever-replenishment of the male gentle might that has descended to him intact through his muscled ancestry and makes sweet his breast; of the phallic daintiness that all the stupid tangle and vulgarity of life in the raw commercial centers cannot wear down in him and brutalize. A thousand delicate and mighty forms of nature are there, to pledge and promise him, the man cut loose from Europe, life abundant.

And Anderson's touch goes to his fellows of the road and the Chicago street. . . . Of a sudden, he is breast to breast with people, with the strange gray American types, men and women he has seen the day previously; men and women, farmers, artisans, shopkeepers, he has not glimpsed in the flesh these five and twenty years. What happens only rarely, instantaneously only, in the most of us, the stretching of a ligament between another creature's bosom and our own, that happens in Anderson swiftly, repeatedly, largely. A visage, strange, gray, dun, floats up out of the dark of his mind. A man is seen doing something, lying face downward in a field, or fluttering his hands like birdwings. A woman is seen making a gesture, or walking down the railway track. The figure may have had its origin in some one long known, in some one seen but a furtive hour, in some one seen merely through hearsay. It may have its origin in the dullest, weariest creatures. But suddenly, the poet is become another person. He is some one who has never before existed, but now, even in a condition of relative colorlessness, has a life of his own as real as those of the strap-hanging men brushed every day in the streetcars. . . . He is a "queer" man working in a shabby little store. The more he strives to explain himself, the more incomprehensible and queer he becomes to his neighbors. He is Melville Stoner, the little long-nosed bachelor of **"Out of Nowhere Into Nothing"**; ironically resigned to the futility of seeking to establish a permanent contact with another creature; tired to his marrow with the loneliness of existence. Or, he is a farm girl mortally stricken in her breast by the insensitiveness and cowardice of men to whom she turns for expression. Or, the face is that of the lanky, cold-footed inventor who cannot channel his passion into human beings. To overcome the profound inner inertia, he sets himself to doing little definite problems. . . . Or, it is the face of **"The Man in the Brown Coat,"** who sits all day inside a book-lined room and knows minutely what Alexander the Great and Ulysses S. Grant did, that floats up before Anderson. Or, it is merely the figure of the officer of the law who strolled by swinging his billy as the author left his office. He is heard muttering to himself his feet ache; seen at night slowly pulling off his shoes and wriggling his stockinged toes.

Then, it is with Sherwood Anderson as it was with the two farmhands of **"The Untold Lie"** who suddenly hear themselves each in the other; hear in the other the voice telling that the assumption of responsibility to women and children is death, the voice telling that the assumption of the responsibility is life. In the people suddenly known to him through the imagination, Anderson recognizes the multiple pulls of his own will; hears speak in the men known the same pulls; hears in those bodies a voice, and in his own body the self-same murmur. Things long since heard in village stores, in factories and offices, spark with significance. Memories appear from nowhere, carry to him the life of a fellow forgotten long since; and the life against the childhood Ohio background is relieved and sharply drawn. Out of the murky, impenetrable limbo, a block, an idea, a shape, has been moved, and in the region of faint gray light stands outlined. What in himself he feared, what he, the fearful rebel in the Yankee flock, thought his own most special insanity, his own pariah marking, that is suddenly perceived an universal trait, present everywhere. His loneliness, that he thought a desolation all his own, is sensed in a million tight, apart bodies. His boastfulness, lust, self-infatuation, his great weariness, promptings of the messianic delusion, despair, they are suddenly perceived everywhere; they, and not the outer mask that men wear in each other's blind sight, are seen the truth. He knows people writhe; sees them, men and women, so hard and realistic, doing the things he does and then is frightened; he knows the many mad chanting voices in each fact-crowded skull. What he is beholding, what he holds in his hands before him in the shape of a scene, a gesture, a history, is the very life in himself. It is himself, Sherwood Anderson, the man who looks like a racing tout and a divine poet, like a movie-actor and a young priest, like a bartender, a business-man, a hayseed, a mama's boy, a satyr, and an old sit-by-the-stove. It is himself as his father and his mother, as the people who moved about him in Clyde, Ohio, in his childhood and moved away from him, the many thousand humble and garish lives he has touched, the men he has done business with, the women he has taken, have made him.

The floating faces insist he attend upon the voice of the mind, without, within. . . . It is too late to avoid humankind with the sentimentalities of the popular authors, or the self-pitifulness of the Main Street men, the cohort of little haters. The heads will have nothing but full entry into lives, even though he perish in the effort of entering. They want the facts of the relationships of men. It is what he really knows of the truth, what he really knows of what has happened to him, what he really knows of what he has done to folk as well as what they have done to him, that is demanded of him now. Anderson has to face himself where Freud and Lawrence, Stieglitz and Picasso, and every other great artist of the time, has faced himself: has had to add a "phallic Chekhov" to the group of men who have been forced by something in an age to remind an age that it is in the nucleus of sex that all the lights and the confusions have their center, and that to the nucleus of sex they all return to further illuminate or further tangle. (pp. 180-86)

Anderson's artistic progress has consisted of the growing faithfulness with which he has given form to his feeling of materials, particularly the material of words. His last allegories and stories chime with overtones of prose, simple words symbolic of the inner state of the protagonists no less than of the outer. At first, in the two early novels, *Windy McPherson's Son* and *Marching Men,* the verbal quality was fairly thin. . . . In the next book, ***Winesburg, Ohio,*** however, form obtains fully. The deep within Anderson utters itself through the prose. The tiny stories of village life are like tinted slits of isinglass through which one glimpses vasty space. The man's feeling for words, present always in him, reënforced one casual day when some one, expecting to produce a raw ha-ha, showed him *Tender Buttons,* is here mature. The visual images, the floating heads, have fleshed themselves, are automatically realized, by marriage with verbal images that had risen to meet them, and that contained, in their turn, the tough, spare, sprawling life in the poet. So this style, even more than the subject matter, is impregnated with the inarticulate American, the man whose inner dance is as the dance of a bag of meal. For in these words, the delicate inner column of Sherwood Anderson has risen to declare itself, to protest against the ugliness that lamed it down, to pour its life out into the unnumbered women and men. And, in his latest work, in the best of the stories in ***The Triumph of the Egg,*** and in the pieces of *A New Testament* [Anderson's collection of prose poems], it works with always simpler means, begins to manifest itself through a literature that approaches the condition of poetry; that is more and more a play of word-timbres, a design of overtones, of verbal shape and colors, a sort of absolute prose.

There has been no fiction in America like this. Small it is indeed by the mountainous side of the masses of Balzac, with their never-flagging volumnear swell, their circling wide contact on life, their beefy hotness. Anderson, to the present, has been most successful in the smaller forms. The short stories show him the fine workman most. . . . The man is not an intellectual critic of society. His range is a fairly limited one. There is a gentle weariness through him. And still, his stories are the truest, the warmest, the most mature, that have sprung out of the Western soil. They are the very stuff of a man; unpremeditated like breath; the stuff of a highly civilized, matured, and coördinating human creature. One has but to compare these fragile, delicate fictions with those of the classic novelists, Poe and Hawthorne, to perceive the bloodfulness of Anderson. The new man is perhaps not as finished an artist as were the older. Nevertheless, he works in flesh. He has experience; he has desire; he has wisdom. It is mature men and women alive and in action that he gives us. The two ante-bellum novelists gave us in place of flesh, as Brooks so trenchantly showed, exquisite iridescent ghosts. They themselves were turned away from their day, and filled the vacuums in which they dwelt with sinister and rainbow-tinted beams. Their people satisfy no lust of experience. Both writers have merely phantasy of a fine quality to offer in its place. Howells, it is true, experienced mature existence. But he was a provincial and handled facts gingerly. He knew his people, but he was afraid of himself and drew characters from the point of view of middle-class conventionality. And Dreiser's characters? Golems, in whose breast the sacred word has not been thrust. Anderson, on the contrary, expresses us. Life of the hour pulses in his ideas. Motives hitherto obscure and unseen are brought by him up to the conscious day. From the first he has possessed the power to create through his prose style protagonists in whom every American can feel himself. . . . The quaint little mushroom-like heads of Anderson's tales, the uneducated, undignified village dreamers, with their queer hops and springs, straggly speech, ineffectual large gestures, they are the little misshapen humans in this towering machine-noisy inhuman land, the aged infants grown a little screw-loose with inarticulateness. The sounds they make as they seek to explain themselves to one another, as they rave and denounce and pray, lie, boast, and weep, might come out of our own throats. They do come out of our own. The author may dub his heads Seth Richmond or Elsie Leander, George Willard or Wing Biddlebaum; they may be seen ever so fitfully; the stories by means of which Anderson has created them may set them out in mid-American farmland thirty years since. But they are flesh of our flesh and bone of our bone; and through them, we know ourselves in the roots of us, in the darkest chambers of the being. We know ourselves in Anderson as we knew ourselves in Whitman. And each new novel, tale and story makes audible an hitherto unheard pulsation of the warm membranes of life. (pp. 187-91)

Paul Rosenfeld, "Sherwood Anderson" in his Port of New York, *1924. Reprint by University of Illinois Press, 1961, pp. 175-98.*

H. L. MENCKEN (essay date 1923)

[*In the following excerpt, Mencken deems* Horses and Men *a vast improvement over Anderson's novel* Many Marriages. *Mencken also reviewed* Horses and Men *favorably in* Smart Set *(see Additional Bibliography).*]

Those partisans of Sherwood Anderson who, on the appearance of *Many Marriages*, retired quietly to their private chapels and there bowed their heads in prayer may now safely emerge again, sinful and defiant. For in this new book [***Horses and Men***] there is at least one story, **"I'm a Fool,"** that comes very close to being a masterpiece, and at least three others that are so simple, so charming and yet so penetrating that they wipe out all memory of the Greenwich Village "psychology" of *Many Marriages*, and leave only a sense of rare and stimulating beauty.

The book is extraordinarily original, but nevertheless Anderson shows his kinship on every page to his master, Dreiser, to whom he dedicates it. What Dreiser introduced into our fiction—and into English fiction in general—was a capacity for seeing poor and miserable people from within, for looking at the world through their eyes. . . .

Anderson's people are nearly all poor folk from the small towns of his native Ohio—boys who run away to follow the races, girls who let the drummers bedazzle them, and village workmen who recreate themselves when their work is done by blowing the cornet. People of narrow lives, and, you will probably add, not much imagination.

Anderson shows how untrue this is. He shows how, like all of us, they are pursued by visions of something better, something nobler, something beyond the skyline, and how, like all of us again, they find that life itself is but little more than a device for making those visions fade. How May Edgley, trying to escape from her sordid home, found only disgrace and death; how the boy, Tom Edwards, felt his world collapsing when they told him he must go to school; how the anonymous old man of **"The Sad Horn Blowers"** suffered because his wife wouldn't let him toot his cornet—into these grotesque transactions Anderson gets something that is almost akin to tragedy. In other hands they would be ludicrous; in his hands they are serious and affecting.

As I have said, the vagueness of *Many Marriages* is not in ***Horses and Men.*** All of the stories are quite simple. One does not have to take any of the psychology on trust: it becomes obvious the moment it is stated. No one does anything that is outlandish and inexplicable. There are no washing-machine manufacturers performing Russian ballets. Instead, Anderson sticks closely to the people that he knows and understands, and shows them in the exercise of their dreadful normalcy. It is a book that conceals all its own artifices; it is full of a high cunning. The author has redeemed *Many Marriages* and leaped far ahead.

H. L. Mencken, "H. L. Mencken Gives Meed of Praise to Anderson's Stories," in The Evening Sun, *Baltimore, December 8, 1923, p. 6.*

ROBERT LITTELL (essay date 1923)

[*Littell, an American literary and drama critic, was an associate editor of* Reader's Digest *magazine. In the following excerpt, he points to strengths and weaknesses in* Horses and Men.]

There is nothing in ***Horses and Men*** half-way as good as **"I Want to Know Why"** or **"The Triumph of the Egg,"** yet these stories are a partial recovery from the heavy, fumbling agony of *Many Marriages*. Mr. Anderson continues, with crude instrument and painful zeal, to work at his unreclaimed land, a fascinating, mysterious place, but a marsh none the less. Why can't he drain it? Why can't he stop his interminable explanations, which affect you, in the long run, as would ceaseless comment from a companion with whom you are listening to music very faintly heard through the wall of the next house? He is too intent on the truth about human beings, something too deep down in its burrow for him to do more than grab the end of its tail. A Sherwood Anderson story at its worst is not much more than several pages of fruitless yanking at the tail.

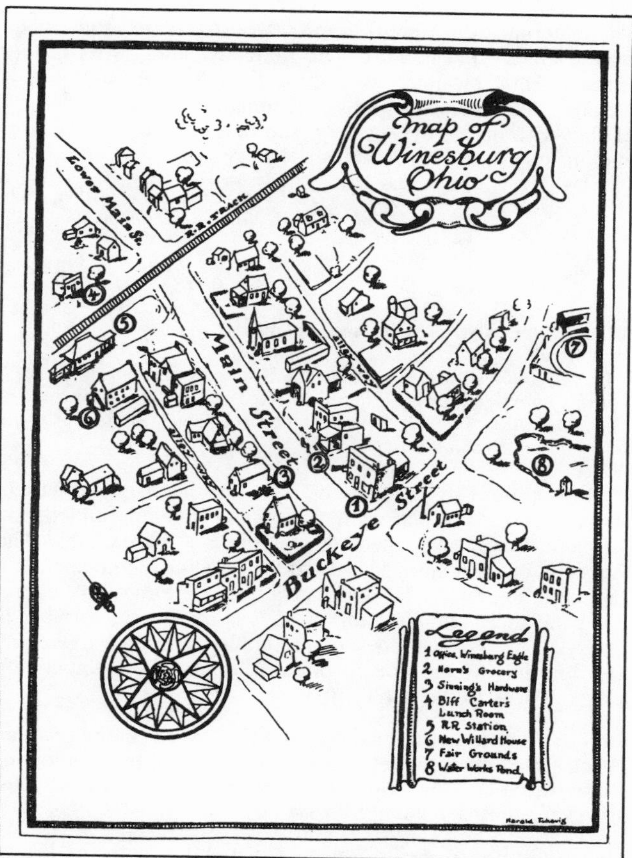

Map of Winesburg that appeared as the frontispiece of Winesburg, Ohio, *by Sherwood Anderson. Copyright 1919 by B. W. Huebsch. Copyright renewed 1947 by Eleanor Copenhaver Anderson. All rights reserved. Reprinted by permission of Viking Penguin Inc. and The Newberry Library.*

At their best (**"The Triumph of the Egg,"** and about three others), his stories have extraordinary poignancy and beauty, and a real grasp of the deepest, strangest things in human nature. At their next best, into which category fall most of the stories in ***Horses and Men,*** they are clumsy, slow-footed, reiterative, but somehow far more disturbing than the work of most far more competent, clear-headed writers. **"'Unused'"** is a good example, moving at times, always disquieting, but distressingly viscous.

In the Foreword Mr. Anderson makes a very revealing confession, solemn to be sure, but utterly sincere. "It may be that my eyes are blind and that I cannot see. It may be I am deaf. My hands are nervous and tremble. . . . With these nervous and uncertain hands may I really feel for the form of things concealed in the darkness?"

The material life [offered] to the novelist contains some good metal, and a great deal of mere mineral matter. Miss Cather extracts from this mass everything that, for her purposes, is precious. Mr. Anderson gives us an appallingly high percentage of slag with the gold. Yet his is the richer mine. Can he ever exploit it as it deserves? (p. 99)

Robert Littell, "Rich and Strange," in The New Republic, *Vol. XXXVII, No. 472, December 19, 1923, pp. 99-100.*

SHERWOOD ANDERSON (essay date 1924)

[In the following excerpt, Anderson discusses his concept of literary realism, touching briefly on Winesburg, Ohio. *This essay was originally published in 1924 in the* Literary Review *of the* New York Evening Post.]

There is something very confusing to both readers and writers about the notion of realism in fiction. As generally understood it is akin to what is called "representation" in painting. The fact is before you and you put it down, adding a high spot here and there, to be sure. No man can quite make himself a camera. Even the most realistic worker pays some tribute to what is called "art." Where does representation end and art begin? The location of the line is often as confusing to practicing artists as it is to the public. (p. 71)

Easy enough to get a thrill out of people with reality. A man struck by an automobile, a child falling out at the window of a city office building. Such things stir the emotions. No one, however, confuses them with art.

This confusion of the life of the imagination with the life of reality is a trap into which most of our critics seem to me to fall about a dozen times each year. Do the trick over and over and in they tumble. "It is life," they say. "Another great artist has been discovered."

What never seems to come quite clear is the simple fact that art is art. It is not life.

The life of the imagination will always remain separated from the life of reality. It feeds upon the life of reality, but it is not that life—cannot be. Mr. John Marin painting Brooklyn Bridge, Henry Fielding writing *Tom Jones,* are not trying in the novel and the painting to give us reality. They are striving for a realization in art of something out of their own imaginative experiences, fed to be sure upon the life immediately about. A quite different matter from making an actual picture of what they see before them.

And here arises a confusion. For some reason—I myself have never exactly understood very clearly—the imagination must constantly feed upon reality or starve. Separate yourself too much from life and you may at moments be a lyrical poet, but you are not an artist. Something within dries up, starves for the want of food. Upon the fact in nature the imagination must constantly feed in order that the imaginative life remain significant. The workman who lets his imagination drift off into some experience altogether disconnected with reality, the attempt of the American to depict life in Europe, the New Englander writing of cowboy life—all that sort of thing—in ninety-nine cases out of a hundred ends in the work of such a man becoming at once full of holes and bad spots. The intelligent reader, tricked often enough by the technical skill displayed in hiding the holes, never in the end accepts it as good work. The imagination of the workman has become confused. He has had to depend altogether upon tricks. The whole job is a fake.

The difficulty, I fancy, is that so few workmen in the arts will accept their own limitations. It is only when the limitation is fully accepted that it ceases to be a limitation. Such men scold at the life immediately about. "It's too dull and commonplace to make good material," they declare. Off they sail in fancy to the South Seas, to Africa, to China. What they cannot realize is their own dullness. Life is never dull except to the dull.

The writer who sets himself down to write a tale has undertaken something. He has undertaken to conduct his readers on a trip through the world of his fancy. If he is a novelist his imaginative world is filled with people and events. If he have any sense of decency as a workman he can no more tell lies about his imagined people, fake them, than he can sell out real people in real life. The thing is constantly done but no man I have ever met, having done such a trick, has felt very clean about the matter afterward.

On the other hand, when the writer is rather intensely true to the people of his imaginative world, when he has set them down truly, when he does not fake, another confusion arises. Being square with your people in the imaginative world does not mean lifting them over into life, into reality. There is a very subtle distinction to be made and upon the writer's ability to make this distinction will in the long run depend his standing as a workman.

Having lifted the reader out of the reality of daily life it is entirely possible for the writer to do his job so well that the imaginative life becomes to the reader for the time real life. Little real touches are added. The people of the town—that never existed except in the fancy—eat food, live in houses, suffer, have moments of happiness and die. To the writer, as he works, they are very real. The imaginative world in which he is for the time living has become for him more alive than the world of reality ever can become. His very sincerity confuses. Being unversed in the matter of making the delicate distinction, that the writer himself sometimes has such a hard time making, they call him a realist. The notion shocks him. "The deuce, I am nothing of the kind," he says. "But such a thing could not have happened in a Vermont town." "Why not? Have you not learned that anything can happen anywhere? If a thing can happen in my imaginative world it can of course happen in the flesh and blood world. Upon what do you fancy my imagination feeds?"

My own belief is that the writer with a notebook in his hand is always a bad workman, a man who distrusts his own imagination. Such a man describes actual scenes accurately, he puts down actual conversation.

But people do not converse in the book world as they do in life. Scenes of the imaginative world are not real scenes.

The life of reality is confused, disorderly, almost always without apparent purpose, whereas in the artist's imaginative life there is purpose. There is determination to give the tale, the song, the painting Form—to make it true and real to the theme, not to life. Often the better the job is done the greater the confusion.

I myself remember with what a shock I heard people say that one of my own books, ***Winesburg, Ohio,*** was an exact picture of Ohio village life. The book was written in a crowded tenement district of Chicago. The hint for almost every character was taken from my fellow-lodgers in a large rooming house, many of whom had never lived in a village. The confusion arises out of the fact that others besides practicing artists have imaginations. But most people are afraid to trust their imaginations and the artist is not.

Would it not be better to have it understood that realism, in so far as the word means reality to life, is always bad art—although it may possibly be very good journalism?

Which is but another way of saying that all of the so-called great realists were not realists at all and never intended being. Madame Bovary did not exist in fact. She existed in the imaginative life of Flaubert and he managed to make her exist also in the imaginative life of his readers.

* * *

I have been writing a story. A man is walking in a street and suddenly turns out of the street into an alleyway. There he meets another man and a hurried whispered conversation takes place. In real life they may be but a pair of rather small bootleggers, but they are not that to me.

When I began writing, the physical aspect of one of the men, the one who walked in the street, was taken rather literally from life. He looked strikingly like a man I once knew, so much like him in fact that there was a confusion. A matter easy enough to correct.

A stroke of my pen saves me from realism. The man I knew in life had red hair; he was tall and thin.

With a few words I have changed him completely. Now he has black hair and a black mustache. He is short and has broad shoulders. And now he no longer lives in the world of reality. He is a denizen of my own imaginative world. He can now begin a life having nothing at all to do with the life of the red-haired man.

If I am to succeed in making him real in this new world he, like hundreds of other men and women who live only in my own fanciful world, must live and move within the scope of the story or novel into which I have cast him. If I do tricks with him in the imaginative world, sell him out, I become merely a romancer. If, however, I have the courage to let him really live he will, perhaps, show me the way to a fine story or novel.

But the story or novel will not be a picture of life. I will never have had any intention of making it that. (pp. 72-8)

Sherwood Anderson, "A Note on Realism," in his Sherwood Anderson's Notebook, *Boni & Liveright, 1926, pp. 71-8.*

WILLIAM FAULKNER (essay date 1925)

[An American novelist and short story writer, Faulkner is a preeminent figure in modern American literature. Throughout his life, Faulkner acknowledged a debt of influence to Anderson, whom he met in 1925 when he was himself a little-known poet and both were living in New Orleans. During that year he became a close friend of Anderson, who encouraged him to try writing fiction, and Anderson subsequently arranged with his publisher, Horace Liveright, to publish Faulkner's first novel, Soldier's Pay *(1926). Anderson drew an affectionate portrait of Faulkner in the character David in his story "A Meeting South," which appeared in the* Dial *in 1925. In the following excerpt from an article that originally appeared in the* Dallas Morning News *in 1925, Faulkner favorably appraises his friend's short fiction.]*

Men grow from the soil, like corn and trees: I prefer to think of Mr. Anderson as a lusty corn field in his native Ohio. As he tells in his own story, his father not only seeded him physically, but planted also in him that belief, necessary to a writer, that his own emotions are important, and also planted in him the desire to tell them to someone.

Here are the green shoots, battling with earth for sustenance, threatened by the crows of starvation; and here was Mr. Anderson, helping around livery stables and race tracks, striping bicycles in a factory until the impulse to tell his story became too strong to be longer resisted.

Winesburg, Ohio

The simplicity of this title! And the stories are as simply done: short, he tells the story and stops. His very inexperience, his urgent need not to waste time or paper taught him one of the first attributes of genius. As a rule first books show more bravado than anything else, unless it be tediousness. But there is neither of these qualities in ***Winesburg, Ohio.*** Mr. Anderson is tentative, self-effacing with his George Willards and Wash Williamses and banker White's daughters, as though he were thinking: "Who am I, to pry into the souls of these people who, like myself, sprang from this same soil to suffer the same sorrows as I?" The only indication of the writer's individuality which I find in ***Winesburg, Ohio*** is his sympathy for them, a sympathy which, had the book been done as a full-length novel, would have become mawkish. Again the gods looked out for him. These people live and breathe: they are beautiful. There is the man who organized a baseball club, the man with the "speaking" hands, Elizabeth Willard, middle-aged, and the oldish doctor, between whom was a love that Cardinal Bembo might have dreamed. There is a Greek word for a love like theirs which Mr. Anderson probably had never heard. And behind all of them a ground of fecund earth and corn in the green spring and the slow, full hot summer and the rigorous masculine winter that hurts it not, but makes it stronger. (pp. 89-90)

Horses and Men

A collection of short stories, reminiscent of ***Winesburg, Ohio,*** but more sophisticated. After reading this book you inevitably want to reread ***Winesburg, Ohio.*** Which makes one wonder if after all the short story is not Mr. Anderson's medium. No sustained plot to bother you, nothing tedious; only the sharp episodic phases of people, the portraying of which Mr. Anderson's halting questioning manner is best at. **"I'm a Fool,"** the best short story in America, to my thinking, is the tale of a lad's adolescent pride in his profession (horse racing) and his body, of his belief in a world beautiful and passionate created for the chosen to race horses on, of his youthful pagan desire to preen in his lady's eyes that brings him low at last. Here is a personal emotion that does strike the elemental chord in mankind. (p. 91)

In this book there are people, people that walk and live, and the ancient stout earth that takes his heartbreaking labor and gives grudgingly, mayhap, but gives an hundredfold. (p. 92)

William Faulkner, "Sherwood Anderson," in The Princeton University Library Chronicle, *Vol. XVIII, No. 3, Spring, 1957, pp. 89-94.*

VIRGINIA WOOLF (essay date 1925)

[An English novelist, essayist, short story writer, and critic, Woolf is considered one of the most important authors of the twentieth-

century. She avidly read and admired Anderson's work, and in the following excerpt she praises his fiction, particularly the stories in The Triumph of the Egg, *for its psychological depth and honesty. This essay originally appeared in 1925 in the* Saturday Review of Literature.]

In ***The Triumph of the Egg*** there is some rearrangement of the old elements of art which makes us rub our eyes. The feeling recalls that with which we read Chekhov for the first time. There are no familiar handles to lay hold of in ***The Triumph of the Egg***. The stories baffle our efforts, slip through our fingers and leave us feeling, not that it is Mr. Anderson who has failed us, but that we as readers have muffled our work and must go back, like chastened school-children, and spell the lesson over again in the attempt to lay hold of the meaning.

Mr. Anderson has bored into that deeper and warmer layer of human nature which it would be frivolous to ticket new or old, American or European. In his determination to be 'true to the essence of things' he has fumbled his way into something genuine, persistent, of universal significance, in proof of which he has done what, after all, very few writers succeed in doing—he has made a world of his own. It is a world in which the senses flourish; it is dominated by instincts rather than by ideas; racehorses make the hearts of little boys beat high; cornfields flow around the cheap towns like golden seas, illimitable and profound; everywhere boys and girls are dreaming of voyages and adventures, and this world of sensuality and instinctive desire is clothed in a warm cloudy atmosphere, wrapped about in a soft caressing envelope, which always seems a little too loose to fit the shape. Pointing to the formlessness of Mr. Anderson's work, the vagueness of his language, his tendency to land his stories softly in a bog, the English tourist would say that all this confirms him in his theory of what is to be expected of an American writer of insight and sincerity. The softness, the shellessness of Mr. Anderson are inevitable since he has scooped out from the heart of America matter which has never been confined in a shell before. He is too much enamoured of this precious stuff to squeeze it into any of those old and intricate poems which the art and industry of Europe have secreted. Rather he will leave what he has found exposed, defenceless, naked to scorn and laughter. (p. 114)

Virginia Woolf, "American Fiction," in her Collected Essays, Vol. II, *Harcourt Brace Jovanovich, Inc., 1967, pp. 111-21.*

CLEVELAND B. CHASE (essay date 1927)

[*Chase, an American author, wrote critical biographies of Anderson and Voltaire. His* Sherwood Anderson *(1927) was the first full-length study of Anderson's life and works. In the following excerpt from that book, he discusses* Winesburg, Ohio, *and selected short stories from* The Triumph of the Egg *and* Horses and Men.]

Winesburg, Ohio is a psychological document of the first importance; no matter that it is an incomplete picture of modern American life, it is an honest and penetrating one done with bold and simple strokes. These stories represent the finest combination Anderson has yet achieved of imagination, intuition and observation welded into a dramatic unity by painstaking craftsmanship. They are one of the important products of the American literary renascence and have probably influenced writing in America more than any book published within the last decade. They made and they sustain Anderson's reputation as an author worthy of comparison with the great short story writers.

It is in no way surprising that Anderson should find his most complete expression in the short story. His very approach to writing leads one to expect it. "I have come," he writes, "to think that the true history of life is but a history of moments. It is only at rare moments that we live." This often reiterated belief of his that only moments of "awareness" are important is much more conducive to the episodic treatment of the short story than to the cumulative continuity of the novel.

Not only does Anderson look at life from the short story point of view, but this medium tends naturally to restrain and to correct . . . two of the great weaknesses in his writing. In such limited space there is little chance for him to become tangled up in profitless philosophic speculations; as a result of being forced to concentrate and focus his attention, Anderson forgets somewhat his worries about ultimate values and devotes himself to the definite and factual present, to the great profit of his writing. The short story also offers fewer temptations to day-dreaming, which may be indulged in more pleasantly in the more leisurely form of the novel.

The first thing to strike one in reading these stories is Anderson's extraordinary technical brilliance. The clumsiness and obvious attempts to imitate various writers which were so noticeable in the first two novels are lacking. Anderson tells these stories with a simplicity and a sureness that show that at last he knows what he is doing and how he wants to do it. He has his medium in such complete control that it is not difficult to be unconscious of his mastery of it. His air of simplicity and ingenuousness, the apparent rambling, the way in which he appears to be haphazardly setting down ideas as they come into his mind in an attempt to discover their meaning, his groping, his artlessness, his naïveté—these are but tricks of the story teller's trade to earn our sympathy for the story which he unfolds graphically and without confusion. To be sure, that groping naïveté betokens a certain self-consciousness on the part of the author, but such self-consciousness is an integral part of Anderson, and rarely does it become obtrusive.

It is in their objectiveness, in their penetration into and interpretation of universal human qualities that these stories differ from most of Anderson's writing. The important creative imaginations have always been interpretive, they have allowed their possessors to get under the surface, to understand life as it is. Thus in this broader sense all valid writing is realistic, whether the approach of the individual writer be allegorical, lyrical, symbolic, or whether it be through the more limited realism of a Zola. Distorting life, reconstructing it as a writer thinks it should be, writing with any view in mind except that of interpreting what is and what has always been is, despite popular misconceptions, not to write with imagination, but without it. Much of Anderson's writing belongs to this latter class. In ***Winesburg, Ohio,*** however, and in a few of his other short stories he shows that he can penetrate objectively into the confused world of emotion and bring back from it at least a part of what he has seen and felt there.

What Anderson is seeking to express in these stories is the intricacy and subtlety that exists in the relationship of an individual to his physical environment and to other people. He is studying the means by which this relationship is established, how it is expressed, the use and the insufficiency of words in expressing it, the effect upon the individual of his failure to establish such relationships. In exploring this field Anderson incidentally shows the loneliness, the essential isolation of all people, however far they may or may not have gone toward orienting themselves in life.

The universality of the emotions Anderson describes is, paradoxically enough, far greater than that of the characters whom he has chosen to be the instruments through which these emotions are depicted. It would be difficult to find another book in which there is such a weird collection of eccentrics, perverts, maniacs, half-wits, frustrated, hopelessly confused people. (pp. 31-4)

Anderson has peopled his mythical Winesburg with strikingly abnormal types; often he goes still further and selects as the basis for his story abnormal events in their lives. It is true that there are such people in most communities and that such events as he pictures do occur; but they are exceptions, not the rule. Anderson would probably be the last to claim that this volume represents a cross section of any American town or village. He has consciously neglected the normal in favor of the sub- or abnormal. But, and in this is the genius of the book, in the neglected "normal" majority there are usually the germs that, unresisted, have caused the abnormality in the people Anderson describes. Those people about whom he does not write are normal because their processes of resistance and of adaptation have made them so.

Thus the universality of ***Winesburg, Ohio*** does not depend upon the frequency with which such types as it describes occur in the world. It goes deeper than that. The emotions and reactions it exposes belong, in varying degrees, to all people. Anderson has dramatized them and made them obvious. He has simplified, focused his attention; in so doing he has produced grotesque people, but they are validly, fundamentally alive people, such as it is the fortune of comparatively few writers to achieve. He has had to sacrifice much to obtain the desired result, but the important thing is that he has obtained it. Most of the stories ring true, even if in a minor key.

Anderson has been widely criticized for the sordidness of ***Winesburg;*** he has been called ignorant, perverted, immoral; even his friend, Paul Rosenfeld, termed him "the Phallic Chekhov" [see excerpt dated 1922]. And there can be no question that he has chosen unpleasant subjects and that he is greatly preoccupied with sex. More than two-thirds of the stories have definitely sexual themes. This is partly due to the influence upon him of D. H. Lawrence and of the psychoanalysts, but even more it is because, using sex as a point of departure, he is able to depict emotions and reactions that are true not only of sex, but of almost all other human relations. It is for this reason that we close a book dealing so largely with sexual problems, not conscious so much of its sexual nature as of the way in which it has exposed the difficulty which the individual experiences in orienting himself in regard to his environment and to the people around him.

Just as the emotions these characters have are more significant than the characters themselves, so these "sexual crises" have implications much wider than those of mere sex. In most of the stories the climax throws light not so much upon the sexual nature of the characters concerned as upon their general emotional make-up. A similar thing might have happened in a realm quite disassociated from sex. Whatever his reason for so doing, Anderson has used sexual examples. To do this constantly is, to my mind, a decided weakness in craftsmanship; it in no important way invalidates the integrity of the conception of the stories. We may question Anderson's taste in concentrating so much upon sex; we cannot question his right to do so. Creative writing cannot be limited by the fickle demands of "good taste."

It is easy enough to pick out flaws in ***Winesburg, Ohio.*** Anderson has lost immeasurably in convincingness by the necessity he has felt himself under to dramatize these stories so highly; he makes his points, but he has to do it by the sledge-hammer method. One longs for a touch of delicacy or restraint. Occasionally the stories call to mind the lists of "awful examples" sent out by welfare organizations, the anti-saloon and anti-cigarette leagues. One also longs for a single fully-rounded character; what Anderson says about these people is true, but it isn't all the truth; there are important phases of their existence about which he seems to know nothing. This comes partly from the over-dramatization and partly from his theory of life as a history of moments. He sometimes neglects important influences that have brought about these moments. It is this lack of roundness, of completeness that must force us to list ***Winesburg, Ohio*** among the minor, if authentic, literary achievements.

In ***The Triumph of the Egg*** and ***Horses and Men*** there are isolated stories that rank with the best of Anderson's work, but neither of these books has the sustained quality of ***Winesburg, Ohio.*** In tone, both are more pleasant. Anderson is no longer entirely preoccupied with sex and suppression. In fact in one story when a character cries out, "Sex. It is by understanding sex I will untangle the mystery (of life)," Anderson, to our astonishment, comments, "It was all very well and sometimes interesting but one grew tired of the subject."

Three of the most successful stories in these two volumes have to do with horse racing, of which the best is, **"I Want to Know Why."** It is told in the first person by a young boy who has run away from home to follow the horses. . . . (pp. 37-40)

There is real quality in that story. Its fumbling inarticulateness is eloquent beyond the power of mere words to convey meaning. . . . In it there is somewhat the same lyric note that one gets in Keats' "Ode to a Nightingale." Anderson recaptures the same emotion, less successfully, in the stories, **"I'm a Fool"** and **"An Ohio Pagan."** But having mentioned Keats, I must hasten to add that Anderson remains at that height but for a fleeting moment. **"I Want to Know Why"** ends in an anticlimax so banal as to make one wonder whether it wasn't by pure chance that Anderson caught the lyric note at all. He concludes what might have been a perfect story by expressing a bewildered astonishment that life can be so lovely and so sordid at the same time; the poet has been replaced by the quack philosopher. (p. 42)

[Of the stories in the two books that are worth attention—**"Seeds," "The Egg," "Unlighted Lamps," "The Man in the Brown Coat," "The Door of the Trap," "The New Englander," "Motherhood," "Out of Nowhere into Nothing," "I'm a Fool," "'Unused,'" "The Sad Horn Blowers,"** and **"An Ohio Pagan"**]—all, with the possible exception of the last, deal directly with the "walls" that separate individuals from each other, with the desire that people have for intimacy and the practical impossibility of their achieving it. It is almost as if Anderson were retelling the same story and merely applying it to different people each time. The lonely young Middle Western old maid, the ineffectual farmer, the country doctor, the writer, the college professor, the prim New England old maid, the young farmer, the intelligent private secretary, the race track swipe, the bright daughter in a degenerate family, all have practically the same difficulty in adjusting themselves to life, the same kind of longings and dissatisfactions. It is merely that the effect of these things on them differs according to the peculiarities of the individual.

These stories are decidedly more mature, less naïve than those in ***Winesburg, Ohio***; technically they are handled better; Anderson hasn't warped and twisted his characters as he did in that first volume of short stories. The characters are no longer such striking gargoyles and grotesques.

But in thus restraining himself, Anderson has lost immeasurably in vividness, convincingness and in what he himself terms "truth to the essence of things." The exteriors of these people are more recognizable; what happens to them is less so. Whatever one's reaction to ***Winesburg, Ohio,*** one could scarcely feel that it was dull or commonplace. One often feels that about these stories. Was not the technique of their telling so well handled, it would be virtually impossible to read many of them. One feels that Anderson is running a little dry; he is having to skimp and to squeeze on his emotions. In ***Winesburg, Ohio,*** one felt that he was writing because he actually had something to say; in most of these stories one wonders if he isn't writing merely because he wants to write and knows how it should be done. (pp. 45-6)

Cleveland B. Chase, in his Sherwood Anderson, *1927. Reprint by The Folcroft Press, Inc., 1969, 84 p.*

DWIGHT MACDONALD (essay date 1928)

[An American essayist and critic, Macdonald was a noted proponent of political causes from the mid-1930s until his death in 1982. In the following excerpt, Macdonald surveys Anderson's career as a short story writer.]

The common man comes into his own in the writings of Sherwood Anderson. In the poignant, memorable figures of Seth Thompson, of Wing Biddlebaum, of May Edgely and Joe Welling he is depicted and as we read these stories of the lives of common people, we realize that none of them are "common," that all become strange, individual, beautifully significant when Anderson draws them from the glare of the noonday world into the clear atmosphere of his imagination. "In the world of fancy even the most base man's actions sometimes take on the forms of beauty." Some of us, persuaded by his artistry, realize the truth of this, but others remain skeptical. They have not found such values among the people as Anderson would have them believe exist there. Speaking of his writings, he himself has made to them the only reply that can be made: "It is likely that I have not, and will not, put into them one truth, measuring by the ordinary standards of truth. It is my aim to be true to the essence of things, that's what I'm after." There is no possibility of settling by discussion this question of truth once the non-rational values enter in, as they must infallibly do in any good art. Whether such and such a character is "true to life" or not depends entirely on the validity of its artistic presentation. A great writer can make the most impossible freak live and breathe where a lesser cannot make a convincing character out of his own father. How often does one hear an unsuccessful writer plead, "But every character in the story is drawn from life." At the most "the facts" serve as little more than a springboard to the higher truths of literature. The great prophets and creators of all ages have seen so profoundly into life that they have been unable to communicate their visions through the reason alone. One may dismiss as mysticism Anderson's conception of humanity if one is unable or unwilling to admit the possibility of truths beyond reason, but one must also impeach as a deceiver a far greater prophet, who exalted the poor in spirit after the same ridiculous fashion. Blessed are the meek, say both, and surely reason was never more gloriously transcended than in this conception of the dignity and worth of humankind. Such ideal concepts are neither above nor below, but apart from reason. Yet it is not accurate to say that Anderson idealizes the common man: he makes him no more strong, or handsome, or intelligent than he would appear to the most literal-minded reader. Rather he sees a significant, noble beauty in the fellow's very weaknesses and imperfections. Here again there is an interesting similarity with the teachings of the New Testament, which exalts the weak and humble for those very qualities. The Christian metaphor of the stone the builders rejected is curiously echoed in the very phrasing of these words from ***Winesburg, Ohio***: "On the trees are only a few gnarled apples that the pickers have rejected. . . . Only the few know the sweetness of the twisted apples."

Anderson is not the first writer to put into his books farmhands and shopkeepers, but he is the first outside the Russians to treat them not as sociological studies or mere clumsy louts, but as fellow mortals with whom he is in personal sympathy. He chooses to write of common people because he is interested in and moved by the happenings of their lives. In this respect he is the natural product of the period: as English literature has developed from century to century its choice of subject has grown more and more democratic. From the kings and princes that alone seemed to the Elizabethans fit subjects for drama it is a far cry to Ray Pearson and Ed Handby of Winesburg, Ohio. Yet this transition is a natural one that takes place in the history of every culture. The reason that Anderson is able to find as good artistic values in his farmhands as the Elizabethans found in their princes is that he is little concerned with the external huskings of time, place, and environment. In this he is the exact opposite of Balzac, Flaubert, Zola, and the other great French realists, who are chiefly preoccupied with the effect of the environment on the individual and who treat their characters largely as expressions of that effect. They face life with clear eyes, attempting to see things as nearly as possible in the light of reason. Anderson, like most Russian and many English writers, has a more cloudy, idealistic vision that tends to separate the individual from his actual surroundings and concentrate on the almost mystical essence of his character. His farmers are individuals who happen to be farmers, and not *vice versa* as in Balzac. The French attempt to explain reality by organizing it with the intellect; Anderson tries to explain it by recreating it in his imagination. For that reason he naturally has a tendency to identify himself with his characters to a much greater extent than the more detached French school. Flaubert, it will be remembered, made this objectivity on the part of the author the foundation of his carefully thought out theory of writing. In Anderson's books, however, the reality is to a great extent inside himself rather than his characters. It is for this reason that his idealistic treatment of the ordinary man is so convincing: he identifies himself with his farmhands and spinsters to some extent, breathing life into them from his own lungs. With the rarest imagination he expresses the common humanity that lies beneath the wrappings of circumstance. Merging himself with his creations, he rejects none as mean or unworthy; he condemns none, perceiving the tragedy behind even the most vicious and insolent lives. (pp. 217-19)

Mid-American Chants is perhaps as direct an expression of Anderson's philosophy as he ever achieved. . . . The relation between his personal philosophy and the purely objective storytelling will vary [in Anderson's succeeding volumes] from the nearly complete dominance of the former to the synthesis of the two in his best productions, notably in the book immediately following [***Winesburg, Ohio***]. It should be noted that the story-telling is never the dominating element when the synthesis is destroyed.

In his next volume this synthesis, achieved more successfully than in any of those preceding or following, produced what is without question Anderson's masterpiece, ***Winesburg, Ohio***. . . . Its publication . . . was the climax of the author's artistic career. One persistent misconception about this book was disposed of by Anderson when he wrote: "I remember with what a shock I heard people say that one of my books, ***Winesburg, Ohio,*** was an exact picture of Ohio village life. The book was written in a crowded tenement district of Chicago. The hint for almost every character was taken from my fellow-lodgers in a large rooming house, many of whom had never lived in a village" [see excerpt dated 1924]. There could be no clearer demonstration of Anderson's primary concern with individuals and his only incidental emphasis on their external environment than the circumstances under which was composed this, his finest work. It is interesting to compare the local color in ***Winesburg, Ohio*** with that of such local color addicts as Sarah Orne Jewett in New England and George W. Cable in the South. The enormous amount of characteristic detail in the work of these two, which makes it impossible for the reader to forget for an instant the precise locale of the story, brings out by contrast the extremely general, so to speak universal, setting of Anderson's work, a setting so lacking in peculiarities and so filled on the contrary with the elementals of the external scene as to bring to mind the simple grass and fields, water and soil of the Old Testament. Anyone who has spent a summer in the country just west of Cleveland, where the mythical Winesburg is situated, knows that the atmosphere of the Ohio small town of reality has done little more than suggest that of the book. The author has evidently idealized and recreated the actual trees and fields and houses of his village to form a suitable background for the people in the book, that is, a background that will be sufficiently vague and universal so as not to distract the reader's attention from the human story working itself out before him by intruding any peculiarity of scene on his consciousness. Also we may be sure that Anderson would not fail to exercise his powers of idealization on the setting as well as on the characters; perhaps he created his setting largely for the sake of its own beauty. At all events, there is a perceptible harmony between the people in Winesburg and the background across which they move, showing that a synthesis of the two elements has been attained. The prose style of Anderson reaches its culmination in these tales. It bears a remarkable resemblance to that of the Bible in its simplicity and in its constant use of imagery. The influence of the Bible on Anderson, by the way, appears to have been considerable both in respect to content and to expression. The simplicity, which is later to degenerate into mannerism, now is clear, sound, and effective. The sentences are often short and usually grammatically simple; in place of subordinate clauses one finds prepositional phrases; there are few long words and many monosyllables. All this simplicity produces an extraordinarily unified effect on the reader so that, undistracted by any of the usual convolutions and ornamentation of modern prose, he feels a direct contact with the characters. The power that at times lifts the style into greatness, however, is that of imagery. This is certainly one of the essentials if not the essential of good literature, and the fact that today writers as feeble in this respect as Hardy and Galsworthy should be considered important figures and that the metaphor and the simile should so generally be assigned to poetry is an indication of the decadence of our prose. The expression of the general in terms of the particular is the primary artistic function and the most effective way to achieve this is by the use of metaphor. From the Homeric simile and the imagery of the Psalms down to the present, the great writers have possessed this power, so that it is no hyperbole to call metaphor the life-blood of literature. In Anderson it upwells as spontaneously as in an imaginative child. He cannot help himself if he would: he must think in terms of the concrete. As for the merit of his prose style, it would be no exaggeration to say that no living writer has better mastered his medium. Every sentence of these stories is artistically valuable; there are no loose ends hanging out, no crudities of phrasing such as mar the work of many modern novelists. With conscious skill Anderson plays on the instrument of language, and if his range is not very wide, he rarely strikes a false note. Each word is carefully, lovingly fitted into place with the craftsman's joy in turning out exquisitely finished work. His style is always in perfect taste because it never intrudes itself at the expense of the subject. There is none of the striving after effect, the vulgar display that mars so much nineteenth century prose. An examination of the nuances and subtleties of his style will convince anyone of the error of those who call Anderson a child-like seeker after beauty who attains it unawares, almost by good luck, according to some of these gentlemen. He is no boy chasing butterflies and catching them by chance. Deciding on the effect he wants to create in each instance, with consummate technical skill he succeeds in capturing with his fine style exactly the fitting tone for the particular story. Such unconscious gropers after truth and beauty as some shallow critics call Anderson and Dreiser may exist, but they would never be able to find a publisher. In respect to form this book also represents the best work of its author. The same simplicity and directness that characterize the style as a feature of the form as well. Each story is told with an almost complete lack of irrelevant detail. It is a remarkable feat of technique, this expressing the essence of an individual life in ten pages without giving the impression of baldness. Each of the tales has in it most of the material for a full-length novel and yet one never feels that the telling is compressed or sketchy or hurried. This is achieved by the use of metaphor on a large scale, in respect to form as well as style: each story suggests the entire existence of an individual through a selection of significant words or actions that are more or less symbols of the whole. Later on this crystallizing of a personality through symbolic action will become at times an obvious, rather annoying trick, but here it is kept within bounds. Anderson is able to compress a life into ten pages without resorting to abstractions largely because instead of analyzing his people he allows them to express themselves: Elmer Cowley beating George Willard to show he is not "queer"; Wash Williams confronted by the nudity of his cast-off wife; the Reverend Curtis Hartman peering through the chink in the window at Kate Swift—it is these moments of significant drama that one remembers the longest. In none of Anderson's books do the characters stand out so sharply as individuals as in ***Winesburg, Ohio.*** Each of them has certain definite external characteristics that impress themselves on the reader because they are indications of the personality within. One cannot think of Curtis Hartman without his thick beard or of Elmer Cowley without his protruding teeth and light blue eyes. One does not feel, as in so much of Anderson's work, especially the novels, that the author has described each character as tall or short or bearded merely to get over with the minimum of physical description that he knows the reader must have, and that the only reason the man is short and bearded is that the author has happened to choose those features for him as arbitrarily as one chooses a suit of clothes for a child. There is an inner necessity here that rules the relationship between the external and the internal personalities, and the inarticulate Ed Handby must remain red-faced and gigantic till the end of time. The reason for this may be that Anderson identifies himself less directly with these characters than with those of his novels, and hence does not conceive of them as being essentially similar people to whom he must arbitrarily give different external characteristics. At any rate, the balance is struck satisfactorily between the subjective and the objective elements in each character. With great imagination Anderson has entered into the personality of each one and patiently searched out the essence that makes him different from all the rest and at the same time forms his chief contact with them. For while they are individuals, Tom Foster and the others are more than that, and it is the glory of their creator that he realizes how much more. They are also figures that represent in their suffering and triumph and bewilderment all humanity, all the lives of men and women. Here Anderson gathers the richest harvest of his gift of imagery, in these people whose lives naturally, without the slightest warping or twisting, become symbols of such universal experiences as are suggested by the titles of the stories: **"Terror," "Sophistication," "Loneliness," "Death."** Bearing the serene light of art these tales move over the troubled darkness of the world, each of them illuminating for an instant the mystery of existence. (pp. 221-25)

The Triumph of the Egg . . . is a book of tales, only three of which, **"Unlighted Lamps," "The New Englander,"** and **"The Egg,"** are comparable in quality to those in ***Winesburg, Ohio.*** The failure of most of these results from the break-down of the synthesis of elements that distinguished the earlier volume. Some of them are too complex and rambling to attain the unity of impression essential to the short story. The loosely organized narrative of **"Out of Nowhere Into Nothing,"** in particular, is surprising after the rigid sense of form apparent in ***Winesburg, Ohio.*** When they are not too full of unassimilated, disorganized material to make a strong impression on the reader, these stories sometimes fail because they are too slight, too lacking in literal body to do so. From sketches of three and four pages to **"Out of Nowhere Into Nothing,"** which occupies a full third of the book, we find Anderson veering. His stories now show more realization of the complexities of life, or perhaps it is merely a less direct and certain grasp of reality; this may be the inevitable result of a maturing mind, and it may be the first signs of degeneration. Certainly this development of his talent, though it inevitably leads to work less pure and perfect than the Winesburg tales, contains in it the potentiality of a fuller and, perhaps, a deeper exploration of human character. The question is whether he will be able to avail himself of this latent possibility or whether this broadening of his field will merely serve to confuse him. That the latter should on the whole be the result seems almost inescapable when we consider that Anderson's greatest strength has always been in the very singleness of vision that this expansion of his horizon is threatening. Some of the failures, as **"The Other Woman,"** come from an excess of subjective analysis. Generally told in the first person, their effectiveness is destroyed by the endless turning in and in on the ego without sufficient connection with external reality. Such excess of introspection is bound to be artistically sterile. The reader soon tires of psychological analysis that exists entirely apart from the world of action. In this volume the style of ***Winesburg, Ohio*** has already degenerated in places to such careless writing as this: "Tom Leander came with his wife and family to visit his father and mother on Sundays. The family appeared at about ten o'clock in the morning. When the wagon turned out of the road that ran past the Russell place, Tom shouted. There was a field between the house and the road and the wagon could not be seen as it came along the narrow way through the corn." This might be called writing in one's shirt sleeves. Unhappily Anderson slips into it more and more until in his last novel [*Dark Laughter*] all pretense of style is abandoned. In **"The Egg,"** by the way, he shows that he can treat a story lightly if he chooses: his skill[ful] blending of the ridiculous and the pathetic gives the tale a delightful human quality. Although in content and even more in expression this book of tales is a come-down from the earlier one, even in the worst of the stories there are still enough moving situations and fine passages to make the fortune of many a lesser writer. (pp. 228-29)

In 1923 ***Horses and Men*** appeared. Like ***The Triumph of the Egg***, it contains several excellent stories and several failures. **"I'm a Fool," "The Sad Horn Blowers," "An Ohio Pagan,"** and **"'Unused'"** are successful examples of the more complex type of story—as compared to the Winesburg tales—upon which Anderson embarked for the first time in ***The Triumph of the Egg***. Certain of these stories fail from a new and significant cause, the abandoning of objective for frankly subjective narration. This has nothing to do with Anderson's identifying himself with his characters; it is purely a matter of technique. Nor does it mean telling the story in the first person of one of the characters, as in **"I'm a Fool"** and **"The Man Who Became a Woman,"** but rather the intrusion into the picture of the author himself *as* author. It is as if Anderson were sitting in an armchair opposite the reader telling him of a story he intended to write. He tries hard to make clear the essentials of the story and by mulling around long enough he succeeds in driving home the point, but he does it by inartistic methods. Although one sees more or less what he is getting at, one remains unmoved because the thing is done not by any skillful arrangement of the material but by a clumsy frontal attack on it. The raw material is all there, perhaps, but it is not worked up into artistic form. In the front of this volume there is a fine two-page tribute to Theodore Dreiser, in which is beautifully expressed Anderson's admiration. The story, **"I'm a Fool,"** is certainly one of the best he ever wrote. Although it is told entirely in the first person by a stable boy, at no time does the style miss richness and harmony. In Anderson's skillful hands the incoherent slangy talk of a boy grows lyrical without at the same time ringing false; there is a singing quality to even the slang in such a writing as this: "Gee whizz [*sic*], Gosh amighty, the nice hickorynut and beechnut and oaks and other kinds of trees along the roads, all brown and red, and the good smells, and Burt singing a song that was called Deep River, and the country girls at the windows of houses and everything." Besides the technical mastery it exhibits, this story is important for its content. In it Anderson has somehow struck way down into the very roots of human nature, and he has succeeded in delineating with sympathy and insight the human boob in all his idiotic, laughable, tragic, stupid, pitiful, sublime boobosity. Here is the very essence of Anderson's portrayal of the common man in this tale of a boy's ridiculous and pathetic failure in a love affair. There is all humanity in the words, "I'm a fool." (pp. 232-33)

Sherwood Anderson is without question a much less significant figure of his age than either Proust or Joyce, and yet I think his books will be read when those writers are no more than names in the histories of literature—in capital letters, to be sure, but still only names. It is his humility and his preoccupation with the humble that has saved him. On account of it he has not marred his work by employing that inhuman scale which is the mark of decadence in art, the scale on which are constructed *Ulysses* and *A La Recherche du Temps Perdu*. A feeling is abroad today that size, complexity, elaboration are in themselves admirable. Secretly conscious of our impotence, we try to escape realizing it by making bigger and bigger corporations, theatres, books. But we are an impotent generation and the more we build hundred-story skyscrapers, the more we go in for million-dollar corporations and billion-dollar mergers, by so much the more we convict ourselves of that very impotence we so desperately deny. Anderson, quietly assured of his own creative power, almost alone of our writers has been content to work on a human scale. Forgetting we are men, we lift up our hands to the stars and try to catch the moon in a net; but he has not been confused by the material vastness and complexity of the times into abandoning the old simple things close to the earth and to men from which all good art must grow. Certainly he is at his best when he is dealing not with the city, but with the village. His nature is provincial: the things he values are precisely those most threatened by the cosmopolitan, industrial trend of the times. "The machines men are so intent on making," he writes, "have carried them very far from the old sweet things." The life of the village, in which each man counts for something in himself and not in the money or power he possesses, where man enters directly into relationship with man and not through some mechanical or industrial medium, it is this life that Anderson understands. He has a feeling for the old sweet provincial things, the vagaries of character, the almost childishly direct expression of emotions, the little homely human features of village life, and his books draw much of their beauty from the expression of his feeling. (pp. 241-42)

Dwight Macdonald, "Sherwood Anderson," in The Yale Literary Magazine, *Vol. XCIII, No. 9, July, 1928, pp. 209-43.*

JOHN CHAMBERLAIN (essay date 1933)

[*Chamberlain is an American editor and critic. At one time the daily book reviewer for the* New York Times, *he has written literary criticism as well as economic and political essays for numerous periodicals. In the following excerpt, he praises Anderson's accomplishment in* Death in the Woods.]

Walking along a country road one day in the South, [Sherwood Anderson] met a man named Boone. "Any kin to Daniel?" asked Sherwood. "Why, my name's Dan'el," the old man said. All of Sherwood Anderson is in the telling of that anecdote: the simple relish of an old man's provincial dignity, the wonder at any expression of individuality. The stories collected in ***Death in the Woods*** are all variations on this eternal theme of wonder. Mr. Anderson remains incapable of irony, of satire, of any studied view of the human comedy.

The trouble with wonder of Mr. Anderson's ingenuous variety is that it is unselective as a principle of literary composition. It gives rise to the shapelessness of his novels, in which the moments of intensified awareness seem no more important to the author than the routine passages. . . . In the short story, however, wonder does better as a touchstone. Some of the stories in ***Death in the Woods*** are in the old Anderson tradition, excellent because the author has hit upon spurts of heightened consciousness that are universally experienced. Some achieve no more than a sort of maundering poetry. And some are downright bad, built out of human circumstances that do not call for any quality of wonder. In the poorer items, Mr. Anderson himself seems trying to be impressed against his own better judgment. This attempt gives rise to an oracular style, with everything unduly emphasized by paragraphing of the single sentence variety—for all the world as if Mr. Anderson were a Scripps-Howard editorial writer taking Blanche Colton Williams's course in the art of the short story.

"Death in the Woods," the best of the present collection, is lifted with but few changes from one of the earlier Anderson books, *Tar: A Midwest Childhood*. It is a simple account of an old woman's death, propped up against a tree in winter, with her dogs running in circles about her, waiting for her to die before they attack the pack in which she has soupbones and liver. The importance of the story derives from the child's point of view from which it is told; like Elizabeth Roberts's "Death at Bearwallow," it emphasizes the mystery which surrounds one's first experience of any of the major emotional encounters. **"The Return"** might be considered the epilogue to an unwritten novel of which **"Departure,"** the last story of ***Winesburg, Ohio,*** is the prologue. It is fully as good as the earlier story. It presents Mr. Anderson standing in wonder before a visit to childhood scenes, a visit in which nothing, of course, happens as planned in the imagination beforehand. Other stories, **"The Fight," "Like a Queen,"** and **"Another Wife,"** are all up to the old Anderson level. As for the rest of the lot, they range from lugubrious Steinesque to mere padded observations. Yet, despite the mixture of poor stuff with the first-rate, it is good to have Mr. Anderson telling stories again.

John Chamberlain, "A Story Teller Returns," in The Saturday Review of Literature, *Vol. IX, No. 41, April 29, 1933, p. 561.*

WILLIAM TROY (essay date 1933)

[*An American critic, Troy is noted for his critiques of works by such literary figures as James Joyce, Henry James, and Gertrude Stein. Underrated in his time, Troy received his greatest recognition for his posthumously published* Selected Essays *(1968). In the following excerpt, he offers a negative review of* Death in the Woods.]

With two important exceptions the stories in this volume [***Death in the Woods***] represent a very definite retrogression on the part of an American writer from whose work one has become accustomed to receive an impression of constant growth and development. Neither the sentimental phallicism of *Perhaps Women* nor the timorous overtones of social consciousness of the more recent *Beyond Desire* are present in this book. The crystallization of one or the other of these attitudes that one had half expected does not take place. Nor is it possible to discover any still newer attitude that is offered in their stead. It is as if Mr. Anderson has at last given up the search for some principle of meaning in life that might give order and scale to his writing. Like one of his characters, the professor who is trying to write a book on values, he seems to have decided, "There are only floods, one flood following another." In a word, Mr. Anderson has relaxed into his old and well-known habit of "groping." Such stories as **"The Return"** and **"The Lost Novel"** mark a return to the thinness of characterization and detail, the diffuse lyricism that we associate with his very earliest work. There is the same monotonous insistence on the inarticulateness of life, the mysterious complexity of even the most ordinary human existences. "There you are. That is all. Life is more like that than people suppose. Little old fragmentary ends of things. That is about all we get.'' If we cannot respond to this philosophy with the same sympathy that we did fifteen or even ten years ago, Mr. Anderson himself is to blame. He has played too long on such a fragile theme. And he has at times played on it so well that nothing but his best will satisfy us. Only two of the stories in this collection can compare with the best in ***Winesburg*** and ***The Triumph of the Egg***.

The title story is marred by the usual self-consciousness of Mr. Anderson when he feels himself in the presence of a character who is somehow exceptional or ''significant.'' We are reminded just a little too often that the recollection of the old woman in the tale is to the author like ''music heard from far off.'' The objective circumstances of her life are what make her come alive; and the reader's only regret is that these are not ''rendered,'' to use Henry James's favorite word, with sufficient directness and completeness. Especially is this true for the scene in which the woman's dead body is set upon by the hungry dogs in the woods. But despite this failure to make the most of its possibilities the story is effectively moving. ''The woman who died was one destined to feed animal life'' is the formula that Mr. Anderson works out for his character; and because he is able to discover so definite a formula the story has more significance than any other in the volume. **''Brother Death,''** which is interesting for a number of different reasons, succeeds chiefly by virtue of the tree symbol, which binds it together with a greater artistic unity than is common in Anderson's work. The distinct superiority of these two tales over the others in the collection merely serves to confirm the feeling that Mr. Anderson is a writer whose triumphs are accidental, whose command over his material is most precarious, and whose greatest need is for some established point of view that will enable him to develop his medium with more certainty.

William Troy, ''Fragmentary Ends,'' in The Nation, *New York, Vol. CXXXVI, No. 3539, May 3, 1933, p. 508.*

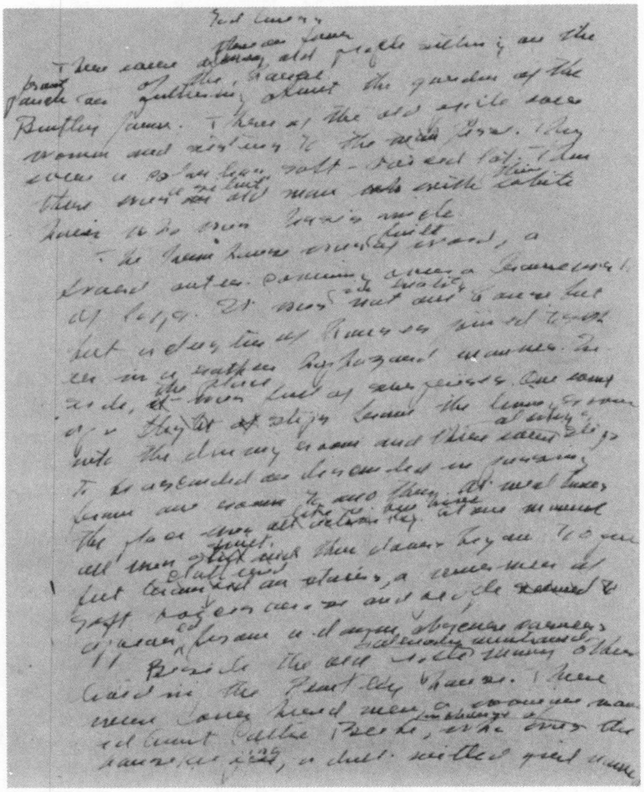

Manuscript page from the Winesburg *story ''Godliness.'' H. L. Mencken once wrote to Anderson: ''Your handwriting is improving. I can now read 40% of it.'' Reproduced by permission of Harold Ober Associates and Sherwood Anderson Papers, The Newberry Library.*

THEODORE DREISER (essay date 1941)

[*Considered among America's foremost novelists, Dreiser was one of the principal exponents of literary Naturalism. He is known primarily for his novels* Sister Carrie *(1901),* An American Tragedy *(1926), and the Frank Cowperwood trilogy (1912-47). In each of these, the author combined his vision of life as a meaningless series of chemical reactions and animal impulses with a sense of sentimentality and pity for humanity's lot. Dreiser and Anderson were longtime friends and admirers of each other's work. Dreiser sent letters of glowing praise to Anderson, once writing, ''I think of many things you have written because I love to think of them—or to put it correctly they compel my temperament to react to them. I think you have* [a] *kindly and a beautiful mind.'' The following excerpt is from Dreiser's tribute to Anderson, which was read at his funeral and published in a special Anderson issue of* Story *magazine in 1941.*]

Anderson, his life and his writings, epitomize for me the pilgrimage of a poet and dreamer across this limited stage called Life, whose reactions to the mystery of our being and doings here (our will-less and so wholly automatic responses to our environing forces) involved tenderness, love and beauty, delight in the strangeness of our will-less reactions as well as pity, sympathy and love for all things both great and small. Whenever I think of him I think of that wondrous line out of ''The Ancient Mariner''—''He prayeth best who lovest best all things both great and small.'' And so sometimes the things he wrote, as well as the not too many things he said to me personally, had the value of a poetic prayer for the happiness and the well being of everything and everybody—as well as the well-outcoming of everything guided as each thing plainly is by an enormous wisdom—if seemingly not always imbued with mercy—that none-the-less ''passeth all understanding.'' He seemed to me to accept in humbleness, as well as in and of necessity in nature, Christ's dictums ''The rain falleth on the just and unjust.'' Also that we are to ''Take no thought for your life, what ye shall eat, or what ye shall drink: nor yet for your body, what ye shall put on. Is not the life more than meat, and the body than raiment?''

As I see him now there was something Biblical and prophetic about him. Through all his days he appears to have been wandering here and there, looking, thinking, wondering. And the things he brought back from the fields of life! *Dark Laughter*! *Many Marriages*! ***The Triumph of the Egg***! *Midwestern Chants*! **Winesburg**!—in which is that beautiful commentary on the strain of life on some temperaments called **''Hands''**! It is to me so truly beautiful, understanding and loving, and weeping, almost, for the suffering of others. (pp. 1-2)

Theodore Dreiser, ''Sherwood Anderson,'' in Homage to Sherwood Anderson: 1876-1941, *edited by Paul P. Appel, Paul P. Appel, Publisher, 1970, pp. 1-2.*

WALDO FRANK (essay date 1941)

[*Frank was an American novelist and critic who was best known as an interpreter of contemporary civilization, particularly that of Latin America. A socialist and supporter of various radical groups in the United States, he was a founding editor of* Seven Arts *(1916-17), a leftist, avant-garde magazine of literature and opinion. He was one of the writers who encouraged Anderson during the latter's early years as a struggling author. In 1916, Frank wrote in* Seven Arts *what has come to be recognized as the first significant appraisal of Anderson's talent, "Emerging Greatness," an essay on the novel* Windy McPherson's Son. *The following year, Frank accepted several of the Winesburg stories for his periodical. The following excerpt is from an essay, originally published in 1941, that is considered one of the most important studies of* Winesburg, Ohio. *Here Frank favorably reappraises the book twenty-five years after first reading it.*]

Sherwood Anderson wrote his most famous book about a generation ago; and it reveals a Mid-American world that already then was a generation dead. A full half century therefore divides the mind that reads the book today from the life it portrays. Since, from this adequate perspective, the work stands firm in its form, true in its livingness, strong in its light upon our present, it is clear that ***Winesburg, Ohio*** is a classic. (p. 41)

It is a dangerous hazard to re-read, after twenty-five years, a book involved in the dreams and fervors of one's youth; it is a blessing when that book stands forth from the test a rediscovery . . . indeed a prophecy and an illumination.

The first impressive realization that came to me with my rereading was that ***Winesburg, Ohio*** has form. The book as a whole has form; and most of the stories have form: the work is an integral creation. The form is lyrical. It is not related, even remotely, to the aesthetic of Chekhov; nor to that of Balzac, Flaubert, Maupassant, Tolstoy, Melville. These masters of the short story used the narrative or dramatic art: a linear progression rising to a peak or an immediate complex of character-forces impinging upon each other in a certain action that fulfilled them and rounded the story. For an analogy to the aesthetic of the Winesburg tales, one must go to music, perhaps to the songs that Schubert featly wove from old refrains; or to the lyric art of the Old Testament psalmists and prophets in whom the literary medium was so allied to music that their texts have always been sung in the synagogues. The ***Winesburg, Ohio*** design is quite uniform: a theme-statement of a character with his mood, followed by a recounting of actions that are merely variations on the theme. These variations make incarnate what has already been revealed to the reader; they weave the theme into life by the always subordinate confrontation of other characters (usually one) and by an evocation of landscape and village. In some of the tales, there is a secondary theme-statement followed by other variations. In a few, straight narrative is attempted; and these are the least successful.

This lyric, musical form has significance, and the tales' contents make it clear. But it is important, first, to note that the cant judgment of Sherwood Anderson as a naive, almost illiterate storyteller (a judgment which he himself encouraged with a good deal of nonsense about his literary innocence) is false. The substance of ***Winesburg, Ohio*** is impressive, is alive, because it has been superbly *formed*. There are occasional superficial carelessnesses of language; on the whole, the prose is perfect in its selective economy and in its melodious flow; the choice of details is stript, strong, sure; the movement is an unswerving musical fulfillment of the already stated theme. Like Schubert, and like the Old Testament storytellers, the author of ***Winesburg, Ohio*** comes at the end of a psychological process; is a man with an inherited culture and a deeply assimilated skill. He is a type of the achieved artist.

The theme of the tales taken as a whole follows the same pattern as the individual "chapters"—although less precisely. **"Hands,"** the first chapter, tells of Adolph Myers, alias Wing Biddlebaum, the unfortunate schoolteacher with sensitive, wandering, caressing hands, who gets into trouble because his loving touch upon his pupils is misinterepreted by a half-wit boy and the crude obscene men of the town. Because the tale is concretely, poetically realized, its symbolism is true; and because this symbolism is not intellectualized, not schematized, it would be false to tear it from its flesh and blood texture. Suffice it to say that the story suggests the tragic ambivalence of hands, which is the fate of all the characters of Winesburg. Hands, at the turn of the century, were making machines, making all sorts of things ("the thing is in the saddle";), making the world that was unmaking the tender, sensitive, intimate lives of the folk in their villages and farms. Hands are made for loving; but hands making mechanical things grow callous, preoccupied . . . fail at love. The second story is a straight variant of the theme: here, it is not the hand, the maker, that goes wrong; it is *thought,* which Doctor Reefy turns into written words—ineffectual scraps of wisdom jotted down, that become paper pills cluttering his pocket. The third chapter, **"Mother,"** completes the theme-statement. Woman, the creator, the lover: the principle incarnate in Wing Biddlebaum's hands and in Doctor Reefy's thoughts, states the theme centrally. The form of the mother, [frustrated], lonely, as last desperate, pervades the variations that make the rest of the book: a continuity of variation swelling, swirling into the corners and crannies of the village life; and at length closing in the mother's death, in the loss forever of the $800 which Elizabeth Willard had kept for twenty years to give her son his start away from Winesburg, and in the son's wistful departure. "He thought of little things—" as the train pulled out; they have become motes and beams carrying a distant sun to the reader.

I have spoken of suggested symbols. Suggestion, if you will *indirection,* is the quality of this lyric form; and no more *direct* expression could have been devised for a book which so precisely portrays a world avid for the expression of eternal truths and forced, by the decay of its old cultural foundation, to seek truth anarchically, hopelessly, indirectly.

It has become a critical commonplace that Winesburg faithfully portrays the midwest village of two thousand souls during the post-civil war pre-motor age. Let us look. . . . No even bearably married couple is to be found in Winesburg; there are few marriages in the book, and these without exception are described as the harnessing together of strangers by the bondage of sex or a morality hostile to the spirit. There is no communion with children. There is no fulfilled sex life, sex being an obsession, a frustration and a trap. There is no normal sociability between men and women: souls lonely as carnivorae for once in their lives burst into melodic plaint to one another, and lapse into solipsistic silence. There is indeed more muttering than talk. There is no congregated worship, and no strength to organized religion except in the sense of a strong barrier; as in the piteous tales of the Reverend Hartman who sins by knocking a piece from his stained-glass church window (part of the figure of Christ) in order to gaze at the body of Belle Robinson in bed. There is almost no joy, beyond the momentary joy of contemplating nature. And the most mature of the characters, Doctor Reefy, Seth Richmond, Elizabeth Willard, the Rev. Hartman, et al., do not evolve beyond a sharp negation of the things that *are,* in favor of a nebulous dream of "life."

Now, these omissions are purposive; and as aesthetically true as they are factually false. The author's art, perhaps unconsciously to himself, traces the frontier of emotional and spiritual action which, in that deliquescence of an agrarian culture which was rotten long ere it was ripe, was a line of *decay*, a domain of deprivation. In those very institutions and traditions which had been the base of the world's health, Winesburg was found wanting.

The positive substance of the book is the solitariness and struggle of the soul which has lost its ancestral props: the energy of the book is the release from these old forms into a subliminal search for new ones. The farms of Robert Frost's *North of Boston* are also peopled by broken, lonely lives; but their despair is hard, heroic. The folk of Winesburg are soft in a tenderness, in a nebulous searchfulness, that have gone farther in decay than the still standing families and churches of Frost's New England. In all the book, only irony—the author's irony—is hard.

This trait of Sherwood Anderson has been too little recognized. Consider the acrid irony in **"Nobody Knows,"** where sex fulfillment ends in the boy's cowardly sigh of relief that "she hasn't got anything on me. Nobody knows"; in **"An Awakening,"** that turns a moment of mystical insight into a brutal, humiliating sexual frustration; in **"The Untold Lie"** (one of the great stories of the world); in the chapters of Jesse Bentley, "the man of God" who is transformed by the sling of his grandchild, David, into a clumsy, puny, ineffectual Goliath. This hardness of irony in the author points to his spiritual transcendence over his subjects. Anderson has inherited intact a strength long since vaporized in Winesburg—and yet the heritage of Winesburg. His sureness of vision and of grasp enable him to incarnate in a form very precise the inchoate emotions of his people. To portray the deliquescence of America's agrarian culture beneath the impact of the untamed machine age required a man spiritually advanced beyond that culture's death. This is a law of art (and of ethic) ignored by the hardboiled Hemingway school, who depict their gangsters *on the level of the gangsters*.

Sherwood Anderson liked to think of himself as a primitive or neo-primitive artist; as a naive unlettered storyteller. The truth is, that he belonged at the end of a cultural process, and shares the technical perfection which, within the limits of the culture's forms, only the terminal man achieves. One book was the pabulum of these people: the Bible. And a Testamental accent and vision modulate every page of Sherwood Anderson's great story. Moreover, the nebulosity of these poor souls' search is an end, a chaos *after* a world. That world was already drooping when it crossed the ocean; it had been, in England, a world of revealed religion and sacramental marriage, of the May dance and the sense of each man's life as mystery and mission. It lives in the past of Winesburg; it has become a beat and a refrain in the blood. In the actual experience of these men and women, it is a recidivism, a lapse away into organic echoes. Thus, of revealed religion and sacramental marriage, of the structures of social and personal responsibilities, nothing remains on the record but the memory and the dynamic yearning. Life has become a Prompter with the text of the dialogue and even the stage missing.

In sum, Sherwood Anderson is a mature voice singing a culture at its close; singing it with the technical skill of, literally, the *past master*. What in Winesburg, Ohio, of the year 1900 was authentic? The old strong concept of marriage? No: only the inherited knowledge that the embrace of man and woman must create a sacrament again. The old dogmas of the churches? No: only the inherited knowledge that there is God—even in sin, there is God; and that for want of a living Body formed of this new world, God is revealed in animistic gods of the corn, and even in the phallus. Thus the artist, distilling the eternal from the old doomed ways, becomes the prophet.

Sherwood Anderson's place at the end of a cultural cycle finds eloquent corroboration in the quality of his immediate imitators and disciples. Ernest Hemingway turned the nebulous seeking softness of the master's characters into a hardshell bravado. Winesburg's men and women are old souls, inheritors of a great Christian culture who have been abandoned and doomed to a progressive emptiness by the invasion of the unmastered Machine. (This is a process now at its nadir in the world.) In Anderson, however, these lives are transfigured by a mature and virile artist who is able to crystallize what is eternal in them as an aesthetic value. (pp. 42-7)

The perfect readability of this book within our agonizing world proves the potential that lived—needing only to be transfigured—within a world already gone when ***Winesburg, Ohio*** was written. Here are intrinsically great stories: as great as any in our language. The author, intellectually bound to the decadence of the agrarian age that he revealed, proves in himself a vital spirit, a creative promise that is ours. The village of these queer men beating the innocent bystander to prove they are not queer, of these sex-starved women running naked through the summer rain, was after all pregnant of the Great Tradition. The tender and humbly precise artist who painted these portraits bespoke the Tradition's still unimagined future. (p. 47)

Waldo Frank, "'Winesburg, Ohio'," in Homage to Sherwood Anderson: 1876-1941, *edited by Paul P. Appel, Paul P. Appel, Publisher, 1970, pp. 41-7.*

HENRY MILLER (essay date 1941)

[*An American novelist, essayist, and critic, Miller was one of the most controversial authors of the twentieth century. The ribaldry and eroticism of such works as his* Tropic of Cancer *(1935) and* Tropic of Capricorn *(1939) made him perhaps the most censored major writer of all time. He was one of the American writers whose works, according to Malcolm Cowley, owe "an unmistakable debt" to Anderson. In the following excerpt from an essay originally published in 1941 in* Story *magazine, Miller praises Anderson's warmth and authenticity as a storyteller.*]

What impressed me about Anderson was his genius for seizing on the trivial and making it important and universal. A story like **"The Triumph of the Egg"** is a classic. (In one of his latest books, *Kit Brandon*, there is another magnificent achievement, a little story in itself about the man who became a horse, who got down on all fours and *was* a horse for ten or fifteen minutes—such a horse as was never seen on land or sea or in the sky or in the myth.) I was extremely happy to be able to tell Anderson how much I enjoyed that book, ***The Triumph of the Egg***. It fell into my hands at a time when, in complete despair over my inability to say what I wanted to say, I was about to give up. That book encouraged me. All Anderson's books did. (Up to *Dark Laughter*, when I practically ceased reading American authors.) He seemed to have the real, the authentic American voice. The style was as free and natural, I thought then, as the glass of ice water which stands on every table in every home and restaurant. Later I learned that it was not so free and natural, that it had been acquired through long apprenticeship.

In Anderson, when all is said and done, it is the strong human quality which draws one to him and leads one to prefer him sometimes to those who are undeniably superior to him as artists. (pp. 114-15)

Henry Miller, "The Storyteller," in Homage to Sherwood Anderson: 1876-1941, *edited by Paul P. Appel, Paul P. Appel, Publisher, 1970, pp. 111-18.*

LIONEL TRILLING (essay date 1947)

[A respected American critic and literary historian, Trilling was also an essayist, editor, novelist, and short story writer. In the following excerpt from a seminal negative appraisal of Anderson, Trilling identifies and discusses the flaws that make Anderson's work, in his opinion, primarily the reading material of adolescents. This essay, originally written in 1941, was expanded in 1947 for publication in the New York Times Book Review.*]*

Anderson's greatest influence was probably upon those who read him in adolescence, the age when we find the books we give up but do not get over. And it now needs a little fortitude to pick up again, as many must have done upon the news of his death, the one book of his we are all sure to have read, for ***Winesburg, Ohio*** is not just a book, it is a personal souvenir. It is commonly owned in the Modern Library edition, very likely in the most primitive format of that series, even before it was tricked out with its vulgar little ballet-Prometheus; and the brown oilcloth binding, the coarse paper, the bold type crooked on the page, are dreadfully evocative. Even the introduction by Ernest Boyd [see Additional Bibliography] is rank with the odor of the past, of the day when criticism existed in heroic practical simplicity, when it was all truth against hypocrisy, idealism against philistinism, and the opposite of "romanticism" was not "classicism" but "realism," which—it now seems odd—negated both. As for the Winesburg stories themselves, they are as dangerous to read again, as paining and as puzzling, as if they were old letters we had written or received.

It is not surprising that Anderson should have made his strongest appeal, although by no means his only one, to adolescents. For one thing, he wrote of young people with a special tenderness; one of his best-known stories is called **"I Want to Know Why":** it is the great adolescent question, and the world Anderson saw is essentially, and even when it is inhabited by adults, the world of the sensitive young person. It is a world that does not "understand," a world of solitude, of running away from home, of present dullness and far-off joy and eventual fulfillment; it is a world seen as suffused by one's own personality and yet—and therefore—felt as indifferent to one's own personality. And Anderson used what seems to a young person the very language to penetrate to the heart of the world's mystery, what with its rural or primeval willingness to say things thrice over, its reiterated "Well . . ." which suggests the groping of boyhood, its "Eh?" which implies the inward-turning wisdom of old age.

Most of us will feel now that this world of Anderson's is a pretty inadequate representation of reality and probably always was. But we cannot be sure that it was not a necessary event in our history, like adolescence itself; and no one has the adolescence he would have liked to have had. But an adolescence must not continue beyond its natural term, and as we read through Anderson's canon what exasperates us is his stubborn, satisfied continuance in his earliest attitudes. (pp. 23-4)

Anderson is connected with the tradition of the men who maintain a standing quarrel with respectable society and have a perpetual bone to pick with the rational intellect. It is a very old tradition, for the Essenes, the early Franciscans, as well as the early Hasidim, may be said to belong to it. In modern times it has been continued by Blake and Whitman and D. H. Lawrence. Those who belong to the tradition usually do something more about the wrong way the world goes than merely to denounce it—they *act out* their denunciations and assume a role and a way of life. Typically they take up their packs and leave the doomed respectable city, just as Anderson did. But Anderson lacked what his spiritual colleagues have always notably had. We may call it *mind,* but *energy* and *spiritedness,* in their relation to mind, will serve just as well. Anderson never understood that the moment of enlightenment and conversion—the walking out—cannot be merely celebrated but must be developed, so that what begins as an act of will grows to be an act of intelligence. The men of the anti-rationalist tradition mock the mind's pretensions and denounce its restrictiveness; but they are themselves the agents of the most powerful thought. They do not of course really reject mind at all, but only mind as it is conceived by respectable society. "I learned the Torah from all the limbs of my teacher," said one of the Hasidim. They think with their sensations, their emotions, and, some of them, with their sex. While denouncing intellect, they shine forth in a mental blaze of energy which manifests itself in syntax, epigram, and true discovery.

Anderson is not like them in this regard. He did not become a "wise" man. He did not have the gift of being able to throw out a sentence or a metaphor which suddenly illuminates some dark corner of life—his role implied that he should be full of "sayings" and specific insights, yet he never was. But in the preface to ***Winesburg, Ohio*** he utters one of the few really "wise" things in his work, and, by a kind of irony, it explains something of his own inadequacy. The preface consists of a little story about an old man who is writing what he calls "The Book of the Grotesque." This is the old man's ruling idea:

> That in the beginning when the world was young there were a great many thoughts but no such thing as a truth. Man made the truths himself and each truth was a composite of a great many vague thoughts. All about in the world were truths and they were all beautiful.
>
> The old man listed hundreds of the truths in his book. I will not try to tell you all of them. There was the truth of virginity and the truth of passion, the truth of wealth and of poverty, of thrift and of profligacy, of carelessness and abandon. Hundreds and hundreds were the truths and they were all beautiful.
>
> And then the people came along. Each as he appeared snatched up one of the truths and some who were quite strong snatched up a dozen of them.
>
> It was the truths that made the people grotesques. The old man had quite an elaborate theory concerning the matter. It was his notion that the moment one of the people took one of the truths to himself, called it his truth, and tried to live his life by it, he became a grotesque and the truth he embraced became a falsehood.

Anderson snatched but a single one of the truths and it made him, in his own gentle and affectionate meaning of the word, a "grotesque"; eventually the truth itself became a kind of falsehood. It was the truth—or perhaps we must call it a simple complex of truths—of love-passion-freedom, and it was made up of these "vague thoughts": that each individual is a precious secret essence, often discordant with all other essences; that society, and more particularly the industrial society, threatens these essences; that the old good values of life have been destroyed by the industrial dispensation; that people have been cut off from each other and even from themselves. That these thoughts make a truth is certain; and its importance is equally certain. In what way could it have become a falsehood and its possessor a "grotesque"?

The nature of the falsehood seems to lie in this—that Anderson's affirmation of life by love, passion, and freedom had, paradoxically enough, the effect of quite negating life, making it gray, empty, and devoid of meaning. We are quite used to hearing that this is what excessive intellection can do; we are not so often warned that emotion, if it is of a certain kind, can be similarly destructive. Yet when feeling is understood as an answer, a therapeutic, when it becomes a sort of critical tool and is conceived of as excluding other activities of life, it can indeed make the world abstract and empty. Love and passion, when considered as they are by Anderson as a means of attack upon the order of the respectable world, can contrive a world which is actually without love and passion and not worth being "free" in.

In Anderson's world there are many emotions, or rather many instances of a few emotions, but there are very few sights, sounds, and smells, very little of the stuff of actuality. The very things to which he gives moral value because they are living and real and opposed in their organic nature to the insensate abstractness of an industrial culture become, as he writes about them, themselves abstract and without life. His praise of the racehorses he said he loved gives us no sense of a horse; his Mississippi does not flow; his tall corn grows out of the soil of his dominating subjectivity. The beautiful organic things of the world are made to be admirable not for themselves but only for their moral superiority to men and machines. There are many similarities of theme between Anderson and D. H. Lawrence, but Lawrence's far stronger and more sensitive mind kept his faculty of vision fresh and true; Lawrence had eyes for the substantial and even at his most doctrinaire he knew the world of appearance.

And just as there is no real sensory experience in Anderson's writing, there is also no real social experience. His people do not really go to church or vote or work for money, although it is often said of them that they do these things. In his desire for better social relationships Anderson could never quite see the social relationships that do in fact exist, however inadequate they may be. He often spoke, for example, of unhappy, desperate marriages and seemed to suggest that they ought to be quickly dissolved, but he never understood that marriages are often unsatisfactory for the very reasons that make it impossible to dissolve them.

His people have passion without body, and sexuality without gaiety and joy, although it is often through sex that they are supposed to find their salvation. John Jay Chapman said of Emerson that, great as he was, a visitor from Mars would learn less about life on earth from him than from Italian opera, for the opera at least suggested that there were two sexes. When Anderson was at the height of his reputation, it seemed that his report on the existence of two sexes was the great thing about him, the thing that made his work an advance over the literature of New England. But although the visitor from Mars might be instructed by Anderson in the mere fact of bisexuality, he would still be advised to go to the Italian opera if he seeks fuller information. For from the opera, as never from Anderson, he will acquire some of the knowledge which is normally in the possession of natives of the planet, such as that sex has certain manifestations which are socially quite complex, that it is involved with religion, politics, and the fate of nations, above all that it is frequently marked by the liveliest sort of energy.

In their speech his people have not only no wit, but no idiom. To say that they are not "real" would be to introduce all sorts of useless quibbles about the art of character creation; they are simply not *there*. This is not a failure of art; rather, it would seem to have been part of Anderson's intention that they should be not there. His narrative prose is contrived to that end; it is not really a colloquial idiom, although it has certain colloquial tricks; it approaches in effect the inadequate use of a foreign language; old slang persists in it and elegant archaisms are consciously used, so that people are constantly having the "fantods," girls are frequently referred to as "maidens," and things are "like unto" other things. These mannerisms, although they remind us of some of Dreiser's, are not the result, as Dreiser's are, of an effort to be literary and impressive. Anderson's prose has a purpose to which these mannerisms are essential—it has the intention of making us doubt our familiarity with our own world, and not, we must note, in order to make things fresher for us but only in order to make them seem puzzling to us and remote from us. When a man whose name we know is frequently referred to as "the plowmaker," when we hear again and again of "a kind of candy called Milky Way" long after we have learned, if we did not already know, that Milky Way is a candy, when we are told of someone that "He became a radical. He had radical thoughts," it becomes clear that we are being asked by this false naïveté to give up our usual and on the whole useful conceptual grasp of the world we get around in.

Anderson liked to catch people with their single human secret, their essence, but the more he looks for their essence the more his characters vanish into the vast limbo of meaningless life, the less they are human beings. . . . The more Anderson says about people, the less alive they become—and the less lovable. Is it strange that, with all Anderson's expressed affection for them, we ourselves can never love the people he writes about? But of course we do not love people for their essence or their souls, but for their having a certain body, or wit, or idiom, certain specific relationships with things and other people, and for a dependable continuity of existence: we love them for being there.

We can even for a moment entertain the thought that Anderson himself did not love his characters, else he would not have so thoroughly robbed them of substance and hustled them so quickly off the stage after their small essential moments of crisis. Anderson's love, however, was real enough; it is only that he loves under the aspect of his "truth"; it is love indeed but love become wholly abstract. Another way of putting it is that Anderson sees with the eyes of a religiosity of a very limited sort. (pp. 24-30)

It is easy enough to understand this crude mysticism as a protest against philosophical and moral materialism; easy enough, too, to forgive it, even when, as in Anderson, the second births and the large revelations seem often to point only to the bosom of a solemn bohemia, and almost always to a lowering rather than a heightening of energy. We forgive it because some part of the blame for its crudity must be borne by the culture of the time. . . . His real heroes were the simple and unassuming, a few anonymous Negroes, a few craftsmen, for he gave to the idea of craftsmanship a value beyond the value which it actually does have—it is this as much as anything else that reminds us of Hemingway's relation to Anderson—and a few racing drivers of whom Pop Geers was chief. It is a charming hero worship, but it does not make an adequate antagonism to the culture which Anderson opposed, and in order to make it compelling and effective Anderson reinforced it with what is in effect the high language of religion, speaking of salvation, of the voice that will not be denied, of dropping the heavy burden of this world.

The salvation that Anderson was talking about was no doubt a real salvation, but it was small, and he used for it the language of the most strenuous religious experience. He spoke in visions and mysteries and raptures, but what he was speaking about after all was only the salvation of a small legitimate existence, of a quiet place in the sun and moments of leisurely peace, of not being nagged and shrew-ridden, nor deprived of one's due share of affection. What he wanted for himself and others was perhaps no more than what he got in his last years: a home, neighbors, a small daily work to do, and the right to say his say carelessly and loosely and without the sense of being strictly judged. But between this small, good life and the language which he used about it there is a discrepancy which may be thought of as a willful failure of taste, an intended lapse of the sense of how things fit. . . . Certainly the precious essence of personality to which Anderson was so much committed could not be preserved by any of the people or any of the deeds his own books delight in.

But what hostile critics forget about Anderson is that the cultural situation from which his writing sprang was actually much as he described it. Anderson's truth may have become a falsehood in his hands by reason of limitations in himself or in the tradition of easy populism he chose as his own, but one has only to take it out of his hands to see again that it is indeed a truth. The small legitimate existence, so necessary for the majority of men to achieve, is in our age so very hard, so nearly impossible, for them to achieve. The language Anderson used was certainly not commensurate with the traditional value which literature gives to the things he wanted, but it is not incommensurate with the modern difficulty of attaining these things. And it is his unending consciousness of this difficulty that constitutes for me the residue of admiration for him that I find I still have. (pp. 30-2)

Lionel Trilling, "Sherwood Anderson," in his The Liberal Imagination: Essays on Literature and Society, *1950. Reprint by Harcourt Brace Jovanovich, 1979, pp. 21-32.*

IRVING HOWE (essay date 1951)

[*A longtime editor of the leftist magazine* Dissent *and a regular contributor to the* New Republic, *Howe is a highly respected American literary critic and social historian. In the following excerpt from his critical biography* Sherwood Anderson, *Howe contrasts the stories he deems Anderson's best, which belong primarily to the "oral" or storytelling tradition, with those he considers less successful, which are obviously "written."*]

Although there is a gap of more than a decade between Anderson's first two volumes of stories and his last one, chronology is of slight consequence to a study of his career as a story writer. ***Death in the Woods,*** which appeared in 1933, contains a few stories quite different in style and subject matter from those in the earlier books, but except for one or two sketches of Southern hillsmen none of these later innovations is particularly important. The one significant line of division in his stories cuts equally through all three books.

Some eight or ten of Anderson's stories, by far the best he ever wrote, can be considered a coherent group. Such stories as **"I Want to Know Why," "The Egg," "Death in the Woods," "I'm a Fool," "The Man Who Became a Woman,"** and to a lesser extent **"The Corn Planting," "A Meeting South,"** and **"Brother Death"** are similar in having as their structural base an oral narration, as their tone a slightly bewildered tenderness, and as their subject matter elemental crises in the lives of simple townspeople. In these stories the central figure is often an "I" who stands at the rim of the action, sometimes looking back to his boyhood and remembering an incident he now realizes to have been crucial to his life, a moment in which he took one of those painful leaps that climax the process of growth. The narrator tells his story in a manner that is an implicit rejection of literary naturalism: he cannot content himself with a catalogue of behavior for he realizes that in the word "behavior" are coiled the greatest enigmas; he stresses the strangeness of his remembered experience because he feels that the ordinary can best be perceived through the intense light cast by the strange; and though he now claims a partial understanding of the incident that persists in his memory, that understanding is itself a humility before the general problem of human experience. Life, as he conceives it, is buried in marshes of sloth and apathy and only in a rare emergence into awareness does one find its epiphany, the *true moment*.

Anderson's narrator senses that in the seemingly simple act of telling his story he enters into a highly complex relation with his audience and that, as one able to shape both the materials of his narrative and the responses of his listeners, he is momentarily in a position of great power. The atmosphere of oral narration, deliberately created by Anderson, is the setting of his best stories, which can be read not merely as imaginative versions of human experience but as renderings of a pervasive pattern of story-telling. Part of the craft of oral narration consists in the narrator's working not only for the usual kinds of interest and suspense, but also to produce in his listeners a vicarious responsibility for the successful completion of the story. The audience quickly senses this relationship and, if the narrator is at all skilled, becomes emotionally involved with his struggle to tell his story almost as much as with the story itself.

The narrator is seen weighing his recollection in his mind, perplexed by the course it has taken and wondering whether it is merely of private significance or of larger emblematic value. As he turns to the memory that is his burden, he seems doubtful that he will be able to extract it from the chaos of the past and give it form. He becomes aware, as well, of the temptations that follow from his power as story teller, but it is a particular virtue of Anderson's short fictions that his narrator does not try to dominate or assert superiority over his audience. Respecting the community of narrator and listener, or writer and reader, Anderson establishes as his controlling point of view the voice of a hesitant human being, one who is anything but omniscient.

In choosing to simulate oral narrative Anderson was aware of the traditional resources he could thereby tap. Sensing that story-telling had once been a ceremony in which the listeners expected the narrator thoroughly to exploit his craft and thus fulfill his communal role, Anderson quite cannily tried to re-establish something of this atmosphere of ritual in his stories. He hoped to lend the act of story-telling a synoptic significance it could not otherwise have, to restore to the story teller a fraction of his role as tribal spokesman or, at least, public figure. But he also sensed, as had Conrad before him, that the most effective story teller is one who is felt to be not merely skillful but also deeply involved in the outcome of his own story. The Andersonian narrator therefore seeks to persuade his audience that the disburdening of his mind has a purpose other than the stimulation of its pleasure; he hints that for him, and perhaps through him for the audience, the recollection of the past provides an occasion for a symbolic cleansing and relief. And, in more private terms, he would certainly have agreed with D. H. Lawrence that "One sheds one's sickness in books—repeats and presents again one's emotions to be master of them."

In those of his stories that follow the oral narrative pattern, Anderson often resorts to a bold sort of artlessness. The narrator of **"The Egg,"** for example, occasionally confesses his perplexity before the events he recalls. Such an intrusion of comment into a narrative is considered a heresy, or at least a fallacy, by certain severe critics; and, indeed, by derailing the story from its guiding point of view an intrusion can immediately destroy every shred of verisimilitude. But in those of Anderson's stories that live, artlessness is usually the veil of conscious craft, and the narrator's intrusion, precisely because it *is* the narrator's and not Anderson's, becomes an integral part of the story. Even while wandering from his narrative line, the oral story teller will drive his apparent divagations toward his climax—and this is exactly the strategy Anderson employs.

It is interesting that the untutored listener will often have a greater regard for this element of narrative contrivance than the sophisticated reader who has been educated to expect "naturalness" in art. The untutored listener realizes that he is supposed to discount, though not disregard, the narrator's claim to be baffled by his own story, for that claim is part of his craft. (This is particularly noticeable in an audience listening to a ghost story.) The listener instinctively senses what the modern critic strives to restate as doctrine: a story, being primarily a story, is not reproducible in any terms but its own, and after the work of exegesis is done there still remains a dimension of unexplicated wonder, to which the story teller will naturally direct his awe and thereby the audience's attention. The narrative device that might be called the protestation to perplexity is a traditional and almost an instinctive way of telling a story, used by Homer and Defoe, Conrad and Twain.

But it is the mark of the good story teller that, even as he confesses to bewilderment about the story's meaning, he is actually presenting the reader with the materials necessary for a total response. Sometimes, as in **"The Egg,"** both Anderson and his narrator seem slightly bewildered by the story's terrible events, but the story is nevertheless there in its entirety and virtual perfection. Sometimes, as in **"Death in the Woods,"** the narrator confesses that "the notes had to be picked up slowly one at a time," but Anderson himself has them all firmly in possession and control. In either instance, all that is important is that the reader not feel that he has been unduly deprived or overloaded; and there is surely no warrant for either feeling with regard to **"The Egg"** or **"Death in the Woods."**

A great deal of cant has been written to the effect that Anderson's stories are "moving" but "formless"—as if a work of art could be moving unless it were formed or form could have any end other than to move. Those who make such remarks are taking form to signify merely the executive plan or technical devices that go into the making of a work of art. But while form includes these it is not reducible to them—unless, of course, one prefers to take the scaffolding as the purpose of the construction. In modern literary discussion form is too often seen as a virtually autonomous and isolable characteristic of a work of art, too often equated with the conscious planning of a James or the elaborate structure of a Proust. And when one tends to think of form largely in terms of the complex and elaborate, one may soon deny it to the simple and primitive. Actually, however, form can be properly apprehended only by relating techniques and strategies to their organic context of emotion and theme, and it is consequently difficult to imagine a work of art with acknowledged authenticity of emotion to be simultaneously lacking in form. Valuable and finely formed fictions, such as some of Anderson's stories and Lawrence's novels, result not merely from the contrivance of skilled intention but also from the flow of released unconscious materials—which is to be taken not as a plea against the use of the blue pencil but as a statement of what it is used on.

In Anderson's best stories, form is achieved through two essential means: tone and perspective. Tone is the outward sign of the emotion resident in a work of art; it is the essence of what a writer communicates, undercutting and simultaneously uniting subject matter and character portrayal. The tone of love, as realized in the best stories and in ***Winesburg, Ohio,*** is the ultimate quality for which Anderson should be read. One reason this tone is so fully present in his best stories is that the structure of the oral narrative, while itself simple, yet permits him a perspective on his material that is both consistent and complex. The consistency is largely derived from his use of the first person as narrator, while the complexity is enforced by an interaction of the four levels of movement in his stories: the events themselves; the feelings of the boy involved in them; the memory of the adult who weighs his involvement in the light of accumulated experience; and the final increment of meaning suggested by the story but beyond the conscious recognition of its narrator. The true action of these stories is thus not the events narrated but the narrator's response, not the perceived object but the perceiving subject. That is why Anderson's stories are so seldom dramatic in the usual sense of the term: their purpose is not to record a resolution of conflict but to refract an enlargement of consciousness.

Somewhat less complex than this abstract model of Anderson's "oral" narratives are his two most popular stories, **"I'm a Fool"** and **"I Want to Know Why."** Though both are written in the first person, their narrators speak, not as men looking back to boyhood, but as boys involved in the immediate present. The result is a rich quality of sensuousness, but also an absence of the irony and complication of vision possible in the stories where the narrator is an adult. (pp. 147-53)

The number of Anderson's stories that can be considered completely first-rate is few, probably no more than half a dozen, and of these almost all come under the heading of what has here been called his "oral" story form. But those of his stories that are first-rate rank only a shade or two below the best of Chekhov and Turgeniev; their life is assured. It is sometimes argued that they are of limited significance because they are restricted to the subject matter of adolescence; but, as should by now be evident, in Anderson's best stories adolescence becomes a commanding vantage point for imaginative statements about all of human life. In any case, even if the objection were accurate it would be of little significance, for only the genuinely mature artist can portray immature life. Anderson's "oral" stories, it is true, do not create the large social world that is often demanded of fiction, and they hardly create the kind of world, as does ***Winesburg, Ohio,*** that is primarily the outer sign of a subjective vision. But this much they do: they impinge irrevocably on the reader's sensibility, enlarging his knowledge of and insight into men—and that is the ultimate test of fiction.

Anderson's remaining stories are, by and large, not so successful as those based on the pattern of oral narrative. When his stories are patently "written," when they do not depend on a central narrator for their movement and meaning, they lack the tonal unity and structural tidiness of the "oral" stories. (The distinction between Anderson's "oral" and "written" stories is not quite the same as that between his stories in the first and third person, for there are several in the third person, such as **"Brother Death"** and **"An Ohio Pagan,"** in which one clearly feels the presence of a narrator's voice.) A few of the stories that do not follow the oral pattern are, of course, successful, notably **"The Untold Lie"** and **"The Return,"** an effective account of a man's disappointing visit to his home town. But in most of the "written" ones there is no sufficiently realized dramatic action or engaging character to replace the oral narrator as a centripetal force. The stories consequently tend to thin into musings or symbolic schemes.

Thematically, this second group of stories is usually concerned with the neurotic costs of the unlived life. In such stories as **"Unlighted Lamps"** and **"The Door of the Trap"** people are locked in their inability to communicate, and experience evades them while they hunger for it. Mary Cochran, who appears in both stories, bears the curse of her father's original failure to warm his marriage with the emotion that "was straining and straining trying to tear itself loose." The theme of unlived life receives two major variations, first as a fear of expressing emotion (**"Unlighted Lamps"**) and then as a hesitation to accept sex from which love might follow (**"The Door of the Trap"**). What the source of this appalling isolation is, Anderson does not feel a need to say; sometimes he hints that it is a heritage of Puritanism or of Midwestern town harshness, but it seems clear that in his deepest feelings he regards isolation as an ineradicable human condition.

Both variations of the theme of unlived life appear in **"Out of Nowhere Into Nothing,"** a long story that is probably his most characteristic expression. Rosalind Westcott returns to her native Iowa town for a brief visit, hoping to talk to her mother and to weigh her life in Chicago, but as she observes the kindly sloth in which her parents live and hears again those terrible "night noises" she had hated as a girl, she realizes that her family cannot help her; she is alone. Like many of Anderson's women, Rosalind Westcott is strong and vital, full of desire for an experience that can engage her emotional capacities. While walking along a railroad track in the corn fields, she meets her next-door neighbor, Melville Stoner, a bachelor who assumes the stance of the reflective observer. She is drawn to him, to his queerness and his trembling wish for companionship. For a moment it seems as if she has found with him "the thing beyond words, beyond passion—the fellowship in living," but Melville Stoner withdraws, pleading that he is too old to abandon his passive role.

Midway, Anderson resorts to long murky flashbacks to Rosalind's Chicago years, and the story slumps badly. But as long as he focuses on Rosalind Westcott and Melville Stoner, who are among his more individualized and memorable characters, the story has a gray, resigned poignancy: the image of these two lonely people walking in the yellow heat of the Iowa corn fields remains fixed in one's mind. The story's greatest strength is as a portrait of male inadequacy, of a good man's refusal to enter the dangerous relationships of love and sex. A woman's desire and a man's loneliness meet, there is a brief parabola of intense feeling and then: parting, each unable to satisfy the other. Of Melville Stoner, Anderson asks, "Did loneliness drive him to the door of insanity, and did he also run through the night seeking some lost, some hidden and half-forgotten loveliness?" Here in one sentence are gathered Anderson's most characteristic and cherished words: *door, run, hidden, half-forgotten, loveliness;* here is his world. The view behind **"Out of Nowhere Into Nothing"** is untenable in itself: to believe life to be a mere occasional explosion in the darkness and to insist so literally on human isolation is a kind of perverse romanticism. But when enough feeling enters into Anderson's fictional rendering of this view, it becomes enlarged and complicated in a way its abstract statement never can be—which is a measure of the artist's triumph.

In most of the stories that deal with the theme of unlived life there is, however, as great an emotional deprivation in their own telling as their characters are supposed to suffer; Anderson allows his dominating notion to weed promiscuously and to choke off the dramatic representation necessary to fiction. When one examines such stories as **"Another Man's Wife," "The Man's Story," "'Unused,'" "The Door of the Trap,"** and **"The New Englander,"** one is struck by how remarkably devoid they are of any account of external experience, how vague in background and hazy in evocation of place and thing. The typical Anderson characters are here all so very familiar: all straining, bursting into nothingness, all lost. Though Anderson's intention is a call to experience, these stories are often evasions of the writer's obligation to focus on particular segments of experience; they create an unprovisioned and unlimned world, a neither-nor area suspended between reality and symbol. Toward his undifferentiated gargoyles Anderson feels and shows the tenderest of loves, but his absorption in a world that is neither descriptively faithful nor symbolically coherent can lead to nothing but a declining sputter of emotion at the end of each story. Having abandoned or rather having never fully accepted realism, he could not find, in these stories, another method for perceiving the objective world. He was trapped in a halfway house: he could neither build realistic structures nor find an adequate means of transcending the need for them.

In this second group of his stories he would often employ elaborate systems of symbolism to sustain his story where neither his action nor his characters could. In **"The New Englander,"** for example, there is an extraordinary skein of symbols but the story itself lacks the conviction of reality; there is nothing viable in relation to which the symbols can act. Anderson is not presenting genuinely conceived characters, he is redecorating the legend of Puritan repression through such symbols as the rock, the trapped rabbit, the imprisoned bird. Here symbols do not enlarge upon reality; they crush it.

Another frequent sign of disintegration in these stories is Anderson's resort to rigid verbal rhythms which he apparently hoped would serve as the controlling and soothing center of his prose. In those pieces where he is most at sea imaginatively, the rhythm is most insistently established, as for example in the story **"'Unused'"**:

> How cruelly the town had patronized May, setting her apart from the others, calling her smart. They had cared about her because of her smartness. She was smart. Her mind was quick, it reached out.

Here the deliberate reiteration of one simple word makes for an increasingly stiff cadence and an irritatingly false simplicity. When Anderson has his writing under control the rhythm is subterranean and bracing; as soon as the relationship between medium and meaning is disturbed, the rhythmic beat becomes a grating staccato responsible for that air of disingenuous folksiness which disfigures so much of his writing.

In Anderson's stories it is thus possible to see most clearly that major contrast in quality which is present in all of his work. The first group of stories, together with ***Winesburg, Ohio,*** is his most valuable achievement, unquestionably an enrichment of the American imagination; the second group is not merely bad in itself but soon comes to seem a portent of the particular kind of badness which is to pervade both Anderson's later novels and much of American fiction in the twentieth century. (pp. 172-77)

Irving Howe, in his Sherwood Anderson, *William Sloane Associates, 1951, 271 p.*

JAMES T. FARRELL (essay date 1954)

[*Farrell was an American novelist, short story writer, and critic who is best known for his grim Studs Lonigan trilogy, a series of novels that describes the life of a lower-class man of Chicago. In the following excerpt, Farrell celebrates Anderson's literary achievement.*]

Sherwood Anderson was one of the most sensitive, significant, and influential American writers in this century. His stories such as **"I Want to Know Why," "I'm a Fool," "Death in the Woods," "The Triumph of an Egg"** [*sic*], and those of ***Winesburg, Ohio*** are among the finest ever written by any American. His use of idiom has a rare flavor and his simple prose rises to a level of poetry. In a few short pages, the hearts and inner lives of his men and women and boys open up for us. He endows his characters with something of his own great creativity. He found a strain of poetry in the experiences of boyhood, and in the spirit of sad, neglected, and queer people. (p. 166)

By and large, much of American humor had been directed against the physically or the socially abnormal, the freak, the odd person, the foreigner, the person who in one way or another deviates from the stereotype of the middle-class regular fellow. But Sherwood Anderson showed most sympathy for those who deviated from the standard stereotypes in one way or another. In fact, he characterized ***Winesburg, Ohio*** as a book of grotesqueries. In these seemingly grotesque people he saw something very human and very common—a spark of creativity. Grotesqueness, freakishness, aggressiveness are treated and interpreted as a substitute, a negative expression for a frustration of the creativity and of the need for love in human beings. The singular humanness of his characters is bound up with insights of this order. The need for creativity and expression, which he himself felt, aided and guided him in perceiving the same need in others, in people who were simple, uneducated, and, sometimes, psychologically or socially peculiar. When Anderson's first stories and books received acclaim he was compared to the Russians. He disavowed their influence. Nonetheless, his stories sometimes suggest those of Chekhov. And his seeming similarity to the Russians, I believe, lies in the fact that with him, as with the Russians, there was a large measure of sympathy for the unfortunate of this world.

It is probable that Anderson never read such a book as Thorstein Veblen's *The Instinct of Workmanship*. Nonetheless, there is some parallel between him and Veblen, an observation Horace Gergory suggested in his excellent introduction to *The Portable Sherwood Anderson,* published by Viking Press [see Additional Bibliography]. In the last years of the nineteenth century and the early ones of this, Veblen observed many of the psychological effects of industrialism on the nature of man. Positing an instinct of workmanship, a conception which bears resemblance with what Anderson saw in the need of human beings to be creative and to express themselves, Veblen analyzed how the development of industrialism was thwarting this so-called instinct. And what Veblen analyzed is similar to what Sherwood Anderson revealed directly and concretely with the insight and feelings of an artist.

Anderson in 1916 or 1917, when several of the Winesburg *stories had already been published in magazines. Reproduced by permission of Harold Ober Associates and Sherwood Anderson Papers, The Newberry Library.*

Similarly, it is fairly certain that Anderson never read any of the philosophical articles of the late George Herbert Mead. But again there is a parallel. Mead saw, much as did the writer, the basis for communication and the development of the self. In Anderson, there is a continuous groping to gain a sense of another. One way of enlarging our understanding of Anderson's work is to see it in terms of the question or problem of identity. Searching and questing for a clearer realization of his own identity, Anderson sought it in others, and he sought for a sense of others in himself. In 1927, he said in a letter to his son: "not to shrink from human life—no matter what its complications—a large order." Anderson did not shrink from this large order. (pp. 166-68)

James T. Farrell, "A Note on Sherwood Anderson," in his Reflections at Fifty and Other Essays, *The Vanguard Press, Inc., 1954, pp. 164-68.*

MALCOLM COWLEY (essay date 1960)

[*Cowley has made valuable contributions to contemporary letters with his editions of important American authors such as Nathaniel Hawthorne, Walt Whitman, Ernest Hemingway, William Faulkner, and F. Scott Fitzgerald; his writings as a literary critic for the* New Republic; *and above all, his chronicles and criticism of modern American literature. Cowley edited a 1960 edition of* Winesburg, Ohio, *making minor, cosmetic changes to the 1919 text. The following excerpt is from that edition's introduction, which is considered an important general essay on* Winesburg, Ohio *and on Anderson's craft and influence.*]

Rereading Sherwood Anderson after many years, one feels again that his work is desperately uneven; but one is gratified to find that the best of it is as new and springlike as ever. There are many authors younger in years . . . who made a great noise in their time, but whose books already belong among the horseless carriages in Henry Ford's museum at Greenfield Village. Anderson made a great noise too, when he published ***Winesburg, Ohio*** in 1919. The older critics scolded him, the younger ones praised him, as a man of the changing hour, yet he managed in that early work and others to be relatively timeless. There are moments in American life to which he gave not only the first but the final expression.

He soon became a writer's writer, the only story teller of his generation who left his mark on the style and vision of the generation that followed. Hemingway, Faulkner, Wolfe, Steinbeck, Caldwell, Saroyan, Henry Miller . . . each of these owes an unmistakable debt to Anderson, and their names might stand for dozens of others. (p. 1)

After finding his proper voice at the age of forty, Anderson didn't change as much as other serious writers; perhaps his steadfastness should make us thankful, considering that most American writers change for the worse. He had achieved a quality of emotional rather than factual truth and he preserved it to the end of his career, while doing little to refine, transform, or even understand it. Some of his last stories—by no means all of them—are richer and subtler than the early ones, but they are otherwise not much different or much better.

He was a writer who depended on inspiration, which is to say that he depended on feelings so deeply embedded in his personality that he was unable to direct them. He couldn't say to himself, "I shall produce such and such an effect in a book of such and such a length"; the book had to write or rather speak itself while Anderson listened as if to an inner voice. (p. 3)

One characteristic of the subconscious is a defective sense of time: in dreams the old man sees himself as a boy, and the events of thirty or forty years may be jumbled together. Time as a logical succession of events was Anderson's greatest difficulty in writing novels or even long stories. He got his tenses confused and carried his heroes ten years forward or back in a single paragraph. His instinct was to present everything together, as in a dream.

When giving a lecture on "A Writer's Conception of Realism," he spoke of a half-dream that he had "over and over." "If I have been working intensely," he said, "I find myself unable to relax when I go to bed. Often I fall into a half-dream state and when I do, the faces of people begin to appear before me. They seem to snap into place before my eyes, stay there, sometimes for a short period, sometimes longer. There are smiling faces, leering ugly faces, tired faces, hopeful faces. . . . I have a kind of illusion about this matter," he continued. "It is, no doubt, due to a story-teller's point of view. I have the feeling that the faces that appear before me thus at night are those of people who want their stories told and whom I have neglected."

He would have liked to tell the stories of all the faces he had ever seen. He was essentially a story teller, as he kept insisting, but his art was of a special type, belonging to an oral rather than a written tradition. It used to be the fashion to compare him with Chekhov and say that he had learned his art from the Russians. Anderson insisted that, except for Turgenev, he hadn't read any Russians when the comparisons were being made. Most of his literary masters were English or American: George Borrow, Walt Whitman, Mark Twain (more than he admitted), and Gertrude Stein. D. H. Lawrence was a less fortunate influence, but only on his later work. His earliest and perhaps his principal teacher was his father, "Irve" Anderson, who used to entertain whole barrooms with tales of his impossible adventures in the Civil War. A great many of the son's best stories, too, were told first in saloons. . . . The best of them retain the language, the pace, and one might even say the gestures of a man talking unhurriedly to his friends.

Within the oral tradition, Anderson had his own picture of what a story should be. He was not interested in telling conventional folk tales, those in which events are more important than emotions. American folk tales usually end with a "snapper"—that is, after starting with the plausible, they progress through the barely possible to the flatly incredible, then wait for a laugh. Magazine fiction used to follow—and much of it still does—a pattern leading to a different sort of snapper, one that calls for a gasp of surprise or relief instead of a guffaw. Anderson broke the pattern by writing stories that not only lacked snappers, in most cases, but even had no plots in the usual sense. The tales he told in his Midwestern drawl were not incidents or episodes, they were *moments,* each complete in itself.

The best of the moments in ***Winesburg, Ohio*** is called **"The Untold Lie."** The story, which I have to summarize at the risk of spoiling it, is about two farm hands husking corn in a field at dusk. Ray Pearson is small, serious, and middle-aged, the father of half a dozen thin-legged children; Hal Winters is big and young, with the reputation of being a bad one. Suddenly he says to the older man, "I've got Nell Gunther in trouble. I'm telling you, but keep your mouth shut." He puts his two hands on Ray's shoulders and looks down into his eyes. "Well, old daddy," he says, "come on, advise me. Perhaps you've been in the same fix yourself. I know what everyone would say is the right thing to do, but what do you say?" Then the author steps back to look at his characters. "There they stood," he tells us, "in the big empty field with the quiet corn shocks standing in rows behind them and the red and yellow hills in the distance, and from being just two indifferent workmen they had become all alive to each other."

That single moment of aliveness—that epiphany, as Joyce would have called it, that sudden reaching out of two characters through walls of inarticulateness and misunderstanding—is the effect that Anderson is trying to create for his readers or listeners. There is more to the story, of course, but it is chiefly designed to bring the moment into relief. Ray Pearson thinks of his own marriage, to a girl he got into trouble, and turns away from Hal without being able to say the expected words about duty. Later that evening he is seized by a sudden impulse to warn the younger man against being tricked into bondage. He runs awkwardly across the fields, crying out that children are only the accidents of life. Then he meets Hal and stops, unable to repeat the words that he had shouted into the wind. It is Hal who breaks the silence. "I've already made up my mind," he says, taking Ray by the coat and shaking him. "Nell ain't no fool. . . . I want to marry her. I want to settle down and have kids." Both men laugh, as if they had forgotten what happened in the cornfield. Ray walks away into the darkness, thinking pleasantly now of his children and muttering to himself, "It's just as well. Whatever I told him would have been a lie." There has been a moment in the lives of two men. The moment has passed and the briefly established communion has been broken, yet we feel that each man has revealed his essential being. It is as if a gulf had opened in the level Ohio cornfield and as if, for one moment, a light had shone from the depths, illuminating everything that happened or would ever happen to both of them.

That moment of revelation was the story Anderson told over and over, but without exhausting its freshness, for the story had as many variations as there were faces in his dreams. (pp. 4-8)

Those moments at the center of Anderson's often marvelous stories were moments, in general, without a sequel; they existed separately and timelessly. That explains why he couldn't write novels and why, with a single exception, he never even wrote a book in the strict sense of the word. A book should have a structure and a development, whereas for Anderson there was chiefly the flash of lightning that revealed a life without changing it.

The one exception, of course, is ***Winesburg, Ohio,*** and that became a true book for several reasons: because it was conceived as a whole, because Anderson had found a subject that released his buried emotions, and because most of the book was written in what was almost a single burst of inspiration, so that it gathered force as it went along. (p. 11)

All the stories were written rapidly, with little need for revision, each of them being, as Anderson said, "an idea grasped whole as one would pick an apple in an orchard." He was dealing with material that was both fresh and familiar. The town of Winesburg was based on his memories of Clyde, Ohio, where he had spent most of his boyhood and where his mother had died at the same age as the hero's mother. The hero, George Willard, was the author in his late adolescence, and the other characters were either remembered from Clyde or else, in many cases, suggested by faces glimpsed in the Chicago streets. Each face revealed a moment, a mood, or a secret that lay deep in Anderson's life and for which he was finding the right words at last.

As the book went forward, more and more of the faces—as well as more streets, buildings, trades, and landscapes—were carried from one story to another, with the result that Winesburg itself acquired a physical and corporate life. Counting the four parts of **"Godliness,"** each complete in itself, there would be twenty-five stories or chapters in all. None of them taken separately—not even **"Hands"** or **"The Untold Lie"**—is as effective as the best of Anderson's later work, but each of them contributes to all the others, as the stories in later volumes are not expected to do. There was a delay of some months before the last three chapters—**"Death," "Sophistication,"** and **"Departure"**—were written with the obvious intention of rounding out the book. First George Willard is released from Winesburg by the death of his mother; then, in **"Sophistication,"** he learns how it feels to be a grown man; then finally he leaves for the city on the early-morning train, and everything recedes as into a framed picture. "When he aroused himself and looked out of the car window," Anderson says, "the town of Winesburg had disappeared and his life there had become but a background on which to paint the dreams of his manhood."

In structure the book lies midway between the novel proper and the mere collection of stories. Like several famous books by more recent authors, all early readers of Anderson—like Faulkner's *The Unvanquished* and *Go Down, Moses,* like Steinbeck's *Tortilla Flat* and *The Pastures of Heaven,* like Caldwell's *Georgia Boy*—it is a cycle of stories with several unifying elements, including a single background, a prevailing tone, and a central character. These elements can be found in all the cycles, but the best of them also have an underlying plot that is advanced or enriched by each of the stories. In ***Winesburg, Ohio*** the underlying plot or fable, though hard to recognize, is unmistakably present, and I think it might be summarized as follows:

George Willard is growing up in a friendly town full of solitary persons; the author calls them "grotesques." Their lives have been distorted not, as Anderson tells us in his prologue, by their each having seized upon a single truth, but rather by their inability to express themselves. Since they cannot truly communicate with others, they have all become emotional cripples. Most of the grotesques are attracted one by one to George Willard; they feel that he might be able to help them. In those moments of truth that Anderson loves to describe, they try to explain themselves to George, believing that he alone in Winesburg has an instinct for finding the right words and using them honestly. They urge him to preserve and develop his gift. . . . All the grotesques hope that George Willard will some day speak what is in their hearts and thus re-establish their connection with mankind. George is too young to understand them at the time, but the book ends with what seems to be the promise that, after leaving Winesburg, he will become the voice of inarticulate men and women in all the forgotten towns.

If the promise is truly implied, and if Anderson felt he was keeping it when writing **"Hands"** and the stories that followed, then ***Winesburg, Ohio*** is far from the pessimistic or destructive or morbidly sexual work it was once attacked for being. Instead it is a work of love, an attempt to break down the walls that divide one person from another, and also, in its own fashion, a celebration of small-town life in the lost days of good will and innocence. (pp. 13-15)

Malcolm Cowley, in an introduction to Winesburg, Ohio *by Sherwood Anderson, revised edition, Penguin Books, 1960, pp. 1-15.*

WALTER B. RIDEOUT (essay date 1962)

[Rideout, an American educator and literary scholar, has written extensively on Anderson's work and is currently preparing what promises to be the definitive biography. In the following excerpt from one of his earlier essays, he explores the subtlety Anderson achieved through the simple story form in Winesburg, Ohio.*]*

It is probably impossible, except impressionistically, to isolate the essential quality of any work of art, but Hart Crane may have come close to isolating that of ***Winesburg, Ohio*** when in another context he wrote of Anderson himself that, "He has a humanity and simplicity that is quite baffling in depth and suggestiveness" [see Additional Bibliography]. Leaving the matter of "humanity" aside, one is indeed struck on first reading the book by its apparent simplicity of language and form. On second or subsequent readings, however, he sees that the hard, plain, concrete diction is much mixed with the abstract, that the sentence cadences come from George Moore and the King James Bible as well as from ordinary speech rhythms, that the seemingly artless, even careless, digressions are rarely artless, careless, or digressive. What had once seemed to have the clarity of water held in the hand begins to take on instead its elusiveness. If this is simplicity, it is simplicity—paradox or not—of a complicated kind. Since ***Winesburg, Ohio*** constantly challenges one to define the complications, I should like to examine a few that perhaps lie closest beneath the surface of the book and the life it describes.

It has been often pointed out that the fictitious Winesburg closely resembles Clyde, Ohio, where Anderson lived from the age of seven to the age of nineteen and which became the home town of his memories. Even now the visitor to the two communities can see that Winesburg and Clyde are both "eighteen miles" south of Lake Erie; in both, the central street of the town is named Main, and Buckeye and Duane branch off from it; both have a Heffner Block and a Waterworks Pond; both lie "in the midst of open fields, but beyond the fields are pleasant patches of woodland." As recently as the summer of 1960, the wooden Gothic railroad station, from which Sherwood Anderson and George Willard took the train for the city and the great world, was still standing; and on the hill above Waterworks Pond, where George walked with Helen White on the darkened fair grounds, one can yet see, overgrown with turf, the banked-up west end turns of the race track. . . . The central village is basically unchanged, and even now to walk through the quiet old residence streets with their white frame or brick houses and wide lawns shaded by big elms and maples is to walk uncannily through a fictitious scene made suddenly real.

The more one learns of the town as it was in the 1890's, the more he sees the actual Clyde under the imagined Winesburg. Anderson was a story teller, of course, not a historian, and the correspondence of the two communities does not have a one-to-one exactness. Nevertheless the correspondences become striking, particularly as one sees that in many instances Clyde names of persons and places appear only faintly disguised in the pages of ***Winesburg, Ohio***. . . . Clyde personal names, it must be noted, are used almost exclusively for the minor characters, and except for one or two debatable possibilities no character, either major or minor, seems to be recognizably based on an actual resident of the town. The important matter, however, is that the "grotesques" of the several tales exist within a physical and social matrix furnished Anderson by his memories of Clyde.

That he should have visualized the locale of his tales so closely in terms of his home town is not surprising, and the reader may dismiss the matter as merely a frequent practice of realistic writers. Yet Anderson is not a realistic writer in the ordinary sense. With him realism is a means to something else, not an end in itself. . . . As he repeats from tale to tale the names of stores and their owners or refers to such elements of town life as the post office, the bank, or the cemetery, there emerges, not a photograph, but at most the barest sketch of the external world of the town. Perhaps even "sketch" implies too great a precision of detail. What Anderson is after is less a representation of conventional "reality" than, to keep the metaphor drawn from art, an abstraction of it.

Realism is for Anderson a means rather than an end, and the highly abstract kind of reality found in Winesburg has its valuable uses. The first of these is best understood in relation to George Willard's occupation on the *Winesburg Eagle*. (Clyde's weekly newspaper was, and still is the *Clyde Enterprise*, but Sherwood Anderson was never its reporter.) It has been suggested that the author may have made his central figure a newspaper reporter in order that he could thus be put most readily in touch with the widest number of people in town and most logically become the recipient of many confidences; yet Anderson's point is that exactly insofar as George remains a newspaper reporter, he is committed to the surface of life, not to its depths. "Like an excited dog," Anderson says in **"The Thinker,"** using a mildly contemptuous comparison, "George Willard ran here and there," writing down all day "little facts" about A. P. Wringlet's recent shipment of straw hats or Uncle Tom Sinnings' new barn on the Valley Road. As reporter, George is concerned with externals, with appearances, with the presumably solid, simple, everyday surface of life. For Anderson the surface is there, of course, as his recurring use of place and personal names indicates; yet conventional "reality" is for him relatively insignificant and is best presented in the form of sketch or abstraction. What is important is "to see beneath the surface of lives," to perceive the intricate mesh of impulses, desires, drives growing down in the dark, unrevealed parts of the personality like the complex mass of roots that, below the surface of the ground, feeds the common grass above in the light.

But if one function of Anderson's peculiar adaptation of realism is, as it were, to depreciate the value of surfaces, a corollary function is constantly to affirm that any surface has its depth. Were we, on the one hand, to observe such tormented people as Alice Hindman and Dr. Parcival and the Reverend Curtis Hartman as briefly and as much from the outside as we view Wesley Moyer or Biff Carter or Butch Wheeler, the lamplighter, they would appear as uncomplicated and commonplace as the latter. Conversely, were we to see the inwardness of Moyer and Carter and Wheeler, their essential lives would provide the basis for three more Winesburg tales. (The real lamplighter of Clyde in the early 1890's was a man named John Becker. It may well have given him the anguish of a "grotesque" that he had an epileptic son, who as a young man died during a seizure while assisting his father in his trade.)

Yet a third function of Anderson's abstract, or shorthand, kind of realism is to help him set the tone of various tales, often a tone of elegiac quietness. Just how this is done will be clearer if one realizes that the real Clyde which underlies Winesburg is the town, not as Anderson left it in 1896, but the town as it was a few years earlier when, as he asserts in **"An Awakening,"** "the time of factories had not yet come." . . . [The] Winesburg tales he conceived of as for the most part occurring in a pre-industrial setting, recalling nostalgically a town already lost before he had left it, giving this vanished era the permanence of pastoral. Here, as always, he avoids the realism of extensive detail and makes only suggestive references, one of the most memorable being the description in **"The Thinker"** of the lamplighter hurrying along the street before Seth Richmond and Helen White, lighting the lamp on each wooden post "so that their way was half lighted, half darkened, by the lamps and by the deepening shadows cast by the low-branched trees." By a touch like this, drawn from his memory of pre-industrial Clyde, Anderson turns the evening walk of his quite ordinary boy and girl into a tiny processional and invests the couple with that delicate splendor which can come to people, "even in Winesburg."

If Anderson's treatment of locale in his tales turns out to be more complex than it seems at first, the same can be said of his methods of giving sufficient unity to his book so that, while maintaining the "looseness" of life as he actually sensed it, the tales would still form a coherent whole. Some of these methods, those that I shall be concerned with, have a point in common: they all involve the use of repeated elements. One such device is that of setting the crisis scenes of all but five of the tales in the evening. In a very large majority of the stories, too, some kind of light partly, but only partly, relieves the darkness. In **"Hands," "Mother,"** and **"Loneliness,"** for example, the light is that of a single lamp; in **"The Untold Lie"** the concluding scene is faintly lit by the last of twilight; in **"Sophistication"** George Willard and Helen White look at each other "in the dim light" afforded, apparently, by "the lights of the town reflected against the sky," though at the other end of the fair grounds a few race trackmen have built a fire that provides a dot of illumination in the darkness. Finally, many of the tales end with the characters in total darkness. Such a device not only links the tales but in itself implies meaning. ***Winesburg, Ohio*** is primarily a book about the "night world" of human personality. The dim light equates with, as well as literally illuminates, the limited glimpse into an individual soul that each crisis scene affords, and the briefness of the insight is emphasized by the shutting down of the dark.

Another kind of repeated element throughout the book is the recurrent word. Considering the sense of personal isolation one gets from the atomized lives of the "grotesques," one would expect a frequent use of some such word as "wall," standing for whatever it is that divides each person from all others. Surprisingly that particular word appears only a few times. The one that does occur frequently is "hand," either in the singular or the plural; and very often, as indeed would be expected, it suggests, even symbolizes, the potential or actual communication of one personality with another. The hands of Wing Biddlebaum and Dr. Reefy come immediately to mind; but, to name only a few other instances, George Willard takes hold of Louise Trunnion's "rough" but "delightfully small" hand in anticipation of his sexual initiation, Helen White keeps her hand in Seth Richmond's until Seth breaks the clasp through overconcern with self, in the field where they are working Hal Winters puts "his two hands" on Ray Pearson's shoulders and they "become all alive to each other," Kate Swift puts her hands on George Willard as though about to embrace him in her desire to make him understand what being a writer means. Obviously the physical contact may not produce mutual understanding. The hand may in fact express aggression. One of the men who run Wing Biddlebaum out of the Pennsylvania town at night "had a rope in his hands"; Elizabeth Willard, who as a girl had put her hand on the face of each lover after sexual release, imagines herself stealing toward her husband, "holding the long wicked scissors in her hand"; Elmer Cowley on the station platform strikes George Willard almost unconscious with his fists before leaping onto the departing train. Nevertheless, the possibility of physical touch between two human beings always implies, even if by negative counterpart, at least the possibility of a profounder moment of understanding between them. The intuitive awareness by George Willard and Helen White of each other's "sophistication" is expressed, not through their few kisses, but by Helen's taking George's arm and walking "beside him in dignified silence."

As for George himself, one can make too much of his role as a character designed to link the tales, unify them, and structure them into a loose sort of *bildungsroman*; on the other hand, one can make too little of it. Granted that Anderson tended to view his own life, and that of others, as a succession of moments rather than as a "figure in a carpet," that his imagination worked more successfully in terms of the flash of insight than of the large design, that his gift was, in short, for the story rather than the novel, still through his treatment of George Willard's development he supplies a pattern for ***Winesburg, Ohio*** that is as definite as it is unobtrusive. This development has three closely related aspects, and each aspect involves again the repetition of certain elements.

The first aspect is obvious. Whatever the outward difference between created character and creator, George's inward life clearly reflects the conflict Anderson himself had experienced between the world of practical affairs, with its emphasis on the activity of money-making and its definition of success in financial terms, and the world of dreams, with its emphasis on imaginative creativity and its definition of success in terms of the degree of penetration into the buried life of others. The conflict is thematically stated in the first of the tales, **"Hands."** Wing Biddlebaum's hands are famous in Winesburg for their berry-picking (hence money-making) skill, but the true story of the hands, as told by "a poet," is of course that they can communicate a desire to dream. Wing declares the absolute opposition of the two worlds by telling George that he is destroying himself because "'you are afraid of dreams. You want to be like others in town here.'" The declaration indicates that George has not yet resolved the conflict, and his irresolution at this point is reinforced by his ambivalent attitude toward Wing's hands. Unlike the other townspeople he is curious to know what lies beneath their outward skill; yet his respect for Wing and his fear of the depths that might be revealed make him put curiosity aside. The conflict between practical affairs and dreams is again made explicit in the third story of the book, **"Mother,"** where it is objectified in the hostility between Tom and Elizabeth Willard and the clash of their influences on their son. ***Winesburg, Ohio*** is not a book of suspense, and thus early in the tales the conflict is in effect resolved when George implicitly accepts his mother's, and Wing's, way, the way of dreams. From this point on both the conflict and George's resolution of it are maintained in a formal sense by the opposition between the "daylight world" of the minor characters and the "night world" of the major ones, the grotesques. George continues to run about writing down surface facts for the newspaper, but his essential life consists in his efforts, some successful, some not, to understand the essential lives of others. From these efforts, from the death of his mother, from his achievement of ''sophistication'' with Helen White, he gains the will to leave Winesburg, committed, as the final paragraph of **''Departure''** asserts, to the world of dreams.

The second of these closely-related aspects of George's development is his growing desire to be a creative writer and his increasing awareness of the meaning of that vocation. George's interest in writing is not mentioned until the book is half over, when, in **''The Thinker,''** it appears to have been an interest that he had had for some time. He talks ''continuously of the matter'' to Seth Richmond, and the ''idea that George Willard would some day become a writer had given him a place of distinction in Winesburg. . . .'' At this point his conception of writing centers on externals, on the opportunities the writer's life offers for personal freedom and for public acclaim. In a remark that suggests a reading of Jack London, George explains to Seth that as a writer he will be his own boss: ''Though you are in India or in the South Seas in a boat, you have but to write and there you are.'' Since writing for George is at this stage mainly a matter of fame and fun, it is not surprising to find him in **''The Thinker''** deliberately, and naively, planning to fall in love with Helen White in order to write a love story. The absurdity, Anderson suggests, is two-fold: falling in love is not something one rationally plans to do, and one does not write thus directly and literally out of experience anyway.

Actually Kate Swift, in **''The Teacher,''** has tried to tell George that the writer's is not ''the easiest of all lives to live,'' but rather one of the most difficult. In one of those scenes where physical touch symbolizes an attempt to create the moment of awareness between two personalities, Kate has tried to explain the demanding principles by which the true writer must live. He must ''know life,'' must ''stop fooling with words,'' must ''know what people are thinking about, not what they say''—all three being principles Anderson was to insist on himself as the code of the artist. That George is still immature both as person and as writer is signified at the end of **''The Teacher''** when he gropes drowsily about in the darkness with a hand and mutters that he has missed something Kate Swift was trying to tell him. This needed maturity comes to him only at the end of ***Winesburg, Ohio.*** When, sitting beside the body of his dead mother, he decides to go to ''some city'' and perhaps ''get a job on some newspaper,'' he is really marked already for the profession of writer, whatever job he may take to support himself, just as Anderson supported himself by composing advertising copy while experimenting with the Winesburg stories. In **''Departure''** the commitment of George Willard to writing unites with his final commitment to the world of dreams. For both George and his creator the two are indeed identical.

The third aspect of George's development provides another way of charting his inward voyage from innocence to experience, from ignorance to understanding, from apparent reality of the face of things to true reality behind or below. Three stories—**''Nobody Knows,'' ''An Awakening,''** and **''Sophistication''**—have a special relationship. They all center on George's dealings with a woman, a different one in each case; they contain very similar motifs; they are arranged in an ascending order of progression. The fact that one comes near the beginning of the book, one about two-thirds of the way through, and one at the end suggests that Anderson was not without his own subtle sense of design.

The first story, **''Nobody Knows,''** is in all ways the simplest. In it George Willard enters traditional manhood by having with Louise Trunnion his first sex experience. In relation to the other two tales in the sequence, the most significant elements of the story, besides the fact of actual sexual conquest, are George's lack of self-assurance at the outset of the affair, his bursting forth with a ''flood of words,'' his consequent aggressiveness and failure to sympathize with his partner, and his action at the end of the story when he stands ''perfectly still in the darkness, attentive, listening as though for a voice calling his name.'' The sexual encounter with Louise has been simply that. It has brought him physical satisfaction and a feeling of entirely self-centered masculine pride. His expectation of hearing a voice, however, would seem to be a projection of guilt feeling at having violated the overt moral code of the community even though ''nobody knows.''

In the second and third stories these elements, or their opposites, appear in a more complex fashion. In both **''An Awakening''** and **''Sophistication,''** George's relation with a woman is complicated by the involvement of another man, though, significantly, Ed Handby in the former story is laconic, direct, and highly physical, while the college instructor in the latter is voluble, devious, and pompously intellectual. In both, too, the final scene takes place on the hill leading up to the fair grounds, close,, incidentally, to the place where Kate Swift tried to explain to George the difficulties that beset the dedicated writer. Yet the two stories have quite different, if supplementary, conclusions.

As George and Belle Carpenter walk up the hill in the final scene of **''An Awakening,''** he feels no more sympathy for her, has no more understanding of her needs, than he had for Louise Trunnion; but before this last walk he has experienced an exaltation that keeps him from any fear of masculine incompetence. Earlier that January night a kind of mystical revelation has come to him when it seems as though ''some voice outside of himself'' announced the thoughts in his mind: '''I must get myself into touch with something orderly and big that swings through the night like a star.''' Unlike the situation at the end of **''Nobody Knows,''** George actually ''hears'' the external voice, and the voice is now the positive one of inspiration, which has replaced the negative one of conscience. Thereafter he talks volubly to Belle, as he had to Louise; but when in **''An Awakening''** his ''mind runs off into words,'' he believes that Belle will recognize the new force in him and will at once surrender herself to his masculine power. Now, in actual fact an insistence on the necessity of universal order—'''There is a law for armies and for men too','' George asserts—is a characteristic of Anderson's own thinking particularly as expressed in the novel, *Marching Men,* which preceded the Winesburg tales in composition, and in the poems, *Mid-American Chants,* which followed; yet George makes this concept ridiculous at the moment because of his intense self-centeredness about his inspiration. As Kate Swift would have said, he is still playing with words, a destructive procedure for the artistic personality as well as for the non-artistic one. Holding the quite uninterested Belle in his arms, he whispers large words into the darkness, until the passionate, non-verbalizing Ed Handby throws him aside, takes Belle by the arm, and marches off. George is left angered, humiliated, and disgustedly disillusioned with his moment of mystic insight when ''the voice outside himself . . . had . . . put new courage into his heart.''

Where **''An Awakening''** records a defeat, **''Sophistication''** records in all ways a triumph. Though Anderson presents the moment in essay rather than dramatic form, there comes to George, as to ''every boy,'' a flash of insight when ''he stops under a tree and waits as for a voice calling his name.'' But this time ''the voices outside himself'' do not speak of the possibilities of universal order, nor do they speak of guilt. Instead they ''whisper a message concerning the limitations of life,'' the brief light of human existence between two darks. The insight emphasizes the unity of all human beings in their necessary submission to death and their need for communication one with another. It is an insight that produces self-awareness but not self-centeredness, that produces, in short, the mature, ''sophisticated'' person.

The mind of such a person does not ''run off into words.'' Hence Helen White, who has had an intuition similar to George's, runs away from the empty talk of her college instructor and her mother, and finds George, whose first and last words to her in the story, pronounced as they first meet, are ''Come on.'' Together in the dimly-lit fair grounds on the hill overlooking the town of Winesburg, George and Helen share a brief hour of absolute awareness. Whereas his relationship with Belle Carpenter had produced in George self-centeredness, misunderstanding, hate, frustration, humiliation, that with Helen produces quite the opposite feelings. The feeling of oneness spreads outward, furthermore. Through his communication with Helen he begins ''to think of the people in the town where he had lived with something like reverence.'' When he has come to this point, when he loves and respects the inhabitants of Winesburg, the ''daylight'' people as well as the ''night'' ones, the way of the artist lies clear before him. George Willard is ready for his **''Departure.''**

Like Hart Crane, other readers will find the simplicity of ***Winesburg, Ohio*** ''baffling''; but it is very probably this paradoxical quality which has attracted and will continue to attract admirers to a book that Anderson himself, with a mixture of amusement, deprecation, defensiveness, and satisfaction, quite accurately termed ''a kind of American classic.'' (pp. 20-31)

Walter B. Rideout, ''The Simplicity of 'Winesburg, Ohio','' in Shenandoah, *Vol. 13, No. 3, Spring, 1962, pp. 20-31.*

REX BURBANK (essay date 1964)

[Burbank is an American educator and literary scholar who has written full-length studies of Thornton Wilder, Jane Austen, Anthony Trollope, and Anderson. In the following excerpt, he analyzes in detail the strengths and weaknesses in selected stories from The Triumph of the Egg *and* Horses and Men.*]*

The stories in ***The Triumph of the Egg*** . . . and in ***Horses and Men*** . . . are uneven, but the best of them represent the pinnacle of Anderson's art. In general, it may be said that their quality rises in proportion to the amount and kind of ironic indirection Anderson employs in style, structure, and narrative action. The most profitable approach to them will be, therefore, to examine the means by which Anderson brings together the devices and techniques of indirection and the degrees to which he renders rather than asserts his meanings.

For convenience, the tales may be divided into two classes, those having to do with adults and those whose chief characters are adolescent boys. The ''adult'' stories generally have in common lonely, sensitive souls who want desperately to break out of the isolation of their inner lives. Among the best of these are the tales which are similar to the stories of Alice Hindman, Kate Swift, and Louise Bentley in ***Winesburg, Ohio;*** tales which portray young women who are defeated by the coarseness, the insensitivity, or the moral cowardice of men and by the hypocrisy behind conventional Puritan moral codes.

The thematic key to these stories lies in the titles: **'''Unused,'''** **''Unlighted Lamps,''** **''Out of Nowhere into Nothing,''** and **''Seeds.''** They present a picture of waste, of human sensitivity never fully developed, of physical and spiritual potential untapped, or of a sensitive nature crushed. The pathetic May Edgely of **'''Unused'''** is the victim of Bidwell's dual standard of morality which allows the stolid Jerome Hadley to boast with impunity of his conquest of her and to degrade her in the eyes of the local gossips. Her death by drowning is an almost merciful release from life in which her longing for sympathetic companionship has brought only a mounting nightmare of terror because of the brutality of men and the sexual hypocrisy of women.

The great reservoir of love in Mary Cochran and her father in **''Unlighted Lamps''** is untouched, for the father fails to the end of his life to say the few simple words that would express his love—would, in fact, give it life—and make the emotional connection that could have saved them both from loneliness. Similarly, Rosalind Wescott of **''Out of Nowhere into Nothing,''** Elsie Leander in **''The New Englander,''** and the unnamed woman in **''Seeds''** are trapped within themselves and unable to satisfy the demands of their inner, imaginative lives for communication with others. The sex impulse, which could be the initial step toward breaking the barrier of loneliness that surrounds them, is reduced to an obstacle by Puritan taboos and by the animal lust these taboos set in motion.

As in ***Winesburg, Ohio,*** Anderson develops the theme of the defeated inner life symbolically; but, where the symbols in ***Winesburg, Ohio*** grew around repeated images of grotesqueness, those in these stories rise out of contrasting motifs of spiritual life and death, communion and isolation, light and dark. Anderson's technique of playing his motifs in a low key and in soft, muted tones, blending discordant moods, disconnected scenes and images, and antithetic themes through a kind of prose pointillism may be seen in one of the best of these tales of lonely women, **''Unlighted Lamps.''**

This story, originally part of the novel titled *Mary Cochran* which Anderson wrote in Elyria but later revised and divided into separate tales, is constructed around the inner impressions of Mary and her father as they examine their lives in the light of his impending death, a narrative situation somewhat similar in its existential implications to Tolstoy's *Death of Ivan Ilych*. Both Mary and her father come to the painful awareness of their failure to break out of their inner isolation and to fulfill their emotional potential. The theme, suggested by the title, of an inner life failing to find outward expression rises from a series of contrasts in style, character, and scene.

The most apparent contrast is between the ''buried'' lives of Mary and her father and the passionate, spontaneous lives of the townspeople, particularly the immigrant laborers whose section of town Mary passes through on her walk into the country. Never having learned to respond to her impulses, Mary is drawn to the poorer district of the town ''where life carried itself off darkly, with a blow and an oath''; but because of the scandal attached to her deceased mother, she cannot come close to the people of the town. She is also repelled by the crude animalism of young Duke Yetter, who misconstrues her casual gesture as an enticement.

Her father, Dr. Cochran, who has spent most of his life attending his patients without ever really entering their lives, conceals his love for Mary—as he concealed his love for his young wife before she left him—under an exterior of cool reserve. He spends his last hours before death, alone, regretfully recalling the failure of his life and resolving to "talk to the girl." "I've been a proud man and a coward," he admits to himself. As he sits alone in his dark room, sounds of a baby crying and of men talking in the livery barn across the street emphasize his isolation.

Supporting the contrasts between the doctor's buried life and the vibrant life of the town are the interrelated motifs of light and dark, of life waxing and waning, and of day fading into evening, all of which blend together, somewhat in the fashion of an impressionistic painting, to form a single impression of unfulfilled potential. The doctor's life has been lived in dimness: "It has been like a stream running always in shadows and never coming out into the sunlight," Mary observes as she watches a slow-moving stream pass along under a bridge. At the end of the story, when the doctor collapses and dies while vainly reaching out for emotional attachment, the sound of a newborn baby and the faint light of a cigarette in the dark stairway where the doctor has fallen bring together the motifs of light and dark, life and death, in ironic fusion.

Anderson's brilliant blending of counterpoints in mood, character, and theme grows almost imperceptibly by means of a shifting narrative perspective. Alternately tracing Mary's and her father's thoughts as they assess their lives, he moves back and forth across the psychological "wall" that separates Mary from her father. These shifts in point of view are abrupt, breaking off timid resolutions to act, little actions just initiated or not undertaken, scraps of life haltingly begun or left untried. The shifts and the breaks carry by indirection the idea that both main characters are afraid to follow their impulses and thus paralyze themselves with indecision.

Anderson further reinforces the theme of action begun and halted with paragraphs balanced and antithetical, such as the following: "Mary sat in the darkness by the office window and saw her father drive into the street. When his horse had been put away he did not, as was his custom, come at once up the stairway to the office, but lingered in the darkness before the barn door. Once he started to cross the street and then returned into the darkness." This paragraph begins with Mary in the darkness and ends with her father returning to the darkness. Between the first and last sentences the father makes a halting effort to leave the darkness, decides against it, and returns—an act that sums up his life, just as Mary's act of sitting apart from life in the darkness typifies hers.

The superiority of **"Unlighted Lamps"** over the longer **"'Unused'"** and **"Out of Nowhere into Nothing"** illustrates the fact that the short tale, where he deftly charged his narratives with the rich intensity of poetry, was the form most suited to Anderson's talent and materials. **"Out of Nowhere into Nothing"** is the longest piece in ***The Triumph of the Egg,*** running to nearly a hundred pages, and it rather tiresomely develops around the inability of Rosalind Wescott, a twenty-seven-year-old girl who has returned from Chicago to her home in Willow Springs, Iowa, to decide whether she should agree to become the mistress of Walter Sayer, her Chicago employer who is a married man. She wants to think over Sayer's proposition as a way to find "meaning" in life and to discuss it with her mother.

The most interesting person in this story is Melville Stoner, Rosalind's neighbor in Willow Springs who is conscious that the frenetic rush of modern city life, the listless resignation to the routine of town and country life, and the dull acceptance of moral convention are but evidences of loneliness and manifestations of a thwarted inner, imaginative life. Paul Rosenfeld observed perceptively that Stoner himself is "ironically resigned to the futility of seeking to establish a permanent contact with another creature; tired to the marrow with the loneliness of existence," while Rosalind is "mortally stricken in her breast by the insensitiveness and cowardice of men to whom she turns for expression" [see excerpt dated 1922]. In a structure built upon contasts between death and life, night and day, shadows and light, dead trees and vibrant plant and insect life, Stoner himself is characterized by resembling alternately a vulture and a sea gull. He appears to Rosalind as death, but he actually holds out to her the promise of life through his imaginative consciousness, which struggles to free itself and needs only the response of her buried imagination. (pp. 88-92)

This story also illustrates the vagueness and lack of focus Anderson's tales fall into when they have no central, unifying symbol. Lacking a controlling symbol, such tales as **"The New Englander," "'Unused,'"** and this one are prolix; the narrative meanders along with foggy characters whose feelings never quite coalesce into concrete, unified thoughts. The point of **"Out of Nowhere into Nothing"** is that Rosalind, like Stoner, craves freedom but is trapped by the dead material facts of life that will not permit her to act in accordance with her nature. While the idea that Stoner is a caged spirit is suggested by the image of a sea gull stranded inland, no such symbol draws together the threads of Rosalind's reflections and weaves them into a unified whole. Unless woven together, the unattached images of an impressionistic presentation become random and vague. Much of Anderson's so-called "mysticism" can be written off, therefore, as a failure to grasp his vision in concrete narrative terms and a consequent tendency to make cloudy perception pass for profundity. Before she leaves for Chicago, Rosalind establishes an almost mystical "fellowship in life" with Stoner, but Anderson gives us no indication that all the impressions that have come to her since leaving Chicago have added up to anything more than a kind of aimless groping, or to any real understanding of life. (pp. 92-3)

Supreme among the adult stories in both volumes is **"The Egg,"** in which Anderson achieves perhaps the most nearly perfect blending of contrasting moods and tones, of absurdity and pathos, symbol and object, and action and theme he was ever to accomplish. Nothing in **"The Egg"** is extraneous to its meaning; nothing in its meaning may be extracted from the facts of the narrative. From the description of the broad swath of baldness on the father's head to the reconstruction of his ridiculous attempt to get an egg into a bottle, and from the passages relating the frustrations of chicken farming to the father's roar of exasperation at the unyielding eggshell, symbol, object, tone, mood, and diction merge in the theme of the defeat of a diffident little man by a world too complicated for him. The egg—a maddeningly fragile, refractory, and intractable thing in itself—is the symbol of those same qualities in life. The narrator's father, groping desperately for what can only be for him a precarious hold upon life as a witty and amusing rustic *bon vivant,* betrays in his efforts to place an egg in a bottle the ludicrous and pathetic chasm between his timid, hesitant nature and the recalcitrance of a perverse world of chance and circumstance. His natural diffidence will not permit him to compete on equal terms in the world of success into which his ambitious wife repeatedly thrusts him. When he tries boldly to enter that dangerous world, he so far exceeds the limitations of his nature that he becomes grotesque, at once comical and pathetic.

"I sang the ugliness of life, the strange beauty of life pressing in on the mind of a boy," Anderson said of the *Mid-American Chants*. Such was to be the theme of his finest fiction. Sudden glimpses of the strange mixture of beauty and ugliness in life had characterized George Willard's growth to maturity in ***Winesburg, Ohio*** and also the slow movement toward sympathetic consciousness of those defeated by the ugliness of life: Sam McPherson, Beaut McGregor, and Hugh McVey. Under the influence of Twain, Anderson brought his vision of the puzzled boy or boy-man to near perfection in a handful of tales that combine a carefully controlled point of view with a painstaking attention to the subtleties of the colloquial diction of the narrator, who betrays both a touching naïveté and a profound sensitivity to the confusing paradoxes of the adult world.

Like [*Huck Finn*], **"I Want to Know Why," "I'm a Fool,"** and **"The Man Who Became a Woman"** are related from the first-person point of view. A boy—or a man looking back upon his youth—has experienced or witnessed a baffling admixture of beauty and ugliness, purity and corruption, success and failure. The narrator himself is either unable to explain precisely what the experience means or—in the case of **"I'm a Fool"**—fails to understand his own role in it and misinterprets it; and, in his groping efforts to explain what he does not fully comprehend, he rambles in his narrative, feeling about for details he vaguely perceives to be significant. Typically his narrative digresses as he searches confusedly for explanations which follow his feelings rather than a logical or chronological sequence, and in his digressions he reveals the pain of entry into adult life in the perplexity he feels at seeing for the first time the ambiguities of life.

Because of his masterly handling of point of view in these tales, Anderson gains the full ironic effect of the discrepancy between what his protagonists say and what they understand or are aware of. The tales may conveniently be grouped together both because their subjects consist of youthful experiences in horse racing and training and because the chief interest in each focuses upon the narrator himself. Each of the three young men is caught up in the perplexing adult world in which the simple values and beliefs of childhood are shaken by discovery that they cannot be maintained in a simple, pure form. All three cling to their youthful privilege of making absolute, categorical judgments of value; and the confusion and the perplexity they experience force them to analyze what happened in retrospect and try to relate their experience—both to themselves and to the listener-reader whom they take into their confidence—in order to understand it.

Though each of the narrators is "crazy about thoroughbred horses," horses are not the central concern of the stories; the horses symbolize, variously, the simplicity of purpose and purity of sense and heart of the natural animal raised to the highest degree of perfection through breeding and training. They represent to the boys a kind of morality based upon simple response to instinct and splendid fulfillment of purpose.The boys hold a simple scale of values grounded in a hierarchy of natural purity: the stallion is more admirable than the gelding; and the swipe and the trainer, who are closer to the horses, are more praiseworthy than is the owner.

In **"I Want to Know Why,"** the boy-narrator loses his comfortable primitivistic moral shroud as he discovers in jockey Jerry Tillford the same reaction to a prostitute that he showed toward the magnificent stallion Sunstreak, a discovery that shatters his faith in the purity of the ecstatic and almost mystical sentiment they had shared after the horse's great race that afternoon. "What did he do it for?" he asks in enraged bafflement. "I want to know why."

Up to the time he sees Jerry with the prostitute, the boy is able to keep his notions of sentiment and instinctual purity neatly separated from questions of lust and depravity. The exhilarating stimulation of the boy's senses and imagination at the track is reminiscent of the idyllic raft scenes in *Huck Finn*. (pp. 96-8)

The boy is innocent in the sense that he himself is free of taint, for he is aware of evil. He knows ugliness exists and tacitly rejects it. He knows, for instance, that the house Jerry and his companions enter is a "place for bad women to stay in"; and he is no stranger to "rotten talk, the kind a kid hears around a livery stable . . . but don't ever expect to hear talked when there are women around." What crushes and baffles him is the realization that untinged purity cannot exist in human nature, a fact which he must thenceforth live with and accept; but this knowledge destroys forever the romantic idealism of his youth. His discovery "spoils looking at horses and smelling things and hearing niggers laugh and everything." The boy's recurrent association of the horses with cleanliness and his uncomplicated love for them suggest his adolescent idealization of sex. Girls are not yet much on his mind, except as disembodied ideals; and in thoroughbreds his emerging sexuality is diffused and "sublimated." "Sunstreak," he says, "is like a girl you think about sometimes but never see. He is hard all over and lovely too. When you look at his head you want to kiss him." The experience with Jerry brings him later to the shocking realization that sentience can mean lust and degradation as well as response to beauty, and his initiation into the puzzling adult world in which ideals of absolute purity and beauty are impossible causes him to respond with the complete disillusionment and bewilderment of the child.

Much of the charm of **"I Want to Know Why"** is the result of Anderson's careful control and balance of the ironic discrepancy between what the boy consciously says and what he unconsciously reveals about himself. His chief characteristic is naïveté, and in using the naïve point of view, so splendidly used by Twain in *Huck Finn,* Anderson is able to reveal the "ugliness of life, the strange beauty of life pressing in on the mind of a boy" without resorting to direct assertion. The perspective of the naïve adolescent caught up in a puzzling conflict of values—the frustrating inability to maintain a simple, inviolate island of purity in a corrupt world—is also utilized in **"I'm a Fool."** In this story the chief character is a groom who, like the boy in **"I Want to Know Why,"** comes from a middle-class family which disapproves of his connection with racing and with the "unrespectable" people associated with it. He too has an uncomplicated, uncritical love for the free, unsophisticated life among the trainers and grooms; and he also becomes initiated into the complexities of life through betrayal of his own simplicity. But whereas the other boy is betrayed by unsuspected depravity in a man he admires, this one is defeated by circumstances and by his own ignorance and inferiority complex. (pp. 99-100)

The plot is simple, but the meaning of the tale lies in the conflict of values that causes the boy to bring about his own dilemma. Until he meets Lucy, he is able to keep his middle-class values separate from those of the track. He has had to live with the values of two conflicting ways of life, for his lower middle-class family, consisting of his mother and his sister, is poor but it also has genteel notions of propriety and respectability which clash with his affinity for the track. The family is fatherless, and the boy has to work; but he is nineteen, so the odd jobs go to others smaller and younger than he. He, therefore, is both driven and drawn to work at the track; and the tension between the demands of his middle-class background and the gratifications of the track comprises the conflict within him that undermines his self-confidence. His attitudes thus vacillate between middle-class respectability and the freedom of the tracks and between his need for self-esteem and his desire for love, which he cannot reconcile in his brief, idyllic romance with Lucy.

He is not bright enough to see the incompatibility of his values. He despises people who ''put on airs,'' yet he has always, he says, believed in putting up ''a good front.'' The free and sentient life of the groom provides him with ''a lot of valuable things for any man to know.'' But he is unable to specify what those things are; and, despite his ''experience'' at the tracks with race-fixing, drinking, brawling and lying, he is basically an innocent who responds with the uncorrupted sensitivity of youth to the immediate life of the senses: ''Gee whiz, Gosh amighty, the nice hickorynut and beechnut and oaks and other kinds of trees along the roads, all brown and red, and the good smells, and Burt [the Negro trainer] singing a song that was called Deep River, and the country girls at the windows of the houses and everything.''

Yet he is not entirely satisfied with the mindless life of the primitive. His assertion that ''You can stick your colleges up your nose for all of me'' betrays his insecurity. Furthermore, the lack of conviction in his insistence upon the superiority of life as a swipe over that of the respectable people in the grandstands is readily apparent in his desire to impress Lucy Wessen, her brother, and her brother's girl friend with his pretended background of wealth and position.

The chief weakness of this story is that the boy's naïveté deteriorates into stupidity. His inability to recognize the broad, palpable inconsistencies in his values makes him an object of contempt as well as pity, and his lack of insight into what should be obvious to a nineteen-year-old deprives the story of the ironic subtlety of **"I Want to Know Why."** In the latter story the boy's bafflement is made understandable by dramatic demonstration of his naïve belief that his adolescent ideal and the facts of life outside the confraternity of life at the track could be kept separated. In **"I'm a Fool"** the swipe's frustrated romance emanates from his stolid inability to discriminate among his allegiances. We cannot help feeling that he is indeed a fool. At times his ignorance comes close to incredibility and Anderson's mastery of rustic Midwestern dialect—which is equal in **"I Want to Know Why"** to the best of Twain—descends into obviousness and loses touch with its purpose. Intended to convey the boy's naïveté, it confirms his ignorance and serves as a substitute for the brilliantly enacted clash in **"I Want to Know Why"** between what the groom says and what he understands. When he advises Wilbur Wessen about betting on ''About Ben Ahem,'' for instance, the boy says: ''Don't bet a cent on this first heat because he'll go like an oxen hitched to a plow, but when the first heat is over go right down and lay on your pile.'' He knows the races are fixed, but he betrays a complete inability to make moral discriminations.

Yet, **"I'm a Fool"** must not be read too gravely, for it is essentially a humorous story, resembling more than anything else Ring Lardner's hyperbolic sketches of ignoramuses who trap themselves by their hilarious persistence in evading the truth. The dialogue of **"I'm a Fool"** is in fact comic in its exaggeration: the initial sentence sets the tone: ''It was a hard jolt for me, one of the most bitterest I ever had to face.'' That there are, however, added dimensions of seriousness and pathos in Anderson's portrayal of the boy raises the story above Lardner's frequently thin satires.

The finest of the horses-and-men tales is **"The Man Who Became a Woman,"** which exceeds **"I Want to Know Why"** in psychological depth and in symbolic richness. In this story the narrator is a man, now well past his adolescence, who is successfully married; and he tells his story not as a naïve, confused boy but as an adult recalling a youthful experience with a sense of shame and degradation and under a compulsion to cleanse himself through confession. (pp. 101-03)

The remarkable Gothic, nightmarish quality—similar to that of Faulkner's *Sanctuary,* later—of the second part of this tale is achieved by Anderson's gradual intensification of symbols of action and atmosphere which culminate in the death of the boy's cherished but doomed innocence in the rib casement of the horse's skeleton. Like the swipe in **"I Want to Know Why,"** Dudley resists entry into adult male sexuality, clinging to his childhood world of untarnished emotional attachments, a fact established in the first part of the story where his association with the writer Tom Means is shown to be based upon their shared love for thoroughbred horses, their joy in the track fraternity, and the boy's admiration for Means's articulate idealization of horses, those untainted aristocrats of nature. With Means present, he is able to expunge the impurities from horse racing and to constrain his emerging sexual longings; for Means gives expression to those noble sentiments the boy feels about thoroughbreds and raises racing to the level of art (Means wants to write ''the way a well-bred horse runs or trots or paces''). In ''loving'' Means, Dudley can hold on to his comfortable pre-adolescent hero worship both of Means himself and of the great Pop Geers.

When Means leaves, however, Dudley is forced to face the more complex facts of the tracks and of his own sexual maturity. Without Means, the imaginative quality that had given meaning to racing and thoroughbreds is lost, and the boy is thrust into the brutal realities of life: the trickery of the horse owners, the lust of the grooms and their ''fly'' girls, and his own physical needs which now turn his dreams to nightmares after which he feels like ''old Harry.'' His resistance to the world of physical fact is a rejection of its ugliness, and it begins when he decides to stay alone at the stables. Shortly, however, he finds it impossible to remain alone; his thoughts of an ideal, undefiled woman, ''slender and like a flower with something in her like a race horse too,'' drive him away from the stables in search of company. Destruction of his impossible ideal begins when he enters the bar, and it ends with his fall into the rib casement, which symbolizes the death of his youth in the grim, skeletal embodiment of his ideal of pure beauty.

Psychologically, he cannot remain in that youthful world and become a man; his resistance to it has already generated a confusion of his sexual longings. But the alternative is acceptance of a sordid outer world utterly lacking in beauty, so his choice is one between nightmares. And Anderson's most masterful achievement in the story is his portrayal of the boy's inner struggle—the irresistible assertion of the dark blood—in concrete dramatic and symbolic terms.

The nightmarish atmosphere of the story both weighs upon the boy's sensibility and mirrors his inner conflict. As Dudley's initial agitation grows to terror, the intensity of his actions increases with the deepening horror of the wasteland images. Matching his own physical impotence and moral confusion are the spiritual impotence and fragmentation of society, as symbolized by the countryside consisting of "stones sticking out of the ground and trees mostly of the stubby, stunted kind"; by the mining town where the long rows of coke ovens at night look "like the teeth of some big man-eating giant lying and waiting . . ."; and by the saloon, whose diabolic atmosphere reflects the brutality of the spiritually emasculated miners. The ugly facts of the outer world combine with the demands of a repressed—or at least a resisted—subconscious to force him to abandon his childhood world of ideal innocence and become a man. In Freudian terms, the "big wave" that hits him releases his male sex drives; and his scream frees him from his verbal and physical paralysis. Entering the haystack naked with the sheep, he is in a figurative sense born again into a new innocence of manhood. When he leaves the track for good, he leaves behind both an ideal impossible to maintain and a sordid reality impossible to ignore. He assumes his role in the adult world where pure non-physical innocence does not exist, where innocence compels a discriminating selection from among complex alternatives.

With the stories in ***The Triumph of the Egg*** and in ***Horses and Men*** Anderson reached the height of his genius. (pp. 104-06)

Rex Burbank, in his Sherwood Anderson, *Twayne Publishers, Inc., 1964, 159 p.*

DAVID D. ANDERSON (essay date 1967)

[*Anderson founded the Society for the Study of Midwestern Literature and edits its annual publication,* MidAmerica. *His critical writings include several important works on Sherwood Anderson, and he is currently preparing* The Four Stages of a Man's Life: A Photo Biography of Sherwood Anderson. *In the following excerpt, he describes the themes underlying the stories in* Death in the Woods.]

In ***Death in the Woods*** Anderson collected the best of the short fiction that he had written during the preceding several years, including the title story. In this book, published in 1933, he dispensed with foreword, preface, introduction, or tone piece, preferring instead that the works themselves be interpreted through their own literary art. Perhaps he no longer felt the need for explaining himself and his works as he had for so long; at any rate, the decision was a wise one. . . . Not only did he change the order and content of the volume after he had received the proofs, eliminating several stories that he felt were unsatisfactory, but he wrote **"Brother Death"** for inclusion. The latter was, he felt, ". . . one of the finest stories I've ever done, and I even dare to say one of the finest and most significant anyone has ever done. Sounds cocky, doesn't it?"

The comment was cocky; hardly in keeping with a mood of desperate uncertainty and fumbling creativity, which Irving Howe maintains was Anderson's state at this time. Not only is the statement cocky, but it is not far from the truth. **"Brother Death"** and **"Death in the Woods"** are two of Anderson's best stories, ranking easily with those in the earlier collections; and the volume as a whole is evidence that in the short story form, Anderson's power in style and execution is at its best.

To give form to the book, Anderson again used a framing technique, leading off with **"Death in the Woods"** and concluding with **"Brother Death,"** companion pieces in mood, theme, and setting. The first story is based on an incident presumably from Anderson's childhood, described at length in *Tar: A Midwest Childhood*. In it Anderson returns to the grotesque castoffs of society that have consistently been his people. The story is that of the life and death of an old woman who is exploited by her brutal husband, her son, and their dogs. (pp. 130-31)

As in Anderson's earlier stories dealing with adolescent initiation [such as **"I'm a Fool"** and **"The Man Who Became a Woman"**], the story transcends that initial theme and becomes a story of adult realization; of recognition that death is inevitable but not terrible, that it can be a release from and a compensation for the brutality and the lack of feeling one encounters in life.

The story has been interpreted as a symbolic presentation of the life and death of Anderson's own mother whom he had earlier pictured as silent and inarticulate, and who had presumbably been sent to her early grave by hard work and selfless devotion. But the story is too harsh and brutal to be representative of the years he had recently seen in perspective as satisfying and rich. Moreover, after having rehabilitated the image of his father in his recent autobiographical writings, Anderson would hardly have returned to a portrayal of him that was as animalistic and as shadowy as the father in this story. Rather, he chose this stark, depersonalized presentation not to symbolize family relations but to commemorate the silent, welcome deaths that occur whenever man reduces his relations with his fellows to the level of the jungle.

In **"The Return"** Anderson counters the grimness of the preceding story with the realization that the machine age had replaced the past recalled by the protagonist. His only choice is to have the machine carry him quickly away from the fears brought on by that realization. **"There She Is—She Is Taking Her Bath"** is a seemingly humorous piece pointing out the inarticulateness of modern life and the resulting folly when man is afraid to penetrate surface barriers. The humor disappears as the impotent protagonist realizes that his fears will continue, that his hands will shake, and that he will spill his dessert.

"The Fight" is another story set in the present. It is an attempt to point out the senselessness and the irrationality at the heart of human rivalry, which no amount of reason can change. Only a change of heart can do this, Anderson points out, an act of love that cannot be intellectualized. **"That Sophistication"** carries this theme through to the Bohemian revolt of the twenties, pointing out that deliberately intellectualized rejection is futile, that it results in a meaningless, ritualized morass. Here again Anderson emphasizes that changes in human relations can come about only by something more far-reaching than merely willing the changes.

The other stories in the collection explore further aspects of the futility of intellectualized human relations. **"In a Strange Town"** points out the uselessness of the attempt to control the human experience through rational action. Such attempts fail, the wanderer in this story shows, because they try to analyze what cannot be analyzed. Human existence can only be understood through empathy and an honest approach to human lives and deaths as extensions of one's self. The mountaineer juror in **"A Jury Case"** realizes this instinctively as he learns that there is a difference between human truth and intellectualized legal truth; and the middle-aged doctor in **"Another Wife"** points out that true feeling transcends things that can be seen, felt, or measured. With true maturity comes wisdom in the form of the realization that appearance, the only thing on which man can focus his intellectual powers, is unimportant and that human emotions, if they are true, perceive this difference and penetrate to the essence of other lives. In **"The Flood"** Anderson points out that the scholar cannot define this ability of the human heart even though he has experienced it and will experience it again.

Through the stories in the collection, Anderson has woven a progressive thematic thread that stresses the inability of the human mind to determine the ultimate reality behind appearance and events. This thread begins with the apparent tragedy, which is not a tragedy at all, in **"Death in the Woods"** by emphasizing man's inability or frightened unwillingness to search for the meaning beneath the surface of human life. This, Anderson points out, results in man's attempts to rationalize his insecurities, knowing all the while that he could find the truth if he were not afraid. The theme reverses itself in the following stories, turning to the side that contains the key to any ultimate fulfillment of man's potential. The answer lies in the rejection of attempts to solve human problems through rational means and in the endeavor to build relationships on the fact that reality can be found only through a determined effort to enter into the lives of others. This, of course, is contingent upon an appreciation of the intrinsic worth not only of human life but also of death, which often provides the fulfillment that life has denied.

This thematic thread leads directly to **"Brother Death,"** the last story in the collection and the one that Anderson wrote as a capstone in order to bring the theme to its logical conclusion. In **"Brother Death"** he completely reverses the conventional roles of appearance and reality. This story, like **"Death in the Woods,"** deals with the realization that death can be life and that life can be death; but again, as in the first story, it is a realization that can come only with maturity. The story has two plots, each an amplification of the same theme. The first plot concerns a young girl and her younger brother who has a heart condition so serious that he may die at any time. In an effort to prolong his life, the family prevents him from playing normally. To the young girl, this is wrong, and finally her protests result in the boy's freedom to play. After a year or two he dies, quietly and peacefully in his sleep.

The second plot centers around the conflict between the father and the oldest son, each of whom has his own ideas about running the family farm. As a focal point for the conflict, Anderson uses two huge oak trees—beautiful and shady but useless—standing in the pasture. The father wants to remove them, but the son protests. Eventually the father has his way, and the son is torn between accepting the decision, thus protecting his position as heir, and leaving the farm. He remains on the farm; and in so doing, he surrenders his individuality to the will of his father. The girl realizes later that the physical death of her younger brother was more humane than the spiritual death suffered by her older brother. Thus, the conventional roles have been reversed: to die is to preserve one's freedom; to live is to relinquish it.

"Brother Death" is Anderson at his best. A microcosm of everything he had experienced in his long observation of America, it shows that he had at last recognized the basic factor that had corrupted American civilization: the inability to distinguish between substance and dross and the all-too-frequent willingness to accept the cheaper substitute rather than search for the more valuable. This concept goes far beyond his earlier dogma that the industrial age is one in which man, through his powers of self-delusion, believes that the standardized machine-made product is as satisfying as that product which has been made not only with skill, but with love, by an artisan who takes pride in his craftsmanship and achieves satisfaction in having made the product. Here Anderson points out that man's willingness to accept material values instead of spiritual values is responsible for the corruption of the American ideal and of the American life.

In **"Brother Death"** as in **"Death in the Woods"** Anderson points out that death of man's body can be his ultimate triumph over his environment, not because he will pass on to a perfect state, but because he is no longer faced with demands that he surrender his individuality. Whereas, to live in a state of compromise with the demands of society is to place one's individuality in danger, eventually surrendering it, and seeing it die. This is the real death that society ignores even while it denies the meaning of the other. This, Anderson says, is the unnecessary and tragic death, while the other should be celebrated as good.

The stories in ***Death in the Woods*** contain Anderson's most cogent and most perceptive comments on American civilization; they are the product of his experiences from boyhood to retirement in the Virginia hills. Coming at this time, as he was trying to find a solution to the Depression, and marking his disenchantment with communism, the collection is the representation of his belief that a reversal of American values was needed. If America was to survive as a nation, she had to look above and beyond the immediate surface of life for the beliefs that she needed so desperately and had lost.

The collection also gives further indication of Anderson's mastery of his craft. Always at his stylistic best in the shorter forms, he again reproduces the flat rhythms of the American Midwest, and constructs his stories in the old, oral tradition that for all its seeming formlessness is carefully controlled. ***Death in the Woods*** is his most consistently high level collection of stories if ***Winesburg, Ohio*** is excluded. . . . (pp. 131-35)

David D. Anderson, in his Sherwood Anderson: An Introduction and Interpretation, *Holt, Rinehart and Winston, 1967, 182 p.*

WILLIAM V. MILLER (essay date 1974)

[*Miller is an American essayist who has written a number of commentaries on Anderson's work. In the following excerpt, he examines Anderson's characterization of women in the short stories.*]

Herbert Gold was not the first to note the limitations of Sherwood Anderson's characterization of women, but his statement offers a starting point for more definitive observations about women in his short fiction: "Except for the poetic school teacher and a few others, women are not women in Anderson's stories. . . . For Anderson women have a strange holy power; they are earth-mothers, ectoplasmic spirits, sometimes succubi, rarely individual living creatures" [see Additional Bibliography]. . . . (p. 64)

For the most part, his female characters are managers, defenders of the home who entrap men, wholehearted givers to men, frustrated gropers after a higher life, or characters in whom these qualities are combined.

There is awe before the wonders of how women manage men in **"Another Wife."** In this story a forty-seven-year-old widower doctor is confused about his relationship with a woman of thirty-seven he has met in the hill country. He thinks he may be in love with the woman, but he is unsure and overly impressed with her culture and her "modernity." Finally, they seemingly blunder into an understanding that they will marry. But the confusion is all male: she is understanding, patient, and sure of what she wants.

Other "managers" include Aunt Sally in **"A Meeting South"**; the doctor's wife in **"Pastoral"**; Gretchen, the nurse in **"The Rabbit-Pen"**; the mother in **"The Egg"**; and the girl in **"Nice Girl."** The latter three characters can serve here to illustrate the managing pattern. In **"The Rabbit-Pen,"** Anderson's first published short story, Gretchen epitomizes all that Joe Harkness, his wife, Ruth and the writer Fordyce are not. Joe hides behind riches and romantic love, Ruth cannot handle her children, and Fordyce can neither understand nor come close to women. But Gretchen manages the entire household with super efficiency and aplomb.

The mother in **"The Egg"** and the girl in **"Nice Girl"** are contrasting types of capable, ambitious women. The former suggests Anderson's image of his mother. "She was a tall silent woman with a long nose and troubled gray eyes. For herself she wanted nothing. For father and myself she was incurably ambitious." . . . First she induced the father to become an independent chicken farmer. Then she got the idea of having a restaurant business, rented a store building, "decided that our restaurant should remain open at night," and tended the restaurant during the day. The father is willing enough, but the mother determines the family moves. Her competence serves as a foil for his poignant frustration in the story's climax.

"Nice Girl," which appeared in 1936, is noteworthy for a potential new direction for Anderson's stories which was never fully exploited: the new note is the objectivity, the irony, and the narrator's lack of sympathy. Agnes Wilson, the unscrupulous protagonist of the story, is unobtrusive and apparently diffident, but behind the scenes she is cunning and manipulating. She secretly arranges for her brother's bootlegger to be arrested and in the course of the story schemes to get her sister's husband.

In one of his typically powerful images, Anderson described the feelings of a young man at the moment he confronts the necessity of getting married. "Some shadowy, lovely thing seemed fleeing out of him and out of her. He felt like a beast who is playing about at night in a forest (and) has suddenly put his foot into a trap. . . . He was held fast, bound down to the earth, not by desire now, but by a strange hesitating sympathy with the thing that bound her to earth." In other stories, too, sex is the bait in the trap of marriage. In this story, **"The Contract,"** and in **"Not Sixteen,"** Anderson could be sympathetic with the necessity of marriage in our culture and with a woman's needs, for he recognized that behind the "trembling figure" of the girl in **"The Contract"** stands "the whole fact of organized life." The frustrated would-be lover of Lillian in **"Not Sixteen"** comes to admire the iron will of Lillian, who is a giving woman but insistent that she will give herself to no one until she is sixteen.

But Anderson could also be very forceful in depicting the trap of marriage. Bill in **"His Chest of Drawers"** is torn between his sexual needs and the needs of self-respect, beauty, and freedom. The small, slender copywriter is left only a chest of drawers in his own house by his wife and four daughters. When most of that space is taken, he gets drunk to regain the illusion of self-respect. "'After all,' he said, 'they do bestow their favors upon us'." . . . For Hugh Walker, the protagonist in **"The Door of the Trap,"** marriage is a prison. We are led to believe that Walker frees Mary, a young girl in the story, from the jeopardy of being emotionally imprisoned when Walker kisses her and sends her off. At a time when Anderson's own marriage to Tennessee Mitchell was disintegrating, he published **"Brothers"** (1921), which includes a bitter description of the murderer's marriage: "His wife in particular was like some strange unlovely growth that had attached itself to his body." . . . (pp. 73-5).

The best presentation of the marriage dilemma is also one of the best tales in ***Winesburg, Ohio***, **"The Untold Lie."** The focus is not on the wife who wants Ray Pearson to "hustle" more but on Ray and what he should tell young Hal Winters about marriage. When the devilish Hal asks him if he should marry Nell Gunther, who is pregnant, there is "only one thing that all his own training and all the beliefs of the people he knew would approve" of his saying. But he cannot tell this "lie." . . . But he remembers also the moments of joy with his thin-legged children as well as the nagging wife and does not tell him; he realizes that "whatever I told him would have been a lie." . . . (p. 75)

The guilt Anderson felt about the exploitation of women by himself and other men is expressed in the characterization of some of the women in the stories as "feeders." He loved the women who freely gave of themselves like, to name a few, Lillian in **"Not Sixteen"** (though she postpones giving physically), Kate in **"Daughters,"** Alice in **"Like a Queen,"** the woman in **"White Spot,"** the wife in **"Brother Earl,"** Kate Swift in **"The Teacher,"** and the woman in **"The Man's Story."** He wrote in *A Story Teller's Story:* "I had always been drawn toward . . . women who gave themselves to physical experiences with grave and fine abandon. . . ."

However, this love is mixed with guilt and the memory of his over-burdened mother. He stated the theme of **"Death in the Woods"** in observations dated 1937: "It seems to me that the theme of the story is the persistent animal hunger of men. There are these women who spend their whole lives, rather dumbly, feeding this hunger. For years I wanted to write this story." The word *feed* and its different forms reverberate through the story. This paragraph illustrates the point: "Then she settled down to *feed* [all italics mine] stock. That was her job. At the German's place she had cooked the food for the German and his wife. . . . She *fed* them and *fed* the cows in the barn, *fed* the pigs, the horses and the chickens. Every moment of every day, as a young girl, was spent *feeding* something." . . . She also fed her husband sexually, but "that hadn't lasted long after their marriage and after the babies came." . . . (pp. 75-6)

Anderson's artist-writers particularly need a woman to feed on, to give them the constant, selfless love that helps sustain their art. Kate Swift and Elizabeth Willard seek passionately to nurture the incipient artist in George. In **"The Yellow Gown"** Mildred is as absorbed in Harold the painter as he comes to be in his masterpiece. Most directly, the woman in **"The Man's Story"** gives her total life to Edgar Wilson, a poet. She leaves her husband; supports Wilson with love and money; and even though mortally wounded, her dying act is to light a fire in the small apartment she shares with him.

Rex Burbank has noted accurately that some of Anderson's best "adult" tales are "similar to the stories of Alice Hindman, Kate Swift, and Louise Bentley in ***Winesburg, Ohio***, tales which portray young women who are defeated by the coarseness, the insensitivity, or the moral cowardice of man and by the hypocrisy behind conventional Puritan moral codes" [see excerpt dated 1964]. What his statement omits is the positive qualities of these women. They are intensely alive, more aware and sensitive than those about them, seekers after a higher degree of self-fulfillment. Once again Anderson appears to dramatize in them his concepts of the buried life of his mother. In doing so, he creates his most successful women. Only Alice in **"Like a Queen"** and Aunt Sally in **"A Meeting South,"** who are unique and seem to draw directly on specific biographical material, have the character dimensions of Elizabeth Willard, Kate Swift, Elsie Leander in **"The New Englander,"** May Edgely in **"'Unused,'"** Mary Cochran in **"Unlighted Lamps,"** and Rosalind Westcott in the long story **"Out of Nowhere into Nothing."**

Kate Swift is characterized through contrasts. With her poor complexion, she was not regarded as a pretty woman in Winesburg. But "alone in the night in the winter streets she was lovely," . . . with a straight back and the "features of a tiny goddess." . . . Her usual attitude in the classroom was one of silent, cold sternness. But like many other Anderson characters, when she tells stories, she becomes animated and virtually hypnotizes her students. "Behind a cold exterior the most extraordinary events transpired in her mind." . . . Although people thought of her as an old maid lacking in human feeling, "in reality she was the most eagerly passionate soul among them." . . . When she thinks George may have a spark of genius in his writing, Kate Swift wants "to blow on the spark." . . . She tells him "to know what people are thinking about, not what they say"; . . . and on another occasion "a passionate desire to have him understand the import of life, to learn to interpret it truly and honestly, swept over her." . . . But her passion becomes physical, both she and George feel the confusion of her intense hopes for him and sexual passion, and she breaks away from George, hitting him in her frustration. Kate Swift is brought to life in but a few pages, but she is one of Anderson's most memorable creations.

Kate Swift is lonely, too; but some of the other questing women we are considering here more keenly seek fulfillment in sex. Before her marriage Elizabeth Willard expressed her restless nature by dreaming of being on the stage, "of joining some company and wandering over the world, seeing always new faces and giving something out of herself to all people." . . . The second expression of her restlessness was giving herself physically to some man. In these ways and others "there was something she sought blindly, passionately, some hidden wonder in life." . . . But this poor woman, who desperately needed to be loved, found release "but twice in her life, in the moments when her lovers Death and Doctor Reefy held her in their arms." . . . (pp. 76-8)

May Edgely in **"'Unused'"** wants to be used, to be connected with the stream of life. Her two sisters are promiscuous, and the males in the family are rough but self-reliant. But May alone competes with the establishment in Bidwell (another Clyde, Ohio). She is an excellent student and berry picker, and she dresses neatly and cares for her mother. However, the year she graduates second in her class, her mother dies; and soon afterwards, in a blatant gesture, she goes into the woods with Jerome Hadley. The town view is that May "who had been treated almost as an equal by the others had wanted to throw something ugly right in their faces:" But they do not know her: she wants only to answer some strong impulse in her personality. The rest of the sad tale is the steady decline and final death of May, victimized by the community.

Rosalind Westcott is warned against men by her taciturn mother; but at the end of **"Out of Nowhere into Nothing,"** she runs toward experience, back to life in a Chicago love affair with a married man which is anything but promising. Elsie Leander, the frustrated title character in **"The New Englander,"** longs for release that is generally sexual in the cornfields of Iowa. And Mary Cochran is the victim of town gossip and her father's inability to communicate. She rejects the young man who misunderstood her actions and determines too late to express her love for her father. The pattern of light imagery in this fine story is epitomized by the image of the title, **"Unlighted Lamps."** Mary poignantly needed some glimpse of her widower father's buried life to illuminate her own identity, but in critical moments he is unable to light the needed lamp.

All of these women—some of his most successful creations (as Gold noted)—have Elizabeth Willard's need: "Like all the women in the world, she wanted a real lover." . . . That Anderson's women never find the sustained, patient love they need is only one dimension of the limitations of their characterization. Rare, indeed, is the character in all of Anderson's fiction who finds such love.

Love is a vital force which permits the men and women of his fiction to escape, if only for the moment, the barrier of conventions and neuroses and find a kind of fulfillment and wholeness lacking in his grotesques and other gropers; but for Anderson "love" differs importantly between the sexes. He could stress the biological role of women with genuine respect: he seemed awed by the capacity of women to create out of their own bodies. Despite the surfacing of deeply felt antagonistic feelings about women in, for example, the story **"Respectability,"** Anderson was not a misogynist. And it is extraordinary that all three of his divorced wives continued long after the divorces to regard him with affection. But as has been noted earlier, Anderson denied to feminine sensibility the realm of the creative imagination. In this realm the artist man, who is not different in kind from other craftsmen, can rise to impersonal love and thus combat what he called the "disease of self." He insisted that this kind of love gives power to art: "Few enough people realize that all art that has vitality must have its basis in love." In a letter to his son dated 1927 he spoke of impersonal love and made a rare reference to religion. "In art there is the possibility of an impersonal love. For modern man it is, I think, the only road to God."

At this point one must exercise great care in generalizing. On the one hand, we have these stated views about women; on the other, the created characters. The personal fulfillment of an individual character is not tantamount to successful characterization. Kate Swift, for example, may be successfully realized and still be terribly frustrated. Furthermore, the "extraordinary events" which "transpired in her mind" suggest an imaginative capacity which Anderson would not allow real women.

Personal fulfillment and "rounded" characterization come together in a few of Anderson's artist men—notably but still not definitely in George Willard, who contrasts with the grotesques in his capacity to get outside himself. However, Anderson's women are circumscribed in their development, fixed in repetitive roles, essentially as they have been described here—managers, defenders of the home, feeders of men, and frustrated gropers after a higher life. These characters reflect both

Anderson's bewildered understanding of women and the expressive basis of his art of characterization. (pp. 78-80)

William V. Miller, "Earth-Mothers, Succubi, and Other Ectoplasmic Spirits: The Women in Sherwood Anderson's Short Stories," in MidAmerica, *Vol. I, 1974, pp. 64-81.*

WELFORD DUNAWAY TAYLOR (essay date 1977)

[*Taylor is an American educator and Anderson scholar who currently serves as editor of the* Winesburg Eagle, *the semiannual publication of the Sherwood Anderson Society. In the following excerpt from his critical biography of Anderson, Taylor discusses several of the short stories from* The Triumph of the Egg, Horses and Men, *and* Death in the Woods.]

One of the few concepts shared by Anderson and literary naturalists, such as Stephen Crane and Theodore Dreiser, is the belief that life is not divinely ordered. This did not mean that he shared their pessimistic conclusion that existence is an absurd experience in which human striving comes to nothing. Rather, Anderson saw the meaning of life in the form of sympathy and understanding among people, and he felt obligated as an artist to bring this about. His characters are often the frustrated, the repressed, the weak, and the broken. But if he is able to understand them through the use of intuitive imagination, and in turn to articulate what he learns, he will have established a sympathetic bond among reader, character, and himself. (pp. 46-7)

Anderson's fiction contains a minimum of detail describing the outward appearance of people, places, and things. Often, there is little indication of a particular time and place in his stories. His stories reveal an impatience to get the surface details out of the way so that he can get quickly to the essence of his subjects. He was exceptionally adept at selecting one or two details that immediately give the impression of the entire subject. (pp. 47-8)

[Anderson] approached his characters from the interior of their beings—from the standpoint of their feelings, emotions, thoughts—rather than from external appearance. This inner terrain shaped Anderson's sense of reality, which he readily admitted was difficult to define:

> I do not know what reality is. I do not think any of us quite know how much our point of view and, in fact, all our touch with life, is influenced by our imaginations.
>
> . . . Having met some person for the first time . . . and having had my first look, I cannot ever see him or her again. . . .
>
> Why is this true? It is true because the moment I meet you . . . my imagination begins to play. Perhaps I begin to make up stories about you.

For Anderson, then, objective facts were less important than "facts" perceived through the imagination. One of his greatest strengths as a storyteller is the ability to perceive "imaginative" facts that offer unique insights into his subjects.

That Anderson could find unique meaning in the most commonplace objects is obvious in **"The Egg"**. . . . Not only does a simple egg suggest to him a bittersweet story of human frustration; it is also used to symbolize the mysterious workings of nature. The youthful narrator, one of several that Anderson employed in his early stories, is prompted by the events of the story to ponder "why eggs had to be and why from the egg came the hen who again laid the egg."

None of the three main characters—the boy and his parents—is ever named. By making them anonymous, Anderson suggests the universality of their plight. Until he was thirty-four, the father was a farmhand. Then he married and was seized with "the American passion for getting up in the world." The means he chose for achieving success was chicken farming. The boy was born during the first year of this disastrous enterprise.

Throughout the story, the boy proves a highly effective point of view. By speaking innocently of the chickens' perilous struggle for survival and of his parents' repeated failure to make money by raising the delicate creatures, a powerful sense of dramatic irony is achieved. A vast gap exists between the innocent relation of details and the far-reaching serious implications that the boy is unaware of. The boy speaks with candor and humor of fluffy chickens "such as you will see pictured on Easter cards" becoming "hideously naked." After eating quantities of food "bought by the sweat of your father's brow," getting diseases like the pip and cholera, "looking with stupid eyes at the sun," the chickens die. To the boy, the droll image of the naked bird looking stupidly at the sun is humorous. But the reader sees reflected in the picture a cruel nature that destroys the very defenseless beings it creates.

After ten years of unsuccessful chicken farming, the family moves to a nearby town in which the parents open a restaurant. But the poultry venture accompanies them in the form of several misshapen chicks that have been preserved in bottles of alcohol. When the father places these freakish specimens on a shelf in his restaurant, an unsavory, bizarre element is introduced into the narrative. They symbolize the cruel workings of nature and foreshadow the futile attempt of a farmer to "get up in the world" by means of the restaurant business.

The farmer is an awkward, uncommunicative man. He has never dealt with the public and does not know how to attract trade to the restaurant. Finally he decides that he should try being jovial to his occasional customers and perhaps entertain them. The story comes to a poignant ending one rainy evening when the farmer tries to entertain a man at the lunch counter by showing him the deformed chicks in the bottles. When the shocked customer attempts to leave, the farmer detains him by proclaiming that he can fit an egg boiled in vinegar through the narrow mouth of a bottle. For more than a half hour he attempts this feat. Then, as his customer is preparing to leave, he pushes the softened shell too hard, and it breaks. The man leaves, laughing loudly.

The farmer, frustrated and angry, curses and hurls another egg after him. Then he gently picks up an egg and climbs the stairs to the family apartment. He gingerly places the egg on a bedside table and drops to his knees beside his wife, sobbing like a baby.

The farmer contains some elements of Anderson's father: he has grandiose ideas; his desire for success seems ill-starred; he brags of being able to do things he cannot accomplish. There can be no question about the boy's compassion for him, however. The boy freely admits that he is "the son of [his] father." Both boy and man stand awed and ineffectual before the paradoxical egg—so seemingly simple, yet so complex in defying man's attempts at understanding.

After seeing the father crying pathetically beside his wife, the narrator admits at the end of the story to "the complete and final triumph of the egg'' over the family's strivings. This admission represents a change in the humor of the story. It now becomes a kind of cosmic laughter—an attitude that suggests laughter as an alternative to man's inability to understand the meaning of existence. Also suggested is the cruelty that nature inflicts upon innocent creatures. The father is as pitiable as the chickens. Both struggle to survive in a world filled with obstacles. The odds are against either succeeding.

"The New Englander" . . . recalls the technique of the ***Winesburg, Ohio*** stories in that its plot is developed by only a few incidents. Elsie Leander, an unmarried woman in her mid-thirties who has grown up on the family farm in Vermont, moves with her mother and father to Iowa. She has lived a sheltered existence with her parents. One day she watches her niece and a farmhand embrace in a cornfield during a storm and suddenly realizes that her protected life has actually been one long episode of repression that has thwarted her feminine impulses to love. (pp. 49-52)

"The Egg" and **"The New Englander"** imply that the lives of average men and women are doomed to frustration, both in attempting to understand and control nature and in the achievement of emotional fulfillment. In these stories Anderson is suggesting that happiness lies in exploring nature to the fullest; in avoiding repression, if possible; and in allowing one's emotions to express themselves.

A frequent character type in Anderson's stories is the person who possesses a strong native capability that is never allowed to develop. In Anderson's view this is a waste, and he gives negative titles to two of his best-known stories containing such characters: **"Unlighted Lamps"** . . . and **"'Unused'"**. . . . (pp. 54-5)

"'Unused'" deals with May Edgley, one of Anderson's most completely developed characters. Early in the narrative May, the youngest girl in the Edgley family, commits an unprecedented act that surprises the town of Bidwell and sets into motion the course of events that leads to her death a short time later. May's two older sisters have become women of the street, causing the family to be shunned by the townspeople. May promises to be different. She is the most intelligent student in her high school and exhibits none of the attributes that have driven her sisters into their sordid lives.

In her seventeenth summer, May works as a picker on a berry farm, where she does her job silently and efficiently. One day, Jerome Hadley, a braggart from the town, joins the pickers, and May becomes talkative and even flirtatious. During the noon hour, while the other workers eat their lunch, May suddenly lays her food on the ground, climbs over a fence, and starts down a lane leading to a wood. After going a little way, she turns around and looks at Jerome, who immediately follows her. They do not return for two hours. Later, he boasts to his cohorts that May was an easy conquest.

This, the only sexual indiscretion in May's life, causes the people in Bidwell to think that she has the same wild blood as her sisters. The sisters themselves upbraid her for her action. Two recurring images are used in describing the reasons for May's lapse and its aftermath. The first is the image of a stream, which is used partially to explain her actions, partially to suggest their ultimate results. After May first met Jerome Hadley in the berry field, and became attracted to him, she allowed her imagination to fantasize about being loved by a man. ''She imagined arms soft and yet firm, strong arms, holding her closely, and sank into a dim, splendid world of emotion.'' Then ''the stream of life in which she had always wanted to float had picked her up—it carried her along.''

Because of the reputation of her sisters and the indifference of her parents, May had never felt loved or accepted despite her native intelligence and high scholastic achievement. She has viewed the affairs of life from the sidelines, never feeling that she was a participant. She had read of but had not experienced love, and had seen it debased by her sisters and disregarded by her parents. Her imprudent act with Jerome Hadley represented an awkward, faltering attempt to enter the stream of life as a participant.

The second recurring image is a tower. It is first mentioned just after a naive character named Maud Welliver enters the story. May, sensing Maud's ingenuousness, tells her that Jerome Hadley had followed her into the woods to ask her advice about a love affair he was having with a married woman. May says that Jerome had intended to kill the woman's husband, but that she talked him out of it. She says that he tried to seduce her, and, because she would not submit, he spread the rumor that she had. This lie, told in order to justify her act to herself and to convince Maud of her chastity, becomes ''the first of the foundation stones'' of ''a tall tower on which she could stand, from the ramparts of which she could look down into a world created by herself, by her own mind.''

From her fertile imagination, May creates a farfetched tale of being courted by an Eastern prince, who is to return and marry her. Although Maud believes this story and comes to regard May as something of a romantic heroine, she invites her to a dance and arranges to have a grocery clerk escort her. In this final scene of the story, May is once again faced with a threatening situation reminiscent of the episode with Jerome Hadley. The dance is held in a seedy roadhouse. May, half believing the romantic fable she has told to Maud, feels quite superior to her escort. She wears her best clothes and a hat decorated with large ostrich plumes that was borrowed from her sister Lillian. As she listens in bored silence to the banal stories her escort tells, May watches the faces of the dancers. Suddenly she thinks of Jerome Hadley and is terrified that he may attend the dance. These thoughts weaken the tower of romance in which she has attempted to live for the past several weeks. She can no longer think of herself as a superior woman in boorish surroundings. She becomes simply a frightened girl trapped in a room full of raucous bumpkins that remind her of the rabble she has known all her life.

These memories mark the turning point in the story. They indicate May's descent to reality from the tower of fantasy that she has built in her imagination. In an attempt to escape from these past associations, she suggests to the grocer that they go outside; but as she rises, six ruffians from Bidwell arrive. One, Sid Gould, has been involved in a fracas over one of May's sisters. When he sees May, he loudly announces that he intends to take her away from the grocer. To quiet his boasting, May accompanies him outside. But as soon as they are a little distance from the roadhouse, she suddenly pulls away from him. (pp. 57-60)

Then, beginning to run, she experiences a moment of self-awareness such as she has never known. She begins to equate the incident with Gould with her encounter with Jerome Hadley. She suddenly realizes that the motive of both men has been not merely sexual gratification but also a malign desire to debase her. Although she had, in an innocent way, given her body to Jerome Hadley, she retained her inner sense of dignity and goodness. She has not made any sort of moral compromise with her seducer; her finest qualities of character remain "unused."

As May continues to run from Sid's boorish friends, who pursue her a long distance, she is overcome by thoughts that the world contains people who wish to destroy the character of others. Within her erupts "a fear of life itself." She stumbles into a stream which, like the stream of life she had sought to enter by enticing Jerome Hadley, has a deceptively strong current. She is swept away, but she seems in a way happy—in being delivered from a hostile world, secure in the realization of having been unused by it.

When May's body is found a few days later, her hand still clutches the plumed hat. As a symbol, the hat has poignant meaning: it represents the life of romance and gaiety of which she had dreamed, and its whiteness suggests the purity she has retained. As a heroine whose physical indiscretions have left her character unsullied, May strongly resembles Gustave Flaubert's Madame Bovary, a nineteenth-century literary heroine with whom Anderson was familiar. Like Emma Bovary, May has dreamed of rising from a base existence into a fulfilling life that offered love and excitement. When this is denied them, both women lose the will to live. Emma commits suicide; May willfully runs into a swift stream, obviously wishing for escape through death.

Unlike numerous Anderson characters who entertain vague dreams of beautiful and pleasant things, May Edgley possesses a high degree of intelligence. Given the opportunity to develop her mind and to pursue meaningful goals, she could have become a productive member of society and a fulfilled individual. Through no fault of her own, she was forced to live in a loveless, ignorant family and to associate with people who wished to take advantage of her innocence. The loss of the successful life that May could have lived is, in Anderson's view, a significant waste for which an uncaring fate can be blamed. (pp. 60-1)

From the mid-1920s onward, Anderson wrote short fiction only occasionally. Though he still sought within common objects for essences that often eluded him and still showed concern for unlived lives, debilitating frustrations, and the pains of growing up, many of the later stories state a marked affirmation of life and a profound respect for nature. [**"Death in the Woods"** and **"Brother Death,"** two stories from Anderson's final collection ***Death in the Woods***] . . . are forceful examples of these principles. In both stories Anderson employs the theme of death to emphasize the values of life and to express his respect for the workings of nature. (p. 67)

Anderson maintained that **"Brother Death"** . . . was his best. In it, he uses death as a means of evaluating the quality of life as it is lived by the John Greys, a farming family in southwestern Virginia. The story successfully answers the question posed by one of the children in the family: "Life, what is it worth? Is death the most terrible thing?"

As the story opens, Ted and Mary, the youngest of the three Grey children, are examining two huge stumps, left from chopping down a pair of giant oaks. The children, who have witnessed the cutting of the trees, innocently feel the stumps. Ted asks whether the trees had felt pain from the saw and whether the stumps had bled—as a man would bleed when one of his limbs was amputated.

The children's conversation points to the major action of the story, which concerns a tense drama within the family. The mother, whose aristocratic Grandfather Aspinwahl planted the trees many decades before, does not want to see them removed. To her they are a symbol of the past grandeur of her family, who have lost most of their wealth and lands. Her husband, John Grey, had decided to cut down the trees because the shade they cast impedes the lawn he is cultivating. (p. 70)

Ted has a serious heart condition that can cause death at any time. His parents and older brother have protected him to the point of preventing him from enjoying play. When he is stopped from playing, he becomes tense, trembles, and turns pale. One day, as he and Mary splash about in puddles during a rain, the mother reprimands them. Ted runs to the barn to escape her, but Mary stands her ground. Facing her mother, she says, "You should have more sense, Mother. . . . You mustn't do it any more. Don't you ever do it again." The mother, torn between her wish to rebuke Mary and her recognition that Mary is right, turns and silently walks into the house. After this confrontation, Mary and Ted are given freedom. Secure in "their own created world," they enjoy doing things that might be potentially injurious to Ted. They no longer fear reprisal from the older family members. Ted does die a couple of years after the puddle episode, but he dies peacefully, in his sleep.

The brother Don, oldest of the Grey children, bears a physical resemblance to Mr. Grey, with "the same lines about the jaws, the same eyes . . . the same curious lack of delicacy of thought and touch—the heaviness that plows through, gets things done." At sixty, John Grey looks forward to the day when Don will take over the large farm. But when Mr. Grey suddenly decides to chop down the trees, Don sides with his mother. The argument that develops between father and son becomes a contest of two strong wills. Don threatens to leave home. The father simply says, "All right. Go then." After the trees are cut down and Don leaves, the family lives in silent tension for several days. Then Don returns.

Mr. Grey's only comment is "It [the farm] will be yours soon now. You can be boss then." Anderson interprets the words to mean that one must assert authority in order to retain authority, but that "something in you must die before you can possess and command." In other words, only by feeling the humiliation of having authority imposed upon you can you ever effectively assert it yourself.

Anderson believes that the price Don has to pay in order to be an effective authoritarian is entirely too high, in terms of its damage to his ego and pride. In fact, he sees Don as having had to endure a living death. Ted, who dies in his sleep and does not live to assume authority over others, as Don presumably does, is far better off than his older brother. For "he never had to make the surrender his brother had made—to be sure of possessions, success, his time to command—would never have to face the more subtle and terrible death that had come to his older brother."

The answer to the question—"Life, what is it worth? Is death the most terrible thing?"—is that life is worthwhile only when one is allowed to actualize himself in his own way, to be free from restrictions imposed by anyone else—whether individuals or society. Having been allowed to live free and untrammeled, if only for a brief time, Ted dies fulfilled. His death is in a sense beautiful, suggesting peace and happiness.

In describing Mr. Grey's decision to chop down the trees, Anderson uses a favorite metaphor: the wall. John Grey's precipitous actions create a wall of estrangement, with Mary and Ted on one side and the rest of the family on the other. Throughout her life, Mary realizes its existence. Anderson calls this process of isolation "a driving destructive thing in life, in all relationships between people." Don is in effect trapped behind the wall because he possesses the same drives of ambition and greed as his father. Having had to endure an ignominious death while he is alive, it follows that for him physical death will be a bitter event because it will separate him from the material things for which he strove.

"Brother Death" is one of Anderson's most powerful statements concerning contemporary America. It denounces materialism not because objects are intrinsically destructive or harmful, but because in the pursuit of material things man turns from human values, such as understanding and concern for his fellow man. To Anderson, the end of material gain does not justify the means of dehumanization. He is saying that America must learn to respect human values if its material achievements are ever to be anything other than empty symbols of selfishness and ruthless avarice. (pp. 71-3)

Welford Dunaway Taylor, in his Sherwood Anderson, *Frederick Ungar Publishing Co., 1977, 128 p.*

JOHN UPDIKE (essay date 1984)

[*Updike is considered one of America's most distinguished men of letters. Best known for his novels, he also writes short stories, poetry, and criticism. In the following excerpt from a general essay on* Winesburg, Ohio, *Updike considers the bittersweet quality for which the work is noted.*]

Sherwood Anderson's ***Winesburg, Ohio*** is one of those books so well known by title that we imagine we know what is inside it: a sketch of the population, seen more or less in cross section, of a small Midwestern town. It is this as much as Edvard Munch's paintings are portraits of the Norwegian middle class around the turn of the century. The important thing, for Anderson and Munch, is not the costumes and the furniture or even the bodies but the howl they conceal—the psychic pressure and warp underneath the social scene. Matter-of-fact though it sounds, ***Winesburg, Ohio*** is feverish, phantasmal, dreamlike. Anderson had accurately called this collection of loosely linked short stories *The Book of the Grotesque;* his publisher, B. W. Huebsch, suggested the more appealing title. The book . . . remains his masterpiece.

"The Book of the Grotesque" is the name also of the opening story, which Anderson wrote first and which serves as a prologue. A writer, "an old man with a white mustache . . . who was past sixty," has a dream in which "all the men and women the writer had ever known had become grotesques." . . . Another writer, an "I" who is presumably Sherwood Anderson, breaks in and explains the old writer's theory of grotesqueness. . . . Having so strangely doubled authorial personae, Anderson then offers twenty-one tales, one of them in four parts, all "concerning," as the table of contents specifies, one or another citizen of Winesburg; whether they come from the old writer's book of grotesques or some different set to which the younger author had access is as unclear as their fit within the cranky and fey anthropological-metaphysical framework set forth with such ungainly solemnity.

"Hands," the first tale, "concerning Wing Biddlebaum," introduces not only its hero, a pathetic, shy old man on the edge of town whose hyperactive little white hands had once strayed to the bodies of too many schoolboys in the Pennsylvania town where he had been a teacher, but also George Willard, the eighteen-year-old son of the local hotelkeeper and a reporter for the *Winesburg Eagle*. He seems a young representative of the author. There is also a "poet," suddenly invoked in flighty passages like:

> Let us look briefly into the story of the hands. Perhaps our talking of them will arouse the poet who will tell the hidden wonder story of the influence for which the hands were but fluttering pennants of promise.

A cloud of authorial effort, then, attends the citizens of Winesburg, each of whom walks otherwise isolated toward some inexpressible denouement of private revelation. Inexpressiveness, indeed, is what is above all expressed: the characters, often, talk only to George Willard, and then only once; their attempts to talk with one another tend to culminate in a comedy of tongue-tied silence. (p. 95)

For Anderson, society scarcely exists in its legal and affective bonds, and dialogue is generally the painful imposition of one monologue upon another. At the climax of the unconsummated love affair between George Willard and Helen White that is one of ***Winesburg, Ohio***'s continuous threads, the two sit together in the deserted fairground grandstand and hold hands:

> In that high place in the darkness the two oddly sensitive human atoms held each other tightly and waited. In the mind of each was the same thought. "I have come to this lonely place and here is this other," was the substance of the thing felt.

They embrace, but then mutual embarrassment overtakes them and like children they race and tumble on the way down to town and part, having "for a moment taken hold of the thing that makes the mature life of men and women in the modern world possible."

The vagueness of "the thing" is chronic, and only the stumbling, shrugging, willful style that Anderson made of Stein's serene run-on tropes affords him half a purchase on his unutterable subject, the "thing" troubling the heart of his characters. Dr. Reefy, who attends and in a sense loves George Willard's dying mother, compulsively writes thoughts on bits of paper. He then crumples them into little balls—"paper pills"—and shoves them into his pocket only to eventually throw them away. "One by one the mind of Dr. Reefy had made the thoughts. Out of many of them he formed a truth that arose gigantic in his mind. The truth clouded the world. It became terrible and then faded away and the little thoughts began again." What the gigantic thought was, we are not told.

Another questing medical man, Dr. Parcival, relates long tales that at times seem to George Willard "a pack of lies" and at others to contain "the very essence of truth." As Thornton Wilder's *Our Town* reminded us, small-town people think a lot about the universe (as opposed to city people, who think about one another). The agonizing philosophical search is inherited from religion; in the four-part story **"Godliness,"** the author, speaking as a print-saturated modern man, says of the world fifty years before: "Men labored too hard and were too tired to read. In them was no desire for words printed upon paper. As they worked in the fields, vague, half-formed thoughts took possession of them. They believed in God and in God's power to control their lives. . . . The figure of God was big in the hearts of men.'' The rural landscape of the Midwest becomes easily confused in the minds of its pious denizens with that of the Bible, where God manifested himself with signs and spoken words. Jesse Bentley's attempt to emulate Abraham's offered sacrifice of Isaac so terrifies his grandson David that the boy flees the Winesburg region forever. Anderson writes about religious obsession with cold sympathy, as something that truly enters into lives and twists them. To this spiritual hunger sex adds its own; the Reverend Curtis Hartman breaks a small hole in the stained-glass window of his bell-tower study in order to spy on a woman in a house across the street as she lies on her bed and smokes and reads. ''He did not want to kiss the shoulders and the throat of Kate Smith and had not allowed his mind to dwell on such thoughts. He did not know what he wanted. 'I am God's child and he must save me from myself,' he cried.'' One evening he sees her come naked into her room and weep and then pray; with his fist he smashes the window so all of it, with its broken bit of a peephole, will have to be repaired.

There are more naked women in ***Winesburg, Ohio*** than one might think. **''Adventure''** shows Alice Hindman, a twenty-seven-year-old spinster jilted by a lover a decade before, so agitated by ''her desire to have something beautiful come into her rather narrow life'' that she runs naked into the rain one night and actually accosts a man—a befuddled old deaf man who goes on his way. In the following story, **''Respectability,''** a fanatic and repulsive misogynist, Wash Williams, recalls to George Willard how, many years before, his mother-in-law, hoping to reconcile him with his unfaithful young wife, presented her naked to him in her (Dayton, Ohio) parlor. George Willard, his chaste relation to Helen White aside, suffers no lack of sexual invitation in Winesburg's alleys and surrounding fields. Sherwood Anderson's women are as full of ''vague hungers and secret unnamable desires'' as his men. The sexual quest and the philosophical quest blend: of George Willard's mother, the most tenderly drawn woman of all, the author says, ''Always there was something she sought blindly, passionately, some hidden wonder in life. . . . In all the babble of words that fell from the lips of the men with whom she adventured she was trying to find what would be for her the true word.'' ***Winesburg, Ohio*** is dedicated to the memory of Anderson's own mother, ''whose keen observations on the life about her first awoke in me the hunger to see beneath the surface of lives.''

The author's hunger to see and express is entwined with the common hunger for love and reassurance and gives the book its awkward power and its limiting strangeness. The many characters of ***Winesburg, Ohio***, rather than standing forth as individuals, seem, with their repeating tics and uniform loneliness, aspects of one enveloping personality, an eccentric bundle of stalled impulses and frozen grievances. There is nowhere a citizen who, like Thomas Rhodes of Spoon River, exults in his material triumphs and impenitent rascality, nor any humbler type, like ''real black, tall, well built, stupid, childlike, good looking'' Rose Johnson of Stein's fictional Bridgepoint, who is happily at home in her skin. Do the Winesburgs of America lack such earthly successes; does the provincial orchard hold only, in Anderson's vivid phrase, ''twisted apples''? No, and yet Yes, must be the answer; for the uncanny truth of Anderson's sad and surreal picture must awaken recognition within anyone who, like this reviewer, was born in a small town before highways and development filled all the fields and television imposed upon every home a degraded sophistication. The Protestant villages of America, going back to Hawthorne's Salem, leave a spectral impression in literature: vague longing and monotonous, inbred satisfactions are their essence; there is something perilous and maddening in the accommodations such communities extend to human aspiration and appetite. As neighbors watch, and murmur, lives visibly wrap themselves around a missed opportunity, a thwarted passion. The longing may be simply the longing to get out. The healthy, rounded apples, Anderson tells us, are ''put in barrels and shipped to the cities where they will be eaten in apartments that are filled with books, magazines, furniture, and people.'' George Willard gets out in the end, and as soon as Winesburg falls away from the train windows ''his life there had become but a background on which to paint the dreams of his manhood.''

The small town is generally seen, by the adult writer arrived at his city, as the site of youthful paralysis and dreaming. Certainly Anderson, as Malcolm Cowley has pointed out, wrote in a dreaming way, scrambling the time and logic of events as he hastened toward his epiphanies of helpless awakening, when the citizens of Winesburg break their tongue-tied trance and become momentarily alive to one another [see excerpt dated 1960]. Gertrude Stein's style, so revolutionary and liberating, has the haughtiness and humor of the *faux-naïve;* there is much genuine naïveté in Anderson, which in even his masterwork flirts with absurdity and which elsewhere weakens his work decisively. ***Winesburg, Ohio*** describes the human condition only insofar as unfulfillment and restlessness—a nagging sense that real life is elsewhere—are intrinsically part of it. Yet the wide-eyed eagerness with which Anderson pursued the mystery of the meager lives of Winesburg opened Michigan to Hemingway, and Mississippi to Faulkner; a way had been shown to a new directness and a freedom from contrivance. Though ***Winesburg, Ohio*** accumulates external facts—streets, stores, town personalities—as it gropes along, its burden is a spiritual essence, a certain tart sweet taste to life as it passes in America's lonely lamplit homes. A nagging beauty lives amid this tame desolation; Anderson's parade of yearning wraiths constitutes in sum a democratic plea for the failed, the neglected, and the stuck. ''On the trees are only a few gnarled apples that the pickers have rejected. . . . One nibbles at them and they are delicious. Into a litle round place at the side of the apple has been gathered all of its sweetness.'' Describing a horse-and-buggy world bygone even in 1919, ***Winesburg, Ohio*** imparts this penetrating taste—the wine hidden in its title—as freshly today as yesterday. (pp. 96-7)

John Updike, ''Twisted Apples,'' in Harper's, *Vol. 268, No. 1606, March, 1984, pp. 95-7.*

CLARE COLQUITT (essay date 1986)

[The following excerpt is from Colquitt's feminist critique of one of Anderson's most acclaimed stories, ''Death in the Woods.'']

''Death in the Woods'' has provoked a varied critical response, ranging from interpretations that see the tale much as Anderson claims he did, as a biological allegory depicting woman as feeder, to more recent interpretations that focus less upon the plight of the old farm woman and more upon the narrative consciousness that constructs her story. This shift of focus has led several critics [among them Sister Mary Joselyn] to conclude that **''Death in the Woods''** is ''a story about the creation of a story'' [see Additional Bibliography]. . . , hence Anderson's many attempts to unveil the mechanics of the creative process through the workings of the tale's narrative center, an older man who looks back to one scene from his childhood

Present-day Clyde, Ohio, Anderson's hometown and his model for Winesburg. © 1987 Lizbeth A. Purdy.

out of which he will spin his yarn. To borrow from the title Anderson gave to his first published memoir, **"Death in the Woods"** has been increasingly viewed as "a story teller's story." (p. 177)

That there exists an intricate bond connecting the "real story" . . . of an old woman's life and death and the "creating" consciousness who narrates her tale has long been acknowledged. Critics have also observed that the relationship between narrator and reader is similarly complex. As early as 1959, Jon Lawry astutely perceived that the narrator's tortuous labors to give meaning to the death he describes are offered as both an interpretative and experiential model for the reader of **"Death in the Woods"** to follow: "The audience is invited to enter as individuals into a process almost identical with that of the narrator . . . to share directly not only the narrator's responses but his act of discovering and creating those responses" [see Additional Bibliography]. . . . What few critics have since examined . . . are the implicatory bonds that result when the reader blindly accepts this enticing invitation; for if the reader succumbs to the narrator's interpretative wiles, he becomes enmeshed in a web of guilt that connects him not only with the "I"/eye of the tale but also with the other men and boys in the woods who pruriently feed upon the body of a dead woman. By further exploring the peculiar design of this web, I hope to illumine the obsessive concern evidenced in this short story with the process of reading and making meaning. (pp. 177-78)

Several critics have noted the somewhat unorthodox alternation of tenses that operates throughout **"Death in the Woods,"** as in the first paragraph of the story: "She was an old woman and lived on a farm near the town in which I lived. All country and small-town people have seen such old women, but no one knows much about them. Such an old woman comes into town driving an old worn-out horse or she comes afoot carrying a basket." . . . Although critics differ as to the effects of such shifts, many would agree with Guerin's explanation that "In this and in the second paragraph of the story the historical present tense of the verbs makes clear the timeless quality of the regularity of such old women and their doings" [see Additional Bibliography]. . . . Diverting the reader's attention from the particular to the general, from the life of one old woman to the experience of "such old women," the narrator strives to "universalize" his story in a timeless setting by removing the "she" of his opening description from history and by granting himself the authority to speak of "all country and small-town people" in categorical terms. Such ahistorical maneuvering complements another effect of this passage that no critic has yet observed: **"Death in the Woods"** begins much like a fairy tale. Further, any reader who reflects upon the tales passed on in childhood may note a slight echo here with one of our culture's most famous allegories of female feeding, the Mother Goose story of the old woman who lived in a shoe. In addition, the reader may come to see Anderson's narrative as cautionary, particularly if other tales of wolves, women, and dark woods come to mind. From this initial description then the reader comes to two important realizations. First, the frame in which the **"Death in the Woods"** occurs is both fanciful and remote, a timeless realm that suggestively resonates with the surreal landscape of children's stories. Second, the reader learns that the tale is not to be interpreted simply as the narrative of an isolated farm woman but rather as a fiction that has universal implications. After all, one of the first statements the narrator makes about the old woman is that she is "nothing special." . . . (pp. 178-79)

Having been thus directed toward the ostensible subject of the story, the reader soon finds that the interpretative process is effectively impeded by obtrusive references the narrator makes concerning his own past. Indeed, in the opening section of **"Death in the Woods,"** the reader learns almost as much about the narrator's childhood as about the plight of old country women. Interestingly, the narrator's allusions to his past closely resemble the boyhood recollections set forth in Anderson's memoirs; yet, despite the similarities that seem to link the story teller with his tale, Anderson himself "persistent[ly]" interpreted the narrative of Mrs. Jake Grimes in thematic, not autobiographical, terms [according to Irving Howe]:

> In a note for an anthology Anderson wrote that "the theme of the story is the persistent animal hunger of man. There are these women who spend their whole lives, rather dumbly, feeding this hunger. . . . [The story's aim] is to retain the sense of mystery in life while showing at the same time, at what cost our ordinary animal hungers are sometimes fed." . . .

Anderson's reading is a superb illustration of what John Berger calls critical mystification—"the process of explaining away what might otherwise be evident" . . .—for as Irving Howe noted more than thirty years ago, this interpretation is "apt, though limited. . . . Anderson could hardly have failed to notice that the story may be read as an oblique rendering of what he believed to be the central facts about his mother's life: a silent drudgery in the service of men, an obliteration of self to feed their 'persistent animal hunger,' and then death." . . . Regardless of the limits of Anderson's analysis, one fact is clear: Anderson, like his narrator, is trying to steer critics of **"Death in the Woods"** away from the realm of history—from the varying records of a writer's conflicted relationship with his mother—to the hallowed domain of myth. Having fastened upon a presumably "safe" and unalterable interpretation of his story, Anderson thereby avoids public confrontation with painful memories of his childhood. (p. 179)

[The narrator] moves quickly to guide the reader's attention away from his apparent subject, an old farm woman, to what is ultimately his larger concern—himself. Particularly jarring is the narrator's first substantial digression concerning the liver he was forced to eat as a child, a digression that interrupts his account of what old women do when they come to town:

> Such an old woman . . . takes [eggs] to a grocer. There she trades them in. . . .
>
> Afterwards she goes to the butcher's and asks for some dog-meat. Formerly the butchers gave liver to anyone who wanted to carry it away. In our family we were always having it. Once one of my brothers got a whole cow's liver at the slaughterhouse near the fair grounds in our town. We had it until we were sick of it. It never cost a cent. I have hated the thought of it ever since.

Clearly, this is a narrator who needs close watch, for as such digressions multiply, the reader becomes increasingly fascinated not with the "real story" . . . of an old woman's death but rather with the peculiar manner in which her story is told. This first digression is peculiar enough, suggesting as it does a puerile hostility on the narrator's part toward his past as well as the bonds of poverty and sickness that bridge the narrator's memories of his childhood with the experience of "nameless" . . . country women. At this juncture, the narrator also reveals that when he first noticed the woman he soon identifies as Mrs. Jake Grimes, he himself was literally sick in bed with "inflammatory rheumatism," . . . a statement that takes on added significance when he subsequently remarks that Mrs. Grimes had journeyed to town even though "she hadn't been feeling very well for several days. . . ." . . . Given the vehemence of these boyhood reflections, the reader might justifiably wonder at this point if the "inflammatory" child has ever fully recovered, for as the unpredictable narrator continues to weave his tale, the reader begins to sense that this man is still none too well.

Following this unsettling digression, the narrator sketches the rough outlines of Mrs. Grimes's life. Through him we learn that in her youth she worked as a "bound girl" . . . for a German farming couple: "At the German's place she . . . cooked the food for the German and his wife. . . . She fed them and fed the cows in the barn, fed the pigs, the horses and the chickens. Every moment of every day, as a young girl, was spent feeding something." . . . That her life was neither one of ease nor happiness becomes plain when the narrator discloses that the "young thing" . . . was sexually abused, perhaps raped, by her employer. Interestingly, however, the reader's knowledge of the bound girl's life is unstable, for the narrator evidences uncertainty concerning the particulars of her story. Thus, in the opening section of **"Death in the Woods,"** the narrator first hesitantly supposes that the young girl was "bound"—"You see, the farmer was up to something with the girl—she was, I think, a bound girl . . ." . . .—whereas only shortly afterwards he claims that he knows the woman was so: "I remember now that she was a bound girl and did not know where her father and mother were." . . . Such wavering causes the reader to question the narrator's confidence in the truth of the tale he says he has only "suddenly" remembered: "I have just suddenly now, after all these years, remembered her and what happened. It is a story." . . . By calling attention in this way to the manipulative possibilities of narration, Anderson directs his audience to larger questions concerning the nature of "story" telling. As Mary Joselyn observes, "the fact that [Anderson] goes out of his way several times to tell us that the story might have been told . . . differently is important, for these statements emphasize that the process of creation is essentially one of choice and of selection." . . . (pp. 180-82)

The role that choice plays in the shaping of fiction is stressed on several occasions in **"Death in the Woods"** when the narrator returns to scenes or conversations that he has previously described. In the opening section of the story, the narrator records two conversations that take place between the bound girl and Jake Grimes, another employee on the German couple's farm. Although the conversations are not identical, the subject of these talks is: both focus upon the sexual abuse that the young girl allegedly suffered on the farm. The narrator first recounts that before Jake became the bound girl's lover, she confided in him that "when the wife had to go off to town for supplies, the farmer got after her. She told young Jake that nothing really ever happened, but he didn't know whether to believe it or not." . . . Between this and a later dialogue occurs a fight involving the German and his hired hand, which the narrator delightfully describes: "They had it out all right! The German was a tough one. Maybe he didn't care whether his wife knew or not." . . . In the midst of this passage, the reader gradually realizes that the narrator could not possibly know all the details he provides of the scene, for there were no witnesses to the brawl. Indeed, the narrator himself seems aware of this problem when he parenthetically inserts: "(I wonder how I know all this. It must have stuck in my mind from small-town tales when I was a boy)." . . . Following this admission, the reader learns of the conversation that takes place after the fight when Jake finds his lover "huddled up . . . crying, [and] scared to death." . . . Now, however, the narrator's phrasing suggests that the bound girl's "stories" are not to be believed: "She told Jake a lot of stuff, how the German had tried to get her, how he chased her once into the barn, how another time . . . he tore her dress open clear down the front." . . . The narrator's unwillingness to grant the woman any degree of credibility in either of these confessions is further emphasized when he reveals that Jake Grimes "got her pretty easy himself, the first time he was out with her," . . . an assertion that may once again lead the reader to wonder how the narrator can possibly "know all this."

What Anderson himself knows of course is how to construct a story, a story that, as its narrative voice becomes increasingly assured, causes the reader to question any interpretation offered concerning the meaning of the life and death of Mrs. Jake Grimes. Indeed, as the description of the fight scene suggests, the narrator identifies himself less with the plight of the "young thing" who is "scared to death" . . . than with the men who are able to bind such women to their will. This is, moreover, not the only occasion in which the narrator reveals his sympathy with brutal forms of masculine expression, as is evident in the second section of the story when Mrs. Grimes makes her last trip to the butcher's:

> she went to the butcher and he gave her some liver and dog-meat.
>
> It was the first time anyone had spoken to her in a friendly way for a long time. The butcher was alone in his shop when she came in and was annoyed by the thought of such a sick-looking old woman out on such a day. . . . [He] said something about her husband and her son, swore at them, and the old woman stared at him, a look of mild surprise in her eyes as he talked. He said that if either the husband or the son were going to get any of the liver or the heavy bones with scraps of meat hanging to them that he had put into the grain bag, he'd seen him [*sic*] starve first. . . .

In spite of the narrator's tacit assumption that his audience will see this interchange as positive, many readers imagining this encounter might question how "friendly" such a conversation would appear to a woman grown accustomed to "the habit of silence" . . . who suddenly finds her family being sworn at and threatened by a man she hardly knows.

Immediately following this passage, the narrator depicts the death that has been anticipated since the opening lines of the story. In this middle section of the narrative, the old woman starts her journey home. Laden with a sack of provisions too heavy for her, Mrs. Grimes decides to take "a short cut over a hill and through the woods. . . . She was afraid she couldn't make it" otherwise. . . . In the midst of her "struggle" . . . home, the old woman "foolish[ly]" allows herself to rest against a tree and "quietly" . . . falls into a sleep from which she never completely awakes. The interest in the "strange picture" her death presents lies with the several dogs that are "running in circles . . . round and round" her sleeping form. . . . (pp. 182-84)

[They] are "all tall gaunt fellows," . . . and when one of them "left the running circle and came to stand before" the half-conscious woman, the "dog thrust his face close to her face. His red tongue . . . hanging out." . . . Bluntly put, in **"Death in the Woods"** . . . the threat Mrs. Grimes faces from these "tall gaunt fellows" is the threat of rape, as becomes plain when the narrator records what happens after the sleeping woman dies.

The seven dogs, which had run round Mrs. Grimes as if operating by "some old instinct, come down from the time when they were wolves," . . . now drag her thinly clad corpse into the open. As they rip the food sack from her back, they tear through her clothing "clear to the hip," . . . conveniently leaving her body unharmed. This last image echoes the earlier "rape" scene in which the German farmer tore the bound girl's "dress open clear down the front," . . . even as it also nicely complements the second section of **"Death in the Woods"** in which the narrator reasserts woman's role as feeder. According to his report, Mrs. Grimes's married life was merely an extension of the monotony she knew on the German couple's farm: "Horses, cows, pigs, dogs, men . . . [all] had to be fed." . . . Even her sexual relations with her husband are imaged by the fixated narrator as a form of feeding when he envisages Mrs. Grimes's relief at no longer being sexually desirable: "Thank heaven, she did not have to feed her husband—in a certain way. That hadn't lasted long after their marriage." . . . (p. 186)

In the final sections of **"Death in the Woods"** the process of reading and interpretation is brought to the fore, for the first person to discover the partially exposed body is a hunter who seemingly "misreads" the scene. "Something, the beaten round path in the little snow-covered clearing, the silence of the place, the place where the dogs had worried the body trying to pull the grain bag away or tear it open—something startled the man and he hurried off to town" to tell "his story": "'She was a beautiful young girl. Her face was buried in the snow'." . . . Once again, the reader notes the narrator's identification not with the woman herself but rather with the man who had been so "frightened" by his discovery that he "had not looked closely at the body": "If something strange or uncanny has happened in the neighborhood all you think about is getting away from there as fast as you can." . . . This rationalization sets the stage for the "mystical" transformations that result when a "crowd of men and boys," including the narrator and his brother, accompany the hunter back into the forest. Following this journey, the young boy knows that he and his brother, like the hunter before them, will "have something to tell." . . . (pp. 186-87)

The "fragments" . . . with which the narrator pieces together his story are modeled upon the hunter's wish-fulfilling vision of the "beautiful young girl":

> She did not look old, lying there in that light, frozen and still. One of the men turned her over in the snow and I saw everything. My body trembled with some strange mystical feeling and so did my brother's. It might have been the cold.
>
> Neither of us had ever seen a woman's body before. It may have been the snow, clinging to the frozen flesh, that made it look so white and lovely, so like marble. . . .

What the narrator remembers from this epiphanic moment is "only the picture there in the forest, the men standing about, the naked girlish-looking figure, face down in the snow. . . ." He further acknowledges that "the scene in the forest had become for me, without my knowing it, the foundation for the real story I am trying to tell. The fragments, you see, had to be picked up slowly, long afterwards." . . . As several critics have observed, this "real story" can be interpreted on one level as the boy's sexual awakening, or as William Scheick has argued, his failure to do so. . . . On another level, however, this experience represents an aesthetic metamorphosis: the "slight thing," who previously moved through town unnoticed, becomes in death a symbol for the feminine ideal, an objet d'art worthy to serve as the "foundation" for a "real story." (p. 187)

Importantly, the narrator returns in the final section of **"Death in the Woods"** to the episode in which he also "had a half-uncanny, mystical adventure with dogs in an Illinois forest." . . . What startles the reader in this passage is not the narrator's repeating himself—he has done that before—but rather the vague confession that prefaces the second reference to the "mystical adventure": "Things happened. When I was a young man I worked on the farm of a German. The hired-girl was afraid of her employer. The farmer's wife hated her. I saw things at that place." . . . If nothing else has previously alerted the reader to the narrator's disturbing identification with the community of males that, within the bounds of this short story, routinely victimizes women, this hesitant admission should; for here the narrator firmly locates himself in a position of power identical to that of Jake Grimes, a position that grants him the ability to "get" frightened "young things" to satisfy his various hungers. Contrary to what William Scheick has argued, the young boy's sexual development clearly has progressed according to the definition of masculinity accepted by "all country and small-town people" [see Additional Bibliography].

Several critics have discerned the shattering effect with which Anderson's male narrators depict their initial sexual encounters with women. Judith Fetterley's analysis of **"I Want to Know Why"** [in her book *The Resisting Reader: A Feminist Approach to American Fiction,* 1978] pertains well to **"Death in the Woods":** "What Anderson's boy resists is not just growing up, it is specifically growing up *male*." . . . Yet as Fetterley demonstrates in her criticism of the earlier story, and as I hope to have shown in my own study of **"Death in the Woods,"** any resistance felt by Anderson's narrators on this score is eventually overcome. Indeed, one might argue of **"Death in the Woods,"** as Fetterley does of **"I Want to Know Why,"** that the story is "infused with the perspective it abhors, because finally to disavow that perspective would be to relinquish power." . . . Or in the terms offered within Anderson's own interpretation of **"Death in the Woods,"** to abandon power is to become like one of those "women who spend their whole lives, rather dumbly, feeding" the "persistent animal hunger of man." Thus, despite the narrator's attempts to sympathize with the "simple story," . . . of Mrs. Jake Grimes, his allegiances are ultimately with the powerful and most definitely closed male community—with the "crowd of men and boys" who go to the woods, with the "frightened" hunter and the "friendly" butcher, and most especially with the two men who strive to "get" the bound girl. Admittedly, the narrator does seem to regard Mrs. Grimes more compassionately than any other man who is fed by her; yet the story he tells deals less with the miserable reality of an old woman's life than with the transforming power of artistic genius. Indeed, it is only *as* an artist that the narrator can justify this woman's life by envisioning her in death as a "slight" but nonetheless "beautiful" "thing." The "foundation" of this "real story" of the artist-as-a-young-man may rest upon the bones of a dead woman, but it certainly little concerns her. In short, the narrator/artist can effectively ignore the political realities facing "such old women" by making of one woman's life a poetical whole, a lyric that suggests that Mrs. Grimes's destiny—and by implication, the destiny of her sex—is biologically determined: "The woman who died was one destined to feed animal life. Anyway, that is all she ever did. She was feeding animal life before she was born, as a child, as a young woman working on the farm of the German, after she married, when she grew old and when she died." . . . The many cyclical images within the story, as well as the narrator's passing references to his own mother and sister . . . reinforce such a constricted view of woman's fate.

The essential hopelessness that pervades Anderson's fiction has long been recognized. As Robert Morss Lovett observed in 1922,

> this hopelessness is not an interpretation playfully or desperately imposed on the phenomena of life from without by thought or reason; it springs from within; it is of the essence of being. . . . It is as if, to use Cardinal Newman's words, man were implicated from birth in some "vast aboriginal calamity"; only instead of placing the fall of man historically in the Garden of Eden Mr. Anderson traces it biologically to the egg . . . [see Additional Bibliography].

To recall that Mrs. Jake Grimes herself takes eggs to market in order to buy food for her family; to recall that this woman dies only when she "foolish[ly]" deviates from her customary route home; to recall that the narrator interprets her existence solely in terms of feeding—to recall these is to realize that Anderson's own aesthetics are most narrowly "bound." Naturally the story proves unsettling to many readers today; for if we are taken in by the interpretative web Anderson's narrator seductively dangles before us, if we also become trembling voyeurs in the woods, then we also implicate ourselves in that "vast . . . calamity" of masculinist convention that proceeds to dehistoricize woman by objectifying her into art. (pp. 188-90)

Clare Colquitt, "The Reader as Voyeur: Complicitous Transformations in 'Death in the Woods'," in Modern Fiction Studies, *Vol. 32, No. 2, Summer, 1986, pp. 175-90.*

ADDITIONAL BIBLIOGRAPHY

Abcarian, Richard. "Innocence and Experience in *Winesburg, Ohio.*" *The University Review* 35, No. 2 (Winter 1968): 95-105.

Traces a pattern of "hope blighted, potential wasted, and innocence lost" in *Winesburg*.

Anderson, David D., ed. *Critical Essays on Sherwood Anderson*. Boston: G. K. Hall & Co., 1981, 302 p.
Reprints significant early reviews of Anderson's works, as well as general and thematic articles on his craft. In addition, several essays appear for the first time in this collection.

Anderson, Maxwell. "A Country Town." *The New Republic* XIX, No. 242 (25 June 1919): 257, 260.
Reviews *Winesburg*, praising it for expressing "the baffled search of every personality for meanings and purposes deeper than anything that may be said or done, answers that will cut under the superficial axioms by which we are judged."

Babb, Howard S. "A Reading of Sherwood Anderson's 'The Man Who Became a Woman'." *PMLA* LXXX, No. 4 (September 1965): 432-35.
Argues that in "The Man Who Became a Woman" Anderson writes about "a particular integrity of being that the youth must experience as a requisite for growing up."

Baker, Carlos. "Sherwood Anderson's Winesburg: A Reprise." *The Virginia Quarterly Review* 48, No. 4 (Autumn 1972): 568-79.
An appreciative general essay on *Winesburg*.

Bort, Barry D. "*Winesburg, Ohio:* The Escape from Isolation." *The Midwest Quarterly* XI, No. 4 (Summer 1970): 443-56.
Examines *Winesburg,* tracing the recurrent theme of despairing loneliness born of the individual's failure to communciate with others.

Boyd, Ernest. Introduction to *Winesburg, Ohio: A Group of Tales of Ohio Small-Town Life,* by Sherwood Anderson, pp. ix-xv. New York: Modern Library, 1919.
Praises Anderson's work as part of "a literature of revolt against the great illusion of American civilization, the illusion of optimism, with all its childish evasion of harsh facts, its puerile cheerfulness, whose inevitable culmination is a school of 'glad' books, which have reduced American literature to the lowest terms of sentimentality."

Bredahl, A. Carl. "'The Young Thing Within': Divided Narrative and Sherwood Anderson's *Winesburg, Ohio*." *The Midwest Quarterly* XXVII, No. 4 (Summer 1986): 422-37.
Examines *Winesburg* as a work written and structured in the tradition of the "divided narrative": one work among many "which struggle structurally to assert a traditional literary unity" while depicting "encountered experience which denies that particular kind of unity."

Campbell, Hilbert H., and Modlin, Charles E., eds. *Sherwood Anderson: Centennial Studies*. Troy, N.Y.: Whitston Publishing Co., 1976, 275 p.
Reprints several of Anderson's letters, lists Anderson's papers, and offers eleven original critical essays written in honor of Anderson's centenary.

Cargill, Oscar. "The Primitivists" and "The Freudians." In his *Intellectual America: Ideas on the March,* pp. 311-98, pp. 537-763. New York: Macmillan Co., 1941.
Discusses Anderson's stories in terms of the author's efforts to understand and utilize primitivist literary techniques and psychoanalytical thought.

Ciancio, Ralph. "The Sweetness of the Twisted Apples." *PMLA* LXXVII, No. 5 (October 1972): 994-1006.
Demonstrates the crucial importance of *Winesburg*'s opening chapter, "The Book of the Grotesque," as the key thematic and philosophical organizing element in the book.

Colum, Mary M. "Literature and Journalism." *The Freeman* IV, No. 90 (30 November 1921): 281-82.
Enthusiastically reviews *The Triumph of the Egg,* finding it superior in craft to the fiction of Theodore Dreiser. Colum considers Anderson "the most significant writer of imaginative prose" in America.

Crane, Hart. "Sherwood Anderson: I and II." *Twice a Year,* Nos. 12-13 (1945): 431-33, 433-38.
Reprints a favorable review of *Winesburg* from a 1919 issue of the *Pagan* and a survey of Anderson's works that originally appeared in 1921 in the *Double Dealer*. In the first essay, Crane concludes that *Winesburg* "constitutes an important chapter in the Bible of her [America's] consciousness"; in the latter, he writes that Anderson "has a humanity and simplicity that is quite baffling in depth and suggestiveness, and his steady and deliberate growth is proving right along the promise it gives of finer works."

Dell, Floyd. "American Fiction." *The Liberator* 2, No. 9 (September 1919): 46-7.
Favorable review of *Winesburg* by the Chicago Renaissance writer who arranged the publication of Anderson's first book, *Windy McPherson's Son*. Dell judges Anderson artistically superior to Dreiser, and praises him for having "broadened the realm of American fiction to include aspects of life of the first importance."

Dreiser, Theodore. *Letters of Theodore Dreiser*. Edited by Robert H. Elias. 3 vols. Philadelphia: University of Pennsylvania Press, 1959.
Numerous approving references to Anderson and his work by a longtime friend.

Fagin, N. Bryllion. *The Phenomenon of Sherwood Anderson: A Study in American Life & Letters*. Baltimore: Rossi Bryn Co., 1927, 156 p.
Overview describing Anderson's works as the product of a fearless, iconoclastic mind.

Fussell, Edwin. "*Winesburg, Ohio:* Art and Isolation." *Modern Fiction Studies* VI, No. 2 (Summer 1960): 106-14.
Perceives *Winesburg* as falling within the tradition of the *Bildungsroman*. Fussell maintains that the work depicts George Willard's intellectual and artistic maturation through his connections with the village's isolated grotesques.

Geismar, Maxwell. "Sherwood Anderson: Last of theTownsmen." In his *The Last of the Provincials: The American Novel, 1915-1925,* pp. 223-84. Boston: Houghton Mifflin Co., 1947.
Describes *Winesburg* as chiefly nostalgic. Geismar defines Anderson as "one of the last to believe in the possibility of civilization in the United States."

———. Introduction to *Sherwood Anderson: Short Stories,* by Sherwood Anderson, pp. ix-xxiii. New York: Hill and Wang, 1962.
An appreciative overview of the major short stories.

Gold, Herbert. "The Fair Apple of Progress." In his *The Age of Happy Problems,* pp. 56-67. New York: Dial Press, 1962.
Discusses Anderson as "one of the purest, most intense poets of loneliness—the loneliness of being an individual and of being buffeted in the current, the loneliness of isolation and that of being swallowed." Gold's essay provides an interesting brief section on the depiction of women in Anderson's stories.

Gregory, Horace. "Editor's Introduction: A Historical Interpretation." In *The Portable Sherwood Anderson,* by Sherwood Anderson, edited by Horace Gregory, pp. 3-31. New York: Viking Press, 1972.
Useful introduction to Anderson's life and work. Gregory surveys the most prominent of the short stories, focusing primarily on "Death in the Woods," which he deems "Anderson's masterpiece among his shorter stories."

Guerin, Wilfred L. "'Death in the Woods': Sherwood Anderson's 'Cold Pastoral'." *The CEA Critic* 30, No. 8 (May 1968): 4-5.
Examines "Death in the Woods" as a "story about how fragments become a whole and have meaning, partly through the workings of the unconscious, partly through the conscious memory."

Hemingway, Ernest. *Selected Letters: 1917-1961,* edited by Carlos Baker, pp. 59ff. New York: Charles Scribner's Sons, 1981.
Numerous references to Anderson, documenting a relationship which steadily deteriorated throughout the authors' lives.

Joselyn, Sister Mary. "Some Artistic Dimensions of Sherwood Anderson's 'Death in the Woods'." *Studies in Short Fiction* IV, No. 2 (Spring 1967): 252-59.

Studies "Death in the Woods" as a work comprising "at least four transformations" in character and form which, according to the critic, together create a well-integrated work of art.

Kazin, Alfred. "The New Realism: Sherwood Anderson and Sinclair Lewis." In his *On Native Grounds: An Interpretation of Modern American Prose Literature,* pp. 205-26. New York: Harcourt, Brace and Co., 1942.

A thoughtful general essay on Anderson's and Lewis's importance as "spokesmen of a new liberation" in American letters.

Lawry, Jon S. "'Death in the Woods' and the Artist's Self in Sherwood Anderson." *PMLA* LXXIV, No. 3 (June 1959): 306-11.

Examines "Death in the Woods," arguing that the narrator's attempts to understand the event he describes serve as an experiential and interpretative model for the reader.

Lorch, Thomas M. "The Choreographic Structure of *Winesburg, Ohio.*" *CLA Journal* XII, No. 1 (September 1968): 56-65.

Argues that *Winesburg* has greater structural unity than most critics have allowed. Because the collection stresses symbol rather than character development or action, the critic suggests that its structure is similar to a choreographed dance.

Love, Glen A. "*Winesburg, Ohio* and the Rhetoric of Silence." *American Literature* XL, No. 1 (March 1968): 38-57.

Studies "how thoroughly Anderson explores the theme of human communication in *Winesburg,* how his treatment of that theme is linked to his attitudes toward silence, words, and talk, and how these attitudes are in turn related to the strong, single idea which runs through all of his work: the loss of human significance in America with the onset of urban, machine civilization."

Lovett, Robert Morss. "The Promise of Sherwood Anderson." *The Dial* LXII, No. 1 (January 1922): 79-83.

Reviews with high praise *The Triumph of the Egg,* perceiving it as a work which reveals "the faith of the artist, the soul of a poet. It is in this evidence of a true vocation that one finds in largest measure the promise of Sherwood Anderson."

McAleer, John J. "Christ Symbolism in *Winesburg, Ohio.*" *Discourse* IV, No. 3 (Summer 1961): 168-81.

Finds in *Winesburg* "a pattern of Christ symbolism which appears throughout the book, touching the life of each person and each time reiterating Anderson's point—in the modern world suffering is the lot of every man."

Mencken, H. L. "Frank Harris and Others." *The Smart Set* LXVII, No. 2 (February 1922): 138-44.

Laudatory review of *The Triumph of the Egg.*

———. "Three Volumes of Fiction." *The American Mercury* I, No. 2 (February 1924): 252-53.

Favorably reviews *Horses and Men.* Perceiving the volume as "largely a set of variations on Dreiserian themes," Mencken pronounces the stories "simple, moving, and brilliantly vivid."

———. "Anderson Great Artist, Says Mencken." *Notes on Modern American Literature* 2, No. 2 (Spring 1978): Item 11.

Reprints a "lost" review of *Winesburg* originally published by Mencken in the *Chicago American* on 28 June 1919, roughly a month before the appearance of his better-known review of the same book in the *Smart Set.* Mencken declares *Winesburg* the work of an artist of "genuine force and originality," whose accomplishment far outstrips that of his contemporaries, "most of them drivellers and cheesemongers."

Miller, William V. "Sherwood Anderson's Unpublished Stories." *MidAmerica* XII (1985): 53-8.

Discusses three of Anderson's unpublished short stories—"Bob," "Fast Woman," and "Brother Earl"—among the eight availablefor study in the Newberry Library archives in Chicago. The Newberry Library is the chief repository of Anderson's papers.

Rosenfeld, Paul. Introduction to *The Sherwood Anderson Reader,* by Sherwood Anderson, pp. vii-xxviii. Boston: Houghton Mifflin Co., 1947.

A moving biographical essay, including an insightful critical interpretation of Anderson's works.

San Juan, Epiphanio, Jr. "Vision and Reality: A Reconsideration of Sherwood Anderson's *Winesburg, Ohio.*" *American Literature* XXXV, No. 2 (May 1963): 137-55.

Examines the form, technique, and style of Anderson's narrative art to determine the secret of the continued "power and significance" of *Winesburg.*

Scheick, William J. "Compulsion toward Repetition: Sherwood Anderson's 'Death in the Woods'." *Studies in Short Fiction* XI, No. 2 (Spring 1974): 141-46.

Discusses how the narrator of "Death in the Woods" uses Mrs. Grimes's simple story toward complex ends.

Schevill, James. *Sherwood Anderson: His Life and Work.* Denver: University of Denver Press, 1951, 360 p.

Detailed critical biography, acclaimed for its comprehensiveness and impartiality.

Schorer, Mark. "Some Relationships: Gertrude Stein, Sherwood Anderson, F. Scott Fitzgerald, and Ernest Hemingway." In his *The World We Imagine: Selected Essays,* pp. 299-382. London: Chatto & Windus, 1969.

A short, valuable overview of Anderson's life and work, touching on Anderson's relationships with Stein and Hemingway.

Tanner, Tony. "Sherwood Anderson's Little Things." In his *The Reign of Wonder: Naivety and Reality in American Literature,* pp. 205-27. Cambridge: Cambridge University Press, 1965.

Examines the significance of the seemingly unimportant, mundane details in Anderson's short fiction.

Weber, Brom. *Sherwood Anderson.* University of Minnesota Pamphlets on American Writers, edited by William Van O'Connor, Allen Tate, Leonard Unger, and Robert Penn Warren, no. 43. Minneapolis: University of Minnesota Press, 1964, 48 p.

General introduction to Anderson's life and works.

West, Michael D. "Sherwood Anderson's Triumph: 'The Egg'." *American Quarterly* XX, No. 4 (Winter 1968): 675-93.

Close, Freudian reading of "The Egg," finding it a story of one man's pathetic, yet heroic, attempt to attack life itself for the sake of his son.

West, Rebecca. Review of *Winesburg, Ohio,* by Sherwood Anderson. *The New Statesman* XIX, No. 484 (22 July 1922): 443-44.

Praises *Winesburg, Ohio* as "an extraordinarily good book" that "delights in places where those who are not poets could never find delight" and "seems persuaded there is beauty in anything, in absolutely anything."

———. "Sherwood Anderson, Poet." In her *The Strange Necessity,* pp. 309-20. New York: Doubleday, Doran, 1928.

Reprint of a 1926 review of *Tar: A Midwest Childhood* that includes favorable comments on *Winesburg* and *The Triumph of the Egg.* West praises the two last-named works as "two of the most interesting books of short stories ever written."

White, Ray Lewis, ed. *The Achievement of Sherwood Anderson: Essays in Criticism.* Chapel Hill: University of North Carolina Press, 1966, 270 p.

Reprints many of the most significant critical examinations of Anderson's works. Contributing essayists include Lionel Trilling, Irving Howe, and William Faulkner, among many others. White's introduction (pp. 3-18) provides a concise, penetrating overview of Anderson's career and critical reputation.

Wilson, Edmund. "The All-Star Literary Vaudeville." In his *The Shores of Light: A Literary Chronicle of the Twenties and Thirties*, pp. 229-47. New York: Farrar, Straus and Giroux, 1952.
Groups Anderson with Hemingway, Stein, and Ring Lardner as superb American short story writers working in the colloquial tradition of Mark Twain.

The Winesburg Eagle I (1975—).
A biannual publication of the Sherwood Anderson Society, edited by Anderson scholar Welford Dunaway Taylor. The periodical includes both original and reprinted articles on Anderson's life and works and occasionally provides a checklist of newly published editions of Anderson's books and pertinent secondary sources.

J(ames) G(raham) Ballard

1930-

English short story writer, novelist, dramatist, and screenwriter.

Ballard is considered one of the most original and distinctive authors of science fiction to emerge in England since the 1960s. Due to the psychological emphasis of his work and his early association with *New Worlds* magazine, a British periodical specializing in avant-garde science fiction, Ballard became known as one of the chief initiators of the "New Wave" in science fiction, which took place in the 1960s and introduced social, psychological, and literary content to a genre previously dominated by a preoccupation with outer space. Ballard stands apart from his contemporaries in his willingness to invert such traditional assumptions as belief in human adaptability and the beneficence of nature and to explore seemingly pessimistic or irrational solutions to catastrophic problems. Ballard typically focuses on the psychological processes by which his characters, faced with the certainty of devolution or entropic decline, gradually accept the extinction of the human species as natural and inevitable and thus attain freedom of mind.

© Jerry Bauer

Ballard was born and raised in Shanghai, China, and during World War II, he was imprisoned there with his parents in a Japanese camp for civilians. Ballard attributes the sources of his imagination to these early years, when he found in the surrealistic wartime landscape of Shanghai "some sort of truth," as he called it, that reverberates in his fiction. Following his move to England in 1946, Ballard studied medicine at King's College, Cambridge, but left without receiving a degree in order to join England's Royal Air Force. Ballard noted in an interview that the many doctor/psychiatrist figures in his writing are his alter egos and reflect his abandoned medical career.

Early in his writing career Ballard began his association with *New Worlds* magazine, where, under the tutelage of editor E. W. John Carnell and later Michael Moorcock, Ballard and other science fiction authors were permitted to experiment with style and theme. In a guest editorial for *New Worlds* in May, 1962, Ballard identified the problems of the present day as the science fiction writer's greatest moral responsibility, dismissing H. G. Wells as "a disastrous influence on the subsequent course of science fiction" and maintaining that the genre "should turn its back on space, on interstellar travel, extraterrestrial life forms, galactic wars and the overlap of these ideas. . . . [It] is inner space, not outer, that needs to be explored."

Ballard's early tales are written in a highly detailed, visual style, influenced by painters of the Surrealist movement, such as Salvador Dali, wherein desolate or unusual landscapes take on psychological dimensions. Several stories in Ballard's first collection, *Billenium, and Other Stories,* describe overpopulated worlds where concepts like flight and privacy have become senseless abstract concepts. In "Billenium," one of Ballard's most frequently anthologized stories, two people discover an unoccupied room in their overcrowded apartment building and invite friends to share in their unprecedented sense of freedom, until the room contains more people than the average congested dwelling. In "The Concentration City," a young man attempts to escape from a multilevel city but finishes at the point he started. *The Disaster Area* contains Ballard's well-known story, "The Subliminal Man," in which alienated citizens of a futuristic metropolis, psychologically enslaved to a vicious system of subliminal advertising, may escape only through catatonia and regression. The title story from the collection *The Overloaded Man* illustrates the moral dangers of solipsism in its narrative about a bourgeois intellectual who destroys the earth by fantasizing the landscape outside his window into meaningless cubist designs.

In *The Voices of Time, and Other Stories,* Ballard establishes his major, recurring theme of entropy. His theory, derived from the second law of thermodynamics, implies the temporal nature of the universe in its assertion that all matter must eventually degrade from order and energy to a state of chaos and inertia. In "The Voices of Time," scientists react with growing lethargy and despair to their awareness of humanity's biological decline. The story's protagonist, confronted with the certainty of a shapeless, disintegrating universe, acknowledges the futility of attempts at survival and dies at the moment of his aesthetic transcendence. According to Brian Ash, this acceptance recalls the Japanese ideal of *Mono no aware,* "the philosophy of sadness brought about by perfection—the idea that beauty contains its own death and that the most beautiful thing is the beginning of decay." In "The Garden of Time," an unusual departure for Ballard into pure fantasy, a feudal lord and his beloved forestall the attacks of barbarians on their castle by picking "time flowers," resulting in a temporary "reversal of time" during which the attackers are thrown back. Both protagonists are finally transformed into crystalline statues, frozen in time and immune to harm. In the title story of *The Terminal Beach, and Other Stories,* an obsessed ex-bomber pilot wanders an abandoned nuclear testing site in search of a "zone of non-time" where he may speak with the dead of past and future wars and where ontological beliefs are negated by the ultimate reality of the bomb. *The Impossible Man, and Other Stories* contains "The Drowned Giant," in which a giant's body is inexplicably washed ashore near a city. The story recalls both Jonathan Swift's *Gulliver's Travels* and Franz Kafka's *The Metamorphosis* in its epigrammatic narrative, which describes the citizenry's initial fear, gradual acceptance, and ultimate denial of the fact of the giant's existence once it has been removed. *Low-Flying Aircraft, and Other Stories* contains Ballard's acclaimed novella, *The Ultimate City,* about a man who rejects the inefficiency of his simple agrarian society and leads his community in restoring technology to a late-twentieth century ghost town. As the city's population grows, however, so do such accompanying problems as pollution, crime, and violence.

In *The Atrocity Exhibition* (published in the United States as *Love and Napalm: Export U. S. A.*), Ballard posits the idea that "perhaps psychopathology should be kept alive as a repository, perhaps the last repository, of the imagination." The book, which is written in a fragmented prose style in the manner of William S. Burroughs's *Naked Lunch,* is narrated by a modern Everyman who describes in detached clinical terms the intermingled violent and sexual responses of human test subjects to situations involving fatal car crashes, sadistic acts, and modern myth figures such as Marilyn Monroe and the Kennedy family. Ballard describes society's modern immunity to immoral subject matter as "the death of affect," and in such stories as "Plan for the Assassination of Jacqueline Kennedy" and "Why I Want to Fuck Ronald Reagan," Ballard examines America's perverse attraction toward and hatred for public and political figures. Following its appearance in England the book attracted heated controversy due to its presumed pornographic treatment of actual persons and immoral subject matter. Despite the support of several prominent critics, the work did not appear in the United States for nearly two years.

Many of Ballard's stories of the 1970s differ from his earlier works in that they present vague, unspecified settings and focus on contemporary figures and events. Some stories in *Myths of the Near Future* address the dangers inherent in technological society through personal, isolated situations more common to mainstream literature than science fiction. In "Motel Architecture," for example, a man who is obsessed with the shower scene in Alfred Hitchcock's film *Psycho* unconsciously recreates the crime.

Many of Ballard's short story collections appear under the same or similar titles in England and the United States, but often contain entirely different, overlapping, or substantially revised stories which date from different periods in his career. *The Best Short Stories of J. G. Ballard* includes many of Ballard's most popular and acclaimed short works, including "Manhole 69," in which three men who have been surgically "cured" of the need for sleep retreat into catatonic states when deprived of sensations such as light, color, and motion.

Unlike most authors of science fiction, Ballard resists the typical Western ideals of progress and evolution. If the purpose of science fiction is to awaken society to its potential for catastrophe as well as achievement, Ballard's contribution to science fiction literature has been to stimulate humanity's awareness of the fallibility of any one or all systems of rational belief. Although he has often been criticized for his presumed pessimism, he has expressed his identification with those of his characters who logically accept the worst of situations as inevitable. Ballard deems his work "*a fiction of psychological fulfillment*. . . . All my fiction describes the merging of the self with the ultimate metaphor, the ultimate image, and that's psychologically fulfilling."

(See also *CLC,* Vols. 3, 6, 14, 36; *Contemporary Authors,* Vols. 5-8, rev. ed.; *Contemporary Authors New Revision Series,* Vol. 15; and *Dictionary of Literary Biography,* Vol. 14.)

PRINCIPAL WORKS

SHORT FICTION

Billenium, and Other Stories 1962
The Voices of Time, and Other Stories 1962
The Four-Dimensional Nightmare 1963
Passport to Eternity, and Other Stories 1963
The Terminal Beach, and Other Stories 1964; revised edition, 1964
The Impossible Man, and Other Stories 1966
The Day of Forever 1967; 1971
The Disaster Area 1967
The Overloaded Man 1968
The Atrocity Exhibition 1970; also published as *Love and Napalm: Export U. S. A.,* 1972
Chronopolis, and Other Stories 1971
Vermilion Sands 1971; revised edition, 1973
Low-Flying Aircraft, and Other Stories 1976
The Best of J. G. Ballard 1977; also published as *The Best Short Stories of J. G. Ballard* [revised edition], 1978
Rolling All the Time 1979?
Myths of the Near Future 1982

OTHER MAJOR WORKS

The Drowned World (novel) 1962
The Wind from Nowhere (novel) 1962
The Burning World (novel) 1964; also published as *The Drought* [enlarged edition], 1965
The Crystal World (novel) 1966
The Assassination Weapon (drama) 1969
Crash (novel) 1973
Concrete Island (novel) 1974
High-Rise (novel) 1975
The Unlimited Dream Company (novel) 1979
Hello America (novel) 1981
Empire of the Sun (novel) 1984

BRIAN W. ALDISS (essay date 1965)

[*Aldiss is an English novelist, short story writer, critic, and editor who is best known for his science fiction novels and criticism. In a favorable review of* The Terminal Beach, *which first appeared in* SF Horizons *in 1965 and is excerpted below, Aldiss examines Ballard's rejection of traditional science fiction themes and his various innovations in the genre.*]

THE WOUNDED LAND

Terminal Beach is a much better collection than we have any right to expect in this wicked world. Not only have the stories virtue in their own right; they show Ballard developing in a way that did not seem likely from his earlier writing.

[Ballard's] ***Four Dimensional Nightmare,*** showed him limited as to subject. There were too many stories about time, more particularly about the stoppage of time. In [***Terminal Beach***], he remains limited as regards theme, but the limitation represents an absorbed concentration and the theme pours forth its rewards, and that in fact is his theme: that limits whether voluntary or imposed bring ample compensation by deflecting attention to occurrences and states of mind not available to the 'normal' world-possessed man. . . .

Some of the best stories in the ***Terminal Beach*** collection hover—as all good SF should—on the verge of being something other than SF. **"The Drowned Giant,"** for instance, is an apparently straightforward eyewitness account of the dismemberment of a gigantic, though otherwise human body cast up on an unspecified shore. The manner of telling recalls such stories of Kafka's as *Metamorphosis* or "The Giant Mole." It begins with this sentence: "On the morning after the storm the body of a drowned giant was washed ashore on the beach five miles to the north-west of the city." The important thing, the narrator tells us, is to remember where the giant appeared, not the fact that he was a giant; to be amazed would be impolite, and by describing the dismemberment of the giant corpse, Ballard weans us of our desire to know where he came from. He concentrates on the important things, and by so doing makes the ends pursued by most SF seem trivial ones. In the hands of the first fifty SF writers you care to name, this story would end with other giants coming down from Akkapulko XIV to rescue him, and the shooting beginning. By eschewing sensationalism, Ballard makes us realise how much SF is given over to sensationalism. (p. 38)

THE UNIFYING WIT

[Ballard] replaces sensationalism with wit. The critics have not noticed how witty Ballard is, yet a unifying wit is his dominant characteristic. Fandom seems to have decided he is the prophet of despondence and let it go at that. Ballard is seldom discussed in fanzines . . . , but the occasional reference tends to be disparaging. Thus a correspondent in *Vector* calls Ballard a "melancholy johnnie." An instance of Ballard's wit is the dry way the pedantry of Pelham is drawn in **"The Reptile Enclosure."** . . . The situation in **"Billenium,"** where seven people move one by one into a small room, is treated with an appreciation of its comic side, while irony is always present in Ballard's writing, often seeming to turn against the author himself, except on the rare occasions when it is dethroned by melodrama. **"Track 12,"** an early story, skilfully combines melodrama and irony, where a man is drowned to the amplified noise of his own adulterous kiss. **"A Question of Re-entry,"** which deals with a Lieutenant in the Amazon, looking for a missing astronaut, has a humorous denouement, if the humour is wry. But Ballard's wit lies chiefly in imagery that, like the imagery of such metaphysical poets as Carew or Donne, can surprise and delight by its juxtaposition of hitherto separate ideas. . . . Such juxtapositional imagery abounds in ***The Terminal Beach.*** (p. 39)

[Ballard's] unifying wit seeks always to combine opposites and incongruities. In **"The Subliminal Man,"** the hideous giant subliminal signs are erected all over town but, as "an appeal to petty snobbery, the lower sections had been encased in mock-Tudor panelling"—a typical wry Ballard joke. In *The Drought,* Catherine strides along with her white lions, a contrast of weak and strong. Mrs. Quilter is buried in the back seat of a limousine. These are typical instances of collage methods, the wit of a cataloguer who is discontented with everyone else's categories. They represent a sensible attempt to deal with the dislocations of our times, and are Ballard's most notable contribution to science fiction. (p. 40)

DETHRONEMENT OF THE HERO

Ballard's attitude is such that we are often reminded of SF by the very things he is ostentatiously not doing. Ballard likes to regard himself as something of an outcast among the SF fraternity. He avoids most other authors, he believes—in sharp distinction to the adulation expressed by other writers—that "H. G. Wells has had a disastrous influence on the subsequent course of science fiction," he seems to regard William Burroughs as the greatest of SF writers, and of course he is the apostle of Inner Space. . . . [In a guest editorial in the magazine *New Worlds*], Ballard said that he believed SF should jettison such ideas as interstellar travel, aliens, and other staple ideas of the genre, turning more towards the biological sciences than the overworked physical ones. "The only truly alien planet is Earth." Not only should subject matter change; style should alter. He says

> Science fiction must jettison its present narrative forms and plots. Most of these are far too explicit to express any subtle interplay of character and theme . . . I think most of the hard work will fall not on the writer and editor but on the readers. The onus is on them to accept a more oblique narrative style, understated themes, private symbols and vocabularies.

This is a conscious reaction against conservative SF. Nor does Ballard, unlike most prophets, fail to practise what he preaches. His central characters, sensitive, sinful, defeated, wounded, wry, are poles away from Heinlein's swaggering heroes, Asimov's world savers, Bester's anger-propelled demons, or Wright's sour conspirators, or of all the snarlingly brave guys with blasters and cloaks and big boots that have been with us since Verne's day. Against the doers, Ballard ranges his non-doers. (pp. 41-2)

In his early stories, his non-doers were also non-runners. His central characters struggle very little against their various worlds: too little, so that we find a faint sense of anti-climax lingering about early stories like **"Prima Belladonna," "Waiting Grounds," "Sound Sweep," "Zone of Terror"** and **"Build-Up."** But at this time, Ballard had still not found his tenor, and was writing stories like **"Mobile," "Escapement,"** and **"Now: Zero,"** all of which are too feeble and derivative to find equivalents in his later work. (p. 42)

Yet, just as he began with such masterly stories as **"Manhole 69"** and **"Track 12,"** so his non-runners still appear in his latest stories. But this is where I think Ballard's development comes in. The non-doing was at first a disadvantage because Ballard had yet to forge the 'oblique narrative style, understated themes, and private symbols' he needed. In the volume called ***The Terminal Beach,*** he presents a series of stories in which the non-doing of the central character is essential to the structure; it has become the structure. His characters, like the characters of Jules Feiffer's cartoons, stand still and give themselves away. Apart from a certain amount of running through a forest in **"The Illuminated Man,"** there is almost no action in the dozen stories. You could hear a finger stir.

This is the effect Ballard needs. He has junked the old types of SF narrative and found space for nuance and for inner space. His settings too have moved from the cities and suburbias into desert places, almost as though this gives Ballard more room for his manoeuvres. Not only is the style more oblique than formerly; the proceedings are looked at from a more oblique angle. The examination now is less of failure than of the private glories often enshrined in failure. This is a major progression in which tales like **"The Subliminal Man"**—where Franklin, the chief character, is torn between doing and non-doing—perhaps mark a transitional stage. The curiously named James B in **"Illuminated Man,"** Pelham in **"The Reptile Enclosure,"** Charles Gifford in **"The Delta at Sunset,"** Traven in **"The Terminal Beach,"** Holliday in **"Deep End,"** Maitland in **"The Gioconda of the Twilight Noon"** can all be regarded as men who are failures from a worldly point of view; but the writer convinces us that there is more of interest to them than that; rejected by or rejecting the world, they are free to discover and suffer in unfrequented ways. (pp. 42-3)

WRECKING THE SPACE STATIONS

It is at this point that Ballard most resembles Ray Bradbury, whose writings he admires, although the ambiguity of his feelings even towards science makes him the more interesting writer. His refuge from life in a scientific age is Bradbury's refuge, a seeking for the childhood world of feeling without thought.

Children are absent from Ballard's stories, sometimes obstrusively (two of the central characters in ***The Terminal Beach*** collection have lost wives and young children in car smashes), but many characters have the childlike trait that they will brave danger to return to the time/place where they feel most intensely. (Their boldness is generally rewarded, for few of them come to grief, even when surrounded with the most inauspicious circumstances). (pp. 44-5)

Perhaps here we have the reason why Ballard, like Bradbury, has become a figure of controversy. Whether his turning away from the striding he-man of SF is an intellectual or an instinctive act (and one must suppose that by its power in Ballard's work it is the latter, aided by intellectual window-dressing), it does not go down smoothly with the addict reader, who wants big tough figures he can identify with. (p. 45)

Ballard is a sensitive writer, and it is hard sometimes not to feel that his stories are written in a perverse spirit. This, of course, is one way to survive the criticism of the ignorant. After the first spate of ill-judged criticisms, Ballard's stories seemed to contain more wrecked space vehicles lying in the sand, more derelict ones orbiting overhead, more modern gadgets going wrong, more motels and hotels sinking in water or dust, more launching ramps and gantries rusting away. In some of the stories in ***Terminal Beach,*** you can almost hear him say "That's one for Arthur Clarke!"

One of his most notable bits of machine-wrecking occurs towards the end of *The Drought,* where Ballard reveals himself as the literary luddite par excellence. He describes a small pavillion, "its glass and metal cornices shining in the sunlight. It had been constructed from assorted pieces of chromium and enamelled metal—the radiator grills of cars, reflectors of electric-heaters, radio cabinets and so on—fitted together with remarkable ingenuity."

This is collage again, and another example of the unifying process at work. It is part Ballard's way of commenting on the meaninglessness of the original gadgets; although they have been perverted from their intended usages, they now make something more worthwhile on a sane scale of values, "a Faberge gem." Analogously, this is what Ballard has done with the materialist values of the average SF tale. He finds most of the usual trappings not worthwhile. His editorial on Inner Space was impatient about "the narrow imaginative limits imposed by the background of rocket ships and planet-hopping," and he is accustomed to refer to fictional space travels as old hat.

Personally, I disagree with much of this, I cannot see how his constant wrecking of the biosphere is to be reckoned as newer than space travel; nor do I think that symbols such as rockets and robots, which have been created as it were by agreement over several decades, should be lightly scrapped. But one welcomes the fact that Ballard has a point of view; it is the only way to create original work. . . . It may be that there is a fallacy in his inner space thesis. If, as I have suggested, his manifesto was conceived to justify his work (and we all need justification), it might be that in times of lower creative pressure, he would fall back on it consciously; on such occasions, the fallacy would be more likely to show through. Ballard's characters are forced to inhabit inner space by their failure to communicate, sometimes to communicate even on an elementary level. Several of his protagonists could be saved or could save themselves just by speaking out. A case in point is Maitland in **"The Gioconda of the Twilight Noon."** We can see no reason why he should not have spoken to the doctor concerning his blindness. Is it convention that keeps him silent, or the conventions of a Ballard story? The same question might be asked of Gifford in **"The Delta at Sunset";** the last we see of him, he is refusing to answer his wife, his one contact with reality. (pp. 45-6)

THE DISLOCATED WORLD

One direction in which [Ballard] has moved is deeper into natural landscapes and away from man-made ones. The enveloping cities of **"Billenium," "Chronopolis," "The Subliminal Man"** (which contains the most brilliant obsolescence-speeding gadgets anyone has dreamed up) and a dozen more stories, are left behind.

One may regret this. At times, subtopia seemed almost like a patent Ballard invention. With his fondness for collages, Ballard should occupy a fallow period by mounting a metropolis novel from shuffled sections of his city stories. It might make his most striking novel yet. . . .

Despite his care to keep within the science fiction framework, Ballard is often careless with his facts. Or perhaps it is more accurate to say that he is rather lordly about his material, just as he is about his readers. (p. 47)

These inaccuracies are not too troublesome in themselves; but Ballard's attitude to inconsistency is less comfortable. I find them easy to forgive when [in *The Drowned World*] . . . we are offered as a result of the draining of Leicester Square, such amusing novelties as the bats "darting from one dripping eave to another," and the scow which "ran aground on the sidewalk, pushed off again and then struck finally on a traffic island." This is how I like my science fiction, with the world topsy-turvy, and something unlikely on every page following from the original premise.

Jim Ballard, in private conversation, enjoys giving the impression that science fiction has little to offer him and that it is a form of cheating, of "unearned experience." I have argued that on the contrary it is often a record of psychic experience. Ballard's writing itself seems to suppport this proposition, even if Ballard won't. . . . [Ballard] uses SF to a fresh end, but it is hard to see what other field of writing would suit his gift for conjuring up vivid and alien landscapes and describing strange and disconnected states of mind.

His witty and nervous worlds, littered with twitching nerves and crashed space stations, carry their own conviction that will eventually win him popular support. For his characters, the worst blow is always over, they are just past their nemesis and consequently free. One can only hope that for Ballard too the worst misunderstanding is over, so that he will be free to create in a more intelligent atmosphere. Despite some shortcomings, his stories represent one of the few stimulating forces in contemporary SF. (p. 48)

Brian W. Aldiss, "The Wounded Land: J. G. Ballard," in J. G. Ballard: The First Twenty Years, *edited by James Goddard and David Pringle, Bran's Head Books Ltd, 1976, pp. 38-48.*

THE TIMES LITERARY SUPPLEMENT (essay date 1970)

[*In the following excerpt, the critic comments on the themes and style in Ballard's* The Atrocity Exhibition.]

[Ballard] presents extreme examples of the private psyche being invaded by public events. The frigid central figure of ***The Atrocity Exhibition*** is haunted by every imaginable modern ill, from the assassination of J.F.K. and a proposed assassination of his widow to the sexual symbolism of car crashes . . . and the code-music of the quasars. Severe anginal spasms and the imaginary sex death of Che Guevara jostle with "the transliterated pudenda of Ralph Nader", in a modern acrostic of despair.

It is hard to see whether the publishers serve their author well by claiming for these pieces a unity beyond a stylistic one. Read separately they have the attraction of oddity and unexpected phrase. Together they offend by repetitive wordiness ("the eucharist of the madonna of the hoardings"), and by the cold plodding sadism masked in jargon which soon becomes self-parody. The last piece, **"The Assassination of J.F.K. Considered as a Downhill Motor Race"**, written several years ago and owing an acknowledged debt to Alfred Jarry, has a wit and style lacking in the other pieces.

The low point is reached in **"Why I Want to Fuck Ronald Reagan"**, with its glum delight in rectal hemorrhages and "the face of L. B. Johnson . . . clearly genital in significant appearance—the nasal prepuce, scrotal jaw, etc."

The subliminal terrors of the present, the austere beauties of dissociation, were displayed to perfection in Mr. Ballard's earlier stories (for instance, in ***The Terminal Beach***). In [***The Atrocity Exhibition***] he earns a title bestowed on one of his splintery mini-chapters, **"Veteran of the Private Evacuations"**.

"Deadly Dials, Queer Quasars," in The Times Literary Supplement, *No. 3567, July 9, 1970, p. 741.*

JAMES FENTON (essay date 1970)

[*Fenton is an English poet and critic. In the following excerpt, he faults Ballard for being intentionally obscure in* The Atrocity Exhibition.]

[***The Atrocity Exhibition***] is an example of a kind of experimental writing which requires of the reader a large amount of concentration and analysis. The temporo-spatial organisation of the work is purposely confused, the scenes or sections being arranged paratactically and in discrete paragraphs. The hero's name (as in a famous Edgar Wallace story, but in this case the change is intentional) changes several times throughout the book. The project of the work is to construct a new schema for the role of violence and sex as communication, using an analysis of a Sixties iconography of politicians, film-stars, car crash victims, assassination victims, etc. There is an obsession with anatomy, especially with the genital areas, and with the body in spaces described by rectilinear planes. Above all, the work is repetitive to a degree, eclectic both in style and ideas, and stunningly pretentious.

James Fenton, "Spoils," in New Statesman, *Vol. 80, No. 2051, July 10, 1970, p. 28.*

PAUL THEROUX (essay date 1972)

[*Theroux is an American novelist, short story and travel writer, and critic best known for his highly acclaimed novel,* The Mosquito Coast *(1981). In the following excerpt, Theroux finds* Love and Napalm: Export U. S. A. *greatly offensive both in style and subject matter.*]

[William Burroughs remarks] in his preface to J. G. Ballard's [***Love and Napalm: Export U. S. A.***], "An auto crash can be more sexually stimulating than a pornographic picture." . . . [In this book Mr. Ballard] weaves a cold-blooded fantasy of aberrant proportions around this idea. The fantasists are a doctor and his patient—or perhaps patients, since the names change even if the nightmares are fairly constant in their hideousness. His Doctor Nathan (a less crazed and more ponderous version of Burroughs's own Doctor Benway) observes that "the car crash may be perceived unconsciously as a fertilizing rather than destructive event—a liberation of sexual energy," and he goes on to describe the sexual element in the deaths of James Dean, Jayne Mansfield, Albert Camus and John F. Kennedy. Indeed, the central idea of this novel is of man as a piece of meat somehow animated by a crack-up.

But this is more than the pornography of auto accidents; in another place "the mysterious eroticism of the multi-story car park" is mentioned, and . . . the erogenous zones of cars are exhibited. Elsewhere . . . sexual possibilities are proposed, the idea of making love with a rear exhaust assembly or "this ashtray, say, or . . . the angle between two walls." Mr. Ballard does not stop there; he does not stop at all. His hero, Travis (sometimes called Talbot, Trabert, Travers, and Tallis) is having a nervous breakdown—a crack-up of his own, you might say—and in the interrelated sections of the book he drools over the arousal potential of Kennedy's assassination, the napalming of peasants, the atrocity movie, science in general ("the ultimate pornography"), radiation burns on one's intended, and finally observations on "the latent sexual character" of the Vietnam war, which lead him to conclude with the deranged imagining that this war, for Americans, is a form of love.

It is a kind of toying with horror, a stylish anatomy of outrage, and full of specious arguments, phony statistics, a disgusted fascination with movie stars and the sexual conceits of American brand names and paraphernalia, jostled by a narrative that shoves the reader aside and shambles forward on leaden sentences strung out with words like "conceptual" and "googolplex" and "quasars" and "blastospheres," one sees his craft (not to mention his Krafft) ebbing, and one is tempted to ridicule or dismiss it. It is a horrible book, and it is even in parts a boring and pointless book. Two chapters spring to mind here, one involving Ronald Reagan (its title unprintable in this newspaper), a speculation of the purest futility, and **"The Assassination of John Fitzgerald Kennedy Considered as a Downhill Motor Race,"** the last an acknowledged lift from Alfred Jarry who wrote the Crucifixion as "An Uphill Bicycle Race."

Although it is, shall we say, unpersuasive as a whole, the details have an undeniable ring of pathological truth. Some people do find pain or human corpses sexually stimulating, or consider their cars as surrogate mistresses and see vulvas in handbags or car grilles, or enjoy atrocity movies and the current issue of sex magazines and, God knows, some sad man may at this minute be contemplating congress with a winsome ashtray or yearning amorously to disembowel a villager.

These things happen—they happen a lot more often than other episodes Mr. Ballard has written of in his science fiction, his rather silly tales of giants and futuristic weirdos with funny names, dramatized in laughable sentences like the opening one in his story **"The Garden of Time"** (in ***Chronopolis***), "Toward evening, when the great shadow of the Palladian villa filled the terrace, Count Axel left his library and walked down the wide rococo steps among the time flowers." . . .***But Love and Napalm: Export U.S.A.*** is not futuristic; here the novelist does more than botanize on the graves of mutilated peasants and famous victims—he blackmails us with our sentiment and outrages our compassion; it is the novel as a form of abuse, the dead-end of feeling.

Man is more than warm meat, but Mr. Ballard's attitude is calculated. He says love when he means sex, and sex when he means torture, and there is nothing so fragile as sorrow or joy in the book. Some men may have an undeniable genius for cruelty and may applaud the parody of pain, . . . [but] if Mr. Ballard was an American he might have found it more difficult to misrepresent a war which, far from arousing us sexually, has made us impervious to suffering. It is not his choice of subject, but his celebration of it, that is monstrous. (pp. 56-7)

Paul Theroux, "The Auto Crash as Sexual Stimulation," in The New York Times Book Review, *October 22, 1972, pp. 56-7.*

BRIAN ASH (essay date 1975)

[*Ash is a respected English critic of science fiction. In the essay excerpted here, he examines Ballard's treatment of entropy in his short story "The Voices of Time."*]

Whether we regard infinity as a continuous process of interrelated events or as an interminable sequence of individual cine stills, the Cosmic influence on time may yet have surprises in store. J. G. Ballard has ingeniously combined the mathematics of physics and the factual discovery of anti-matter to foresee, in *The Crystal World,* the final annihilation of time. . . . All that ever happened, happened yesterday—but a kind of human consciousness lives on in an appreciation of universally static crystalline beauty.

In an earlier story, **"The Voices of Time,"** Ballard has written movingly of this long deterioration in temporal vitality. To the individual specialists at work in an experimental research station, the awareness of decay takes different forms. For one, it is the slowing-down in the frequencies of radio signals emitted by distant stars; for another, who finds himself sleeping longer each day, it is a matter of biochemistry. . . . His extending periods of sleep, which could easily be taken superficially as a neurotic escape from the pressures of late twentieth-century existence, are, he argues, in keeping with a general biological decline that ranges from a continuing fall in world wheat-production to the increasing drop in birthrate which confounds the neo-Malthusian projections made during the 1960s. In the same way that the life of one particular organism is limited, so is the duration of the entire biosphere:

> It's always been assumed that the evolutionary slope reaches for ever upwards, but in fact the peak has already been reached, and the pathway now leads downwards to the common biological grave. . . . Five thousand centuries from now our descendants, instead of being multi-brained starmen, will probably be naked prognathous idiots . . . grunting their way through the remains of this Clinic like Neolithic men caught in a macabre inversion of time. . . .
>
> (pp. 162-63)

The haunting quality of universal decay which Ballard has instilled into **"The Voices of Time,"** as if to ennoble the tale with an atmosphere of aesthetic sorrow, calls to mind—as few stories in the genre can—the ancient Japanese concept of *Mono no aware*. This is the philosophy of sadness brought about by perfection—the idea that beauty contains its own death and that the most beautiful thing is the beginning of decay. Therefore, by long Japanese association, everything in decline—because it is dying—is beautiful. It summons echoes of the terrible beauty found by Wells's Time Traveller in the far future, as it does—in a similar sense—of the ephemeral glory of the sparks which Kingsley Martin suggested Wells could see flying off the wheels of cause and effect as they turn.

If the inexorable grinding of those wheels is predetermined ultimately to close the temporal circle, it will only reinforce the suspicion that time has never been on humanity's side, manipulate it how we will. (p. 163)

Brian Ash, "The Destruction of Time," in his Faces of the Future: The Lessons of Science Fiction, *Taplinger Publishing Co., Inc., 1975, pp. 145-64.*

DEREK MAHON (essay date 1976)

[*Mahon is an Irish poet, editor, critic, and essayist. In the following excerpt, he calls* Low-Flying Aircraft and Other Stories *a success.*]

Ballard's method is that of H. G. Wells. He takes the known facts of contemporary history, the observable nature of the world, and makes logical deductions until he is in the realm of fantasy or, in Wellsian parlance, 'romance'. Personal character has little interest for him, and personal histories exist only in relation to an historical phase. . . . There are nine stories in [***Low-Flying Aircraft, and Other Stories***]. Some are *jeux d'esprit,* like **"The Greatest Television Show on Earth"**, in which the invention of 'time vision' has enabled the TV networks to cover, and even to improve upon, actual historical events. When they come to do **"The Flight of the Israelites"**, however, the camera crews, surprised by the force of the resurgent Red Sea, are lost in the swirling maelstrom and the world's screens go blank.

All of this is good fun, though not on the same level as the powerful novella, ***The Ultimate City,*** with which the collection opens. Here we have Ballard at his best—genuinely inventive, sharply observant and highly plausible. We are in the post-technological age. The cities lie deserted, 'like an abandoned dream waiting to be reoccupied'. The streets are lined with cars parked on flattened tyres; deer roam through lower Manhattan. Halloway, driven by curiosity, comes over in his glider from Garden City across the Sound, a place of greenhouses and windmills powered by solar energy, to investigate the metropolis abandoned in despair by his parents' generation. It is an Icarian flight. Intrigued by the possibilities, he reneges on the pastoral quietism of home to start a new, old-style colony in the city, and the history of urban man is briefly re-enacted, from the turning on of the lights to street muggings and terminal pollution. But what sticks in the mind is the description of Halloway's aerial ballet before the vast, reflecting windows of a silent office block, until 'colliding with his own image, he fell with the broken machine among the cars a hundred feet below'. (pp. 812-13)

Derek Mahon, "Crash," in New Statesman, *Vol. 92, No. 2385, December 3, 1976, pp. 812-13.*

GEORGE GARRETT (essay date 1977)

[*Garrett is an American novelist, short story writer, poet, and critic noted for his mastery of many forms of fiction. In the following excerpt, Garrett offers a brief consideration of* Rolling All the Time.]

James Ballard, though not in the least a "slick" writer (he has too much energy and power for that), belongs with those writers to whom the validity and implications of an experience mean more than any display of personal artistic sensibility. . . . [In ***Rolling All the Time,*** Ballard] starts from the "old-fashioned" presumption or strategy that the world is reasonable, if not rational, and is urgently threatened by the wicked and the absurd. Add, for the special flavor of his stories, a strong democratic bias (none of your urban elitism here), a remarkable understanding of the *work* that people do, the joys and sorrows of working, and, not least, the hard glint of unflinching integrity, and you come up with a first-rate story writer. . . . **"The Feast of Crispian"** is one of the best war stories that I've ever read, and as an account of the U.S. Merchant Marine in those days it stands with the best of them, right there with *Dark Sea Running*. (p. 107)

George Garrett, "Fables and Fabliaux of Our Time," in The Sewanee Review, *Vol. LXXXV, No. 1, Winter, 1977, pp. 104-10.*

MICHAEL IRWIN (essay date 1977)

[*In this excerpt from his favorable review of* Low-Flying Aircraft, and Other Stories, *Irwin praises the effective use of landscapes in Ballard's fiction.*]

[The stories in ***Low-Flying Aircraft***], set in a "post-technological" future, leave haunting pictures in the mind. Certain images recur: cars or aeroplanes half-submerged in sand, broken bridges, empty cities, shattered buildings, decaying machines. It is hard to think of another writer whose visions would be so nearly expressible as paintings. J. G. Ballard's landscapes—the word is unavoidable in discussion of his work—seem to convey more of his meaning than do the stories enacted against them. Several of these tales would make striking films, but the films could almost be silent—or, rather, wordless. The strange scenery fascinates because while hyperbolic, surrealistic, it is yet curiously familiar. One has repeatedly a sense of having seen something very like the blighted cities and dying seaside resorts that Mr. Ballard describes. He taps our memories of disused railway-stations or airstrips, dumped cars, derelict cinemas or factories. The world he creates seems credible because it has already begun to exist.

The author's attitude to that world is intriguingly ambivalent. He shows the human race crippled and dwindling through its own violence, negligence or blind self-gratification. Nature seems well rid of us and of our detritus. . . . [Yet] even mechanical relics can seem touching. There is exhilaration when an ancient car, long inert, is made to move again, or when a juke-box, silent for a quarter of a century, is brought back to raucous life. . . . [Ballard's] stories contrive to be both stark and wistful.

The Ultimate City, much the longest piece in the collection, is virtually a novella. Halloway, the hero, leaves his gentle agrarian community, all cycling, recycling and solar energy, to revisit a nearby city abandoned years before "when the world's reserves of fossil fuels had finally been exhausted". With the aid of a few strangers he meets among the ghostly office blocks and department stores he sets out to revitalize the town, or at any rate part of it. He collects enough petrol from abandoned lorries and cars to work a number of generators. Offices and shops are restocked. Rubbish is cleared. Traffic lights, neon signs and pinball machines are put back in action. Soon young people come flowing to the town to relish the forgotten pleasures; but as the population multiplies so do the problems: pollution, road accidents, crime, even inflation. Halloway and his helpers variously represent all the main forces that founded, developed and will eventually destroy our towns. In a few months the entire history of Halloway's city is reenacted at high speed, up to and including its collapse. The sequence is perhaps too tidy, too allegorical, but the backgrounds are often superb, and it is the backgrounds that do the work of the story.

With the exception of **"The Beach Murders"**—an ingeniously fragmented mystery that the reader must assemble like a jigsaw puzzle—the four stories that lack background, that deal only in ideas, are no more than decently entertaining. But the remaining five, which constitute three-quarters of the volume, are works of real imaginative force, dreamlike, vivid, unpredictable in their effect. Eerie and elegiac as they are they do not lack an element of hope. . . .

Michael Irwin, "On the Scrapheap," in The Times Literary Supplement, *No. 3905, January 14, 1977, p. 26.*

DUNCAN FALLOWELL (essay date 1977)

[*Fallowell is a prominent English critic. In the following excerpt, he presents a caustic analysis of Ballard's "weaknesses," focusing on characterization, prose style, technical structure, and intellectual content.*]

Accidie, ennui, malaise—the French have more words to describe the prevailing breeze in Mr. Ballard's [***Low-Flying Air-***

craft and Other Stories]. The breeze is a light one, nagging, and blows across sand dunes and derelict cities and abandoned seaside resorts like the Vengeance of Warhol, the wind from nowhere going nowhere. What remains of a population in this latest Ballard doomscape is one of listless biodegradable people, magazine archetypes gazing out to sea from the crumbling concrete balcony of a deserted hotel on the Spanish coast—the woman tucks a strand of hair behind her ear and sips at a dry martini, the man reverts to a second Boy's Own Paper adolescence in a desperate attempt to appear virile. Fate has finally overtaken both of them; and their impotence is exposed.

Against this dismal backdrop Mr. Ballard releases his heroes and the occasional heroine. They take to the air (literally in many of the stories, in patched-up aeroplanes salvaged from the Last Days of Technology) as proof that the spirit of man goes on and on and on. If they fail, it serves as a warning that the same old thoughts applied in the same old way, however changed the circumstances, only produce more of the same old problems.

Mr. Ballard's cleverness used to lie in casting a smoke-screen across his weaknesses as a writer with one ingenious imaginative idea. This was in the days when he was content to be known as a writer of science fiction adventure stories. Now that he is being set up as a literary prophet the weaknesses become more obvious. They are:

(1) Characterisation. He is quite hopeless at this. Nowhere in his writing can I recall a name actually turning into a face. . . . Ballard's men are either strong or weak, mostly strong. His women are either strong or weak, mostly weak (if strong they are usually quasi-lesbian or sado-masochistic). A tabulation of names in three short story collections, including this one, will establish the point.

Low-Flying Aircraft. Men: Melville, Forrester, Halloway, Buckmaster, Sherrington, Hamilton, Hathaway. Women: Judith, Miranda, Helen Winthrop (butch), Judy. Except when talking among themselves, which they sometimes do in a language called Middle Chappy, the men are known by their surnames and the women by their christian names: official pre-war adventure story etiquette. The men are invariably dactyls (—⏑⏑), and if they are not it is perhaps because they are common or in some other way inadequate, *eg* "foreign". On the other hand, the women are never common. They have strayed here from the genteel de-odourised suburbs of the novelette, with a nomenclature to prove it. So:

The Overloaded Man. Men: Burlington, Cameron, Shepley, Carter, Harcourt, Sheringham. Are you beginning to catch the drift? Women: Marion, Margot, Helen, Eve, meagre tokens in a male world.

The Terminal Beach. Men: Connolly, Sherrington, Springman, Pelham, Maitland, Rossiter—the archetypal Ballard name as in "Rossiter lifted one eyebrow," "Rossiter pulled himself off the bed," "Rossiter pounded the counter-ledge," and "Rossiter was right." The Rossiters of this author's world are never wrong. It is their chief shortcoming. Even where the men are mere trochees (—⏑), they are of the kind who if ever they did succeed in committing a conscious sin would go off to the Empire somewhere and help build it with a good grace which might almost amount to relish. They are vaguely bogus too (even when fighting the rotters), slightly raffish and wishful-suave, the sub-Bond species—minus sex. It is true that Mr. Ballard quite often gives them sex but they rarely convey the impression of caring one way or the other about it. These characters would rather tinker with machines than with people—a trait which exposes them as strong and active men who are nonetheless sexually, emotionally and intellectually in a pre-natal stage of their development. Surely this explains why they cannot fire the imagination of the reader. And the women: Mildred, Judith, Louise—as in "For God's sake, Louise." The women never begin to happen at all, unless they are first de-sexed (as an aviator or scientist for example) so that they can behave like men. Insofar as Mr. Ballard writes about a dehumanised world of helpless ill-fortune, these mechanical nameplates can be said to populate it convincingly, *faute de mieux*.

(2) Prose Style. This is more than conventional, it is decidedly old-fashioned. Ballard is a 'period' writer in the sense of writing about a period (the fact that he writes about the future is simply to define which one) and also in the sense of typifying popular fiction of a certain generation. He can be placed somewhere between Rider Haggard and Ian Fleming without discomfort. Perhaps the biggest disappointment in him is his failure to develop a prose style which does not constantly trivialise his underlying obsessions. (pp. 59-60)

In every sense of the word [Ballard's] prose wants for taste. It lacks suppleness, grace, quick wits and complexity. Basically it lacks instinct. It fails to rise to the occasion and the consequent discrepancy is very irritating, especially when men of noted opinion repeatedly put forward Mr. Ballard as the one chosen by the Fates to raise science fiction into the arena of rich, adult art.

(3) Prose Style/Technical Structure. The amount of nonsense written about Ballard the Innovator is legion. Literary revolutions, like all others if genuine, are technical. They are involved with the development of newly accurate modes of objective perception and communication. Hence they imply a moral repercussion upon a system of ultimate reality. They happen at the interface of form and content (itself an artificial distinction). They have nothing whatever to do with subject matter as such. **"The Beach Murders"** is the only example of a modern story in ***Low-Flying Aircraft***. . . . The innovation is that the reader is invited to play games with twenty-six alphabetical clues relating to the solution of the crime. What is most interesting about it is not the explicit nature of the device employed but the effect it has on the quality of Mr. Ballard's writing. Suddenly there is so much more going on. The images are stronger, the gaucheries fewer, the energy flowing within the story is more fertile—and of course it is slightly less 'easy to read'.

Few of the other stories stray far from the punch-line method, of which Somerset Maugham was the most brilliant exponent. In this, the last paragraph will explain the events of the story, as with the punch-line of a joke. Since Maugham's time—despite any moodish influence Katherine Mansfield might have had—this has become the standard method for straight, commercial short stories. There is no reason at all why Ballard should not use it. Now and again. In [**"Low-Flying Aircraft"**] it works extremely well.

However, if he proposes to do what he is so often claimed to be doing, *ie* reflecting the contemporary world by positing a future one, then the punch-line method is not true to it. Since it requires an adhesion to the sequences of "easy" linear fiction for its effect, it is inadequate for monitoring a world in which Einstein long ago made space itself curved and time one of the relative dimensions. The fact that older people especially choose to disregard this in their daily lives, seeking refuge in a perceptual nostalgia, explains why so much of mankind appears to have lost control over its own actions and their consequences. Mr. Ballard's essence lives in this perceptual nostalgia too. So be it. But it being so, one is right to question the legitimacy of a reputation based upon an altogether profounder grasp of our world.

Which brings us to (4) Intellectual weakness. If science fiction is going to become literature proper then it is because its level of operation is raised and its sphere of understanding or "compassion" enlarged. This has not so far taken place. To have 'nightmare visions of the future' and to write them out in an entertaining way—and Mr. Ballard's stories are very entertaining, if you like the *genre*—is not a worthless activity. They will encourage us to think about the future. It daily becomes more urgent to do so, apparently. But one way or the other, for better or for worse, *everything* makes us think. What is significant however is *the way* our mentation works. And literature affects this—the collective unconscious thinking aloud and so evolving itself. I do not think Mr. Ballard affects this. Prophets of doom are prophets in no useful sense, even if their predictions are true. They do nothing but gluttonise on disaster and encourage us to do likewise.

As a professional writer of some standing, Mr. Ballard should be concerned about this at a far more subtle level than he has yet demonstrated. When he really does make the effort—**"The Beach Murders"** is a minor example—it pays off. That is a law of nature. His usual, mechanical and slip-shod style on the other hand (at its worst here in ***The Ultimate City,*** a pedestrian yawn degenerating from a good idea) only grows more portentous and shallow as his themes, under pressure from the claims of his apologists, grow more epic. . . .

Of course Mr. Ballard still has flashes of speculative ingenuity. The best example of this is in [**"Low-Flying Aircraft"**] and no wonder it gives its title to the entire volume. But by and large this is a messy collection which will surprise even his devotees, of which there are quite a number. As a quick read the stories have their justification. But one had been encouraged to expect rather more than that. (p. 60)

Duncan Fallowell, "Ballard in Bondage," in Books and Bookmen, *Vol. 22, No. 6, March, 1977, pp. 59-60.*

ANTHONY BURGESS (essay date 1978)

[*Considered one of the most prolific and versatile English novelists of his generation, Burgess has written such widely divergent works as* Tremor of Intent *(1966), an eschatological espionage story;* Nothing Like the Sun *(1964), a fictional version of William Shakespeare's life; and* A Clockwork Orange *(1962), an account of a futuristic dystopia narrated by a violent teenage criminal. In addition, Burgess is recognized for his vast knowledge of music and linguistics and, in particular, for his erudite criticism of James Joyce's works. In the following excerpt from his laudatory introduction to* The Best Short Stories of J. G. Ballard, *Burgess commends Ballard's writing for both content and style, placing two of his stories among "the most beautiful stories of the world canon of short fiction."*]

The first thing to say about J. G. Ballard is not that he is among our finest writers of science fiction but that he is among our finest writers of fiction *tout court* period. Ballard himself might retort that, granted the first claim, the second is redundant, since the only important fiction being produced today is science fiction. . . . I understand that the only living writers Ballard really admires are Isaac Asimov and William Burroughs. This can be interpreted negatively as a rejection of the kind of fiction that pretends there has been no revolution in thought and sensibility since, say, 1945. And this, alas, means the greater part of contemporary fiction, which remains thematically and stylistically torpid, limiting itself, as to subject matter, to what can be observed and inferred from observation and, as to language, what might be regarded by George Eliot as a little advanced but, on the whole, perfectly intelligible. Ballard considers that the kind of limitation that most contemporary fiction accepts is immoral, a shameful consequence of the rise of the bourgeois novel. Language exists less to record the actual than to liberate the imagination. To go forward, as Ballard does, is also to go back—scientific apocalypse and pre-scientific myth meet in the same creative region, where the great bourgeois novelists of tradition would not feel at home.

Ballard is a writer who accepts thematic limitations, but they are his own. His aesthetic instinct tells him that the task of the science fiction writer is not primarily to surprise or shock with bizarre inventions but, as with all fiction writers, to present human beings in credible, if extreme, situations and to imagine their reactions. Ballard's characters are creatures of the earth, not from outer space. Why devise fanciful new planets when we have our own planet, on which strange things are already happening, on which the ultimate strange happening is linked to present actualities or latencies by cause and effect? There is nothing in the evolutionary theory that denies living things the ability to develop leaden carapaces as a protection against nuclear fallout. . . . Our response to Ballard's visions is twofold: we reject this impossible world; we recognize that it is all too possible. The mediator between that world and this is a credible human being in a classic situation—tragic-stoical: he fights change on our behalf, but he cannot win. Faulkner, in **"The Overloaded Man,"** comes closest to victory by devising an epistemological trick—reducing the objects of the detestable world to sense-data, turning the sense-data to ideas, then killing the ideas by killing himself.

It would be too easy to call Ballard a prophet of doom. . . . Both H. G. Wells and Aldous Huxley built their utopias (eutopias, dystopias) on unassailable scientific knowledge. Ballard's own authority in various specialist fields seems, to this non-scientist, to be very considerable: I never see evidence of a false step in reasoning or a hypothesis untenable to an athletic enough imagination. The intellectual content of many of the stories is too stimulating for depression and so, one might add, is the unfailing grace and energy of the writing.

In my view, two of the most beautiful stories of the world canon of short fiction are to be found in this selection [***The Best Short Stories of J. G. Ballard***]. They are not, in the strictest sense, science fiction stories: their premises are acceptable only in terms of storytelling as ancient as those of Homer. In **"The Drowned Giant"** the corpse of a colossus of classical perfection of form is washed up on the beach. Children climb into the ears and nostrils; scientists inspect it; eventually the big commercial scavengers cart it off in fragments. The idea, perhaps, is nothing, but the skill lies in the exactness of the observation and the total credibility of the imagined human response to the presence of a drowned giant. Swift, in *Gulliver,* evaded too many physical problems, concerned as he was with a politico-satirical intention. Ballard evades nothing except the easy moral: to say that his story means this or that is to diminish it. In **"The Garden of Time"** a doomed aristocrat, aptly named Axel,

Paperback American edition of Ballard's Best Short Stories. *Washington Square Press, 1985. Cover artwork © 1985 Carlos Ochagavia.*

plucks crystalline flowers whose magic holds off for a while the advancing hordes that will destroy his castle and the civilized order it symbolizes. In an older kind of fairy story, the magic of the flowers would be potent but unspecified, vaguely apotropaic. In Ballard the flowers drug time into a brief trance—specific and, if one is a little off one's guard, almost rationally acceptable. The rhythms of poignancy which animate both stories are masterly: Ballard is a *moving* writer.

There are three short pieces at the end of this selection [**"The Atrocity Exhibition," "The Assassination of John Fitzgerald Kennedy Considered as a Downhill Motor Race,"** and **"Why I Want to Fuck Ronald Reagan"**] which show Ballard moving in a new direction. . . . These little sketches, highly original in form as well as content (though Burroughs seems to be somewhere underneath) play grim love-death games with public, or pubic, figures. They will serve as a reminder that Ballard, master of traditional narrative styles, is restless to try new things. Through him only is science fiction likely to make a formal and stylistic breakthrough of the kind achieved by Joyce, for whom Vico's *La Scienza Nuova* was new science enough. That Ballard is already important literature this selection will leave you in no doubt. (pp. vii-ix)

Anthony Burgess, in an introduction to The Best Short Stories of J. G. Ballard *by J. G. Ballard, Holt, Rinehart and Winston, 1978, pp. vii-ix.*

H. BRUCE FRANKLIN (essay date 1979)

[*Franklin, an American professor of English and American literature, is also a noted critic and historian. In the following excerpt from his analysis of the future of Western civilization as portrayed in science fiction, Franklin questions the limited historical view and the pessimism inherent in Ballard's fiction.*]

More than any other writer, J. G. Ballard incarnates the apocalyptic imagination running riot in Anglo-American culture today. Ballard began projecting multiform visions of the end of the world in the late 1950s, even before these became the rage, and he has been consistently, in fact obsessively, at it ever since. Along with other British and, somewhat later, American purveyors of literary gloomanddoom, Ballard has been a symbol of the ascendancy of the "New Wave" in science fiction. And the "New Wave" has been a leading force in the broad and deep expansion of a doomsday mentality in our culture. (p. 82)

Doomsday visions have been around for many centuries, if not millenia, but they become ascendant only during certain historical epochs and for specific historical reasons. J. G. Ballard and the other creators of an apocalyptic science fiction thrive because of certain conditions of the present era. One main goal of this essay is to investigate these conditions.

From the outset, we must understand the enormous significance of science fiction in the most developed capitalist nations. Science fiction has attained a modicum of academic respectability in the last decade, but those of us who teach it still find ourselves constantly on the defensive. . . . [The] simple fact is that science fiction is the major non-realistic literary form of the twentieth century, intricately related to all areas of social, historical, and scientific thought. Another object of this essay is to show that a single science fiction writer, in this case J. G. Ballard, reveals to us—whether deliberately or not remains to be seen—insights essential to our well-being if not our survival. For Ballard is not some oddity or aberration, but a representative Anglo-American intellectual who has chosen to write science fiction because it is the most suitable vehicle for the expression of ideas he holds in common with many other Anglo-American intellectuals.

Ballard makes little pretense that his fantasies of the death of the world or the human species are scientific, plausible, or even possible. The forms of his catastrophes are, in fact, mutually contradictory. There may be too many people, as in **"Billenium"**, or too few people, as in **"The Impossible Man."** . . . The end may come about through hydrogen bombs, solipsism, suicide, ceaseless urbanization, or in a world-wide "autogeddon" of car crashes. Even within a single work there is often no consistent explanation of why the cataclysm is occurring other than some vague pseudo-scientific theory, presented like a magician's patter and perhaps offered to satisfy the conventional expectations of the readers of science fiction. (pp. 83-4)

Let me try to penetrate at once to the heart of Ballard's imaginative creation. . . . [In one of Ballard's earliest short stories], **"The Overloaded Man"**, he prefigures the most recent forms of his imaginings and provides us with a precis for the underlying content of them all. In this story he shows quite explicitly that the source, or at least one crucial source, of the central problem of all his fiction is the historical dichotomy between subject and object, a dichotomy which he perceives as becoming catastrophic as bourgeois society itself disintegrates. In **"The Overloaded Man"** it is explicitly the lone petty bourgeois intellectual who destroys the entire world not by bombing it with nuclear weapons or too many people but by withdrawing himself from it. The protagonist's solipsism is equated with suicide, murder, and global catastrophe. In short, **"The Overloaded Man"** is a paradigm for Ballard's artistic opus.

The story is set in the near future, subtly indicated by the slight increase in automatic domestic appliances, a slight exaggeration of late 1950s suburban plastic architectural trends, a somewhat more leisured existence for the technocratic social class, and a small deterioration of social relationships within that class. The first sentence summarizes the story of the title character: "Faulkner was slowly going insane." Two months have passed since he resigned from his job as "a lecturer at the Business School," and he has been lying around the house, pretending to his wife that he is "still on creative reflection." As soon as his wife, dressed in "the standard executive . . . brisk black suit and white blouse," leaves for her job, Faulkner is free "to begin his serious work." . . . (p. 87)

This consists of turning all of objective reality into meaningless abstractions, "systematically obliterating all traces of meaning from the world around him, reducing everything to its formal visual values." He finds it "pleasant to see the world afresh again, to wallow in an endless panorama of brilliantly coloured images. What did it matter if there was form but no content?" His method is the same as that used by the main character in ***The Atrocity Exhibition (Love and Napalm)***; Faulkner is able to convert houses, trees, people, whatever, into "geometric units," pieces of a gigantic "cubist landscape." In this early story, Ballard takes us step by step, in simple narrative, through the whole process. Faulkner has his first success with consumer goods, for reasons explicitly related to the essence of capitalism, which converts all good things into "goods"; that is, commodities. . . . After he has then "obliterated the Village and the garden," he begins "to demolish the house." He sinks "deeper and deeper into his private reverie, into the demolished world of form and colour which hung motionlessly around him." Soon he has "obliterated not only the world around him, but his own body, and his limbs and trunk seemed an extension of his mind, disembodied forms whose physical dimensions pressed upon it like a dream's awareness of its own identity." . . . (pp. 87-8)

In other words, he has achieved solipsism, reducing all objective reality to an appearance of his own mind. Solipsism is a danger inherent in bourgeois ideology right from the start, in its Cartesian assertion that *I* exist because *I* think. . . . Faulkner plunges down his chosen path to annihilation, converting his wife into "a softly squeaking lump of spongy rubber" as he murders her, and drowning himself in order to become, in the very last word of the story, "free." (p. 88)

In his early works, Ballard sometimes offers a wishful alternative to alienation and solipsism. It is a vision of cosmic unity with intelligent beings throughout the macrohistory of the universe. This vision, reminiscent of Olaf Stapledon and carried forward in different ways, in the works of Arthur C. Clarke and Ursula Le Guin, is expressed as a revelation in **"The Waiting Grounds"**: "Meanwhile we wait here, at the threshold of time and space, celebrating the identity and kinship of the particles within our bodies with those of the sun and the stars, of our brief private times with the vast periods of the galaxies, with the total unifying time of the cosmos . . ." Before long, this unity between the microcosm and the macrocosm will be lost for Ballard and it will become the object of an endless quest, always reducing itself to the jungles and deserts of the entrapped and tormented individual psyche.

In **"Build Up,"** another of these revealing early stories, Ballard projects an endless three-dimensional city whose economy is based on the final commodity: space, which sells for about one dollar a cubic foot. The protagonist, trying to locate what he calls "free space" ("in both senses") discovers that time itself has become nullified by this ultimate form of capitalist super-development. His odyssey toward some limit of the boundless city leaves him right back where he started, defined with utmost precision in the final words of the story: "$*SHELL* × 10n." (p. 89)

[Ballard's fiction] is ultimately a literature of despair, negation, and death. Kerans' impulses [in *The Drowned World*], however cloaked in fantasies of embodying the sun and the sea, are merely another form of the madness incarnated by Faulkner in **"The Overloaded Man."** Kerans, and through him his author, is expressing a dying society.

Ballard of course knows this. . . . The symbols of our age are for him its most horrifying historical events, and the progress of his fiction is largely into a deepening exploration of the psychological content of these events. The nuclear bombs of ***Love and Napalm*** were already the annihilating symbols of **"The Terminal Beach"**; the auto crashes of *Crash* and *Concrete Island* were just as universally final in **"The Impossible Man."** . . . My criticism is that Ballard does not generally go down far enough below the unconscious to the sources of the alienation, self-destruction, and mass slaughter of our age. He therefore remains incapable of understanding the alternative to these death forces, the global movement toward human liberation which constitutes the main distinguishing characteristic of our epoch. The real nemesis of militarism, exploitation, and the rape of the environment is not the insane overloaded man who is seeking to be "free" by obliterating the entire world. . . . Nor is it the main figure of ***Love and Napalm***, a doctor trying to cure the world by rearranging its pieces. . . . Beyond the scope of Ballard's death-worshipping imagination are the people rescuing the world from the state of being that determined that imagination.

Of all Ballard's works, the one in which he comes closest to perceiving the rising forces of our epoch is a short story, **"The Killing Ground,"** written in 1966 during the American invasion of Vietnam and clearly intended in part as propaganda against it. But even in this story he ends by turning away from his own best insights. The time is "thirty years after the original conflict in south-east Asia," and "the globe was now a huge insurrectionary torch, a world Viet Nam." The scene is the Kennedy Memorial at Runnymede on the banks of the Thames, and the point-of-view is that of Major Pearson, leader of a scraggly band of "rebel" guerrillas harassing the technologically superior American invasion forces. In one striking passage, Ballard briefly imagines the masses of people creating a better future out of this holocaust:

> . . . the war had turned the entire population of Europe into an armed peasantry, the first intelligent agrarian community since the 18th Century. *That* peasantry had produced the Industrial Revolution. This one, literally burrowing like some advanced species of termite into the sub-soil of the 20th century, might in time produce something greater.

But that seems a shadowy hope, and certainly Ballard is unable to imagine not only that future but the present society of his insurrectionary peasantry. They, like the impotent Major Pearson and his ragged soldiers, are dominated by the "immense technology" of the American invaders, who seem like "some archangelic legion on the day of Armageddon." . . . The Americans had won in Vietnam, had then "occupied the world," and at the end of the story they have killed Major Pearson and destroyed his unit. We must remind ourselves who did win in Vietnam. American technology was not invincible; the Tet offensive took place a little over a year after this story was published; within five years the vaunted American military machine was a shambles; and in less than a decade a socialist society.

We can grasp the ironies of Ballard's misunderstanding of history if we take a close look at [**"The Garden of Time"**]. . . . **"The Garden of Time"** is almost pure allegory, a rarity for Ballard. It shows the last stand of feudalism, incarnated by Count Axel, a figure apparently derived both from *Axel,* the symbolist closet drama by Villiers de l'Isle Adam and from Edmund Wilson's interpretation of the play in *Axel's Castle.* In **"The Garden of Time"** Axel's castle, garden, and exquisite life with his flawless wife are besieged by "an immense rabble" appearing on the horizon and ineluctably advancing upon him across the plains and hills. Variously described as "the mob," a "horde," and "a vast concourse of laboring humanity," this army of "limitless extent" obviously represents the revolutionary masses storming the final symbolic bastion of feudal privilege, grace, and beauty. Axel's only defense is the crystal flowers of time in his garden. While growing, each crystal flower seems "to drain the air of its light and motion." When picked, each flower begins "to sparkle and deliquesce," causing an abrupt "reversal of time." As this happens, the entire revolutionary concourse is "flung back" away from the castle. Time, in the form of the crystal flowers, of course runs out for the Count, and he and his wife are left to stand as stone statues surrounded by the vulgar mob that overwhelms his ruined estate. (pp. 94-5)

[Ballard's later fiction] takes the form of a bizarre attempt to achieve "a new sexuality born from a perverse technology." ***Love and Napalm: Export U.S.A.*** sets forth this "new sexuality" as the equation of human sex and "love" with car crashes, assassinations, napalm, B-52 raids, thermonuclear weapons, disembodied fragments of the human body, and the lines and angles of freeways, machines, wounds, and buildings (the sexiest structure is a multi-level parking garage that suggests both rape and death). The central symbol of this quest is the automobile.

Back in the short story **"The Subliminal Man,"** Ballard had projected the automobile and the concrete milieu we construct for it as the basic economic and psychological fact of decaying capitalist society:

> Whatever other criticisms might be levelled at the present society, it certainly knew how to build roads. Eight, ten and twelve-lane expressways interlaced across the continent, plunging from overhead causeways into the giant car parks in the centre of the cities, or dividing into the great suburban arteries with their multiacre parking aprons around the marketing centres. Together the roadways and car parks covered more than a third of the country's entire area. . . .

In **"The Subliminal Man"** Ballard did something extraordinary for him and unusual for any Anglo-American writer of science fiction: he subjected this future automobilized monopoly capitalist society to a rigorous analysis, showing how the psychology of the people within it is determined by the political economy. The vast forces of production, still ruled by capitalist social relations, become a colossal alien power, constantly producing more and more commodities and increasingly incapable of satisfying real human needs. If the commodities turned out by capitalist production actually satisfied human needs, they could be sold through rational description. Since this is clearly not the case, in capitalist society today advertising attempts to evade or manipulate our rational thought processes and to stimulate irrational desires. . . . In **"The Subliminal Man"** Ballard merely extrapolates from one advertising technique already utilized to reach the subconscious directly, subliminal messages beamed directly into the retina too fast to be recognized consciously. In a few pages, Ballard creates a nightmare vision of a monopoly capitalist society using this technique on a grand scale, successfully reducing each person to an automaton of mindless consumption, endlessly working, purchasing, and driving back and forth to jobs and supermarkets in a shiny new automobile on vast expressways under gigantic subliminal advertising signs whose shadows swing back and forth "like the dark blades of enormous scythes."

The alienation of people within such a society and their increasing obsession with catastrophic death is a subject for deep exploration, and this is the primary subject of Ballard's subsequent fiction. The greatest strength of this late fiction is that it penetrates profoundly into the morbid psychology that comes from living in such a society; its most critical weakness is that in pursuing this exploration, Ballard loses sight of the underlying causation of the psychopathology of everyday life in decaying capitalism. He leaves behind his own best insights, in stories such as **"The Overloaded Man," "The Impossible Man," "Build-Up,"** and **"The Subliminal Man,"** which show the individual human being as the victim of an inhuman social structure, and begins to stand the world on its head, making the psychology of the individual the cause rather than the product of the death-oriented political economy.

Underlying the elaborate verbal structure of the late fiction are some fairly simple, in fact simple-minded, ideas about social reality. Indeed, the formal pyrotechnics disguise as much as they reveal of the ideational content. Clad in an elegant costume is the tired old idea that human nature is basically brutish and stupid, that people are inherently perverse, cruel, and self-destructive, and that's why the modern world is going to hell. . . . Such a vision, I believe, is merely a projection of Ballard's own class point of view, a myopia as misleading as the national and racial point of view in the earlier novels and intimately related to that narrow outlook.

Now some may think it unfair or inappropriate to discuss Ballard's late fiction as essentially political statement, but Ballard's recent art is profoundly political; in fact its content is most intensely political when its form is most "surreal." For example, ***Love and Napalm: Export U.S.A.,*** the most plotless, fragmented, surrealist, and anti-novelistic of his long fictions, includes the following as explicit primary subjects: the Vietnam War; Hiroshima and Nagasaki; the massacres in Biafra and the Congo; the presidential candidacy of Ronald Reagan. . . . An author who did not want his work to be discussed politically would (or should) choose different subject matter.

In ***Love and Napalm*** Ballard presents the fashionable liberal idea that "America is a land of violence"; that's the fundamental lesson, he tells us, of Hiroshima and Dallas, Los Angeles and Memphis, Hollywood and Saigon. . . . This is summed up commonly in that cliche we've been hearing since 1963: "Oswald may have pulled the trigger, but wasn't it all that hate and violence in America that loaded the gun?" With all its fancy tricks, this is one of the dominant messages of ***Love and Napalm,*** which actually ends with these final words: "Without doubt Oswald badly misfired. But one question still remains unanswered: who loaded the starting gun?" The implied answer is that we did, with our morbid psychology, which will lead to the first word of the book, "Apocalypse." (pp. 99-101)

Although Ballard's brilliant imagination penetrates deeply into the symbolic significance of the automobile, it is determined by his class outlook and therefore operates within very narrow limits. From his class point of view, automobiles exist only as objects of consumption—first economic and now primarily psychological—and destruction. . . . In *Concrete Island* they are not only the vehicle of self-destruction but of willful self-isolation in the cellular island prison formed by a society of speeding machines, concrete speedways, and "normal" individuals who race back and forth to work and empty relationships with other individuals. The millions upon millions of automobiles just appear ready-made on the scene. With the notable and revealing exception of **"The Subliminal Man,"** in which Dr. Franklin has to augment his income by working Sundays as "visiting factory doctor to one of the automobile plants that had started Sunday shifts," there is no sense whatever that automobiles and their milieu are physically constructed by the tens of millions of people around the world extracting raw materials from the earth [for manufacture]. . . . Ballard, because his outlook is that of a minority sub-class of petty bourgeois intellectuals rather than that of the vast majority of people who work in the mines, mills, factories, . . . and forests of the world, sees the automobile only as something that is consumed or consumes. Hence the exquisite symbolic logic of the cannibalistic and ritualistic re-arrangement of the pieces of cars. In ***Love and Napalm*** and *Crash,* this primarily takes the form of the sexual fantasies of mingled human and mechanical parts in car crashes. (pp. 103-104)

The working people of Ballard's own society rarely appear in his field of view, and when they do, they resemble Morlocks. In fact, when Ballard imagines a society "where," he tells us, "I would be happy to live," it is the world of ***Vermilion Sands,*** a weird hedonistic playground and sandbox for infantile artists who resemble incipient Eloi, safely isolated from the terrors of the city and totally untroubled by the intrusion of any workers except chauffeurs, maids, butlers, and personal secretaries. The working people of the rest of the world are no longer presented as the superstitious, treacherous, terrifying savages of *The Drowned World* and *The Crystal World;* they simply had disappeared from view altogether.

Hence Ballard's imagined world is reduced to the dimensions of that island created by intertwined expressways on which individuals in their cellular commodities hurtle to their destruction or that apartment complex in which the wealthy and professional classes degenerate into anarchic tribal warfare among themselves. And hence Ballard accurately, indeed magnificently, projects the doomed social structure in which he exists. What could Ballard create if he were able to envision the end of capitalism as not the end, but the beginning, of a human world? (pp. 104-05)

H. Bruce Franklin, "What Are We to Make of J. G. Ballard's Apocalypse?" in Voices for the Future: Essays on Major Science Fiction Writers, Vol. II, *edited by Thomas D. Clareson, Bowling Green University Popular Press, 1979, pp. 82-105.*

THOMAS SUTCLIFFE (essay date 1982)

[*In the following excerpt from his favorable review of* Myths of the Near Future, *Sutcliffe focuses on Ballard's use of language, his polemics, and his vital imagination.*]

Retrospection is obviously not a cardinal virtue for science-fiction writers, but few avoid it as conspicuously as J. G. Ballard. He writes as though he never looks back, with the concentration of a tunnel-visionary on what is about to be written. The vision itself is no longer a particularly singular one. . . . Where Ballard does stand apart—and this creates the continuing interest of his work—is in allowing the psychic shocks of his imagined worlds to disturb his own prose. That prose is often marked by what seems to be an unconsciousness about its own effects and direction, as though it were the product of an obsessive mind rarely pausing to check how erratic its progress is. . . .

[***Myths of the Near Future***] proves that Ballard has not lost his nerve. There are still repetitions, and there is no sense that these recurrences are the formal elaborations of a theme. Attention is not drawn to them in that way. Ballard has abandoned that least realistic device of realism, the insistence on continual modification, the novelty of the novel, in order to show characters who are at the point of giving up the rationality of language in order to gain access to a new and anarchic physics.

There are repetitions in another sense. **"Myths of the Near Future"** and a companion story **"News from the Sun"** both explore a characteristic Ballard theme, the pathological effect of modern "advancement" on the modern psyche. They return quite clearly to earlier rhapsodies from the novels and make use of a familiar repertoire of effects, desolate bars and empty motels, deserted streets ceding to sand or jungle and littered with the relics of an over-extended technology which has instituted its own dereliction. But the fascination with what happens to language when it loses its foundation hasn't become stale. "So called articulate speech is an artefact of time" says one of Ballard's characters, about to embrace a babbling condition of timelessness. Ballard's prose hovers uneasily between the visionary and the ludicrous. His similes are like nothing on this constrained earth. "Around him the bright winds were like the open jaws of a crystal bird, the light flashing between its teeth." This kind of thing can easily go wrong; there is something coyly anthropomorphic in his description of "hills waiting with the infinite guile of the geological kingdom for the organic world to end and a more vivid mineral realm to begin," but in general the risks he takes to present the decay of time and space are worth taking.

Ballard is not much interested in emotions. His characters are like abandoned buildings themselves, with the sharp architecture of their rationality remaining after feeling has fled. They record the details of their own dissipation with a scientific accuracy, and they are all animated by the "remorseless logic of madness" which is attributed to the one character in the stories who is diagnosed as insane. They are at their most sympathetic when, like the reader, they are assailed by the sense that there is meaning locked in the dislocated world around them ''like the forgotten codes of a discarded geometric language.''

Other stories are less ambitious but rarely less effective. Ballard is still a master of aggressively polemical writing, sending despatches from the near future intended to turn our minds back. In **''Theatre of War''** he presents the shooting script for a *World in Action* documentary on an English civil war. The United States has intervened on a massive scale to bolster a corrupt British government and the economy is sagging under the weight of dollar scrip. Any doubts that the parallels with Vietnam are too laborious, that there is something too obvious about the device of bringing the war home to English readers, are silenced by the dead-pan acknowledgment, in a final footnote, to General Westmoreland, President Thieu and various US and ARVN troops for providing the chilling dialogue. In **''Motel Architecture''** and **''Intensive Care Unit''** he treats with deadly seriousness the old cliché about television killing the art of conversation. Here too language stands on the border between logic and irrational.

In some senses these stories remain limited; they have specialized effects and specialized intentions. In some cases they are exhausted by one reading. But they never show the lifeless ingenuity of some science fiction, and their imaginative intelligence and readiness to take risks make it clear that in Ballard's case the term writer needs no additional qualification.

Thomas Sutcliffe, ''Leaving Language Behind,'' in The Times Literary Supplement, *No. 4147, September 24, 1982, p. 1031.*

PETER BRIGG (essay date 1983)

[In the following excerpt, Brigg offers a survey of the stories in Myths of the Near Future.*]*

When an acknowledged master of the science fiction short story publishes his first collection in six years it merits attention. The ten stories in ***Myths of the Near Future*** merit considerable praise as well, for in them the remarkable Ballard style does not falter and one cannot help be impressed by the continued ranging flexibility of his imagination. (p. 19)

[**''Myths of the Near Future''**] and **''News from the Sun''** continue Ballard's probe of the space age, suggesting man is venturing in the wrong evolutionary direction in the extraordinary technologies of space unaugmented by psychological growth. In both stories space has been abandoned but those connected with it suffer from increasing narcomas until they are awake for only a few moments each day. In nearly deserted landscapes the characters find meanings and equivocal ''new lives'' in the sleep worlds which signal their physical deaths.

''The Intensive Care Unit'' and **''Motel Architecture''** are television futures. The ''unit'' in the former is a family, united for the first time after living out their entire lives connected only by video. The descriptions of courtship by video and lives drained by physical contact are wickedly pathological images of repulsion for all human contact. Physical contact leads to carnage in the story and the narrator awaits a final attack from his scissors-wielding son. In **''Motel Architecture''** an isolated aesthete spends his time endlessly replaying the shower sequence from *Psycho,* mimics it unconsciously by murdering the girl sent to service his multiple televisions and tracks the murder to himself through a series of traps.

''Having a Wonderful Time'' is a series of postcards from a Mediterranean vacation island which reveal that the visitors will get their wish ''to stay here forever'' because their governments are coping with excess populations by stranding them. In **''Zodiac 2000''** a mental patient, apparently from an inverse universe, escapes, is involved with terrorists, and murders one. The story is structured around a contemporary zodiac with the scales replaced by the psychiatric couch, the ram by the vibrator, etc.

Two of the scientific fantasies are sexual, **''The Smile''** and **''A Host of Furious Fancies.''** In **''The Smile''** a man sets up a life-like mannequin as his mistress and, carrying the theme to its limits through love, intimacy and jealousy Ballard arrives at a man trapped by a dumpy dummy wife who can only wait eagerly for her ''demise.'' **''A Host of Furious Fancies''** is much nastier, as one of Ballard's doctor-narrators outsmarts himself and is sucked into a trap by a mad heiress whose incestuous advances had driven her father to suicide. By seducing the doctor the girl makes him the slavish replacement for her father, fulfilling her fancy at his expense.

Outlines can only communicate the wide range of subjects and approaches without touching the tense, flat, yet superbly evocative styles of which Ballard is master. His ''futures'' always evoke present concerns through their psychological insight and projections, and ***Myths of the Near Future*** is as frightening and perceptive a collection of them as has yet been made. (pp. 19-20)

Peter Brigg, in a review of ''Myths of the Near Future,'' in Science Fiction & Fantasy Book Review, *No. 15, June, 1983, pp. 19-20.*

ROBERT L. PLATZNER (essay date 1983)

[In the following excerpt, Platzner offers an appreciative survey of Ballard's catastrophic fiction and also comments on the failure of his political satire.]

Recognized as one of the leading writers of apocalyptic science fiction, J. G. Ballard is probably one of the most widely read literary catastrophists of our time. In four major novels and dozens of short stories Ballard has effectively and repeatedly extinguished all life on this planet, and while not all of his books are doomsday books, the apocalyptic mode clearly suits him and undoubtedly represents a commitment to a personal obsession. The intensity of his writing often seems to be in direct proportion to the magnitude of the horrors he invokes, and like the author of the Book of Revelations, Ballard occasionally exhibits signs of grim satisfaction at the spectacle of world annihilation. However, it is my contention that the droughts, the floods, and the radiation storms that Ballard has loosed upon the world are not the real subject of his fables so much as preconditions of fabulation, and that at the heart of Ballard's eschatology is a vision of irreversible, regressive transformation—of entropy as a form of galactic and psychic metamorphosis. For as energy dissipates and the life-force diminishes—the stylized scenario of nearly any Ballardian apocalypse—and human life forms become at once simpler and less recognizable, we enter a fictional realm in his novels where individual identity and sexuality become increasingly ambiguous or diffuse, and where all processes inexorably run down. And when given a choice between a big bang and a little whimper, Ballard almost always chooses the latter, placing his fin-de-siècle characters in a twilight kingdom, where only change is constant, and constantly degenerative.

Unlike such contemporary SF figures as Heinlein, Asimov, or Herbert, Ballard appears to have little interest in the technology of survival. In nearly all of his future societies, human civilization (or, more precisely, advanced industrial capitalism) is given only a marginal chance, at best, of adapting to a changing environment whose destructive powers have become overwhelming. What he seems to be saying in narrative after narrative is that man's time is up: we cannot maintain our productive energies much longer, and we certainly cannot sustain the Faustian will-to-power upon which Western civilization has nourished itself for centuries. Cursed, then, by a profound disbelief in human creativity and in Nature's beneficence, Ballard is left at last with very little to write about except the inhuman and the inorganic—for such is the logic of his obsession. It is little wonder, therefore, that so many of his stories seem like so many variations upon a single theme.

The terrors of temporality in an entropic universe would seem to be the greatest of Ballard's apocalyptic anxieties, though by no means the only one, and to judge from the number and variety of narrative contexts in which this theme appears, one would have to conclude that "time's lease" is the one obsession that unlocks the secret of cosmic abandonment for Ballard's chronophobes. In **"The Voices of Time,"** for example, a dying neurosurgeon whose greatest achievement has been a surgical technique for releasing the body from its need for sleep—thereby rescuing consciousness from temporal-biological rhythms—suddenly finds himself sinking gradually towards terminal narcosis, as does most of the human race. Determined to secure a vision of cosmic evolution he believes is somehow locked up within a pair of mysteriously "silent" genes before the End, he constructs a huge mandala at whose center he perceives, at last, the voices of the Heraclitean stream of universal time he has so long pursued. . . . Unable to withstand the mind-shattering impact of this epiphany, Powers dies at the very moment of psychic transcendence, a mad, latter-day Dante gazing raptly upon the disintegrating core of a formless universe. But the whole point of Ballard's tale is that the protagonist's culminating vision of galactic tidal flow is no delusion; the cosmic clock is, indeed, running down, galaxies are breaking up, and the Jodrell Bank Observatory has already begun to compute the precise moment of universal collapse. One premonitory symptom of this collapse, at the biological level, is the extended need for sleep that has been evident for centuries, and as the hours of waking consciousness diminish, our need for some last evolutionary breakthrough into a higher consciousness becomes increasingly urgent—hence, the mandala.

But even mysticism, Ballard hints, will not suffice to release us from the sentence of doom that hangs over the entire sentient universe, and as one scientist in **"The Voices of Time"** puts it: "My total failure, my absolute lack of any moral or biological right to existence, is implicit in every cell of my body. . . ." No biophysical rationale for this sentence of doom—and Ballard provides none, incidentally—could possibly carry sufficient conviction to justify so sweeping and so hopeless a vision of world-annihilation. What we have fallen into, in fact, in stories like **"The Voices of Time,"** is Ballard's version of the Slough of Despond, a metaphysical Slough of Despond to be precise, in which the human sense or measure of time becomes irrelevant. Georges Poulet has described this condition as a loss of being that is brought on by a perception of the "infinite deficiency of the present moment." For Poulet, such "deficiencies" arise out of the historical loss of eternity, or rather out of a loss of faith in that absolute atemporal realm whose transcendence of human time endowed the latter with meaning. For Ballard, however, it is not the loss of heaven, or eternity, or "divine causality" that precipitates this crisis of time and being. Instead, it is the second law of thermodynamics that creates a metaphysical vacuity at the heart of things into which time, space, energy, and matter can escape into nothingness. Ballard's universe quite simply wills itself into a condition of terminal stasis; and in this state of deathly equilibrium, time ceases to exist because there is no motion (or even potentiality of motion) left to measure. (pp. 209-11)

For those whom Ballard has poised on the metaphysical brink of time or of sanity, psychosis often serves as a necessary stratagem for determining what, if anything, is left of reality. The traumatized ex-bomber-pilot of **"Terminal Beach,"** for example—known only as Traven and probably the most self-consciously visionary of all of Ballard's philosophical suicides—retires, St. Anthony-like, to an abandoned atoll in the Pacific (a deserted nuclear test site) in search of what Ballard calls a "zone of non-time." There, through a series of increasingly insane meditations, he summons up both the remembered dead and the not-yet-annihilated mass victims of World War III. The spiritual climax of this mad hermit's quest is achieved only after Traven has reanimated, ventriloquistically, the corpse of a Japanese doctor he has found wedged into the crevice of a sand dune. For what the corpse reveals to Traven is that he, and all of us, are as truly dead as all of the victims, real and projected, of all of the atomic wars that have been or ever will be fought. The only reality is the Bomb, and in its shadow all ontological distinctions of being and nonbeing have been rendered meaningless. To exist, Traven learns, is to be swept up into a "world of quantal flux" in which there are no coordinates of either time or identity. Only madmen can even entertain the possibility of order in such a universe, since they alone perceive that order is merely artifice.

For Traven the sole reminder on this "terminal" island of the rationality that was once civilization is a maze of concrete blocks, a maddening, labyrinthine structure, suggestive, perhaps, of the Cretan labyrinth, but without apparent function or significance. Traven nearly dies within this mind-trap at one point, and he is forced to admit at last that its insane intricacies have defeated his intellect. There is no thread that will lead us out of this nightmare we call the universe, Ballard insists, only a series of interminable delusions culminating in death.

The limits of metaphysical change in a story like **"Terminal Beach"** or in some of the even more experimental narratives that follow it are identical with whatever transformation of narrative materials and perspective the author is able to achieve. The more dissociative the relationship between the fictional protagonist and his environment becomes, the more the reader is inclined to doubt the ontological status of all events and perceptions within that narrative. Thus, the ultimate effect of the enveloping and self-obliterating surrealism of Ballard's later stories and novels is that of discrediting the reality base to which all science fiction must finally relate. The ultimate metamorphosis which Ballard attempts, therefore, is the metamorphosis of the tale itself, and not simply its characters or setting. What is perhaps Ballard's most ambitious attempt to date to achieve a new narrative form in which transformation of the self will be total and continuous is to be found in the pages of ***The Atrocity Exhibition.*** More a novel kit in pieces than a continuously developed narrative, ***The Atrocity Exhibition*** invites its reader to assemble and reassemble its serial fragments into any one of a number of possible permutations. Directionality as such does not exist, or rather exists only as a function of whichever set the reader decides to place first. A completed series of such sets constitutes, therefore, only one possible interpretation of the data placed before us.

Provisionally, then, ***The Atrocity Exhibition*** concerns itself with the mental breakdown of a physician whose last, relatively sane act was the assembling of an exhibit of paintings, photographs, and films on the subject of "world cataclysm." The purpose of this exhibit and its approximate contents remain something of a mystery throughout the novel, as does the name of the marginally psychotic protagonist. Identified variously as Travis, Talbot, Traven, Tallis, Trabert, Talbert, and Travers, "he" may be a doctor impersonating an ex-bomber-pilot, or a would-be assassin, or the amnesiac victim of a car-crash, or a psychopathic murderer, or a spy, or quite possibly none of the above. The modality of imagined events or persons is all but impossible to fix in a world where nothing stays put long enough to be identified and where every relationship undergoes an indeterminable number of permutations. The only trace of what might be called a subsistent reality underlying all this confusion is to be found in the recurrent emphasis given to images of sex and violence, whatever the context or pretext. . . . If violence or sexuality, then, form the matrix of any communicative act, it follows quite logically (and perversely) that every act of physical or psychological union is a terminal act, whether real or fantasied. Further, every gesture of personal violence becomes a microcosm of some apocalyptic event "out there"—wherever "out there" may be in a functionally solipsistic universe. In fact, it may no longer be possible to speak of a microcosm in a narrative where the extensions of the self are infinite, and the structure of the self non-existent.

For Talbot, or Traven, or whatever his name may be, nothing exists discretely. Phenomena are given to us only in combination or juxtaposition, and so a car crash may, for all we know, be an orgasm, or an ashtray a sex organ. Ballard's world of regressive change has finally become a world of private nightmares—of private phenomenological nightmares, to be precise. If matter exists at all, it exists only in those transient moments when the combinations and permutations of the dissociative consciousness fail to structure the data our minds are constantly processing; in those moments the phenomenal world comes rushing in to fill the vacuum of mental space. In ***The Atrocity Exhibition*** Ballard tends to fill that vacuum with the debris of contemporary American politics and pop culture perceived exclusively from the perspective of conspiracy theory and paranoia. And since death and mutilation, as Ballard repeatedly assures us, are primarily conceptual realities, practically anything can be done to anyone, and for almost any reason:

> Maximal arousal was provided by combined torture and execution sequences. Montage newsreels were constructed in which leading public figures associated with the Vietnam war, e.g. President Johnson, General Westmoreland, Marshall Ky, were substituted for both combatants and victims. On the basis of viewers' preferences an optimum torture and execution sequence was devised involving Governor Reagan, Madame Ky and an unidentifiable eight-year-old Vietnamese girl napalm victim. Paedophiliac fantasies of a strangely sadistic character, i.e. involving repeated genital penetration of the perineal wounds, were particularly stimulated by the child victim. Prolonged exposure to the film was found to have notable effects on all psychomotor activity. The film was subsequently shown to both disturbed children and terminal cancer patients with useful results. . . .

Ballard is clearly attempting something like political satire in passages like these, but it does not quite succeed, and the reasons are not too obscure to figure out. For one thing, his indignation over American war-crimes notwithstanding, he is obviously enjoying himself too much to be particularly concerned about the precise target of his abuse, and even more disconcertingly, he is unable to screen out his own fetishistic obsessions from those he ridicules in others. But as the number of such projections increases, it soon becomes obvious that the reality content of such passages is almost coincidental, and what really matters is the intensity of loathing such images are capable of expressing, whatever their origin or point of reference.

In fact, ***The Atrocity Exhibition*** is best approached, I would argue, not as political satire, but as a form of sublimated and abstracted Gothic fantasy, minus of course the period costumes and decor. Admittedly Ballard goes to great lengths to make his nightmare novel relentlessly up to date (circa 1970), with endless references to movie stars, Presidential assassins and, of course, the omnipresent Vietnam war, but the real setting of this novel is the haunted castle of the mind, where the hero with a thousand names contemplates obsessively a constantly shifting landscape of pure terror. Here is the ultimate apocalypse, where the mind implodes under the stress of an environment supersaturated with maniacal aggression. To dispute the accuracy of these perceptions on the political or the historical plane is to misunderstand the modality of Ballard's fiction, as well as the obsessional sources from which he has consistently drawn his material. ***The Atrocity Exhibition*** and other kindred novels within the Ballard canon represent a distinctly gnostic strain in contemporary science fiction, positing a world without conceivable order or meaning. That Ballard has chosen subjective rather than cosmic paranoia as the premise of his private myth merely suggests that he, like so many of his American counterparts in the 60's (Barth, Barthelme, Coover), has come to regard the *gnosis* of madness as the only credible perspective from which to view contemporary culture. But the sheer hopelessness of Ballard's metamorphic future (or fantasied present) expresses only his own conviction that modern life offers no resistance to the self-shattering force of total doubt. (pp. 213-16)

Robert L. Platzner, "The Metamorphic Vision of J. G. Ballard," in Essays in Literature, *Vol. X, No. 2, Fall, 1983, pp. 209-17.*

J. G. BALLARD (INTERVIEW WITH THOMAS FRICK) (essay date 1984)

[In an interview with Thomas Frick, excerpted below, Ballard discusses various aspects of his fiction—imagination, his view of society, and artistic technique—while also commenting on his own background, particularly as a boy in Shanghai during World War II.]

INTERVIEWER: Let's start with obsession. You seem to have an obsessive way of repeatedly playing out permutations of a certain set of emblems and concerns. Things like the winding down of time, car crashes, birds and flying, drained swimming pools, airports, abandoned buildings, Ronald Reagan. . . .

BALLARD: I think you're completely right. I would say that I quite consciously rely on my obsessions in all my work, that I deliberately set up an obsessional frame of mind. In a paradoxical way, this leaves one free of the subject of the obsession. It's like picking up an ashtray and staring so hard at it that one becomes obsessed by its contours, angles, texture, et cetera, and forgets that it is an ashtray—a glass dish for stubbing out cigarettes. (pp. 135-36)

INTERVIEWER: You've written about Salvador Dali and Max Ernst, and in particular the surrealists seem to have fired your imagination the most.

BALLARD: Yes, the surrealists have been a tremendous influence on me, though, strictly speaking, corroboration is the right word. The surrealists show how the world can be remade by the mind. In Odilon Redon's phrase, they place the logic of the visible at the service of the invisible. They've certainly played a very large part in my life, far more so than any other writer I know. (p. 139)

INTERVIEWER: How did this interest arise? Were you taken to museums as a child?

BALLARD: It has always puzzled me, because there were no museums in the Shanghai where I was brought up.

INTERVIEWER: Perhaps Shanghai itself was a kind of museum?

BALLARD: I assume that I looked back on Shanghai and the war there as if it were part of some huge nightmare tableau that revealed itself in a violent and gaudy way . . . that remade world that one finds in surrealism. Perhaps I've always been trying to return to the Shanghai landscape, to some sort of truth that I glimpsed there. I think that in all my fiction, I've used the techniques of surrealism to remake the present into something at least consonant with the past. . . .

INTERVIEWER: How does a book take shape for you?

BALLARD: That's a vast topic, and, to be honest, one I barely understand. Even in the case of a naturalistic writer, who in a sense takes his subject matter directly from the world around him, it's difficult enough to understand how a particular fiction imposes itself. But in the case of an imaginative writer, especially one like myself with strong affinities to the surrealists, I'm barely aware of what is going on. Recurrent ideas assemble themselves, obsessions solidify themselves, one generates a set of working mythologies, like tales of gold invented to inspire a crew. I assume one is dealing with a process very close to that of dreams, a set of scenarios devised to make sense of apparently irreconcilable ideas. Just as the optical centers of the brain construct a wholly artificial three-dimensional universe through which we can move effectively, so the mind as a whole creates an imaginary world that satisfactorily explains everything, as long as it is constantly updated. So the stream of novels and stories continues. . . . (pp. 140-41)

INTERVIEWER: Do you map out your way with any kind of outline or notes before you begin?

BALLARD: Yes, always. With short stories I do a brief synopsis of about a page, and only if I feel the story works as a story, as a dramatic narrative with the right shape and balance to grip the reader's imagination, do I begin to write it. Even in the ***Atrocity Exhibition*** pieces, there are strong stories embedded in the apparent confusion. There's even the faint trace of a story in **"Why I Want to Fuck Ronald Reagan,"** and the other sections at the end of the book. (p. 143)

INTERVIEWER: Burroughs wrote an eccentric and laudatory, in its way, introduction to the American edition of ***Atrocity Exhibition.*** Do you know him?

BALLARD: Burroughs, of course, I admire to the other side of idolatry, starting with *Naked Lunch,* then *Ticket, Soft Machine,* and *Nova Express*. . . . I admire Burroughs more than any other living writer, and most of those who are dead. It's nothing to do with his homosexual bent, by the way. I'm no member of the "homintern," but a lifelong straight who prefers the company of women to most men. The few homosexual elements in *Crash* and ***Atrocity Exhibition,*** fucking Reagan, et cetera, are there for reasons other than the sexual—in fact, to show a world beyond sexuality, or, at least beyond clear sexual gender. (p. 148)

INTERVIEWER: How about aleatory methods, à la Burroughs? There was a drawing of you in *Ambit* magazine in which I noticed a pair of scissors on the front of your desk.

BALLARD: The artist requested those scissors in order to cut up his sheets of paper. He then placed them on the desk and incorporated them into the drawing. On the whole, no. I need to rework my material to too great an extent to allow intact foundpieces to appear. However, as in Dali's paintings, there are more elements of collage than might meet the eye at first glance. A large amount of documentary material finds its way into my fiction.

INTERVIEWER: Can you give me some examples?

BALLARD: Well, certainly ***Atrocity Exhibition,*** where I adopt a style of pseudoscientific reportage closely based on similar scientific papers. And there's the piece **"Theatre of War,"** in ***Myths of the Near Future,*** where all the dialogue except for the commentator's is taken from Viet Nam newsreel transcripts. (p. 154)

INTERVIEWER: What about the piece **"The Generations of America,"** which consists entirely of a list of names, connected alternately by the words "and" and "shot"—as opposed to "begat"?

BALLARD: Lists are fascinating; one could almost do a list novel. Those names were taken from the editorial mastheads of *Time, Newsweek,* and *Fortune*—that was part of the joke, of course, as the first two publications played a large role in the sensationalizing of violent death and assassination that I described.

INTERVIEWER: Given that a certain center of your work's themes and imagery lies in the events and personalities of the sixties, and given that your work was more available in the States then than now, what would you say were the major alterations in the Zeitgeist?

BALLARD: I'm not sure I have anything to add to what everyone has been saying for years. The sixties were a time of endlessly multiplying possibilities, of real selflessness in many ways, a huge network of connections between Viet Nam and the space race, psychedelia and pop music, linked together in every conceivable way by the media landscape. We were all living inside an enormous novel, an electronic novel, governed by instantaneity. In many ways, time didn't exist in the sixties, just a set of endlessly proliferating presents. Time returned in the seventies, but not a sense of the future. The hands of the clock now go nowhere. Still, I've hated nostalgia, and it may be that a similar hot mix will occur again. On the other hand, being quite serious, the future may be boring. It's possible that my children and yours will live in an eventless world, and that the faculty of imagination will die, or express itself solely in the realm of psychopathology. In ***Atrocity Exhibition*** I make the point that perhaps psychopathology should be kept alive as a repository, probably the last repository, of the imagination. (p. 155)

INTERVIEWER: In one sense, in the midst of technological decay and overload, you uphold a conservative yet paradoxically pro-technological view. . . .

BALLARD: I'm certainly no Luddite. The whole drift of my mind is pretty clearly stated in my work; basically, one has to immerse oneself in the threatening possibilities offered by modern science and technology, and try to swim to the other end of the pool. I think my political views were formed by my childhood in Shanghai and my years in a detention camp. I detest barbed wire, whether of the real or the figurative variety. Marxism is a social philosophy for the poor, and what we need badly now is a social philosophy for the rich. To Americans that means Ronald Reagan, but I'm thinking of something else, some moderating set of values, whether the *noblesse oblige,* the obligation owed to the less fortunate by the old English upper classes, or the Buddhist notion of gaining merit. Apart from anything else, the modern communications landscape creates a different system of needs and obligations. I've written about that in much of my fiction. (pp. 157-58)

J. G. Ballard, in an interview with Thomas Frick, in The Paris Review, *Vol. 26, No. 94, Winter, 1984, pp. 133-60.*

LORENZ J. FIRSCHING (essay date 1985)

[In the following excerpt, Firsching discusses Ballard's interweaving of three levels—environmental, interpersonal, and intrapsychic—with patterns of birth and death in "Low-Flying Aircraft" and The Ultimate City.*]*

The Ultimate City is closely related to **"Low-Flying Aircraft"** (both appeared in 1976). It also articulates some of the concerns that Ballard expresses in the novels which made his early reputation: *The Wind from Nowhere, The Drowned World, The Drought,* and *The Crystal World.* In particular, each of the four, as it depicts present-day civilization being destroyed by one of the classical elements (by air, water, fire, and earth, respectively), has in common with ***City*** and **"Aircraft"** certain structural features as well as an apocalyptic theme.

An analysis of their structure and of the themes connected with it is a necessary step towards understanding what I believe to be one of Ballard's central preoccupations: the ambiguous nature of modern life. . . . [In] the two short stories mentioned above, Ballard has designed the fiction to frustrate conventional expectations so as to confront the reader with uncertainty and doubt, with a world of multiple meanings . . . or perhaps of no meaning at all. Elsewhere Ballard uses other means to achieve this end; but . . . [here] he repeatedly structures the plot elements to evoke a deep sense of ambiguity. It is therefore appropriate to consider these stories together, as forming a distinct and highly important part of Ballard's opus. (p. 297)

[The stories center] upon the experiences of one main character; and these experiences may be parcelled out, for the sake of analysis, into three distinct but related levels. First, there is the "exterior" (or "historical," or "objective") level. This level comprises the protagonist's experiences of his physical environment and the events taking place within that environment. Ballard's four earliest novels evince broad similarities in this regard: in each some apocalyptic change in the human environment has taken place or is beginning.

Experiences on the first level can affect those on the second, the "intermediatory" level, consisting of the main character's interpersonal relationships, especially with his wife, lover, and/or parents. This connection between the "exterior" and the "intermediatory" is at least part of what Ballard is getting at when he remarks in *The Drought* that the failure of Ransom's marriage "was a failure of landscape." . . . (p. 298)

Finally, there is the "interior," or (to adopt Ballard's term) "psychic," level, involving the deepest psychological experiences of the protagonist. Ballard has characterized his first four novels as stories of "psychic transformation," . . . and this is equally true of **"Low-Flying Aircraft"** and—albeit in a different sense—of ***The Ultimate City.*** Furthermore, such "psychic" transformations are variously related to changes on the "exterior" and "intermediatory" levels—as we will soon discover.

Ballard brings these levels of the fiction together in two ways. Primarily he structures the movement of events on any one level to parallel that on the others. As a rule, the sequence of "exterior" events proceeds from the familiar, ordered world of the present to an alien and chaotic future through the effects of some apocalyptic environmental change. That environmental change, which severs the protagonist's ties to the present world, is correlated with what goes on on the "intermediatory" level, where the bonds linking him to other people begin to dissolve (sometimes even before worldwide disaster begins). On the "psychic" level, however, the sequence of events moves in the opposite direction; from the confusion and alienation at the outset towards the appearance of a new psychic state, a "new psychology" (the term occurs in *The Drowned World*), as contemporary civilization disappears. Thus the three levels of experience form an intricate pattern of disintegration and rebirth.

Complex patterns of birth (or rebirth) and death, linked in a variety of ways to an urban environment, may be found on each of the three levels, thus reinforcing their structural connection. In fact, birth and death are major themes in Ballard, and figure both on a grand scale, as the death of modern civilization or the birth of a "new psychology," and as they apply to the individual . . . ([e.g.,] Judith's pregnancy in **"Low-Flying Aircraft"**). In addition, the themes of birth and death have a "formal dimension": they play a role in Ballard's structuring of his fiction. In ***The Ultimate City,*** for instance, they dictate and give meaning to the sequence of events on the "exterior" level (the rebirth and death of the city), the "intermediatory" level (Halloway's relationship with Miranda, who is an ambiguous symbol of birth and fertility), and the "psychic" level (Halloway's psychic "death"). (p. 298)

[The] city enters into the structure of these works in a variety of ways. It serves not only as a locus but as a nexus of the "exterior," "intermediatory," and "psychic" (e.g., the landscape that causes Ransom's marriage to fail in *The Drought* is urban); and at the same time, like the symbols of birth and death, it vehiculates the ideas Ballard wishes to convey.

The multiple functions of the city in Ballard's opus may be seen most clearly in ***The Ultimate City.*** The story takes place in the 21st century, after the urban populations of the late 20th century, driven by "some unconscious perception of their own extinction," have abandoned cities and formed low-technology garden communities. Halloway, after the death of his parents, becomes dissatisfied with his life in one of these communities, builds a glider, and flies to a nearby city. There he meets Olds, the industrialist Buckmaster and his daughter Miranda, and Buckmaster's helper, Stillman. Halloway conceives the idea of bringing the city back to life, and with the help of Olds he succeeds. A party from the nearby garden community tries but fails to stop Halloway; soon small groups of immigrants begin to arrive in Halloway's city, and crime, pollution, and inflation—"real sign[s] of his success, a confirmation of all he had dreamed about"—appear. Rioting breaks out, Stillman is killed, Buckmaster and Miranda leave to seek another city, the immigrants drift away, and Olds flies off in Halloway's glider. As the story closes, Halloway, alone in the again abandoned city, dreams of following Buckmaster and Miranda, to aid in the industrialist's mission to build monuments to the vanished Age of Technology.

A change in the "intermediatory" level of his experience—the death of his parents—triggers Halloway's decision to leave the garden community, and brings to the surface his fascination with technology (his glider is based on plans left by his father). Once in the city, two key relationships shape the "intermediatory" level of the story. The first is Halloway's relationship with Miranda. He is clearly attracted to Miranda; but as he becomes increasingly obsessed with bringing the city back to life, he loses touch with her. Halloway uses a defoliant to destroy the exotic plants with which she has seeded the city, thus intertwining the themes of death and birth (or fertility). In the final scene between the two, Halloway sees her standing on a balcony wearing a wedding dress; she beckons to him, but between them is an impenetrable barrier of deadly nightshade, planted by Miranda (again fusing birth and death on several levels, and with marvelous economy). As the story ends, Halloway dreams that he might "come to terms with Miranda," and that then "she would wear her wedding dress again for him;" but this hope is clearly forlorn.

Halloway's relationship with Miranda shows the complex connections in Ballard among the "external," "intermediatory," and "psychic" levels. As the urban environment changes ("exterior" level), approaching the vacuous state of 20th-century life, Halloway's mental state ("psychic" level) deteriorates; he loses the ability to understand and communicate with other people, and thus his relationship with Miranda ("intermediatory" level) also deteriorates. On each level, the sequence of events reinforces—and complicates—the numerous symbolic figurations of the themes of birth and death, as the rebirth (and eventual death) of the city moves for the most of the story in the opposite direction from the death (or disintegration) of Halloway's personality and his relationship with Miranda.

Even more important to an understanding of ***The Ultimate City*** is Halloway's relationship with Olds. What binds them together is a common interest in flight. Here, and in several of Ballard's other recent works, flight ambivalently stands for freedom and psychic transformation as it compounds flying and fleeing. Halloway's flight from the garden community is at once a physical escape and the beginning of his psychic transformation. In the city, Halloway meets Olds, who has devoted his life to the service of machinery and who, significantly, is mute. Olds becomes fascinated with the concept of flight, and Halloway is able to enlist his aid in bringing the city back to life only by promising to teach him to fly. As the urban environment changes, Halloway becomes caught up in the mentality conditioned by such an environment; like the main character in **"Chronopolis,"** Halloway becomes obsessed with the clock: "So much of life here depends on time—hours of work, rates of pay, and so on, they're all hitched to the clock." Olds meanwhile grows further and further away from Halloway, becoming less and less the servant of the clock and other machinery.

The climax of the psychic transformation of Halloway (and Olds—another example of structural unity by opposite movement) comes at the conclusion of ***The Ultimate City.*** Olds has equipped Halloway's glider with an engine; he leaves a final message for Halloway: "I can—. Fulmar, albatross, flamingo, frigate-bird, condor . . . IGNITION!" Above, as Olds flies off, the city's neon signs proclaim his psychic breakthrough: "I CAN FLY!" And what of Halloway? His last hope, as he prepares to leave the city in quest of Buckmaster and Miranda, tells the story: "And perhaps, too, Olds would teach him how to fly." Halloway's psychic transformation is complete: he has lost both Miranda and Olds . . . and he has lost the power to fly.

I have deliberately avoided the question of ambiguity in ***The Ultimate City*** to this point, in order to concentrate on the structure of the story. But this very structure raises certain problems for the reader. How and why should an environmental change (the rebirth of the city) have such a decisive effect on personal relations and mental states? ***The Ultimate City*** is told in a quiet, unaffected style, yet the conclusion is almost mystical: Halloway, presumably because of his obsession with the city, has mysteriously lost the power to fly. The reader is left to guess at both the mechanism and the meaning of this psychic transformation.

Nor is this the only uncertainty that Ballard introduces into his story. The city, and the technology associated with it, are always shown in an unfavorable light; the rebirth of the city is described in terms of crowding, crime, pollution, and inflation, and as such it leads to Halloway's breakdown on the "intermediatory" and "psychic" levels. Hence, the reader might naturally assume that the low-technology garden communities represent Ballard's utopian alternative to the city. Yet Halloway and (later) scores of others are so dissatisfied with life in these communities as to abandon them and return to the city. And no wonder, Halloway's parents died as the result of a fire; they might have been saved, but the garden communities' ban on all engines prevented them from reaching medical aid in time. Ballard in fact presents the reader with an alternative, neither side of which seems acceptable. (pp. 299-301)

Lorenz J. Firsching, "J. G. Ballard's Ambiguous Apocalypse," edited by Robert M. Philmus, in Science-Fiction Studies, *Vol. 12, No. 37, November, 1985, pp. 297-310.*

ADDITIONAL BIBLIOGRAPHY

Brigg, Peter. *J. G. Ballard.* Mercer Island, Washington: Starmont House, 1985, 138 p.

A general introduction to Ballard's works and an overview of early and later phases in his career.

Burroughs, William S. Preface to *Love and Napalm: Export U.S.A.*, by J. G. Ballard, pp. 7-8. New York: Grove Press, 1972.

An appreciation of Ballard's fiction by an author whom Ballard greatly admires.

Goddard, James, and Pringle, David, eds. *J. G. Ballard: The First Twenty Years,* Hayes, Middlesex, England: Bran's Head Books, 1976.

Selection of thematic essays, book reviews, and an interview with Ballard, drawn from several contributors.

Pringle, David. *Earth Is the Alien Planet: J. G. Ballard's Four-Dimensional Nightmare*. San Bernardino, California: Borgo Press, 1979, 63 p.

An innovative study of Ballard's career and works up to *Low-Flying Aircraft and Other Stories*.

John Cheever

1912-1982

American short story writer and novelist.

Cheever is considered one of the most important twentieth-century American writers of short fiction. He has been called "the Chekhov of the exurbs" for his well-crafted chronicles of upper-middle-class manners and mores. Characterized by skillful portrayals of a world of cocktail parties, backyard barbeques, and commuter trains, Cheever's short stories describe the tensions underlying this suburban idyll. Although such stories as "The Swimmer," "The Enormous Radio," and "The Housebreaker of Shady Hill" established Cheever as a fine storyteller and a trenchant social commentator, only in recent years has his work been recognized as serious literature. The republication of sixty-one of his best stories in the 1978 collection *The Stories of John Cheever* has led to more scholarly reappraisals of his works. Critics note particularly the importance of Cheever's themes of human morality and spirituality and praise his compassion and his abiding belief in the redemptive power of love.

Cheever was born in Quincy, Massachusetts. His New England background is evident in his writing, not merely in the settings of his stories, but in the traditions and values that inform them. He attended Thayer Academy, a preparatory school in Massachusetts, but his formal education ended when he was expelled at seventeen. The short story he wrote about the experience—"Expelled"—was published October 1, 1930 in the *New Republic*, and Cheever's literary career had begun. During the next several years, Cheever lived for the most part in New York City, supporting himself with odd jobs, including writing an occasional book synopsis for Metro-Goldwyn-Mayer. His own fiction, however, was always Cheever's primary occupation. Throughout the 1930s his short stories appeared in such magazines as the *Atlantic, Colliers, Story,* the *Yale Review,* and, especially, the *New Yorker*. Cheever's connection with the *New Yorker* began in 1935 and lasted all his life; well over one hundred of his stories were originally published in that magazine. Despite its advantages, this alliance also had a detrimental effect on Cheever's reputation, for critics associated his stories with the stereotypical *New Yorker* style: slick, facile, and self-conscious. Cheever was serving in the U.S. Army during World War II when his first collection, *The Way Some People Live,* was published in 1943. Composed of thirty stories, many of them little more than sketches, the book garnered some positive critical attention. After the war, Cheever wrote scripts for television series, including "Life with Father," and his fiction appeared regularly in periodicals. In 1953 his second collection appeared. Approximately the same length as *The Way Some People Live, The Enormous Radio, and Other Stories* consists of only fourteen stories, each exemplifying Cheever's movement toward longer, more fully developed works.

In the years that followed, Cheever diversified his writings, and his fame and reputation grew. He published his first novel, *The Wapshot Chronicle,* in 1957, and the following year saw the appearance of *The Housebreaker of Shady Hill, and Other Stories,* which includes "The Five-forty-eight" and "The Country Husband," stories that had previously won the Benjamin Franklin Award and the O. Henry Award. Another collection, *Some People, Places, and Things That Will Not Appear in My Next Novel,* was published in 1961, followed three years later by the sequel to *The Wapshot Chronicle, The Wapshot Scandal*. Also in 1964 appeared *The Brigadier and the Golf Widow,* which contains one of Cheever's most celebrated short stories, "The Swimmer." In the years following the 1969 publication of the novel *Bullet Park*, Cheever suffered depression and bad health, including a near-fatal heart attack in 1972, and he became increasingly addicted to alcohol. Although his personal problems did not compromise the quality of his next collection, *The World of Apples*, his condition worsened until 1975 when, at the insistence of his wife and three children, Cheever successfully underwent alcohol rehabilitation. His novel *Falconer,* published in 1977, abandons the usual suburban Cheever milieu to depict a drug-addicted prison convict and is widely acclaimed as one of his finest achievements. The next year *The Stories of John Cheever* met with immense success, both popular and critical. On the *New York Times* best-seller list for six months, *Stories* received the Pulitzer Prize, the National Book Award, the National Book Critics Circle Award, and the Edward McDowell Medal. Cheever's last work, the novella *Oh What a Paradise It Seems,* was published in 1982, the year of his death from cancer.

© 1977 by Nancy Crampton

Cheever's fictional world commonly portrays individuals in conflict with their communities and often with themselves. His stories are remarkably homogeneous, and most share similar settings and characters. The typical Cheever protagonist, affluent, socially prominent, and emotionally troubled, is an upper-middle-class WASP who commutes to his professional job in the city (usually New York) from his home in suburbia. In the evenings he and his wife attend neighborhood cocktail parties, and once a year the family vacations on the East Coast. Cheever's description of his milieu is realistic, but his stories are more than merely accurate portrayals of a particular way of life. Into each picture of idyllic suburbia, Cheever injected an element of emotional tension arising from the gap between the serene environment and individual passion and discontent. While this tension may take many forms, the most common problem in a Cheever story concerns marital conflict. Adultery, real or fantasized, is a recurrent motif, as Cheever's characters struggle with their simultaneous desires for emotional fulfillment and domestic and societal order. Cheever does not judge his middle-class characters, critics note, rather, he treats them with understanding and compassion. Although he obviously intended to satirize the stifling and hypocritical aspects of the life-style he depicts, Cheever clearly recognized that while the values of upper-middle-class suburbia may not address the individual's deepest concerns, they do reflect an admirable effort to impose stability on a chaotic world. Commentators point out that as Cheever's characters are ambivalent in their desires, so the stories themselves are ambiguous, and the author presents no clear resolution. The stories are generally realistic in setting and technique, but they are less complete tales with a beginning and end than they are isolated slices of life briefly illuminated.

Recent critics have noted subtle but important phases in Cheever's short fiction career, citing distinctions among the collections. From the very short pieces in *The Way Some People Live,* Cheever moved to more fully realized stories in *The Enormous Radio*. The stories in these two collections generally have New York City as their setting; with *The Housebreaker of Shady Hill* Cheever moved to the suburban world commonly associated with his work. Irony and wit become more evident in this collection, as does Cheever's narrative detachment. In *Some People, Places, and Things That Will Not Appear in My Next Novel,* stories with European settings begin to appear. Critics observed a darker note in *The Brigadier and the Golf Widow,* in addition to a more experimental technique, as in "The Swimmer." *The World of Apples* has likewise been termed somber, but some critics dispute this description, for the title story is clearly a celebration of the triumph of human decency.

Although Cheever's short fiction was regularly published both in magazines and in collections, and although he received many literary awards throughout his career, critical appraisal of his work was for years limited. Most early reviewers praised Cheever's prose style and his descriptive talent, but faulted his stories for their irresolution and what was considered their essential pessimism. A few early critics gave high praise to Cheever's work, but even these warned of the danger that his fiction would harden into a predictable formula in accordance with the *New Yorker* style, and the *New Yorker* association continued for many years to color critical response to Cheever's work. The critical success of the novel *Falconer,* however, and the republication of much of Cheever's best short fiction in *The Stories of John Cheever* sparked the appearance of serious academic criticism. Critics began to reappraise Cheever's work and to reach new conclusions about his fictional vision; perhaps the most radical change is the view of Cheever as optimist rather than pessimist. It is now generally accepted that Cheever's stories, while they can evoke pathos and despair, contain a core of hope, even of idealism. Recognized now are Cheever's frequent use of light imagery, his sensuous delight in nature and beauty, and his belief that such things carry positive moral force. Far from being thought a chronicler of hopelessness, Cheever is now regarded as a champion of basic human decency and morality. Moreover, critics contend that his precise representation of a particularized milieu does not restrict Cheever's artistic vision. Many agree with William McPherson, who wrote: "The world John Cheever renders is a narrow one . . . but it has a universal resonance."

Cheever is therefore recognized as one of the most significant of modern short fiction writers. Critics maintain that *The Stories of John Cheever,* a distillation of his best work, proves his mastery of the short story genre and secures him a distinguished place in American letters. In such representative stories as "The World of Apples" and "The Season of Divorce," Cheever compassionately treated universal human emotions and moral dilemmas, and thus fulfilled his artistic intention, described by Saul Bellow as "not only to find evidence of a moral life in a disorderly society but also to give us the poetry of the bewildering and stupendously dreamlike world in which we find ourselves."

(See also *CLC,* Vols. 3, 7, 8, 11, 15, 25; *Contemporary Authors,* Vols. 5-8, rev. ed., Vol. 106 [obituary]; *Contemporary Authors New Revision Series,* Vol. 5; *Dictionary of Literary Biography,* Vol. 2; *Dictionary of Literary Biography Yearbook:* 1980, 1982; and *Concise Dictionary of American Literary Biography,* Vol. 1.)

PRINCIPAL WORKS

SHORT FICTION

The Way Some People Live 1943
The Enormous Radio, and Other Stories 1953
The Housebreaker of Shady Hill, and Other Stories 1958
Some People, Places, and Things That Will Not Appear in My Next Novel 1961
The Brigadier and the Golf Widow 1964
The World of Apples 1973
The Stories of John Cheever 1978
Oh What a Paradise It Seems 1982

OTHER MAJOR WORKS

The Wapshot Chronicle (novel) 1957
The Wapshot Scandal (novel) 1964
Bullet Park (novel) 1969
Falconer (novel) 1977

WILLIAM DuBOIS (essay date 1943)

[In the following excerpt, DuBois claims that Cheever shows promise, but he perceives serious flaws in The Way Some People Live.*]*

There are thirty sketches in [***The Way Some People Live***]; all of them are worth at least five minutes of your time, even though the majority are exercises in marital frustration, hag-ridden dipsomania, poverty, or plain and fancy jitters. Most of them appeared between the covers of the *New Yorker*. Perhaps this accounts for their peculiar epicene detachment, and facile despair.

If the short-story is merely a character in a crisis, Mr. Cheever's attempts fulfil the definition. This is not intended as a churlish comment; his talent is fine and incisive, he is definitely a writer to watch. But the crisis in any story, once it is stated, must be resolved in a way that touches off emotional responses in the reader, and this Mr. Cheever, for the most part, obstinately refuses to do. His people are seldom really angry, and almost never gay. When disaster impends, they usually run away from it, mix another Manhattan, or keep their reactions hidden from both the reader and themselves. . . .

Unfortunately, this avoidance of anything resembling a climax, plus the author's misanthropic view of the human race, can only make for boredom, if you take your Cheever in large doses. Somewhere in this world (including the New York whose surface he scratches so brilliantly) Mr. Cheever could discover children who love their parents, people whose business doesn't fail, marriages that do not require twenty years of agony to build into a divorce, old folks whose minds are not as stuffy as New England attics, ladies who fall in love from uncomplicated motives, satyrs who are not suffering from vitamin deficiency.

Certainly such people must exist, but Mr. Cheever will have none of them. As a result, the characters in his own unhappy world have an astonishing and tortured similarity. For all that, you will begin each of these stories with genuine interest. How else can you approach an opening sentence like "He put his felt hat, his white shirt, and the Tripler tie his mother-in-law had given him for Christmas into the trash can"? ***The Way Some People Live*** is the perfect book for an up-and-coming dentist's ante-room. A few of those tense moments spent with Mr. Cheever's people and their off-center agonies will buck you up no end for the ordeal ahead.

William DuBois, "Tortured Souls," in The New York Times Book Review, *March 28, 1943, p. 10.*

DIANA TRILLING (essay date 1943)

[*An American writer on literary and social topics, Trilling was fiction critic for the* Nation *from 1942 to 1949. In the following excerpt, she explains her frustration with the vagueness of the stories in* The Way Some People Live. *This essay was first published in a slightly different form in the* Nation *in 1943.*]

John Cheever's stories, which for the most part have appeared in the *New Yorker* and which are even more talented than the average stories printed in that magazine, are now collected in a volume called ***The Way Some People Live***. To read them out of their usual reassuring context is an exceedingly frustrating experience, a bit like holding a conversation in a language in which one has been well-schooled, but in which one is still not fluent. For even the best of Mr. Cheever's stories, such as **"The Pleasures of Solitude"** or **"The Edge of the World,"** are strongly-worded hints rather than completely communicated statements. No doubt this is explained by the fact that even more than our novelists our present-day writers of short fiction not only choose inarticulate characters to write about but refuse to be articulate *for* them. It is an artificial, and wholly self-imposed, limitation of a piece with the time-limitation in the contemporary short story. The sooner it is got rid of, the better for this branch of fiction.

Diana Trilling, in a review of "The Way Some People Live," in Reviewing the Forties, *Harcourt Brace Jovanovich, 1978, pp. 26-9.*

STRUTHERS BURT (essay date 1943)

[*Burt was an American man of letters whose short story collections include* John O'May, and Other Stories *(1918) and* The Scarlet Hunter *(1925). In the following excerpt from a review of* The Way Some People Live, *he hails Cheever as an important new writer.*]

Unless I am very much mistaken, when this war is over, John Cheever—he is now in the army—will become one of the most distinguished writers; not only as a short story writer but as a novelist. Indeed, if he wishes to perform that ancient triple-feat, not as popular now as it was twenty years ago in the time of Galsworthy and Bennett and their fellows, he can be a playwright too, for he has all the necessary signs and characteristics. The sense of drama in ordinary events and people; the underlying and universal importance of the outwardly unimportant; a deep feeling for the perversities and contradictions, the worth and unexpected dignity of life, its ironies, comedies, and tragedies. All of this explained in a style of his own, brief, apparently casual, but carefully selected; unaccented until the accent is needed. Meanwhile, he has published the best volume of short stories I have come across in a long while [***The Way Some People Live***], and that is a much more important event in American writing than most people realize.

The short story is a curious and especial thing; a delicate and restricted medium in which many have walked, but few succeeded. . . . Its strength, like the sonnet's, comes from deep emotion and perception, and, when necessary, passion, beating against the inescapable form that encircles it. As in the sonnet, as indeed in all good poetry, not a word or line, or figure of speech, or simile, must be amiss or superfluous. The author has just so many minutes in which to be of value, and the contest—the selection—in his mind is between what he would like to say, and what he should say; the search is for the inevitable phrase and sentence and description that contain the final illumination but which, at the same time, seem inevitable and natural.

As a result, probably not more than a score of truly great short stories have ever been written. . . .

The present volume consists of thirty short stories and one can see the compression used, for the book is only two hundred and fifty-six pages long. Many of the stories are only a few pages in length, a thousand, twelve hundred words; and at least half of them are eminently successful; a quarter are far above the average; all are well done; and only a couple fail. **"Of Love: A Testimony,"** except for its title, is one of the best love stories I have ever read. There is a curious and interesting development in the book, and in the procession of the stories—the way they are placed—that ties the volume together and gives it almost the feeling of a novel despite the inevitable lack of connection between any short stories. The earlier stories have to do with the troubled, frustrated, apparently futile years of 1939 and 1941; and then there are some beautifully told stories of the average American—the average American with a college degree, the same suburbanite—actually at war, but still in this country. This gives the book the interest and importance of a progress toward Fate; and so there's a classic feeling to it. . . .

John Cheever has only two things to fear; a hardening into an especial style that might become an affectation, and a deliberate casualness and simplicity that might become the same. Otherwise, the world is his.

Struthers Burt, "John Cheever's Sense of Drama," in The Saturday Review of Literature, *Vol. XXVI, No. 17, April 24, 1943, p. 9.*

ARTHUR MIZENER (essay date 1953)

[*Mizener is the author of highly respected biographies of F. Scott Fitzgerald and Ford Madox Ford. In the following excerpt from a review of* The Enormous Radio, and Other Stories, *Mizener explains why he finds the collection clever but lacking in depth.*]

[Mr. Cheever] is not a writer of any great talent, but the stories in [***The Enormous Radio and Other Stories***] are all skillfully worked out and loaded with carefully observed manners. Congreve, who might, for a while at least, have been a great success in the *New Yorker,* once remarked that he selected a moral and then designed a fable to fit it. It seems unlikely, though great works have been written in even queerer ways than that. It is the glaring fault of Mr. Cheever's stories that they all appear to have been produced in that way. He does not so much imagine experience as have clever ideas for stories. There are the ingenious camera-angles, the elevator operators (two of these) and the apartment-house superintendents, very cute and innocent and staring wide-eyed at quality folk. There are the neat discoveries of commonplace morals in sophisticated lives. When Mr. Cheever tries for the big idea, his stories waver toward a formally—and therefore morally—ambiguous melodrama, as in **"Torch Song"** where a girl who appears, magically, never to grow old (shades of Dorian Gray) turns out to love dying people, or in **"O City of Broken Dreams,"** where a pair of hicks who are said to be from Indiana but are really from Ring-Lardner-land are fantastically diddled by blasé theatrical people. These are the stories of a clever short-story manufacturer, a man who has ideas about experience but has never known these ideas in experience. Their language and technique are highly refined; their feeling is crude. They are as well-made as any conscientious editor could demand; you cannot blame the doctor for their having been born with a very minimum of vitality. (pp. 19-20)

Arthur Mizener, "In Genteel Traditions," in The New Republic, *Vol. 128, No. 2008, May 25, 1953, pp. 19-20.*

MORRIS FREEDMAN (essay date 1953)

[*Freedman is an American educator whose writings include* Confessions of a Conformist *(1961) and* Chaos in Our Colleges *(1962). In the following excerpt from a review of* The Enormous Radio and Other Stories, *he discusses Cheever's vision of life.*]

Cheever, a product of the Hebraic New England conscience, implacable as a Kafkaesque judge, cuts through the layers of tawdry pretense and elaborate alibi while arraigning his defendants—all of them guilty, often as vaguely and as profoundly as Kafka's people—of some breach against the mysterious deity of honest grace and lightness and self-understanding. Cheever's intelligence is startling and disturbing in its cold superiority as he bares a human problem to the bone, but his fine and controlled compassion is deep and thoughtful and genuine. . . .

Cheever's *bête noir* is New York City. It is a place that has the quality of hell, almost literally at some moments: "They sat together with their children through the sooty twilights, when the city to the south burns like a Bessemer furnace, and the air smells of coal, and the wet boulders shine like slag, and the Park itself seems like a strip of woods on the edge of a coal town." The havoc the city works on genuine human beings is Cheever's theme. The insanities connected with city life are simultaneously harrowing and hilarious. Perhaps the most moving story in [***The Enormous Radio and Other Stories***], **"O City of Broken Dreams,"** is also the funniest. A small-town bus driver and his family are lured to the big city by an irresponsible, fancy-talking Broadway producer who has read two acts of a play the driver has written. While the driver is waiting for an executive in a Radio City office, the secretary offers to sell him fresh farm eggs or costume jewelry wholesale; the unpaid butler of a Park Avenue establishment trails a bloody bandage from his finger over the carpets as he berates his employer who, at the moment, is occupied in a floating crap game in Harlem.

At first reading, one comes away with a sense that Cheever's characters are sunk in a mire of unrelieved hopelessness. (p. 390)

But the volume as a whole yields the secret of coping with the eternal imminence of disaster which is living. In three stories Cheever transcends the bleakness of Kafka; the other stories, then, must be read as demonstrations not of what Cheever believes life must inevitably be, but of what it should not be, of what we should fight against it becoming. **"The Pot of Gold"** concludes with the husband turning to his family for richness and away from the mad schemes for success which have driven him for so long. In **"The Cure,"** a husband separated from his wife is slowly disintegrating in his loneliness, succumbing to a series of personal horrors in the improbable and therefore all the more macabre settings of Madison Avenue and suburbia, until he goes back to her and his children to save himself. In **"Goodbye, My Brother,"** the first story, Cheever movingly attacks the narrow-minded enemies of instinct and self-fulfillment. Salvation lies in meeting the unavoidable horror head on, and engaging it with one's best talents, not obscuring it or fleeing from it. (pp. 390, 392)

Cheever, by reason of his New England background, has breathed into his system that Biblical concentration on the moral nature of reality, on the inescapable essence of a word or an act, which we find in Hawthorne, Melville, and James. (p. 392)

Morris Freedman, "New England and Hollywood," in Commentary, *Vol. 16, No. 4, October, 1953, pp. 389-90, 392.*

GRANVILLE HICKS (essay date 1958)

[*Hicks was an American literary critic whose famous study* The Great Tradition: An Interpretation of American Literature since the Civil War *(1933) established him as the foremost advocate of Marxist critical thought in Depression-era America. After 1939, Hicks sharply denounced communist ideology, which he called a "hopelessly narrow way of judging literature," and in his later years adopted a less ideological posture in critical matters. In the following excerpt, he describes successful aspects of Cheever's writing in* The Housebreaker of Shady Hill.]

[Cheever's chosen segment of American life in ***The Housebreaker of Shady Hill and Other Stories***] is suburbia, than which nothing, according to a widely held opinion, can be duller. Nor can it be said that Cheever seeks to contradict the general impression. Saturday night parties and Sunday hangovers figure in several of the stories, and he does not suggest that they are particularly glamorous. As for the other side of life in Shady Hill—"a regular Santa Claus's workshop of madrigal singers, political discussion groups, recorder groups, dancing schools, confirmation classes, committee meetings, and lectures on literature, philosophy, city planning, and pest control"—the glimpses he gives of it are not inviting.

If, then, Cheever's stories are rich and exciting, the explanation lies not in his material but in what he is able to make of it. In one of the stories, describing Shady Hill at night, he writes: "The village hangs, morally and economically, from a thread; but it hangs by its thread in the evening light." The figure of speech suggests his vision of the quality of the life he is writing about. For his characters, life in Shady Hill, whatever its limitations, represents stability. The hero of the title story sees this clearly: "Shady Hill is, as I say, a *banlieue* and open to criticism by city planners, adventurers, and lyric poets, but if you work in the city and have children to raise, I can't think of a better place." Thus Johnny Hake is awakened to an appreciation of what Shady Hill means to him because he has become, in his own mind, an outcast. He knows he can lose what he has, and it is therefore dear to him. But of course everyone is vulnerable; every life "hangs, morally and economically, from a thread."

The best of the stories are concerned with this vulnerability. Johnny Hake loses his job and finds himself a common thief. Francis Weed in **"The Country Husband"** is subjected to a series of unusual emotional experiences, and is able to re-achieve stability only by virtue of a psychiatrist's advice and woodwork as therapy. Marcie Flint is led into adultery by the least predictable of paths. Cash Bentley in **"O Youth and Beauty!"** and Will Pym in **"Just Tell Me Who It Was"** are victims of the encroaching years. The thread breaks or it almost breaks, and the result is a crisis that absorbs the readers's attention.

I am not suggesting that Cheever's success can be explained solely in terms of his sense of vulnerability. He is one of the sharpest of observers, and some of his descriptions of suburban scenes are a pure joy. He has also developed an admirable technique for handling a complex series of incidents, so that such a story as **"The Trouble of Marcie Flint"** has a remarkable density. But his great gift is for entering into the minds of men and women at crucial moments. Johnny Hake's relief when he is pulled back from the abyss, Charles Flint's euphoric state just before disaster hits him, Francis Weed's delayed response to an airplane accident—it is in such passages as these that Cheever shows his mastery. Cheever knows where drama is to be found, and he has taught himself how to make the most of it. (pp. 33, 47)

Granville Hicks, "Cheever and Others," in The Saturday Review, *New York, Vol. XLI, No. 37, September 13, 1958, pp. 33, 47.*

RICHARD GILMAN (essay date 1958)

[*Gilman is an American literary and dramatic critic whose works include* The Confusion of Realms *(1969) and* Decadence: The Strange Life of an Epithet *(1979). In the following excerpt, he concludes that Cheever expresses adolescent values in* The Housebreaker of Shady Hill.]

Consider the situation of John Cheever, whose prophetic role it is to call suburbia to repentance, but whose artist's soul must kick against the pricks. . . .

He is more likely uncomfortable in the role of culture-hero to the barbecue and Volkswagen set, though whatever distress he feels he keeps to himself. Still, that is what he is, the Dante of the cocktail hour, and if he deserves, for his craftsmanship and uncommon satirical gifts, another name to go under, it is also true that he has laid himself open to his followers. . . .

The tension in [the stories in ***The Housebreaker of Shady Hill and Other Stories***] about the mythical suburban community of Shady Hill arises, as in all art, from the space between appearance and reality, or the data of existence and its possibilities. In this town where existences receive the most brittle nourishment, like paper flowers in a martini glass, there storms up the dream of love. Here where the good life is pursued as by sleepwalkers there supervenes, like a hand on the shoulder, the temptation of a shattering about-face.

"God preserve me," a character in one story prays, "from women who dress like toreros to go to the supermarket, and from cowhide dispatch cases, and from flannels and gabardines. Preserve me from word games and adulterers, from basset hounds . . . and Bloody Marys and smugness and syringa bushes and P.T.A. meetings."

And "amen" the readers on the 5:18 may say. And an amen at each moment in these chapters of the moral history of Shady Hill when with grace and economy the revelation is offered—that all is sand, that no felicity has been snared, that life has reneged on its promises. But they do not get off in the Bronx and throw their attaché cases away, and who could expect them to? Still, literature has been known to bring about such things.

Cheever's will not bring it about, nor anything symbolic of it, because if you wait patiently enough and hearken between the lines you will hear, often faintly it is true, the all-clear sounding.

For Cheever, with all his wit and sophistication and his coldness of eye, is essentially a sentimentalist and usually contrives to let his fish off the hook. It is never clearer than when he is opposing something to the toreador pants and sterile parties and waspishness of suburban marriages. The land of deliverance he prays for is wholesome and American: "the trout streams of our youth," a light-hearted game of softball, bright welcoming lights behind the picture window. Or else it is romantic and "deep"—the "churches of Venice" or islands in the "purple autumn sea."

Cheever's women are always loved for their blondeness or bosom line and his men because they are lithe. They have a nostalgic need for mountains (not high), sailboats at twilight and tennis with new balls. It is all adolescent at bottom and not simply because Cheever is portraying a world of adolescent values. In the end he shares them. At least he shares them enough so that in these stories sadness never mounts to tragedy or feeling to passion. To smell red meat is a vague hope in a universe of frozen canapés, and the jungle is far, far from the cropped lawns.

Richard Gilman, "Dante of Suburbia," in Commonweal, *Vol. LXIX, No. 12, December 19, 1958, p. 320.*

IRVING HOWE (essay date 1959)

[*Howe is one of America's most highly respected literary critics and social historians. In the following excerpt, he points to Cheever's limitations in* The Housebreaker of Shady Hill.]

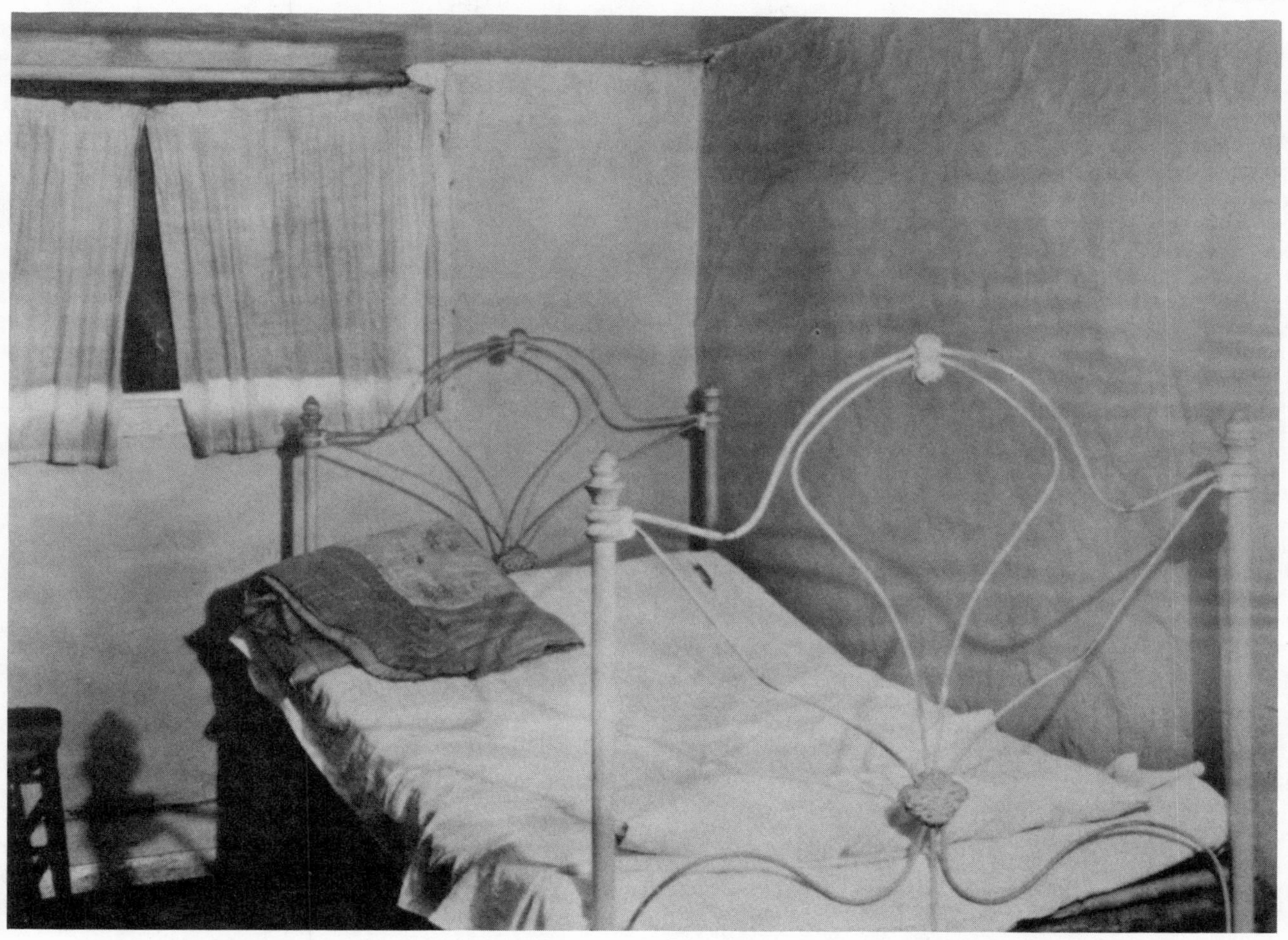

Walker Evans's photograph of the room where Cheever spent his first months in New York City.

John Cheever is one of the *New Yorker*'s most canny and skillful hands, an expert at regulating the delicate psychic relations between the magazine and its public. Undeceived as to the troubles of suburbia, Cheever stands before his readers somewhat like a cautious therapist making sure the patients don't fly into a rage and tear apart the modern furniture.

The stories in ***The Housebreaker of Shady Hill and Other Stories*** have a recurrent pattern. They start with a release of some trouble in the life of a suburbanite: the hero is short of cash, he wants to neck with the babysitter, he is ready to vomit up a throatful of boredom. Reading the first page or two leads to a surge of expectation—the sense of danger is genuine enough, reality is breaking past the world of gadgets and ranch houses, even past the surface of Cheever's greying prose. But, alas, this reality proves to be a canary, not an eagle, and a canary soon caged. The adorable fantasy of escape is squashed in a mild whimsy of resignation; the emotion that had been pinched into vitality becomes a mere dribble of weariness. And though defeat may well be the greatest of literary subjects, Cheever never allows his characters to face either the desperateness or dignity of defeat: he murders their vital core before they have a chance to.

Cheever really knows a great deal about suburban life; but he cheats. He systematically refuses to face the meaning of the material he has himself brought to awareness and then suppressed. A toothless Thurber, he connives in the cowardice of contemporary life; the resignation which constitutes his stock of wisdom is nothing but advice to his readers that, dying slowly, they also die quietly. (pp. 130-31)

Irving Howe, in a review of "The Housebreaker of Shady Hill," in Partisan Review, *Vol. XXVI, No. 1, Winter, 1959, pp. 130-31.*

GENE BARO (essay date 1961)

[*Baro comments on strengths and weaknesses in* Some People, Places, and Things That Will Not Appear in My Next Novel.]

There is something of the virtuoso performance in the writings of John Cheever, particularly in his short stories. The reader is seldom, if ever, allowed to forget the author or to lose himself in the matter of the work; instead, he is invited at almost every turn to recognize the shaping intelligence and subtle sensibility of the writer himself. . . .

In story after story, the reader is gripped by poignance or terror or surrenders himself to a humanitarian idealism or to a social criticism expressed as ironic comedy, only to have the rug pulled out from under him by Mr. Cheever. Suddenly, the reverse of what appeared to have been affirmed seems true.

Almost entirely, Mr. Cheever is concerned with middle-class values, with the orderly and comfortable life that has been made apparently by rational self-interest. We meet well-to-do families at home and abroad; we see the promise of privileged lives; but somehow the promise is not working out: the dark pressures of the irrational underlie the everyday performance. . . .

At the same time, there are moments in virtually all of [the stories collected in ***Some People, Places, and Things That Will Not Appear in My Next Novel***] when, so to speak, the promises of suburbia, of the orderly life of the monied middle class, seem real, seem truly to point to something more desirable just ahead. In fact, Mr. Cheever plays variations on what this life might be and on what it seems to be. His stories are parables of some complexity, and his rather teasing methods with the reader are an admirable means of showing us on yet another level how gullible we are, how disposed to believe readily in the surface of things.

One does not need to point out that Mr. Cheever writes very well indeed. A less than first-rate talent could not manage convincingly these quick changes of appearance, these sleights-of-mood. In practice, we are always taken in; Mr. Cheever's disciplined imagination is one move ahead of us; for the moment, he so controls his material and our interest that everything seems possible.

Mr. Cheever is addressing the very audience he is writing about; it is a weakness of his method—virtuoso performance though it is—that he seems to be playing at writing. All the problems he points to are real, all the values, with their implications, are in genuine debate, yet the result is of an intricate trick performed with consummate skill. It is as if the writer were saying, "Watch me! I can make you feel this or that about the life you lead, the things you cherish." At the end, the world of Mr. Cheever's concern remains intact. This is because he does not follow his insights far enough; his work lacks intellectual passion or an enlarged vision of reality—though it suggests both these qualities. In the final analysis, it is as if he had hypnotized us at a suburban house party rather than compelled our greater understanding of ourselves.

Gene Baro, "Mr. Cheever's Sleights-of-Mood Performed with Consummate Skill," in Lively Arts and Book Review, *April 30, 1961, p. 29.*

FREDERICK BRACHER (essay date 1964)

[*Bracher surveys Cheever's work and discusses the author's dominant themes and concerns.*]

American fiction in the Forties and Fifties was dominated by the towering figures of Hemingway and Faulkner; the lesser writers—the foothill range from which the peaks emerged—were apt to be taken for granted, despite the very high level they achieved. Among these, John Cheever may well prove to have been the most sensitive to the temper of his times. Without attempting either a realistic picture or critical analysis of American life, Cheever used his remarkable literary gift to catch the ephemeral quality and feel of life in a period of accelerating change. In his stories and novels he has demonstrated an acuteness of sensibility which establishes him among our most significant writers of comedy.

Cheever's early stories, collected in ***The Way Some People Live***, are wry sketches of urban middle-class life, understated and occasionally sardonic. The stories in ***The Enormous Radio*** and ***The Housebreaker of Shady Hill*** show more warmth of feeling, a bittersweet sense of the absurdities of human life. In the novel *The Wapshot Chronicle* (1957) the humor is more apparent and more grotesque. The wry wit persists, but beyond the surface ironies that made Cheever's early stories "amusing," lies a view of life colored by the original, basic assumptions of comedy: a moral vision of continuity in which a tragic conclusion is not merely an unhappy ending but may be, also, a new beginning in the never-ending cycles of human existence.

Cheever's most recent work—***Some People, Places, and Things That Will Not Appear in My Next Novel*** and *The Wapshot Scandal* (1964)—has become more somber in tone and more critical of our mechanized civilization. The atmosphere is reminiscent of Kafka—at once familiar, preposterous, and faintly sinister. Cheever has moved from the rich aura of the railroad station at St. Botolph's, where the dark smells of "coal gas, floor oil, and toilets" somehow magnify the lives of passengers, to the shiny emptiness of the glass-domed air terminal, efficient, unreal, and diminishing to the human spirit. To evoke such an atmosphere, Cheever pushes satire to the edge of burlesque, but he is clearly not content with a sardonic picture of a moral wasteland. Though the springs of human sensibility may be drying up in the desert of automated non-living, Cheever seems to be working toward the kind of implicit moral statement which distinguishes the serious writer of comedy from the mere entertainer.

Moral earnestness has been a pervasive element in all of Cheever's writing. Morris Freedman noted this is in 1953: "Cheever, by reason of his New England background, has breathed into his system that Biblical concentration on the moral nature of reality . . . which we find in Hawthorne, Melville, and James" [see excerpt dated 1953]. He might have added that Cheever's moral vision—as is appropriate for a writer of comedy, unwilling to rest in the depressingly familiar facts of human bondage—has been characteristically affirmative. In *The Wapshot Chronicle,* as in his earlier stories, Cheever is more concerned with man's possibilities than with his limitations; and throughout his fiction he depicts the sensuous surface of life "with candor and with relish" and celebrates love in all its forms. The novel also reminds us, despite its nostalgic evocation of the past way of life at St. Botolph's, that man has always had to face new and inhospitable environments and that change, with its concomitant reactions of surprise and shock, can be tonic as well as disturbing. Taken as a whole, Cheever's fiction constitutes, like the life of Leander Wapshot, "a gesture or sacrament toward the excellence and continuousness of things."

A basic metaphor for Cheever's vision of life is the voyage. . . . Cheever's characters move through experience, instead of resting in it. No matter how absorbing the present, it is flowing toward an unpredictable future and carrying the individual to a new stage of growth, to new possibilities of experience. Love and pain, passion and sorrow, are intense but transitory; nothing finally endures but the pattern of movement and change. (pp. 47-9)

In his most recent collection of stories, Cheever explicitly turns his back of some elements of his past writing. The superficial trappings of social comedy—glamor girls, scornful descriptions of the American scene, explicit accounts of sex, drunks, and homosexuals—are among the things that will not appear, if one takes the title at face value, in his next novel. They "throw so little true light on the way we live." Cheever singled them out to demonstrate "the unimportance that threatens fiction'' if it continues to concern itself chiefly with the external events and outward surface of society. ''We live at deeper levels than these and fiction should make this clear.''

The deeper levels are personal and internal, and Cheever's new approach is defined in stories like **"The Bella Lingua," "Events of That Easter," "A Vision of the World,"** and **"The Embarkment for Cythera."** In these a realistic setting is only a framework, a point of departure for an expedition into the inner world of dream and fantasy. If successful, such explorations may arrive at truths that will redeem and give some reality to the preposterous surface of the mechanized suburbia in which most of us live. The writer's perpetual struggle ''seems to be to tell the truth without surrendering the astringent atmosphere of truthfulness.'' As the actual world—supermarkets with piped-in music, highways lined with Smorgorama and Giganticburger stands, TV commercials advertising Elixircol for ''wet-fur-coat-odor''—becomes increasingly unreal, the writer must turn inward to discover a vision of the world which has the atmosphere of truthfulness. (pp. 50-1)

In his most recent fiction, Cheever seems less concerned than in his earlier stories with the actual ''taste of death''; his new material is more reminiscent of T. S. Eliot's unreal city: the sense of dissociation produced by living in the urban Wasteland. The setting has changed from the comfortable, if transitory, security of Shady Hill to the half-sinister irrationality of Proxmire Manor, a suburb so exclusive and conventional that within its boundaries it is illegal to die. Key images for the new stories are the supermarket and the superhighway—two inhumanly efficient devices for satisfying basic human needs. Life in the supersuburb, where the Moonlight Drive-In has replaced old churches and homesteads, is disjointed and discontinuous; and the structure of the new stories makes a virtue of accidental or casual associations, the ''broken lines of communication in which we express our most acute feelings.'' (pp. 51-2)

The difficulty of an adequate emotional response to our blaring mechanized environment is at least an implicit theme in all of Cheever's recent stories. (p. 52)

Before we can feel truly, we must be able to define the people, places, and things toward which our feeling is directed. In the past, language and literature have helped man to make some order out of the chaos of his external environment; but what language can do justice to the violence of recent change, the unreality of the supermarket? . . .

To sustain a vision of a world in which life flows freely, Cheever is relying more and more on the mythopoeic imagination. (p. 53)

For model and guide, Cheever reminds us, we have always had the dream—a nightly vision of the world which flouts the rational limitations of the waking mind and yet has its own authenticity. To grant our dreams their legitimacy means, ultimately, to accept the incomprehensible, as myth has always done, and to adapt ourselves, with the sanction of ritual if possible, to the next stage of the cycle. . . . Whether our desires are realizable or not, the important thing is to move ahead, to continue the cycle. On the moral level, Cheever would seem to agree with T. S. Eliot's imperative: ''Not fare well, but fare forward, voyagers.''

The last of the characters to be ousted in Cheever's **"A Miscellany of Characters That Will Not Appear"** is an aging writer in a shabby pensione in Venice. In an account of what this writer has lost, Cheever gives a strong hint of his own intentions for the future. He will try to preserve and exercise ''the gift of evoking the perfumes of life: sea water, the smoke of burning hemlock, and the breasts of women.'' But this is no longer enough. ''To celebrate a world that lies spread out around us like a bewildering and stupendous dream,'' one must manage to comprehend it through the imagination. The nearly impossible task of the writer is to make the world of the supermarket, in which we must live, congenial to the sensibility that makes life worth living. To reestablish the continuity of human experience, the writer must fare inward as well as forward, into the territory where the senses and the sensibility are reinforced by ''the ear's innermost chamber, where we hear the heavy noise of the dragon's tail moving over the dead leaves.'' (pp. 56-7)

Frederick Bracher, ''John Cheever: A Vision of the World,'' in Claremont Quarterly, *Vol. 11, No. 2, Winter, 1964, pp. 47-57.*

JOHN W. ALDRIDGE (essay date 1964)

[*Aldridge is an American literary critic whose works include* After the Lost Generation *(1951) and* Time to Murder and Create: The Contemporary Novel in Crisis *(1966). In the following excerpt, Aldridge comments that the important and incisive qualities of Cheever's fiction are often negated by the author himself. This essay was originally published in the* New York Herald Tribune Book Week, *25 October 1964.*]

If you have searched as I have for critical discussion of John Cheever that goes beyond the mere review and treats of his special gifts with some real thoroughness and force, you will probably already share my conviction that Cheever is one of the most grievously underdiscussed important writers we have at the present time. (p. 171)

Cheever has, of course, all along been unfortunate in the company his work has kept. His lengthy association with the *New Yorker,* in which ever since the early thirties the bulk of his fiction has appeared, has not helped to attract serious critics to his work, and as his image has come over the years to be more and more closely identified with that of the magazine, he must long ago have resigned himself to the fact that if recognition should one day come, it would very probably take the form of some such damning encomium as the *Time* profile. For the *New Yorker* air of blasé superciliousness and the *Time* air of blasé sanctimoniousness are both generated by the same wind machine, and a writer can hardly expect to be buoyed up on the one without sooner or later being borne off on the other. It was no accident that *Time* should have offered Cheever to the world as a kind of crew-cut, Ivy League Faulkner of the New York exurbs, who could be both artistically sincere and piously right-thinking about the eternal verities, and who was somehow so stalwartly imaginative that he could parlay even the eternal banalities into a disturbing yet comforting, whimsical yet tragic fable of immense significance for the present age.

But the question is not whether the *Time* profile was an accident, but whether it was altogether mistaken, and one is compelled to admit that it was not. There are moments, to be sure, when Cheever does indeed seem to resemble Faulkner—in his distinguished story-telling gifts, his obsession with, and creative mastery of, a cultural territory of which he has made himself the sole owner and proprietor, even in his essential integrity and toughness of mind, which have enabled him to be consistently better than the medium he writes for and more serious than his middlebrow admirers would be able to recognize. There are also moments when he seems extraordinary in his power to infuse the commonplace and often merely dyspeptic metaphysical crises of modern life with something of the generalizing significance of myth, particularly at a time when it is precisely the ability to deal with the modern social experience in terms of any principle of imaginative coherence that seems to be missing in so many of our most important writers.

Certainly, more thoroughly than anyone else now at work in the field of the American short story, Cheever has explored the troubled surfaces of the new affluent society in which so many of us now live and cannot quite find our being; and as the best of the stories in ***The Brigadier and the Golf Widow*** make clear, he has also penetrated beneath the surfaces into the special conditions of psychic purgatory that we have been able to afford to create for ourselves. He understands just what happens when a man making too much money awakens to the fact that there is nothing left to spend it on except some form of anesthesia against the knowledge that there is nothing left to spend it on. His people are all exempt, at least in his later stories, from the problems of economic insufficiency; hence they are open to all the torments of economic surfeit. They drink too much, fornicate when they can, and then with all guilt and no pleasure, and the men ride commuter trains with the feeling that they are being borne along on fur-lined conveyor belts from somebody else's fabrication of Happiness to somebody else's merchandising image of Success, with no chance that anything ever again will happen to them. So they are obliged to take refuge in small arbitrary or merely ceremonial rebellions, in nostalgia for a past that they may not particularly have liked but in which they at least had something to feel, and in daydreams, not of Walter Mittyish grandiosity, but of almost girlish modesty and poignance.

Yet on the rare occasions when they do open their eyes to the real world, they tend to find themselves in another dream in which the most incredible things are likely to happen or *appear* to be happening. A beautiful woman without any clothes on combs her long golden hair in the window of a passing Pullman car; a husband and wife, also naked, chase each other around the terrace of the house across the street; the teenage babysitter suddenly turns into a siren of unspeakable loveliness, awakening in them quaint, implacable longings to flee with her across the Atlantic on the old *Mauretania* and settle down in some sex-smelling Bohemian garret. Or just as incredibly, they feel their identities slipping away, and *others* notice: the elevator operator mistakes them for deliverymen; the train conductor thinks they are waiters; when they arrive home, they are attacked in the driveway by their own dogs. Or they decide it would be fun to swim home from a party by way of various friends' pools, until they discover that everything they had always taken for granted is beginning to seem untrue, that they have all along been swimming from some crazy illusion of the real into some horrible hallucination that just happens to *be* the real, and in which the reassuring image of the four beautiful daughters safely at home playing tennis, the popularity enjoyed in the community, the affluence and the martini parties, are all revealed to be a lie, part of some fantastic and unnamable hoax perpetrated, oddly enough, on themselves by themselves.

These are some of the typical projections of Cheever's sense of the contemporary world, and I hope I will not seem unfaithful to my own sense of their importance if I say that showing through them are the qualities that have made Cheever likable to the *New Yorker* and *Time,* and which have helped to obstruct his breakthrough into genuine excellence and serious reputation. Somehow the nightmare tonalities of his work come to seem after a while a little too coy and cloying, the postures of psychic torment a little too much like the smartly macabre decor of some Fifth Avenue shop window in which creepy mannequins stand around draped in the latest creations by Charles Addams. For Cheever's vision of all the exactly right contemporary horrors comes perilously close to expressing itself in the stereotypes and platitudes, rather than in the perceived actualities, of experience, and one wonders if he is any longer capable of dealing with his materials in any other way, so that his characters and situations, his Proxmire Manors, Shady Hills, and Bullet Parks, will cease to seem interchangeable, and his resolutions predictable and harmless because stylish.

One also notices, particularly in his novels, and more particularly in *The Wapshot Scandal,* that his most aberrant effects are not only represented in the clichés of aberration—in nymphomania, dipsomania, paranoia, and sexual narcissism—but are often neutralized by some last-minute withdrawal from the full implication of their meaning, some abrupt whimsical detour into palliating fantasy. And while less obvious in his stories, the same tendency is discernible in them. All discordant extremes of conduct and perception are finally absorbed into a fundamentally equable view of life, in much the same way that the *New Yorker* tends to substitute for the distasteful realities a kind of gloss or meringuey confection of the real, which provides us with a faint sickening flavor without actually disturbing our psychic digestion.

It may be that Cheever is temperamentally the sort of writer who prefers to give comfort rather than to educate and transform consciousness. After all, he has been quoted as saying that "one has the impulse to bring glad tidings to someone." Sometimes he even seems to be registering certain grotesqueries simply because he thinks he ought to, or that they are expected of a writer who wishes to be taken seriously, or quite blatantly because he imagines them to be the going literary thing this season. Certainly, his work always seems on the verge of escaping from under its weight of nightmare into an almost Dionysian celebration of the joys of clean living and positive thinking, and of course this is the quality that *Time,* with its stethoscopic sensitivity to the uplifting rhythms of the heart, was able to make serve its pietistic ends.

In any case, it is obvious that Cheever needs both to strengthen and to expand his imaginative grasp, and there is some evidence in this new collection [***The Brigadier and The Golf Widow***] that he has at least tried to do the latter. The stories here are more varied in situation and locale than those in his previous two volumes. Several have to do with expatriate life, and there are some experimental pieces and character sketches that show that he has become aware of a world that is not entirely regulated by the arrival and departure every weekday morning of the 9:14. But they are also more uneven in quality, and the touch is very often unsure, even rather mechanical, as if Cheever were writing at times from habit or falling back on certain effects that he knows by now will do because they served him well in the past. He also seems to be experiencing some difficulty in telling his good work from his bad. A really fine story like **"The Swimmer"** is followed by the group of vignettes in **"Metamorphoses,"** some of which are vapid beyond belief, and the last and best story in the book, **"The Ocean,"** is forced to work hard to overcome the pointlessness of **"A**

Vision of the World," which immediately precedes it. Perhaps three or four of the stories at most come up to the level of the best in ***The Enormous Radio*** and ***The Housebreaker of Shady Hill.***

There is, in short, still very little to convince one that Cheever is moving on. He still needs to find something more and, above all, something different to say about his subject. In fact, he needs to be more drastic than that. He needs to break out of his present mode and rearrange or retool his imaginative responses, not only so that he will be able to confront squarely the full implications of his vision, but so that his vision can become in fact a vision and not simply a congeries of shy and whimsical glances through a glass darkened by a pessimism not quite his own, not quite earned by his imagination. One wishes to say to him now what Gertrude Stein once said to Hemingway: begin over again and concentrate. For he does not yet disturb us enough. He does not yet rouse enough fear. And until he does, he seems destined to remain a writer best known and most admired by all the wrong people for his comforting limitations. (pp. 172-77)

John W. Aldridge, "John Cheever and the Soft Sell of Disaster," in his Time to Murder and Create: The Contemporary Novel in Crisis, *David McKay Company, Inc., 1966, pp. 171-77.*

CLINTON S. BURHANS, JR. (essay date 1969)

[*Burhans analyzes the themes of cultural continuity and human alienation in Cheever's short stories.*]

Many qualities make John Cheever's writing appealing and interesting. Sinuous, mellow, evocative, capable of a surprising range of effects, his prose moves without apparent effort and convinces without fireworks. He has a keen eye for the bizarre and the eccentric; for the left-overs, the left-behinds, the left-outs; but more than this, a quiet acceptance of them all growing from an understanding that everyone is warped by life either more or less and in one way or another. He is a major chronicler of contemporary absurdity, especially in its upper middle-class urban and suburban manifestations; and he is a trenchant moralist who sees all too clearly into the gap between men's dreams and what they make of them. But in illuminating this absurdity and uncovering this gap, he neither derides the human beings trapped in both nor belittles their dreams. He has the long view of man: he sees that what we call progress has only drawn man deeper into the quicksand of his basic condition; that men are born more than ever into a world of chance, complexity, and ultimate loneliness; and that whatever the contemporary terminology, harpies still hover over man and devils ride his back. Cheever reflects this world in whimsy and fantasy, in irony and extravagance, but never at the cost of his deep compassion for those who must live in it with him; an unobtrusive decency shines everywhere in his writing.

Beyond these values and closely related to them, a provocative and significant theme seems to be emerging in Cheever's work, especially in the stories and novels of the past ten years or so. [In a 1959 essay included in *Fiction of the Fifties*] he pinpoints a shaping change in the attitudes underlying his thought and art:

> The decade began for me with more promise than I can remember since my earliest youth. . . . However, halfway through the decade, something went terribly wrong. The most useful image I have today is of a man in a quagmire, looking into a tear in the sky. I am not speaking here of despair, but of confusion. I fully expected the trout streams of my youth to fill up with beer cans and the meadows to be covered with houses; I may even have expected to be separated from most of my moral and ethical heritage; but the forceful absurdities of life today find me unprepared. Something has gone very wrong, and I do not have the language, the imagery, or the concepts to describe my apprehensions. I come back again to the quagmire and the torn sky. . . .

The image is a powerful one; and Cheever's writing since the mid-fifties, especially in the Wapshot novels and in the stories collected in ***The Brigadier and the Golf Widow,*** seem at their deepest levels of meaning and value to be his groping both for a conceptual framework to explain his apprehensions and also for a language and forms to express them.

As Cheever's feeling that "something has gone very wrong" has deepened, so too has his sense of the past and of the indelible relationship between human beings and their sociocultural matrix. His concern with contemporary absurdity is not that of an existentialist; his vision is not that of a Sartre or a Camus. He has the traditionalist's sense of a human nature and of its continuance in time and in experience; and he increasingly views man as a creature industriously but blindly cutting away the roots from which he grows and tearing up the soil which nurtures him. (pp. 187-88)

[For Cheever], man is a creature of the past both in his unchanging and unchangeable existential conditions and also in the tissue of historical, social, and familial forces and relationships which shape his responses to these conditions. (p. 189)

As the complex product of this tissue of interrelationships, of an immutable existential condition shaped by particular backgrounds in time and place, man pays a price and often a terrible one, Cheever feels, if he tries to deny his backgrounds and become something different or if he is cut off from these sources of his identity and values. Self-exiled from America because of a scandal, Anne Tonkin in **"A Woman Without a Country"** tries to make herself into an Italian, "but the image was never quite right. It seemed like a reproduction, with the slight imperfections that you find in an enlargement—the loss of quality. The sense was that she was not so much here in Italy as that she was no longer there in America." Refusing to be taken as a tourist, she claims to be Greek, and "the enormity, the tragedy of her lie staggered her. . . . Her passport was as green as grass, and she traveled under the protectorate of the Great Seal of the United States. Why had she lied about such an important part of her identity?" (p. 191)

This profound and complex sense of the past informs the deepest levels of Cheever's apprehensive concern with the present and the future and explains his perplexed feeling of standing "in a quagmire, looking into a tear in the sky." Given man's permanent existential condition and his inescapable relationship to his particular past, what, Cheever wonders, is man doing to himself in the present and what does it forebode for the future? Exploring these questions, Cheever centers on two predominant problems: *one,* the vast and unparalleled changes which characterize the contemporary world; and *two,* the rate of change which these reflect and its frightening significance.

In **"The Angel of the Bridge,"** the narrator recounts his mother's, his brother's, and his own bizarre responses to a contemporary world whose changes they find incomprehensible and subliminally unbearable. At seventy-eight, his mother skates at Rockefeller Center dressed like a young girl; she had "learned to skate in the little New England village of St. Botolphs . . . and her waltzing is an expression of her attachment to the past. The older she grows, the more she longs for the vanishing and provincial world of her youth. She is a hardy woman . . . but she does not relish change." She is afraid to fly, and "her capricious, or perhaps neurotic, fear of dying in a plane crash was the first insight I had into how, as she grew older, her way was strewn with invisible rocks and lions and how eccentric were the paths she took, as the world seemed to change its boundaries and become less and less comprehensible." Reflecting similar deep-seated anxieties, the narrator's brother is unable to use elevators because he is afraid the building will collapse while he is riding in one.

At first amused by these aberrations and feeling superior to them, the narrator suddenly finds himself terrified by large bridges. Convinced they will fall if he tries to drive across them, he goes out of his way to find "a small old-fashioned bridge that I could cross comfortably" and he feels "that my terror of bridges was an expression of my clumsily concealed horror of what is becoming of the world." (pp. 192-93)

Even more than by the nature of contemporary change, Cheever is disturbed by its velocity, by the rate of change and its chasmal incoherence. Shopping at a supermarket, the narrator of **"A Vision of the World"** thinks that "you may need a camera these days to record a supermarket on a Saturday afternoon. Our language is traditional, the accrual of centuries of intercourse. Except for the shapes of the pastry, there was nothing traditional to be seen at the bakery counter where I waited." Later, at the country club, he watches the daughter of a millionaire funeral director dancing with an indicted stock-market manipulator who had paid his fifty-thousand-dollar bail from the money he carried in his wallet. The band plays songs from the 1920's, and "we seemed," the narrator remarks, "to be dancing on the grave of social coherence." (p. 193)

The price contemporary man pays for too much and too rapid change appalls Cheever. The urban-suburban sprawl and the moral-esthetic collapse which the narrator of **"The Angel of the Bridge"** ultimately cannot stomach are more than simple ugliness evoking a good-old-days nostalgia: they reflect a way of life without roots or meaning or values, a quantitative life lacking any qualitative dimension. (p. 194)

For Cheever, then, the major casualties in the disruption of social coherence are traditional human values and relationships and the process by which they are sustained and extended. In **"A Vision of the World,"** the narrator is constantly struck and increasingly disturbed by the meaninglessness and incoherence of the contemporary world. Its chaotic discontinuities have the quality of a dream world; and, paradoxically, only in his dreams can he establish any relationship to the past and its traditional values. (pp. 194-95)

His dreams are largely of past events or people and traditional figures; and in each dream, someone speaks the words, "'*porpozec ciebie nie prosze dorzanin albo zyolpocz ciwego*." These apparent nonsense syllables are actually broken Polish and other Slavic derivatives from which relevant meaning can be extrapolated: "there are many good things in life; you should not search for the things that do not exist in life," or perhaps, "you have a good and pleasing life and should not cry for things you do not need." The relevance of these strange words becomes clear in the narrator's last dream:

> I dream that I see a pretty woman kneeling in a field of wheat. Her light-brown hair is full and so are the skirts of her dress. Her clothing seems old-fashioned—it seems before my time—and I wonder how I can know and feel so tenderly toward a stranger who is dressed in clothing that my grandmother might have worn. And yet she seems real—more real than the Tamiami Trail four miles to the east, with its Smorgorama and Gigantic-burger stands, more real than the back streets of Sarasota.

She begins to speak the mysterious eight words, and he suddenly awakes to the sound of rain. Sitting up, he too speaks eight words: "'Valor! Love! Virtue! Compassion! Splendor! Kindness! Wisdom! Beauty!' The words seem to have the colors of the earth, and as I recite them I feel my hopefulness mount until I am contented and at peace with the night." The strange unfocussed words have become sharp and clear; they are "the virtues of conservatism," the "good things in life," the traditional values the narrator wants to make legitimate "in so incoherent a world." (p. 195)

In this complex feeling for the past, for man's relationship to his backgrounds and his deep need for social coherence, Cheever is neither a nostalgic traditionalist nor a naturalistic determinist. He is thoroughly aware that man cannot return to or repeat the past, especially an imaginary past, however tempting an escape it may seem; and he views man in more than animal terms. To Cheever, man is the complicated product of his past, of heredity shaped by natural and cultural environment, and he is convinced that the identity and the values man lives by are rooted with him in that past. If man cannot return to or repeat the past, neither can he with impunity move very far beyond a coherent relationship to it. Deeply disturbed by his perceptions of vast change exploding in an apparently geometric progression, Cheever senses that man may be incurring a catastrophic penalty for progress, that the brilliance and power which have given man dominion over the earth may finally be operating to eliminate him from it.

Working at the heart of Cheever's complex concern with the past, then, is a profound insight into the contemporary human condition, a potentially tragic view of man which seems both electrifyingly relevant and poignantly accurate. As Cheever implictly defines him, man is a biological creature who survives, like all organic life, by adapting to his environment. But man is also a cultural creature, a unique being who changes his environment; and in this uniqueness lies the potential for tragedy which Cheever has sensed. For if man changes his environment faster than he is capable of adapting to it, he is inevitably and self doomed.

Here is the "something" which for Cheever "has gone very wrong" in our time; man has released energies and developed technologies which together are changing his world far beyond his capacity to endure such change. . . . What can save a world, Cheever wonders, in which the needs and angers once vented in spears and arrows can now find outlet in nuclear missiles?

But life can end with a whimper as well as with a bang; and man can destroy himself just as surely, if more slowly, by violating the organic relationship to his natural and social environments through which he understands himself and his world and derives the values he lives by. . . . How, Cheever asks, can man adapt to a world he is changing faster than his capacity for comprehending and humanizing change?

In this provocative insight, which seems increasingly to be shaping his recent work, Cheever becomes more than the whimsical *New Yorker* satirist of urban and suburban absurdities, more than an austere but compassionate New-England moralist. . . . Fearing that contemporary man in his obsession with progress is destroying "the excellence and continuity of things," Cheever sees that he may ultimately pay the price of survival for the very brilliance of his own success. Emerging in Cheever's thought and art, this insight suggests a thoroughly contemporary and potentially major tragic vision of man and the human condition. If Cheever has not yet fully articulated it, if he has not yet found the most effective forms to express it, the promise is rich and worth exploring. (pp. 197-98)

Clinton S. Burhans, Jr. "John Cheever and the Grave of Social Coherence," in Twentieth Century Literature, Vol. 14, No. 4, January, 1969, pp. 187-98.

JOHN LEONARD (essay date 1973)

[*An American critic, Leonard was editor of the* New York Times Book Review *from 1971 to 1976. In the following excerpt from a review of* The World of Apples, *he highly praises Cheever, coining a now-famous term for him, the "Chekhov of the exurbs."*]

I happen to believe that John Cheever is our best living writer of short stories: a Chekhov of the exurbs. This view is not commonly shared. Critics tend to take an avuncular attitude toward Cheever; they have already written their one review of him and stashed it away in a drawer, waiting for the next book. Anyone who writes so clearly and so well, about such ordinary matters as marriage and children, cannot be presumed to be highly serious. He must be trying to glide by on charm.

See how effortlessly he goes about his business in this new collection [***The World of Apples***]. He enters his stories the way the rest of us leave our homes, opening the door, stepping out, getting rained on by the day. The awareness of each story seems random; it is composed of what is noticed. But watch: the noticing begins to fix on discrepancies. What is perceived is out of synch with what is felt. What is said is so often wholly inappropriate to the circumstances—women, usually, say those awful things in Cheever's fiction—that the story becomes a mugging. It's as if we had agreed to pretend that politeness is reality; then rudeness, aggression, attack not only our notion of ourselves but our notion of how the universe is supposed to be organized. Yeats asked, "How but in custom and ceremony/ Are innocence and beauty born?" Cheever was after something similar in *Bullet Park* when he talked about "that sense of sanctuary that is the essence of love." The people whom he allows to tell his stories—men, always, in ***The World of Apples***—find no sanctuary. Custom and ceremony are in shambles. Innocence and beauty are remembered, not experienced; and even the memories are suspect: what is being remembered is the desire for innocence, beauty, and sanctuary, rather than the fulfillment. And what remains after the stories have gone is the watermark on the day's page, the blood-vein in the mugger's eyelid: chance and terror.

And yet it is all accomplished with a casual left-handedness. (p. 112)

I like these words, and the emotions they invoke—love, humor, serenity, sweetness, strength, clemency, intelligence, ardor, soul. They aren't used much, or they are not used honestly, in books by Cheever's peers. Irony has deformed these words; they have become indices of simplemindedness; their profession is excused, or tranduced, as a black joke. There is, of course, no escaping irony. It is an indispensable tool for writers of twentieth-century fiction, part of the surgical bag, like sex, ennui, paranoia, and a contempt for your readers. But it isn't absolutely necessary to use irony as a club for bludgeoning your characters into submission; writers who use truncheons are fearful of themselves.

Irony *can* be used the way Cheever uses it: protectively, on behalf of ardor and intelligence and clemency, even while these words, these values really, are inadequate to cope with a world of chance, of evil. Inside Cheever's irony, love and humor are preserved, not abused. A sadness obtains. His fiction has consistently been about a certain failure of reciprocity in our relations with the rest of the universe. (Women, especially, are unknowable and chancy; I suppose someone will write a tract about it, missing the point.) What we don't know, didn't expect, and can't understand overwhelms our decent impulses. We lose. We are not, however, ugly for losing. (p. 114)

John Leonard, "Cheever to Roth to Malamud," in The Atlantic Monthly, *Vol. 231, No. 6, June, 1973, pp. 112-16.*

ROBERT PHILLIPS (essay date 1973)

[*Phillips is an American writer whose works include short stories, criticism, and poetry. The following, which details Phillips's disappointment in Cheever's* A World of Apples, *is drawn from a comparison of that collection with Bernard Malamud's* Rembrandt's Hat. *(1973)*]

The World of Apples is as important to the Cheever canon as a carbon copy is to its bright original. (p. 245)

Even the title story, which focuses upon a poet's loss of faith in the world and therefore in himself, does not move the reader in the way Malamud's spiritual pilgrims do. Is this due to Cheever's determined eccentricities? His indefatigable good humor? With one or two exceptions, these stories chronicle the sadness and futility of suburban and moneyed existences. In several the sound of the rain is intended as a balm for the bruised spirits of those grown more accustomed to the sounds of traffic. And perhaps this is one of Cheever's shortcomings. Writing strictly of one class, his books cannot compare with those attempting a Balzacian cross-section of humanity. Malamud is no Balzac, and writes most often about the poor. But *Rembrandt's Hat* is also populated with successful architects and professors, doctors and students. Cheever's humor and irony make him a greater writer than, say, Louis Auchincloss, whose humorless novels also examine the professional classes to the exclusion of all others. But the limitation is there.

Loneliness of course knows no class barrier, and it is this state which is Cheever's subject. The husband who loses his wife to the off-Broadway stage, the American tourist who loses his Russian beloved through interference of the State Department, and the husband who loses his wife to a phantom lover are all outdone by the hero of **"The Chimera,"** whose marriage is so unhappy he conjures up a demon lover of his own, but whose masochism is also so great he loses even her. Another protagonist, in **"The Geometry of Love,"** desperately seeks "radiance, beauty, and order, no less," and all he finds is a world in which kittens get murdered in Waring blenders.

That kitten in the blender is symptomatic of what else might be "wrong" with this collection. What formerly had been the telling detail for Cheever has, in these late stories, become a mannerism. (Would any woman *really* hang her diamonds out on the line to dry?) The eccentric actions in these rambling reminiscences have become almost Gothic: full chamberpots are thrown in husband's faces, husbands defecate in their wive's dresser drawers; daughters unwittingly murder their mothers. Moreover, in four of these twelve stories, Cheever's plots depend upon the meanest kind of trick for their denouement: a servant discerns the employer she has hated all her days is her mother; a man trying to proposition a woman on an airplane is actually her husband; etc.

Ah, but the title story! I can hear those say who already have read most of the reviews of ***The World of Apples.*** For it is said to be one of Cheever's best. Well, it is and it isn't. In its portrait of old Asa Bascomb, expatriate American poet comprised of ¾ Frost and ¼ Pound, Cheever has created a potentially remarkable character, and one quite different from his melancholy suburban husbands. Asa, whose poetry is said to contain "the pungency, diversity, color, and nostalgia of the apples of the Northern New England he had not seen for forty years," suddenly finds himself smitten by a compulsion for smut. He writes dirty limericks, ballads, finally nothing at all but dirty words. Fair enough. It is in his overnight conversion back to the pontifical Santa Claus of American poetry which strains credibility. Such rapid changes in character do, we know, sometimes occur in life. But life is, as someone said, stranger than fiction. As a cautionary tale for one man's search to recapture that which he has lost—in Asa's case, the capacity for spirituality—the story is ambitious. But ultimately lacks credibility. Just possibly the quick-change act which has become Cheever's stock-in-trade—the suburban housewife suddenly turned off-Broadway nude actress, the promising pianist who comes to hate music—has become affectation and self-imitation. ***The World of Apples*** is an enormously entertaining book, but it is a throwback to the somewhat trivial ***The Way Some People Live,*** rather than a companion volume to ***The Enormous Radio,*** which in retrospect is Cheever's best. (pp. 246-47)

Cheever at home with his dogs. © 1981 Thomas Victor.

Robert Phillips, in a review of "The World of Apples," in Commonweal, *Vol. XCIX, No. 9, November 30, 1973, pp. 245-47.*

ALFRED KAZIN (essay date 1973)

[A highly respected American literary critic, Kazin is well known for such essay collections as The Inmost Leaf *(1955),* Contemporaries *(1962), and particularly for* On Native Grounds *(1942), a study of American prose writing since the era of William Dean Howells. In the following excerpt from an equally acclaimed, more recent work, Kazin describes Cheever's short fiction as "social lament."]*

Cheever—Salinger and Updike were to be like him in this respect—began and somehow has remained a startlingly precocious, provocatively "youthful" writer. But unlike Salinger and Updike, he was to seem more identifiable with the rest of *The New Yorker,* just as his complaint about American life was more concrete and his fiction more expectable. His stories regularly became a form of social lament—writing never hard to take. What they said, and Cheever openly *said* it, was that America was still a dream, a fantasy; America did not look lived in, Americans were not really settled in. In their own minds they were still on their way to the Promised Land. In story after story Cheever's characters, guiltily, secretly disillusioned and disabused with their famous "way of life" (always something that could be put into words and therefore promised, advertised and demonstrated), suddenly acted out their inner subversion. They became "eccentrics," crazily swimming from pool to pool, good husbands who fell in love with the baby-sitter. Sometimes, like "Aunt Justina," they even died in the living room and could not be moved because of the health laws and restriction by the zoning law on any funeral parlors in the neighborhood.

Acting out one's loneliness, one's death wish—any sudden eccentricity embarrassing everybody in the neighborhood—these make for situation comedy. Life is turning one's "normal" self inside out at a party. The subject of Cheever's stories is regularly a situation that betrays the basic "unreality" of some character's life. It is a trying-out of freedom in the shape of the extreme, the unmentionable. Crossing the social line is one aspect of comedy, and Cheever demonstrates it by giving a social shape to the most insubstantial and private longings. Loneliness is the dirty little secret, a personal drive so urgent and confusing that it comes out a vice. But the pathetic escapade never lasts very long. We are not at home here, says Cheever. But there is no other place for us to feel that we are not at home.

In these terms the short story becomes not the compression of an actual defeat but the anecdote of a temporary crisis. The crisis is the trying-out of sin, escape, the abyss, and is described by Cheever with radiant attention: *there* is the only new world his characters ever reach. . . . The "country husband" in [the] most brilliant of Cheever's stories returns home to find that his brush with death is not of the slightest interest to his family, so he falls in love with the baby-sitter. He does not get very far with the baby-sitter, so he goes to a therapist who prescribes woodworking. The story ends derisively on the brainwashed husband who will no longer stray from home. But who cares about this fellow? It is Cheever's clever, showy handling of the husband's "craziness," sentence by sentence, that engages us. Each sentence is a miniature of Cheever's narrative style, and each sentence makes the point that Cheever is mastering his material, and comes back to the mystery of why, in this half-finished civilization, this most prosperous equitable and accomplished world, everyone should seem so disappointed. So there is no mastery in Cheever's story except Cheever's. It is Cheever one watches in the story, Cheever who moves us, literally, by the shape of his effort in every line, by the significance he gives to every inflection, and finally by the cruel lucidity he brings to this most prosperous, equitable and accomplished world as a breaking of the heart.

My deepest feeling about Cheever is that his marvelous brightness is an effort to cheer himself up. His is the only impressive energy in a perhaps too equitable and prosperous suburban world whose subject is internal depression, the Saturday night party, and the post-martini bitterness. Feeling alone is the air his characters breathe. Just as his characters have no feeling of achievement in their work, so they never collide with or have to fight a society which is actually America in allegory. All conflict is in the head. People just disappear, as from a party. . . . Cheever is such an accomplished performer of the short story that the foreshortening of effect has become second nature with him. There is the shortest possible bridge between cause and effect. *The New Yorker* column is still the inch of ivory on which he writes. (pp. 111-13)

Alfred Kazin, "Professional Observers: Cozzens to Updike," in his Bright Book of Life: American Novelists & Storytellers from Hemingway to Mailer, *Atlantic-Little, Brown, 1973, pp. 95-124.*

WILLIAM PEDEN (essay date 1975)

[Peden is an American critic who has written on the American short story and on such American historical figures as Thomas Jefferson and John Quincy Adams. In the following excerpt, he surveys Cheever's career as a short story writer from the publication of The Way Some People Live *to that of* The World of Apples.*]*

Much of the most important recent American short fiction has been in [the] province of the usual and the unexceptional. John Cheever, John O'Hara, Peter Taylor, and John Updike seem to me among the most representative of the many talented and perceptive writers who have for the most part concerned themselves with incidents in the lives of ordinary men and women in familiar or immediately recognizable situations, and have created a contemporary fiction of manners characterized by skill, urbanity, and insight.

Of these chroniclers of the unexceptional, perhaps the most distinguished is John Cheever. . . . [Many of the stories in his first collection, ***The Way Some People Live,***] are brief fictional anecdotes or narrative sketches about a few moments or hours in the lives of a character or a group. Typical are **"Summer Theatre,"** in which a group of amateur prima donnas displays higher than average pre-opening-night jitters; **"Problem No. 4,"** in which a draftee training in South Carolina concentrates more on his wife back in New York than on his lieutenant's earnest adjurations concerning a security mission; **"The Law of the Jungle,"** with its effective contrast between older and younger generations in pre-World War II New York; and **"The Peril in the Streets,"** essentially a monologue delivered by an unhappy drunk in the presence of a bartender and a draftee. Longer, somewhat more ambitious stories include **"Of Love: A Testimony,"** a restrained and melancholy description of a love affair doomed to failure.

Though some of the stories in ***The Way Some People Live*** border on the trivial, the collection on the whole is an impressive one, and indicates the direction the author's subsequent stories were to take. Cheever writes in a relaxed, seemingly casual but thoroughly disciplined manner; his general mood is a compound of skepticism, compassion, and wry humor; he is concerned with the complexities, tensions, and disappointments of life in a strictly contemporary world of little men and women, unheroic, unspectacular, unexceptional. Loneliness, perhaps the dominant mood of the short fiction of the forties, fifties, and early sixties, permeates the collection. (pp. 30-1)

[***The Enormous Radio and Other Stories***] was published ten years later, in 1953. It is unquestionably one of the major collections of the period. Gone are the occasional triviality and the sometimes studied informality of the earlier stories. With only isolated exceptions, Cheever has gained complete control of his medium; he is at all times and in all places on top of his materials. ***The Enormous Radio*** stories concern individuals similar to the people of his first collection, though they are often older and more mature—university graduates, World War II alumni, young businessmen on the way up or slightly older ones on the way down, and their anxious, frequently harried women. The scene is contemporary, usually in or around New York City. Cheever's subject matter continues to be the usual, but his treatment of it is far from commonplace. He is concerned with the loneliness that festers beneath the façade of apparently "happy" or "successful" individuals; he suggests the potential terror or violence inherent in the metropolitan apartment dweller's condition. Beneath the often placid, impeccably drawn surfaces of his stories there is a reservoir of excitement or unrest that is capable of erupting into violence; his well-mannered characters walk a tightrope that at any moment may break; the vast, shining city masks cruelty, injustice, and evil. (pp. 31-2)

Most of the people of ***The Enormous Radio*** stories are decent, respectable, fundamentally likable. Sometimes they win a temporary victory, like Ralph and Alice Whittemore of **"The Pot of Gold"**; only rarely do they become malignant, like Joan Harris of **"Torch Song,"** a "big, handsome girl" who leaves the Middle West to become a New York model. A modern vampire, Joan thrives on sickness and disaster, and well merits the cry of the man she helps destroy: "What kind of an obscenity are you that you can smell sickness and death the way you do?" For the most part the characters exist between these extremes, frightened and to all intents and purposes terribly alone, lost in a metropolitan no man's land from which most of the traditional guideposts have been removed; among the most memorable are the characters in **"The Season of Divorce," "The Summer Farmer," "The Superintendent,"** and, perhaps the best story Cheever has yet written, **"Goodbye, My Brother."**

Four of Cheever's pieces, written after the publication of ***The Enormous Radio,*** are included in *Stories: Jean Stafford, John*

Cheever, Daniel Fuchs, William Maxwell (1956). Except for **"The Bus to St. James's,"** with its account of the corrosive effect of big city mores and tensions, these stories display an extension of subject matter and theme and a considerably more leisurely technique than most of their predecessors. My own personal favorite, and I think the best of these stories, is **"The Day the Pig Fell into the Well,"** a warm-hearted and robust re-creation of the Nudd family at Whitebeach Camp in the Adirondacks. The story possesses a variety of character and incident more usually associated with the novella or the novel than with the short story; over this "chronicle of small disasters" hovers a kind of Indian summer warmth, as Cheever portrays the American equivalent of the English middle class with Galsworthian compassion and dislike, affection and irony. Almost as good are **"The National Pastime,"** part essay, part short story, a nostalgic re-creation of a New England boyhood, and the prizewinning **"The Country Husband,"** one of the best of Cheever's excursions into the suburbia, which was to furnish subject and theme for his next collection, ***The Housebreaker of Shady Hill.*** (pp. 33-4)

The title piece of the Shady Hill stories, with its mingling of humor, effective characterization, serious commentary, and suspense, is characteristic of the collection as a whole. (p. 34)

Except for the sadistic organization man of the merciless **"The Five-forty-eight,"** most of Cheever's nonheroes are essentially amiable men: one-time track star Cash Bentley, forty, who provides the climax for many a Saturday night Shady Hill party by hurdling sofas, tables, and firescreen; Francis Weed, who becomes infatuated with the Weed's babysitter but eventually, at the advice of a psychiatrist, finds solace through woodwork; Will Pym, whose only sin was marrying a flirtatious woman considerably younger than himself; and Charles Flint, "fugitive from the suburbs of all large cities" whose plea, written in his journal aboard ship, suggests the real villain of Cheever's world, Shady Hill itself, with its culture vultures, its inane activity, its joyless parties and meaningless love skirmishes, its pretentiousness and unending striving for status. (p. 35)

Like Johnny Hake or Charles Flint, some of these unheroic protagonists win a partial victory through love or by demonstrating a kind of courage or integrity; very rarely are they destroyed, like Cash Bentley. Most of the time they see things through; they muddle along, a little balder, a bit more short of breath, somewhat sadder today than they were yesterday. Sorrow and disappointment pervade the book: sadness for the loss of youth and love, for the gradual dimming of the dreams of the past, and for the nagging awareness of entrapment in an often comfortable present built upon an extremely flimsy moral foundation. Usually this is implicit within the narrative framework of character and incident; only rarely does Cheever indulge in commentary like that of the misunderstood child of **"The Sorrows of Gin"**: "the pitiful corruption of the adult world; how crude and frail it was, like a piece of worn burlap, patched with stupidities and mistakes, useless and ugly."

Cheever's fourth collection, ***Some People, Places, and Things That Will Not Appear in My Next Novel,*** contains **"The Death of Justina"** and **"Boy in Rome,"** which are among his best work; and even the slightest pieces in the book display Cheever's hallmarks, urbanity, wit, intelligence, and technical dexterity. As a whole, however, the book is a letdown, fatigued and written in an overcasual manner—at times almost a parody—of Cheever's earlier work. **"A Miscellany of Characters That Will Not Appear"** is a moving manifesto and declaration of intent, as much essay as short story. Among the clichés and bromides of character and incident that Cheever wishes to see eliminated from fiction—his own and that of his contemporaries—are "all scornful descriptions of American landscapes with ruined tenements, automobile dumps, polluted rivers . . . diseased elm trees . . . unclean motels, candle-lit tearooms, and streams paved with beer cans," all explicit descriptions of sexual commerce, all lushes, all parts for Marlon Brando, all homosexuals, all fake artistry. Cheever's exhortation, in spite of its levity of manner, is admirable; it would have more significance if it were not embedded in a collection that is the most uneven of Cheever's books, markedly inferior to ***The Enormous Radio*** and ***The Housebreaker of Shady Hill,*** and in some ways less impressive than ***The Way Some People Live.***

On the other hand, his fifth collection of short stories, ***The Brigadier and the Golf Widow*** . . . , is perhaps Cheever's best. Over the years. Cheever's narrative method loosened up considerably, became more varied, more flexible: he is as adept in a brief anecdotal episode involving a son's last meeting with his divorced father (**"Reunion"**) as he is in relatively traditional narratives of people and incidents (the title story or **"A Woman without a Country"** and several others), or pieces like **"The Seaside Houses"** or **"Just One More Time,"** which are essentially fictional essays in which narrative hardly exists. In the setting, too—past or present, actual or filtered through the narrator's memories—we find considerable variety; it ranges from such familiar Cheever territory as Manhattan (**"Reunion"**) to suburbia (in **"Metamorphoses,"** Bullet Park, the scene of his novel of the same name) to the small New England village of St. Botolph's (**"The Angel of the Bridge"**).

Several of these stories are as good as any that Cheever has ever written: the title story with its expert delineation of a country-club militarist—"Bomb Cuba! Bomb Berlin! Let's throw a little nuclear hardware at them"—and the "other woman," for whom, as for so many of the author's female characters, adultery is replacing bridge as the favorite national pastime; **"The Swimmer,"** one of the most conceptually interesting stories in the Cheever canon; though this story of Neddy Merrill's plan to "reach his home by water" hovers somewhat uneasily between realism and metaphor, it is nonetheless unforgettable; **"The Angel on the Bridge,"** memorable as much in the deft creation of the narrator's ice-skating-in-Rockefeller-Plaza mother, his brother, and the young hitchhiker he encounters as it is in the portrayal of the central character, who suddenly develops an obsessive fear of bridges; **"The Seaside Houses,"** a marvelous evocation of the influence of rented houses on those who own them and those who rent them, beautifully executed, with not a false word or jarring note until what seems to me an ending in which Cheever suddenly loses his touch; and **"The Music Lesson,"** too delicious to be summarized, perhaps the collection's most interesting variation of the tensions-of-marriage syndrome with which he has often concerned himself.

At the conclusion of **"Clementina"** the central character contemplates some of the recent events in her life: ". . . remembering the cold on her skin and the whiteness of the snow and the stealth of the wolves, she wondered why the good God had opened up so many choices and made life so strange and diverse." The last words can be applied to the author himself. With over a hundred successful stories behind him, Cheever has lost none of his zest, none of his wonderment in celebrating what he has termed "a world that lies spread out around us like a bewildering and stupendous dream."

The same can be said about Cheever's 1974 National Book Award fiction nominee, ***The World of Apples.*** **"The Jewels of the Cabots,"** a saga in miniature of life in St. Botolph's, is Cheever at his best, beautifully controlled, illuminated throughout by the effective juxtaposition of the trivial and the significant, the tragic and the comic. In the midst of the narrator's reminiscences of minor childhood experiences or recollections of love, adultery, and murder, we tend to remember most distinctly such asides and gratuitous comments as "when the ship sinks I will try to reach the life raft with an overhand and drown stylishly, whereas if I had used a Lower-Class sidestroke I would have lived forever."

Then there is the title story, a far remove from the world of St. Botolph's, a masterly portrait of an aging but very vigorous American poet in Italy. Or, in more familiar Cheever country, **"The Fourth Alarm,"** full of suburban *angst* and strain, growing out of a wife's sudden decision to perform in an off-Broadway skin show, or **"The Geometry of Love,"** in which the engineer protagonist is destroyed by the failure of his marriage.

The narrator of **"The Jewels of the Cabots"** comments that "Children die, beautiful women are mangled in automobile accidents, cruise ships founder, and men die lingering deaths in mines and submarines, but you will find none of this in my accounts." The statement is applicable to the body of Cheever's short stories. He is concerned with large contemporary and universal problems—hypocrisy, individual and societal idiocy, the absurdity of sham and pretentiousness, the need for love and understanding—but his approach to them is sophisticated, low-keyed, subtle. One of the most entertaining storytellers and one of the most perceptive and urbane commentators on the contemporary scene, Cheever is a wry observer of manners and customs, more saddened than amused by the foibles he depicts with such understanding and grace. And in spite of the failures of so many of his characters and the disruptions in their personal and professional lives, the overall effect, particularly of his more recent work, is anything but somber. In its entirety it is animated by the sense of wonder implicit in Clementina's previously quoted comment and in the author's statement in an interview a few years ago:

> I know almost no pleasure greater than having a piece of fiction draw together disparate incidents so that they relate to one another and confirm that feeling that life itself is a creative process, that one thing is put purposefully upon another, that what is lost in one encounter is replenished in the next, and that we possess some power to make sense of what takes place.

(pp. 35-9)

William Peden, "Metropolis, Village, and Suburbia: The Short Fiction of Manners," in his The American Short Story: Continuity and Change, 1940-1975, *revised edition, Houghton Mifflin Company, 1975, pp. 30-68.*

SAMUEL COALE (essay date 1977)

[*Coale is an American writer. In the following excerpt, he illustrates three aspects of Cheever's work—portraits of suburbia, darkness, and "lyric vision"—with discussions of a representative story for each: "The Country Husband," "The Swimmer," and "Goodbye, My Brother."*]

In his early sketches Cheever was very much the sharp observer of manners, the chronicler of urban and suburban social mores. For Cheever the suburban experience also created a specific attitude in its inhabitants, a point of view from which to observe and judge the rest of the world. It also, however, was to become a condition of the soul, a spiritual outlook or understanding that came to epitomize modern man's alienated yet sporadically hopeful state. It is this deeper or broader concern that the later Cheever stories explore, a vision that lies beyond mere social chronology. (pp. 11-12)

At first the plot of **"The Country Husband"** seems to be merely an assortment of random episodes. (p. 28)

There is a deeper, broader pattern of experience, however, revealed in **"The Country Husband."** Francis Weed's narrow escape from death jars his sense of life. The normal routines of his life, which he has taken for granted for so long, are suddenly interrupted, and he recognizes swiftly the true fragility and precariousness that all life embodies. He returns to the elegant suburban community of Shady Hill with a reawakened sense of his own uncertain mortality and observes everything around him in this new, sensitive manner. For one thing he realizes the very real beauty that Shady Hill can offer. . . . It is as if against the black backdrop of his own imminent death, the light of such a polished world must shine miraculously brighter.

At the same time Weed realizes that the beauty of such a scene precludes intimations of death. Its very elegance seems to cancel out or override any deeper concerns and fears, as if it were challenging the entire concept of death altogether. In such a place his recent experience must necessarily go untold. Yet he has passed through that ominous brush with death, and the world around him cannot appear to him in the same innocent manner, in the same self-satisfied and contented way, that it had before. His vision of life and death has been transformed.

The usual routine delights of Shady Hill—old Mr. Nixon yelling at the squirrels in his bird-feeding station, Donald Goslin's overtly sentimental and self-pitying rendition of Beethoven's Moonlight Sonata on his piano, the Mercer's black retriever, Jupiter, galloping around the neighborhood—do not delight Francis Weed on the evening of his return. At the Farquarsons' party he recognizes the maid whose hair had been cropped and sees in her an emblem of human dignity in its most naked and socially exposed moment. The memory deepens his own awareness of death, his own deepened regard for the human condition, but it seems suddenly out of place in the social comforts of Shady Hill. . . . Shady Hill appears to him suddenly as a refuge and retreat from reality, a false sanctuary that can regard such a desperate display of human dignity as only an unseemly impoliteness.

It is after this realization that Francis falls desperately in love with Anne Murchison, the baby sitter. "The image of the girl seemed to put him into a relationship to the world that was mysterious and enthralling," and he was "struck by the miraculous physicalness of everything." Her image invigorates his own renewed sense of life's beauty, renewed as it is also by his awareness of ever-present death. He has passed through a dark night of the soul and is emerging, however foolishly at the moment, into an exaggerated sense of life's offerings.

Francis's vision, however flawed and comic, focusing as it does upon the unenlightened baby sitter, does strike at the heart of that state of spiritual grace and purity that Cheever could not help but admire and celebrate. . . . Here may be the heart of Cheever's own vision of the world, a physical and spiritual moment of grace and beauty.

Francis Weed's romanticized view of his surroundings clashes with the realities of those surroundings. (pp. 29-32)

Gradually Francis cannot abide this growing abyss. He feels cut off from the world he once knew and loved and is unable to cross the border into his new romantic world of passionate delight. His decision to seek finally the advice of a psychiatrist shatters his private self-esteem, but he admits to Dr. Herzog that he is desperately in love.

The plot of the story leaps suddenly from Weed's declaration of love in Dr. Herzog's office to a glimpse of him at some point in the future. When last we see Francis Weed, all seems back to normal. Woodworking has provided the cure: "Francis finds some true consolation in the simple arithmetic involved and in the holy smell of new wood." The suburban routines—old Mr. Nixon's shouting, Goslin's sonata-playing, and Jupiter's rampaging—continue uninterrupted. In Francis's vision the suburban world itself is restored to a world filled anew with possibility and delight.

Francis Weed realizes the precariousness of life and of Shady Hill, that his suburban sanctuary may be more precarious than even life itself: "The village hangs, morally and economically, from a thread; but it hangs by its thread in the evening light." Shady Hill maintains its promise of a fragile beauty, no matter how unreal, precarious, and false it may appear to be at times. It may suggest escape and a false sanctuary, but it also is a realm of aesthetic delight and creature comforts.

Cheever recognized the constantly ambiguous character of his suburban landscape, and in the final lyric line of **"The Country Husband"** seemed to celebrate and comically castigate it at once: "Then it is dark; it is a night where kings in golden suits ride elephants over the mountains." Fantasy and promise, delusion and delight, balance each other in Cheever's vision of suburbia, the promise and delusion of permanent security, the fantasy and delight of beautiful comfort. Within that precarious balance the suburban landscape lies. (pp. 32-3)

Cheever's stories are filled with the carefully observed manners, emotions, and objects of the suburban landscape. These points of reference provide the stylistic texture, the realistic surface, of his fiction and suggest the themes of his work—middle-class uncertainties, an overall sense of loss and loneliness, a pervasive aura of guilt and self-indulgence. The style creates an urbane and skillful gloss or polish within which the zany absurdities of life can be viewed from a safe and careful distance. The effect achieved—a gleaming surface of carefully balanced and elegantly lucid sentences that make the world a tidier and more ordered place—even suggests a certain insulation on the writer's part.

In Cheever's darker tales objects often seem to overwhelm the characters' sense of well-being, as if these people were living in a strange and alien world of obstacles and mysteriously laid traps. Things suddenly appear threatening, disconnected from any meaningful pattern or experience. The atmosphere that surrounds them suggests a malevolent universe, unassimilated into man's desire for order and serenity. Cheever's manner of describing these objects reflects the spiritual rootlessness and unease, even fear, that his often aimless characters experience.

Characters themselves undergo strange transformations in Cheever's darker stories. The usual dispassionate tone of his style suggests a disinterested but sympathetic observer observing the habits and gestures of people he may know. The listlike shape of the prose suggests the manner in which these habits and routines are accomplished, one by one, carefully, decorously. Both tone and shape reveal the manners of the characters, the customs and ceremonies within which they lead their lives, and the kinds of customs and ceremonies they enact. When these customs are suddenly disrupted for no apparent reason, the fear of chaos threatens to overwhelm the characters' sensibility. A kind of demonic force or inexplicable terror seems to have abruptly shattered the superficial patina of their lives. (pp. 35-6)

One fine day Neddy Merrill [protagonist of **"The Swimmer"**] decides to swim from a friend's house to his own home eight miles away by way of the swimming pools in the area. (p. 43)

[When he eventually reaches home his] own house is dark, deserted, and locked up. No one has lived there for a long time.

The startling revelation of the deserted house sheds new light on the events that have preceded it. Neddy's celebration of suburbia has really been a reaching out for things already lost, for time already past. His voyage reveals not only the beauty of the landscape, as well as the self-righteous and snobbish social hierarchy of the place, but also his expulsion from it. Financial reverses of some kind have exiled him in some way. In returning to recapture that sense of place that is no longer his, he realizes that he is an outsider now. He has been expelled from that beneficent world, from its comfortable surroundings, and from the social regulations that go with it.

Where has he returned from? What has happened to him? Cheever only hinted at the personal disasters that have befallen him—no money, no family, the misfortunes to which the naked Mrs. Halloran has referred—but the stunning truth of these disasters at the end of the story undercuts totally Neddy's own self-gratifying celebration of the suburban existence. Money and position dominate that existence. Without them all beauty rings hollow there. Neddy is now a mere wanderer involved in a perpetual journey; as far as his relationship to suburbia is concerned, he can only look backwards.

The dark empty house signified not grace and comfort but loss and desolation, and from that perspective the brilliance and natural beauty of suburbia can only be the galling reminder of some lost paradise. It is a false paradise, however, based all too obviously on money and social position. Neddy can celebrate the water and the sunlight all he wants, but disconnected from that suburban realm, of which he had been a part, they are too easily overcome by thunder and the darkness of that closed deserted house.

The developing recognition on the reader's part that all is not what it seems with Neddy Merrill and his voyage is carefully established by Cheever as the story moves on from pool to pool. The casual, calm prose, reflecting Neddy's own mind, gradually darkens as Neddy's memory becomes suspect. Beneath that lucid, almost lyric prose style darker moments intrude—Neddy's loss of memory, Mrs. Halloran's warnings, the gathering thunder, the autumnal chill in the air. The story begins to take on a dreamlike effect, as though Neddy were trapped in some ongoing quest that can only lead to some dark and terrible revelation. Cheever carefully laid the trail toward the deserted house, so that when the reader arrives there, he is stunned at the transformation that takes place between his first impressions of Neddy Merrill and his final understanding.

In **"The Swimmer,"** Neddy Merrill has fallen from grace, but there is no restoration here. Suburbia may be limited in its moral scope and social pretensions, but outside its pale all remains darkness and dissolution. (pp. 45-7)

About being a writer of fiction, Cheever once said, "One has an impulse to bring glad tidings to someone. My sense of literature is a sense of giving, not a diminishment." This sense of giving glad tidings suggests the comic or good-humored aspects of Cheever's fiction. The curious episodes and patterns of our frenetic contemporary experience and the odd objects and cultural bric-a-brac of our disposable contemporary society have always fascinated him. They provide the materials for his fiction of manners, in which his characters are always observed in the social roles thrust upon them by the strict decorum of suburban living. Cheever created characters who were trapped in the often outrageous and bizarrely funny social demands of the suburban brave new world. All of this Cheever recorded meticulously in his even-tempered, pleasantly ironic, and understated style with the discerning but dispassionate eye of a camera.

The reader is always aware of Cheever's style, of the way in which he describes his characters' actions and dilemmas. People in his stories tend to be used as examples of a particular theme or situation, such as suburban social values, the moral pretensions of the affluent upper-middle-class, or the often eccentric happenings of chance that may occur unexpectedly to them during the most ordinary of days. His stories often suggest that he is more interested in the carefully contrived outlining of overall situations than in the representation and creation of well-rounded characters.

Cheever seemed more interested in viewing situations from the outside, from a detached and distanced point of view, than from the inside, from a particular character's personal point of view. Such detachment accounts for the comic or humorous aspects of his style: to watch an old lady slip on a banana peel may be funny from a distance; to experience that slip from the interior point of view of the old lady herself certainly would not be.

One of Cheever's essential stances as a writer is as an ironic observer of the world around him. He observes and describes behavior, not the depth of feeling that may accompany it. From this often witty and determinedly detached point of view, he does not attempt to penetrate the darker and desperate depths of life but eagerly delights in the absurdities and arcane episodes of life. Cheever may often appear to be skating on thin ice in many of his weaker stories, but he delights in the intricate and filagreed patterns and designs he can create on the smooth, clear surface of that ice. The shapes and patterns of these episodes delight him—the inversions, unexpected turns, transformations, reversals, ironic twists—and often the delight itself, generated by his gentle ironies, becomes the most memorable aspect of the stories.

In the best of Cheever's stories he seems to be celebrating his own decorative language and "glad tidings," even in the face of (or perhaps because of) certain death and chaos. The reader, because of the quiet beauties of the prose, becomes aware of the artist's encounter with experience and with the materials of contemporary society and realizes that even within the boundaries of our throw-away, no-deposit, no-return world, genuine moments of spiritual renewal and natural beauty can appear. At the heart of Cheever's "glad tidings" lie these beautiful moments, these lyrical instances of calm and renewed hope. These rare moments of spiritual transcendence coincide in and with the presence of natural beauty, and the graceful lyricism of Cheever's style created and celebrated such occasions. We might call this Cheever's lyric vision.

This momentary state of grace often created in Cheever's characters the experience of spiritual elevation and moral uplift. At these moments his prose expresses their and his own personal emotions and sentiments, in the lyric poet's accustomed manner, rather than merely recounting external events. Such lyricism moves beyond the comic stance of the stories and into the realm of celebration. These moments come as the culmination of an ordered existence within which the universe momentarily exists, not as a mad poetic ecstasy, not as a strange mystical illumination. They are, therefore, moral, for they carry with them the age-old virtues that Cheever as a man and as a writer believes in—order, compassion, virtue, kindness. In Cheever's eyes, these alone can redeem the comfortable suburban landscape from its own spiritual deadness and self-indulgence. (pp. 49-51)

The scene [of **"Goodbye, My Brother"**] is set at the Pommeroy family's summer place at Laud's Head, on an island off Massachusetts. The disruptive intruder on the otherwise happy Pommeroy reunion is the youngest brother, Lawrence, who has been away from them for several years. He is always observing the worst in everything and everyone around him. He reminds the narrator, his older brother, of a Puritan cleric because of his gloomy outlook and constant search for malevolent forces beneath the appearances of things. (p. 61)

His older brother is sick of [Lawrence's] constant depressed and depressing outlook and tells him that such prevailing pessimism is really a distortion of reality. In his anger the older brother strikes Lawrence on the back of the head with a root. Lawrence is not badly hurt, and the narrator binds his wound with his shirt. That evening Lawrence, full of self-pity and reproach, rails aginst his older brother's actions. Lawrence and his family (his wife and two children have come to the island with him to join in the family reunion) leave for the mainland in the morning.

The narrator on that morning after Lawrence has left observes keenly the beauty that the summer day has to offer. For him, this is the true reality of life, this almost lyric celebration of the natural beauty of the world around him. In his own mind he poetically links the aroma of the roses with the smell of strawberry jam. In the presence of such beauty, Lawrence's sad and gloomy vision appears false and unrealistic. . . . (pp. 61-2)

Lawrence clearly represents that New England Puritan outlook that the narrator is trying to overcome and discredit. The seemingly casual directness and deliberate urbanity of Cheever's style itself undercuts the darker seriousness of Lawrence's consciousness, portraying Lawrence's pessimistic outlook as ridiculous superstition when seen in the light of common day. When stated so baldly and simplistically, the Puritan ideas and observations on doom and mortality tend to wither and look downright silly.

The purity and gracefulness of Cheever's style capture that natural beauty of the summer's day. The narrator glories in going swimming in the sea, "as if swimming had the cleansing force claimed for baptism. . . . We would all go swimming and shed our animus in the cold water." The swim suggests an initiation rite that allows one to participate in such a lyric vision of beauty and serenity. It is the ceremony, the ritual, through which one must pass to share this vision. "The curative powers of the open sea," even though perhaps an "illusion of purification,'' work their magic on the narrator and on the reader. We are convinced of the reality of the narrator's celebration of natural beauty and of the unreality of Lawrence's morbid concerns.

Ritual is very important to the narrator. After he hits Lawrence on the head with the root and wishes him dead and buried, he adds, ''not buried but about to be buried, because I did not want to be denied ceremony and decorum in putting him away, in putting him out of my consciousness.'' The exorcism must be accomplished ceremoniously and decorously to have any meaning whatsoever. In essence, the style, with its reassuring rhythms and calmness, its rhetorical purities and grace notes, and its lucid observations of natural beauty, creates that sense of decorous ceremony.

On the day of Lawrence's departure the narrator describes the vision he sees at the side of the sea:

> The sea that morning was iridescent and dark. My wife and my sister were swimming—Diana and Helen—and I saw their uncovered heads, black and gold in the dark water. I saw them come out and I saw that they were naked, unshy, beautiful, and full of grace, and I watched the naked women walk out of the sea.

The final image, of course, suggests the rising of Venus from the sea. In Roman mythology Venus was the goddess of spring, rebirth, and love, and rose from the sea at birth. Cheever often uses many classical and Christian allusions and images in his stories. Their echoes add depth and resonance to his present scenes, as here the image of Venus rising from the sea broadens and strengthens the narrator's lyric vision as contrasted to Lawrence's image as a Puritan cleric.

The final image of natural beauty in **"Goodbye, My Brother,"** redolent as it is with the innocence of nakedness, the rich colors of black and gold, and the reassuring and almost hypnotically repetitive rhythms of ''I saw,'' creates and embodies Cheever's lyric vision. The lines create that moment, ''full of grace,'' and establish that spirit of renewal and redemption, of rejuvenation and rebirth, as suggested by the sea and the classical overtones, that underlies the full-bodied lyricism of Cheever's best stories. (pp. 62-4)

Samuel Coale, in his John Cheever, *Frederick Ungar Publishing Co., 1977, 130 p.*

JOHN CHEEVER (essay date 1978)

[*In the following excerpt from his preface to* The Stories of John Cheever, *Cheever describes his fictional world and reminisces about the composition of his stories.*]

Cheever (center) with fellow authors Yevgeny Yevtushenko and John Updike. © Nancy Crampton.

These stories [in ***The Stories of John Cheever***] seem at times to be stories of a long-lost world when the city of New York was still filled with a river light, when you heard the Benny Goodman quartets from a radio in the corner stationary store, and when almost everybody wore a hat. Here is the last of that generation of chain smokers who woke the world in the morning with their coughing, who used to get stoned at cocktail parties and perform obsolete dance steps like "the Cleveland Chicken," sail for Europe on ships, who were truly nostalgic for love and happiness, and whose gods were as ancient as yours and mine, whoever you are. The constants that I look for in this sometimes dated paraphernalia are a love of light and a determination to trace some moral chain of being. Calvin played no part at all in my religious education, but his presence seemed to abide in the barns of my childhood and to have left me with some undue bitterness. (pp. ix-x)

Any precise documentation of one's immaturity is embarrassing, and this I find from time to time in the stories, but this embarrassment is redeemed for me by the memories the stories hold for me of the women and men I have loved and the rooms and corridors and beaches where the stories were written. My favorite stories are those that were written in less than a week and that were often composed aloud. I remember exclaiming: "My name is Johnny Hake!" This was in the hallway of a house in Nantucket that we had been able to rent cheaply because of the delayed probating of a will. Coming out of the maid's room in another rented house I shouted to my wife: "This is a night when kings in golden mail ride their elephants over the mountains!" The forbearance of my family has been inestimable. It was under the canopy of a Fifty-ninth Street apartment house that I wrote, aloud, the closing of **"Goodbye, My Brother."** "Oh, what can you do with a man like that?" I asked, and closed by saying, "I watched the naked women walk out of the sea!" "You're talking to yourself, Mr. Cheever," the doorman said politely, and he too—correct, friendly, and content with his ten-dollar tip at Christmas—seems a figure from the enduring past. (pp. x-xi)

John Cheever, in a preface to his The Stories of John Cheever, *1978. Reprint by Ballantine Books, 1981, pp. ix-xi.*

ISA KAPP (essay date 1978)

[*Kapp comments on the somber outlook on life in Cheever's stories.*]

For three decades the legato Cheever prose has remained as urbane and tempting as an ad in the *New Yorker,* sharing with the magazine that has published nearly all his stories a zealous attention to surfaces, a scrupulous rendition of speech and, not the least of its attractions, a supercilious tone that separates its uncommon reader from the gaucheness and banality of common experience.

Cheever has been called the American Chekhov, and it is true that both writers have a ruminative manner, dwell wistfully on lost opportunities, and are masters at conjuring up a mood, an excitation of the nerves, a vapor of unstated emotion hanging in the air. But when they undertake their favorite identical subject, the seesaw between tranquility and disturbance in marriage, we see how enormous a role the accident of disposition plays in creating the hierarchy of art. Chekhov's plain and pliant responses make us feel that marital disharmony is only one aspect of life, part of the natural order of things, rather than an occasion for outrage. We sense the Russian writer's intuitive sympathy with all of his characters. Cheever's sympathies spring unaccountably back to the observer, as if he were personally affronted, violated in his finer sensibilities by the shabby tales he relates. His heroes and heroines are usually caught in a spirtual flagrante delicto, a bit awkward and pathetic as they come into view through a light frost of derision. (p. 16)

The affable husband of **"The Chimera"** brings his mate breakfast in bed, only to find her haggard-eyed, avowing "I cannot any longer endure being served . . . by a hairy man in white underwear." A reader may well wonder whether this would have seemed sufficient provoction to Chekhov, Henry James or even Fannie Hurst, but he will discover in [***The Stories of John Cheever***] stories with no motivation at all, like **"A Vision of the World."** . . . If Cheever is no analyst of motive, it may be because he regards the battle of the sexes as too ferocious for psychological interpretation, rooted instead in some primal biological antagonism or some malevolent caprice of the universe.

Can the author of all this domestic infelicity really believe, as he says in his Preface, that the constants he looks for are "a love of light and a determination to trace some moral chain of being"? [see excerpt dated 1978]. We have to suppose that he simply does not recognize his own saturnine bent of mind, his speedy susceptibility to the faintest intimations of discord, and to the sorrows of gin. He is like the narrator of **"The Seaside Houses,"** who hardly turns the key of his rented vacation home before he discerns from the dimness of a bulb that his landlord is parsimonious, and from the whiskey bottles in the piano bench that he is a secret drinker and an unhappy man.

Perhaps it is to make amends to himself and us for the disproportion in his focus that so many of Cheever's stories launch into lyrical transports when the human outlook is particularly grim. The hero of **"A Vision of the World,"** whose wife is perpetually sad, does a considerable amount of dreaming, and sits up in bed exclaiming: "'Valor! Love! Virtue! Compassion! Splendor! Kindness! Wisdom! Beauty!' The words seem to have the colors of the earth, and as I recite them I feel my hopefulness mount until I am contented and at peace with the night." A baffling transfiguration indeed, as is the final image in the story about poor Francis Weed trying to recover from his passion for the babysitter by taking up woodwork therapy: A black dog prances through the tomato vines and "Then it is dark; it is a night where kings in golden suits ride elephants over the mountains."

Despite the rhapsodic thrill of the language, it seems to me one of the least wholesome elements in Cheever's fiction that he so often juxtaposes the pleasing prospect of nature and the disagreeable one of men and women, and lurches so readily from cynicism to exaltation. He does much better when he comes to terms with the blackness in himself, which may be why *Falconer,* for all the abrasiveness of its cat slaughters and brutalities among prisoners, is a strong and plausible novel.

Similarly, because Cheever moves head-on into a harsh situation without either exaggerating or poeticizing it, **"Goodbye, My Brother,"** written early in his career, is one of his finest stories. It takes place in a big summer house on an island off the coast of Massachusetts, and is about a family reunion dampened by the arrival of the youngest brother, a censorious New England Savonarola who sees the worst in everyone. The narrative is garnished with evocative details, such as the shadow of the maid in a dark garden and the backgammon games after coffee; and for once the landscape—dunes, coarse grass, open sea—enhances rather than diverts us from the austere emotions.

A sense of humour can do wonders for a bilious outlook, and luckily Cheever is diverse enough a writer to give way more than once, in the midst of his disenchantments, to a comic phrase or notion. (pp. 16-17)

No unhappy ending can stop Cheever's spirits from soaring . . . once Italy enters the scene. Like himself, most of his fictional characters have traveled in closed circuits that go from the bar of Grand Central Station to the suburbs of New York and New England. In 1956 Cheever spent a year in Italy, and what an infusion of red blood and charm the change in setting gives to his writing! In the Italian stories—e.g. **"The Bella Lingua"** and **"The Duchess"**—the swimming pools and adulteries of Shady Hill are far behind him and Cheever turns into the most likeable of writers. He leans back, develops perspective, takes a robust interest in other people's lives. **"The Golden Age"** is a delightful memoir of an American television writer who rents a castle in Tuscany and is known in the vicinity as "il poeta." He is embarrassed because his situation comedy (Cheever once wrote scripts for *Life with Father*) is to be shown that night on Italian TV and he will, in this country of simple habits and high art, be exposed as a commercial hack, a harbinger of barbarism and vulgarity. But when the moon comes out he sees some figures ascending toward him. A little girl gives him flowers and the Mayor embraces him. "Oh, we thought, signore," the Mayor says, "that you were merely a poet."

In Italy Cheever grows more springy, outgoing and natural, and the melancholy fog of "pain and sweetness" lifts from his fiction. His lens to the world seems to be set at a more secure point, midway between triumph and disappointment. What an accomplishment it would have been if he could have added that comfortable frame of mind to the rest of his clear and elegant prose. (p. 17)

Isa Kapp, "The Cheerless World of John Cheever," in The New Leader, *Vol. LXI, No. 18, September 11, 1978. pp. 16-17.*

ROBERT TOWERS (essay date 1978)

[*Towers examines several aspects of* The Stories of John Cheever, *including the work's verisimilitude, its author's moral purpose, and his narrative technique.*]

For years many of us have gone around with bits and pieces of John Cheever stories lodged in our minds—oddities of character or situation, brief encounters, barely remembered passages of special poignancy or beauty. . . .

A reading of [***The Stories of John Cheever***] usefully corrected certain misconceptions of mine that had grown up over the years. Influenced no doubt by the popularity of **"The Swimmer"** and by the four novels, I had come to think of Cheever's work as far more surrealistic and bizarrely plotted than it turns out to be. Of the sixteen or so stories that seem to me clearly first-rate (a high percentage, given the size of the *oeuvre*), twelve are distinctly within the bounds of realism, observing the conventions of causality, chronology, and verisimilitude, with no untoward intrusions of the arbitrary or the fantastic.

Though Cheever disclaims a documentary purpose and (rightly) resents comparison to a social nit-picker like the later John O'Hara, his stories do have a powerful documentary interest—and why not? Documentation of the way we—or some of us—live now has been historically one of those enriching impurities of fiction that only a mad theorist would wish to filter out. Less grand than Auchincloss, subtler and cleverer than Marquand, infinitely more generous than O'Hara, Cheever has written better than anyone else of that little world which upper-middle-class Protestants have contrived to maintain. . . .

Of course, Cheever, for all his fascination with manners, has never been primarily a documentary writer. His response to experience is essentially that of an old-fashioned lyric poet. In his preface to the new collection, he writes, "The constants that I look for in this sometimes dated paraphernalia are a love of light and a determination to trace some moral chain of being" [see excerpt dated 1978]. While one might question Cheever's profundity as a moralist, there can be no doubt about his preoccupation with—and celebration of—the shifting powers of light. His stories are bathed in light, flooded with it; often his characters appear slightly drunk with it, their senses reeling.

Light, for Cheever, seems to have distinctly moral or religious properties. . . . Light seems to be associated with a blessing, with a tender maternal smile fleetingly experienced, with all that is clean, tender, and guiltless, with the barely glimpsed immanence of God within His creation. At times Cheever appears to soar like Shelley's skylark toward the source of light, a belated romantic beating his luminous wings in the void.

But while the lyric impulse sometimes leads him into a slight (and often endearing) silliness—"The light was like a blow, and the air smelled as if many wonderful girls had just wandered across the lawn"—he is for the most part a precisionist of the senses. Though his imagery of light has the strongest retinal impact, Cheever's evocation of color and texture and smell is also vivid and persistent. He shares with two very different writers, Lawrence and Faulkner, an extraordinary ability to fix the sensory quality of a particular moment, a particular place, and to make it function not as embellishment but as an essential element in the lives and moods of his characters. (p. 3)

The introduction of an element of the weird into a densely realistic setting is an old trick of Cheever's, going back to his beginnings as a storyteller. Nowhere does it work better than in **"The Enormous Radio."** . . . The social texture is every bit as thick and as accurately rendered as in any of the realistic stories; the husband's indictment of his wife, when at last the contagion spreads to the couple, is as grimly factual, as "class-specific," as if magic had nothing to do with the situation. The stories in which the two elements are successfully interwoven are among Cheever's most brilliant; they include not only the famous **"Torch Song"** and **"The Swimmer"** but also that superbly macabre piece, **"The Music Teacher,"** in which a husband, driven to despair by a chaotic household and regularly burned meals, resorts to an elderly piano teacher who has been recommended by a neighbor; she gives him a musical formula with which to tame his wife and then dies the ugly death of a witch. But on a re-reading they seem to me to veer toward slickness, to stand up less well than, say, a strongly felt and quietly impressive piece like **"The Summer's Farmer"** or **"The Bus to St. James's."**

Cheever is a writer whose faults have an unusually close connection to his strengths. The imaginative identification with the upper-middle class which allows him to depict their mores and dilemmas with such vivacity entails a narrowness of social range and a sentimental snobbery which can get the best of him when his guard is down. Unlike Faulkner, whose Snopeses and Bundrages are as lovingly rendered as his Compsons, Cheever is not at ease when he enters the thoughts and feelings of one of those retainers—usually an Irish-Catholic—who service the elevators and the doors of the East Side apartment houses. In

"Clancy in the Tower of Babel," "Christmas Is a Sad Season for the Poor," and **"The Superintendent,"** he settles for faintly embarrassing stereotypes of those workers while displaying his usual keenness of observation and sympathy for the apartment dwellers for whom they work. The absence of Jews in Cheever's New York world is striking; at times it seems a deliberate avoidance, as in **"O City of Broken Dreams,"** where a bus-driver-turned-playwright from Indiana is brought into a thicket of producers and theatrical agents of whom not even one has a Jewish name.

The most serious embarrassments occur when he attempts an identification with a really alien figure, as in **"Clementina,"** his story of a simple-hearted Italian girl who emigrates to America, or **"Artemis, the Honest Well-Digger,"** a late story in which he introduces a young digger of artesian wells to a sexually predatory matron of suburbia and then whisks him off on an implausible tour of Russia. His condescension to these characters is well meant, full of good will, and hard to swallow.

The snobbery is fairly innocent as snobberies go, attaching itself mostly to well-bred or even aristocratic ladies and causing little damage beyond a maudlin blurring of Cheever's usually sharp vision. (pp. 3-4)

Cheever's role as narrator is always obtrusive. He has, of course, never had any truck with the notion—once a dogma among certain academic critics—that an author should keep himself as invisible as possible, that he should show rather than tell. Cheever-as-narrator is regularly on stage, rejoicing in his own performance, commenting upon—often chatting about—his characters, dispatching them on missions, granting them reprieves or firmly settling their hash. At his most effective he can tell us things about a character with such authority that we never for a moment doubt that his comprehension is total, final. . . . He loves to generalize: "Walking in the city, we seldom turn and look back"—or: "It is true of even the best of us that if an observer can catch us boarding a train at a way station. . . ."

From these and a myriad other touches a composite image of Cheever-as-a-narrator emerges. . . . Cheever-as-a-narrator is a personable fellow—debonair, graceful, observant, and clever. His sympathies are volatile and warm. He is a good host—one who likes to entertain, to amuse, to turn a phrase. He is also a bit of a show-off, an exhibitionist. Beneath the gaiety and charm of his discourse, deep strains of melancholy and disappointment run. He is not, however, a cynic. Nor is he a profound moralist. He has no fundamental quarrel with the family or society as they now exist. For the ills of the flesh and spirit his sovereign remedy is the repeated application of love, love, love. . . .

Thanks to this volume, the best of Cheever's stories are now spread glitteringly before us. In our renewed pleasure in these, we can let the others—the trivial and the miscalculated—recede to their proper place. Cheever's accomplishment in his exacting art is proportionally large, as solid as it is brilliant, and likely to endure—a solemn thing to say (however true) of a writer who has so often flaunted the banner of devil-may-care. (p. 4)

Robert Towers, "Light Touch," in The New York Review of Books, *Vol. XXV, No. 17, November 9, 1978, pp. 3-4.*

LYNNE WALDELAND (essay date 1979)

[In the following excerpt from her full-length biographical and critical study of Cheever, Waldeland compares Cheever with other American authors and summarizes his career and talent.]

Cheever's career is varied enough that it is possible to see links between him and a number of American writers and movements. It seems to me, however, that beneath the realistic surface of most of his novels and stories, beneath the careful delineation of manners, a representational American milieu, and historical and cultural facts, Cheever is basically a romantic and a moralist. He is a romantic in that his interest finally is in the individual. However much he may write about behavior in New England small towns, Eastern big cities, and the American suburb, he is really most concerned about the reverberations of that behavior in the individual human soul. And he is a moralist in that despite the comic texture of his works, the toleration for all manner of human foibles, and the general affirmation which most of his works finally reach, he is always aware of right and wrong, better and worse, life-enhancing and life-diminishing qualities both in people and in the world which can thwart the full humanity of his characters. In these qualities he seems most to resemble James and Fitzgerald. He is like James in his understanding of the interplay between the individual and society, between inner morality and outer manner, and because he can successfully capture that connection in fiction. He is like Fitzgerald in the lyrical elegance of his style and in his use of that style to contain the pain of the perception that the world often frustrates and even destroys the best possibilities of human beings. There is also a little echo of Hawthorne in Cheever's work in his New England moral toughness, his wish that people reach their best human potential despite a lack of cooperation by society. It seems to me that Cheever in his own time has no close peer. He is less naively romantic than Salinger, less simply a chronicler of manners than Auchincloss, less egocentric than Mailer, less narrowly focused than Malamud or Roth, less gimmicky than Vonnegut. His combination of attention to the individual and awareness of the facts and the power of society connect him more with classic American authors like Hawthorne, James, and Fitzgerald; and despite his own New England background and East Coast life-style, he has resisted the post-World War II tendency of American writers to divert American fiction toward a narrow exploration of their own individual religious, racial, or geographical roots. (pp. 142-43)

The single most remarkable aspect of Cheever's career so far is, I think, the beauty and consistency of his style. It is lyrical without being flowery; it is precise without being coldly analytical. But in good fiction, style is intrinsic rather than an extra element troweled on over plot, character, and setting; it convinces us that it proceeds inevitably from the inner being of the writer. When we are thus convinced, we feel confident in developing a sense of the writer from the quality and nature of the style. I think one can safely, accurately come to just such a sense of John Cheever. . . . Cheever's great contribution to contemporary American literature is that when he brings his formidable gifts of observation and language to bear upon life in our time, he doesn't diminsh it but instead leaves us with a sense of increased possibility and even, at times, joy. (pp. 144-45)

Lynne Waldeland, in her John Cheever, *Twayne Publishers, 1979, 160 p.*

JOHN UPDIKE (essay date 1982)

[Considered a perceptive observer of the human condition and an extraordinary stylist, Updike is a distinguished American man of letters. Best known for such novels as Rabbit Run *(1960) and* Rabbit Is Rich *(1981), he is, like Cheever, a chronicler of life in*

Protestant, upper-middle-class America. Updike also shares Cheever's affiliation with the New Yorker, *which regularly publishes Updike's fiction, criticism, and poetry. In the following excerpt from a review that originally appeared in the* New Yorker *in 1982, Updike discusses* Oh What a Paradise It Seems, *concentrating on the elements of transcendentalism in the novella and Cheever's pervasive use of water imagery.*]

Water as well as light has figured in John Cheever's work as an essence palpable, as a manifestation of the natural good that bubbles and pours and glints around us. The first short story that he saw fit to include in [***The Stories of John Cheever***], **"Goodbye, My Brother,"** dissolves its murderous fraternal tensions in the beatific vision of two women walking naked out of the "iridescent and dark" sea, and one of the most recent tells of **"Artemis, the Honest Well Digger"**: water is Artemis's "livelihood as well as his passion," and he reflects, "Man was largely water. Water was man. Water was love." In between, **"The Swimmer"** traverses eight miles of swimming pools while his life ebbs away, and poor Nerissa Peranger is turned *into* a swimming pool, and many a man and woman lie awake with the seductive sound of rain in their ears. Cheever has called his latest book, ***Oh What a Paradise It Seems,*** an "ecological romance;" the main action traces the rapid (and what in Cheever's fiction is not rapid?) alteration of a body of water called Beasley's Pond, "shaped like a bent arm," from a splendid skating spot and piece of untroubled nature into a landfill zone—"a heap of rubbish, topped by a dead dog"—and, thanks to some swift and obscure political and technological heroics, back again to its former paradisiacal condition. (p. 189)

[The hero of ***Oh What a Paradise It Seems***] is Lemuel Sears, an "Old man but not yet infirm," with a smooth skater's stroke and a young man's erotic susceptibility. His battle in behalf of Beasley's Pond runs parallel with the ups and downs of his romance with one Renée Herndon, a younger if not girlish woman encountered in a line at a bank teller's window. When she, wanton nymph that she is, halts the gush of her favors, Sears turns for consolation, so fluid is his own sexual nature, to a homosexual fling with her elevator operator. These events take place in New York City and the not far-off but old-fashioned hamlet of Janice. In Janice, we witness some crisp suburban comedy involving the Salazzos and the Logans, neighbors on Hitching Post Lane with differing opinions upon not only land use but wind chimes and proper deportment in supermarket checkout lines. In addition to these characters, vivid and lovable as mayflies as they twirl for their moment in the sunshine, there is an unusually strong narrator's voice that promises us at the outset "a story to be read in bed in an old house on a rainy night" and presents us throughout with friendly *discursi* on matters as unexpected as Balkan villages, the archeology of fortresses and market-places, the evolution of the ice skate, the democratization of Freudian parlance, the antiquity and ubiquity of fried food, the possibility of a world wherein even the tenderest intentions will be communicated by means of signal lights on automobiles, and the decline of queues and caste sense—all of which, briskly interposed, enhance without hindering the flow of this tumbling, plashing little narrative, which chance or ingenious design has caused to be printed upon exactly one hundred pages.

The book is too darting, too gaudy in its deployment of artifice and aside, too disarmingly personal in its voice, to be saddled with the label of novel or novella; it is a parable and a tall tale—both sub-genres squarely within the Judeo-Christian tradition, North American branch. Cheever has lately taken the mantle of that tradition ever more comfortably upon his shoulders, and now unabashedly assumes the accents of a seer. Indeed, Sears, his hero, meets a seeress, in one of the most tangential episodes of this brief but wide-ranging narrative. It happened years ago, in Eastern Europe. The prophetess occupied a cave beneath an extinct volcano. Sears's official interpreter was terrified of encountering this fabled person, but Sears was "either too tired or too drunk or too solaced by the beauty of the farmland" to feel anxious. And, when they did meet, the seeress, who was prosaically middle-aged and wore nothing more esoteric than a clean cotton dress, felt his wallet (she was blind) and began to smile, began to laugh, and announced, *"La grande poésie de la vie."* Then Sears laughed, and they embraced, and parted still laughing. Ever more boldly the celebrant of the grand poetry of life, Cheever, once a taut and mordant chronicler of urban and suburban disappointments, now speaks in the cranky, granular, impulsive, confessional style of our native wise men and exhorters since Emerson. The pitch of his final page is positively Transcendental:

> The thought of stars contributed to the power of his feeling. What moved him was a sense of those worlds around us, our knowledge however imperfect of their nature, our sense of their possessing some grain of our past and of our lives to come. It was that most powerful sense of how singular, in the vastness of creation, is the richness of our opportunity. The sense of that hour was of an exquisite privilege, the great benefice of living here and renewing ourselves with love. What a paradise it seemed!

If such root affirmations ring, in this late age of median strips and polluted ponds, with a certain deliberate and wry gallantry, that, too, is accommodated in the tale—in the burlesque of its consumerism, the ogreish farce of its politics, the chemical pranks of its natural resurrection. The smooth phraseology of praise and idyll are suddenly roughened by a heartfelt qualification: Sears, remembering the "utter delight of loving" his lost Nereid, Renée, then admits that this utter delight "seemed, in his case, to involve some clumsiness, as if he carried a heavy trunk up a staircase with a turning." Cheever's instinctive belief in the purity and glory of Creation brings with it an inevitable sensitivity to corruption; like Hawthorne, he is a poet of the poisoned. His American landscape is dotted with tiny atrocities—back-yard charcoal braziers and "stand-up" swimming pools and domestic architecture that "was all happy ending" and in whose sad living rooms people pass one another "a box of crackers that the label promised would stimulate conversation." The tinge of snobbishness in his dismay is redeemed by the generosity with which Cheever feels, like an American of a century and a half ago, the wonder of this land of promises.

He loves nature—light, water, human love. . . . Were Cheever less a New Englander than he is, with the breath of Thoreau and Emily Dickinson in his own lovely quick light phrasing, he might fail to convince us that a real glory shines through his transparent inventions. The gap in *Falconer* between the circumstantial prison and the spiritual adventure that it allegorized certainly took a reader's indulgence to bridge. But in ***Oh What a Paradise It Seems*** there are no more gaps than between the blades of a spinning pinwheel. All is fabulous from the start; all is fancy, praise, and rue, seamlessly. Janice, that oddly named village, receives postcards from all the territories that Cheever's imagination has been happy in—Italy,

Eastern Europe, the St. Botolph's of the Wapshot chronicles, and the Shady Hill and Bullet Park where America's dream of space and plenty and domestic bliss has come to so fragmentary a realization. The paradisiacal elixir has a chalky taste but in this testament survives its contaminants and is served up sparkling. (pp. 189-90, 193)

John Updike, "On Such a Beautiful Green Little Planet," in his Hugging the Shore: Essays and Criticism, *Alfred A. Knopf, 1983, pp. 291-99.*

RICHARD H. RUPP (essay date 1982)

[*Rupp surveys the thematic evolution of* The Stories of John Cheever, *categorizing the stories by setting and composition date.*]

In the 1978 edition of his collected short fiction [***The Stories of John Cheever***], John Cheever arranged the sixty-one stories chronologically, and it makes sense to read them that way. These stories span a generation of writing, from the mid-forties to the early seventies. . . . They chronicle the social, spiritual, and geographical mobility of Cheever's people—the eastern Protestant middle class—and they chronicle loss and change. . . . (p. 231)

Cheever's stories dramatize rites of passage, the ceremonies of youth and middle age, a life style that changes and vanishes to be succeded by another. They chronicle the ephemeral and the eternal in American life—what has passed, what is passing, what is to come. The places are New York City, suburbia (apotheosized in innocent Shady Hill and its sinister neighbor, Bullet Park), Rome, and Italy, St. Botolphs and the Massachusetts islands. As he traces the passions and wanderings of his fellow Americans, Cheever gives us a comprehensive, compassionate account of the way some people live.

John Cheever is a middle-class writer who describes middle-class experience: the relocation from urban origins to suburban disenchantment. Cheever's heroes are less individuals than types or versions of the same experience; his innocents are either born into or move into a specious Eden. Discovering there a corruption both personal and social, they struggle toward some spiritual reintegration, usually through marriage and the family. Frequently the Cheever hero faces up to some universal human quirk or ailment and accepts himself and his life as he finds it. His experience is illustrative, representative, and communal—for Cheever is writing, as Emerson wrote, of representative men. His voice as he speaks to us—and he characteristically comments on the situations he creates—is wry, compassionate, and detached, that of the sympathetic observer.

Much of the appeal in these stories derives from Cheever's perceived relationship with his readers. Like another great New Yorker before him [Walt Whitman], he speaks of Americans and for them. . . . (pp. 231-32)

Although he claims to be a provincial writer in his Preface to these stories. Cheever treats America's soul as well as it suburbs. Wherever Americans have grown up in cities and fled to the uneasy Edens outside them, there stands John Cheever, like Walt Whitman.

His audience, then, is not restricted to New Yorkers and *New Yorker* readers; he speaks to civilized Americans everywhere. As Cheever posits him, the reader is intimately familiar with America's upward mobility and footloose life style. Like his characters, Cheever's reader was born in a small town, has spent some of his working life in a big city, and now lives in a suburb. He has traveled to Europe—preferably by boat—is married, male, middle-aged, commutes to work by train, belongs to the Episcopal Church, drinks too much; vexed by his own sexuality he wanders an erratic path between fidelity and infidelity (but always back again); is literate, bemused, ironic, and nostalgic for the better time and place that never was. Not since J. D. Salinger discovered American teenagers has a writer so identified and identified with his audience. At his best, Cheever's reader shares the community of his fellow sufferers on the five-forty-eight.

Finally, the ideal reader, like the characters, is himself capable of violence, insanity, even cruelty to animals. He is deterred from the abyss of isolation and egoism only by the bizarre, the unique, the unexpected in his own character. He is strengthened if at all by an appetite for life, an eye for its pied beauty, a taste for the eccentric. Cheever's narrator, like a slightly drunken celebrant, weaves towards the high altar of American innocence to offer there a sacrifice of praise for the goodness and vitality of this life, here and now; for, at heart, Cheever knows his America to be decent, pious, loving, committed to the eternal verities of love, family, and community.

His stance is basically religious and conservative. He has inverted the transcendentalism of his spiritual forbears, Hawthorne and Emerson, opting instead for the immanence of salvation in the here and now, for the community of love in the temple of Mammon. A brief look at some of these stories will, I hope, bear out these extravagant contentions.

The stories invite classification by setting. The New York stories seem to fall into two groups, early and late. In the earlier group, Cheever's characters live in Manhattan apartment buildings—vertical conclaves where community is at best difficult. In the later group, New York is no longer a place to live but only an arena for bizarre actions. The two suburbs, Shady Hill and Bullet Park, are similarly demarcated between apparent community and grim isolation. Rome and Italy offer interesting variations on the theme of American isolation, while St. Botolphs and its offshore islands chronicle the strains inherent even in real communities.

To begin with the "early" New York stories, let us consider [**"The Enormous Radio"** and **"Torch Song"**]. . . . Cheever knows and gives us the rituals of the elevator and the lobby, the quirks of diverse tenants, the balkiness of machinery. Typically, Cheever finds a simple, natural action and enlarges it to absurd dimensions for both comic and pathetic effects. A major source of his comic effects can be found in what Henri Bergson has called "mechanical inelasticity." Whenever humans begin to act like simple machines, we laugh at them.

"The Enormous Radio," for instance, shows the effect of a strange, balky machine on a susceptible, lonely housewife, who becomes in effect its human extension. Irene Westcott listens with increasing horror and fascination to the domestic affairs of her neighbors, thereby bringing the sorrows of the world into her marriage to Jim. . . . (pp. 232-33)

From external to internal sorrow is only a short, inevitable step. Accusations about mishandled money, stolen jewels, and an aborted child fly between the Westcotts while the newscaster on the enormous radio speaks in noncommittal tones about a railroad disaster in Tokyo and a fire in a Buffalo hospital, extinguished by nuns. Like Young Goodman Brown, the Westcotts have lost an illusory faith and must begin again to find a real one with each other. Cheever enlarges on this catalogue of woes to incorporate the Westcotts in the community of suffering. (p. 233)

"Torch Song" . . . speaks to the perverse innocence of American dreams. The setting is New York during the late thirties and forties. Jack Lorey and Joan Harris "came from the same city in Ohio and had reached New York at about the same time in the middle thirties."

Over the years Joan drifts in and out of Jack's life as they drift from one job and one lover to another. They meet at odd and unexpected moments. Joan is always with a different man—first a drug-addicted Swedish count, then with a brutal German, then with a succession of drunken and doomed men: with Philip, an RAF pilot; with Pete, an aspiring ad man; with Ralph, a music-loving heart specialist; with Stephen, an English anthropologist; with Stanley, who kept a filthy room in Chelsea. Finally, after the war, a failed marriage, and failing health, Jack meets Joan again, dressed always in black. Sweet, patient, innocent as always, the Black Widow has come for him at last, and her visit frightens him out of self-pity and lassitude. . . . The pattern of mechanical inelasticity this time has gone beyond the comic to the grotesque. Joan Harris, like Chekhov's Darling, drains the life from her lovers. Joan's affinity for doomed Europeans may suggest a wider significance as well. This is Cheever's parable of World War II, and Joan is the Angel of Death. (p. 234)

The later New York stories focus less on apartment living than on experiences in the city at large. New York in the fifties and sixties has become less a place to live than a place to make a living. Put simply, New York is now the stage for some human action, ridiculous, mythical, or strange, which dramatizes the plight of deracinated man. . . .

[**"The Angel of the Bridge"**] describes a miraculous action, and miracle is never far from the realistic surface of Cheever's stories. The narrator's family, transplanted from St. Botolphs, Massachusetts, consists of the narrator's seventy-eight-year-old mother who ice skates at Rockefeller Center and fears airplanes, his older brother, who fears elevators, and himself, seemingly normal. The narrator, who may be Coverly Wapshot, develops acute pontophobia, however, while crossing the George Washington Bridge in a thunderstorm. He imagines the bridge collapsing and hurling "the long lines of Sunday traffic into the dark waters below us." (p. 235)

The bridge symbolizes a disaffection of man for his creations, a disaffection so deep as to induce paralysis. The city of man is almost Augustinian in its iniquity. With its airplanes, its elevators, its bridges, the city has become literally oppressive and threatening.

The miracle occurs on the approaches to the Tappan Zee Bridge. He thinks he might negotiate something at water level, but as he approaches the bridge, he cannot go through with it. He pulls off to the side, utterly distraught, and imagines himself in a psychiatric ward, "screaming that the bridges, all the bridges in the world, were falling down." Then she appears at the door, this nameless angel of the bridge, a young girl with long, straight brown hair, a cardboard suitcase, and a harp, hitch-hiking. As they start up again, she plays the harp and sings "The Riddle Song" ("I gave my love a cherry. . . .")

> She sang me across a bridge that seemed to be an astonishingly sensible, durable, and even beautiful construction designed by intelligent men to simplify my travels, and the water of the Hudson below us was charming and tranquil. It all came back—blue-sky courage, the high spirits of lustiness, an ecstatic sereneness. Her song ended as we got to the toll station on the east bank, and she thanked me, said good-bye, and got out of the car.

The miracle is not the heavenly being but the earthly touch, the sense of community, however fleeting, that makes the girl's song an act of ritual praise for creation. The story stands in dramatic contrast to Joan Harris's torch song. It instances the immanence of God's love for the narrator and enables him to relate to his terrified brother and mother. Things haven't changed—he has. He can accept his family's frailties without condemning them. "My brother is still afraid of elevators, and my mother, although she's grown quite stiff, still goes around and around and around on the ice." (p. 236)

In . . . **"The Fourth Alarm,"** a man is forced to choose between his identity and his wife. The protagonist, a patient, decent, middle-aged suburbanite, must come to terms with his stage-struck wife, Bertha, who has landed a starring role in the all-nude review, *Ozamanidas II*.

At the climax of the show—one hesitates to use the word—the cast invites all the audience to shed their clothes and join them on stage in a group grope. At first the narrator cooperates, but he carries his wallet, wristwatch, and keys with him towards the stage. One actor, then the whole cast encourage him to "put down his lendings." But to do so would involve a surrender, not just of money and the certainty of getting home to the suburbs, but of his very identity. . . . And so he puts his clothes on and goes home.

In contrast to the Sutton Place stories of New York at mid-century, these [stories] give us vignettes of a fantastic, unlivable environment. If we are to take the action of **"The Fourth Alarm"** as illustrative, the best a sane man can manage is a strategic withdrawal. New York is no longer habitable.

Although he began his writing career in the thirties with stories about New York life, Cheever first reached national prominence in the late fifties and early sixties with the Wapshot novels. By the time he won the National Book Award, he was writing of Shady Hill, an idealized Westchester suburb. A consideration of his two suburban settings. Shady Hill and Bullet Park, reveals the same kind of contrasts observable in his New York stories—a gradual darkening of vision as the possibilities of full, authentic life in contemporary America seem to lessen. At the same time, his outlook has become more clearly and specifically religious.

Shady Hill first appears in **"O Youth and Beauty!"** Once again Cheever employs the pattern of the simple action, repeated to the level of absurdity, which so often characterizes his comic imagination in these stories. The protagonist, Cash Bentley, feels compelled to defend his youth and beauty at the tag end of cocktail parties. While Trace Bearden fires his starter's gun out the window, Cash runs the high hurdles over the living room furniture: "There was not a piece of furniture in Shady Hill that Cash could not take in his stride. The race ended with cheers, and presently the party would break up."

The Bentleys cling precariously to their suburban life; beset with unpaid bills and high expenses at the country club, Cash drinks too much and quarrels with Louise, his wife. The obstacle races are his tenacious claim on a receding youth. At the Farquarsons, Cash catches his foot on a piece of furniture

Dust jacket of Cheever's acclaimed 1978 collection, The Stories of John Cheever. *Copyright © 1978 by John Cheever. Reproduced by permission of Alfred A. Knopf, Inc.*

and falls, gashing his head and breaking his leg. His fall is also a fall from grace. Once popular, Cash now sits at home beside Louise, "who is sewing elastic into the children's underpants." Cash begins to turn jealous of young lovers, grows moody, drinks too much. His youth and beauty are passing.

Then one night the Bentleys return to the country club with the Beardens; after too many drinks Cash begins the obstacle race once more. He clears all the furniture in the lounge but collapses on the floor at the other end. His public appearances are over—but not his career. The next night, at home, he drags the furniture into the shape of the race course. Louise is called upon to fire the starter's pistol, which she has never done before.

> "Hurry up," he said, "I can't wait all night."
>
> He had forgotten to tell her about the safety, and when she pulled the trigger nothing happened.
>
> "It's that little lever," he said. "Press that little lever." Then, in his impatience, he hurdled the sofa anyhow.
>
> The pistol went off and Louise got him in mid-air. She shot him dead. . . .

This passionate clinging to a passing stage of life is fatal. Cheever seems to be re-writing "The Short Happy Life of Francis Macomber" as a cautionary tale for aging suburbanites. (pp. 237-39)

"The Housebreaker of Shady Hill" suggests that not all the denizens of the town are . . . spiritually dark, however, Johnny Hake, for one thing, knows where he was born and raised, where he belongs, and despite his frailty under financial pressure, what he believes in. He is tested early. When called upon to fire the boss's front man, he cannot bring himself to do it. His visit to the bedside of Gil Bucknam is warning enough for the man, however; as soon as Bucknam pulls himself together, he fires Johnny. Johnny strikes out on his own, does miserably at soliciting sales over the phone, and resorts to stealing nine hundred dollars from a sleeping neighbor's trousers. . . .

Johnny Hake has broken "all the unwritten laws that hold a community together." With the stolen money he is able to pay his bills—bills were smaller in those days—but the financial reprieve has left him spiritually bankrupt. Once his eyes are darkened, however, he sees theft everywhere—a customer takes a thirty-five cent tip from a lunch counter; a friend offers to "steal" money from a trusting customer; he remembers stealing fifty dollars from his father's pocket in a New York hotel room; the newspapers are suddenly replete with accounts of international thefts and swindles. Like Irene Westcott and Goodman Brown before him, Johnny Hake has fallen from innocence.

But he will not succumb to self-pity. He echoes one of the cardinal tenets in Cheever's code of conduct, the need to seize one's identity and to live it out regardless of consequences: "If there is anybody I detest, it is weak-minded sentimentalists—all those melancholy people who, out of an excess of sympathy for others, miss the thrill of their own essence and drift through life without identity, like a human fog, feeling sorry for everyone."

That identity, even though it includes housebreaking, stands him in good stead. Ultimately the old man at Parablendum dies, and Gil Bucknam calls him back to his job. He takes an advance on his salary, repays the Warburtons (a Jamesian echo), and whistles his way back home past the Shady Hill police. Thus corporate bonds are only a special form of communal bonds; Johnny's bonds with Parablendum restore him to financial and spiritual health. The essential principle here and throughout Cheever's stories is belief in self-worth and respect for the communal obligation which derives from that belief. (pp. 240-41)

If innocence, forgiveness, and community serve to support the continuity of life in Shady Hill, no such meliorating forces are at work in Bullet Park. Man is isolated, unsupported by marital love, family, or a strong community. Even the climate seems to have turned colder. Bullet Park is, first of all, the setting for Cheever's third novel. The story of Mr. Hammer and Mr. Nailles recapitulates the sacrifice of Isaac and the crucifixion of Christ. Bullet Park witnesses no resurrection, however; it is a grim place which deprives its inhabitants of that community they need to come fully alive.

The place has its comic moments, of course. The narrator of **"The Ocean"** suspects that his wife is putting pesticide on his cutlets. He has lost his job after successfully negotiating a takeover by a larger company. His daughter Flora has dropped out of college and lives in Greenwich Village with her unemployed boyfriend, pasting costly butterflies on a skeleton. The narrator seeks refuge in dreams and memories. He remember's Cora's beauty when he married her. He wakes beside her at three in the morning, seized by the desire to love all those who have slighted him. He sees a green meadow and a sparkling stream, thatched-roof cottages and a square Saxon church tower. He looks for his wife and daughter in the village but cannot find them. He falls into a deep sleep on the grass, like Piers Plowman. Perhaps he will wake to love, but the prospects are not promising. (p. 242)

"Another Story" plays a variation on the theme of bare, unaccommodated man. The narrator has befriended a threadbare Italian prince, Marcantonio Parlapiano ("Mark Anthony, speak softly"), who generally goes by "Boobee." Boobee is transferred by his company from Verona to New York with his American wife, Grace. Boobee has a language problem, though, and doesn't adapt well to American ways. While his neighbors speak of balky machines (rotary lawn mowers) and of chemical fertilizers, Boobee "praises the beauty of the landscape, the immaculateness of American women, and the pragmatism of American politics, and spoke of the horrors of a war with China. He kissed me goodbye on Madison Avenue. I think no one was looking."

The medium of Boobee's confusion is language. He has not and seemingly cannot learn the language of the tribe. To compound his confusion, Grace decides to take up opera. Boobee thinks she is mad but finds no solace from the narrator, who tells him that American husbands do not complain about their wives. Shortly after this scene, Boobee is injured in an automobile accident. When the narrator goes to see him in the hospital, he learns that Boobee and Grace are separated. He cries as he recounts the ultimate indignity: Grace wants him to change his name. Rather than do that, he decides to return to Verona, where unhappy love is a long tradition.

The coda offers a parallel experience. The narrator runs into a friend in Moscow. At the airport he hears a story about the friend's ex-wife, who found her identity as a terminal announcer at Newark Airport. Unfortunately she brings the language and intonation of the terminal home to the dinner table. This loss of language destroys their intimacy and their marriage. . . . (pp. 243-44)

In each of these Bullet Park stories, a marriage has failed. In each, people are cut loose from their moorings and drift on the ocean of life without direction, without love, without community. Like the later New York stories, Cheever's Bullet Park evidences a darkening of vision, a reduction of hope, an awareness of the fragility of love and the confusion of life against which art is only a momentary stay. One thinks again and again while reading these stories of another New Englander, Wallace Stevens, for whom the writing of poems is the pressing back of the imagination from within against the pressure of news from without. We are not far in either case from art as desperation.

Cheever is no suburban Céline, however. Balance is everything for him. Balance, and humor, and an appetite for life, and a capacity to celebrate the world and the individual. He seems to find a partial order between the individual and his world in the Italian stories—but that order does not include expatriated Americans, with rare exceptions. Having lived there for some time in the fifties, Cheever loves Rome and Italy. The country offers tangible evidence that man has lived on harmonious terms with his world for centuries.

"The Bella Lingua" is an example of a kind of Italian order from which Americans are excluded. Wilson Streeter—the name sounds suspiciously like Lambert Strether—is an expatriate statistician, divorced, who wants to learn the beautiful language. He finds a succession of Italian teachers no help to him. Finally he comes upon Kate Dresser, who is willing to teach him. He comes weekly to an Italian palace for his lesson. Periodically a group of aging Italian nobles shuffle through the apartment on the way to tea at the Baronessa Tarominia's, at the other end of the palace.

Kate, a widow, has a fifteen-year-old son, Charlie, who has found some companionship with Embassy children. All of them are aggressively American. They wear blue jeans and black leather jackets; they carry baseball mitts. "They are Embassy children, and the children of writers and oil-company and airline employees and divorcees and Fulbright Fellows. Eating bacon and eggs, and listening to the jukebox, they have a sense of being far, far from home that is a much sweeter and headier distillation than their parents ever know."

Streeter, on the other hand, thinks that he has acclimated himself to Italy. He visits friends in the country and enjoys the song of an Italian peasant girl with flowers in her hair, but he still doesn't understand what she is singing. He makes halting progress with his Italian lessons, but his knowledge of the language is only secondary and literary. The American counterpart of Boobee, he knows not the language of the tribe.

Into this world comes Uncle George, from Krasbie, Iowa. Uncle George serves as a catalyst and foil to Streeter. George is tricked, robbed, and exasperated by Italians, but his innocence is inviolable. Streeter, by contrast, is fooling himself. His pathetic efforts to acclimate himself to the bella lingua and to Roman life takes him nowhere. Seeing a whore, a corpse, and a churl who is feeding firecrackers to stray cats, Streeter knows that he does not want to die in Rome.

It is Uncle George then, and not Streeter, who comes as the ambassador to take Charlie home with him. Kate will have her Rome if she insists and so will Streeter, as Strether had his Paris before him, but all the life, the vigor, and the future are drained from that life when Uncle George (the name is surely symbolic) takes Charlie back to Krasbie. Streeter and Kate begin the study of Dante, but the great *Commedia* is only a linguistic substitute for the life of Americans in America. Cheever implies that America's future lies less in Bullet Park than in Krasbie. It certainly doesn't lie in Rome, with its threadbare aristocrats. (pp. 244-45)

"The World of Apples" celebrates the joyous reconciliation of conflicting tendencies that beset every man's life. If one is to live authentically, he makes a similar reconciliation, thus fulfilling the potential of his own life. Such a reconciliation involves a harmony between man and his world with its waters, its mountains, its light, and air. Cheever's Asa Bascomb emerges from his ordeal as the worthy son of great poetic sires—Walt Whitman, Prospero, and St. Francis. He observes the filial pieties with reverence, and his reward is joy in life.

One final locale for Cheever's stories deserves attention, St. Botolphs. It figures prominently in *The Wapshot Chronicle,* less so in *The Wapshot Scandal*. Few of these stories are set in Massachusetts, but those that are shed light on the mythic origins of Cheever's imagination. (p. 246)

[In **"The Lowboy,"** the] family dispute centers on a lowboy, a family heirloom that the narrator has received from Cousin Mathilda. Richard wants the lowboy and comes to make his claim. His desire is simply greater, thus more authentic than the narrator's. He must have the piece, so the narrator gives it to him.

Unfortunately, the piece is damaged. The man who repairs the splintered leg discovers that this is the famous Barstow lowboy, made by the celebrated Sturbridge cabinetmaker in 1780: it is worth ten thousand dollars. As time passes, Richard reconstructs both the lowboy and the room in Cousin Mathilda's house, with another Turkish carpet, heavy brasses, and a silver pitcher to cover the water stain left by the pitcher.

It would seem that Richard is paying his pieties to the family, but he is not. In his idolatry of heirlooms, he has underestimated the lives which they were made to enhance, and those lives come back in ghostly procession to haunt him. The narrator watches this parade of prickly individualists who will not be reduced to the status of furniture custodians. First comes Grandmother De Lancey, who campaigned for women's rights and cheered fire engines. Then Aunt Louisa, who painted huge canvases and smoked cigars (like Amy Lowell). Then Timothy, a child pianist who played with an orchestra at twelve and killed himself at fifteen. Uncle Tom, whose conquests numbered in the thousands, appears, carrying his crippled son up the stairs. Next comes Aunt Mildred, the poet who took a lover and left Uncle Sidney with the housework. Sidney himself, stinking of liquor, sits beside Richard on the sofa. He spills whiskey, inflames it with his lighted cigarette, and watches the whole macabre Christmas fantasy go up in flames.

Richard learns nothing from the masque. He has committed himself to the lowboy. At Thanksgiving Dinner he quarrels with his wife and children, sending the narrator home to smash and discard all the heirlooms that have hedged his own life. . . . (pp. 247-48)

So the family and marital love are first and last Cheever's subject, the magnetic north of his compass and ours. He calls attention to his limitations but doesn't apologize for them. Not for him the world of, say, Joyce Carol Oates. His stories are parables, fairy tales for grown-ups, but they celebrate love, the wonders and beauties of the natural world. He portrays the contrary forces at work within this world of love, to be sure. His characters struggle for balance between a vigorous individuality that threatens to warp itself in grotesque isolation and a need for community that may degenerate into mindless defense of the zoning regulations. Balance is not easily won, but it is everything.

Cheever has placed himself squarely in the New England tradition of our national literature. His roots go back to Emerson, Thoreau, and Hawthorne and beyond them to his colonial forbears. He reminds us that not only Jewish-American writers have families; tradition and filial piety apply to Yankee stock as well.

Individuality may be rugged, bizarre, or pathetic, but it does evidence the struggle towards identity which all of us must undergo. The community may be idealized and increasingly difficult to find, particularly in the later stories, but it is there nonetheless—most of all in the community of understanding that Cheever projects with his readers. For through it all, the ugliness of individual acts is muted by the charm of the narrative voice—beguiling, understanding, bemused, generalizing, incantatory.

Perhaps the most remarkable of Cheever's achievements is his simple conviction that he will be read and understood. He speaks to our need for heroes and heroism, our desire to affirm ourselves, to find harmony between our inner and outer landscapes. In reading him sympathetically, we see ourselves and our America, imperiled not so much by violence without as violence within—the loss of faith, the loss of hope, the loss of love.

John Cheever celebrates our mortality in these stories, as his fellow New Englander Wallace Stevens celebrates it in "Sunday Morning." As recurrent as are his New York, his Shady Hill, his Bullet Park, his Rome, and his St. Botolphs, they instance not so much clinical analyses of places and mores as glimpses of an ideal; not places and times, but an attitude of accommodation, of compassion, of a celebration both sacred and profane. Cheever raises them in a wry, tongue-in-cheek, hard-curled-around-the-glass toast to the human frailties that are our fate and our glory. (pp. 249-50)

Richard H. Rupp, "Of That Time, of Those Places: The Short Stories of John Cheever," in Critical Essays on John Cheever, *edited by R. G. Collins, G. K. Hall & Co., 1982, pp. 231-51.*

MICHAEL BYRNE (essay date 1983)

[*In the following excerpt, Byrne describes Cheever's "optimistic imagination" in the novella* Oh What a Paradise It Seems.]

For those critics who have consistently found John Cheever a sentimental, narrow chronicler of the minor epiphanies and trials of surburbia, ***Oh What A Paradise It Seems*** will be fuel for the fire (and judging from the tepid reviews given the book, "fire" might be too strong). This complaint, usually directed against "New Yorker writers," has a corollary in regard to a Cheever novel: structural clumsiness. With the exception of *Falconer,* the argument suggests that the acknowledged master of the short story fails at longer fictions, that the Cheever novel unconsciously aspires to the condition of a short story collection. By this estimate *Falconer* was a felicitous masterpiece and ***Oh What A Paradise It Seems*** a reversion to type. Ostensibly, this criticism applies. The novella tells the story of Lemuel Sears, an old man outraged over the pollution of a skating pond of his youth. Sears, despite a society unconcerned with preserving the ecology and a sinister conspiracy concerned with turning the pond into profit, wins the day and saves Beasley's Pond. The Yankee virtues (celebrated in *The Wapshot Chronicle)* of breeding, tenacity and respect for nature triumph. In the era of James Watt, Cheever's optimism seems outrageous. Moreover, in alternating chapters of the one hundred page novella, Cheever juxtaposes the main story with a tale of two feuding housewives, Sears' love affair with a younger woman, Sears' first homosexual affair, and the tragic end of an idealistic environmentalist. The story shifts and races with the speed of a scenario rather than a novel. Finally, Cheever brings the principals together in a town hall scene, reminiscent of the "well-made" courtrooms of Galsworthy. And, still at a breakneck pace, Cheever concludes: "But, you might ask, whatever became of the true criminals, the villains who had murdered a high-minded environmentalist and seduced, bribed and corrupted the custodians of municipal welfare? Not to prosecute these wretches might seem to incriminate oneself with the guilt of complicity by omission. But that is another tale, and as I said in the beginning, this is just a story meant to be read in bed in an old house on a rainy night." A brief description of this work does seem to evoke an image of a dying writer tossing craft aside, straining for a final statement of affirmation, whatever the cost. Seen in the context of Cheever's total body of work, however, ***Oh What A Paradise It Seems*** actually marks the great strides his fiction was taking, thematically and technically. Through its controlling principle of the "optimistic imagination,'' the book reveals a writer closer in temperament to the Post-Modernists than Chekhov. (p. 38)

Both a statement of Cheever's vision and the novella's technical foundation, the ''optimistic imagination'' allows Cheever self-consciously to eschew the probability of action that largely governed his prior work. In ***Oh What A Paradise It Seems,*** when the narrator acknowledges the fictionality of the work, when he himself intrudes in the action, when mysteries are left unexplained, when subplots inexplicably evaporate, and when the main action is resolved more quickly than the eye can read, this ''optimistic imagination'' is at work.

I take the term from Cheever's description of Lemuel Sears: ''[his] imagination was inclined to be optimistic.'' Indeed, after the cozy opening of the novella (''This is a story to be read in bed in an old house on a rainy night''), Sears' imagination is put to a test. After he learns that Beasley's Pond has been declared a dump site, he writes letters to two advocates to end the dumping. His letter is ridiculed by the mayor (a member of the dumping conspiracy) and the two advocates are murdered. Yet, if the conspiracy reiterates Cheever's long concern with evil, this is an evil that remains shadowy and abstract (as is not the case in *Bullet Park* and *Falconer*). The conspiracy is hinted at and alluded to, but never identified or shown working. And the novella's conclusion (cited earlier) demonstrates that Cheever intended his images of benevolence and optimism to eclipse their dark counterparts. In this respect, a contrast between ***Oh What A Paradise It Seems*** and *Bullet Park* is telling. The earlier work is divided between the narrative of Elliot Nailles and the interior monologue of Paul Hammer. The point of view of Nailles' story is omniscient, cynical and tired. Nailles, the fundamentally decent suburbanite, almost loses his son to a strange malaise and later to the murderous imagination of Hammer. But because of the narrative tone, Tony's rescue and the restoration of order in Bullet Park are neither convincing nor compelling. Hammer's monologue, however, is profoundly disturbing and real; the point of view is passionate and earnest. Through technique Cheever's portrait of evil and chaos in *Bullet Park* totally dominates the idea of order. In ***Oh What A Paradise It Seems*** tone serves the opposite purpose. Sears' nostalgia for Beasley's Pond is treated without sentimentality, and his naive efforts to stop the pollution are treated affectionately rather than ironically. Likewise, the environmentalist Horace Chisholm, eventually murdered by the conspiracy, is lionized without sentimentality. Cheever's delicate balance in tone toward the optimists in his story emerges in this typical passage on Chisholm: ''Then he seemed lost. He was lost. He had lost his crown, his kingdom, his heirs and armies, his court, his harem, his queen and his fleet. He had, of course, never possessed any of these. He was not in any way emotionally dishonest and so why should he feel as if he had been cruelly stripped of what he had never claimed to possess? He seemed to have been hurled bodily from the sanctuary of some church, although he had never committed himself to anything that could be called serious prayer.'' The tonal effect of caricaturing the conspirators (or not showing them at all) and objectively characterizing Sears and Chisholm is that order and benevolence are made compelling; chaos and evil, lifeless.

So total is Cheever's insistence on benevolent order that any sinister element in the plot is summarily resolved or cryptically abandoned. Along with the concluding dismissal of the conspirators' fates are two unresolved subplots. The first concerns Sears' love affair with Renee, a young, attractive woman. Her continual admonition to Sears, ''You don't understand the first thing about women,'' is underlined by the mysterious meetings she attends. Neither Sears nor the reader ever learns the nature of these meetings, and Renee's departure in the middle of the book assures Sears he never will. Similarly, the subplot involving Betsey Logan, a housewife also enraged at the pollution of Beasley's Pond, ends inconclusively. After the murder of Chisholm, Betsey decides to blackmail the conspiracy by poisoning the food at the local supermarket. Following several cases of poisoning, the dumping ceases. Here Cheever glosses over the ethical implications of her act, insisting only on Sears' vision of benevolent mystery as he gazes at the restored pond: ''What moved him was a sense of those worlds around us, our knowledge however imperfect of their nature. . . . The sense of that hour was of an exquisite privilege, the great benefice of living here and renewing ourselves with love.'' Further, the deliberate abandonment of the unsavory in the plot has a counterpart in Horace Chisholm's felicitous rescue of the Logans' child (accidentally abandoned on the turnpike!). The child lost and found is a familiar incident for Cheever's audience. Often it figures as his analogue for grace; in ***Oh What A Paradise It Seems*** it is one more instance of the serendipitous restoration of order. A pond restored; a child saved.

If the plot of ***Oh What A Paradise It Seems*** trots happily along sidestepping probability and creating more questions than answers, there is the narrator's repeated declaration that he is reporting a plot, an imaginative artifice. He frequently prefaces a chapter or a paragraph with ''This is a story,'' ''At the time of which I am writing,'' or ''this is just a story.'' This insistence on fictionality urges the reader to delight in rather than to scrutinize the narrative eccentricities. Persons attempting to find a coherent plot will be shot.

Or will they? The question is raised in the narrator's remarkable opening of chapter three:

> I wish the story I'm telling began with the fragrance of mint growing along a stream bed where I'm lying, concealed with my rifle, waiting to assassinate a pretender who is expected to come here, fishing for trout. What I can see of the sky is blue. The smell of mint is very strong and I hear the music of water. The pretender is a well-favored young man and thinks himself quite alone. There is, he seems to think, some blessedness in fishing trout with flies. He sings while he assembles his rod and looks up at the sky and around at the trees to reassure himself of the naturalness of this garden from which, unknown to him, he is about to be dismissed. My rifle is loaded and I put it to my shoulder take the location of his heart in my cross-sights. The smell of mint seriously challenges the rightness of this or any other murder. . . . Yes I would much sooner be occupied with such matters than with the death of the Salazzos' dog Buster, but at the time of which I am writing the purity of the water was of inexorable interest—far more important than dynasties—and the Salazzos are linked to the purity of Beasley's Pond.

Here the narrator's insistence on artifice is wholly realized: he (like other Post-Modern narrators) fully reveals himself. Who is the ''well-favored young man''? Why is he a ''pretender''? Why is he about to be dispatched? More mysteries left unanswered. But this narrative intrusion dramatizes the heart of ***Oh***

What A Paradise It Seems: an Edenic world (the stream bed / Beasley's Pond) is threatened with mysterious violence (the narrator / the conspiracy), a violence averted by some benevolent, imaginative imperative.

This imperative is a moral order and it forms the theme and structure of Cheever's novella. Not only does he insist throughout the book on a vision of optimism, natural order, and the "great benefice of living here", he imaginatively shapes that order. It would be a serious error to call ***Oh What A Paradise It Seems*** a Post-Modernist work, but Cheever's improbable plot, self-conscious narrator and unresolved mysteries demonstrate the contemporaneity of his technique. That he uses these techniques for an assertion of order reveals the distance between him and many Post-Modernists. I have paraphrased Cheever in calling this order the "optimistic imagination." And I think his work as a novelist inevitably led him to this vision of regeneration and redemption. It was predicated on faith in *Falconer;* in ***Oh What A Paradise It Seems*** it is an act of will. (pp. 39-42)

Michael Byrne, "The Optmistic Imagination: John Cheever's 'Oh What A Paradise It Seems'," in The CEA Critic, *Vol. 45, Nos. 3 & 4, March & May, 1983, pp. 38-42.*

ADDITIONAL BIBLIOGRAPHY

Adams, Robert M. "Chance-taker." *The New York Review of Books* XXIX, No. 7 (29 April 1982): 8.
Review of *Oh What a Paradise It Seems,* concentrating on the novella's elusive qualities.

Auser, Cortland P. "John Cheever's Myth of Man and Time: 'The Swimmer'." *CEA Critic* XXIX, No. 6 (March 1967): 18-19.
Characterizes "The Swimmer" as "a myth of time and man as it is also a modern myth of metamorphosis."

Bellow, Saul. "On John Cheever." *The New York Review of Books* XXX, No. 2 (17 February 1983): 38.
Eulogy of Cheever.

Broyard, Anatole. Review of *Oh What a Paradise It Seems,* by John Cheever. *The New York Times* (3 March 1982): C28.
Favorable review. Broyard writes: "I find myself still mulling over *Oh What a Paradise It Seems,* still feeling my way through it, and I believe that's what John Cheever intended."

Cheever, John. "Why I Write Short Stories." *Newsweek* XCII, No. 18 (30 October 1978): 24-5.
Explains the lasting attraction of the short story genre.

———. "'Fiction Is Our Most Intimate Means of Communication'." *U.S. News & World Report* LXXXVI, No. 20 (21 May 1979): 92.
Thoughtful remarks on the role and meaning of literature in contemporary life. Cheever writes that in his own work, "urgency is what I principally seek," and that "I want to share with [the] reader the excitement of being alive or of comprehending the human condition."

———, and Cowley, Susan Cheever. "A Duet of Cheevers." *Newsweek* LXXXIX, No. 11 (14 March 1977): 68-70, 73.
Interview with Cheever conducted by his daughter, then a writer at *Newsweek.* Although the conversation is primarily concerned with personal subjects—touching on Cheever's childhood, his family, and his former drinking problem—Cheever's literary career is referred to throughout.

Cheever, Susan. *Home Before Dark: A Biographical Memoir of John Cheever by His Daughter.* Boston: Houghton Mifflin Co., 1984, 243 p.
Personal memoirs of Cheever by his daughter, who writes in her preface: "I wanted to tell the story of a man who fought to adhere to some transcendent moral standard until the end of his life." The book includes excerpts from John Cheever's private journals as well as several pages of photographs.

Collins, R. G. "Beyond Argument: Post-Marital Man in John Cheever's Later Fiction." *Mosaic* XVII, No. 2 (Spring 1984): 261-79.
Concentrates on "The World of Apples," the novel *Falconer,* and *Oh What a Paradise It Seems* in a study of Cheever's treatment of sexual relationships.

———. "Fugitive Time: Dissolving Experience in the Later Fiction of Cheever." *Studies in American Fiction* 12, No. 2 (Autumn 1984): 175-88.
Explores Cheever's treatment of time in the later short stories and in *Oh What a Paradise It Seems.*

——— ed. *Critical Essays on John Cheever.* Boston: G. K. Hall & Co., 1982, 292 p.
Collection of critical work on Cheever. The book includes interviews with Cheever, a representative selection of short reviews of his stories and novels, and a number of longer critical studies on various aspects of Cheever's fiction, among them Samuel Coale's comparison of Cheever and Nathaniel Hawthorne and Burton Kendle's analysis of nostalgia in the short stories.

Crews, Frederick C. "Domestic Manners." *The New York Review of Books* 111, No. 5 (22 October 1964): 7.
Examines characterization in *The Brigadier and the Golf Widow.*

De Feo, Ronald. "Cheever Underachieving." *National Review* XXV, No. 19 (11 May 1973): 536-37.
Tepid praise for *The World of Apples,* which De Feo considers inferior to Cheever's earlier work.

Didion, Joan. "A Celebration of Life." *National Review* X, No. 15 (22 April 1961): 254-55.
Praises Cheever's fiction as "a celebration of life."

Donaldson, Scott. "The Machines in Cheever's Garden." In *The Changing Face of the Suburbs,* edited by Barry Schwartz, pp. 309-22. Chicago: University of Chicago Press, 1976.
Analyzes Cheever's use of transportation technology as a symbol of the destructive, dehumanizing elements of modern life.

DuBois, William. Review of *The Enormous Radio, and Other Stories,* by John Cheever. *The New York Times* (1 May 1953): 19.
Objects to the limitations of the characters, setting, and general themes of the stories in *The Enormous Radio.*

Gerlach, John. "Closure in Modern Short Fiction: Cheever's 'The Enormous Radio' and 'Artemis, the Honest Well Digger'." *Modern Fiction Studies* 28, No. 1 (Spring 1982): 145-52.
Measures the sense of closure achieved by "The Enormous Radio" and "Artemis, the Honest Well Digger" against the standards established for the short story genre by Edgar Allan Poe. Gerlach concludes that while the ending of "The Enormous Radio" satisfies traditional expectations, that of "Artemis" reveals closure only in a "formal" sense.

Heyen, William. Review of *The Brigadier and the Golf Widow,* by John Cheever. *Studies in Short Fiction* III, No. 1 (Fall 1965): 79-80.
Praise for Cheever's rendering of the "essential ambiguity of human experience" in *The Brigadier and the Golf Widow.*

Hill, Doug. "The Bite of the Termite." *Books in Canada* 8, No. 2 (February 1979): 19-20.
Discusses the style and themes of Cheever's short fiction. According to Hill, "the tension between opposing modes gives Cheever's work its character—both its special bite and its special limitations."

Hunt, George. "Beyond the Cheeveresque." *Commonweal* CVI, No. 1 (19 January 1979): 20-2.
Focuses on Cheever's imaginative and stylistic qualities as a short story writer.

Irving, John. "Facts of Living." *Saturday Review* 5, No. 25 (30 September 1978): 44-6.
High praise for *The Stories of John Cheever,* emphasizing Cheever's sympathetic humanity. Irving contends: "In the darkest of his stories there shines a light; that light is Cheever's loyalty to human beings—in spite of ourselves."

Kendle, Burton. "Cheever's Use of Mythology in 'The Enormous Radio'." *Studies in Short Fiction* IV, No. 3 (Spring 1967): 262-64.
Explication of "The Enormous Radio" as an Edenic fable.

King, Francis. "Making It New." *Spectator* 242, No. 7876 (23 June 1979): 29-30.
Comments on Cheever's fundamental optimism and concludes that he is "the greatest of his country's writers at the present."

Lehmann-Haupt, Christopher. "In Defense of John Cheever." *The New York Times* (10 May 1973): 43.
Examines the eccentricities and emphasizes the merits of the stories in *The World of Apples.*

Leonard, John. Review of *The Stories of John Cheever,* by John Cheever. *The New York Times* (7 November 1978): 43.
Explicates how Cheever's characters carry their author's moral message.

———. "Cheever Country." *The New York Times Book Review* (7 March 1982): 1, 25-6.
Characterizes *Oh What a Paradise It Seems* as "minor art," but considers admirable Cheever's affirmation of human goodness and faith.

Locke, Richard. "Visions of Order and Domestic Disarray." *The New York Times Book Review* (3 December 1978): 3, 78.
Compares Cheever's stories to "the piano sonatas of Schubert in which an inexpressibly poignant theme returns again and again in slightly different forms and contexts."

McPherson, William. "Cheever by the Dozen." *The Washington Post Book World* (22 October 1978): 1, 6.
Describes the world of Cheever's short fiction as "narrow," but of "universal resonance." The essay includes extensive quotes from Cheever about his work.

Moore, Stephen C. "The Hero on the 5:42: John Cheever's Short Fiction." *Western Humanities Review* 30, No. 2 (Spring 1976): 147-52.
Recognizes moral heroism in Cheever's short story characters.

Pawlowski, Robert S. "Myth as Metaphor: Cheever's 'Torch Song'." *Research Studies* 47, No. 2 (June 1979): 118-21.
Analysis of the mythic elements of "Torch Song."

Schickel, Richard. "The Cheever Chronicle." *Horizon* 21, No. 9 (September 1978): 28-33.
Combines critical commentary and quotes from Cheever to create a portrait of both the writer and the man.

Shaw, Irwin. "Cheever Country." *Bookviews* 2, No. 2 (October 1978): 56-7.
Review of *The Stories of John Cheever,* extolling Cheever's talent and achievement. Shaw describes Cheever as "a prober of the hidden, and a judge of stern moral standards. . . ."

Ten Harmsel, Henrietta. "'Young Goodman Brown' and 'The Enormous Radio'." *Studies in Short Fiction* IX, No. 4 (Fall 1972): 407-08.
Compares "The Enormous Radio" with Nathaniel Hawthorne's "Young Goodman Brown." Ten Harmsel maintains that "like Hawthorne, Cheever deals basically with the universal dilemma of maintaining a balanced humanity in a world where evil seems to overwhelm the good."

Theroux, Paul. "Treasons." *New Statesman* 87, No. 2242 (8 March 1974): 334.
Unreservedly praises *The World of Apples,* claiming that "the book is a joy."

Towers, Robert. "Light Touch." *The New York Review of Books* XXV, No. 17 (9 November 1978): 3-4.
Studies several aspects of Cheever's work, including verisimilitude, narrative technique, and evidence of moral purpose.

Wain, John. "Literate, Witty, Civilized." *The New Republic* 168, No. 21 (26 May 1973): 24-6.
Attests to Cheever's championship of "old-style" values "like love and loyalty and kindness and consideration for others and protectiveness toward the weak." Wain focuses on "The World of Apples" in emphasizing Cheever's moral decency.

Warnke, Frank J. "Cheever's Inferno." *The New Republic* 144, No. 20 (15 May 1961): 18.
Contends that "Cheever's vision is more of nightmare than of promise," and faults the author for failure to follow through on this vision in *Some People, Places, and Things That Will Not Appear in My Next Novel.*

Wood, Ralph C. "The Modest and Charitable Humanism of John Cheever." *The Christian Century* 99, No. 36 (17 November 1982): 1163-66.
Underscores the humanism and spirituality of Cheever's short fiction. Wood concludes: "At its best Cheever's fiction serves magnificently to enlarge our lives by giving renewed witness to the primordial human truths, yet without pretending that they are sufficient to deliver us from evil. And in his extraordinary presence as a companionable and forgiving narrator, Cheever offers a literary parable of God's own unstinted grace."

G(ilbert) K(eith) Chesterton

1874-1936

English novelist, short story writer, critic, essayist, journalist, and poet.

Regarded as one of England's premier men of letters during the first half of the twentieth century, Chesterton is best known today as a witty essayist, a formidable Christian polemicist, and, more popularly, as the creator of mystery stories, particularly the Father Brown series. These stories, featuring the cleric who is an authority on human nature, are among the most highly praised and popular works of detective fiction.

The son of a middle-class London family, Chesterton enjoyed a happy childhood, which he recalled with affection, claiming his early years gave him an essentially religious insight into life. Chesterton later studied literature and art at London's Slade School of Art. His interest in drawing and painting played a key role in his later writing career, and critics frequently praise the visual artistry of his descriptions. During his studies at the Slade School from 1892 to 1895, Chesterton suffered a severe emotional and philosophical crisis that threatened his sanity. Fearful that the external world did not exist and might be only a projection of his mind, he endured intense anguish for a long period, though he recovered thoroughly. This experience fostered Chesterton's understanding of the dark side of human nature—its horrors, evils, and madnesses—which is pertinent to his writings and a major force in his detective fiction.

Chesterton first gained public attention as a social and literary critic. With his book *What's Wrong with the World* he achieved recognition, along with Hilaire Belloc, as a leading exponent of Distributism, a social philosophy that proposed a property-owning democracy in which private property is divided into the smallest possible units, thereby creating small communities and neighborliness among people. Chesterton devoted his journalistic and editorial skills throughout his life to the cause of reformist political ideas. In 1916 he began editing the magazine *New Witness,* which later, as *G. K.'s Weekly,* served as an organ of Distributism. The periodical didn't sell well, and to support its publication, which continued until his death, Chesterton began writing the immensely popular Father Brown stories.

Committed as he was to influencing the thinking and feelings of his age, Chesterton in most of his writings did not fail to be the teacher as well as the artist. Using paradox and parable, symbol and allegory, Chesterton strove to effect social change that would embody his religious convictions: the divine revealed in the ordinary, the value of life, childlike wonder, and a sense of community. Though his detective stories were the least serious of all his works, they were nevertheless imbued with the essence of these beliefs. Father Brown, his most successful creation, served as a mouthpiece for Chesterton, and critics note that in each of these stories some lesson on Christian humanism is dispatched.

Originally printed in the *Saturday Evening Post,* the Father Brown stories spanned three decades, the early 1900s to the 1930s, and were collected in *The Innocence of Father Brown, The Wisdom of Father Brown, The Incredulity of Father Brown, The Secret of Father Brown,* and *The Scandal of Father Brown,*

The Bettmann Archive/BBC Hulton

as well as in *The Father Brown Omnibus*. Loosely based upon Chesterton's friend, the Roman Catholic priest John O'Connor, the character of Father Brown is a seemingly absent-minded cleric of unkempt appearance who possesses a profound understanding of evil. Brown's knowledge is derived from the confessional, where he has heard the countless transgressions of his "flock," and, more importantly, from his ability to search his own heart for the potential for evil. Father Brown explains, "when I tried to imagine the state of mind in which such a thing could be done, I always realized that I might have done it myself under certain mental conditions, and not others, and not generally the obvious ones. And then, of course, I knew who really had done it; and he was not generally the obvious one."

It is this seemingly intuitive solving of the mystery that has been most challenged by afficionados of the detective genre. Arguing that good detection requires a deductive method, some critics note that Chesterton's detective stories fail because Father Brown's method is transcendental. They concede that Chesterton usually provides some clues but object that these are few and often unclear or lost among the stories' descriptive passages. Others insist that Father Brown is successful as a detective because he relies on common sense and on his powers of observation. These critics praise Chesterton for not endowing his creation with some esoteric knowledge that is used to solve crimes, as do many mystery and detective writers.

Chesterton's detective fiction further departs from standard formula of the genre by examining motives of the criminal rather than the crime and its consequences. In fact, commentators note that in many Father Brown stories there is no crime. As Erik Routley demonstrates, Father Brown considers the criminal a good person gone wrong, and his intent is to reach the heart of the individual to arrest the evil rather than the perpetrator. Some critics have pointed out that Chesterton's story formula was to establish a crime or mystery, then propose irrational, supernatural, or magical explanations, and finally to resolve the mystery by very natural solutions, thus exposing folly, exploding superstition, and dispelling darkness. As a thinker whose ideas and beliefs were rooted in the eighteenth century, Chesterton rejected atheism and occultism and detested the increasing dominance of science in the twentieth century; he held that scientific explanations of phenomena could in the extreme be superstitious and that courting the irrational is misguided theology.

Several commentators have spoken of the darker aspects of Chesterton's imagination, noting in particular his suggestion of a nightmarish reality. Some have seen this dimension as an integral part of Chesterton's sensibility; Jill Brown argues that Chesterton used his writings to prove that this irrational dimension can be controlled by common sense and faith. Closely tied with Chesterton's fascination with horror is his concern for the meaning of sanity. Chesterton derided rationality that posed as sanity, averring it was in fact a deranged lunacy. In the stories of *The Poet and the Lunatics,* for example, as Maurice Evans contends, Chesterton especially plays with the theme of reason that leads to madness. Here the detective hero is Gabriel Gale, who, like Father Brown, is more a philosopher and psychologist than a detective. Gale searches out not the sinner, but the lunatic. He numbers among his madmen the artist, the scientist, the curate, the psychologist, the business man—any who are immersed in their own self-importance. Focusing on these various fields, Chesterton could attack what he believed to be the subtle causes of the madness of his era. Gale, like his predecessor Father Brown, could see into the madman's heart; the character muses, "the man of imagination alone, who can see himself in the lunatic's shoes, is the man who can save the lunatic's sanity. The man who can imagine himself committing a crime is the man who can solve it—or who can prevent its commission." Although Chesterton employed the same formula in several other works, including *Four Faultless Felons, Daylight and Nightmare, The Man Who Knew Too Much,* and *The Paradoxes of Mr. Pond*—his other detectives—Horne Fisher, Mr. Pond, and Gabriel Gale—never captured the imagination of the reading public as Father Brown did.

Though Chesterton did not consider his Father Brown stories important, he has been credited with adding a more literary cast to the detective story genre with his moral fervor, vivid imagination, and rich, descriptive style. Most critics acknowledge Chesterton as a master of detective fiction and one of its primary innovators, who, according to Howard Haycraft "perfected the *metaphysical* detective story." Thus while much of his more "serious" writing is currently considered occasional or eccentric, most critics would agree with the assessment of R. L. Megroz: "Chesterton was certainly a romanticist, often escaping from reality by fantasies, among which may be included his medievalism; but always one comes back to his great sanity, his poetic insight, his sweetness, which redeem all his propaganda, illuminate his poetry, and could fill even the detective story with a wisdom akin to mysticism."

(See also *TCLC,* Vols. 1, 6; *Contemporary Authors,* Vol. 104; and *Dictionary of Literary Biography,* Vols. 10, 19, 34.)

PRINCIPAL WORKS

SHORT FICTION

The Club of Queer Trades (1905)
The Innocence of Father Brown (1911)
The Wisdom of Father Brown (1914)
The Man Who Knew Too Much (1922)
Tales of the Long Bow (1925)
The Incredulity of Father Brown (1926)
The Secret of Father Brown (1927)
The Poet and the Lunatics (1929)
The Father Brown Omnibus (1933)
The Scandal of Father Brown (1935)
The Paradoxes of Mr. Pond (1937)
G. K. Chesterton: Selected Short Stories (1972)
Daylight and Nightmare: Uncollected Stories and Fables (1986)

OTHER MAJOR WORKS

The Wild Knight, and Other Poems (poetry) 1900
The Defendant (essays) 1901
Twelve Types (essays) 1902
Robert Browning (criticism) 1903
The Napoleon of Notting Hill (novel) 1904
Heretics (essays) 1905
Charles Dickens (criticism) 1906
The Man Who Was Thursday (novel) 1908
Orthodoxy (essays) 1908
George Bernard Shaw (criticism) 1909
The Ball and the Cross (novel) 1910
What's Wrong with the World (essays) 1910
The Ballad of the White Horse (poetry) 1911
Manalive (novel) 1912
The Victorian Age in Literature (criticism) 1913
The Flying Inn (poetry) 1914
Wine, Water, and Song (poetry) 1915
The Ballad of St. Barbara, and Other Verses (poetry) 1922
Eugenics and Other Evils (essays) 1922
St. Francis of Assisi (biography) 1923
The Everlasting Man (essays) 1925
The Return of Don Quixote (novel) 1927
St. Thomas Aquinas (biography) 1933
Autobiography (autobiography) 1936

DIXON SCOTT (essay date 1911)

[In the following excerpt from an article originally published in 1911 in the Manchester Guardian, *Scott, an English critic, suggests that the wild fantasy and sometimes extravagant sense of evil portrayed in* The Innocence of Father Brown *are due to the fact that Chesterton's literary gifts are too great for light fiction.]*

"The criminal is the creative artist; the detective only the critic," mourns Valentin, chief of the Paris police, on the ninth page of this blood-red fairy-book [***The Innocence of Father Brown***]. There's a nasty implication in the thought, perhaps—yet it isn't mere professional resentment that makes one sternly retort that ***The Innocence of Father Brown*** fairly proves the guilt of Mr. Chesterton. He has been accused of many crimes by our literary Valentins—of undue flippancy, of undue earnestness, of a proneness to platitude, of a weakness for paradox; but perhaps the true charge against him, underlying all these, is that he is too big for his books. That, on the face of it, might not seem much more culpable than palming off sovereigns for shillings—and, indeed, there are extenuating circumstances. For the first four or five of these dozen "detective" tales are really simply goluptious; not since the brave old days of Notting Hill, when Auberon Quin gravely stood on his head in sight of his loyal subjects, have we had such a farrago of magnificent nonsense. **"The Blue Cross," "The Secret Garden," "The Queer Feet," "The Flying Stars"**—their names alone are enough to set the blood simmering. . . . The centre of each is some madcap, incredible crime, worked out with a lunatic exactness and intricacy, and then hidden cunningly away in the midst of conspicuously meek and mild accessories—among sweetshops in Camden Town, placid villas in Putney, policemen and postmen and matter-of-fact porters. This done—solution safe, and relying on his own ready wit to bring the wildest irrelevance to heel—"G.K.C." fairly lets himself go. Round we are rattled, pelted with puns and wild poetry, at the heels of little moon-faced Father Brown, till at length in some blind alley, with reason on the verge of revolt, the baffling eye of the problem blandly opens and executes a solemn wink. And the effect of fantasy is famously heightened . . . by the vivid realism of the figures and scenes. Mr. Chesterton has the poet's gift for seeing the most commonplace things—moons or men's faces, hills, street-lamps, and houses—with a startling freshness and suddenness, as though they had been but that instant made; and since epithet and object leap into his mind together—since he has, undeniably, the power of seizing the one golden word and planking it down with a rollicking bang—the old familiar places past which the rout pours shed their old shabbiness wondrously, shine out with the sudden significance of places washed by a dawn. . . . It is true, no doubt, that some of these qualities will simply exasperate the downright democrats whom Mr. Chesterton wants specially to cheer, and that they will tickle the palates of precisely the people whom in his heartiness he affects to despise. True, too, perhaps, that we have here a repetition of the great Notting Hill blunder [in the novel *The Napoleon of Notting Hill*]. Adam Wayne wanted to prove modern London romantic, but adopted the curiously cumbrous and expensive process of painting its buildings with hot blood. Mr. Chesterton, too, would drive home to us the unconquerable queerness of things—the picturesqueness of sweetshops and suburbs—but tries to do it by cramming daft fairy-tale crimes into the middle of the unregarded streets. Somehow, he will *not* realize that his fingers flourish a weapon far more effective in such affairs than Wayne's big sword; that his cool picture of that "quaint, quiet square" brings out all its elfin magic like a spell; that a pantomime troupe pouring into it simply turns it back into a bit of stage scenery.

But these are little errors and ironies that the reader, carried away by the pantomime, will not allow to sadden him unduly. It is when he is half-way through the book that he becomes aware of a sudden change—a change so sinister that he may very well wonder whether the madness has not mounted to his head. He gets the dark, indescribable sensation of being in the presence of something actually evil. All this violence and vividness become horribly akin to the insane lucidity of nightmare. Yet, queerly, as he perceives on reflection, this change coincides with another which seems a pure triumph of virtue. Flambeau, the great criminal, the author of the fantastic crimes he has been tracking hitherto, suddenly repents; and Father Brown is at liberty to roam more largely about the world, holding Flambeau by the hand, a brand snatched from the burning, like a little dumpy Dante tripping beside a big blond Virgil. But instead of the light from this Flambeau falling on sins of an ever-increasing freshness and fantasy—outrages so utterly outrageous that we laugh at them as at the red-hot pokers and battered policemen of pantomime—we pass into places where things unspeakable prowl and spawn, as though we were indeed winding down the circles of some hell. "Mud-stains, blood-stains." There are dipsomaniacs and blotched paramours; the lost faces of idiots leer out of the darkness, blind women are murdered, there are new and more fearful forms of fratricide; and in this heavy atmosphere of horror quiet details swell and twist like things seen in an ill dream. The physical uglinesses are bad enough—Norman Bohun's smashed head "a hideous splash like a star of blackness and blood." But far more dreadful is the way some peaceful secondary thing—a group of trees, or a distant passer-by, or a quiet country church—will suddenly writhe out of its place and rush into the foreground, waxing horribly, like a face in a fever, as though struggling to express something too monstrous for speech. . . . (pp. 184-87)

It is a violence that seems somehow daemonic. It is a vividness like the unclean clarity that comes with drugs. It is like moving in a world of gargoyles, among the devils on Notre Dame. Now the change may be merely due to sudden spurts of real energy—Mr. Chesterton's true gifts, tired of tomfoolery, bursting out into mutinous roars. Or there may be something in it of that kind of devil-worship, that fascinated insistence on evil, which goes along with some fiery sorts of religion. Or, again, it may be only the result of lashing an invention tired of its nice new game. These are matters for the moralists. But the technical crime, which is all a mere Valentin may deal with, is in any case the same; and it is that technical transgression which produces this atmosphere of evil, this sense of unlawful powers. It is the evil of ugliness, of deformity—and the deformity is fundamentally due to the disparity between energy and outlet. It is this inadequacy that drives the perspectives mad and fills the trees with a frightening energy—hints at solemn significance where there is none and darkens impossible crimes till they swell into symbols of Sin. "Pooh!" cries Mr. Chesterton cheerily. "You are too easily terrified nowadays. The men who carved gargoyles did it out of jollity, sitting in the sun and drinking ale like brothers." Maybe; but at least they did it to lighten an ancient faith, not to give weight to a joke. That, indeed, was the true superiority of the Middle Ages: they did give their dreamers and carvers a task even bigger than their power. And even later on, with cathedrals all cut and dried, lyrics could still be complemented with campaigns—or, better still, the blood and the ink could be blended by writing books which relied on men's living bodies as much as they did on dead words. Born too late for campaigns, Mr. Chesterton has to try to satisfy the militant side of him by letting out in polemical battles that are only a little less unreal than villanelles. Whilst lacking a public as eager as the Elizabethan for blank verse and drama, he tries to pack his energies into tushery like this. Perhaps it isn't such an innocent thing to give away sovereigns for shillings. There is such a thing as degrading the currency. (pp. 188-89)

Dixon Scott, "The Guilt of Mr. Chesterton," in his Men of Letters, *Hodder and Stoughton, 1916, pp. 184-90.*

JULIUS WEST (essay date 1915)

[In the following excerpt from his full-length study of Chesterton, West discusses the characteristics of Chesterton's detective fiction to date.]

Chesterton may be held to have invented a new species of detective story—the sort that has no crime, no criminal, and a detective whose processes are transcendental. ***The Club of Queer Trades*** is the first batch of such stories. *The Man who was Thursday* is another specimen of some length. More recently, Chesterton has repeated the type in some of the ***Father Brown*** stories. In ***The Club of Queer Trades,*** the transcendental detective is Basil Grant, to describe whom with accuracy is difficult, because of his author's inconsistencies. Basil Grant, for instance, is "a man who scarcely stirred out of his attic," yet it would appear elsewhere that he walked abroad often enough. The essentials of this unprecedented detective are, however, sufficiently tangible. He had been a K.C. and a judge. He had left the Bench because it annoyed him, and because he held the very human but not legitimate belief that some criminals would be better off with a trip to the seaside than with a sentence of imprisonment. After his retirement from public life he stuck to his old trade as the judge of a Voluntary Criminal Court. "My criminals were tried for the faults which really make social life impossible. They were tried before me for selfishness, or for an impossible vanity, or for scandal-mongering, or for stinginess to guests or dependents." It is regrettable that Chesterton does not grant us a glimpse of this fascinating tribunal at work. However, it is Grant's job, on the strength of which he becomes the president and founder of the C.Q.T.—Club of Queer Trades. Among the members of this Club are a gentleman who runs an Adventure and Romance Agency for supplying thrills to the bourgeois, two Professional Detainers, and an Agent for Arboreal Villas, who lets off a variety of birds' nest. The way in which these people go about their curious tasks invariably suggests a crime to Rupert Grant, Basil's amateur detective brother, whereupon Basil has to intervene to put matters right. The author does not appear to have been struck by the inconsistency of setting Basil to work to ferret out the doings of his fellow club-members. The book is, in fact, full of joyous inconsistencies. The Agent for Arboreal Villas is clearly unqualified for the membership of the Club. Professor Chadd has no business there either. He is elected on the strength of having invented a language expressed by dancing, but it appears that he is really an employee in the Asiatic MSS. Department of the British Museum. Things are extremely absurd in **"The Eccentric Seclusion of the Old Lady."** At the instigation of Rupert, who has heard sighs of pain coming out of a South Kensington basement, Basil, Rupert, and the man who tells the story, break into the house and violently assault those whom they meet.

> Basil sprang up with dancing eyes, and with three blows like battering-rams knocked the footman into a cocked hat. Then he sprang on top of Burrows, with one antimacassar in his hand and another in his teeth, and bound him hand and foot almost before he knew clearly that his head had struck the floor. Then Basil sprang at Greenwood . . . etc. etc.

There is a good deal more like this. Having taken the citadel and captured the defenders (as Caesar might say), Basil and company reach the sighing lady of the basement. But she refuses to be released. Whereupon Basil explains his own queer trade, and that the lady is voluntarily undergoing a sentence for backbiting. No explanation is vouchsafed of the strange behaviour of Basil Grant in attacking men who, as he knew, were doing nothing they should not. Presumably it was due to a Chestertonian theory that there should be at least one good physical fight in each book.

It will be seen that ***The Club of Queer Trades*** tends to curl up somewhat (quite literally, in the sense that the end comes almost where the beginning ought to be) when it receives heavy and serious treatment. I should therefore explain that this serious treatment has been given under protest, and that its primary intention has been to deal with those well-meaning critics who believe that Chesterton can write fiction, in the ordinary sense of the word. His own excellent definition of fictitious narrative (in *The Victorian Age in Literature*) is that essentially "the story is told . . . for the sake of some study of the difference between human beings." This alone is enough to exculpate him of the charge of writing novels. The Chestertonian short story is also in its way unique. If we applied the methods of the Higher Criticism to the story just described, we might base all manner of odd theories upon the defeat (*inter alios*) of Burrows, a big and burly youth, by Basil Grant, aged sixty at the very least, and armed with antimacassars. But there is no necessity. If Chesterton invents a fantastic world, full of fantastic people who speak Chestertonese, then he is quite entitled to waive any trifling conventions which hinder the liberty of his subjects. As already pointed out, such is his humour. The only disadvantage, as somebody once complained of the Arabian Nights, is that one is apt to lose one's interest in a hero who is liable at any moment to turn into a camel. None of Chesterton's heroes do, as a matter of fact, become camels, but I would nevertheless strongly advise any young woman about to marry one of them to take out an insurance policy against unforeseen transformations. (pp. 29-33)

The transcendental type of detective, first sketched out in ***The Club of Queer Trades,*** is developed more fully in [***The Innocence of Father Brown*** and ***The Wisdom of Father Brown***]. In the little Roman priest who has such a wonderful instinct for placing the diseased spots in people's souls, we have Chesterton's completest and most human creation. Yet, with all their cleverness, and in spite of the fact that from internal evidence it is almost blatantly obvious that the author enjoyed writing these stories, they bear marks which put the books on a lower plane than either *The Napoleon of Notting Hill* or *The Ball and the Cross*. In the latter book Chesterton spoke of "the mere healthy and heathen horror of the unclean; the mere inhuman hatred of the inhuman state of madness." His own critical work had been a long protest against the introduction of artificial horrors, a plea for sanity and the exercise of sanity. But in ***The Innocence of Father Brown*** these principles, almost the fundamental ones of literary decency, were put on the shelf. Chesterton's criminals are lunatics, perhaps it is his belief that crime and insanity are inseparable. But even if this last supposition is correct, its approval would not necessarily license the introduction of some of the characters. This is Israel Gow, who suffers from a peculiar mania which drives him to collect gold from places seemly and unseemly, even to the point of digging up a corpse in order to extract the gold filling from its teeth. There is the insane French Chief of Police, who commits a murder and attempts to disguise the body, and the nature of the crime, by substituting the head of a guillotined criminal for that of the victim. In another story we have the picture of a cheerful teetotaller who suffers from drink and suicidal mania. There is also a doctor who kills a mad poet, and a mad priest who drops a hammer from the top of his church-tower upon his brother. Another story is about the loathsome treachery of an English general. It is, of course, difficult to write about crime without touching on features which revolt the squeamish reader, but it can be done, and it has been done, as in the Sherlock Holmes stories. . . . The harnessing of the horror into which the discovery of insanity reacts is a favourite device of the feeble craftsman, but it is illegitimate. It is absolutely opposed to those elementary canons of good taste which decree that we may not jest at the expense of certain things, either because they are too sacred or not sacred enough. . . . For example, the whole story **"The Wrong Shape"** is filled with decadent ideas; one is sure that Baudelaire would have entirely approved of it. It includes a decadent poet, living in wildly Oriental surroundings, attended by a Hindoo servant. Even the air of the place is decadent; Father Brown on entering the house learns instinctively from it that a crime is to be committed.

Considered purely as detective stories, these cannot be granted a very good mark. There is scarcely a story that has not a serious flaw in it. A man—Flambeau, of whom more later—gains admittance to a small and select dinner party and almost succeeds in stealing the silver, by the device of turning up and pretending to be a guest when among the waiters, and a waiter when among the guests. But it is not explained what he did during the first two courses of that dinner, when he obviously had to be either a waiter or a guest, and could not keep up both parts, as when the guests were arriving. Another man, a "Priest of Apollo," is worshipping the sun on the top of a "skyscraping" block of offices in Westminster, while a woman falls down a lift-shaft and is killed. Father Brown immediately concludes that the priest is guilty of the murder because, had he been unprepared, he would have started and looked round at the scream and the crash of the victim falling. But a man absorbed in prayer on, let us say, a tenth floor, is, in point of fact, quite unlikely to hear a crash in the basement, or a scream even nearer to him. But the most astonishing thing about **"The Eye of Apollo"** is the staging. In order to provide the essentials, Mr. Chesterton has to place "the heiress of a crest and half a county, as well as great wealth," who is blind, in a typist's office! The collocation is somewhat too singular. One might go right through the Father Brown stories in this manner. But, if the reader wishes to draw the maximum of enjoyment out of them, he will do nothing of the sort. He will believe, as fervently as Alfred de Vigny, that L'Idée C'est Tout, and lay down all petty regard for detail at the feet of Father Brown. This little Roman cleric has listened to so many confessions (he calls himself "a man who does next to nothing but hear men's real sins," but this seems to be excessive, even for a Roman Catholic) that he is really well acquainted with the human soul. He is also extremely observant. And his greatest friend is Flambeau, whom he once brings to judgment, twice hinders in crime, and thenceforward accompanies on detective expeditions.

The Innocence of Father Brown had a *sequel,* ***The Wisdom of Father Brown,*** distinctly less effective, as sequels always are, than the predecessor. But the underlying ideas are the same. In the first place there is a deep detestation of "Science" (whatever that is) and the maintenance of the theory incarnate in Father Brown, that he who can read the human soul knows all things. The detestation of science (of which, one gathers, Chesterton knows nothing) is carried to the same absurd length as in *The Ball and the Cross*. In the very first story, Father Brown calls on a criminologist ostensibly in order to consult him, actually in order to show the unfortunate man, who had retired from business fourteen years ago, what an extraordinary fool he was.

The Father Brown of these stories—moon-faced little man—is a peculiar creation. No other author would have taken the trouble to excogitate him, and then treat him so badly. As a detective he never gets a fair chance. He is always on the spot when a murder is due to be committed, generally speaking he is there before time. When an absconding banker commits suicide under peculiar circumstances in Italian mountains, when a French publicist advertises himself by fighting duels with himself (very nearly), when a murder is committed in the dressing-room corridor of a theatre, when a miser and blackmailer kills himself, when a lunatic admiral attempts murder and then commits suicide, when amid much incoherence a Voodoo murder takes place, when somebody tries to kill a colonel by playing on his superstitions (and by other methods), and when a gentleman commits suicide from envy, Father Brown is always there. One might almost interpret the Father Brown stories by suggesting that their author had written them in order to illustrate the sudden impetus given to murder and suicide by the appearance of a Roman priest. (pp. 51-7)

In summing up, it may be said of Chesterton that at his best he invented new possibilities of romance and a new and hearty laugh. It may be said of the decadents of the eighteen nineties, that if their motto wasn't "Let's all go bad," it should have been. So one may say of Chesterton that if he has not selected "Let's all go mad" as a text, he should have done. Madness, in the Chestertonian, whatever it is in the pathological sense, is a defiance of convention, a loosening of visible bonds in order to show the strength of the invisible ones; perhaps, as savages are said to regard lunatics with great respect, holding them to be nearer the Deity than most, so Chesterton believes of his own madmen. (p. 58)

Julius West, "The Romancer," in his G. K. Chesterton: A Critical Study, *Martin Secker, 1915, pp. 23-58.*

LOUISE MAUNSELL FIELD (essay date 1922)

[The following excerpt is from a generally favorable review of The Man Who Knew Too Much.*]*

Gilbert K. Chesterton's Horne Fisher [from ***The Man Who Knew Too Much***] is to a quite surprising extent what the publishers announce him as being—a new type of detective. His newness, however, consists not in any peculiar or revolutionary analytical or deductive methods, nor in his languid manner, but in his family and social connections. "The Prime Minister is my father's friend. The Foreign Minister married my sister. The Chancellor of the Exchequer is my first cousin," as he presently informs his friend Harold March, the young newspaper man. Horne Fisher knew all the secrets of the powerful; he was intimately acquainted with their hidden vices—and with their hidden virtues as well. In fact, he knew too much to act as another would have done in the curious cases which chance brought his way; he usually foresaw important consequences to which one who knew less would have been blind. And so the wrongdoer, whoever he might be, was never brought to justice by this ***Man Who Knew Too Much.***

In adopting this formula for the eight tales in which Horne Fisher is the central figure—that the criminal shall never pay the penalty for his crime—Mr. Chesterton has given himself a somewhat heavy handicap. It is not the easiest of tasks to invent a murder mystery—and all but two of the eight stories are murder mysteries—which shall be ingenious, plausible, perplexing and also possess some credible reason why the wrongdoer shall be permitted to escape. Two of the stories—the two murder mysteries which are very much the best of the Horne Fisher tales—fulfill all these requirements. **"The Bottomless Well"** is an excellent story, with a well-managed solution, and so is **"The Fad of the Fisherman,"** whose conclusion has a neat twist and surprise. **"The Vanishing Prince"** follows fairly closely on the heels of these two, but **"The Face in the Target"** has several very obvious weaknesses, and in **"The Hole in the Wall"** Mr. Chesterton frankly throws up the sponge, not even pretending to give a reason why the murderer should not have been prosecuted. The two closing tales depend on the almost unfailing cleverness of Mr. Chesterton's style; their plots have at once too much and too little of the fantastic. One feels that the author's invention had begun to run low.

Besides the eight stories in which Horne Fisher appears, there is one very long tale, almost a novelette, which takes up about a fourth of the volume, **"The Trees of Pride."** Like the others, it is a detective story, but it is no detective, amateur or professional, who reveals the truth about the so-called peacock trees and the strange disappearance of Squire Vane. . . . The tale has several twists and surprises, and will succeed in bewildering almost any reader.

The robust exuberance, the all but incessant sparkle of epigram and paradox which marked so much of Mr. Chesterton's earlier work, have been much subdued of late. One need only compare [***The Man Who Knew Too Much***] with ***The Club of Queer Trades,*** for instance, to note the difference. But Mr. Chesterton is always clever; he knows how to turn a phrase, to give freshness to an old truth, to express one of those facts which are so very obvious that we usually fail to notice them. He has the gift of being almost invariably entertaining, and very uneven in merit as these stories are, nevertheless they all have in them something that is worth while, and the best are very good indeed.

Louise Maunsell Field, in a review of "The Man Who Knew Too Much," in The New York Times Book Review, *December 10, 1922, p. 10.*

G. K. CHESTERTON (essay date 1936)

[*In an excerpt from his autobiography, Chesterton describes the real-life model for Father Brown and recounts the incident that inspired him to create the character.*]

Some time ago, seated at ease upon a summer evening and taking a serene review of an indefensibly fortunate and happy life, I calculated that I must have committed at least fifty-three murders, and been concerned with hiding about half a hundred corpses for the purpose of the concealment of crimes; hanging one corpse on a hat-peg, bundling another into a postman's bag, decapitating a third and providing it with somebody else's head, and so on through quite a large number of innocent artifices of the kind. It is true that I have enacted most of these atrocities on paper; and I strongly recommend the young student, except in extreme cases, to give expression to his criminal impulses in this form; and not run the risk of spoiling a beautiful and well-proportioned idea by bringing it down to the plane of brute material experiment, where it too often suffers the unforeseen imperfections and disappointments of this fallen world, and brings with it various unwelcome and unworthy social and legal consequences. . . . This being my strict principle, from which I have never wavered, there has been nothing to cut short the rich accumulation of imaginative corpses; and, as I say, I have already accumulated a good many. . . . Any who have come upon traces of this industry may possibly know that a large number of my little crime stories were concerned with a person called Father Brown; a Catholic priest whose external simplicity and internal subtlety formed something near enough to a character for the purposes of this sketchy sort of storytelling. And certain questions have arisen, especially questions about the identity or accuracy of the type, which have not been without an effect on more important things. (pp. 320-21)

The notion that a character in a novel must be "meant" for somebody or "taken from" somebody is founded on a misunderstanding of the nature of narrative fancy, and especially of such slight fancies as mine. Nevertheless, it has been generally said that Father Brown had an original in real life; and in one particular and rather personal sense, it is true. (p. 321)

When a writer invents a character for the purposes of fiction, especially of light or fanciful fiction, he fits him out with all sorts of features meant to be effective in that setting and against that background. He may have taken, and probably has taken, a hint from a human being. But he will not hesitate to alter the human being, especially in externals, because he is not thinking of a portrait but of a picture. In Father Brown, it was the chief feature to be featureless. The point of him was to appear pointless; and one might say that his conspicuous quality was not being conspicuous. His commonplace exterior was meant to contrast with his unsuspected vigilance and intelligence; and that being so, of course, I made his appearance shabby and shapeless, his face round and expressionless, his manners clumsy, and so on. At the same time I did take some of his inner intellectual qualities from my friend, Father John O'Connor of Bradford, who has not, as a matter of fact, any of these external qualities. He is not shabby, but rather neat; he is not clumsy, but very delicate and dexterous; he not only is but looks amusing and amused. He is a sensitive and quick-witted Irishman, with the profound irony and some of the potential irritability of his race. My Father Brown was deliberately described as a Suffolk dumpling from East Anglia. That, and the rest of his description, was a deliberate disguise for the purpose of detective fiction. But for all that, there is a very real sense in which Father O'Connor was the intellectual inspiration of these stories. . . . I cannot do better than tell the story of how the first notion of this detective comedy came into my mind. (pp. 322-23)

I had gone to give a lecture at Keighley on the high moors of the West Riding, and stayed the night with a leading citizen of that little industrial town; who had assembled a group of local friends such as could be conceived, I suppose, as likely to be patient with lecturers; including the curate of the Roman Catholic Church; a small man with a smooth face and a demure but elvish expression. I was struck by the tact and humour with which he mingled with his very Yorkshire and very Protestant company; and I soon found out that they had, in their bluff way, already learned to appreciate him as something of a character. (pp. 324-25)

Next morning he and I walked over Keighley Gate, the great wall of the moors that separates Keighley from Wharfedale, for I was visiting friends in Ilkley; and after a few hours' talk on the moors, it was a new friend whom I introduced to my old friends at my journey's end. He stayed to lunch, he stayed to tea; he stayed to dinner; I am not sure that, under their pressing hospitality, he did not stay the night; and he stayed there many nights and days on later occasions; and it was there that we most often met. It was in one of these visits that the incident occurred, which led me to take the liberty of putting him, or rather part of him, into a string of sensational stories. (pp. 325-26)

I mentioned to the priest in conversation that I proposed to support in print a certain proposal, it matters not what, in connection with some rather sordid social questions of vice and crime. On this particular point he thought I was in error, or rather in ignorance; as indeed I was. And, merely as a necessary duty and to prevent me from falling into a mare's nest, he told me certain facts he knew about perverted practices which I certainly shall not set down or discuss here. I have confessed on an earlier page that in my own youth I had imagined for myself any amount of iniquity; and it was a curious experience to find that this quiet and pleasant celibate had plumbed those abysses far deeper than I. I had not imagined that the world could hold such horrors. If he had been a professional novelist throwing such filth broadcast on all the bookstalls for boys and babies to pick up, of course he would have been a great creative artist and a herald of the Dawn. As he was only stating them reluctantly, in strict privacy, as a practical necessity, he was, of course, a typical Jesuit whispering poisonous secrets in my ear. When we returned to the house we found it full of visitors, and fell into special conversation with two hearty and healthy young Cambridge undergraduates, who had been walking or cycling across the moors in the spirit of the stern and vigorous English holiday. They were no narrow athletes, however, but interested in various sports and in a breezy way in various arts; and they began to discuss music and landscape with my friend Father O'Connor. I never knew a man who could turn with more ease than he from one topic to another, or who had more unexpected stores of information, often purely technical information, upon all. The talk soon deepened into a discussion on matters more philosophical and moral; and when the priest had left the room, the two young men broke out into generous expressions of admiration, saying truly that he was a remarkable man, and seemed to know a great deal about Palestrina or Baroque architecture, or whatever was the point at the moment. Then there fell a curious reflective silence, at the end of which one of the undergraduates suddenly burst out: "All the same, I don't believe his sort of life is the right one. It's all very well to like religious music and so on, when you're all shut up in a sort of cloister and don't know anything about the real evil in the world. But I don't believe that's the right ideal. I believe in a fellow coming out into the world, and facing the evil that's in it, and knowing something about the dangers and all that. It's a very beautiful thing to be innocent and ignorant; but I think it's a much finer thing not to be afraid of knowledge."

To me, still almost shivering with the appallingly practical facts of which the priest had warned me, this comment came with such a colossal and crushing irony, that I nearly burst into a loud harsh laugh in the drawing-room. For I knew perfectly well that, as regards all the solid Satanism which the priest knew and warred with all his life, these two Cambridge gentlemen (luckily for them) knew about as much of real evil as two babies in the same perambulator.

And there sprang up in my mind the vague idea of making some artistic use of this comic yet tragic cross-purposes; and

Chesterton's caricature of himself, drawn while he was at the Slade School, 1893-1895.

constructing a comedy in which a priest should appear to know nothing and in fact know more about crime than the criminals. I afterwards summed up the special idea in the story called **"The Blue Cross,"** otherwise very slight and improbable, and continued it through the interminable series of tales with which I have afflicted the world. In short, I permitted myself the grave liberty of taking my friend and knocking him about; beating his hat and umbrella shapeless, untidying his clothes, punching his intelligent countenance into a condition of pudding-faced fatuity, and generally disguising Father O'Connor as Father Brown. The disguise, as I have said, was a deliberate piece of fiction, meant to bring out or accentuate the contrast that was the point of the comedy. There is also in the conception, as in nearly everything I have ever written, a good deal of inconsistency and inaccuracy on minor points; not the least of such flaws being the general suggestion that Father Brown had nothing in particular to do, except to hang about in any household where there was likely to be a murder. A very charming Catholic lady I know once paid my detective priest the appropriate compliment of saying: "I am very fond of that officious little loafer." (pp. 326-28)

G. K. Chesterton, "The God with the Golden Key," in his Autobiography, *1936. Reprint by Hutchinson of London, 1969, pp. 320-43.*

MAURICE EVANS (essay date 1938)

[In the following excerpt from his book-length study written in 1938, Evans demonstrates how Chesterton explores motive rather than consequence in his detective fiction. He also illustrates Chesterton's method of expressing his ideas allegorically, particularly in The Poet and the Lunatics.*]*

[The interest in Chesterton's detective stories] is primarily in the motives which produced an action rather than in the consequences of that action; and Father Brown in unravelling the mystery, discovers at the same time the heretical philosophy which produced it. We may quote **"The Hammer of God"** in illustration (***The Wisdom of Father Brown***). The profligate squire has been killed by a mighty blow of a hammer; and the village blacksmith is suspected because he alone seems strong enough to deal such a blow. But Father Brown traces the crime to the squire's ascetic brother, the village parson, who dropped the hammer on to his head from the top of the church tower. Seeing his brother far below in his green riding coat, the murderer imagined him as a foul green beetle to be crushed, and was seized with the sin of Pride. This story is a good detective mystery, reasonably solved; and at the same time, an analysis of sinful motives. Father Brown, besides being an ordinary Catholic priest, is a symbol of the wisdom of the Catholic Church, and crime is treated as heresy. There are many more examples of a complete realism which continues at the same time to be religious propaganda, but no further illustration need be given. The popularity of these stories is a proof that they are successful. (pp. 73-4)

The Poet and the Lunatics contains allegorical treatment of a variety of Chesterton's beliefs. The title implies his favourite antithesis between imagination that is sane, and reason that leads to madness. Gabriel Gale, the hero, has all the right beliefs and is contrasted with a variety of heretical types, after the fashion of Father Brown, but the characters are more frankly allegories. Gale himself, for example, expresses his humility by his trick of standing on his head; and like St Tiller, who was crucified in that position, he is rewarded with a vision of the world as it really is in all its strangeness, "with the stars like flowers and the clouds like hills, and all men hanging on the mercy of God." He has in the opening chapter a queer companion, James Hurrel the business man, who induces all who come into contact with him to commit suicide. This is followed by **"The Yellow Bird"**, a treatment of the doctrine of liberty and limitation. Mallow the artist finds his fullest expression in painting small things; beginning with a picture of the whole valley, he ascends to the garden and finally feels himself worthy to paint the creeper under the window. Ivanhov, on the contrary, hates all limitation and has a mania for destroying boundaries. He begins by setting the canary free from its cage, and it is killed by wild birds: he breaks the bowl in which the goldfish are contained, and they, too, die. Finally, after throwing open all the windows and breaking the creeper which Mallow loved, he blows up the house in an attempt to free himself of its restriction. Gale states the moral of the action, "liberty is the power of a thing to be itself . . . we are limited by our brains and bodies, and if we break out, we cease to be ourselves and perhaps to be anything". Similarly, **"The Crime of Gabriel Gale"** is a treatment of that scepticism which believes things to exist only in mind. It is symbolized by a young man who through a series of uncanny coincidences comes to believe that he is God and can make things happen according to his will. Gale cures him by pinning him to a tree between the prongs of a pitch-fork, and leaving him in agony for two hours. The reality of pain convinces the young man that he is not omnipotent and cures him of his obsession. Gale once more applies the parable: "It is the only answer to the heresy of the mystic, which is to fancy that mind is all. It is to break your heart. Thank God for hard stones; thank God for hard facts." By them alone do we know that "the stars will stand and the hills will not melt at our word." (pp. 79-81)

It is not unusual . . . to associate the detective story with allegory, yet Chesterton has contrived to fuse the two in ***The Poet and the Lunatics.*** The effect is achieved, as we have already indicated, by a study of motives rather than actions, so that the detective becomes a philosopher and psychologist combined. Father Brown, Basil Grant and Gabriel Gale are all well studied in the dangers of heresy as well as the course of crime. The characters are allegorical; and yet are commonly allowed to behave like ordinary human beings, to whom no special significance is attached, for large tracts of the novel. For example, Gabriel Gale, in the opening episodes of ***The Poet and the Lunatics,*** is emphatically an allegory of Catholic humility moving among a proud or practical world. James Hurrel, his companion, is the spirit of big business producing ruin everywhere, rather than an ordinary business man. Yet some of the later episodes are completely realistic, and the book ends by treating everyone as an ordinary person. Gale's connection with Hurrel is explained, and he gets married like any other hero. (p. 89)

A few points may be made about the more purely literary value of Chesterton's [works]. His detective stories are excellent of their type, and his solutions both simple and unexpected. He scorns the strange Chinaman or the newly discovered death ray, and always plays fair with his readers. For example, in ***The Innocence of Father Brown,*** a man is murdered, though half a dozen people watching the door see no one enter. Father Brown realizes that someone must have entered who was too familiar for any one to notice and, consequently, traces the crime to the postman. Chesterton's solutions indeed are generally overlooked by their very simplicity. One of his favourite tricks is to blind the reader's eye by suggestions of the supernatural and fantastic, and then to produce a very obvious explanation which had been missed in the *mêlée*. **"The Shadow of the Shark"** (***The Poet and the Lunatics***) is a good example of this. A murder is committed on the seashore and no footprints are left in the sand. Suspicion is naturally attached to a rather wild member of the company who has knowledge of strange cults and who perpetually talks of some cruel sea god whom he worships. Such a man, it is argued, would naturally commit a murder in such a place to propitiate his god, and an ingenious solution is suggested, by which he slew his victim from the cliff top, with the help of a boomerang. But Gale, keeping a completely open mind and blinded by none of these suggestions, discovers a much more obvious method. The victim was killed by someone who paddled up just below the level of high-tide, so that his footprints were washed away.

The solutions are always completely fair, but the method of detection is not. The clues are given, but are of such a nature that only somebody on the spot could interpret them. For example, in **"The Yellow Bird"** (***The Poet and the Lunatics***) the main clue is a small yellow bird which is attacked by other birds among the trees. Gabriel Gale, seeing it, realizes that it is a canary freed from its cage, and so deduces Ivanhov's mania for breaking limitations which ultimately drives him to blow the house up. But a reader unable to see the bird would never realize that it was a canary and so see its significance. Again, in **"The Story of the Queer Feet"** (***The Innocence of Father Brown***) the only clue is the sound of feet in a passage which pass one way in a slow and measured tread, and then scurry hastily back. Father Brown, hearing the footsteps, realizes that it is someone playing the parts of both guest and waiter at a dinner, for the purpose of deceiving both and stealing a famous set of fish knives. But once more, we cannot deduce the answer because we cannot hear the feet. There is no question of setting the reader a mental problem to unravel: the pleasure comes entirely from seeing it done for us.

But even in the stories themselves, the clues are extremely scanty, and Chesterton's detectives all have amazing powers of intuition. The assumptions are that people act logically according to their philosophies, and that certain heretical philosophies inevitably lead to sin. Gabriel Gale has only to hear a scientist make a few stray remarks on animalcule to know that he is capable of murder. There are certain infallible signs of innocence or guilt in Chesterton's characters which one can recognize after a little practice. There is no significance in whether a man is kind to animals or not, but whether he is humble or has a sense of wonder or a love of small things. (pp. 93-6)

Maurice Evans, in his G. K. Chesterton, *Cambridge at the University Press, 1939, 157p.*

JORGE LUIS BORGES (essay date 1952)

[*An Argentine short story writer, poet, and essayist, Borges was one of the leading figures in contemporary literature. His writing is often used by critics to illustrate the modern view of literature as a highly sophisticated game. Justifying this interpretation of Borges's works are his admitted respect for stories that are artificial inventions of art rather than realistic representations of life. Here Borges, who himself wrote detective fiction, suggests that Chesterton's detective stories reveal his essential attraction to the dark and demoniacal. This essay was originally published in 1952.*]

Each story in the Father Brown Saga presents a mystery, proposes explanations of a demoniacal or magical sort, and then replaces them at the end with solutions of this world. Skill is not the only virtue of those brief bits of fiction; I believe I can perceive in them an abbreviation of Chesterton's life, a symbol or reflection of Chesterton. The repetition of his formula through the years and through the books (***The Man Who Knew Too Much, The Poet and the Lunatics, The Paradoxes of Mr. Pond***) seems to confirm that this is an essential form, not a rhetorical artifice. (p. 82)

Chesterton restrained himself from being Edgar Allan Poe or Franz Kafka, but something in the makeup of his personality leaned toward the nightmarish, something secret, and blind, and central. Not in vain did he dedicate his first works to the justification of two great gothic craftsmen, Browning and Dickens; not in vain did he repeat that the best book to come out of Germany was *Grimm's Fairy Tales*. He reviled Ibsen and defended Rostand (perhaps indefensibly), but the Trolls and the creator of *Peer Gynt* were the stuff his dreams were made of. That discord, that precarious subjection of a demoniacal will, defines Chesterton's nature. For me, the emblems of that struggle are the adventures of Father Brown, each of which undertakes to explain an inexplicable event by reason alone. [A footnote states: "Most writers of detective stories usually undertake to explain the obscure rather than the inexplicable."] That is why I said, in the first paragraph of this essay, that those stories were the key to Chesterton, the symbols and reflections of Chesterton. That is all, except that the "reason" to which Chesterton subjected his imaginings was not precisely reason but the Catholic faith or rather a collection of Hebrew imaginings that had been subjected to Plato and Aristotle.

I remember two opposing parables. The first one is from the first volume of Kafka's works. It is the story of the man who asks to be admitted to the law. The guardian of the first door says that there are many other doors within, and that every room is under the watchful eye of a guardian, each of whom is stronger than the one before. The man sits down to wait. Days and years go by, and the man dies. In his agony he asks, "Is it possible that during the years I have been waiting, no one has wanted to enter but me?" The guardian answers, "No one has wanted to enter this door because it was destined for you alone. Now I shall close it." (In the ninth chapter of *The Trial* Kafka comments on this parable, making it even more complicated.) The other parable is in Bunyan's *Pilgrim's Progress*. People gaze enviously at a castle guarded by many warriors; a guardian at the door holds a book in which he will write the name of the one who is worthy of entering. An intrepid man approaches the guardian and says, "Write my name, sir." Then he takes out his sword and lunges at the warriors; there is an exchange of bloody blows; he forces his way through the tumult and enters the castle.

Chesterton devoted his life to the writing of the second parable, but something within him always tended to write the first. (pp. 84-5)

Jorge Luis Borges, "On Chesterton," in his Other Inquisitions: 1937-1952, *translated by Ruth L. C. Simms, 1964. Reprint by University of Texas Press, 1984, pp. 82-5.*

MAISIE WARD (essay date 1955)

[*In a brief overview, Ward traces the Christian basis of Chesterton's detective fiction.*]

[Chesterton searched] below the obvious to discover the deepest reality. And indeed he saw the whole of life as a great detective story, especially for the Christian. Christ was discovered in a stable by wise men who had first visited the palace where the King of the Jews should in all probability have been found. God was hidden in the manhood of the crucified. Truth, which is reality, has always to be sought, is never obvious.

All this Chesterton translated into the realm of the detective story. . . . Father Brown, though suggested to Chesterton by a priest friend of his, was also to a great extent unconscious self-portraiture. The author of the stories like the hero with his peering myopic eyes saw so much more than he appeared to see, and so much of what he saw was in the soul. Conan Doyle created a detective—Sherlock Holmes—who discovered his criminal by the ashes of his favourite cigar or the mud on his shoes. . . . Father Brown's detecting is almost wholly psychological and, if in the course of it, he has occasion to hear the confession of a criminal, G. K.'s phrase about the Founder of Christianity might well apply to its priest. Diogenes, he once reminded us, took a lantern and for long searched vainly for an honest man—but Christ sought for and found one where Diogenes had never thought to look: inside the thief to whom he promised Paradise.

Other books in the same genre as Father Brown are: ***Four Faultless Felons***, ***The Man Who Knew Too Much***, and ***The Poet and the Lunatics***. The first of these though containing some good stories does not stick in the mind like the Father Brown books because the heroes are not distinctive personalities like the little priest. But ***The Man Who Knew Too Much*** is a very interesting study, again suggested by life to Chesterton. An intimate friend of his who belonged both to the aristocracy and the intelligentsia of England had from a worldly point of view made very little of his opportunities. G.K.C. believed that this was indeed because he knew too much to try very hard for the prize of that sort of success, knew too much both of the soiling of one's honour that may attend success and of the passing of the years and the realisation they bring to the thoughtful of how poor a thing it really is.

But of these three books by far the most interesting is ***The Poet and the Lunatics***. If Gabriel Gale had occurred to him earlier Chesterton might have made of him as famous a figure as Father Brown. For the long lounging poet with his yellow hair is the expression of a profound psychological fact which Chesterton again recognized in himself. The man of imagination alone, who can see himself in the lunatic's shoes, is the man who can save the lunatic's sanity. The man who can imagine himself committing a crime is the man who can solve it—or who can even prevent its commission. The poet, as always in Chesterton, is far more practical than he who is called "the practical man." To my mind one or two of these stories surpass all but the supreme best of Father Brown. (pp. 28-9)

Maisie Ward, "G. K. Chesterton," in Books on Trial, *Vol. XIV, No. 1, August-September, 1955, pp. 27-30.*

R. A. KNOX (essay date 1958)

[*In an excerpt from an essay devoted to Father Brown, Knox explores the many aspects that distinguish Father Brown stories from typical detective fiction, including Father Brown's psychological rather than logical deductions, Chesterton's lyrical descriptions, and the moral didacticism sometimes implicit in the tales.*]

When you take to writing detective stories, the measure of your success depends on the amount of personality you can build up round your favourite detective. Why this should be so, is not immediately obvious; it might have been supposed that this kind of fiction had a merely mathematical appeal. But, whether because Sherlock Holmes has set the standard for all time, or because the public does not like to see plots unravelled by a mere thinking-machine, it is personality that counts. You are not bound to make your public *like* the Great Detective; many readers have found Lord Peter Wimsey too much of a good thing, and I have even heard of people who were unable to appreciate the flavours of Poirot. But he must be real; he must have idiosyncrasies, eccentricities; even if he is a professional policeman, like Hanaud, he must smoke those appalling cigarettes, and get his English idioms wrong. And if possible—perhaps that is where Lord Peter fails—he must appeal to us through weakness; when he appears on the scene of the tragedy, the general reaction must be "A man like that will never be able to get at the truth." It is because he drops his parcels and cannot roll his umbrella, because he blinks at us and has fits of absent-mindedness, that Father Brown is such a good publisher's detective. He is a Daniel come to judgment. (p. 171)

There was to be nothing of the expert about Father Brown; he should have no knowledge of obscure poisons, or of the time required to let the *rigor mortis* set in; he was not to be the author of any treatise about the different kinds of cigarette ashes. All his knowledge was of the human heart; he explains, in **"The Secret of Flambeau,"** that he is only capable of detecting murder mysteries because he was the murderer himself—only, as it were, *in petto*. "What I mean is that, when I tried to imagine the state of mind in which such a thing would be done, I always realized that I might have done it myself under certain mental conditions, and not under others; and not generally the obvious ones. And then, of course, I knew who really had done it; and he was not generally the obvious person." He could put himself inside the other man's skin. He could even put himself inside an animal's skin—no, the dog did not know the murderer by instinct and spring at him, that was sentimental mythology. The important thing about the dog was that it howled when the sword-stick was thrown into the sea—howled because the sword-stick didn't float.

The real secret of Father Brown is that there is nothing of the mystic about him. When he falls into a reverie—I had almost said, a brown study—the other people in the story think that he must be having an ecstasy, because he is a Catholic priest, and will proceed to solve the mystery by some kind of heaven-sent intuition. And the reader, if he is not careful, will get carried away by the same miscalculation; here, surely, is Chesterton preparing to shew the Protestants where they get off. Unconsciously, this adds to the feeling of suspense; you never imagine that Poirot will have an ecstasy, or that Albert Campion will receive enlightenment from the supernatural world. And all the time, Father Brown is doing just what Poirot does; he is using his little grey cells. He is noticing something which the reader hasn't noticed, and will kick himself later for not having noticed. The lawyer who asks "Where was the body found?" when he is told about the Admiral's drowning has given himself away as knowing too much, already, about the duck-pond; if he had been an honest man, he would have assumed that the Admiral was drowned at sea. The prophet who goes on chanting his litany from the balcony, when the crowd beneath is rushing to the aid of the murdered woman, gives himself away as the murderer; he was expecting it. We had all the data to go upon, only Father Brown saw the point and we didn't. (pp. 172-73)

Father Brown began life as short stories in the *Saturday Evening Post*, and short stories he remained; for an author so fertile in ideas, perhaps it was the simplest arrangement. But it must be confessed that this enforced brevity produces a rather breathless atmosphere; the more so, because Chesterton was an artist before he became an author, and occupies a good deal of his space with scene-painting. And the scene-painting takes up room—valuable room, the pedantic reader would tell us.

What scene-painting it is! The Norfolk Broads, and the house full of mirrors standing on its lonely island; or that other island on the Cornish estuary, with its wooden tower—you would expect the second of these pictures to be little more than a repetition of the first, but in fact it is nothing of the kind; in the one case you have the feeling of being in Norfolk, in the other you have the feeling of being in Cornwall. The atmosphere of that dreadful hotel in **"The Queer Feet"**; the atmosphere of a winter-bound summer resort in **"The God of the Gongs"**; the (quite irrelevant) effect of bitter cold in **"The Sign of the Broken Sword"**—what a setting they give to the story! Flambeau explains, at the beginning of **"The Flying Stars,"** that in his criminal days he was something of an artist; "I had always attempted to provide crimes suitable to the special seasons or landscapes in which I found myself, choosing this or that terrace or garden for a catastrophe"; and if the criminal, so limited in his choice of means, can be expected to provide a suitable *décor,* how much more the writer of stories! Yet it is only Chesterton who gives us these effects, the "topsy-turvydom of stone in mid-air" as two men look down from the tower of a Gothic church; the "seas beyond seas of pines, now all aslope one way under the wind" on the hill-side of Glengyle; the "green velvet pocket in the long, green, trailing garments of the hills" on to which Mr. Harrogate's coach overturns, ready for the coming of the brigands. Did Chesterton pick out these landscapes with his artist's eye, and then, like Flambeau, invent crimes to suit them?

But it does take up room. And, if only because the canvas is so overcrowded, you must not expect in these stories the mass of details which you would expect of Freeman Wills Crofts; the extracts from Bradshaw, the plan of the study with a cross to shew where the body was found. Hence the severely orthodox readers of detective stories, who love to check and to challenge every detail, must be prepared for a disappointment; Chesterton will not be at pains to tell us whether the windows were fastened; how many housemaids were kept (in defiance of modern probabilities), and which of them dusted the room last; whether a shot in the gun-room would be audible in the butler's pantry, and so on. Even the unities of time and place are neglected; you can never be quite sure whether it is next morning, or a week later, or what. Consequently, you never quite feel "Here am I, with all the same data at my disposal as Father Brown had; why is it that his little grey cells work, and mine don't?" Not that there is any deliberate concealment of clues, but the whole picture is blurred; the very wealth of detail confuses you. All you can do is to set about eliminating the impossible characters in the hope of finding, by a process of exhaustion, the villain. Women can be ruled out; there is only one female villain in the whole series—it is part of Chesterton's obstinate chivalry that he hardly ever introduces you to a woman you are meant to dislike. People with Irish names (how unlike Sherlock Holmes!) are fairly certain to be innocent. But, even so, the characters of the story elude you; you do not feel certain that you have been told quite enough about them.

For Chesterton (as for Father Brown) the characters were the really important thing. The little priest could see, not as a psychologist, but as a moralist, into the dark places of the human heart; could guess, therefore, at what point envy, or fear, or resentment would pass the bounds of the normal, and the cords of convention would snap, so that a man was hurried into crime. Into crime, not necessarily into murder; the Father Brown stories are not bloodthirsty, as detective stories go; a full third of them deal neither with murder nor with attempted murder, which is an unusual average nowadays; most readers demand a corpse. The motives which made it necessary for Hypatia Hard to elope with her husband, the motives which induced the Master of the Mountain to pretend that he had stolen the ruby when he hadn't—the reader may find them unimpressive, because there is no black cap and no drop at the end of them. But, unless he is a man of unusual perspicacity, he will have to admit that he also found them unexpected.

The truth is that what we demand of a detective story is neither sensations, nor horrors, but ingenuity. And Chesterton was a man of limitless ingenuity. What really contents us is when we see at last, and kick ourselves for not having seen before, that the man who was murdered in the Turkish bath without any trace of a weapon was stabbed with an icicle; that the poisoner did drink the tea which accounted for her victim, but took a stiff emetic immediately afterwards; that the time of a particular incident was given wrongly, not because the witness was in bad faith, but because she saw, not the clock, but the reflection of the clock in a looking-glass. All those brilliant twists which a Mason and an Agatha Christie give to their stories, Chesterton, when he was in the mood for it, could give to his. How to dispose of the body? If it was only for a short time, you could hang it up on the hat-stand in a dark passage; if you wanted to get rid of it altogether, you could bury it in the concrete floor of a new set of flats. A ship could be lured to its doom by lighting a bonfire which would confuse the appearance of the lights in the tideway; you could gag a ruler so securely that he would be unable to answer the challenge of his own sentries, and would be shot. They are all ideas we might have thought of, and didn't.

Whether such expedients would be likely to be adopted in real life is perhaps more questionable. But then, how far is the writer of mystery stories bound by the laws of probability?

Chesterton and Frances Blogg during their engagement.

Nothing could be more improbable than Father Brown's habit of always being on the spot when a crime is committed; but he shares this curious trick of ubiquity with Hercule Poirot. The thing is a literary convention; it may not be a good one, but it is well worn. No, when we open a detective story we leave the world of strict probability behind us; we must be prepared for three or four quite independent pieces of shady business happening to happen in the same country house on the same evening. And Chesterton's imagination was flamboyant; he was like a schoolboy on holiday, and could sit as light to realism as P. G. Wodehouse. If you meet him on his own ground—that is, halfway to fairyland—you will have to admit that for sheer ingenuity he can rival Miss Sayers herself. Cast your mind back to your first reading of the Father Brown stories, and ask yourself whether you saw what was the missing factor which linked all the various exhibits in Glengyle Castle, or why **"The Insoluble Problem"** was insoluble.

No, if we are to judge the Father Brown cycle by the canons of its own art, we shall not be disposed to complain that these are something less than detective stories; rather, that they are something more. Like everything else Chesterton wrote, they are a Chestertonian manifesto. And it may be reasonably maintained that a detective story is meant to be read in bed, by way of courting sleep; it ought not to make us think—or rather, it ought to be a kind of *catharsis,* taking our minds off the ethical, political, theological problems which exercise our waking hours by giving us artificial problems to solve instead. If this is so, have we not good reason to complain of an author who smuggles into our minds, under the disguise of a police mystery, the very solicitudes he was under contract to banish?

I am inclined to think that the complaint, for what it is worth, lies against a good many of the Father Brown stories, but not all, and perhaps not the best. Where the moral which Chesterton introduces is vital to the narrative, belongs to the very stuff of the problem, the author has a right, if he will, to mystify us on this higher level. In the over-civilized world we live in, there are certain anomalies which we take for granted; and he may be excused if he gently mocks at us for being unable, because we took them for granted, to read his riddle. There is something artificial in a convention which allows us to say that nobody has entered a house when in fact a postman has entered it, as if the postman, being a State official, were not a man. There is something top-heavy about a society in which a fellow guest is indistinguishable from a waiter if he cares to walk in a particular way. And there is something lacking in the scientific investigator who can be taken in when his own secretary disguises himself in a false beard, simply because he has sat opposite his secretary day after day without noticing what he looked like. But it must be confessed that in some of the stories, especially the later ones, the didactic purpose tends to overshadow, and even to crowd out, the detective interest: such stories as **"The Arrow of Heaven,"** and **"The Chief Mourner of Marne."** If we read these with interest, it is not because they are good detective stories, but because they are good Chesterton. When he wrote ***The Incredulity of Father Brown*** and ***The Secret of Father Brown,*** Chesterton had perhaps rather written himself out, and publishers pressed him for copy faster than even he could supply it. At the end of his life, he seemed to get a second wind, and ***The Scandal of Father Brown*** contains some of his most ingenious plots. But how seldom does an author manage to spin out a formula indefinitely; how signally Conan Doyle failed to do it! But—those first six stories Chesterton contributed to the *Saturday Evening Post*! How could that level have been maintained? (pp. 174-79)

R. A. Knox, "Father Brown," in his Literary Distractions, *Sheed and Ward, 1958, pp. 170-79.*

W. W. ROBSON (essay date 1969)

[In the following excerpt Robson offers a detailed thematic and stylistic discussion of the Father Brown stories. The critic stresses that Chesterton used his superficially light or casual stories to express serious ideas.]

Chesterton himself did not attach great importance to the Father Brown stories. Ordered in batches by magazine editors and publishers, they were written hurriedly for the primary purpose of helping to finance his distributist paper, *G. K.'s Weekly.* And though they have proved to be the most popular of Chesterton's writings, critical attention to them has been casual. This is partly because they are, of course, detective stories; and the detective story is commonly dismissed, without argument, as a very low form of art. That it is also a very difficult and demanding form, in which many clever writers have failed, is not regarded as relevant. Nor is there much respect for the innovators in this genre, or much comment on their remarkable rarity. If there were, Chesterton's reputation would stand very high; for his detective stories, while they may not be the best ever written, are without doubt the most ingenious. But to show ingenuity and originality in the detective story is for the superior critic merely to have a knack for a particular sort of commercial fiction. It is not the sort of thing he takes seriously. And Chesterton himself, it seems, would have agreed with him.

My contention will be that these stories, together with Chesterton's novel *The Man Who Was Thursday,* are the best of his writings, and I will try to give reasons why they should be taken seriously. (p. 611)

What is Chesterton *saying* in the Father Brown stories? In what follows I shall discuss their manifest meaning, and I shall carry the discussion as far as the borders of their latent meaning, leaving it to others, if they are interested, to explore that. This manifest meaning must be understood in terms of their genre. Whatever else these stories may turn out to be, they are certainly, on the face of it, light fiction, in a recognizable genre. (p. 615)

Chesterton, like all detective story writers, derives from Poe. Indeed, it might be said that he derives from a single story of Poe: many of the Father Brown stories can be regarded as ingenious variations on the theme of "The Purloined Letter." The suggestion of realistic police work, which we have in "The Murders in the Rue Morgue" and "The Mystery of Marie Roget," did not attract him. Father Brown keeps away from the secular authorities. . . . There are no chemical analyses or careful checking of alibis in these stories. Nor is there the dry intellectuality of Dupin. For between Poe and Chesterton comes Conan Doyle. It is, of course, Sherlock Holmes who humanized the figure of the Great Detective, the symbol of reason and justice. (p. 616)

Chesterton, Stevenson, Doyle—are disciples of Dickens, the great master of the unfamiliarity in the familiar. But Chesterton was perhaps the closest of them all to the detective story side of Dickens. The novel of Dickens that has most in common with Chesterton is *The Mystery of Edwin Drood.* It will be said that this is not merely a detective story, that it has imagination and moral seriousness. All the same, it *is* a detective story, and as such it is genuinely mysterious. And this is not only because it is unfinished. . . . The quality of Chesterton's work at its best, in the Father Brown stories, is comparable to that of *Edwin Drood*. It is true to its genre: it is full of suspense, sensation, genuine clues, red herrings, "atmosphere," real mystery and spurious mystery. But Chesterton, though he might talk lightheartedly about batches of corpses despatched to the publisher, is serious, as Dickens is serious in *Edwin Drood*. In these stories murder is murder, sin is sin, damnation is damnation. Every imaginative writer must choose his genre, and every genre has limitations. The detective tale has obvious limitations. The most serious is this: no character can have depth, no character can be done from the inside, because any must be a potential suspect. It is Chesterton's triumph that he turned this limitation of the genre into an illumination of the universal human potentiality of guilt and sin. No character in the stories matters except Father Brown. But this is not a fault, because Father Brown, being a man, epitomizes all their potentialities within himself. "Are you a devil?" the exposed criminal wildly asks. "I am a man," replies Father Brown, "and therefore have all devils in my heart."

This ability to identify himself with the murderer is the "secret" of Father Brown's method. Some readers have misunderstood Chesterton's intention here. They suppose that Father Brown is credited with special spiritual powers, pertaining to his rôle as a priest. They see him as a thaumaturgic Sherlock Holmes. One adverse critic saw in Father Brown's ability to divine the truth, where plodding mundane detectives fail, a typical dishonest trick of the Catholic apologist. But it is made quite clear that Father Brown owes his success not to supernatural insight but to the usual five senses. He is simply more observant, less clouded by conventional anticipations and prejudices, than the average man. The kind of clue he notices is not cigar ash or footprints, but something like this:

> "I am sorry to say we are the bearers of bad news. Admiral Craven was drowned before reaching home. . . ."
>
> "When did this happen?" asked the priest.
>
> "Where was he found?" asked the lawyer.

A moment later the priest realizes that the lawyer has murdered Admiral Craven. If you are told that a seaman, returning from the sea, has been drowned, you do not ask where his body was "found." Admiral Craven was found in a landlocked pool; Father Brown realized that Mr. Dyke could only know that because he had put him there. Most of the clues in the stories are of this kind. It is true that at the end of this story (**"The Green Man"**) Father Brown does show some knowledge which, in the terms of the story, he could not have acquired by natural means; he knows that Mr. Dyke committed the murder because his client, the Admiral, discovered that he had been robbing him. This is a fault in the story. But the same sort of fault can be found in greater writers when they are winding up the plot. Shakespeare makes Iago confess that he dropped Desdemona's handkerchief in Cassio's chamber. Surely a man like Iago would never have confessed anything. The essential discovery that Father Brown makes in this story is the identity of the murderer, not his motive. It should have been left to the police to find that out.

Chesterton takes pains to emphasize that Father Brown has no supernatural powers, by frequently contrasting him with false images who claim them. (Examples are to be found in stories like **"The Song of the Flying Fish"** or **"The Red Moon of Meru."**) Their characteristic sin is spiritual pride. They are quite happy to be accused of ordinary crimes, which they have not committed, if the crimes are thought miraculous. For contrast, we have a story like **"The Resurrection of Father Brown,"** in which Father Brown is subjected to the overwhelming temptation to claim credit for a false miracle: that he has risen from the dead. Without hesitation, dazed as he is, he discredits the story.

Father Brown is, then, not a thaumaturge. But it must be granted that, apart from his powers of observation, he has exceptional moral insight. . . . But Chesterton's aim is not really a psychological study of such a man. Almost at once Father Brown becomes largely a mouthpiece for Chesterton's own wit and wisdom. . . . The artistic reason for Father Brown's powers of repartee, and his wittiness in general, is that we look straight at him as we do not look at Sherlock Holmes, who is reflected in the—sometimes exasperated—admiration of Dr. Watson. Chesterton has dispensed with a Dr. Watson; and so Father Brown has to seem brilliant to *us*. And the only way this can be done is by making him brilliant. . . . Father Brown by himself has no solidity. He is not a credible priest; he seems to be away from his parish as often as Dr. Watson was away from his practice. He comes and goes from nowhere. The temptation to make him a semi-symbolic figure must have been great. Agatha Christie succumbed to a similar temptation in her stories about *The Mysterious Mr. Quin*. But this is false to the genre. Chesterton's stories, though often fantastic, are not fantasies. Again and again it is emphasized that Father Brown in himself is an ordinary man: an extraordinarily ordinary man.

But Father Brown's ordinariness is ordinariness *à la* Chesterton. He shares his creator's aesthetic sense. Indeed, his detective powers are closely connected with his aesthetic sense. He knows what is the "right" crime for the "right" criminal. The whole remarkable story called **"The Wrong Shape"** is built around this aesthetic criminology. The reformed criminal Flambeau, hunted and converted by Father Brown in the early stories, has similarly an aesthetic sense about his crimes. He chooses the right sort of crime for the right setting, as in **"The Flying Stars."** (Some memories of the fabled exploits of Vidocq, who fascinated Balzac, must have gone into Flambeau's creation.) It is an aesthetic sense that sometimes provides Father Brown with an essential clue; as in **"The Worst Crime in the World,"** where his perception of the balanced arrangement of a hall enables him to spot that one suit of armor, out of what must have been a pair, is missing. And Chesterton, as often, notes the curious and sometimes topsy-turvy relationship between aesthetic fitness and moral fitness:

> "It's a wonder his throat isn't cut," said Mr. Smart's valet Harris, not without a hypothetical relish, almost as if he had said, in a purely artistic sense, "It's a pity."

That "hypothetical relish" explains a good deal of our pleasure in the fantasies and atrocities of the stories.

Finally, Father Brown's detective skill owes much to that linguistic sensitivity which he shares with his creator. He finds himself thinking of foreign voyages in a house in Cornwall.

> Besides the butler, the Admiral's only servant were two negroes, somewhat quaintly clad in tight uniforms of yellow. The priest's instinctive trick of analysing his own impressions told him that the colour and the little neat coattails of these bipeds had suggested the word "Ca-

> nary,'' and so by a mere pun connected them with Southward travel.

Other characters share it at times.

> He was a man with more literary than direct natural associations; the word ''Ravenswood'' came into his head repeatedly. It was partly the raven colour of the pine-woods; but partly also an indescribable atmosphere almost described in Scott's great tragedy; the smell of something that died in the eighteenth century; the smell of dank gardens and broken urns; of wrongs that will never now be righted; of something that is none the less incurably sad because it is strangely unreal.

Such things show the literary critic in Chesterton, the power of verbal analysis which we associate with a critic of our own day like William Empson, and which Empson himself has praised in Chesterton. But sometimes this linguistic sensitiveness is employed in the interests of logical clarity. Chesterton has a feeling for the niceties of idiom, and their conceptual implications, which recalls a philosopher like the late Professor Austin. (pp 617-22)

Father Brown, then, is represented as at the same time an ordinary man, of simple tastes, who enjoys simple pleasures, and a clever, shrewd person, with observation and sensitiveness beyond the ordinary. But he is not a mystic. He remains true both to traditional theology, and to the genre of the detective story, in never decrying reason. It is when Flambeau, disguised as a priest, does this that Father Brown is certain he is a fraud. Of course, Father Brown is represented as a religious man. It is not by accident, and not merely to find a new twist to the Sherlock Holmes formula, that Chesterton makes him a priest. But once again Chesterton is at pains to dissociate him from anything exotic, any suggestion of the allegedly subtle lures of Rome. (p. 623)

Again and again in these stories Chesterton shows how much the common dislike of Catholicism is (or was) due to dislike of ''religious externals.'' But the deeper religious meaning of these stories is to do with something more important than cultural considerations. The abundance of quacks, mystagogues, sorcerers in them is not only due to the desire to point a contrast with Father Brown. It is to illustrate, in terms proper to the genre in which Chesterton is writing, his belief that what Christianity has shown is that the age-old effort of man to grasp the Divine is bankrupt. Man cannot come to God. Christianity says that God came to man. This was what Chesterton was saying over and over again, in different tones and with varying degrees of humor or earnestness. Orwell claimed that writers like Chesterton seem to have only one subject: that they are Catholics. One might as well retort that Orwell's only subject seems to be that he was not one. Either the Catholic faith is relevant to the whole of life, or it is relevant to none of it. That, at any rate, was Chesterton's position.

In the end, then, the priest's ''steady humble gaze'' owes its power to more than observation. When he realized that the doctor did the murder, he ''looked him gravely and steadily in the face''; and the doctor went away and wrote his confession. He is an atheist, and he begins his confession: ''*Vicisti, Galilaee!*'' But he goes on at once ''In other words, damn your eyes, which are very remarkable and penetrating ones.''

The religious meaning is central in the best of these stories. But some of them contain a good deal of effective social satire also. I have already mentioned **''The Invisible Man,''** that ingenious fable of the people who ''don't count.'' Wells, we know, had another idea of the ''invisible man''; and Ralph Ellison has another. Seeing the invisible in Chesterton's story means what Ellison means: keeping a sense of human brotherhood. Some of the incidental themes in this story are interesting, especially considering its date. We note that the victim Isidore Smythe is a characteristically modern man, who not only has a fast car, but, more remarkably, a complete staff of robots to wait on him. Another parable, with a keen edge of social satire, is another well-known story, **''The Queer Feet.''** The point of this story, as a detective story, is that a gentleman's coat looks the same as a waiter's; but the stratagem of Flambeau, the owner of the ''queer feet'' which now saunter like a gentleman and now scurry like a waiter, is possible only because of the great gulf fixed between gentlemen and waiters. It is the ''outsiders,'' first of all Death (the dead waiter at the beginning of the story), then the crook Flambeau, and finally the shabby Father Brown, who point the satire on the Twelve True Fishermen. Chesterton, like Kipling, vividly describes the ritualism of English upper-class life; but he sees it more ironically than Kipling. They parody the twelve apostles, who were fishermen, and fishers of men like Father Brown, who can bring the reformed criminal back from the ends of the earth with ''a twitch upon the thread.'' Light and amusing as the story is, it is an exposure, not only of social class, but of plutocracy employing the traditions of social class, to eliminate humanity and brotherhood. Yet all the Fishermen are very likeable, and the story ends with an amusing touch. After their silver has been recovered, thanks to Father Brown, their first thought is to invent a new addition to their ritual by way of commemorating its recovery. The members will in future wear green coats, to distinguish them from waiters.

But the most memorable of the stories are not witty parables like these, but imaginative fairy tales. What some readers remember most in the Father Brown stories is Chesterton's powers of description. His liking for a twilight setting—dawn or dusk—has been noted; and so has the constant sense we have that the action is taking place in a toy theater, where the weird and wonderful backcloth dominates everything, and the tiny puppets that gesticulate in fight or dance in front of it seem faceless and featureless. And these backcloths have a décor which links Chesterton to Swinburne and the Decadents. His moral and religious outlook could not be more different from theirs; but his imagination has been formed on their work. Lurid, or fanciful, or grotesque decoration dominates stories like **''The Wrong Shape''** or **''The Dagger with Wings.''** Of course this decoration is there in part to distract us. . . . It is Chesterton's task as conjurer to arrange this scene, with bizarre figures in a bizarre setting, so that we shall miss the explanation of the mystery, which always turns on some straightforward, mundane motive. (In more than half the stories the motivation for the crime is nothing more metaphysical or *outré* than greed.)

However, I think the unforgettable descriptions of gardens, houses, landscapes, and the effects of *light* in these stories are not mainly there for camouflage, or merely for scene painting. I think they have something to do with the latent meaning of the stories; and this in turn has something to do with the attraction of the detective story, as a genre, both to Chesterton himself and to his readers. But first of all let us note that, even at the level of the plot, the descriptions are highly relevant. This passage from **''The Hammer of God,''** read in its context, contains the explanation of the mystery. Two men look down from the top of a church.

> Immediately beneath and about them the lines of the Gothic building plunged outwards into the void with a sickening swiftness akin to suicide. There is that element of Titan energy in the architecture of the Middle Ages that, from whatever aspect it be seen, it is always running away, like the strong back of some maddened horse. This church was hewn out of ancient and silent stone, bearded with old fungoids and stained with the nests of birds. And yet, when they saw it from below, it sprang like a fountain at the stars; and when they saw it, as now, from above, it poured like a cataract into a voiceless pit. For these two men on the tower were left alone with the most terrible aspect of Gothic; the monstrous foreshortening and disproportion, the dizzy perspectives, the glimpses of great things small and small things great; a topsy-turvydom of stone in the mid-air.

This is the sort of passage that we feel is too good for a detective story. Yet it is surely an artistic virtue, if only a minor one, that the height of the church and the way the landscape below it looks like "a map of the world" should, for the attentive, explain both the crime's motive, and the method of its commission.

But my main reason for quoting the passage is to call attention to the phrases about "monstrous foreshortening and disproportion," "dizzy perspectives," "glimpses of great things small and small things great." These are clues to Chesterton's imagination. First of all, it was intensely visual. He began as a painter, and we can find the painter's eye in all his descriptions. But—more important—it was child-like. . . . This child-like quality in Chesterton attracts some readers and repels others. Those whom it repels dislike the association he makes between childish fantasies about winged daggers and flying vampires, and serious themes of good and evil. They feel that the former degrade the latter. . . . I cannot answer this objection, except by saying that Chesterton himself seems to have been aware of it, and tries to answer it in his story **"The Dagger with Wings."** Here the real mystery of nature is contrasted with the spurious mystery, the "white magic," which the criminal mystagogue exploits. Father Brown, as usual, appears as the agnostic: "I do believe some things, of course, and therefore, of course, I don't believe other things." The wickedness of the mystagogue and murderer Strake is explained as the perversion of a good thing: his power as a story-teller. He enjoys his masquerade as the man he has murdered. "He enjoyed it as a fantasy as well as a conspiracy." The monistic mumbo-jumbo with which he tries to deceive Father Brown is recognized by Father Brown as "the religion of rascals." In contrast, the cold of the air, as Father Brown walks home after the exposure and arrest of Strake, "divides truth from error with a blade like ice." Crime and insanity in this story are associated with changing colors, pantheistic unities, mixed-upness; goodness and innocence with the whiteness of snow, the dualism of black and white, truth and error, artifice and nature. The villain Strake has the wilfulness, the perversity, the distortions, of a naughty child. It is the normal imagination of the child that shows him up.

We might say, then, that Father Brown is imagined by Chesterton as a child whose vision is undistorted. The psychological critic will no doubt see in the contrasting distortions of perspective, the "wrong shapes," the murderous yet strangely unheated fantasies of the stories, some relationship to the child's bizarre notions of the sexual behavior of adults. And this may be the latent appeal of all classic detective stories. For reasons of temperament, period, and literary mode, Chesterton avoids overtly sexual themes in the Father Brown stories. Yet it was presumably the real Father Brown's knowledge of sexual depravities that shocked Chesterton [see excerpt by Chesterton dated 1936]. And in **"The Secret of Father Brown"** the priest confides to his interlocutor that he "acted out" in his imagination all the crimes that he had investigated. What renders Father Brown invulnerable is precisely this playacting. But whether this makes the stories entirely wholesome is not certain. The oddities in them must tempt psychological criticism. Chesterton's fascination with the way things look upside down—as in an unpleasant story, **"The Vanishing of Vaudrey"**—seems to be intimately related to his love of paradox. We remember how Dean Inge, with a note of animosity that Chesterton rarely provoked in his opponents, called him "that obese mountebank who crucifies truth head downwards." Inge was thinking, of course, of Chesterton's paradoxes. . . . Chesterton's love of the paradoxical amounts to an obsession. Perhaps more than anything else it has turned readers away from him. And we cannot but relate it to what appear to be morbid and pathological elements in these stories.

But these do not predominate. On the whole Chesterton is quite clear about what he is doing. And what he is doing is to play a game with the reader. Some of his funniest stories are those in which he "sends up" his own genre, as in **"The Purple Wig,"** or **"The Absence of Mr. Glass."** In others he debunks the thriller motifs of other writers, such as the supernatural curse (**"The Doom of the Darnaways," "The Perishing of the Pendragons," "The Salad of Colonel Cray"**). It is very characteristic of Chesterton to point out that the doom of the Darnaways would lose all its spell if it were the doom of the Browns. It is also very characteristic that he also loves to pull the legs of scientific investigators (**"The Blast of the Book," "The Mistake of the Machine"**). Chesterton is not hostile to science because it is inhuman. On the contrary, science, to *be* science, has to be inhuman. But it is out of this, precisely, that Chesterton extracts his comedy.

We may think it a pity that wit and wisdom and such remarkable (if idiosyncratic) descriptive power were wasted on these little detective tales. On the other hand, it may be that they served to focus psychological and moral and religious preoccupations which Chesterton happened to have at the time, and which he could not have discharged in any other form. At any rate, these stories seem to have survived in the affections of ordinary readers, while Chesterton's more ambitious works are forgotten. But I suppose the superior critic will say this is because all the ordinary reader cares about is whodunit. (pp. 623-29)

W. W. Robson, "G. K. Chesterton's 'Father Brown' Stories," in The Southern Review *(Louisiana State University), Vol. V, No. 3, Summer, 1969, pp. 611-29.*

RUSSELL KIRK (essay date 1969)

[An American historian, political theorist, novelist, journalist, and lecturer, Kirk is considered one of America's most eminent conservative intellectuals. His works, particularly The Conservative Mind *(1953), have provided a major impetus to the conservative revival that has developed since the 1950s. In the following excerpt from a lecture delivered in October 1969, Kirk*

explores lunacy in Chesterton's fiction, particularly The Poet and the Lunatics *and* Four Faultless Felons.]

No man of his time defended more passionately the cause of sanity and "centricity" than did G. K. Chesterton, despite his aversion to watches and his uncalculated picturesqueness of dress. But no imaginative writer touched more often than did Chesterton upon lunacy, real or alleged: a prospect of his age with the madhouse for its background.

"It is, indeed, an absurd exaggeration to say that we are all mad," Chesterton writes in *Lunacy and Letters,*

> "just as it is true that we are none of us perfectly healthy. If there were to appear in the world a perfectly sane man, he would certainly be locked up. The terrible simplicity with which he would walk over our minor morbidities, our sulky vanities and malicious self-righteousness; the elephantine innocence with which he would ignore our fictions of civilization—these would make him a thing more desolating and inscrutable than a thunderbolt or a beast of prey. It may be that the great prophets who appeared to mankind as mad were in reality raving with an impotent sanity."

What Burke called "metaphysical madness," the delusions of the ideologue and the neoterist, was the modern affliction against which Chesterton contended. The Library of the British Museum, Chesterton remarks, "discharges a great many of the functions of a private madhouse." Against the sort of lunacy encountered in libraries, and the sort encountered in public affairs, Chesterton took his stand. Madhouses, public or private, loom large in seven of his fantastic romances; madmen pop up in high places. In our era, his argument runs, some of the wisest and best men may find themselves in Bedlam: for the madman and the rogue manipulating madmen are in power. (pp. 33-4)

As we slide away from the normality that Chesterton upheld, we fall into a kind of rationalistic insanity. Starving the moral imagination (which must be nurtured early by myth, fable, allegory, and parable), we find ourselves upon the alienist's couch. Chesterton chose fantasy as his weapon for defending common sense, knowing that defecated rationality—private judgment carried to its extreme—is the enemy of the higher reason. (pp. 34-5)

Chesterton set out to reinvigorate the moral imagination through fable: by "supposal," creating a fiction to impart a moral. "It is only in our exhausted and agnostic age," he wrote late in life, "that the idea has been started that if one is moral one must not be melodramatic." The Greeks, the medieval scholars, the Protestant moralists, and the eighteenth-century rationalistic moralists all knew better. Fantastic melodrama—from the shape-shifting of the gigantic being called Sunday (Nature incarnate) to the purposeful groping of Father Brown—was Chesterton's instrument for the recovery of moral order. And of melodramatic subjects, none is more compelling than the madman and the madhouse. (pp. 35-6)

In her biography of Chesterton [see Additional Bibliography], Maisie Ward does not mention ***The Poet and the Lunatics***. . . . Yet I rate that series of fantastic tales high in Chesterton's fiction.

Gabriel Gale, its intuitive hero, has a talent for mollifying madmen and moderating their excesses. The whole book is about lunacy and its subtle causes in this century.

"Genius oughtn't to be eccentric!" Gale exclaims. "Genius ought to be centric. It ought to be the core of the cosmos, not on the revolving edges. People seem to think it a compliment to accuse one of being an outsider, and to talk about the eccentricities of genius. What would they think if I said I only wish to God I had the centricities of genius?"

The maddest of all maniacs is the man of business, as Gale discovers from a considerable acquaintance among madmen. Also there is the Russian psychologist who believes in emancipation, expansion, the elimination of limits: he begins by liberating a caged bird (to its destruction), next frees goldfish from their bowl, and ends by blowing up himself and the house where he has been a guest.

"What exactly is liberty?" Gale inquires, just before the explosion. "First and foremost, surely, it is the power of a thing to be itself. In some ways the yellow bird was free in the cage. . . . We are limited by our brains and bodies; and if we break out, we cease to be ourselves, and, perhaps, to be anything. . . ." (pp. 43-4)

In these stories, one encounters the scientific maniac, purged of conscience, ready to kill for the sake of a museum's endowment; the artistic maniac, murderous when disabused of his pet fallacy; the anti-superstition maniac, more fanatical than any witch-doctor. One encounters, again, the solipsist who begins to fancy that he is God, and who can be saved only through intense pain:

> There is no cure for that nightmare of omnipotence except pain; because that is the thing a man *knows* he would not tolerate if he could really control it. A man must be in some place from which he would certainly escape if he could, if he is really to realize that all things do not come from within. I doubt whether any of our action is really anything but an allegory. I doubt whether any truth can be told except in a parable.

Therefore Gale pinned a poor self-intoxicated curate to a tree during a fierce storm, until the man recognized his own puniness, and that he was not sitting in the sky, and that he had no angelic servants going "to and fro in colored garments of cloud and flame and the pageant of the seasons." Lacking forcible parables, we are swallowed up by the monstrous ego.

Because he ridiculed certain powerful interests, Gale himself escapes being committed to a madhouse only through liberation by an armed genuine lunatic. The corrupt and treacherous psychologists who would put Gale behind walls tell him that he is a megalomaniac expressing himself in exaggeration. (pp. 44-5)

At the end of ***The Poet and the Lunatics,*** the more criminal of [the] two mad-doctors has set up a private asylum in Wimbledon, its garden very like the splendid grounds of the madhouse in *The Ball and the Cross*. But the pretended patients are not mad at all: they are professional criminals, Dr. Starkey's agents, feigning insanity to gain immunity from prosecution. Somewhat as Chesterton the journalist found out rascals in high political places, Gale finds out Dr. Starkey and his crew. . . .

The novelettes of ***Four Faultless Felons*** contain Chesterton's last studies in lunacy. **"The Moderate Murderer"** has a religious maniac for a foil, and a homicidal builder of empire who is madder and more dangerous. Hume, a dominie, averts the assassination of the Governor of Polybia by interrupting the Governor's stroll—his instrument of interruption, in the emergency, being a bullet through the Governor's leg. Had the Governor continued his walk, he would have been killed on the rifle-range by the no-nonsense-with-natives Deputy Governor. (p. 46)

In the same volume, **"The Honest Quack,"** a Dr. Judson, endeavors to commit his friend Walter Windrush to an asylum, that he may save him from a charge of murder. Judson concocts a Theory of Arboreal Ambidexterity, expressly to prove that Windrush (whose life centers round a rare tree he guards in his walled garden) is an anthropoid sport, not responsible for his own actions, because suffering from the rare mental affliction of Duodiapsychosis. (p. 47)

To obtain a colleague for committing Windrush, Dr. Judson successfully butters up that whited sepulchre Dr. Doone, the high authority on Arboreal Man, who signs the document of committal. After all, though, Windrush is found innocent by the police, and the real murderer takes poison—Dr. Doone himself. Walter Windrush is restored to his guardianship of the unique sprawling tree—under which, unknown to him, a murdered man's bones had lain for many a year. Dr. Judson wonders how Windrush can bear dwelling beside the tree now.

> "My dear fellow, and you are the cold and rational man of science," said Windrush lightly. "In what superstitions you wallow! In what medieval darkness you brood all your days! I am only a poor, impracticable, poetic dreamer, but I assure you I am in broad daylight. In fact, I have never been out of it, not even when you put me in that pleasant little sanatorium for a day or two. I was quite happy there, and as for the lunatics, well I came to the conclusion that they were rather saner than my friends outside."

Privately, Windrush really believes that the garden of his Tree is the Garden of Eden; and he is not wrong. The skeptical Judson and his love Enid Windrush discover it for themselves. . . . (pp. 47-8)

Gardens are what men make of them. Maclan and Turnbull, entrapped, found themselves in the apocalyptic garden of Professor Lucifer's madhouse; Judson and Enid found themselves the new Adam and Eve, in the first of all gardens. And Chesterton, like Owen Hood, was resolved that some private gardens must endure. Wrath against the sophisters of lunacy—those pairs of cunning doctors committing sane men to Bedlam—runs through these stories: wrath against the devastators of gardens. (p. 48)

If all of our actions are allegories, men may apprehend reality only through parables. Of possible parables, Chesterton—he being sane and free—was haunted by the parable of the confining madhouse, and by the opposed parable of the garden. The madhouse is sterile, the prison of the solipsist; the garden, proliferating, expresses an immortal continuity and community, realized in time and place. If we burst out of the garden, we burst into the madhouse. (p. 50)

G. K. Chesterton, decidedly a man alive, strove in parable to defend the hedges of that one spot which is Eden. If those hedges should be swept away, we would not find ourselves rejoiced by the elimination of limits. Instead, we should find ourselves bounded by the walls of that one spot, forever parched, which is Hell. (p. 51)

> *Russell Kirk, "Chesterton, Madmen, and Madhouses," in* Myth, Allegory and Gospel: An Interpretation of J. R. R. Tolkien, C. S. Lewis, G. K. Chesterton, Charles Williams, *edited by John Warwick Montgomery, Bethany Fellowship, Inc., 1974, pp. 33-51.*

KINGSLEY AMIS (essay date 1972)

[*A distinguished English novelist, poet, essayist, and editor, Amis was one of the Angry Young Men, a group of British writers of the 1950s whose writings expressed bitterness and disillusionment with society. His first and most widely praised novel,* Lucky Jim *(1954), is characteristic of the school and demonstrates his skill as a satirist. Amis has since rejected categorization or alliance with any literary group and maintains that he is only interested in following his artistic instincts. Although Amis wrote the first James Bond adventure after Ian Fleming's death, he did not become Fleming's successor, with critics charging that he made Bond too human. In the following excerpt from his introduction to* G. K. Chesterton: Selected Stories, *which he edited, Amis reviews Chesterton's strengths and weaknesses as a writer of short fiction. He criticizes some lapses in detection and credibility in the stories, while singling out Chesterton's descriptive power as his greatest strength.*]

[It] is in his fiction that I find Chesterton's genius best and most characteristically displayed. (Here I am far from sure I have the majority with me.) The novels and stories, especially the stories, dramatize virtually the whole range of the themes and interests met with in his other work. Further, the polemical tone and forensic style of much of that other work reappear—modified, to be sure—in the fiction, alongside the elements of narrative, in which he was only periodically interested, and of description, at which he was a master.

Lack of concern to narrate, readiness to depict or argue or float paradoxes instead, are the twin flaws of his less successful fictional efforts. In his later novels, these non-narrative and non-dramatic concerns, together with perished satire on fashionable fads of his day, reduce the story to a mere vehicle, and a boneshaker at that. Implausibility and facetiousness abound. His worst volume, ***Tales of the Long Bow***, chronicles the escapades of a group of friends set on bringing about the enactment of common sayings. Thus Colonel Crane literally eats his hat (he has taken to wearing a scooped-out cabbage on his head), Captain Pierce literally gets pigs to fly (well, he has some dropped on parachutes). The result is quite as painful as it sounds. (pp. 13-14)

[A feature of the early novel *The Napoleon of Notting Hill*] that links it to its author's other fiction is its use of a kind of rhetoric, stylized almost to the point of the theatrical, in both dialogue and narration. A sufficient example from the novel would need a solid page or more of prefatory explanation, so I will point instead to the closing few sentences of **"The Blue Cross"** and of **"The Yellow Bird"**, and to any of Father Brown's periodic tirades. There is something vulgar and faintly absurd about this effect, which, to my taste, comes an embarrassing cropper at the end of **"The Oracle of the Dog"**, but there is something rather grand as well, qualities which co-exist happily and naturally enough in a Chestertonian universe. (pp. 14-15)

What I will risk calling nightmarishness is another characteristic Chestertonian effect, an air of unreality that is not the same thing as implausibility (though there is implausibility here and there as well), a feeling that the world we see and hear and touch is a flimsy veil that only just manages to cover up a deeper and far more awful reality, a sense, in fact, of impending ''apocalypse'' in the literal meaning of ''uncovering''. Many of the stories distil this impression, most notably, perhaps, that little masterpiece, **"The Honour of Israel Gow"**—a masterpiece in other ways too, as I hope to show. (p. 15)

[Father Brown] is one of the greatest of all great-detective figures. For many, he will always be *the* greatest, largely because he does without those adventitious eccentricities—solitary violin-playing, obsessive orchid-growing—that other contenders need in order to stiffen their personalities. He also scorns his rivals' tendency to happen to be an expert in whatever specialized field of knowledge is required for solving the case. His field of knowledge is human nature, and his skills are observation, reason and common sense. I have heard it said that he is sometimes too much a mouthpiece for his author's religious beliefs; their shared enemy, however, is not any kind of Protestantism nor even atheism as such, but bogus mysticism, superstition and folly. To have such nuisances spiritedly and accurately denounced is, in our day quite as much as in theirs, a little better than endurable.

To revert: whatever else he may or may not be, Brown is a detective, not (of course) a professional, just someone who happens to be about when a crime has been committed, but a detective none the less; and all these stories, like most of the ninety-odd stories Chesterton wrote, are detective stories. They are, very arguably, detective stories ''with a difference.'' . . . (p. 16)

Some sort of defining gesture seems called for at this point. Most people would probably agree that a detective story without a difference, so to speak, involves a crime, normally murder, of which the perpetrator is not immediately apparent, some clues to his identity, method, etc., some deduction from these, and the exposure of the criminal. Where such people divide is over the deduction part, how valid it needs to be and how important it should be made. To the more permissive wing, form rather than substance—a bit of speculation about why the body was moved, a couple of minutes' pondering about those footsteps in the snow—is all that is required; the author can deceive the reader, withhold vital information, proceed by revealing totally new facts instead of linking established ones together, and get away with it if his story moves well, his detective is fun and his dénouement sufficiently unexpected. To the more rigorous party, in whose moderately liberal section I myself belong, deduction is of the essence, whatever else may be stirred in: the author may mislead the reader, but he must not cheat him or lie to him; the detective is entitled to a certain amount of luck, but not to second sight; the unravelling must be consequential; and no twin brothers, poisons unknown to science, previously undisclosed secret passages or other conjuror's rabbits are permitted.

I have said I favour the second view; but holders of the first could certainly plead that their kind of story has always been far more widespread and popular than mine, and further, by way of starting to move back to the main issue, that at the time when Father Brown entered on his career the deduction-before-everything school of writing hardly existed: none of the supposedly marvellous chains of reasoning devised by Poe's Dupin stands up to scrutiny, and Dupin's great successor, Sherlock Holmes, went on about deduction far more regularly than he used it. Only a very few of his exploits, ''The Red-Headed League'' and ''Silver Blaze'' among them, satisfy my criteria; Holmes was much likelier to produce the criminal out of nowhere at all in the last couple of pages.

Chesterton never descended to that kind of thing, but there is a nasty rabbit in **"The Secret Garden"**, and he does annoyingly withhold clues that he could have slipped in easily and unobtrusively. ''Didn't you notice,'' asks Brown towards the end of one of the stories in this collection, ''the [murderer] played with a pen and not with a paper-knife; though he had a beautiful bright steel paper-knife [on his desk]? . . . There are limits to the irony of assassins.'' No, I didn't notice, because I wasn't told about the knife at the time. Elsewhere, there is a piece of implausibility or illogic nearer the heart of the plot, vulnerable to a simple question or two, as follows.

"The Secret Garden"—how could the murderer have been so certain that one of the other characters was going to bring a vitally important object with him on the fatal evening? And, even if the murderer was just gambling on a good chance, how could he expect to find the object unattended exactly when he needed it?

"The Invisible Man"—would not at least one of the witnesses simply have happened to mention seeing the man?

"The Oracle of the Dog"—what would have happened to the game on the beach if Miss Druce had cried out a little later than she did?

And so on. Nevertheless, others of the stories, apart from everything else they do, will satisfy the strictest deductive precisian—or rather should make him cheer. Brown's apparently insane, but really pedantically accurate, answers to sane questions; his own apparently insane, but really vitally relevant questions; the clue in four words that identifies a murderer at once and unmistakably—to Brown, though to very few of us; the desert well that indicated the solution of a crime by having nothing to do with it; all such strokes take their place in what I see as the finest detective-story tradition. They do more than that: they are models, helping to shape that tradition as well as adding lustre to it.

"The Honour of Israel Gow" (to specify further) would have been a remarkable story in any era. Its Edwardian date makes it astonishing. The deductive rules and limitations, at that time still only half-shaped, are more than adhered to, they are exploited with the panache of a master. The setting-up of the main body of clues—the strange assortment of objects littering Glengyle Castle—is skilful and inventive enough; the profusion of the false explanations suggested by Father Brown sustains that level; the process whereby it is the most macabre event that establishes the rationality of the true explanation ascends higher; the explanation of that explanation is a kind of wild, spendthrift bonus, and the way in which the most essential clue of all is not merely introduced, but spotlighted, on the second page has the impudence of genius.

In short, here is a detective story as well as a detective story with a difference, or several differences. One of these I will leave it to the reader to discover. Another is the emphatic presence of that air of unreality I alluded to earlier, leading Brown, no hysteric, to suggest in the middle of a violent storm that ''the great devil of the universe may be sitting on the top tower of this castle at this moment, as big as a hundred elephants, and roaring like the Apocalypse''. Yet another difference—an addition, not a subtraction or a substitution—lies in the use of Chesterton's descriptive gift, most notably as regards the landscape surrounding the castle. The painter he at first intended, but failed, to become could hardly have bettered his prose depictions of the effects of light.

This particular difference also distinguished the story that, to me, shares first place in this volume, **"The Blue Cross".** Chesterton was fascinated not just by light, but by changes in light, as also by the changes in feeling that accompany them. This overriding interest leads him, here as elsewhere, to play ducks and drakes with the passage of time. He wants a busy, sunlit, prosaic morning joined on to a mysterious evening twilight that leads into a sinister darkness under the stars, so that his characters have to move at snail's pace while these changes come about. Poor Valentin and his policemen are condemned to take what I compute as six hours to cover the six or so miles from Victoria to somewhere near Hampstead: unbelievably slow going even by horse-omnibus.

I find it hard to care, while sternly refusing any comfort along the lines of, "Well, it all helps to build up the atmosphere of fantasy". Such helps are gross, and fantasy, in the sense of abandonment of reasonableness, is out of place in a tale that, among other things, celebrates reason. My consolation, or distraction, lies in Chesterton's bold use of a different sort of unlikelihood that manages (for once: it could only be done once) to use million-to-one-against coincidence—Valentin's finding and following of Father Brown's trail—as its strategy, and to pull it off. And who could forget that sublimely rhetorical moment at which Brown tells the great thief Flambeau that there is no escape from God's laws anywhere in the universe?—"On plains of opal, under cliffs cut out of pearl, you would still find a notice-board, 'Thou shalt not steal.'"

Other Chestertonian differences include his exaltation of now tattered virtues like honour, courage, loyalty and chivalry, or chivalrousness; his capacity to go on demonstrating that murder or other violence is not an indispensable ingredient of the detective story—in five of [the thirteen stories in ***G. K. Chesterton: Selected Stories***], no crime ever gets committed; his constant ability to suggest, without ever repeating himself, that the crime, or apparent crime, has been committed with the aid of magic. (pp. 17-20)

What above all pervades these pieces, indeed the whole of his fiction, is Chesterton's inexhaustible fascination with the outward appearance of things, not only with the effects of light upon them, but with the things in themselves: landscape and seascape, streets, shops, gardens, the outsides and insides of houses, ornaments, knick-knacks of every possible kind, details of dress and costume—and, more than any of these, the lineaments of the human being inside the costume. Nobody, I think, would call Chesterton a great characterizer of the inner selves of men and women, but one would have to turn to a writer on the scale of his beloved Dickens to find a better representer of how they look. Of all the thousands of people who appear in his fiction, even those with the merest walk-on parts, not one recalls another in his face or body. Every time, the author rises exultantly to the occasion and draws someone new.

If Chesterton was an optimist (no bad thing to be anyway, I should have thought, if it can be managed), it was largely because he loved the world his God had made, and never ceased to enjoy that vitally important aspect of the entire creation: its surface. (p. 21)

Kingsley Amis, in an introduction to G. K. Chesterton: Selected Stories *by G. K. Chesterton, edited by Kingsley Amis, Faber & Faber, 1972, pp. 11-21.*

ERIK ROUTLEY (essay date 1972)

[*In an excerpt from his appreciation of the detective genre, Routley investigates the Father Brown stories, finding them to be a celebration of the virtues of the ordinary person, as exemplified by Father Brown. Routley also explores morality and religion in the stories.*]

Father Brown is the Catholic Church impersonated as the church of the common man. The stories about him in the first four of the five collections are almost all moral theology presented as detection. It is, therefore, impossible in writing about him to avoid a certain amount of language that recalls moral theology in its popular form. Detective literature is seventy-five per cent moralism anyhow; but here it is entirely moralism.

But it is moralism of a certain kind, which Chesterton was supremely good at stating. It is the sort of moralism in which the morality of the common man is presented as contradicting the morality of sophistication, and as being nearer to that morality of eternity in which the profoundly anti-relativist (and as we should now say anti-existentialist) Chesterton believed. Himself the most sophisticated of writers and the most mannered, Chesterton succeeded in holding his readers in whatever he wrote because he was the one man alive who could write in so mannered a fashion and yet not become a bad writer. He perfected this piece of jugglery more skilfully than any writer, perhaps in any language, ever did; he was a master of fantasy and romance, and a master of literary rhythm and proportion. Consequently nearly all the best written jokes in all literature are his. 'The human race, to which so many of my readers belong. . . .'

This sophistication he turned to the purpose of championing the common man as citizen of state and of church. When he began to write the Father Brown stories, and up to the time when he finished the first twenty-four of them, he was already a well-known apologist for the Catholic Church, but not himself a Catholic. He was received into the Church near the end of the interval which separates the two halves of the Father Brown collection (the year was 1925). This makes no difference. So far as his interpretation of Catholicism to Englishmen went (or, as his detractors preferred to say, his propaganda), the fact of his being personally received into the Church was hardly more than an historical detail. He made it his business to represent Catholic teaching as sane, commonplace, cheerful, colourful and above all English, to a readership the majority of whom still thought of it as dark, contorted, forbidding, drab and above all foreign.

So his priest was small, inconspicuous, physically negligible, entirely ordinary. He was Father J. Brown. Whenever he was involved in a problem which people who conformed to and were misled by normal ways of thinking had mishandled, Brown cleared up the mystery by cutting through the artificialities with which misdirected thinking had surrounded it, and exposed it as something quite normal and human. He is therefore as concerned as any puritan to strip away 'the supernatural' when it means 'the superstitious' from people's view of a situation. Again and again he does that. He was liable to do it by speaking, in his flat and dull voice, some epigram which in the space of a few words upset the accepted, but erroneous, order of things. He sometimes spoke with passion. But he spoke for that ordinary person whom Chesterton wanted to liberate—for the original man hidden under the chocolate-and-biscuit dado of Victorian and agnostic convention.

What really places this humble clerical Quixote in territory all his own is that in these episodes, which may involve crimes as clear-cut as murder, his moral sense has almost nothing to do with what some believe to be the moral sense behind detective stories. Now much that is said about this is entirely beside the point. The fact that crime is inseparable from detective stories is no argument for their inherent immorality: but it is equally true to say that the fact that crime is found out and punished is not ground on which one can build a respectable argument in their favour. They are 'about' something which is not identifiable by so confined a description as that. It is true—and one can say so, provided one does not inflate the truth into a sort of virtue—that detective stories enshrine the moral axiom that it is wrong to murder, or blackmail, or steal. Father Brown, being a priest of the church of the New Testament, says, in effect, 'We know that: we assume that. But there is a great deal of another kind of wrong about; there is the wrong that preceded the crime, and there is the wrong that has so perverted people's minds that they are now looking in the wrong place for the criminal.' In all the forty-eight stories, there is just one description of even the arrest of a criminal. That is not Father Brown's business.

But then, the crime is by no means always murder. . . . It is murder in twenty-four of the first forty stories, attempted murder in one; in six it is theft, in one, blackmail. There are two suicides, one case of sacrilege; in four cases no crime has been committed, and in one it is prevented. Restitution in one case annuls an actually committed theft. Two of the murders are historical enigmas solved by Father Brown in the course of conversation long after they took place (**"Fairy Tale"** and **"Broken Sword"**).

At the end of many stories you find the clue gently and often evasively given by the priest as he is turning away to go about some routine duty like visiting a deaf school (**"Three Tools"**). In these parting epigrams, which solve the only mystery Father Brown is interested in (that of how people's minds work), there is almost invariably exposed some error which common custom and carelessness of mind have represented among society to be an axiom. We do not here have to judge whether Chesterton's insights were always right or even whether we agree with them.

Take for example **"The Invisible Man,"** a story which has become so famous as to be proverbial. Here the puzzle to be solved is how a murderer entered a place into which quite positively nobody was observed to go by the only possible entrance. The answer is that it was the postman—a person whom, because of his uniform and his absolutely regular visits, nobody thought of observing. Now John Dickson Carr, that master of locked-room puzzles who owes so much to Chesterton, would have presented his solution as something which neither the readers nor the characters in the story noticed. Chesterton says, not 'You didn't notice that', but 'You wouldn't notice that'. In that subjunctive the whole business of uncovering the deeper strata of detective literature is implied.

> "Nobody notices postmen, somehow," he said thoughtfully; "yet they have passions like other men, and even carry large bags where a small corpse can be stowed quite easily."

Half a sentence for moralism, the other half for method: that is Father Brown's way. The story ends not with an arrest but with (in the Catholic sense) a confession. (pp. 91-4)

Pursuing the subject of superficial quirks in human character which provide a moral pattern for some of the lighter stories in this collection, we may note the pleasant irony of **"The Oracle of the Dog,"** in which a dog, when invested with mysterious perceptive powers such as dog-sentimentalists are apt to bestow on him, points to one person as the criminal, whereas, when he is treated as a dog, he points to another. (p. 96)

Again, there is a world of social and psychological comment in the climax of **"The Man in the Passage,"** where a series of witnesses at a trial are invited to describe a strange-looking person whom they claimed to have seen in the dark passage behind a theatre. Father Brown demonstrates that what they saw was their own reflection in a mirror which had been slid out into the passage (part of the mechanism of an ingenious crime). (p. 97)

Bogus religion, or the belief that all religions or any mixture of religions are as good as Catholic Christianity, forms the surprising background of several other stories. **"The Wrong Shape,"** which contains some pleasant Holmes-like detection through detail, contains also an indictment of nature-worship and humanism, and, for good measure, it brings in a mysterious Indian for the usual purpose of throwing mystical dust in the reader's eyes. **"The Hammer of God"** is an unusually grave and haunting exposure of the symbolism of towers—the exaltation of a church spire perverted into the kind of pride which William Golding so memorably handled in his novel *The Spire*. **"The Eye of Apollo"** is a commentary on that sun-worship which formed the background (to mention only one very distinguished example) of the religion of Constantine the Great.

Caricature of Chesterton drawn by Thomas Derrick for G. K.'s Weekly.

In this story the high-priest of a revived sun-worship gains such ascendancy over a naïve woman that he persuades her to stare at the sun until she goes blind. (p. 98)

"The Secret Garden" is, of course, based on the fanatical and materialistic anti-clericalism of classical post-Revolutionary France. The chief of police has murdered a millionaire who was about to make a dramatic donation to the Church. The millionaire is a 'scatterbrained sceptic' but is 'drifting to' the Church; as for Valentin, the murderer, 'he would do anything, *anything,* to break what he called the superstition of the Cross. He has fought for it, he has starved for it, and now he has murdered for it.' Only by understanding what a man of this temper would do to bring down the Church could the priest solve that particular mystery.

Then there is that hilarious business called **"The Resurrection of Father Brown."** Outwardly this has something of the Reichenbach Falls in its atmosphere; for a few pages we are in no doubt that Father Brown is dead, murdered at the mission station in Latin America where he is doing special duty. During the ceremonial lying-in-state he comes to life and sits up comically in his coffin, and everybody thinks that he has indeed risen from the dead, to which, as soon as he can find a voice, he can only splutter, 'Oh, you *silly* people . . . God bless you and give you more sense.'

It turns out to have been a hoax. Drugged, given out to be dead, he 'comes back to life': the people take it for a miracle: then the sceptical enemies of the Faith will expose the whole story and show the whole town how the church has deceived it. Behind it all is (guess what) an American journalist. (p. 99)

All this indicates that in Chesterton's stories there is a very powerful religious interest. This need be no disadvantage in the secular age which during Chesterton's lifetime was beginning, and which has since his death thoroughly set in. For the message always is that true religion is as rational and as human and as popular as a detective story, and that its business is to release the truth from the prison in which bogus religion has locked it. In the books which he was writing at the same time as the Father Brown stories, Chesterton was constantly saying that religion is not an esoteric activity proper for specialists or the bourgeois or the anti-socially pious, but a commonplace thing as familiar, as rugged, as uncompromising and as admirable as the common man himself. As might be expected from a Catholic apologist, the English puritan habit of mind was often his target, and surface-puritanism was normally the best example for his purpose of bogus religion. Chesterton rarely expressed a hatred of Protestantism such as his friend Hilaire Belloc constantly expressed, but like Ronald Knox he was really angered by what he took to be puritanism. In one weird and terrible story, **"The Sign of the Broken Sword,"** Father Brown demolishes the reputation of a local hero by examining his character, starting from his puritanism. . . . This is one of the best Father Brown stories, partly because of the effortless and inevitable inclusion of so many memorable sayings. To put together two separated passages in it:

> "Where does a wise man hid a pebble?"
>
> "On the beach."
>
> "Where does a wise man hide a leaf?"
>
> "In the forest."
>
> "But what does he do if there is no forest? He grows a forest to hide it in. A fearful sin."

But as the story goes on it provides two false solutions to the mystery (which is the reason for the legendary broken sword always associated with General St Clare and reproduced on the statue they are standing under). Flambeau, Father Brown's closest friend, proposes first that the General went mad. The priest replies:

> "A horrid story . . . but not the real story . . . Yours is a clean story, a sweet, pure, honest story, as open and white as that moon. Madness and despair are innocent enough. There are worse things, Flambeau."

Second, when it is made clear that St Clare had reason to seek the death of one of his officers who could expose him, Flambeau suggests that he murdered him under cover of battle.

> "You are still full of good and pure thoughts," said the other. "It was worse than that."

Then follows the passage about ignorantly reading the Bible—the attack on puritan values; then the truth—that St Clare murdered his enemy first, then arranged a suicidal battle to cover it, thus planting the forest in which to hide his leaf.

That is a dark business in which we are told that Father Brown was "deeply moved." A much more light-hearted affair, but one whose narration uses the same technique of "false solutions," and the same background of ignorant Protestantism (but this time honest protestantism), is **"The Honour of Israel Gow,"** which is the only story situated in Scotland. The strange secret burial of the last of the Glengyles and the weird collection of miscellaneous treasures laid out in the house by the half-witted gardener, Gow, provide the starting point. Father Brown, challenged to show any rational connection between some heaps of snuff, some torn manuscripts, the inner machinery of a clock and a collection of jewels without their settings, produces off-hand two plausible explanations neither of which he supposes for a moment to be the right one. He is up to that point urging his hearers not to be over-hospitable to mystery and spookery. But the true explanation is a story of literal honesty, beginning with an illiterate village lad who, given a sovereign for a tip in mistake for a farthing, returned with nineteen shillings and elevenpence three farthings change, and ending with that same lad in old age, having been left for his pains 'all the gold of the Glengyles', systematically removing the gold from every object Glengyle had—even the gold from his teeth—and leaving in the house everything that the removal of the gold had left—the machinery of gold watches, the stones that had gold settings, the pages that had gold illuminations, the snuff that had been in gold snuff boxes. It is a study in fundamentalist honesty, beginning with a nobleman's obsession with it and ending with a peasant's response to it. There is no crime. The literalism of the Scottish presbyterian peasant is followed to its lunatic conclusion: it looks fantastic, but not ignoble. (pp. 99-102)

Without reprinting the whole Father Brown series *in extenso* I see no way of demonstrating beyond question Chesterton's innocence of the charge of dragging moralism in so that Father Brown may be given a chance to preach. But innocent he is. The artistry of the stories is not in their moralism, but in the skill which makes the reader miss the moralism altogether until his third or fourth reading. That is why the Father Brown stories are almost universally misunderstood. (pp. 108-09)

The careless reader finds [Father Brown's] paradoxes tiresome, and the reader who neither shares nor accepts his values is at a loss to understand what he is talking about, and is mystified by the notion that it can be important. It is nonsense to say that Father Brown reaches his solutions by the exercise of some esoteric, even psychic, gift that can express itself only in oracular utterances of delphic ambiguity. I know of a few unsafe paradoxes in Chesterton's more exuberant essays: I can find none in Father Brown. He represents not paradox but plain dissent. He firmly rejects what is bogus in humanistic and materialistic thought, representing Catholic doctrines as, precisely, common sense. It is found always to be sentimental materialism which has thrown people off the track. It is always entertaining, therefore, when materialists in the stories are prepared to invoke the supernatural, only to be brought back by the priest of the exotic mysteries of the Church to an earthly, natural, solution. (p. 109)

Nowhere else does Father Brown indulge in such epic clowning as in that heroic chase of Flambeau [in **"The Blue Cross"**] which is made to appear like a leisurely excursion through London. There are moments here that the creator of Holmes might well have given a year's royalties for.

> "'Here," I says to the chap, who was nearly out of the door, "you've paid too much."
>
> "'Oh," he says, "have we?" . . . "Sorry to confuse your accounts, but it'll pay for the window."
>
> "What window?" I says.
>
> "'The one I'm going to break," he says, and smashes that blessed pane with his umbrella.'

That is the stuff out of which *The Man Who Was Thursday* and *The Flying Inn* were made. It introduces Father Brown as an inconspicuous little Quixote who is going to be one too many for the magnificent Flambeau; it introduces Aristide Valentin, Chief of the Paris Police, who is chasing Flambeau but cannot find him without encountering Father Brown and using Father Brown's clues. It is the very next story in which Valentin's materialistic passions bring him to his death, and the next but one after that brings Flambeau on to the side of the angels. But that opening story is symbolic of the principle of dissent from the obvious and accepted conventions of life that is the junction between the Father Brown stories and the main line of detective fiction. Father Brown is in his way as romantic (by the same canons we used in judging Holmes romantic) as Holmes himself. The décor is rarely anything but distant, impressionistic, and slightly uncanny. The names are as evocative as Doyle's, "Pendragon," "Saradine," "Boulnois," "Bohun," to say nothing of Flambeau himself. It is the 'dissent against convention' colour in romanticism that Father Brown supplies in his own person, leaving the rest to the subsidiary characters and exotic background of the scenes into which he makes his way. For Chesterton human life always was like that—a counterpoint between the familiar and the fantastic. (His devotees will remember his special love for such adjectives as 'wild' and such images as 'sword'); and indeed the Church and its faith were likewise for him a counterpoint between reason and romance—the reason of St Thomas Aquinas and the pageantry of the mass.

So when the dogmatic content of the stories is relatively distant, they usually turn on the detective writer's device of 'misdirection', which is almost universal, and on secular detection, which it is only Chesterton's distinction to have related so intimately with morality. In **"The Duel of Dr Hirsch," "The Perishing of the Pendragons," "The Strange Crime of John Boulnois," "The Song of the Flying Fish"** and **"The Worst Crime in the World"** the point is entirely gained through misdirection. Nobody is made to appear a moral illiterate because he did not see the point; Father Brown is no more than the only person present who follows the Holmesian maxim of accepting the improbable as true when every alternative is clearly impossible, and he does not need to be a priest to do that. On two occasions only do we get anything approaching the '140 varieties of cigar ash'—the display of special knowledge. In **"The Actor and the Alibi"** the solution is plain to Father Brown because he alone of those present sees the suggestiveness of the play's being *The School for Scandal* (in which one actor is for some time on stage but invisible), while in **"The Doom of the Darnaways"** the title of a book on a bookshelf, *The History of Pope Joan,* suggests, because of its non-existent subject, a non-existent book, a dummy bookshelf, and a secret passage. (This was a shade risky: some people have believed in the existence of a Pope Joan, and Brown's disbelief was dogmatic rather than historical.) But those two very mild displays of special knowledge are the only examples of their kind, and the Father Brown stories are therefore the purest examples in the whole field of detection through faculties which are common to everybody. (pp. 110-12)

Father Brown neither looks nor behaves like a superman, and any attempt to build him up into a superman arouses his alarm and anger (as in **"The Resurrection"**). He does not detect crime by making himself larger than the criminal, nor confound the established police force by demonstrating greater skill or education than its members have. There are two layers, as it were, in the structure of thought he always erects to solve a mystery. One is common to him and Holmes—reason, but Father Brown's reason is far less vulnerable than Holmes's. He certainly protests against the distortions of reason which lead others to false conclusions, and this is what all the other classic detectives do. That is one layer. But the other is this direct contradiction of the superman tradition; he pursues his object by making himself less, not greater, than the criminal, by 'getting inside him', as he puts it: by never allowing himself to say, 'That's a thing I could never have done'.

This isn't a brilliant *tour-de-force* by Chesterton; it is no more than an accurate observation of human nature and human communications. You may outwit a criminal by superior skill, but you do not identify him or vindicate an innocent person by superior moral goodness—the very idea makes nonsense. This is the same kind of operation that Chesterton was engaged in in all his other writings. At the bottom of it is a comprehensive cosmic optimism which has its roots in the eighteenth century and which he shared with nobody else in the twentieth. He really did believe in the fundamental goodness of the common man. Evil in the common man was an exception to the design. That was what nobody else really believed, and what to a much greater extent everybody positively disbelieves now. The normal belief is that man is evil and that goodness is an exception or an accident. To Father Brown any criminal is a good man gone wrong. He is not an evil man who has cut himself off from the comprehension or sympathy of those who labour to be good. Consider the laborious rectitude of all the characters in **"The Chief Mourner of Marne,"** and how vulnerable and brittle the priest shows it to be. The way he talks makes it perfectly plain that if they were the people accused of a crime his patience with them would be as unflappable as is his patience with the man they are now accusing.

One effect of noticing this is to explain the unusual attitude to violence which these stories show. Violence is the ground on which many well-intentioned and sentimental critics attack the detective story. Here anyhow is the evidence for saying that it is an accident of such stories, not a property; for here there is virtually none, apart from that which produced the crime. Who could be less of an apostle of violence than Father Brown? Where in all the literature is violence so certain not to be met with violence? (pp. 113-14)

Chesterton . . . was the only author of detection who has written so much else in so many literary forms. Other detective authors have written non-detective fiction, and one or two others have written even theology; and a few people have written one or two detective tales as a sideline from the main track of quite different work. Only with Chesterton do we have a major contribution to detective literature which is doing the same thing as his other work is doing—using fantastic means instead of argumentative means to get the same thing said about something of primary importance, in this case his optimism about the common man's common sense. (pp. 114-15)

It was this, then, that made Chesterton, through the accident of his hitting on a successful detective form, a major contributor to the literature. Having found his way into this field, he managed in the Father Brown stories to raise all the most awkward questions which make it difficult to dismiss the form as a trivialisation of the novelist's art. Having said that, I should be prepared to defend the proposition that his lighter tales, ***The Club of Queer Trades*** and ***The Paradoxes of Mr Pond,*** are just as much 'pure' Chesterton as Father Brown is. They, like the last, and in some ways (compared with the earlier ones) apocryphal Father Brown stories, ***The Scandal of Father Brown,*** are amiable intellectual leg-pulls, studies in the resolution of incongruities, fantasies in logic that nobody else could have written. At the same time it has to be said that had he written them but not created Father Brown, Chesterton would not have qualified as a detective writer, while had he written the Father Brown tales but not those others, he would not have diminished his reputation as a crusader against humbug.

No: there is humbug in Holmes, but there is none here. It will remain an open question whether the Father Brown stories lifted themselves, by their own distinction, clean out of the detective field, or whether we may use them as evidence for arguments yet to come about the literature. I am assuming the second answer to be right, but having done so I have made everything much more difficult than it otherwise would have been. (p. 116)

Erik Routley, "The Mystery of Iniquity" and "The Fairy Tale and the Secret," in his The Puritan Pleasures of the Detective Story: A Personal Monograph, *Victor Gollancz Ltd., 1972, pp. 89-103, 104-16.*

THOMAS E. PORTER (essay date 1984)

[In the following excerpt, Porter likens the Father Brown stories to biblical parables and terms Father Brown a model of "Christianity in action."]

It is evident, even to the casual reader [of the Father Brown stories], that each tale illustrates a truth or set of truths or highlights a principle of common sense or an insight that has application beyond the solution of a particular mystery. As the tales include such illustrations, they move, in function, toward a venerable literary genre: the parable.

Using the obvious Biblical analogue, the parable proper is a story drawn from common experience that leaves the mind in sufficient doubt about its precise application to provoke thought. Gospel narratives like the Good Samaritan or the Prodigal Son come immediately to mind. The purpose of the parable is to teach by vivid illustration. Critics have not overlooked this dimension of Chesterton's work; Hugh Kenner, amplifying a remark of Hilaire Belloc's, states that the parable is "Chesterton's chosen form." In the Father Brown stories the "common experience" on which the author draws is the familiar whodunit formula; he weaves his teaching into the data, illustrating as he goes. The lessons of the tales, that the Old Testament is an Oriental book needing careful interpretation, that scientific explanations, zealously adopted, can become superstitions, that the irrational makes for bad theology, that capitalism can be as heretical a doctrine as communism are properly thought-provoking. These lessons, and others similar to them, unfold along with the solution to the crime.

Given this parabolic effect in the tales, Father Brown emerges, not only as sleuth, but as teacher. By and large, his *dicta* carry the burden of the parable's impact; he is the one who points out, for example, that the Puritan general misreads the Old Testament and that heredity may be as magical an explanation of evil as a curse is. Chesterton makes it clear that, though Father Brown's virtues are his own, he teaches also by reason of his office. That is, in action and attitude Father Brown represents a Christian point of view. He speaks of "sin" and of "charity" and, while his truths often reflect plain common sense, they are shaped by religious perspectives. The suicidal old man, for instance, who could not feel grief is labeled a "devotee of the Religion of Cheerfulness." All this suggests that a principal "truth" of Chesterton's detective stories is the revelation of the detective as a model of Christianity in action.

Thus in the parabolic aspect of the tales Father Brown is the Christian confronting the world. Much of what would ordinarily fit that kind of model is missing in that nothing of his interior life or his sacramental ministry (with the exception of occasional references to confession) appears. The collar and the Roman hat announce his affiliation and specify a source for both his attitudes and his teaching. Just as the Christian as such does not belong to any special class or race, so the priest's activities cut across all such barriers. He goes about, doing good, dispensing justice and teaching the truth to all comers in all climates.

Chesterton's Christianity, as exemplified in Father Brown, is not everybody's. While most Christians might agree with his rejection of scientism, atheism and occultism, not all would agree with the substance of his critiques. Father Brown is too much the humanist and his teaching somewhat too rationalistic for broad acceptance among certain types of believers. He relies very heavily on common sense and reason. Those denominations that hold to basic tenets of Reformation theology tend to view the intellect as essentially corrupted by the Fall and logic as an instrument of prideful self-justification. They would doubt that repentance is possible without a dramatic and explicit experience of grace. Conversions like Flambeau's are too intellectual to be genuine and Father Brown's advocacy of them too "natural." For those sectaries who see a sharp dichotomy between the sacred and the profane, the little priest's traffic with the world (in the Pauline sense) would be suspect. He belongs in the pulpit, the sacristy and the rectory, dispensing spiritual counsel, not abroad in the marketplace, on the rostrum or in the pub. In significant ways, Father Brown is not only in the world, but also of it.

In contemporary theological terms, then, Chesterton's Christian is an incarnationalist, a believer who sees nature and mankind as redeemed in all its aspects and the potential for evil in human beings as repressible. This is why Father Brown's Christianity seems sensible and attractive and why his opponents, the ideologues, appear to be short-sighted, narrow and mean-spirited. This humanness is catalogued by the sum of the priest-detective's virtues: innocence, trust in reason, investigative incredulity, belief in individual freedom to choose and change. If Father Brown is a model Christian, then these qualities are presumably indispensable to the type. If more spiritual qualities are required, then they must build on these. At the very least, the priest represents a humanizing and Christianizing force in a society threatened by inhumane systems and attitudes.

The rhetoric of the tales, Chesterton's narrative voice, promotes this incarnational view; the fictive world of Father Brown fits him as he fits it. The landscape is humanized, indeed, romanticized, with rich and varied impressions that sometimes verge on the baroque:

> Outside, the last edges of the sunset still clung to the corners of the green square but inside a lamp had already been kindled; and in the mingling of the two lights the coloured globe glowed like some monstrous jewel and the fantastic outlines of the fiery fishes seemed to give it indeed something of the mystery of a talisman; like strange shapes seen by a seer in the crystal of doom.

High color and chiaroscuro typify the descriptive passages; vivid images highlight the characterizations of the personae: "Everything about [Dr. Hood] and his room indicated something at once rigid and restless, like that great Northern Sea by which (on pure principles of hygiene) he had built his home." Chesterton describes the perspective of his narrator in his autobiography: "[The primary problem for me was] how men could be made to realize the wonder and splendor of being alive in environments which their own daily criticism treated as dead-alive, and which their imagination had left for dead." This lively imagination produces, in the tales, strongly defined impressions and sensations rather than a distanced reproduction of phenomena. The country manors, the village streets, pubs and sitting rooms are not Raymond Chandler's "mean streets" or Agatha Christie's homogeneous parlors. A feature of Chesterton's parables is this highly colored picture of a world invested with feeling and pregnant with life. (pp. 83-6)

Finally, then, Father Brown's reasonable Christianity depends on a creative imagination that humanizes the landscape. The conventional formula itself proclaims ultimate intelligibility; by virtue of the whodunit structure the crime is explained and the criminal discovered. The basic mission of the detective is "to make narrative sense out of the data." The assumption underlying the mission is patent, to wit, that sense *can* be made of the data. Father Brown's mission is to make common sense of the data and Christian sense of its implications. In a world of the "live" imagination he can comment on the roots of evil, principally the propensity to construct a closed system in which the architect is god. Chesterton's narrative style creates a cosmos with a human impress and so one with the potential for christianization. Whatever one thinks of this kind of cosmos, it does not fade noticeably with the passage of time. Like the parables of the New Testament, Chesterton's tales and his hero retain their savor. (p. 86)

Thomas E. Porter, "Gilbert Keith Chesterton," in Twelve Englishmen of Mystery, *edited by Earl F. Bargainnier, Bowling Green University Popular Press, 1984, pp. 64-87.*

NOEL O'DONOGHUE (essay date 1986)

[The following is drawn from a review of Chesterton's previously uncollected stories that appeared in 1986. O'Donoghue explores the role of nightmare and the consciousness it reflects.]

At this stage of G. K. Chesterton's posthumous career, a new book of uncollected pieces may well seem like the kind of "Concluding Postscript" that may be left to scholars to collect and to peruse. . . . However, just as Soren Kierkegaard's *Concluding Unscientific Postscript* contains the essence of his Existentialist understanding of man and God, so this much more modest Postscript takes us straight to the centre of Chesterton's no less original and profound—and no less disturbing—understanding of man and God. Essential to both Kierkegaard and Chesterton is the profound almost annihilating, consciousness that between man and God there is not so much an angel with a flaming sword—that, too, of course—but a nightmare of irrationality and terror, the private terror of annihilation, eternal and incalculable.

Daylight and Nightmare is largely a record of how Chesterton coped, or tried to cope, with the world of nightmare and with the dragon or dragons that dominate that world. One typically Chestertonian approach is to see nightmare as literally a mare whose habitat is in a mountain fastness where the hero of the story—none other than "Little Jack Horner"—finds the Mare's Nest and manages to make a friend of nightmare. This is an early story and it has all the sudden twists and turns of a George MacDonald fantasy. More than the later stories of this collection, which are more readable as *stories,* this early piece (1892), entitled **"The Taming of the Nightmare"** is worthy of close study from the point of view of the healing of the "Nightmare Imagination" by way of the fairy-tale imagination.

In the later stories, that is to say, in those written after 1920, the nightmare element tends to serve the author's own philosophy of the wonder of common things, the technological destruction of Hebbdom. Indeed the story in which the dragon holds the centre of the stage (**"The Dragon at Hide and Seek"**) is almost the least successful piece both as a story and as dealing with the nightmare (by entering within it, rather than, as in the early story, by making common cause with it). One story in this selection should not be missed: **"A Real Discovery"** shows Chesterton at his most funny-profound. Reading these finished and unfinished stories, one cannot help realising what a very good story teller our author was. Even when, as in the final story **"The End of Wisdom,"** one sees the happy ending from afar off, yet both character and situation keep a firm hold on the reader. (pp. 535, 537)

Noel O'Donoghue, in a review of "Daylight and Nightmare: Uncollected Stories, Fables," in The Chesterton Review, *Vol. 12, No. 4, November, 1986, pp. 535-37.*

JILL BROWN (essay date 1987)

[Brown centers her appraisal of Chesterton on a discussion of the bright and dark elements in his imagination and their expression in his works of short fiction.]

Chesterton and his wife, Frances Blogg Chesterton. The Granger Collection, New York.

Chesterton's imagination was a very odd thing indeed. Reading his childhood memories, one begins to wonder seriously whether there was not something abnormal about his eyesight. The abnormality, however, was not in his optic nerves—but in his imagination. Wordsworth's "light that never was on sea or land" was literally part of his earliest consciousness:

> To me my whole childhood has a certain quality . . . a sort of white light on everything, cutting things out very clearly . . . and rather emphasising their solidity. The point is that the white light had a sort of wonder in it, as if the world were as new as myself; but not that the world was anything but a real world. I am much more disposed *now* to fancy that an apple-tree in the moonlight is some sort of ghost or grey nymph. . . . But when I was a child I had a sort of confident astonishment in contemplating the apple-tree.

In the same way, the small boy enjoyed the bold outlines of his cardboard cut-out figures for his toy theatre: they had this same satisfying clarity. There was also a hobby-horse's head, painted white—"almost archaic in its simplification"—and just as intensely delightful. Sixty years later, Chesterton recognised these first responses to shape and colour as the origin of his adult beliefs:

> All my life I have loved edges; and the boundary line that brings one thing sharply against another. All my life I have loved frames and limits, and I will maintain that the largest wilderness looks larger seen through a window. . . . I have also a pretty taste in abysses and bottomless chasms and everything else that emphasises a fine shade of distinction between one thing and another. . . . And I believe that in feeling these things from the first, I was feeling the fragmentary suggestions of a philosophy I have since found to be the truth.

This passage is of the first importance in understanding Chesterton's mind. All his later characteristics as a writer begin here. The child, however, was not bothered by philosophical inferences; he was simply interested and happy. When, as a disgruntled Art student, Chesterton rejected Impressionist painters because their pictures were vague and grey, he was passionately re-asserting this childhood instinct for the bright and solid. (pp. 15-16)

Chesterton's aesthetic instinct for "frames and limits" suffused his mature thinking. This is what he loves in people, too, their incisive, flamboyant qualities. The characters in his stories shout, argue passionately, tear through the countryside in fast cars. They are violent, ecstatic in their loyalties. (p. 18)

Chesterton has been criticised—probably rightly—for political naïveté in his championing of "the little man" and the small business through Distributism; but on non-political grounds, his awareness of clear solid reality is anything but simple.

The first indication of the complexity of Chesterton's imaginings comes in the jumble of brilliant, rag-bag images. In "On Running after one's hat," for instance, we start with flooded Battersea as a new Venice: toothache: burnings at Smithfield: railway signals in red and green: the butcher in a gondola: a man running after a silk hat: anglers sitting by dark pools: a gentleman struggling with a jammed drawer. *"Belles-lettres"* essays were always characterised by lightness of touch; but Chesterton's flicking, dazzling vitality was exceptional. (p. 19)

Chesterton's sense of the kaleidoscopic quality of life is so acute that it implies that pre-requisite for seriousness—the perception that disparate forces co-exist in the universe. And an honest mind which realises this will eventually be forced to engage with such forces at a deeper level. Chesterton worked out his deeper ideas in the early novels. In each of these, two opposing forces achieve a fine, tense balance by the last page: scepticism and romanticism in *The Ball and the Cross;* detachment and commitment in *The Napoleon of Notting Hill;* law and freedom in *The Man Who Was Thursday*. This is Chesterton's most exciting perception: that the very dynamic of life comes from its opposing forces. (pp. 19-20)

People are duplex, too; the success of Chesterton's detective stories lies partly in the enigmatic nature of many characters: Flambeau, the reformed criminal; Israel Gow, the silent gardener; Wilfred Bohun, the criminal clergyman. Is Innocent Smith a good or a bad man?—this is the great question of *Manalive*. In Chesterton's later writing, this idea of the "irregular equilibrium" lacks the early resilience; sometimes we merely feel the clever old journalist is up to his tricks again. But where Chesterton is most sensitive to this disturbing idea, his imagination rouses and he does his best work. (p. 20)

But, Chesterton's bright miraculous world also had its darker side.

Out of the corners of his eyes, as it were, he continually caught glimpses of something terrifyingly alien, a world of uncanny evil. If we praise him for his "childlike" quality, we have to acknowledge that that quality includes, on occasion, a singularly nasty imagination, and that he had a strong sense of guilt. When he was considering becoming a Catholic in 1922, he wrote a long letter to Ronald Knox which includes the revealing phrase, "All the morbid life of the lonely mind of a living person with whom I have lived"—and he wasn't referring to [his wife] Frances. Evelyn Waugh comments that, in Catholicism, Chesterton sought not primarily Authority "but, surprisingly in a man of such transparent innocence. Absolution"; and there is in Chesterton's writing the persistent suggestion of a very private and unspeakable nightmare. (p. 22)

Throughout his life Chesterton described physical horror with verve. There is plenty in the Father Brown stories (curiously, often to do with dead, with the mutilated or with otherwise ghastly heads). In **"The Invisible Man,"** for instance, there is an eerie room full of humanoid robots; there are also bloodstains, but no corpse: "'Eaten him?' said the nightmare at his ear; and he sickened at the idea of rent, human remains absorbed and crushed into all that acephalous clockwork." Nevertheless, the physical is a small element of the range of uncanny effects in these stories. The formula never varies—a Catholic priest dispels illusions of evil and darkness. There is an obvious meaning of "Good conquers Evil," but the unfailing nastiness of the central images suggest something more personal to Chesterton. I believe the stories correspond to some deep *and continuously felt* process going on in Chesterton's mind. Christianity exorcising his own darker imaginings. They are a safety-valve releasing him from himself, a device of the subconscious mind; and much of their success depends on the imaginative power generated by this compulsion. This said, the richness and delicacy of Chesterton's imagination is remarkable; for instance, in the evocation of extreme cold in **"The Sign of the Broken Sword."** He orchestrates a number of tiny effects, so that the midnight chill conveys a dimension of meaning for which the mechanical plot is itself inadequate.

In a Chesterton story, the uncanny starts off with ordinary things: a hall mirror, a river landscape. Suddenly, the whole world becomes charged with the numinous; he is particularly good at the moment when the scalp begins to crawl. He writes: "But so long as a tree is a tree, it does not frighten us at all. It begins to be alien, to be something strange, only when it looks like ourselves. When a tree really looks like a man our knees knock under us." This is the recurrent dread which haunted Chesterton: that his solid, good world would slip away, leaving either a reflection of his own face, or a nothingness. (pp. 23-4)

Some readers are disappointed because Chesterton's eerie happenings turn out to have natural explanations. Dr. Stephen Medcalf [in an essay published in John Sullivan's critical collection *G. K. Chesterton: A Centenary Appraisal* (see Additional Bibliography)] has seen this as symptomatic of a major weakness; Chesterton is arbitrarily putting up "a defence against the shadowland of [his] mind." Certainly, Chesterton had been so frightened by his experience of the occult that he insisted that the writer refuse to explore it seriously lest he be damaged as Blake was damaged. If an artist refuses to explore because he thinks perception of truth depends on *not* exploring, we may regret his decision, but we can hardly call him "arbitrary." Chesterton would have promptly admitted to being scared, but I do not detect dishonesty either to himself or to the reader. He has been frightened by what he *thought* he saw; these experiences cannot be denied; and he is not denying them. Horror is a real thing in the mind of man and always returns; Father Brown may dispel one patch of darkness, but in the nature of things another will gather to need exorcising.

The horror of the uncanny persists not only in the fiction—where it could have been simply a money-spinning excitement—but in the non-fiction, which shows how deep it was in Chesterton's sensibility. (pp. 24-5)

All these examples of Chesterton's imagination, bright and dark, are what he called "the pristine revelation," which he saw as the artist's primary task. He himself struggled for the right words to catch those fading, devastating moments. The nightmare, which he controlled so carefully and only allowed to spurt out spasmodically in fearful shapes, is a real part of that "revelation" for him; it makes, behind the hearty bulk of the genial "G.K.C.," a shadow which throws that figure into sharper perspective.

We are bound to ask, did Chesterton as a child really see "a sort of white light" in nature; or did he merely recognise as an adult, when he had read his Wordsworth and MacDonald, that his early perceptions were like theirs? I am inclined to answer "the first," if only because I doubt whether any writer could create so complex an aesthetic and intellectual structure, and live with it so happily for sixty years as Chesterton did, if it did not have deep roots in his subconscious. And how good *is* Chesterton's imagination? I have been arguing that it is remarkable; but the fact remains that he left no one great visionary work to show for it: no *Prometheus Unbound,* no *Passage to India.* Was he too lazy to discipline his marvellous gift? Part of the answer to this is in Chesterton's habit of scattering his good things, a scattering which I do not think was accidental. Certainly he refused to take his "art" seriously, because he believed that people are more important than books. But he can hardly be regarded as a fine imagination gone to waste; too many people have read him with delight. When Coleridge wanted to praise Wordsworth, he said that he had

> above all the original gift of spreading the tone, the atmosphere, and with it the depth and height of the ideal world around forms, incidents and situations of which, for the common view, custom had bedimmed all the lustre, had dried up the sparkle and the dewdrops.

This is what Chesterton did for his Edwardian public. As he amused and dazzled them with his journalism, day by day he evoked "the tone, the atmosphere" of his visionary universe, poised, fearfully and wonderfully, on the edge of miracle. (p. 26)

Jill Brown, "'Unearthly Daylight': The Light and the Dark in Chesterton's Imagination," in The Chesterton Review, *Vol. 13, No. 1, February, 1987, pp. 15-28.*

ADDITIONAL BIBLIOGRAPHY

Barker, Dudley. *G. K. Chesterton: A Biography.* New York: Stein & Day, 1973, 304 p.

Biographical study that, drawing upon notebooks kept by Chesterton as a young man, presents the subject as one whose life and work reflect the scars of an extended period of nervous collapse suffered during his student days at the Slade School.

Belloc, Hilaire. *On the Place of Gilbert Chesterton in English Letters.* New York: Sheed & Ward, 1940, 84 p.

Overview of the beliefs and literary characteristics of Chesterton by one of his closest friends and coreligionists.

The Chesterton Review I— (1974—).

The quarterly periodical of the Chesterton Society, edited since its inception by the Society's founder, the distinguished Chesterton scholar Father Ian Boyd. Each number carries literary and biographical essays on the subject and his coreligionists, previously uncollected essays by Chesterton himself, and reviews of recently published books on Chesterton. Special issues have been devoted to Christopher Dawson, Hilaire Belloc, Eric Gill, and the Father Brown stories.

Churchill, R. C. "The Man Who Was Sunday: G. K. Chesterton, 1874-1936." *Contemporary Review* 224, No. 1296 (January 1974): 12-15.

An appreciative biographical and critical essay written for the centenary of Chesterton's birth.

Clemens, Cyril. "Father Brown." In his *Chesterton as Seen by His Contemporaries,* pp. 137-43. 1939. Reprint. New York: Haskell House Publishers, 1969.

Discusses the Father Brown mysteries, reprinting the favorable critical impressions of S. S. Van Dine, Mary Roberts Rinehart, and Hesketh Pearson, among others.

Ffinch, Michael. *G. K. Chesterton.* London: Weidenfeld & Nicolson, 1986, 369 p.

Illustrated biography that draws heavily from unpublished archival material.

Gillespie, Robert. "Detections: Borges and Father Brown." *Novel* 7, No. 3 (Spring 1974): 220-30.

Compares the Father Brown stories with Jorge Luis Borges's mysteries, offering evidence that "Chesterton and Borges both play with similar notions of contradiction, necessity, circular time, and transcendental reality."

Hollis, Christopher. *G. K. Chesterton.* London: British Council, 1950, 32 p.

A short biographical and critical survey.

———. "The Irish Question and Father Brown." In his *The Mind of Chesterton,* pp. 168-83. London: Hollis & Carter, 1970.

Explores the Father Brown stories, noting the horror present in some of them, and refuting the perception of Chesterton as a man ignorant and insensitive to the effects of evil.

Haycraft, Howard. "England: 1890-1914 (The Romantic Era)." In his *Murder for Pleasure: The Life and Times of the Detective Story,* pp. 62-82. New York: D. Appleton-Century Company, 1941.

Summarizes the strengths and weaknesses of Chesterton's short stories.

Hynes, Samuel. "A Detective and His God." *The New Republic* 190, No. 5 (6 February 1984): 39, 41-2.

Review-essay on *The Father Brown Omnibus.* Hynes concludes that Chesterton "put his lost causes into his Father Brown stories, and made them into parables of his vision—of one insignificant man of faith confronting the lunacies, the nightmares, and the follies of the world, and not failing because his faith doesn't fail. And that, I take it, is why we read Father Brown, instead of other, more serious Chesterton books."

Jago, David. "The Metaphysician as Fiction-Writer: G. K. Chesterton's Narrative Techniques." *The Antigonish Review* 22 (Summer 1975): 85-99.

Examines Chesterton's melding of fictional techniques and metaphysics in the Father Brown stories, *The Club of Queer Trades,* and several novels.

Kenner, Hugh. *Paradox in Chesterton.* New York: Sheed & Ward, 1947, 156 p.

Study of Chesterton's canon that seeks "to justify paradox as Chesterton used it, as a means to truth and as a means to art, understanding by art all making." An insightful introduction to the book is provided by Marshall McLuhan.

Lea, F. A. "G. K. Chesterton." In *Modern Christian Revolutionaries: An Introduction to the Lives and Thought of Kierkegaard, Eric Gill, G. K. Chesterton, C. F. Andrews, Berdyaev,* edited by Donald Attwater, pp. 87-155. New York: Devin-Adair Co., 1947.

An in-depth examination of Chesterton's social, political, and religious beliefs, and of their expression in his writings.

"The Strength and Weakness of Father Brown." *Life & Letters* IV, No. 21 (February 1930): 157-72.

Review-essay of *The Father Brown Stories* which discusses the detecting technique of Father Brown and the literary technique of Chesterton.

Macaulay, Rose. "Personalities and Powers: Mr. G. K. Chesterton." *Time & Tide* 2, No. 5 (4 February 1921): 106-07.

An admiring overview of Chesterton's accomplishments.

Noyes, Alfred. "The Centrality of Chesterton." *The Quarterly Review* 291, No. 595 (January 1953): 43-50.

General essay on Chesterton's importance.

O'Connor, John. *Father Brown on Chesterton.* London: Frederick Muller, 1937, 173 p.

Biographical sketch of Chesterton by his longtime friend, Father O'Connor, after whom Father Brown was loosely modeled.

Person, James E., Jr. Review of *Daylight and Nightmare: Uncollected Stories and Fables,* by G. K. Chesterton. *National Review* XXXIX, No. 15 (14 August 1987): 53.

Perceptive review of Chesterton's uncollected writings.

Poston, Lawrence, III. "'Markheim' and Chesterton's 'The Hammer of God'." *Nineteenth-Century Fiction* 12 (1957): 235-36.

Posits the influence of R. L. Stevenson's story "Markheim" on the concluding scene of Chesterton's "The Hammer of God."

Seven: An Anglo-American Literary Review I— (1980—).

An annual periodical, founded and edited by Barbara Reynolds, that publishes scholarly essays on the works of seven distinguished authors of similar and/or related outlook: George MacDonald, Charles Williams, J. R. R. Tolkien, Dorothy L. Sayers, Owen Barfield, C. S. Lewis, and Chesterton.

Sullivan, John, ed. *G. K. Chesterton: A Centenary Appraisal.* New York: Harper & Row, 1974, 243 p.

A collection of critical essays by such distinguished contributors as W. H. Auden, P. N. Furbank, and Kingsley Amis.

Symons, Julian. "The Short Story: The First Golden Age." In his *Bloody Murder: From the Detective Story to the Crime Novel, a History,* pp. 74-85. New York: Viking, 1985.

Contains a favorable discussion of the Father Brown stories. Symons concludes: "A reading of Chesterton reinforces the truth that the best detective stories have been written by artists and not by artisans."

Titterton, W. R. *G. K. Chesterton: A Portrait.* 1936. Reprint. New York: Haskell House Publishers, 1973, 235 p.

An anecdotal biography focusing on the development of Chesterton's social, economic, and religious beliefs, and on his work as a journalist—particularly as editor of *G. K.'s Weekly.*

Ward, Maisie. *Gilbert Keith Chesterton.* New York: Sheed & Ward, 1943, 685 p.

Critically affirmed as the most detailed, informative, and useful of all the biographies of Chesterton yet written.

Wills, Garry. *Chesterton: Man and Mask.* New York: Sheed & Ward, 1961, 243 p.

Considered one of the essential studies of Chesterton's career.

William (Cuthbert) Faulkner

1897-1962

American novelist, short story writer, poet, dramatist, screenwriter, and essayist.

A preeminent figure in modern American literature, Faulkner created a profound and complex body of work that reflects the heritage of the American South. Mississippi, where Faulkner lived all of his life, provided the geographical and cultural background for the Yoknapatawpha County of his novels and short stories, but only in a superficial sense can Faulkner be considered a regional writer: his radical stylistic innovations and his moral depth give his works a universality that places him among the major figures of world literature. Faulkner is more highly regarded for his novels than for his short fiction; he himself occasionally disparaged his short stories as commercial efforts, leading critics for many years to ignore them as serious literary works. Nevertheless, Faulkner's most successful stories are now considered to be among the best that the twentieth century has produced, and such widely anthologized stories as "A Rose for Emily," "That Evening Sun," and "The Bear" are generally acclaimed as masterpieces.

The Bettmann Archive, Inc.

Faulkner began writing and publishing short fiction in 1925 while living in New Orleans. There he met Sherwood Anderson, who convinced him to turn from poetry to fiction. While working on his first novel, *Soldiers' Pay*, Faulkner published several sketches and short stories for a local paper and a magazine. They were later collected in the volumes *Salmagundi* and *New Orleans Sketches*, and though clearly apprentice efforts, some suggest themes which were to appear in Faulkner's more mature writing. His early novels soon attracted literary attention and admiration, but Faulkner encountered serious financial trouble due to the lack of popular interest in his work. He turned to producing short stories for "the slicks"—popular, general-interest magazines such as *The Saturday Evening Post*—to earn enough money to continue work on his novels. As late as 1946, Faulkner wrote to Harold Ober: "Thank you for the Ellery Queen check. What a commentary. In France I am the father of a literary movement. In Europe I am considered the best modern American and among the first of all writers. In America I eke out a hack's motion picture wages by winning second prize in a manufactured mystery story contest." Nevertheless, Faulkner's short stories were never weak commercial efforts, and their importance in the Yoknapatawpha legend is illustrated by Faulkner's care when collecting them in volumes. In 1930 Faulkner published the first such collection, *These Thirteen,* composed of several previously published stories and a few unpublished ones. Although the stories are uneven in quality, the volume contains three of Faulkner's most highly acclaimed stories: "Red Leaves," "A Rose for Emily," and "That Evening Sun." Faulkner designed a structural unity for *These Thirteen* by framing six Yoknapatawpha stories between four concerning World War I and three set in Europe. Thus, according to critics, the Mississippi stories form the heart of the book and draw resonance from each other through recurring subjects, themes, and characters.

After another short story collection, *Doctor Martino, and Other Stories,* Faulkner began to extend the technical virtuosity he had displayed in his novels to his short fiction. He created an intermediate genre: novels composed of separate but interrelated short stories or novellas. Several of the stories had appeared first in magazines and were later modified, sometimes extensively, to fit into the structure of the novel. Faulkner had already used the published story "Wash" and the unpublished "Evangeline" as material for his novel *Absalom, Absalom!*, but both were fully integrated into the text of the novel. In *The Unvanquished, The Wild Palms, Go Down, Moses, and Other Stories,* and *Knight's Gambit,* each chapter of the work is individually titled and forms a distinct story, but also contributes to the thematic unity of the whole. *The Unvanquished* is a series of stories concerning the Civil War and Reconstruction, unified by chronological progression, the single narrative voice of Bayard Sartoris, and the moral development of Bayard as he passes through adolescence into adulthood. *The Wild Palms* is composed of alternating chapters from two separate and ambiguously related novellas, "Wild Palms" and "Old Man." While some critics find parallel situations and dramatic foils between the two novellas, others consider each, particularly "Old Man," to be more successful when considered separately. *Knight's Gambit,* a collection of detective stories originally published in magazines and unrevised for book publication, is considered the least unified of the group and is most often regarded as simply a short story collection. The stories are connected, however, by the character of the detective Gavin

Stevens and by the inclusion of the long title story, which Faulkner wrote in an attempt to gather elements of the previous stories into a cohesive finale.

Go Down, Moses is widely considered one of Faulkner's greatest works and his most successful effort in combining the novel and short story. When the book was originally published as *Go Down, Moses, and Other Stories,* the subtitle was inserted by the publisher without Faulkner's knowledge, and Faulkner pressed to have "and Other Stories" dropped in the book's second printing because he considered it a novel. The book is a narrative spanning five generations of the white and black descendants of Lucius Quintus Carothers McCaslin, who founded the McCaslin plantation: "bought the land, took the land, got the land no matter how, held it to bequeath, no matter how." McCaslin is a shadowy figure behind the narrative: all but one of the stories are concerned with his descendants, and none are set within his lifetime. The stories are concerned with the effects of his actions as they are felt by his descendants, primarily in his abuse of the land, participation in slavery, and miscegenation, creating two family lines, one illegitimate, unacknowledged, and under subjection to the other. The twin themes of the gradual loss of the wilderness and the exploitation of black people unify the book. The stories, however, are not arranged chronologically and do not share a common narrator or common protagonists; critics disputing the book's classification as a novel note that one story, "Pantaloon in Black," does not involve any of McCaslin's descendants. Nevertheless, the stories are thematically coherent, and the centrality of Isaac McCaslin serves to unify the work. The emotional climax of the novel, entitled "The Bear," is considered to be one of Faulkner's greatest achievements and is discussed as both a short story and the concluding section of the novel.

The remaining short story collections that Faulkner assembled include *Collected Stories of William Faulkner* and *Big Woods. Collected Stories* reprints all the stories from *These Thirteen* and all but two from *Doctor Martino, and Other Stories,* as well as seventeen stories that had previously appeared only in magazines. Faulkner organized *Collected Stories* by gathering the separate narratives into six sections, thereby suggesting a unity within each section: "The Country," "The Village," "The Wilderness," "The Wasteland," "The Middle Ground," and "Beyond." Scholars have begun to study Faulkner's careful arrangement of collections such as *These Thirteen* and *Collected Stories* and to judge his success in producing a unified narrative. *Big Woods,* Faulkner's last collection, consists of four of Faulkner's best hunting stories, including a version of "The Bear" different from the one included in *Go Down, Moses. Uncollected Stories of William Faulkner* is a posthumous book incorporating stories not included in previous collections. It contains several that were later revised for inclusion in novels, as well as uncollected magazine fiction, and several unpublished stories of interest to Faulkner scholars or enthusiasts.

"A Rose for Emily," one of Faulkner's most-often anthologized stories, concerns the life of Emily Grierson, a spinster whose isolation from her community forms the tension of the narrative. While some of Faulkner's early critics dismissed the work as merely the exploitation of horror for the sake of sensationalism, later critics perceived a deeper meaning in the story. Cleanth Brooks and Robert Penn Warren found Emily's madness to be an excessive assertion of individuality over community standards, and her fate, therefore, a tragedy. Ray B. West, Jr. interpreted the story as a conflict between the old South represented by Miss Emily, a "lady" in the aristocratic tradition, and the new South influenced by the industrialized North, represented by her lover Homer Barron. Emily's downfall was her inability to accept change, as evidenced by her refusal to accept the deaths of Colonel Sartoris and her father and by her resorting, apparently, to murder and necrophilia to keep Homer from leaving her.

"That Evening Sun" is considered a brilliant and enigmatic tale leaving many unresolved questions for the reader. The story of a black woman, Nancy, who becomes terrified that her estranged husband Jesus has come back to town to murder her, "That Evening Sun" poses the question of whether Nancy's fear is justified or not, and whether Jesus actually does murder her on the night the story ends. Critics are divided on this issue. Laurence Perrine demonstrates that this ambiguity is the culmination of a series of factual questions that are left unanswered. Other critics raise issues such as the degree to which the Compson family for whom Nancy works and to whom she appeals for protection, is responsible for her safety. Another question concerns the narrative persona of Quentin Compson, who tells the story fifteen years after its events have occurred. Quentin was nine years old at the time of the story and would be twenty-four years old when he narrated it; yet the same character commits suicide at the age of twenty-one in the novel *The Sound and the Fury.* Faulkner was guilty of more blatant inconsistencies than this, however, and he offered the following justification: "I can move these people around like God, not only in space but in time too." Nonetheless, Quentin s narration after the fact raises a question: since he must know whether Nancy died fifteen years before, why does Quentin withhold this information from the reader? One possible solution is to recognize that the story focuses on Nancy's fear and the Compson's response to it, rather than the fact or fallacy of Nancy's impending death. With such a purpose, any resolution of the story's ambiguities would only weaken it.

Many commentators point to "The Bear" as a concentrated exploration of themes that recur in Faulkner's work: the mistreatment of blacks, miscegenation, incest, the ownership of land, and the problem of guilt. The first three sections of the story form a hunting narrative which culminates in the killing of the legendary bear, Old Ben. The crucial fourth section is not a part of the hunting story: constituting almost half of the novella, it narrates Isaac McCaslin's repudiation of the McCaslin plantation, of which he is the heir. One reason for his repudiation is his belief in communal use, rather than private ownership, of land. A deeper reason, however, lies in his discovery that his grandfather Lucius McCaslin had impregnated one of his slaves, Eunice, and later sexually abused the daughter he had fathered by her, driving Eunice to suicide. Haunted by guilt, Isaac refuses his inheritance as a protest against his grandfather's misconduct. Critics are divided concerning their view of Isaac's action. Many commentators consider his repudiation heroic, even Christlike, and assert the value of patient suffering that Isaac exemplifies. Others point out that ownership of the plantation was not relinquished but merely transferred to Isaac's cousin McCaslin Edmonds, and that when Isaac accepts a monthly stipend from the plantation he disowned, he nullifies his intended effect.

Significantly, Faulkner cut the fourth section from the story when it was reprinted separately as part of *Big Woods*. Some critics believe the fourth part should have been retained, claiming it illustrates the further moral development of Isaac McCaslin—a process central to the rest of the story—and that there are important analogies between the fourth section and the hunting narrative of the first three. Other critics, agreeing with Faulkner that the fourth section belonged to the novel rather than to the story, note that much of the section is incomprehensible when isolated from *Go Down, Moses,* that the hunting story alone forms a complete and coherent unit, and that the addition of the fourth section apart from the context of *Go Down, Moses* serves to break the unity of the story. Most of the criticism of "The Bear" focuses on Isaac's repudiation of his inheritance, however, and most critics believe it is this complex and moving passage which makes "The Bear" such a central work in Faulkner's Yoknapatawpha saga and one of his most impressive stories.

Although Faulkner's short stories were long considered a minor contribution to his work, they are now receiving greater recognition and critical attention. Faulkner himself had great respect for the genre, considering the short story the most demanding form of writing after poetry. His short stories fill an important place in the Yoknapatawpha legend, and the best of them stand alone as brilliant examples of Faulkner's art. They, together with his novels, establish Faulkner as one of the great prose writers of modern literature.

(See also *CLC,* Vols. 1, 3, 6, 8, 9, 11, 14, 18, 28; *Contemporary Authors,* Vols. 81-84; *Dictionary of Literary Biography,* Vols. 9, 11, 44; and *Dictionary of Literary Biography Documentary Series,* Vol. 2.)

PRINCIPAL WORKS

SHORT FICTION

These Thirteen 1930
Salmagundi 1932
Doctor Martino, and Other Stories 1934
The Unvanquished 1938
The Wild Palms 1939
Go Down, Moses, and Other Stories 1942; also published as *Go Down, Moses,* 1949
Knight's Gambit 1949
Collected Stories of William Faulkner 1950
Big Woods 1955
New Orleans Sketches 1958
Uncollected Stories of William Faulkner 1979

OTHER MAJOR WORKS

The Marble Faun (poetry) 1924
Soldiers' Pay (novel) 1926
Mosquitoes (novel) 1927
Sartoris (novel) 1929; also published as *Flags in the Dust* [unabridged edition], 1973
The Sound and the Fury (novel) 1929
As I Lay Dying (novel) 1930
Sanctuary (novel) 1931
Light in August (novel) 1932
A Green Bough (poetry) 1933
Pylon (novel) 1935
Absalom, Absalom! (novel) 1936
The Hamlet (novel) 1940
Intruder in the Dust (novel) 1948
Requiem for a Nun [first publication] (drama) 1951
A Fable (novel) 1954
The Town (novel) 1957
The Mansion (novel) 1959
The Reivers (novel) 1962

LIONEL TRILLING (essay date 1931)

[*A respected American critic and literary historian, Trilling was also an essayist, editor, novelist, and short story writer. In the following excerpt, he reviews Faulkner's first short fiction collection,* These Thirteen, *commending Faulkner's technique and emotional power while reproaching him for lack of import.*]

Mr. Faulkner has the tone and emotional impact of a major writer. But despite the dramatic stress and portentousness of his work its implications are too frequently minor. It has so often been pointed out that Mr. Faulkner "creates his own world" that one at first assumes that his work tends to be minor simply because it is idiosyncratic. Yet one has only to take the example of Baudelaire to understand how even an esoteric symbolism may be consistent with that largeness of implication which we feel to be one of the primary requirements of major writing. In the work of Mr. Faulkner the absence of this largeness of reference seems to be the result of his particular social point of view rather than of the symbols that express it.

But for the present reviewer Mr. Faulkner is most interesting when he avoids social implications entirely. When he can exploit emotion in some strange and hitherto unexplored setting of mind or place he seems most at ease. Such settings are the minds of the children as they come into contact with primitive fear in the story **"That Evening Sun,"** or the lost and fantastic colony of Negro-owning Indians in **"Red Leaves"** and **"A Justice,"** or again the fear-hazed mind of the platoon and the caving chalk-field over which it wanders in **"Crevasse."** These scenes and moods, isolated from common reality, self-defined, not a little fantastic, offer Mr. Faulkner the possibility of complete success.

Such stories, depending as they do on mood, scene, and melodrama, are perhaps as unimportant as those of a writer like A. E. Coppard, but this question becomes irrelevant before their technical perfection. However, when Mr. Faulkner's material is not isolated, but is the material of the daily world, perfection dissipates. Pure event, pure emotion, acceptable enough in a special world, are given the lie by a common world which cries out for understanding as well as for rendition. **"A Rose for Emily,"** the story of a woman who has killed her lover and lain for years beside his decaying corpse, is essentially trivial in its horror because it has no implications, because it is pure event without implication; and for the same reason the hero of **"Hair"** is, with his endless self-abnegation, little more than quaint—a "character," an "original." Moreover, when Mr. Faulkner does wish to hint implications, when he deals with philosophical emotions, the world in which he sets them has no vital contact with the world of common experience. In **"Ad Astra"** and **"All the Dead Pilots"** he uses an isolated society of inarticulate young men who in civilian life were separated from many of the realities of existence by their aristocracy, and who in the war are yet more isolated by the aristocracy of the flying corps and their love of death. Here, because the philosophical importance of emotions depends on their articulateness and their universality, Mr. Faulkner's emotions fail of final meaning and become high-flown and sentimental. (pp. 491-92)

In the present volume perhaps the two best stories are **"Dry September"** and **"Victory."** The first is the story of a lynching, the second of a Scotch shipwright whom the war makes a gentleman and who remains one in waxed mustache and pressed suit even when reduced to selling matches. These stories seem best because they are aerated by contact with the common world, by the writer's acceptance of the common, an acceptance which by no means limits the originality, even idiosyncracy, of their vision and style. Beside them the rest of the stories, for all their success in their own terms, have a subtle kind of stuffiness, shut off as they are in their interesting but hermetically sealed universes. (p. 492)

Lionel Trilling, "Mr. Faulkner's World," in The Nation, *New York, Vol. CXXXIII, No. 3461, November 4, 1931, pp. 491-92.*

MALCOLM COWLEY (essay date 1942)

[*An American critic, editor, poet, translator, and historian, Cowley has made valuable contributions to contemporary letters with his writings as a literary critic for the* New Republic, *his chronicles and criticism of modern American literature, and his editions of the works of such American authors as Nathaniel Hawthorne, Walt Whitman, and Faulkner. In the following excerpt, Cowley reviews* Go Down, Moses, *judging it to be an intermediate genre between the novel and the short story collection; he also discusses its contribution to Faulkner's Yoknapatawpha legend.*]

We have grown used to reading collections of short stories that masqueraded as novels so as to have a wider sale. Here is another sort of hybrid: a loosely jointed but ambitious novel masquerading as a collection of stories, possibly because William Faulkner was too proud or indifferent to call them chapters in a book.

Six of the seven episodes in ***Go Down, Moses*** deal with the McCaslin family, on its big plantation in northwestern Mississippi. These six have the same underlying theme, which is the price paid by many generations for the first McCaslin's relations with a slave girl who was also—trust Faulker for this added detail—his illegitimate daughter. Four of the stories are concerned with his white grandson, Isaac McCaslin; they deal respectively with his parentage, his training as a hunter, his abnegation—if that is the word for what he did when he surrendered his plantation for the humbler inheritance he received from a half-Indian guide—and his last hunting trip into the wilderness. Two other stories deal with the first McCaslin's colored descendants, who also appear more briefly in the tales about old Isaac. One of them bears a child by her white cousin; another is electrocuted for shooting a Chicago policeman, and the white merchants of Jefferson pay for bringing his body home. Only one story, **"Pantaloon in Black,"** has nothing to do with the McCaslin clan; it describes a murder and a lynching as a sequence of tragic events beyond good and evil.

The first story, **"Was,"** comes close to being Faulkner's funniest, and the first half of **"The Bear"** is almost the best hunting yarn I have ever read. The trouble is that the book as a whole is a little too formless and repetitive to make a satisfactory novel, just as the seven episodes are a little too interdependent to stand completely alone. And there is another sense, too, in which ***Go Down, Moses*** is a hybrid. Most of the stories were first published in various magazines and met the strict rules they set for contributors; then afterwards they were revised and fitted together to meet the equally strict but quite different rules that Faulkner sets for himself. The magazine sections can still be recognized; they are straightforward prose, concerned only with telling a story. The later additions are in the curious idiom which Faulkner invented and sometimes writes magnificently, but which he writes at other times with no consideration for the reader.

Perhaps the best way to judge the book is neither as a novel nor as a series of novellas; neither as magazine nor as personal writing; but simply as another instalment of the Mississippi legend on which Faulkner has now been working for more than fifteen years. It is, as everyone knows by this time, the story of an imaginary county called Yoknapatawpha—area, 2,400 square miles; population, 15,611 by Faulkner's last census, which was printed at the end of *Absalom, Absalom!* At least a fifth of its people, Negro and white, have by now appeared in one or more of his stories. And these stories, although they differ in quality, and although the seven in ***Go Down, Moses*** are only his second-best, have each the effect of making the legend as a whole seem more impressive. There is no other American writer, and not many novelists anywhere, who have succeeded in presenting the life of a whole neighborhood, with all its social strata, all its personal conflicts, all its humor and much more than its share of violent crimes.

Malcolm Cowley, "Go Down to Faulkner's Land," in The New Republic, *Vol. 106, No. 26, June 29, 1942, p. 900.*

RAY B. WEST, JR. (essay date 1949)

[*West is an American short story writer, poet, and critic. In the following excerpt from an essay originally published in* Perspective *in 1949, he interprets "A Rose for Emily" as an allegory in which Emily represents the Old South and Homer Barron represents the new order influenced by the North. West's thesis was later disputed by William Van O'Connor (see excerpt dated 1952).*]

The first clues to meaning in a short story usually arise from a detection of the principal contrasts which an author sets up. The most common, perhaps, are contrasts of character, but when characters are contrasted there is usually also a resultant contrast in terms of action. Since action reflects a moral or ethical state, contrasting action points to a contrast in ideological perspectives and hence toward the theme.

The principal contrast in William Faulkner's short story **"A Rose for Emily"** is between past time and present time: the past as represented in Emily herself, in Colonel Sartoris, in the old Negro servant, and in the Board of Aldermen who accepted the Colonel's attitude toward Emily and rescinded her taxes; the present is depicted through the unnamed narrator and is represented in the *new* Board of Aldermen, in Homer Barron (the representative of Yankee attitudes toward the Griersons and through them toward the entire South), and in what is called "the next generation with its more modern ideas."

Atmosphere is defined in the *Dictionary of World Literature* as "The particular world in which the events of a story or a play occur: time, place, conditions, and the attendant mood." When, as in **"A Rose for Emily,"** the world depicted is a confusion between the past and the present, the atmosphere is one of distortion—of unreality. This unreal world results from the suspension of a natural time order. Normality consists in a decorous progression of the human being from birth, through youth, to age and finally death. Preciosity in children is as monstrous as idiocy in the adult, because both are *unnatural*. Monstrosity, however, is a sentimental subject for fiction unless it is the result of human action—the result of a willful attempt to circumvent time. When such circumvention produces acts of violence, as in **"A Rose for Emily,"** the atmosphere becomes one of horror.

Horror, however, represents only the extreme form of maladjusted nature. It is not produced in **"A Rose for Emily"** until the final act of violence has been disclosed. All that has gone before has prepared us by producing a general tone of mystery, foreboding, decay, etc., so that we may say the entire series of events that have gone before are "in key"—that is, they are depicted in a mood in which the final violence does not appear too shocking or horrible. We are inclined to say, "In such an atmosphere, anything may happen." Foreshadowing is often accomplished through atmosphere, and in this case the atmosphere prepares us for Emily's unnatural act at the end of the story. Actually, such preparation begins in the very first sentence:

> When Miss Emily Grierson died, our whole town went to her funeral: the men through a sort of respectful affection for a fallen monument, the women mostly out of curiosity to see the inside of her house, which no one save an old manservant—a combined gardener and cook—had seen in at least ten years.

Emily is portrayed as "a fallen monument," a *monument* for reasons which we shall examine later, *fallen* because she has shown herself susceptible to death (and decay) after all. In the mention of death, we are conditioned (as the psychologist says) for the more specific concern with it later on. The second paragraph depicts the essential ugliness of the contrast: the description of Miss Emily's house "lifting its stubborn and coquettish decay above the cotton wagons and the gasoline pumps—an eyesore among eyesores." (A juxtaposition of past and present.) We recognize this scene as an emblematic presentation of Miss Emily herself, suggested as it is through the words "stubborn and coquettish." The tone—and the contrast—is preserved in a description of the note which Miss Emily sent to the mayor, "a note on paper of an archaic shape, in a thin, flowing calligraphy in faded ink," and in the description of the interior of the house when the deputation from the Board of Aldermen visit her: "They were admitted by the old Negro into a dim hall from which a stairway mounted into still more shadow. It smelled of dust and disuse—a close, dank smell." In the next paragraph a description of Emily discloses her similarity to the house: "She looked bloated, like a body long submerged in motionless water, and of that pallid hue."

Emily had not always looked like this. When she was young and part of the world with which she was contemporary, she was, we are told, "a slender figure in white," as contrasted with her father, who is described as "a spraddled silhouette." In the picture of Emily and her father together, framed by the door, she frail and apparently hungering to participate in the life of her time, we have a reversal of the contrast which has already been presented and which is to be developed later. Even after her father's death, Emily is not monstrous, but rather looked like a girl "with a vague resemblance to those angels in colored church windows—sort of tragic and serene." The suggestion is that she had already begun her entrance into that nether-world (a world which is depicted later as "rose-tinted"), but that she might even yet have been saved, had Homer Barron been another kind of man.

By the time the deputation from the new, progressive Board of Aldermen wait upon her concerning her delinquent taxes, however, she has completely retreated into her world of the past. There is no communication possible between her and them:

> Her voice was dry and cold. "I have no taxes in Jefferson. Colonel Sartoris explained it to me. Perhaps one of you can gain access to the city records and satisfy yourselves."
>
> "But we have. We are the city authorities. Miss Emily. Didn't you get a notice from the sheriff, signed by him?"
>
> "I received a paper, yes," Miss Emily said. "Perhaps he considers himself the sheriff. . . . I have no taxes in Jefferson."
>
> "But there is nothing on the books to show that, you see. We must go by the—"
>
> "See Colonel Sartoris. I have no taxes in Jefferson."
>
> "But Miss Emily—"
>
> "See Colonel Sartoris." (Colonel Sartoris had been dead almost ten years.) "I have no taxes in Jefferson. Tobe!" The Negro appeared. "Show these gentlemen out."

Just as Emily refused to acknowledge the death of her father, she now refuses to recognize the death of Colonel Sartoris. He had given his word, and according to the traditional view, "his word" knew no death. It is the Past pitted against the Present—the Past with its social decorum, the Present with everything set down in "the books." Emily dwells in the Past, always a world of unreality to us of the Present. Here are the facts which set the tone of the story and which create the atmosphere of unreality which surrounds it.

Such contrasts are used over and over again: the difference between the attitude of Judge Stevens (who is over eighty years old) and the attitude of the young man who comes to him about the "smell" at Emily's place. For the young man (who is a member of the "rising generation") it is easy. For him, Miss Emily's world has ceased to exist. The city's health regulations are on the books. "Dammit, sir," Judge Stevens replied, "will you accuse a lady to her face of smelling bad?" Emily had given in to social pressure when she allowed them to bury her father, but she triumphed over society in the matter of the smell. She had won already when she bought the poison, refusing to comply with the requirements of the law, because for her they did not exist.

Such incidents seem, however, mere preparation for the final, more important contrast between Emily and Homer Barron. Emily is the town's aristocrat; Homer is a day laborer. Homer is an active man dealing with machinery and workmen—a man's man. He is a Yankee—a Northerner. Emily is a "monument" of Southern gentility. As such she is common property of the town, but in a special way—as an ideal of *past* values. Here the author seems to be commenting upon the complex relationship between the Southerner and his past and between the Southerner of the present and the Yankee from the North. She is unreal to her compatriots, yet she impresses them with her station, even at a time when they considered her *fallen:* "as if (her dignity) had wanted that touch of earthiness to reaffirm her imperviousness." It appeared for a time that Homer had won her over, as though the demands of reality as depicted in him (earthiness) had triumphed over her withdrawal and seclusion. This is the conflict that is not resolved until the final scene. We can imagine, however, what the outcome might have been had Homer Barron, who was not a marrying man, succeeded, in the town's eyes, in seducing her (violating her world) and then deserted her. The view of Emily as a monument would have been destroyed. Emily might have become the object of continued gossip, but she would have become susceptible to the town's pity—therefore, human. Emily's world, however, continues to be the Past (in its extreme form it is death), and when she is threatened with desertion and disgrace, she not only takes refuge in that world, but she also takes Homer with her, in the only manner possible. (pp. 192-95)

Miss Emily's position in regard to the specific problem of time is suggested in the scene where the old soldiers appear at her funeral. There are, we are told, two views of time: (1) the world of the present, viewing time as a mechanical progression in which the past is a diminishing road, never to be encountered again; (2) the world of tradition, viewing the past as a huge meadow which no winter ever quite touches, divided from (us) now by the narrow bottleneck of the most recent decade of years. The first is the view of Homer Barron and the modern generation in Jefferson. The second is the view of the older members of the Board of Aldermen and of the confederate soldiers. Emily holds the second view, except that for her there is no bottleneck dividing her from the meadow of the past.

Emily's small room above stairs has become that timeless meadow. In it, the living Emily and the dead Homer have remained together as though not even death could separate them. It is the monstrousness of this view which creates the final atmosphere of horror, and the scene is intensified by the portrayal of the unchanged objects which have surrounded Homer in life. Here he lay in the roseate atmosphere of Emily's death-in-life: "What was left of him, rotted beneath what was left of the nightshirt, had become inextricable from the bed in which he lay; and upon him and upon the pillow beside him lay that even coating of the patient and biding dust." The symbols of Homer's life of action have become mute and silent. Contrariwise, Emily's world, though it had been inviolate while she was alive, has been invaded after her death—the whole gruesome and unlovely tale unfolded.

In its simplest sense, the story says that death conquers all. But what is death? Upon one level, death is the past, tradition, whatever is opposite to the present. In the specific setting of this story, it is the past of the South in which the retrospective survivors of the War deny changing customs and the passage of time. Homer Barron, the Yankee, lived in the present, ready to take his pleasure and depart, apparently unwilling to consider the possibility of defeat, either by tradition (the Griersons) or by time (death) itself. In a sense, Emily conquered time, but only briefly and by retreating into her rose-tinted world of the past, a world in which death was denied at the same time that it is shown to have existed. Such retreat, the story implies, is hopeless, since everyone (even Emily) is finally subjected to death and the invasion of his world by the clamorous and curious inhabitants of the world of the present.

In these terms, it might seem that the story is a comment upon tradition and upon those people who live in a dream world of the past. But is it not also a comment upon the present? There is some justification for Emily's actions. She is a tragic—and heroic—figure. In the first place, she has been frustrated by her father, prevented from participating in the life of her contemporaries. When she attempts to achieve freedom, she is betrayed by a man who represents the new morality, threatened by disclosure and humiliation. The grounds of the tragedy is depicted in the scene already referred to between Emily and the deputation from the Board of Aldermen: for the new generation, the word of Colonel Sartoris meant nothing. This was a new age, a different time; the present was not bound by the promises of the past. For Emily, however, the word of the Colonel was everything. The tax notice was but a scrap of paper. (pp. 196-97)

Manuscript page of Faulkner's story "A Rose for Emily." Courtesy of Jill Faulkner Summers.

Perhaps our specific dilemma is the conflict of the pragmatic present against the set mores of the past. Homer Barron was an unheroic figure who put too much dependence upon his self-centered and rootless philosophy, a belief which suggested that he could take whatever he wanted without considering any obligation to the past (tradition) or to the future (death). Emily's resistance is heroic. Her tragic flaw is the conventional pride: she undertook to regulate the natural time-universe. She acted as though death did not exist, as though she could retain her unfaithful lover by poisoning him and holding his physical self prisoner in a world which had all of the appearances of reality except that most necessary of all things—life. (p. 197)

"A Rose for Emily" would seem to be saying that man must come to terms both with the past and the present; for to ignore the first is to be guilty of a foolish innocence, to ignore the second is to become monstrous and inhuman, above all to betray an excessive pride (such as Emily Grierson's) before the humbling fact of death. The total story says what has been said in so much successful literature, that man's plight is tragic, but that there is heroism in an attempt to rise above it. (p. 198)

Ray B. West, Jr., "Atmosphere and Theme in Faulkner's 'A Rose for Emily'," in William Faulkner: Four Decades of Criticism, *edited by Linda Welshimer Wagner, Michigan State University Press, 1973, pp. 192-98.*

LESLIE A. FIEDLER (essay date 1950)

[An American critic, novelist, short story writer, essayist, poet, and editor, Fiedler is a controversial commentator on American literature who approaches modern literature from primarily Marxist and Freudian perspectives. Fiedler is praised for his Love and Death in the American Novel *(1960), an insightful, provocative, highly individual landmark in literary criticism. In the following excerpt, Fiedler terms Faulkner "essentially a short story writer" and likens him to Charles Dickens in his success with both a popular audience and serious critics.]*

It is a strange experience for those of us to whom Faulkner's name is associated with the critical journals in which his fiction almost never appears, to find his stories, dressed up with the obvious pictures of the weekly family magazine, flanked not by a Kafka or Joyce, but by the dismal hacks whose names I cannot even now (though I have just looked) remember. Sometimes Faulkner writes for *Harper's,* but never for anything even as pretentious as the *New Yorker.* The only "little magazine" which has printed any of the present stories is *Sewanee Review,* in which first appeared the charming but utterly slick **"A Courtship."**

If Faulkner's stories were the work of his left hand, their appearance in popular magazines would be of little consequence (a man has to live!), but Faulkner is essentially a short story writer. He has no special talent for sustained narrative, though twice he has brought off a *tour de force* in long fiction. (pp. 384-85)

Faulkner as a storyteller is apparently short-breathed by nature, and his years of writing for the stringent space limits of the magazines has confirmed his tendency to write in gasps. What look like novels at first glimpse, *The Hamlet* or ***The Unvanquished,*** for instance, come apart into loosely linked short narratives; *Light in August* achieves substance by intertwining two separate stories, and *Sanctuary,* slim enough in finished form, consists of various sub-plots out of the Sartoris-Snopes background, tacked onto the original money-making shocker. Only in *Absalom, Absalom!* and *The Sound and the Fury* has Faulkner worked out genuine full-length narratives by extension rather than patchwork; and even in these two books, he attains novelistic thickness not by inventing a long, complex fable, but by revealing in a series of strict "point of view" accounts of the same experience the amount of narrative material proper to a short story. It is this experiment with "point of view," a virtue made of a short-breathed necessity, that has concealed somewhat the essentially popular nature of Faulkner's work, and has suggested to his critics comparisons with Proust or Joyce or James, rather than Dickens, whom he so strikingly resembles. The inventor of Popeye and the creator of Quilp have a great deal in common besides an obsession with the grotesque, and especially they have a demonic richness of invention (typified by their equal skill at evoking names that are already myths before the characters are drawn) and a contempt for the platitudes of everyday experience.

Like Dickens, Faulkner is primarily, despite his intellectual *obiter dicta,* a sentimental writer; not a writer with the occasional vice of sentimentality, but one whose basic mode of experience is sentimental, in an age when the serious "alienated" writer emblazons anti-sentimentality on his coat of arms. In a writer whose very method is self-indulgence, that sentimentality becomes sometimes downright embarrassing, as in the stories of World War II in [***Collected Stories***], **"The Tall Men," "Two Soldiers,"** etc., in which the soupiest clichés of self-sacrifice and endurance are shamelessly worked; he is not above the crassest "happy endings," stage-managing creakily the fulfillments that we had hoped for against all logic and probability. Even in so good a story as **"Uncle Willy"** the subtlety of tone and the ingenuity of development serve the conventional soft tale of the town lush opposed to the embattled forces of spinsterhood in a struggle for the old man's life and a boy's soul. Since Romanticism, the reservoir of the sentimental has been nostalgia, and in popular American literature this reservoir has been preeminently the nostalgia for boyhood and for our only homegrown Middle Ages, the ante-bellum South. (p. 385)

The detective story is the inevitable crown of Faulkner's work; in it (the six stories in ***Knight's Gambit*** and *Intruder in the Dust*) many strains of writing find fulfillment, not least his concern with the "switcheroo" and the surprise ending. Such devices are generally regarded these days as old-fashioned and factitious, but Faulkner has always shared with the mass public a sneaking fondness for them. **"A Rose for Emily,"** in some ways the best of his short stories, is marred by the last-minute use of such machinery, and many of his other pieces good or bad (**"Hair," "A Courtship"**) employ that disreputable device, presumed to have died with O. Henry. In the sub-literature of the detective novel the "switcheroo" has not only survived, but has become its very point; and it is therefore inevitable that Faulkner turn more and more to that form, as, indeed, Dickens was doing at the end of his career. (p. 386)

That Faulkner is an uneven writer everyone knows; but the good and bad in his work cannot be equated with the popular and highbrow elements. The two distinctions cut through his achievement on different planes; he is neither a natural storyteller confusing his talent with forays into the "literary," nor a great artist prostituting his talents for a living. His successes and failures are alike rooted in each level; and, indeed, he is often a "bad" writer, both by purely slick standards and in light of the higher criticism.

Why he is such a super-eminently good "bad" writer, surmounting excesses of maudlin feeling and absurd indulgences in overripe rhetoric alike, is a mystery. We can only cite the astonishing richness of invention and specification, the ability to realize characters and tensions with a power to coerce our credence that has nothing to do with a resemblance to "real" life or the technical standards we had fondly supposed would be demanded of any first-rate fiction in our time. It is only the just and delightful final turn of the screw that so baffling a writer has pleased over twenty-five years two audiences, each unaware of the fact, much less the grounds, of the other's appreciation. (p. 387)

Leslie A. Fiedler, "William Faulkner: An American Dickens," in Commentary, *Vol. 10, No. 4, October, 1950, pp. 384-87.*

WILLIAM VAN O'CONNOR (essay date 1952)

[An American critic who is associated with Robert Penn Warren and Cleanth Brooks, O'Connor was a practitioner of the New Criticism, which dictates that literature must be examined as an object in itself through close analysis of symbol, image, and met-

aphor. In the following excerpt, from an essay originally published in Sewanee Review *in 1952, he refutes Ray B. West's "historical emphasis" in his interpretation of "A Rose for Emily" (see excerpt dated 1949).*]

[Stressing] or rather over-stressing historical and sociological, or regional, aspects of Faulkner's fiction, even when the mythic qualities are acknowledged, leads to distorting the more basic intention of many, perhaps most, of the stories—to reading them somehow as documents in a legendary history of the South. (I am not of course trying to say that one can ignore these aspects. They are inevitably and powerfully interwoven with the themes; they may have brought some of the themes sharply to his consciousness; and certainly the regional characteristics modify and qualify the ways in which the themes are developed.) Perhaps a review of Ray West's account of **"A Rose for Emily"** will indicate the dangers in the "historical" emphasis. West reads the story as a conflict between the values of the Old South and the new order, business-like, pragmatic, self-centered. But it can't be read in these terms because the Old South and the new order are merely a part of the flavor and tone of the story, *not* the poles of conflict. The theme is that a denial of normal emotions invites retreat into a marginal world, into fantasy. The severity of Miss Emily's father was the cause of her frustrations and her retreat. The past becomes a part of her fantasies, just as the present does. It is incidental that her relationship to the Old South makes her a part of the town's nostalgia; it was the nostalgia, not her being a "lady," which caused her to be treated reverently by the town's board when she refused to acknowledge her taxes; presumably even ladies paid their taxes in the Old South. If the conflict is between the two orders it seems curious indeed that Miss Emily would choose Homer Barron, Yankee, amoral, and without loyalty, as her beloved. And her murder of the new order, Homer Barron, is the reverse of what actually happened, the destruction of the old order by the new. The story is simple enough when read as an account of Miss Emily's becoming mad as a consequence of her frustrations, the denial to her of normal emotional relations. That the Old South, which as a physical presence (in its houses, memories, and so on) lingers in the new order and in doing so seems unreal, has its parallel, obviously, in Miss Emily, who was most strangely detached from reality. But this is a parallel only—it is not the dramatic pull or struggle that composes the action. (pp. 44-5)

William Van O'Connor, "History in 'A Rose for Emily'," in A Rose for Emily *by William Faulkner, edited by M. Thomas Inge, Charles E. Merrill Publishing Company, 1970, pp. 44-5.*

WILLIAM FAULKNER (INTERVIEW WITH **ROBERT A. JELLIFE**) **(interview date 1955)**

[*In the following excerpt from a 1955 interview, Faulkner answers questions concerning "A Rose for Emily" and "The Bear."*]

Q: Mr. Faulkner [the young lady who asked the question] likes to know if Emily [in **"A Rose for Emily"**] is your ideal woman, or do you like Emily or not?

FAULKNER: I feel sorry for Emily's tragedy; her tragedy was, she was an only child, an only daughter. At the time when she could have found a husband, could have had a life of her own, there was probably some one, her father, who said, "No, you must stay here and take care of me." And then when she found a man, she had had no experience in people. She picked out probably a bad one, who was about to desert her. And when she lost him she could see that for her that was the end of life, there was nothing left, except to grow older, alone, solitary; she had had something and she wanted to keep it, which is bad—to go to any length to keep something; but I pity Emily. I don't know whether I would have liked her or not, I might have been afraid of her. Not of her but of anyone who had suffered, had been warped, as her life had probably been warped by a selfish father.

Q: Mr. Faulkner, what does the loss symbolize in the story?

FAULKNER: Why, it's the loss which, the grief which might come to anyone, and one must have the training to face loss and griefs.

Q: Mr. Faulkner, I think she means "rose."

FAULKNER: Oh, that was an allegorical title; the meaning was, here was a woman who had had a tragedy, an irrevocable tragedy and nothing could be done about it, and I pitied her and this was a salute, just as if you were to make a gesture, a salute, to anyone; to a woman you would hand a rose, as you would lift a cup of *sake* to a man. (p. 127)

[Q:] Could you make any comment or explanation about **"The Bear"**? It's very famous and, what shall I say, it's very popular among Japanese scholars. I wonder if you could make any comment or explanation about that wonderful piece. I mean, **"The Bear."**

FAULKNER: Yes, that was symbolism. That was the story of not just a boy but any human being to grow, as he grows up, to compete with the earth, the world, the bear representing not evil, but an old obsolescence that was strong, that held to the old ways, but because it had been strong and lived within its own code of morality, it deserved to be treated with respect. And that's what that little boy did. He learned not about bears, from that bear, but he learned about the world, he learned about man. About courage, about pity, about responsibility, from that bear.

Q: I keep thinking that piece is the boy's initiation to life and nature.

FAULKNER: That's right, his discovery of the world, of life.

Q: What did you mean by the bear? Taking it this way, the bear is symbolic of nature itself?

FAULKNER: Yes, symbolic of nature in an age when nature in a way is being destroyed. That is, the forests are going, being replaced by the machine, and that bear represented the old tradition of nature.

Q: Does that nature include both evil and good?

FAULKNER: Yes, sure. Its own morality. It did things that were evil, by a more intelligent code, but by its own code they were not evil and it was strong and brave to live up to its own code of morality. (pp. 139-40)

William Faulkner and Robert A. Jellife, in an interview in Lion in the Garden: Interviews with William Faulkner, 1926-1962, *edited by James B. Meriwether and Michael Millgate, Random House, 1968, pp. 127-41.*

WILLIAM FAULKNER (INTERVIEW WITH **CYNTHIA GRENIER**) **(interview date 1955)**

[*In the following excerpt from an interview Grenier conducted in Paris in September, 1955, Faulkner comments on his story "The Bear" and on several of his characters.*]

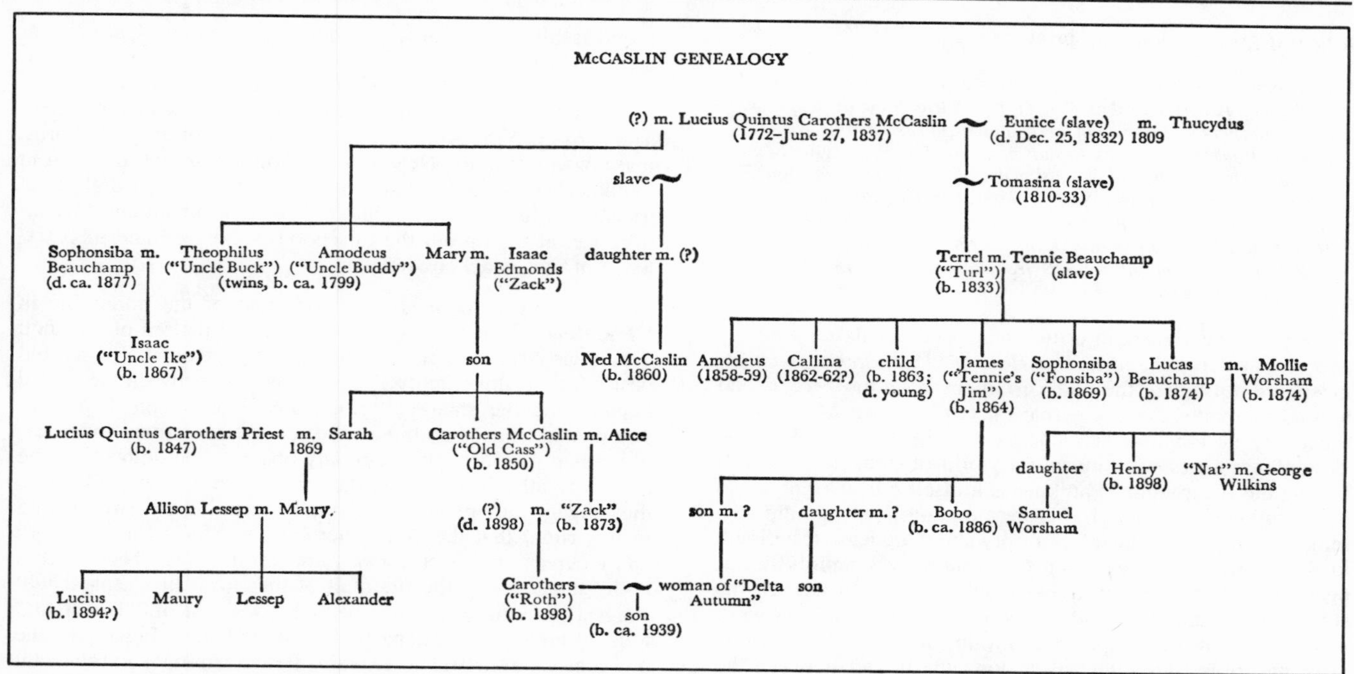

The McCaslin family genealogy chart. From William Faulkner: The Yoknapatawpha Country, *by Cleanth Brooks. Reprinted by permission of Yale University Press.*

Q: I was reading over **"The Bear"** the other night, and though I don't know much about hunting or anything like that, I liked the feelings in the story. I thought it was a very good story.

FAULKNER: (Appraising look, and almost a smile. Waits.)

Q: Tell me, was there a real Big Ben and a Lion?

FAULKNER: Yes. There used to be a bear like Big Ben in our county when I was a boy. He'd gotten one paw caught in a trap, and 'cause of that, folks used to call him Reel Foot, 'cause of the way he walked. He got killed too, though not so spectacularly as I killed him in the story of course. . . . (Drawing on pipe reflectively.) I took Hogganbeck from a fella that worked for my father. He was about thirty, but had the mind of a fourteen-year-old. I was about eight or nine. 'Course, me being the boss's son, we always did what I wanted to do. It's a wonder we survived, some of the things we got into. It's a wonder.

Q: I imagine from what you've said, and from what's known from your writing and life, that you've taken quite a lot from your own experience to put into your books. Like the parts in your books on aviation for instance. Did those come out of your own experience?

FAULKNER: No. They came from the imagination and experience of anyone who had much to do with airplanes at that time.

Q: Who are your favorite literary characters in your own work?

FAULKNER: Dilsey and Ratliff, the sewing-machine agent.

Q: Why?

FAULKNER: Well, Dilsey is brave, courageous, generous, gentle and honest. She's much more brave and honest and generous than I am. . . . Ratliff is wonderful. He's done more things than any man I know. Why, I couldn't tell some of the things that man has done. . . . (Pause. Sudden and direct.) And who are *your* favorite characters?

Q (startled): Isaac McCaslin in **"The Bear."**

FAULKNER (smiling a little, very quick and direct): Why?

Q: Because he underwent the baptism in the forest, because he rejected his inheritance.

FAULKNER: And do you think it's a good thing for a man to reject an inheritance?

Q: Yes, in McCaslin's case. He wanted to reject a tainted inheritance. You don't think it's a good thing for him to have done so?

FAULKNER: Well, I think a man ought to do more than just repudiate. He should have been more affirmative instead of shunning people.

Q: Do you think that any of your characters succeed in being more affirmative?

FAULKNER: Yes, I do. There was Gavin Stevens. He was a good man but he didn't succeed in living up to his ideal. But his nephew, the boy, I think he may grow up to be a better man than his uncle. I think he may succeed as a human being.

Q: And who is your unfavorite character?

FAULKNER: Jason. Jason Compson. (pp. 224-25)

William Faulkner and Cynthia Grenier in an interview in Lion in the Garden: Interviews with William Faulkner, 1926-1962, *edited by James B. Meriwether and Michael Millgate, Random House, 1968, pp. 215-27.*

R.W.B. LEWIS (essay date 1959)

[*A prominent American critic, Lewis is the author of the noted study,* The American Adam *(1955), which traces the development of the archetypal American hero and explores various writers' contributions or reactions to that myth. In* The Picaresque Saint *(1959), excerpted below, he outlined a type of saintly but roguish hero common to the works of Alberto Moravia, Ignazio Silone, Albert Camus, Graham Greene, André Malraux, and Faulkner. Here Lewis likens the action of the fourth section of "The Bear" to an epic descent into Hades from which Ike is reborn as a Christ-like or heroic character.*]

[If], as several European critics suggested, Faulkner's novels and stories through, say, *The Hamlet* (1940) possess an atmosphere not unlike the Old Testament in its most tragic and baffled moments, we can perhaps take ***Go Down, Moses***—and especially its longest and richest component, **"The Bear"**—as Faulkner's first venture into a world of light like that following the Incarnation. Faulkner is himself our warrant for so heady an analogy; though, before pursuing it, we should also remember that **"The Bear"** is a story about the American South in the eighteen-eighties when the frontier was rapidly disappearing; and the vividly invoked setting is the ground of the story's being and of all that it becomes. **"The Bear"** is a work in the tradition of Cooper and Twain; another tale of a boy growing up and growing wiser along the border between the civilized and the still unspoiled; and it partakes, too, of that even more widespread drama of American literature, the effort of youth to mature in the face of all the obstacles our culture has erected. Historical and traditional elements provide a fertile base. None the less, it is in **"The Bear"** that we meet Faulkner's first full-fledged hero in the old heroic meaning of the word; and he is a young man who quite self-consciously takes up carpentering, once he has accepted his peculiar moral mission, because

> if the Nazarene had found carpentering good for the life and ends He had assumed and elected to serve, it would be all right too for Isaac McCaslin. . . .

"The Bear" is a canticle or chant relating the birth, the baptism, and the early trials of Isaac McCaslin of Yoknapatawpha County in Mississippi. It is ceremonious in style, and it is not lacking in dimly seen miraculous events. We get moreover *an* incarnation, if not *the* Incarnation. Or better, we get a reincarnation; and we witness an act of atonement which may conceivably flower into a redemption. . . . (pp. 193-94)

What we discover first, along with young Ike McCaslin, and what determines his and our subsequent judgments is not strident evil, but the qualities of an archetypal or ideal being. A cluster of virtues is unambiguously present from the start, as qualities to be striven for, prizes to be won: proving their efficacy in the mastery of self and the victorious confrontation of evil: pity and humility and courage and pride and the will to endure and the rest. Their names recur with musical regularity, like the burden of a song. And together they comprise what we may call the honorable: something Roman and a trifle stiff, to some degree traditionally Stoic and to a greater degree unmistakably Virgilian. It is the honorable that permeates the wilderness, scene of the main action and home of the main actors in the drama. Old Ben, the bear, patriarch of the wilderness, embodies the virtues in some undefined and magical way; and like Old Ben, the honorable exists as an ethical reality before the story opens, "before the boy was born"—as a glimpse of immortality. This reality is independent of shifting urban moral fashions; it is an ideal prior to civilization. But it is not an uncivilized ideal; its priority is logical rather than temporal; it is prior because it is ideal, not so much older as timeless. It has nothing to do with "primitivism," or with noble savagery, or even the American Adamic dream of unspoiled original innocence in the New World—nothing except this, that in Faulkner's handling of it the honorable emerges by a dialectical transformation, a "transvaluation" of that dream and that innocence: at the instant the falsehood is exposed and the existence of evil is acknowledged.

The humanly recognizable embodiment of the honorable in **"The Bear"** is an action, a repeated ritual pattern of conduct: "the yearly rendezvous . . . the yearly pageant-rite of the old bear's furious immortality," the annual duel between the skilled hunters and the shaggy, tremendous, indomitable Old Ben. The duel is enacted within a solid set of conventions and rules, older than memory and faultlessly observed on both sides, the men *hunt* all other bears in the wilderness, but with Old Ben they engage rather in a kind of ritual dance. It is by participating in this ritual that the young hero, Isaac McCaslin, is reborn and receives, as it were, a sacramental blessing. That process is the substance of the first half of the story. In a sense I will suggest, it is the whole of the story; the rest of **"The Bear"** tells us how a hero, if properly initiated, may behave in the presence of evil. But to explain these seemingly extravagant remarks, and to take hold of the experience more firmly, we need to examine the experience in its actual and living form: its artistically realized form, unabstracted. To do so is to look closely at the story's structure.

The difficulty of most of Faulkner's stories lies in the order of their telling. He has always provided us with lots of action; and if his unconventional arrangement of the incidents sometimes resembles a random shuffle through a fateful crazy-house, it at least avoids another extreme of modern fiction. It never evaporates into atmosphere or aesthetic self-indulgence. What *happens* in a Faulkner story is the most important thing in it, except perhaps the moral excitement that produces the happening. But we are let in on the event secretively, gradually, almost grudgingly, from different viewpoints and at different times. This is to say that Faulkner's structural experiments—like his verbal ones—are significant, but not significant in themselves; only in what they are intended to disclose. . . . (pp. 196-97)

"The Bear" has a plot relatively simpler than some of Faulkner's earlier writings; but here again Faulkner has played weird tricks with the temporal ordering. He has concluded his tale, for instance, with an episode that occurs at a moment earlier in time than several episodes that have preceded it in the telling. . . . (pp. 197-98)

André Gide, when he was writing *The Counterfeiters,* confided to his journal a desire to render the events of his novel *légèrement déformés,* so that the reader's interest might be aroused in an effort to restore the original aspects; the reader becoming thereby the author's collaborator. Faulkner's motive may in part be the same. His alleged contempt for his reader has the effect, anyhow, of involving the reader nearly to the extent of devouring him. No other American writer engages his readers so mercilessly; and except for those who fear and resent him on quite other grounds, readers of Faulkner can and do get an immense satisfaction from that participation with him that verges on the creative. This is one of the first generation features of Faulkner—one that links him with Gide and Joyce. But the aim of Faulkner's deliberate deformations is not finally aesthetic; he wants the reader to participate not in a creative act but in a moral act. He wants to define a moral experience of mythological proportions and of ambiguous reality: an aim that of necessity makes heavy demands on the reader. Conrad, for example, asks no less of us when he makes his arduous way through the thickets to release his prophetic myth of modern history in *Nostromo*; nor, to name a writer even closer in feeling to Faulkner, does Virgil in his myth of Roman history. In the *Aeneid,* the last event of the poem—the duel between Aeneas and Turnus—occurs many centuries before some of the events already described: the long course of Roman history across the centuries and up to the battle of Actium, as given in the preview by Anchises in Book VI and in the pictures engraved on the shield of Aeneas in Book VIII. In the *Aeneid,* of course, the chronologically later events appear explicitly as prophecies, almost as dreams. But that, I propose, is exactly the nature of the fourth section of **"The Bear,"** with its narrative of Ike's twenty-first and later years.

Before I press the suggestion, some mechanical observations may be helpful. The fourth section has the same formal organization and is roughly the same length as the first three sections combined. This gives it, suitably, the appearance and function of a counterweight. Both of these two large parts begin at certain moments in Ike's life (when he is sixteen and twenty-one, respectively), retreat to earlier moments, and then spiral back through their starting points. The recurring insistence of Faulkner upon his hero's age is too striking to be overlooked; it is almost a plea: "He was sixteen then . . . then he was sixteen." Ike's age is the chief structural element; and his sixteenth year was his *annus mirabilis*. The story flows through that year on three distinct occasions; as though only by this means could the contradictory richness of the year's experience be made manifest. . . . (pp. 199-200)

The story begins in Ike's sixteenth year, the year he is to complete his rite of initiation. Till this moment, he has grasped the importance but not the meaning of the experience.

> It seemed to him that there was a fatality in it. It seemed to him that something, he didn't know what, was beginning; had already begun. It was like the last act on a set stage. It was the beginning of the end of something, he didn't know what except that he would not grieve. He would be humble and proud that he had been found worthy to be a part of it too or even just to see it too.

"The beginning of the end of something"—an end *and* a beginning, in fact: which is why Ike has reason to be humble and proud. For the drama he is engaged in is a vast drama of death and birth: the death of Old Ben, of Sam Fathers (Ike's foster-parent and tutor), of the dog Lion, of the wilderness and the companionship Ike had known there, of an entire world; and the birth and rebirth of Isaac McCaslin as the solitary reincarnation of those dead and the lone witnesses (very much in the second generation "tradition") to that world and its truth. This is what Ike is disciplined to perceive, as the story returns to the great year in section three. When Old Ben dies in that section, he dies metaphorically in childbirth. He has, indeed, many features in common with the "terrible mother" of heroic mythology; and in this context, the name of Sam Fathers, Ike's spiritual guide, is intrusively significant. It requires only a twist of the tongue to convert the story's title into "The Birth."

In the fourth section we find that it was also during Ike's sixteenth year, on a December night after the last bear hunt, that he solved the riddle of his family's history. The section begins with the sentence, ominously uncapitalized: "then he was twenty-one." The defining occasion of most of it is a conversation between Ike and his cousin Cass Edmonds in the plantation commissary on the date of Ike's legal coming-of-age. But, while the entire span of Ike's very long life is touched upon, it is the discoveries of his sixteenth year that account for the intensity of his speech and the resoluteness of his decision to reject his inheritance. With the conversation as foreground, those discoveries pass through Ike's memory like shadows on the wall behind—shadows themselves in a ghostly conversation; for they appear as remembered entries in the commissary ledgers, written in a question-and-answer style. The entries had been made decades earlier by Ike's uncle and his father, and they had been pieced together with amazement and horror by Ike five years before the present moment. Their language has the sparse, foreshortened quality of memory:

> [Uncle Buck:] *Eunice Bought by Father in New Orleans 1807 $650. Marrid to Thucydus 1809 Drownd in Crick Cristmas Day 1832*
>
> [Uncle Buddy:] *June 21th 1833 Drownd herself*
>
> [Uncle Buck:] *23 Jun 1833 Who in hell ever heard of a niger drownding himself*
>
> [Uncle Buddy:] *Aug 13th 1833 Drownd herself*

The motivation for Eunice's suicide is revealed only in its impact upon Ike's oddly mythopoeic imagination. It is up to us, collaborators in the hunt, to discover that Eunice had been the mistress of the grandfather, Carrothers McCaslin (Uncle Buck's "Father"), bought by him and—when she was pregnant by him with the child Tomasina—married off to another slave, Thucydus; and that Eunice drowned herself twenty-three years later when she realized that her daughter, too, had become pregnant by Carrothers McCaslin: by her own father, by Eunice's lover. For Ike, the tragic event has the formality of legend:

> . . . he seemed to see her actually walking into the icy creek on that Christmas day six months before her daughter's and her lover's (*Her first lover's,* he thought. *Her first*) child was born, solitary, inflexible, griefless, ceremonial, in formal and succinct repudiation of grief and despair who had already had to repudiate belief and hope

Ike has a shocking revelation of the literal fact of human brotherhood: Turl, the child Tomasina bears, and Jim, the child Turl later begets, are actually Ike's cousins, and have their rights in the legacy he renounces.

The first essential link between the two large parts I have been discussing—the first three sections taken together, and the fourth as their counterweight—is the near simultaneity of the death of Old Ben and the discovery of mixed blood and incest in the McCaslin clan. The fourth section of **"The Bear"** is not merely the further adventures of Isaac McCaslin. The harmony of the parts may be summarized in ancient formulas: the birth into virtue, and the vision of evil. Only the person adequately initiated can have the vision at all; and only the potency of the initiation enables the reborn individual to withstand the evil when it is encountered. The action in section four (the discovery and the renunciation) is made possible by the experience that preceded it; the ritual in the wilderness *contains,* implicitly, the decision in the commissary.

This leads to a somewhat more complex view of the relationship. It is true that the fourth section is contained within the sections that have the wilderness as their setting: the containment achieved when Faulkner brings his story back to the wilderness in the fifth and final section, returning to the life of Ike before he has reached the age of decision, returning to the atmosphere and the rhythms of the hunting world. The fifth section reverts to the style—relatively straightforward, though highly orchestrated and charged with autumnal splendor—of the first, second, and third sections; picking up that style where it had been left almost sixty pages before, and so enveloping and containing the very different style in between. We may illustrate by quoting from the last lines of section four and the first of section five, breaking in anywhere on the endlessly flowing matter of section four:

> . . . and on their wedding night she had cried and he thought she was crying now at first, into the tossed and wadded pillow, the voice coming from somewhere between the pillow and the cachinnation: 'And that's all. That's all from me. If this dont get you that son you talk about, it wont be mine': lying on her side, her back to the empty rented room, laughing and laughing.
>
> He went back to the camp one more time before the lumber company moved in and began to cut the timber. Major de Spain himself never saw it again.

Faulkner has even gone to the extreme, as we notice here, of employing a single quotation mark in the conversations of the fourth section: the conventional sign of the speech contained within the speech—as against the double quotation mark elsewhere. It is the sort of device peculiarly trying for those not already persuaded by Faulkner; but it is an instance of his anxiety that we should recognize the mode of existence of that phase of the whole experience.

Its *mode* of existence is as important as its content. For what we are given in the fourth section is not so much a narrative of events that have happened, as an intense, translucent vision of the future. Its appearance between the third and fifth sections—between the episodes of Ike's sixteenth and eighteenth years—allows us to suppose that it is a dream; perhaps a dream that occurred during the year between. It is a true dream, to be sure, a true prophecy, issuing securely from the gate of horn; but passing before our eyes incidents that at the moment of perception exist only in a state of possibility. The sense of something not yet realized is carried in the prose itself. We are struck by the decrease in visibility. Against an immeasurably vast setting, actions and dialogue have curiously hazy outline. Sentences spray out in all directions, almost never (within our hearing) reaching their probable periods. Everything is potential, unfinished, pushing toward completion. But the experience is not a *mere* possibility, in the sense that a quite different experience is equally possible. We have to reckon with Faulkner's notions about time and reality: according to which events become real not when they occur but only when they are looked back upon in memory. The fourth section creates the real by dreaming how it will eventually be remembered. *Forsan et haec olim meminisse iuvabit*. Aeneas can say no more than that; and if Faulkner permits Ike to dream in some detail how these things will later seem to be, it is partly because Faulkner has dared assume (as Mme. Magny has observed) something like the divine viewpoint. But not altogether. The events are certain, but not yet. They are only partially visible to the human perception. A spirit or a goddess might see them whole, as ghostly Anchises and Venus can see the future of Rome; but the most illuminated human perception is fully competent only with the past; and the dream remains dreamlike. And beyond all that, the *content* of the dream is such that the most illuminated human art can—or should—present it only through a liquid mist of prophecy.

To justify the latter contention, we must come back to actualities, to the national and provincial traditions it is Faulkner's role in these pages to represent. It is a long way from ancient Rome to nineteenth century Mississippi; and it is time to take account of the boundaries within which Ike acts out his backwoods drama; the force of the larger implications is derived from Faulkner's artistic conversion of specifically American materials. Like *Moby-Dick,* **"The Bear"** is most in tune with perennial rhythms of experience when it is most solidly American; and if we close in on the particular portion of America that provides its scene, we recognize its significant prototype in *Huckleberry Finn*. Both are narratives of boys growing up in the nineteenth century South; both record a sense of the troubled kinship between white and black, though Twain does not carry that kinship literally into the blood streams. Both suggest an ironic reversal of the conventional morality that legitimizes social injustice—though, again, Twain's humor is in charge of his outrage and prevents him from intruding lectures on social legislation and warnings to the government up north, as it protects Huck himself from a pretentious awareness of his own virtue. But the central insight Faulkner shares with Twain is one that both share with many another American writer: a sense of the fertile and highly ambiguous possibility of moral freedom in the new world. . . . In so far as **"The Bear"** is a story about death, it is about the death of the frontier world and its possibility, of the new unspoiled area where a genuine and radical moral freedom—a kind of original innocence—could again be exercised.

But to say so without fundamental qualification would be to ascribe to Faulkner a view of innocence and the New World almost exactly opposite the one finally revealed in **"The Bear."** It would be to forget how often Faulkner has engaged in the ritual slaughter of the animal innocent—how he has penetrated the veil of innocence to arrive at the tragic fact, performing an operation on the hopeful world of his time similar to the one Hawthorne felt impelled to perform a century ago on Emerson. A part of the history Ike McCaslin rehearses for Cass Edmonds, on his twenty-first birthday, seems to echo the cheerful story Emerson and his colleagues used to tell each other:

> 'He [God] made the earth first and peopled it with dumb creatures, and then He created man to be His overseer on the earth and to hold suzerainty over the earth and the animals on it in His name, not to hold for himself and his descendants inviolable title forever . . . and all the fee He asked was pity and humility and sufferance and endurance. . . . He watched it. And let me say it. Dispossessed of Eden. Dispossessed of Canaan and those who . . . devoured their ravished substance ravished in turn again and then snarled in what you call the old world's worthless twilight over the old world's gnawed bones, blasphemous in His name until He used a simple egg to discover to them a new world where a nation of people could be founded in humility and pity and sufferance and pride of one another. . . .'

The identification of the New World as a divinely offered second chance for humanity after the first opportunity had been so thoroughly muffed in the Old World—the association of America with Eden—has never been more eloquently made. But Faulkner's hero is examining the myth precisely to see where it went wrong; and Faulkner himself, in writing **"The Bear,"** was returning to the wilderness for the reason Graham Greene had gone to the Liberian jungle: driven, as Greene said in *Journey Without Maps,* by a "curiosity to discover . . . from what we have come, at what point we went astray." It is the familiar moment in the career of the second-generation novelist, when he returns to the sources to understand the bewildering fatalities of his age. Faulkner and Isaac McCaslin conclude that the mistake was inherent in the myth; that the New World was not ever devoid of evil, from the moment of its settling—that it was 'already tainted even before any white man owned it by what Grandfather and his kind, his fathers, had brought into the new land . . . as though in the sailfuls of the old world's tainted wind which drove the ships.' It was the evil of slavery, rooted in the sin of spiritual pride and the lust of possession. What Grandfather and his kind brought with them into the New World was themselves; what they brought was the nature of man.

After probing to the falsity of the myth, **"The Bear"** goes on, by way of atonement, to construct a new and more durable image of innocence and moral freedom: a new image of a new kind of New World. Qualities undergo a profound dialectical transformation in **"The Bear"**—and of a nature indicated at once in the opening sentences:

> There was a man and a dog too this time. Two beasts, counting Old Ben, the bear, and two men, counting Boon Hogganbeck, in whom some of the same blood ran which ran in Sam Fathers, even though Boon's was a plebeian strain of it and only Sam and Old Ben and the mongrel Lion were taintless and incorruptible.

The change is already apparent in the paradoxical attribution to a mongrel dog of "taintless" and "incorruptible" qualities. It is there, too, though we do not immediately know it, in the same attribution to the man, Sam Fathers, who is also a mongrel, the half-breed offspring of a Negro slave and a Chicasaw Indian. The purity transcended is, in short, a physical purity, a matter of blood, something misleadingly suggested by the physical purity of the land—a very dangerous illusion. What takes its place is a tougher kind of purity, of innocence, of moral freedom; virtues not of a historical and accidental but of an ideal and permanent kind; qualities not given but achieved, by conduct and by art, through discipline and submission. The new innocence is not other than conscience.

"The Bear" thus moves toward a "transvaluation of values" at once large and homely. . . . The two achievements have a good deal in common; for both manage to take hold of the mystery of power, in order to subdue it and transcend it: as Camus would do also in *The Plague,* and Greene (as his very title suggests) in *The Power and the Glory*. In assessing Faulkner's tale, we may permit ourselves still broader references; for it belongs to a still broader tradition, the tradition of heroic legend. In that tradition, where power is always a major factor, the special character of the hero's power is often represented by a "magic weapon," and by the use made of it. We may contemplate a significant range from the great bow of Odysseus, with which he ruthlessly slays a houseful of political and domestic rivals, to, say, St. Martin of Tours telling the pagan Emperor that, "Armed only with the Cross, in the forefront of the enemy, I will fear no evil." Aeneas enters his supreme battle wearing on his shield the recorded destiny of Rome, a predestined power that makes him invulnerable to the mightiest of the Latins; and the secret source of Ahab's power is the giant harpoon baptized "not in the name of the father, but in the name of the devil." Isaac McCaslin's weapon is nothing so grandiose; but it is not much less meaningful. It is, of course, his hunter's rifle.

His first gun is too big for him, a man's weapon in a boy's hand. Then at eleven years old, the year he first encounters Old Ben, he receives his own gun, "a new breech-loader, a Christmas gift; he would own and shoot it for almost seventy years. . . ." The imagery of the gun is diffused through the story, one of its unifying motifs; an association is noted with the taintless mongrel dog, whose color is gunmetal gray. But what is important is the use Ike makes of his gun in his relation with Old Ben. The first time he meets the bear, Ike has abandoned his rifle, along with his watch and compass, to present himself in humility before the ancient patriarch: an act of communion, verging on the holy. The second time, he throws his gun aside and risks his life to rescue a little fyce who was barking helplessly in the bear's path: an act of charity. That, I think, is the main symbolic movement of the narrative. For what we comprehend in **"The Bear"** is a movement generically similar to that of *Bread and Wine*. It is the transmutation of power into charity.

That is what the conversion of innocence amounts to, and Faulkner's artistic conversion of the historical image of America. In it, power suffers no real loss, but undergoes a sea-change. It comes under the control of moral understanding; a kind of grace enters into it. More concretely: Ike does not give up his weapon of destruction; on the contrary, we have swift glimpses of him in his later years as the greatest hunter in Yoknapatawpha County. But he uses his power with restraint and fidelity; he uses it with conscience. Boon Hogganbeck is the vulnerably innocent man, in the inferior sense of the word, and he is last seen nearly out of his head and rabidly dismantling his own gun. Ike continues to live near and in the dwindling forest, as close as possible to the source of his moral energy: a Natty Bumppo who is also an imitator of Christ. But Ike is not intended to represent Christ in a second coming; it is only that he seems to move in a world of light—a meager light but definite enough, for instance, to read the past by (in a way Quentin Compson could not); a new world in which values are confirmed only by raising them to a higher power; not the historical and physical New World—this is precisely what is transcended—but a world so perpetually new that Ike appears to be its only living inhabitant. . . . (pp. 200-08)

The transcendence enacted in **"The Bear"** . . . was if anything too successful and complete. It carried Ike out of the quicksands of history, but at the same time it nearly carried him out of the company of mortal men. He has moved dangerously close to the person of the savior-god, to the person of Jesus: dangerously close, at least, for the purposes of fiction. It is worth insisting that the life of Christ is not under any circumstances a fit subject for literature: not because such a subject would be irreverent, but because within the limits of literature it would be impossible; or, what is the same thing, it would be too easy. And this is exactly why the quality of the fourth section of **"The Bear"**—the mode of its existence—is so uncannily appropriate to its content. It was perhaps Faulkner's most extraordinary poetic intuition to present the affinities between a human being and a divine—a Mississippi hunter and the figure of Christ—not as an actuality, but as a foggily seen prophetic possibility: something longed for and even implicit in present circumstances and character, but something that has decidedly never yet happened. **"The Bear,"** reaching to the edge of human limits, does the most that literature may with propriety attempt to do. (p. 209)

R.W.B. Lewis, "William Faulkner: The Hero in the New World," in his The Picaresque Saint: Representative Figures in Contemporary Fiction, *1959. Reprint by Victor Gollancz Ltd., 1960, pp. 179-219.*

CLEANTH BROOKS AND ROBERT PENN WARREN (essay date 1959)

[Brooks and Warren, both noted American authors, are considered two of the most prominent figures of the school of New Criticism. In the following excerpt from their guide to fiction for students, Brooks and Warren interpret "A Rose for Emily" as a tragic struggle between an individual and the society that attempts to restrict her.]

[**"A Rose for Emily"**] is a story of horror. We have a decaying mansion in which the protagonist, shut away from the world, grows into something monstrous, and becomes as divorced from the human as some fungus growing in the dark on a damp wall. Miss Emily Grierson remains in voluntary isolation (or perhaps fettered by some inner compulsion) away from the bustle and dust and sunshine of the human world of normal affairs, and what in the end is found in the upstairs room gives perhaps a sense of penetrating and gruesome horror.

Has this sense of horror been conjured up for its own sake? If not, then why has the author contrived to insert so much of the monstrous into the story? In other words, does the horror contribute to the theme of Faulkner's story? Is the horror meaningful?

In order to answer this question, we shall have to examine rather carefully some of the items earlier in the story. In the first place, why does Miss Emily commit her monstrous act? Is she supplied with a proper motivation? Faulkner has, we can see, been rather careful to prepare for his dénouement. Miss Emily, it becomes obvious fairly early in the story, is one of those persons for whom the distinction between reality and illusion has blurred out. For example, she refuses to admit that she owes any taxes. When the mayor protests, she does not recognize him as mayor. Instead, she refers the committee to Colonel Sartoris, who, as the reader is told, has been dead for nearly ten years. For Miss Emily, apparently, Colonel Sartoris is still alive. Most specific preparation of all, when her father dies, she denies to the townspeople for three days that he is dead. "Just as they were about to resort to law and force, she broke down, and they buried her father quickly."

Miss Emily is obviously a pathological case. The narrator indicates plainly enough that people felt that she was crazy. All of this explanation prepares us for what Miss Emily does in order to hold her lover—the dead lover is in one sense still alive for her—the realms of reality and appearance merge. But having said this, we have got no nearer to justifying the story: for, if Faulkner is merely interested in relating a case history of abnormal psychology, the story lacks meaning and justification as a story. . . . If the story is to be justified, there must be what may be called a moral significance, a meaning in moral terms—not merely psychological terms.

Incidentally, it is very easy to misread the story as merely a horrible case history, presented in order to titillate the reader. Faulkner has been frequently judged to be doing nothing more than this in his work.

The lapse of the distinction between illusion and reality, between life and death, is important, therefore, in helping to account for Miss Emily's motivation, but merely to note this lapse is not fully to account for the theme of the story.

Suppose we approach the motivation again in these terms: what is Miss Emily like? What are the mainsprings of her character? What causes the distinction between illusion and reality to blur out for her? She is obviously a woman of tremendous firmness of will. In the matter of the taxes, crazed though she is, she is never at a loss. She is utterly composed. She dominates the rather frightened committee of officers who see her. In the matter of her purchase of the poison, she completely overawes the clerk. She makes no pretense. She refuses to tell him what she wants the poison for. And yet this firmness of will and this iron pride have not kept her from being thwarted and hurt. Her father has run off the young men who came to call upon her, and for the man who tells the story, Miss Emily and her father form a tableau: "Miss Emily a slender figure in white in the background, her father a spraddled silhouette in the foreground, his back to her and clutching a horsewhip, the two of them framed by the back-flung front door." Whether the picture is a remembered scene, or merely a symbolical construct, this is the picture which remains in the storyteller's mind.

We have indicated that her pride is connected with her contempt for public opinion. This comes to the fore, of course, when she rides around about the town with the foreman whom everybody believes is beneath her. And it is her proud refusal to admit an external set of codes, or conventions, or other wills which contradict her own will, which makes her capable at the end of keeping her lover from going away. Confronted with his jilting her, she tries to override not only his will and the opinion of other people, but the laws of death and decay themselves.

But this, still, hardly gives the meaning of the story. For in all that has been said thus far, we are still merely accounting for a psychological aberration—we are still merely dealing with a case history in abnormal psychology. In order to make a case for the story as "meaningful," we shall have to tie Miss Emily's thoughts and actions back into the normal life of the community, and establish some sort of relationship between them. And just here one pervasive element in the narration suggests a clue. The story is told by one of the townspeople. And in it, as a constant factor, is the reference to what the community thought of Miss Emily. Continually through the story is it what "we" said, and then what "we" did, and what seemed true to "us," and so on. The narrator puts the matter even more sharply still. He says, in the course of the story, that to the community Miss Emily seemed "dear, inescapable, impervious, tranquil, and perverse." Each of the adjectives is important and meaningful. In a sense, Miss Emily because of her very fact of isolation and perversity belongs to the whole community. She is even something treasured by it. Ironically, because of Emily's perversion of an aristocratic independence of mores and because of her contempt for "what people say," her life is public, even communal. And various phrases used by the narrator underline this view of her position. For example, her face looks "as you imagine a lighthouse-keeper's face ought to look," like the face of a person who lives in the kind of isolation imposed on a lighthouse-keeper, who looks out into the blackness and whose light serves a public function. Or, again, after her father's death, she becomes very ill, and when she appears after the illness, she has "a vague resemblance to those angels in colored church windows—sort of tragic and serene." Whatever we make of these descriptions, certainly the author is trying to suggest a kind of calm and dignity which is super-mundane, unearthly, or "over-earthly," such as an angel might possess.

Miss Emily, then, is a combination of idol and scapegoat for the community. On the one hand, the community feels admiration for Miss Emily—she represents something in the past of the community which the community is proud of. They feel a sort of awe of her, as is illustrated by the behavior of the mayor and the committee in her presence. On the other hand, her queerness, the fact that she cannot compete with them in their ordinary life, the fact that she is hopelessly out of touch with the modern world—all of these things make them feel superior to her, and also to that past which she represents. It is, then, Miss Emily's complete detachment which gives her actions their special meaning for the community.

Miss Emily, since she is the conscious aristocrat, since she is consciously "better" than other people, since she is above and outside their canons of behavior, can, at the same time, be worse than other people; and she *is* worse, horribly so. She is worse than other people, but at the same time, as the narrator implies, she remains somehow admirable. This raises a fundamental question: why is this true?

Perhaps the horrible and the admirable aspects of Miss Emily's final deed arise from the same basic fact of her character: she insists on meeting the world on her own terms. She never cringes, she never begs for sympathy, she refuses to shrink into an amiable old maid, she never accepts the community's ordinary judgments or values. This independence of spirit and pride can, and does in her case, twist the individual into a sort of monster, but, at the same time, this refusal to accept the herd values carries with it a dignity and courage. The community senses this, as we gather from the fact that the community carries out the decencies of the funeral before breaking in the door of the upper room. There is, as it were, a kind of secret understanding that she has won her right of privacy, until she herself has entered history. Furthermore, despite the fact that, as the narrator says, "already we knew that there was one room in that region above stairs which no one had seen in forty years, and which would have to be forced," her funeral is something of a state occasion, with "the very old men—some in their brushed Confederate uniforms—on the porch and the lawn, talking of Miss Emily as if she had been a contemporary of theirs, believing that they had danced with her and courted her perhaps. . . ." In other words, the community accepts her into its honored history. All of this works as a kind of tacit recognition of Miss Emily's triumph of will. The community, we are told earlier, had wanted to pity Miss Emily when she had lost her money, just as they had wanted to commiserate over her when they believed that she had actually become a fallen woman, but she had triumphed over their pity and commiseration and condemnation, just as she had triumphed over all their other attitudes.

But, as we have indicated earlier, it may be said that Miss Emily is mad. This may be true, but there are two things to consider in this connection. First, one must consider the special terms which her "madness" takes. Her madness is simply a development of her pride and her refusal to submit to ordinary standards of behavior. So, because of this fact, her "madness" is meaningful after all. It involves issues which in themselves are really important and have to do with the world of conscious moral choice. Second, the community interprets her "madness" as meaningful. They admire her, even if they are disappointed by her refusals to let herself be pitied, and the narrator, who is a spokesman for the community, recognizes the last grim revelation as an instance of her having carried her own values to their ultimate conclusion. She would marry the common laborer, Homer Barron, let the community think what it would. She would not be jilted. And she would hold him as a lover. But it would all be on her own terms. She remains completely dominant, and contemptuous of the day-to-day world.

It has been suggested by many critics that tragedy implies a hero who is completely himself, who insists on meeting the world on his own terms, who wants something so intensely, or lives so intensely, that he cannot accept any compromise. It cannot be maintained that this story is comparable to any of the great tragedies, such as *Hamlet* or *King Lear,* but it can be pointed out that this story, in its own way, involves some of the same basic elements. Certainly, Miss Emily's pride, isolation, and independence remind one of factors in the character of the typical tragic hero. And it can be pointed out that, just as the horror of her deed lies outside the ordinary life of the community, so the magnificence of her independence lies outside its ordinary virtues. (pp. 350-54)

Cleanth Brooks and Robert Penn Warren, in an interpretation of "A Rose for Emily," in Understanding Fiction, *edited by Cleanth Brooks and Robert Penn Warren, second edition, Appleton-Century-Crofts, Inc., 1959, pp. 350-54.*

JOSEPH J. MOLDENHAUER (essay date 1960)

[*Moldenhauer is a German-born American critic specializing in nineteenth-century American writers. In the following excerpt he discusses thematic parallels between the novellas "Wild Palms" and "Old Man" and the juxtaposition of the two in* The Wild Palms.]

When Faulkner's double novel, ***The Wild Palms,*** appeared in 1939, its peculiarity of structure—the alternating chapters of two long stories whose plots, characters, settings, and themes seemed completely unrelated—provoked a number of reviewers to express bewilderment and outright dissatisfaction with the work as a whole. They were virtually unanimous in their praise of one of the tales, **"Old Man,"** and unenthusiastic though not bitterly hostile toward the other, **"The Wild Palms."** But they gravely denounced the coupling of the stories as arbitrary, artificial, and detrimental to both narratives. Conrad Aiken raised his voice in the wilderness when he admired the book's "fugue-like alternation of viewpoint", but he did not suggest the relationship between this structure and the themes and characters of the stories. (p. 305)

Among the inevitable results of the contemporary "discovery" of Faulkner has been a renewed interest in ***The Wild Palms.*** **"Old Man"** and **"The Wild Palms"** have been studied individually, and critical attempts to explain the curious form of the original edition have in the past decade produced several imaginative though somewhat unconvincing hypotheses. In any case, it has been firmly established that the reader should recognize ***The Wild Palms*** as a structural experiment and that each of the stories might be profitably read in terms of the other.

"Old Man," with its chronological plot and seeming lack of philosophical complexity, has always been the more popular work. Early critics were quick to appreciate the fundamentally allegorical qualities of this story: the nameless protagonist, the parable-like beginning, the heavy elements of fate and coincidence, the archetypal material of a voyage on water, and the ostensibly direct moral recommendation of the hero, who endures cyclopean hardships with singleness of mind and will. While **"Old Man"** is not so systematic an allegory as *Pilgrim's Progress,* it will survive comparison with works like *Mardi* and *Huckleberry Finn*. . . . Moreover, **"Old Man"** has much in common with Faulkner's earlier saga, *As I Lay Dying,* particularly that the physical obstacles faced by the voyagers in each tale are so huge and frustrating that they give the work an integral quality of grotesque humor. An allegorical reading of **"Old Man"** is unquestionably enlightening; but Faulkner's pairing of **"The Wild Palms"** with the river tale suggests that the former story might set limits of interpretation upon the latter.

What has unfortunately been overlooked is that **"The Wild Palms"** itself contains many allegorical elements. It also portrays a physical and spiritual voyage. Fate and coincidence are highly instrumental to its plot. The name of the protagonist, Harry Wilbourne, embraces rich denotative possibilities, among which are "will burn" (will suffer some infernal punishment), "burning with will," and "bourne-ed (limited) by will." Just as **"Old Man"** invites comparison with *Huckleberry Finn* (although the dominant values of Mark Twain's novel are in fact inverted in **"Old Man"**), **"The Wild Palms"** might easily be called a hysterical or inverted *Scarlet Letter*. While the symbolic content of Faulkner's story can be in part traced to such disparate sources as Dante and Hemingway, the characterizations and the theme—the complex, often destructive demands upon one another of the physical or spiritual or psychological elements in man—are immediately suggestive of Hawthorne's novel. Furthermore, Faulkner's double-edged use of allegorical materials, with its accompanying delight in the manipulation of points of view, is at least a close cousin to Hawthorne's method. Both writers employ the moral and aesthetic weapon of puritanism, the concept of correspondence between the emblem and the thing symbolized, in making critical judgments upon the puritan's own mental anatomy. In effect, they ironically reverse allegorical expectations to illustrate the awesome pitfalls which allegorical thinking and moral preconception place in the way of human sympathy.

In both **"The Wild Palms"** and **"Old Man"** the relationship of the protagonist to the moral framework of Southern puritanism is of central importance. Neither story was intended to stand alone, and if they are separated one sacrifices not simply a clever structural device but a vital dimension of meaning. It is in the interaction of the two equivocally allegorical tales, one, like *The Scarlet Letter,* approaching fearful tragedy, and the other, like *Huckleberry Finn,* verging upon burlesque in its humor, that the reader must seek any final statement by the novelist. (pp. 305-07)

Irving Howe, who in his *William Faulkner* made the first serious effort to explain and justify the alternation of chapters in ***The Wild Palms,*** submitted the following pattern for the interweaving of plot elements:

"The Wild Palms"	**"Old Man"**
1. Failure of abortion, Charlotte close to death.	2. Convict leaves for flood.
3. Flashback: Charlotte and Harry leave New Orleans.	4. "Lost" in flood.
5. Flashback: drifting from country to Chicago.	6. Drifting with pregnant woman on flood waters.
7. Flashback: haven in a mining camp.	8. Haven with Cajun.
9. Charlotte's death, Harry's imprisonment.	10. Return to prison.

Howe supplements his design with this statement: "Even a glance at the . . . parsing of the novel should show rough parallels between the stories and the possibility that if taken together they might yield a tone of dissonant irony which neither could alone. . . . Each story charts an escape from confinement to a temporary and qualified freedom, and then to an ultimate, still more confining imprisonment." But his conceptions of "freedom" and "imprisonment" and his reading of the two stories as basically identical in moral statement cast severe limitations upon his search for "dissonant irony," and his argument that "the two parts of the book are genuinely bound together by theme and atmosphere" does not thoroughly convince the reader of the need for chapter alternation. Howe even lowers his colors somewhat in the last paragraph of his essay: "Probably of little use to anyone but himself, Faulkner's device . . . may be judged a *tour de force* that partly works."

In an article entitled "The Unity of **'The Wild Palms,'**" W. R. Moses presents the provocative idea that "Themes—and plots are . . . mirror twins of an almost embarrassing degree of similarity." He picks up Howe's equation of the "drifting" motifs of chapters five and six, and observes that "the convict struggles to escape a material flood," whereas "Harry and Charlotte struggle to remain immersed in an immaterial one, which in spite of its immateriality is just as destructive as the raging Mississippi." This promising hypothesis is weakened, however, by the critic's strained efforts to discern symbolic parallels. He neatly isolates three instances of mirror-contrast but fails to exploit their inherent meaning. Despite his early promise that the reading of the two stories as a single novel with a double plot is "a rich experience," he does not assay the wealth.

Yet Moses' pairing of episodes and Howe's parsing of chapters hold great value; once the fundamental ironic contrast between the stories is appreciated, the plot-alternations justify themselves. To Howe's schematization of the literary design I should like, then, to add the ideas I have developed in my study:

"The Wild Palms"	**"Old Man"**
1. Major characters introduced; not identified or fully named. Major symbol (wind) presented. Charlotte near death. Doctor contrasted with Harry.	2. Major character introduced; identified but not named. Major symbol (river) suggested. Convict contrasted, by implication, with Harry.
3. Flashback: chronological beginning of lovers' journey; Harry willingly renounces his monastic life for what he believes will be freedom. Harry's guilt stressed toward end of episode.	4. Chronological beginning of convict's journey; convict unwillingly thrown into the river or imprisoning reality. Irony of convict's "freedom" stressed at end of episode.
5. Flashback: Harry and Charlotte feel repressed in Chicago and go to Wisconsin.	6. Convict burdened by woman; river frustrates his efforts to return to levee.

Harry tries to abandon Charlotte but cannot. Another failure to reconcile guilt and sensuality in Chicago. Lovers leave for Utah, seeking again for freedom.	Convict tries twice to surrender, is twice rejected and fired upon. Convict defeated in efforts to abandon his ''freedom.''
7. Flashback: Charlotte becomes pregnant. Unsuccessful search for employment in Texas. Harry punishes himself and Charlotte with shoddy operation. Return to gulf coast for final four days of ''freedom.''	8. Convict helps woman bear child. Successful employment with Cajun. ''Cosmic joker'' punishes convict as flood resumes. Return to Parchman and ''imprisonment.''
9. Charlotte dies. Harry given fifty years in prison to enjoy remorse for his freedom.	10. Convict victimized by law officers. Convict given ten years in prison for his ''escape'' from the levee.

Not only the ''mirror opposites'' of plot but the consistent ironic contrasts of motivation, incident, and theme are revealed by this structural representation. The relative simplicity and directness of **"Old Man"** may be seen, moreover, to throw the tragedy of **"The Wild Palms"** into sharp relief. In spite of the heavy ironies which appear in a comparative reading of the stories and Faulkner's apparent sympathy with the convict rather than Wilbourne, it is clear that **"Old Man"** serves primarily to parody the tragic theme of the other tale. Faulkner's major concern seems to be with Wilbourne, a credible modern character whose incubus—guilt—is the author's special interest. On the other hand, the convict in **"Old Man"** is really a grotesque, a petrified man, an automaton who manages to reject experience and flee from the problem of existence. With his neurotic indecisiveness, Wilbourne fails not because he is diametrically opposed to the ''successful'' convict but because neither resource, the convict's faith in the divinity of rules or Charlotte's faith in the power of love to deny all rules, is accessible to him. Harry's tragedy (the thesis of the novel) is caused not by the implacable forces of external nature nor by Charlotte's ''powerful sexual needs,'' (as Howe has said) but by his own inner weakness. His struggle throughout the story is internal. **"Old Man"** serves as the antithesis of the novel; the convict succeeds because his struggle is almost purely external; his morality and mentality are all of a piece; his herculean duel with the river is never tragic. Irving Howe has provided this working definition of the Faulknerian tragic theme: ''cursed by the tragic need to compromise his freedom, man can still redeem himself through a gesture which may not mitigate his defeat but will declare his humanity in defeat.'' While **"The Wild Palms"** clearly meets the requirements of this formula, the other story just as clearly avoids them. Its mode is the comic.

The reading of ***The Wild Palms*** which I have presented seems, finally, to harmonize with Faulkner's latest and most challenging statement about the book. Asked by an interviewer whether he had brought the two stories together for ''any symbolic purpose,'' Faulkner replied:

> That was one story—the story of Charlotte Rittenmeyer and Harry Wilbourne, who sacrificed everything for love, and then lost that. I did not know it would be two separate stories until after I had started the book. When I reached the end of what is now the first section of ***The Wild Palms,*** I realized suddenly that something was missing, it needed emphasis, something to lift it like counterpoint in music. So I wrote on the ***Old Man*** story until ***The Wild Palms*** story rose back to pitch. Then I stopped the ***Old Man*** story at what is now its first section, and took up ***The Wild Palms*** story until it began again to sag. Then I raised it to pitch again with another section of its antithesis, which is the story of a man who got his love and spent the rest of the book fleeing from it, even to the extent of voluntarily going back to jail where he would be safe. They are only two stories by chance, perhaps necessity. The story is that of Charlotte and Wilbourne.

(pp. 319-22)

Joseph J. Moldenhauer, ''The Edge of Yoknapatawpha: Unity of Theme and Structure in 'The Wild Palms','' in William Faulkner: Three Decades of Criticism, *edited by Frederick J. Hoffman and Olga W. Vickery, 1960. Reprint by Harcourt Brace Jovanovich, 1963, pp. 305-22.*

ALFRED KAZIN (essay date 1961)

[*A highly respected American literary critic, Kazin is best known for such essay collections as* On Native Grounds *(1942),* An American Procession *(1984), and* Contemporaries *(1962), from which the following excerpt is drawn. Kazin discusses Faulkner's short story career and comments on several stories included in his* Collected Stories. *This essay was originally published in 1961.*]

Faulkner's short stories are not of the kind that has made the *New Yorker* famous; they are not even the stories of a writer who often writes stories; many of them are not really ''short stories'' as that peculiarly contemporary branch of literature has been invented, patented, and mechanically imitated in the United States—tight, deft, wholly dramatic and polished fables of social life that present symbols rather than characters whose uniqueness is the prime concern of the writer. So little is Faulkner a short story writer, in fact, that several of these stories [in ***Collected Stories***]—and by no means the best!—were written for the slicks: something that could never be done by the kind of short story writer who specializes in the art of the miniature, and for whom each short work has to be perfect.

Faulkner has often turned to the short story in order to relax. There is a hammy and grandiloquent side to his imagination—as well as to his rhetoric—a kind of sodden and mischievous looseness of manner that easily spills into his stories. It reminds me of W. C. Fields presiding over a banquet. One side of Faulkner's literary manner is that of the temperamental impresario presiding over his created world—a manner that recalls the gigantic confidence of Dickens and Balzac working away at their great blocks of marble. The fact that there is no other American novelist today who suggests such impressions to the reader is an instance of the power and breadth of Faulkner's imaginative world. Faulkner has an abiding sense that the whole human race can be fitted into his own native spot of Mississippi earth, no larger ''than a postage stamp.'' The characters in these stories range from Indians on the old Mississippi frontier, who had *their* Negro slaves, down to Midwesterners who have been transplanted from their frontier into houses, in Southern California, backed ''into a barren foothill combed and curried into a cypress-and-marble cemetery dramatic as a stage set and topped by an electric sign in red bulbs which, in the San Fernando valley fog, glared in broad sourceless ruby as though just beyond the crest lay not heaven but hell.''

As such fiercely inimical phrases suggest, Faulkner pays out steady moral judgment on all that has unfolded in his *comédie humaine* of American life. Moving from the Indian swamps to Hollywood (past the South before and after the war, the clash of the poor Snopeses with the haughty De Spains and Sartorises, the young aviators in the Royal Flying Corps, traveling air circuses in the 1920s), the reader has a constant sense, in Faulkner's work, not of ''America'' but of world history on this soil, from the time when ''New Orleans was a European city.'' A whole procession of races, clans, tribes, and classes moves through these stories, and you sense that you are reading not from story to story, from ''gem'' to ''gem,'' as they say of collections by Katharine Anne Porter or J. D. Salinger or Hemingway (these are really virtuosi of the short story and perhaps exclusively of the story), but from anecdote to anecdote fallen from the novels that are themselves recurrent stories of what has happened on this ''postage stamp'' of land in Mississippi.

Of course there are stories in [*Collected Stories*] like **''A Rose for Emily,''** that are famous anthology pieces—stories that show all too clearly how airily Faulkner can reproduce the manipulation of the reader's emotions that is the real aim of the commercial short story. **''A Rose for Emily''** is the story of the old maid who fell in love with a Northerner but resisted being jilted once too often; only after her death, when the curious townspeople were able to enter her house at last, did they discover that she had kept her dead lover in the bed where she had killed him after their last embrace. But even in **''A Rose for Emily,''** the intended Gothic touch of horror counts less with Faulkner than the human drama of the Southern gentlewoman unable to understand how much the world has changed around her. And in a far greater story, **''That Evening Sun,''** in which the characters are the Compson children from Faulkner's great novel, *The Sound and the Fury,* the emotion of the Negro servant, Nancy, who is pregnant by another man and lives in terror of being killed by her husband, is built up with such skill and communicates so well the bewilderment and anxiety of the children themselves (Quentin, the oldest, is the narrator) that the terror of the woman becomes the atmospheric center of the story, communicating itself to the children as the first absolute fact they must learn to recognize.

''That Evening Sun'' begins with a description of ''old'' Jefferson in the days when Negro laundresses still walked about carrying baskets of wash on their heads, and were able to stoop under fences without dropping their load. And the use of this opening comes back to us when young Quentin describes Nancy telling a story to him and the children—''. . . like she was living somewhere else, waiting somewhere else. She was outside the cabin. Her voice was inside and the shape of her, the Nancy that could stoop under a barbed wire fence with a bundle of clothes balanced on her head as though without weight, like a balloon, was there.''

This concern with emotion as a fact in itself, virtually an absolute, that stands apart from history and survives it—this is nowhere more pronounced than in **''Red Leaves,''** probably the high point of this collection. An Indian chief has died, and his Negro slave, knowing that by custom the dog, the horse, and the body servant of a chief must be buried with him, runs off to the swamp. Faulkner indulges in a certain amount of mischievous humor, Southern white man's humor, at the expense of Negro slaves. With his marvelous sense of costume, he describes an old Indian, barefoot, in a long linen frock coat and a beaver hat, busily complaining that ''This world is going to the dogs. It is being ruined by white men. We got along fine for years and years, before the white men foisted their Negroes upon us. In the old days the old men sat in the shade and ate stewed deer's flesh and corn and smoked tobacco and talked of honor and grave affairs; now what are we to do? Even the old wear themselves into the grave taking care of them that like sweating.'' And the torpid, tubby Indians go after the runaway with a kind of sadness—they are vaguely sorry for him, but sorrier that he cannot understand and accept fully the ritual that obliges him to be buried with his master, thus putting Indians to exertions that are undignified and useless. These Indians are philosophical-minded, yet they are so detached in their fatalism (the world moves as it must and men must die) that they can insist on their ritual without, as it were, having to respect it. The Negro slave, by contrast, is portrayed as *misunderstanding* his proper function as a man; he seems to find satisfaction in the exertion of flight itself (as does Joe Christmas in *Light in August*). When he gets panicky, he identifies himself with the animals in the woods, and all in all is shown operating on a level that causes the Indians to shake their heads. Yet as in his great novel, *Light in August,* Faulkner rises above these reflections on the race his own class so long held in servitude; the story ends on a concentrated image of the slave, begging for water before his end and unable to swallow it. On capturing the slave, who had nowhere to run but back home again, this Indian had said, ''Come. You ran well. Do not be ashamed.'' Now he simply says, in a final, not unkindly order—''Come.'' It is a marvelous story, and not the least for the sense of fatality in human affairs that unites the Negro and Indian at last; this sense of what *must be* is always the deepest element in Faulkner's imaginative sense of things.

Perhaps it is this quality that interests me in a story, **''Beyond,''** that is admittedly slight and even a bit forced in emotion. But Faulkner, portraying a dead father who in a brief interlude of consciousness after death has been searching for his son, who died at ten, has the man say, ''. . . anyway, there is a certain integral consistency which, whether it be right or wrong, a man must cherish because it alone will ever permit him to die.'' At times, as in the story **''The Tall Men,''** this classical understanding in Faulkner, his insistence on the supremacy of character over everything, tends to get propagandized. In this story an old Southern law officer says to a stranger: ''Yes, sir. A man gets around and he sees a heap; a heap of folks in a heap of situations. The trouble is, we done got into the habit of confusing the situations with the folks.'' And Faulkner practically smirks as the old fellow says it. Still, the fact remains: it *is* ''folks,'' not ''situations,'' that make up the real life of fiction. ''Situations'' make short stories, but ''folks'' make life. Faulkner is interested in ''folks.'' No wonder that his interest sometimes gets too big for the mold to which stories are fitted. (pp. 154-58)

Alfred Kazin, ''Old Boys, Mostly American: William Faulkner, The Short Stories,'' in his Contemporaries, *Little, Brown and Company, 1962, pp. 154-58.*

EDMOND L. VOLPE (essay date 1964)

[*In the following excerpt, from an essay originally published in 1964, Volpe analyzes ''Barn Burning'' as an examination of evil personified by the character Ab Snopes.*]

"Barn Burning," published in 1939, is one of Faulkner's finest short stories and one of his most profound. In a sensitive exploration of the troubled psyche of a child, Faulkner defines the nature of evil. The story is deceptive in its apparent simplicity. It is easy to misunderstand the moral significance of the boy's emotional conflict if we fail to recognize metaphor as metaphor, ignore the subtlety of Faulkner's narrative technique and miss the implications of the imagery. On the surface, the young boy's emotional struggle seems to be equated with a conflict between an aristocracy representing ethical order and a sharecropper, Ab Snopes, representing moral entropy.

The protagonist is the youngest son of Ab Snopes. The child's given name is Colonel Sartoris. In the opening scene, in which the boy's emotional conflict is identified, the justice declares: "'I reckon any boy named for Colonel Sartoris in this country can't help but tell the truth, can they?'" As Faulkner's narrator defines the boy's anxiety, he is trapped between the "old fierce pull of blood" and a thrust towards justice and truth. The external correlatives of the moral forces tearing the boy in two would therefore seem to be his father, the sharecropper, and De Spain, the aristocrat. Ab Snopes is a barn burner, a violent, destructive man. De Spain's plantation house, on the other hand, provides the child an objective image for the moral thrust generating his rebellion against his father. His immediate reaction to the sight of the house is to compare it to a symbol of justice, the courthouse. The white, ante-bellum manor evokes in the boy a surging sense of dignity and peace, and he feels certain, for a moment, that it must be safe from the malevolent touch of his father.

The opposition of sharecropper and aristocrat suggests social as well as moral implications. And, in fact, certain elements in the story support the possibility. Ab makes the valid point that De Spain's house is built with "nigger sweat" as well as the white sweat of the sharecropper. Ab views himself, the narrator seems to suggest, as a continually violated victim of an unjust socio-economic system. He "burns with a ravening and jealous rage." The "element of fire," the narrator authoritatively informs us, speaks to "some deep mainspring" of Ab's being "as the element of steel or powder spoke to other men, as the one weapon for the preservation of integrity, else breath were not worth the breathing, and hence to be regarded with respect and used with discretion."

"Barn Burning" however is not really concerned with class conflict. The story is centered upon Sarty's emotional dilemma. His conflict would not have been altered in any way if the person whose barn Ab burns had been a simple poor farmer, rather than an aristocratic plantation owner. The child's tension, in fact, begins to surface during the hearing in which a simple farmer accuses Ab of burning his barn. The moral antagonists mirrored in Sarty's conflict are not sharecropper and aristocrat. They are the father, Ab Snopes, versus the rest of mankind. Major De Spain is not developed as a character; his house is important to Sarty because it represents a totally new and totally different social and moral entity. Within the context of the society Faulkner is dealing with, the gap between the rich aristocrat and the poor sharecropper provides a viable metaphor for dramatizing the crisis Sarty is undergoing. Ab Snopes is by no means a social crusader. The De Spain manor is Sarty's first contact with a rich man's house, though he can recall, in the short span of his life, at least a dozen times the family had to move because Ab burned barns. Ab does not discriminate between rich and poor. For him there are only two categories: blood kin and "they," into which he lumps all the rest of mankind. Ab's division relates to Sarty's crisis and only by defining precisely the nature of the conflict the boy is undergoing can we determine the moral significance Faulkner sees in it. The clue to Sarty's conflict rests in its resolution.

In the story's climactic scene, Ab Snopes orders his wife to hold her son to prevent him from warning De Spain that Ab intends to burn his barn. Sarty fights free of his mother's arms and rushes to the manor house. After De Spain passes him on the horse, he hears shots ring out and at once begins to think of his father as dead. The nature imagery which Faulkner introduces in the concluding paragraphs of the story does not suggest that Sarty's rebellion has meant a triumph for morality and justice. In the chill darkness, on the crest of the hill, the boy sits with his back towards home, facing the woods. His fear and terror of his father are gone. Only grief and despair remain. By aligning himself with De Spain, the boy destroys his father and gains his freedom. At the story's end, he moves into the future without looking back, responding, independent and alone, to the call of the "rapid and urgent beating of the urgent and quiring heart of the late spring night." The imagery suggests a feeling of unity with the world of nature, a sense of wholeness as if the boy, at last, has found himself. The quiescent, enveloping nature imagery contrasts sharply with the threatening, rigid, metallic imagery which Faulkner uses to convey the child's sense of his father as a living force. The contrast clearly indicates that Sarty's struggle is against the repressive and divisive force his father represents. The boy's anxiety is created by his awakening sense of his own individuality. Torn between strong emotional attachment to the parent and his growing need to assert his own identity, Sarty's crisis is psychological and his battle is being waged far below the level of his intellectual and moral awareness.

Faulkner makes this clear in the opening scene with imagery that might be described as synesthesia. The real smell of cheese is linked with the smell of the hermetic meat in the tin cans with the scarlet devils on the label that his "intestines believed he smelled coming in intermittent gusts momentary and brief between the other constant one, the smell and sense just a little of fear because mostly of despair and grief, the old fierce pull of blood." The smells below the level of the olfactory sense link the devil image and the blood image to identify the anxiety the father creates in the child's psyche. Tension is created by the blood demanding identification with his father against *"our enemy* he thought in that despair; *ourn! mine and hisn both! He's my father!"* Sarty's conflict is played out in terms of identification, not in moral terms. He does not think of his father as bad, his father's enemies as good. (pp. 75-7)

Ab unjustly accuses Sarty of intending to betray him at the hearing, but he correctly recognizes that his son is moving out of childhood, developing a mind and will of his own and is no longer blindly loyal. In instructing the boy that everyone is the enemy and his loyalty belongs to his blood, Ab's phrasing is revealing: "'Don't you know all they wanted was a chance to get at me because they knew I had them beat?'" Ab does not use the plural "us." It is "I" and "they." Blood loyalty means total identification with Ab, and in the ensuing scenes, Snopes attempts to make his son an extension of himself by taking him to the De Spain house, rise up before dawn to be with him when he returns the rug, accompany him to the hearing against De Spain and finally make him an accomplice in the burning of De Spain's barn.

The moral import of Ab's insistence on blood loyalty is fully developed by the satanic imagery Faulkner introduces in the scene at the mansion. As they go up the drive, Sarty follows his father, seeing the stiff black form against the white plantation house. Traditionally the devil casts no shadow, and Ab's figure appears to the child as having "that impervious quality of something cut ruthlessly from tin, depthless, as though sidewise to the sun it would cast no shadow." The cloven hoof of the devil is suggested by Ab's limp upon which the boy's eyes are fixed as the foot unwaveringly comes down into the manure. Sarty's increasing tension resounds in the magnified echo of the limping foot on the porch boards, "a sound out of all proportion to the displacement of the body it bore, as though it had attained to a sort of vicious and ravening minimum not to be dwarfed by anything." At first Sarty thought the house was impervious to his father, but his burgeoning fear of the threat the father poses is reflected in his vision of Ab becoming magnified and monstrous as the black arm reaches up the white door and Sarty sees "the lifted hand like a curled claw." (pp. 78-9)

The satanic images are projected out of the son's nightmarish vision of his father, but they are reinforced by the comments of the adult narrator. Sarty believes Snopes fought bravely in the Civil War, but Ab, we are told, wore no uniform, gave his fealty to no cause, admitted the authority of no man. He went to war for booty. Ab's ego is so great it creates a centripetal force into which everything must flow or be destroyed. The will-less, abject creature who is his wife symbolizes the power of his will. What Ab had done to his wife, he sets out to do to the emerging will of his son. Ab cannot tolerate any entity that challenges the dominance of his will. By allowing his hog to forage in the farmer's corn and by dirtying and ruining De Spain's rug, he deliberately creates a conflict that requires the assertion of primacy. Fire, the element of the devil, is the weapon for the preservation of his dominance. Ab's rage is not fired by social injustice. It is fired by a pride, like Lucifer's, so absolute it can accept no order beyond its own. In the satanic myth, Lucifer asserts his will against the divine order and is cast out of heaven. The angels who fall with Lucifer become extensions of his will. In the same way, Ab is an outcast and pariah among men. He accepts no order that is not of his blood.

All centripetal will, Snopes can have no feeling for any other being. He is incapable of recognizing what Faulkner in *Absalom, Absalom!* describes as each person's sense of self, the "I Am" of his being. In the crucial scene on the slope, the narrator interprets Sarty's resistance to his father's description of "they" as the enemy: "Later, twenty years later, he was to tell himself, 'If I had said they wanted only truth, justice, he would have hit me again.'" Sarty's resistance constitutes a recognition of an entity beyond his father, a correlative of his own emerging sense of individuality. The truth and justice "they" the enemy want is nothing more than acknowledgment of their rights as individual entities. Ab would have hit Sarty again because such a statement would have been a challenge to Ab's will, identical with the challenge of the enemy. The "they" referred to in this passage are simple farmers, not aristocrats. Sarty is struggling to be himself. He responds with such intensity to the sight of De Spain's house not because it corresponds to some innate moral sense but because he sees it as an entity, powerful and completely isolated from his father's will. The mansion makes him forget "his father and the terror and despair both." The surge of joy has the effect of diminishing the terrifying image of Ab to little more than a "buzzing wasp." The "they" who belong to the house he feels certain, must be safe from his father, their barns "impervious to the puny flames he might contrive." (pp. 79-80)

In the ensuing scenes, Ab moves inexorably to a collision with De Spain that must terminate in barn burning. Sarty's increasing anxiety as he watches Ab respond to the challenge De Spain represents corresponds to the escalating threat to his own identity that Ab poses as he forces the boy to submit to the pull of blood by making him his accomplice. When De Spain fines Snopes an extra twenty bushels, Sarty tries to stave off the barn burning by insisting to Ab that they will not pay. He will hide the bushels. Sarty's daydreams express a hope that somehow his father will change. In the field plowing, his bare feet in the rich soil, he dreams that Ab has accepted the fine. Acceptance would mean that Ab has acknowledged the integrity of an order beyond his own and is willing to live with it rather than striking out with his destructive violence. If that were true, if his father were indeed changed, then the boy's own terror and grief would be at an end, the *"being pulled two ways like between two teams of horses"* would cease.

At the hearing of Ab's suit against De Spain, the boy momentarily feels defiant and even exultant. He believes his father is charged with barn burning, and Sarty knows Ab is innocent. His cry, protesting his father's innocence, expresses the desperate hope that Ab's innocence is proof that he has changed. The fear and terror immediately return. Ab's suit, Sarty recognizes, is an assertion of will that must end in barn burning. After the hearing, the child again insists to his father that they do not have to pay even the ten bushels. Ab's statement that they will wait until October to see what happens lulls the child's anxiety and the following scene has the quality of an idyll. For the first time, Ab appears human. The terrifying images of rigidity and blackness are gone. The boy listens to his father telling a story at the blacksmith's. At lunch, Ab divides the food with his two sons. During the slow afternoon they loiter along a fence watching the horse trading.

This peaceful interlude ends abruptly that evening with the mother's anguished cry. Again, Sarty sees the figure of his father stiff in the black suit "as though dressed carefully for some shabby and ceremonial violence." When Ab orders him to get the oil from the barn, Sarty responds to the pull of blood, at the same time dreaming of running away and never returning. But he does return. When he dares, for the first time, to express opposition to his father, he is made a prisoner. The scene is right out of a child's nightmare. Ab grabs Sarty by the back of the shirt and holds him helpless with just his toes touching the floor, thrusting him into the bedroom and ordering the boy's mother to hold him. Ab will not allow the aunt to hold the struggling child. Sarty must fight free of the grasp of Ab's surrogate, the terrified creature whose will has become an extension of Ab's. By warning De Spain, Sarty identifies himself with an entity other than his father, and only by violating his blood does he gain his freedom. Whether Ab is actually killed we do not know. The detail is unimportant. For Sarty, Ab is dead. Significantly, the boy feels grief but no guilt. He has destroyed the crushing force that threatened his awakening identity and, at last, the fear and terror are gone. His nightmare ended, Sarty, appropriately, falls into a dreamless sleep, from which he awakens whole and at peace, ready for the future. (pp. 80-1)

Edmond L. Volpe, "'Barn Burning': A Definition of Evil," in Faulkner, the Unappeased Imagination: A Collection of Critical Essays, *edited by Glenn O.*

Carey, The Whiston Publishing Company, 1980, pp. 75-82.

THOMAS R. GORMAN (essay date 1966)

[In the following excerpt, Gorman presents a system of ethical and moral values that he discerns in Faulkner's short stories.]

It is certainly by now a cliché to depict our age as an age of crises, a time of decay and disintegration. Many . . . in all fields have sketched the stresses in our culture and our civilization. They have portrayed them variously as the end of the road for man, or the beginning of a new order. Fewer . . . have seen this collapse of order as a conflict not of ideologies and systems, but rather as a Calvary of the human heart, a Crucifixion of man as man. Fewer artists still have endeavored to assay this Crucifixion within the short story. William Faulkner was one of these few.

The range of his some seventy-five short stories is overwhelming. In nature, or type, they fall roughly into four classes: the conventional commercial story, the tragic, the comic, and finally stories that are a blending of pathos and honor. Their subject matter is as vast as that of any modern short story writer. The majority of them are pieces of the tremendous Saga Faulkner wove about the South. Some cover the Indians in Mississippi at the time of Andrew Jackson; others the time before, after, and during the Civil War; others the time before, after, and during the First World War; others the depression; and still others the Second World War. There are stories of artists, stories of hunting, and detective stories. Faulkner's work with the short story was one of the great imaginative ventures of the century. (p. 4)

Throughout these short stories Faulkner aims at a complex moral lesson—a lesson of *knowing*. His insight is so complicated that it seems best described as a multi-dimensional moral truth. Despite the difficulty of abstracting philosophical or ethical principles from works of art, this esthetic view can be approximated in four moral evaluations:

First, to understand himself and his nature, man must know what the forces of personal psychology and the forces of history are, and also how their interlocking may complicate and, to some extent, determine human behavior;

Second, man to live in society must realize that both the natural man—the man who lives merely by his natural impulses and instincts—and the man who lives under a code that has been allowed to atrophy—the man who lives by the letter and not the spirit—will both prove asocial, positing their own destruction;

Third, man must recognize that nature herself will avenge injustice—that is to say that for Faulkner the forces of history and the laws of biology and natural selection will collaborate to destroy the vain, proud and arrogantly unjust man and the society he builds;

and Fourth, there are eternal truths and values which man and society must incorporate into their personal and social structuring to endure and prevail.

The initial stage of Faulkner's multiple moral insight deals with complex interweavings of history and psychology. Faulkner portrays the impossibility of understanding, much less judging men without comprehension of this subtle determinism, but he definitely insists that human actions must be qualified by knowledge of interior and exterior forces before they can be grasped.

His approach to this problem takes two forms in his short stories. First, he is constantly preoccupied with the interior forces and their consequences. In **"The Brooch,"** the story of an overly possessive mother who destroys her son's marriage and drives him to suicide, the man himself sees his life as previously patterned in *Green Mansions,* a book he has cherished since childhood. Shortly before he seals himself in the bathroom to destroy himself—to the Freudian, a womb symbol—he thinks about the book, "Yes—it seems to have been right all the time about what I will do." His great response to the book arises because it mirrors to him his own inner nature. In **"Barn Burning,"** part of the Snopes saga told twice—once from the point of view of the young son as a tragedy and once by a third party as humorous pathos—the young son, while contemplating his father's habit of contracting as a share cropper only to burn his employer's barn if he feels his dignity and honor have been besmirched, thinks, "Maybe it [his new job] will change him now from what he couldn't help but be." Here the son is perceiving that his father's asocial tendencies spring from some inner necessity. When Gavin Stevens, in **"Tomorrow,"** suffering a hung jury because one man won't vote free a man who performed an entirely justifiable killing, learns that the killed man was, as a child, raised by this obstinate juror; his nephew and he have the following conversation:

> "Of course he wasn't," Gavin said "the lowly and invincible of the earth—to endure and endure and then endure, tomorrow and tomorrow and tomorrow. Of course he wasn't going to vote Bookwright free."
>
> "I would have," the nephew said. "I would have freed him. Because Buck Thorpe was bad. He—"
>
> "No, you wouldn't," Uncle Gavin said.—"It wasn't Buck Thorpe, the adult, the man. He would have shot that man as quick as Bookwright did, if he had been in Bookwright's place. It was because somewhere in that debased and brutalized flesh which Bookwright slew there still remained, not the spirit maybe, but at least the memory, of that little boy,—though the man the boy had become didn't know it, and only Fentry did. And you wouldn't have freed him either. Don't ever forget that. Never."

Here a man's strange conduct is made comprehensible by an understanding of his psychology, but that in turn is only understandable in terms of his history.

Another approach to this first stage of his moral insight puts the stress on exterior social forces. In **"A Rose for Emily"** and throughout ***Go Down, Moses,*** it is a combination of personal psychology and socio-historical forces precipitating tragedy that intrigues Faulkner. Few writers are more conscious of historical flux. His stories weave back and forth in time, both from story to story and in themselves, demonstrating that man is not an isolated unit, but is concretized by his own personality, and by the conditions and history of the time and place within which he resides. Speaking in **"Monk,"** the story of a convict imbecile, Gavin Stevens says, "It is only in literature that the paradoxical and even mutually negating anecdotes in the history of a human heart can be juxtaposed and annealed by art into verisimilitude and credibility." Faulkner throughout his stories tries to show that unless man understands the outer and inner forces that beset the heart of any man, he can understand neither that individual, nor himself.

There is a second stage to the over-all moral lesson running through this literature. In essence it is spiritually akin to the theme of the Byron who wrote *Don Juan*. It asks the questions posed in different language by the modern existentialists. How should man live? What is the good life for man? It manifests itself in Faulkner's constant visitation to various black depths of human behavior and his violent and unrelenting assault upon the atrophied Southern Culture. Too much has been made critically of Faulkner's sensationalism and also far too much of the fact that he writes about the South. Faulkner may particularize about the things he knows and experiences, but ultimately he is always writing about the universal condition of being man. Faulkner like Byron has two related convictions that have remained constant. The first is that the nature of man is such that he is incapable of living by his natural impulses alone and maintaining either sanity or stability in society. The other is that though man must establish a Code for living, that Code must be organic and built upon justice, for if the Code when lived coalesces and becomes stagnant, or if it is founded upon the sands of injustice, man and his society will go mad and crumble. Faulkner postulates that to be human is to be part, or mostly, animal, but to live humanly man must have a hierarchy of values to channel his activities. However, this Code, if it should be called that, must be founded upon transcendental and eternal values yet be malleable to the changing conditions of human living.

Again, from another point of view, he returns to his concern with history and the individual man. Faulkner visits the depths to see how man living by whim and impulse will react and also to show that the conduct of men who live arrogantly and pridefully and unjustly under a supposedly civilized code is not far different, and perhaps more reprehensible. But his treatment of what he finds is blatantly that of a moralist. Perhaps the thing that most indicates his positive, moral approach to his materials is his humor.

In the stories of the Snopes saga which just about reach the ultimate in portraying the life of a man in its most black caverns, the prevailing note is humor—a wild comic humor which at first is almost offensive. However, this humor seems to make the material bearable and to point out that even in the wretchedly dark night of the soul man is still man and preserves a dignity which is infinite. This humor is not just folk humor, but is beyond that a terrible, sophisticated folk humor. It is some of the most shocking and violent humor possible, yet it is not satire for it has a poignant tenderness about it. Possibly it is ultimately the humor of democracy for it does not ridicule any man, but pities them all. It is a genuine humor based on what the existentialist Gabriel Marcel calls Sympathy—that realization that what happens to one man may happen to all men.

One of the best examples of a combined focusing of these two ideas about the nature of man's life pattern appears in **"Wash."** This is the story of Wash Jones who is simply a nobody. He is lower than the low since even Negro slaves abuse him. He is the prime example of a man without breeding who just lives the life of a happy savage. He, however, is aware of his position and has compensated for his own lack of nobility by giving hero worship to his lifelong friend Cornel Sutpen, a hero of the Civil War. Here is the polarity between the natural man and the man of supposed principle. Wash expresses his worship of a man embodying a Code of Conduct he is incapable of maintaining by telling Sutpen that, "it ain't that you were brave at one minute one day of your life and got a paper to show hit from General Lee. But you air brave, the same as you air alive and breathing." He serves this man even to the point of ignoring Sutpen's seduction of his granddaughter because he blindly believes that the "kernel will make hit right." When the "kernel" fails and treats the granddaughter as if she were less important than one of his horses, Wash kills him and later his granddaughter and her illegitimate child. Finally, he literally commits suicide. This he does indirectly through a type of despair, but more directly because it is the only manner which a man like himself has to preserve his integrity in the face of a supreme injustice. Meditating upon their situation shortly after he has killed his best friend and before his further violence, he thinks:

> Brave,—Better if nara one of them had never rid back home in '65—Better if his kind and mine too had never drawn the breath of life on this earth. Better that all who remain of us be blasted from the face of the earth than that another Wash Jones should see his whole life shredded from him and shrival away like a dried shuck thrown into the fire.

It is as if Faulkner would obliterate all society that fails to render justice to its fellow man.

Thirdly, there is Faulkner's terrible indictment of society as expressed in his preoccupation with decay. If he had been an ancient Jew, he would have spoken of the hand of Providence, but here he only seems to find in nature proof of the saying that the wages of sin are death. Everywhere he sees societies which were highly developed coming to a bad end because they have ignored Justice. His treatment of the Southern aristocracy and the Indian tribes is the same. The same dreadful moral judgment is worked out in history: decay, destruction and death follow for those who violate the basic laws of decency, who turn against the "fitness of things." He possesses a strange vision in which the laws of biology and natural selection combine with other forces of history to wreak nature's vengeance upon the unjust, arrogant, and prideful man. Imbeciles and degenerates flow across his pages. Always they are the offspring of a clan or race that has violated first principles of decency. This is the theme of ***Go Down, Moses*** with only the hope at the end of five generations that there may come a new race founded in justice that will prevail—that will endure and re-bless the land and the people. In **"Delta Autumn"** Uncle Ike finds that his grand-nephew is the grandson of a slave he once set free. Though he feels such marriage is impossible in America for another hundred years, to this child he hesitantly passes the symbol which the hunters have used to signify manhood. Later musing upon the time of his life, in which he has seen the land gutted and betrayed by his race and others, he comes to the conclusion that "the people who have destroyed it will accomplish its own revenge." His conclusion is the same as the one that Faulkner reiterates again and again; that there is an order of nature and nature itself will punish the violators of that order and their sons and their sons.

With all this emphasis upon decay and with his belief that the natural man and the atrophied social man can not build a society that will last and which will not be its own undoing, it has been easy for some critics to see in Faulkner only a nightmare of nihilism, but from first to last in his writing career Faulkner has been writing a literature of affirmation. He has been affirming that men are immortal, that they all, no matter how decadent, have a dignity that is greater than anything upon the earth. The same uncle Ike also says:

> There are good men everywhere, at all times. Most men are. Some are just unlucky! because most men are a little better than their circumstances give them a chance to be. And I've known some that even circumstances couldn't stop.

and

> God created man and he created the world for him to live in and I reckon He created the kind of world He would have wanted to live in if He had been a man—the ground to walk upon, the big woods, the trees and the water, and the game to live in it.

Critics have loved to make passing reference to Faulkner's "Romanticism and Despair," to allude to the "dark shape of doom" being omnipresent and eternal in his writings, and to point out quickly that he is constructing "a vast savage, Demonic, *Tragedie Humaine* of the American South. Robert Penn Warren, however, noted that not "man's doom, but his manhood in the face of that doom is what is important."

Faulkner expresses over and over again in his short stories two emotions. He is possessed with a titanic rage against any manner of injustice, vanity, arrogance and pride and an overwhelming compassion, sympathy and love for the lowly and humble of the earth. In **"Golden Land,"** a bitterly ironic story of a man who comes from the plains of Nebraska to make his fortune in California only to collapse personally into alcoholism and to witness the decay of his children into nymphomania and homosexuality, suddenly remembers his long forgotten youth. Thinking of his parents, he almost finds the clue to his destruction for "they—his mother and father—had tried to explain it to him—something about fortitude, the will to endure." In **"The Bear,"** Uncle Ike as a young boy makes the discovery that "Truth is one. It doesn't change. It covers all things which touch the heart—honor and pride and pity and justice and courage, and love."

Faulkner, 1936. The Bettmann Archive, Inc.

Granville Hicks has said of [Faulkner's] work that "He never tried to deceive us into thinking we knew these characters well for that we cannot know anyone is part of his philosophy." This is clearly a mis-reading. Faulkner's main emphasis seems to be that man can know himself, his fellow man and his time and knowing these things build in justice and humility a new society that will endure and prevail. Perhaps Faulkner himself never stated his vision and aim in writing in these terms, but outside of the experience of his art they are a close approximation of his aesthetic moral judgment on his time.

It is as if besides writing upon all the complexities to the statements "Know Thyself," and "Man, fear thyself, thine arrogance and vanity and pride," Faulkner was composing an artistic transliteration of two old beatitudes: Blessed are they who hunger and thirst for justice, for they shall be satisfied and Blessed are the meek, for they shall possess the earth. (pp. 4-6)

Thomas R. Gorman, "Faulkner's Ethical Point of View," in The CEA Critic, *Vol. XXVIII, No. 8, June, 1966, pp. 4-6.*

MALCOLM COWLEY (essay date 1967)

[*In the following, excerpted from the introduction to his edition of selected works by Faulkner, Cowley asserts that Faulkner's novels are less successful than his novellas and discusses the author's love and concern for the South.*]

It had better be admitted that almost all [Faulkner's] novels have some obvious weakness in structure. (p. xxiv)

Faulkner seems best to me, and most nearly himself, either in long stories like **"The Bear,"** in ***Go Down, Moses,*** and **"Old Man,"** which was published as half of ***Wild Palms,*** and **"Spotted Horses,"** which was first printed separately, then greatly expanded and fitted into the loose framework of *The Hamlet* . . .; or else in the Yoknapatawpha saga as a whole. That is, he has been most effective in dealing with the total situation always present in his mind as a pattern of the South, or else in shorter units which, though often subject to inspired revision, have still been shaped by a single conception. It is by his best that we should judge him, as every other author; and Faulkner at his best—even sometimes at his worst—has a power, a richness of life, an intensity to be found in no other American writer of our time. He has—. . . I am quoting from Henry James's essay on Hawthorne—"the element of simple genius, the quality of imagination."

Moreover, he has a brooding love for the land where he was born and reared and where, unlike other writers of his generation, he has chosen to spend his life. It is ". . . this land, this South, for which God has done so much, with woods for game and streams for fish and deep rich soil for seed and lush springs to sprout it and long summers to mature it and serene falls to harvest it and short mild winters for men and animals." So far as Faulkner's country includes the Delta, it is also (in the words of old Ike McCaslin)

> . . . this land which man has deswamped and denuded and derivered in two generations so that white men can own plantations and commute every night to Memphis and black men own plantations and ride in jimcrow cars to Chicago and live in millionaires' mansions on Lake Shore Drive, where white men rent farms and live like niggers and niggers crop on shares and live like animals, where cotton is planted and grows man-tall in the very cracks of the sidewalks, and usury and mortgage and bankruptcy and measureless wealth, Chinese and African and Aryan and Jew, all breed and spawn together.

Here are the two sides of Faulkner's feeling for the South: on the one side, an admiring and possessive love; on the other, a compulsive fear lest what he loves should be destroyed by the ignorance of its native serfs and the greed of traders and absentee landlords. (pp. xxv-xxvi)

In the group of novels beginning with ***The Wild Palms*** . . . , which attracted so little attention at the time of publication that they seemed to go unread, there is a quality not exactly new to Faulkner—it had appeared already in passages of *Sartoris* and *Sanctuary*—but now much stronger and no longer overshadowed by violence and horror. It is a sort of homely and sober-sided frontier humor that is seldom achieved in contemporary writing (except sometimes by Erskine Caldwell, also a Southerner). The horse-trading episodes in *The Hamlet,* and especially the long story of the spotted ponies from Texas, might have been inspired by the Davy Crockett almanacs. **"Old Man,"** the story of the convict who surmounted the greatest of the Mississippi floods, might almost be a continuation of *Huckleberry Finn*. It is as if some older friend of Huck's had taken the raft and drifted on from Aunt Sally Phelps's farm into wilder adventures, described in a wilder style, among Chinese and Cajuns and bayous crawling with alligators. In a curious way, Faulkner combines two of the principal traditions in American letters: the tradition of psychological horror, often close to symbolism, that begins with Charles Brockden Brown, our first professional novelist, and extends through Poe, Melville, Henry James (in his later stories), Stephen Crane, and Hemingway; and the other tradition of frontier humor and realism, beginning with Augustus Longstreet's *Georgia Scenes* and having Mark Twain as its best example.

But the American author he most resembles is Hawthorne, for all their polar differences. They stand to each other as July to December, as heat to cold, as swamp to mountain, as the luxuriant to the meager but perfect, as planter to Puritan; and yet Hawthorne had much the same attitude toward New England that Faulkner has to the South, together with a strong sense of regional particularity. The Civil War made Hawthorne feel that "the North and the South were two distinct nations in opinions and habits, and had better not try to live under the same institutions." In the spring of 1861 he wrote to his Bowdoin classmate Horatio Bridge, "We were never one people and never really had a country." "New England," he said a little later, "is quite as large a lump of earth as my heart can really take in." But it was more than a lump of earth for him; it was a lump of history and a permanent state of consciousness. Like Faulkner in the South, he applied himself to creating its moral fables and elaborating its legends, which existed, as it were, in his solitary heart. Pacing the hillside behind his house in Concord, he listened for a voice; one might say that he lay in wait for it, passively but expectantly, like a hunter behind a rock; then, when it had spoken, he transcribed its words—more cautiously than Faulkner, it is true; with more form and less fire, but with the same essential fidelity. "I have an instinct that I had better keep quiet," he said in a letter to his publisher. "Perhaps I shall have a new spirit of vigor if I wait quietly for it; perhaps not." Faulkner is another author who has to wait for the spirit and the voice. He is not so much a novelist, in the usual sense of being a writer who sets out to observe actions and characters, then fits them into the framework of a story, as he is an epic or bardic poet in prose, a creator of myths that he weaves together into a legend of the South. (pp. xxviii-xxx)

Malcolm Cowley, in an introduction to The Portable Faulkner *by William Faulkner, edited by Malcolm Cowley, revised edition, The Viking Press, 1967, pp. vii-xxx.*

ELMO HOWELL (essay date 1970)

[In the following excerpt, Howell views "Red Leaves" as Faulkner's exploration of the dark side of human nature.]

Faulkner's aim in **"Red Leaves"** is to create, without regard to the facts of history, a horror in the wilderness unmitigated by any recognizable moral system. The immolation of the Negro is only a dramatic instance of the amorality of the Indians, most powerfully represented by the figure of their new chief Moketubbe, son of Issetibbeha. As a young man, Issetibbeha brought back from a trip to France, among other useless finery, a pair of slippers with red heels, which he wore as a badge of his office. Even as a boy, the secretive Moketubbe was caught trying to wear the shoes, though they were already too small for him. Later when he stole them, his intent was clear. "Yao," said Issetibbeha. "I too like being alive, it seems." He gave the shoes to Moketubbe, lived five years longer and died quite suddenly one morning, "though the doctor came in a skunk-vest and burned sticks." In spite of the concern for custom and usage and an elaborate ceremonial, Faulkner's Chickasaw compound is governed by the tooth and claw principle of the jungle. (p. 297)

[Spurning] the romantic view of nature, Faulkner looks back on what life might have been like in his part of the country before the white men came and conjures up a wilderness as fascinating and terrifying as the Darwinian forests of Maine. The Negro slaves of the Indians contribute their part to the general picture of savagery, the majority of them leading lives "transplanted whole out of the African jungles." Faulkner makes no effort to pierce their racial mask, not even that of the victim, a Guinea man who was taken at fourteen by a trader off Kamerun, before his teeth were filed. "They seemed to be musing as one upon something remote, inscrutable. They were like a single octopus. They were like the roots of a huge tree uncovered, the earth broken momentarily upon the writhen, thick, fetid tangle of its lightless and outraged life." (p. 298)

In *The Sound and the Fury*, Quentin Compson says that a Negro is not a person so much as the "obverse reflection of the white people he lives among." The Negroes in **"Red Leaves"** stand in a similar relation to their Indian masters. They are raised like animals, kept at first in a communal pen with a lean-to roof over one corner, "like a pen for pigs." Later they are placed in cabins, in pairs, to breed, so that after a few years Issetibbeha is able to sell forty head to a Memphis trader. The lane between the cabins is littered with "fetish-shaped objects" made of wood and rags and feathers, lying among bones and broken gourd dishes. Their tribal life is intact, beginning at nightfall in the largest cabin and removed after dark to the creek bottom where the drums are kept. A mute guards them by day, a boy of fourteen, naked except for the mud caked on his body to keep off mosquitoes. They have about them a smell, "rank, violent," and their faces are like "the death masks of apes."

Thus in their more expressive, visceral way, the Negroes reflect the barbarism of their Indian masters, which is more refined and consequently more terrible. But to what purpose does Faulkner create this picture of savagery? The title suggests something beyond mere sensation, and in one of his interviews he tried to make the implication clear. The title indicates "the deciduation of Nature which no one could stop," by which he apparently means red leaves to suggest red men or men in general, all of whom, men and leaves alike, follow in an inexorable course of life and death. Consequently, the point of the story has nothing to do with the institution of slavery nor with the treatment of one Negro by his Indian masters, but with life in general terms, which Faulkner portrays as a jungle, where to eat is hardly less inevitable than to be eaten.

In **"Red Leaves,"** Faulkner is venturing into the same region that Conrad explores in *Heart of Darkness:* that element of human nature that civilized man would prefer to forget. The moral facade is lifted and life is exposed in its barest terms. Faulkner's debt to Conrad is profound, as he was free to admit. In different ways, they were both exiles from home, from a defeated country, whose remoteness in time or place fostered a romantic view and an attachment to what Faulkner called the old verities of the heart. They both adored the simple fellow who is honest and true, but they were aware of how often the simple fellow is taken in. They had no illusions about human nature. If they had been orthodox Christians, they would have written about original sin; in secular terms, it was a matter of being civilized, of being as far as possible from the jungle, which at best is never far away.

In *Heart of Darkness,* Conrad's theme is clearly stated: Mr. Kurtz steps "over the edge" to find the meaning in life—its horror—and at the moment of his death fixes it in the mind of Marlow where it grows into a mania. (pp. 298-300)

"Red Leaves" is about the same horror, though no European consciousness intervenes to register it as Marlow's does. Conrad's descriptions of African savagery are restrained, his "monstrous passions" and "unspeakable rites" left mostly to the imagination. Faulkner, on the other hand, rejoices in the garish details of Indian life, which may be short and brutish but never dull. Moketubbe is a source of excitement as well as solemn thought, as his retainers suggest when they skirt the subject of his father's death and his involvement in it.

> "Yao," the second said. "He is the Man now. He used to wear the shoes behind Issetibbeha's back, and it was not known if Issetibbeha knew this or not. And then Issetibbeha became dead, who was not old, and the shoes are Moketubbe's, since he is the Man now. What do you think of that?"
>
> "I don't think about it," Basket said. "Do you?"
>
> "No," the second said.
>
> "Good," Basket said. "You are wise."

Yet they adore him, in a childish way, squiring him about the woods in a litter, having him wear the absurd shoes as often and as long as nature can bear. They recall the search for the slave of the last chief, Issetibbeha's father, and reflect on the curious ways of the black people, who would rather work and sweat than enter the earth honorably with a chief. "They are savages; they cannot be expected to regard usage." They allow the Negro to live for almost a week, savoring his struggle for life and loving him for it, like the cat's playful excitement with the mouse. In the meantime, the other Indians have been coming in on horseback, afoot, and in wagons to eat the funeral feast of baked dog and succotash and yams baked in ashes and most of all to witness the final ceremony. The dog and the horse are waiting—the dog that has been howling for a week; and as the panting Negro is brought in, the people move towards the final scene, "patient, grave, decorous, implacable."

The horror is not less real than in Conrad's Congo but tempered by a certain animal excitement. The Negro suffers—in the due course of things it is time for him to suffer—but his death gives pleasure to the Indians in heightening their own awareness of being alive. "Come," they tell him. "You ran well. Do not be ashamed." He quits life with decorum, and the consummation provides, aside from the spectacle of sudden death, the satisfaction of a tragedy, where joy and pain are mixed. It is a solemn but not a somber story. (pp. 300-01)

In Faulkner's wilderness, joy and pain go hand in hand; the Indians who admire the Negro and give him time to eat and drink also want to watch him die. Faulkner gives his jungle a dimension that Conrad's lacks, a suggestion that in spite of the horror the spectacle of life is worthwhile. The Negro seeks death from the rattlesnake, but the suffering only makes him want to live. Critics err when they condemn the Indians for killing him, for the Negro himself does not condemn them. **"Red Leaves"** goes back to the time before man separated himself from nature, with his particular gods and creeds. He is still part of the "normal deciduation" and exults in the pain as well as the joy. Mr. William Van O'Connor calls the Negro's death a scene of "implacable cruelty." So it seems to the European eye, but from the point of view established in the story it has no significance beyond the Negro's awareness of suffering and the pleasure it gives the Indians. It is all a part of the process of nature, which is neither kind nor cruel.

The mouse, says the naturalist Joseph Wood Krutch, has a natural life span of two years, although it is usually eaten long before that time. It is one of the most defenseless of creatures, its place in the economy of nature apparently being to reproduce itself quickly and then provide food for some larger animal. To the speculative mind . . . , this horrid thought provides amusement and a sense of participation in some cosmic plan quite beyond our comprehension. "What we would like to do," says Mr. Krutch, "is to realize the sum of the earth's energy and joy. The most that we can usually do is to participate in the opening of one flower or in a rabbit's running of his race. There is too much beauty and too much joy for us to take in." It is in this sense that **"Red Leaves"** is an exultant story.

Although Faulkner's main achievement must inevitably be associated with the South, he had a natural bent in another direction which his Indian stories represent. When he turned to regions beyond the South, to the North or to Europe of the First World War, he failed; the human comedy came to him only in the idiom of North Mississippi. But he was always close to the natural world, and in spite of the frustration which so much of his early work suggests—the frustration that comes in trying to be separate from nature—his pages are suffused with the joy of which Mr. Krutch speaks. He never quite despairs because he sees man in a larger perspective than any of his moral systems can project him. **"Red Leaves"** is one of his most satisfying stories because it shows him working in harmony with that natural law which underlies all system and governs alike all created things. (pp. 302-03)

Elmo Howell, "William Faulkner's Chickasaw Legacy: A Note on 'Red Leaves'," in Arizona Quarterly, *Vol. 26, No. 4, Winter, 1970, pp. 293-303.*

FORREST L. INGRAM (essay date 1971)

[*In the following excerpt, Ingram, an American critic, discusses several themes explored in* The Unvanquished, *Faulkner's chronicle of the impact of the Civil War.*]

The central theme of [***The Unvanquished***] is an involved one. The exigencies of war introduce serious disorder into human living on several levels: on the physical level—the ravaging of land and property; on the moral level—habits of lying, stealing, cheating, killing; on the psychological level—depersonalization, limiting the variety of human responses to a single kind of response, distortion of character; on the political level—gun rule, justice through vengeance, disregard for law; on the sociological level—the breakdown of family life, and the disruption of Negro-White relations. As the war continues, the unnatural conditions under which its participants must live become the custom, the rule rather than the exception. The deeds of disorder which war encourages in men become habits which, even after the last cannon stands silent and the last Yankee soldier has departed, remain imbedded in the Southerner's soul, ready to rise to the surface at the drop of a challenger's threat. In such men as Colonel John Sartoris, the habits of war become so deeply ingrained that, despite his determined effort, he is unable to break them—just as the drunkard cannot turn from his drink. Nevertheless, the conditions of war can be alleviated, the habits of war can be replaced by habits of peace; an order can be established which is neither the pre-war order come back to life, nor the war order itself continuing unabated. In the person and committed action of Bayard Sartoris—The Sartoris—the South (and "man"—who will prevail) succeeds in reestablishing order—a new order solidly based in responsible moral choice and buttressed by an understanding of civil law, of the dignity of the human being, of the worth of the land, of the character of Southern Negroes, and of the nature of courage.

The book leads us through the most brutal years of the Civil War—the only one of Faulkner's works to do so. In **"Ambuscade,"** war begins as a game Ringo and Bayard play behind the smokehouse. The feel it as little more than a game when they lift down the long musket and fire on the Yankee soldiers who have come onto the Sartoris homestead. In this story, only a horse dies and a mere pile of wood chips behind the smokehouse lies in ruin, demolished by the sweep of Loosh's arm. In **"Retreat,"** however, the meaning of war begins to intrude more and more on the consciousness of Granny and the two boys. A chest of silver and a team of mules are stolen; two Negro slaves pack a bundle and march toward freedom; the little white lies Granny was forced to tell in **"Ambuscade"** have ceased to shock her. War theft acquires the polite name "borrowing." John Sartoris wears a price on his head like an outlaw. And when the Yankees burn the Sartoris house, Granny joins Ringo and Bayard in their rhythmic cursing: "The bastuds! The bastuds!"

As Granny and the two boys ride toward Hawkhurst in **"Raid,"** they see more burned houses, families uprooted, Whites crouched now in Negro cabins. The house of Granny's sister is in ashes. The railroad that used to run through Hawkhurst lies in ruin. On the road, displaced Negroes tramp in stunned groups toward "Jordan" and freedom. They rush the bridge over which the Yankees have just marched, only to have it blown up. Negroes, mules, and captured supplies flood the Yankee camp. "Damn this war!" Colonel Dick mutters when he sees Granny, who has just been rescued from the river. "Damn it. Damn it."

Colonel Dick tries to repair some of the damage the Union troops have wreaked on the Southern people. He requisitions a hundred and ten mules and Negroes to Granny, along with ten chests of silver. But Granny makes use of his generosity and of the wartime situation to establish a business. Forgery replaces the lying, borrowing, and cursing of the early stories. Granny makes a virtue of necessity—her business actually is stealing on a broad basis, but is justified (she believes) by wartime conditions. Nevertheless, those who live by trickery may die by it. Granny conquers the Yankees, but is vanquished by "southern gentlemen"—"because she still believed that what side of a war a man fought on made him what he is."

As the war ends, the breakdown of all order affects Bayard profoundly. No legal system, no civil court of justice, no representative of law and order can be found to retaliate against the crime of Grumby and his band of thieves and murderers. With some help, Bayard tracks down his man, scares his companions out of Mississippi into Texas, and kills his grandmother's murderer. Then he and Ringo nail Grumby's body to the compress door and his hand to Granny's grave marker. Later, Bayard remarks that in being forced by circumstances to have to kill Grumby he had had to perform "more than should be required of children because there should be some limit to the age, the youth at least below which one should not have to kill."

In **"Skirmish at Sartoris,"**—an important linking story, and not merely an appendage, as some commentators have thought—Faulkner clearly shows that the ruthless habits of war have not been rooted out of a people pursuing peace. Bloodshed and lawlessness hover like hawks above the new young life which peacetime should bring. Neither the North nor the South had found a successful means of making the transition from war to peace. The election—in which a Negro is apparently the sole candidate for marshall—merely provides another kind of battlefield. Still, the opponents fight with guns, not ballots. Ironically, after John Sartoris has shot the two carpetbaggers, he makes bond to the sheriff while overriding George Wyatt's objections with the query, "Don't you see we are working for peace through law and order?"

Each time John Sartoris surmounts peace-time problems by wartime tactics, the narrator Bayard notes that the cheers which follow his success resemble the cheers that followed his heroic escapades during the war. It was "like the Yankees used to hear it.'' Further, John does not wait upon the formalities and legalities of that ''law and order'' through which he is striving to obtain peace. He forces the carpetbaggers to fire first so that his case will stand as self-defense. He appoints Drusilla (by what authority Faulkner does not say) to be the ''voting commissioner until the votes are cast and counted,'' and proclaims that the election will be held at his home. There, he stands brazenly over the ballot box and then proclaims the outcome of the election without counting the votes. Father's troops express their approval of his actions in war-whoops: ''It came back high and thin and ragged and fierce, like when the Yankees used to hear it out of the smoke and the galloping: 'Yaaaaay, Drusilla! . . . Yaaaaaay, John Sartoris! Yaaaaaaay!''

The events of **''An Odor of Verbena''** transpire nine years after those of **''Skirmish at Sartoris.''** Flashbacks fill in motivational gaps by relating incidents which shaped Bayard's character during that interval. The distance and increased knowledge of Bayard's character help make believable Bayard's dissociation of himself from the community's atmosphere of gallant unconcern for true peace and from his father's attitude of dictatorial supremacy. Bayard, the law student of the University of Mississippi, enters the scene from a background of education and cultivated sensibility. From that vantage point, he can initiate the real reconstruction of a war-torn South.

By the time Bayard reaches manhood, the recultivation of the soil has already begun. Verbena grows in the garden, the pastures are covered with grass, flowers bloom in the yard. Then, too, John Sartoris has built a railroad to replace the one the Yankees destroyed, and the Sartoris house, burned to the ground in **''Retreat,''** stands once again on its old landsite.

Disorders on many other levels, however, still run rampant. Shortly before the story opens, John Sartoris has killed two carpetbaggers and a neighboring hill man. Bayard clearly rejects his father's ruthlessness and disregard for human life. In Bayard's dream for the South, concern for human dignity would surely be the cornerstone.

Many Southerners regretted John Sartoris' treatment of Redmond. His constant taunting of a man with a clear record, the backbiting and slandering he employed not even as an election tool, but merely because it had become a habit with him, all this repelled Bayard. John had acquired Redmond's share of the railroad, too, by means which were more suited to a Snopes than to a Sartoris. This, too, Bayard rejected. Colonel John Sartoris talked a good game of ''moral house-cleaning.'' He said that he would not be armed when he went to meet Redmond, yet he wore his derringer under the coat-sleeve of his right arm, even if, as George Wyatt testifies, he made no move to fire it. Bayard wore no weapon when he confronted Redmond.

Colonel John Sartoris has come to regard law as an intellectual battlefield. He prepares himself to give up killing only because he feels that with Bayard's prowess at law, he will be able to obtain what he wants THROUGH legal means rather than OVER them. ''I have not needed you in my affairs so far,'' he tells Bayard,

> but from now on I shall. . . . What will follow will be a matter of consolidation, of pettifogging and doubtless chicanery in which I would be a babe in arms but in which you, trained in the law, can hold your own—our own. . . .

Bayard rejects this notion of law too. The first law is the law of personal responsibility and of respect for others. ''Thou shalt not kill,'' he feels is solidly based in man's nature. He would probably feel the same about lying, stealing, and cheating as he does about killing.

Throughout the early phases of the war, a tendency to regard other human beings not as persons but as forces or things begins to twist the Southern personality. Bayard and Ringo consider the Yankees merely as ''the bastuds,'' for which expression they are made to wash out their mouths with soap. Granny sees a difference between officers and the regular soldiers until, at the command of one officer, her house is burned. The she joins the two boys in her depersonalized judgment of all Northern forces as ''the bastuds.''

The Negroes go through a similar depersonalization: from ''Loosh and Philadelphy'' they become the singing, trudging mass, void of all personality, of all individuality. They are herded together with mules, requisitioned along with the mules and trunks of silver. In **''Skirmish at Sartoris,''** Ringo says ''They ain't no more niggers, in Jefferson nor nowhere else,'' because ''niggers'' have been abolished. Still the South treated Cassius Q. Benbow not as an individual, but as a ''nigger.'' And so Ringo remarks, ''This war ain't over. Hit just started good.'' In all these instances of depersonalization, only Bayard's relation with Ringo stresses individuality above racial qualities: ''What counted was, what one of us had done or seen that the other had not. . . .''

Bayard's emphasis on the dignity of the human being, his stress of individual worth, becomes most obvious in the flashback conversations with Drusilla recorded in **''An Odor of Verbena.''** Drusilla says Father's dream is to benefit all the people of the South. Bayard replies, ''But how can they get any good from what he wants to do for them if they are—after he had—.'' ''Killed some of them?'' Drusilla asks; ''I suppose you include those two carpetbaggers he had to kill to hold that first election, don't you?'' Bayard answers: ''They were men. Human beings.'' Drusilla will not grant the point. ''They were northerners, foreigners. . . . They were pirates.''

Bayard's method of handling his father's murderer again shows a tremendous respect for the individual. Though he could not have walked unarmed into Grumby's den, he feels he can enter Redmond's office carrying no weapon. Redmond shot his father in front, not in the back. His father was armed and expected trouble. Redmond was courageous; he had almost been forced, because of John's brutal taunting, to take the course he did in order to salvage his reputation. Redmond was one of those few men Bayard could face unarmed and escape unscathed.

If Bayard concretizes the new South's respect for the individual, so also does he direct the South toward a new respect for law. In **''Skirmish at Sartoris,''** we see mock elections, stolen ballot boxes, infiltration of carpetbaggers, and the countermeasures of violence agreed on by the Southern Whites. Bayard himself, in **''Vendée,''** had considered himself a minister of justice. Now, in the time of the new peace, law and order need to be reestablished. Gun rule must be relegated to the crises of war; vengeance must yield to due process of law; even the prewar custom of death-dueling must fall into the dead past. Redmond, ironically, is an attorney-at-law; Bayard, a law student. Yet no trial is held; no arrest is made. They merely confront one another—without bloodshed. The code-law of ''a life for a life'' crumbles and on its ruins can emerge a new South, respecting law and order rather than trying to control the processes of law.

Bayard, indeed, solves few problems in the course of the stories. But his process of maturation embodies the kind of maturation necessary to the South, if it is ever to create a new order on those several levels of human living treated above, where disorder had raged. (pp. 121-26)

Forrest L. Ingram, "William Faulkner: 'The Unvanquished'," in his Representative Short Story Cycles of the Twentieth Century: Studies in Literary Genre, *Mouton, 1971, pp. 106-42.*

HERBERT A. PERLUCK (essay date 1972)

[*In the following excerpt, Perluck departs from the usual reading of "The Bear" as a story of expiation, viewing Ike's repudiation of his inheritance as a flight from responsibility.*]

The usual reading of **"The Bear"** makes of Isaac McCaslin a kind of saint who, by repudiating his inheritance—the desecrated land upon which a whole people has been violated—performs an act of expiation and atonement which is a model for those acts that must follow before the curse upon the land is lifted. Ike's repudiation of the land, at twenty-one, with which the tortuous inner section of **"The Bear"** opens, and over which he and his cousin, McCaslin Edmonds, debate in the commissary, is seen in terms of what the reader understands Ike to have learned and attained under the influence of Sam Fathers in the untainted Wilderness: the "freedom and humility and pride." The story is of one man's repudiation of the forces of greed and materialism that have all but extinguished God's hope for man of freedom and generosity.

The whole sequence of the commissary, the Beauchamp legacy, and the later life of Isaac McCaslin, is thus ordinarily taken as a sort of complementary sequel to what may be called the hunt-narrative; Part IV in the total structure and intention of the work is a filling-out, past and future, of the "story proper," as it is sometimes regarded: the hunt-narrative and especially the episode of the fyce, in which the later renunciation, at twenty-one, is prefigured.

There is much, however, in this difficult portion of the work that suggests a contrary view. Instead of a romantic Christian pastoral of redemption, in which the repudiation of the land and earlier the apparently selfless rescue of the fyce from under the erect bear are seen as almost sanctifying gestures of renunciation, a searing tragedy of human desire and human limitation evolves, chiefly through ironic means. From McCaslin's scornful skepticism as he listens to Ike's account of God's circuitous providence, and the "lip-lift" of contempt when he realizes that even Ike does not wholly believe in his "freedom," to the almost hysterical laughter with which Part IV concludes, the principal effects are ironic.

The central thematic irony, however, upon which these effects are grounded, is slowly constructed of larger elements. The repudiation in the commissary *is* prefigured in the hunt-narrative; something of a parallel does develop between the selfless non-possession of Ike's gesture at twenty-one and the repudiation of passion earlier—that effort to preserve the idyll of the Big Woods, in the reluctance of both Ike and Sam Fathers to slay Old Ben. But the point of the parallel is not merely to provide background and extension to the "story-proper"; it is drawn and pressed home by McCaslin Edmonds on Ike because in both gestures there is weakness and something even sinister which cannot become clear to McCaslin, or to the reader, until the dense and complex drama of the debate in the commissary is enacted.

The terrible irony of Part IV develops in the growing awareness in the reader, as well as in the characters, of the discrepancy between what we and Ike supposed him to have achieved, to have attained to, and what in fact his repudiations actually represent. The whole inner section of **"The Bear"** reflects back on the hunt-narrative and forward into the last sequence: Ike's return at eighteen to the woods, which are being destroyed by the lumber company; his vague, troubled guilt at the sight of the nearly demented, grieving Boon. Coming where it does in the story structure, Part IV has the effect of making the reader, as it makes Ike and McCaslin, remember and painfully reinterpret the earlier events as of some dream-idyll of human perfection, of perhaps a kind of angelic pre-existence, now dissipated in the wakeful glare of the human reality. Slowly and relentlessly, Faulkner's intention takes hold in Part IV, in the tragic incompleteness of man, as the gulf is drawn between action, life as lived, and the memory of action and events, in which our dreams of life, our poems, are created.

"The Bear" is no Saint's Life; on the contrary, what it expresses ultimately is that there is no "freedom" in renunciation, no sanctity through repudiation—that actually there is no such thing as human sainthood as we have conceived it. If Isaac McCaslin is a saint at all, it is not in the traditional ascetic sense of a successful renunciation of the world and the flesh in atonement and expiation; it is rather a "sainthood" of *un*success, an unwitting, unwilled elevation produced in the tragic *defeat* of spirit and soul in the "uncontrollable mystery" of the world which men and "saints" must live in perforce. In much the same way that Kafka's Bucketrider is unaccountably (to him) "upraised" into the "regions of the icy mountains and [is] lost forever," Isaac McCaslin ascends without comprehending wherein that only "sainthood" man is allowed resides: in the anguished, complex heart. **"The Bear"** is a story of a renunciation that fails, as they all must. It is also the story of man's ineluctable fate of being only man. And on another level, it is a parable of man's pride, in his trying to be more than man, and of the evil this pride accomplishes in its condescending ascription of all that man does not want to see in himself to a certain few untouchables, the Boons of the world. (pp. 173-75)

McCaslin tried to explain to Ike, by quoting the "Ode [on a Grecian Urn]," why Ike saved the fyce instead of killing Old Ben, or at least what McCaslin had thought then—that the humility and pride Ike had wanted to learn in order to become worthy of the Wilderness and of a manhood in which the Bear was hunted by men like Sam Fathers, Major de Spain, Walter Ewell, and McCaslin, that these he had just learned, had come to possess, through forbearance and selfless courage, through, in short, a kind of renunciation, *non*possession. McCaslin's purpose in quoting Keats had been to show Ike how we may pursue bravely and fiercely and yet not kill, out of pity and love; how we may love by not loving; how we may be proud and humble, fierce and gentle, at the same time; how by not possessing in the heart we may possess all. (p. 177)

Ike's failure to kill Old Ben was a way out, an escape from himself; . . . Keats had only helped him to repudiate, and so think he had *freed* himself from, what being human and alive in time imposes on a man. McCaslin hadn't told him that what we may know in the heart is not what we are allowed to live. The non-possession, the renunciations, and thus the "freedom" which may be realized in the heart—this Ike has tried to *live*. "Sam Fathers set me free," he protests to McCaslin. . . . But the freedom he had indeed obtained was only the "freedom of the heart," which Sam Fathers showed him how to achieve by virtue of giving himself up to the Wilderness, as he does when he "relinquishes" his gun and compass and goes alone to see and be seen by Old Ben—much as Henry Fleming, in that other story of a boy's initiation into manhood, comes to touch the great god Death and discovers it is only death after all. He momentarily relinquishes self and pride, in effect—the way they are relinquished provisionally in a poem—the better to confront that naked red heart of the world, the Wilderness of the human heart, which is "free" only when it is so confronted and acknowledged. This "freedom" is from the blind, uncomprehending *fear* of the "Wilderness" and its creatures, but is not, as Ike would desire it—a confusion that leads to his agony in the commissary—a freedom from the necessary human commitment in acts and time. The moral freedom to choose *not* to act does not exist, except in the heart, where it is not a moral but a spiritual or aesthetic freedom. Sam Fathers set Ike free only in the sense of his enabling him to look at *all* that a man can feel and do, *all* that the "Wilderness" contains; he could not free him from himself. So it was not the fyce that had kept him from shooting—out of love and forbearance; he had, in fact, blanched from that full sight of himself as a man, who at the same time he was humble and loved the thing he pursued, was a slayer and ravener.

The "poem," as it were, that Ike has tried to live is one in which his hunting of Old Ben but his not having to kill him is the chief symbol—as it is even now in the commissary. And it *was* very much like the girl and the youth on the Urn, although Ike had not quite been able to see the analogy. He has wished, Hamlet-like, to kill and yet not kill, to realize fully a state of "being" out of time, which is realized only in a play, in art, and in the complex heart. But the Prince must slay, the hunter must slay; they cannot, if they would be princes and hunters, preserve that moment of excruciated sensibility in the timeless drama of the heart. The "Old Free Fathers" were aware of this painful human paradox of action, in which man commits himself in the irrevocable, and they celebrated it in the sacramental gesture of grief and responsibility (but there was also pride) for the life they spilled: a consecrating gesture—the smearing the warm blood of a youth's first kill on his forehead—which absolved a man from *regret* but not from *grief*. (pp. 178-79)

Faulkner's meaning in **"The Bear"** is that if man would live, he must be prepared for the dying too; if he would love, he must also grieve for the spilled life that loving and living require. Simply to repudiate the spilling, to relinquish the grief, by relinquishing the passion, is to remove oneself from life, and from love, which, like the hunt, necessarily involves us in blood. There is no renunciation of life and the world which we can choose to make, and there can be no "acceptance" of the inevitabilities; we may only choose life. What we may renounce is only renunciation itself, and what we may attain to is not a regenerate state, sainthood, being, but our humanity. We gain life by "losing" it only in the sense of having it *taken away,* of trying to live what is in the heart, and failing. Renunciation, "acceptance," is to surrender life to live in the "pretty rooms" of sonnets ("and Isaac McCaslin, not yet Uncle Ike . . . living in one small cramped fireless rented room in a Jefferson boarding-house . . . with his kit of brand-new carpenter's tools . . . the shotgun McCaslin had given him with his name engraved in silver . . . and the bright tin coffee-pot." We prefer to think the Boons of this world do the slaying, and our renunciations are our way of *allowing* them to. We construct our "pretty rooms" right in the Wilderness where we play at virtue and perform our purification rites, just as Major de Spain, Walter Ewell, McCaslin Edmonds and the rest did each year. The Negroes and their white masters, at the camp site, lived under an entirely different dispensation from the one which ordinarily prevailed in town, in real life, where they were virtually slaves. In the Big Woods they could play at being untainted, guiltless—there one felt free. The pursuit of Old Ben over the years is unsuccessful, not merely because he is a wily old beast, almost supernatural, but because they didn't want to kill him, and not killing him is the ritual of purification; by this, and by the altered relationship of Negro and white master, they could free themselves, for a while at least. Sam Fathers had begun, long before, to live at the camp site all year round, but when they approach him after he has collapsed, he murmurs, "Let me out, master," knowing that only death can really free him, that he hasn't been free at all in the white man's lodge and woods. The Boons, with the hard button eyes—the insensitive, un-human destroyers and raveners, as we conceive them—are there at the last, almost by design, to shatter the pretty glass room of this dream of redemption: we create them and then sacrifice them in our condescensions and our renunciations in this last act of the ritual. (pp. 193-94)

Herbert A. Perluck, "'The Bear': An Unromantic Reading," in Religious Perspectives in Faulkner's Fiction: Yoknapatawpha and Beyond, *edited by J. Robert Barth, S.J., University of Notre Dame Press, 1972, pp. 173-201.*

WALTER TAYLOR (essay date 1974)

[*In the following excerpt, Taylor discusses the difficulty of reconciling elements of nostalgia for ante-bellum life with the evil of racism in the story "Was."*]

[**"Was"**] is told through the point of view of Cass Edmonds, Faulkner's most articulate defender of the plantation ethic in ***Go Down, Moses.*** A youthful orphan at the time of the action, living with his aging twin uncles, Amodeus ("Buddy") and Theophilus ("Buck"), Cass is just becoming aware of his surroundings. It is natural that he should remember the story sentimentally, and that is the way it proceeds.

The reader is affectionately introduced to the genial disorder of the McCaslin household as a pet fox runs a frantic race for his life with the McCaslin dogs, who have their own room in the house. This, however, is the least of the twins' problems. Tomey's Turl has run away, and Buck is sure he is headed for nearby Beauchamp plantation to see his girl, Tennie. That means Hubert Beauchamp will bring him back, and with him for an extended visit, Hubert's husband-hunting sister, Sophonsiba. Buck has no alternative but to prevent such a disaster by catching Turl himself, even if it means temporary exposure to this formidable enemy. But nothing seems to work for Buck. When he sets the Beauchamp dogs on Turl, the pack recognizes an old friend, and quarry and dogs disappear nonchalantly into the woods together. That night, weary from the chase, Buck climbs into a bed in the first unlocked room he can find in the Beauchamp house—only to find Miss Sophonsiba occupying it. Thus captured, he must be won back from the Beauchamps by means of his twin's only competitive talent—poker. At last, thanks to Turl's crafty dealing (if Buddy wins, Turl is to get Tennie), the McCaslins gain a tenuous victory, preserving for the moment the purity of their rustic retreat from at least one of the two women who would defile it.

Such is ante-bellum life at the McCaslins, as remembered by Cass Edmonds. The mood of sentimental nostalgia always predominates. In spite of slavery, everyone lives a casual, semi-serious life, and the worst tragedy imaginable is marriage. (p. 75)

But if this attitude of genial nostalgia seems to predominate in **"Was,"** the story carries a substratum of suggestion which invites the reader to see the action differently. This other way of looking at the events of **"Was"** is only hinted at in the story, but the hints are difficult to ignore. In Faulkner's version of the paradise of bachelors old Buck and Buddy are not "wise innocents" before the fall. . . . Isaac McCaslin's mythology of the New Eden—developed in **"The Bear"**—indicates that evil was brought into the land before their time. But there is no necessity to turn to the remainder of the novel to learn that there has already been a tragedy in the McCaslin paradise which involved women and a kind of sin, a tragedy which has had a profound effect on the twins. **"Was"** itself leaves the matter perfectly plain.

The reader is made aware throughout the tale that all is not right with Tomey's Turl. Youthful Cass is very conscious of Turl's pigmentation. His hands are "saddle colored," he notices on one occasion; on another that Turl deals the cards with "arms that were supposed to be black but were not quite white." There are other hints. Turl refers to Buck as "old Buck," rather than, according to plantation custom, "Mr. Buck." He has, Cass reflects, "maybe . . . been running off from Uncle Buck for so long that he . . . [has] even got used to running away like a white man would do it." Hubert Beauchamp is the first to speak of the situation openly. Asked to buy Turl as husband for Tennie, he refuses to "have that damn white half-McCaslin on his place even as a free gift." Mr. Hubert, however, is the only character in the story who calls Turl "McCaslin." It is clear from **"Was"** that Turl is close kin to the twins—if not a half-brother, then at least a cousin—and that the subject, though no secret, is taboo. (p. 76)

Faulkner, furthermore, repeatedly introduces material which is calculated to shock a great many readers. The twins insist—perhaps to an abnormal degree—on demonstrating that Turl is a slave by treating him like one. Over and over Buck refers to his illegitimate brother as "my nigger." Turl is the butt of much of the story's humor. Buck hunts him as though he were wild game. "You stay back where he wont see you and flush," he tells Cass. "I'll circle him through the woods and we will bay him at the creek ford." Or again, "He's going to earth. We'll cut back to the house and head him before he can den." The climax of all this comes with Turl "treed" in Tennie's cabin. When Cass bangs on the back door with a stick, Turl explodes out the front past the helpless Buck, who lands on the whiskey bottle he carries in his rear pocket, refusing "to move until he knew for certain it was just whiskey and not blood" that he feels. Then, with chilling objectivity, he blames himself for his failure. "Afterward," Cass relates, "Uncle Buck admitted that it was his own mistake, that he had forgotten when even a little child should have known: not ever to stand right in front of or right behind a nigger when you scare him; but always to stand to one side of him." If the prevailing mood of **"Was"** is genial reminiscence, in short, there is nothing genial about what all this implies. Hence it should not be altogether surprising that . . . [many critics] have found **"Was"** "horrifying."

The problem here is that **"Was"** persuasively renders two conflicting sets of values. On one level we laugh with Cass at the brusque burlesque of Buck's and Turl's capers; on another, we are repelled by the same antics. For critics who do not ignore this dual perspective, a natural reaction has been to search the text for a point at which the opposed themes are reconciled. [The critic] Volpe, for whom Turl's fate is "horrifying," believes he has found a "catalyst that transforms a horror story into a humorous warm, nostalgic tale of the Old South": it "is a feeling of security" which Faulkner shows "rooted in the formalized and accepted pattern of Negro-white relations." But many readers will react less optimistically; will find themselves unable to reconcile a situation in which slavery and miscegenation are ridiculed. (pp. 76-7)

On being questioned, . . . Faulkner spoke freely of the tragedy of Turl's plight. Asked if Turl was "on the same plane as the fox," he replied that the twins "by instinct knew that slavery was wrong, but they didn't know quite what to do about it. And . . . in daily life, they would use the terms in which the Negro was on a level with the dog or the animal they ran." This was true "especially in the heat of a race." Their attitude was not without a certain odd sense of values; Turl "would have received the same respect that the bear or the deer would. . . . They wouldn't have betrayed him, tricked him. . . . They would have run him all fair with the dogs and if he could escape, could kill the dogs and get away, good for him." But that was all—"If he couldn't, it was too bad." What that amounted to was that Turl was indeed "at that time" no more to the twins than the fox; and this was true "at the very same time that these twin brothers had believed that there was something outrageous and wrong in slavery and they had done what they could" about that problem.

Unsystematic as they are, these comments suggest much about **"Was."** The last statement, in particular, seems clearly to indicate that the reader is expected to hold conflicting opinions simultaneously in a kind of suspended judgement. The key phrase in it is "at the very same time." Taken together, Faulkner's comments imply (1) that the twins have genuinely done the best they were capable of about slavery; (2) that there is an unplanned cruelty which is nonetheless quite real; and (3) that the situation is somehow very funny. Of equal interest is the fact that Faulkner made no more effort in his interviews than he seems to make in the story to reconcile these views. I do not believe Faulkner intended to ignore any of the implications of his story, and I do not believe that he intended to reconcile them. . . . (p. 78)

Walter Taylor, "Horror and Nostalgia: The Double Perspective of Faulkner's 'Was'," in The Southern Humanities Review, *Vol. VIII, No. 1, Winter, 1974, pp. 74-84.*

EBERHARD ALSEN (essay date 1977)

[Alsen is a German-born American critic. In the following excerpt, he analyzes Rider in "Pantaloon in Black" as an existential hero who rejects the Christian concept of a just and merciful God and engineers his own lynching in order to expose the injustice of white oppression.]

[Rider's death by lynching in **"Pantaloon in Black"**] is not a tragic "catastrophe" but a triumphant assertion of Rider's individuality and freedom, an act that, paradoxical as it may seem, gives meaning to his existence.

The first and longer part of the two-part story opens with the funeral of Mannie, to whom Rider, a giant of a sawmill worker, had been married for only six months. In the first scene, Rider mystifies his family, his friends and the reader by his strange behavior. After placing the first shovelful of earth on Mannie's coffin, he refuses to let go of the shovel and insists on filling Mannie's grave singlehandedly. Then he rejects invitations to dinner by his aunt and to a drinking bout by his friends and stalks off. During this scene we see Rider only from the outside, but from the second scene on, and for most of Part 1, we are allowed insight into his emotions and motivations. The last scene of Part 1, the scene which describes Rider's killing of a white man, is again narrated objectively and thus creates similar puzzlement as the first scene. And although Part 2 of the story is told by an obtuse outsider, a sheriff's deputy who has no understanding of Rider's personality, this part nevertheless answers many of the questions that Part 1 raises.

As Rider walks from the cemetery to his cabin and as we begin to get glimpses of his thoughts, there occurs a very significant flashback which reveals much of Rider's character and which associates him for the first time with the dice game, a metaphor that later becomes very important for an understanding of Rider's view of life. In this passage we learn that Rider had led a meaningless life before he fell in love with Mannie, a life whose primary rewards were "the women bright and dark and for all purposes nameless" and "the Saturday and Sunday dice and whiskey." Then one day, when he saw Mannie, he said to himself: "'Ah'm thu wid all dat'," and married her. Under the influence of Mannie, who kept his clothes exceptionally neat, served his dinner exactly on time every day, and saved some of Rider's pay every Friday, Rider became an extremely reliable and respected man. He paid his rent promptly, he refloored the porch and rebuilt the roof of his rented cabin, and he was put in charge of all the timber workers at the sawmill because "the gang he headed moved a third again as much timber between sunup and sundown as any other moved. . . ." Thus, because of his commitment to another human being, Rider changed from an undistinguished and undistinguishable person to an outstanding individual who commanded dignity and respect.

But after Mannie's death Rider allows his meticulously clean clothes to become dirty, he crams food in his mouth with both hands, he returns to drinking liquor, spilling it all over himself, and he eventually even returns to shooting dice. But this change is not really a relapse, nor is it merely the result of overpowering grief, as most critics have assumed. Instead, it masks Rider's spiritual and intellectual crisis, his quarrel with God, or better, his re-evaluation of his view of life. And in this crisis lies the key to the meaning of the story.

Rider acts so strangely at the funeral because he wants to get away from the cemetery as quickly as possible in order to be alone and to be able to think, and because he wants to get away from the talk about a God who, without provocation, has destroyed Mannie's life and thereby deprived Rider's existence of its purpose and meaning. For as is revealed later on, Rider considers Mannie's death to be proof of God's senseless cruelty. (pp. 169-71)

The final change in Rider's beliefs is illustrated in his conversation with his aunt just before he goes to the fatal dice game. As Rider arrives at his aunt's cabin, still carrying his jug of whiskey, his aunt asks him to "come home, whar we kin help you" and tells him that liquor won't do him any good. But Rider asserts: "'Hit done awready hope me. Ah'm awright now'." By "awright" Rider means, as his subsequent comments show, that he is now able to repudiate his old notion of God. The change in Rider's view of life is indicated by his changing his mind about whether or not the liquor has done him any good. For it was not liquor but thinking that has brought about this change in him:

> Then he said it. It was his own voice, without either grief or amazement, speaking quietly out of the tremendous panting of his chest which in a moment now would begin to strain at the walls of this room too. But he would be gone in a moment.
>
> "Nome," he said. "Hit aint done me no good."
>
> "And hit cant! Cant nothing help you but Him! Ax Him! Tole Him about hit! He wants to hyar you and help you!"
>
> "Efn He God, Ah dont needs to tole Him. Efn He God, He awready know hit. Awright. Hyar Ah is. Leff Him come down hyar and do me some good."

In this crucial passage, Rider reveals that his thinking has led him to the point where he can no longer believe in the just and benevolent God in whom he has been brought up to put his "faith and trust." Instead, Rider has begun to see this God as the "big boy" who has challenged him, a deceitful and calculating enemy who is playing with loaded dice. (p. 172)

It is during this conversation with his aunt that Rider's plan to foil the diceman apparently takes shape. For when his aunt gets upset about Rider's repudiation of God, he simply walks off and goes straight to the sawmill where he kills Birdsong. By doing that he determines the shape of his fate and thus gives meaning to an existence which God had robbed of meaning by taking away Mannie.

As soon as Rider arrives at the sawmill, it becomes clear that he is planning to kill Birdsong in order to get himself lynched. When he knocks at the door of the toolroom where the crap game is in progress, he says: "'Open hit. Hit's me. Ah'm snakebit and bound to die'." What Birdsong and the other diceplayers take for drunken raving—and with good reason, for Rider has finished his jug by now and is staggering—has actually much deeper significance. Rider's comment about the snakebite, which he repeats twice more, refers on the surface to "snake poison," a Southern slang term for bootlegged whiskey. Rider might also be alluding to the biblical snake, to Satan. For like Satan, Rider now considers himself God's enemy. And thirdly, Rider's reference to the snakebite also suggests an allusion to "snake eyes" in craps, for Rider is "out of the game" of life now because he has decided to bring about his own death. (pp. 172-73)

As soon as Rider confronts Birdsong, we find that he is not as drunk as he seems and that he is, in fact, plotting against the white man. For when Birdsong doesn't want to let Rider in on the game because he is drunk, Rider plays on the man's greed and says: "'Ah aint drunk. Ah just cant wawk straight fer dis yar money weighin me down'"; and once in the game, Rider raises the stakes twice in order to make cheating attractive to Birdsong. What Rider has expected, promptly happens. As he spots Birdsong trying to substitute loaded dice for the regular ones, he seizes his wrist and holds it "until the white man's hand sprang open and the second pair of dice clattered onto the floor beside the first two and the white man wrenched free and sprang up and back and reached the hand backwards towards the pocket where the pistol was.'' But ''in the second before the half drawn pistol exploded [Rider] actually struck at the white man's throat'' with his razor, slashing his neck clear to the bone.

Although the killing of Birdsong is premeditated, it is technically not murder. For as the passage clearly indicates, Rider kills the man in self defense. But this is the Deep South of 1940, and Rider knows that when a black man kills a white man, self defense or not, the black man is just asking to be lynched. (p. 173)

That we see the white people in the story as corrupt and inhuman is largely due to the fact that earlier we have been allowed insight into Rider's character, that we have learned of his change after he married Mannie, and that we have witnessed his spiritual and intellectual crisis after Mannie's death. Because we understand Rider's character much better than does the deputy, we realize that the white man's obtusity and inhumanity are the direct result of his belief that blacks ''aint human.'' But although most readers will have a better understanding of Rider's behavior than the deputy who tells the story, they will be just as puzzled as he is by what Rider does and says during his struggle with the chaingang that Ketcham uses to subdue him and lock him up again.

An understanding of the story hinges on an understanding of this last scene. This is how the deputy describes Rider's battle with the chaingang:

> . . . for a full minute that nigger would grab them as they come in and fling them clean across the room like they was rag dolls, saying, ''Ah aint trying to git out. Ah aint trying to git out,'' until at last they pulled him down—a big mass of nigger heads and arms and legs boiling around on the floor and even then Ketcham says every now and then a nigger would come flying out and go sailing through the air across the room, spraddled out like a flying squirrel and with his eyes sticking out like car headlights, until at last they had him down and Ketcham went in and begun peeling away niggers until he could see him laying there under the pile of them, laughing, with tears big as glass marbles running across his face and down past his ears and making a kind of popping sound on the floor like somebody dropping bird eggs, laughing and laughing and saying, ''Hit look lack Ah just cant quit thinking. Look lack Ah just cant quit.''

As on the day before, when he lifted a ten foot cypress log, and as earlier in the last scene, when he ripped his cot out of the floor of his cell and tossed it against the wall, Rider is once more resorting to superhuman exertion in an effort to calm his restless mind and to ''quit thinking'' about the loss of his wife, the loss of his ''faith and trust'' in God, and the resulting meaninglessness of his life. And while he has made up his mind to get himself lynched and thereby give his existence some meaning, it stands to reason that he would have preferred life with Mannie to any kind of death, no matter how meaningful.

But although Rider can't ''quit thinking'' disturbing thoughts, he laughs and laughs and laughs. This laughter is perhaps more ambiguous than anything else in the story. The simplest interpretation would be that Rider is laughing at himself, at his inability to ''quit thinking'' of Mannie's death and of the injustice of God and man. Seen this way, his laughter would suggest that he realizes that it is only with his death that he will be able to overcome the idea of God in his mind and thereby become free. I find this explanation unsatisfactory because there is really nothing humorous about the things that Rider can't ''quit thinking'' about.

While the causes of Rider's present situation are nothing to laugh about, there is, however, a certain irony and even absurdity in the situation itself. The irony of the situation is that the white sheriff and jailer are pretending to protect Rider from the lynching party, while Rider is trying to make it easier for them to lynch him. Rider might therefore be laughing at the inability of the white people to see that by planning his own lynching, he is robbing it of significance as punishment. Rider might also be laughing about the absurdity of the position he is in, the paradox that it is only by choosing the time and nature of his death that he can determine the shape and meaning of his existence.

This is to me the most satisfactory interpretation of Rider's laughter. It is suggested by the way in which Rider has changed his view of life after Mannie's death. As we have seen, he has repudiated his Christian upbringing because God has shown himself to be as hostile and unfair as the white man. For like Birdsong and other racist whites, God has loaded the dice against Rider to make sure that a black man does not win in the game of life. Therefore Rider has decided to wrest control of his life away from God, and in order to accomplish that he first of all tries to kill the idea of a God in his mind and then plans and brings about his own death. As a result, he becomes, for the first time in his life, truly free. Just as Camus' Sisyphus accepts his damnation proudly and achieves victory over the gods by embracing his fate, so Rider becomes the master of his destiny by determining the time and manner of his death. Unlike Sisyphus, however, Rider deliberately puts himself into the hands of his oppressors so he can make them his instruments in asserting his freedom and individuality.

But Rider's death has not only philosophical significance. The way in which his death is reported and the way in which Part 2 of the story retells, from the white people's point of view, most of the incidents already narrated in Part 1, makes us aware of the degradation and oppression of blacks like Rider. The shift in point of view makes apparent the bigotry and inhumanity not only of the deputy who tells the story of the events leading to Rider's death, but also of Birdsong, Maydew, Ketcham, the coroner, and, in fact, of all the whites in the story. Thus it is because of the story's narrative structure that we become aware of the possibility that in killing Birdsong, Rider may have been striking out not merely at one exploiter, but at white oppression in general, and that, by being lynched for it, he becomes a hero and martyr.

For Rider's killing of Birdsong not only challenges the entire social order that the whites in the story represent, but it also makes the whites demonstrate the cruelty and inhumanity of the attitudes on which that order is based. By killing one oppressor and by showing that he is not afraid of being lynched, Rider serves notice to the white community that they cannot always count on blacks to accept white oppression in the spirit of Christian passivity and humility. Rider's bringing about his own death through the killing of Birdsong is therefore not only an act that has philosophical or personal meaning but an act that has social significance as well. (pp. 176-78)

Eberhard Alsen, "An Existentialist Reading of Faulkner's 'Pantaloon in Black'," in Studies in Short Fiction, *Vol. 14, No. 2, Spring, 1977, pp. 169-78.*

JAMES B. CAROTHERS (essay date 1983)

[In the following excerpt, Carothers asserts that Faulkner's short stories deserve greater critical attention than they have received in the past. He focuses his discussion on the character of the trickster in Faulkner's short fiction.]

[We] have been a long time in coming to the view that Faulkner's short stories deserve the same careful, systematic, and respectful attention that has been accorded to his novels, and that view is by no means common today. Though we have recently come a long way from the time when a critic could omit discussion of the short stories from his guide to Faulkner on the grounds that they "do not appreciably add to our knowledge of Faulkner's techniques and ideas," much of the recent work on the short stories continues to manifest the same critical attitudes and habits of mind that caused the vast majority of Faulkner's short stories to be ignored, denigrated, or simply misread during the earlier years.

Simplified to primer class, my thesis is that short stories were, for Faulkner, considerably more than a way to make money or a way to make novels, and . . . , while some significant and encouraging work has been done on the short stories in recent years, we are going to have to question, and to modify or discard some of the prevailing notions, habits, and practices of the past if we are to deal responsibly with the short stories in the future. (pp. 205-06)

As a general procedure, I suggest that we ought to approach individual Faulkner short stories with an openness to the possibility that each of them has a coherent and discoverable narrative structure, a setting in place and time appropriate to the narrative situation, characters who are rendered with sufficient precision, solidity, and depth to stand up on their hind legs and cast shadows, and serious thematic purpose to reward close reading. We should approach each story, in other words, prepared to believe that it may have meaning and value independent of its eventual place in a Faulkner novel, a short story volume, or his income ledger. (p. 211)

At the risk of seeming to offer a formulaic reduction of my own, I want now to sketch a Faulkner formula that occurs repeatedly in his short fiction and his novels. As I suggested earlier, I believe that interest in the poetics of Faulkner's short story collections has sometimes led us to neglect the poetics of individual Faulkner short stories. Faulkner himself said that his stories often began with an image or picture in his mind, or with a situation or character, but always with the aim of rendering "some moving passionate moment of the human condition distilled to its absolute essence." While this general formulation is useful and important, it does not help us to identify the source of the *substance* of Faulkner's fiction, and so, for a portion of that substance, I wish to call attention to a character type that occurs almost ubiquitously within the Faulkner canon, particularly in his comic and humorous fiction, and most particularly in his short stories.

The character is the trickster, by which I mean any individual who practices deceit for personal gain. In the trickster Faulkner had ready to hand a character, a situation, and a vehicle for plot development from the beginning to the end of his career. The Faulkner trickster is at once a generalized type and a very particular individual, and probably owes something to a variety of sources. His Indian and black tricksters—Ikkemotubbe and Crawford in **"A Justice,"** Lucas Beauchamp in **"A Point of Law"** and **"Gold Is Not Always,"** for example—have close affinities with clearly identifiable character types within their respective ethnic traditions, but Faulkner's knowledge of the trickster figure undoubtedly owes something to other sources, Mark Twain and the Southwestern humorists, Shakespeare, Cervantes, and the Greek drama, to name some of the most likely. And the variety of possible sources is reflected in the fact that Faulkner himself added substantially to the trickster tradition.

A trickster appears in Faulkner's very first published short story, **"Landing in Luck,"** in the person of Cadet Thompson, a thoroughly dislikable individual who seeks to represent his amazingly fortunate landing as proof of his aeronautical skill. Other early trickster figures appear in **"The Liar"** and **"Sunset"** among the New Orleans pieces, though the figures there are not rendered with particular skill or sympathy. But about this time Faulkner also began to write *Father Abraham,* in which, by creating the consummate trickster, Flem Snopes, he opened for himself a rich mine of humor that he never truly exhausted. Flem, we are told in *Father Abraham,* "had reduced all human conduct to a single workable belief: that some men are fools, but all men are no honester than the occasion requires." Flem's success at foisting the untamable ponies on Frenchman's Bend while escaping legal responsibility for the havoc and destruction they wreak there derives from this precept, and the pattern is maintained consistently through the versions of this incident that were recounted in *Father Abraham,* **"Spotted Horses,"** and *The Hamlet*. Flem functions as trickster in unloading the Old Frenchman's place in both **"Lizards in Jamshyd's Courtyard"** and *The Hamlet,* and Flem's trickster nature is apparent throughout the Snopes trilogy.

A number of other stories that Faulkner eventually adapted for his Snopes saga, such as **"Fool About a Horse"** and **"The Hound,"** have significant trickster elements, and a large number of Faulkner's short stories develop the plot of the trickster tricked. Where Faulkner's earliest trickster stories describe characters who simply trick others, or who are simply tricked themselves, this later group shows more sophisticated development and comic reversals, as when Pap in **"Fool About a Horse"** is gulled by Pat Stamper with a fish hook, a bicycle pump, and some shoe blacking into buying back at a dear price a horse he had traded cheaply away earlier in the day. Surratt's practical joke on Luke Provine in **"A Bear Hunt"** is compounded by the tricks of Uncle Ash and the Indians so that the result is not only a good scare for Provine, but a sound thrashing for Surratt as well. Ernest Cotton's murderous treachery in **"The Hound"** is betrayed by his own guilt and ineptitude as well as by the howling of his victim's dog. More complexly comic reversals occur in **"Mule in the Yard"** and in **"Centaur in Brass,"** two excellent stories that are unusual in that they were included in ***Collected Stories,*** even though Faulkner already had plans for them in subsequent volumes of the Snopes trilogy.

Trickster figures and plots abound in the stories of ***The Unvanquished*** as well, with Granny's silver-and-mule business being the most obvious. Granny serves as a trickster also in **"Ambuscade"** when she saves Bayard and Ringo by hiding them under her skirts. John Sartoris proves himself to be an accomplished trickster by capturing sixty Yankees virtually without assistance and by escaping from the Yankees himself

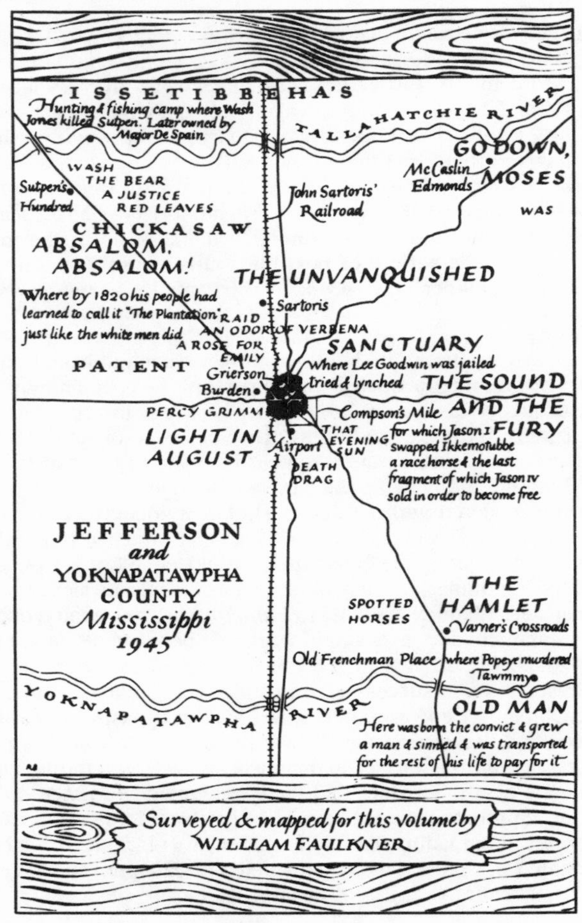

Faulkner's map of Jefferson and Yoknapatawpha County, noting the locales of his various novels and stories. Courtesy of Jill Faulkner Summers.

by pretending to be lame, hard-of-hearing, and dull-witted. And Granny's death at the hands of Grumby is, among other things, the result of her own overreaching as a trickster.

Faulkner also wrote trickster stories in the latter portion of his career, as evidenced by **"Shingles for the Lord," "A Courtship,"** *Notes on a Horsethief,* **"Hog Pawn,"** and **"By the People."** In several of these later stories he developed a theme that was also sounded in the later novels: that the respectable community must occasionally resort to trickery to overcome threats from within or without. This is particularly evident in a story like **"By the People,"** when Ratliff thwarts Clarence Snopes, but it had also been demonstrated by the supposedly bumbling Gavin Stevens as early as 1932 in **"Smoke."**

Such variations on the trickster character, subject, and theme suggest, I hope, the incredible variety of Faulkner's short fiction. Some of his tricksters are successful, some are unsuccessful. Some trick themselves, and some are tricked by others in turn. Some of them are essentially harmless, some are dangerous, and some are even murderous. Some are subversive and some are reputable. Trickster characters and situations appear in Faulkner's apprentice fiction, in short stories that he reworked for novels, and in stories that continue to stand splendidly in their own right. I do not mean to suggest that the trickster is the essential figure in Faulkner's humor, for it is simply one of a number of elements of his humor, but I would insist that Faulkner's tricksters can be examined in extensive variety and in careful isolation within the texts of his short stories.

The same must also be said for many of the other more or less traditional topics of Faulkner studies: Faulkner's attitudes towards women or towards blacks, the Civil War, World War I, aviation, Christianity, literature, marriage, love and death, his use of point-of-view, his handling of narrative chronology, his characteristic settings in place and time, his prose style. In addition, some other possible areas for future study seem to be unique to the short stories. We need, I think, to know a good deal more than we currently do about Faulkner's reading within the short story form, both classics and contemporaries, and we would benefit particularly from more detailed knowledge of Faulkner's reading of such writers as Poe, Hawthorne, Henry James, Joyce, and Hemingway, to list some of the obvious possibilities. We need guides to the short stories as detailed and comprehensive as the various guides to his novels. And I have little doubt that these things will be accomplished, if we can cease viewing the short stories as "lesser Faulkner," or the key to the solution of some other problems. Given proper attention, Faulkner's short stories reveal of their author what Faulkner himself wrote of the autobiographical character in the story fragment from which I have taken my title: "There was a giant in him. . . ." (pp. 224-27)

James B. Carothers, "Faulkner's Short Stories: 'And Now What's to Do'," in New Directions in Faulkner Studies: Faulkner and Yoknapatawpha, 1983, *edited by Doreen Fowler and Ann J. Abadie, University Press of Mississippi, 1984, pp. 202-27.*

W. E. SCHLEPPER (essay date 1984)

[In the following excerpt, Schlepper discusses Faulkner's use of the detective story to explore the themes of truth and justice in Knight's Gambit.]

The six stories collected in Faulkner's ***Knight's Gambit,*** written between 1932 and 1940, were not greeted with much critical enthusiasm upon publication, nor have they received a great deal of attention since, although Faulkner's fame has, of course, caused some interest in them. What attention they have received has mainly concentrated on Gavin Stevens, who figures prominently in each of the stories and provides a link with several of the novels, thus placing ***Knight's Gambit*** in the context of Yoknapatawpha County—sufficient reason, it would seem, for asking whether these stories add to our understanding of that world.

Gavin Stevens remains the obvious starting-point. But although he plays an important part in ***Knight's Gambit,*** he can hardly be claimed to be the protagonist—in the sense that his existence is at stake—with the exception, perhaps, of the title story of the collection [**"Knight's Gambit"**]. . . . My stress here is upon the thematic structure of the book rather than the development of Stevens' personality, emphasizing the themes of truth and justice.

One type of detective story, exemplified by Agatha Christie's, rests on the understanding that (a) the detective's superior intelligence and insight will correlate details of the data in a way not thought of at the time by the other characters or the reader, but which later, when explained, will instantly fall into place, and (b) that once the detective has discovered the truth and presented his reasoning to the baffled audience, justice ensues and social order is restored. Faulkner initially proceeds on the same assumptions—for example, in **"Smoke":** "It seems to me now that we must have known all the time" and the last paragraph of the story; in **"Monk"**; and in **"Hand upon the Waters":**

> The sheriff rose. ". . . Just what made you suspect something was wrong? What was it the rest of us seem to have missed?"
>
> "It was that paddle," Stevens said.
>
> "Paddle?"
>
> "Didn't you ever run a trotline, a trotline right at your camp? You don't paddle, you pull the boat hand over hand . . . and the paddle stayed in his house. If you had ever been there, you would have seen it. But the paddle was in the skiff when that boy found it."

At the end of **"Smoke,"** after the murderer has convicted himself, there is general agreement as to what is to follow. Life in Jefferson will be in order again. This conclusion seems to explain why Faulkner included the story in the collection, placing it first, a fact which critics have found puzzling.

What seems to be fact at first in **"Smoke"** is revealed as misinterpretation or illusion when Stevens shows that the observed details have been connected wrongly (the stick marks; the impossibility of passing Uncle Job) and that the first confession is also wrong. The reason for the confusion is jumping to conclusions, or, as Faulkner puts it:

> But men are moved so much by preconceptions. It is not realities, circumstances, that astonish us; it is the concussion of what we should have known, if we had only not been so busy believing what we discover later we had taken for the truth for no other reason than that we happened to be believing it at the moment.

In **"Smoke,"** it takes Stevens' putting his finger on the relevant facts and relating them correctly for the truth to be revealed. After that, the technicalities of Granby Dodge's arrest and sentence are left out. Truth entails justice and general satisfaction. But **"Smoke"** is the only story in which truth and justice are virtually identical. **"An Error in Chemistry"** states explicitly what the others also show:

> "I'm interested in truth," the sheriff said.
>
> "So am I," Uncle Gavin said. "It's so rare. But I am more interested in justice and human beings."
>
> "Ain't truth and justice the same thing?" the sheriff said.
>
> "Since when?" Uncle Gavin said. "In my time I have seen truth that was anything under the sun but just, and I have seen justice using tools and instruments I wouldn't want to touch with a ten-foot fence rail."

In **"Monk"** Faulkner deals with truth first, saying in the opening paragraph that "it is only in literature that the paradoxical and even mutually negativing anecdotes in the history of a human heart can be juxtaposed and annealed by art into verisimilitude and credibility," and then, in the second paragraph, he deals with justice: "he should never have gone to the penitentiary at all." Poirot would have been highly suspicious of the first claim—use your skills, by all means, to discover the truth, but not art to make truth.

Stevens becomes involved in the events at a stage when justice has already miscarried after Faulkner states that Monk, "a moron, perhaps a cretin," is, even more radically than Shakespeare's Barnardine, "unfit to live or die": "he never should have lived." This is borne out both by the way in which he is induced physically to join the community (when "the man, whoever it was, came along . . . and said, 'All right, Monk. Jump in,' he got into it exactly as the homeless dog would have, and came to Jefferson," and by the attempt he makes at mental and verbal communication: "He just kept on trying to say whatever it was that had been inside him for twenty-five years and that he had only now found the chance (or perhaps the words) to free himself of"; "It was as though he were trying to postulate something, using this opportunity to bridge the hitherto abyss between himself and the living world." In the seven years that Monk has lived in Jefferson he has not become a member of the community, and he again fails in his new environment, the penitentiary, although at the time of Stevens' visit there with the pardon, it appears that he has. Not only can society not undo the earlier injustice, but it also fails to prevent his committing a senseless crime when he appears to be adjusted and integrated. The death sentence that follows is doubtful justice again, and though Stevens gets to the bottom of the matter he fails to achieve visibly just results. At the end of the story three men have died, and in no case does one feel that the person responsible has been brought to justice. But the detective knows, and the narrator can tell that he knows, the truth.

There is no need to go into the other stories in detail. What they show is not only that Truth is not always Justice, but that abstract Justice is too general a concept to be of use when it comes to the lives of individuals, because it cannot usually be expected to fit the individual human condition. So there are different kinds or degrees of justice after the initial case of perfect justice in **"Smoke"** and the complete lack of it in **"Monk."** (pp. 365-69)

The prerequisite for justice—no less than for retribution—is, of course, possession of the truth. How does Stevens come by it? His position is that "'It adds up, all right,'" so his task is to get "the right ciphers" and put them together correctly. His methods are somewhat haphazard, rarely relying on deduction in the Sherlock Holmes style (though to some extent he does in **"Smoke"**), sometimes resembling the tirelessly driving and interviewing detective like Ross MacDonald's Lew Archer (in **"Tomorrow"**), and often being enlightened "by accident" (as in **"Monk,"** and **"An Error in Chemistry"**).

But more important than his methods of detection is the assumption underlying his efforts, namely that the crimes can be brought home to their perpetrators, because people's actions can be understood. Faulkner's position in ***Knight's Gambit*** is that the truth about people can be known and made visible. But it is truth of a restricted kind. Compared with the complexities of Joe Christmas, Quentin Compson or the Sutpen family, Monk, the Holland brothers and Jackson Fentry are no more than outlines of characters, not to speak of Boyd Ballenbaugh or Bookwright, who are merely agents to set the plots in motion. So it takes either a close-knit community, whose members agree on all the important issues (**"Smoke"**), or first-hand knowledge resulting from personal involvement (**"Knight's**

Gambit") to achieve more than partial justice (which satisfies one claim at the expense of another), and more than the partial and superficial truth of "Who did it?" and "How was it done?" either of which fails altogether to answer the deeper probe of "What was it that made him do it?" or instead offers an unsatisfying abstract answer, like "greed." So while **"Smoke"** and **"Knight's Gambit"** seem to support the viability of the approach, the six stories together suggest that the more difficult methods chosen in the novels, leading to ambiguous results, are yet likely to provide more rewarding insights. (pp. 370-71)

W.E. Schlepper, "Truth and Justice in 'Knight's Gambit'," in The Mississippi Quarterly, *Vol. XXXVII, No. 3, Summer, 1984, pp. 365-75.*

JAMES G. WATSON (essay date 1984)

[In the following excerpt, Watson discusses Faulkner's short-story career and examines in detail several stories from Go Down, Moses.*]*

The first, indisputable fact about William Faulkner's career as a writer of short stories is that he was first a novelist. No perspective on his short fiction would be complete without recognizing that his stories exist as part of a body of fiction in which the broadest outlines and deepest significance are defined by his nineteen novels. But no perspective would be complete, either, without the fact that the novels are intimately related, often indebted, to short stories. Sometimes Faulkner used short stories as preliminary sketches for ideas, characters, and techniques he later appropriated for his novels: the germinal materials from which *Absalom, Absalom!* (1936) grew are an unpublished story, **"Evangeline,"** and a published one, **"Wash."** At other times he used stories as separate episodes or chapters in extended fictions: *The Hamlet* (1940) incorporates revised versions of five stories published in the 1930s, and ***The Unvanquished*** . . . and ***Go Down, Moses*** . . . are novels made up entirely of short story chapters, most of them revised from separate publications. *Notes on a Horsethief* (1951), published as a separate book, is a story extracted from a work in progress, the novel *A Fable* (1954). And, of course, Faulkner wrote stories that were stories in their own right, autonomous fictions designed and crafted to stand alone, and the best of these are among the best short stories ever written: **"A Rose for Emily"** and **"Red Leaves"** and **"Dry September,"** to name a few. Probably it is true that many of them were written to earn the money Faulkner needed for uninterrupted work on his novels, but there are very few stories of second quality in the canon. Indeed, if they were written for money, they were less successful for that than they were aesthetically. Given the intricacy and experimental qualities that characterize Faulkner's short stories as well as his novels, it is surprising that some of the stories were published at all. (p. 126)

Was the novelist who described himself as a "failed poet" a failed short story writer as well? He was not. His own earliest judgment is suggested by a passage in a letter written to his mother from Paris in 1925. "I have just written such a beautiful thing that I am about to bust," he told Maud Faulkner; "2,000 words about the Luxembourg gardens and death. It has a thin thread of plot, about a young woman, and it is poetry though written in prose form. I have worked on it for two whole days and every word is perfect."

That sounds a little like the young Hemingway describing the vignettes he wrote in Paris for *In Our Time,* and Faulkner's piece, which was to become the concluding scene of *Sanctuary,* is like those prose poems. But the similarity ends there. It was Hemingway's dictum, set forth in his *Death in the Afternoon,* that the short story writer must "put down what really happened in action; what the actual things were which produced the emotion that you experienced." That simply does not describe a story like **"A Rose for Emily,"** where half a century of communal observation and speculation are reposited with a narrator confronting the present fact that most of it is terribly, terrifyingly wrong. Faulkner himself was not much concerned with facts: he said they didn't cast shadows. Instead, it was the tellers in the tale, and their tellings, that captured his imagination. His stories and novels commonly portray the reactions to what may or may not have really happened from a variety of points of view which produce, in their totality, the emotional impact of single events. And since Faulkner's own impulse as author was to muse upon those musing characters—"with the same horror and the same astonishment," Cash Bundren says in *As I Lay Dying*—Faulkner's voice is often one dimension of the several in any story. Hemingway's much admired objectivity, in Faulkner, is subjectivity; what Hemingway cut, Faulkner compressed for inclusion. This may help to explain why Faulkner's short stories often seem novelistic in scope while Hemingway's novels, by contrast, are extended short stories—*The Old Man and the Sea* being only the most obvious example. In **"A Rose for Emily,"** to cite only one of several distinguishing characteristics, there are seven named and specified characters, plus the narrator, plus significant townspeople who affect the action—aldermen, doctors, a Baptist minister, two female cousins, a druggist, and Confederate war veterans. In the 139 pages of *The Old Man and the Sea,* there are two, not counting Joe DiMaggio and the fish, and some random fishermen, two American tourists, and a writer.

There are at least two important results of such configurations in Faulkner's short fiction, both of which were immediately apparent. First, as we have seen, the magazines that paid high prices for stories could not be counted on to publish his because of the way they were made. Partly because of that, very early in the thirties, Faulkner began gathering unpublishable stories with published ones into short story collections, ***These 13*** in 1931 and ***Doctor Martino and Other Stories*** in 1934. Second, because those stories were made as they were, of stories within stories and times within the present time, they effectuated a complex, contrapuntal unity in the extended narratives where they served as separate but interrelated units of structure. Their adaptability to these still larger stories is due to a synecdochic assumption that underlies much of Faulkner's work, short stories and story collections as well as novels. Hugh Kenner explains it this way in his book, *A Homemade World:*

> Faulkner's root need was not to symbolize (a condensing device) but to expand, expand: to commence with the merest glimpse and by way of wringing out its significance arrange voices and viewpoints, interpolate past chronicles, account for just this passion in just this ancillary passion, and tie the persons together, for the sake of intimacy, intensity, plausibility, with ties of blood and community and heritage.

As the impulse to expand forced him beyond the limits of a single story set at a single place and time, Faulkner's own place, the still closed society of the South, provided him a subject and a way of telling. Kenner says, "What the Old South gave him, what is inseparable from his preferred way of working, making possible in fiction what is essentially a method for poetry, was a society of which he could plausibly postulate that everything in it affects everyone.'' Thus the opening sentence of **"A Rose for Emily":** ''When Miss Emily Grierson died, our whole town went to her funeral''; and of **"Dry September":** ''Through the bloody September twilight, aftermath of sixty-two rainless days, it had gone like a fire in dry grass—the rumor, the story, whatever it was''; and of **"That Evening Sun":** ''Monday is no different from any other weekday in Jefferson now,'' with that ''now'' echoing once in the next sentence and once more in the opening paragraph before Quentin turns to ''then,'' fifteen years in the past, and the differences *then* that prompt his story *now*.

Stories like these are born of the legend maker's art, not the journalist's. Yoknapatawpha County, it is well to remember, is a region of the imagination, and its history, if it can be said to have a factual history, exists exclusively in the fictions where it is made and remade by characters directly, subjectively involved with the history they create. **"A Justice,"** for example, is in one sense a document in the history of old Indian times in Yoknapatawpha County, the story of a contest between an Indian and a Negro slave for the slave's wife and of Chief Ikkemotubbe's belated intercession on behalf of the slave. Sam Fathers, the old half-Indian, half-Negro offspring of that contest, tells the story to Quentin as he heard it from his father's friend, Herman Basket. ''This is how Herman Basket told it,'' he begins, ''when I was big enough to hear talk.'' All three tellers are legend makers: Herman who told the tale, Sam who is the product of the tale he tells of Herman's telling, and Quentin who tells the story of Sam and his tale. The past interpenetrates the present in this fictional configuration in the form of an oral text, conserved by its tellers, and of a living artifact, the old man Quentin describes as ''definite, immobile, and complete, like something looked upon after a long time in a preservative bath in a museum.'' That Quentin is too young to understand the tale he hears and retells is a favorite strategy of Faulkner's for extending the implications of bare facts. Like communal memory, in **"A Rose for Emily"** and detective stories such as **"Tomorrow"** and **"Knight's Gambit,"** the child narrator involves the reader at an extratextual level of the story as assumed rememberer, deducer, theorizer. The great example of the technique is Benjamin Compson's chapter of *The Sound and the Fury,* the ''short story'' from which Faulkner said the novel developed. There Benjy ''tells'' what he can neither articulate nor comprehend, and the reader pieces a mosaic from the fragments. Modifications of the same inform the stories. At the end of **"A Justice,"** for example, Quentin flees the facts of Sam's story in confusion, leaving the reader to confront what Sam knows but never says—that no court of appeal holds jurisdiction over lovers, that there is no ''justice'' in the conflicts of the heart.

"A Justice" was submitted to magazines five times without luck before Faulkner published it in ***These 13***. But **"A Justice,"** and stories like it that employ two or more dimensions of time and levels of understanding, proved uniquely suited to the short story collections Faulkner was constructing. Although there is disagreement about the theme of ***These 13,*** there is no disagreement that the stories work together to approximate the unity of extended narrative. The book is composed of three groups of stories: the four World War I stories, the six set at various times in Jefferson and Yoknapatawpha County, and three final ones set abroad. In this arrangement, the Yoknapatawpha stories at the core of the book serve as a keystone that draws strength from the framing stories it draws together. In his fine book *The Achievement of William Faulkner,* Michael Millgate says that ''The experience of reading the central section according to Faulkner's scheme is one of continual recognition and awareness of reverberation: the recurrence of characters, setting, situations, and themes provokes the recollection and hence the continuing coexistence of the earlier story or stories and produces a total effect of progressive enrichment.'' Millgate finds in that progression Faulkner's constant reiteration of the power and presence of death. I have argued that the subtle transformations from war stories of Part I, through the Yoknapatawpha stories, to the stories of love and imagination in Part III reaffirm the regenerative motion of life and that the climax of that progression is in the transcendent imaginative vision of the final story, the poetic coda **"Carcassonne."** In **"Carcassonne,"** the nameless poet of Rincon, longing *to perform something bold and tragical and austere,''* soars outward in imagination, ''a dying star upon the immensity of darkness and of silence within which, steadfast, fading, deep-breasted and grave of flank, muses the dark and tragic figure of the Earth, his mother.'' Whatever their themes, Faulkner was speaking of just such books when he wrote to Malcolm Cowley in 1948 about his plan for ***Collected Stories of William Faulkner.*** He said there that ''even to a collection of short stories, form, integration, is as important as to a novel—an entity of its own, single, set for one pitch, contrapuntal in integration, toward one end, one finale.'' That principle describes the form of stories such as **"A Rose for Emily"** and **"A Justice"** as well as the books in which they are collected. It is a reminder of what Faulkner took to be the insufficiency of bare facts, simple causes, and single contexts.

The principle of counterpoint proved a source of some confusion, however, when stories like those in Faulkner's short story collections were elevated to chapters in novels composed of stories. Faulkner told Random House editor Robert Haas in 1948 that he wanted *Collected Stories* to have ''an integrated form of its own, like the Moses book if possible, or at least *These 13*.'' But ***Go Down, Moses*** had been published in 1942 as a collection, subtitled ''and Other Stories,'' not as a novel. Writing to Haas in 1949 about reissuing the book, Faulkner insisted that the new edition conform to his first intention. The letter documents the scope and significance of short story structures in Faulkner's longer fictions.

> Moses is indeed a novel. I would not eliminate the story or section titles. Do you think it necessary to number these stories like chapters? Why not reprint exactly, but change the title from GO DOWN, MOSES and other stories, to simply: GO DOWN MOSES, with whatever change is necessary in the jacket description. We did THE UNVANQUISHED in this manner, without either confusion or anticipation of such; and, for that matter, THE WILD PALMS had two completely unrelated stories in it. Yet nobody thought it should be titled THE WILD PALMS and another story. Indeed, if you will permit me to say so at this late date, nobody but Random House seemed to labor under the impression that GO DOWN, MOSES should be titled ''and other stories.'' I remember the shock (mild) I got when I saw the printed page. I say, reprint it, call it simply GO DOWN, MOSES, which was the way I sent it in to you 8 years ago.

In the second printing and subsequent reissues, Faulkner's title was restored.

Go Down, Moses is a multiple narrative, composed of seven story-chapters that tell the history of the McCaslin family in Yoknapatawpha County from the early 1800s to 1942. Each chapter is a self-contained story connected to the other stories by common setting, situations, and the characters' ties of common blood. In **"Was,"** for example, Buck McCaslin is the white half-brother of his father's slave, Turl; Isaac McCaslin and Lucas Beauchamp, the protagonists of the novel, are Buck's and Turl's sons. Like their biblical analogues, Isaac and Ishmael, Isaac and Lucas are far from equal inheritors of the patriarch's largess, and accordingly their separate stories are told in separate, if often parallel and overlapping, narrative units. The counterpointed story-chapters allow for the omission of details from one character's tale by the remembrance of it in another, and the interposition of collective memory, and hence of legend, casts the McCaslins in a progressive structure of telling, hearing, and retelling. The book opens with this remarkable sentence from **"Was"**:

> Isaac McCaslin, "Uncle Ike," past seventy and nearer eighty than he ever corroborated any more, a widower now and uncle to half a county and father to no one this was not something participated in or even seen by himself, but by his elder cousin, McCaslin Edmonds, grandson of Isaac's father's sister and so descended by the distaff, yet notwithstanding the inheritor, and in his time the bequestor, of that which some had thought then and some still thought should have been Isaac's, since his was the name in which the title to the land had first been granted from the Indian patent and which some of the descendents of his father's slaves still bore in the land.

The interrupted chronology in the arrangement of the stories complements the alternating narrative focus of the book and reinforces repetitions that dramatize the past as a force of motion in the present—Isaac's reading of the McCaslin ledgers in **"The Bear,"** for example, and the recurrence of miscegenatic love from generation to generation. In ***Go Down, Moses,*** as in the spiritual from which it takes its title, all the characters, white and black, feel the pull of their one blood and appeal to Pharaoh to "let my people go." By these means, the single but collective stories of the McCaslins and their "people" are carried forward. Representative moments in their history and represented lives gradually reveal the patterns and sequences that form parts of a larger, causal progression encompassing all time in this space—mythic and real, past and present, and even future.

Such effects, and Faulkner's stated intention to produce them, define the kind of stories he wrote. The uses to which he put those stories demonstrate their considerable contribution to the making of that rival world he called a "cosmos of my own." His modernism, refined from sources as various as the symbolist poets and James Joyce at one extreme and Herman Melville and Sherwood Anderson at the other, had long posited the book as a world in the world, and Yoknapatawpha County is, in fact, a world made in books. Committed to the integral relation of meaning to fictional form, he found in the cosmos he created a way of telling by which, as he said, he might arrest the motion of life "by artificial means and hold it fixed so that 100 years later when a stranger looks at it, it moves again since it is life." Short stories were essential to that aesthetic, first, because the multiple perspectives of separate stories approximate the fullness of a world and, second, because by their interaction together in a significant form they establish and sustain the lifelike motionlike conditions of the fictional cosmos.

Faulkner worked consciously to shape such a world from the stories that became ***Go Down, Moses.*** He made **"The Fire and the Hearth"** from three existing stories and wrote the 1935 story **"Lion"** into **"The Bear,"** which he published in the *Post* without Part IV, claiming that Isaac's renunciation of his McCaslin heritage belonged to the novel and had no part in the short story. These changes and additions provide narrative balance, consistency, and connections between the story-chapters. They caulk the seams of the book. But there are changes of another kind in the transition from story-as-story to story-as-chapter in ***Go Down, Moses.*** In the slow float of shifting light and shadow, separate stories like separate lives are transformed by the force of context alone, without strategic revision. The stories alter the new environment and are altered by it. Expressive in themselves of Faulkner's need to expand, they are the stuff of larger expansions, building blocks of the fictional world he called "a kind of keystone in the Universe."

The title story, **"Go Down, Moses,"** is one such, and it illustrates the wonderful elasticity of Faulkner's short fiction. **"Go Down, Moses"** was published in *Collier's* In January 1941, and that text, with some stylistic revisions, was incorporated as the final chapter of the novel. It is the story of how Mollie Beauchamp appealed to the county attorney, Gavin Stevens, to arrange the funeral of her grandson, Butch Beauchamp, "sold . . . into Egypt" by Roth Edmonds for local crimes and executed in Chicago for murder. To portray Jefferson, Faulkner uses the devices and strategies that give his short stories their characteristic scope and depth. Names without faces evoke imagined memories, peopling the town with characters and events from the actual present and an imaginary past—Roth Edmonds and Hamp Worsham, a storekeeper named Rouncewell and the Negro murderer who fathered Butch on Mollie's eldest daughter, long since dead. Facts, modified in combination, are gleaned from disparate sources—a Chicago census taker, a Memphis newspaper, and old Miss Worsham, whose grandfather owned Hamp's and Mollie's parents. In the story-as-story, Stevens is the protagonist in whose consciousness the past is gradually called forth, fragmentary and incomplete, suggesting by implication a depth of experience never detailed. In this broad, artifical context, he is the benevolent, indulgent representative of white southern paternalism. Mollie herself is portrayed in stereotypical terms that accord with his preconceptions about "darkies." To him she is "a little old negro woman with a shrunken, incredibly old face beneath a white headcloth and a black straw hat which would have fitted a child." He is concerned with Law and all the associated formulas of social order. She is the instrument of his partial and delayed understanding that social rites and forms are expressions of human feeling. Only when Butch Beauchamp's body has been returned, the newspaper obituary prepared, and the cortege has wound through the town square toward the McCaslin burying ground does Stevens realize that *"she doesn't care how he died. She just wanted him to come home, but she wanted him to come home right. She wanted that casket and those flowers and the hearse and she wanted to ride through town behind it in a car."*

This makes a good story—the kind of story, in fact, that Faulkner soon would write in *Intruder in the Dust*—and *Collier's* paid $1,000 for it. But it is not precisely the same story we read as the concluding chapter of ***Go Down, Moses,*** where Beauchamp and Edmonds are by now familiar names and Stevens's partially remembered facts are fragments to be measured against a fuller history. Stevens appears in the book only in **"Go Down, Moses,"** in context one of several minor functionaries, usually white, always peripheral, the repositories of conventional understandings and communal misconceptions. The puzzled Deputy who tries to retell Rider's story at the end of **"Pantaloon in Black"** is another. In the story-as-chapter, Stevens is the near-stereotype, not Mollie: he represents the Law, but she is history's own living artifact, "child" of nothing less than her massed and portentous past. Beyond Stevens's understanding of her as "darkie," beyond even the heroic resignation he finally accords her, Mollie's appeal to him places her in that richer, legendary context.

> "It was Roth Edmonds sold him" she said.
> "Sold him in Egypt. I dont know whar he is.
> I just knows Pharaoh got him. And you know
> the Law. I wants to find my boy."

Go Down, Moses is a multiple narrative, and it is a tragic one, where lives are so intertwined in time and place and blood that the most ennobling acts are self-defeating, the commonest gestures noble. Mollie's "my boy" echoes "my people" and God's injunction to Moses. Stevens is instrument of Mollie's will, agent of her re-enactment of other appeals in the novel and hence of other lives. As protagonist of the final story-chapter, Mollie Beauchamp is coessential with Buck and Buddy McCaslin, who freed hers and their own people from slavery in 1837 but could not free them from themselves, and with their long line of McCaslin and Beauchamp people similarly bound. Faulkner dedicated the novel to "Mammy Caroline Barr, Mississippi, 1840-1940, Who was born in slavery and who gave to my family a fidelity without stint or calculation of recompense and to my childhood an immeasurable devotion and love." Mollie is her analogue, and although the story **"Go Down, Moses"** ends with Gavin Stevens's well-meant tribute, the novel ***Go Down, Moses*** ends with her as it began. (pp. 129-37)

James G. Watson, "The American Short Story, 1930-1945," in The American Short Story, 1900-1945: A Critical History, *edited by Philip Stevick, Twayne Publishers, 1984, pp. 103-46.*

LAURENCE PERRINE (essay date 1985)

[*In the following excerpt, Perrine discusses several ambiguous elements in "That Evening Sun" that lead to conflicting interpretations.*]

Just as Caddy throughout [**"That Evening Sun"**] keeps asking questions which are seldom answered by the adults, so the story itself keeps raising questions for which no sure answers are provided by its author. We may always, of course, conjecture, and sometimes infer, but rarely can we rest in certainty, though we sniff like bloodhounds back and forth through the story searching for clues.

That many of these questions are deliberately raised and left unanswered can be demonstrated. Faulkner's resurrection of dead Quentin to narrate the story, rather than using an omniscient narrator, is part of his method. It is not that Quentin is an unreliable narrator. Indeed he has remarkably precise recall of what he has seen or heard or smelled. Uncertainties arise not because of defects in his memory but because of gaps in his knowledge. He can report accurately what was reported to him, he can repeat precisely what people have said, but these abilities do not guarantee the truth of their saying. In addition there is much that Quentin has not heard and does not know. And some matters, like motivation, may be unknowable *except* to an omniscient narrator.

Here is a partial list of questions raised by the story which cannot be certainly answered: (1) Why is Nancy so often late for cooking breakfast? (2) Why is she arrested? (3) Why does she attempt suicide? (4) Has Nancy slept with more than one white man? (5) Who fathered Nancy's unborn child? (6) Does she know? (7) Does Jesus know? (8) Why does Mr. Compson tell Jesus to stay off their place? (9) Why does Jesus leave Nancy? (10) Where does he go? (11) How long does he stay? (12) Does he come back? (13) What causes Nancy's disturbance in the kitchen? (14) Is Aunt Rachel Jesus' mother? (15) Why might Jesus be "mad" at Nancy? (16) Why does Nancy think he is angry with her? (17) For what does Nancy feel guilty? (18) Why did Mrs. Lovelady commit suicide? (19) What happened to her child? (20) What happened to Nancy's pregnancy? (21) Is Nancy alive next morning?—I shall address some, but not all of these questions. (p. 297)

Why does Nancy attempt suicide? The reasons are probably multiple, may be unknown to Nancy herself, and are best left to the imagination of the reader. The function of her attempt in the story is clearer. The depth of her despair here, put beside the violence of her jealous reaction to Mr. Compson's suggestion that Jesus has probably "got another wife" in St. Louis, reveals Nancy's emotional extremes and prepares for her paroxysm of fear when she hears that Jesus has returned.

Who fathered Nancy's unborn child? Several commentators confidently name Mr. Stovall as the father, since he is the only candidate named; others more cautiously attribute paternity only to an unknown white man, their caution validated by Mr. Compson's rebuke to Nancy, "If you'd just let white men alone." We cannot be sure, however, whether Mr. Compson speaks from certain knowledge, or whether his rebuke simply combines the universal tendency to generalize from one instance with the Southern white's tendency to give black behavior the least favorable interpretation. Moreover, Jesus' claim that he can "cut down the vine" that Nancy's "watermelon" came off of is a valid threat only if Mr. Stovall is the only white man she has slept with. How else would he know whose "vine" to cut? A third possibility, that Jesus himself is the father, is seldom considered. Yet how can Nancy know who made her pregnant if she was living with Jesus while having sexual relations with another? That Nancy and Jesus have been living together is indicated by the general acceptance of them as husband and wife, by the children's approaching no nearer than the ditch to Nancy's house, by Jesus' taking breakfast in the Compson kitchen when Nancy begins cooking there, by Jesus' eloquent statement that "when white men want to come in my house, I aint got no house," and by Nancy's announcement of Jesus' departure: "one morning she woke up and Jesus was gone." On the basis of the published story alone, we must acknowledge a possibility that Nancy, in declaring that her "watermelon" didn't come off Jesus' "vine," is baiting Jesus with a possibility, not a certainty.

Evidence from outside the story, however, does certify Faulkner's intention as being that Jesus should *know* the child not to be his. In submitting the story for publication in the *American Mercury,* Faulkner modified the passage about Nancy's pregnancy (in response to its editor H. L. Mencken's protest that it was "somewhat loud for a general magazine") as follows:

> When Dilsey was sick in her cabin and Nancy was cooking for us, we could see her apron swelling out; . . . [Jesus] said it was a watermelon that Nancy had under her dress. And it was Winter, too.
>
> "Where did you get a watermelon in the Winter?" Caddy said.
>
> "I didn't," [Jesus] said. "It wasn't me that give it to her. But I can cut it down, same as if it was."

Faulkner restored the original wording—both more effective and more ambiguous—for the story's first book publication in ***These Thirteen*** later that year.

Why does Jesus leave Nancy? Nancy wakes up one morning "and Jesus was gone." The almost casual way she tells it does not suggest that they had quarreled. Nancy says, "He quit me. Done gone to Memphis, I reckon. Dodging them city *po*-lice for a while." Had Jesus simply tired of dodging the Jefferson "*po*-lice" and sought temporary respite in the larger city? Later, Nancy says, "He said I done woke up the devil in him and aint but one thing going to lay it down again." But Nancy makes this remark after the presumed return of Jesus; if he said it to her, he must have said it sometime *before* he left, for there has been no communication between them since. The threat (presuming Jesus actually made it and Nancy has correctly interpreted it) would explain Nancy's outbreak of fear on hearing of his return. But if Jesus intends to murder her, why must he go away first and then come back to do it? And why does Nancy's fear not date from his making the threat? Might she not have "invented" the remark to rationalize the fear that has arisen in her *after* his departure?

Where does Jesus go? Nancy says, "Done gone to Memphis, I reckon." Father says, "He's probably in St. Louis now." (pp. 300-01)

Why might Jesus be "mad" at Nancy? Why does she think he is? When Mr. Compson suggests to Nancy that Jesus has "probably got another wife by now," Nancy's reaction is immediate: "If he has, I better not find out about it. I'd stand right there over them, and every time he wropped her, I'd cut that arm off. I'd cut his head off and I'd slit her belly and I'd shove—". Reacting this way, Nancy might very well think that Jesus would react the same way when the cases are reversed and she sleeps with another man. But, as critics have pointed out, when Jesus is told that the watermelon is not off his vine, he threatens the father, not Nancy. Moreover, he must have known about her prostitution earlier, for his speech about "When white man want to come in my house, I aint got no house" voices a sense of injustice that must have been smouldering for a long time. Not until the moment when he tells Nancy, *if* he does, that she "done woke up the devil in him" does Jesus manifest any anger toward Nancy. The problem is to explain the delay. But the parallel between Jesus' sleeping with a hypothetical "St. Louis woman" and Nancy's sleeping with Mr. Stovall is inexact. In the one case Jesus is loving a new woman and has forgotten Nancy. In the other, Nancy is sleeping with Mr. Stovall for money and has not at all forgotten Jesus. Still, Jesus feels the indignity keenly and makes a violent threat, just as Nancy does, though against the father, not against Nancy. We hear nothing of his attempting to carry out that threat, however. The only violence in the story is committed by whites against blacks. And even supposing that Jesus knows who the father is, there is little possibility of his being able to carry out the threat, so supreme is white power in Jefferson. Though Mr. Stovall has slept with Nancy several times, has refused to pay her, has knocked her down and kicked her teeth out, and possibly fathered her child, Jesus has pretty clearly never attacked Mr. Stovall. Nancy continually protects herself against Jesus by sleeping in the Compsons' house or surrounding herself with Compson children, knowing that Jesus is unlikely to attack her in their presence. Meanwhile, we may conjecture, Jesus' anger and frustration seethe inside him, and his indignity is daily pressed upon him as Nancy's belly swells. Such being the case, is it illogical to believe that the anger originally directed toward the unknown father might be redirected toward Nancy? Nancy herself undergoes an emotional transition, from blaming others to blaming, at least partially, herself. At the beginning of her terror, she says, "I aint nothing but a nigger. It aint none of my fault." But near the end she says, "I reckon it belong to me, I reckon what I going to get aint no more than mine." Nancy is capable of changing from an initial defiant taunting of Jesus ("It aint off your vine") to a feeling of guilt over her physical infidelity to the man who "always been good" to her. Whether we accept a change in Jesus' feelings or not will depend on how much credence we give to Nancy's report that he said she "done woke up the devil in him and aint but one thing going to lay it down again." Nancy's feelings change; there are good reasons why Jesus' feelings *might* change; and there are reasons why Nancy should believe they have changed, whether they have or not. The mere act of his leaving her would explain *that*.

What happens to Nancy's pregnancy? It is puzzling that Nancy's pregnancy, forced so vividly on our attention early in the story, should never be mentioned again. There are three possibilities: Nancy has had an abortion; she has had a miscarriage or stillbirth; she is still pregnant at the end of the story.

A recent critic contends that "the following enigmatic paragraph can hardly be read in any other way than as a symbolic confirmation of an abortion":

> "Father said for you to go home and lock the door, and you'll be all right," Caddy said. "All right from what, Nancy? Is Jesus mad at you?" Nancy was holding the coffee cup in her hands again, her elbows on her knees and her hands holding the cup between her knees. She was looking into the cup. "What have you done that made Jesus mad?" Caddy said. Nancy let the cup go. It didn't break on the floor, but the coffee spilled out, and Nancy sat there with her hands still making the shape of the cup.

There is nothing enigmatic about this paragraph. It is simply a graphic description of Nancy's terror. Nancy's sitting with her hands still making the shape of the cup she has dropped, like other symptoms of her terror, exhibits a violent disjunction between the signals received and sent out by her brain. In her suicide attempt, after putting the noose around her neck, she can't make her hands let go of the window ledge. In her cabin she keeps her hand on the hot lamp without realizing that the hand is burning. But if one insists on reading the paragraph symbolically, it is a much apter symbol for miscarriage than for abortion, for Nancy's dropping the cup and spilling its contents is involuntary. But, indeed, the abortion-theory must be dismissed. In Mississippi, before the turn of the century, a black woman of Nancy's class and education would not have had access to abortion at her stage of pregnancy. Still, if Nancy has had either abortion or miscarriage, it is strange that Quentin, keenly observant of physical detail, should not mention that Nancy's belly was "flat" again. A colleague of mine suggests that the sentence "Jason's legs stuck straight out of his pants where he sat on Nancy's lap" . . . may be intended to convey this information. Possibly so. We can not be certain.

Does Jesus come back? So strong is Nancy's conviction of Jesus' return that few commentators question it, yet all the reasons supporting it are undermined by uncertainty.

Our first news of Jesus' return is received on the night that Nancy sits by the cold stove in the Compsons' kitchen, scared to go home:

> "I am going to walk down the lane with Nancy," [father] said. "She says that Jesus is back."
>
> "Has she seen him?" mother said.
>
> "No. Some Negro sent her word that he was back in town."

What we are given here is *at the very least* a fourth-hand report. Quentin tells us that father said that Nancy said that "some Negro" said. Though there is not need to question the reliability of Quentin or of father, the last two members in the series are increasingly unreliable. The phrase "sent her word" (rather than "told her") suggests moreover the probability of one or more additional intermediaries. What evidence the first Negro had, how the word was sent, what the word was, whether it was transmitted accurately, and whether Nancy interpreted it correctly—all these factors are left undetermined.

The next suggestion of Jesus' return is the disturbance in the kitchen when the Compson household is awakened by Nancy's terrified ululation. When Caddy asks, "Was it Jesus? Did he try to come into the kitchen?" Nancy can only answer, "I aint nothing but a nigger. God knows." Whether Nancy was frightened by an intruder, whether that intruder was Jesus, or whether the whole affair was a bad dream—these matters are left unresolved. Nancy herself seems not to know the answers.

The chief support for Jesus' return seems simply the intensity of Nancy's own subjective conviction. Dilsey asks, "How do you know he's back? You aint seen him." "I can feel him," Nancy says. "I can feel him laying yonder in the ditch." "Tonight?" Dilsey asks. "How come you know it's tonight?" "I know," Nancy replies. "He's there waiting. I know. I done lived with him too long. I know what he is fixing to do fore he know it himself." Nancy may well have lived with Jesus long enough to have a feeling for how his mind works; but this hardly gives her absolute power to predict his actions, let alone the precise *time* of his actions. There is no evidence that she had foreseen Jesus' leaving her, and there is some suggestion that she was surprised when it happened. She woke up one morning "and Jesus was gone." If she failed to predict this event when she went to bed with him the previous evening, why should one think she could predict the date on which Jesus would attempt to kill her when she has been out of communication with him for weeks? Dilsey's question is crucial: "How come you know it's tonight?" There is no rational answer to Dilsey's question. There *is,* however, a strong psychological reason why Nancy's terror should peak this night. Dilsey's return to work has deprived Nancy of the security offered by the Compson house. For the first time in weeks she is faced with the prospect of spending the night alone in her cabin.

Nancy's intuitions are, for her, convictions; and she expresses them with such force that many readers accept them as truth. Yet it is difficult to believe that, in the lapse of time between the first report of Jesus' return and Nancy's night of terror, there would be no confirmation of his return. If Jesus is back, why has nobody seen him? It is also hard to imagine why Jesus would lie for hours in an uncomfortable ditch in order to take his revenge. There are easier ways. And Nancy's words strain credulity when she tells Mr. Compson, "He looking through that window this minute, waiting for yawl to go," just as they strain it when Mr. Compson escorts her home on the first night after she has heard of Jesus' return: "I can feel him now, in this lane. He hearing us talk, every word, hid somewhere, waiting." In Nancy's mind, after his "return," Jesus is omnipresent.

A final piece of evidence for Jesus' return would seem, at first sight, objective enough. "I got the sign," Nancy says. "It was on the table when I come in. It was a hogbone, with blood meat still on it, laying by the lamp." But *when* did she get the sign? If she means when she returned to the cabin with the children, the children would have seen it too, as would Mr. Compson when he arrived. (If she had removed it, the children would have seen her remove it, and she could not have removed it so far that she could not have *showed* it to Mr. Compson.) If she refers to sometime earlier in the day, why had she not mentioned it to Dilsey when Dilsey asked, "How do you know he's back? You aint seen him?" We are left with strong reasons to believe that the "sign" is a desperate last-ditch invention of Nancy's feverish mind designed to keep Mr. Compson in the cabin. (It should be pointed out that Mr. Compson's "He's not here. I would have seen him" is equally an invention—a display of false confidence designed to calm Nancy down. When Nancy replies, "He waiting in the ditch yonder," Mr. Compson first says, "Nonsense," but then, "Do you know he's there?" Even *he* is impressed by the force of Nancy's conviction.)

Is Nancy alive next morning? It is now time to construct the most plausible account of the story we can imagine for each of the two suppositions about its ending:

(A) Nancy, washerwoman, cook, and prostitute, is made pregnant by a white man. Her violent husband, Jesus, angered by the pregnancy, makes what is either a castration or a murder threat against the father, and voices his indignation in a fine speech about "I cant hang around white man's kitchen. But white man can hang around mine. . . ." Frustrated, however, by his powerlessness to carry out his threat, he gradually turns his anger against Nancy and tells her she "done woke up the devil" in him and only her death will "lay it down again." Perhaps to prevent himself from carrying out his threat, he leaves town. His anger, still frustrated, drives him back. Nancy, hearing of his return, knowing his violent nature, and aware of his threat, knows he has come back to kill her, and is so overcome by fear that Mr. Compson feels obliged to escort her home at night. When Mrs. Compson objects to being left alone, a pallet is fixed for Nancy in the kitchen. After Jesus makes an unsuccessful attempt one night to break into the house, Nancy's fear turns to terror. Denied the protection of the Compson house after Dilsey's return, she entices the children to come home with her and pretends that their father is with them. She knows Jesus will strike this night because she is unprotected and because he has left a "sign," which, in her disturbed state, she had not mentioned to Dilsey. When Mr. Compson, who has come after the children, refuses to stay with her, her will breaks, and she resigns herself to the death that surely awaits her.

(B) Nancy's suicide attempt, to which her pregnancy is a contributing cause, displays the conflicting impulses and emotional extremes to which she is subject. In the kitchen sometime later, she taunts Jesus with the assertion that the "watermelon" under her skirt "never came off [his] vine." Jesus' anger is directed, not against her, however, but against the unknown father and against white men in general. When Jesus leaves her, her response is at first casual, but during his absence she questions the reasons for his departure and her own role in it. She is torn between the desire to relieve herself of responsibility ("I aint nothing but a nigger. It aint none of my fault") and a need to acknowledge her guilt ("Jesus always been good to me. Whenever he had two dollars, one of them was mine"). She shows that her feelings toward Jesus run deep when she tells Mr. Compson what she'd do if she caught Jesus with another wife. The false rumor that Jesus has returned intensifies her inner conflicts and feelings of guilt, and she convinces herself that Jesus has come back to kill her ("I aint going to see him but once more, with that razor in his mouth"). She imagines that Jesus had threatened her life before he left ("He done say I woke up the devil in him"), and she irrationally feels him lurking everywhere, waiting, hearing all she says. She so vividly hallucinates an attempted attack by Jesus in the Compsons' kitchen one night that afterwards she is unsure what actually happened. Her terror psychologically peaks on the day when Dilsey returns to the kitchen, depriving her of her sanctuary. Her guilt and her fear mount together ("I hellborn," she tells Jason. "I going back where I come from soon"), and she turns to the desperate expedient of enticing the Compson children to her cabin. When Mr. Compson dismisses her fears as "Nonsense," her imagination creates the "proof" of the hog-bone with blood meat still on it. When this too fails, her will breaks, and she resigns herself to what she falsely believes her fate, now fully accepting her guilt ("I reckon it belong to me. I reckon what I going to get ain't no more than mine").

The first account is the more emotionally compelling, as demonstrated by the reactions of commentators. The second bears up better, I think, under rational scrutiny of the facts. But neither account can be proved. Each rests on undemonstrable assumptions, each embraces long sequences of conjecture (the first, especially, about the progress of Jesus' feelings; the second about Nancy's).

If we ask ourselves Faulkner's *intention* in the story, we must conclude that Faulkner wished to end it with an unresolvable question mark. First, Faulkner takes great pains to emphasize that question mark. On the final three pages of the story, the question is put before the reader six separate times. Nancy four times asserts that Jesus is waiting in the ditch, and Mr. Compson four times dismisses the assertion as "Nonsense." After that, Mr. Compson twice answers Caddy's questions with assurances that nothing is going to happen and that Jesus has gone away. Even so, Quentin is unpersuaded. "Who will do our washing now, Father?" he asks. The Compson family are divided on the answer. Second, the uncertainty about the ending is *not* caused by any gap in Quentin's knowledge. Quentin certainly knows whether Nancy was alive or not the next morning. This uncertainty exists because Faulkner deliberately stops the story before Quentin reaches the next morning. Finally, the question of Nancy's survival is the crowning uncertainty in a story whose consistent method is uncertainty. The other uncertainties lead up to and feed into the final uncertainty. (pp. 301-07)

Laurence Perrine, "'That Evening Sun': A Skein of Uncertainties," in Studies in Short Fiction, *Vol. 22, No. 3, Summer, 1985, pp. 295-307.*

ADDITIONAL BIBLIOGRAPHY

Allen, Dennis W. "Horror and Perverse Delight: Faulkner's 'A Rose for Emily'." *Modern Fiction Studies* XXX, No. 4 (Winter 1984): 685-96.

A psychological examination of Emily's character.

Backman, Melvin. "'The Bear' and *Go Down, Moses.*" In his *Faulkner: The Major Years,* pp. 160-74. Bloomington: Indiana University Press, 1966.

A general explication of 'The Bear' in the context of the other stories in *Go Down, Moses.* Backman sees the story as a "public admission of sin" and views both Faulkner and Isaac McCaslin as "fragmented by unbearable guilt." He considers Isaac's repudiation of his inheritance an ineffectual response to the racial injustice that it was meant to atone.

Bassett, John. *William Faulkner: An Annotated Checklist of Criticism.* New York: David Lewis, 1972, 551 p.

A comprehensive annotated list of reviews and criticism on Faulkner through 1970.

———. *Faulkner: An Annotated Checklist of Recent Criticism.* Kent, Ohio: Kent State University Press, 1983, 272 p.

An annotated compilation of criticism and scholarship on Faulkner from 1971 to 1982.

Beauchamp, Gorman. "The Rite of Initiation in Faulkner's 'The Bear'." *The Arizona Quarterly* XXVIII, No. 4 (Winter 1972): 319-25.

Discusses Isaac McCaslin's experiences in "The Bear" as an example of an initiation ritual common to primitive religious systems passed on to Isaac by Sam Fathers.

Beck, Warren. "Short Stories into Novels." In his *Faulkner,* pp. 275-333. Madison: University of Wisconsin Press, 1976.

Discusses novels such as *The Unvanquished* and *Go Down, Moses* that are composed of short stories. Beck also discusses the relationship between the novels and short stories in which the same characters figure, such as *The Sound and the Fury* and "That Evening Sun," and *The Hamlet* and "Barn Burning."

Bethea, Sally. "Further Thoughts on Racial Implications in Faulkner's 'That Evening Sun'." *Notes on Mississippi Writers* VI, No. 9 (Winter 1974): 87-92.

Refutes Scottie Davis's interpretation of 'That Evening Sun' (see Additional Bibliography), contending that Nancy's downfall is not merely due to her irrational fears and her character flaws, but rather that Faulkner intended to indict the white community for its offenses against blacks in general and Nancy in particular.

Blotner, Joseph. *Faulkner: A Biography.* 2 vols. New York: Random House, 1974.

An authoritative biography.

Brooks, Cleanth. "The Tradition of Romantic Love and *The Wild Palms.*" *Mississippi Quarterly* XXV, No. 3 (Summer 1972): 265-87.

The text of a discussion concerning *The Wild Palms.* Brooks begins the discussion by exploring the "erotic heresy" that causes Charlotte and Wilbourne to abandon all other social ties in order to be with each other. This is followed by a symposium of scholars examining both Faulkner's novel and the western tradition of chivalric or romantic love.

———. "Sketches, Early Stories, and an Abortive Novel." In his *William Faulkner: Toward Yoknapatawpha and Beyond,* pp. 100-28. New Haven: Yale University Press, 1978.

Discusses the sketches and stories Faulkner wrote in New Orleans, comparing some of them with his later work. Brooks also discusses the unfinished novel *Elmer,* a *bildungsroman* about the childhood and adolescence of a painter, which Faulkner wrote during a trip to Europe in 1925.

———. "His Somewhat Lesser Sound and Fury." *Saturday Review* VI, No. 22 (10 November 1979): 51-3.

A review of *Uncollected Stories of William Faulkner.*

———. *William Faulkner: First Encounters.* New Haven and London: Yale University Press, 1983, 230 p.

Essays on the short stories and several novels designed to introduce Faulkner to the reader.

Brown, May Cameron. "Voice in 'That Evening Sun': A Study of Quentin Compson." *Mississippi Quarterly* XXIX, No. 3 (Summer 1976): 347-60.

Examines extant versions of the text of "That Evening Sun." Brown discusses Quentin's role as narrator of the story and defends Quentin's sensitivity to Nancy's plight.

Campbell, Harry Modean, and Foster, Ruel E. "Humor in 'A Rose for Emily'." In *William Faulkner: A Critical Appraisal,* pp. 99-100. Norman: University of Oklahoma Press, 1951.

Finds a surrealistic humor in "A Rose for Emily."

Creighton, Joanne V. *William Faulkner's Craft of Revision: The Snopes Trilogy, "The Unvanquished," and "Go Down, Moses."* Detroit: Wayne State University Press, 1977, 182 p.

Discusses Faulkner's revisions from the short story versions of his tales to the versions found in his novels.

Dabney, Lewis M. "'Red Leaves'" and "Sam Fathers and *Go Down, Moses.*" In his *The Indians of Yoknapatawpha: A Study in Literature and History,* pp. 90-117, pp. 118-57. Baton Rouge: Louisiana State University Press, 1974.

Explicates "Red Leaves" and *Go Down, Moses,* with special attention given to Faulkner's portrayal of Indians and of the half-Indian Sam Fathers. Dabney compares details of Faulkner's fiction with historical information on Mississippi Indian tribes.

Davis, Scottie. "Faulkner's Nancy: Racial Implications in 'That Evening Sun'." *Notes on Mississippi Writers* V, No. 1 (Spring 1972): 30-2.

Asserts that Nancy is not a victim of prejudice, but causes her own undoing through deficiencies in her character. This view is challenged by Sally Bethea (see Additional Bibliography).

Early, James. *The Making of "Go Down, Moses."* Dallas: Southern Methodist University Press, 1972, 127 p.

Discusses the extant versions of the stories included in *Go Down, Moses,* examining changes from published magazine versions to the versions found in the novel.

Folks, Jeffrey J. "Honor in Faulkner's Short Fiction." *The Southern Review* XVIII, No. 3 (July 1982): 506-16.

Examines the ironic view of honor portrayed in the stories "Shingles for the Lord" and "Honor."

Fowler, Virginia C. "Faulkner's 'Barn Burning': Sarty's Conflict Reconsidered." *CLA Journal* XXIV, No. 4 (June 1981): 513-21.

Examines the internal struggle of Sarty Snopes in the story.

Funk, Robert W. "Satire and Existentialism in Faulkner's 'Red Leaves'." *Mississippi Quarterly* XXV, No. 2 (Summer 1972): 339-48.

Asserts that in "Red Leaves" Faulkner satirizes the cultural effects of slavery and makes an existential point of the Negro's struggle to survive, even if in slavery.

Harter, Carol Clancey. "The Winter of Isaac McCaslin: Revisions and Irony in Faulkner's 'Delta Autumn'." *Journal of Modern Literature* I, No. 2 (1970-71): 209-25.

Discusses revisions in "Delta Autumn" for inclusion in *Go Down, Moses.* In Harter's view Faulkner's revisions emphasize Ike's role as an ironic Christ figure, and connect the narrative with the whole of *Go Down, Moses,* thereby achieving more depth and significance.

Heller, Terry. "The Telltale Hair: A Critical Study of William Faulkner's 'A Rose for Emily'." *Arizona Quarterly* 28, No. 4 (Winter 1974): 301-18.

Examines the reader's response to "A Rose For Emily," the town's and narrator's attitude toward Emily, and conflicting narrative cues about the action of the story.

Holland, Norman N. "Fantasy and Defense in Faulkner's 'A Rose for Emily'." *Hartford Studies in Literature* IV, No. 1 (1972): 1-35.

A psychoanalytic examination of "A Rose for Emily."

Howell, John M. "Hemingway, Faulkner, and 'The Bear'." *American Literature* LII, No. 1 (March 1980): 115-26.

Demonstrates that 'The Bear' contains a parallel thematic development to that found in Hemingway's *For Whom the Bell Tolls,* and compares similarities and differences in treatment by the two authors.

Inge, M. Thomas, ed. *William Faulkner: A Rose for Emily.* Columbus, Ohio: Charles E. Merril Publishing Co., 1970, 140 p.

Includes the text of "A Rose for Emily" as well as several excerpts from critical essays concerning that work and two thematically related short stories by other authors.

James, Stuart. "The Ironic Voices of Faulkner's *Go Down, Moses.*" *South Dakota Review* XVI, No. 3 (Autumn 1978): 80-101.

Asserts that Faulkner intended Isaac McCaslin to be seen as an ironic character.

Kinney, Arthur F. "Faulkner's Narrative Poetics and *Collected Stories.*" *Faulkner Studies: An Annual of Research, Criticism, and Reviews,* No. 1 (1980): 58-79.

Discusses the arrangement and sectional division of *Collected Stories of William Faulkner.*

Kuyk, Dirk, Jr.; Kuyk, Betty M.; and Miller, James A. "Black Culture in William Faulkner's 'That Evening Sun'." *Journal of American Studies* 20, No. 1 (April 1986): 33-50.

Considers "That Evening Sun" within the context of black culture. The critics assert that the story's ambiguities result from Faulkner's inability to fully enter the black cultural experience.

Limon, John. "The Integration of Faulkner's *Go Down, Moses.*" *Critical Inquiry* XII, No. 2 (Winter 1986): 422-38.

Asserts that "Pantaloon in Black" was placed in *Go Down, Moses* by Faulkner to deliberately break the cohesion of the book.

Lydenberg, John. "Nature Myth in Faulkner's 'The Bear'." *American Literature* 24, No. 1 (March 1952): 62-72.

Traces a mythic symbolism in the characters and events portrayed in "The Bear."

McHaney, Thomas L. *William Faulkner: A Reference Guide.* Boston: G. K. Hall & Co., 1976, 568 p.

An annotated bibliography of criticism on Faulkner arranged chronologically.

Mickelson, David. "The Campfire and the Hearth in *Go Down, Moses.*" *The Mississippi Quarterly* XXXVIII No. 3 (Summer 1985): 311-27.

Examines an opposition in *Go Down, Moses* between the hearth, representing a female world of marriage and domesticity, and hunts and games, representing a male world of competition and solitude.

Muller, Gilbert H. "The Descent of the Gods: Faulkner's 'Red Leaves' and the Garden of the South." *Studies in Short Fiction* XI No. 3 (Summer 1974): 243-49.

A theological reading of "Red Leaves."

O'Brien, Edward J. "'That Evening Sun Go Down' by William Faulkner." In his *The Short Story Case Book,* p. 324. New York: Farrar & Rinehart, 1935.

A commentary for students. O'Brien reprints "That Evening Sun Go Down" and provides a paragraph by paragraph commentary on the text, with questions to provoke thought.

O'Connor, William Van. "The Wilderness Theme in Faulkner's 'The Bear'." *Accent* XIII, No. 1 (Winter 1953): 12-20.

Discusses Faulkner's revisions of "The Bear," his creation of a symbol of the wilderness in Old Ben, and his recognition that adherence to the spirit of the wilderness does nothing to alleviate the other great problem of the book, that of racial injustice.

Pascal, Richard. "Love, Rapacity, and Community in *Go Down, Moses.*" *Ariel* XV, No. 3 (July 1984): 63-79.

Discusses the dichotomy between love and debased sexual dominance explored in *Go Down, Moses.*

Perry, Menakhem. "Literary Dynamics: How the Order of a Text Creates Its Meanings (With an Analysis of Faulkner's 'A Rose for Emily')." *Poetics Today* I, No. 2 (Autumn 1979): 35-64, 311-61.

A discussion of the ways in which the order and presentation of elements in a literary text can affect its reading, and a discussion of "A Rose for Emily" in which its nonchronological sequence of episodes functions to affect the reader's perception of the story.

Phillips, K. J. "Waste Land in Faulkner's *Go Down, Moses*." *The International Fiction Review* IX, No. 2 (Summer 1982): 114-19.

Relates elements of *Go Down, Moses* to myths that formed the basis for T. S. Eliot's "The Waste Land."

Pinsker, Sanford. "The Unlearning of Ike McCaslin: An Ironic Reading of William Faulkner's 'The Bear'." *Topic: A Journal of the Liberal Arts* XII (Spring 1972): 35-51.

Views Isaac's repudiation of his inheritance as an impotent gesture.

Pitcher, E. W. "Motive and Metaphor in Faulkner's 'That Evening Sun'." *Studies in Short Fiction* 18, No. 2 (Spring 1981): 131-35.

Suggests that at the climax of "That Evening Sun," Nancy is no longer afraid of dying, but fears losing her soul because she has had an abortion.

Pounds, Wayne. "Symbolic Landscapes in 'The Bear': 'Rural Myth and Technological Fact'." *The Gypsy Scholar* IV, No. 1 (Winter 1977): 40-52.

Contrasts the world of the wilderness with the world of the plantation as represented in "The Bear."

Ragan, David Paul. "'Belonging to the Business of Mankind': The Achievement of Faulkner's *Big Woods*." *The Mississippi Quarterly* XXXVI, No. 3 (Summer 1983): 301-17.

Discusses the arrangement of the stories and connecting interludes of *Big Woods*, as well as revisions within the stories themselves for inclusion in this volume.

Ricks, Beatrice. *William Faulkner: A Bibliography of Secondary Works*. Metuchen, N.J.: Scarecrow Press, 1981, 657 p.

A list of criticism on Faulkner arranged topically with occasional annotations.

Sachs, Viola. "The Bear." In her *The Myth of America: Essays in the Structures of Literary Imagination*, pp. 125-42. Paris: Mouton, 1973.

An analysis of mythic and symbolic elements in "The Bear."

Sartre, Jean-Paul. "William Faulkner's *Sartoris*" and "On *The Sound and the Fury:* Time in the Work of Faulkner." In his *Literary and Philosophical Essays*, pp. 78-83, 84-93. New York: Collier Books, 1962.

Examines various technical devices and themes in Faulkner's work. These essays, written in the late 1930s, are among the earliest that acknowledge Faulkner as a major writer.

Schleifer, Ronald. "Faulkner's Storied Novel: *GDM* and the Translation of Time." *Modern Fiction Studies* XXVIII, No. 1 (Spring 1982): 109-27.

Views initiation themes as Faulkner's attempt to create meaning for past experiences in present time.

Sederberg, Nancy B. "'A Momentary Anesthesia of the Heart': A Study of the Comic Elements in Faulkner's *Go Down, Moses*." In *Faulkner and Humor: Faulkner and Yoknapatawpha, 1984*, edited by Doreen Fowler and Ann J. Abadie, pp. 79-96. Jackson: University Press of Mississippi, 1984.

Examines humorous episodes in *Go Down, Moses* and their relation to the underlying tragic theme of the work.

Sequeira, Isaac. "'The Bear': The Initiation of Ike McCaslin." *Osmania Journal of English Studies* 9, No. 1 (1972): 1-10.

Analyzes "The Bear" as a rite of initiation in which Isaac McCaslin fails to complete the process of adjusting to the adult world and assuming a place in society.

Skei, Hans H. *William Faulkner: The Short Story Career*. Oslo, Norway: Universitetsforlaget, 1981, 164 p.

A compendium of publication information and information concerning revisions of short stories as they were published in magazines and collections or incorporated into novels.

———. *William Faulkner: The Novelist as Short Story Writer*. Oslo, Norway: Universitetsforlaget, 1985, 330 p.

An unsystematic but detailed examination of Faulkner's short stories from the first known sketches to the last stories Faulkner published.

Slabley, Robert M. "Quentin Compson's 'Lost Childhood'." *Studies in Short Fiction* I No. 3 (Spring 1964): 173-83.

Discusses reasons for Quentin's narration of "That Evening Sun" fifteen years after the events take place, and relates that short story to "A Justice" and to *The Sound and the Fury*.

Trilling, Lionel. "The McCaslins of Mississippi." *The Nation* 154, No. 22 (30 May 1942): 632-33.

An early review of *Go Down, Moses*. Trilling disparages Faulkner's prose, but praises his description of the racial division of the South.

Utley, Francis Lee; Bloom, Lynn Z.; and Kinney, Arthur F. *Bear, Man, and God: Seven Approaches to William Faulkner's "The Bear."* New York: Random House, 1964, 429 p.

Includes the text of "The Bear" and various biographical, historical, and critical texts relating to the story. The volume also includes "Lion," an earlier story which Faulkner used as material for "The Bear," and a shortened version of "The Bear," which was published in *The Saturday Evening Post* concurrently with the publication of *Go Down, Moses*.

Voss, Arthur. "Virtuoso Storyteller: William Faulkner." In his *The American Short Story: A Critical Survey*, pp. 242-61.

Gives plot summaries of many of Faulkner's short stories.

Wagner, Linda W., ed. *William Faulkner: Four Decades of Criticism*. East Lansing: Michigan State University Press, 1973, 374 p.

A collection of major critical essays dating from the 1930s to the early 1970s.

Welty, Eudora. Review of "The Bear." In her *Short Stories*, pp. 39-47. New York: Harcourt, Brace, and Co., 1949.

Compares "The Bear" with D. H. Lawrence's "The Fox." Welty concentrates on the hunting story, ignoring part four of "The Bear" included in the *Go Down, Moses* version; she also comments on Faulkner's literary style.

Mary (Eleanor) Wilkins Freeman

1852-1930

(Also wrote under pseudonym of Constant Reader) American short story writer, novelist, poet, and dramatist.

Freeman was a late nineteenth- and early twentieth-century American short story writer and novelist. Her critical reputation rests primarily on *A Humble Romance, and Other Stories,* and *A New England Nun, and Other Stories,* the short story collections that first won her acclaim for their depiction of the small New England villages Freeman knew, and for her realistic and unsentimental portrayal of the inhabitants of this specific region. Although much of Freeman's work is unread and unexamined today, Perry D. Westbrook maintains that "two or three volumes of her early short stories and one or two novels, all written before 1900, form as valuable a study of New England rural and village life as we have." These books launched Freeman's career as a significant commentator on conditions prevailing in post-Civil War New England. Since the 1970s Freeman has been the subject of renewed attention from feminist critics examining those of her works that explore the scope of women's lives during her era.

Freeman was born in Randolph, Massachusetts, and moved with her family to Brattleboro, Vermont, when she was fifteen, living there until her middle thirties. After the deaths of her parents she returned to Randolph to reside with friends. As a young woman, Freeman had published stories and verse in the children's magazines *Wide Awake* and *St. Nicholas;* faced with the necessity of supporting herself and an aunt, she resumed writing fiction. Her stories began appearing in such periodicals as *Harper's Monthly* and the *New York Sunday Budget,* which published her first nonjuvenile short story, "A Shadow Family," in 1882. She continued to place short fiction in various journals, and once she was established as a successful and popular short story writer, she began to write novels, which appeared serially in magazines before publication in book form. Most of her volumes of short stories were compiled from works previously published in magazines. The collections *A Humble Romance* and *A New England Nun,* as well as the novels *Jane Field*, *Pembroke*, and *Jerome, a Poor Man*, established Freeman as a prominent writer of local color fiction and a preeminent short story writer.

In the early 1890s Freeman met Charles M. Freeman, a doctor seven years her junior whom she married in 1902. Although she continued writing, Freeman abandoned regional fiction and ventured into new genres, such as ghost stories, dramas, and historical and romance novels. These later efforts were never as critically successful or as popular as her earlier work, and commentators generally agree that such honors as the William Dean Howells Medal she was awarded in 1925 for distinguished work in fiction and her 1926 election to the National Institute of Arts and Letters were based on her early accomplishments. Freeman's marriage too proved unsuccessful. Her husband, an alcoholic, was periodically confined to mental institutions, and Freeman herself, long dependent on tranquilizers and sleeping medications, increasingly relied on such aids. She separated from her husband and spent her last years living with friends and relatives.

"A young writer should follow the safe course of writing only about those subjects she knows thoroughly," Freeman wrote, and her most highly regarded works are those that depict life in the small rural New England villages of her own experience. "What directed me to the short story?" she wrote. "I think the answer is very simple. The short story did not take so long to write, it was easier, and of course I was not *sure* of my own ability to write even the short story, much less a novel." Freeman's short stories chronicle a particular point in New England history. The combined effects of westward expansion and Civil War fatalities had left the area with a disproportionately female and elderly population; further, urban expansion and industrialization had lured many of the more vital and ambitious people of both sexes away from the rural Eastern villages. Freeman was concerned with setting down her observations about life under these conditions and was further interested in exploring the peculiarities of the New England temperament. The region was originally settled by pioneers sustained by a strict Calvinist faith and rigid adherence to a Puritan ethic of hard work and sacrifice. Their descendents, inheriting a tamed wilderness, were not as well served by this religious orthodoxy as their forebears, and according to Westbrook, "a study of the lingering Puritanism of her own times" interested Freeman.

The short story collections *A Humble Romance* and *A New England Nun* are considered Freeman's best and most representative works. Larzer Ziff has noted that in plotting her stories, Freeman depended "upon some dramatic complication, usually the behavior of a character who goes against the grain of the community." The title stories of these collections, as well as "The Revolt of 'Mother'," "A Village Singer," and "A Conflict Ended," earned Freeman critical notice as a "student of the will." Fred Lewis Pattee has noted that "her favorite theme is revolt," and in these stories, the principal characters assert themselves against friends, family, or an existing social order. Her protagonists, usually women, are generally one of two types: either deeply conventional persons who are driven to commit one uncharacteristically daring and rebellious act, or avowed eccentrics who staunchly and often successfully resist the community's insistence on conformity. Probably the best example of the first type appears in the story "The Revolt of 'Mother'." Mrs. Penn, the "Mother" of the title, lives forty years in a ramshackle house while her husband promises her a more suitable dwelling but channels all the family's funds into the care of his livestock. Exasperated, she moves her family and furnishings into a newly built barn, astonishing her neighbors, disconcerting her husband, but finally compelling him to provide the family with a comfortable home. Examples of the second type occur in such stories as "Christmas Jenny," "A Gala Dress," and "A Solitary." In these stories the protagonists, though recognized as village "characters," gain acceptance despite their differences from their neighbors.

Freeman's almost exclusive use of New England settings and her explorations of New England character types led to her early classification as a local color writer. A "local color movement" had developed in American literature around 1880, with writers exploiting the dialect, dress, customs, and mannerisms of certain regions, often with photographic attention to detail. Most recent literary critics and historians writing about Freeman, however, have focused primarily on her differences from such prominent New England local colorists as Sarah Orne Jewett, with whom she was often compared, and Harriet Beecher Stowe. Although Freeman's regional fiction is often considered realistic, her realism is not that of Jewett and Stowe, who faithfully reproduced the physical details of their particular settings. Rather, Freeman's New England, as Ziff noted, "could be anywhere rural and neglected," and her themes are generally considered more universal than those of these other regional writers. For example, although she used New England place and family names in her stories, she eschewed the meticulous physical description that was characteristic of much local color fiction in favor of using symbolic details. Westbrook has noted that in this Freeman resembles Nathaniel Hawthorne, who shared Freeman's interest "in general aspects of New England life rather than in its shadings from county to county or from state to state." Critics believe that she preferred to use generalized rather than specific locales and characters because this gave her greater opportunity to treat such broad themes as individual revolt and societal pressure toward conformity. Some commentators maintain that classifying Freeman as a local color or regional writer not only limits her appeal, but also overlooks the fact that her primary themes were more universal than those commonly dealt with in local color fiction.

Freeman's novels, though generally well-received at the time of their publication, have not garnered the sustained critical attention of her early short stories, and in fact, much of her post-1900 short fiction has been similarly disregarded. Many critics maintain that while she was skilled at creating a short story around the idiosyncrasies of a leading character, this method was too weak to sustain a novel. Freeman's later attempts at subjects outside her New England regional fiction, such as the historical novel *The Heart's Highway,* the social-problem novel *The Portion of Labor,* and the detective novel *An Alabaster Box,* coauthored with Florence Morse Kingsley, display the same weaknesses, and are further flawed by her unfamiliarity with these genres. Charles Miner Thompson has called her novels "experiments" that were for the most part failures, "obviously outside the range of her abilities."

Recently Freeman's short fiction has received renewed critical attention from feminist literary critics who are concerned with her explorations of women's lives. The solitary but self-sufficient unmarried women protagonists of the stories "A New England Nun," "An Honest Soul," and "A Church Mouse," for example, as well as the defiant and often successfully rebellious women characters central to "The Revolt of 'Mother'," "A Poetess," and "A Mistaken Charity" have been interpreted as positive depictions of strong women making unconventional choices. In choosing to write about the rebels and outcasts of her time, Freeman left an enduring record of a period of decline in the rural New England way of life, a record that with its psychological insights and historical perspective holds a lasting appeal to readers. Freeman's insight into the strong and sometimes eccentric personalities of her New England neighbors was extensive, and she portrayed these people and their era vividly and with sympathy.

(See also *Twentieth Century Literary Criticism,* Vol. 9; *Contemporary Authors,* Vol. 113; and *Dictionary of Literary Biography,* Vol. 12.)

PRINCIPAL WORKS

SHORT FICTION

A Humble Romance, and Other Stories (1887)
A New England Nun, and Other Stories (1891)
Young Lucretia, and Other Stories (1892)
Silence, and Other Stories (1898)
The Love of Parson Lord, and Other Stories (1900)
Understudies (1901)
Six Trees (1903)
The Wind in the Rosebush, and Other Stories of the Supernatural (1903)
Edgewater People (1918)
The Best Stories of Mary E. Wilkins (1927)
Collected Ghost Stories (1974)
Selected Stories of Mary E. Wilkins Freeman (1983)

OTHER MAJOR WORKS

Jane Field (novel) 1893
Pembroke (novel) 1894
Madelon (novel) 1896
Jerome, a Poor Man (novel) 1897
The Jamesons (novel) 1899
The Heart's Highway (novel) 1900
The Portion of Labor (novel) 1901
The Debtor (novel) 1905
By the Light of the Soul (novel) 1906
The Shoulders of Atlas (novel) 1908
The Butterfly House (novel) 1912
An Alabaster Box [with Florence Morse Kingsley] (novel) 1917

[WILLIAM DEAN HOWELLS] (essay date 1887)

[Howells, an American novelist, short story writer, and dramatist, is recognized as one of the nineteenth century's major literary figures and one of its most influential literary critics. A pioneer of American literary realism, he is credited with successfully distancing American literature from the sentimental romanticism of its infancy. In the following excerpt, Howells offers a favorable review of A Humble Romance, and Other Stories.*]*

Take . . . a number of studies like ***A Humble Romance, and Other Stories,*** by Miss Mary E. Wilkins, and you have the air of simple village life as liberally imparted as if all the separate little dramas were set in a single frame and related to one another. The old maids and widows aging and ailing and dying in their minute wooden houses; the forlorn elderly lovers; the simple girls and youths making and marring love; the husbands and wives growing apart and coming together; the quarrels and reconciliations; the eccentricities and the heroisms; the tender passions and true friendships; the funerals and weddings; the hates and spites; the injuries; the sacrifices; the crazy consciences; the sound commonsense—are all suggested and expressed in a measure which, we insist, does not lack breadth, though each sketch is like the sentences of Emerson, "an infinitely repellent particle," and will having nothing to do with any other, so far as community of action is concerned. Community of character abounds: the people are of one New England blood, and speak one racy tongue. It might all have been done otherwise; the lives and fortunes of these villagers might have been interwoven in one texture of narrative; but the work would not necessarily have gained breadth in gaining bulk. Breadth is in the treatment of material, not in the amount of it. The great picture is from the great painter, not from the extensive canvas. Miss Wilkins's work could hardly have given a wider sense of life in a Yankee village and the outlying farms if it had greater structural unity. It has unity of spirit, of point of view, of sympathy; and being what the author intended, we ask no other unity of it; many "broader" views lack this unity which is so valuable. Besides, it has humor of a quaint, flavorous sort, it has genuine pathos, and a just and true respect for the virtues of the life with which it deals. We are tempted to give some passages illustrative of a very remarkable freshness in its description; they are abundant, but perhaps we had better content ourselves by referring the reader to the opening of the touching sketch, **"A Far-away Melody."** What is notable in all the descriptions is the absence of literosity; they are as unrhetorical as so many pictures of Tourguénief's, or Björnson's, or Verga's, and are interesting proofs of the fact that the present way of working is instinctive; one writer does not learn it from another; it is in the time, in the air, and no critic can change it. When you come to the motives of these little tales, the simplicity and originality are not always kept; sometimes they ring false, sentimental, romantic; but even then they are true in the working out of character, though this does not redeem them from the original error. For the most part, however, they are good through and through, and whoever loves the face of common humanity will find pleasure in them. They are peculiarly American, and they are peculiarly "narrow" in a certain way, and yet they are like the best modern work everywhere in their directness and simplicity. They are somewhat in the direction of Miss Jewett's more delicate work, but the fun is opener and less demure, the literature is less refined, the poetry is a little cruder; but there is the same affectionate feeling for the material, a great apparent intimacy with the facts, and a like skill in rendering the Yankee parlance. We have our misgivings, however, about "thar" and "whar" on New England tongues, though we are not ready to deny that Miss Wilkins heard them in the locality she evidently knows so well. (p. 640)

[William Dean Howells], "Editor's Study," in Harper's New Monthly Magazine, *Vol. 75, No. 448, September, 1887, pp. 638-42.*

THE ATLANTIC MONTHLY **(essay date 1891)**

[In the following, an anonymous critic praises the originality and compressed style of Freeman's short stories, which display her "power of packing a whole story in a phrase."]

[It is] the disposition of Miss Wilkins to single out for her subjects highly accented phases of New England life. . . . In [***A New England Nun, and Other Stories***] Miss Wilkins has included twenty-four stories. The book is charged with tender sentiment, yet once only, so far as we remember, at the close of the moving story of **"Christmas Jenny,"** does the author introduce anything which may be likened to an artistic use of sentiment. In this story the figures of the girl and her lover make the kind of foil which we are used to in German sentimental literature. The touch here, however, is so slight as almost to escape notice. It serves chiefly to remind one how entirely Miss Wilkins depends for her effects upon the simple pathos or humor which resides in the persons and situations that are made known through a few strong, direct disclosures. The style is here the writer. The short, economical sentences, with no waste and no niggardliness, make up stories which are singularly pointed, because the writer spends her entire strength upon the production of a single impression. The compression of these stories is remarkable, and almost unique in our literature, and it is gained without any sacrifice of essentials and by no mere narrowness of aim, but by holding steadily before the mind the central, vital idea, to the exclusion of all by-thoughts, however interesting they may be. Hence it happens frequently that the reader, though left satisfied on the main issue, is piqued by the refusal of the storyteller to meet his natural curiosity on other points. (p. 847)

Miss Wilkins, with her passion for brevity, her power of packing a whole story in a phrase, a word, although she gives her characters full rein sometimes, naturally relies chiefly upon her own condensed report of persons, incidents, and things. Sententious talk, though not unknown in New England, runs the risk of being unnaturally expressive, and Miss Wilkins shows her fine artistic sense by not trusting to it for the expression of her characters. As a rule, the speech of the New England men and women in her stories is very simple and natural; her art lies in the selection she makes of what they shall say, the choice of a passage which helps on the story. Thus the brevity of speech which is in itself a characteristic of New England people is not made to carry subtleties or to have a very full intrinsic value, nor is it a mere colloquialism, designed to give color and naturalness, but it is the fit expression which conveys a great deal to the reader, because, like the entire story, it is a condensation, an epitome.

Of the genuine originality of these stories it is hard to speak too strongly. There is, indeed, a common character to the whole series, an undertone of hardship, of loss, of repressed life, of sacrifice, of the idolatry of duty, but we suspect this is due more to the prevailing spirit of New England life than to any determining force of Miss Wilkins's genius. For the most part, she brings to light some pathetic passage in a strongly marked individuality, and the variety of her characterizations is noticeable. Now and then she touches a very deep nature, and opens to view a secret of the human heart which makes us cry out that here is a poet, a seer. Such an effect is produced by the most powerful story in the book, **"Life Everlastin'."** More frequently she makes us exclaim with admiration over the novelty, yet truthfulness, of her portraitures, as in **"The Revolt of 'Mother'"** and the story which gives the title to her book [**"A New England Nun"**]. Always there is a freedom from commonplace, and a power to hold the interest to the close which is owing, not to a trivial ingenuity, but to the spell which her personages cast over the reader's mind as soon as they come within his ken. He wonders what they will do; and if he is surprised at any conclusion, the surprise is due, not to any trick in the author, but to the unexpected issue of an original conception, which reflection always shows to be logical and reasonable.

The humor which is a marked feature of Miss Wilkins's stories is of a pungent sort. Every story has it, and it is a savor which prevents some, that otherwise would be rather painful, from oppressing the reader unduly. (pp. 847-48)

"New England in the Short Story," in The Atlantic Monthly, *Vol. 67, No. 6, June, 1891, pp. 845-50.*

MARY E. WILKINS FREEMAN (essay date 1917)

[*In the following excerpt, Freeman lightheartedly bemoans the fact that she is best known for the short story "The Revolt of 'Mother'," claiming that the characters and action of the story are not true to life, as fiction should be.*]

It occurs to me that I have never read a severe criticism of an author's own work by the author, and that it may be an innovation. I am therefore proceeding to criticize the story by which I consider myself lamentably best known, and that is **"The Revolt of 'Mother'."** It was in an evil day I wrote that tale. It exposed me to much of which I could not dream. This very morning I have a letter concerning that story. Somebody wishes to use it in a book. I fear I am mostly known by **"The Revolt of 'Mother'."** My revolt against the case is perfectly useless. People go right on with almost Prussian dogmatism, insisting that **"The Revolt of 'Mother'"** is my one and only work. It is most empahtically not. Were I not so truthful, having been born so near Plymouth Rock, I would deny I ever wrote that story. I would foist it upon somebody else. It would leave me with a sense of freedom I have not known since that woman moved into her husband's barn in print.

In the first place all fiction ought to be true, and **"The Revolt of 'Mother'"** is not in the least true. When I wrote that little tale I threw my New England traditions to the winds and trampled on my New England conscience. Well, I have had and still have retribution. It is not a good thing to produce fiction which is not true, although that sounds paradoxical. The back bone of the best fiction is essential truth, and **"The Revolt of 'Mother'"** is perfectly spineless. I know it, because I am of New England and have lived there. I had written many true things about that cluster of stainless states and for a change I lied.

Sometimes incessant truth gets on one's nerves. It did on mine. There never was in New England a woman like Mother. If there had been she most certainly would not have moved into the palatial barn which her husband had erected next the mean little cottage she had occupied during her married life. She simply would have lacked the nerve. She would also have lacked the imagination. New England women of that period coincided with their husbands in thinking that sources of wealth should be better housed than consumers. That Mother would never have dreamed of putting herself ahead of Jersey cows which meant good money. Mother would have been to the full as thrifty as Father. If Mother had lived all those years in that little cottage she would have continued to live there. Moving into the new barn would have been a cataclysm. New England women seldom bring cataclysms about their shoulders.

If Mother had not been Mother, Father would never have been able to erect that barn. (pp. 25, 75)

It is a dreadful confession, but that woman called "Mother" in **"The Revolt of 'Mother'"** is impossible. I sacrificed truth when I wrote the story, and at this day I do not know exactly what my price was. I am inclined to think gold of the realm. It could not have been fame of the sort I have gained by it. If so I have had my punishment. Not a story since but somebody asks "Why not another **"Revolt of 'Mother'"**? My literary career has been halted by the success of the big fib in that story. Too late I admit it. The harm is done. But I can at least warn other writers. When you write a short story stick to the truth. If there is not a story in the truth knit until truth happens which does contain a story. Knit, if you can do no better at that than I, who drop more stitches than any airplane in Europe can drop bombs. You can at least pull out the knitting, but a story printed and rampant is a dreadful thing, never to be undone. (p. 75)

Mary E. Wilkins Freeman, "Who's Who—And Why: Mary E. Wilkins Freeman, an Autobiography," in The Saturday Evening Post, *Vol. 190, No. 23, December 8, 1917, pp. 25, 75.*

HAMLIN GARLAND (essay date 1925)

[*Garland was an American literary critic who stressed the importance of regional writing to the growth and development of a vital and original national literature. During a transitional period in late nineteenth-century American letters, when romanticism was giving way to literary realism and naturalism, Garland championed the works of Freeman, Howells, Jewett, and other local color fiction writers. The following excerpt is drawn from the speech Garland gave when Freeman received the first William Dean Howells Medal for Fiction in November 1925.*]

In the choice of Mary E. Wilkins Freeman as the recipient of the first Howells Medal for Fiction, I perceive an especial fitness, for she was not only a neighbor and a friend of William Dean Howells but the frequent subject of his approving comment. He considered her one of the leaders in the school of writers whose pens were at that time recording the characteristic color of American life.

Book after book flowed from her pen, each containing unfaltering portraits of lorn widowhood, crabbed age and wistful youth. She dramatized cheerful drudgery, patient poverty, defiant spinsterhood and many other individual but related types of character, each with its proper background of hill-town or village street; and in her books she has made an unparalleled study of New England life.

Almost without knowing it, she was the New England representative of the nation-wide group of Local Color fictionists; for at this time Joel Chandler Harris of Georgia, Thomas Nelson Page of Virginia, George W. Cable of Louisiana, Mary N. Murfree of Tennessee, Joseph Kirkland of Illinois, Alice French

Freeman (foreground) at a party celebrating the seventieth birthday of Mark Twain (left foreground) at Delmonico's, New York City.

of Arkansas, Sarah Orne Jewett of Maine, and many others were delineating the distinctive customs and characters of their several localities and sharing in the awakened interest of the public. None of these social recorders surpassed Mary Wilkins, and few equalled her in the art of the short story. Her concise diction, her unwavering use of phrase, her humor, her restraint, and her sympathetic understanding make her books not only delightful reading, but enduring pictures of an era which may be taken as the reverse side of the movement which was building cities and settling the far West.

Forty years ago no short-story writer was corrupted by overpayment. Money was a consideration, of course, but it was not an overwhelming lure. Our lives were simple, and our desires of moderate scope. I well remember the modest cottage home in Randolph in which Mary Wilkins lived, and in which I took tea with her—awed by the knowledge that she was not only earning her entire living by her pen but receiving for each of her sketches several times the sum of my noblest check. Nevertheless I can truthfully say that I did not envy her prosperity although I did envy her the security of her position and the quiet poise of her art.

Howells was to her, as to me, kindly critic as well as friend, but there was no thought of imitation in her mind. His reviews gave her helpful suggestion and encouragement, but there was no call for a discipleship. Miss Wilkins pursued her own way as we all wished her to do, feeling that in her pages the record of a melancholy yet heroic period of our ancestral life was being imperishably recorded, a record which was all the better, perhaps, for being unconsciously historical.

On that judgment I still rest. In the thousand pages of her short stories as well as in her longer novels the historian of the future will find set down the era of abandoned old age as well as of abandoned farms.

It has its poetry as well as its pathos, and the art of our honored novelist did not fail to include the scent of cinnamon roses and the laughter of village girls. Along with her pictures of obdurate deacons, kitchen colonels, defiant church mice and revolting mothers, she has pictured aspiring youth and genial middle age. But they are all of the old New England, the New England before the coming of the French Canadian and the Italian peasant. If, toward the last of her work, these alien elements entered, they did so by way of contrast. The body of her work remains of the Anglo-Saxon order. (pp. 318-21)

Hamlin Garland, "The Howells Medal," in his Afternoon Neighbors: Further Excerpts from a Literary Log, *The Macmillan Company, 1934, pp. 317-27.*

GRANVILLE HICKS (essay date 1935)

[*Hicks was an American literary critic whose famous study* The Great Tradition: An Interpretation of American Literature since the Civil War *(1933) established him as the foremost advocate of Marxist critical thought in Depression-era America. Throughout the 1930s he argued for a more socially engaged brand of literature and severely criticized such writers as Henry James, Mark Twain, and Edith Wharton, because he believed they failed to confront the realities of society. In the following excerpt, Hicks examines some reasons for the decline of regional fiction with specific reference to Freeman.*]

Freeman accepting from Hamlin Garland the first William Dean Howells Medal for outstanding work in fiction, 1925.

By the end of the seventies Rose Terry Cooke had begun her mild studies and Sarah Orne Jewett had entered upon her apprenticeship. The former, for all her sentimentality, could portray the more salient traits of the New England character, and the latter reflected with extraordinary subtlety the fragile beauties of that bleak land. Neither, however, made any effective recognition of whatever was ignoble or sordid or otherwise unpleasant in the life of New England, and it remained for Mary Wilkins Freeman, who joined their ranks in the eighties, to display the lonely spinster, the toil-bent farmer, and the worn-out workman. She at least saw that the small town had sometimes warped its inhabitants and that the intrusion of industrialism had increased the difficulties of these simple people. She could not, it is true, resist the temptation of the happy ending; her unfortunates are always compensated for their sufferings. But she had an eye for varieties of character and types of experience that her contemporaries ignored, and her stories made the record of New England life more nearly complete. (p. 56)

The promise of regionalism was never kept. Scarcely was the movement under way before its dangers were apparent; before it reached its apogee, its failure was inevitable. (p. 57)

One thinks of Mary Wilkins Freeman, following ***A New England Nun, A Humble Romance,*** and *Pembroke* with the soggy sentiment and inept symbolism of ***Six Trees,*** with so clumsy a venture into new fields as *The Portion of Labor,* with the repetitiousness, the stylistic pretentiousness, the unconvincing complacency of any of her later collections. Like Harte and Cable, she could not find another subject so congenial to her powers as that she had begun by attacking, and that subject proved incapable of extension and unfriendly to literary growth. (pp. 58-9)

The aim of the sectional writers, it is to be remembered, was to make imaginative use of the kind of life that was familiar to them, and their strength should have lain in a steady progress from an understanding of that life to a comprehension of the larger issues of American civilization. But how could such growth take place if they were not willing to examine the section as they found it, if their attention was fastened not on the present but on the past? (p. 60)

For the truth is that the kind of life these writers described no longer existed. (p. 61)

Concentration on the past also encouraged the attempt to exploit sectional peculiarities and thus invited the writer to concern himself with the superficial mannerisms of his region. Though at the outset the interest in dialect held out the hope that literature might be rooted in the realities of everyday speech, as time went on dialect was cultivated for its own sake, as a kind of literary ornament, and attention was distracted from the fundamental tasks of fiction. In the same way the description of local scenery and the introduction of local customs became ends in themselves. (pp. 62-3)

Of course it cannot be argued that there was any easy alternative open to the regionalists. The understanding of historical forces that would have explained actual conditions in any given section in the decades after the war was difficult to attain. When, as sometimes happened, a writer sought that understanding, he was almost certainly doomed to disappointment. . . . So Mrs. Freeman discovered when she wrote *The Portion of Labor,* with its strange mixture of insight into New England character and childish ignorance of industrial conditions. These writers were what they were, and they carried with them into any literary field the burden of habits that regionalism had fostered. Mrs. Freeman had all her life been dealing with essentially tragic materials that she had refused to treat as tragic. She had, for example, furnished *Pembroke,* as sharp a study of New England crabbedness as has ever been written, with a happy ending that violated every premise she had laid down. It is no wonder, then, that she disposed in *The Portion of Labor* of problems of shop conditions, wage cuts, and strikes by ending the book with a collection of engaged couples, a meaningless conversion, and a handful of platitudes. (pp. 63-4)

Granville Hicks, "A Banjo on My Knee," in his The Great Tradition: An Interpretation of American Literature Since the Civil War, *revised edition, Macmillan Publishing Company, 1935, pp. 32-67.*

LARZER ZIFF (essay date 1966)

[*Ziff is an American critic who has examined the combined effect of social and literary influences on American culture in his studies* The American 1890s: Life and Times of a Lost Generation *(1966),* Puritanism in America: New Culture in a New World *(1973), and* Literary Democracy: The Declaration of Cultural Independence *(1981). In the following excerpt, he discusses some deficiencies in Freeman's short fiction, most notably the lack of a strongly delineated sense of place and her substitution of action for analysis.*]

At the same time that Miss Jewett was exploring the vital meaning still resident in New England rural life, Mary Wilkins Freeman was writing stories and novels of the region. These, however, spoke of "that black atmosphere of suspicion and hatred, which gathers nowhere more easily than a New England town." Her critical pictures of a region which was dying, unlike those of Miss Jewett, suggested not a genial afterglow of great days, but the piercing northern night which had descended on a land now barren. By 1895 . . . Mrs. Freeman was established as the realist most likely to succeed Howells as leader of the school, but, although her writing career was to continue until 1918, she had already achieved her best work. (p. 292)

She was well aware of the changing times and considered the developments they brought important. But Mrs. Freeman was quick to criticize what she disliked before she understood it, and to apply the theories of the day to her fiction before she had made them her own. She was far less of an artist than Miss Jewett, and, in her concern for action and its immediate consequences rather than its relation to setting, she was careless in her diction and all too ready to help herself out of difficulties with a forced ending. The New England of her stories and novels does not convey the sense of place carried by Sarah Jewett's Maine; it could be anywhere rural and neglected: flora, speech, customs do not figure strongly in her plots. She depends, rather, upon some dramatic complication, usually the behavior of a character who goes against the grain of the community, and she devotes herself to working this out as a tale rather than following its reverberation as a metaphor of the quality of the life lived, as did Miss Jewett.

But Mrs. Freeman, though she failed to record the harmonies that Sarah Jewett saw, was concerned with rebellion. Her village folk are petty and grudging. They are materialists whose religion confirms their stinginess rather than relieving it, and her sympathetic characters are forced to act against the narrowness of folkways rather than in concert with them as do Miss Jewett's. Spinsterhood is a prison for Mary Freeman, and in place of the ruddy old age of the single woman in Miss Jewett she clearly presents the single state as a frustrated existence, since in it a woman is deprived of what Mrs. Freeman considers to be her birthright—a man. The heroine of the title story in her best collection, ***A New England Nun and Other Stories,*** is an example of sexual sublimation, and she pursued this theme in its various guises through a number of tales. The hesitant, reticent New England suitors are far from the charming beings they appear to be in Miss Jewett's pages, but they are always, for Mrs. Freeman, preferable to no man at all. Since Mrs. Freeman's villagers set far more store by their possessions than do Miss Jewett's, poverty is a far more important fact in her stories, as it was in her life. For a man, being jobless is what being manless is for a woman, a horrifying state of uselessness and poverty to be avoided at all costs, and Mrs. Freeman's happy endings usually feature a man landing a job or a woman landing a man. Although not so fully realized—episodes too often substituting for the art of the story—Mary Wilkins Freeman's work aims at a range of impressions well beyond Miss Jewett's ken. While today it takes on an artificiality from which Miss Jewett is almost entirely free, its greater popularity in its own day is understandable.

Since Mary Freeman was at odds with the setting about which she wrote, her work is at its best when she has as her central character somebody who has a legitimate complaint about that environment. In following such a character she can achieve a fusion of her contempt with the psychology of the hero or heroine. Her many volumes are laden with near misses; she seems not to have had a sense of her craft and not to have grown with it. But every now and again there is a rewarding hit like the story **"Life Everlastin'."** Here Mrs. Freeman has found an ideal alter ego, the hardworking, poor but honest woman who is the village agnostic and is therefore simultaneously respected and an outcast. Measured against her gossipy, homely churchgoing sister, this woman is a saint, but her career of going against the mean grain of her village is threatened finally by her accidental detection of the hiding place of a man who has committed a brutal murder. She knows him: he is John Gleason, one of the wastrel hired men whom she has helped out from time to time, but she cannot permit either her loyalty to him or her scorn for the community to allow her to shield him from the consequences of his act, and she reveals his hiding place to the sheriff. Then this woman, betrayed by life into finally acting according to the standards of her petty village, faces the consequences of her own act and, for the first time in twenty-five years, appears in church. Barabbas, not Jesus, sent her there, and the story closes with her saying: "I've made up my mind that I'm goin' to believe in Jesus Christ. I ain't never, but I'm goin' to now, for . . . *I don't see any other way out of it for John Gleason.*"

The elements which make up this stunning story are often present in Mrs. Freeman's other work in the nineties, but they all too seldom combine, and, especially in her novels, they come forth only spasmodically. In her sustained fiction her failure to penetrate to the psychological workings of her central characters is destructive, because, while a metaphoric act may serve as a substitute for analysis in a short story, the novel calls for a closer examination of the person who goes against the grain. (pp. 292-94)

Larzer Ziff, "An Abyss of Inequality: Sarah Orne Jewett, Mary Wilkins Freeman, Kate Chopin," in his American 1890s: Life and Times of a Lost Generation, *The Viking Press, 1966, pp. 275-305.*

ABIGAIL ANN HAMBLEN (essay date 1966)

[Hamblen discusses Freeman's powerful characterizations in her early short stories.]

Mary Wilkins' first two books of adult fiction, ***A Humble Romance and Other Stories*** and ***A New England Nun and Other Stories*** do much to establish her place in American literature. For these early collections are actually source material for anyone interested in early nineteenth century American life and thought, giving concrete and vivid details of a way of life that, presumably dead, still has noticeable repercussions.

It is true that a good many writers have concentrated on rural New England: Sarah Orne Jewett, Rose Terry Cooke, Margaret Deland, Alice Brown are only the most nearly typical of these, and perhaps the best known. They had their vogue for a time, Miss Jewett's delicate art earning special (and lasting) respect. And yet Mary Wilkins achieved something more. Granville Hicks explains: "Neither [Rose Terry Cooke nor Sarah Orne Jewett]," he says, "made any effective recognition of whatever was ignoble or sordid or otherwise unpleasant in the life of New England. . . . Mary Wilkins Freeman . . . at least saw that the small town had sometimes warped its inhabitants . . . she had an eye for varieties of character and types of experience her contemporaries ignored, and her stories made the record of New England more nearly complete" [see excerpt dated

1933]. That expression "made the record of New England life more nearly complete" is really the key to her significance; the reader cannot help seeing that **"A Humble Romance"** and the tales that came after are from life; their great value is in their straightforward unromantic portrayal of a certain culture, a certain way of thinking and living in a certain American corner of the earth.

The people Mary Wilkins writes about are almost symbolic of what later generations have taken to mean "Yankee" traits of character. Mainly these people are women, young women whose shy hopes of love are early killed or thwarted, older women unloved and alone, bereft of all they had desired. Most of them are poor with a poverty that makes the reader wince. Betsey Dole, for instance, plans how to use her saucer of cold potatoes, her tiny scrap of pork, her slice of bread to make three meals; Inez Morse carefully meditates on the unheard-of luxury of a bow of crimson ribbon; ancient Martha Patch faints from hunger, with only a teaspoon of tea leaves left in the house.

But poor or not-quite poor, one thing each of them possesses is a will coupled with an endurance that resembles the grey, weatherbeaten outcroppings of rock in their pastures. These women are descendants of the Puritan fathers who believed in a God of pure Will, and unconsciously modelled themselves upon Him. They are the descendants of men who forced their way into a gloomy wilderness and established their way of life and let it be known to all comers that no other way would be acceptable.

Through the generations the bitter winters and the stingy soil have had their effect, but the steadfastness of temperament remains. Inez Morse (**"A Taste of Honey"**) sets herself to pay off the pitiful six-hundred-dollar mortgage her father had failed to erase after a lifetime of toil. She denies herself everything possible in the way of pleasure and luxury, even marriage. She works and pinches and saves, and she does pay the mortgage off, though her fiancé, tired of waiting, leaves her for another girl. In **"Louisa"** a young woman almost starves, and, worse, watches her complaining mother and feeble grandfather suffer, when an available marriage would end privation for them all. But she will not feign love for gain; she keeps her integrity. **"The Revolt of 'Mother'"** shows Sarah Penn, determined upon having a decent home for her children, even if it means moving into the enormous new barn her husband has built instead of her long-dreamed-of house. (pp. 19-20)

One fact the reader cannot escape is that in many cases the steadfastness of the Puritan has, in these his descendants, degenerated into an unlovely obstinacy so mean and pinched that it has nothing of the heroic in it. **"A Conflict Ended"** is an excellent illustration. Here is Marcus Woodman sitting, Sunday after Sunday, on the steps of the church instead of going in to the service. For ten years he does this, keeping a vow made when the present minister was engaged against his wishes. . . .

Side by side with the strong will, reinforced and sustained by it, is pride. The religion of these people may enjoin humility, but how can humility be forced on men and women (especially women) whose very life-sustenance is pride? Nancy Pingree, the last of a once fine and prosperous family, barely ekes out existence in her ancient mansion, but she holds up her head, allowing no one to acknowledge her poverty. She is a Pingree, and she will one day take her place with the others in the gloomy old Pingree family lot in the cemetery. The money for her funeral, saved a few cents at a time over a period of twenty years, is carefully hidden away in her bureau drawer. (p. 21)

Nor is pride confined to those who come from a once-rich family. Jenny Stevens, upstairs in Miss Pingree's mansion, has her standards of self-respect; she tries to support her dying mother and herself by sewing, but obtains very little work, and her landlady knows it. Still the rent of fifty cents a week is paid faithfully. Then one Saturday, after a particularly lean week, Jenny comes to pay as usual, and Nancy Pingree, wanting to help, tells her to let this week go: she, Miss Pingree, is in no need of the money. Jenny, embarrassed but firm, stands offering the money, and still the other refuses it. After a silent moment the girl lays the money on the window seat, saying, "'You can do just what you've a mind to do with it. . . . I certainly shan't take it back.'" (pp. 21-2)

And **"A Gala Dress"** shows extreme pride; the Misses Babcock are much reduced in circumstances; indeed, they have barely enough to eat. But they come from a "better class" than many of their neighbors, and they hold up their heads as Miss Pingree does hers. To appear at any public function wearing anything but black silk is unthinkable, and they have between them just one fine black silk gown, the last remnant of their former prosperity. They share this dress, wearing it turn and turn about, each sister sewing on her own trimming so no one will notice. (p. 22)

[The] reader is shown that these nineteenth-century Puritans range themselves into two classifications, those of the first resembling more nearly their ancestors of two hundred years before. These are "religious" to the core, and their salient trait is an uncompromising intolerance for anyone deviating from their code. **"An Independent Thinker"** offers an excellent example of this intolerance. Esther Gay is almost stone-deaf, so on Sundays she stays away from church and—crowning horror—*knits!* This is something so scandalous that it cannot be overlooked by her neighbors. Old Lavinia Dodge, across the street, is forbidden by her ancient mother to visit Esther; the young man who is courting Esther's granddaughter is told by his mother that he is not to marry into the Gay family. (pp. 24-5)

But Esther is adamant; she will not go against her principles: "'Then I s'pose you think it would be better for an old woman that's stone deaf, an' can't hear a word of the preachin', to go to meetin', an' set there doin' nothin' two hours, instead of staying to home an' knittin' to airn a little money to give the Lord. All I've got to say is, you kin think so then. I'm agoin' to do what's right, no matter what happens.'"

Her arguments do not help the situation. When old Mrs. Dodge dies, the unfortunate Lavinia, terribly crippled with rheumatism, has to go to the poorhouse; there is no money left. Esther offers her a home with her, and the old woman, in spite of the horror and shame of the poor-house, refuses. *Esther works on Sundays!*

How Esther, without giving in, cannily solves the problem of Lavinia's home and her granddaughter's courtship makes up the little plot. But what gives the story significance here is the picture of a code so rigid that the slightest deviation is considered an abomination. Esther Gay is honest, industrious, generous; she supports herself and looks after her granddaughter. Yet she must suffer the disapproval of all who know her because she does not keep the Sabbath in the prescribed manner. (p. 25)

It is not important here to make more than a passing note of [the stories'] structure. Some are hardly more than expanded sketches, plotless accounts of happenings in the lives of a handful of characters. In some of them, circumstances cause a change of heart or of opinion, and once in a while a man or woman works his or her way out of a dilemma, or takes positive and daring action and battles with life. Usually there is a happy ending, sometimes quite obviously contrived.

It may be that these happy endings have something to do with the civilization the stories describe, the civilization that began with the Puritans. Professor [Fred Lewis] Pattee has an interesting theory: Mary Wilkins herself came to Puritan stock, he says, and the Puritan always anxious to justify the ways of God to man, to show that this is a moral universe, inexorably weighted on the side of good. Hence all complications must end felicitously.

But the endings do not matter. What matters is that here is an artist whose work is of lasting value because of its minutely detailed, unglamorized truth. On the basis of these stories alone Mary Wilkins deserves to be acknowledged as a significant writer, one who saw the life about her clearly, and who recorded it for all time. (p. 33)

Abigail Ann Hamblen, in her The New England Art of Mary E. Wilkins Freeman, *The Green Knight Press, 1966, 70 p.*

JAY MARTIN (essay date 1967)

[In the following excerpt, Martin discusses characterization in a number of Freeman's short stories.]

Charles Miner Thompson, in pointing to her largely suppressed romanticism, called Mary E. Wilkins a disguised idealist [see *TCLC*, Vol. 9]. For nearly a decade Mary E. Wilkins made a career of producing stories and poems for children. But with ***A Humble Romance*** and ***A New England Nun,*** she abruptly turned about to criticize New England decadence more sternly and comprehensively than any of her peers had dared. . . . Rejecting the remnants of the Puritan village tradition that for Harriet Stowe and Rose Cooke still remained viable material; unconcerned with the consolations that Sarah Jewett found in nature or memory; unwilling to sentimentalize the fading and yellowing antique, as Lucy Larcom, Celia Thaxter, Annie Trumbull Slosson, and others did; uninterested in the Concord idealism these others inherited, Mary E. Wilkins delineated in full the humorless, vacant, mindless, narrow New Englander who had appeared as only one aspect of the work of her predecessors. (p. 148)

[The story **"A Conflict Ended"**] suggests the stylistic and tonal paradoxicalness at which Miss Wilkins ordinarily aims. Ten years before the story begins, Marcus Woodman has objected to the investiture of a new pastor and, in a burst of stubborn self-assertion, vows never to set foot in the church again. For ten years each Sunday he has sat on the church steps—while, with an equally self-assertive vow, his betrothed has refused to marry him so long as he continues his folly. Even though the story ends happily, Miss Wilkins insists on the tragedy of ten years made dull and painful; with all the villagers we feel, as the narrator says, "the pathos in the comedy." Mary Wilkins's characters would be comic if they were not so hopelessly pathetic. . . . The wills of her characters are diseased by exaggeration and incongruity and betrayed into ludicrous commitments.

In **"Gentian,"** for instance, a farmer refuses to let his wife cook for him because she secretly gave him medicine in his tea when he was dangerously ill. When she returns home after leaving him for nearly a year, he sends her away again—then appears at her sister's house to ask her to come home, as he had been intending to do when she first appeared. He surrenders his self-will in one direction even as he asserts it in another. In **"A New England Prophet"** Miss Wilkins delineates the pathetic absurdity of the Millerite craze, much as Eggleston had done in *The End of the World*. As in that novel, a shrewdly skeptical critic reveals the high comedy in the absolutely serious millennial conviction. Similarly, Candace Whitcomb in **"A Village Singer"** revolts against being displaced as choir soloist by playing her own organ and singing loudly from her house next to the church. David and Maria, in **"Two Old Lovers,"** have been keeping company together for twenty-five years. Certainly, as Miss Wilkins says, "There was something laughable, and at the same time rather pathetic, about [their] . . . courting," for David has never overcome his reticence so far as to ask her to marry him. In **"The Revolt of 'Mother,'"** too, emotional contraries intermingle. After living for forty years in a shack, Sarah Penn watches incredulously and sullenly the construction of a new barn—a second barn—by her husband. Pleading and expostulation having failed, she revolts against her flinty New England husband and moves her furniture and family out of the house and into the new barn. She has lived an animal existence for forty years, the symbolism suggests, and now she insists on living at least as well as the stock.

In her best stories Mary Wilkins has an admirable control of her art. . . . Her best story is undoubtedly **"A New England Nun."** Louisa Ellis, the "New England Nun" who has been waiting fourteen years for her lover, Joe Dagget, to return from making his fortune in Australia, is shocked by his masculine presence—which now seems crude to her—when he finally comes back to claim her hand. For, in the intervening years, she has "turned into a path . . . so straight and unswerving that it could only meet a check at her grave": unwittingly she has become another in the tradition of New England solitaries. Her path is described by the adverbs modifying her unconscious modes of action—"peacefully sewing," "folded precisely," "cut up daintily." . . . Into this delicately ordered world, Joe comes bumbling and shuffling, bringing dust into Louisa's house and consternation into her heart. Whenever he enters her house, Louisa's canary—the symbol of her delicacy as well as of her imprisonment—awakes and flutters wildly against the bars of his cage. Joe's masculine vigor is symbolized by a great yellow dog named Caesar, which Louisa has chained in her back yard for fourteen years, and fed corn mush and cakes. Joe threatens to turn him loose, which suggests to Louisa a picture of "Caesar on the rampage through the quiet and unguarded village." At last, accidentally overhearing Joe and Lily Dyer confess their love for each other—while yet Joe sadly but sternly remains true to Louisa—she gently rejoices that she can release him, and herself, from his vows. In contrast to the wild, luxuriant fertility—the fields ready for harvest, wild cherries, enormous clumps of bushes—surrounding the scene between Joe and Lily stands the gently passive sterility of Louisa's life, who looks forward to "a long reach of future days strung together like pearls in a rosary." In contrast to the fervid summer pulsating with fish, flesh, and fowl, is Louisa's prayerful numbering of days in her twilight cloister.

Beginning with the comic stereotype in New England literature of the aging solitary . . . Mary Wilkins transmutes Louisa into an affectionately pathetic but heroic symbol of the rage for passivity. Much like Nicholas Gunn in **"A Solitary,"** she consecrates her whole being to acquiescence. Nicholas, whose stony self-denial Wilkins compares to a Buddhist monk's, also shows the paradoxical tropical intensity of the cold New England character in the sudden dawning in him of passionate sympathy for a sick man. The same intensity is to be found in the other characters mentioned here: the various revolts of "Mother," Candace Whitcomb, Narcissa Stone (in **"One Good Time"**), of Delia Caldwell (in **"A Conquest of Humility"**), or of Marcus Woodman are documents of the smoldering violence in the New England character, recalling the energy which once subdued a wilderness and settled a land. Now, not what they do, but what they essentially are in their passionate commitments—though they have no purpose worthy of commitment—suggests the true measure of their heroism. Lacking a heroic society, Mary Wilkins's heroes are debased; noble in being, they are foolish in action. (pp. 149-51)

Jay Martin, "Paradises Lost: Mary E. Wilkins," in his Harvests of Change: American Literature, 1865-1914, *Prentice-Hall, Inc., 1967, pp. 148-52.*

PERRY D. WESTBROOK (essay date 1981)

[Westbrook, an American critic, is the author of the biographical and critical study Mary Wilkins Freeman *(see Additional Bibliography). In the following excerpt from his book on Jewett and her contemporaries, he examines several of Freeman's short stories that demonstrate peculiarities of the will, conscience, and spirit in her characters.]*

Mary Wilkins Freeman saw New England life through the dusky lenses of Salem Puritanism. For the oddities of New England character she had no such simple explanation as inbreeding, or climate, or the influence of a former frontier life. To her the New England mind was a complex of morbidly sensitive conscience and overdeveloped will. She went farther than either Harriet Beecher Stowe or Rose Terry Cooke in tracing the scars left by over two centuries of Calvinism, and often she found these scars to be still festering. As with Hawthorne, her own interest in matters of conscience and will is a hangover of an ancestral preoccupation with the state of the soul. (p. 88)

Though Hawthorne dealt primarily with the Puritan soul as it existed in the past, the younger writer adapted her methods to a study of the lingering Puritanism of her own times. There is disagreement as to whether Freeman's characters are indigenous to Brattleboro or to Randolph. But to argue the matter is to misunderstand the author's purposes. Like Hawthorne, she was interested in general aspects of New England life rather than in its shadings from county to county or from state to state. Thus, while the names of the towns in her stories correspond to those around Randolph—Dover, Canton, Pembroke—the descriptions of landscape are no more specific than those in *Twice-Told Tales*. In fact, there is little emphasis at all on description beyond the sketching in of a typical New England setting—a marked divergence from the methods of the other local-color writers, who described their regions with photographic realism down to the last tree or crossroads. The characters, too, are generalized rather than individualized; they are symbols, caricatures, like Hawthorne's Ethan Brand or the Reverend Mr. Hooper in "The Minister's Black Veil," each one representing some quality or bent, rather than being a fully-rounded human being. As in Dante's *Inferno,* even their physical appearance reflects their inner state—a hunched back, for example, signifying a crooked will. A writer with such purposes and methods would not wish to particularize her settings. Freeman's stories could have taken place in the hills of Vermont or the flatlands of eastern Massachusetts, or anywhere else where the influences of a dying Puritanism lingered.

Her style, too, is affected by this Hawthorne-like approach to her subject matter. A highly localized dialect like that of Rowland Robinson, for example, would be out of place. Her characters speak a typical, only slightly colored rural New England speech. One would recognize them as New England country people but could not place them in any one region as one could Jewett's Maine fishermen or Rose Terry Cooke's Connecticut farmers. Freeman's descriptive and narrative style is even less obtrusive than the rather formally impersonal style of Hawthorne. At times she has all the directness and simplicity of Hemingway, without the impression of a forced ease. (pp. 88-9)

[Freeman's] analysis of the peculiarities of the New England character had gone one step farther than that of either Rose Terry Cooke or Harriet Beecher Stowe, who had come to the conclusion that the disappearance of frontier conditions forced the vigorous New England will to find an outlet in petty and ignoble ends—squabbling with one's neighbor, pinching pennies, browbeating one's wife and children. To Mary Wilkins Freeman the New England character had been molded by its religion rather than by the frontier. The steady and strenuous development of the conscience and the will among the Puritans had reached its culmination in the settlement of North America. Pioneering and Calvinism went hand in hand, but Calvinism led the way. The spreading of Protestant Christianity would be considered a sacred obligation; in fulfilling that obligation—in fighting and converting the hostile heathen and in wringing a livelihood out of a sterile, frozen land—what greater assets could there be than a will trained in iron self-denial and a conscience, a sense of duty, that dared not flinch before death itself?

Freeman would agree with Stowe and Cooke that the comparative ease of New England farm life after the coming of the railroads released much spiritual energy that for want of better outlets was expended in meanness and "cussedness." (p. 89)

During the last hundred years the Puritan conscience has become as vestigial an organ in the American mind as is the appendix in the body. But, like the appendix, the vestigial conscience is subject to disease. In Mary Wilkins Freeman's stories this disease usually takes the form of a pitiable worrying over trivialities. One of her earliest and best stories, **"An Honest Soul,"** is typical. The heroine is Martha Patch, an unmarried sempstress who is so poor that, though she wishes for a window opening on the street, she can't afford it and has to be content with a view into her backyard. One day two customers each give her bundles of rags to be made into quilts, for which she will receive a dollar apiece. On completing the job she finds that she has used in one customer's quilt a bit of cloth belonging to the other. A normal person would ignore this fact; a meticulously honest person would point it out to the customers, even though realizing it could make no possible difference to them; but Martha Patch tears the quilts apart and resews them. But this second time too she has confused two pieces of rag. Again she rips the quilts and again she sews them together. Much time has now elapsed in which Martha has earned no money; and having earned no money, she hasn't eaten. On the morning she is going to deliver the finally completed quilts, she faints and spends the day on her floor, unable to arise till a neighbor eventually finds and resuscitates her.

Sarah Orne Jewett would have considered this woman an example of commendable New England self-reliance and individualism. Freeman is not so sure.

> It is a hard question to decide, whether there were any real merit in such finely strained honesty, or whether it were merely a case of morbid conscientiousness. Perhaps the old woman, inheriting very likely her father's scruples, had had them so intensified by age and childishness they they had become a little off the bias of reason.
>
> (pp. 90-1)

In Mary Wilkins Freeman's stories disease of the conscience is usually accompanied by disease of the will. The old woman who remade her patchwork quilts twice was stung by a morbidly sensitive conscience and driven on in her futile task by volition so terrific that it defied starvation itself. But as in this story our attention is focused primarily on the freakish conscience, in other stories it is focused on the workings of the lopsided will. In the selection entitled **"A Conflict Ended"** the villager Marcus Woodman quarrels with the rest of his parish over the choice of a minister who is not "doctrinal." Though no one ever knew exactly what Marcus meant by the word "doctrinal," he swore that if this man were called he would never go inside the church door as long as he lived. Some one commented that he would have to sit on the steps, then. Marcus answered, "I will set on the steps fifty years before I'll go into this house if that man's settled here." And he is true to his word. (p. 91)

The stock condition surrounding [Freeman's] characters' lives is poverty—sometimes a poverty as grim as that of *Tobacco Road* or *As I Lay Dying;* sometimes that even more grinding poverty of a decayed gentry trying to keep up appearances, such as we find in *The Sound and the Fury*. In painting the economic and cultural bankruptcy of the New England village she uses the somber pigments of a merciless realism; the rosy tints of sentiment are applied sparingly and then only when reality calls for them, as it sometimes does. (p. 96)

To read life solely in terms of economics would be impossible for one with her background. The economics are always present in her work, but quite rightly she does not make them the main thing. The chief question to her is not how many cows or silk dresses one of her characters may have, but how much peace of mind, self-expression, feeling of oneness with God and humanity. If New England life were bankrupt in these commodities of the soul, then it was bankrupt indeed. If there were an abundance of such goods, then the stony soil, the one best dress for the wear of a lifetime, the diet of beans and potatoes were irrelevant.

More often than not Freeman found a hopeless spiritual bankruptcy. Sometimes, as we have seen, the conscience and will were diseased beyond expectation of recovery. At other times the New England soul was too feeble to be stimulated even by disease into any activity whatsoever. It simply lay in the stream of life like a rotted log, refusing to stir till disintegrated by complete decay. Such is the case in the story of **"Sister Liddy,"** which is laid in a poorhouse. One would be tempted to lump this story with the dozens of others of similar setting by the various authors of New England. But Freeman's treatment of the theme is uniquely grim for the times. A story without a plot, it is reminiscent of the naturalism of Chekhov or Gorky. The characters are a half-dozen female derelicts living in the dreary bareness of a New England poor farm. (p. 97)

The women are always talking and boasting of their pasts—the people they knew, the places they had been to, the one fine dress they had owned. But Polly Moss, the dreariest of the lot, has never had anything; her life has never been less drab and hopeless than at present. Aroused by the bragging of the others, she invents a sister named Liddy who had known glories, luxuries, and honors, unsurpassable by the pitiful realities of the others' former lives. In the fictitious radiance of Sister Liddy's splendors Polly has her single brief hour in the sun. But being old and broken in health, she is soon on her deathbed, where she confesses her subterfuge. . . .

The home of Mary Wilkins and Charles Freeman in Metuchen, New Jersey. By permission of the Metuchen Edison Historical Society.

Two types of poverty are described here—material and spiritual; both are presented with unflinching regard for facts. But by emphasizing the spiritual poverty above the material Mary Wilkins Freeman has added an element of horror to the bleakness of these lives. . . . The empty purse, the empty larder, the empty stomach are objects of compassion to the materialist. But the empty soul is an object of infinitely greater compassion, even of terror, to the idealist.

This spiritual or psychological probing distinguishes Freeman among her New England contemporaries. Of all the stories about almshouses, for example, none in this period has quite caught the mood of such places, the state of mind of the inmates, so convincingly as the story of **"Sister Liddy."** Freeman was able to detach herself more fully from her subject and see it as it was rather than as she would like it to be according to her theories. (p. 98)

Freeman found that the void of the soul extended into economic levels higher than the poorhouse. In her famous story **"A New England Nun"** a thrifty woman who has waited fifteen years for her fiancé to return from Australia realizes, when he finally does return, that she is no longer capable of going through with the marriage. During all the barren time a large part of her humanity has parched out of her. She is only able to continue her limited life, "like an uncloistered nun," finding in it a vegetable contentment. "Serenity and placid narrowness had become to her as the birthright itself." So far had she lost her femininity that she welcomes her lover's breaking their engagement in favor of a young and very womanly schoolteacher.

In a higher social sphere, Freeman shows us Caroline Munson, the elderly and genteel heroine of **"A Symphony in Lavender,"** contenting herself with a similar half-life. A dream that Caroline had concerning the man who later proposed to her caused her to turn him down. But the dream is a rationalization of an inner lack—a psychological rather than sexual sterility—that makes her incapable of a full life. Henceforward she lives alone with an old servant in her ancestral mansion, satisfied with an insipid guardianship of the family silks and teacups.

Freeman was almost the sole writer of her time who was willing to face the complete insolvency of the older order in New England life. (p. 99)

In her Puritanic preoccupation with the soul—or, since modern readers like the Greek word better, the psyche—Freeman was always seeking for some spiritual compensation in the barren and arid lives that her characters so often lived. Frequently her search was unsuccessful, as in *Pembroke* or stories like **"Sister Liddy."** But sometimes in the case of even the gauntest old maid she would find moments of spiritual elevation that went far to balance the lopsided budget of empty days. This compensation came generally as a brief upsurge of long dormant vitality—an hour's triumphal reassertion of the personality, sweeping all pettiness and frustrations before it.

In the famous story **"The Revolt of 'Mother',"** . . . a farm woman has grown tired of waiting for years for her inconsiderate husband to fulfill his promise of enlarging their cramped dwelling. The climax comes when he starts work on an enormous and luxurious barn. One day, while the husband is away, his wife simply moves her family into the barn, setting up her housekeeping in the stables, which she correctly considers much more commodious than the farmhouse. After decades of being browbeaten it is the woman's moment of triumph. Public opinion is shocked; the minister attempts to mediate; but she holds her ground. When her husband, Adoniram, returns he is

> like a fortress whose walls had no active resistance, and went down the instant the right besieging tools were used. "Why, mother," he said hoarsely, "I hadn't no idee you was so set on't as all this comes to."

This is a typical example of the triumphal moment that comes to the lives of so many of even the drabbest of Freeman's characters. But she herself did not consider **"The Revolt of 'Mother'"** realistic—and she was a firm believer in realism. The act described in the story she considered too daring and too imaginative for a New England woman. Another of her characters, Candace Whitcomb, heroine of **"A Village Singer,"** is perhaps more lifelike. For forty years Candace has been the paid soprano in the village choir. When her voice begins to crack, she is given a surprise party at which she is presented with a photograph album. Enclosed in the album is a note announcing the church's purpose of relieving her of the strain of her musical duties. The first Sunday on which her successor, Alma Way, sings, Candace, who lives next door to the church, plays her organ as boisterously as she can and sings at the top of her cracked vocal chords. Needless to say, Alma's performance is spoiled and the service is ruined. When Mr. Pollard, the minister, calls to expostulate with Candace he finds a raging Medea rather than the mousy choir singer he had known so long.

> He was aghast and bewildered at this outbreak, which was tropical, and more than tropical, for a New England nature has a floodgate, and the power which it releases is an accumulation. Candace Whitcomb had been a quiet woman, so delicately resolute that the quality had been scarcely noticed in her, and her ambition had been unsuspected. Now the resolution and the ambition appeared raging over her whole self.
> (pp. 102-03)

A lifetime of outraged self is at last finding expression, and one cannot condemn her. Her abrupt towering over her frustration is heroic; one feels the same admiration as for a caged animal suddenly set free. But the triumph is evanescent. . . . In the morning she awakes, her fires burnt out, but she has had her moment. . . . [There] is nothing left for her to do but die. In her few hours of fierce revolt there has been a compensation, a justification, for the humdrum years of her restrained and frustrated life. (p. 103)

Freeman's contribution has been a psychological insight hitherto unknown in New England literature with the exception of Hawthorne. The volume of her important work, as has been already said, was slight—consisting of the two or three collections of short stories and . . . one or two novels. . . . The general level of her work is far below that of Sarah Orne Jewett, for example, who maintained her high literary standards through more than a dozen books. But at her best, Freeman has seen more deeply into the life of her region than has Jewett. Of a less well-to-do family, she experienced New England life on a drabber level, and she was much more critical of it than any of the writers thus far considered. In the impressive line of analysts of the New England mind—beginning with Jonathan Edwards and continuing through Frost—Freeman occupies a secure position. More adept than Hawthorne, Emily Dickinson, or Robinson in standing outside her environment, she was able to bring to her work an objectivity that in part compensates for her obvious artistic inferiority to these other writers. One must turn to Frost to find the equal of her calm, dispassionate probing. (p. 104)

Perry D. Westbrook, "The Anatomy of the Will: Mary Wilkins Freeman," in his Acres of Flint: Sarah Orne Jewett and Her Contemporaries, *revised edition, The Scarecrow Press, Inc., 1981, pp. 86-104.*

MARJORIE PRYSE (essay date 1983)

[*In the following excerpt, Pryse examines several of Freeman's depictions of human relationships in her short fiction, focusing on relationships between women, a prevalent theme in her works.*]

For contemporary readers, Mary Wilkins Freeman's interest lies in her depiction of the lives of women in late nineteenth-century New England, for in the variety of those portraits she stands unsurpassed in American literature [of] her time. In some of these stories, Freeman portrays life for women alone; in others, Freeman's fiction analyzes bonds between sisters or close friends, and between mothers and daughters or women who become surrogate mothers, daughters, or sisters to each other. In several of the most dramatic stories, she depicts women in conflict with men, and [a few] of the stories . . . , she examines life as men alone experience and view it. (p. 315)

Freeman's first significant publication, **"Two Old Lovers,"** establishes her interest in patterns and in the ways men and women separately live their lives. The story suggests that the habit of life in Leyden, rather than David Emmons's particular idiosyncrasy, explains his slowness in asking Maria Brewster, his apparent lover of more than twenty-five years, to marry him. Beginning with a description of Leyden, in which the houses are "built after one of two patterns," the story creates a fictional world in which even the patterns of human lives are fixed. The men inhabit the world of the town's shoe factories during the day while the women stay at home and keep the cottages, and the shoe factories resemble clumsy angels "tempered with smoke or the beatings of the storms." Like the town itself, the "two old lovers" have both chosen a different pattern by which to live, and throughout, the story sets their lives in juxtaposition. Maria is stronger than David, and her affection is more "mother-like" than "lover-like." David, on the other hand, is compared to the poet Robert Herrick, and his courtship, prolonged even to his deathbed, partakes of the sixteenth century's idealization of the beloved rather than the "eminently practical" feeling Maria has for him.

Maria perceives both her need for a human kinship and David's need for mother-love, whereas David sees nothing. Therefore she thrives and he declines. The story focuses on a world in which mother-love is not absent but unrecognized. The clumsy angels—the shoe factories to which the men of Leyden turn for inspiration—become angels of destruction. The men making shoes become so worn that their paths and those of the women do not cross. Even on his deathbed, David Emmons does not ask Maria to marry him but only says that he "'allers meant to—have asked.'" Despite the overtones of romance, then, **"Two Old Lovers"** portrays the effects of an industrializing culture that has destroyed all but the idealized, courtly forms of love between men and women.

In subsequent stories, Freeman would turn to the lives of women in order to explore the nature of vision, affection, and human conflict obscured by her culture's insistence on divergent patterns of life for men and women. **"An Honest Soul"** presents a situation emblematic of that in which many women in Freeman's fiction find themselves. After the death of her hardworking parents, Martha Patch has struggled to eke out her survival alone, by taking in quilting and living frugally. The story anatomizes the seventy-year-old woman's pride, as she believes she has switched pieces for two separate quilts and in her confusion restitches them not once but twice. But the elderly woman's strength of will forms the backdrop for another drama—one that Freeman suggests is more significant to Martha's life and health than her want of food. For the house she inhabits—never completed in her father's lifetime—lacks both door and window in front; and living without a front window becomes symbolic of her life's burden.

Many women in Freeman's fiction lack front windows in a symbolic sense—focusing their sights on back views and domestic struggles in lieu of connection with the outside world, which Martha's idea of having a front window implies. Yet Martha contents herself with watching the progress of the grass—which, she thinks, grows much greener in the spot she can see from inside her house than elsewhere in the yard. The story implies a connection between that green grass and Martha's own transforming gaze; for despite her lack of a front window on the passing world, Martha Patch yet possesses a vision. When she lies collapsed in a sunbeam at the end of the story and a neighbor discovers her, the neighbor offers her husband's skill at carpentry in payment for needlework. Now Martha will have her front window, but the view that remains real for her is the one she has intensified by her own watching—the greener spot of grass. With or without a front window, the woman has found a form for vision. (pp. 315-17)

The desire to find a form for vision and to protect that vision establishes a sisterhood of sorts in many of Freeman's stories. . . . **"A Patient Waiter"** epitomizes the historical position of the late nineteenth-century New England woman—Fidelia Almy waits in vain forty years until she dies for a letter from her departed lover—but specifically characterizes the nature of the vision as that of "mother's " legacy. For although Fidelia takes center stage in the story, her orphaned niece, Lily, who lives with her and whom she mothers, achieves the story's vision. Like her aunt, Lily has a departed lover for whose letters she waits in vain—until he writes announcing his plans to return just as Fidelia lies on her deathbed. The arrival of this letter seems to confirm Lily's own faith, but in witnessing the final shattering of her aunt's—when the latter arrives, Fidelia thinks her long-lost Ansel Lennox has written at last—Lily receives a vision that offers her a realistic perception of the "awful pitifulness" of life. The absence of mail for Fidelia evokes years of broken promise. Only in her death can Fidelia pass the post office on her way to the green graveyard without caring whether or not there is a letter for her. And amid all the "fair, wide possibilities of heaven," Lily loses her faith in Providence. In that loss, she discovers that the real sky—despite her imminent marriage to her own lover—yields no male but only her "dear, poor aunty." Fidelia's "faithful soul" could not force the heavens to fulfill their own promises, and in the image of mortality that her aunt's death leaves Lily, the young woman recognizes the depths of her loss: she regains her lover but loses the only mother she ever knew.

This story . . . may be seen as transitional fiction that bridges stories of women alone and the larger group of stories in which Freeman explores relatedness among women. (pp. 318-19)

The search for "mother," or for a tie with another woman that will allow them to replicate that experience in some visionary way, links several of the protagonists in . . . [Freeman's stories]. **"On the Walpole Road,"** from ***A Humble Romance,*** is one of Freeman's best stories, as well as one in which the narrator explores connecting links between women who are related by blood ties or by surrogate motherhood and sisterhood. The story's narrative frame depicts two women trying to get home before a storm hits. On the way, the older one, Mrs. Green, tells a story about her Aunt Rebecca's unhappy marriages to Uncle Enos and a man named Abner Lyons. Several related stories embedded within the narrative imply, by the story's end, that Mrs. Green and her younger listener, Almiry, have found outside of marriage what Aunt Rebecca could not achieve within it—a community of women. For Rebecca (who once served as surrogate mother to Mrs. Green), life became a tragedy of isolation from such a community. Forced by her own mother to marry Enos, then forcing her second husband Abner into a masculine role to which he is unsuited (androgynous by nature, he prefers to share domestic tasks), Rebecca perversely perpetuated the lack of sympathy between women and androgynous men, a sympathy that might have eased her alienation. By the story's end, Mrs. Green seems to be consoling the unmarried Almiry, and Freeman implicitly links the two women as surrogate mother and daughter.

Stories about sisters and sisterhoods serve as variations on the same theme. In **"A Gala Dress,"** for example—another of Freeman's strongest stories—two women, Emily and Elizabeth Babcock, share a black silk dress, which means that they can never appear at church or social gatherings together. One sister trims the dress in black velvet; the other sister rips off the velvet and sews on black lace when it is her turn to wear the dress. In their secret sharing, the sisters approach the closest possible symbiosis, seeming to inhabit the same (dress) body. They practice this deception to hide their poverty from the town and from their closest neighbor, Matilda Jennings, who lives alone and who, in the sisters' eyes, belongs to an inferior social class.

In their treatment of Matilda throughout the story, Emily and Elizabeth Babcock limit the potential of their sisterhood to include other women—until, as a result of an accident at the Fourth of July picnic, the sisters and Matilda manage to confess their deepest secrets to each other. The story portrays their mutual discovery that in their impoverishment of spirit they have cut themselves off from deep friendship. When they offer Matilda the damaged though mended dress (after receiving a windfall inheritance of two new ones), they offer her much more than a garment. They reject their formerly exclusive "sorority" and extend the symbol of their own shared body to Matilda, in the process transforming the "coarse old face" of their new friend with a "fine light," which the reader of these stories will recognize as emblematic of the vision that results from new relatedness between women in Freeman's fiction. The theme of "mother" becomes transposed in this story about sisters, but the qualities of the vision are familiar. (pp. 320-22)

[Women] in Freeman's fiction have available to them, whether or not they recognize it, a community that sustains their spirit and validates their vision. (p. 335)

Marjorie Pryse, in an afterword to Selected Stories of Mary E. Wilkins Freeman *by Mary E. Wilkins Freeman, edited by Marjorie Pryse, W. W. Norton & Company, 1983, pp. 315-42.*

ADDITIONAL BIBLIOGRAPHY

Bader, Julia. "The Dissolving Vision: Realism in Jewett, Freeman, and Gilman." In *American Realism: New Essays,* edited by Eric J. Sundquist, pp. 176-98. Baltimore: The Johns Hopkins University Press, 1982.

Examines Freeman's short fiction to establish a correlation between "the psychological condition of particular characters" and "the degree of realism of which they are capable," finding especially that "the initial description of the locale is often the most significant clue to the nature of her heroines."

Brooks, Van Wyck. "Country Pictures." In his *New England: Indian Summer,* pp. 455-73. New York: E. P. Dutton & Co., 1940.

Considers the variety of approaches used by Freeman, Robert Frost, Rudyard Kipling, E. A. Robinson, Edith Wharton, and Eugene O'Neill to portray aspects of New England life.

Donovan, Josephine. "Mary E. Wilkins Freeman." In her *New England Local Color Literature: A Women's Tradition,* pp. 119-38. New York: Frederick Ungar, 1983.

Feminist interpretations of some of Freeman's short stories, finding that the death of a maternal figure, or the decline of a matriarchal society, is a major theme.

———. "Silence or Capitulation: Prepatriarchal 'Mothers' Gardens' in Jewett and Freeman." *Studies in Short Fiction* 23, No. 1 (Winter 1986): 43-8.

Examination of fiction by Freeman and Jewett that depicts the chasm that appeared between two generations of women at the close of the nineteenth century due to changes in women's traditional roles.

Foster, Edward. *Mary E. Wilkins Freeman.* New York: Hentricks House, 1956, 229 p.

Biography of Freeman, using extensive quotes from her letters. Foster provides some critical comment on the principal works and includes a useful bibliography.

Glasser, Leah Blatt. "Mary E. Wilkins Freeman: The Stranger in the Mirror." *The Massachusetts Review* 25, No. 2 (Summer 1984): 323-39.

Contends that Freeman is "miscategorized as a local colorist" and maintains that the study of the psychology of women attempting to rebel is central to Freeman's work.

Hirsch, David H. "Subdued Meaning in 'A New England Nun'." *Studies in Short Fiction* 2, No. 2 (Winter 1965): 124-36.

Interprets one of Freeman's best-known and most anthologized short stories in psychoanalytic and mythic terms.

Kendrick, Brent L. Introduction to *The Infant Sphinx: Collected Letters of Mary E. Wilkins Freeman,* by Mary E. Wilkins Freeman, edited by Brent L. Kendrick, pp. 1-37. Metuchen, N.J.: Scarecrow Press, 1985.

Biographical and critical overview. In prefatory essays to each of five sections of letters, Kendricks provides further information about Freeman's life and career.

O'Brien, Edward J. "The Early Regionalists." In his *The Advance of the American Short Story.* Rev. ed., pp. 151-75. Folcroft, Pa.: Folcroft Press, 1931.

Notes the "stark and bitter realism" of Freeman's short stories, which "form as complete a study of suppressed desire as Sherwood Anderson's stories, but somehow they fail in their desperate reality to offer a solution, or even to plumb the essential depths of knowledge, the first step necessary toward spiritual liberation."

Pattee, Fred Lewis. Introduction to *A New England Nun, and Other Stories,* pp. vii-xxvi. New York: Harper & Brothers Publishers, 1920.

Comments on the characteristics of Freeman's early short fiction.

Pryse, Marjorie. "The Humanity of Women in Freeman's 'A Village Singer'." *Colby Library Quarterly* XIX, No. 2 (June 1983): 69-77.

Interprets the protagonist's death in "A Village Singer" as inevitable. According to the critic, Freeman's commitment to realism would not permit her to portray a rebellious woman who defied social mores successfully.

———. "An Uncloistered 'New England Nun'." *Studies in Short Fiction* 20, No. 4 (Fall 1983): 289-95.

Feminist interpretation of Freeman's well-known and widely reprinted story, contending that the protagonist's rejection of marriage represents a positive, transcendent "alternative pattern for living" that was intended as a model for other women.

Quina, James H. "Character Types in the Fiction of Mary Wilkins Freeman." *Colby Library Quarterly* IX, No. 8 (December 1971): 432-39.

Divides Freeman's typical characters into four groups: the control groups who maintain the societal status quo, the ascetics who have withdrawn from life, those in rebellion against the status quo, and those who moderate between the second and third types. Quina draws examples from Freeman's principal works of fiction.

Romines, Ann. "A Place for 'A Poetess'." *The Markham Review* 12 (Summer 1983): 61-4.

Close examination of the short story "A Poetess." Romines finds it distinct from the other stories in the collection *A New England Nun* in that its protagonist does not act to fulfill those of her needs that conflict with an existing social order, but instead modifies her behavior.

Sherman, Sarah W. "The Great Goddess in New England: Mary Wilkins Freeman's 'Christmas Jenny'." *Studies in Short Fiction* 17, No. 2 (Spring 1980): 157-64.

Mythic interpretation of Freeman's well-known occasional story. The critic perceives the title character as an archetypal maternal figure or fertility symbol.

Toth, Susan Allen. "Mary Wilkins Freeman's Parable of Wasted Life." *American Literature* XLII, No. 4 (January 1971): 564-67.

Comparison of Freeman's "The Three Old Sisters and the Old Beau" with Nathaniel Hawthorne's "The Wedding Knell," stressing the authors' differing approaches to similar plots.

———. " 'The Rarest and Most Peculiar Grape': Versions of the New England Woman in Nineteenth-Century Local Color Literature." In *Regionalism and the Female Imagination: A Collection of Essays,* edited by Emily Toth, pp. 15-28. University Park, Pa.: Human Sciences Press, 1985.

Discusses Freeman's local color fiction as a source for the study of women's changing roles at the end of the nineteenth century.

Tutwiler, Julia R. "Two New England Writers—In Relation to Their Art and to Each Other." *Gunton's Magazine* 25, (November 1903): 419-25.

Discusses contrasting characteristics of Freeman's and Jewett's writing styles and principal themes.

Wagenknecht, Edward. Introduction to *Collected Ghost Stories,* by Mary E. Wilkins Freeman, pp. viii-xii. Sauk City, Wis.: Arkham House, 1974.

Briefly characterizes Freeman as a writer of local color fiction and discusses some of her supernatural works.

Westbrook, Perry D. *Mary Wilkins Freeman.* Boston: Twayne, 1967, 191 p.

Critical and biographical study of Freeman focusing on her principal works of fiction.

Williams, Blanche Colton. "Mary Wilkins Freeman." In her *Our Short Story Writers,* pp. 160-81. New York: Dodd, Mead & Co., 1920.

Biographical and critical essay discussing Freeman's short fiction and analyzing some of her characters.

Wood, Ann Douglas. "The Literature of Impoverishment: The Women Local Colorists in America, 1865-1914." *Women's Studies* 1, No. 1 (1972): 3-45.

Discusses Freeman in relation to other women local color fiction writers of the late 1800s and early 1900s, including Jewett, Rose Terry Cooke, and Kate Chopin.

[Woolf, Virginia.] Review of *The Debtor,* by Mary E. Wilkins Freeman. *The Times Literary Supplement,* No. 201 (17 November 1905): 396.

Largely favorable review of one of Freeman's novels in which Freeman's short stories are characterized as "very brief and delightful," "unpretentious in theme and slight in construction," but notable for "the skill and charm of the workmanship."

Ernest (Miller) Hemingway

1899-1961

American short story writer, novelist, essayist, nonfiction writer, memoirist, journalist, poet, and dramatist.

The Granger Collection, New York

Hemingway is recognized as one of the preeminent American fiction writers of the twentieth century. His novels and stories, predominantly concerned with disillusionment and personal loss, heroic tests of physical and emotional courage, and stoic resolve in the face of an apparently meaningless world, are distinguished by an evocative, deceptively simple style. Although Hemingway's literary achievement has been measured largely by his novels *The Sun Also Rises* and *A Farewell to Arms,* his short stories have increasingly won critical acclaim. In his first major publication, the short fiction collection *In Our Time,* Hemingway formulated the stylistic and thematic concerns which mark all his later fiction. This book is particularly important because it introduces Hemingway's most fully drawn protagonist, Nick Adams, a Midwestern youth whose apprenticeship to life's travails Hemingway developed here and in the later collections *Men without Women* and *Winner Take Nothing.* The best-known Adams stories include "Big Two-Hearted River," "Indian Camp" and "The Killers," all of which objectively document the effect of harsh reality on a sensitive mind. Equally well-regarded are such stories as "A Clean, Well-Lighted Place," "The Snows of Kilimanjaro," "Hills Like White Elephants," and "The Short Happy Life of Francis Macomber," through which Hemingway depicted a range of ironic and heroic responses to the human condition. Nowhere in his work is the theme of individual integrity more thoroughly treated than in the novella *The Old Man and the Sea,* the last work to appear in his lifetime. This work, which earned him a Pulitzer Prize and helped secure for Hemingway the Nobel Prize for Literature, is widely considered one of the most masterfully wrought and meaningful tales in American fiction.

Perhaps to a larger degree than that of any other twentieth-century writer, criticism of Hemingway's work has been colored by his own mythical persona. Indeed, he helped promote his larger-than-life reputation as a robust, belligerent American hero who sought to experience violence as well as to write of it. He was a schooled expert in the arenas of war, bullfighting, deep-sea fishing, boxing, big-game hunting, and reckless, extravagant living, experiences which he often recounted in his fiction. Although he spent much of his life in foreign countries—France, Spain, Italy, and Cuba, in particular—he was, once established as a major writer, continually in the public eye. His passion for fistfighting and quarrels and his weakness for hard liquor became legendary, as did his ties to Hollywood personalities. Yet, beneath this flamboyance was a man who viewed writing as his sacred occupation, one which he strove always to master. Although he loved fame and never shunned his mythical status, he was disenchanted in his later years with the vulnerable position created by his literary success. His life was marred by three failed marriages, a debilitating addiction to alcohol, and marked periods of literary stagnation.

Born and raised in Oak Park, Illinois, by strict, Congregationalist parents, Hemingway led a fairly happy, upper-middle-class childhood, though as he grew older he felt bitter toward both his parents, particularly his mother, whom he viewed as selfish and domineering. By his teens he had become interested in literature, and he wrote a weekly column for his high school newspaper and contributed poems and stories to the school magazine. Upon his graduation in 1917, he took a junior reporter position on the *Kansas City Star,* covering the police and hospital beats and writing feature stories. It was here that he began consciously refining his prose according to the *Star*'s guidelines of compression, selectivity, precision, and immediacy. In his journalism, Hemingway demonstrated a proclivity for powerful yet utterly objective stories of violence, despair, and emotional unrest, concerns that dominated his fiction. Of tremendous impact to Hemingway's development as a writer was his ensuing participation in World War I as a Red Cross ambulance driver in Italy. Wounded in both legs by a shrapnel explosion near the front lines, he fell in love with the American nurse who cared for him; however, she abruptly left Hemingway for an older man. He returned to the States a decorated hero, but his triumph was overshadowed by the disillusionment of his broken romance and a stifling relationship with his parents. At Oak Park, and also in northern Michigan where his family owned a summer cottage, Hemingway drafted stories drawn from boyhood, adolescence, and wartime experiences that captured his awakening realization of life's inherent misfortunes. He eventually returned to journalism to support himself, contributing features to the *Toronto Star.*

Following his first marriage in 1921, Hemingway returned to Europe to launch a writing career. Sherwood Anderson, who had met and befriended Hemingway earlier in Chicago, provided him with letters of introduction to several notable writers living in Paris, the literary capital of the twenties. For the next seven years, Hemingway resided principally in France though he travelled frequently, covering the Greco-Turkish War of 1922 and writing special-interest pieces for the Toronto paper. During this period Hemingway matured as a writer, greatly aided in his artistic development by his close contact with several of the most prominent writers of the time, including Gertrude Stein, James Joyce, Ezra Pound, Ford Madox Ford, and F. Scott Fitzgerald. He eventually quit journalism, though he periodically returned to the medium, serving as a correspondent during several major wars.

Hemingway's first publication, *Three Stories and Ten Poems,* included an Anderson-inspired story, "My Old Man," that was chosen for Edward J. O'Brien's *The Best Stories of 1923*. Hemingway's power and originality as a writer of compressed, impressionistic sketches became apparent with his next publication, *in our time* (the lowercased form an affectation of the publisher). A series of eighteen brief untitled chapters stemming from Hemingway's war and journalistic experiences, this work was revised, greatly expanded, and published in America in 1925 as *In Our Time*. The American version included fifteen complete short stories with the remaining vignettes serving as interchapters. By the appearance of his next story collection, *Men without Women,* Hemingway's literary reputation—as the author of *The Sun Also Rises* and consequent chronicler of the "lost generation"—was all but solidified. Following the immense success of *A Farewell to Arms,* he was recognized as a major force in literature.

While the 1930s was Hemingway's most prolific decade, he published little of lasting significance, save for the short story collection *Winner Take Nothing* and an assembly of forty-nine stories, published with the play *The Fifth Column,* which incorporated such widely anthologized stories as "The Short Happy Life of Francis Macomber" and "The Snows of Kilimanjaro." The 1940s was a fallow decade for Hemingway. After the publication of his variously received long novel of the Spanish Civil War, *For Whom the Bell Tolls*, his major achievement was his participation as reporter and paramilitary aide in the liberation of France from German occupation in 1944. Surprisingly, the fifties was for Hemingway nearly as productive as the thirties, though most of the work from this period was published posthumously. By the middle of the decade, however, a variety of recurrent physical ailments had severely curtailed his creative energy. In 1960, Hemingway suffered a mental breakdown and was admitted to the Mayo Clinic for electrotherapy treatments. His depressive behavior and other illnesses persisted, resulting in Hemingway's suicide the following year.

In his short fiction Hemingway depicted a brutal, disillusioning environment in which his protagonists learn bitter lessons about the precariousness of existence, the evanescence of happiness, and the universality of suffering. As Irving Howe has written, "Hemingway struck to the heart of our nihilism through stories about people who have come to the end of the line, who no longer know what to do or where to turn: nihilism not as an idea or a sentiment, but as an encompassing condition of moral disarray in which one has lost those tacit impulsions which permit life to continue." Hemingway's most conspicuous treatment of this concern occurs in the story "A Clean, Well-Lighted Place," in which an aging Spanish waiter affirms that the essence of life is "nada" ("nothing") and that the individual survives best by conducting oneself in a courageous, quiet, and dignified manner. This implied presence of a strict moral code to guide the protagonist—in the words of Jeffrey Meyers "a steadfast, traditional code of honor" that "emphasizes dignity, solidarity, self-sacrifice, and stoicism"—unifies nearly all Hemingway's stories. Hemingway's intent was to contrast the corrupt, chaotic world with the one ideal which he believed humanity could, and should, still attain: "grace under pressure." The most memorable expression of this theme occurs in "The Short Happy Life of Francis Macomber," a story of an unhappy man's display of cowardice, his wife's retaliatory love affair, and his ultimate recovery of integrity as he bravely faces a charging buffalo. His now happy life is cut short when his wife—fearful of her husband's newfound potency—fires a bullet through the back of his head. The tense reportorial style, the ironic dialogue of his characters, and the understated tone of the denouement to this story are considered ideal technical components through which Hemingway's themes attained penetrating focus.

As with virtually all his fiction, the dramatic tension and thematic movement of this story are founded upon the laconic dialogue of the characters. Hemingway's economical use of dialogue and physical description to expose the strengths, weaknesses, and inner tensions of his characters is considered one of his foremost contributions to fiction and is perhaps nowhere better displayed than in "Hills Like White Elephants," a masterfully compressed story of a couple's discussion concerning a husband's proposal that his wife submit to an abortion. The detached, objective voice in this story is characteristic of Hemingway's work and serves to maintain a constant tension between narration and subject matter.

Although Hemingway's writing has occasionally been viewed as glorified journalism, his style is considered highly mannered and is said to owe much to the artistic currents of the time. Critics beginning with Edmund Wilson in 1924 have demonstrated Hemingway's obvious debt, particularly in *In Our Time,* to the modernist stylistic innovations introduced in such works as Stein's *Three Lives* (1919), Anderson's *Winesburg, Ohio* (1919), and Joyce's *Portrait of the Artist as a Young Man* (1914-15). Yet most commentators have discerned Hemingway's originality in his ability to fuse these influences into a distinctively individual whole. As Wilson first wrote of Hemingway, "he is rather strikingly original, and in the dry compressed little vignettes of *in our time* has almost invented a form of his own." His style may be characterized as one of extreme concision, heightened by prominent imagery, incantatory repetition, and cool, lucid description.

Detractors of Hemingway complain primarily of two weaknesses in his writing: his style of contrived rhythms and ostentatiously simple diction—in which he is said to mimic Stein's peculiar style to detrimental excess—and his limited subject matter. Although these criticisms are generally well supported, most Hemingway adherents assert that in the majority of his stories, particularly the apprenticeship tales of Nick Adams's adolescent and early adult years, Hemingway presented a rich fictional world through which he addressed life's most burdensome concerns with consummate narrative skill. Leo Gurko has defended, in particular, Hemingway's seeming preoccupation with loss and death: "Loss and approaching death may be the unavoidable fact of human existence. The central lesson of existence, however, is that death must be accepted, faced without demoralization, and thereby mastered. Hemingway's stories are as much a demonstration of the lesson as they are of the fact; their drama arises from the tension between them.'' Hemingway's most extensive treatment of this overriding concern in the short prose form appears in *The Old Man and the Sea*. In this work, which has been likened to fable, parable, and myth, Hemingway pitted an aged Cuban fisherman named Santiago against a gigantic marlin and documented their epic struggle amidst an indifferent sea. The story is at once a confirmation of the naturalistic state of human existence and a celebration of the sacred interdependence between the human and the natural world. Although Santiago eventually loses the marlin to sharks, he maintains a purposive, peaceful resolve with his fate, epitomizing the ''victory in defeat'' ideal that Hemingway recurrently addressed in his fiction. An immensely popular work, the novel has nonetheless received considerable criticism for what some consider its obtrusive Christian symbolism and mundane monologues. Yet the work continues to receive much critical attention.

Indeed, all Hemingway's short fiction has benefited from a massive amount of scholarship and, with the exception of a small number of negative reactions, notably by Virginia Woolf, Wyndham Lewis, and Leon Edel, has been largely favored. Perhaps Wilson has provided the best reason for such enduring appeal: ''[Hemingway] has responded to every pressure of the moral atmosphere of the time, as it is felt at the roots of human relations, with a sensitivity almost unrivalled.'' With such stories as ''The Snows of Kilimanjaro,'' ''The Killers,'' ''The Short Happy Life of Francis Macomber,'' *The Old Man and the Sea,* ''Big Two-Hearted River,'' and others, Hemingway's reputation as a master of the short fiction form and as one of the finest and most influential writers of this century is firmly established. Robert P. Weeks sums up Hemingway's contribution in this way: ''Hemingway has won his reputation as an artist of the first rank by operating within limits that would have stifled a lesser writer. But within and because of these limits, he has in his best work uttered a lyric cry that—although it may not resemble the full orchestra of Tolstoy or the organ tones of Melville—is nonetheless a moving and finely wrought response to our times.''

(See also *CLC,* Vols. 1, 3, 6, 8, 10, 13, 19, 30, 34, 39, 41; *Contemporary Authors,* Vols. 77-80; *Dictionary of Literary Biography,* Vols. 4 and 9; *Dictionary of Literary Biography Yearbook: 1981;* and *Dictionary of Literary Biography Documentary Series,* Vol. 1.)

PRINCIPAL WORKS

SHORT FICTION

Three Stories and Ten Poems 1923
in our time 1924
In Our Time 1925; revised edition, 1930
Men without Women 1927
Winner Take Nothing 1933
The Fifth Column and the First Forty-Nine Stories 1938; also published as *The First Forty-Nine Stories* [abridged edition], 1956
The Portable Hemingway 1944
The Old Man and the Sea 1952
The Hemingway Reader 1953
The Fifth Column and Four Stories of the Spanish Civil War 1969
The Nick Adams Stories 1972
The Complete Short Stories of Ernest Hemingway 1987

OTHER MAJOR WORKS

The Torrents of Spring: A Romantic Novel in Honor of the Passing of a Great Race (novel) 1926
The Sun Also Rises (novel) 1926; also published as *Fiesta,* 1927
A Farewell to Arms (novel) 1929
Death in the Afternoon (nonfiction) 1932
Green Hills of Africa (nonfiction) 1935
To Have and Have Not (novel) 1937
For Whom the Bell Tolls (novel) 1940
Across the River and into the Trees (novel) 1950
A Moveable Feast (autobiography) 1964
Islands in the Stream (novel) 1970
The Garden of Eden (novel) 1986

EDMUND WILSON (essay date 1924)

[*Wilson is one of twentieth-century America's foremost men of letters. A prolific reviewer, creative writer, and social and literary critic, he exercised his greatest literary influence as the author of* Axel's Castle *(1931), a seminal study of literary symbolism, and as the author of widely read reviews and essays in which he introduced the best works of modern literature to the reading public. The following review, which greatly promoted Hemingway's reputation as a significant new writer, focuses on the merits of* Three Stories and Ten Poems *and* in our time.]

Mr Hemingway's poems [in ***Three Stories and Ten Poems***] are not particularly important, but his prose is of the first distinction. He must be counted as the only American writer but one—Mr Sherwood Anderson—who has felt the genius of Gertrude Stein's *Three Lives* and has been evidently influenced by it. Indeed, Miss Stein, Mr Anderson, and Mr Hemingway may now be said to form a school by themselves. The characteristic of this school is a naïveté of language often passing into the colloquialism of the character dealt with which serves actually to convey profound emotions and complex states of mind. It is a distinctively American development in prose—as opposed to more or less successful American achievements in the traditional style of English prose—which has artistically justified itself at its best as a limpid shaft into deep waters.

Not, however, that Mr Hemingway is imitative. On the contrary, he is rather strikingly original, and in the dry compressed little vignettes of ***in our time*** has almost invented a form of his own:

> They shot the six cabinet ministers at half-past six in the morning against the wall of a hospital. There were pools of water in the courtyard. There were dead leaves on the paving of the courtyard. It rained hard. All the shutters of the hospital were nailed shut. One of the ministers was sick with typhoid. Two soldiers carried him downstairs and out into the rain. They tried to hold him up against the wall but he sat down in a puddle of water. The other five stood very quietly against the wall. Finally the officer told the soldiers it was no good trying to make him stand up. When they fired the first volley

he was sitting down in the water with his head
on his knees.

Mr Hemingway is remarkably successful in suggesting moral values by a series of simple statements of this sort. His more important book is called ***in our time,*** and below its cool objective manner really constitutes a harrowing record of barbarities: you have not only political executions, but criminal hangings, bull-fights, assassinations by the police, and all the cruelties and enormities of the war. Mr Hemingway is wholly unperturbed as he tells about these things: he is not a propagandist even for humanity. His bull-fight sketches have the dry sharpness and elegance of the bull-fight lithographs of Goya. And, like Goya, he is concerned first of all with making a fine picture. He is showing you what life is, too proud an artist to simplify. And I am inclined to think that his little book has more artistic dignity than any other that has been written by an American about the period of the war.

Not perhaps the most vivid book, but the soundest. Mr Hemingway, who can make you feel the poignancy of the Italian soldier deciding in his death agony that he will "make a separate peace," has no anti-militaristic *parti pris* which will lead him to suppress from his record the exhilaration of the men who had "jammed an absolutely perfect barricade across the bridge" and who were "frightfully put out when we heard the flank had gone, and we had to fall back." It is only in the paleness, the thinness of some of his effects that Mr Hemingway sometimes fails. I am thinking especially of the story called **"Up in Michigan,"** which should have been a masterpiece, but has the curious defect of dealing with rude and primitive people yet leaving them shadowy. (pp. 340-41)

Edmund Wilson, "Mr. Hemingway's Dry-Points," in The Dial, *Vol. LXXXII, No. 4, October, 1924, pp. 340-41.*

ERNEST WALSH (essay date 1925)

[*An expatriate American poet, Walsh helped influence the course of modern literature through his editorship, with Ethel Moorhead, of the avant-garde Paris journal* This Quarter, *which during the 1920s published seminal works by such writers as Gertrude Stein, William Carlos Williams, and Hemingway. In the following excerpt, Walsh extols the artistry and integrity of Hemingway's style and short story construction.*]

Everyone talks about the beauty of Hemingway's prose. It is a dirty low-down critic's trick to speak of a man's heart as *prose*. It is time it was written that *beautiful prose* as written by Ernest Hemingway is not an accomplishment like playing the piano and which anyone can acquire by sufficient practice and moral application and the possession of a piano. The genius of Hemingway's writing lies somewhere around his getting ready to write since some time back. The rest happened. Hemingway managed to get born in America and born with more sensitiveness than most young men born in America. And then he used that sensitiveness to face life rather than to avoid it. (pp. 319-20)

There are lines in Hemingway's stories *that come at one reading them as if they had grown in the reader's heart* out of an old memory or an old wish to remember. It doesn't matter that Hemingway's characters all talk alike regardless of age or race or sex and that in each case the language is Hemingway's language. I say it doesn't matter because this is surmounted by an important contribution to the letters of this day. *Hemingway's characters don't all think alike*. But they all think and think as they ought to think. Thinking characters is a new thing in letters. We have all felt that most of the books of today were so many words put in an order of some sort by a puzzle fixer who played a game. We have looked for a long time for a book of thoughts that held a handful of easy language together. There is something behind each word in a Hemingway story that tells us Hemingway was thinking of more than grammar and publishers when he put it down. There is a great deal of talk these days about MACHINE-AGE and the end of art and literature. When Conrad died someone spoke about the end of the good days of writing. Someone else spoke about the close of the late *renaissance* in literature. Yes, that is closed. Now the good days are beginning. The good days are here. But this is no *renaissance*. This is the beginning.

You can read Hemingway from beginning to end without the dictionary. Hemingway's vocabulary is mean and bare as a poor monastery and out of this he makes patterns of monastic austerity and richness. His stories are a triumph over material. He has accepted his world. He is the most indigenous of our writers and the least detached, the only young man writing who holds opinions and for that I could pray in a barber shop.

A Hemingway story is told from the inside of the characters not from without. There is not that annoying space between author and characters. One doesn't feel one is reading a book while the author looks over one's shoulder and breathes heavily into one's ear. One is alone with a story by Hemingway. One confesses a pleasure in reading him with more privacy afforded than the confessional box affords. There is no one about but the reader and the words on the printed page. Hemingway is the shyest and proudest and sweetest-smelling story-teller of my reading. His method of simplicity in word and sentence structure is the first thing to catch the critic's eye but other writers have been simple without getting his tone and strength. It is obvious that the use of words with few syllables gives a concentrated effect but Hemingway's strength is not merely in having made use of this truth for that would be just a trick of style. It is the piling up of word for word in the right order to give a homely word more than its meaning, it is the use of *speech* as distinguished from *language* that puts Hemingway among the first men writing today. He can make the slang word *"swell"* purchase more meaning in the mind of his reader than one would think possible without tiring the word. He is no dilettante in slang. He is no snobbish didapper seeking prey in shallow water. Hemingway selected his audience. His rewards will be rich. But thank God he will never be satisfied. He is of the elect. He belongs. It will take time to wear him out. And before that he will be dead. (pp. 320-21)

Ernest Walsh, "Mr. Hemingway's Prose," in This Quarter, *Vol. 1, No. 2, Autumn-Winter, 1925, pp. 319-21.*

LOUIS KRONENBERGER (essay date 1926)

[*A drama critic for* Time *from 1938 to 1961, Kronenberger was a distinguished historian, literary critic, and author highly regarded for his expertise in eighteenth-century English history and literature. A prolific and versatile writer, he also wrote plays and novels and edited anthologies. In the following excerpt, Kronenberger stresses Hemingway's powers of observation in the* In Our Time *stories.*]

Ernest Hemingway's first book of short stories [***In Our Time***] comes fortified with the praise of men like Sherwood Anderson, Ford Madox Ford, Waldo Frank, and John Dos Passos.

The praise of such men fosters deduction. It indicates that Mr. Hemingway must have merit; it implies that his work is experimental, original, modernistic; it may even suggest that his work stems in part from the modes set by their own creation. All these deductions are to some extent true, but only the first is important. There are obvious traces of Sherwood Anderson in Mr. Hemingway and there are subtler traces of Gertrude Stein. His work is experimental and very modern. But much more significantly, it has sound merit of a personal, non-derivative nature; it shows no important affinity with any other writer, and it represents the achievement of unique personal experience.

I think it should be emphasized that Mr. Hemingway's stories are as much an achievement as they are an experiment. Already he has succeeded in making some of them finished products, whose form is consonant with their substance and whose value is not an implication for the future but a realization in the present. It is true that he has no power of emotion or deep quality of cerebration, but the way he has observed people and things, speech, surroundings, atmosphere, the spirit of our times, constitutes sufficient accomplishment for the moment. When translated into words, this power of observation is doubly effective: it is precise and direct, it is also suggestive and illuminating. Almost wholly through his sense of observation, he gets life into these pages: life at any moment, life at a vivid moment, life at a high and crucial moment. At his best, getting it there for a moment's duration, he somehow sends it running backward and forward, so that whatever must be understood is comprehensible by a discerning reader.

For the rest, his stories are experiments demanding further discipline and art. Between each two he interposes a paragraph of bare incident which further suggests the spirit of our time. Unfortunately some of the stories themselves, in their form and meaning, are like these paragraphs. They imply significance but they do not attain it; their lacunae are greater than their substance. They are not without life, but they lack meaning and intensity. Mr. Hemingway is in some respects an "intellectual" writer—in his culture, his humor, his implicit sophistication, his objectivity; but his work itself is finest when it portrays life, conversation, action. He is a synthetic observer, not an analyst.

Louis Kronenberger, "A New Novelist," in The Saturday Review of Literature, *Vol. II, No. 29, February 13, 1926, p. 555.*

F. SCOTT FITZGERALD (essay date 1926)

[*The author of such classic American novels as* The Great Gatsby *(1925) and* Tender Is the Night *(1934), Fitzgerald was the spokesman for the 1920s Jazz Age, America's decade of prosperity, excess, and abandon. Fitzgerald and Hemingway met in Paris shortly after the publication of* The Great Gatsby *and shortly before the publication of* In Our Time. *Fitzgerald was instrumental in introducing Hemingway to his own editor at Scribner's, Maxwell Perkins, with whom Hemingway subsequently established close ties. Hemingway and Fitzgerald's friendship eventually became a literary rivalry, and their relationship degenerated into one of enmity, distrust, and scorn. In the following excerpt, Fitzgerald presents an enthusiastic appraisal of* In Our Time.]

In Our Time consists of fourteen stories, short and long, with fifteen vivid miniatures interpolated between them. When I try to think of any contemporary American short stories as good as **"Big Two-Hearted River"**, the last one in the book, only Gertrude Stein's "Melanctha", Anderson's "The Egg", and Lardner's "Golden Honeymoon" come to mind. It is the account of a boy on a fishing trip—he hikes, pitches his tent, cooks dinner, sleeps, and next morning casts for trout. Nothing more—but I read it with the most breathless unwilling interest I have experienced since Conrad first bent my reluctant eyes upon the sea.

The hero, Nick, runs through nearly all the stories, until the book takes on almost an autobiographical tint—in fact **"My Old Man"**, one of the two in which this element seems entirely absent, is the least successful of all. Some of the stories show influences but they are invariably absorbed and transmuted, while in **"My Old Man"** there is an echo of Anderson's way of thinking in those sentimental "horse stories", which inaugurated his respectability and also his decline four years ago.

But with **"The Doctor and the Doctor's Wife"**, **"The End of Something"**, **"The Three-Day Blow"**, **"Mr. and Mrs. Elliot"**, and **"Soldier's Home"** you are immediately aware of something temperamentally new. In the first of these a man is backed down by a half breed Indian after committing himself to a fight. The quality of humiliation in the story is so intense that it immediately calls up every such incident in the reader's past. Without the aid of a comment or a pointing finger one knows exactly the sharp emotion of young Nick who watches the scene.

The next two stories describe an experience at the last edge of adolescence. You are constantly aware of the continual snapping of ties that is going on around Nick. In the half stewed, immature conversation before the fire you watch the awakening of that vast unrest that descends upon the emotional type at about eighteen. Again there is not a single recourse to exposition. As in **"Big Two-Hearted River"**, a picture—sharp, nostalgic, tense—develops before your eyes. When the picture is complete a light seems to snap out, the story is over. There is no tail, no sudden change of pace at the end to throw into relief what has gone before.

Nick leaves home penniless; you have a glimpse of him lying wounded in the street of a battered Italian town, and later of a love affair with a nurse on a hospital roof in Milan. Then in one of the best of the stories he is home again. The last glimpse of him is when his mother asks him, with all the bitter world in his heart, to kneel down beside her in the dining room in Puritan prayer.

Anyone who first looks through the short interpolated sketches will hardly fail to read the stories themselves. [Here Fitzgerald arbitrarily names several of the untitled sketches.] **"The Garden at Mons"** and **"The Barricade"** are profound essays upon the English officer, written on a postage stamp. **"The King of Greece's Tea Party"**, **"The Shooting of the Cabinet Ministers"**, and **"The Cigarstore Robbery"** particularly fascinated me, as they did when Edmund Wilson first showed them to me in an earlier pamphlet, over two years ago.

Disregard the rather ill considered blurbs upon the cover. It is sufficient that here is no raw food served up by the railroad restaurants of California and Wisconsin. In the best of these dishes there is not a bit to spare. And many of us who have grown weary of admonitions to "watch this man or that" have felt a sort of renewal of excitement at these stories wherein Ernest Hemingway turns a corner into the street. (pp. 264-65)

F. Scott Fitzgerald, "How to Waste Material: A Note on My Generation," in The Bookman, *New York, Vol. LXIII, No. 3, May, 1926, pp. 262-65.*

VIRGINIA WOOLF (essay date 1927)

[*An English novelist, essayist, and short story writer, Woolf is considered one of the most prominent literary figures of twentieth-century English literature. A discerning and influential critic and essayist as well as a novelist, Woolf began writing reviews for the* Times Literary Supplement *at an early age. In the following excerpt, Woolf compares* Men without Women *with Hemingway's novel* The Sun Also Rises *and finds the short story collection inferior.*]

The first thing that the mind desires [in the practice of literary criticism] is some foothold of fact upon which it can lodge before it takes flight upon its speculative career. Vague rumors attach themselves to people's names. Of Mr. Hemingway, we know that he is an American living in France, an "advanced" writer, we suspect, connected with what is called a movement, though which of the many we own that we do not know. It will be well to make a little more certain of these matters by reading first Mr. Hemingway's earlier book, *The Sun Also Rises,* and it soon becomes clear from this that if Mr. Hemingway is "advanced" it is not in the way that is to us most interesting. A prejudice of which the reader would do well to take account is here exposed; the critic is a modernist. Yes, the excuse would be because the moderns make us aware of what we feel subconsciously; they are truer to our own experience, they even anticipate it, and this gives us a particular excitement. But nothing new is revealed about any of the characters in *The Sun Also Rises*. They come before us shaped, proportioned, weighed, exactly as the characters of Maupassant are shaped and proportioned. They are seen from the old angle; the old reticences, the old relations between author and character are observed. (p. 1)

[It] would appear from his first novel that this rumor of modernity must have sprung from his subject matter and from his treatment of it rather than from any fundamental novelty in his conception of the art of fiction. It is a bare, abrupt, outspoken book. Life as people live it in Paris in 1927 or even in 1938 is described as we of this age do describe life (it is here that we steal a march upon the Victorians), openly, frankly, without prudery, but also without surprise. The immoralities and moralities of Paris are described as we are apt to hear them spoken of in private life. Such candor is modern and it is admirable. Then, for qualities grow together in art as in life, we find attached to this admirable frankness an equal bareness of style. (pp. 1, 8)

Of character, there is little that remains firmly and solidly elucidated. Something indeed seems wrong with the people. If we place them (the comparison is bad) against Tchekhov's people, they are flat as cardboard. If we place them (the comparison is better) against Maupassant's people they are crude as a photograph. If we place them (the comparison may be illegitimate) against real people, the people we liken them to are of an unreal type. They are people one may have seen showing off at some cafe; talking a rapid high-pitched slang, because slang is the speech of the herd, seemingly much at their ease, and yet if we look at them a little from the shadow not at their ease at all, and, indeed, terribly afraid of being themselves, or they would say things simply in their natural voices. So it would seem that the thing that is faked is character; Mr. Hemingway leans against the flanks of that particular bull after the horns have passed.

After this preliminary study of Mr. Hemingway's first book, we come to the new book, ***Men Without Women,*** possessed of certain views or prejudices. His talent plainly may develop along different lines. It may broaden and fill out; it may take a little more time and go into things—human beings in particular—rather more deeply. And even if this meant the sacrifice of some energy and point, the exchange would be to our private liking. On the other hand, his is a talent which may contract and harden still further! it may come to depend more and more upon the emphatic moment; make more and more use of dialogue, and cast narrative and description overboard as an encumbrance.

The fact that ***Men Without Women*** consists of short stories, makes it probable that Mr. Hemingway has taken the second line. But before we explore the new book, a word should be said which is generally left unsaid, about the implications of the title. As the publisher puts it . . . "the softening feminine influence is absent—either through training, discipline, death, or situation." Whether we are to understand by this that women are incapable of training, discipline, death, or situation, we do not know. But it is undoubtedly true, if we are going to persevere in our attempt to reveal the processes of the critic's mind, that any emphasis laid upon sex is dangerous. Tell a man that this is a woman's book, or a woman that this is a man's, and you have brought into play sympathies and antipathies which have nothing to do with art. The greatest writers lay no stress upon sex one way or the other. The critic is not reminded as he reads them that he belongs to the masculine or the feminine gender. But in our time, thanks to our sexual perturbations, sex consciousness is strong, and shows itself in literature by an exaggeration, a protest of sexual characteristics which in either case is disagreeable. Thus Mr Lawrence, Mr. Douglas, and Mr. Joyce partly spoil their books for women readers by their display of self-conscious virility; and Mr. Hemingway, but much less violently, follows suit. All we can do, whether we are men or women, is to admit the influence, look the fact in the face, and so hope to stare it out of countenance.

To proceed then—***Men Without Women*** consists of short stories in the French rather than in the Russian manner. The great French masters, Mérimée and Maupassant, made their stories as self-sufficient and compact as possible. There is never a thread left hanging; indeed so contracted are they, that when the last sentence of the last page flares up, as it so often does, we see by its light the whole circumference and significance of the story revealed. The Tchekov method is, of course, the very opposite of this. Everything is cloudy and vague, loosely trailing rather than tightly furled. The stories move slowly out of sight like clouds in the summer air, leaving a wake of meaning in our minds which gradually fades away. Of the two methods, who shall say which is the better? At any rate, Mr. Hemingway, enlisting under the French masters, carries out their teaching up to a point with considerable success.

There are in ***Men Without Women*** many stories which, if life were longer, one would wish to read again. Most of them indeed are so competent, so efficient, and so bare of superfluity that one wonders why they do not make a deeper dent in the mind than they do. Take the pathetic story of the Major whose wife died—**"In Another Country"**; or the sardonic story of a conversation in a railway carriage—**"A Canary for One"**; or stories like **"The Undefeated,"** and **"Fifty Grand"** which are full of the sordidness and heroism of bullfighting and boxing—all of these are good trenchant stories, quick, terse and strong. If one had not summoned the ghosts of Tchekov, Mérimée and Maupassant, no doubt one would be enthusiastic. As it is, one looks about for something, fails to find something, and so is brought again to the old familiar business of ringing impressions on the counter, and asking what is wrong?

For some reason the book of short stories does not seem to us to go as deep or to promise as much as the novel. Perhaps it is the excessive use of dialogue, for Mr. Hemingway's use of it is surely excessive. A writer will always be chary of dialogue because dialogue puts the most violent pressure on the reader's attention. He has to hear, to see, to supply the right tone, and to fill in the background from what the characters say without any help from the author. Therefore, when fictitious people are allowed to speak it must be because they have something so important to say that it stimulates the reader to do rather more than his share of the work of creation. But, although Mr. Hemingway keeps us under the fire of dialogue constantly, his people, half the time, are only saying what the author could say much more economically for them. At last we are inclined to cry out with the little girl in **"Hills Like White Elephants"** "Would you please please please please please please stop talking?"

And probably it is this superfluity of dialogue which leads to that other fault which is always lying in wait for the writer of short stories; the lack of proportion. A paragraph in excess will make these little craft lopsided and will bring about that blurred effect which when one is out for clarity and point so baffles the reader. And both these faults, the tendency to flood the page with unnecessary dialogue and the lack of sharp, unmistakable points by which we can take hold of the story, come from the more fundamental fact that, though Mr. Hemingway is brilliantly and enormously skillful, he lets his dexterity, like the bullfighter's cloak, get between him and the fact. For in truth story writing has much in common with bullfighting. One may twist one's self like a corkscrew and go through every sort of contortion so that the public thinks one is running every risk and displaying superb gallantry. But the true writer stands close up to the bull and lets the horns—call them life, truth, reality, whatever you like,—pass him close each time.

Mr. Hemingway, then, is courageous; he is candid; he is highly skilled; he plants words precisely where he wishes; he has moments of bare and nervous beauty; he is modern in manner but not in vision; he is self-consciously virile; his talent has contracted rather than expanded; compared with [*The Sun Also Rises*] his stories are a little dry and sterile. So we sum him up. (p. 8)

Virginia Woolf, "An Essay in Criticism," in New York Herald Tribune Books, *Vol. 9, No. 4, October 9, 1927, pp. 1, 8.*

JOSEPH WOOD KRUTCH (essay date 1927)

[*Krutch is widely regarded as one of America's most respected literary and drama critics. A conservative and idealistic thinker, he was a consistent proponent of human dignity and the preeminence of literary art. In the following excerpt, Krutch describes Hemingway's use of deceptively simple dialogue to convey profound insights into human nature.*]

Spiritually the distinguishing mark of Mr. Hemingway's work is a weariness too great to be aware of anything except sensations; technically it is an amazing power to make the apparently aimless and incompetent talk of his characters eloquent, to make them say what they seem too inarticulate or too lazy to define with words.

Two men have descended after a winter's skiing in the higher Alps [in **"An Alpine Idyll"**]. "You oughtn't to ever do anything too long," says one. "No," says the other, "we were up there too long"; and something about the moment at which these remarks are introduced makes the reader suddenly weary both physically and spiritually. In another story [**"Hills Like White Elephants"**] a man and a woman are discussing (so we gather from oblique evidence) an abortion which the former is eager to have performed and to which the latter is wearily consenting. They have just tried a new drink. "'It tastes like licorice,' the girl said and put the glass down. 'That's the way with everything.' 'Yes,' said the girl. 'Everything tastes of licorice. Especially all the things you've waited so long for, like absinthe.'" Each of these conversations is in some sense quotable and therefore not entirely typical; each, too, involves the same trick (again repeated in the story of the drug addict who replies "They haven't got a cure for anything" to the suggestion that "they" have a cure for his disorder), and the trick consists in making the weary response to an individual situation imply a general hopelessness in the face of all situations; but much of the conversation is effective for reasons more difficult to analyze. It is apparently meandering and endlessly repetitious; it seems to require a page to make articulate the simplest idea; and yet this dialogue, standing almost by itself, is sufficient to make fourteen mostly very short stories both vivid and convincing. It appears to be the most meticulously literal reporting and yet it reproduces dulness without being dull.

Here, if you like, is art upon its last legs. For all his scrupulous detachment and his care never to say one word in his own person, Mr. Hemingway tells us both by his choice of subject and by the method which he employs that life is an affair of mean tragedies, and he tells us it as plainly as if he were devoting a treatise to the exposition of his ideas. In his hands the subject matter of literature becomes sordid little catastrophes in the lives of very vulgar people and its language the most undistinguished which can possibly be made by the most skilful manipulation to convey a meaning. And yet he possesses a virtuosity not short of amazing; once begun, none of his stories will allow themselves to be laid down unfinished. Mr. Hemingway's range may be narrow and his art "unimportant," but within the limits of what he undertakes in the present volume [***Men without Women***] he is a master. These stories are painfully good. No one, whatever his artistic creed may be, can escape their fascination during the moments it takes to read them; and no one can deny their brilliance.

Joseph Wood Krutch, "The End of Art," in The Nation, *New York, Vol. CXXV, No. 3254, November 16, 1927, p. 548.*

CYRIL CONNOLLY (essay date 1927)

[*Connolly, an English novelist and critic who reviewed books for the* New Statesman, *the* Observer, *and the* Sunday Times *was also the founding editor of the respected literary monthly* Horizon *(1939-50). In the following excerpt, Connolly offers a qualified positive assessment of* Men without Women.]

Men Without Women is a collection of grim little stories told in admirable colloquial dialogue with no point, no moral and no ornamentation. They are about bull-fighters, crooks, crook prize-fighters, crook peasants, dope fiends, and soldiers in hospital. The title is intended to strike the note of ferocious virility which characterises the book, which is, however, by no means free from the strong silent sentimentality latent in this attitude. They are, in fact, a blend of Gertrude Stein's manner, Celtic childishness, and the slice of life (the real thing!) redeemed by humour, power over dialogue and an obvious knowledge of the people he describes. . . . Mr. Hemingway really represents an acute phase of post-war dissatisfaction. Unfortunately the post-war period is nearly over; the violent and exciting confusion of those years has passed and with it the vogue for those talented authors who substituted impatience for ambition and struggled bravely on without the great driving power of tradition. The literature of the future will be in the hands of a bland and orderly generation about which absolutely nothing is known. Meanwhile Mr. Hemingway remains easily the ablest of the wild band of Americans in Europe and is obviously capable of a great deal of development before his work reaches maturity. At present this work is irritating, but very readable and full of a power and freshness that will interest anyone who prefers the terser examples of American realism to the laborious chronicles of dull families and dull crimes. Mr. Hemingway is considered, falsely, a second Joyce in America; at present he is more of a dark horse than a white hope, but his book makes a good test of one's own capacity to appreciate modernity. In descriptions of bull fights and of the normal life of unromantic Spain he is unexcelled.

Cyril Connolly, in a review of "Men without Women," in New Statesman, *Vol. 30, No. 761, November 26, 1927, p. 208.*

[H. L. MENCKEN] (essay date 1928)

[*Mencken was one of the most influential social and literary critics in the United States from the eve of World War I until the early years of the Great Depression. In the following excerpt, Mencken favorably appraises Hemingway's short fiction.*]

Mr. Hemingway and Mr. Wilder have made huge successes of late, and received a great deal of uncritical homage. I believe that both are too sagacious to let it fool them. It is technical virtuosity that has won them attention; it is hard and fundamental thinking that must get them on, if they are to make good their high promise. I gather from both of them the feeling that they are yet somewhat uncertain about their characters—that after their most surprising bravura passages they remain in some doubt as to what it is all about. As a result, their work often seems fragmentary: it charms without leaving any very deep impression. But that is a defect that the years ought to cure. Meanwhile, Mr. Hemingway's [***Men without Women*** stories] **"Fifty Grand,"** first printed in the *Atlantic,* and **"The Killers,"** first printed in *Scribner's* and Mr. Wilder's "The Marquesa de Montemayor" and "Uncle Pio" are things to be sincerely thankful for. They may not be masterpieces, but masterpieces might surely be written in their manner.

[H. L. Mencken], in a review of "Men without Women," in American Mercury, *Vol. 14, No. 53, May, 1928, p. 127.*

CLIFTON FADIMAN (essay date 1933)

[*Fadiman became one of the most prominent American literary critics during the 1930s with his insightful and often caustic book reviews for the* Nation *and* New Yorker *magazines. In the following excerpt from an open letter to Hemingway, Fadiman gently admonishes the writer for the shortcomings he discerns in* Winner Take Nothing.]

DEAR MR. HEMINGWAY: I have this week enjoyed the great pleasure of reading your latest collection of stories, ***Winner Take Nothing.*** Nobody needs to tell you that they are good stories. Unless you started to imitate your imitators, I don't suppose you could write a bad one. It is true that the volume as a whole (more later) seems to me less satisfactory than ***Men Without Women.*** It is true also that not one of the stories approaches **"The Killers."** Still, even Maupassant wrote only one "Boule de Suif," they tell me.

The stories are so good, however, that the testier among your admirers may well inquire why they are not better. The way we figure is that while honesty and skill may get an ordinary writer by, they are not enough for us in Ernest Hemingway. Now that your school has been let out for a long recess, and your imitators are growing less conscious of the importance of being Ernest, and the atmosphere of controversy is dying down, it seems only legitimate to take a little informal inventory.

Here's the point: It seemed to many of us that *A Farewell to Arms* marked a triumphant advance over *The Sun Also Rises.* After your second novel, we began to place heavy bets on you for the great American Literary Sweepstakes. For me, certainly, *The Sun Also Rises* was the finest novel of the year. Somebody, nevertheless, is still holding my bet. It didn't seem to me that the odds were tilted one way or the other by *Death in the Afternoon,* which was perhaps something you simply had to get out of your system.

Well, here are these short stories, as honest and as uncompromising as anything you've done. But that's not enough. Somehow, they are unsatisfactory. They contain strong echoes of earlier work. They mark time, whereas *A Farewell to Arms* was a magnificent leap forward. Maybe, like Walter de la Mare's poor Jim Jay, you are allowing yourself, perhaps out of a certain very interesting wilfulness, to get stuck fast in yesterday. Naturally, you have a perfect right to stick fast wherever you damned please, but so have your readers a right to raise thin cries of dismay.

I can't believe that in ***Winner Take Nothing*** you are giving your talents a fair show. Nobody ever doubted your ability to provide us with a novel shudder. Why bother to redemonstrate it? A man who could write the billiard-room scene in *A Farewell to Arms* has too much on the ball to worry excessively about third-position exercises in the macabre (**"A Natural History of the Dead"**), no matter how perfectly done they are.

Then there is this business of dating. It seems a shame that eyes as wide-open and penetrating as yours should continue to fix themselves on things which smell of the early 1920's. Frigidly objective studies of Lesbians and sentimental whores, coldly shocking tales of self-mutilation and sacrilege—aren't they beginning to get just a litle high in flavor?

Your irony, too, is something that you appear to have developed to its full possibilities. You can pass beyond it. Your brilliant trick of incongruous juxtaposition—placing two apparently unrelated aspects of life side by side so that each will unobtrusively bring out the horror of the other—it's a good device, beloved of young writers, but it should be only a vestibule leading to a deeper and more inclusive kind of irony. It is true enough that the face of life is grotesque, but surely you are fit for something more than merely showing us its grotesquerie. As a matter of fact, the trouble is that you yourself have educated us so completely in your own peculiar irony that now we almost know it by heart and continued demonstrations of it move us only as brilliant bravura performances. I think that's why stories like **"Homage to Switzerland"** and **"The Mother of a Queen"** and **"One Reader Writes"** leave us, or me at any rate, a bit cold.

So many of the stories, particularly **"Fathers and Sons,"** contain a kind of youthful Red Indian brutality which everyone is happy to admit only you can make interesting. But at bottom it doesn't seem to me very different from the atmosphere surrounding college-boy fraternity initiations. Nobody objects to brutality *per se,* but the trouble is its roots lie in our childhood and they say that among the things good artists do is to help us outgrow our childhood. That's why I can't feel that your stories about sport and sudden death lead to anything large or profound. As literary material, you have developed these things to the saturation point. Why not go on with something else?

May I close with a reference to a friend of mine, a very good critical writer, who is enormously engaged by ping-pong. He plays it as if it were a matter of life and death, and while playing it he gets out of it certain physical and emotional values of an intense order. Come up some time and take a look at him. You might turn into a ping-pong *aficionado.* I merely wish to remark that though my friend's ping-pong overcasts and electrifies his life, no hint of it seems to get into his writing.

Mr. Hemingway, we are still betting on you.

Sincerely and in all admiration.

CLIFTON FADIMAN
(pp. 58-9)

Hemingway fishing in Horton Creek in northern Michigan, August 1904. The Granger Collection, New York.

Clifton Fadiman, "A Letter to Mr. Hemingway," in The New Yorker, *Vol. III, No. 37, October 28, 1933, pp. 58-9.*

WYNDHAM LEWIS (essay date 1934)

[Lewis was an English novelist and painter, who, with T. S. Eliot, Ezra Pound, and T. E. Hulme, was instrumental in establishing the anti-Romantic movement in literature during the first decades of the twentieth century. He has remained a highly controversial figure due to his unpopular political stances, savage literary attacks on many of his contemporaries, and the generally vituperative, iconoclastic cast of his nonfiction. In the following excerpt from one of the most damning reviews Hemingway received in his lifetime, Lewis asserts that Hemingway's fiction is seriously marred by Gertrude Stein's influence, and he questions its artistic worth.]

Ernest Hemingway is a very considerable artist in prose-fiction. Besides this, or with this, his work possesses a penetrating quality, like an animal speaking. (p. 17)

A quality in the work of the author of ***Men Without Women*** suggests that we are in the presence of a writer who is not merely a conspicuous chessman in the big-business book-game of the moment, but something much finer than that. Let me attempt to isolate that quality for you, in such a way as not to damage it too much: for having set out to demonstrate the political significance of this artist's work, I shall, in the course of that demonstration, resort to a dissection of it—not the best way, I am afraid, to bring out the beauties of the finished product. This dissection is, however, necessary for my purpose here. "I have a weakness for Ernest Hemingway," as the egregious Miss Stein says: it is not agreeable to me to pry into his craft, but there is no help for it if I am to reach certain important conclusions.

But *political significance!* That is surely the last thing one would expect to find in such books as ***In Our Time,*** *The Sun Also Rises,* ***Men Without Women,*** or *Farewell to Arms.* And indeed it is difficult to imagine a writer whose mind is more entirely closed to politics than is Hemingway's. I do not suppose he has ever heard of the Five-Year Plan, though I dare say he knows that artists pay no income tax in Mexico, and is quite likely to be following closely the agitation of the Mexican matadors to get themselves recognized as 'artists' so that they may pay no income tax. I expect he has heard of Hitler, but thinks of him mainly, if he is acquainted with the story, as the Boche who went down into a cellar with another Boche and captured thirty Frogs and came back with an Iron Cross. He probably knows that his friend Pound writes a good many letters every week to American papers on the subject of Social Credit, but I am sure Pound has never succeeded in making him read a line of *Credit-Power and Democracy.* He is interested in the sports of death, in the sad things that happen to those engaged in the sports of love—in sand-sharks and in Wilson-spoons—in war, but *not* in the things that cause war, or the people who profit by it, or in the ultimate human destinies involved in it. He lives, or affects to live, *submerged.* He is in the multitudinous ranks of *those to whom things happen*—terrible things of course, and of course stoically borne. (pp. 17-18)

[With] Mr. Hemingway, the story is told in the tone, and with the vocabulary, of the persons described. The rhythm is the anonymous folk-rhythm of the urban proletariat. Mr. Hemingway is, self-consciously, a folk prose-poet in the way that Robert Burns was a folk-poet. But what is curious about this is that the modified *Beach-la-mar* in which he writes, is, more or less, the speech that is proposed for everybody in the future—it is a volapuk which probably will be ours tomorrow. (pp. 23-4)

It is very uncomfortable in real life when people become so captivated with somebody else's tricks that they become a sort of caricature or echo of the other: and it is no less embarrassing in books, at least when one entertains any respect for the victim of the fascination. (pp. 24-5)

If we blot out Gertrude Stein, and suppose she does not exist, does this part of Hemingway's equipment help or not? We must answer *Yes* I think. It does seem to help a good deal: many of his best effects are obtained by means of it. It is so much a part of his craft, indeed, that it is difficult now to imagine Hemingway without this mannerism. He has never taken it over into a gibbering and baboonish stage as has Miss Stein. He has kept it as a valuable oddity, even if a flagrantly borrowed one—ever present it is true, but one to which we can easily get used and come to like even as a delightfully clumsy engine of innocence. I don't mind it very much.

To say that, near to communism as we all are, it cannot matter, and is indeed praiseworthy, for a celebrated artist to take over, lock, stock and barrel from another artist the very thing for which he is mainly known, seems to me to be going too far in the denial of the person, or the individual—especially as in a case of this sort, the trick is after all, in the first instance, a *personal* trick. Such a practice must result, if universally indulged in, in hybrid forms or monstrosities.

And my main criticism, indeed, of the *steining* of Hemingway is that it does impose upon him an ethos—*the Stein ethos,* as it might be called. With Stein's bag of tricks he also takes over a *Weltanshauung,* which may not at all be his, and does in fact seem to contradict his major personal quality. This infantile, dull-witted, dreamy stutter compels whoever uses it to conform to the infantile, dull-witted type. He passes over into the category of *those to whom things are done,* from that of those who execute—if the latter is indeed where he originally belonged. One might even go so far as to say that this brilliant Jewish lady had made a *clown* of him by teaching Ernest Hemingway her baby-talk! So it is a pity. And it is very difficult to know where Hemingway proper begins and Stein leaves off as an artist. It is an uncomfortable situation for the critic, especially for one who 'has a weakness' for the male member of this strange spiritual partnership, and very much prefers him to the female. (pp. 27-8)

[Reading Hemingway's fiction] is like reading a newspaper, day by day, about some matter of absorbing interest—say the reports of a divorce, murder, or libel action. If you say *anyone could write it,* you are mistaken there, because, to obtain that smooth effect, of commonplace reality, there must be no sentimental or other heightening, the number of words expended must be proportionate to the importance and the length of the respective phases of the action, and any false move or overstatement would at once stand out and tell against it. If an inferior reporter to Hemingway took up the pen, that fact would at once be detected by a person sensitive to reality.

It is an art, then, from this standpoint, like the cinema, or like those 'modernist' still-life pictures in which, in place of *painting* a match box upon the canvas, a piece of actual match box is stuck on. A recent example of this (I choose it because a good many people will have seen it) is the cover design of the French periodical *Minotaure,* in which Picasso has pasted and tacked various things together, sticking a line drawing of the Minotaur in the middle. Hemingway's is a poster-art, in this sense: or a *cinema in words. The steining* in the text of Hemingway is as it were the hand-made part—if we are considering it as 'super-realist' design: a manipulation of the photograph if we are regarding it as a film.

If you say that this is not the way that Dante wrote, that these are not artistically permanent creations—or not permanent in the sense of a verse of Bishop King, or a page of Gulliver, I agree. But it is what we have got: there is actually *bad* and *good* of this kind; and I for my part enjoy what I regard as the good, without worrying any more about it than that.

That a particular phase in the life of humanity is implicit in this art is certain. It is one of the first fruits of the *proletarianization* which, as a result of the amazing revolutions in the technique of industry, we are all undergoing, whether we like it or not. But this purely political, or sociological side to the question can be brought out, I believe, with great vividness by a quotation. Here, for instance, is a fragment of a story of a mutiny at sea. . . .

> About 5.30 Green, the boatswain, came down first, and French Peter, Big Harry, and all the other lot followed. The deck was left without anybody, and the wheel too, they came into the cabin; Trousillot was there as well. They did not speak at first. The first thing they did was to rub me over. They could not feel anything. I had the two revolvers with me, but they did not feel them. French Peter and Big Harry felt me over. All the others were present. Green said, 'Well, steward, we have finished now.' I said, 'What the hell did you finish?' He said, 'We have finished captain, mate and second.' He said, 'We got our mind made up to go to Greece; if you like to save your own life you had better take charge of the ship and bring us to Greece. You bring us to Gibraltar, we will find Greece: you bring us there you will be all right, steward. We will take the boats when we get to Greece, and take the sails and everything into the boats, and sell them ashore and divide the money between ourselves. You will have your share, the same as anybody else; the charts and sextants, and all that belongs to the navigation, you can have. Me and my cousin, Johny Moore, have got a rich uncle; he will buy everything. We will scuttle the ship. My uncle is a large owner there of some ships. We will see you right, that you will be master of one of those vessels.' I said, 'Well, men, come on deck and get them braces ready, and I hope you will agree and also obey my orders!' The other men said, 'All right, steward, very good, very good, steward, you do right.' That was all I could hear from them, from everybody. The conversation between me and Green was in English, and everybody standing round. He spoke to the other men in Greek. What he said I don't know. I said, 'Where are the bodies? Where is the captain?' Green said, 'Oh they are all right, they are overboard,' and all the men said the same. . . .

That is not by Hemingway, though it quite well might be. I should not be able to tell it was not by Hemingway if it were shown me as a fragment. But this is by him:

Across the bay they found the other boat beached. Uncle George was smoking a cigar in the dark. The young Indian pulled the boat way up the beach. Uncle George gave both the Indians cigars. They walked up from the beach through a meadow that was soaking wet with dew, following the young Indian who carried a lantern. Then they went into the woods and followed a trail that led to the logging road that ran back into the hills. It was much lighter on the logging road as the timber was cut away on both sides. The young Indian stopped and blew out his lantern and they all walked on along the road.

They came around a bend and a dog came out barking. Ahead were the lights of the shanties where the Indian bark-peelers lived. More dogs rushed out at them. The two Indians sent them back to the shanties. In the shanty nearest the road there was a light in the window. An old woman stood in the doorway holding a lamp.

Inside on a wooden bunk lay a young Indian woman. She had been trying to have her baby for two days. All the old women in the camp had been helping her. The men had moved off up the road to sit in the dark and smoke out of range of the noise she made. She screamed just as Nick and the two Indians followed his father and Uncle George into the shanty. She lay in the lower bunk, very big under a quilt. Her head was turned to one side. In the upper bunk was her husband. He had cut his foot very badly with an axe three days before. He was smoking a pipe. The room smelled very bad.

Nick's father ordered some water to be put on the stove, while it was heating he spoke to Nick.

'This lady is going to have a baby, Nick,' he said.

'I know,' said Nick.

'You don' know,' said his father. 'Listen to me. What she is going through is called being in labour. The baby wants to be born and she wants it to be born. All her muscles are trying to get the baby born. That is what is happening when she screams.'

'I see,' Nick said.

Just then the woman cried out.

The first of these two passages is from a book entitled *Forty Years in the Old Bailey*. It is the account of a mutiny and murder on the high seas, the trial occurring on May 3 and 4, 1876. It was evidence verbatim of one Constant von Hoydonck, a Belgian, twenty-five years of age, who joined the vessel *Lennie* at Antwerp, as chief steward, on October 22. This is a *Querschnitt*, a slice, of 'real life': and how close Hemingway is to such material as this can be seen by comparing it with the second passage [from the story **"Indian Camp"**] out of ***In Our Time***.

That, I think, should put you in possession of all that is essential for an understanding of the work of this very notable artist: an understanding I mean; I do not mean that, as a work of art, a book of his should be approached in this critical and anatomizing spirit. That is another matter. Where the 'politics' come in I suppose by this time you will have gathered. This is the voice of the 'folk,' of the masses, who are the cannon-fodder, the cattle outside the slaughter-house, serenely chewing the cud—*of those to whom things are done,* in contrast to those who have executive will and intelligence. It is itself innocent of politics—one might almost add alas! That does not affect its quality as art. The expression of the soul of the dumb ox would have a penetrating beauty of its own, if it were uttered with genius—with bovine genius (and in the case of Hemingway that is what has happened): just as much as would the folk-song of the baboon, or of the 'Praying Mantis.' But where the politics crop up is that if we take this to be the typical art of a civilization—and there is no serious writer who stands higher in Anglo-Saxony today than does Ernest Hemingway—then we are by the same token saying something very definite about that civilization. (pp. 36-41)

Wyndham Lewis, "Ernest Hemingway (The 'Dumb Ox')," in his Men without Art, *1934. Reprint by Russell & Russell, Inc., 1964, pp. 17-41.*

HOWARD BAKER (essay date 1938)

[In the following excerpt, Baker discusses the artistry of Hemingway's stories, particularly "The Snows of Kilimanjaro."]

Ernest Hemingway has demonstrated his powers in the short story so often that his work quite naturally and rightfully calls forth superlatives. The superlatives, I think, ought not to be limited to the generally liked stories in ***Men Without Women;*** they are just as appropriate to his earliest prose, to the Indian sketches and the **"Big Two-hearted River"** in ***In Our Time,*** as well as to the fiercely honest paragraphs set between the stories. And they are possibly even more appropriate to a recent story, **"The Snows of Kilimanjaro."** . . . (p. 585)

Not that Hemingway has won his preëminence easily. Every aspect of his talent has been under fire from one angle or another; his brutality and his tenderness, his sportsman's life and his city life, his short and his long sentences, his habit, as some critics said, of spinning bull in the afternoon, or, as others said, of writing calamity in cablegrams. What was really under fire, I think, was his ideas of value or his attitudes towards life; Hemingway's severest critics, say what they would about his sentence structure, really disliked what the sentences said, the calamity rather than the structure of the cablegram. This implies an ethical foundation in criticism which Hemingway might justly complain was handled a little obscurely by his opponents.

It is never easy to assay the values in writing as fine and as complex as Hemingway's; yet one must try. Looking back, we can see clearly now that Hemingway at no time gave expression to a facile, an easily grasped and immediately acceptable attitude towards his experience; he said nothing that could be reduced to a formula; he never said what he was expected to say; one could imitate his manner and matter but never his final effects—he was in these respects unlike Anderson or Cabell or Lewis or the host of others.

In saying what he really thought and felt, he was original, of course; but originality is a means to an end rather than an end. His principal end seems to me to have been something at once so simple and so difficult as commentary on living satisfactorily in our world. Given that you find yourself in a war, how shall you live and keep sane? The answers that Hemingway has given, shocking though they may be, with their intricate blending of whiskey and action and cruelty and pity, I suspect are the only good answers. Given peace, how shall you live? The answers naturally become many-sided. But in the long run they put the highest value on the practice of human skills. These skills range from sports to arts, from making love to making books; if some, at first glance, seem to be worth much more than others, we must consider that Hemingway has a way of seeing sports which raises them to the status of arts: he finds in the practice of them the same passion and deftness and comprehension that the arts demand. In this respect we could say that a dominant theme in his work is much like that which Caroline Gordon employs in her splendid novel *Aleck Maury, Sportsman*.

When a sport assumes the characteristics of an art, it begins raising ultimate problems, demanding a response to questions about life and death, good and evil; thus Hemingway sees the crest of life, as it were, in the superb practice of a skill, and over that crest he sees death. Or to put much the same thing in simpler terms, Hemingway appears to have had born in him a powerful prevailing consciousness of death, and it comes out strongest when he is most conscious. This is what gives his work, it seems to me, its extraordinary intensity—that intensity which is often mistaken for brutality. When a man's best work is overshadowed by a *memento mori* created by his own spirit, you may be sure that his work will be moral, though it may well be troubling to the spirits of his readers: the behavior of his characters, as distinct from their basic morals, has caused a good deal of stormy prudishness to be directed against him.

Hemingway's work is peculiarly of his times; in writing always in one way or another about the artist, the artist and death, he gives expression to the same urges which have been most powerful in Thomas Mann. To find value so exclusively in artistic experience, excellent though it is, is also a limitation, for the artist stands so much alone in the world that the world itself is taken for granted. Hemingway has started out too easily with, given a war, given a time of peace, given wealth and leisure—what then of the artist? We may justly balk at these givens; the sportsman may, but the serious artist ought never to take the world for granted. It is hasty, though probably not wrong, to rush to the conclusion that Hemingway, in his recent activities and in his last novel (*To Have and Have Not*), gives evidence of enlarging the range of his talent.

Still, take Hemingway at his best, and it is clear that his range was never seriously limited. In **"The Snows of Kilimanjaro"** he is at his best, and in a variety of ways. The story is about the death of an artist, a writer; the dying man tortures himself by reviewing in his mind the fine work he should have done, had he not dissipated his time and skill in the ease which his wealthy wife provided for him. The conversations between the man and his wife are most complicated and sensitive, rich with the irritability and disappointment and affection of the man, and with the fear and love and uncomprehension of the woman; and in the midst of these conversations are set, in fiercely focused paragraphs, sketches of the things the dying artist knows he could have and should have treated. Nothing could bespeak an austere morality better than this story. It also displays the sweep of Hemingway's powers—the old ability to tell a chapter of experience in a single sentence, the later ability to encompass the most complex of relationships between people by using dialogue, and besides these, a splendid organizational ability; for by pursuing the mind of the dying man objectively and then by switching at the last moment to the point of view of the woman, Hemingway circumvents the difficulty in telling a story in which the only possible narrator has been killed off. (pp. 586-88)

Howard Baker, "The Contemporary Short Story," in The Southern Review, *(Louisiana State University), Vol. III, No. 3, Winter, 1938, pp. 576-96.*

EDMUND WILSON (essay date 1941)

[*In the following excerpt from one of the most influential assessments of Hemingway's fiction, Wilson provides a survey of Hemingway's artistic development.*]

Ernest Hemingway's ***In Our Time*** was an odd and original book. It had the appearance of a miscellany of stories and fragments; but actually the parts hung together and produced a definite effect. There were two distinct series of pieces which alternated with one another: one a set of brief and brutal sketches of police shootings, bullfight crises, hangings of criminals, and incidents of the war; and the other a set of short stories dealing in its principal sequence with the growing-up of an American boy against a landscape of idyllic Michigan, but interspersed also with glimpses of American soldiers returning home. It seems to have been Hemingway's intention—***'In Our Time'***—that the war should set the key for the whole. The cold-bloodedness of the battles and executions strikes a discord with the sensitiveness and candor of the boy at home in the States; and presently the boy turns up in Europe in one of the intermediate vignettes as a soldier in the Italian army, hit in the spine by machine-gun fire and trying to talk to a dying Italian: *'Senta,* Rinaldi. *Senta,'* he says, 'you and me, we've made a separate peace.'

But there is a more fundamental relationship between the pieces of the two series. The shooting of Nick in the war does not really connect two different worlds: has he not found in the butchery abroad the same world that he knew back in Michigan? Was not life in the Michigan woods equally destructive and cruel? He had gone once with his father, the doctor, when he had performed a Caesarean operation on an Indian squaw with a jackknife and no anaesthetic and had sewed her up with fishing leaders, while the Indian hadn't been able to bear it and had cut his throat in his bunk. Another time, when the doctor had saved the life of a squaw, her Indian had picked a quarrel with him rather than pay him in work. And Nick himself had sent his girl about her business when he had found out how terrible her mother was. Even fishing in Big Two-Hearted River—away and free in the woods—he had been conscious in a curious way of the cruelty inflicted on the fish, even of the silent agonies endured by the live bait, the grasshoppers kicking on the hook.

Not that life isn't enjoyable. Talking and drinking with one's friends is great fun; fishing in Big Two-Hearted River is a tranquil exhilaration. But the brutality of life is always there, and it is somehow bound up with the enjoyment. Bullfights are especially enjoyable. It is even exhilarating to build a simply priceless barricade and pot the enemy as they are trying to get over it. The condition of life is pain; and the joys of the most innocent surface are somehow tied to its stifled pangs.

The resolution of this dissonance in art made the beauty of Hemingway's stories. He had in the process tuned a marvelous prose. Out of the colloquial American speech, with its simple declarative sentences and its strings of Nordic monosyllables, he got effects of the utmost subtlety. F. M. Ford has found the perfect simile for the impression produced by this writing: 'Hemingway's words strike you, each one, as if they were pebbles fetched fresh from a brook. They live and shine, each in its place. So one of his pages has the effect of a brook-bottom into which you look down through the flowing water. The words form a tesellation, each in order beside the other.'

Looking back, we can see how this style was already being refined and developed at a time—fifty years before—when it was regarded in most literary quarters as hopelessly non-literary and vulgar. Had there not been the nineteenth chapter of *Huckleberry Finn*?—'Two or three nights went by; I reckon I might say they swum by; they slid along so quick and smooth and lovely. Here is the way we put in the time. It was a monstrous big river down there—sometimes a mile and a half wide,' and so forth. These pages, when we happen to meet them in Carl Van Doren's anthology of world literature, stand up in a striking way beside a passage of description from Turgenev; and the pages which Hemingway was later to write about American wood and water are equivalents to the transcriptions by Turgenev—the *Sportsman's Notebook* is much admired by Hemingway—of Russian forests and fields. Each has brought to an immense and wild country the freshness of a new speech and a sensibility not yet conventionalized by literary associations. Yet it *is* the European sensibility which has come to Big Two-Hearted River, where the Indians are now obsolescent; in those solitudes it feels for the first time the cold current, the hot morning sun, sees the pine stumps, smells the sweet fern. And along with the mottled trout, with its 'clear water-over-gravel color,' the boy from the American Middle West fishes up a nice little masterpiece.

In the meantime there had been also Ring Lardner, Sherwood Anderson, Gertrude Stein, using this American language for irony, lyric poetry or psychological insight. Hemingway seems to have learned from them all. But he is now able to charge this naïve accent with a new complexity of emotion, a new shade of emotion: a malaise. The wholesale shattering of human beings in which he has taken part has given the boy a touch of panic. (pp. 174-76)

[In ***Men Without Women***] Hemingway has mastered his method of economy in apparent casualness and relevance in apparent indirection, and has turned his sense of what happens and the way in which it happens into something as hard and clear as a crystal but as disturbing as a great lyric. Yet it is usually some principle of courage, of honor, of pity—that is, some principle of sportsmanship in its largest human sense—upon which the drama hinges. The old bullfighter in **"The Undefeated"** is defeated in everything except the spirit which will not accept defeat. You get the bull or he gets you: if you die, you can die game; there are certain things you cannot do. The burlesque show manager in **"A Pursuit Race"** refrains from waking his advance publicity agent when he overtakes him and realizes that the man has just lost a long struggle against whatever anguish it is that has driven him to drink and dope. 'They got a cure for that,' the manager had said to him before he went to sleep; "'No,' William Campbell said, 'they haven't got a cure for anything.'" The burned major in **"A Simple Enquiry"**—that strange picture of the bedrock stoicism compatible with the abasement of war—has the decency not to dismiss the orderly who has rejected his proposition. The brutalized Alpine peasant who has been in the habit of hanging a lantern in the jaws of the stiffened corpse of his wife, stood in the corner of the woodshed till the spring will make it possible to bury her, is ashamed to drink with the sexton after the latter has found out what he has done. And there is a little sketch of Roman soldiers just after the Crucifixion: 'You see me slip the old spear into him?—You'll get into trouble doing that some day.—It was the least I could do for him. I'll tell you he looked pretty good to me in there today.'

This Hemingway of the middle twenties—*The Sun Also Rises* came out in '26—expressed the romantic disillusion and set the favorite pose for the period. It was the moment of gallantry in heartbreak, grim and nonchalant banter, and heroic dissipation. The great watchword was 'Have a drink'; and in the bars of New York and Paris the young people were getting to talk like Hemingway. (pp. 178-79)

In [***Winner Take Nothing***] he deals much more effectively than in *Death in the Afternoon* with that theme of contemporary decadence which is implied in his panegyric of the bullfighter. The first of these stories, **"After the Storm,"** is another of his variations—and one of the finest—on the theme of keeping up a code of decency among the hazards and pains of life. A fisherman goes out to plunder a wreck: he dives down to break in through a porthole, but inside he sees a woman with rings on her hands and her hair floating loose in the water, and he thinks about the passengers and crew being suddenly plunged to their deaths (he has almost been killed himself in a drunken fight the night before). He sees the cloud of sea birds screaming around, and he finds that he is unable to break the glass with his wrench and that he loses the anchor grapple with which he next tries to attack it. So he finally goes away and leaves the job to the Greeks, who blow the boat open and clean her out.

But in general the emotions of insecurity here obtrude themselves and dominate the book. Two of the stories deal with the hysteria of soldiers falling off the brink of their nerves under the strain of the experiences of the war, which here no longer presents an idyllic aspect; another deals with a group of patients in a hospital, at the same time crippled and hopeless; still another (a five-page masterpiece) with a waiter, who, both on his own and on his customers' account, is reluctant to go home at night, because he feels the importance of a 'clean well-lighted cafe' as a refuge from the 'nothing' that people fear. **"God Rest You Merry, Gentlemen"** repeats the theme of castration of *The Sun Also Rises;* and four of the stories are concerned more or less with male or female homosexuality. In the last story, **"Fathers and Sons,"** Hemingway reverts to the Michigan woods, as if to take the curse off the rest: young Nick had once enjoyed a nice Indian girl with plump legs and hard little breasts on the needles of the hemlock woods.

These stories and the interludes in *Death in the Afternoon* must have been written during the years that followed the stock-market crash. They are full of the apprehension of losing control of oneself which is aroused by the getting out of hand of a social-economic system, as well as of the fear of impotence which seems to accompany the loss of social mastery. And there is in such a story as **"A Clean, Well-Lighted Place"** the feeling of having got to the end of everything, of having given up heroic attitudes and wanting only the illusion of peace.

And now, in proportion as the characters in his stories run out of fortitude and bravado, he passes into a phase where he is occupied with building up his public personality. He has already now become a legend, as Mencken was in the twenties; he is the Hemingway of the handsome photographs with the sportsmen's tan and the outdoor grin, with the ominous resemblance to Clark Gable, who poses with giant marlin which he has just hauled in off Key West. And unluckily—but for an American inevitably—the opportunity soon presents itself to exploit this personality for profit: he turns up delivering Hemingway monologues in well-paying and trashy magazines; and the Hemingway of these loose disquisitions, arrogant, belligerent and boastful, is certainly the worst-invented character to be found in the author's work. If he is obnoxious, the effect is somewhat mitigated by the fact that he is intrinsically incredible. (pp. 182-84)

You may fear, after reading *The Fifth Column,* that Hemingway will never sober up; but as you go on to his short stories of this period, you find that your apprehensions were unfounded. Three of these stories have a great deal more body—they are longer and more complex—than the comparatively meager anecdotes collected in ***Winner Take Nothing.*** And here are his real artistic successes with the material of his adventures in Africa, which make up for the miscarried *Green Hills:* **"The Short Happy Life of Francis Macomber"** and **"The Snows of Kilimanjaro,"** which disengage, by dramatizing them objectively, the themes he had attempted in the earlier book but that had never really got themselves presented. And here is at least a beginning of a real artistic utilization of Hemingway's experience in Spain: an incident of the war in two pages which outweighs the whole of *The Fifth Column* and all his Spanish dispatches, a glimpse of an old man, 'without politics,' who has so far occupied his life in taking care of eight pigeons, two goats and a cat, but who has now been dislodged and separated from his pets by the advance of the Fascist armies. It is a story which takes its place among the war prints of Callot and Goya, artists whose union of elegance with sharpness has already been recalled by Hemingway in his earlier battle pieces: a story which might have been written about almost any war.

And here—what is very remarkable—is a story, **"The Capital of the World,"** which finds an objective symbol for, precisely, what is wrong with *The Fifth Column.* A young boy who has come up from the country and waits on table in a pension in Madrid gets accidentally stabbed with a meat knife while playing at bullfighting with the dishwasher. This is the simple anecdote, but Hemingway has built in behind it all the life of the pension and the city: the priesthood, the working-class movement, the grown-up bullfighters who have broken down or missed out. 'The boy Paco,' Hemingway concludes, 'had never known about any of this nor about what all these people would be doing on the next day and on other days to come. He had no idea how they really lived nor how they ended. He did not realize they ended. He died, as the Spanish phrase has it, full of illusions. He had not had time in his life to lose any of them, or even, at the end, to complete an act of contrition.' So he registers in this very fine piece the discrepancy between the fantasies of boyhood and the realities of the grown-up world. Hemingway the artist, who feels things truly and cannot help recording what he feels, has actually said good-bye to these fantasies at a time when the war correspondent is making himself ridiculous by attempting to hang on to them still.

The emotion which principally comes through in **"Francis Macomber"** and **"The Snows of Kilimanjaro"**—as it figures also in *The Fifth Column*—is a growing antagonism to women. Looking back, one can see at this point that the tendency has been there all along. In **"The Doctor and the Doctor's Wife,"** the boy Nick goes out squirrel-hunting with his father instead of obeying the summons of his mother; in **"Cross-Country Snow,"** he regretfully says farewell to male companionship on a skiing expedition in Switzerland, when he is obliged to go back to the States so that his wife can have her baby. The young man in **"Hills Like White Elephants"** compels his girl to have an abortion contrary to her wish; another story **"A Canary for One,"** bites almost unbearably but exquisitely on the loneliness to be endured by a wife after she and her husband shall have separated; the peasant of **"An Alpine Idyll"** abuses the corpse of his wife (these last three appear under the general title ***Men Without Women***). Brett in *The Sun Also Rises* is an exclusively destructive force: she might be a better woman if she were mated with Jake, the American; but actually he is protected against her and is in a sense revenging his own sex through being unable to do anything for her sexually. Even the hero of *A Farewell to Arms* eventually destroys Catherine—after enjoying her abject devotion—by giving her a baby, itself born dead. The only women with whom Nick Adams' relations are perfectly satisfactory are the little Indian girls of his boyhood who are in a position of hopeless social disadvantage and have no power over the behavior of the white male—so that he can get rid of them the moment he has done with them. Thus in *The Fifth Column* Mr. Philip brutally breaks off with Dorothy—he has been rescued from her demoralizing influence by his enlistment in the Communist crusade, just as the hero of *The Sun Also Rises* has been saved by his physical disability—to revert to a little Moorish whore. Even Harry Morgan, who is represented as satisfying his wife on the scale of a Paul Bunyan, deserts her in the end by dying and leaves her racked by the cruelest desire.

And now this instinct to get the woman down presents itself frankly as a fear that the woman will get the man down. The men in both these African stories are married to American bitches of the most soul-destroying sort. The hero of **"The Snows of Kilimanjaro"** loses his soul and dies of futility on a hunting expedition in Africa, out of which he has failed to get what he had hoped. The story is not quite stripped clean of the trashy moral attitudes which have been coming to disfigure the author's work: the hero, a seriously intentioned and apparently promising writer, goes on a little sloppily over the dear early days in Paris when he was earnest, happy and poor, and blames a little hysterically the rich woman whom he has married and who has debased him. Yet it is one of Hemingway's remarkable stories. There is a wonderful piece of writing at the end when the reader is made to realize that what has seemed to be an escape by plane, with the sick man looking down on Africa, is only the dream of a dying man. The other story, **"Francis Macomber,"** perfectly realizes its purpose. Here the male saves his soul at the last minute, and then is actually shot down by his woman, who does not want him to have a soul. Here Hemingway has at last got what Thurber calls the war between men and women right out into the open and has written a terrific fable of the impossible civilized woman who despises the civilized man for his failure in initiative and nerve and then jealously tries to break him down as soon as he begins to exhibit any. (It ought to be noted, also, that whereas in *Green Hills of Africa* the descriptions tended to weigh down the narrative with their excessive circumstantiality, the landscapes and animals of **"Francis Macomber"** are alive and unfalteringly proportioned.)

Going back over Hemingway's books today, we can see clearly what an error of the politicos it was to accuse him of an indifference to society. His whole work is a criticism of society: he has responded to every pressure of the moral atmosphere of the time, as it is felt at the roots of human relations, with a sensitivity almost unrivaled. Even his preoccupation with licking the gang in the next block and being known as the best basketball player in high school has its meaning in the present

Hemingway at Shakespeare & Company, the Paris bookstore owned by his friend Sylvia Beach. Princeton University Library. Papers of Sylvia Beach.

epoch. After all, whatever is done in the world, political as well as athletic, depends on personal courage and strength. With Hemingway, courage and strength are always thought of in physical terms, so that he tends to give the impression that the bullfighter who can take it and dish it out is more of a man than any other kind of man, and that the sole duty of the revolutionary socialist is to get the counter-revolutionary gang before they get him.

But ideas, however correct, will never prevail by themselves: there must be people who are prepared to stand or fall with them, and the ability to act on principle is still subject to the same competitive laws which operate in sporting contests and sexual relations. Hemingway has expressed with genius the terrors of the modern man at the danger of losing control of his world, and he has also, within his scope, provided his own kind of antidote. This antidote, paradoxically, is almost entirely moral. Despite Hemingway's preoccupation with physical contests, his heroes are almost always defeated physically, nervously, practically: their victories are moral ones. He himself, when he trained himself stubbornly in his unconventional unmarketable art in a Paris which had other fashions, gave the prime example of such a victory; and if he has sometimes, under the menace of the general panic, seemed on the point of going to pieces as an artist, he has always pulled himself together the next moment. The principle of the Bourdon gauge, which is used to measure the pressure of liquids, is that a tube which has been curved into a coil will tend to straighten out in proportion as the liquid inside it is subjected to an increasing pressure. (pp. 191-96)

Edmund Wilson, "Hemingway: Gauge of Morale," in his The Wound and the Bow: Seven Studies in Literature, *1941. Reprint by Farrar, Straus, and Giroux, 1978, pp. 174-97.*

CLEANTH BROOKS AND ROBERT PENN WARREN (essay date 1943)

[Brooks is the most prominent of the New Critics, an influential movement in American criticism that also included Allen Tate, John Crowe Ransom, and Robert Penn Warren, and which paralleled a critical movement in England led by I. A. Richards, T. S. Eliot, and William Empson. For Brooks, metaphor was the primary element of literary art and the effect of that metaphor of primary importance. Brooks's most characteristic essays are detailed studies of metaphoric structure, particularly in poetry. Warren, a poet and novelist as well as critic, is considered one of the most distinguished men of letters in America today. Warren's deep interest in history and his conception that art is a vital force in contemporary society inform all his work. In the following excerpt from their Understanding Fiction, *first published in 1943, Brooks and Warren define the Hemingway hero and the Hemingway world through a discussion of the action in "The Killers."]*

[In addition to the structure of **"The Killers,"** as it concerns the relations among incidents and with regard to the attitudes of the characters,] there remain as important questions such items as the following: What is Hemingway's attitude toward his material? How does this attitude find its expression?

Perhaps the simplest approach to these questions may be through a consideration of the situations and characters which interest Hemingway. These situations are usually violent ones: the hard-drinking and sexually promiscuous world of *The Sun Also Rises;* the chaotic and brutal world of war as in *A Farewell to Arms, For Whom the Bell Tolls,* or **"A Way You'll Never Be"**; the dangerous and exciting world of the bull ring or the prize ring as in *The Sun Also Rises, Death in the Afternoon,* **"The Undefeated," "Fifty Grand"**; the world of crime, as in **"The Killers,"** *To Have and Have Not,* or **"The Gambler, the Nun, and the Radio."** Hemingway's typical characters are usually tough men, experienced in the hard worlds they inhabit, and apparently insensitive: Lieutenant Henry in *A Farewell to Arms,* the big-game hunter in **"The Snows of Kilimanjaro,"** Robert Jordan in *For Whom the Bell Tolls,* or even Ole Andreson. They are, also, usually defeated men. Out of their practical defeat, however, they have managed to salvage something. And here we come upon Hemingway's basic interest in such situations and such characters. They are not defeated except upon their own terms; some of them have even courted defeat; certainly, they have maintained, even in the practical defeat, an ideal of themselves, formulated or unformulated, by which they have lived. Hemingway's attitude is, in a sense, like that of Robert Louis Stevenson. . . . (p. 307)

[For Stevenson, the world] is, objectively considered, a violent and meaningless world—"our rotary island loaded with predatory life and more drenched with blood . . . than ever mutinied ship, scuds through space." This is Hemingway's world, too. But its characters, at least those whose story Hemingway cares to tell, make one gallant effort to redeem the incoherence and meaninglessness of this world: they attempt to impose some form upon the disorder of their lives, the technique of the bullfighter or sportsman, the discipline of the soldier, the code of the gangster, which, even though brutal and dehumanizing, has its own ethic. . . . The form is never quite adequate to subdue the world, but the fidelity to it is part of the gallantry of defeat.

It has been said above that the typical Hemingway character is tough and, apparently, insensitive. But only apparently, for the fidelity to a code, to a discipline, may be an index to a sensitivity which allows the characters to see, at moments, their true plight. At times, and usually at times of stress, it is the tough man, for Hemingway, the disciplined man, who actually is aware of pathos or tragedy. The individual toughness (which may be taken to be the private discipline demanded by the world), may find itself in conflict with some more natural and spontaneous human emotion; in contrast with this the discipline may, even, seem to be inhuman; but the Hemingway hero, though he is aware of the claims of this spontaneous human emotion, is afraid to yield to those claims because he has learned that the only way to hold on to "honor," to individuality, to, even, the human order as against the brute chaos of the world, is to live by his code. This is the irony of the situation in which the hero finds himself. Hemingway's heroes are aristocrats in the sense that they are the initiate, and practice a lonely virtue.

Hemingway's heroes utter themselves, not in rant and bombast, but in terms of ironic understatement. This understatement, stemming from the contrast between the toughness and the sensitivity, the violence and the sensitivity, is a constant aspect of Hemingway's method. . . . Just as there is a margin of victory in the defeat of the Hemingway characters, so there is a little margin of sensibility in their brutal and violent world. The revelation arises from the most unpromising circumstances and from the most unpromising people—the little streak of poetry or pathos in **"A Pursuit Race," "The Undefeated," "My Old Man,"** and, let us say, **"The Killers."** (pp. 308-09)

[Ole Andreson of **"The Killers"**] fits into this pattern. Andreson won't whimper. He takes his medicine quietly. But Ole Andreson's story is buried in the larger story, which is focused on Nick. How does Nick Adams fit into the pattern? Hemingway, as a matter of fact, is accustomed to treat his basic situation at one or the other of two levels. There is the story of the person who is already initiated, who already has adopted his appropriate code, or discipline, in the world which otherwise he cannot cope with. . . . There is also the story of the process of the initiation, the discovery of evil and disorder, and the first step toward the mastery of the discipline. This is Nick's story. (But the same basic situation occurs in many other stories by Hemingway, for example, **"Up In Michigan," "Indian Camp,"** and **"The Three-Day Blow."**)

It has been observed that the typical Hemingway character is tough and apparently insensitive. Usually, too, that character is simple. The impulse which has led Hemingway to the simple character is akin to that which led a Romantic poet like Wordsworth to the same choice. Wordsworth felt that his unsophisticated peasants or children, who are the characters of so many of his poems, were more honest in their responses than the cultivated man, and therefore more poetic. Instead of Wordsworth's typical peasant we find in Hemingway's work the bullfighter, the soldier, the revolutionist, the sportsman, and the gangster; instead of Wordsworth's children, we find the young men like Nick. There are, of course, differences between the approach of Wordsworth and that of Hemingway, but there is little difference on the point of marginal sensibility.

The main difference between the two writers depends on the difference in their two worlds. Hemingway's world is a more disordered world, and more violent, than the simple and innocent world of Wordsworth. Therefore, the sensibility of Hemingway's characters is in sharper contrast to the nature of his world. This creates an irony which is not found in the work of Wordsworth. Hemingway plays down the sensibility as such, and sheathes it in the code of toughness. . . . The typical character is sensitive, but his sensitivity is never insisted upon; he may be worthy of pity, but he never demands it. The underlying attitude in Hemingway's work may be stated like this: pity is only valid when it is wrung from a man who has been seasoned by experience, and is only earned by a man who never demands it, a man who takes his chances. Therefore, a premium is placed upon the fact of violent experience. (pp. 309-10)

Cleanth Brooks and Robert Penn Warren, "'The Killers', Ernest Hemingway: Interpretation," in Understanding Fiction, *edited by Cleanth Brooks and Robert Penn Warren, second edition, Appleton-Century-Crofts, Inc., 1959, pp. 306-25.*

MALCOLM COWLEY (essay date 1944)

[*An American critic, editor, poet, translator, and historian, Cowley has made valuable contributions to contemporary letters with his literary criticism, his chronicles of modern American literature, and his editions of the works of such American authors as Nathaniel Hawthorne, Walt Whitman, and Hemingway. His introduction to* The Portable Hemingway, *published in 1944, is considered a landmark, albeit controversial, study for its thesis that a "personal demon" rules and unites all of Hemingway's fiction. In the following excerpt from that work, Cowley discusses the thematic unity in the short stories and assesses Hemingway's achievement.*]

Going back to Hemingway's work after several years is like going back to a brook where you had often fished and finding the woods as deep and cool as they used to be. The trees are bigger, perhaps, but they are the same trees; the water comes down over the black stones as clear as always, with the same dull, steady roar where it plunges into the pool; and when the first trout takes hold of your line you can feel your heart beating against your fishing jacket. But something has changed, for this time there are shadows in the pool that you hadn't noticed before, and you have a sense that the woods are haunted. When Hemingway's stories first appeared, they seemed to be a transcription of the real world, new because they were accurate and because the world in those days was also new. With his insistence on "presenting things truly," he seemed to be a writer in the naturalistic tradition (for all his technical innovations); and the professors of American literature, when they got around to mentioning his books in their surveys, treated him as if he were a Dreiser of the lost generation, or perhaps the fruit of a misalliance between Dreiser and Jack London. Going back to his work in 1944, you perceive his kinship with a wholly different group of novelists, let us say with Poe and Hawthorne and Melville: the haunted and nocturnal writers, the men who dealt in images that were symbols of an inner world.

On the face of it, his method is not in the least like theirs. He doesn't lead us into castles ready to collapse with age, or into very old New England houses, or embark with us on the search for a whale that is also the white spirit of evil; instead he tells the stories he has lived or heard, against the background of countries he has seen. But, you reflect on reading his books again, these are curious stories that he has chosen from his wider experience, and these countries are presented in a strangely mortuary light. In no other writer of our time can you find such a profusion of corpses: dead women in the rain; dead soldiers bloated in their uniforms and surrounded by torn papers; sunken liners full of bodies that float past the closed portholes. In no other writer can you find so many suffering animals: mules with their forelegs broken drowning in shallow water off the quay at Smyrna; gored horses in the bull ring; wounded hyenas first snapping at their own entrails and then eating them with relish. And morally wounded people who also devour themselves: punch-drunk boxers, soldiers with battle fatigue, veterans crazy with "the old rale," Lesbians, nymphomaniacs, bullfighters who have lost their nerve, men who lie awake all night while their brains get to racing "like a flywheel with the weight gone"—here are visions as terrifying as those of "The Pit and the Pendulum," even though most of them are copied from life; here are nightmares at noonday, accurately described, pictured without blur, but having the nature of obsessions or hypnagogic visions between sleep and waking.

And, going back to them, you find a waking-dreamlike quality even in the stories that deal with pleasant or commonplace aspects of the world. Take, for example, **"Big Two-Hearted River,"** where the plot—or foreground of the plot—is simply a fishing trip in the northern peninsula of Michigan. Nick Adams, who is Hemingway's earliest and most personal hero, gets off the train at an abandoned sawmill town; he crosses burned-over land, makes camp, eats his supper, and goes to sleep; in the morning he looks for bait, finds grasshoppers under a log, hooks a big trout and loses it, catches two other trout, then sits in the shadow and eats his lunch very slowly while watching the stream; he decides to do no more fishing that day. There is nothing else in the story, apparently; nothing but a collection of sharp sensory details, so that you smell or hear or touch or see everything that exists near Big Two-Hearted River; and you even taste Nick Adams' supper of beans and spaghetti. "All good books are alike," Hemingway later said, "in that they are truer than if they had really happened and after you are finished reading one you will feel that all that happened to you and afterwards it all belongs to you: the good and the bad, the ecstasy, the remorse and sorrow, the people and the places and how the weather was." This story belongs to the reader, but apparently it is lacking in ecstasy, remorse, and sorrow; there are no people in it except Nick Adams; apparently there is nothing but "the places and how the weather was."

But Hemingway's stories are most of them continued, in the sense that he has a habit of returning to the same themes, each time making them a little clearer—to himself, I think, as well as to others. His work has an emotional consistency, as if all of it moved with the same current. A few years after **"Big Two-Hearted River,"** he wrote another story that cast a retrospective light on his fishing trip (much as *A Farewell to Arms* helps to explain the background of Jake Barnes and Lady Brett, in *The Sun Also Rises*). The second story, **"Now I Lay Me,"** deals with an American volunteer in the Italian army who isn't named but who might easily be Nick Adams. He is afraid to sleep at night because, so he says, "I had been living for a long time with the knowledge that if I ever shut my eyes in the dark and let myself go, my soul would go out of my body. I had been that way for a long time, ever since I had been blown up at night and felt it go out of me and go off and then come back." And the soldier continues:

> I had different ways of occupying myself while I lay awake. I would think of a trout stream I had fished along when I was a boy and fish its whole length very carefully in my mind; fishing very carefully under all the logs, all the turns of the bank, the deep holes and the clear shallow stretches, sometimes catching trout and sometimes losing them. I would stop fishing at noon to eat my lunch; sometimes on a log over the stream; sometimes on a high bank under a tree, and I always ate my lunch very slowly and watched the stream below me while I ate. . . . Some nights too I made up streams, and some of them were very exciting, and it was like being awake and dreaming. Some of those streams I still remember and think that I have fished in them, and they are confused with streams I really know.

After reading this passage, we have a somewhat different attitude toward the earlier story. The river described in it remains completely real for us; but also—like those other streams the soldier invented during the night—it has the quality of a waking dream. Although the events in the foreground are described with superb accuracy and for their own sake, we now perceive what we probably missed at a first reading: that there are shadows in the background and that part of the story takes place in an inner world. We notice that Nick Adams regards his fishing trip as an escape, either from nightmare or from realities that have become a nightmare. Sometimes his mind starts to work, even here in the wilderness; but "he knew he could choke it because he was tired enough," and he can safely fall asleep. "Nick felt happy," the author says more than once. "He felt he had left everything behind, the need for thinking, the need to write, other needs. It was all back of him." He lives as if in an enchanted country. There is a faint suggestion of old legends: all the stories of boys with cruel stepmothers who wandered off into the forest where the big trees sheltered them and the birds brought them food. There is even a condition laid on Nick's happiness, just as in many fairy tales where the hero must not wind a certain horn or open a certain door. Nick must not follow the river down into the swamp. "In the swamp the banks were bare, the big cedars came together overhead, the sun did not come through, except in patches; in the fast deep water, in the half light, the fishing would be tragic. In the swamp fishing was a tragic adventure. Nick did not want it. He did not want to go down the stream any further today."

But fishing is not the only activity of his heroes that Hemingway endows with a curious and almost supernatural value. They drink early and late; they consume enough beer, wine, anis, grappa, and Fundador to put them all into alcoholic wards, if they were ordinary mortals; but drinking seems to have the effect on them of a magic potion. Robert Jordan, in *For Whom the Bell Tolls,* is the soberest of Hemingway's heroes, the child, as it were, of middle age. Nevertheless he finds that a cup of absinthe "took the place of the evening papers, of all the old evenings in cafés, of all the chestnut trees that would be in bloom now in this month . . . of all the things he had enjoyed and forgotten and that came back to him when he tasted that opaque, bitter, tongue-numbing, brain-warming, stomach-warming, idea-changing liquid alchemy." There is much that he wants to remember, but also the fear of death that he wants to forget, and he personifies liquor as "the giant killer." On one occasion he reflects that writing about his fears might help him even more than drowning them in absinthe. He says to himself, after worrying about all the lives that have been lost as a result of his activities behind the Fascist lines: "But my guess is you will get rid of all that by writing about it. . . . Once you write it down it is all gone." Hemingway himself sometimes seems to regard writing as an exhausting ceremony of exorcism. And, as a young man after the First World War, he had painful memories of which he wanted to rid himself by setting them all down. (pp. 40-3)

Considering his laborious apprenticeship and the masters with whom he chose to study; considering his theories of writing, which he has often discussed, and how they have developed with the years; considering their subtle and highly conscious application, as well as the very complicated personality they serve to express, it is a little surprising to find that Hemingway is almost always described as a primitive. Yet the word really applies to him, if it is used in what might be called its anthropological sense. The anthropologists tell us that many of the so-called primitive peoples have an extremely elaborate system of beliefs, calling for the almost continual performance of rites and ceremonies; even their drunken orgies are ruled by tradition. Some of the forest-dwelling tribes believe that every rock or tree or animal has its own indwelling spirit. When they kill an animal or chop down a tree, they must beg its forgiveness, repeating a formula of propitiation; otherwise its spirit would haunt them. Living briefly in a world of hostile forces, they preserve themselves—so they believe—only by the exercise of magic lore.

There is something of the same atmosphere in Hemingway's work. His heroes live in a world that is like a hostile forest, full of unseen dangers, not to mention the nightmares that haunt their sleep. Death spies on them from behind every tree. Their only chance of safety lies in the faithful observance of customs they invent for themselves. (pp. 47-8)

Sometimes his stories come close to being adaptations of ancient myths. His first novel, for example, deals in different terms with the same legend that T. S. Eliot was not so much presenting as concealing in *The Waste Land.* When we turn to Eliot's explanatory notes, then read the book to which they refer as a principal source—*From Ritual to Romance,* by Jessie L. Weston—we learn that his poem is largely based on the legend of the Fisher King. The legend tells how the king was wounded in the loins and how he lay wasting in his bed while his whole kingdom became unfruitful; there was thunder but no rain; the rivers dried up, the flocks had no increase, and the women bore no children. *The Sun Also Rises* presents the same situation in terms of Paris after the First World War. It is a less despairing book than critics like to think; at times it is gay, friendly, even exuberant; but the hero has been wounded like the Fisher King, and he lives in a world that is absolutely sterile. I don't mean to imply that Hemingway owes a debt to *The Waste Land.* He had read the poem, which he liked at first, and the notes that followed it, which he didn't like at all; I doubt very much that he bothered to look at Jessie L. Weston's book. He said in 1924, when he was paying tribute to Joseph Conrad: "If I knew that by grinding Mr. Eliot into a fine dry powder and sprinkling that powder over Mr. Conrad's grave Mr. Conrad would shortly appear, looking very annoyed at the forced return, and commence writing, I would leave for London early tomorrow with a sausage grinder." And yet when he wrote his first novel, he dealt with the same legend that Eliot had discovered by scholarship; recovering it for himself, I think, by a sort of instinct for legendary situations.

And it is this instinct for legends, for sacraments, for rituals, for symbols appealing to buried hopes and fears, that helps to explain the power of Hemingway's work and his vast superiority over his imitators. The imitators have learned all his mannerisms as a writer, and in some cases they can tell a story even better than Hemingway himself; but they tell only the story; they communicate with the reader on only one level of experience. Hemingway does more than that. Most of us are also primitive in a sense, for all the machinery that surrounds our lives. We have our private rituals, our little superstitions, our symbols and fears and nightmares; and Hemingway reminds us unconsciously of the hidden worlds in which we live. Reading his best work, we are a little like Nick Adams looking down from the railroad bridge at the trout in Big Two-Hearted River:

> many trout in deep, fast-moving water, slightly distorted as he watched far down through the glassy convex surface of the pool, its surface pushing and swelling smooth against the resistance of the log-driven piles of the bridge. At the bottom of the pool were the big trout. Nick did not see them at first. Then he saw them at the bottom of the pool, big trout looking to hold themselves on the gravel bottom in a varying mist of gravel and sand.

During the last few years it has become the fashion to reprimand Hemingway and to point out how much better his work would be (with its undoubted power) if only he were a little more virtuous or reasonable or optimistic, or if he revealed the proper attitude toward progress and democracy. Critics like Maurice Coindreau (in French) and Bernard DeVoto have abused him without bothering to understand what he plainly says, much less what he suggests or implies. Even Maxwell Geismar, who is one of the few professors with a natural feeling for literary values, would like to make him completely over. "What a marvelous teacher Hemingway is," he exclaims,

> with all the restrictions of temperament and environment which so far define his work! What could he not show us of living as well as dying, of the positives in our being as well as the destroying forces, of 'grace under pressure' and the grace we need with no pressures, of ordinary life-giving actions along with those superb last gestures of doomed exiles!

Or, to put the matter more plainly, what a great writer Hemingway would be, in Geismar's opinion, if he combined his own work with equal parts of Trollope and Emerson.

And the critics have some justice on their side. It is true that Hemingway has seldom been an affirmative writer; it is true that most of his work is narrow and violent and generally preoccupied with death. But the critics, although they might conceivably change him for the worse, are quite unable to change him for the better. He is one of the novelists who write, not as they should or would, but as they must. Like Poe and Hawthorne and Melville, he listens to his personal demon, which might also be called his intuition or his sense of life. If he listened to the critics instead, he might indeed come to resemble Trollope or Emerson, but the resemblance would be only on the surface and, as he sometimes says of writing that tries hard to meet public requirements, it would all go bad afterwards. Some of his own writing has gone bad, but surprisingly little of it. By now he has earned the right to be taken for what he is, with his great faults and greater virtues; with his narrowness, his power, his always open eyes, his stubborn, chip-on-the-shoulder honesty, his nightmares, his rituals for escaping them, and his sense of an inner and an outer world that for twenty years were moving together toward the same disaster. (pp. 49-51)

Malcolm Cowley, "Nightmare and Ritual in Hemingway," in Hemingway: A Collection of Critical Essays, *edited by Robert P. Weeks, Prentice-Hall, Inc., 1962, pp. 40-51.*

MARK SCHORER (essay date 1952)

[*Schorer is an American critic and biographer who wrote the definitive life of Sinclair Lewis. In his often-cited essay "Technique as Discovery" (1948), Schorer argued that fiction deserves the same close attention to diction that the New Critics had applied to poetry. In the following excerpt from a review of* The Old Man and the Sea, *he favorably discusses the novella as a timeless parable of the cycle of life.*]

Everywhere [***The Old Man and the Sea***] is being called a classic. In at least one sense, the word cannot be applied, for here and there, where the writing wavers, its pure lucidity is muddied by all that hulking personality which, at his worst, Hemingway has made all too familiar. . . . [A] murky paragraph that has to do with "mysticism about turtles" is a case in point. Or a sentence such as this: "He did not truly feel good because the pain from the cord across his back had almost passed pain and gone into a dullness that he mistrusted"—is it a quibble to suggest that the word "truly" and its location spoil this sentence, jar us out of the mind of the old man whom we are coming to know into the reflection that we've read Hemingway before? Or a brief passage such as this:

> After he judged that his right hand had been in the water long enough he took it out and looked at it.
>
> "It is not bad," he said. "And pain does not matter to a man. . . .
>
> "You did not do so badly for something worthless," he said to his left hand. "But there was a moment when I could not find you."
>
> Why was I not born with two good hands? he thought. Perhaps it was my fault in not training that one properly. But God knows he has had enough chances to learn. He did not do so badly in the night, though, and he has only cramped once. If he cramps again let the line cut him off.

The last sentence tells us with dramatic concreteness what the generalization, "pain does not matter to a man," which is really Hemingway's, does not tell us at all. It should not have been written, precisely because what *is* written must make *us* speak that conclusion, it should be our generalization from his evidence.

But the old man seldom lapses into dramatic falseness. In his age, alone at sea, he has taken to speaking aloud, and instead of dialogue between characters by which most fictions move, this story moves by little dialogues in the old man himself, the exchange of what is spoken and what is not spoken. This is almost a running drama between that which is only possible and that which is real:

> "Fish," he said, "I love you and respect you very much. But I will kill you dead before this day ends."
>
> Let us hope so, he thought.

The threat of over-generalization is almost always in the spoken words, which, then, are immediately rooted in actuality by the reservations of the unspoken. And of course, Hemingway's incredible gift for writing of the natural life serves the same function. Whether he is describing plankton, jelly fish, the sucking fish that swim in the shadow of the marlin, the gutting of a dolphin that contains two flying fish, or turtles, they are all always there before us, actualities, and the old man is an actuality among them.

The novel is nearly a fable. The best fiction, at its heart, always is, of course, but with his particular diction and syntax, Hemingway's stories approach fable more directly than most, and never so directly as here. It is the quality of his fiction at its very best, the marvelous simplicity of line. ("'Be calm and strong, old man', he said.") There has been another strain in his fiction, to be sure—his personal ambition to become a character in a tall tale, folklore as opposed to fable. That is the weaker man pushing aside the great novelist. The strain glimmers once in this story, when we are told of the old man's feat of strength in his youth: "They had gone one day and one night with their elbows on a chalk line on the table and their forearms straight up and their hands gripped tight." Take it away.

The true quality of fable is first of all in the style, in the degree of abstraction, which is not only in some ways Biblical but is always tending toward the proverbial rhythm. ("The setting of the sun is a difficult time for fish.") Next, it is in the simplicity of the narrative, and in the beautiful proportion (about three-fourths to one-fourth) of its rise and fall. Finally, of course, it is in the moral significance of the narrative, this fine story of an ancient who goes too far out, "beyond the boundaries of permitted aspiration," as Conrad put it ("You violated your luck when you went too far outside," the old man thinks), and encounters his destiny:

> His choice had been to stay in the deep dark water far out beyond all snares and traps and treacheries. My choice was to go there to find him beyond all people. Beyond all people in the world. Now we are joined together and have

been since noon. And no one to help either one
of us.

In this isolation, he wins a Conradian victory, which means destruction and triumph. We permit his martyrdom because he has earned it. His sigh is "just a noise such as a man might make, involuntarily, feeling the nail go through his hands and into the wood." He stumbles under the weight of his mast when he carries it across his shoulder, up a hill. He sleeps, finally, "with his arms out straight and the palms of his hands up." There is more than this, and for those who, like this reviewer, believe that Hemingway's art, when it is art, is absolutely incomparable, and that he is unquestionably the greatest craftsman in the American novel in this century, something that is perhaps even more interesting. For this appears to be not only a moral fable, but a parable, and all the controlled passion in the story, all the taut excitement in the prose come, I believe, from the parable. It is an old man catching a fish, yes; but it is also a great artist in the act of mastering his subject, and, more than that, of actually writing about that struggle. Nothing is more important than his craft, and it is beloved; but because it must be struggled with and mastered, it is also a foe, enemy to all self-indulgence, to all looseness of feeling, all laxness of style, all soft pomposities.

"I am a strange old man."

"But are you strong enough now for a truly
big fish?"

"I think so. And there are many tricks."

Hemingway, who has always known the tricks, is strong enough now to have mastered his greatest subject. "I could not fail myself and die on a fish like this," the old man reflects. They win together, the great character, the big writer. (pp. 19-20)

Mark Schorer, "With Grace under Pressure," in The New Republic," *Vol. 127, No. 14, October 6, 1952, pp. 19-20.*

WILLIAM FAULKNER (essay date 1952)

[*An American novelist and short story writer, Faulkner is one of the preeminent figures in modern American literature. His most renowned works, such as* The Sound and the Fury *(1929),* Light in August *(1932), and* Absalom! Absalom! *(1936), reflect the distinct heritage of the American rural South while they display radical stylistic innovations as well as psychological and moral depth. In the following excerpt from an article originally published in* Shenandoah *in 1952, Faulkner pronounces* The Old Man and the Sea *a major achievement.*]

His best. Time may show [***The Old Man and the Sea***] to be the best single piece of any of us, I mean his and my contemporaries. This time, he discovered God, a Creator. Until now, his men and women had made themselves, shaped themselves out of their own clay; their victories and defeats were at the hands of each other, just to prove to themselves or one another how tough they could be. But this time, he wrote about pity: about something somewhere that made them all: the old man who had to catch the fish and then lose it, the fish that had to be caught and then lost, the sharks which had to rob the old man of his fish; made them all and loved them all and pitied them all. It's all right. Praise God that whatever made and loves and pities Hemingway and me kept him from touching it any further.

William Faulkner, in a review of "The Old Man and the Sea," in Essays, Speeches & Public Letters *by William Faulkner, edited by James B. Meriwether, Random House, 1965, p. 193.*

LEON EDEL (essay date 1955)

[*An American critic and biographer, Edel is a highly acclaimed authority on the life and work of Henry James. In the following excerpt, Edel questions Hemingway's status as a major American author, contending that Hemingway's works lack a distinctive style and deal with "superficial action." Edel does, however, find Hemingway a superior short story writer, an "artist of the small space, the limited view."*]

I would like to offer a mild dissent in the current cheering for our poet of big-game hunting and bull-fighting. Doubtless we rejoice, as Americans, that once again our literature has been honored by the Swedish Academy; and it is pleasant to feel that a writer as ebullient and myth-making as Ernest Hemingway should have been selected. Nevertheless the Swedish Academy has not been very brilliant, on the whole, in its choice of Nobel prize-winners; the list, going back to the beginning of the century, is filled with forgotten names and redolent with omissions. (p. 18)

Ernest Hemingway, I hold, belongs to the second shelf of American fiction, not the first: he can safely sit beside Sinclair Lewis rather than beside Hawthorne, Melville, or James. But my dissent at this moment is not in matters of classification. It stems from the Academy's discernment of the award on the grounds of Hemingway's Style—his "mastery of the art of modern narration." I am not, of course, sure what the Swedish Academy means by "modern narration"—unless indeed it is thinking of brisk journalism, the most characteristic form of narration of our time. But the award has generally been interpreted as an award for Style.

Now Style, I agree, is virtually everything in literature. The writer who forges a Style places himself, in the very nature of things, in the forefront of his period, and provides himself with a shining pass-key to posterity. But we must be careful here—both myself and the critics who have been embalming Hemingway—to be sure we speak of the same thing. A Style involves substance as well as form. No writer has received his key for swaddling meagre thought in elegant flowers. Such flowers fade easily. I would argue that Hemingway has not created a Style: he has rather created the artful illusion of a Style, for he is a clever artist and there is a great deal of cleverness in all that he has done. He has conjured up an *effect* of Style by a process of evasion very much as he sets up an aura of emotion by walking directly away from emotion.

What I am trying to suggest is that the famous Hemingway "Style" is not organic. And any Style worthy of the name must be; the much-worn, but nevertheless truthful *mot,* that *Style is the man,* testifies to this. Is Hemingway's Style the man? At the risk of vulgarly punning, I would answer no, it is the mannerism! It is an artifice, a series of charming tricks, a group of clevernesses. Gertrude Stein taught Hemingway that one can obtain wry effects by assembling incongruities, and Hemingway early learned how to juxtapose these with high effect. "There were many more guns in the country around and the spring had come." Now the coming of spring is a *non sequitur*. It has nothing to do with the guns. Spring occurs in many parts of the world where there are no guns. And yet this juxtaposition underlines the ironic effect that in spring, and in this particular time and place, men could still shed blood, at the very season of the year when everything around us is reborn. This is very good, and there are many such examples in Hemingway. There are others which are mere incongruity, as when he writes "The river ran behind us and the town had been captured very handsomely." This is quite simply *mish-mash*. It is easily imitated, as a whole school of junior Hemingways has demonstrated. It's a fine trick. But it doesn't add up to a Style. Neither do the long tagged-together sentences reminiscent of Molly Bloom's internal monologue.

What of the substance? In Hemingway's novels people order drinks, they are always ordering drinks, then they drink, then they order some more; they make love, and the love-making is "fine" and "nice" and it is "good" and it is of course sufficiently romantic, as in the pulps, that is, sufficiently adolescent. There is some killing. There is some fine riding and shooting and sailing. It is a world of superficial action and almost wholly without reflection—such reflection as there is tends to be on a rather crude and simplified level. It will be argued that all this is a part of life and has validity in fiction. I do not dispute this for a moment. It is my contention merely that such a surface view, dressed out by a series of prose mannerisms, does not constitute a Style and that the current emphasis on this side of Hemingway tends, in effect, to obscure the rather hollow qualities residing in his total production. He has created a world of Robinson Crusoes, living on their lonely islands, with bottle and gun for companions, and an occasional woman to go with the drinks.

I have said that Mr. Hemingway belongs to the second shelf of our literature, or at least that is where I would put him, and it would be precisely on this ground: that he has not written an adult novel, but that he has contrived with great cleverness some very good novels. He is happier, in reality, in the short story. The short story by its very nature demands simplification; characters need not be developed, plot and drama need not be created—a mood, a nostalgia, a moment of experience, suffice. Hemingway is an artist of the small space, the limited view. And I am not sure that what I have called "evasion" in his work will not be borne out if we search for its roots in his life, from which, after all, an artist's work always springs. To be able to cope with emotion only by indirection, or to write prose which seeks surface expressly to avoid texture—is this not a little like escaping from life by big-game hunting or watching violence in a bull-ring or day-dreaming through long hours of fishing? These are all fascinating pursuits for our hours of leisure or when given a proper perspective and taken in proper proportion (unless indeed one earns one's living by fighting bulls or is a career-fisherman). When they become a substitute for other forms of life—and granted that they themselves are part of life and partake of it—they can become an evasion of life.

But Hemingway is not as old as his Old Man. There have been striking examples in the history of literature of artists in whom, only at the end, is there a great melting together of experience and of expression that culminates in a large, mature, and durable work. And a Style. We must not at all exclude the possibility that Hemingway may yet write a book for the top shelf of our literature. But let us not put him there until he does. (pp. 18-20)

Leon Edel, "The Art of Evasion," in Folio, *Vol. XX, No. 2, Spring, 1955, pp. 18-20.*

SEAN O'FAOLAIN (essay date 1956)

[O'Faolain, one of Ireland's most distinguished men of letters, is highly regarded for his short stories. In the following excerpt from a study first published in 1956, O'Faolain examines the narrative and thematic constraints of Hemingway's fiction.]

Most novelists deal with character, or characterization. Hemingway does not. He may think he does, but that is irrelevant. What he deals with is personality. Character is a public, social thing formed almost always by society. Personality is a private, secret thing formed almost always by the man and the woman alone. It is a distinction which has been observed by many people who have written about the individual and the soul. Yeats made it, saying that personality is what remains when the dross of outward things falls away in moments of great tragedy and personality burns with a pure adamantine flame. Catholic thinkers, like Garrigou Lagrange and Maritain, have insisted on the same distinction, pointing out that the modern worship of "individualism" is often completely false and deluded, since what is worshiped in the end is a mere digit, a cipher in a bureaucrat's blueprint, not a personal man; and that all that really matters is this unique personal thing which makes each soul incapable of being duplicated. This is why novelists who deal with character rather than personality seek always for the external indications and stress them. One is told what politics a man has, what tobacco he smokes, what dress he favors, what his ideas are, where he lives. The color of his hair, his ties, his idiosyncrasies are exploited. In the end one may see a man as one might know him in the club or on a ship. Writers who are interested in personality despise these trappings. They are thinking so hard about the noumenal flame in the man that they cannot be bothered with the external phenomena. If we examine Hemingway's stories we will find that he never bothers very much about externals of this order. What do we know, of this order, about, say, Nurse Barkley? Or Jordan? Or recall that fine story **"The Undefeated,"** about the all-but-undefeated bull and the all-but-defeated matador? We cannot visualize the matador, tell anything about him except that he is at once half a coward and altogether a hero. Hemingway does not care about anything else pertaining to him. He is concerned only with the essences of people as they reveal themselves—and only as they reveal themselves—in certain testing moments, great and small.

He is not interested in anything that could be called reasonable, or that could be tested by what the world calls common sense. He is after another sort of common sense: that gallant form of common sense which is the acceptance of the facts of danger and death. Otherwise he might seem deliberately, and challengingly, to have chosen the sort of conflicts in which reason has no place. . . . He knows that the behavior of the unhappy Francis Macomber is quite devoid of our sort of common sense. He forces us to see, in ***The Old Man and the Sea,*** that the whole point of the old man's fight with the fish is that his gallant struggle is pointless, rationally speaking, since he will return at the end of it all with nothing but a skinned skeleton.

To this we must reply that Hemingway either cheats or is blithely inconsistent. We may recall, for example, the Fascist captain who is killed by Sordo's stratagem on the hilltop [in *For Whom the Bell Tolls*]. Hemingway, as if he were remembering the fun Bluntschli makes of the heroic ass in *Arms and the Man,* presents this captain to us not as a hero but as a foolhardy fanatic.

This is where his *mystique* of heroism becomes ankle-deep. For we suddenly realize that heroism for heroism's sake is not quite good enough, and we begin, uneasily, to probe into the nature of heroism itself. We ask: Is a gangster not also a brave man? In other words, we come to the point where we feel that it is impossible for any writer to deal satisfyingly with heroism without considering values, which means the weighing up of motives, which means the development of an implicit criticism of the forces that produce these motives, which means in the long run that the author has to imply his own norm. (pp. 129-32)

The Hemingway *mystique* has sometimes been called, in a superficial, conversational way, a form of Stoicism. The comparison only serves to expose his shallowness. Indeed, it is to do grave injustice to Hemingway to evoke the complexity and variety of that noble philosophy, with its simultaneous belief in a wise and well-ordaining divinity and its frank acceptance of the facts of pain and practical evil; its concurrent belief in the power of the mind to control and enjoy the urges of the body, to partake in the Epicureans' "beautiful arrangement of things," and to "pass from Nature to Nature's God"; its effective blending of a life of useful activity in service to others with a quasi-Oriental love of contemplation. To invite thoughts of that full and complex *mystique* is only to be obliged to think what an unvarious wash of color even the best of Hemingway's work has drawn across the landscape of life. We must not invite such comparisons. Hemingway is not a thoughtful man. He has no evident interest in social, moral or philosophical ideas at all. He is not and never pretended to be an intellectual. He is a man who loves gallant men and gallant animals. He is also a man, and it is this which gives him his real stature also as an artist who loves the gallant spirit, and he has roved the world in search of that flame of the spirit in men and beasts. To capture that flame, to record the moments in which it burns most brightly, has been his life's design. But to explain to us the origins of such moments, to give us their pedigree, is beyond his power. (pp. 137-38)

It might seem that, having said that Hemingway has wisely and shrewdly chosen his ground and his gamut in accordance with his instinct for what he can do and cannot do, I am now complaining that he has not done something quite different. On the contrary, while properly pointing out the limitations of his gamut I am trying to draw attention to the excellence of what he actually has achieved by insisting again that what he has achieved has nothing whatever to do with the naturalism with which he is usually associated, for which he is widely read, and which is the source of his widespread popularity. (pp. 138-39)

He is, within his honestly stated limits, and despite the weaknesses and idiosyncrasies that belong to the coarser element of his mind, a writer whose subject is *l'essence de l'homme et son tragique immuable*. I dare to say that Racine would have been shocked by his stories, but that if he were patient enough he would have come to understand and admire what Hemingway is seeking. Zola would not have been in the least shocked by him, and would never have been able to understand what he is seeking. I place Hemingway, in his own modest way, in the great and now almost defunct classical tradition.

By his denial of the past and his concentration on the present (the captive now), Hemingway has succeeded in rediscovering in men a greater dignity than, I suspect, he had ever hoped to find in them. This is his achievement, and how few, how very few, modern writers have arrived so far! Had he not made this discovery he would have been confined to those graphic short stories and sketches which were his first stunned reactions to his experience of life. He persisted and he discovered. When any man does something like this he has won a great primal victory within his personality over all the enemies of promise: he has found a way out towards writing; he has conquered the blank page. After that the rest is a matter of a growing skill in the writing, and of an ever-developing personality.

I am not sure that Hemingway's personality has gone on developing. If it is to develop further he will now have to face up to the limitations of his central device, get more room to spread, humanize his *mystique* by considering—I choose that word—a greater variety of human problems. To do this he will have to summon up the energies of his soul for the greatest act of courage in his long and gallant struggle—the courage to face that past which he has so far buried away in the cupboard with the old dance programs, piles of letters and faded photographs, memories hitherto too painful to handle. If he can do this without injury to his great technical gifts as an apparently naturalistic writer his popularity will not suffer. The trouble will be that he may well have to sacrifice something of his pseudorealism that the populace so loves, and his colonels instead of calling abruptly for another Martini at the sight of anything in the nature of an intellectual problem—the Martini is Hemingway's magical trap door—may have to pause and endure the less easy and more troublesome experience of considering more carefully whatever matter may be on hand. His work could thereby (or in some other way which it is his task to invent) become finer, and stronger, and take on much more depth. His popular appeal would be almost certain to decline at once—unless his critics fight for him in a full understanding of his problem as a writer, and as a man. (pp. 142-44)

The moral of Hemingway is that the only possible Hero of our times is the lone wolf. It is an idea wholly in accord with the spirit of the twenties, which he so well represents. (p. 145)

Sean O'Faolain "Ernest Hemingway: Men without Memories," in his The Vanishing Hero: Studies in Novelists of the Twenties, *1956. Reprint by Little, Brown and Company, 1957, pp. 112-45.*

ROBERT P. WEEKS (essay date 1962)

[An American scholar of modern literature, Weeks has specialized in the work of John Dos Passos and Hemingway. In the following excerpt, he considers and defends the limitations of Hemingway's fictional world.]

The best of [Hemingway's] critics recognized that though he dealt with a limited range of characters, placed them in quite similar circumstances, measured them against an unvarying code, and rendered them in a style that epitomized these other limitations, it was precisely this ruthless economy that gave his writing its power. And when Hemingway himself commented on his aims, it was clear that he knew what he was doing. He knowingly restricted himself in order to strip down, compress, and energize his writing. Prose, he once said, is not interior decoration but architecture, and the Baroque is over. His best work stands as a striking application to writing of Mies van der Rohe's architectural maxim: "Less is more."

On the other hand, Hemingway's detractors, many of whom are well-qualified, have doggedly insisted—and sometimes with a certain logic—that less is simply less: Hemingway is too limited, they say. His characters are mute, insensitive, uncomplicated men; his "action" circles narrowly about the ordeals, triumphs, and defeats of the bull ring, the battlefield, the trout stream, and similar male proving grounds; his style (some deny Hemingway's writing the benefit of this term) has stripped so much away that little is left but "a group of clevernesses"; and his "code" is at best a crudely simple outlook, in no sense comparable to the richer, more profound Stoicism which it is sometimes thought to resemble. (pp. 1-2)

The critics who disparage Hemingway's characters because they lack inwardness are probably outnumbered by those who disparage his fictional situations for the narrowness of their range. . . . This is not only a world of men without women, but of men without jobs, men without parents or children, men without homes or even communities. It is a world in which the soldiers desert or else operate as guerillas, for there are no lasting affiliations in this world of isolates. (pp. 2-3)

His characters go into battle, but never to the ballot box; they are constantly being tested but never in a social context. According to this view, raw physical courage is not only the supreme value in his fictive world but practically the only one.

As a direct consequence of limiting his characters to certain types and severely limiting the situations in which he places them, Hemingway works with a relatively narrow group of ethical problems. On this account, some deny that his writing has any moral sense whatever. (p. 3)

The objections to Hemingway's style, like those to his characters and situations, rest ultimately on the belief that it, too, is sterile. Too much has been stripped away, leaving the diction pale, the syntax weak, the verbs without energy, the adjectives colorless. (p. 4)

But the . . . characteristic response [of critics defending Hemingway] has been to maintain that this world—like Homer's—is less limited than it appears to be; that Hemingway has succeeded in making war—and the other forms of violence that interest him—a moral equivalent of life. The soldiers, boxers, and bullfighters are tested and found to behave under stress not as Republicans, intellectuals, Spaniards, or expatriates behave, but as men do. Seen in this light, Hemingway is a classicist. His achievement is not merely that he has rendered the here and now with the authority of a candid photograph; he has also given us a glimpse of eternal and universal truth. (p. 5)

In much the same way that the limited world of Hemingway's fiction can be shown to imply a much broader one, his spare, economical style can be revealed as a precise instrument of implication. "The dignity of movement of an iceberg is due to only one-eighth of it being above water." So Hemingway himself has written, effectively characterizing the immense power of the unsaid. (p. 6)

[The] power and distinctiveness of Hemingway's fiction derive from the combination of his various limitations. Considered singly, any one of them is crippling. How could one hope to write serious literature about characters and situations so bare, in a style that is quite inflexible and spare, only designed, it would seem, to celebrate the virtue of the stiff upper lip? The effect of the "less is more" principle can be experienced only when one looks at the whole façade or some large feature of a building, for only then can the absence of ornamentation be apprehended as a value in itself.

The power of this effect can be demonstrated if we look at a scene in which his various limitations all work together. An ideal scene is one which Hemingway evokes again and again. It appears in . . . [many] of his finest stories, and he uses it to end five of his six novels. It is the scene in which the hero has finally been cornered, but as he gallantly suffers his defeat he is not alone; he is in the presence of others who either do not even notice him, or if they do are unaware of his ordeal and of the gallantry with which he endures it. Here, in short compass, Hemingway brings to bear his most powerful and distinctive skills. . . . (pp. 11-12)

Hemingway's fishermen, soldiers, waiters, and other limited and seemingly unpromising characters are generally elevated by this strategy to persons deserving our attention. They are not dumb oxen chewing their cuds at the door of the slaughterhouse, but gallant men enduring their suffering with grace in a cold, empty universe. Occasionally they have one companion who recognizes and values their admirable stoicism, but this only emphasizes the rarity of such recognition in this world. And, anyway, it is made clear that the hero is beyond such help. (p. 12)

Hemingway understood suffering, like the Old Masters in Auden's poem "Musée des Beaux Arts"—that it occurs "while someone else is eating or opening a window or just walking dully along"—or watching carts hurrying down a slope. (p. 15)

With consummate art in these works and stories—art so unobtrusive as to elicit the charge of not being art at all—Hemingway confers on a seemingly routine experience affecting ordinary people a cosmic significance. And his style, far from being a series of surface mannerisms, reveals itself to be a way of looking at the world and expressing an attitude of tense resignation in the face of inevitable suffering and defeat. In the characters that do not share the secret, either because they are insensitive . . . , or have no way of knowing it . . . , Hemingway mirrors man's fate as he sees it and shows us that suffering and death, even when heroically endured, are a lonely and personal affair. (pp. 15-16)

Hemingway's art does lack a broad base. He has won his reputation as an artist of the first rank by operating within limits that would have stifled a lesser writer. But within and because of these limits, he has in his best work uttered a lyric cry that—although it may not resemble the full orchestra of Tolstoy or the organ tones of Melville—is nonetheless a moving and finely wrought response to our times. (p. 16)

Robert P. Weeks, in an introduction to Hemingway: A Collection of Critical Essays, *edited by Robert P. Weeks, Prentice-Hall, Inc., 1962, pp. 1-16.*

CARLOS BAKER (essay date 1963)

[An American scholar, Baker has written and edited several books on Hemingway, including the authorized biography, Ernest Hemingway: A Life Story *(1969; see Additional Bibliography), and* Ernest Hemingway: Selected Letters 1917-1961 *(1981). In addition, Baker assisted Mary Hemingway in the editing of the posthumous novel* Islands in the Stream. *In the following excerpt from his most extensive interpretive study of Hemingway's work, he explores symbolic unity and meaning in* The Old Man and the Sea.]

During over a quarter-century of experiment and speculation, Hemingway discovered ways of opening out the literature he wrote, of universalizing the significance of the stories he has to tell. We have heard much in our time about open and closed universes, and open and closed societies. Such a book as ***The Old Man and the Sea*** clearly demonstrates by example the difference between open and closed literatures. It is characteristic of a closed literature to be fact-bound. Its factual texture may be so tightly woven, so impenetrable to light, so opaque to the contemplation, that we are unable to see through it to any larger implications. The distinction is naturally a matter of degree: no literature is entirely closed. But one knows by experience the kind of book which too seldom offers the imagination a constructive opening, the book by which one feels bound or uncomfortably limited. In the midst of such a work the reader may find himself squirming with esthetic claustrophobia.

Open literature is the literature of agoraphilia. It recognizes the necessity of fenestration. Out through its windows we continually catch glimpses of a larger world than that immediately encompassed by the story we are reading. We look out towards the sea that is all around us, the vast waters crowded with life and joined forever, as Melville tells us, to contemplation. Hemingway early discovered and then steadily experimented with the means by which closed literature could be converted into open literature. The particular kind of fenestration he provides began to develop at that point where the sensibility of the artist revolted against the limits which factualistic naturalism necessarily imposes. In *Death in the Afternoon,* he asserted that the writer of prose ought to aim at "architecture, not interior decoration." Hemingway's study, as one of the architects of modern prose, has not been wholly devoted to this matter of fenestration. But in the process of the development of his powers, he has plainly promoted it to the rank of a key element.

One characteristic of open literature is its tendency to take on certain stylistic overtones of the parable. Readers of ***The Old Man and the Sea*** appear to have been impressed by its parable-like aspects, an impression traceable in part to echoic resemblances between the language of the novel and that of the Bible. The language is not in fact truly Biblical, as anyone can discover by reading the story of Jonah immediately before or after an encounter with Santiago. Yet the language does share two qualities with that of the Old and New Testaments: first, a slightly stylized vocabulary and movement long familiar to readers of the King James or the Douai translations, and secondly, what D. H. Lawrence once called the essence of poetry—"a stark, bare, rocky directness of statement." It is this latter quality which brings the story of Santiago closest in tone to such parables in the synoptic gospels as those of the sower, the lost sheep, the laborers in the vineyard, or the Pharisee and the publican.

Novels do not commune or communicate only by style or tone any more than men live only or commune mainly by the utterances of the logical intellect. What ***The Old Man and the Sea*** carries for the close reader is the conviction, sporadically renewed, that this story means more than it directly says. Those off-the-cuff allegorists who suggested that there was, for example, a one-for-one correspondence between Santiago, his marlin, and the sharks and Hemingway, his fiction, and the critics seem to have been content to rest triumphantly on this perception. A far more careful statement of the matter may be found in the words of Mark Schorer [see excerpt dated 1952]. "For those who, like this reviewer, believe that Hemingway's

the author wood-cut from portrait by henry strater

in our time

by

ernest hemingway

A Girl in Chicago: Tell us about the French women, Hank. What are they like?

Bill Smith: How old are the French women, Hank?

paris:

printed at the three mountains press and for sale at shakespeare & company, in the rue de l'odéon; london: william jackson, took's court, cursitor street, chancery lane.

1924

The frontispiece and title page of in our time. *Three Mountains Press, 1924.*

art, when it is art, is absolutely incomparable, and that he is unquestionably the greatest craftsman in the American novel in this century," ***The Old Man and the Sea*** may well appear to be "not only a moral fable, but a parable, and all the controlled passion, all the taut excitement in the prose come, I believe, from the parable. It is an old man catching a fish, yes; but it is also a great artist in the act of mastering his subject, and, more than that, of actually writing about the struggle. Nothing is more important than his craft, and it is beloved; but because it must be struggled with and mastered, it is also a foe, enemy to all self-indulgence, to all looseness of feeling, all laxness of style, all soft pomposities."

Such a view of Santiago's adventure can be made to stand up fairly well under hard-bitten scrutiny. Yet even so forthright a statement falls into the possible error of too greatly constricting the available meanings of the story. (pp. 320-22)

The voyage Santiago undertakes seems, in fact, naturally ordered for the illustration of a larger experience of life than was even intended in some of the New Testament parables. Its theme has been well pointed up by the Christian stoic Samuel Johnson, both in the title and the substance of his poem on the vanity, which is to say the vain-ness, of human wishes. The story of Santiago shows not only a natural tragic pattern, as the individual human life may do when seen as a whole; it also can stand as a natural parable. In this story, as in the life of man, the battle commences, grows, and subsides between one sleep and another. In human experience there are many forms of both marlin and shark. Much is to be endured, and perhaps relatively little is to be enjoyed between our human setting-forth and our return to port. A provisional means of describing the effect of Hemingway's novel may be found in Yeats's opinion that "the more a poet . . . purifies his mind with elaborate art, the more does the little ritual of his verse resemble the great ritual of nature, and become mysterious and inscrutable. He becomes, as all the great mystics have believed, a vessel of the creative power of God."

Although Hemingway might have questioned the temerity of Yeats's last sentence, he could not, after ***The Old Man and the Sea,*** deny the first. For his best work, like that of any great creative artist, is in a happy conspiracy with permanence. The language, the subjects, the underlying symbolic structures all belong to that area of human thought and belief which survives virtually without change from age to age. This area, this continuum, this current flowing unchanged below the surface disturbances, is the true artist's gulf stream. After his return from the green hills of Africa in 1934, he found an image for his point of view among the blue depths of Atlantica.

> When, on the sea, [he wrote] you are alone with it and know that this Gulf Stream you are living with, knowing, learning about, and loving, has moved, as it moves, since before man . . . [then] the things you find out about it, and those that have always lived in it, are permanent and of value because that stream will flow as it has flowed, after the Indians, after the Spaniards, after the British, after the Americans and after all the Cubans and all the systems of governments, the richness, the poverty, the martyrdom, the sacrifice and the venality and the cruelty are all gone as the high-piled scow of garbage . . . spills off its load into the blue water. . . . The stream, with no visible flow, takes five loads of this a day when things are going well in La Habana and in ten miles along the coast it is as clear and blue and unimpressed as it was ever before the tug hauled out the scow; and the palm fronds of our victories, the worn light bulbs of our great discoveries and the empty condoms of our great loves float with no significance against one single, lasting thing—the stream.

In all things as permanent as this blue river in the sea, the writer who means his work to last must sink his nets, cast his lines, and bring his giants to the gaff. Let the garbage go. It will disappear as all such things have always gone. But the stream will last. This is the area where Hemingway, the compleat angler, has chosen to fish. (pp. 323-25)

Carlos Baker, in his Hemingway: The Writer as Artist, *third edition, Princeton University Press, 1963, 379 p.*

JOSEPH DEFALCO (essay date 1963)

[In the following excerpt, DeFalco characterizes the Hemingway hero through a discussion of individuation and affirmation of ideals in the short story playlet "Today Is Friday" and the stories "The Snows of Kilimanjaro" and "Fathers and Sons."]

Hemingway's clearest presentation of man's attempt to preserve an ideal is reflected in a group of stories called here, rather loosely, the Hemingway hero stories. Most of them examine the manifold difficulties encountered on the journey toward individuation, and a few examine the process in its totality. Here men face the ultimate test, or some symbolic reflection of that test, by trying to rise above the contingencies of life. Some of the stories point to a final, almost transcendental element in Hemingway's thought which at first glance seems at odds with his naturalistic technique.

In Hemingway's treatment of the ideals a man may hold, he forces consideration of the efficacy of the commitment to an ideal in a world where values have been prostituted to other gods, chiefly Mammon and unfaith. The man who commits himself to these false ideals is personified by Hemingway as "Noman." Those who adhere to the ideal of self-fulfillment are in the minority, and their very existence becomes intolerable to the majority who follow another course. The outcome of such a situation is always the same: persecution of those who hold the individual ideal. In most of Hemingway's stories he consistently champions the ideal of individuality. In those stories where other forces seem to emerge victorious, there is an underlying author sympathy which laments the fate of man in a world which can no longer accept a valid ideal.

The journey toward individualism in Western culture is best personified by the life of Christ, and Hemingway resorts to this motif in a number of ways. In **"Today is Friday,"** Hemingway constructs a capsule drama saturated with ironic commentary about the Crucifixion. He does not resort to preciosity to mock the ideal represented by Christ, nor is his dramatization condemnatory of Christianity in any way. His attitude is clearly illustrated by the refrain repeated several times by one of the Roman soldiers who witnesses the Crucifixion: "He was pretty good in there today." The reiteration establishes a sustained tone of wonder, and it more effectively reveals the narrative purpose than any direct sentiment. The approach to the myth of Christ is one of a lament for the passing of a system of life which could foster such a hero. Other heroes many times reflect the model of Christ in their search for some mode of self-fulfillment in a world which has already indicated that for those who follow the ideal, crucifixion will be the end result. (pp. 185-86)

The figure of Christ crucified for the sins of mankind as a central character in any dramatization might force the subject matter to the level of sentimentality. Such an element would be ludicrous in relation to the situational connotations and the magnitude of the Crucifixion theme. Hemingway rarely falls into such a trap, no matter what the subject matter. In **"Today is Friday"** he avoids all such pitfalls by approaching his subject obliquely. The three soldiers who were present at the Crucifixion occupy the center of the stage, but the focus is elsewhere. The drama is hardly more than a vignette, and its length, coupled with the wine-shop setting and the colloquialisms of the dialogue, forces a cataclysmic event into an almost absurd compression. Yet the effect of the employment of these stylistic devices is such that, working on the correlative cultural conditioning of his audience, Hemingway achieves a subtlety of emotional response and evokes a tremendous reader sympathy for his subject.

The title of the piece implies an authorial comment upon the complicity of contemporary man in the events described within the drama. The casting of the dialogue into "tough-guy," soldier jargon ("Hey, what you put in that, camel chips?") translates the episode into a modern idiom. Hemingway also gains his purpose through characterization, since the soldiers as well as the Hebrew wine-seller are all disinterested persons. In this way the dramatic perspective suggests an objective treatment of the subject matter. Still, two of the characters, the "1st Roman Soldier" and the "3d Roman Soldier," reveal their sympathy with Christ's actions on the cross.

The admiration of the two Roman soldiers contrasts with the skepticism of the '2d Roman Soldier': "'You guys don't know what I'm talking about. I'm not saying whether he was good or not. What I mean is, when the time comes. When they first start nailing him, there isn't none of them wouldn't stop if they could." One further contrast is illustrated by George, the Hebrew wine-seller and prototypes of the disinterested bartender: "'No, I didn't take any interest in it, Lootenant." (pp. 189-90)

The obvious view of Christ taken by the characters within the drama is that He was human. This device serves Hemingway's ends. In a reflex of the surface irony, an underlying level of muted irony reveals the author's tone and sheds light on the stories patterned after the motif of the *imitatio Christi*. The fact that Christ's performance on the cross has aroused sympathy on the part of the two soldiers suggests the possibility that Christ is a pertinent symbol for society in His role as the redeeming hero. The reference is slight, but it is supported in the drama by the illness of one of the soldiers. The suggestion is that the event he has witnessed has disturbed him more deeply than he can say. "'I got a gut-ache,'" he tells his companions. This statement reflects the nausea of other Hemingway characters who become ill after witnessing events that probe to the core of their emotional responses.

The direct treatment of the Crucifixion as a theme in **"Today is Friday"** gathers importance in its relation to the themes of many of Hemingway's other short stories. In particular it provides a parallel for those which treat a central character who holds an ideal not compatible with that of his world. (p. 190)

[In **"The Snows of Kilimanjaro"** the] form of the story is that of the traditional lament for a lost life. In its approach the story is not dissimilar to the Old English "Deor," "Wanderer," and "The Wife's Lament." That is, it is part of the tradition in literature of the lament for the passing of life and for missed opportunities. From the authorial perspective and because of the author's personal situation at the time of writing, the story may be a kind of prose elegy, following that traditional form. Whatever the tradition, the form of the story conveys the tale of a dying man lamenting a misused life. It is this fictional structure which points to the theme of individuation.

The story fits into the pattern of stories which involve an intense focus upon a single, central character, and it examines by subjective response the events of a past life as this character reviews them. A more important theme in relation to the individual emerges here, for the thematic vehicle rests upon a question: What is the nature of death? As it turns out, death comes in many guises, and the symbols which depict it are a catalogue of the central character's life: buzzard, hyena, women, and money. The final approach to death, however, relates to none of these, for it comes in the form of "Old Compie," the pilot who "saves" Harry at the end of the story. It is Harry's ascendence into death in an almost ironic fashion upon which the entire theme of the story hinges.

Each of the death symbols reflects some role Harry has played in his life or represents some attachment which has led him into a life of sterility. The pilot of the long awaited plane functions somewhat differently, for he appears in the dream sequence at the end and carries Harry off toward Kilimanjaro: "And then he knew that was where he was going." Kilimanjaro is identified in the epitaph appended to the story as: "The Masai 'Ngàje Ngài,' the House of God." The transporting of Harry to Kilimanjaro reveals that Compie is the final guide who will lead him, at least within the logic of his own inner drama, to a kind of redemptive Avalon now that he has recognized all his failings.

As Harry approaches each stage of self-realization, the death symbols enter as a kind of mockery of his past and underline his development. His whole purpose in journeying to Africa to achieve some sort of renewal is stated directly in the narrative: "Africa was where he had been happiest in the good time of his life, so he had come out here to start again." The buzzards and the hyena function as the two natural symbols of death. The fact that they are scavengers parallels Harry's self-accusation that he has betrayed his real self for women and money. (pp. 207-09)

Death finally comes to Harry in an unexpected way. Throughout, he watches the figures of the birds and the hyena in anticipation that they are the harbingers of death. At times he even reflects upon the many guises of death and the way it will finally arrive: "He lay still and death was not there. It must have gone around another street. It went in pairs, on bicycles, and moved absolutely silently on the pavements." Yet the irony of the mode in which death arrives evolves into a resolution of the question posed throughout. Death may be a form of transcendence if the subject has undergone an ordeal of suffering and if he has achieved insight and illumination. The plight which Harry laments is symptomatic of the same "disease" which afflicts all of the Hemingway heroes in the short stories who would strive for the ideal. Having missed the ideal throughout his life, Harry recaptures the view of his youthful strivings. Death, therefore, is anti-climactic.

Although couched in bitter and naturalistic terms, the lament of Harry is nonetheless a tragic one which posits an ideal of truth. Harry's situation at the literal level is a pathetic one, to be sure, but his mental journey, his recapitulation of his misspent life, purges him of his errant ways. Compie's entrance at the conclusion of the narrative indicates that a transformative process has taken place. Had the situation remained in the realm of the literal, death might have been depicted by the hyena symbol. As it turns out, the appearance of the hyena is more of a comment on the world Harry has left than on Harry himself. Harry is thus more properly identified with the leopard mentioned in the epitaph which was seeking the summit.

Pandering to the representative forces of materialism and its various offspring too long, or having been exposed to life's contingencies and having "adjusted" to them, may suddenly force the individual into a situation where he must "take up his cross," as it were, and suffer the fate of those who live directly the life that leads to crucifixion. In fact the adjusted state may itself become a kind of ideal, although it is never the purest in Hemingway's hierarchy. The figure who appears in the stories as "the one who knows," a Zurito [in **"The Undefeated"**] or a Wilson [in **"The Short Happy Life of Francis Macomber"**], may have had to make compromises en route in order to stay alive in the world, but he still has that degree of strength and self-knowledge which fits him for the task of the ideal when he is forced. (pp. 209-11)

In **"Fathers and Sons,"** Hemingway describes an older Nick Adams who re-examines his life. The presence of Nick's son in the story points out the theme of reconcilement of the past with the present and the future. It is an appropriate conclusion to Hemingway's arrangement of ***The First Forty-Nine.*** The most relevant point of the story to the theme of individuation is that it asks some important questions concerning the possibility of continuity for man. Nick reassesses the learning experiences he has undergone as a youth and the role which his father played in that learning. The father taught him things about hunting, but he failed to give him the more vital information that leads a child into adulthood. The real learning came from the experiences with the environment. Nick evidences his concern for the loss suffered, and he indicates the need for reconcilement in a remark to his son, who has just told him, "'Well, I don't feel good never to have visited the tomb of my grandfather.' 'We'll have to go,' Nick said. 'I can see we'll have to go." (pp. 217-18)

The final acceptance of the father figure as necessary to the continuity of life is in reality a reconcilement with the forces of authority. No matter what the reason for the original loss of attachment, Nick finally becomes at one with the father and thereby becomes the father himself. The reconcilement represents a return from isolation and dissociation. Nick's acceptance of his own father is tantamount to his becoming a self-realized man. He is a man who recognizes that he too will pass away and that the only hope for personal immortality rests in the continuity from his father to his own son.

The stories with a strong hero as the central character illustrate the falseness of the notion that Hemingway projects in his fiction a view of life typified by the "nada" prayer of **"A Clean, Well-Lighted Place."** To assign nihilistic tendencies to the author because of the attitudes of the characters in the stories is to misread Hemingway. Too often his objectivity and naturalistic style is confused with authorial viewpoint. . . . Throughout the short stories Hemingway depicts man in his strife with contingent forces in the local environment and in the cosmos. The true man of ideals may be in harmony with ultimate causality, but in Hemingway's stories his doom in this world is a foregone conclusion. The man who can get along in the world, however, is also represented. He is the one who recognizes the hopelessness of following the ideal to its logical extension. These adjusted ones are the characters like Zurito and Wilson, but they are not the true Hemingway heroes. Only those who grasp the ideal and follow it, whether through innocent ignorance or through full acknowledgement of the ideal, are truly the "undefeated" in Hemingway's terms. (pp. 218-19)

Joseph DeFalco, in his The Hero in Hemingway's Short Stories, *University of Pittsburgh Press, 1963, 226 p.*

FRANK O'CONNOR (essay date 1963)

[*O'Connor, an acclaimed Irish short story writer and man of letters, suggests in the following excerpt that Hemingway's fine stylistic technique may be in need of better material.*]

Ernest Hemingway must have been one of the first of Joyce's disciples. Certainly, so far as I can ascertain, he was the only writer of his time to study what Joyce was attempting to do in the prose of *Dubliners* and *A Portrait of the Artist as a Young Man* and work out a method of applying it. It took me years to identify Joyce's technique and describe it with any care, and by that time I realized that it was useless for any purpose of my own. So far as I know, no critic had anticipated me, but Hemingway had not only anticipated me; he had already gone into business with it on his own account, and a handsome little business he made of it. (p. 156)

[When] you really know *A Portrait of the Artist as a Young Man* you recognize exactly where the beautiful opening of Hemingway's **"In Another Country"** came from.

> In the *fall* the war was always there, but we did not go to it any more. It was *cold* in the *fall* in Milan, and the dark came very early. Then the electric lights came on, and it was pleasant along the streets looking in the windows. There was much game hanging outside the shops, and the snow powdered in the fur of the foxes and the *wind blew* their tails. The deer hung stiff and heavy and empty, and small birds *blew* in the *wind,* and the *wind* turned their feathers. It was a *cold fall* and the *wind* came down from the mountains.

There! You have realized how cold and windy it was that fall in Milan, haven't you? And it didn't really hurt, did it? Even if you were not very interested to begin with, you have learned one or two very important things that you might otherwise have ignored. Quite seriously, this is something you don't recall from other famous passages of literature, written by predecessors of Joyce and Hemingway, because in . . . [this passage there is not] what you could call a human voice speaking, nobody resembling yourself who is trying to persuade you to share in an experience of his own, and whom you can imagine yourself questioning about its nature—nothing but an old magician sitting over his crystal ball, or a hypnotist waving his hands gently before your eyes and muttering, "You are falling asleep; you are falling asleep; slowly, slowly your eyes are beginning to close; your eyelids are growing heavy; you are—falling—asleep."

Though Joyce was the most important single influence on Hemingway, and one can trace him even in little pedantries like placing the adverb immediately after the verb when usage requires it either to precede the verb or to follow the object, as in "he poured smoothly the buckwheat batter," he was not the only influence. Gertrude Stein and her experiments with language were also of some importance. Her experiments—usually rather absurd ones—were intended to produce a simplification of prose technique like the simplification of forms that we find in the work of certain modern painters. Her mistake—a blatant vulgarization of Joyce's fundamental mistake—was to ignore the fact that prose is a very impure art. Any art which formally is practically indistinguishable from a memorandum issued by a government office is necessarily impure. "Prosaic" is a term of abuse, though in fact it should have a connotation as noble as "poetic."

As practiced by Hemingway, this literary method, compounded of simplification and repetition, is the opposite of that we learned in our schooldays. We were taught to consider it a fault to repeat a noun and shown how to avoid it by the use of pronouns and synonyms. This led to another fault that Fowler christened "elegant variation." The fault of Hemingway's method might be called "elegant repetition." His most elaborate use of it is in **"Big Two-Hearted River."**

> There was no underbrush in the island of *pine trees*. The *trunks* of the *trees* went straight up or slanted toward each other. The *trunks* were straight and *brown* without *branches*. The *branches* were *high above*. Some interlocked to make a solid *shadow* on the *brown forest floor*. Around the grove of *trees* was a bare space. It was *brown* and soft underfoot as Nick walked on it. This was the over-lapping of the *pine*-needle *floor,* extending out beyond the width of the *high branches*. The *trees* had grown tall and the *branches* moved *high,* leaving in the sun this bare space they had once covered with shadow. Sharp at the edge of this extension of the *forest floor* commenced the sweet fern.
>
> Nick slipped off his pack and lay down in the *shade*. He lay on his *back* and looked up into the *pine trees*. His neck and *back* and the small of his *back* rested as he stretched. The earth felt good against his *back*. He looked up at the sky, through the *branches,* and then shut his eyes. He opened them and looked up again. There was a wind *high* up in the *branches*. He shut his eyes again and went to sleep.

This is part of an extraordinarily complex and simple-minded literary experiment in which Hemingway sets out to duplicate in prose a fishing trip in wooded country, and it is constructed with a minute vocabulary of a few dozen words, like "water," "current," "stream," "trees," "branches," and "shadow." It is an elaboration of the device I have pointed out in *A Portrait of the Artist as a Young Man*. In some ways it anticipates Joyce's "Anna Livia Plurabelle" though in general it resembles more an experiment in Basic English. The curious thing is that I have worked with scores of young Americans—people who knew their Hemingway far better than I did—and they had never noticed the device. Perhaps this is what Hemingway and Joyce intended; perhaps I read them in the wrong way, but I do not know of any other way to read prose. And I feel quite sure that even Joyce would have thought **"Big Two-Hearted River"** a vulgarization of his rhetorician's dream. However, Hemingway went one better than his master when he realized that precisely the same technique could be applied to dramatic interludes, and that the repetition of key words and phrases in these could produce a similar simplification with a similar hypnotic effect. (pp. 157-61)

The advantages and disadvantages of a style like this are about evenly divided. The principal advantage is clear. Nobody is ever likely to get the impression that he is accidentally reading a government memorandum or a shorthand report of a trial. If Goethe is right in saying that art is art because it is not nature, this is art. Even in very good stylists of the older school of storytelling there is often a marked struggle at the beginning of the story before the author can detach himself from what is not storytelling and the story becomes airborne; a paragraph or more of fumbling prose like the tuning up of an orchestra, but in Hemingway the element of stylization cuts off the very first sentence from whatever is not storytelling, so that it rings out loud and clear like music cutting across silence. Turgenev's "Living Relic" begins with the words "A French proverb runs: 'A dry fisherman and a wet hunter present a sorry sight.' Never having had any predilection for fishing . . ."—a leisurely enough opening in the manner of his period. Chekhov's "Sleepy" begins with the single word "Night," which is more urgent though perhaps a little trite. The first sentence of **"In Another Country"** is a perfect opening phrase, mannered enough to jolt the reader awake without making him go to see if the front door is locked: "In the fall the war was always there, but we did not go to it any more." In the same way, when Hemingway ends a story it stays ended, without giving us the feeling that perhaps we have bought a defective copy.

The obvious disadvantage is that it tends to blur the sharp contrast that should ideally exist between narrative and drama, the two forms of which storytelling is compounded. Ideally, the former should be subjective and persuasive, the latter objective and compulsive. In one the storyteller suggests to the reader what he believes happened, in the other he proves to him that this in fact is how it did happen. In a good story the two aspects are nearly always kept in balance. In a Hemingway story drama, because it is stylized in the same way as the narrative, tends to lose its full impact. Dialogue, the autonomous element of drama, begins to blur, and the conversation becomes more like the conversation of alcoholics, drug addicts, or experts in Basic English. In Joyce's "Grace," the author's irony gives the conversation of the men in the sick room the same dull, claustrophobic quality, but there one can excuse it on the ground that his aim is comic. There is no such excuse for the conversation in Hemingway's story.

Of course you may say if you please that the drama there is implicit rather than explicit, and that it is made sufficiently clear that the man does not love the girl—after all he indicates it by saying "I love you now" and "I love it now" too close together—and that she knows it and is offering up her unborn child for the sake of a man she feels sure will leave her, but the dialogue by which two people communicate or try to communicate with one another is missing. And here, I think, we may be touching on a weakness in both Joyce and Hemingway. To the rhetorician dialogue must so often seem unnecessary since he knows so many ingenious ways of evading it.

Not that Hemingway often took his rhetoric to the fair as Joyce did. In fact, if we exclude **"Big Two-Hearted River,"** which is only a caricature of a literary method, there never was much of the real experimenter in him. He was a practical writer, not a research worker, and he took from the research workers like

Joyce and Gertrude Stein only what he felt he needed, in the spirit of an American efficiency expert studying the tests of a group of scientists to discover how he can knock a second or two off the time it takes to move a lever. When you compare [*A Portrait of the Artist as a Young Man* with] . . . **"In Another Country"** you can see that Joyce is already letting his own theory run away with him, while Hemingway uses precisely as much of it as he needs to create the effect that he himself has in mind.

In fact, from a purely technical point of view, no other writer of the twentieth century was so splendidly equipped. He could take an incident—any incident, no matter how thin or trivial—and by his skill as a writer turn it into something one read thirty years ago and can still read today with admiration and pleasure.

One can see his skill better when the material *is* skimpy and he has to rely on his ability as a writer. There is nothing in **"Che Ti Dice La Patria?"** that could not have been observed just as well by any journalist reporting on a hasty trip through Fascist Italy—someone is rude, a young man in a shady restaurant says that the two Americans are "worth nothing," an insolent policeman holds them up for fifty lire, that is all—but no journalist could have given us the same feeling of the sinister quality of life in Italy at the time. And when Hemingway ends his description of it in a final poker-faced sentence it stays ended—"Naturally, in such a short trip we had no opportunity to see how things were with the country or the people." **"Fifty Grand"** is just about as dull a subject as a writer's heart could desire but the story itself can still be reread.

But the real trouble with Hemingway is that he so often has to depend upon his splendid technical equipment to cover up material that is trivial or sensational. For much of the time his stories illustrate a technique in search of a subject. In the general sense of the word Hemingway has no subject. Faulkner shows a passion for technical experiment not unlike Hemingway's, and, like Hemingway's, picked up in Paris cafés over a copy of *transition,* but at once he tries to transplant it to Yoknapatawpha County. Sometimes, let us admit, it looks as inappropriate there as a Paris hat on one of the Snopes women, but at least, if we don't like the hat we can get something out of the woman it disguises. Hemingway, on the other hand, is always a displaced person; he has no place to bring his treasures to.

There are times when one feels that Hemingway, like the character in his own **"A Clean, Well-Lighted Place,"** is afraid of staying at home with a subject. In his stories one is forever coming upon that characteristic setting of the café, the station restaurant, the waiting room, or the railway carriage—clean, well-lighted, utterly anonymous places. The characters, equally anonymous, emerge suddenly from the shadows where they have been lurking, perform their little scene, and depart again into shadows. Of course, one has to realize that there is a very good technical reason for this. The short story, which is always trying to differentiate itself from the novel and avoid being bogged down in the slow, chronological sequence of events where the novel is supreme, is also seeking a point outside time from which past and future can be viewed simultaneously, and so the *wagon lit* setting of **"A Canary for One"** represents a point at which wife and husband are still traveling together though already apart—"we were returning to Paris to set up separate residences"—and the railway station setting of **"Hills Like White Elephants"** the point where the abortion that must change everything for the lovers has already been decided on though it has not yet taken place. The story looks backward and forward, backward to the days when the girl said that the hills were like white elephants and the man was pleased, and forward to a dreary future in which she will never be able to say a thing like that again.

But though this is perfectly true, it forces us to ask whether the technique is not limiting the short-story form so as to reduce it to an essentially minor art. Any realistic art is necessarily a marriage between the importance of the material and the importance of the artistic treatment, but how much of the importance of the material can possibly seep through such rigid artistic control? What has happened to the familiar element in it? If this girl, Jig, is not American, what is she? Does she have parents in England or Ireland or Australia, brothers or sisters, a job, a home to go back to, if against all the indications she decides to have this baby? And the man? Is there any compelling human reason why he should feel that an abortion is necessary or is he merely destructive by nature?

Once more, I know the formal answer to all these questions: that Hemingway's aim is to suppress mere information such as I require so as to concentrate my attention on the one important thing which is the abortion. I know that Hemingway has been influenced by the German Expressionists as well as by Joyce and Gertrude Stein, and that he is reducing (or enlarging) these two people into the parts they would play in a German Expressionist tragedy—*Der Mann* and *Die Frau*—and their problem into the tragedy itself—*Das Fehlgebären*. But I must respectfully submit that I am not German, and that I have no experience of Man, Woman, or Abortion in capital letters.

I submit that there are drawbacks to this method. It is all too abstract. Nobody in Hemingway ever seems to have a job or a home unless the job or the home fits into the German scheme of capital letters. Everybody seems to be permanently on holiday or getting a divorce, or as *Die Frau* in **"Hills Like White Elephants"** puts it, "That's all we do, isn't it—look at things and try new drinks?" Even in the Wisconsin stories it comes as a relief when Nick's father keeps himself out of harm's way for an hour or two by attending to his profession as doctor.

Even the submerged population that Hemingway writes of is one that is associated with recreation rather than with labor—waiters, barmen, boxers, jockeys, bullfighters, and the like. Paco in **"The Capital of the World"** is a waiter with a soul above waitering, and he dies by accident in an imitation bullfight that I find comic rather than pathetic. In the later stories the neurotic restlessness has developed out of the earlier fishing and shooting into horse racing, prize fighting, bull fighting, and big-game hunting. Even war is treated as recreation, an amusement for the leisured classes. In these stories practically no single virtue is discussed with the exception of physical courage, which from the point of view of people without an independent income is usually merely a theoretical virtue. Except in war it has little practical application, and even in war the working classes tend to regard it with a certain cynicism: the hero of the regiment is rarely a hero to the regiment.

In Hemingway the obsession with physical courage is clearly a personal problem, like Turgenev's obsession with his own futility, and it must be recognized and discounted as such if one is not to emerge from one's reading with a ludicrously distorted impression of human life. In **"The Short Happy Life of Francis Macomber"** Francis runs away from a lion, which is what most sensible men would do if faced by a lion, and his wife promptly cuckolds him with the English manager of their big-game hunting expedition. As we all know, good wives admire nothing in a husband except his capacity to deal with lions, so we can sympathize with the poor woman in her trouble. But next day Macomber, faced with a buffalo, suddenly becomes a man of superb courage, and his wife, recognizing that Cressida's occupation's gone and that for the future she must be a virtuous wife, blows his head off. Yet the title leaves us with the comforting assurance that the triumph is still Macomber's, for, in spite of his sticky end, he had at last learned the only way of keeping his wife out of other men's beds.

To say that the psychology of this story is childish would be to waste good words. As farce it ranks with "Ten Nights in a Bar-Room" or any other Victorian morality you can think of. Clearly, it is the working out of a personal problem that for the vast majority of men and women has no validity whatever.

It may be too early to draw any conclusions about Hemingway's work: certainly it is too early for one like myself who belongs to the generation that he influenced most deeply. In a charitable mood, I sometimes find myself thinking of the clean well-lighted place as the sort of stage on which Racine's heroes and heroines appear, free of contact with common things, and carrying on their lofty discussions of what to Racine seemed most important. The rest of the time I merely ask myself if this wonderful technique of Hemingway's is really a technique in search of a subject or a technique that is carefully avoiding a subject, and searching anxiously all the time for a clean well-lighted place where all the difficulties of human life can be comfortably ignored. (pp. 162-69)

Frank O'Connor, "A Clean, Well-Lighted Place," in his The Lonely Voice: A Study of the Short Story, *The World Publishing Company, 1963, pp. 156-69.*

IRVING HOWE (essay date 1963)

[*Howe is one of America's most highly respected literary critics and social historians. In the following excerpt, he delineates Hemingway's artistic vision, moral code, and concise style.*]

Of all the writers who began to print after the First World War, Hemingway seems best to have captured the tone of human malaise in an era of war and revolution; yet it is noteworthy that, while doing so, he rarely attempted a frontal or sustained representation of life in the United States, for he seems always to have understood that common experience was not within his reach. By evoking the "essence" of the modern experience through fables of violence that had their settings in Africa and Europe, Hemingway touched the imagination of American readers whose lives, for all their apparent ordinariness, were also marked by the desperation which would become his literary signature and which is, indeed, central to all "modernist" writing. These readers, in turn, often tried to endow their lives with meaning and value by copying the gestures of defiance, the devotion to clenched styles of survival, which they found in Hemingway's work. Because he had penetrated so deeply to the true dilemmas of the age, Hemingway soon began to influence its experience—not for the first time, life came to imitate art.

Who, by now, is not familiar with the shape and colors of Hemingway's world? His recurrent figures are literary expatriates in the wastes of *nada,* bullfighters who have lost their nerve and skill, rich young men without purpose, wounded soldiers who would sign "a separate peace" in order to withdraw from the world's battles, distraught young women grasping at physical sensations as if they were a mode of salvation, tired gangsters, homeless café-sitters, stricken Spaniards: men and women always on the margin, barely able to get by from day to day. There emerges from this gallery the characteristic hero of the Hemingway world: the hero who is wounded but bears his wound in silence, who is sensitive but scorns to devalue his feelings into words, who is defeated but finds a remnant of dignity in an honest confrontation of defeat. In almost all Hemingway's books there is a tacit assumption that the deracination of our life is so extreme, everyone must find a psychic shelter of his own, a place in which to make a last stand.

But note: to make a last stand—for if defeat is accepted in Hemingway's world, humiliation and rout are not. His fictions present moments of violence, crisis and death, yet these become occasions for a stubborn, quixotic resistance through which the human capacity for satisfying its self-defined obligations is both asserted and tested. "Grace under pressure": this becomes the ideal stance, the hoped-for moral style, of Hemingway's characters. Or as he puts it in describing Romero's bullfighting in *The Sun Also Rises:* "the holding of his purity of line through the maximum of exposure." All of Hemingway's novels and stories can be read as variants upon this theme, efforts to find improvised gestures and surrogate codes for the good, the true, even the heroic.

The Hemingway hero is a man who has surrendered the world in order to remake a tiny part of it, the part in which he can share honor and manner with a few chosen comrades. Jake Barnes, Frederick Henry, most of Hemingway's heroes, are men who have seen too much, who want no more of this world and now seek to act out the choregraphy of heroism as a kind of private charade. The bull-ring becomes, for some of them, a substitute for the social world; the combat with the bull, a version of the manly testing which this world does not allow; the circle of *aficionados,* a monastic order of crippled heroes.

It may be true, as Edmund Wilson claims, that Hemingway shows a taste for scenes of killing, but at his best he wishes to squeeze from them some precarious assertion—or perhaps more accurately, some credible facsimile—of value. The Hemingway hero turns to his code, a mixture of stylized repression and inarticulate decencies, so that manners become the outer sign of an inexpressible heroism and gestures the substance of a surviving impulse to moral good. And what is this code? The determination to be faithful to one's own experience, not to fake emotions or pretend to sentiments that are not there; the belief that loyalty to one's few friends matters more than the claims and dogmas of the world; the insistence upon avoiding self-pity and public displays; the assumption that the most precious feelings cannot be articulated and that if the attempt is made they turn "rotten"; the desire to salvage from the collapse of social life a version of stoicism that can make suffering bearable; the hope that in direct physical sensation, the cold water of the creek in which one fishes or the purity of the wine made by Spanish peasants, there will be found an experience that can resist corruption (which is one reason Hemingway approaches these sensations with a kind of propitiatory awe, seldom venturing epithets more precise than "fine" and "nice," as if he feared to risk a death through naming). Life now consists in keeping an equilibrium with one's nerves, and that requires a tight control over one's desires, so that finally one learns what one cannot have and then even not to want it, and above all, not to make a fuss while learning. As Jake Barnes says in *The Sun Also Rises:* "I did not care what it was all about. All I wanted to know was how to live in it."

Hemingway was always a young writer, and always a writer for the young. He published his best novel *The Sun Also Rises* in his mid-twenties and completed most of his great stories by the age of forty. He started a campaign of terror against the fixed vocabulary of literature, a purge of style and pomp, and in the name of naturalness he modelled a new artifice for tension. He struck past the barriers of culture and seemed to disregard the reticence of civilized relationships. He wrote for the nerves.

In his very first stories Hemingway struck to the heart of our nihilism, writing with that marvellous courage he then had, which allowed him to brush past received ideas and show Nick Adams alone, bewildered, afraid and bored, Nick Adams finding his bit of peace through fishing with an exact salvaging ritual in the big two-hearted river. Hemingway struck to the heart of our nihilism through stories about people who have come to the end of the line, who no longer know what to do or where to turn: nihilism not as an idea or a sentiment, but as an encompassing condition of moral disarray in which one has lost those tacit impulsions which permit life to continue. There is a truth which makes our faith in human existence seem absurd, and no one need contemplate it for very long: Hemingway, in his early writing, did. Nick Adams, Jake Barnes, Lady Brett, Frederick Henry, and then the prizefighters, matadors, rich Americans and failed writers: all are at the edge, almost ready to surrender and be done with it, yet holding on to whatever fragment of morale, whatever scrap of honor, they can.

Hemingway was not so foolish as to suppose that fear can finally be overcome: all his best stories, from **"Fifty Grand"** to **"The Short Happy Life of Francis Macomber"** are concerned to improvise a momentary truce in the hopeless encounter with fear. But Hemingway touched upon something deeper, something that broke forth in his fiction as the most personal and lonely kind of experience but was formed by the pressures of 20th Century history. His great subject was panic, the panic that follows upon the dissolution of nihilism into the blood-stream of consciousness, the panic that finds unbearable the thought of the next minute and its succession by the minute after that. We all know this experience, even if, unlike Jake Barnes, we can sleep at night: we know it because it is part of modern life, perhaps of any life, but also because Hemingway drove it into our awareness.

Hemingway's early fiction made his readers turn in upon themselves with the pain of measurement and consider the question of their sufficiency as men. He touched the quick of our anxieties, and for the moment of his excellence he stood ready to face whatever he saw. The compulsive stylization of his prose was a way of letting the language tense and retense, group and regroup, while beneath it the panic that had taken hold of the characters and then of the reader kept spreading inexorably. The prose served both as barrier and principle of contrast to that shapelessness which is panic by definition, and through its very tautness allowed the reader finally to establish some distance and then perhaps compassion.

The poet John Berryman once said that we live in a culture where a man can go through his entire life without having once to discover whether he is a coward. Hemingway forced his readers to consider such possibilities, and through the clenched shape of his stories he kept insisting that no one can escape, moments of truth come to all of us. Fatalistic as they often seem, immersed in images of violence and death, his stories are actually incitements to personal resistance and renewal.

A code pressing so painfully on the nervous system and so constricted to symbolic gratifications is almost certain to break down—indeed, in his best work Hemingway often shows that it does. After a time, however, his devotion to this code yields him fewer and fewer psychic returns, since it is in the nature of the quest for a moral style that the very act of approaching or even finding it sets off a series of discoveries as to its radical limitations. As a result the later Hemingway, in his apparent satisfaction with the moral style he has improvised, begins to imitate and caricature himself: the manner becomes that of the tight-lipped tough guy, and the once taut and frugal prose turns corpulent. (pp. 65-70)

Irving Howe, "Contours of American Fiction: The Quest for Moral Style," in his A World More Attractive: A View of Modern Literature and Politics, *Horizon Press, 1963, pp. 59-76.*

LEO GURKO (essay date 1968)

[*In the following excerpt, Gurko examines violence and loss in "Fifty Grand" and "The Killers."*]

While Hemingway's novels explore the nature of heroism, his short stories are devoted to loss and the resultant melancholy. Their brief incidents, single moods, isolated conversations, are perfectly suited to defining human limitations. The process of affirmation and achievement, especially in a skeptical age like the present, requires more time, detail, and preparation than the short story can naturally or comfortably embrace. The affinity between the short story and the presentation of life on the negative side is as evident in Hemingway as it is in the locked-in structure of the earlier masters, Poe, Maupassant, Chekhov, and Joyce.

Hemingway's period as a short-story writer was the fifteen-year stretch between 1921 and 1936. The stories, whether early or late, simple or complex—whether, like **"My Old Man,"** written under the influence of Sherwood Anderson or, like **"In Another Country,"** under the influence of James Joyce—are alike in their delineation of loss. The father in **"Indian Camp,"** the writer in **"The Snows of Kilimanjaro,"** the American hunter in **"The Short Happy Life of Francis Macomber,"** the boy in **"The Capital of the World,"** the Swede in **"The Killers,"** lose their lives. The bullfighter in **"The Undefeated"** loses his license to fight. In **"Hills Like White Elephants,"** a couple agree to lose their baby through an abortion. The aging father in **"Fifty Grand"** loses his championship. Nick Adams, in **"The End of Something,"** loses his first love, and in **"The Doctor and the Doctor's Wife"** witnesses his father's humiliation at the hands of a local lumberjack. The boy in **"My Old Man"** discovers that his idolized father, a jockey, was a crook. The deep-sea diver in **"After the Storm"** comes within a hair's-breadth of the salvage treasure but is turned back. In **"The Gambler, the Nun, and the Radio,"** the Mexican gambler has bad luck all the time and in all things. The aged Spaniard in **"Old Man at the Bridge,"** victimized by the civil war, has lost everything. In **"Big Two-Hearted River"** the movement, to be sure, is toward life, yet the reader is tensely aware throughout that one false step on Nick's part and he will slide all the way back to the unnamed psychic nightmare he is struggling away from.

If loss can be described as a kind of death, then Hemingway's stories, at least on the surface, are powerfully concerned with death. This is made clear in the first collection ***In Our Time,*** by the brief italicized scenes inserted between the stories. There are fourteen of them, numbered as chapters, to go with the fourteen tales, and their importance is indicated by the fact that the first edition of ***in our time,*** published in Paris, contained only these little "chapters." The stories themselves were added later in the first American edition.

The keynote of the interchapters is violence. One describes the flight of Greek refugees in the rain and mud of Thrace during the Greco-Turkish War of 1922. Another deals with German soldiers being shot one by one as they climb over a garden wall in France during the First World War. In another, six cabinet ministers are executed in the rain. In another, Nick Adams, shot in the spine, is dying near some dead Austrian soldiers in an Italian village street. In another, a soldier during a fierce bombardment frantically begs Christ to save him. In another, a policeman shoots two burglars robbing a cigar store. The last six deal with various bullfighting scenes, winding up with the death of a badly gored matador. The message is plain. In our time, the young Hemingway is saying in the early twenties, violence is the essential condition. And violence contains the threat of death in its most aggressive form.

Underneath the surface show of violence, however, there is the struggle to control it. Loss and approaching death may be the unavoidable fact of human existence. The central lesson of existence, however, is that death must be accepted, faced without demoralization, and thereby mastered. Hemingway's stories are as much a demonstration of the lesson as they are of the fact; their drama arises from the tension between them.

A superb instance of this is **"Fifty Grand,"** where vitality and the will to to endure carry Jack Brennan, the aging welterweight champion, through his ordeal. The surface of the story is gray, bleak, and forbidding. In the gritty, dirty milieu of big-time boxing, with crooked fighters, crooked managers, and crooked gamblers, Brennan has managed to survive only by being as dirty as the next man. He has a wife and two daughters who live in a normal world far away; he seldom sees them; but the longing to accumulate enough money, retire from the ring, and make his escape to them is the dream that has sustained him for years. Now his last chance has come. When approached by gamblers to throw his scheduled fight with Walcott, he agrees, bets fifty thousand of his own money on his opponent, a bet on a sure thing as he believes, and plans to retire for good.

But in the thirteenth round he is suddenly and deliberately fouled by the challenger. As he staggers back in agony, he realizes he has been double-crossed. The gamblers have secretly bet on him to win. If he falls to the canvas, the referee will award the fight to him on a foul, and he will lose his money. Though in extreme pain he manages to summon the will to go on fighting and the wit to foul Walcott with equal viciousness. Walcott does fall, is awarded the fight, and Brennan finally does make a successful escape. But at heavy cost. "I'm all busted inside," he says after the fight. Hurt though he is, he can still reflect, "It's funny how fast you can think when it means that much money."

The story is told with ruthless honesty. Brennan is a cold, surly, stingy man, and no attempt is made to sentimentalize him even though he loves his wife and children, or to idealize him even when he displays supreme courage in a moment of crisis. He lives in a harsh world, described with an extraordinary fidelity to the lingo of trainers, fighters, and their assorted hangers-on. The story is narrated by Brennan's handler and only friend in a hard-bitten, slightly melancholy tone that is perfectly suited to the occasion. Ring Lardner had been Hemingway's model for his high-school pieces. **"Fifty Grand,"** published ten years after its author's graduation from Oak Park High School, stands comparison with any of Lardner's somber little masterpieces about sports figures. Put next to "Champion," Lardner's most famous boxing tale, it is clear that while Lardner has drawn a compelling portrait of a monster, Hemingway has drawn an equally compelling one of a man. (pp. 175-79)

Perhaps the most famous of [Hemingway's longer stories] is **"The Killers,"** Symbolists have had a field day with this story, seeing in it a reworking of Christian legend, with Ole Andreson (son of man) the Christ figure pursued and killed by the Devil's agents, while Nick Adams (Adam—the original man) tries vainly to prevent it.

Original man or not, Nick is once again the protagonist. He rushes off to warn Ole that the killers are after him. Andreson may or may not be Christ, but he is certainly an ex-prizefighter being chased by gangsters for having once double-crossed them. Yet it is true that in six places Hemingway says, "he turned to the wall," a variant of the Old Testament expression, to indicate that Ole is ready to die. The name of the town in the story is Summit (the peak, climax, or highest point where the ultimate confrontation takes place?). The killers are dressed exactly alike and are faceless men. Killing Ole is just another impersonal transaction to them (the absence of the human element suggesting the superhuman?). There are enough tantalizing clues in the story to encourage symbol-hunting, and if **"The Killers"** were not so eminently satisfactory on its own immediate terms, every reader would undoubtedly join the hunt.

But within its concrete frame no story of Hemingway's is more satisfying. As a straightforward account of a young man's first discovery of evil, it is powerfully rendered. Nick has had previous experiences with humiliation and pain. He has been slugged by a mean-tempered brakeman and threatened by an unstable ex-pugilist. He has seen his father faced down and has witnessed an Indian committing suicide. He has been wounded in the war and suffered a nervous breakdown. But he has never before encountered the face of evil as a naked, impersonal, unavoidable, and unalterable aspect of the moral universe, like floods and hurricanes in the physical sphere. The two killers, precisely because they lack individuality and commit murder as a matter of business (nothing personal intended; they do not even know their victim), embody destructiveness in its purest form.

Nick is severely jarred by the experience, and the details of the story are so arranged as to communicate the jarring effect at every turn. The clock in the diner does not keep the right time. The two killers wrangle with George, the waiter, about the food and drink, keep up a barrage of wisecracks that have a nasty undertone, insult everyone around and even each other, and produce a menacing atmosphere even before they draw their guns. Nick is tied back to back with the cook under the muzzle of a shotgun. Later he goes off to warn Ole, who adds to his agitation by refusing to flee or fight back or go to the police. The Swede just gives up.

Everything in the story has another face. The ordered, normal world of diners, ham sandwiches, small towns is abruptly replaced by the disordered world of gangsters and callous murder. The clock reads twenty after five, but it is really only five. The menu features chicken croquettes but all George has on hand is sandwiches. The lunch counter was not always a lunch counter; it was once a saloon. Even Ole's landlady turns out to be somebody else, a substitute taking the real landlady's place for the day. The two killers are dangerous men, yet they look like a vaudeville team. They expect Ole to appear at six; when he does not, they leave in a rage; even *their* normal routine has been upset. Ole had been a heavyweight fighter, yet he lies on his bed inert and helpless. By the time Nick gets back to the diner after his fruitless errand of warning, he no longer inhabits the same universe he did at the start. He has been inexpressibly shocked by the double discovery of annihilating wickedness and his own helplessness to do anything about it. He wants only to run away.

Before he leaves, George advises him not to think about what has happened. The advice is characteristic of Hemingway, and George's attitude throughout sets the standard. He talks back to the killers and, though bowing to superior force, never loses his dignity or nerve. His attitude contrasts with Nick's and with the Negro cook's. Nick, young and naïve, is hard hit and wants to leave town, as though he will get away from it somewhere else, as though what the killers stand for is localized. The cook wants to stay out of it altogether. George rejects noninvolvement; at the same time he keeps his balance and composure. **"The Killers"** is something more than a story about gangsters in the 1920s, something less than a re-creation of Christianity. It is an extraordinary account of the emotional shock that comes to all of us when we discover that the familiar world has an aspect other than the smiling and benign, an aspect of savagery and horror. (pp. 188-91)

The terseness and brevity of [Hemingway's] writing are the natural characteristics of the short story. It lends itself without strain to the limited emotion of sadness, which is the chief psychological residue of Hemingway's harsh view of life. Yet he manages to work into this emotion its exact opposite, the sense that all is not loss, that perhaps a meaningful though not total recovery can be made. In the novels this becomes a major theme. In the stories it is not much more than a suggestion, but a suggestion strong enough to soften their otherwise annihilative impact. (p. 203)

Leo Gurko, in his Ernest Hemingway and the Pursuit of Heroism, *Thomas Y. Crowell Company, 1968, 247 p.*

JACKSON J. BENSON (essay date 1969)

[Benson is a prominent American scholar of Hemingway literature. In the following excerpt, he discusses the central function of irony in Hemingway's fiction.]

[The] importance of irony in Hemingway's work can hardly be overstated. It affects his sense of the comic, his use of allusion, and his employment of verbal wit, and it leads him into various associated modes of satire and parody. It is irony also that leads him into his worst failures of emotional control when his attack on sentimental attitudes becomes so extreme that it causes him to approximate the same emotional excesses in his own work. (p. 25)

In "Chapter III" [**"The Garden at Mons"**], from ***In Our Time,*** a soldier recalls ambushing German soldiers as they climb over a garden wall:

> The first German I saw climbed up over the garden wall. We waited till he got one leg over and then potted him. He had so much equipment on and loooked awfully surprised and fell down into the garden. Then three more came over further down the wall. We shot them. They all came just like that.

The central irony of this paragraph is contained in its lack of overt emotion, a simple, almost childlike acceptance of horror as a perfectly natural part of life. Like some awful, yet matter-of-fact reversal of *A Child's Garden of Verses,* the surface ritual described reminds us of a children's game like hide-and-seek—the soldier who is killed "looked awfully surprised." The implicit emotion arising from this treatment of the situation is a childlike delight in the success of the surprise. The surface ritual is in turn opposed by the reality of the situation: we realize that the narrator, who in this case frames the ritual in his mind, was actually killing people; we realize that the jolly term *potted* is equivalent to a calculated, cold-blooded killing. But the point I want to make here in particular is the timelessness which is so effortlessly achieved, so that the emotional force of the passage cannot be escaped by assigning this event to the convenient pigeonhole of a particular moment or set of circumstances. The passage is like a bad dream that comes back again and again to haunt us and from which we cannot release ourselves.

There is a very profound irony in the working of this style, it seems to me, between all the mechanisms that humanity has invented to rationalize the terror of existence (including the whole area of propaganda, ritual, and mass media sentimentality) and the stark insistence, as implemented by this stylistic technique, that the dark part of human existence is not momentary or accidental, but continuing and as real as anything else in man's experience. (pp. 113-14)

There is something in Hemingway's storytelling posture very similar to the posture of the satirist who recounts absurdities with a straight face. Perhaps there is a strain, too, of the straight-faced storyteller of the American frontier, with the significant difference that Hemingway shows life producing its own exaggerations and its own absurdities. (p. 114)

Hemingway's use of irony can be said to contrast two fundamentally different world views, one that he feels is moral with one that he feels is immoral. Either the irrationality which surrounds the individual, which lies outside the circle of the light that Jake Barnes burns at night or beyond the willing hands of Frederic Henry at Catherine's deathbed, can be recognized, and on the basis of such a recognition lead to meaningful behavior, or the irrationality can be ignored or explained away, leading to behavior which is negative or destructive and making it impossible for man to love, empathize with, or become committed to his fellow man.

Just as, in Hemingway's doctrine, man does not stand in the center of the universe, so too is his morality not God-given but man-created. This man-created morality is metaphorically represented in Hemingway's works by the structure I have termed "game." This view of man's place and his moral responsibility is the reason why Christianity never becomes a very important factor in the thinking of the Hemingway protagonist. Christianity, in Hemingway's design, must be considered to be aligned with sentimentality: Christianity is both ego-centered (centered on man's welfare, conduct, and beliefs) and anthropomorphic. What is the use of praying, Frederic Henry seems to be saying in the desperation attending Catherine's death, if one cannot ask and expect to have the omnipotent Being stem the tide? If He has any relationship with man at all, it must be in terms of what is asked for in reason.

But whatever is "outside," beyond the sphere of man-created order, has little regard for man's reason: Catherine dies—for no man-centered "reason." There is no higher court. There is no appeal from the necessity of courage.

Thus, in what is probably one of the best short stories ever written, **"A Clean, Well-Lighted Place,"** the older waiter knows "it all was nada . . . Our nada who art in nada." There is no help for man except the "clean, well-lighted places" that he carves out of the darkness for himself. The other waiter, who has "youth, confidence, and a job," is unaware of everything except his own desires. He sees no meaning in providing such a clean well-lighted place as their cafe to the old man. The young waiter does not observe the dignity of the old man who, being the last customer, delays the closing of the cafe. The younger waiter can see no difference between the *bodegas,* where one must stand at a bar, and a clean and pleasant cafe. For him, the consequences of the night do not exist. For him, the old man who from "despair" of "nothing" tried to kill himself the week before "should have killed himself." Although the structure of the irony is perfect, it is played at almost whisper-intensity so that many a reader has passed over the irony. The younger waiter is so real, so normal, so average, so characteristic. How then should we characterize his lack of concern, his selfishness, his lack of empathy, his shallow cynicism, his blindness?

Although the young waiter "wouldn't want to be that old," it remains a distinct possibility, just as it is possible that he, like the old man, will outlive the wife he is so impatient to go home to. It may be that he will live to be alone and be in despair over "nothing." But it is clear that he has not yet been required to face the darkness with courage or even to recognize its existence (and thus gain awareness and compassion for others faced with the same task). For now, the younger waiter lies outside the moral community; how well he will pass the tests of future disasters remains to be seen. As for the two who are joined together with "all those who need a light for the night," the very old man who is clean and maintains his dignity and the older waiter who empathizes with those who may need the cafe, the implication in the story is very strong that they have done all that it is within them to do and they are to be admired for it.

Many recent discussions of this story emphasize Hemingway's presentation of "nothingness" as a real entity, a presentation which appears to involve a strikingly profound intuitive proposal by a writer who has been thought to be so unphilosophic in his orientation to life. Commented on less, but equally important to the theme of the story, is the emphasis placed on the awareness of the older waiter. In looking back over the story, the reader should note how much of the story is devoted to the older waiter's clear and accurate perceptions of himself, of the other two characters, and of what might generally be termed "the situation." The fundamental irony of the story lies in the skillfully balanced and controlled contrast between the attitude of boredom (self-absorption) displayed by the young waiter, who has "everything," and the active concern and essential "aliveness" of the older waiter, who has "nothing." The ironic paradox that results is that only through the awareness of nothing or non-meaning can meaning be created. (pp. 115-17)

Blindness versus awareness is Hemingway's most pervasive theme, and it is borne on a rippling wave of irony into almost everything he writes. Seeing oneself, others, and the situation clearly is the basic requirement for the creation of meaning—genuine concern or love for others. Illusion and self-centeredness are the enemies of meaning, just as the younger waiter is hostile to the old man and impatient with the older waiter. A wonderfully ironic metaphor for the hostility of unawareness to meaningful human relationships is the deafness of the American lady in another short story, **"A Canary for One."** The American lady, through selfishness and irrational prejudice against all "foreigners," has broken up her daughter's love affair with a young Swiss engineer. Ironically, she decides to substitute a caged canary for the engineer, thinking (in parallel with her own caging of her daughter) that the canary will adequately compensate the girl for her loss. It becomes clear that the woman is not only physically deaf but emotionally deaf. She participates in and becomes an enforcer of non-meaning, much like the carabinieri (who are also deaf) at the bridge in *A Farewell to Arms*. Although her physical disability is more literal, it has a distinct relation to the blindness of the younger waiter who, although standing in the light, cannot see what is in the light or even perceive that there is a difference between the light and the darkness.

Although in these two stories, **"A Clean, Well-Lighted Place"** and **"A Canary for One,"** love of one kind or another is considered, and even recommended, this subject is handled without sentiment: emotion is examined without emotionalism. Compare Hemingway's handling of this theme with that of Dickens in *A Christmas Carol*. (p. 118)

Hemingway does arouse emotions by his use of irony, but generally the emotions aroused remain unconnected with sentimentality. Usually the emotions aroused are those we traditionally attach to tragedy and to satire. The tragic emotions are associated with the ironies inherent in Hemingway's "world picture," whereas the satiric emotions are associated with those ironies that result from the contrast of Hemingway's view of man and his place in the world with the sentimental view of man and his place in the world. Thus, the satiric pattern of emotion is dependent on an initial establishment of the tragic pattern so that a second set of contrasts, between the tragic and the sentimental, can be set up.

The emotional values of satire are produced by Hemingway when he contrasts his value system, or game, with sentimental or ego-centered value systems. This contrast specifically opposes awareness with blindness, commitment with selfishness, courage with cowardice. The satiric pattern is really a part of the larger, over-all pattern of tragic irony except for one significant difference: the tragic emotions are evoked by necessary circumstances. Injustice, cruelty, and stupidity need not be a part of man's behavior, and when these are demonstrated in the actions of *specific* characters in opposition to the values held by the central protagonist, they arouse the reader's indignation and anger if the threat posed by them is potent, or they arouse our scornful laughter on those few occasions when the threat posed by them is impotent. So it is that we become very angry with the carabinieri at the bridge and indignant with Miss Van Campen and Lady Brett, whereas we laugh at the antics of Robert Cohn and the braggadocio of Ettore.

The irony of tragedy and the irony of satire in general are very closely allied. Both are based on a conflict of value systems, and both flow from an author who maintains a strong moral position. We can see in Hemingway's work that the tragic and the satiric frequently overlap, and we can see that the tragic and the satiric are based on the same terms—that is, of contrast: the positive individual is seen in opposition to negative forces which threaten to injure or crush him. We can see, too, that

Hemingway in the ring, 1944. The Granger Collection, New York.

the combinations of sympathy, recognition of terror, and indignation are at work in "Chapter V" [**"The Shooting of the Cabinet Ministers"**] from ***In Our Time***. Our sympathy is drawn to the sick minister, who appears to be in the grip of forces which, with overwhelming and relentless power, would destroy his human dignity. A sense of terror is evoked by the inevitability of misfortune suggested by the rain and the typhoid and by the timelessness created by the prose style. But we are also made indignant by specific suggestions of human blindness: the use of the hospital for the shooting, the mechanical adherence to ritual by the firing squad, and the attempt by the soldiers to force the sick minister into a ritual that he cannot participate in.

In Hemingway's fiction the forces of tragedy are necessarily impersonalized, whereas the threats posed by ego-centered individuals are usually vehicles of satire. In *For Whom the Bell Tolls* the threatened foul-up of the Republican Army of which we are made conscious from the very beginning, though representing a human rather than a natural threat of disaster, becomes necessary and unavoidable; as a threat, it plays a crucial part in the tragic irony surrounding the blowing up of the bridge, as does the Fascist gunfire which disables Jordan. On the other hand, the unnecessary egocentricity, blindness, waste, stupidity, and selfishness associated with such individuals as Comrade Marty and Pablo are vehicles for the satiric emotions of anger and indignation.

The story examined earlier in this chapter, **"A Clean, Well-Lighted Place,"** contains both tragic and satiric irony. The tragic irony is seen in the contrasts between the power of man to create a circle of light and the vulnerability of man and the light he creates to the omnipresent power of darkness, between the courage man shows and the certain defeat the reader knows lies in wait for man. We are sympathetic with the older waiter. We see him in opposition to forces completely beyond human power to resist except temporarily and in a very small way. He maintains the light of the cafe as long as he can until the lateness of the hour and the insistence of the younger waiter force him to return to the voracious darkness. We do not identify with the older waiter's specific condition, but we can identify emotionally and intellectually with his general condition: his awareness of others, his sympathy for the old man who needs the cafe, and his ability to see the need for the cafe to provide light and dignity and protection for the old man from the forces of non-meaning. We can also experience in reading this story a very powerful recognition of the power of that non-meaning. We can feel the very fabric of the terror that awaits the old man who seeks the protection of the light for as long as possible and who does not want to go home to face the emptiness that is there, the emptiness that has led him to attempt suicide because of "nothing." We feel indignant, too. We want to shake the younger waiter who cares so little, who is so blind, who through his own selfishness contributes to the powers of the darkness that lie in wait for all of us. (pp. 119-21)

Some of the best examples of Hemingway's overuse of irony can be found at the ends of his novels. The end of a story is the place where it is difficult for nearly any writer to maintain an emotional equilibrium in his writing, and Hemingway usually finds the temptation to overdramatize man's inevitable defeat too much for him. *A Farewell to Arms* is better balanced emotionally at the end than most of the novels that follow it, but there is one passage, the one describing the callous unawareness of the two nurses, that is unnecessarily melodramatic. Henry's suffering during Catherine's ordeal in the hospital is already sufficiently established without the episode of the nurses. Particularly effective in dramatizing this suffering is a passage pointed out by Ray B. West, Jr., as a masterpiece of indirect and restrained depiction of emotional intensity: When Catherine is in extreme danger and Henry is trying to serve her in some way by administering the anesthetic gas, Catherine cries out that it isn't doing any good, that it doesn't seem to be working. In three short sentences, Hemingway suggests Henry's anxiety and Catherine's severe danger: "I turned the dial to three and then four. I wished the doctor would come back. I was afraid of the numbers above two." As West points out, "Another author might have examined in great detail both Catherine's illness and the emotion which Frederic was experiencing at that time; but from the simple, quiet statement, reinforced by the dial registering the numbers above two, we get the full force of Frederic's terror in a few strokes." The delicacy with which Hemingway leads his reader here to create the emotion for himself is in sharp contrast to the satiric impact of the cruel giggling and delight of the two nurses on their way to a Caesarean operation who pass Henry waiting anxiously in the corridor. Henry's pain and aloneness are brought too much into relief: our sympathy is overtaxed.

This passage in *A Farewell to Arms* is reminiscent of another, parallel passage in ***The Old Man and the Sea***—a passage which concerns the ironic unawareness of the tourists who mistake the marlin which has been destroyed by sharks for a large shark. This inadvertent transposition of the marlin (which, in the terms I have established here, roughly symbolizes meaning) and the shark (non-meaning—blind, voracious ego-satisfaction) contains, through the prior dramatization of Santiago's experience, more than enough emotional dynamite of itself, yet the transposition's emotional punch is further intensified by being made by well-fed, secure tourists (a synonym in Hemingway for "unawareness") who are *eating*—blindly. The episode contrasts sharply with the condition of Santiago, who, having already suffered from the sharks of nature, is now caused to suffer lack of recognition at the hands of human sharks. As explained earlier, "lack of recognition" is a sentimental trigger. An already established sympathy has been over-reinforced.

As a matter of fact, there are really three major ironies (and several smaller touches) which contribute to what strikes me as an excessively emotional ending to a basically fine story. The emotional contrast central to ***The Old Man and the Sea*** consists of Santiago's courage, persistence, faith, and skill in opposition to his bad luck, his loss of the boy, and his old age (in connection with his stressed condition of being alone in a hostile element). The controlling irony of the dramatization is firmly tragic. At the end, however, Hemingway has seen fit to increase the emotional impact of the basic contrast (which, in terms of the heroic suffering and courage displayed, is emotional enough as it is) by adding several boosters. Only one of the ironic patterns that emerge at the end of the novel is dramatically justified—the pattern which emerges from the implicit comparison of the conditions of the young boy and the old man. This comparison involves the boy's youth, which of course emphasizes the old man's age and present exhaustion as well as the burden of life which he has carried so well, and the boy's devotion, which emphasizes the lonely ordeal that the old man has gone through and the hostility that he has survived without becoming bitter or hostile himself. In addition to this pattern, interjected into the ending, is the ironic unawareness of the tourists, and, in the last line of the novelette, the irony of the old, exhausted fisherman who, although deprived of his winnings by forces beyond his control, has won the battle of the human spirit—battered, he still dreams of the lions.

Before the ending of the novel, the lion has been established as a symbol of the beauty as well as the strength of youth and the lithe, regal courage that the lion traditionally represents. The old man no longer dreams of "storms, nor of women, nor of great occurrences, nor of great fish, nor fights, nor contests of strength, nor of his wife," but only of places and of "the lions on the beach." As with the example of Joe DiMaggio, who played to the limit of his ability despite the pain of a bone spur, the lions provide a sense of heroic perspective to the old man's struggle, as well as acting to unify a novel which deals with man's relationship with the natural world. Nevertheless, the final touch of the lions proves too much for us; it should never fail to provide a moist eye and a lump in the throat: "Up the road, in his shack, the old man was sleeping again. He was still sleeping on his face and the boy was sitting by him watching him. The old man was dreaming about the lions." Although I have reservations about the inclusion of the lions here, one could argue that these last lines constitute an effective summary of man's tragic condition—the heroic will of commitment in opposition to necessary defeat. But in combination with the passage concerning the tourists that comes immediately before it, the emotional emphasis of the ending becomes satiric rather than tragic. The introduction of an exterior element, the tourists, changes the perspective, making Santiago more like a misunderstood, still noble, victim. The emotional underlying of the contrast of conditions, the tourists' and the old man's, boosts our sympathy for the old man out of proportion to the dramatic context itself. In effect, Hemingway forces the reader first to lose his objectivity by making him indignant and second to become personally involved by a strong demand for the reader's sympathy in the face of a threat to deny Santiago the sympathy he deserves. The sympathy is demanded less on the basis of man's tragic condition than on man's tragic condition unrewarded by recognition—an entirely different matter. In short, it is an emotional trick, the very thing which Hemingway had dedicated himself to fight and expose as false and a violation of "true emotion." (pp. 123-26)

Hemingway's abuse of the power of irony is most likely in those situations in which he gets carried away in satisfying his own emotional investments. Hemingway is not a sentimental writer, but a writer who for the duration of his career was locked in a struggle between his attraction for tragic irony and his attraction for satiric irony and sentiment. Too often, when his attraction to satire overcame his general preference for tragedy, his work lost its tragic impact and became personal, bitter, and sentimental. Such a tendency is probably the eternal trap for all writers who care too much. (p. 128)

Hemingway's work, because of its apparent simplicity, seems destined to attract simplistic labels. The root cause for much of the confusion and misjudgment is Hemingway's use of irony, which has been much more extensive and complex than most readers at first recognized—and more than some, filled with personal antagonism, were willing to recognize. Connected to this use of irony (and often a part of the ironic structure itself) is a loading process similar to the employment of metaphor in contemporary poetry, wherein levels of meaning are achieved through the use of image, symbol, and allusion. This loading is usually accompanied by a simplified diction and sentence structure that both ironically denies the possibility of complexity and contrasts sharply with the other levels of meaning. The hard, direct style often possesses a surface tension that, like good poetry, resists immediate penetration even after the loading has been discovered.

Hemingway's "narrowness" is another part of the simplistic fallacy. It has never, to my knowledge, been noted how very diverse much of Hemingway's art is. No two of his novels really have much in common; certainly his book-length nonfiction is very different in subject matter and technique; and the range of subject and technique in his stories is also amazingly broad, particularly if one stops to think how many single stories explore a manner that is never repeated or a context that is never used again. Very few prominent writers of fiction have achieved such a variety, even though their over-all scope may not have been so limited as Hemingway's was by his own intense emotional preoccupations. The fact that Hemingway has seldom been given credit for continuous experimentation and change has severely inhibited our apprehension of his work. (pp. 187-88)

In an age when most people have abandoned the concept that what an individual does can have any importance, Hemingway's message is that what each man does is important, if not to anyone else, at least to himself. If a man is courageous enough, he can win himself; man's selfhood is sacred and must not be abandoned to self-pity or lost in the morass of those forces in modern life which seek to castrate man—rendering him sexless, faceless, and fearful. Although Hemingway's direction in literature followed a path largely dictated by his own emotional need to achieve a masculine independence from a cultural atmosphere dominated by feminine respectability and by a smug, middle-class parochialism, it was a direction that fitted the needs for our literary and emotional condition more often than not. (p. 191)

The emotional intensity which led Hemingway into his excesses also led him to his victories and fostered those qualities of character that made his victories possible: self-discipline, self-honesty, and a very real courage. He was locked in mortal combat all his life with an opponent, art, which grants no quarter and never allows total victory. The artist can be, will be, and must be destroyed by such a conflict, but he need not be defeated. In this sense, destruction is the function of man's material and temporal limitations, the words and paper of the artist, whereas defeat is a function of the spirit, the essence of art. Art can be a true transcendence from the limitations of form, yet form—and this is the pity and irony of it—will always destroy, in one way or another, the hand of the artist. If the artist brings too much courage to this world, the world has to kill him to break him, so of course it kills him. (pp. 191-92)

Jackson J. Benson, in his Hemingway: The Writer's Art of Self-Defense, *University of Minnesota Press, 1969, 202 p.*

PHILIP YOUNG (essay date 1972)

[*A prominent American scholar, Young is most noted for his influential critical study* Ernest Hemingway: A Reconsideration *(see Additional Bibliography) and for his editorship of the controversial* Nick Adams Stories *(1972). In the following excerpt from an essay originally intended as an introduction to the latter work, Young asserts that the Adams stories are unified through one hidden element: the author's rebellion from his family and his Oak Park environment.*]

[As we follow Nick in ***The Nick Adams Stories***] across the span of a generation in time we have got a story worth following. As it turns out, Hemingway arranged it (consciously or otherwise) in five distinct stages—that is, the original fifteen stories occur in five segments of Nick's life, three stories to each part. "The Northern Woods," as the first section is called, deals with heredity and environment, parents and Michigan Indians. "On His Own" is all away from home, or on the road, and instead of Indians, prizefighters. "War" is exactly that, or as the author put it later on, "hit properly and for good." Then "A Soldier Home": Michigan revisited, hail and farewell. And fifth, "Company of Two": marriage, Europe revisited, and finally looking backward, a sort of coda.

Maybe it will also appear now and at long last that in Nick Hemingway gave us the most important single character in all his work—the first in a long line of fictional self-projections, the start of everything. Later protagonists from Jake Barnes and Frederic Henry to Richard Cantwell and Thomas Hudson were shaped by Nick, were all to have (if only tacitly) his history behind them. So had Hemingway. Not that everything that happens to Nick had happened to him. Indeed the author remarks right here, in the fragment called **"On Writing,"** that "Nick in the stories was never himself. He made them up." To an extent that is of course true; the autobiography is transmuted. But it is bemusing that at the very moment when the writer is categorically disassociating himself from his persona he makes him interchangeable with himself, as the "he," the consciousness of the piece, shifts from Nick to Hemingway back to Nick again. . . . But the real point is that this extended and disciplined self-portrait became a significant story in its own right: the story of an American born with the century, complicated in boyhood and badly hurt in a war, who came to terms with what happened and turned it to lasting fiction. (p. 6)

"It is the account of a boy on a fishing trip," . . . [wrote] Scott Fitzgerald . . . about **"Big Two-Hearted River."** "Nothing more—but I read it with the most breathless unwilling interest I have experienced since Conrad first bent my reluctant eyes upon the sea" [see excerpt dated 1926]. In 1926 Hemingway was happy to settle for such published praise. But Fitzgerald might have asked himself why nothing more than a fishing trip should have galvanized his attention. If he had done so he might have discovered that he was responding perfectly to what Hemingway called in those days "my new theory that you could omit anything if you knew that you omitted . . . and make people feel something more than they understood." The things he had left out before were never really crucial, but this time an omission made all the difference. As he pointed out years later, "The story was about coming back from the war but there was no mention of the war in it."

There is no doubt, however, that the perilous state of Nick's nervous system, unmentioned in the story, accounts for the intensity of the writing, which is what arrested Fitzgerald. Here is the quintessential Hemingway style: simplicity, forged under great pressure, out of complexity. The trout, "keeping themselves steady in the current with wavering fins," reflect Nick as in a mirror. . . . Acting, and not thinking, his trip proves a remarkable success. He will carry his scars, but will never be badly shaken again. Fishing is better therapy than Milan's; for Nick the war in Italy ended in Michigan. (pp. 13-14)

[In **"Fathers and Sons"**] Nick looks backward to his boyhood and rounds it off. Nick is now thirty-eight and a writer; [his] son is about the age of Nick when he first appeared in **"Indian Camp."** The action has covered a generation. The doctor who discussed suicide with his boy in the first story has now committed it, though we are told only that he is dead—another important omission. And as Nick remembers how useless his father was on the subject of sex, which he learned about from Trudy instead, so now he cannot talk to his boy about the doctor's death, though he knows that sooner or later they will have to visit "the tomb of my grandfather" (the boy has been raised abroad). A son is now father to the son, things have come full circle, and in his collected ***First Forty-Nine Stories*** Hemingway put this one forty-ninth.

The tale is told, but if Nick's history seems in retrospect to amount to slightly more than the sum of its chapters it may be because his progress through the first third of our century is at once representative, distinctive, and personal. Representative as a national passage from the innocence of a shaky prewar security through the disillusionment of a European ordeal-by-fire, and the rejection of much that a previous age had stood for, to "normalcy." Distinctive for memories of specific experiences the exact like of which we never had. And personal as the recreated autobiography of a culture hero of his time. But if anyone still feels more than he can account for in remembering Nick, he might ask what if anything Hemingway omitted from the story as a whole. The answer is so obvious that it might never dawn on us. The Nick Adams fiction is about leaving Oak Park, but there is no mention of Oak Park in it.

The text may be taken from [his sister] Marcelline. When Ernest was flopping loose in their suburban house on his return from the war he spoke to her one day about "all the other things in life that aren't here. . . . There's a whole big world out there. . . ." What he omitted is what he escaped from. What he escaped to, for the rest of his life and all of his career, moves against a background he expunged. Oak Park was rejected for Michigan, and when that became a small world it was in turn put behind for a greater one. All that is simple to understand. But it is hard to realize today how great was the *need* for rebellion—how preposterous were things *At the Hemingways,* the name of Marcelline's affectionate book. (pp. 17-18)

What Hemingway called "Mr. Young's trauma theory of literature" is not retracted: the wounds in Italy are still climactic and central in the lives of Hemingway and all his personal protagonists. Nor is there any reason to withdraw the notion, which the author also objected to, that he wrote chiefly about himself; he was not lacking in imagination, but to live his life as he wished, then to write about it, was the way he basically operated. Neither is there any reason to abandon the idea that the adventures of Nick Adams were foreshadowed by *The Adventures of Huckleberry Finn.*

But a different emphasis can be put on this combination. Huck's rebellion was of course from Aunt Sally—and St. Petersburg, which Twain did not omit. Nick's rebellion is a given—omitted but as basic as the wound, and prior to it. Almost nothing Hemingway ever wrote could be set in Oak Park; it is extremely doubtful that he could have written a "wonderful novel" about the place. What he could write about happens "out there"—an exact equivalent for what, departing "sivilization" for the last time, Huck called "the territory." In the overall adventure, life becomes an escape to reality. No reward whatever is promised, and the cost in comfort and security is high. Out there can kill you, and nearly did. But it beats "home," which is a meaner death, as Ernest tried to tell Marcelline. (pp. 18-19)

Philip Young, "'Big World Out There': 'The Nick Adams Stories'," in Novel: A Forum on Fiction, *Vol. 6, No. 1, Fall, 1972, pp. 5-19.*

ARTHUR WALDHORN (essay date 1972)

[*An American scholar of English literature, Waldhorn is the author of a wide cross section of literary and linguistic studies. In the following excerpt, Waldhorn discusses Nick Adams's apprenticeship as he learns the bitter lessons of life.*]

Nick Adams and Hemingway are not identical twins but they are intimately related. They share like—sometimes exact—experiences and recall obsessively whatever has scraped their sensibilities. They grow rather tougher as they mature and learn how to guard against the furies. But they can never quell them. Both the character and his creator are at last master apprentices, skilled in the trade of living, knowing in its complex minutiae, but not quite able to accomplish the job of survival professionally. Nonetheless, Nick served Hemingway by allowing him distance from the disabling force of his traumatic memories and by shielding him (and us) from the devastating truth that writing it does not really get rid of it. Nick Adams is, in one sense, the first scapegoat led to the abattoir to assure Hemingway's survival. Apart from his biographical function, Nick has his own dimension. In the twelve stories in which he is identified by name, as well as in at least a half-dozen others in which he is recognizable though nameless, the outlines of a *Bildungsroman* may be discerned or, as several critics have titled the scattered sequence, of "The Education of Nick Adams." If ***in our time*** first defines the world, the Nick Adams stories first define a way to live in it. Most of the stories are narrated externally but the center of consciousness is always Nick. Usually, as might be expected of an apprentice, his role is that of spectator, but behind the physical passivity there is continuous psychic activity as Nick absorbs and assesses experience, clinging to what protects, trying to shuck what threatens.

Nick's father and the Indians appear in the opening story as they do in the last, **"Fathers and Sons,"** forming a frame whose emblem might read 'In the beginning was the end.' What happens in **"Indian Camp"** is prototypic of the disasters etched on Nick's consciousness during the more than twenty-five years depicted in these stories. **"Indian Camp"** starts as an idyl (or a rite of passage), father and young son journeying by canoe to an Indian settlement in the forest. In one of the cabins, the boy watches his physician father perform a Caesarean delivery on a squaw—using a jackknife, fishing gut, and no anesthetic. In the bunk above, her husband, driven frantic by her screams, slits his throat.

The boy does not return from the forest "idyl" initiated into manhood. A caul of innocence protects him from more than partially comprehending the tragedy he has witnessed. His questions to his father are sensitive but, predictably, childlike, curious rather than searching: "Do ladies always have such a hard time having babies?" "Is dying hard, Daddy?" His father's answers are wisely brief, honest, and comforting. Yet the hideous introduction to birth, suffering, and death demands a surer solace, one Nick finds in childish fancy: "he felt quite sure that he would never die." Comfort drawn from others and self-indulgent flights from reality mark the early stages of apprenticeship for several of Hemingway's characters. A more substantial resource for both apprentice and exemplar appears for the first time in **"Indian Camp."** At the end of the story, sandwiched between his questions to his father and his fantasy of immortality is a brief paragraph of sheer sensation: "The sun was coming up over the hills. A bass jumped, making a circle in the water. Nick trailed his hand in the water. It felt warm in the sharp chill of the morning." Unconscious of feelings he will comprehend years later, Nick already plucks from nature a sense of renewal and reassurance. There are a few "good" places, Nick will learn, where reality is tolerable even though fantasies of immortality must be abandoned.

For his sensitivity to nature, Nick is indebted to his father, Dr. Henry Adams, a debt he acknowledges in some detail in **"Fathers and Sons."** As Nick later realizes, not all his debts to his father deserve gratitude. In the stories of boyhood, however, the reader perceives more clearly than Nick Dr. Adams's complexity. In **"Indian Camp,"** for example, the reader recoils from Dr. Adams's callous indifference to the squaw's agony and his schoolboy exultation in his own skill. Whether Nick recognizes these crudities is unstated. What is certain is, as he says in **"Fathers and Sons,"** that he "loved him very much for a long time." And he preferred to be with him rather than with his mother, who, as he remembers in **"Now I Lay Me,"** was "always cleaning things out," and had once charred, while burning household debris, her husband's prized boyhood collection of arrowheads and stone axes. Nick is not witness to his father's partly deserved humiliation in **"The Doctor and the Doctor's Wife"** as an arrogant Indian hired hand forces him to back down from a fight. Nor does he hear his mother's priggish Christian Scientist's defense of the Indian. But when his father, leaving for a walk, tells Nick his mother wants him, the boy firmly responds, "I want to go with you . . . I know where there's black squirrels." And off they go as the story ends. The genius and intent buried in the tale surface in these final moments when Nick first appears and speaks his only words in the entire story. To that point, each parent's shortcomings have been sharply outlined for the reader. Nick has not even been present and, one suddenly realizes, need not have been, for, like any perceptive child, he has already on like occasions watched, absorbed, and formed his preference. When called upon to choose, he does so unhesitatingly. (pp. 53-6)

Not an exemplary hero (his tutelage marred by a narrow Victorian morality), Dr. Adams functioned as Nick's sole preceptor until the boy was fifteen. After that, as Nick recalls in **"Fathers and Sons,"** his father "shared nothing with him." Indeed, Nick symbolically discards his father when he suffers a whipping rather than don Dr. Adams's underwear. He "hated the smell of him," of all his family except one sister, and he walks alone in the dark to the Indian camp to rid himself of the smell.

The end of parental influence frees Nick for the next stage in the *Bildungsroman,* his initial encounter with society. As in boyhood, Nick is again more acted upon than active. In his adventures along the road, he is perplexed and unsettled by the ugliness of experience, barely able to cope with the profaneness of the world. One motif in the stories of this period is flight, a direct disengagement. Another motif, however, marks an advance in his education—the appearance of characters who play variations on the role of exemplary hero. A particularly shabby lot they are too in these stories, but they thrust Nick beyond the near horizon of Dr. Adams's shrunken vision and instruct him variously in techniques of survival he must learn to master.

In each of the stories about Nick's vagabondage, events move swiftly and their import is resolutely withheld. In **"The Battler,"** Nick is thrown off a speeding train, first welcomed, then threatened by a punch-drunk ex-fighter, saved by the fighter's guardian, an almost too courteous Negro, and goes on his way. In **"The Light of the World,"** one of Hemingway's noisiest stories, a nameless seventeen-year-old, probably Nick, lingers with an older friend at a railroad waiting room in northern Michigan. The room is crowded with five whores and ten men, four of them silent Indians. The "action" is all talk, loud, vulgar, and comic: the whores and several of the men crudely bait a homosexual cook; and two of the whores raucously debate which of them has been the true love of a famous prizefighter. Nick is briefly attracted to the fattest of the tarts but is led away by his friend. In **"The Killers,"** Nick vainly tries to save another boxer, this one the intended target of two comically prototyped but grimly real Chicago gunmen. Although Nick warns the boxer, he cannot persuade him to escape. His stoic passivity unnerves Nick, who decides to get out of town.

Each of the characters Nick encounters has been hurt by society and discarded as dross. Ad Francis in **"The Battler"** had been a lightweight champion until he married the girl who managed him and had, for publicity purposes, passed as his sister. Howls of public outrage wrecked their marriage and, along with too many beatings in the ring, sped his fall. "He just went crazy," his friend Bugs explains to Nick. "He was busting people all the time after she went away and they put him in jail." Now the two men just "move around," Bugs, as Philip Young suggests, a less than innocent Nigger Jim [see Additional Bibliography], alternately blackjacking his charge and maternally coddling him. Whatever Ad's former status, he is now crazy and dangerous. Hardly an exemplary hero, he exemplifies the fate of those—even champions—who try to battle the world. Ad is a warning in the guise of a physically disfigured, mentally distorted wreck that a "separate peace" is not always self-willed. These outcasts squatting near a swamp beside the railroad track have no choice and little more than tattered fragments of dignity. For Nick, who has taken to the road to learn what middle-class life had failed to teach, the lesson is appalling, the shock so acute that, as Young observes, he does not even realize until he has left the two men and walked some distance along the track that he carries in his hand a sandwich Bugs had given him. (pp. 57-9)

Hemingway writing while on safari in Kenya, 1953. The Granger Collection, New York.

Hemingway's most frequently analyzed and anthologized story, **"The Killers,"** brings Nick's adolescence to a bruising close. A comic spirit informs **"The Killers"** as it does **"The Light of the World"** but dwells here in the precincts of death rather than life. The stereotyped whores, lumberjacks, and wooden Indians at the rail depot are harmless enough, but the movie-style Chicago gangsters Al and Max (complete with derbies, chest-buttoned black overcoats, silk scarves, and gloves, which they wear while eating) pop out of the imaginary screen intent upon actual murder. As ridiculous and unreal as Kafka's expressionistic "undertakers" in *The Trial,* their purpose is as serious and sinister. Along the length of this razor's edge between the comic and the tragic Nick is painfully stretched.

Nick's reactions to Ole Andreson's imminent death contrast sharply, as several critics have shown, with those of the other characters. Sam, the Negro short-order cook, simply shuts himself off from the reality and advises Nick to do the same. George, the counterman, acknowledges the horror and even sends Nick to warn Ole, but later urges Nick not to think about what has happened. Ole, disciplined in the "code," faces the wall and stoically resigns himself to the inevitable. Nick's effort to persuade Ole to save himself is a rare shift from his wonted role as passive observer. Though he fails, Nick's short journey from the diner to the boarding house marks an important milestone in his educational progress. The diner is not Nick's first sight of the world but through Ole he has his first full glimpse of how a man lives and dies in it. Awed and dizzied by the sight, Nick must turn away. "I can't stand to think about him waiting in the room," he says later to George, "and knowing he's going to get it." Almost a cliché of terror, Nick's words reveal how language fails to sound his nameless dread. Again, his refuge is flight: "I'm going to get out of this town."

As with even more conventional modes of primary and secondary education, Nick's curriculum informs him about the world without adequately preparing him to adjust to it. The end of innocence always arrives too suddenly, sometimes destructively for the hypersensitive. Despite some useful instruction, Nick emerges from his adolescence unable to protect himself, still too tender to avoid psychic contusion. War damages his body as well as his spirit, scarring the tissues of both forever. Healing inward wounds takes even longer, for Nick at least to his thirty-eighth year, the farthest Hemingway leads him. By the end of the war, the third stage of the *Bildungsroman,* Nick will have learned nearly all he must know about living with pain. He will even have the protection of a calloused inner skin. But he will also have the dubious "boon" of memory to penetrate that hardened surface, to keep him vulnerable, always an apprentice. (pp. 61-2)

Arthur Waldhorn, in his A Reader's Guide to Ernest Hemingway, *Farrar, Straus and Giroux, 1972, 284 p.*

LINDA W. WAGNER (essay date 1975)

[An American critic, Wagner has written widely on twentieth-century American literature, including the works of William Carlos Williams, Edgar Lee Masters, and John Dos Passos. In addition, she has made significant contributions to Hemingway scholarship through her bibliographic study Ernest Hemingway: A Reference Guide *(1977) and the 1974 collection* Ernest Hemingway: Five Decades of Criticism, *which she edited (see Additional Bibliography). In the following excerpt from an essay on* In Our Time, *Wagner examines Hemingway's use of juxtaposition in the story.]*

Hemingway's first collection of stories and vignette interchapters is perhaps his most striking work, both in terms of personal involvement and technical innovation. Thematically, all the later Hemingway writing is here in embryo—the fruitless if still polite marriages, the understated agony of war (both military and personal), veneration for the old but unbeaten, censure for the uncaring and unjust, and the fascination with the way man meets death. The Nick Adams/Hemingway persona, regardless of his fictional name, is as effective in these early stories as he is ever to be; and Malcolm Cowley, for one, thinks this collection may be Hemingway's best, most fully realized, work.

Technically, too, the book is a masterpiece of that most intriguing device, juxtaposition. Brought to artistic attention early in the century through movies and graphic art, this practice of essentially omitting transition, of placing one concrete image against another, edge on edge, was also an outgrowth of Joyce's *Ulysses* and Pound's *Cantos*. The position of each story, and its relationship to what surrounds it, is crucial in creating the total effect of ***In Our Time,*** just as it had been in Hemingway's 1924 vignette collection, the lower case ***in our time.*** Situating his longer stories within the vignettes of this earlier book was effective partly because it placed the burden of association on the reader, and partly because the more formal stories—which usually concerned personal and relatively slight happenings—were thus coupled with the pieces that focused on war, honor, man against death. As Hemingway had explained to Edmund Wilson, the arrangement was intended "to give the picture of the whole between examining it in detail. Like looking with your eyes at something, say a passing coast line, and then looking at it with 15x binoculars."

Hemingway's progression in ***In Our Time*** combines a chronological arrangement (the stories) with a largely thematic one (the vignettes). The shorter sketches move from World War I to bullfighting, thus taking the reader from the question of man's honor as determined by the relatively impersonal forces of war, to man's honor as self-determined. The order of the vignettes varies somewhat from their sequence in the earlier ***in our time;*** Chapter IX, for example, originally appeared as Chapter II, as bullfighting was paired with war in order to give what were presumably the author's first views of each: war, in Chapter I, appears at first to be a huge, unruly drunk to the new kitchen corporal; bullfighting, conversely, seems to be an unpleasant blood ritual. Successive glimpses of each, however, educate the observer more fully.

The studies of war emphasize death and the way men, including Nick, prepare to meet it. But another theme in ***in our time;*** is that of man's fear, stemming often from his ignorance—the soldier's fear during the shelling, Sam Cardinelli's and the typhoid victim's, the Chicago policeman's fear of the very "wops" Hemingway admired so greatly. And a further connecting theme is that of man's responsibility. It is the bull that gores Maera, but *men* let him die. All the deaths that Hemingway records in the vignettes occur because of men, whether they are performing under the guise of patriotism or justice.

In the 1925 ***In Our Time,*** the stories trace these same themes but more obliquely. The first stories reflect Nick's boyhood response to his parents, then his broken romance; Hemingway takes us briefly to war, then to a marriage, and finally to Nick's trying in **"Big Two-Hearted River"** to re-establish himself, ostensibly after his war experience but perhaps too after his years of battering loves. At the end of ***In Our Time,*** Nick is alone, happily alone. And it is this essential tranquility that in retrospect heightens the tension and sorrow of the preceding pieces. By finally seeing what is possible for Nick, we can better understand the real torment of Krebs, Nick, or Maera. The calm of **"River"** would be much less moving were it not surrounded by the deaths of Maera and Sam Cardinelli: Nick is managing to save himself; other men—for various reasons—could not. A further dimension to Nick's endurance in this two-part story is given in the recently-published section **"On Writing,"** which was once included as the ending of **"River,"** Part II. Here Nick speaks movingly of his future life as writer and we see that as much of his composure comes from his belief in his writing as in his pleasure from fishing.

What occurs in ***In Our Time,*** as in the best collections of fiction, is that the powerful cumulative effect of the prose obscures the force of many single pieces. The book is unified, finally, by its organ base of tone—a mood of unrelieved somberness if not outright horror. The mood is even more striking because it is given the reader so objectively, with such control that he is caught in the tension resulting from the discrepancy between what is said and how it is said. The short reportorial nature of the prose in the vignettes is particularly effective in creating the objective tone.

Throughout the collection, Hemingway's arrangement contributes a great deal to the creation of this mood. **"On the Quai at Smyrna,"** the preface vignette that was added in the 1930 edition, makes explicit both the devastation of war/life and man's protective coldness toward it. This detached recounting of incredible human misery during evacuation intensifies the tragedy, once the reader realizes the gap between what is meant and the understatement of the narrator. Here Hemingway doubles on his irony; the speaker is not one of Hemingway's heroes but a refined dolt—British, as in Chapter V—who may not really see the horror. His detachment is consequently open to question, unlike the self-protective attitudes of Krebs or Nick later. "You couldn't get the women to give up their dead babies. They'd have babies dead for six days. Wouldn't give them up. Nothing you could do about it." The effect here of death and bereavement *en masse* prepares the reader for the close-up stories to follow, and for their parallel tone.

While the vignettes deal with death, and subconsciously make us search for our joys, most of the stories proper deal with kinds of love—yet, because their outlook is often so bleak, we realize that the stories too are studies of death. (pp. 243-45)

Fittingly, at the very center of the book Hemingway has placed **"Soldier's Home,"** the powerful story that so well summarizes his primary theme in ***In Our Time,*** one man's alienation from his culture, even from—or especially from—those who love him. Yet the story is not a romantic hero-against-society indictment; the values of the parents and the culture are not entirely to blame for his isolation. Krebs is himself bewildered; it is too soon after his war experience; he recognizes the games he will have to play, but he is not yet ready to play them. Krebs needs time. And Hemingway gives him time by placing Nick's resolution in **"River"** as far away as possible, at the end of the book. What Krebs sees as tentative—that he will someday have to find a job and a girl and a place in this world—Nick has accepted. (He *will* carry those heavy cans of spaghetti and beans so that he can enjoy them for supper, knowing he has paid the price.)

"Soldier's Home" is a central story too in that Hemingway here first expresses his ethic of virtue: "All of the times that had been able to make him feel cool and clear inside himself when he thought of them; the times so long back when he had done the one thing, the only thing for a man to do, easily and naturally, when he might have done something else. . . ." Most of his later characters will rise or fall on the basis of that ethic. So long as man had choice, his heroism had to depend on his resolution of that choice—thus, Jake's decision to introduce Brett to Pedro; Jordan's decision to blow the bridge, even with its great risks to the people he loved; Morgan's decision to turn in the bank robbers; Santiago's decision to stay with the marlin—each man has choice. Each man acts as he needs to act. (p. 246)

"Cat in the Rain," "The End of Something"—many of the stories in ***In Our Time***] are sometimes maligned because of their lack of "plot," of resolution. The problem . . . seems to be one of terminology. *Plot* to mean prescriptive action, action that points a moral, was too artificial to appeal to either Ezra Pound or Hemingway. As Pound had written, "Life for the most part does not happen in neat little diagrams and nothing is more tiresome than the continual pretence that it does." Hemingway would favor using *plot* to mean motion. He seldom wrote a static story. Its movement might be circular, might bring the reader back—or at least close to—its initial mood, but the very motion would be the means of telling the story, just as the fact that the story did circle would be integral to its "meaning." The exhilaration of skiing in **"Cross-Country Snow"** both opens and closes the story, yet within its brief compass Hemingway has conveyed the tension in the young marriage because of the coming of the child (a situation so expertly foreshadowed in the behavior of the pregnant waitress). The story suggests the change in life style, the change in the marriage and the change in Nick and George's friendship, all through the objective correlative of skiing. That act itself is described by Hemingway as the epitome of physical freedom in its "rush and sudden swoop," the very freedom that in other ways forms the theme of the story. In 1955 Hemingway described his concept of movement in fiction: "Everything changes as it moves. That is what makes the movement which makes the story. Sometimes the movement is so slow it does not seem to be moving. But there is always change and always movement."

With Hemingway, there is also always a reason for his inclusion—as, above, the fact that the surly waitress was pregnant, and that it was Nick in his sensitivity to the situation who was aware of her pregnancy. No character, no scene, no line of description remains in a story without some credible justification (the chief difference between his fiction and nonfiction seems to be the discursiveness of the latter). He often complained about some modern writing as being "crude and defective in art": "Many of their novels are without unity of plot and action. The story is at times tediously spun out, running on and on like the tale of a garrulous storyteller. They seem to have little idea of what the next chapter of their novel will contain. And sometimes they drag in strange and unnecessary scenes with no apparent reason whatever."

Hemingway's insistence on justifying everything in the story can also be seen in his choice of titles. Titles are of two kinds: either they signal the objective focus of the fiction, or they contain definite and expressible irony, as with **"The Revolutionist,"** who is shy and gentle or **"The Battler,"** pathetic instead of fierce. With deeper irony, Hemingway chooses **"Indian Camp"** so that he can play on the connotations of the supposedly dirty and insensitive Indians in the opening of the story, and thus reverse our expectations of their behavior in the course of the action. That his father had no anaesthesia (as well as no sympathy) for the woman surely stemmed in part from his reaction against her race. And **"Soldier's Home"** with its echo of "old folks' home" or "veterans' home" catches the reader off-balance twice—first when he realizes that Krebs is in his own home, where people love him, and therefore better off than someone in a "home"; and again, when he realizes that his first take is wrong, and that in Krebs' home love is used—albeit unintentionally—to control instead of to protect.

Such separation in kinds of titles is, with Hemingway, arbitrary at best, for even the simpler titles carry double weight. **"Three-Day Blow"** and **"Cross-Country Snow"** refer to Nick's emotional state as well as to the weather, just as **"The End of Something"** describes three things, the mill, the love affair, and Nick's illusions; and **"Cat in the Rain,"** both the woman and the animal.

The result of this extremely tight writing is that the reader must value every word, every scene, every character in his reaction to the fiction. Hemingway's comment about his writing being "suggestive" is, of course, helpful; so too is his remark to

William Seward that his short stories were of two kinds, "tough" and "as delicate as they come." What he meant by *tough* were stories like **"The Light of the World," "Indian Camp,"** or the Paco story, **"The Capital of the World,"** where the sensational characters or actions nearly obliterate any less pleasant philosophical meaning. Hemingway always felt called to defend these "unpoetic" kinds of subjects, even though he was constantly using them to capture the most basic of truths.

In contrast, the "delicate" stories are the relationship stories—**"The End of Something," "The Doctor and the Doctor's Wife," "Out of Season"**—and Hemingway is again accurate in his choice of term: *delicate* in the sense of suggestive (although even his tough stories are primarily suggestive); but *delicate* also in his approach to subject matter. What easier focus in stories of love and marriage than sex scenes, yet there is almost no sex anywhere in ***In Our Time***. What easier means of characterization than a conflict between two characters, but Hemingway instead presents two characters' reactions to an outside force, as with George and the doctor to the Indians, or with Bill and Wemedge to literature and romance. Such an approach is oblique perhaps, but it is also much closer to reality, where everyday events comprise the fabric of most lives. Yet from mundane and trivial happenings, something dramatic does happen: lives are formed, as Hemingway's stories so expertly show. His selection of episodes in a way parallels his objective presentation. What easier way to draw character than to tell a reader what a man is like? Hemingway instead relies almost entirely on dialogue and action. . . . With Hemingway, dialogue can convey information, establish character, present theme, and create tempo—even while it appears to be only repeating itself.

In **"Cat in the Rain,"** the differences in the apparently repetitious dialogue pattern signal the quickening pace of the story. Early scenes used generally short speeches and relatively polite responses; here the wife's longer, more impassioned sentences provoke George's more abrupt answers.

> "I want to pull my hair back tight and smooth and make a big knot at the back that I can feel," she said. "I want to have a kitty to sit on my lap and purr when I stroke her."
>
> "Yeah?" George said from the bed.
>
> "And I want to eat at a table with my own silver and I want candles. And I want it to be spring and I want to brush my hair out in front of a mirror and I want a kitty and I want some new clothes."
>
> "Oh, shut up and get something to read," George said. He was reading again. . . .
>
> (pp. 249-51)

Like the varying pace of **"Cat,"** the pace of ***In Our Time*** as a whole slows as it progresses, moving as it has from the war deaths and the shock of **"Indian Camp"** to these relationship stories where very little happens, except under the surface. Lest we miss the real tension, Hemingway employs his masterful juxtaposition; the stories occur amid bullfighting vignettes, which in themselves stress man's choice of the life and death struggle. The bullfighter struggles to live with honor; similarly, the marriage in question struggles to live—also with honor. But the bullfighting sequence goes on to an end with the great Maera dead, whereas Hemingway spares us the end of this marriage and swings back to an earlier period for the last three stories, **"My Old Man"** and the two parts of **"Big Two-Hearted River."** By ending with these stories, Hemingway broadens his interest in romantic love to include different kinds of love—one man's responsibility for another (man for son in **"My Old Man"** and for himself in **"River"** as Nick searches again to find his separate peace). The stories also remind us of the opening and recurring motifs of death. That the deaths in ***In Our Time*** are as often figurative ones, resulting from love as frequently as from war, foreshadows one part of the enduring Hemingway vision. And that Nick is able to find his life even after experiencing some of the inevitable dying foreshadows another side of his composite. (p. 252)

Linda W. Wagner, "Juxtaposition in Hemingway's 'In Our Time'," in Studies in Short Fiction, *Vol. XII, No. 3, Summer, 1975, pp. 243-52.*

JOSEPH M. FLORA (essay date 1982)

[Flora is an American critic who has published books on Vardis Fisher, William Ernest Henley, and Frederick Manfred, in addition to his study on Hemingway's Nick Adams, excerpted below. Flora here explicates Nick's recovery of identity and hope in "Big Two-Hearted River."]

The reader of ***In Our Time*** has a large frame of reference against which he should evaluate **"Big Two-Hearted River"**—the war experience for Nick and others being major in that background. Probably no other Nick story illustrates how greatly Hemingway was concerned with Nick's career as a whole, as an ongoing thing, as "work in progress." (p. 147)

Understandably, **"Big Two-Hearted River"** has been anthologized frequently, for anthologizers like to include the best of a writer if they can get it. But if the reader does not already know Nick, he will miss much of the story's impact—even though he would probably enjoy reading it. He could get a great deal from the story by itself—and still not think of World War I. **"Big Two-Hearted River"** gains immeasurably from the context that Hemingway meant us to have.

The opening of Part I recalls **"The Battler"**—where Nick also had been traveling alone by train. There Nick's destination was vague, but here it is precise, and his purpose is precise. He intends to go fishing alone on the Big Two-Hearted River. Previously Nick had been hoboing; this time he has paid his fare, and he does not need to pick himself up from the ground. Indeed, the action here is quite the reverse. The baggageman pitches his baggage to him from the baggage car. But almost immediately Nick sits down—and from shock. The opening anticipates the course he will take in Part II when he is actually fishing. The narrator does not tell us that Nick is shocked, but we know that he is. We experience the shock with him. Sheridan Baker puts it effectively: "It is almost as if the Nick of this story, not Ernest Hemingway, had written **'The Big Two-Hearted River'**" [See Additional Bibliography: *The Short Stories of Ernest Hemingway: Critical Essays,* Jackson J. Benson, editor]. And if we have read **"A Way You'll Never Be"** the shock also takes us backward in time, for it is like the shock at the start of that story where we see what Nick Adams saw at Fossalta. The first sentence of the story leaves Nick alone surrounded by destruction: "The train went up the track out of sight, around one of the hills of burnt timber." Sitting on the bundle, Nick, almost like some Waste Land fisher king, surveys the wreckage around him. Seney, Michigan, has been burned to the ground. Only the foundation of the Mansion House hotel shows above the ground. "Even the surface had been burned off the ground.'' This destruction perforce reminds Nick of the earlier destruction he has seen. His journey has begun ominously, for he has not found what he expected, but what he sought to forget. He is immediately tested.

The river of the title, never mentioned in the story, counteracts the image of the destruction of the opening paragraph. The river is there and the railroad bridge. The fire has not, after all, destroyed everything man-made. Nick reaffirms the conviction that started him on this journey; he has to build his life on what is there, not on what is not. The quest is to find what is there, what he can be certain of. In this frame, the simplest sentence can take on the profoundest meaning. ''The river was there.'' More, it is alive, moving. It swirls against the log spiles of the bridge. Having returned to the States from Europe (which his training had presented as possessing the greatest traditions of civilization), Nick turns to nature to see if he can find there a sustaining force. (pp. 148-50)

Nick's search becomes more significant as we sense what he leaves behind. Even though he journeys to an unnamed destination, he could hardly seem to be acting more precisely by directive. There is no grail image for what he seeks, but his quest is nonetheless religious. The other Nick stories—continually suggestive in their titles and imagery and motifs of the problem of good and evil and the possibilty of faith—should help to prepare us for consideration of **"Big Two-Hearted River"** in terms of religious quest. Even the very act of fishing has established symbolic value for Western civilization, especially the challenge of Jesus to become fishers. The fish is an established icon for Jesus. (pp. 150-51)

It may be helpful to see Nick's experience in terms of that of René Descartes, the first of the modern philosophers. Descartes' method was philosophical and abstract. Nick's approach is to suspect the abstract, to deal with the concrete. (Because the reader experiences Nick's progress so vividly, he will hesitate using a label like primitivism which seems to lessen the experience.) Nevertheless, Nick and Descartes are not far apart.

In seeking to prove God's existence, Descartes started by doubting everything that could be doubted. He decided that he could not even trust his senses, for they gave him conflicting information about a single piece of data. Finally, Descartes was left with only himself. He could not doubt his own existence. ''I think,'' he declared, ''therefore, I am.'' Having reduced everything to an undeniable assertion, Descartes felt that he could then move forward. At least to his own satisfaction, he was subsequently able to verify God's existence.

Nick is not interested in syllogisms. Thinking is what he wishes to avoid. But he is modern man in the sense that faith in the Old World and in himself has been taken from him. Hence he has tried to reduce life as much as he can, to get away from people, memories, his personal needs: ''He felt he had left everything behind, the need to think, the need to write, other needs. It was all back of him.'' Nick will rely on his senses, on what he feels. He will start where Descartes started, with what he could absolutely trust. Then—like Descartes—he can move forward, to find—perhaps—what he cannot lose, maybe even God.

Despite the setback at Seney, all the evidence mounts to indicate to us that Nick's program of reduction before advancement is working. As the trout moves, Nick feels ''all the old feeling.'' There are things he has not lost, despite the trial by fire. Nick bears a heavy burden, even ''too heavy'' a burden the staccato rhythms insist, as he begins the walk ''up-hill,'' leaving the burned country. Paradoxically, the burden becomes easy, even a joy. Twice we are told that Nick feels happy.

There is a complex poetry here, and the repetitions are an important part of it. They function to make us share in shouldering Nick's burden in his climbing and in the joys of his success. (pp. 153-54)

As Nick commences his climb, the description is at once precise and suggestive: ''He hiked along the road, sweating in the sun, climbing to cross the range of hills that separated the railway from the pine plains.'' He is a man against the sky, although more immediately rendered than any character in Robinson's philosophical poem. He is Bunyan's Christian, although the allegorical is replaced with a naturalism and we see Nick clearly as a creature of our time. The descriptions of Nick's climb can also remind us of another famous climb up a hill—even as we sense echoes of promises of easy burdens. Hemingway's handling of scene in **"Big Two-Hearted River"** is unmistakably assured, and the scenes are never mere photographic realism. From the top of the hill Nick's view reveals the joy of accepted challenge. From the height, Nick can put Seney (and Fossalta) in perspective. He is like Descartes, now ready to move forward: ''Seney was burned, the country was burned over and changed, but it did not matter. It could not all be burned. He knew that.'' Nick has completed an important piece of thinking.

Having made such judgment, Nick is ready for advancement, and he proceeds, like the road, ''always climbing.'' The pictorial aspect of the story shifts. We have been aware of Nick as a character in the scenes. The country is made to be majestic and to call for the hand of a painter. Now we look with Nick, who already has a part of his reward: ''Ahead of him, as far as he could see, was the pine plain. The burned country stopped off at the left with the range of hills. On ahead islands of dark pine trees rose out of the plain. Far off to the left was the line of the river. Nick followed it with his eye and caught glints of the water in the sun.'' Nick can see nothing but the pine plain until far in the distance arise the ''far blue hills'' of the Lake Superior height of land. Because of the heat-light, the vista reminds us even more of a painting—perhaps of a Cézanne. If Nick looks too steadily, the blue hills are gone, but if he only half-looks, they are there, ''the far off hills of the height of land.'' (pp. 154-55)

Hemingway makes the importance of Nick's view of this wilderness country unmistakable. Nick sits down, as he had earlier upon arriving at Seney. The destruction he witnessed there is perforce recalled to our minds. Nick will take in this scene, too. In his epigraphs to *The Sun Also Rises* Hemingway would later play off Gertrude Stein's famous ''lost generation'' indictment against the affirmation of the statement from Ecclesiastes, ''but the earth abideth forever.'' Here, for similar effect, we contrast the two scenes Nick views.

The second scene looks forward as well as backward. Nick now sits leaning against a charred stump, and his legs are stretched out in front of him. Both details recall the description of war in interchapter VI where Nick sat against the wall. Here he notices a grasshopper and then many other grasshoppers—to discover that they have been made black by the burned-out country side. (Sheridan Baker reports that in realistic terms this is an improbability: the detail is not likely to disturb the reader since it is so symbolically right) [See Additional Bibliography: *The Short Stories of Ernest Hemingway: Critical Essays,* Jackson J. Benson, editor]. Nick, wondering how long they would stay that way, may make us think not only of his state but that of other soldiers. The grasshoppers also bring to mind Nick's lecture on them in **"A Way You'll Never Be."** Since his attention is here on a particular grasshopper, we are also reminded of Nick's experience with a particular salamander in **"Now I Lay Me"** when he engaged in his ritualistic night fishings. The salamander seemed too human as he "tried to hold on to the hook" with his tiny feet. **"Now I Lay Me"** also echoes because Nick smokes a cigarette as he sits. His smoking reinforces our idea of the tautness of his nerves.

Smoking also anticipates other events of the story. Nick will smoke whenever he wishes to slow down his responses. The vista Nick surveys is given a special punctuation by his stopping to smoke. Hemingway's "war" story that does not mention war creates country; it creates country as antidote to the horrors of destruction.

Nick shows compassion to the grasshopper he has so carefully examined—as in **"Now I Lay Me"** he had decided not to use the crickets for bait because of the way they were about the hook. Nick is hypersensitive to the simplest forms of life after his encounter with mass destruction. That hypersensitivity is emphasized when Nick speaks to the grasshopper, for there is almost no use of speech in this longest of the Nick stories. When used, speech must then receive more than ordinary attention. "Go on, hopper . . . Fly away somewhere." Nick tosses the hopper into the air and watches him sail away. He has seen himself in that hopper. As soon as Nick sees the hopper land, he arises and again commences to travel. Provocatively, Hemingway repeats the opening sentence of **"The Battler"**: "Nick stood up."

There is something at work other than Nick's earlier war memories. We know there has been no speech in the story before the episode with the grasshopper, and Hemingway calls that lack of speech to our attention, stating that Nick was "speaking out loud for the first time." He is, in part, telling us to pay heed to later speaking, but he is not giving us new information. More important, he is emphasizing the verbal atmosphere of the whole story. **"Big Two-Hearted River"** is Hemingway's account of Genesis. That "for the first time" is haunting. The biblical and religious overtones of the story are insistent.

Nick will need no map as he goes into the country he has just viewed. Like Adam, he will keep his direction by the sun. He starts walking again, and soon the road and the fire line are behind him. Nick makes judgments on his experience that have a pristine quality: "Underfoot the ground was good walking." The word *good* comes in for frequent play in Part I. *Good* in Genesis is God's verdict on the world He has created. Nick's senses will likewise continuously assert that life is good: "Then it was sweet fern, growing ankle high, to walk through, and clumps of jack pines; a long undulating country with frequent rises and descents, sandy underfoot and the country alive again." . . . (pp. 156-58)

Few stories attempt to call all of the reader's senses into play as fully and as continuously as does **"Big Two-Hearted River."** Usually a story seems to be underway when the dialogue starts, when what characters say engages us intellectually. Even Hemingway stories sometimes work that way. Not here. We feel the heat of the day, the weight of Nick's pack, and we come with Nick to look with primordial wonder at the world. We rediscover our senses. The fern smells sweet, and Nick makes that good count. He breaks off some sprigs and puts them under his straps so that he can relish the smell as he walks. Only the sense of sound is underplayed: there is little attention to forest or river sound in **"Big Two-Hearted River."** Consequently, as we have seen, the breaking of the silence by the human voice has a powerful effect, partly Adamic but also useful for reminding us of Nick's past. Ultimately, the muted sounds of **"Big Two-Hearted River"** are a powerful means of reminding us of the clamor of war, of the sounds that Nick means to forget or minimize on this trip. The silences of **"Big Two-Hearted River"** contrast with the sounds of the Nick war stories . . . , stories that often build on the sounds of war and depend on dialogue to carry large sections of the narrative. (p. 158)

On a hasty judgment, **"Big Two-Hearted River"** is sometimes described as a story in which nothing happens. Actually, a great deal happens, as attention to such details as bait reveals. **"Big Two-Hearted River"** might more precisely be termed a story of significant action. Therein lies its true distinction. (p. 166)

But action is always different from the anticipation of action, and Hemingway's simplicity in describing the moment of Nick's entry into the stream is powerfully suggestive: "He stepped into the stream. It was a shock. His trousers clung tight to his legs. His shoes felt the gravel. The water was a rising cold shock." The big trout who kept themselves steady in the current challenged Nick's imagination at the bridge in Seney. Now Nick is in the destructive element with the fish. He cannot control events in the way he could on the journey to the good camp; he has to wade "with the current." How destructive the element can be, Nick at once *sees* as a grasshopper jumps out of the bottle to be sucked under in a whirl. The hopper surfaces, then floats "rapidly, kicking" until he disappears when a trout takes him. A part of Nick is feeling with the hopper.

The second hopper goes on Nick's hook. What might have been merely a precise detail is surely more than that to the reader who knows **"Now I Lay Me"**: "The grasshopper took hold of the hook with his front feet, spitting tobacco juice on it." Even though **"Now I Lay Me"** was written after **"Big Two-Hearted River,"** it is clear that by establishing Nick's faith in the sacred in nature, by showing similarities between Nick and the hoppers, Hemingway meant us to see Nick's action with the second hopper as affirmative, an important gain. Nick not only feels professionally, he now can act professionally. Although he is killing the hopper, he respects the hopper's life. Nick has a sense of communion with the creatures different only in degrees, not kind, from what Santiago will later demonstrate in ***The Old Man and the Sea*** when he kills the marlin. Nick in looking at the first hopper has seen the rhythm of the Big Two-Hearted River—the rhythm of life and death. War is a violation of this sacred rhythm. Here Nick reaches below the conscious levels of his mind and touches the sacredness of the intended order. By dropping his line into the river, Nick finds that order good.

Hemingway does not let us miss the religious aspects of Nick's fishing, for his first strike is more than an ecological lesson. The first trout is small, but he is the essence of life. Nick sees "the trout in the water jerking with his head and body against the shifting tangent of the line in the stream." He brings him to the surface, and the trout appears a thing of beauty: "His back was mottled the clear, water-over-gravel color, his side flashing in the sun." Nick is careful to wet his hand before he lets the trout—too small to keep—off the hook; thereby Hemingway gives the reader a practical lesson in fishing. If the hand is not wet, a fungus will attack the part where the delicate mucus has been disturbed. To instruct in the art of fishing is not the purpose, however. Nick's consciousness reaches back to previous times when he found many dead trout in the river because of careless fishermen. Moreover, the passage—the only one to make direct reference to other human beings in Part II—is an image of life in our time when the sacredness of life has been wantonly violated. Nick recalls that "again and again" he had come upon dead trout. By keeping the memory general, Hemingway increases the symbolic value of the reference. We may indeed be reminded of World War I and the horrors Nick has witnessed. For Nick, and precisely because of what he has seen in war, life is sacred. He not only sees the beauty of the small trout, he *feels* it, and then his conscious mind works: "As Nick's fingers touched him, touched his smooth, cool, underwater feeling he was gone, gone in a shadow across the bottom of the stream. He's all right, Nick thought. He was only tired." . . . (pp. 167-69)

The Big Two-Hearted river is the river of life and death, and each implies the other. In terms of the image of the very first day that Hemingway has built upon, it is the river of both morning and evening. The joy of morning implies the journey to the darker shadows.

There is something enticing about the swamp scene Nick is watching. It seems to call to him even as he pulls away from it. It is like the woods in Frost's "Stopping By Woods on a Snowy Evening." They are lovely, dark and deep. But the time has not yet come for the speaker of the poem to enter them. He has promises to keep. Youth, especially, pulls back from the entry, but it too can feel the pull. Nick tries to check thoughts of the swamp. He wishes, for the first time, that he had brought something to read. A book could challenge him to another view of experience. But he has no book, and his thoughts revert to the swamp. Nick's conscious mind has to check the pull the thrice-stated decision that he does not want to go into the swamp partly belies: "in the fast deep water, in the half light, the fishing would be tragic. In the swamp fishing was a tragic adventure. Nick did not want it. He did not want to go down the stream any further today." (pp. 173-74)

The way to check the call of the deep woods or the dark swamp is to resort to action. Frost's persona must put his horse back into motion towards the fulfillment of his obligations. Nick will tend to the fish he has caught. He "whacks" the necks of the trout, cleans them, tossing the offal ashore "for the mink to find." He completes the proper care of his trout, a deed of pleasure that surely confirms the accomplishment of this day.

The ending of the story is sober, but convincingly affirmative. Nick gives the "yes" to life that means he will write truly of war and life. The final paragraph reverses the first paragraph of the story. There "Nick sat down." Now "Nick stood up." He becomes man in motion as he climbs the bank and cuts into the woods. He is going back to camp—the good place, to fortify himself for the challenge of fishing in future days. He looks back: "The river just showed through the trees." Nick knows about that river and accepts its two-heartedness. The final sentence is not whistling in the dark: "There were plenty of days coming when he could fish the swamp." This is the affirmation that the artist needs, a belief that the future matters, a belief that he will have the chance to create work that will have a life beyond life. All of that is implied in the ending of **"Big Two-Hearted River."** What is most immediately before us is the large sense of miracle, or recovery of the wounded Nick. On that level the title of the story affirms the religious tone that has marked the whole. The river is two-hearted because it creates for Nick the second chance, the miracle of beginning—as it were—all over again. (pp. 174-75)

Joseph M. Flora, in his Hemingway's Nick Adams, *Louisiana State University Press, 1982, 285 p.*

BICKFORD SYLVESTER (essay date 1986)

[*In the following excerpt, Sylvester discusses* The Old Man and the Sea *as the full, calculated expression of Hemingway's artistic vision.*]

Cleanth Brooks wrote recently that the early story, **"Fifty Grand,"** "presents Hemingway's basic theme quite as well as ***The Old Man and the Sea.***" "Nor do I think," he continued, "that Hemingway in his most recent story now finds the world any more meaningful than he once found it." For once Mr. Brooks was following rather than initiating opinion. Ever since ***The Old Man and the Sea*** was published, critics have admitted that in its effect upon the reader the book is somehow different from Hemingway's earlier work. Those who like the difference and those who do not have tried to account for it in many ways, most of them familiar to readers of the early reviews and of the surprisingly few later readings of the story. But to a man commentators have assumed that whatever the story's new impact—whatever the nature of that affirmative power most readers have felt—it reflects no essential change in Hemingway's view of an inscrutable natural order in which, ultimately, man can play no part. I want to suggest, on the contrary, that ***The Old Man and the Sea*** reveals Hemingway's successful achievement at last of a coherent metaphysical scheme—of a philosophical naturalism which, although largely mechanistic in principle, embraces the realm of human affairs and gives transcendent meaning to the harsh inevitabilities Hemingway has always insisted upon recording.

I think it is precisely the failure to recognize the presence of this informing scheme that has hampered the most searching students of the story. And what is equally important, I think this oversight largely accounts for several recent interpretative extremes. On the one hand we have Clinton S. Burhans with his well-intentioned portrayal of the aging Hemingway as an apologist for conventional views of human solidarity [see Additional Bibliography (1960)], and on the other hand we have Robert P. Weeks supporting the *Encounter* critics by insisting that because the style and attitude of ***The Old Man and the Sea*** is different from that in Hemingway's earlier work, the book is a fuzzy-minded failure, inferior to the first short stories [see Additional Bibliography]. (p. 130)

There is indeed in ***The Old Man and the Sea*** a greater tolerance shown toward the total community than ever before in Hemingway's work. Burhans, like many reviewers, is right in perceiving this much. But rather than interdependence, there is implied the dependence of the many upon the one, of the passive community upon a potent individual redeemer who, in his dependence upon a principle basic to universal order, is independent of all men. (p. 131)

[It] is entirely wrong to regard Santiago's individual experience as valuable only as a lesson in the folly of isolated activity, and to suggest, therefore, that Santiago's reward comes at the end of his journey as he rejoins the community. For Santiago's reward comes, not on land but at the farthest point in his circular voyage, at the moment of his greatest isolation from other men. It comes when he plunges his lance into his quarry.

As Santiago concludes his awesome chase, the fish leaps high out of the water and dies. The marlin seems at the summit of his death leap "to hang in the air" above his slayer. Surely this is another of the moments of cessation occurring at the high points in the circular experiences of all Hemingway's major heroes, and serving to define the achievement of transcendent experience. . . . The contest in which Santiago has been engaged is presented as a pattern of action in time so exactly in accord with what has always happened everywhere that there is no discrepancy between the immediate enactment and the eternal act. As the "now" and the perpetual become fused, relativity ceases; thus for the participants in the action all sensation of motion disappears. Santiago's reward for his struggle is, therefore, not in the nature of a lesson at all. It is that Lear-like perception of the eternal which the very rare creature can wrest from the round of existence, the one boon that cannot be reclaimed by the sea which has provided it.

But what is of greater importance is that Santiago's moment of "strangeness" marks the first time in Hemingway's major fiction in which the experience of ultimate participation culminates a hero's main endeavor. There are Jake Barnes' peaceful fishing trip above Burguete, and Lieutenant Henry's idyllic winter interlude away from the war; and Robert Jordan's ecstasy occurs, of course, during a lull in his preparation for the bridge. Thus each earlier case clearly suggests that the rest of the universe operates only according to the frictionless concord implicit in moments of ideal love—as a Shelleyan cosmos, actually—and that man's manifest dedication to violence must leave him ultimately cut off from consonance with all that is universal and abiding, merely tantalized and diminished by what he has glimpsed. But Santiago's vision culminates his commitment to worldly struggle. Thus the compassionate violence implicit in his slaying of the marlin he loves is revealed as the key to a universal harmony in which man may partake. Hemingway has at last been able to employ the central paradox of the bullfight and the hunt so as successfully to reconcile the forces of love and violence which have hitherto remained ironically separated in his major works of fiction.

His achievement is partly foreshadowed by two incidents in *For Whom the Bell Tolls*. As Jordan sets up a machine gun, soon after his experience of sexual transport with Maria, she begs him to tell her that he loves her and at the same time to let her help him shoot. But Jordan still lives in the world of all Hemingway's earlier heroes, a world in which there can be no meeting ground for love and killing. . . . (pp. 132-34)

Now the fact that Hemingway is able at last to see the world "clear and as a whole" only by perceiving that love and violence may be simultaneously expressed—and that in order to do so he has had to replace the protective aspect of Jordan's love by Santiago's sense of identification with a respected adversary—leaves his new conception obviously vulnerable to all sorts of value judgments. His vision of something rather like a cosmic bull ring invites us to question whether there are not metaphysical, social, and even biological complexities which cannot be crowded into such an arena. But I am concerned here with the specific way in which Hemingway extends *his* view of reality so as to discover a harmony between human and natural affairs as he sees them. And there is evidence beyond his published work that Hemingway was preoccupied during the last of his productive period with employing the paradoxical fusion of affection and violence more centrally in his fiction than he ever had earlier. In 1951 Professor Harry Burns of the University of Washington read manuscripts of

Hemingway in later years. The Granger Collection, New York.

The Old Man and the Sea and of the novella now tentatively entitled *The Sea Chase*, one of the series of works that we have heard Hemingway originally intended to publish with ***The Old Man and the Sea.*** Professor Burns has given me permission to report that Hemingway had been working back and forth between these other units and ***The Old Man and the Sea*** intermittently for ten years. He had indeed thought of publishing the whole group together. And *The Sea Chase*, the other unit most nearly in finished form in 1951, dealt with an anti-submarine captain in the Caribbean whose animosity toward an enemy submarine commander developed into grudging admiration and finally into love, even as he intensified a deadly pursuit of his unseen undersea victim. The thematic parallel to ***The Old Man and the Sea*** is striking, of course.

But to return to ***The Old Man and the Sea*** itself, Santiago's epiphany is not our only indication that in their tense struggles the champions in the story act in accord with natural order. The marlin's fight lasts exactly forty-eight hours; it is seventy-two hours, from morning to morning, between Santiago's departure and his resurgence of vitality at the story's end; and another great primitive up against invincible odds, the "Great negro from Cienfuegos" whom Santiago defeats in "the hand game," struggles just twenty-four hours even—from dawn to dawn. Thus the champions' ordeals achieve temporal synchronization with the larger units of natural order. Furthermore, the marlin's "strange" death occurs at noon. He dies at the crest of a leap as the sun is at its apex. And we are reminded that for the sun, too, the moment of defeat is also one of supreme victory. [Sylvester adds in a footnote: "It is perhaps worth remembering also that while Christ did not die at noon,

His ordeal began then, as does the marlin's, and that the observers of His death also had a strange vision.''] The sun also falls, but like the marlin, the Negro, and the fisherman, it has lasted all the way around. Nor can we forget the shape of Santiago's entire sea-journey, far out to the moment of brief stasis in which victory and defeat are in fleeting balance—and then the return to port. This temporal and spatial coincidence between the journey of the sun and the various rounds of combat implies consonance with an order which is supra-animate—which is universal in the observable physical world.

Moreover, the emphasis upon temporal completion suggests specifically that nature sanctions the champions' intuitive maintenance of a precise degree of intensity—the source of that good pain, "the pain of life." . . . The marlin's aggressive reaction to the current is tempered by his calmness. He does not seek brief balance, but a prolonged approximate balance. Rather than run himself out in a futile flurry as do lesser fish, or break the line and immediately free himself, Hemingway makes clear, he seems to accept his inevitable sacrifice and, like Santiago against the sharks, seek rather to endure than to prevail—to last a certain amount of time while fighting all the way. It is this ideal degree of force—not great enough to end the tension, and yet enough to keep up as much tension as possible—which earns him his harmony with the sun, and which emerges as the final dynamic principle of natural perpetuity. (The fishing line, stretched just under the breaking-point throughout the chase, is a suggestive symbol.) The fish has left just enough strength for his great leap as he dies, and Hemingway remarks, "Then the fish came *alive,* with his *death* in him" (italics mine). The marlin has found the most intense life in this kind of death—in having lasted all the way around while retaining enough strength to meet the final thrust of the harpoon with the same resolute aggression he has shown toward the stream and the weight of the boat.

And the sharks are to the man what the man and current have been to the fish. Led by the champion shark, they are the final overwhelming natural odds against which a champion must pit himself. As they do their work Santiago's material gain and his strength are eaten away as had been the marlin's heading against the Gulf Stream, so that the reader feels a parallel between the old man's continued struggle after his marketable take is gone and the marlin's stubborn resistance even when he is turned "almost east" with the current. But like the fish the man has paced himself. He fights the sharks until "something" in his chest is broken (just as the fish's heart had been pierced by the harpoon) and he notices the "coppery" taste of his blood in his mouth. Yet even at the end of the story, as he tells the boy of his broken chest, he undergoes a resurgence of life and plans another trip. He, too, comes alive "with his death in him." He will die. That is why the boy is "crying again" as he leaves the old man sleeping. Death is the final concomitant of life in a champion's combat with nature. And the only reason Santiago's death is not portrayed within the story is that his heart, like that of the great turtle he loves, will continue to beat "for hours after he has been cut up and butchered." (pp. 134-36)

But what matters is that as a champion he has contributed to the order of the universe: that like the great creatures he has opposed he possesses innate qualities which have permitted him to bring his struggle to cyclical completion without relaxing the tension of life even though he has felt his death in him. I doubt that Hemingway could have found a more felicitous representation of this orderly opposition of forces than the twenty-four-hour hand-game which ends the great Negro's competitive career. As we have observed at length, the mechanistic principle of life objectified in that scene reverberates throughout the story. It insinuates itself kinesthetically into our nerves and muscles as we read. And this is what accounts, I suggest, for much of that extraordinary artistic impact which has for so long intrigued interpreters and eluded definition.

Clearly, then, the value of the rare act is found in the act itself, not in a reaction against it, as Burhans' thesis demands, nor even primarily in its power to inspire others in the community or yield satisfaction for its participants, as Earl Rovit has suggested. Such an act—such a life—on the part of its exceptional creatures is valuable as the only means whereby each species is permitted its contribution to the systematic tension of the universe. And this contribution is the object of that mythic quest which Rovit quite rightly perceives in Santiago's journey. (p. 136)

What is new in ***The Old Man and the Sea,*** let me repeat, is Hemingway's discovery that the need for extended effort in the face of inevitable darkness is not merely a man-made hypothesis, not a masochistic sop to the unmoored human ego, but the reflection of a natural law man is permitted to follow. The idea of an immanent order based upon the tension between opposed forces is in one formulation or another a familiar one, of course. We think of Heraclitus, and Hegel, as well as of more recent philosophers. But the idea has perhaps never been so consummately concretized in a work of art as it is in ***The Old Man and the Sea,*** where its presence is in all likelihood almost entirely a product of Hemingway's life-long observation of man and nature. The order with which Santiago achieves consonance is indeed limited to the natural world. But within the observable physical universe of this story man is seen to play his part in a way which has not yet been sufficiently articulated by any critic.

We can see a way, then, in which Mr. Weeks is wrong to be disturbed by the several errors in factual observation in the story. Hemingway is working here partly with new artistic means to match his new vison. Formerly, convinced of the absence of a perceptible order in the world, Hemingway made a fetish of presenting objects exactly as they appeared, so that any latent meaning could shine through them without distortion. But here, convinced of the principle behind the facts, he can occasionally take poetic license and present objects for any kind of associational value they may have. Mr. Weeks thinks it merely a lazy error on Hemingway's part, for example, that Rigel, the first star Santiago sees one night, actually appears close to midnight in the Caribbean. But Rigel, after all, is a first-magnitude star in the constellation of Orion, the hunter. And it is entirely appropriate, symbolically, to call attention to Santiago's attunement with the stars in this way. Hemingway is in this story at last attempting to pull the world together, rather than to reveal its ironic division. Thus "the way it was" need no longer be his sole guide as an artist.

If we are accurately to assess Hemingway's total achievement—and it is now our responsibility to begin that task—we must recognize that he was a writer who neither abandoned nor helplessly parodied his essential vision, but who significantly extended it, finding in paradox and symbolism the artistic means to do so. However we may evaluate his advance, we must severely qualify our tendency to regard him as the champion of mindlessness in literature. For we have evidence in the last great published work of his lifetime that either consciously or unconsciously he eventually became as concerned with perfecting what he had to say as he had always been with polishing his way of saying it. (pp. 137-38)

Bickford Sylvester, "Hemingway's Extended Vision: 'The Old Man and the Sea'," in PMLA, *81, Vol. 81, No. 1, March, 1986, pp. 130-38.*

ADDITIONAL BIBLIOGRAPHY

Astro, Richard, and Benson, Jackson, J., eds. *Hemingway: In Our Time*. Corvallis: Oregon State University Press, 1974, 214 p.
Contains eleven essays originally presented as addresses at a 1973 literary conference. Notable essays covering Hemingway's short fiction include Delbert E. Wylder's "Internal Treachery in the Last Published Short Stories of Ernest Hemingway" and John Griffith's "Rectitude in Hemingway's Fiction: How Rite Makes Right."

Baker, Carlos. *Ernest Hemingway: A Life Story*. New York: Charles Scribner's Sons, 1969, 697 p.
Exhaustive, authorized biography of Hemingway.

Baker, Sheridan. *Ernest Hemingway: An Introduction and Interpretation*. New York: Holt, Rinehart and Winston, 1967, 150 p.
Concise introduction to Hemingway's life and work.

Bates, H. E. "American Renaissance." In his *The Modern Short Story: A Critical Survey*, pp. 163-93. Boston: The Writer, 1941.
Discussion of Sherwood Anderson's initial impact on Hemingway's work and of Hemingway's successive development of the American short story.

Benson, Jackson J., ed. *The Short Stories of Ernest Hemingway: Critical Essays*. Durham, N.C.: Duke University Press, 1975, 375 p.
Twenty-five reprinted essays which focus both on individual and thematically unified Hemingway stories.

Black, Frederick. "The Cuban Fish Problem." *New Mexico Quarterly* 23, No. 1 (Spring 1953): 106-08.
Parodic response to *The Old Man and the Sea*.

Bloom, Harold, ed. *Hemingway: Modern Critical Views*. New York: Chelsea House Publishers, 1985, 233 p.
Includes essays on Hemingway's fiction by several major critics and reprints George Plimpton's 1958 *Paris Review* interview with Hemingway.

Brenner, Gerry. *Concealments in Hemingway's Works*. Columbus: Ohio State University Press, 1983, 279 p.
Comprehensive, psychoanalytic interpretation of Hemingway's fiction.

Burgess, Anthony. *Ernest Hemingway and His World*, New York: Charles Scribner's Sons, 1978, 128 p.
Heavily illustrated, brief popular biography.

Burhans, Clinton S., Jr. *"The Old Man and the Sea:* Hemingway's Tragic Vision of Man." *American Literature* 31 (January 1960): 446-55.
Studies Hemingway's novella as a symbolic tour de force in which the willful individualism of Santiago is shown to be a punishable transgression against society and the ideal of community living.

———. "The Complex Unity of *In Our Time*." *Modern Fiction Studies* 14, No. 3 (Autumn 1968): 313-28.
Demonstrates the thematic unity of *In Our Time*. Burhans asserts: "Better than any other single work, more than any one or few of its stories and vignettes, the unified whole of *In Our Time* introduces Hemingway's world and the art in which he creates it."

Canby, Henry Seidel. "Farewell to the Nineties." In his *Seven Years' Harvest: Notes on Contemporary Literature*, pp. 150-54. New York: Farrar & Rinehart, 1936.
Emphasizes the affinity of the *Winner Take Nothing* stories with Rudyard Kipling's fiction.

Donaldson, Scott. *By Force of Will: The Life and Art of Ernest Hemingway*. New York: Viking Press, 1977, 367 p.
Comprehensive biographical and critical study of Hemingway.

Fenton, Charles A. *The Apprenticeship of Ernest Hemingway*. New York: Viking Press, 1954, 302 p.
Examines how Hemingway's journalism affected his creative development. Fenton details the evolution of Hemingway's earliest sketches and vignettes from their initial journalistic form to their final appearance in *In Our Time*.

Fiedler, Leslie A. "The Revenge on Woman: From Lucy to Lolita." In his *Love and Death in the American Novel*, pp. 291-336. New York: Dell Publishing Co., 1966.
Contains a brief, critical discussion of Hemingway's portrayal of women in his fiction.

Fitzgerald/Hemingway Annual I-XI (1969-79).
Edited by Matthew Bruccoli; was the standard source for new material by and about F. Scott Fitzgerald and Hemingway.

Gabriel, Joseph F. "The Logic of Confusion in Hemingway's 'A Clean, Well-Lighted Place'." *College English* 22, No. 8 (May 1961): 539-46.
Addresses the debate regarding Hemingway's problematic shift of speakers in "A Clean, Well-Lighted Place." Gabriel posits that ambiguity was Hemingway's intent and that the reader's attention to the story's central concept of "nothingness" is thereby heightened.

Griffin, Peter. *Along with Youth: Hemingway, the Early Years*. Oxford: Oxford University Press, 1985, 275 p.
First volume of a planned three-part biography which traces Hemingway's development through 1920. Printed here for the first time is a sampling of Hemingway's short fiction juvenilia: five unpublished short stories written during 1919 and 1920 whose originals are housed in the Hemingway collection in the John F. Kennedy Library in Boston. Also included are a number of letters exchanged between Hemingway and his first wife Hadley Richardson during their courtship.

Hamilton, John Bowen. "Hemingway and the Christian Paradox." *Renascence* 24, No. 3 (Spring 1972): 141-54.
Explores Christian symbol and the theme of suffering and grace in *The Old Man and the Sea*.

Hanneman, Audre. *Ernest Hemingway: A Comprehensive Bibliography*. Princeton: Princeton University Press, 1967, 568 p.
Descriptive bibliography that precisely documents the publishing data and contents of all Hemingway's work as well as principal secondary sources.

———. *Supplement to Ernest Hemingway: A Comprehensive Bibliography*. Princeton: Princeton University Press, 1975, 393 p.
Updates Hanneman's 1967 bibliography and includes selected excerpts from reviews following the appearance of new Hemingway material, including *The Fifth Column and Four Stories of the Spanish Civil War* and *The Nick Adams Stories*.

Hannum, Howard L. "Nick Adams and the Search for Light." *Studies in Short Fiction* 23, No. 1 (Winter 1986): 9-18.
Detailed reading of "The Light of the World" that focuses on Nick Adams's actions and development throughout the story.

Hemingway Review I— (1981—).
Semiannual periodical, formerly titled *Hemingway Notes*, that publishes literary criticism and reviews of Hemingway's work.

Hovey, Richard B. *Hemingway: The Inward Terrain*. Seattle: University of Washington Press, 1968, 248 p.
Freudian approach to Hemingway's life and work.

Howell, John M., ed. *Hemingway's African Stories: The Stories, Their Sources, Their Critics*. New York: Charles Scribner's Sons, 1969, 169 p.
Research anthology that reprints "The Short Happy Life of Francis Macomber," "The Snows of Kilimanjaro," and selected comments by Hemingway on the art of writing, followed by scholarly

essays on the African context of Hemingway's work and nine interpretive essays of the two stories.

Jobes, Katharine T., ed. *Twentieth-Century Interpretation of "The Old Man and the Sea": A Collection of Critical Essays,* Englewood Cliffs, N.J.: Prentice-Hall, 1968, 120 p.

Assembly of thematic, stylistic, and comparative interpretations of Hemingway's novella.

Kazin, Alfred. "A Dream of Order: Hemingway." In his *Bright Book of Life: American Novelists and Storytellers from Hemingway to Mailer,* pp. 1-20. New York: Dell Publishing Co., 1971.

Examines Hemingway's pursuit of ordered existence in his fiction and relates Hemingway's worldview to those of other prominent American and European writers of the time.

Kerner, David. "Counterfeit Hemingway: A Small Scandal in Quotation Marks." *Journal of Modern Literature* 12, No. 1 (March 1985): 91-108.

Reviews the critical controversy surrounding Hemingway's unattributed dialogue in "A Clean, Well-Lighted Place" and laments that Hemingway's original text has been widely emended to compensate for the difficulty of reading it as originally published.

Lawrence, D. H. Review of *In Our Time,* by Ernest Hemingway. In his *Phoenix: The Posthumous Papers of D. H. Lawrence,* pp. 365-66. New York: Viking Press, 1936.

Favorable review of *In Our Time* as a vivid, fragmentary novel of a man's life.

Lee, A. Robert. *Ernest Hemingway: New Critical Essays,* edited by A. Robert Lee. Totowa, N.J.: Barnes & Noble, 1983, 216 p.

Features ten commissioned essays on Hemingway, including Colin E. Nicholson's "The Short Stories after *In Our Time*: A Profile," Eric Mottram's "Essential History: Suicide and Nostalgia in Hemingway's Fictions," and Faith Pullin's "Hemingway and the Secret Language of Hate."

Light, Martin. "Of Wasteful Deaths: Hemingway's Stories about the Spanish War." *Western Humanities Review* 23, No. 1 (Winter 1969): 29-42.

Discusses the shared themes of "The Butterfly and the Tank," "The Denunciation," "Night Before Battle," "Nobody Ever Dies," and "Under the Ridge," relating the stories to their historical context and to Heminway's artistic development.

Lynn, Kenneth S. "Hemingway's Private War." *Commentary* 72, No. 1 (July 1981): 24-33.

Asserts that critical analysis of Nick's trauma in the Adams stories has been misguided. Lynn stresses that the hidden tension of such stories as "Big Two-Hearted River" stems not from the experience of war but from a son's hatred of his mother.

McCaffrey, John K. M., ed. *Ernest Hemingway: The Man and His Work,* New York: Cooper Square Publishers, 1969, 351 p.

Extensive collection of biographical and interpretive essays.

Meyers, Jeffrey. *Hemingway: A Biography,* New York: Harper & Row, 1985, 644 p.

Comprehensive critical biography which details Hemingway's tumultous personal relationships, complex psychological makeup, and protracted literary and physical decline. Meyers devotes several pages to interpretive and biographical analysis of Hemingway's fiction and notes, in particular, the affinity of Hemingway's life and art with Rudyard Kipling's.

———, ed. *Hemingway: The Critical Heritage,* London: Routledge & Kegan Paul, 1982, 612 p.

Selective anthology of reviews of Hemingway's works from 1923 through 1970.

Moore, Harry T. "An Earnest Hemingwaiad." *Encounter* 10, No. 6 (June 1958): 15-18.

Mock-epic poem recounting Hemingway's artistic decline.

Reader, Constant [pseudonym of Dorothy Parker]. "Reading and Writing." *The New Yorker* III, No. 37 (29 October 1927): 92-7.

Appreciation of Hemingway's literary beginnings and enthusiastic review of *Men without Women.* Parker labels Hemingway "the greatest living writer of short stories."

Reynolds, Michael S. *Critical Essays on Ernest Hemingway's "In Our Time."* Boston: G. K. Hall & Co., 1983, 273 p.

Collection of new and previously published essays treating numerous aspects of *In Our Time.*

Rovit, Earl. *Ernest Hemingway.* New York: Twayne, 1963, 192 p.

Highly regarded survey study of Hemingway's career.

Rubinstein, Annette T. "Brave and Baffled Hunter." *Mainstream* 13, No. 1 (January 1960): 1-23.

General, judicious survey of Hemingway's career.

Saturday Review, Special Issue: Hemingway, A World View 44 (29 July 1961): 6-38.

Includes a pictorial review of Hemingway's life, assessments of his work and world stature by such prominent international critics as Salvador de Madariaga, Carlo Levi, and Ilya Ehrenburg, and appreciative essays by John Ciardi, Carlos Baker, and Harold Loeb.

Smith, Julian. "'A Canary for One': Hemingway in the Wasteland." *Studies in Short Fiction* V, No. 4 (Summer 1968): 355-61.

Analyzes this story as one of Hemingway's "most explicit portrayals of the post-World War I European wasteland."

Spender, Stephen. "Writers and Revolutionaries: The Spanish War." *New York Review of Books* XIII, No. 5 (25 September 1969): 3-6, 8.

Contains a brief discussion of Hemingway's involvement in the Spanish Civil War and two stories that stemmed from it: "The Denunciation" and "Under the Ridge."

Steinke, James. "Hemingway's 'In Another Country' and 'Now I Lay Me'." *Hemingway Notes* 5, No. 1 (Fall 1985): 32-9.

Contrasts the characters, events, and effect of two closely linked Hemingway stories.

Stephens, Robert O. "Hemingway's Old Man and the Iceberg." *Modern Fiction Studies,* 7, No. 4 (Winter 1961-62): 295-304.

Explores the theme of biological struggle in *The Old Man and the Sea.*

———, ed. *Ernest Hemingway: The Critical Reception.* New York: Burt Franklin, 1977, 502 p.

Sourcebook of early to recent reviews of Hemingway's work.

Wagner, Linda Welshimer. *Ernest Hemingway: Five Decades of Criticism.* East Lansing: Michigan State University Press, 1974, 328 p.

Contains essays on individual novels, on Hemingway's style and technique, on his work as a whole, and on his literary development. Of especial interest is George Plimpton's 1958 *Paris Review* interview with Hemingway on the theory and practice of his craft.

———. "'Proud and Friendly and Gently': Women in Hemingway's Early Fiction." *College Literature* VII, No. 3 (Fall 1980): 239-47.

Assesses Hemingway's depiction of women in his early and later fiction.

———, ed. *Ernest Hemingway: A Reference Guide.* Boston: G. K. Hall & Co., 1977, 363 p.

Annotated bibliography of reviews and studies from 1923 to 1975 on Hemingway and his works.

Wain, John. "Ernest Hemingway: Aim and Achievement." *The Observer* (London), No. 8871 (9 July 1961): 21.

Sympathetic, interpretive summary of Hemingway's oeuvre.

Watts, Emily Stipes. *Ernest Hemingway and the Arts.* Chicago: University of Illinois Press, 1971, 243 p.

Contains numerous references to Hemingway's short fiction and his assimilation of the techniques and concepts of modern painting, architecture, and sculpture.

Weeks, Robert P. "Fakery in *The Old Man and the Sea.*" *College English* 24, No. 3 (December 1962): 188-92.

Asserts that Hemingway's typically objective style and worldview have softened radically in this work.

Wilson, Douglas. "Ernest Hemingway, *The Nick Adams Stories.*" *Western Humanities Review* 27, No. 3 (Summer 1973): 295-99.

Representative essay opposing the editorial judgments made by Philip Young when compiling *The Nick Adams Stories*.

Witherington, Paul. "To Be and Not To Be: Paradox and Pun in Hemingway's 'A Way You'll Never Be'." *Style* 7, No. 1 (Winter 1973): 56-63.

Discussion of Nick Adams's relationship to the motifs of action, inaction, aimlessness, and direction in "A Way You'll Never Be."

Young, Philip. *Ernest Hemingway: A Reconsideration*. University Park: Pennsylvania State University Press, 1966, 297 p.

Analysis of major traits in Hemingway's fiction, including the Hemingway moral code, the wounded hero, and the Hemingway style.

(Henri René Albert) Guy de Maupassant

1850-1893

(Also wrote under the pseudonyms of Joseph Prunier, Guy de Valmont, and Maufrigneuse.) French short story writer, novelist, journalist, poet, dramatist, and travel writer.

Maupassant is considered one of the finest short story writers of all time and a champion of the realist approach to writing. His short stories, noted for their diversity and quality, are characterized by the clarity of their prose and the objective irony of their presentation, as well as their keen evocation of the physical world. To the realist's ideal of scrupulous diction Maupassant added an economy of language and created a narrative style outstanding in its austere power and simplicity and vivid sensuousness.

Maupassant was born in Normandy of wealthy parents, and both the setting and character of his childhood are clearly reflected in his fiction. His father and mother separated when he was eleven years old after a bitter and unhappy life together, and Maupassant was raised under the influence of his strong, domineering mother. His stories, such as ''Le Papa de Simon,'' often center around the dilemma of a rejected woman and the children of an ill-fated liaison, exploring the problems of identity and the individual's place in a rigid social structure. In addition, Maupassant's experiences as a soldier in the Franco-Prussian War inform some of his finest stories, such as his masterpiece, ''Boule de suif,'' which expresses the author's disgust for the degradation and folly of war. After the war, due to financial problems in the Maupassant family, the author was forced to accept a position as a clerk in the Naval Office. This experience provided the setting for such stories as ''L'heritage'' in which he depicted the hopeless, tedious existence of the civil servant.

Perhaps the greatest influence on Maupassant's life and career was Gustave Flaubert, a childhood friend of his mother, who served as a friend and mentor to the author during his young adulthood. In the company of Flaubert and his circle, which included Ivan Turgenev, Alphonse Daudet, and Émile Zola, Maupassant was truly at the center of European thought, and his work bears its legacy. ''Boule de suif,'' which was his first published story, was part of a collaborative effort, *Les soirees de Medan,* which included the work of several young French Naturalists under the influence and direction of Zola. The work proved a minor success for the young Naturalists, but Maupassant's story was so clearly superior to those of his fellow contributors that it established him immediately as a strong young talent in short fiction. He subsequently broke with the Naturalist school, turning instead to the precepts of realism. These principles, forged by Flaubert, called for a scrupulous concern with form and a dedication to precision of detail and exact description. Maupassant also shared with his mentor a severe pessimism toward life, as well as a disdain for bourgeois values, which are reflected throughout his work.

Maupassant spent several years on the staffs of two Parisian newspapers, the *Gil-Blas* and the *Gaulois,* often working under pseudonyms. From 1880 to 1890 he published nearly 300 short stories and six novels, a prodigious literary feat, although Maupassant made full use of his material by constantly reshaping and reworking existing stories and duplicating scenes, descriptions, and vignettes from his newspaper pieces in his stories and novels. His creative life was cut short by a degenerative condition stemming from syphillis, which he had contracted as a young man. The disease led to recurrent problems with his eyesight and eventually to a complete physical and emotional collapse. Struggling with bouts of debilitating mental illness, Maupassant attempted suicide in 1892 and was subsequently confined to a sanatorium in Passy, where he died.

Maupassant's critical reception has focused on several major areas, among them his morality, the nature of his realism, the influence of Flaubert on his work, and the autobiographical aspects of his fiction. The morality of Maupassant's work was questioned as early as 1880, when his poem ''Au bord de l'eau'' shocked and offended bourgeois sensibilities, sparking threats of a lawsuit. Henry James, one of Maupassant's most perceptive commentators, called Maupassant a ''lion in the path'' of moralistic nineteenth-century critics because of the frankly erotic element in his work. A central concern of critics during his own time, Maupassant's sensuality continues to be remarked upon by such modern critics as Martin Turnell, who find his emphasis on sexuality evidence of his limited artistic vision.

Maupassant's realism has also provided a focal point for critics. Early commentators were often appalled at what they detected as his lack of compassion for his characters. Later critics have dismissed this contention in favor of commentary on the technical virtuosity of Maupassant's prose, praising the purity of his narrative style and the absence of authorial commentary so much in vogue among novelists of his era.

Discussions of Maupassant's realism often cite the influence of Flaubert on his apprentice, prompting a variety of responses. Some, including Turnell, see in such works as "Boule de suif" many parallels in structure, theme, and exposition. Edward Sullivan, on the other hand, argues that Maupassant made no effort toward Flaubertian objectivity in his most famous short story, and that his bitterness is rather a clear and subjective response to the Franco-Prussian War.

Some of Maupassant's critics have focused on what they find to be an autobiographical element in his work. These commentators find in the short stories that deal with madness, such as "Le Horla" and "Lui?," evidence of Maupassant's mental instability. This approach is countered by others, who find in these same stories, although written very near the time of Maupassant's physical collapse, a clarity of style and perspective that indicates that he was fully in charge of his faculties, and that it was an artistic and not a confessional motivation that led him to explore madness and the supernatural.

Maupassant wrote six novels, and in the past twenty years these have become a center of critical interest for commentators on his work. However, his reputation will continue to be based on his contribution to the short story genre. For their variety, concision, clarity of prose style, and realistic approach, Maupassant's short stories have earned him a place among the finest exponents of the genre.

PRINCIPAL WORKS

SHORT FICTION

La Maison Tellier 1881
Mademoiselle Fifi 1882
Contes de la bécasse 1883
Miss Harriet 1884
Contes et nouvelles 1885
Yvette 1885
Monsieur Parent 1886
La petite roque 1886
Toine 1886
Le Horla 1887
L'inutile beauté 1890
The Complete Short Stories of Guy de Maupassant 1955

OTHER MAJOR WORKS

Une vie (novel) 1883
[*A Woman's Life,* 1888]
Bel-Ami (novel) 1885
[*Bel-Ami; A Novel,* 1891]
Mont-Oriol (novel) 1887
[*Mont-Oriol; A Novel,* 1891]
Pierre et Jean (novel) 1888
[*Pierre et Jean; The Two Brothers,* 1889]
Sur l'eau (travel sketches) 1888
Afloat (Sur l'eau) (travel sketches) 1889
Fort comme la mort (novel) 1889
[*Strong as Death; A Novel,* 1899]
Notre coeur (novel) 1890
[*Notre Coeur (The Human Heart),* 1890]
La vie errante (travel sketches) 1890
Musotte (drama) 1891
The Life Work of Henri René Guy de Maupassant, Embracing Romance, Travel, Comedy, & Verse, for the First Time Complete in English (short stories, novels, plays, poetry, travel sketches) 1903

GUSTAVE FLAUBERT (letter date 1880)

[*The most influential French novelist of the nineteenth century, Flaubert is remembered primarily for the stylistic precision and dispassionate rendering of psychological detail in his masterpiece,* Madame Bovary. *Flaubert was a close friend of Maupassant's mother and acted as both mentor and father figure to him. In the excerpt below, Flaubert praises "Boule de suif."*]

I have been longing to tell you that I consider **"Boule de Suif"** a *masterpiece*. Yes, young man, nothing more nor less than a masterpiece. The idea is quite original, magnificently worked out and excellent in style. The setting and the characters are brought before one's eyes, and the psychology is grand. I am delighted with it, in short; and two or three times I laughed aloud. (p. 231)

That little tale will *live,* I promise you. What a grand bunch your bourgeois are. Not a single failure. Cornudet is immense and life-like. The nun pitted with smallpox is perfect, and the count with his 'my dear child', and the ending. The poor girl crying while her friend sings the Marseillaise; that is grand, too. I should like to hug you for a quarter of an hour on end. But, really, I *am* pleased with it. I enjoyed it, and I admire it. (p. 232)

Gustave Flaubert, in a letter to Guy de Maupassant in 1880, in his Letters, *translated by J. M. Cohen, 1950. Reprint by Philosophical Library, Inc., 1951, pp. 231-32.*

JULES LEMAÎTRE (essay date 1885)

[*Lemaître was a prominent French critic of the late nineteenth and early twentieth centuries. In the excerpt below, he outlines the bitterness, brutality, and pessimism he finds in Maupassant's short stories, while acknowledging the classic perfection of their form. This essay was originally published in 1885.*]

[The] tale, in M. de Maupassant's hands, has become realistic. Glance through its themes. You will see in almost all of them some little fact seized in passing, interesting for some reason or other, as evidence of stupidity, unthinkingness, egoism, sometimes even of human goodness, or pleasing by some unexpected contrast, some irony of things, at all events something that has *happened,* or at least an observation made from life, which little by little has assumed in the writer's mind the living form of a short story. (pp. 164-65)

One consequence of this realism is that these tales are not always gay. Some of them are sad, and some are extremely brutal. This was inevitable. Most of the subjects are taken from classes and 'environments' in which instincts are stronger and blinder. (p. 165)

Add to this that in spite of his natural gaiety, M. de Maupassant, like many writers of his generation, affects a moroseness, a misanthropy that gives an excessively bitter flavour to several of his narratives. It is evident that he likes and searches for the most violent manifestations of love reduced to desire, of egoism, of brutality, of simple ferocity. (p. 166)

M. de Maupassant searches out with no less predilection the most ironical conjunctions of ideas or of facts, the most unexpected and most shocking combinations of feelings, those most likely to wound in us some illusion or some moral delicacy. The comic and the sensual mingling in these almost sacrilegious combinations, not precisely to purify them, but to prevent them from being painful. While others depict for us war and its effects on the fields of battle or in families, M. de Maupassant, hewing out for himself from this common material a portion that is indeed his own, shows us the effects of the invasion in a special world and even in houses which we usually designate by euphemisms. You remember Boule-de-Suif's astonishing sacrifice, and the unheard-of conduct of those whom she obliged, and, in **"Mademoiselle Fifi,"** Rachel's revolt, the stab, the girl in the steeple who is afterwards brought back and embraced by the parish priest and at last married by a patriot who has no prejudices. Remark that Rachel and Boule-de-Suif are certainly, along with Miss Harriet, little Simon, and the parish priest in **"Un Baptême"** (I think that is all), the most sympathetic characters in the tales. (pp. 167-68)

There is in these stories and in some others a triumphant brutality, a determination to regard men as sad or comical animals, a large contempt for humanity, which becomes indulgent, it is true, immediately when there comes into play *divûmque hominumque voluptas, alma Venus:* all this saved in most cases by the rapidity and frankness of the narrative, by the out-and-out gaiety, by the perfect naturalness, and also (I scarcely dare say it, but it will explain itself) by the very depth of the artist's sensuality, which at least always spares us mere smuttiness. (p. 169)

M. de Maupassant is extraordinarily sensual; he is gladly, feverishly, and enthusiastically sensual; he is as it were haunted by certain images, by the memory of certain sensations. . . . To the initial and crude sensations are added the impressions of surrounding objects, landscape, lines, colours, sounds, perfumes, the hour of the day or night. He enjoys odours thoroughly (see **"Une Idylle," "Les Soeurs Rondoli,"** etc.), for in fact sensations of this sort are particularly voluptuous and enervating. But, to tell the truth, he enjoys the entire world, and in him feeling for nature and love are invoked and blended. (pp. 172-73)

Thus we see how many new elements are added to the old and eternal foundation of smuttiness—observation of reality, and more readily of dull or violent reality; instead of the old wantonness, a profound sensuality enlarged by the feeling of nature and often blended with sadness and poetry. All these things are not encountered at the same time in all M. de Maupassant's tales. I give the impression left by them taken as a whole. Amidst his robust jollities, he has sometimes, whether natural or acquired, a vision similar to that of Flaubert or of M. Zola; he also is attacked by the most recent malady of writers, I mean pessimism and the strange mania for making out the world to be very ugly and very brutal, for showing it governed by blind instincts, for thus almost eliminating psychology, the good old 'study of the human heart,' and for endeavouring at the same time to represent in detail and with a relief that has not yet been attained this world which is of so little interest in itself and only of interest as material for art; so that the pleasure of the writer and of those who enjoy him and enter fully into his thought consists only of irony, pride, and selfish pleasure. No concern about what used to be called the ideal, no preoccupation with morality, no sympathy for men, but perhaps a contemptuous pity for absurd and miserable humanity; on the other hand, a subtle skill in enjoying the world in so far as it falls within the senses and is of a nature to gratify them; the interest that is refused to things themselves fully granted to the art of reproducing them in as plastic a form as possible; on the whole, the attitude of a misanthropical, scoffing, and lascivious god. (pp. 174-76)

[M. de Maupassant] joins to a vision of the world, to feelings and preferences of which the classics would not have approved, all the external qualities of classic art. Moreover, this has been also one of Flaubert's originalities; but it seems to be more constant and less laborious in M. de Maupassant.

'Classical qualities, classical form,' are easy words to say. What exactly do they mean? They imply an idea of excellence; they imply also clearness, sobriety, the art of composition; they mean, finally, that reason, rather than imagination and sensibility, presides over the execution of the work, and that the writer dominates his material.

M. de Maupassant dominates his material marvellously, and it is through this that he is a master. (pp. 176-77)

His prose is excellent, so clear, so direct, so unstudied! He has, like everybody to-day, skilful conjunctions of words, lucky hits in expression, but they are always so natural with him, so pat to the subject, and so spontaneous that one only notices this too late. Notice also the fullness, the good disposition of his phrasing, when it happens to stretch out a little, and how it falls back 'squarely' on its feet. (p. 178)

Classic by the naturalness of his prose, by the good standard of his vocabulary, and by the simplicity of the rhythm of his phrases, M. de Maupassant is classical also by the quality of his comedy. . . . In brief, if M. de Maupassant is more than moderately brutal, he is also more than moderately gay. And his comedy comes from the things themselves and from the situations; it does not reside in the narrator's style nor in his wit. M. de Maupassant has never been witty, and perhaps never will be, in the sense in which the word is understood by men about town. But he has the gift by plainly telling stories, without hits, without witticisms, without efforts, without contortions, of exciting unmeasured gaieties and bursts of inextinguishable laughter. Read again only **"Boule-de-Suif," "La Maison Tellier," "La Rouille," "Le Remplacant," "Décoré," "La Patronne,"** the end of **"Les Soeurs Rondoli,"** or the episode of Lesable and the handsome Maze in **"L'Héritage."** Now, there you have great art employed on little subjects, and, as nothing is more classical than to obtain powerful effects by very simple means, you will find that the epithet of classic is not out of place.

M. de Maupassant displays extreme clearness in his narratives and in the drawing of his characters. He distinguishes and brings into relief, with a great power of simplification and singular sureness of touch, the essential features in the physiognomy of his characters. (pp. 179-81)

M. de Maupassant has yet another merit, which, without being confined to the classics, is more frequently found in them and is becoming rather rare with us. He has in the highest degree the art of composition, the art of subordinating all else to something that is essential, to an idea, to a situation, so that in the first place everything prepares for it, and that afterwards everything contributes to render it more striking and to draw out all its effects. . . . Just as much description or landscape as is needed 'to give the setting' as the phrase runs; and descriptions themselves very well composed, not made up of details of equal value interminably heaped up together, but brief and taking from things only those features that stand out and give an epitome of the whole. . . . Clear, simple, connected, and vigorous, succulent in their deep-seated drollery, such are almost all these little tales; and how rapid is their action!

It is rather curious that, of all the story-tellers and novelists who have a vogue to-day, it should be perhaps the most daring and the most indecent who approaches closest to the sober perfection of the venerable classics; that one is able to observe in **"Boule-de-Suif"** the application of the excellent rules inscribed in books of rhetoric, and that **"L'Histoire d'une Fille de Ferme,"** though it may alarm their modesty, is of a sort to satisfy those humanists who are best furnished with precepts and doctrines. And yet this is the case. (pp. 182-84)

Need I now say that, although a faultless sonnet is as good as a long poem, a short story is doubtless a cheaper masterpiece than a novel; that, moreover, in M. de Maupassant's tales one would find, by making a careful search, some faults, especially forced effects, and here and there excesses of style (as when, in order to obtain a stronger effect, he shows us in **"La Maison Tellier"** children who are making their first Communion 'thrown on the flagstones by a burning devotion' and 'shivering with a divine fever'—this in the country! in a Norman village! little Normans!)? Need I add that one cannot have everything, and that I cannot at all imagine him writing *La Princesse de Clèves* or even *Adolphe*? Assuredly also there are things which one is allowed to love as much as the **"Contes de la Bécasse."** One may even prefer to the author of **"Marroca"** some artist at once less classic and less brutal, and love him, I suppose, for the very refinement and distinction of his faults. But M. de Maupassant remains a writer almost irreproachable in a literary form that is not irreproachable, so well is he able to disarm the austere and doubly to please those who are not austere. (pp. 185-86)

Jules Lemaître, "Guy de Maupassant," in his Literary Impressions, *translated by A. W. Evans, Daniel O'Connor, 1921, pp. 154-86.*

ANATOLE FRANCE (essay date 1887)

[France was a French novelist and critic of the late nineteenth and early twentieth centuries. According to contemporary literary historians, France's best work is characterized by lucidity, control, and tolerance. In the excerpt below, he praises the clarity of Maupassant's prose style and discusses the realism of his narrative perspective. This essay was originally published in the journal Le Temps *on 13 February 1887.]*

M. de Maupassant is one of the most whole-hearted story-tellers of this country in which so many and such good stories have been told. His strong, simple, and natural language has a flavour of the soil that makes us love him dearly. He possesses the three great qualities of the French writer, first clearness, then again, clearness, and lastly, clearness. He has the feeling of proportion and order which is the feeling of our race. He writes as a good Norman landowner lives, with economy and joy. Sly, pawky, a good fellow, something of a boaster, a little foppish, ashamed of nothing but his large native kindliness, careful to hide what is most exquisite in his soul, full of sound sense, no dreamer, little curious of the things beyond the tomb, believing only what he sees, and reckoning only on what he touches, the man belongs to us, he is a fellow countryman. Hence the friendship which he inspires in everybody throughout France who can read. And in spite of this Norman flavour, in spite of this cornflower perfume which we inhale in all his work, he is more varied in his types, richer in his subjects, than any other story-teller of our time. There hardly exists an imbecile or a vagabond who is not to his purpose and whom he does not put, as he passes, into his bag. He is the great painter of the human grimace. He paints without hate and without love, without anger and without pity, the miserly peasants, drunken sailors, lost women, cheap clerks dazed by their toil, and all those humble beings whose humility is as devoid of beauty as of virtue. He shows us all these grotesques and all these unfortunates so distinctly that we believe we see them before our eyes and find them more real than reality itself. He makes them live, but he does not judge them. We do not know what he thinks of those scoundrels, rogues, and blackguards whom he has created and who haunt us. He is a skilful artist, and he knows that he has done all that is needed when he has given life. His indifference is equal to that of nature; it astonishes me, it irritates me. I would like to know what is the inner belief and feeling of this pitiless, robust, and good-natured man. Does he like fools for their stupidity? Does he like evil for its ugliness? Is he jovial? Is he sad? Does he amuse himself while he amuses us? What does he believe about man? What does he think of life? What does he think of Mademoiselle Perle's chaste grief, of Miss Harriet's foolish and fatal love, and of the tears shed in the Church of Virville by Rosa when she remembers her first communion? Does he say to himself: Perhaps life after all is good? At least he appears here and there to be very pleased with the way in which it is given. Perhaps he says to himself that the world is well made since it is full of ill-made and ill-behaving beings about whom stories may be written. That would be, all things considered, a good philosophy for a story-teller. Nevertheless, we are, on the contrary, free to think that M. de Maupassant is at heart melancholy and compassionate, lacerated by profound pity, and that he inwardly laments the miseries which he exposes before our gaze with so superb a tranquillity. (pp. 47-9)

Does not M. de Maupassant . . . suffer when he sees men as his eyes and his brain show them to him, so ugly, so evil, and so cowardly, bounded in their joys, their griefs, and even in their crimes, by an irremediable misery? I do not know. I only know that he is practical, that he does not cry for the moon, and that he is not a man to seek remedies for incurable ills. (p. 50)

Anatole France, "M. Guy de Maupassant and the French Story-Tellers" in his On Life & Letters, first series, *translated by A. W. Evans, Dodd, Mead and Company, 1924, pp. 41-50.*

HENRY JAMES (essay date 1888)

[James was an American-born English novelist, short story writer, critic, and essayist of the late nineteenth and early twentieth centuries. He is regarded as one of the greatest novelists of the English language and is admired as an insightful critic. His criticism is informed by his sensitivity to European culture, particularly English and French literature of the late nineteenth century. Francis Steegmuller has called the following essay by James the "best discussion of (Maupassant's) work in English." In the ex-

cerpt below, James states that Maupassant is an artist of the senses: of smell, sight, and sexuality. Because of this, James concludes, Maupassant is "embarrassing" for a moralist; he is a "lion in the path," a writer who cannot be ignored or dismissed.]

[As] a commentator M. de Maupassant is slightly common, while as an artist he is wonderfully rare. Of course we must, in judging a writer, take one thing with another, and if I could make up my mind that M. de Maupassant is weak in theory, it would almost make me like him better, render him more approachable, give him the touch of softness that he lacks, and show us a human flaw. The most general quality of the author of ***La Maison Tellier*** and *Bel-Ami,* the impression that remains last, after the others have been accounted for, is an essential hardness—hardness of form, hardness of nature; and it would put us more at ease to find that if the fact with him (the fact of execution) is so extraordinarily definite and adequate, his explanations, after it, were a little vague and sentimental. (p. 245)

[Maupassant's] gifts are remarkably strong and definite, and . . . he writes directly *from* them, as it were: holds the fullest, the most uninterrupted—I scarcely know what to call it—the boldest communication with them. . . . M. de Maupassant neglects nothing that he possesses; he cultivates his garden with admirable energy; and if there is a flower you miss from the rich parterre, you may be sure that it could not possibly have been raised, his mind not containing the soil for it. He is plainly of the opinion that the first duty of the artist, and the thing that makes him most useful to his fellow-men, is to master his instrument, whatever it may happen to be.

His own is that of the senses, and it is through them alone, or almost alone, that life appeals to him; it is almost alone by their help that he describes it, that he produces brilliant works. They render him this great assistance because they are evidently, in his constitution, extraordinarily alive; there is scarcely a page in all his twenty volumes that does not testify to their vivacity. Nothing could be further from his thought than to disavow them and to minimise their importance. He accepts them frankly, gratefully, works them, rejoices in them. . . . M. de Maupassant's productions teach us, for instance, that his sense of smell is exceptionally acute—as acute as that of those animals of the field and forest whose subsistence and security depend upon it. It might be thought that he would, as a student of the human race, have found an abnormal development of this faculty embarrassing, scarcely knowing what to do with it, where to place it. But such an apprehension betrays an imperfect conception of his directness and resolution, as well as of his constant economy of means. Nothing whatever prevents him from representing the relations of men and women as largely governed by the scent of the parties. Human life in his pages (would this not be the most general description he would give of it?) appears for the most part as a sort of concert of odours, and his people are perpetually engaged, or he is engaged on their behalf, in sniffing up and distinguishing them, in some pleasant or painful exercise of the nostril. (pp. 249-51)

Not less powerful is his visual sense, the quick, direct discrimination of his eye, which explains the singularly vivid concision of his descriptions. These are never prolonged nor analytic, have nothing of enumeration, of the quality of the observer, who counts the items to be sure he has made up the sum. His eye *selects* unerringly, unscrupulously, almost impudently—catches the particular thing in which the character of the object or the scene resides, and, by expressing it with the artful brevity of a master, leaves a convincing, original picture. If he is inveterately synthetic, he is never more so than in the way he brings this hard, short, intelligent gaze to bear. His vision of the world is for the most part a vision of ugliness, and even when it is not, there is in his easy power to generalise a certain absence of love, a sort of bird's-eye-view contempt. He has none of the superstitions of observation, none of our English indulgences, our tender and often imaginative superficialities. (pp. 251-52)

As regards the other sense, the sense *par excellence,* the sense which we scarcely mention in English fiction, and which I am not very sure I shall be allowed to mention in an English periodical, M. de Maupassant speaks for that, and of it, with extraordinary distinctness and authority. To say that it occupies the first place in his picture is to say too little; it covers in truth the whole canvas, and his work is little else but a report of its innumerable manifestations. These manifestations are not, for him, so many incidents of life; they are life itself, they represent the standing answer to any question that we may ask about it. He describes them in detail, with a familiarity and a frankness which leave nothing to be added; I should say with singular truth, if I did not consider that in regard to this article he may be taxed with a certain exaggeration. M. de Maupassant would doubtless affirm that where the empire of the sexual sense is concerned, no exaggeration is possible: nevertheless it may be said that whatever depths may be discovered by those who dig for them, the impression of the human spectacle for him who takes it as it comes has less analogy with that of the monkeys' cage than this admirable writer's account of it. I speak of the human spectacle as we Anglo-Saxons see it—as we Anglo-Saxons pretend we see it, M. de Maupassant would possibly say. (pp. 253-54)

If he is a very interesting case, this makes him also an embarrassing one, embarrassing and mystifying for the moralist. I may as well admit that no writer of the day strikes me as equally so. To find M. de Maupassant a lion in the path—that may seem to some people a singular proof of want of courage; but I think the obstacle will not be made light of by those who have really taken the measure of the animal. We are accustomed to think, we of the English faith, that a cynic is a living advertisement of his errors, especially in proportion as he is a thorough-going one; and M. de Maupassant's cynicism, unrelieved as it is, will not be disposed of off-hand by a critic of a competent literary sense. . . . It is easy to exclaim that if he judges life only from the point of view of the senses, many are the noble and exquisite things that he must leave out. What he leaves out has no claim to get itself considered till after we have done justice to what he takes in. It is this positive side of M. de Maupassant that is most remarkable—the fact that his literary character is so complete and edifying. (pp. 254-55)

M. de Maupassant would probably urge that the right thing is to know, or to guess, how events come to pass, but to say as little about it as possible. There are matters in regard to which he feels the importance of being explicit, but that is not one of them. . . . He deprecates reference to motives, but there is one, covering an immense ground in his horizon, as I have already hinted, to which he perpetually refers. If the sexual impulse be not a moral antecedent, it is none the less the wire that moves almost all M. de Maupassant's puppets, and as he has not hidden it, I cannot see that he has eliminated analysis or made a sacrifice to discretion. His pages are studded with that particular analysis; he is constantly peeping behind the curtain, telling us what he discovers there. The truth is that the admirable system of simplification which makes his tales so rapid and so concise (especially his shorter ones, for his novels in some degree, I think, suffer from it), strikes us as not in the least a conscious intellectual effort, a selective, comparative process. He tells us all he knows, all he suspects, and if these things take no account of the moral nature of man, it is because he has no window looking in that direction, and not because artistic scruples have compelled him to close it up. The very compact mansion in which he dwells presents on that side a perfectly dead wall.

This is why, if his axiom that you produce the effect of truth better by painting people from the outside than from the inside has a large utility, his example is convincing in a much higher degree. A writer is fortunate when his theory and his limitations so exactly correspond, when his curiosities may be appeased with such precision and promptitude. . . . M. de Maupassant is remarkably objective and impersonal, but he would go too far if he were to entertain the belief that he has kept himself out of his books. They speak of him eloquently, even if it only be to tell us how easy—how easy, given his talent of course—he has found this impersonality. (pp. 257-59)

He feels oppressively, discouragingly, as many another of his countrymen must have felt—for the French have worked their language as no other people have done—the penalty of coming at the end of three centuries of literature, the difficulty of dealing with an instrument of expression so worn by friction, of drawing new sounds from the old familiar pipe. . . . Everything seems to him to have been done, every effect produced, every combination already made. (p. 261)

If it be a miracle whenever there is a fresh tone, the miracle has been wrought for M. de Maupassant. . . . He has taken his stand on simplicity, on a studied sobriety, being persuaded that the deepest science lies in that direction rather than in the multiplication of new terms. . . . Nothing can exceed the masculine firmness, the quiet force of his own style, in which every phrase is a close sequence, every epithet a paying piece, and the ground is completely cleared of the vague, the ready-made and the second-best. Less than any one to-day does he beat the air; more than any one does he hit out from the shoulder. (pp. 262-63)

He has produced a hundred short tales and only four regular novels; but if the tales deserve the first place in any candid appreciation of his talent it is not simply because they are so much the more numerous: they are also more characteristic; they represent him best in his originality, and their brevity, extreme in some cases, does not prevent them from being a collection of masterpieces. (They are very unequal, and I speak of the best.) (p. 264)

For the last ten years our author has brought forth with regularity these condensed compositions, of which, probably, to an English reader, at a first glance, the most universal sign will be their licentiousness. They really partake of this quality, however, in a very differing degree, and a second glance shows that they may be divided into numerous groups. It is not fair, I think, even to say that what they have most in common is their being extremely *lestes*. What they have most in common is their being extremely strong, and after that their being extremely brutal. A story may be obscene without being brutal, and *vice versâ,* and M. de Maupassant's contempt for those interdictions which are supposed to be made in the interest of good morals is but an incident—a very large one indeed—of his general contempt. A pessimism so great that its alliance with the love of good work, or even with the calculation of the sort of work that pays best in a country of style, is, as I have intimated, the most puzzling of anomalies (for it would seem in the light of such sentiments that nothing is worth anything), this cynical strain is the sign of such gems of narration as **"La Maison Tellier," "L'Histoire d'une Fille de Ferme," "L'Ane," "Le Chien," "Mademoiselle Fifi," "Monsieur Parent," "L'Héritage," "En Famille," "Le Baptême," "Le Père Amable."** The author fixes a hard eye on some small spot of human life, usually some ugly, dreary, shabby, sordid one, takes up the particle, and squeezes it either till it grimaces or till it bleeds. Sometimes the grimace is very droll, sometimes the wound is very horrible; but in either case the whole thing is real, observed, noted, and represented, not an invention or a castle in the air. M. de Maupassant sees human life as a terribly ugly business relieved by the comical, but even the comedy is for the most part the comedy of misery, of avidity, of ignorance, helplessness, and grossness. When his laugh is not for these things, it is for the little *saletés* (to use one of his own favourite words) of luxurious life, which are intended to be prettier, but which can scarcely be said to brighten the picture. I like **"La Bête à Maître Belhomme," "La Ficelle," "Le Petit Fût," "Le Cas de Madame Luneau," "Tribuneaux Rustiques,"** and many others of this category much better than his anecdotes of the mutual confidences of his little *marquises* and *baronnes*.

Not counting his novels for the moment, his tales may be divided into the three groups of those which deal with the Norman peasantry, those which deal with the *petit employé* and small shopkeeper, usually in Paris, and the miscellaneous, in which the upper walks of life are represented, and the fantastic, the whimsical, the weird, and even the supernatural, figure as well as the unexpurgated. These last things range from **"Le Horla"** (which is not a specimen of the author's best vein—the only occasion on which he has the weakness of imitation is when he strikes us as emulating Edgar Poe) to **"Miss Harriet,"** and from **"Boule de Suif"** (a triumph) to that almost inconceivable little growl of Anglophobia, **"Découverte"**—inconceivable I mean in its irresponsibility and ill-nature on the part of a man of M. de Maupassant's distinction; passing by such little perfections as **"Petit soldat," "L'Abandonné," "Le Collier"** (the list is too long for complete enumeration), and such gross imperfections (for it once in a while befalls our author to go woefully astray), as **"La Femme de Paul," "Châli," "Les Soeurs Rondoli."** To these might almost be added as a special category the various forms in which M. de Maupassant relates adventures in railway carriages. Numerous, to his imagination, are the pretexts for enlivening fiction afforded by first, second, and third class compartments; the accidents (which have nothing to do with the conduct of the train) that occur there constitute no inconsiderable part of our earthly transit.

It is surely by his Norman peasant that his tales will live; he knows this worthy as if he had made him, understands him down to the ground, puts him on his feet with a few of the freest, most plastic touches. M. de Maupassant does not admire him, and he is such a master of the subject that it would ill become an outsider to suggest a revision of judgment. He is a part of the contemptible furniture of the world, but on the whole, it would appear, the most grotesque part of it. His caution, his canniness, his natural astuteness, his stinginess, his general grinding sordidness, are as unmistakable as that quaint and brutish dialect in which he expresses himself, and on which our author plays like a virtuoso. . . . If it is most convenient to place **"La Maison Tellier"** among the tales of the peasantry, there is no doubt that it stands at the head of

Chateau de Miromesnil, birthplace of Maupassant. From Maupassant: A Lion in the Path, *by Francis Steegmuller. Random House, 1949. Copyright 1949, © renewed 1977 by Francis Steegmuller. Reprinted by permission of McIntosh and Otis, Inc.*

the list. . . . Every good story is of course both a picture and an idea, and the more they are interfused the better the problem is solved. In **"La Maison Tellier"** they fit each other to perfection; the capacity for sudden innocent delights latent in natures which have lost their innocence is vividly illustrated by the singular scenes to which our acquaintance with Madame and her staff (little as it may be a thing to boast of), successively introduces us. The breadth, the freedom, and brightness of all this give the measure of the author's talent, and of that large, keen way of looking at life which sees the pathetic and the droll, the stuff of which the whole piece is made, in the queerest and humblest patterns. The tone of **"La Maison Tellier"** and the few compositions which closely resemble it, expresses M. de Maupassant's nearest approach to geniality. Even here, however, it is the geniality of the showman exhilarated by the success with which he feels that he makes his mannikins (and especially his woman-kins) caper and squeak, and who after the performance tosses them into their box with the irreverence of a practised hand. (pp. 265-69)

M. de Maupassant evidently knows a great deal about the army of clerks who work under government, but it is a terrible tale that he has to tell of them and of the *petit bourgeois* in general. . . . In **"Monsieur Parent," "L'Héritage," "En Famille," "Une Partie de Campagne," "Promenade,"** and many other pitiless little pieces, the author opens the window wide to his perception of everything mean, narrow, and sordid. The subject is ever the struggle for existence in hard conditions, lighted up simply by more or less *polissonnerie*. (pp. 271-72)

"L'Héritage" is a drama of private life in the little world of the Ministère de la Marine—a world, according to M. de Maupassant, of dreadful little jealousies and ineptitudes. Readers of a robust complexion should learn how the wretched M. Lesable was handled by his wife and her father on his failing to satisfy their just expectations, and how he comported himself in the singular situation thus prepared for him. The story is a model of narration, but it leaves our poor average humanity dangling like a beaten rag.

Where does M. de Maupassant find the great multitude of his detestable women? or where at least does he find the courage to represent them in such colours? . . . They are a large element in that general disfigurement, that *illusion de l'ignoble, qui attire tant d'êtres,* which makes the perverse or the stupid side of things the one which strikes him first, which leads him, if he glances at a group of nurses and children sunning themselves in a Parisian square, to notice primarily the *yeux de brute* of the nurses; or if he speaks of the longing for a taste of the country which haunts the shopkeeper fenced in behind his counter, to identify it as the *amour bête de la nature*. . . . (pp. 275-76)

[Maupassant has] yet remained, for those who are interested in these matters, a writer with whom it was impossible not to reckon. This is why I called him, to begin with, so many ineffectual names: a rarity, a "case," an embarrassment, a lion in the path. He is still in the path as I conclude these observations, but I think that in making them we have discovered a legitimate way round. If he is a master of his art and it is discouraging to find what low views are compatible with mastery, there is satisfaction, on the other hand in learning on what particular condition he holds his strange success. This condition, it seems to me, is that of having totally omitted one of the items of the problem, an omission which has made the problem so much easier that it may almost be described as a short cut to a solution. The question is whether it be a fair cut. M. de Maupassant has simply skipped the whole reflective part of his men and women—that reflective part which governs conduct and produces character. He may say that he does not see it, does not know it; to which the answer is, "So much the better for you, if you wish to describe life without it. The strings you pull are by so much the less numerous, and you can therefore pull those that remain with greater promptitude, consequently with greater firmness, with a greater air of knowledge." (pp. 284-85)

The erotic element in M. de Maupassant, about which much more might have been said, seems to me to be explained by the same limitation, and explicable in a similar way wherever else its literature occurs in excess. The carnal side of man appears the most characteristic if you look at it a great deal; and you look at it a great deal if you do not look at the other, at the side by which he reacts against his weaknesses, his defeats. . . . Let us not be alarmed at this prodigy (though prodigies are alarming) of M. de Maupassant, who is at once so licentious and so impeccable, but gird ourselves up with the conviction that another point of view will yield another perfection. (pp. 286-87)

Henry James, "Guy de Maupassant," in his Partial Portraits, *Macmillan and Co., Limited, 1888, pp. 243-87.*

LEO TOLSTOY (essay date 1898)

[*Tolstoy is regarded as one of the greatest novelists of all time. His* Voina i mir (War and Peace) *and* Anna Karenini (Anna Karenina) *are considered all-encompassing documents of the human condition and outstanding examples of the realistic novel. In the excerpt below, Tolstoy posits that Maupassant lacks one of the most important elements indispensable to a work of art: morality. However, he notes that as Maupassant matured as an artist, his stories took on a growing sense of moral concern, and he claims that in his later years Maupassant abandoned the sensual life.*]

[Maupassant] possessed that special gift, called genius, which consists in the faculty of intense, strenuous attention, applied, according to the author's tastes, to this or that subject; and by means of which the possessor of this capacity sees the things to which he applies his attention in some new aspect overlooked by others. This gift of seeing what others do not see was evidently possessed by Maupassant. But, to judge by the little volume I read [***La Maison Tellier***], he was unfortunately destitute of the chief of the three qualifications which, in addition to genius, are indispensable to a true work of art. These are: (1) A correct, that is, a moral, relation of the author to his subject; (2) perspicuity or beauty of expression (the two are identical); and (3) sincerity, *i.e.*, an unfeigned feeling of love or hatred to the subject depicted. Of these three Maupassant possessed only the last two, and was utterly without the first. He had not a correct, that is, a moral, relation to the subjects he described.

Judging by what I read, I came to the conclusion that Maupassant possessed genius, that gift of attention revealing in the objects and facts of life properties not perceived by others; that he possessed a beautiful form of expression, uttering clearly, simply, and with charm what he wished to say; and that he possessed also the merit of sincerity, without which a work of art produces no effect, that is, he did not merely pretend to love or hate, but did indeed love or hate what he described. But, unhappily, being destitute of the first and perhaps most important qualification for a work of art, of a correct, moral relation to what he described—that is, lacking a knowledge of the difference between good and evil—he loved and described that which he should not have loved and described, and did not love that which he should have loved and described. Thus, in this little volume, the author described with great minuteness and fondness how women seduce men, and men women; he even, as in **"La Femme de Paul,"** referred to certain obscenities difficult to understand. And not only with indifference, but even with contempt, he described the country labouring people as he would animals.

This ignorance of the distinction between good and evil is especially striking in the story, **"Une Partie de Campagne."** In this, as a most charming and amusing joke, is related a minute account of how two gentlemen, rowing with bare arms in a boat, seduced at the same time, one of them an elderly mother, the other a young girl, her daughter.

The sympathy of the author is evidently all the time so much on the side of these two villains, that he, I will not say ignores, but simply does not see what must have been experienced by the seduced mother and maiden daughter, by the father, and by the young man evidently engaged to the daughter. And, therefore, we not only have the revolting description of a disgusting crime represented as an amusing joke, but, moreover, the event itself is described falsely, in that only one side of the subject is presented, and that the most insignificant one, namely, the pleasure taken by the scoundrels.

In this same little volume there is a story, **"Histoire d'une Fille de Ferme,"** which was specially recommended to me by Tourgenief, and which specially displeased me by again this incorrect relation of the author to his subject. He evidently sees in all the working folk whom he describes, only animals rising no higher than sexual and maternal love, and therefore his descriptions produce an impression of incompleteness and artificiality.

Lack of understanding of the life and interests of the working people, and the representation of them as semibrutes moved only by sensuality, spite, and greed, constitute two of the greatest and most serious deficiencies of most of the latest French authors, and, in their number, of Maupassant, who, not only in this story, but in all those others in which he treats of the people, always describes them as coarse, dull animals at whom one can only laugh. (pp. 2-5)

So repugnant to me were the stories, **"Une Partie de Campagne," "La Femme de Paul,"** and **"L'histoire d'une Fille de Ferme,"** that I did not then remark the pretty story, **"Le Papa de Simon,"** and the story, excellent in its description of the night, **"Sur l'eau."** (p. 6)

[With] the exception of the first two (strictly speaking, excepting only the first one), all the novels of Maupassant, as novels, are weak; and had Maupassant left us only these, he would have been merely a remarkable illustration of how a brilliant genius may perish on account of the abnormal society in which it is developed and those false theories about art which are invented by people who do not love art and therefore do not understand it. But, fortunately, Maupassant wrote short stories in which he did not subject himself to the false theory he had accepted; writing, not *"quelque chose de beau,"* but what touched or revolted his moral feeling. And in these stories (not in all, but in the best of them), it is observable how this moral feeling grew in the author, and how by degrees, and unconsciously, that which formerly constituted the chief meaning and happiness of his life was for him dethroned and assessed at its true value. (p. 25)

A powerful moral growth in the author during his literary activity, is written in indelible letters in these exquisite short stories, and in his best book, **"Sur l'eau."**

Not only in this dethronement of sexual love (involuntary, and therefore so much the more complete) is this moral growth of the author seen; it is seen in all those increasingly higher moral demands which he applies to life.

Not in sexual love alone does he see the innate contradiction between the demands of the animal and rational man; he sees it in all the organisation of the world.

He sees that the world as it is, the material world, is not only not the best of worlds, but, on the contrary, might be quite different, (this idea is wonderfully expressed in **"Horla"**), and that it does not satisfy the demands of reason and love; he sees that there is some other world, or at least, the demand for such another world in the soul of man.

He is tormented, not only by the unreasonableness of the material world and its ugliness, but by its unlovingness, its disunity. I do not know a more heartrending cry of despair from a strayed man feeling his loneliness, than the expression of this idea in that most exquisite story, **"Solitude."**

The thing that most tormented Maupassant, to which he returns many times, is the painful state of loneliness, spiritual loneliness, of man; of that bar which stands between man and his fellows; a bar which, as he says, is the more painfully felt, the nearer the bodily connection.

What then, torments him, and what would he have? What will destroy this bar? What suppress this loneliness? Love. Not that love of woman, a love with which he is disgusted; but pure, spiritual, divine love.

And it is that which Maupassant seeks; it is towards this saviour of life long ago plainly disclosed to man, that he painfully strives amid those fetters in which he feels himself bound. (pp. 27-8)

Maupassant attained that tragic moment in life when commenced the struggle between the falsehood of the life about him and the true life of which he began to be conscious. The first throes of spiritual birth had already commenced in him.

And it is these anguishes of birth that he expressed in his best work, especially in his short stories.

Had it been his, not to die in the anguish of birth, but to be born, he would have given us great instructive works; but, as it is, what he has given us in his birth struggle is much. Let us therefore be thankful to this powerful, truthful man for what he has given us. (p. 32)

Leo Tolstoy, in his Guy de Maupassant. *Translated by V. Tcherkoff, 1898. Reprint by Haskell House Publishers Ltd., 1974, 32 p.*

JOSEPH CONRAD (essay date 1904)

[Conrad was born and raised in Poland and later resided in England. A major novelist, he is considered an innovator of novel structure as well as one of the finest stylists of modern English literature. In the excerpt below, taken from his 1904 introduction to Yvette and Other Stories, *Conrad discusses the nature of Maupassant's artistic vision, stressing the truthfulness of his art and defending him against charges of cynicism and immorality.]*

To introduce Maupassant to English readers with apologetic explanations as though his art were recondite and the tendency of his work immoral would be a gratuitous impertinence.

Maupassant's conception of his art is such as one would expect from a practical and resolute mind; but in the consummate simplicity of his technique it ceases to be perceptible. This is one of its greatest qualities, and like all the great virtues it is based primarily on self-denial. (p. 25)

We are at liberty . . . to quarrel with Maupassant's attitude towards our world in which, like the rest of us, he has that share which his senses are able to give him. But we need not quarrel with him violently. If our feelings (which are tender) happen to be hurt because his talent is not exercised for the praise and consolation of mankind, our intelligence (which is great) should let us see that he is a very splendid sinner, like all those who in this valley of compromises err by over-devotion to the truth that is in them. His determinism, barren of praise, blame and consolation, has all the merit of his conscientious art. (pp. 25-6)

The interest of a reader in a work of imagination is either ethical or that of simple curiosity. Both are perfectly legitimate, since there is both a moral and an excitement to be found in a faithful rendering of life. And in Maupassant's work there is the interest of curiosity and the moral of a point of view consistently preserved and never obtruded for the end of personal gratification. The spectacle of this immense talent served by exceptional faculties and triumphing over the most thankless subjects by an unswerving singleness of purpose is in itself an admirable lesson in the power of artistic honesty, one may say of artistic virtue. The inherent greatness of the man consists in this, that he will let none of the fascinations that beset a writer working in loneliness turn him away from the straight path, from the vouchsafed vision of excellence. He will not be led into perdition by the seductions of sentiment, of eloquence, of humour, of pathos. . . . This is not to say that Maupassant's austerity has never faltered; but the fact remains that no tempting demon has ever succeeded in hurling him down from his high, if narrow, pedestal.

It is the austerity of his talent, of course, that is in question. Let the discriminating reader, who at times may well spare a moment or two to the consideration and enjoyment of artistic excellence, be asked to reflect a little upon the texture of . . . **"A Piece of String,"** and **"A Sale."** How many openings the last offers for the gratuitous display of the author's wit or clever buffoonery, the first for an unmeasured display of sentiment! And both sentiment and buffoonery could have been made very good too, in a way accessible to the meanest intelligence, at the cost of truth and honesty. Here it is where Maupassant's austerity comes in. He refrains from setting his cleverness against the eloquence of the facts. There is humour and pathos in these stories; but such is the greatness of his talent, the refinement of his artistic conscience, that all his high qualities appear inherent in the very things of which he speaks, as if they had been altogether independent of his presentation. Facts, and again facts are his unique concern. That is why he is not always properly understood. His facts are so perfectly rendered that, like the actualities of life itself, they demand from the reader the faculty of observation which is rare, the power of appreciation which is generally wanting in most of us who are guided mainly by empty phrases requiring no effort, demanding from us no qualities except a vague susceptibility to emotion. . . . Now, Maupassant, of whom it has been said that he is the master of the *mot juste,* has never been a dealer in words. His wares have been, not glass beads, but polished gems: not the most rare and precious, perhaps, but of the very first water of their kind.

That he took trouble with his gems, taking them up in the rough and polishing each facet patiently, the publication of the two posthumous volumes of short stories proves abundantly. I think it proves also the assertion made here that he was by no means a dealer in words. On looking at the first feeble drafts from which so many perfect stories have been fashioned, one discovers that what has been matured, improved, brought to perfection by unwearied endeavour is not the diction of the tale, but the vision of its true shape and detail. (pp. 27-8)

Maupassant's renown is universal, but his popularity is restricted. It is not difficult to perceive why. Maupassant is an intensely national writer. He is so intensely national in his logic, in his clearness, in his aesthetic and moral conceptions, that he has been accepted by his countrymen without having had to pay the tribute of flattery either to the nation as a whole, or to any class, sphere or division of the nation. The truth of his art tells with an irresistible force; and he stands excused from the duty of patriotic posturing. He is a Frenchman of Frenchmen beyond question or cavil, and with that he is simple enough to be universally comprehensible. What is wanting to his universal success is the mediocrity of an obvious and appealing tenderness. He neglects to qualify his truth with the drop of facile sweetness; he forgets to strew paper roses over the tombs. The disregard of these common decencies lays him open to the charges of cruelty, cynicism, hardness. And yet it can be safely affirmed that this man wrote from the fulness of a compassionate heart. He is merciless and yet gentle with his mankind; he does not rail at their prudent fears and their small artifices; he does not despise their labours. It seems to me that he looks with an eye of profound pity upon their troubles, deceptions and misery. But he looks at them all. He sees—and does not turn away his head. As a matter of fact he is courageous. (p. 29)

It cannot be denied that he thinks very little. In him extreme energy of perception achieves great results, as in men of action the energy of force and desire. His view of intellectual problems is perhaps more simple than their nature warrants; still a man who has written **"Yvette"** cannot be accused of want of subtlety. But one cannot insist enough upon this, that his subtlety, his humour, his grimness, though no doubt they are his own, are never presented otherwise but as belonging to our life, as found in nature, whose beauties and cruelties alike breathe the spirit of serene unconsciousness. (p. 30)

Maupassant was a true and dutiful lover of our earth. He says himself in one of his descriptive passages: *"Nous autres que séduit la terre . . ."*. It was true. The earth had for him a compelling charm. He looks upon her august and furrowed face with the fierce insight of real passion. His is the power of detecting the one immutable quality that matters in the changing aspects of nature and under the evershifting surface of life. To say that he could not embrace in his glance all its magnificence and all its misery is only to say that he was human. He lays claim to nothing that his matchless vision has not made his own. This creative artist has the true imagination; he never condescends to invent anything; he sets up no empty pretences. And he stoops to no littleness in his art—least of all to the miserable vanity of a catching phrase. (p. 31)

Joseph Conrad, "Guy de Maupassant," in his Notes on Life and Letters, *Doubleday, Page & Company, 1921, pp. 25-31.*

BENEDETTO CROCE **(essay date 1922)**

[*Croce was an Italian philosopher, historian, editor, and literary critic who wrote during the first half of the twentieth century. According to Croce, the only proper form of literary history is the* caratteristica, *or critical characterization, of the poetic personality and work of a single artist; its goal is to demonstrate the unity of the author's intention, its expression in the creative work, and the reader's response. In the following excerpt from an essay first published in 1922 in the* London Mercury, *he describes Maupassant as "ingenuous" and discusses the short stories in this context, touching also upon the lyricism of Maupassant's style.*]

If any one of modern poets especially deserve the title of "ingenuous" poet, that one seems to me to be the most Parisian, liberal, malicious, jesting, sarcastic story writer, Guy de Maupassant.

He is ingenuous and innocent in his own way, as one without any suspicion of what is called human spirituality or rationality, faith in the true, in purity of the will, in the austerity of duty, the religious conception of life, of the moral struggles and intellectual conflicts, by means of which those ideals develop and maintain themselves. He is all sense—he suffers and enjoys,—suffering far more than he enjoys,—only as sense. (p. 344)

It may be said of Maupassant that his view of reality is the precise opposite of the religious view, which is consciousness of union with all other beings and with God, of communion with the Whole. God is absent from his world of pleasure and of pain of pleasure: true, a form of the extraordinary and portentous does sometimes appear there, but it is altogether a natural phenomenon, consisting of strange fears and wanderings of mind, of hallucinations, of incubi, of the portentousness of madness, which always threatens.

But the contracted heart of Maupassant does frequently become distended and softened in a sort of dolorous calm or calm dolorousness, a feeling of pity, of a pity that is without justice or redemption, because justice and redemption are linked with the moral consciousness, and his pity is due, on the contrary, to sympathy, to vibration in tune with the vibration of others, and is also sensuality, but of the tenderest quality, which weeps over others as over itself. It is a lament inspired by the infinitude of human misery. . . . (pp. 348-49)

The pity is spontaneous and effective: it is not sought or provoked, and the laugh too is spontaneous, another form of reaction momentarily calming. This laughter sometimes alternates with pity, as in **"Boule de suif,"** sometimes with an ironical feeling for things, as in the **"Maison Tellier"** or the **"Pain maudit"**; at other times it has a tinge of contempt, as in certain parts of *Bel Ami,* and the stories of **"L'Héritage"** and **"En famille."** But in many other cases it is simple, frank hilarity, as in certain stories dealing with Norman customs (**"Le lapin," "L'aveu"**), in some dealing with war (**"L'aventure de Walter Schnafs"**), in the making fun of masonic stupidity (**"Mon oncle Sosthène"**) or of the English who infest the hotels (**"Nos Anglais"**), in certain erotic adventures (**"Les Épingles," "Décoré," "Bombard," "Les tombales,"** and the like), or bizarre (**"En wagon," "Boitelle"**). (p. 351)

Ingenuous and candid in his hedonism, in his amoralism, in his irreligion, in his tears and in his laughter, he cannot and does not make any claim either before others or before himself to sociological, evangelical or ethical reforms. Indeed, ethical-historical reality remains extraneous to him to such an extent that for him it can hardly be said to exist, so much so that on the rare occasions when he does refer to it, he gives proof of his obtuseness for that aspect of the world, as when he talks of war, which to him seems to be nothing but ferocious human stupidity. . . . Exquisite in his sense for form, Maupassant was very slightly preoccupied with the technical side of composition, he was ''literary'' only to a very small extent.

His artistic activity arose from an abundance of feeling and experience, which had been maturing within him between 1870 and 1880, bursting forth in an impetuous torrent during the following decade, now shining in the sun in the silver streamlets of his most limpid stories, now assembling itself in the broad lakes of his novels, or breaking its banks and almost losing itself in the hundreds of brooks and becks of the short tales, the anecdotes, the diversions. Sometimes in this wide and rapid course appears the vice of superabundant power, which is regardless of waste. This may be observed in the over great length of some of his stories in respect of their artistic motive, and its opposite in the excessive brevity and too summary treatment of certain little sketches and anecdotes, which bear traces of journalistic improvisation, or indulge the taste of readers for the salacious. He usually attains to perfection in the stories of moderate complexity. But Maupassant never once falls into the artificial or empty in these ups and downs of artistic intensity. Hardly anything of his lacks the imprint of artistic talent, however slight or trifling it may seem. He never once allows himself to be oppressed and suffocated by external observation and by the accumulation of details, or follows abstract schemes.

He was a poet, far more of a poet in his prose narrative than in his verse, employed in early youth, but abandoned later. Everyone who knows admires the altogether poetical form of such stories as . . . **''Le Port,''** where not one word, nor rhythm, nor inflexion of voice but converges to the final and total effect. (pp. 352-54)

Maupassant's stories are lyrical stories, not because they are written with emphasis and lyricism (things of which they show themselves to be altogether free), but because the lyric is really intrinsic to the form of the narrative, and shapes each part of it, without mixtures and without leaving any residue. In like manner those parts which are pointed to as especially lyrical, in the rhetorical sense of the word, never separate themselves from the narrative and discursive tone of prose, and speaking thus simply, gradually accelerate the rhythm, and rise spontaneously to poetry. (pp. 354-55)

And Maupassant, because he is a poet, although he kows nothing but matter and sense, and portrays nothing but the obscure tremblings of matter and the spasms of the senses, yet employs so much objective truth in his portrayal, that he makes present the ethical ideal, by means of pain, pity and displeasure; by means of the comical and laughter, the superiority of the sagacious intelligence; by means of desolation and desperation, the claim of religion. I see quite clearly why Tolstoi separated him at once from all the French artists of his time and held him to be moral in spite of appearances [see excerpt dated 1898]. He is moral in his results, and his most audacious tales leave behind them an impression of purity, just because, as has been said, he is a poet. He distinguishes himself and emerges from the company of his contemporaries and compatriots, the Zolas, Daudets and their like, themselves endowed with noteworthy qualities and possessors of certain artistic forms, but not fundamentally and essentially poetical like him. Such he truly was born, pouring forth poetry with potent facility and consuming his short life. He entered and left the literary world (as he himself one day remarked when he was already infirm and meditating suicide) ''like a meteor.'' (pp. 357-58)

Benedetto Croce, ''Maupassant,'' in his European Literature in the Nineteenth Century, *translated by Douglas Ainslie, Alfred A. Knopf, 1924, pp. 344-58.*

ERNEST GEORGE ATKIN (essay date 1927)

[In the excerpt below, Atkin explores the supernatural in several of Maupassant's short stories.]

There is much appearance of paradox in linking the supernatural with the name of this arch-realist [Maupassant], the supremely objective artist in that nineteenth-century French school which found common inspiration in a materialistic philosophy or naturalistic view of life. Maupassant's supernaturalism has been obscured by his naturalism, somewhat as Balzac's short stories have been overshadowed by the imposing mass of his novels, or Zola's romantic tales by his larger, naturalistic creations. And for other reasons which will presently appear, Maupassant's stories of supernatural fear have not been accorded due attention and estimation, whether in relation to his personality, or to his work in general, or again, independently and for their intrinsic value as his contribution to a special *genre*.

Really, I believe, neither paradox nor derogation from his prevailing standards is evidenced by these productions. So far from showing Maupassant in contradiction with himself, they bear a strict relation to a phase of his personality that is not at all inconsistent with his more familiar aspects. And where a less gifted realist might have been driven to compromise between reality and supernatural effect, Maupassant has made no compromise, whether in conception or in technique. (pp. 185-86)

The traditional marvelous of literature had its ultimate roots in the superstitious beliefs of the past. Advancing science pushed those beliefs further and further into the background; with every step, the existence of the *genre* which dealt in the genuine supernatural was made more precarious. But the old fear—man's age-long dread of incalculable forces with immeasurable capacity for harm—has survived belief in the supernatural and lives on today. If science has not done away with all mysteries, still less does reason banish the sense of mystery; least of all do modern nerves and imaginations rule out fear from the presence of the mysterious. Whether we think of this susceptibility as something innate and ineradicable, or as something from which we shall not escape so long as the ultimate essence of things is a mystery, or as something merely which has been lodged in our imaginations by oral and literary tradition, the susceptibility and the thrill are undoubted facts of experience. Maupassant, then, seizes on this survival as valuable art-material, and with its aid brings about a notable modernization of supernatural fiction. Admirable in itself, his rendering of the fear of the incomprehensible appears no less remarkable as an adaptation of art to altered conditions. The demand, at the moment, for more realism in every branch of literature pressed with peculiar force upon the supernatural *genre*. To meet the requirement in spite of the rationally restricted scope of supernaturalism, to add more realism without corresponding loss of the unique emotional effect which is of the story's essence—this was a difficult feat, and a hazardous one for an extreme realist to attempt. That Maupassant successfully achieved such a *tour de force* by means of the artistic objectification of his conception of "true fear," is a view which calls for substantiation in some detail, since . . . the stories of fear have not usually been regarded in this light by his critics. (pp. 194-95)

Maupassant's problem was severely conditioned by the prime requirement—the harmonizing of realism with uncanny suggestion. Even so, his principle of fear was broad enough to allow considerable latitude in respect to material or treatment. Stated somewhat abstractly, his case was this: he had at his disposal two highly variable quantities, represented by "ce qu'on ne comprend pas" and "la vraie peur" respectively; he might vary his portrayal of either at will, subject solely to a kind of inverse proportion between realism and suggestion. (p. 195)

The story **"Sur l'eau,"** despite its revelation of a gruesome secret, has but a slight plot. A man spends a night alone in his boat on the Seine, because he is unable for some reason to pull up his anchor. A growing sense of some mysterious force at work develops through the hours into an agony of fear, until morning, when two passing fishermen come to his aid. When they finally manage to raise the anchor, they find it fastened to the corpse of an old woman. (p. 197)

The portrayal of fear in **"Sur l'eau"** is reinforced and heightened with traits of nightmare experience and of the abnormal imaginings induced by drink, and with unearthly descriptions of the surroundings. Through the skilful blending of atmosphere and psychological realism, the story secures a striking emotional effect.

In **"La Peur"** of 1882, the narrator relates two adventures which exemplify his notion of true fear. . . . In both of his experiences the cause of his fear was for the time incomprehensible, while attendant circumstances bore in upon his senses and imagination the irresistible contagion of supernatural terror. (p. 199)

A conspicuous trait of the second account in **"La Peur"** is the *dramatization,* to a greater degree than in the first episode or in **"Sur l'eau,"** of the impressionistic factor which is, as the title suggests, the real nucleus of the narrative. There is, to be sure, impressionism of the usual sort (though without romantic emphasis) in the preliminary atmosphere of the setting—a storm-lashed forest and a ranger's lonely cabin, at night. But the impressionism which deserves special attention is to be found elsewhere, incorporated as action proper—a series of stimuli and emotional reactions whereby the seasoned adventurer, who has never known fear in real danger, is gradually forced to relax his hold on the distinction between reality and unreality, and to become a prey at last to the authentic ghostly thrill. (pp. 199-200)

"La Peur," demonstrating the power of supernatural suggestion over a stout heart and a skeptical mind, makes the reader himself become partner to its demonstration—the best possible tribute to the story's artistry. Yet this suggestiveness has been obtained by realistic means. Irrespective of the final "explanation" on physical grounds, we are from the beginning never conscious of a departure from reality on the part of the author. Given his realistic conception of fear, there can be no question of bidding for our assent to something frankly supernatural; no question either, in a dramatization of this fear, of resorting to the indirect, subjective appeal of frequent *mots d'auteur*—that impressionistic device familiar in Daudet, for instance. Objective without the tangible horrors on which Poe is fond of dwelling, **"La Peur"** is also without the emotionalism conspicuous in many of the latter's tales.

Dramatized emotion, again, is the main structural feature of **"L'Auberge."** The story further resembles **"Sur l'eau"** and **"La Peur,"** actually combining traits from both. The solitary wildness of scene in the second episode of **"La Peur"** is matched, in **"L'Auberge,"** by a wintry Alpine wilderness and an inn which is cut off from the world during half the year by snow. . . . In the present story, the author speaks from the "omniscient" standpoint, not through another person as narrator. Either method, in Maupassant's hands, yields a realistic effect. (pp. 201-02)

The dramatization of fear in **"Sur l'eau," "La Peur"** and **"L'Auberge"** imparts objective consistency and convincing realism to a supernatural that is primarily atmospheric and psychological. In **"Apparition,"** the supernatural motive is more tangible and circumstantial, more dramatic in the ordinary sense. Instead of embodying the successive stages of gradually mounting emotion, **"Apparition"** unfolds a tale of mysterious adventure to its formidable culmination, and introduces at this climactic point the participant-narrator's description of his sudden shock of terror. The swift reflex is rendered, appropriately, by the massing of graphic psychological details in a few sentences; the drama of fear is presented in miniature—a scene within the larger drama of mystery. . . . Evidently, Maupassant planned something different from the cumulative emotional effect which was his objective in **"Sur l'eau"** and our other examples of that type: his mysterious situation was designed to provoke a more than ordinary curiosity, a supersensitive awareness in which suspense should be strongly tinged with fear. It is also apparent that, while he has varied the patterns of the two types in obedience to different preconceived effects, he has conformed his procedure in each case to realistic requirements, and has created an irresistibly realistic impression.

A third type of story, being largely introspective, is *psychological* drama in a much stricter sense than the other two types. There is here, as in **"Apparition,"**a mysterious happening which presents itself with dramatic suddenness and is so abnormal as to seem supernatural. However, the occurrence does not constitute the climax of the narrative as it does in **"Apparition"**; it is placed early in the story, and serves to motivate the narrator's intimate confession and analysis of his fears and thoughts; he writes in the shadow of his experience, in the dread of a menacing Unknown which he feels is still near. **"Lui?"** and **"Le Horla"**may be cited as good specimens of this introspective type. (pp. 202-04)

"Le Horla" develops a psychology of supernaturalism commensurate with the utmost emotional and logical scope of the author's idea of fear. The helpless narrator of **"Lui?"** knowing that he did not exist, yet unable to reason himself out of the fear that would assail him when he was alone, felt that his only salvation lay in companionship. The "halluciné raisonnant" of [**"Le Horla"**] pushes his feverish analysis to a point where subjective manifestations become, to his distraught mind, objective proof of the existence and the unseen presence of a Being with superhuman powers. And with the discovery that he is dominated by the tyrannous "Horla" comes the crushing realization that his own existence—in time all human existence even—is doomed; suicide alone will release him. The successive stages of his introspection are more numerous and more searching than in **"Lui?."** They deal with his fear in connection with nightmare, somnambulism, hypnotism and hallucination; the brooding fear that he may be going mad compels self-examination and an analysis of madness; refusing to believe that his senses have deceived him, he makes a supreme effort to reconcile the mysterious manifestations with the laws of reason and nature; he inquires into the cause of all supernatural beliefs and fears. As he surveys the mass of traditional superstitions, he sees in all these inventions the straining of human intelligence to penetrate a mysterious Unknown, to comprehend an unseen Presence of which men have always been conscious. . . . The nature of the thing called the Horla is, by definition, unknowable in any ordinary sense, and must therefore continue to terrify. The terror is greater than that of **"Lui?"** because the mystery is greater. The half-materialized phantom of that story was directly traceable to an hallucination. The Horla, less tangible but endowed with a more formidable personality, is symbolic not of a particular mystery like hallucination but of the mysteriousness of universal, ultimate reality—the reality that lies beyond the reach of our perception. In the light of Maupassant's previous supernaturalism, this impressive creation is clearly nothing less than the imaginative concrete personification of his abstract Unknown, of his *"ce qu'on ne comprend pas"* in its widest signification. (pp. 205-07)

According to expert testimony, both Poe and Maupassant are scientifically accurate in their analysis of fear. But, over and above accuracy of analysis, there can be little question that Maupassant's portrayal goes beyond Poe's in its extraordinary fusion of subtle uncanny suggestion with the strictest *vraisemblance*. Poe's supernaturalism, when realistic, is too apt to make its appeal to terror through repulsive details, through fulsome descriptions of physical horror rather than fearsome suggestion. With full awareness of the grosser aspects of Maupassant's naturalism in general, one may say that his stories in this special field contain far less that pertains to bodily corruption and the graveyard than those of Poe, far more of "the shudder at the veiled Unknown." (p. 209)

[My study of Maupassant] is meant to suggest the realist more than the naturalist; but one who is not content with the revelation, afforded by his marvelous perceptive powers, of all the teeming reality in the life about him; who, although he may be aware of the peril involved, bends his gaze none the less keenly toward the confines of Reality itself, fascinated by the "veiled Unknown." Such a man, assuredly, is not to be dismissed simply as *morbid*. Nor is it morbid on his part to become impatient of the restriction, or even afraid of that which baffles his scrutiny. Realist that he is, he analyzes his fear: it is the same, in essence, as the supernatural terror which is as old as humanity. He formulates its meaning in a simple realistic principle: "true fear" is the fear of the unknown. Artist also that he is, he sees its fictional possibilities, which are not conditioned on superstitious belief either real or assumed, but flow directly from the fact that this "reminiscence of fantastic terror" lives on in our imagination and thus may be imaginatively evoked. If his stories of fear may, in a limited sense, be said to represent the capitalization of his own experience, they are, more truly still, the dramatization of an emotion to which none of us can claim to be wholly a stranger and immune. In technique, they are thoroughly realistic; they are founded upon a realistic conception of supernatural terror, the situations are honestly motivated, and the psychology of fear is objectified in scenes which are remarkable for their truthfulness and force. With but few exceptions, this whole group of fictions measures up to the level of Maupassant's gifts as a story-teller. From another viewpoint, finally, we must give credit to Maupassant for his share in revitalizing a *genre* which was threatened, if not with actual destruction, with serious danger of becoming an anachronism.

Thus it appears that the phrase which at first glance seemed like a contradiction in terms. . . . the *supernaturalism* of *Maupassant!*. . . . is no paradox after all, but designates something real and valuable in this great artist's personality and his work. (pp. 219-20)

Ernest George Atkin, "The Supernaturalism of Maupassant," in PMLA, *42, Vol. XLII, No. 1, March 1927, pp. 185-220.*

VIRGINIA WOOLF (essay date 1929)

[An English novelist, essayist, and short story writer, Woolf is a preeminent twentieth-century author. Her works, noted for their subjective explorations of characters' inner lives and their delicate poetic quality, have had a lasting effect on the art of the novel. She was a discerning and influential essayist as well as a novelist. Her critical writings, termed "creative, appreciative, and subjective" by Barbara Currier Bell and Carol Ohmann, cover a wide range of literature and comprise some of her finest prose. In the excerpt below, Woolf discusses Maupassant's realism.]

In English fiction there are a number of writers who gratify our sense of belief—Defoe, Swift, Trollope, Borrow, W. E. Norris, for example; among the French, one thinks instantly of Maupassant. Each of them assures us that things are precisely as they say they are. What they describe happens actually before our eyes. We get from their novels the same sort of refreshment and delight that we get from seeing something actually happen in the street below. (p. 124)

Above all, Maupassant is the most promising at the moment, for Maupassant enjoys the great advantage that he writes in French. Not from any merit of his own, he gives us that little fillip which we get from reading a language whose edges have not been smoothed for us by daily use. The very sentences shape themselves in a way that is definitely charming. The words tingle and sparkle. As for English, alas, it is *our* language—shop-worn, not so desirable, perhaps. Moreover, each of these compact little stories has its pinch of gunpowder, artfully placed so as to explode when we tread on its tail. The last words are always highly charged. Off they go, *bang*, in our faces and there is lit up for us in one uncompromising glare someone with his hand lifted, someone sneering, someone turning his back, someone catching an omnibus, as if this insignificant action, whatever it may be, summed up the whole situation forever.

The reality that Maupassant brings before us is always one of the body, of the senses—the ripe flesh of a servant girl, for example, or the succulence of food. . . . It is all concrete; it is all visualized. It is a world, then, in which one can believe with one's eyes and one's nose and one's senses; nevertheless, it is a world which secretes perpetually a little drop of bitterness. Is this all? And, if this is all, is it enough? Must we, then, believe this? So we ask. Now that we are given truth unadorned, a disagreeable sensation seems attached to it, which we must analyze before we go further.

Suppose that one of the conditions of things as they are is that they are unpleasant, have we strength enough to support that unpleasantness for the sake of the delight of believing in it? Are we not shocked somehow by *Gulliver's Travels* and **"Boule de Suif"** and **"La Maison Tellier?"** Shall we not always be trying to get round the obstacle of ugliness by saying that

Maupassant and his like are narrow, cynical and unimaginative when, in fact, it is their truthfulness that we resent—the fact that leeches suck the naked legs of servant girls, that there are brothels, that human nature is fundamentally cold, selfish, corrupt? This discomfort at the disagreeableness of truth is one of the first things that shakes very lightly our desire to believe. Our Anglo-Saxon blood, perhaps, has given us an instinct that truth is, if not exactly beautiful, at least pleasant or virtuous to behold. (p. 126)

Virginia Woolf, "Phases of Fiction," in The Bookman, *New York, Vol. LXIX, No. 2, April, 1929, pp. 123-32.*

MAUPASSANT CRITICISM IN FRANCE: 1880-1940 **(essay date 1938-41)**

[Maupassant Criticism in France: 1880-1940 *is a major study by Artine Artinian, a noted Maupassant scholar and bibliographer. While he was preparing his book, he wrote to many of the premier writers of the day—American, English, and European—asking them to discuss the importance and influence of Maupassant on their work. The following series of excerpts is taken from the responses he received.*]

SHERWOOD ANDERSON (1938)

I have your very interesting letter about Maupassant and having received it I have been trying to think out my attitude. To tell you the truth I cannot say how much Maupassant I have read. At one time I read and liked him a very great deal but later my admiration rather waned. I came to feel that Maupassant had asserted a tremendous influence on the American short story, that for example, our Mr. O'Henry stemmed directly from him but that on the whole the influence was not good. I have felt that what I think of as the plot short story—I almost said the trick short story—came from this influence. It seemed to me that Maupassant was very, very insistent upon technique and that in this insistence upon technique, the human element often pretty much got lost.

I am glad to write you about this but as I said in the beginning it is a matter that I may not have thought through and as I also said, I have not read Maupassant for a long time now. I did, however, come to have the feeling suggested here and I am giving it to you for what you may think it is worth. (pp. 129-30).

GERTRUDE ATHERTON (1941)

It is a good many years since I read Guy de Maupassant's stories—it being all one can do to keep up with current books—but I have a very clear recollection of their clarity, conciseness, drama, often unexpected climax and beauty of style. With all that—to say nothing of his characterization and the fact that he had interesting stories to tell—I don't see how he can fail to hold a high and permanent place in the history of letters. I should say it is quite certain that many young writers read, study, and do their best to imitate him. He has fathered a large brood.

One of these "some days" I shall read him again.

ERSKINE CALDWELL (1938)

I have read a handful of Maupassant in translation, and I'm sure I'm all the better for it. It is my belief that there could be no substitute for Maupassant, and consequently his work will always be among the essential items in the catalog of literature.

HENRY SEIDEL CANBY (1938)

I think you may safely state that Maupassant had a most extraordinary influence upon young Americans who like myself were trying to write short stories in the early nineteen hundreds. He is widely read, widely imitated, and extremely influential in establishing the type of short story which was successful for so many years.

THEODORE DREISER [taken from a letter from his secretary] (1938)

Mr. Dreiser has your letter with regard to Maupassant and has asked me to answer it. He has read a great deal of Maupassant, in English, and considers him one of the world's great writers. He feels that Maupassant is too much neglected today, and that he has had far more influence with modern writers, especially with those who write popular magazine stories, than is generally recognized. He feels that this influence has not been of great value, however, inasmuch as these newer writers have tried to imitate Maupassant's tone, and have missed his peculiar insight and emotional sincerity.

JAMES T. FARRELL (1938)

I fear that I cannot be of much help to you. I have not read much of de Maupassant in years now, and in order to answer your letter properly, I should have to reread him—which I haven't the time to do. I have always admired his stories, and considered him to have been a master of the short story form—so-called. However, I think that he is a bit cold. His perfection of form and his clarity have, sometimes, impressed me as having been won at the expense of feeling. Personally, I do not believe that your attempt to get opinions of writers of today on de Maupassant is likely to be of much importance in your work. You will undoubtedly get suggestive insights and these will be valuable. However, I believe that more fruitful efforts can be gained from a comparative study on the following lines. A—to make a study, not merely of de Maupassant, but also of his times, and of the immediate past in France out of which he developed. The aim of this study should be to come to a grasp of the tendencies which were at work in that period. B—to consider modern literature in its relationship to and its reflection of modern life. C—to evaluate on the basis of this comparison, how de Maupassant is or is not an influence today in the body of modern writing. This comparative study would demand a consideration of French painting, the class construction of French society, etc. An influence of de Maupassant is undoubtedly to be found in hundreds of short stories, even of writers who may never have read him. The question in part is that of seeking to estimate to what degree French naturalism of the nineteenth century survives as an influence in American writing, and to what degree American realism and naturalism stem from other sources. Further, I think that there is a definite relationship between realism and naturalism in nineteenth century French writing and the eighteenth century French materialists. Naturalism and realism in writing presuppose a materialistic outlook on life, and nineteenth century materialism was predominantly French in its sources. I doubt if de Maupassant has much direct influence in French literature today. . . . I believe that one of the contributions of de Maupassant is his sense of form. There is an orderliness about French writing, a kind of logic and a form which is one of the products of French tradition. De Maupassant's stories are very orderly and cleanly put together. At times, they seem to me so orderly that they are cold. (pp. 145-46)

BRUNO FRANK (1938)

I know, of course, how every writer should read every single line by Guy de Maupassant, and read him in French.

I never cared very much for his novels, not even for the famous ones, like *Fort comme la mort* or *Notre Coeur* (And his early poems are scarcely worth mentioning.) But he always seemed to me the unsurpassed and unsurpassable master of the short story. His incredibly abundant imagination, his deep and acute knowledge of the human soul, his miraculous technique in starting and building up a plot, the vigor and limpidness of his style, make him the lasting model for every short story writer. But among our contemporaries there is, in my opinion, but *one* man whose art (though not his prolificness) can be compared to his. This is Mr. W. Somerset Maugham, the eminent English narrator, who himself, repeatedly and emphatically, professed to be Maupassant's disciple.

F. L. LUCAS (1938)

I have read most of Guy de Maupassant, because I find him (unlike so many distinguished writers) always readable. Literary snobs, no doubt, think the less of him for being thus readable; so much the worse for them. Let them continue to grub in Acrostic Land, or dance on the Steppe with temperamental Slavs.

I have read him in French. A person who cannot read *his* French is hardly literate.

I put him high—which simply means, of course, that, liking him, I think other people ought to. But I like him because he could invent, or steal (I do not care which) so many good plots, and tell them so well; because he has a vast range and variety of characters; because I like his view of life—its frank pessimism, its hate of cruelty and sham—and like also his way of not pushing his view of life at the reader, but leaving it implied between the lines; because his style is good, even for French prose; and because he can make me *see* his scenery.

I do not think he ever wrote anything as supreme as *Madame Bovary*; I don't think he was as subtle and delicate at catching the shades of the soul as his great rival Tchekov; his is the clear French sunlight, with no mists. But one cannot have everything. (pp. 162-63)

HEINRICH MANN (1938)

Guy de Maupassant is an author whom I started to read in his language in my early twenties and whom I have continued to read ever since. His two hundred short stories present a summary of his age as well as a syllabus of its literary tools.

Life and letters have seldom, if ever, attained such complete harmony as they have in his works. He knew that we write because others wrote before us. A dough of words,—so he calls himself and people of his type in the preface to *Pierre et Jean*. That is the discernment of the man who always unerringly described what he saw, portrayed only what had been actually experienced, and remained true to the very end of his life.

He was an heir. For him the prose writers of the century, from Stendhal to Flaubert, had heaped up a treasure; he had to exert himself in order to possess it. He increased it by the gift which none of his predecessors had attained—ease—which, according to Stendhal, is the highest achievement. It certainly is that—*la facilité*—with which a master in his short ten years produces a work such as Maupassant's. (pp. 163-64)

THOMAS MANN (1938)

I will answer your question regarding my attitude toward Maupassant by the following simple statement: I consider the work of this Frenchman immortal in the true sense of the word, and I am convinced that through the ages he will be regarded as one of the greatest masters of the *Novelle* who shine in the entire galaxy of illustrious writers.

WILLIAM SAROYAN (1938)

A strange coincidence: only five days ago I wrote a few paragraphs about Guy de Maupassant. I am attaching what I wrote, which you will see is entitled Guy de Maupassant. This was to have been a short story; I abandoned the work because it began to be an essay and I didn't want to write an essay; but what I have written is valid by itself, essay or no essay, or story or no story.

I will now make specific replies to your questions:

1. I read almost all of Guy de Maupassant's stories as a boy; that is, I discovered him when I was fourteen and went on reading him until I was twenty; at twenty I stopped reading altogether, except fragments of all writers; nothing of any great length; no novels, no books straight through. No time to read; only time to write.

2. I feel very strongly about Guy de Maupassant. I must tell you sincerely that to me he is truly one of the giants not only of literature but of living. I feel personally related to him; that is, to the kind of writer and human being he was. To me even his inferior stories are more important than the works of writers who worked harder but weren't his equal. I have read him only in translation; I understand he has been poorly translated; but even so, I got the message.

These replies are brief, I know; I am not a scholar; I am a writer. I hope this material will do. Will you be good enough to return the piece I am attaching when you have had a copy made? And please ask anything more you like; I shall be pleased to try to answer your questions. . . .

Guy de Maupassant

The grief I felt as a boy for dumb people whose betrayal by the world I could not fail to see and regret was not articulated for me until I discovered the French writer Guy de Maupassant, who, in one story after another, told me about everything. That discovery took place in the dead of winter, at a time of great stillness within myself, a speechlessness that was the consequence partly of the time of year, the dullness of the city in which I lived, the emptiness and hopelessness of the people, and partly because I was fourteen years old, very poor, friendless, lonely, and desperately eager to understand.

Instead of ending the stillness within myself, the stories intensified and deepened it, and instead of making me happy, they made me even sadder than I had been. It was a sadness of a different order, however, and contained within itself a power and joyousness which I believed to be more important to me than anything else in the world that I might discover, inherit, earn, or steal.

I was grateful that such a man had lived and written, so that in seeking meaning there might be some to find. And I was grateful that I had had the personal good luck of finding Guy de Maupassant. His writing gave me the world, and gave my life a specific beginning which seemed to have some chance of continuing for a while. I knew that he and I were not a great deal different from one another and that what he could do, I could do. I was always a writer; but Guy de Maupassant put me to work in earnest. (pp. 178-79)

FRANK SWINNERTON (1938)

Many thanks for your interesting letter. I am not competent to express any serious opinion upon Guy de Maupassant; but I have read (in French) two of his novels, *Pierre et Jean* and *Une Vie,* while I own and have read (also in French) six or seven volumes of his short stories, containing perhaps seventy-five of them. I have also this year read, for purposes of review, a volume of about thirty stories, translated into English, with which I was unfamiliar. In my opinion he "dates" as a novelist, and in that field is definitely second-rate, owing to deficiency in the power of sustained narrative. But as a writer of short stories he is, at his best, so magnificent as to surpass everything in that kind of writing except the best of Anton Tchekov. Tchekov had, I think, a loftier irony; Maupassant greater power, greater adroitness, greater pungency.

But how impossible to "place" him in world letters! When one thinks of Dante, or Shakespeare, Maupassant shrinks. He won't compare with Blake, or Keats, or Coleridge. He hasn't, really, the size of Tolstoy, or even Balzac or Dickens, whom he more nearly approaches. But in his own line, as a writer of short stories, where art and skill are of more account than vision or grandeur, he pretty well stands by himself; and that is as far as I should be inclined to go without giving the subject far more intense thought than this hasty exchange of letters permits. I hope you will therefore excuse me for not venturing a critical opinion upon this point. (pp. 184-85)

HUGH WALPOLE (1938)

My idea of de Maupassant is that, at his best, he is perfect—in his own way—which is raw, crude, over-coloured. They are stories of a brilliant, observant, gesticulating animal in the Zoo.

When he isn't at his best, he misses badly. The great thing about him is that he taught his successors. And it isn't his fault that a lot of his stories now are faded specimens under rather dusty glass. This is of course my *personal* feeling—not at all dogmatic.

FRANZ WERFEL (1938)

Guy de Maupassant is to me one of the most original writers of all time. He created a new form which had not existed before him, and filled it with an essence which is as voluptuous and dangerous, as crude and tender, as dusky and clear as Nature herself. Only very, very few artists have ever succeeded in achieving that. Maupassant is truly one of the most incorruptible masters of truth. (p. 188)

ARNOLD ZWEIG (1938)

My answer to your interesting question was delayed so long only because I spent several months in Europe, and returned to Palestine only the day before yesterday. But I start now immediately—because of my interest in the subject—to describe to you my relation to Guy de Maupassant.

I had already begun to read his first short stories as a student in Obersekunda. They were translations,—small booklets which I had bought with money earned by myself. In those early years of the century German literature attracted masters of the short form from all languages, short stories of Tchekov and Andrejev, Hamsun and Bang, Kipling and Gogol, and, first of all, Maupassant. My predilection for the short form came undiminished from the fairy tale books of my youth and has continued to this day. I understood instinctively two things: first, that there was mastery in the artistic formation in which Maupassant took everyday material over into his stories. And second, that only that author who was able to handle the short form would master great epic themes. Stories like **"The Barrel," "Boule-de-Suif"** and dozens of others gave me the highest delight for reasons then still quite unclear. Almost at the same time I started to read them in French, and have continued that habit. When getting acquainted with **"Le Horla,"** I may have been a student and beginner of about twenty. I still remember my emotion and admiration. I do not even need to close my eyes to see the white ship passing his country-house from which the strange guest, the split ego, invaded the life of the sick person. From then on I sought for facts about the life Maupassant and the whole group to which he belonged, and found them in the journal of the Goncourts, as far as it had been published by then. This world of great writers included him as the youngest next to Flaubert and Zola. He has remained for me the young writer in the trinity of the late nineteenth century, who was second to none in vigor, artistic ability and insight, and who portrayed an epoch in his short stories as did Rembrandt or Goya in their etchings and drawings. The courage of his morale and the unerringly firm hand with which he caught the unpolished life of his time and his nation and, thereby, of all time and every nation, make him worthy of such great comparisons. His place in universal literature? He stands shoulder to shoulder with the classic masters of the short form, with Boccaccio, Cervantes, H. von Kleist and E. A. Poe. Jack London then became his heir. (pp. 189-90)

T. A. Steinlen's illustration for "Une partie de campagne," originally printed in the Gil-Blas.

STEFAN ZWEIG (1938)

I am delighted indeed that you are writing a more comprehensive study of Guy de Maupassant. For I feel that he is not justly treated in France to-day. Nor do I know of any important critical or biographical work dealing with him,—but that is, perhaps, my fault.

In very early years, I read Maupassant in French. I always measure my impression of authors according to the intensity of the recollections which I have of scenes and figures. That is why I can state sincerely that I have remained faithful to few novelists of modern times as much as I have to him. I always saw the genius of Maupassant in his ability (he has been my model in that to this day) to avoid the superfluous and never to become talkative, boring, rambling or inexact. Other writers would have made novels out of three quarters of his *contes*. They would have expanded the story into the unlimited by descriptions of landscapes, by small talk and mediocre philosophy. But Maupassant had a rather mysterious sense of the right measure. He shows a figure by ten strokes, describes a fate in twenty pages. For that reason he achieves real perfection in two or three dozen small works of art, because in these short stories each line gives as constant and unchangeable an impression as in a poem. I am convinced that his time will come again. Perhaps it is about to come just now, since you feel more and more urgently the need for condensing larger and diffuse works. His tempo belongs to our own, his plastic and realistic way of writing to any generation. He will conquer readers again and again. And he will have us as his disciples and friends, for we admire both his knowledge of the human soul and his power of literary imagination. (pp. 191-92)

Sherwood Anderson and others, "'Inquiry' into the Present Fame of Maupassant in Europe and the United States," in Maupassant Criticism in France: 1880-1940 *by Artine Artinian, 1941. Reprint by Russell & Russell, 1969, pp. 129-92.*

SEAN O'FAOLAIN (essay date 1948)

[*An Irish fiction writer and critic, O'Faolain is considered a master of the short story form. In the excerpt below, he examines Maupassant's subject matter, technique, and approach in his short stories, labelling him a realist.*]

[Maupassant] is the most uncompromising of all the French realists: he presents, that is to say, the more bitter element in French literature and French character with a devastatingly quiet assumption that no other way of regarding life is possible. He does not preach or moralize, or praise, or condemn: he simply presents. His main quality is persuasiveness combined with chilliness. He is so cold that even if we feel that he is being hateful we cannot be angry; we can only laugh uncomfortably without even the comfort of feeling that he responds with a smile, since, if that stolid Norman face ever does smile, it is with the famous *sourire caché* of his great teacher Flaubert. Compared to his immobile features the 'Mona Lisa' grins from ear to ear. Nor has this misanthropic sangfroid any of the modern American's swagger of toughness. Somebody has called him a *Huron de génie*. (pp. 138-39)

In any case something of the young 'Huron' emerges from his books themselves: his evident sympathy for strong masculine peasant types, such as old Hautot in that excellent story **"Hautot père et fils"**; the satisfaction with which he describes physical sounds, colours, smells—**"Une Idylle," "Les Sœurs Rondoli"**; the sense of oneness between man and nature, especially in regard to the passions; see those strangely affecting passages of natural description which lighten the savagery of **"L'Héritage"**; add the fact that he skipped the reflective side of man, as Henry James has pointed out [see excerpt dated 1888], or at any rate reflection as addressed to anything higher than the gratification of an instinct, and that, even so, he addresses himself to the most elementary instincts—for instance, Norman avarice, as in **"Le Diable"**; and that his line was as hard and clear as a diamond on glass; add that in all he did one feels his own enormous pride and self-assurance. All this builds up a general impression of clean, muscular force. Beside him Flaubert smells of the study; and there is a mustiness as of accumulated note-books about Zola; both seem (as indeed they are) paunchy and preserved. As for any suggestion that this writer was a subjective, or introspective or dreamy romantic soul—what mainly emerges is what Henry James called 'the hardness of form, the hardness of nature'. (p. 140)

Wrong, crass, savage, simpliste in his view of life; absurd, mad with arrogance—we may feel him one or all of these things, but we cannot feel that he is evil or touched by evil since this is a term that simply does not enter into his vocabulary. On the contrary, in this man's writings, whose life was certainly far from chaste and pure, we feel the sheerness and coldness of early morning light—of March, or perhaps November—for one cannot suggest that there is anything in him even so near the sunny season as to be autumnal or of the spring. There are no suggestive half-lights in Maupassant. We see the prostitute, the beastly peasant, the timid bourgeois, the civil servant—his favourite subjects—in an unpitying light that exposes their wrinkled faces, their painted gums, their frayed cuffs, their shifty eyes, their hearts that have dried like peas. There is in his tales nothing of the diaphanous prurience of de Kock, the wet lips of Zola, the sense of sin that is all over Mauriac. Indeed there is in much of Maupassant the healthy disgust and contempt of what somebody has called a Pagan puritan.

But in many other ways he is the most ascetic of writers—no prolonged descriptions, no indulgence in 'atmosphere', no elaborate psychology, the simplest of subjects, the most unexceptional characters, a classical discipline of the imagination that not so much prunes as excludes all irrelevancies, and rigidly subordinates everything to the indicated aim, as complete an effacement of self as seems possible this side of a *procès-verbal,* and a style as laconic as a judgment from the bench. He touched the uttermost boundaries of classical realism. Anybody who persisted beyond him could only do what Zola did, round the world and find himself back in the romantic morass. (pp. 141-42)

What one questions about Maupassant's stories is not what this or that one over-emphasizes or under-emphasizes: it is that the bulk of his work passes such an exclusively bitter and misanthropic judgment on life. He ignores all social and philosophic generalizations—those large conclusions and positions which assuage away the sharp detail of existence under benign or optimistic abstractions. Agreed that in doing so he is based on a position, himself; and that this position is almost piratical in its primitiveness; beyond and outside all those refinements, and elaborations, and disinfections of crude human nature that we call civilized life. For it is his satisfaction to peel off every shred of convention, in thought and action, and to reveal the elemental passions hidden but boiling beneath it. The elemental passions are his *métier*. (pp. 150-51)

[As] every reader of his stories knows, the marks of his realism are marks common to all realism, what he did was to select the three main paths of the tradition, each naturally leading into the next one, and follow them farther than anybody before or since. They are individualism, scepticism and elementalism. He followed these three roads or sections of the same road to the cliffs's edge, there built his house, and faced the abyss. (p. 156)

To see how Maupassant exhausts these three elements, let us turn to another of his stories and consider there just one of the characteristics of his method—his 'elementalist' refusal to indulge in elaborate psychology. Let us test this by one of his more feeling and more subtle tales, **"Miss Harriet"**. (pp. 160-61)

Maupassant handles his painful story with extreme cunning. To begin, he draws back a little from the scene; he sinks it into the personality of a narrator which is a useful, however risky, device whenever a theme is too crude or harsh for direct impact. Next he surrounds the theme with a more elaborate and lyrical atmosphere of natural beauty than is usual with him. We note, however, how spare and sharp his technique is in these natural descriptions. There is no description for description's sake; no luxuriating in irrelevant beauty. (p. 161)

There can scarcely be any need to underline the individualism, scepticism and elementalism of Maupassant's treatment of this unhappy theme; beyond, perhaps, the need to remark that it is unusually kind, for him, and that, before him, nobody except Flaubert would have dared either to select such a subject or to treat it with such cold unelaboration. I doubt if, even today, any writer would be either so cold in choice of subject or so laconic in treatment. . . . (p. 167)

As to our specific point—Maupassant's refusal to indulge in elaborate psychology: somebody has called this picture of Miss Harriet 'a bizarre silhouette' and the adjective seems fair, but 'silhouette' is less just. The woman is persuasive; her emotions are sufficiently elaborate; her conflict sufficiently disturbing. What prompted the word was, probably, Maupassant's interest in elemental passion and his almost savage insistence on keeping to that plane. This is where he pursues his path to the cliff's edge, as he does consistently throughout his work. This is where he forces people to call him such names as *un Huron de génie*. This is where, at the end, we are in a position to appraise his power and measure his weakness—his price that he willingly pays, believing it to be not a weakness but a final and irrefragable strength.

The truth is that Maupassant saw life as a puritan moralist: he saw it, as he believed, without sentiment, and only with sensual eyes; he saw what a Christian would call the seven deadly sins, and he saw little else. He saw men and women ridden by pride, covetousness, lust, anger, gluttony, envy and sloth: Norman farmers, Parisian civil-servants, small-town bourgeoisie. What he denied was the slightest trace of soul in any one of them, the least speck of godliness, all hope of redemption here or hereafter. That was *his* reality, and it was in pursuit of it that he reduced human nature to its most elemental passions. Miss Harriet might be a Pantheist; she would die as a dog dies; the most that even an artist could strew on her grave was pity and flowers, and the thought that she would persist as a flower or as grass and as the flesh of an ox and the flesh of those after her who would eat her body and drink her blood. He reduced life to the senses and he revelled in them as a man and as a writer—not gaily, though he could be gay. . . . (pp. 167-68)

Maupassant may have softened a little towards the end. The mass of his work is clean and classical in its raillery, its optimism, its stoical acceptance of a most ascetic and uncompromising view of life.

One's quarrel with such a writer, and one's admiration of him, will never be purely literary: they will be coloured by what, for short, one may call our philosophies, our own personal view of life, and we will approve or disapprove of Maupassant not as a writer but as a man with a similar, or with another (and unacceptable) view of life. It would not have troubled him, but the fact remains that he challenges such approvals and disapprovals more than any other writer of short stories. There is room in the house of Chekhov, Stevenson or Henry James for men of many philosophies. Maupassant invites a select company or else a very tolerant one. That was his choice. He chose his way; he never diverged from it; he succeeded in it. He defined his own notion of reality early in his career—in **"Boule de Suif"**, his first published story; which is to say he defined his own temperament and its needs. When he had finished he looked into the abyss and it received him. (pp. 169-70)

Sean O'Faolain, "Guy de Maupassant, or 'The Relentless Realist'," in his The Short Story, *1948. Reprint by The Mercier Press, 1972, pp. 129-70.*

FRANCIS STEEGMULLER (essay date 1949)

[*Steegmuller's* Maupassant: A Lion in the Path *is considered an outstanding critical biography; he takes his title from Henry James's study of Maupassant (see excerpt dated 1888). In the excerpt below, Steegmuller discusses several of the major short stories, identifying predominant themes and varieties of narrative technique. In his conclusion, he ranks Maupassant with Anton Chekhov as a master of the short story form.*]

The beauty and power of **"Boule de Suif"** are the result of the successful combination—by means, of course, of technical narrative skill—of the two themes, both close to Maupassant's heart: the theme of the humiliation of a woman, already fruitful in **"Le Papa de Simon,"** and the theme of the humiliation of France. The national humiliation is painted in the story's opening words:

> For several days in succession remnants of the defeated army had been crossing the city. They were no longer troops, but disbanded hordes. Their beards were long and dirty, their uniforms in rags, they moved slackly. There were no flags, no grouping by regiments. . . .

And the essential attribute of Boule de Suif herself is humiliation: for not only is she hideously treated by her companions as the story progresses, but she is a prostitute to begin with—and it was always Maupassant's belief that a career of prostitution has its origin in a woman's betrayal. Maupassant was subsequently to write numerous stories laid against the background of the Franco-Prussian war—so many, indeed, that the theme of France's defeat can be called one of his predominant themes, almost obsessive. Not only in **"Boule de Suif,"** but in general throughout his life, it somehow allied itself, almost became fused, with that larger, more fundamental theme that was already, with the double success of **"Le Papa de Simon"** and **"Boule de Suif,"** showing signs of becoming the great underlying theme of his work, as it was of his life: the humiliation that had been suffered by [his mother] Laure. (pp. 108-09)

[**"La Maison Tellier"**] is the first of Maupassant's stories to contain touches of his personal humor—a wildish, fly-away, fantastic, non-respectable humor which to those who care for such things is like the taste of a favorite wine. A French photograph of the time, which purports to be that of "the Rouen brothel on which Maupassant based **"La Maison Tellier"** [see accompanying illustration] and which in any case does depict the staff of *a* Rouen brothel, a provincial establishment of the kind described in the story, illustrates both Maupassant's material and what he did with it. He well knew any brothel's combination of grimness and gaiety, both of which are clearly visible in the faces and gestures of the originals in the photograph: but whereas in the raw material grimness rather dishearteningly prevails and a capacity for comedy and farce barely suggests itself, in the story those suggestions blossom into Maupassant humor and even the grimness of the women's existence is comically (that does not mean unsympathetically) conveyed by means of the sobbing in church. (p. 152)

In the three chief stories in ***La Maison Tellier*** [**"La Maison Tellier", "En Famille," and "Histoire d'une Fille de ferme"**] Maupassant had obviously been following, and following successfully, the course charted for him by Flaubert at the time of **"Boule de Suif":** "Try to write a dozen like it and you'll be a man." As Zola indicated in his review, the stories were indeed like **"Boule de Suif"**; they were of the same general character, the same weight and pace; even **"La Maison Tellier"**, for all its humor, is full of the grave and measured influence of Flaubert. They were infinitely superior to Maupassant's newspaper work, and it is easy to understand that Laure might wish her son to give up journalism because "his serious work would be the better for it."

But Laure had reckoned without the influence of the *Gil-Blas*.

At the time she expressed her wish, her son was still writing chiefly articles for his newspapers, and the few tales that he had published in them could not compare with those that he had written for his volume. In the months immediately following, however, he began to write for the *Gil-Blas* a series of very different tales, tales characterized above all by the article-writer's qualities of "good humor, lightness of touch, vivacity, wit and grace": **"Un Coq Chanta"** . . . , with its huntsman too sleepy for love; **"Farce Normande,"** with its wedding-night horseplay **"Mon Oncle Sosthène,"** about the Freemason converted by the Jesuit sent him as a joke by an unlucky nephew; **"La Rouille"** . . . , whose title describes the condition an old bachelor finds himself to be in when belatedly contemplating marriage. These stories and the others like them which appeared in the *Gil-Blas* during the months just after Laure [expressed her wish that her son give up journalism] all partake pungently of the newspaper's character; they are of far greater interest than the stories appearing in the *Gaulois* at the same time; they mark the triumphant climax of the evolution of Maupassant's anecdote-studded articles into stories. The raffishness of the *Gil-Blas* had led him to discover one side of his genius: his supremacy in the light, risqué story.

This is the type of story that has come to be known as Maupassantian, and that comes to mind as soon as his name is mentioned. . . . (pp. 157-58)

Proprietors and staff of a Rouen brothel alleged to be Maupassant's model for the Maison Tellier.

Very quickly, this new, lighter style blending beautifully with his own temperament, Maupassant began to use it also in stories that were not risqué; and soon not only little comedies and farces, but also little tragedies, dramas and satires were appearing at the rate of one a week. They were presented in a variety of forms with apparently equal ease: straight third-person narrative, monologue, reminiscence, conversation, entries in a diary, exchange of letters. Frames are absent, simple, elaborate, or over-elaborate; consisting most frequently of conversation at dinner in a house, a club, or a hunting lodge; or perhaps at a funeral. Sentences flow, crackle, glitter or sparkle, at the author's desire; characters make their entrances gracefully, though often with a certain daring and violence; they induce, suffer, or react violently or subtly to situations from the most delicate to the most baroque; and closings range from quiet fade-aways to brutal shocks.

These stories, the direct outcome of the journalism so despised by Flaubert, make it seem likely that not only Flaubert's life, but also his death, contributed to Maupassant's maturing into artistic "Manhood." Along with the grief, which was certainly deep and sincere—after Flaubert's death Maupassant was never again so close to anyone, always excepting Laure—the foster-father's disappearance must have brought with it a sense of hitherto unknown independence. During his eleven-year writing career Maupassant was to obey Flaubert and produce a dozen or more tales "like" **"Boule de Suif."** But he was also to produce dozens more *unlike* it, many of them very unlike it indeed, and numbers of them considerably superior to it. And notable among the non-Flaubertian traits which he developed were the rapidity and ease with which he learned, from his work for the *Gaulois* and the *Gil-Blas,* to write—a faculty which resulted, when everything turned out well, in a fluidity and freshness that make his style the perfect expression of the extreme vivacity of his imagination. (pp. 159-60)

Maupassant's work contains many missed opportunities like **"Les Bijoux."** Any writer as prolific as he, particularly any writer so constantly productive of short stories, each one of which represents a fresh approach, a new attack, without the gradually accumulating drive and unity that can make more uniformly successful an equal number of pages in a novel, must be expected to fail some of the time, to produce pale approximations or foolish burlesques of his best work, or departures from it that arrive nowhere; and his reputation suffers accordingly. But the strange feature of Maupassant's case is that his considerable number of failures has done very little harm indeed to his reputation as compared with the damage dealt it by one of his greatest successes—**"La Parure."** (pp. 208-09)

Unquestionably it is the extreme familiarity and popularity of this single story, gradually built up over the years, that has resulted in Maupassant's unjustified reputation as a specialist in trick endings. And many critics and readers, perceptive but not quite *sufficiently* perceptive or familiar with Maupassant's work, have in their irritation been even more unjust: the immense lowbrow popularity of the tale has resulted in the assumption that Maupassant is a writer for lowbrows only, that he has little or nothing to offer the more discriminating. This identification of the author with his most popular tale, plus the swing of the highbrow pendulum away from tales with surprise endings, has resulted in the dismissal of a large body of Maupassant's work: not only his many successful tales on the superior pattern of **"Les Bijoux,"** but also those of his tales which are plotless or all but plotless, whose patterns are so loose and unobtrusive as to be all but imperceptible, and which are pungent and iridescent with character, atmosphere, sentiment, and subtle comment on human life both individual and collective. (pp. 209-10)

"Le Horla" is as universally known as **"La Parure,"** but its excellence is of a subtler kind. In it Maupassant's skill is devoted to gradually communicating a sense of fear, rather than leading brilliantly up to a brutal shock; and the greater dependence on subtleties of language in achieving the effect causes the story to suffer more gravely in translation. In certain English versions it reads like one of the less successful products of a pulp-writer; in the original it is an absorbing and exciting study of insanity, with the beauties of Maupassant's language unobtrusively fulfilliing the task imposed by the subject.

Its success is all the more remarkable in that it is not a "psychological" story: that is, little if any explanation for its supernatural events can be sought in traits or actions attributed by the author, more or less as clues, to his characters—the kind of explanation or solution that can be suggested, for example, in the case of Henry James's *The Turn of the Screw.* In **"Le Horla"** the super-natural is imposed from without. . . . (p. 251)

The external aspect of **"Le Horla"**—the imposing of the supernatural from without—is exemplified in the title itself. The French word *hors* means outside, without; in *Une Vie* and **"La Bête à Maît' Belhomme** there are characters named respectively Horslaville and Horlaville (outoftown); and Horla, a word invented by Maupassant, combines that sense of *hors* with a suggestion of the first syllable of *horrible*. . . . (p. 252)

[**"Mouche"**, **"Le Champ d'Oliviers,"** **"Qui Sait?"** and **L'Inutile Beauté"** are each] an example of a different, contrasting, Maupassant genre. In **"Mouche,"** which he is said to have written in three hours, he returned to the rowdy days of the '70's beside the Seine; there is not the slightest lessening of verve, but the style is marvelously changed, free, impressionistic, non-naturalistic, its structure almost not to be analyzed. **"Le Champ d'Oliviers,"** with its unforgettable figures of a passionate priest and his criminal son, is one of Maupassant's or anyone's noblest productions; Taine pronounced it worthy of Aeschylus. **"Qui Sait?"** is the last of the supernatural stories, and **"L'Inutile Beauté"** the best serious work with a highlife background. (pp. 312-13)

Only with Chekhov (as has so often been said) has the short story reached comparable heights. For some reason none of the many gifted writers of the present century has been able to renew and transform it as radically and vitally as Maupassant and Chekhov did. (p. 324)

In thus being with Chekhov a culmination (unfortunately) in the development of the short story—a block, since no one has been able to go beyond the power and life with which he endowed the form—Maupassant well merits the epithet applied to him by Henry James in the *Partial Portraits* essay: "a lion in the path." James was referring to something else when he used the phrase: to the fact that Maupassant's purely sensual point of view made him a "case" that was "embarrassing and mystifying for the moralist." Perhaps James's phrase can be used to carry, today, a third meaning: that "M. de Maupassant, who is at once so licentious and so impeccable," is a highly imposing figure in the literary path, considerably more imposing than many critics since James have been inclined to admit. (p. 325)

Francis Steegmuller, in his Maupassant: A Lion in the Path, *Random House, 1949, 430 p.*

G. HAINSWORTH (essay date 1951)

[*Hainsworth discusses Maupassant's use of symbolism and its effect on narrative technique in his short stories.*]

Maupassant's first important prose work, **"Boule de Suif,"** presents problems of form similar to those of [Flaubert's] *L'Éducation sentimentale*. It has however been evaluated purely in terms of its subject-matter, often limited arbitrarily to Boule de Suif herself, who has been lucky when she has not been simply identified with Adrienne Legay [the alleged real-life model for the character] or interpreted, in the teeth of the evidence, as a *courtisane sublime*. But no more than Flaubert's does Maupassant's aesthetic allow for 'heroes', and his attack here on 'les honnêtes gens autorisés qui ont de la Religion et des Principes' must obviously extend to Boule de Suif herself. The old device of the stage-coach journey, used to bring in a miniature of society, serves to express, over and beyond satire, a whole world-view, and it is precisely in this that Maupassant's tale most differs from the rest of the *Soirées de Médan*.

We may divide **"Boule de Suif"** into four parts, each of which offers, as a recurrrent theme, at least one shifting of moral attitude brought about by circumstances and the play of instincts. The sum of the tale, with its insistence on externals and various explicit allusions to the imbecility of human reason, amounts to the asseveration of a complete determinism in which moral values—patriotism, religion, class-consciousness—dissolve into nothingness.

In such circumstances, what are we to make of the massive introductory paragraphs in the imperfect tense, describing the retreating troops, paragraphs which seem to cry out for explanation? Their parallelism with the concluding paragraphs of the tale must be felt by every reader, and an intended symmetry is obvious. In view of our definition of the theme, may we not consider that the fleeing army and the fleeing coach are related in the author's mind to this conception of human behaviour as an endless and aimless drift, something like the sailor in the storm of Schopenhauer's image? To sum up, and without entering into detail on this or other aspects of the work, **"Boule de Suif"** represents three or four repetitions of the same theme, it is symmetrical as to its beginning and ending, and the opening pragraphs may be said to figure forth indirectly the whole.

Without analysing them in detail, let us note certain aspects of other early tales of his, as they appear in the 1881 volume, ***La Maison Tellier***. The title-piece itself is less a study of the pious *proxénète* (like Celestina, or Michel Masson's *Bonne Mère*), than the juxtaposition of two institutions, the 'Maison Tellier' and the 'Maison de Dieu', both seen from a curious angle. The most striking feature is the recurrence of comparisons and of highlights (chiefly conversational remarks) tending to bring out the *respectability* of Mme Tellier and her staff, and which weld the different scenes into a whole imbued with a spirit comparable to that of Montaigne's *Cannibales*. **"En Famille"** is closer in plan to **"Boule de Suif."** The theme here, in widest terms, is the monotonous repetition of existence. Adverbial expressions of the type *toujours* occur, for example, some forty times, and there is even a monotony, which may be looked upon as intentional, in the repetition of certain conjunctions and of sentences presenting a ternary pattern. The considerable degree of symmetry which characterizes the general plan is largely explained by the repetition of scenes involving similar incidents. (pp. 3-4)

Such features as we have noted above persist in much of Maupassant's later work. After the fashion of **"La Maison Tellier,"** many of his tales resolve themselves into more or less artful juxtapositions. The combination patriotism-prostitution, which is one aspect of **"Boule de Suif,"** continues in **"Mlle Fifi"** and **"Le Lit 29,"** a satiric group to which **"La Moustache"** (agriculture, patriotism, the relation of the sexes) should be assimilated. Elsewhere, in a series which is more purely comic, love-making is brought somehow in parallel with one topic or another: with rabies (**"Enragée"**), with murder (**"Le Crime au père Boniface"**), hunting (**"La Rouille"**), poaching (**"Le Lapin"**), *tourisme* (**"Les Soeurs Rondoli"**), spa-treatment (**"Mes vingt-cinq jours"**), the act of cutting a cake (**"Le Gâteau"**). . . .

[Frequently] the explicit theme is *prefigured* indirectly in the first paragraphs, or, in the text, a detail is preceded by a symbol which becomes comprehensible in the light of the whole tale.

Sometimes, although the introduction is striking in itself, its symbolism is such that it may appear to contribute but little to the expressiveness of the manifest theme, as when two chimneys standing in a cloudy valley announce the mental confusion of a woman hesitating between two lovers (**"Réveil"**), or an aged office-worker, about to see life 'as it really is', steps out of the gas-light of his office and is dazzled by the afternoon sunshine (**"Promenade"**). . . . (p. 5)

In other cases the introductory paragraphs can be looked upon as enriching tangibly the emotional content of the following narration. So in **"Une Passion,"** where the presentation of ships entering harbour as howling monsters in process of being eaten alive preludes the story of a woman who devours, metaphorically speaking, not only her lover but her husband, and in **"L'Ivrogne,"** where, before relating how the drunken fisherman commits murder in his jealous rage, the author describes at some length a storm raging against the coast. One of the most striking examples of this procedure is the one offered by **"Un Soir":** all the protagonist's misogyny is first expressed indirectly, but with admirable energy, in the description of his savage extermination of an octopus.

In such tales as **"La Bûche,"** where the falling of a log from the fire introduces the question of an abortive love-affair, **"Le Fermier,"** whose opening paragraphs insist on a skittish horse which must be connected with the heroine, or **"Le Masque,"** the story of the man who will not resign himself to old age, led up to by a description of dancers desperately attempting to defy the laws of gravity, it might seem a matter of doubt whether the symbol should be classified as formal or as lending solidity and resonance to the anecdote.

These problems are raised most acutely by tales like **"Une Fille de Ferme,"** where the author, in a way which seems to us characteristic of him, makes use—whether in the introduction or in the body of the narrative—of symbols, usually animal, of a relatively simple order, with cows, horses, hens, the earth or part of it taken as female, and fish, birds, ships, the sun, taken as male. **"Mes vingt-cinq jours"** and **"L'Aveu,"** where a mention of cows precedes the appearance of the female protagonists, offer simple examples of this kind of procedure. **"Miss Harriet"** presents a more complex case. The intimate connection of the *cadre* here with the story itself has passed unnoticed, and yet there can be little doubt that the picture of the hare in the introduction and the evocation of the sun rising over the earth, personified as female, correspond respectively (*a*) to the whole trend of the description of Miss Harriet herself in the text (outline, coloration, gait, timidity), (*b*) to the symbolic use of nature in the text, where the sun stands for the male in the eyes of Miss Harriet herself, and the earth is taken as female, notably by Chenal. In intention then, this *cadre,* at the same time, obviously, as it suggests by what association of ideas Chenal is reminded of Miss Harriet, has an intimate relation with the theme. (pp. 5-6)

The better to understand such *procédés,* let us glance at that considerable body of tales where the brute creation plays a part which it would not always be possible to describe as symbolic in the ordinary sense. Here Maupassant takes pleasure in showing the hunter as hunted or evokes, by the side of human suffering, that of animals. **"Coco",** for example, where Isidore, persecuted by the other rustics, kills the horse which, having eaten the grass, is eaten by it, and **"Deux Amis"** in which the protagonists catch fish and are in turn caught, correspond to a vision in which creation appears as an endless play of quasi-mechanical forces presenting in each aspect a fundamental similarity. In other words, Maupassant seems congenitally incapable of viewing the activities of the individual in isolation. He is not merely haunted by the repetition and ultimate aimlessness proper to them, but is constantly prompted by the rest of animate and inanimate nature despondently to recognize here too the working of an inexorable determinism. He is in his own way obsessed by the problem of 'les deux infinis' and sees each detail *sub specie aeterni,* as he conceives eternity.

Most of the analogies and symbols his work presents can be looked upon as having for primary object the communication of this point of view. The intentions that lie behind them are ultimately the same as those which prompt him elsewhere to preface a discussion of paternity by an explicit reference to a tree shedding its pollen (**"Un Fils"**), [or] to accompany some brutal episode by an evocation of the starry heavens (**"Le Père", "Mohammed Fripouille"**). . . . (p. 7)

[Our] distinctions between juxtaposition and transposition, formal or expressive symbol and non-symbol could be looked upon as resolving themselves into a higher unity since, literally for Maupassant if not for us, one thing *is* another. In any event Maupassant's use of the symbolic or explicit detail evoking a parallel and suggesting, pessimistically in most cases, behind what is particular what is general, must be taken as his most chracteristic tendency. Now confining itself to a brief hieroglyph expressng the brevity of happiness or of life or to the mere evocation, in opening and conclusion, of some swirling stream (**"La Petite Roque"**), now luxuriating in the symbolism of **"L'Inutile Beauté,"** where the queenly, ornamental heroine (resembling the spirited animals evoked in the beginning, after having been the *jument poulinière* mentioned further on) is shown (wearing a diadem) on the background of the Arc de Triomphe and of the Opera, while summarizing in her person the whole of civilization interpreted as whatever runs contrary to nature; now expressing itself in all forms at once as in **'Yvette",** where the change in the heroine's outlook, her awakening to grim reality, is set against the flowing river, punctuated by descriptions of the lightning and of dreams, and accompanied by the evocation of a whole fauna calculated to suggest the idea of a human ant-hill—this tendency, in one shape or another, runs through the major part of his work and constitutes its true signature. (pp. 8-9)

G. Hainsworth, "Pattern and Symbol in the Work of Maupassant," in French Studies, *Vol. V. No. 1, January, 1951, pp. 1-17.*

MARTIN TURNELL (essay date 1959)

[Turnell has written widely on French literature and has made significant translations of the works of Jean-Paul Sartre, Blaise Pascal, Paul Valéry, and Maupassant. In the excerpt below, he acknowledges that "Boule de suif" is a masterpiece, but faults the limitations he discerns in Maupassant's artistic vision.]

Although Maupassant wrote a few stories in the 'seventies, his apprenticeship did not bear real fruit until the appearance of the prodigious **"Boule de Suif"** a few months before his master's death in 1880. It remains his masterpiece and it stamps him as Flaubert's disciple. He was no imitator; he learnt from Flaubert, but he adapted what he learnt to the particular needs of the short story. It is not a disparagement to say that like all his best work **"Boule de Suif"** is profoundly Flaubertian in conception, structure and style.

All Flaubert's novels are based on sharp contrasts which lead to a position of complete negation. These contrasts are reproduced in Maupassant's work. The short story made a certain degree of simplification unavoidable. In his less successful stories the contrasts become facile and mechanical, but this is not a criticism which can fairly be made of **"Boule de Suif."** It crystallizes around the theme of prostitution-patriotism. It may appear to be no more than the story of the good-natured little prostitute who first refuses the enemy out of genuinely patriotic motives, then yields from motives which she mistakenly believes to be patriotic; but in their context the terms acquire a much larger significance. They come to stand not merely for the motives of an individual or a group of individuals, but for the political and moral confusion of a nation.

Flaubert's novels owe much of their effectiveness to his brilliant powers of construction. Although *Madame Bovary* is divided into three parts, there are five distinct movements: the prologue describing Charles Bovary's early years, the unfortunate marriage, the two disastrous love affairs, and the epilogue dealing with the aftermath of disaster. We find the same divisions in miniature in **"Boule de Suif."** There is a prologue which provides a brief account of defeat and occupation, the expedition to Dieppe, the hold-up at Tôtes, the fall of Boule de Suif, and the epilogue with the coach disappearing into the dark. In both novel and short story we find the same symmetry, the same interlocking of events, the same shifting of moral attitudes, and travel plays the same vital part in welding them into wholes. (p. 201)

[Maupassant's] style is deliberately unspectacular. It depends on economy, compactness and sobriety, on the perfection of its phrasing and the writer's gift of ironical understatement; the horrors which are suddenly revealed by the cool, clear, unemphatic prose. He seldom describes nature decoratively in the manner of Flaubert, and when he does he becomes commonplace. Nature is functional. There is not a superfluous word in the opening of **"Histoire d'une fille de ferme."** The physical details are carefully built into a mosaic. The sweltering heat, the blinding light, the farmyard smells, the frolics of the animals and the apple blossom all lead up to Rose's feeling of 'un bien-être bestial', and its consequences.

Maupassant's openings are among his most brilliant feats. They are organic wholes. Nothing sticks out. Every sentence, every word comes in exactly the right place and depends on its context. In the first two pages of **"Boule de Suif"** he gives a remarkable picture of a defeated occupied country:

> Pendant plusieurs jours de suite des lambeaux d'armée en déroute avaient traversé la ville. Ce n'était point de la troupe, mais des hordes débandées. Les hommes avaient la barbe longue et sale, des uniformes en guenilles, et ils avan-

> çaient d'une allure molle, sans drapeau, sans régiment.
>
> [For several days on end the remnants of a defeated army had been passing through the town. They were no longer troops, but disorganized hordes. The men had long, dirty beards, their uniforms were in rags, and they marched with a shambling step, without a flag, without a regiment.]

In three sentences he places the routed, demoralized army before us. He has an unerring eye for the graphic detail. Once again there is not a word too many. Each adds something to the picture, while the phrase, 'd'une allure molle, sans drapeau, sans régiment', conveys perfectly the weary shambling gait of the shattered troops. It is like watching the beginning of a film. The camera 'pans' over the plain giving a bird's-eye view of the exhausted, straggling soldiers, pausing now and then for a close-up of individuals, nosing in and out of the dark corners of the city. (pp. 202-03)

The story is shaped like concentric and contracting circles. The wide circle of the open country encloses the army and the city, which in turn encloses the citizens. Shape and movement are conveyed by the rhythms of the prose. The ternary rhythms reflect the movements of the troops milling helplessly round and round, wondering at which point on the circle of the horizon the enemy will apppear. The ternary rhythms alternate with, and sometimes enclose, binary rhythms or the sharp antitheses which reveal the divisions and disorders inside the circle. . . .

We see the raw recruits oscillating violently between extremes, prepared instinctively to follow anyone who will give a lead in any direction. It is something more than a picture of instability; it is a picture of positive and negative impulses cancelling out. (p. 204)

The spectacle of the ex-tradesmen, who have been commissioned because of their bank balances or their superficially martial appearance, is a sign of the corruption which is the source of the débâcle.

We pass naturally from the ex-tradesmen, who have bought or intrigued themselves into positions they are unfit to hold, to their opposite numbers on the civilian side in the little group who are about to break out of the circle on their journey to Dieppe. There are ten people in the party: three married couples, two nuns, and two individuals—Cornudet and Boule de Suif. (p. 205)

The expedition provides Maupassant with an opportunity of studying a corner of society, and of introducing his own brand of moral comedy with its bitter bawdy flavour. The aristocrats and the bourgeois are condemned out of hand, but no one escapes Maupassant's irony. Cornudet, who seems cast for the role of chorus and who hums the Marseillaise unceasingly after the fresh start, is far from unblemished. He tried, unsuccessfully, to seduce Boule de Suif on the first night, did nothing to strengthen her resistance, and did not offer her food when she was vanquished and hungry. The Marseillaise is a comment on the cowardice of the middle classes certainly, but also on Boule de Suif who panders to it, on the nuns, disregard of Christian teaching, and on the neutrality of the singer.

The flight to Dieppe repeats the movement of the defeated armies and emphasizes the moral patterns which were outlined in the prologue. We have been shown a cross-section of society. Soldiers and civilians divide into broad groups: the brave and the cowardly, the patriots and those 'on the make', *résistants* and *attentistes*. 'Résistance-attentisme' is . . . simply a particular aspect of prostitution-patriotism. Patriotism and prostitution cancel out. The coach with its load of discredited individuals, like the disintegrating armies, disappears into the void to the strains of the Marseillaise. The story has the neatness of an equation. Whatever its terms, whether you add, subtract, divide or multiply, the answer in Maupassant always comes to zero.

The brothel possessed an extraordinary fascination for nineteenth-century French writers. It was an obvious stick to beat the bourgeois, an easy way of exposing their hypocrisy and scoring off the 'old goats' who escaped from their pious, long-faced wives for an evening's fun among the gilt and the plush. It also had a deeper significance. It was a reflection of the fundamental nihilism of the age. The writers imagined that they had got rid of religion. The next step was to get rid of man, to reduce him to a bundle of instincts, to turn love into a commodity which was bought and sold, into the tangle of hairy legs and frilly bloomers among the rumpled sheets that we find in one of Maupassant's bolder illustrators.

In **"La Maison Tellier,"** as in other stories, Maupassant adapts the *conte leste* to his particular purposes. It is an account of a school treat transposed into a somewhat unexpected setting. The visit of Madame and her staff to her brother's, for the First Communion of her niece, fulfils the same object as the expedition in **"Boule de Suif."** It enables him to study a corner of society at close quarters. It also provides ample scope for his comedy. . . . (pp. 205-06)

The story is built round the familiar contrasts: the House of God and the House of Love, the *curé* and Madame with their respective flocks which are significantly united in the moment of hysteria, the fragrant open countryside and the hot, fetid, noisy brothel. The theme of prostitution-patriotism re-emerges as respectability-prostitution. From the outset, Maupassant goes to considerable lengths to establish the 'respectability' of Madame and the decorousness of her establishment. (pp. 206-07)

Although Maupassant's aim is clearly to make her into an adequate foil for the *curé,* to link respectability and religion, his real interest is in the denouement. On the last page she makes an assignation with the local judge. It is another equation. The foolish *curé* mistakes hysteria for a miracle; respectability and prostitution cancel out; the answer is another zero. (p. 207)

"La Maison Tellier" is written with Maupassant's customary dexterity, but the theme was a temptation rather than an opportunity. Far from being one of his most notable achievements, the story exhibits all his characteristic vices—his crudity, his facile cynicism, a fundamental lack of intelligence. (pp. 207-08)

"L'Héritage" is one of Maupassant's successes certainly, but it is not a success of the order of **"Boule de Suif."** He is concerned in it with little people—with petty spite, petty avarice, sham respectability—because he was a little man himself who was normally incapable of dealing with great actions or great issues. **"Boule de Suif"** is superior to anything else he did because history had provided him with a theme which, for a moment, turned his little people into actors in a vast drama. That is why this one story has overtones, a resonance, a meaning for which we shall look in vain in any of his other works. (p. 209)

Flaubert's novels leave us with the impression of a disparity between their technical accomplishment and the quality of the writer's experience. Maupassant creates precisely the opposite impression. Henry James put it very well. 'A writer is fortunate', he said, 'when his theory and his limitations so exactly correspond' [see excerpt dated 1888]. For at bottom it was his poverty of experience which made him concentrate on a short-range art form and turned him into a supreme craftsman. He was in no sense a writer of the calibre of Flaubert. He was doing something smaller, but in spite of his debt to Flaubert he was doing something different. It is impossible to read the best of the *contes* without perceiving that their economy and their shapeliness belong essentially to the short story. We know that the majority of them first appeared in periodicals, and if they are read in bulk they soon become wearisome. Those which deal with the Norman peasantry, the Franco-Prussian War, the lower reaches of the bureaucracy and the banks of the Seine, which are almost as much the Maupassant country as Normandy, are excellent of their kind; but when he tried, with the ill-considered encouragement of Taine and Bourget, to write about more complex personalities the results were poor. (pp. 209-10)

'You are the true and only successor of my dear Flaubert', Taine said to Maupassant. But history has proved him wrong. Whatever his short-comings, Flaubert has been one of the most potent as well as one of the most beneficial influences in the contemporary novel. Without him it is difficult to see how James, Proust or Conrad could have achieved all they did, not to speak of the lesser figures like Zola and Joyce. Maupassant's progeny is more numerous, but much less distinguished. Far from possessing a first-rate brain, as Mr. Steegmuller has so recklessly asserted, he did not possess either the moral or the intellectual qualities which are essential to the great writer. But he knew all the tricks. That is why he was the inventor of the commercial short story whose descendants must be sought in the glossy magazines—the professional entertainers who start somewhere near the front and who finally pull off their modest tricks somewhere in the back pages among the advertisements for cosmetics, underwear and aphrodisiacs. (p. 220)

Martin Turnell, "Maupassant," in his The Art of French Fiction: Prévost, Stendhal, Zola, Maupassant, Gide, Mauriac, Proust, *Hamish Hamilton, 1959, pp. 197-220.*

J. H. MATTHEWS (essay date 1962)

[*In the excerpt below, Matthews argues that Maupassant used narrative structure to project his own attitudes about life and that he deliberately manipulated the reader's point of view to conform with his own.*]

We have witnessed for too long a real injustice towards Maupassant short stories. While his novels have gradually earned the respect of the critics—to such a point that commentary upon *Pierre et Jean* has become a minor, but eminently respectable, industry in academic circles—his *contes* have been set aside, though they offer a convenient and enlightening introduction both to the man and his work. It is to give some substance to this claim that this study of theme and structure in Maupassant's short stories has been undertaken.

A very necessary definition of terms must precede any such examination. The term 'narrative structure' is self-explanatory; I refer to the form Maupassant uses, and may reasonably be claimed to have chosen, as best suited to carry the theme he has in mind. But with the word 'theme' we must go more cautiously. In my examination of **"Pierrot,"** I have already suggested that the theme of a Maupassant *conte* is not necessarily the story it tells. The theme, as the term is used here, is the thought, idea, or emotion which underlies the 'story'. That is to say, the theme takes advantage of the story to objectify itself. Seen in this light, the 'story', the narrative structure, is simply an excuse, serving to invite the reader's response. This response will be the result of his perception of the *true* meaning of the *conte*. (p. 136)

It would seem that we can do much to correct the false impression of Maupassant's work which is prevalent, by grouping his *contes* according to another kind of classification, a classification which really is by themes—using the term as it is understood here. For, as I hope to show, it is only by approaching Maupassant's work in this way that we cease to find our attention diverted by suppositions regarding convenience, habit, negligence or cynicism on Maupassant's part. Much that has been readily accepted as valid criticism of his work drops away when we do so. And it is only then that we become aware of recurrent preoccupations, whose reappearance points not to facility but to obsessive compulsion.

Words as strong as these require some support and cannot be fully justified without an exhaustive examination of all Maupassant's short stories. But the validity of the thesis finds considerable confirmation, I believe, if we consider only a few of the major themes which characterize Maupassant's work, and examine how the obsessive themes under discussion are reflected in the very structure of the *conte* in which they find their development and a noteworthy enrichment.

There is, without doubt, an objection which presents itself immediately. To seek to establish a certain complexity in Maupassant's narrative structures seems to point to unnecessary complication of what is, apparently, quite a straightforward issue. After all, is it not true that Maupassant proposed a very simple plan for the writer of realistic fiction?. . . No one would question the fact that the simply rectilinear structure is serviceable enough in, for instance, **"Mon Oncle Jules,"** or even in a much better story, like **"Une Vendetta."** But we may fairly say that, to perceive the full quality of Maupassant's art, we must keep in mind that he was not always satisfied just to tell a tale. (p. 137)

Even in stories which follow a rectilinear pattern we frequently observe something of what I mean. The only adornment may be the addition of a preliminary section and of a concluding one: the story is 'framed' between an introductory section, designed to evoke a suitable mood or otherwise prepare the reader's emotional or rational response, and a closing section, through which certain crucial conclusions suggest themselves to us. It is these conclusions which embody the story's theme. And so introduction and conclusion are both necessary if Maupassant is to ensure that his readers become sensitive to the import of his theme, which is the *conte's* justification.

It will be appreciated that it is not here a question of the means which Maupassant borrows so readily, to furnish himself with a neat *entrée en matière*. . . . A more pertinent example is **"La Mère Sauvage."**

Returning to Virelogne after fifteen years' absence, the narrator sees a burnt-down cottage which provokes from him the remark, "Quoi de plus triste qu'une maison morte, avec son squelette debout, délabré, sinistre?" It is in the passage from which these lines are taken that Maupassant evokes the mood he requires, so as to prepare for the tale of Mère Sauvage. She loves her son. When he is killed at the front, she takes revenge on the Prussian soldiers billeted in her house: she burns it down one night, while they are asleep. Proudly admitting her guilt, she is summarily executed. This is the 'story'. It is when we read the concluding section that we fully appreciate that this narrative is simply a vehicle—not to say an excuse—through which Maupassant seeks to express his theme, which does not become explicit until the very last lines: "Moi, je pensais aux pères des quatre doux garçons brûlés là-dedans; et à l'héroïsme de cette autre mère, fusillée contre ce mur. Et je ramassai une petite pierre, encore noircie par le feu." (p. 138)

The effect provoked by this narrative tone is reinforced by the final image with which Maupassant leaves his readers: all that remains of so much suffering is a blackened pebble in the hand of a stranger, suggesting all the futility and sterility of war. So that it is only now that we fully understand the function of the frame within which Maupassant has placed his narrative. Reported unemotionally by the narrator's friend Serval, the unhappy history of Mère Sauvage stands between the remarks which introduced the necessary mood and the final comment, which changes the focus, setting the tale in perspective. The effect is to require the reader to view events from a distance, and thus to become aware of the futile waste which is one of the tragic consequences of war (one of the themes Maupassant was to develop fervently in **"Sur l'Eau."** The significant feature of **"La Mère Sauvage"** is this change of focus, which provokes reflection and leads the reader to the conclusions dictated by this *conte*'s theme. So then it may be said that it is the necessity to make us responsive to his fundamental theme which both leads Maupassant to utilize the narrative structure he uses and is the justification for its use. (pp. 138-39)

[The] effect produced by [several of the] *contes* is increased for any reader who is responsive to the deliberately symbolic value of the circular structure within which the narrative is related. Like **"Pierrot"** with its hole—the marl-pit—these stories are constructed around a central image. In **"À Cheval"** and **"En famille"** it is the image of the circle which exemplifies the impossibility of progress,the uselessness of attempting to escape; the endlessly repetitive round of meaningless existence. Indeed, it seems fair to claim that the image of the circle is essential to a writer with an outlook like Maupassant's, working in the medium of the short story. A straight-line development typifies more commonly optimism—the sort of optimism expressed through the energetic progress of Balzac's Rastignac. It indicates—when not used for specifically tragic purposes—an optimism regarding the world (society) and man's place in it. In Maupassant, certainly, the circle is the symbol of defeat, of the impossibility of advancement.

We sense this unmistakably in **"La Parure."** It is true that Maupassant does show us, here, people capable of energetic action and dedicated purpose. Placed in a situation which demands effort on their part, they are revealed to be capable of such effort. Madame Loisel devotes ten years to making good the loss of a borrowed necklace. So her example of patient hard work seems to be a salutary one. Indeed, the atmosphere of this *conte*—in which a deliberately muted tone underplays emotionalism—is in contrast with the stories already mentioned. But this is true only up to a point; a point reached when the owner of the necklace reveals that the original was an imitation. In reality, then, **"La Parure,"** although apparently developing in a straight line, so to speak, evokes once more a circular effect as soon as the ironic import of the tale is made plain to us. (p. 141)

[Maupassant's] main concern in his best stories is to involve his readers by any means which present themselves within the framework of the *conte,* and to leave us inescapably with the same conclusions he himself has drawn about life. In this context his frequent recourse to circular structures becomes especially indicative of his outlook and of the view of life he seeks to suggest to us. Similarly, his elaborate use of irony which sometimes, but by no means always, is allied with pity, tends to empty life of real meaning. The irony of our attempts to escape, the repetitious character of human existence marked by cruelty and inexplicable suffering—these are among the recurring themes of Maupassant's stories, just as they were major preoccupations in his own life. . . . (pp. 141-42)

It appears incontestable that many of the stories he wrote, apparently with such effortless ease, were not an end in themselves. They were a means, rather. Maupassant's activity as a writer owes its prompting to something more than the mere instinct for financial reward. He contrives, instead, to project into the world around him his own "sensation de désenchantement", in many typical *contes* which leave with the reader "comme une traînée de tristesse". This is why so frequently, in stories like **"Menuet"** and **"Amour,"** Maupassant concentrates upon the evocation of a mood—profound sadness, or nostalgia for a past gone for ever. (p. 142)

I think it worth remarking that the surprise-ending as it is used by Maupassant is rarely, as it is in O. Henry, just a matter of technical trickery, supporting a wry but shallow comment upon life. **"La Parure"** shows that Maupassant aims deeper than this. In his work, the surprise-ending marks the moment of revelation, for the reader, or for the characters, or for both. This is the point at which incidents, attitudes, conduct, are all shown for what they really are. So that, although Maupassant quite often turns the device to comic effect, laughter is far from being the sole motive behind his use of this technique. (p. 143)

[Careful] reading can only strengthen our opinion that the fundamental impetus which resulted in his short stories was of a deeply personal nature, so that the techniques he was led to adopt stem from a genuine *pudeur* rather than from cynical indifference. Yet, though Maupassant succeeded in hiding his feelings, he could never manage to suppress them altogether. They are betrayed as much in his treatment of his material as in its choice. What others may seek to achieve by assertion, Maupassant wishes to infer by example. What others may try to prove, Maupassant is content to illustrate. His stories invite not acquiescence but complicity. Giraudoux's definition of the theatre as designed to convince minds already convinced permits of easy adaptation here. For we do not find ourselves succumbing to proof. Instead we feel ourselves to be recognizing, in the evidence produced with apparent negligence, the confirmation of conclusions we willingly believe to be our own. Pierre Cogny has shown convincingly how much of Maupassant's power comes from his being "l'écrivain de son destin". A detailed analysis of the themes and structures of Maupassant's stories might well lead us to the conclusion that the appeal his *contes* still hold for us today lies in the fact that he is not only the writer of his own destiny but also of ours. (p. 144)

J. H. Matthews, "Theme and Structure in Maupassant's Short Stories," in Modern Languages, *Vol. XLIII, No. 4, December, 1962, pp. 136-44.*

EDWARD D. SULLIVAN (essay date 1962)

[In the excerpt below, Sullivan provides a thorough analysis of Maupassant's short stories, dividing them into two main cate-

gories, the contes, or shorter pieces, and the nouvelles, or more extended short fictions. In addition, the critic explores Maupassant's major themes and techniques.]

The world created by a short-story writer has its own coherence, its own identifying characteristics, its own structure, but when we try to examine it closely we are faced with a set of problems that are quite different from those involved in the analysis of an individual play, a short novel, or even a volume of poetry. Guy de Maupassant wrote over 300 short stories in a period of about ten years, roughly between 1880 and 1890; and, while it would be convenient if we could take one story and show that it embodies the characteristics of all the others, to do so would produce something either highly artificial or hopelessly misleading. Maupassant wrote many different kinds of stories—different in subject, in length, in technique, and in their impact on the reader; his interest changed with the passage of time, as he encountered new experiences, and he rewrote and re-used just about everything that he ever produced. To deal with this large and varied body of work we shall need to examine carefully a number of representative stories and make reference to a good many others if we are to discover the full meaning and value for ourselves of Maupassant's singularly sharp-eyed exploration of the world as he knew it. (p. 7)

[It is the] sensual aspect of Maupassant, his overriding emphasis on the sexual impulse, which has disconcerted and dismayed a number of readers. It bothered both Henry James and Tolstoy [see excerpts dated 1888 and 1898] who admired the artist in Maupassant but were shocked by his total unconcern for moral questions. (p. 8)

Maupassant has been undervalued for some time now, as writers and readers have preferred the Chekov-type story with its greater margin of mystery, its delicate, but enigmatic insights. It is not surprising that an age like ours, which cherishes its own bewilderment and prefers puzzles to solutions, would be rather scornful of a man who felt he could express some clear perception of a truth—however limited. He cultivated a very small garden indeed, but he assumed somewhat arrogantly, and somewhat inconsistently perhaps, that he could speak with authority in his own domain; and although he believed in neither God nor Man—and still less in women—without faith and without illusions, he sought endlessly to expose a truth that his own philosophy told him was not there.

If, in his stories, Maupassant strikes some of us as old-fashioned, it is not only because we have lived for some time nearer to the Chekov end of the spectrum, but because of his old-fashioned arrogance in believing that he could express his own intuition directly. The closer we examine his stories the more we realize that he did not seek to express in his fictions his puzzlement and his problems, but concentrated on communicating to us his insights. . . . His effort was to communicate matters that he knew something about, provide a brief look behind the mask of pretence that people commonly wear. When one reads a large number of his stories one can guess that certain subjects must have obsessed him since they recur so frequently; the question of paternity is one such theme treated with innumerable variations in dozens of stories, yet we learn nothing from the stories and very little from his biography about his own specific relationship to this subject. Similarly, many of his stories are concerned with hallucinations and madness, but they are written in a singularly lucid prose, and if we would learn of his own intimate madness we must rely on his biographers and doctors for our information. (pp. 8-9)

Maupassant's greatest virtue lies in the fact that his narratives sustain the readers' interest and that he develops them with economy and concision, selecting 'unerringly, unscrupulously, almost impudently', as Henry James put it, the precisely pertinent details and excluding all verbal flourishes or elaborate enumeration. But these are exactly the kind of qualities that make him seem all too clear, quite uncomplicated, and possessing none of those particular asperities which offer a handhold to critics and which abound in writers like Flaubert or James. Maupassant was limited, as we all are, but more than most writers he deliberately refused to acknowledge the existence of a moral dimension and denied anyone's capacity to penetrate deeply into the psychological domain. . . . Yet one is sometimes convinced that his limitations result not from a lack of a window but from an overwhelming fear of looking through it into what he guessed must be an unspeakable abyss.

In any case, he gives the appearance of being clear and uncomplicated, yet for all the apparent simplicity—perhaps because of it—he is an exceedingly difficult writer to deal with. We shall need to look clearly and unobstructedly at his work and re-examine the clichés that cling to him as well as the complexities which may be observed, surprisingly, in so simple a writer. (p. 10)

The severe domain of the *conte,* with its strict limitations of length, seems to put intolerable burdens on a writer: a slightly misplaced detail, a single false note can damage the story beyond repair. Here there was no room for the development which enriched his *nouvelles,* yet Maupassant worked easily and gladly within the restrictions of the form. By temperament he was inclined to strip off details rather than to accumulate them, to concentrate on the significant line rather than on the diverting image, to drive directly, relentlessly towards a single effect. (p. 11)

The short form was not an unbearable constraint for Maupassant; it was probably congenial to his vision of the world, which he tended to see in any case as fragmented, disjointed, partial, and lacking in fundamental connections.

Many of Maupassant's stories begin with a preliminary discussion or scene which serves to introduce the main action he wishes to relate. This technical device, called a framework or *cadre,* has been frequently used by tellers of tales in all periods as a way of establishing with some authenticity at the beginning of a story the circumstances under which it is being told. The author may introduce a narrator, either himself (or someone speaking in the first person) or another person, and usually he specifies the kind of audience which hears the tale. This is, of course, an ancient device, reminding us of the oral traditions of story-telling and pretending to simulate them. . . . Maupassant took it over quite naturally and used it for a variety of purposes, although many of his stories get along without any such introduction of a specific narrator. The framework involves also, in most cases, a concluding statement, some kind of conclusion drawn by the narrator or one of his listeners, which brings us out of the world of the tale and back into the society which has been listening to it.

According to one count more than 160 of Maupassant's stories begin by establishing the circumstances of the narration, usually an oral situation, although he had a fondness also for the device of finding a document which reveals its own story. That is to say, more than half his stories have some kind of clearly designated narrator, but it should be borne in mind that there are almost as many which get along without such a scheme. (pp. 11-12)

One can easily attribute altogether too much importance to this question of the framework and its function. As a fictional technique it has now a somewhat old-fashioned air and strikes the modern reader as an outworn convention; when used now it is most frequently handled as a piece of deliberate irony or to evoke a particular atmosphere. It was accepted by Maupassant as a congenial and workable convention which he felt no compulsion to use in every instance. . . .

Oddly enough, in spite of the extensive use of the narrator-device, Maupassant never built up a narrator who could be repeatedly used, and apparently had no desire to create someone like Conrad's Marlow who has a special authority with the reader by virtue of our familiarity with him and his ways. (p. 13)

[In **"Un Soir"**] the effect of the *cadre* is extraordinary because there is a substantial narrative to which the preliminary elaboration is keyed and there is an effective interplay of symbols and images between frame and story. The framework is so detailed, so leisurely in pace, that we are not really sure whether we are already involved in the main line of the story or are only moving towards it. Maupassant, who is justly noted for his swift, direct technique of narration, can be extremely deliberate when he chooses, as here, to create a particular effect. (pp. 15-16)

[In **"Un Soir"** the] elaborate *cadre* has been integrated into the story and used to enhance the effect of an otherwise banal account of suspicion and discovery; it is not a story of adultery, but centres rather on the violent emotions that lie just beneath the undistinguished surface of ordinary men. Maupassant's role was to reveal those aspects, however base or unpleasant, and he used here all the elements of his story to that end. (p. 17)

Maupassant saw the task of the literary artist as something more than putting words together to narrate an action; the artist's great gift—acquired by diligent practice—is immediate perception of the undercurrents of life which pass unnoticed by others. His glance is more penetrating, simple objects are more revealing to him; the single glimpse of his friend in **"Le Rosier de Madame Husson"** is enough for the narrator's imagination, '. . . et en une seconde toute la vie de province m'apparut'. An unexpected casual encounter, as in **"Un Soir,"** may lay bare an abyss of violent emotions. His fondness for using the framework in so many stories may be nothing more than the desire of a man about to explore the depths who wants to leave a marker on the surface which plots his point of entry and to which he may return. Maupassant, as we shall see when we look into a number of his stories, is fearful of what his explorations might produce and hesitates before the vast uncharted regions of the subconscious or of the irrational lest he be carried away completely. The *cadre* at least ensures that he can climb back out of his own story. (pp. 18-19)

Like **"La Parure"**, **"A Cheval"** and a great many other stories, [**"Le Protecteur"**] relies on plot almost entirely for its effect, the anecdote itself has an interest and a meaning independently of the way it is told; Maupassant's art in such stories consists in keeping out of the way of the narrative as it plunges forward. This is a line-drawing: he strips off everything that blurs the line, and of character gives us only what is needed to support the tale. . . . (p. 22)

Maupassant wrote many such anecdotes on all sorts of subjects, frequently supporting or justifying them by an introductory *cadre:* **"Ma Femme"** is nothing more than an after-dinner story and that is the setting he arranges for it; **"En Voyage"** with an elaborate setting on a train is a sentimental anecdote which is kept from disaster by the sense of reality imposed by the *cadre*. In all of them he achieved, usually very skilfully, the line that he sought; the question then arises whether there is more that can be accomplished. Can he also achieve in this limited scope a greater solidity, a greater complexity, some sense of characters who might conceivably exist outside of their function in the tale?

Certain stories of Maupassant take us beyond plot and beyond the process of revelation inherent in plot into a domain where the dimensions are broader, the characters less single-minded, and where curious resonances are audible. In many of these there is a lack of that scorn and irony which marks his attitude towards the *conseiller d'état* and the unhappy horseman or that monumental indifference which polishes the hardness of **"La Parure."** The narrator, canons of objectivity to the contrary, allows his sympathetic understanding of his people to be felt, a firmly controlled but evident tenderness and pity for the tricks chance plays and the way they bear their burdens. The counterpart of his disclosure of fakery is his sympathy for unpretentious honesty. **"Miss Harriet"** could so easily have become a satire of the English spinster abroad, but is a deeply moving portrait which, without seeming to do more than describe her actions for a brief period in a Norman inn, conveys the sense of her whole life and a sympathetic and pitying awareness of its meagreness. **"Hautot Père et Fils,"** is another where the humble people involved are treated with tenderness and dignity in a plot which could easily have been handled cynically or farcically: when the father dies, the son takes over his mistress. (pp. 22-3)

To abandon plot for the creation of atmosphere or mood, to suggest through seemingly purposeless dialogue or random details a world of feeling—this is the domain of Chekov, the kind of story which stands at the opposite pole from Maupassant's brisk anecdote. Maupassant, too, could create atmosphere and evoke feeling from the simplest scenes, and he has done so frequently; but he rarely let the creation of atmosphere carry the whole burden of narration, and we sometimes fail to see it clearly because we are busily following plot. A few examples will suggest ways of exploring an aspect of Maupassant's art that serious students of his stories could pursue with profit.

"Amour" is probably the most extreme example, being almost devoid of any anecdotal interest. It is compounded of two elements: the joy of hunting and an awareness of what love can be, as glimpsed in the behaviour of birds: the attachment unto death of the male bird for the female just killed. It is a powerful hunting sketch, a brilliant evocation of the bitter cold, the frozen swamp, the desperate discomfort, and the wild unreasoning joy of the human animal as he plunges back into nature. His ferocity is aroused for he is there to kill—and kill he does even as he observes with sharply contained emotion the affecting behaviour of the birds. It is a story which creates the same kind of direct communication with nature as the huntsman knows it that we find in Turgenev's *A Sportsman's Sketches* or, more highly developed, in William Faulkner's *The Bear*. (pp. 26-7)

The *conte* was originally a fairy tale, an account of something marvellously non-realistic, but this is too narrow a definition

T. A. Steinlen's illustration for "La Maison Tellier," originally published in the Gil-Blas.

to apply to the wide range of stories written in the nineteenth and twentieth centuries and neither useful nor generally accepted as a way of distinguishing *conte* from *nouvelle*. Yet the *conte* never entirely lost its ancient feeling for the fairy story and supernatural occurrences, and such stories now form a recognizable sub-division of the genre. In Maupassant's work the number of stories devoted to the supernatural and the inexplicable reminds us that the *conte* in its original sense survives and that it has great significance for the student of Maupassant's stories.

Maupassant's earliest efforts in the short story, before **"Boule de Suif"** was written and while he was still Flaubert's pupil, were more nearly romantic fairy tales than the crisp observation of ordinary life one would expect. **"Le Donneur d'eau bénite,"** written about 1877, is full of well-observed details, but tells a traditionally impossible story—a child stolen by gypsies, brought up by a wealthy childless lady, many years later finds his true parents who are old and poor, his father having become a 'donneur d'eau bénite'. Here, too, very early in the game when Maupassant was only twenty-seven, the theme of paternity appears—the child discovering his parents—which was to be the subject of so many of his stories. (p. 28)

There is still another variety of Maupassant story which goes back to an earlier form of the *conte,* and which Maupassant handles with great brilliance. It is not the fairy tale so much as the tale involving folklore and farce, nearer in spirit to the *fabliau* than to Perrault. Many of the stories he wrote about peasants have this genial humour, an exhilarating sense of not beng bound to the pretences of life and of dealing with unrestrained primitive folk whose activities are frequently situated on the edge of farce. **"La Bête à Maît' Belhomme"** is a very funny story of the peasant who had a flea in his ear (literally) and of the efforts of all hands to remove it. The story is made up of wonderful dialogue and keen observation, has the atmosphere of farce and folklore but with a grand ring of sharply observed truth. (p. 30)

More directly related to a continuous tradition are the stories which involve, or seem to involve, the supernatural. Critics have generally been inclined to connect Maupassant's stories of terror, hallucinations and the supernatural more with his biography and his eventual madness, than with the very rich tradition of such tales. Without attempting to solve the biographical problem and without trying to explore the vast literary tradition behind these stories, they can be examined as part of Maupassant's concern for the old problem of appearance and reality, of his persistent effort to remove the outer wrappings, to take off the mask. We depend on our senses, but what if there are phenomena that our senses cannot perceive? His stories are a series of elaborations of such a hypothesis. (pp. 30-1)

Most of Maupassant's stories in this area are not about the supernatural but about the unknown. He was profoundly impressed by the notion that we are strictly limited by the capacity of our senses, that many things must exist which escape our imperfect organs. . . . It is a basic article of faith and leads him to an interest in all efforts to penetrate into the hidden mysteries of life, the whole area of parapsychology involving hypnotism, magnetism, mesmerism and the like. His narrators are usually sceptical men of the world, not inclined to be taken in by charlatans, and they seek a rational explanation for the phenomena they have observed. (p. 31)

Various themes are joined as we follow in more detail and with specific illustrations the progress from the story with a rational explanation to the frankly supernatural, touching fear, futility, and hallucination on the way. In January 1883 **"Auprès d'un mort"** has the simplest explanation imaginable why, after Schopenhauer's death, the smile on his face changed to a grimace: his false teeth slipped out! In **"Apparition,"** a few months later, we are left not knowing whether we have seen a ghostly apparition or a sequestered female. In December 1883 **"La Main,"** which was a reworking of the much earlier **"La Main d'Ecorché,"** makes no commitment as to the supernatural aspect of the mummified hand; the narrator insists at the beginning that it is not 'surnaturel' but simply 'inexplicable', and this kind of hedging understandably irritates one of the ladies in the audience who exclaims at the end: 'Mais ce n'est pas un dénouement cela, ni une explication!' (p. 32)

His interest in the realm beyond our senses is closely akin to his interest in . . . humble suicides, for his deeply rooted assumption seems to be that the unknown when revealed must be horrible, and this is the source of his diagnosis of fear. It is not the realm of the occult, uniquely, but the sense that reality is even worse than appearance if only we could see it; and even more disturbing is the knowledge that our senses are *constantly* deceiving us. (p. 33)

The very powerful story **"Lui?,"** based on the themes of fear and solitude, carries us one step further into the unknown. This time a man, suffering from a genuine hallucination, sees someone sitting in his room, and this drives him into marriage in order not to be alone. It is not the supernatural as such that bothers him but: 'J'ai peur surtout du trouble horrible de ma pensée, de ma raison qui m'échappe brouillée, dispersée par une mystérieuse et invisible angoisse.' The story is completely credible; it does not depend on any suspension of disbelief, it simply suggests that there may be something more than meets the eye—something disturbing—and furthermore one's eye is not reliable. To say that the man suffers from an optical illusion or an hallucination does not settle the question for him, because what troubles him is that one never knows how much one suffers from such illusions or how radical is the error of the senses. At the bottom of the anxiety and even the madness that Maupassant never ceased to explore is the abominable knowledge that our instruments of perception are hopelessly unreliable. (p. 34)

Nothing that Maupassant wrote before 1880—a few stories, a couple of plays, a great deal of verse, some articles—gives any hint of the precisely engineered perfection of **"Boule de Suif."** After years of laborious and tentative efforts under the tutelage of Flaubert, he discovered his real genius with a single stroke, and found at the same time the literary form that was most exactly suited to his particular talents. For **"Boule de Suif"** is a *nouvelle,* long enough to allow development without undue haste, yet limited enough to channel our interest in one very specific direction, excluding the exploration of issues, however interesting, which would turn us away from the hard clear line which is relentlessly followed to the end.

That line is the simple line of a journey—a journey by carriage of a small group of people and for no great distance—in the course of which one small drama is played out. The thin line which Maupassant laid out between Rouen and the little town of Tôtes in Normandy becomes a taut string which he plucks with effortless skill to produce surprising overtones and resonances. He is not attempting here the complex counterpoint of the novel, nor is he bound to the simple percussive effect of the *conte*. Here he has a single string and a single theme, but he has time to work out the simple variations and suggest relationships with other themes.

The length of **"Boule de Suif"** was determined in part by the fact that it was to appear as one of six stories by six different authors making up a volume to be called *Les Soirées de Médan''*. (p. 36)

The theme of *Les Soirées de Médan* was to be anti-patriotic, anti-chauvinist and anti-war. The irony and satire contained in **"Boule de Suif,"** however, turn out to be directed not at patriotic sentiments as such but at hypocritical professions of patriotism by the cynical and the selfish. Maupassant wrote, as his character Boule de Suif acts, from a deep sense of national feeling and the humiliation of the defeat of the Franco-Prussian War. Reading the first few pages one cannot take seriously the doctrine of objectivity preached by Flaubert and adopted by Maupassant. The author makes no effort to conceal his opinions from the reader, and in fact he makes them forcefully and bitterly clear. (pp. 36-7)

It is a disturbing story because it is not about Boule de Suif's activities but about the values a society lives by and the terrible gap between the values that society professes and those it uses. Everything is turned upside down, nothing is what it seems to be, and, although Boule de Suif is not that durable literary type, the prostitute with a heart of gold, she has a simple honesty that reveals the sham of the others. Maupassant's rage at the humiliation of military defeat is expressed in the savagery of his delineation of those who accommodate themselves effortlessly and profitably to that defeat. (p. 37)

[The] whole story is built on the revelation of a total reversal. Boule de Suif exercises a profession which puts her on the outside of this society, but she is the only one who possesses the values most esteemed by that society but which none of these established pillars, her companions, can claim. She is patriotic, courageous and religious; the others pretend to be, act the role when possible, but clearly are not. (p. 39)

Maupassant in his first important work sounds clearly the fundamental theme that will be heard in various forms throughout his whole career. He is obsessed by the difference between appearance and reality, between the outer mask and the inner face, and he saw his task as that of a story-teller who catches us by his art and by his narrative skill and reveals to us not life as it appears (as 'realists' are supposed to do) but rather all the aspects of life that are carefully and deliberately concealed from our view by convention, habit, ignorance or timidity. This is pointed up in a dozen ways, by images or brief references that ride smoothly on the surface of his prose; the French officers, for example, we learn from the first pages, although they are dressed in fine military uniforms, are really 'anciens commerçants en drap ou en graines, ex-marchands de suif ou de savon'. The phrase 'marchands de suif' turns out to be a programme for the rest of the story. We learn, too, again as a thought suggestive for the coming action, that the inhabitants of Rouen find it prudent to be friendly with the German officers billeted with them, but maintain the illusion of aloofness in public. Maupassant hated masks—any kind of mask, even Carnival masks—and whenever he told a story he not only developed a narrative but he lifted a mask. **"Boule de Suif"** was a general indictment and he was to spend some ten years in amplifying and illustrating that indictment, looking sometimes with revulsion, sometimes with amusement, frequently with little evidence of any emotion at matters long concealed and which many preferred not to have brought to light.

"La Maison Tellier," another of Maupassant's most celebrated *nouvelles,* appeared in May 1881, just about a year after the publication of **"Boule de Suif,"** and, although its chief characters are prostitutes and it does give some surprising views of what goes on behind the façade of respectability, the tone is quite different. Maupassant is not indignant at injustice and hypocrisy as he was in **"Boule de Suif,"** but amused at working out the possibilities inherent in what is essentially a farcical situation. Again everything hinges on a reversal: prostitutes play the role of *grandes dames,* but it is all carried on in the most light-hearted manner imaginable, far different from the stresses and strains of **"Boule de Suif."**

Maupassant, who gives ample evidence of being a sharply critical, even cynical, observer of the foibles of his fellow men, and who found little to admire in what he saw, reserved his sympathy almost exclusively for prostitutes, peasants, and primitives. (pp. 40-1)

The movement of the story is extraordinary, and we are pulled by the narrator's art to accept an astonishing variety of situations; one leads to another so cunningly that we are unable to protest at scenes which, coldly summarized, are simply outrageous. (p. 41)

"La Maison Tellier" is a brilliantly conducted story: we are moved unprotesting to accept what the author chooses to put before us. He pulls us from sociological observation to what gives every appearance of being a comic narrative, to a zestful comic incident in the train, to a serio-comic masquerade, to a moment of deep feeling, and then a return by easy stages to the *status quo ante* after one last fling. (p. 42)

[In both **"Boule de Suif"** and **"La Maison Tellier"**] the story line is simple; it could have been handled much more swiftly, but given greater scope, less hurried, he is able to concentrate on establishing an atmosphere, a tone, and a precise visual image of the scene. Everything in these tales depends on developing the exact tone—the sombre mood of wintry defeat and sharp criticism in **"Boule de Suif,"** the wholly different tone of **"La Maison Tellier."** He takes time to develop this, precisely plotting scenes and images, revealing flashes of insight, and the result is a *nouvelle*. He did not bother in either of these stories, it should be noted, to use any *cadre,* or present a narrator to tell the story. Both are straight third-person reporting. (p. 43)

[A pair of stories] provides an example of a subject requiring ample scope for development which benefits from the space allowed: the very brief **"Yveline Samoris"** (1400 words), which appeared in the *Gaulois* in December 1882, and the longest of Maupassant's *nouvelles,* **"Yvette"** (27,000 words), which was serialized in the *Figaro* in August and September 1884.

"Yveline Samoris" sets up a framework in the form of a brief dialogue between two unidentified men; one points out 'la Comtesse Samoris', remarks that she killed her daughter, and then explains. His account is a flat illustration of the proposition set up in the *cadre:* '. . . Mme Samoris, née courtisane, avait une fille née honnête femme, voilà tout.' And that is just about all. The innocent daughter, discovering her mother's true status and source of income, melodramatically threatened to kill herself unless her mother changed her mode of life. The Countess shrugged and after a month Yveline killed herself. 'Voilà tout.' (p. 48)

Maupassant could hardly have been satisfied with the story: he never included it in any collection of stories published during his lifetime, but he kept it in mind as something to be reworked. **"Yvette"** is a very successful attempt to develop on the basic *donnée* a wholly different approach and tone, to consider the matter from a different angle, and change not only the dénouement but the whole focus of interest. (p. 49)

Given the situation of a woman who appears to have a position in society but is really a *courtisane* or *demi-mondaine* and who has a daughter who is ignorant of her mother's status, the *nouvelle* develops a question of character. What is Yvette like? Is she innocent or wily, terribly naïve or instinctively sophisticated? The movement of the story carries us not from ignorance to discovery as in **"Yveline Samoris,"** but from innocence to sophistication. This is not at all about loss of innocence in the conventional fictional sense, but the discovery, on the part of a sensitive young girl, of how much of life is a deceptive mask, and her response, by which she accommodates herself to this newly acquired knowledge. To make such a transition meaningful requires a great deal of preparation, the atmosphere and background have to be carefuly established, and all of this cannot be crammed into a few brief pages. (pp. 49-50)

For Maupassant, the higher one goes in the social scale, the more elaborate is the mask that conceals the blunt truth: Mme Tellier's establishment may not be an admirable institution in all respects, but it does not pretend to be much more than it is; Mme Obardi's salon is false in every respect, her name, her wealth, her position. And it is entirely natural, from Maupassant's point of view, that her daughter, having reached a crisis upon discovering the reality behind her mother's appearance, should resolve her crisis by a subterfuge of her own, the simulation of suicide. In the short story **"Yveline Samoris"** the girl's innocence is accepted as a premise and nothing contradicts it: she is thus led swiftly to take her own life by the logic of the tale. With Yvette, since we see more of her, know her better, matters are much less categorical: her innocence is more complex, we are not always certain how to judge her, we have the sense of dealing with an unknown being, which corresponds to Maupassant's idea of the *jeune fille,* and Yvette takes on thereby a greater complexity involving us in an awareness of the uncertainty and ambiguity of human existence.

After **Yvette** Maupassant wrote four other *nouvelles,* all of them first-rate and all of them suffused with a feeling of pity for the poor human creatures involved. The observation is just as keen, and the narration as well controlled as in **"L'Héritage,"** without the brittleness of that story and others like it where the author remains, not out of sight, but sardonically indifferent to the lives he explores. **"La Petite Roque," "Monsieur Parent," "Le Horla," "Le Champ d'Oliviers"** are all stories of considerable length written by a man in full control of his talent who has allowed himself all the room he needs. It is customary to invoke Maupassant's illness at this point in his life, an illness that ended in madness and an asylum, but all we can infer from this group of stories, incuding **"Le Horla,"** is that he was capable of great insight and great human sympathy.

"La Petite Roque," which appeared in December 1885 in the *Gil Blas,* treats a deliberately shocking subject—the rape and murder of a little girl—but the story is really about remorse for a crime—any crime—and a desire to end the terrible hallucinations which are produced by a guilty conscience. Once again the mask of respectability is pierced: it is the mayor of the town who is guilty of this terrible crime. Once again there is no *cadre,* and we are presented directly with a mysterious crime. . . . What gives the story its quality, in addition to the sense of unsentimental pity for the man, is the deep feeling for nature that is expressed: the countryside—the trees, the flowers, the brooks—is vibrantly beautiful in contrast to the horrors committed by men. It is not a pleasant story, but it is intensely powerful and superbly controlled; there are no false notes, no sneers, no leers, nothing to get in the way of a strongly felt apprehension of the dreadful potential for evil that exist behind the façade of social respectability and hidden by the beauties of nature. (pp. 52-4)

In a number of instances, some of which we have just seen, Maupassant felt that a given story had been told too quickly and went back to rework it, expand its dimensions, flesh out its bare bones. In most cases he improved his story immeasurably and found himself in the domain of the *nouvelle* where he left some very durable achievements. His ten longest stories are the most frequently remembered and include a remarkable proportion of first-rate tales; only **"Les Soeurs Rondoli"** seems out of place and of radically inferior quality, and although **"L'Héritage"** is overextended it none the less has a hardness and brilliance that wins our admiration.

Maupassant was a *conteur* as well as a *nouvelliste,* and we have divided his stories on this basis in order to observe the operation of his techniques in both forms. It should be noted that it is in his *contes* that the *cadre* or framework is extensively used; in his ten *nouvelles* he used a *cadre* only once, in **"Les Soeurs Rondoli"**; and in several instances when he transformed a *conte* into a *nouvelle* he abandoned the narrative framework and plunged directly into the story without preamble. (p. 56)

The examination we have just made of Maupassant's stories, looking closely at some and gathering others in groups about them, has shown how frequently that author repeats certain subjects and how persistently a few major themes recur. The most strikingly repeated theme is that of *paternity* revealed or discovered, treated in all variations and from all points of view. Somewhere behind there stories, as well as many others, is the general theme of *betrayal*—betrayal in the form of marital infidelity, deceit of any sort in human relations. Closely related is the pervading sense of *hypocrisy,* of the system of pretence that society has established for the conduct of its operations. It is clear from the stories we have studied that the one great premise which underlies his whole art is his belief in the utter disproportion between appearance and reality—everywhere and in all forms. His stories are written out of a need to correct that disproportion, if only fragmentarily, to lift the mask of appearance, to expose hypocrisy, to provide an unobstructed view of a piece of the world as it is, not as it is purported to be.

Such a view of life, when held by an indignant optimist, generally results in high-minded attempts at reform. For Maupassant the result is sadness, and sometimes even fear; the reality that lies behind appearance is no more comforting—probably even less so—than the outer falsity itself. To lift the mask is not lightly to be undertaken by one who believes that the face revealed will be ugly. . . . This perpetual turning over of all manner of stones to see what is under them has even more serious consequences: the obsessive need to see clearly, not to be duped, never to be taken in, leads also to horror at the thought of what one may find. This is what marks deeply the stories which explore the supernatural and the terror that accompanies it and, as we saw when we examined them as a group, revelation can be terrible; anyone who seeks to explore the heart of darkness must, even as in Conrad's terms, be prepared to face 'the horror'.

In such a dark and disillusioned view of life, some relief is indispensable, and Maupassant willingly and frequently sought such relief, but even this is related to his basic vision. Not all of his tales can be attached to the theme of appearance *v.* reality or the lifting of the mask; often he liked to show those areas of human life where the usual masks do not exist, the lives of the simple, the primitive, and, above all, the peasant, who provides comic activity and undisguised passions. (pp. 57-8)

One has the sense that Maupassant is at his most relaxed in the many stories which relate the comical, farcical behaviour of peasants and in the stories, like **"Mouche"** written nostalgically late in his career, of the gay, rowdy life on the Seine, which was like everything else 'pleine de mirage et d'immondices', but a life gloriously uncomplicated. Here he relaxed, but for the most part, in story after story, the insistence on the main theme of the mask is obsessive. (pp. 58-9)

In Maupassant's view there is no way out of the trap: innocence which is ignorance, an uncritical acceptance of appearance, is intolerable; but disillusioned exploration of the realities of existence leads to sadness, bitterness and even to fear. The primitives are not really attractive in themselves, it is just that their violent simplicity is engaging; and the comic peasants whose farces amuse are the same grimly brutal folk who casually let a baby freeze in **"Le Baptême."** As an artist Maupassant perfects his senses in order to reveal life as it is, but at the same time he believes his senses to be deceptive. He is haunted both by what he may miss and by what he may find, but all he can do is continue his exploration to the end. (p. 59)

When Ernest Hemingway died in the summer of 1961, William Faulkner spoke of him as a dedicated craftsman and defined his craft thus: '. . . to arrest for a believable moment the antics of human beings involved in the comedy and tragedy of being alive.' Maupassant practised this same craft and wrote his beautiful, lean narratives, so closely related to Hemingway's own (and so far removed from the intricacies of Faulkner's prose), which mercilessly probe beyond the crust of human activity and into realms which are only just beginning to be explored. (p. 60)

Edward D. Sullivan, in his Maupassant: The Short Stories, *Barron's Educational Series, Inc., 1962, 64 p.*

JOHN RAYMOND DUGAN (essay date 1973)

[Dugan explores Maupassant's handling of description, setting, and character development in the short stories.]

The short stories of Guy de Maupassant present to the critic certain rather complex problems. The two hundred and seventy odd tales which are known to be his, present such a variety of subject matter and technique that it is extremely difficult to pin him down. Some readers, judging from such well known pieces as **"La parure"** or **"La ficelle"** see him as the master of the trick ending, while others will consider **"Le Horla"** or **"L'endormeuse"** as sufficient evidence to call him an explorer of hallucination. As Sullivan so aptly points out, no such sweeping generality can even hope to approximate the truth [see excerpt dated 1962]. (p. 11)

The problem of the physical world is given a great deal of attention by Maupassant, as one might logically expect from an artist of his period and formation. By assigning to it a special function with regard to fictional problems of character and situation, he too will seek to bridge the gap. If our observations of his opinions are borne out in his own works, then reality must be developed according to some kind of discernible pattern.

On the simplest level this reality is obviously the décor in which the narrative is placed. This external world deals with a relatively small number of geographical locations, variations on which can be traced through his work from beginning to end. (pp. 11-12)

A child of Normandy, of that rich green countryside astride France's most important river and wedded to the sea, Maupassant exploits the area to great advantage. Landscapes, rural and maritime settings, are perhaps the richest and most varied descriptive elements in his work. (p. 12)

It is perfectly justifiable to expect that Normandy will dominate Maupassant's interest in non-Parisian France. Out of the stories reviewed, I have found that somewhere over half the total, or about one hundred and fifty, contain some reference, direct or otherwise to this geographical area—the Norman countryside, the Seine Valley, or the principal urban centres of this region that the author knew so well, Rouen, Le Havre, Etretat or Fécamp. . . . But nowhere does the author focus our attention for any extended duration on this element. The characters in such stories as **"Le Père Amable"** (1886), **"Le diable"** (1886) or **"Le petit fût"** (1884), are closely bound up with their fields and crops, yet again Maupassant does not indulge in extensive passages of description of external nature. The farm in these three is always there, but any description of the natural setting is brought into the narrative only as an adjunct of development of plot and character. (pp. 12-13)

Exterior description has still another variation in these essentially rural stories. Vial points out an interesting fact concerning

Maupassant's method of presentation—that in about half his stories he uses as a point of departure, or as an introduction, an incident which is only remotely connected with the main body of the tale, such as an after-dinner conversation, a train journey, or a courtroom situation, to mention only three general types. . . . In a number of rural tales this element is entirely contained within this framework, and is thus set apart from the development of plot and character. The fairy tale effect the "cadre" produces is most effective for example in **"La légende du Mont-Saint-Michel"** (1882), in which the description of the setting encases the narrative, thereby providing both the backdrop and the link between a timeless mythological tale and the real contemporary world of Maupassant the observer and the writer. This "cadre" description appears as well in such works as **"Le fermier"** (1886), in which it links people of distinct social classes, or in **"Le retour"** (1884), where we find an opening seascape which evokes the past life and the hardships of the principal participants in the action. By setting the description apart from the main action, Maupassant not only stresses the value of it within the story, but deepens its meaning and intensifies its relationship to the work as a whole. (p. 13)

[A] masterpiece such as **"Miss Harriet"** (1883), as much a rejection of "objectivity" as any work of Maupassant, depends for most of its impact on the significance of the setting. Both in the framework introduction and throughout the ensuing narrative, landscape and seascape are vitally important. The link is direct and immediate. The natural setting joins the "present" of the introductory cadre with the past of the central story by means of a visual image, a panoramic view of the coast and is complicated by the narrator's painting to which Miss Harriet reacts so strikingly. (p. 16)

Normandy, Provence, Auvergne, Corsica, Algeria all essentially non-urban, if not in the strictest of senses rural backdrops for a very large number of Maupassant's stories, all showiing similar variations in the use to which exterior description is put, and all revealing a similar concern with the sea, the sky, panoramic vistas. In the vast majority of cases the descriptive element somehow links the fictional world the author is creating to that of his own direct experience. Maupassant too is bridging a gap. This is supremely evident in the framework stories in which, by means of description, or less frequently an unexpected event, there is a sudden shift and immediate jumping of the time sequence. The framework represents the present, the story itself usually the past. But what about those stories which are basically urban in nature?

I have briefly mentioned certain works which are concerned both with the Norman seacoast and with Paris. The urban stories, mostly of course Parisian, must be regarded separately from these others. (pp. 17-18)

[What] is striking about these stories as a group is the relative infrequency with which Maupassant refers to the external aspects of the city. While our investigation shows that about one hundred stories make direct reference to Paris, about two-thirds of these offer only the briefest mention of the exterior world of urban life, if indeed they mention it at all. The importance of the outdoors is very much reduced with them although as we have seen, not entirely lost. If Maupassant seeks a "link", then surely a simple examination of outdoor description will not provide us with all the answers to this important relationship.

But obviously descriptive passages in Maupassant's short stories are not limited to the exterior world, whether the natural settings of land and sea or the cityscapes of late nineteenth century France. If the external world of Maupassant is dual, the natural and the man-made, so too is the internal—the interior *décor* and man himself. From a descriptive point of view both the appearance of his characters and their habitat will occupy his attention in no small way. Both these subjects focus our eye on the small detail; they are restricted and restrictive in scope, not expansive as was the external world. They are inward rather than outward probings, and in that sense, internal in nature. (p. 22)

Certainly one of the clearest illustrations of the power of interior descriptions in Maupassant's short stories is provided by **"Hautot père et fils."** After the accidental death of his father, Hautot fils travels hesitantly to Rouen, carrying out his parent's death-bed instructions, to break the news to his father's mistress. As he enters the apartment, this is what we see:

> Il n'osait plus parler, les yeux fixés sur la table dressée au milieu de l'appartement, et portant trois couverts, dont un d'enfant. Il regardait la chaise tournée dos au feu, l'assiette, la serviette, les verres, la bouteille de vin rouge entamée et la bouteille de vin blanc intacte. C'était la place de son père, dos au feu! On l'attendait. C'était son pain qu'il voyait, qu'il reconnaissait près de la fourchette, car la croûte était enlevée à cause des mauvaises dents d'Hautot. Puis, levant les yeux, il aperçut, sur le mur, son portrait, la grande photographie faite à Paris l'année de l'Exposition, la même qui était clouée au-dessus du lit dans la chambre à coucher d'Ainville.

It would seem from this, and indeed from a multitude of other passages . . . that Maupassant had learned much from Flaubert. One might say that, in their context, these objects have a whole story to tell. Selective detailed description and precise notation of fact preserve a seeming objectivity, a common enough device of Maupassant. Indeed we are witnessing this scene through the eyes of a fictional character, and thus the creator is doubly concealed. But in this fact lies an essential difference between the junior and the senior artists. By viewing the scene exclusively through the eyes of César Hautot, we the readers are much more immediately concerned with the people involved and their reactions to the situation, than with the objects. Unlike Charles Bovary's celebrated cap or Salammbô's anklet, these things speak only subjectively to the personnages directly involved, and not objectively to the outsider. The significant detail conveys meaning directly to the characters, and only indirectly to us. We must proceed through *them* to the object. The presence of the photograph underlines the basically introverted nature of the description. It is as if the father were physically present at this scene, viewing the confrontation of the two strangers whose lives are linked through him alone. The description is thus not objective at all in the true sense. To the reader it is in itself meaningless without the reactions of the fictitious characters who view it. It is as if these objects had no existence at all except that conferred on them by Hautot and family. This is the same relationship which exists between Miss Harriet, the landscape, and the painting. . . . (pp. 24-5)

The "real" world thus tends to be relegated in significance, through artistic presentation, to a secondary position. For if objects rely totally on personalities instead of the contrary, then they need not be introduced at all to establish character. The *rôle* of the *décor* becomes something quite distinct from

Flaubert's concept. Perhaps **"Le Horla"** will serve to clarify this point further. As the tension increases, the world of the narrator narrows down to his own bedroom. He lies in wait for this "being" to make its presence felt, and we see the following:

> En face de moi, mon lit, un vieux lit de chêne à colonnes; à droite, ma cheminée; à gauche, ma porte, fermée avec soin, après l'avoir laissée longtemps ouverte, afin de l'attirer; derrière moi, une très haute armoire à glace, qui me servait chaque jour pour me raser, pour m'habiller, et où j'avais coutume de me regarder, de la tête aux pieds, chaque fois que je passais devant.

What could appear to be more objective? And again the author conceals himself behind his protagonist. But like the carafe, the milk, and the turning pages of the book, these things, particularly the mirror, will take on new meanings for him, which we the spectators can only indirectly share. Again the objects are turned inwards. We do not interpret them as we do Félicité's parrot in **"Un coeur simple"**. The narrator does this himself.

Setting is frequently reduced in importance in Maupassant's short stories, yielding to a single object set apart from its physical context, and dominating the lives of the people concerned. And in many cases of this type the object itself is the title of the story. A list of these would include some of the author's best known works—**"Les bijoux"** (1883), **"La parure"** (1884), **"Les épingles"** (1888), **"Le gâteau"** (1882), **"Le masque"** (1889), **"Le parapluie"** (1884), and **"La ficelle"** (1883), to mention only some of the most popular. In every one, it is the object which is to mould the lives of the people and can even decide their fate. Poor Maître Hauchecorne's whole existence is destroyed by that cursed piece of string which he innocently salvaged; the Loisel couple struggle to pay for the lost necklace; Monsieur Lantin only discovers his dead wife's infidelity through the presence of the jewels; and Monsieur Oreille's insecurity is intensified by that seemingly innocent umbrella. Much more than simply described, these objects take on a kind of life of their own, and speak by their very presence or absence (as is the case in **"La parure"**) to their victims. They have far greater vitality than the famous "zaïmph" of Salammbô. And again the same contrast with Flaubert's technique is self-evident. Félicité's approach to life leads her inevitably and inexorably towards her parrot, whereas Maître Hauchecorne and the Loisels are destroyed by the seemingly inert thing which increasingly controls their lives. Félicité bestows life on her parrot, whereas Maupassant's people are affected by things which take on a kind of independent vitality because of the unique relationship between them and their possessors. It is the fact that they are the possessors of a kind of life which indicates that Maupassant's position is veering away from a narrow and conventional determinism. The movement is not outward, drawing our attention to the object that instigates the conflict, but rather inward to the person affected by that object. They speak not of the person but to the person. Reality itself turns inward. Victims as these people inevitably are, they all struggle with their situation. If Maupassant finds himself in a corner, he is not going to abandon life without a fight.

It would follow that he could create stories while dispensing almost totally with setting. This is certainly visible on the literal level in his courtroom narratives such as **"Tribunaux rustiques"** (1884), **"Le cas de Madame Luneau"** (1883), **"Rosalie Prudent"** (1886) or **"Un cas de divorce"** (1886). In all of these we have a method of presentation basically the same as that of some of the landscape. The courtroom testimony or the lawyer's summing up represent a kind of cadre in which the story unfolds. But only in the first of the stories mentioned is there any attention at all paid to description of this "real" setting. The narrative develops in a kind of physical void, and thus heightens the fictitious nature of the situation with which the plot is concerned. The lack of description diminishes the immediate veracity of the subsequent testimony and again turns it inward onto itself rather than outward towards the reader. The comedy or the pathos depends on the individual's interpretation of his own world, not on ours. (pp. 25-7)

I have reserved for special attention one type of setting often used by Maupassant, the interior of a travel conveyance, since it demonstrates perhaps more clearly than any other the significance of the interior setting in conjunction with the exterior. Be it train, boat or coach, in every case the milieu in which the narrative is rooted is significantly walled off from the outside world. At its most complete it represents a kind of microcosm, a self-sufficient little unit, set apart for detailed study. From **"Boule de Suif"** (1880) to **"L'inutile beauté"** (1890), that is to say from the beginning to the end of Maupassant's publishing career, this environment is of great value to him.

At its simplest, the travel interior provides still another type of framework or cadre into which the story can be placed, and thus a connective between the narrator's present and his past. Of such a type is of course **"Miss Harriet"** (1883), in which the storyteller is inspired to relate his curious experience to his fellow travellers as they pass through the area in which these events occurred. In the initial paragraphs of the piece we are given this setting in which the actual narration takes place. But of course the exterior setting is vividly set forth here, and represents a kind of point of departure for the intrigue itself. It is as if the little group in the break were witnessing a recreation of a series of incidents through imagination and memory against a backdrop of exterior reality from which they are physically separated by their means of locomotion, and the reality which is visually present is not a part of their first-hand experience. There is a theatrical quality to the physical world in its function as a link between past and present. (pp. 27-8)

Maupassant's most celebrated work, **"Boule de Suif"** is concerned with a coach, and once the characters are seated in the conveyance, we have no further reference to the setting itself. Our curiosity is aroused simply by the juxtaposition of such an unlikely group of people, perhaps . . . a little too carefully selected to give a cross-section of society. They are in an exceedingly confined space, seated in very strict order, under conditions of fear and tension. It is the fact that they are so confined that gives rise to the development of the narrative. Extracted from their respective physical and social environments and thrown briefly together by the need to escape from Prussian hands, they are thrown into an intensity of contact which is almost physical, and their undescribed surroundings are the major contributing factor to the story's intrigue, once the situation has been established.

This kind of setting then is an essential, as we can see, for the creation of certain situations in which the characters are removed from their own world. The travel cadre represents a technique by which the author separates certain phenomena from their environment in order to juxtapose them with specimens from other backgrounds and deal with the resultant conflict, or in other cases to consider them in isolation. The physical world often passes by the window, but in all cases it is clearly isolated from the narrative situation under examination. An excellent illustration of this may be found in the development of the marital conflict of the first chapter of **L'inutile beauté.''** As the elegant couple ride in the direction of the Bois de Boulogne, we catch glimpses of the Arc de Triomphe and the setting sun, of the flow of people and carriages, and generally of the activity perceivable outside. But our interest lies entirely with these two people and the reasons for their friction.

The travel setting is a rather special sort of ''interior'' setting for two rather obvious reasons which I have already suggested. In none of the stories and novels in which it is used is there a detailed presentation of the interior of the conveyance in question, so that our interest in that interior is exclusively directed towards the people of the narrative. It is thus the clearest manifestation of this general lack of concern which we have already seen in Maupassant for immediate physical reality in which one might call a photographic sense. Selection is very discriminating indeed. Simply compare the use of the train in Maupassant with Zola's presentation in *La bête humaine,* or Boule de Suif's coach journey with Emma Bovary's ride through Rouen with Léon. The purpose of selection is quite different here.

Secondly, the travel setting often, but not always, links the interior with the exterior as it passes by the vehicle, as indeed it does in both Flaubert and Zola. The inside setting which interests the reader seems quite stationary be comparison. In other words there is, as well as a bond between the two, a barrier which inhibits the intermingling of them. The settings are viewed and admired, but not contacted directly. The reaction of the character to external nature is an experience in which we the readers are concerned more with the mood and the dramatic tension than with the exterior objects which do admittedly contribute to them. Here again we might conclude that the rôle of the physical world has been shifted to some extent, since again external reality imposes itself on the characters in such a way that it is reduced in significance and only serves to intensify and clarify other aspects of the story. The movement is retractive, not expansive.

One must not forget, in dealing with the physical world of Maupassant, that for each individual in his stories, other individuals too are part of his reality. It therefore becomes important to glance briefly at how they reveal themselves, and how Maupassant chooses to present them. Here too there emerges a basic pattern and a curious development of technique. **''Boule de Suif''** offers an excellent starting point for the consideration of this factor.

The story is introduced by a rather lengthy and very effective description of the Prussian arrival in Rouen, and proceeds to the particular series of events which occupy the major portion of the narrative. Our first introduction to the occupants of the coach is the voices of three unidentified men who meet in front of the Hôtel de Normandie. It is not until the coach is well under way and until the dawn appears, that their shadowy forms are brought into clear focus. First, the three married couples are introduced, with fairly complete indications of their social backgrounds, and some slight indication of their physical appearance. Following this, there is reference to the nuns, then to Cornudet and his past, and finally to Boule de Suif herself. And it is only this last named who merits a detailed physical portrait.

Both **''Mademoiselle Fifi''** and **''La maison Tellier''** are begun in a similar fashion. There is at first an indication of the setting, and then the characters, one by one, are introduced. In the case of the former, we see the major first in a reclining position reading his mail, and then are given descriptions of him and his subordinates in some detail, terminating with the appearance of Mademoiselle Fifi. In the latter story we learn first of Madame's background, then we see her in some detail. After an introduction to their establishment, physical descriptions of the employees follow one after the other.

In all three of these relatively early pieces, Maupassant attaches a good deal of importance to the presentation of his personages before the story *per se* can be really launched. It is quite obvious that, in his emulation of his illustrious predecessors, the younger author is using a tried and true technique in order to set his story in motion. The characters are methodically catalogued, introduced one by one, before we can have any clear indication as to the nature of the story. Their physical appearance, whether presented in minute detail, or rapidly sketched in, is placed in a position of emphasis and would appear to vary in detail in direct proportion to his or her significance in the subsequent development. (pp. 29-31)

Out of this general review of descriptive material within the short stories there emerges then a series of patterns which, when considered in the broader context of all of Maupassant's prose work becomes helpful in ascertaining his major artistic contribution.

The frequent landscape and seascape passages seem to share certain general characteristics. Whether it be the Norman coast of **''Miss Harriet''** the Seine Valley of **''Le Horla''** or the city

Caricature of Maupassant.

of Rouen as we find it in **"Un Normand"** (1882) or the Mediterranean coast of **"Les soeurs Rondoli"** we can discern an underlying, one might say almost abstract pattern of strong horizontal and vertical sweeps. The movement here is generally outward, reaching towards a horizon, towards an infinity which is given depth by the sudden intervention of masts, rocks, steeples or other striking verticals.

The means by which Maupassant integrates these passages into the fabric of the story also has significance. The more elaborately detailed descriptions come generally in one of two important locations. They may occur in the introduction or conclusion, that is to say in the "cadre" such as we find in **"La peur"**, or **"La légende du Mont Saint-Michel"**, and thus attempt to link two distinct time sequences, the "real" one of the narrator and the fictional one of the story itself, or indeed we may discover them within the context of the narrative, where again they have a certain linking function. In **"Les soeurs Rondoli"** description links the interiorized situation of the railway carriage with the outdoor world of the passing Mediterranean coast. In **"La petite Roque"** it links the internal suffering of the criminal with the deed itself. Generally speaking the descriptive passage attempts to underline and give lasting value to a particular moment in the narrative. Time again is intimately bound up with description and deserves careful consideration.

The interior descriptions too fall into a broad pattern. In his fidelity to the Flaubertian concept, Maupassant too attaches much value to the little significant detail—the photo in **"Hautot père et fils"**, the pictures on the wall in **"La chambre 11"**, the piece of string in **"La ficelle"**. In each case the descriptive material is scrupulously pertinent to the characters and situation at hand. Indeed we see a tendency away from the materialistic, essentially visual rendition of real objects towards a more internalized vision in which these objects, like the jewels of **"Les bijoux"**, the necklace of **"La parure"** or indeed the mysterious, invisible **"Horla"** become meaningful only through the internal life of the characters present, and not through some objective external communication between the described world and the reader. Here too we have a quest for a new dimension, a new interpretation of man's universe. The dominant object, the travel setting, the interior décor, the hallucination, the landscape in the short stories all point in the direction of a deepening interrogation of the meaning of existence itself.

Generally one can conclude then that the descriptive element in the short stoies indicates a shift in emphasis, a change in perspective on the part of the artist. Techniques of the "realistic" tradition, impressionistic presentation, the little significant detail are maintained in Maupassant, but there is the suggestion of a new dimension not clearly discernable in the conventional interpretation of sense perceptions. (pp. 32-3)

John Raymond Dugan, in his Illusion and Reality: A Study of Descriptive Techniques in the Works of Guy de Maupassant, *Mouton, 1973, 209 p.*

MARY DONALDSON-EVANS (essay date 1981)

[Donaldson-Evans discusses three thematic subcodes in "Boule de suif"—the nutritional, the politico-economic, and the military—and she explores the way in which these interact with the main thematic code of sexuality.]

At the risk of being dismissed as a subscriber to what in recent criticism has been called the "referential illusion", I should like to suggest that a full appreciation of **"Boule de suif"** is possible only if one takes into account the "hors-texte" of the Franco-Prussian War of 1870-71, for it provides both background to the story and a vital part of its symbolism. Historians have suggested that this tragic year, with its three-part catastrophe (the battles of the Empire against Prussia, the Republic against Prussia, and Versailles against the Commune) marked the end of the French self-image of grandeur, that after the devastating defeats suffered at the hands of the enemy and the fratricidal bloodbath which followed, France was no longer able to look upon herself as "la Grande Nation". Maupassant, a young idealist at the time of the war, had enlisted a year before he was obliged to, so eager was he to participate in a French victory which he felt to be imminent. For him too, the disastrous outcome was a turning point, an end to his youthful optimism and naïveté. He was to spend the next several years meditating upon the causes of 'l'Année Terrible", a meditation which would bear fruit in the writing of **"Boule de suif"**. (pp. 16-17)

"Boule de suif" is constructed upon the interplay of three thematic "sub-codes"—the nutritional, the politico-economic and the military—with the main code which is sexual. To understand the way in which these codes function, it is necessary to consider the text in both its diachronic and synchronic dimensions. It is also useful, although not essential, to place **"Boule de suif"** in the context of Maupassant's war stories, on the one hand, and his 'whore" stories, on the other. It is not by chance that the two themes frequently collide, and that his most unforgettable prostitutes are war heroes as well.

Let us begin, then, with the sexual code. As a prostitute, Boule de suif is the incarnation of sexuality. She is a "marchande d'amour", her *marchandise* being her body. Aggression is the *sine qua non* of her trade. In the eyes of society, she is immoral, ignoble; yet, . . . Boule de suif, like many of Maupassant's prostitutes, has managed to retain her self-respect by transferring her moral sensibility to a domain other than the sexual. She thus possesses a sense of dignity despite public opinion, and when the whispered insults reach her ears at the outset of the journey, she is not intimidated; rather, she looks directly at her insulters with "un regard tellement provocant et hardi qu'un grand silence aussitôt régna". That they let themselves be silenced by her is not an indication of respect, however, and the epithets used to describe the prostitute as seen through their eyes ("honte publique", "vendue sans vergogne") make it quite obvious that at this point in the story she is held in low esteem indeed. In fact, a study of the terms used for the prostitute throughout the story reveals that they follow a curve, corresponding closely to the rise and fall of her "value" in their eyes. Her proper name, Elisabeth Rousset, is used only four times, in each case by the innkeeper Follenvie in transmitting the Prussian's message. To the others, and to the narrator, she is Boule de suif, an *objet de consommation* in the eyes of all. (pp. 19-20)

If the women are, or pretend to be, shocked by the presence of a harlot in the carriage, the men are clearly aroused. The vulgar Loiseau is the only one not to lower his eyes under the prostitute's provocative gaze; rather, he continues to look at her "d'un air émoustillé". Cornudet, the only male traveller unaccompanied by a woman, can afford to be bolder. The first night in Tôtes, he openly propositions her in the hotel corridor and only reluctantly returns to his own room after her adamant refusal. . . . The other two male characters, prevented by their class consciousness from any overt reaction to the prostitute's sexuality, effect a similar transfer the last night when, during the "celebration" dinner, they engage in a seemingly innocent flirtation with one another's partners. . . . (p. 20)

Nor do the other women play a completely passive role. Even the nuns, whose position places them beyond sexuality, are involved. Maupassant's ingenuity in using a nun to weaken the prostitute's resistance must not be forgotten, and the elder nun's *emportement* is not unlike Boule de suif's own. In fact, a study of Maupassant's lexicon reveals the presence of a contiguous relationship between Boule de suif and the nuns. For example, the prostitute's chubby fingers, "pareils à des chapelets de courtes saucisses" evoke both the literal *chapelets* of the two nuns and the *saucisson* upon which they lunch during the final stage of the journey. Moreover, the nuns are characterized as "de saintes filles habituées à toutes les soumissions", and are the first to obey the Prussian officer when he asks the voyagers to exit from the carriage upon their arrival in Tôtes. Only the epithet "saintes" apparently subverts the equation nuns = prostitutes, and one senses that, in the case of the elder nun at least, it is merely an accident of nature (the disfiguring smallpox) which made of her a "sainte fille en cornette" rather that a "fille" *tout court*. (pp. 21-2)

Among the male travellers, the prostitute's ostracization on sexual grounds is mirrored by Cornudet's politico-economic isolation. . . . Just as the women are sisters in their supposed "virtue", the men draw together against Cornudet, "frères par l'argent". In actual fact, however, the distance which separates the moneyed males from Cornudet is travelled as quickly as that separating the "virtuous" women from the prostitute. Cornudet has inherited a large sum of money from his bourgeois father. Unlike the other bourgeois, however, he was not imbued with the bourgeois ethic. Rather than invest his money to increase his wealth, he had spent it; rather than work, he had played. Now a "have not", he is associated with the prostitute who is by definition *déclassée*. Unlike her, however, he is untrue to himself, and his passive role in the collaboration (he does nothing to alert Boule de suif to the plot and only expresses his dismay after it has succeeded) makes a mockery of the ideals embodied in his loudly proclaimed Republicanism. In his case, too, liberty, equality and fraternity have sold out to egotism. As eager as the others to reach Le Havre, he has sacrificed Boule de suif just as surely as they have. For him, too, the prostitute has a *valeur marchande*. (p. 23)

The nutritional code is present at all levels of the text. The alimentary uses of animal fat are well-known, and Boule de suif is the first to be assimilated to the nutritive, both literally and metaphorically. . . . If the metaphorical alliance of the sexual and culinary can be considered a literary commonplace, . . . Maupassant's exploitation of the theme is far from hackneyed, thanks to the constant *va-et-vient* between the literal and the figurative. As a prostitute Boule de suif is to be bought and consumed, much as one would buy a cutlet from a butcher shop. Moreover, it is clear that her bourgeois travelling companions are voracious consumers, and Maupassant's description of the contagious yawning which is transmitted from one to another places the emphasis, not upon the various "styles" of yawns dictated by etiquette and social class, but rather upon the common "trou béant d'où sortait une vapeur". . . . the rapidity with which the travellers empty the strumpet's basket, and the savagery of their appetites are suggestive of a cannibalistic carnage, the victim of which is Boule de suif herself. . . . (pp. 24-5)

In Tôtes (which suggests "tôt" and "toast", both derivatives of the Latin *tostus*, meaning "grilled" or "cooked") the metaphorical union of the sexual with the nutritional is again underlined by the fact that each of the Prussian officer's three "invitations" to the prostitute is extended, through the intermediary of the aptly named Follenvie, at dinnertime. The fifth dinner, which we have characterized as a celebration dinner, is, as we have seen, consumed in the absence of Boule de suif who is otherwise engaged upstairs, this time quite literally sacrificing herself for the good of her compatriots. But unlike the previous nutritional sacrifice, this giving of herself had not been spontaneous; rather it had been wrenched from her through a carefully planned and skilfully executed verbal aggression. The scenario of the conspiracy had been sketched the previous day while Boule de suif attended a baptism. Thus, while the prostitute, ostensibly the symbol of vice, prayed, the married couples, apparent bastions of all that is proper and "moral", plotted against her, the women in particular deriving vicarious pleasure from their planning. . . . Assimilated at once to the food itself and to the gluttonous cook, it is these women who, beneath their veneer of sophistication and righteousness, are the true *marchandes d'amour*. (pp. 25-6)

The final betrayal of Boule de suif, the arrogance which the bourgeois display as they continue their journey, and their insensitivity and egoism in eating in her presence and without offering her even their leftovers (the nuns wrap up their remaining sausage after having eaten their fill) once again evoke the culinary. (pp. 26-7)

This discussion of the nutritional code would be incomplete were we to fail to evoke the most arresting metaphor of all, that of the pigeons pecking at the horses' steaming excrement in the final scene at Tôtes. . . . The solemnity and decorum with which the coprophagic pigeons feed upon the horses' dung is clearly symbolic of the arrogance and outward "dignity" with which the travellers had committed the most shameful and undignified of betrayals. The double evocation of the digestive in this passage (the pigeons ingesting what is in fact the residue—one is tempted to say "end-product"—of the alimentary process) in addition to suggesting the repulsive nature of the bourgeois' treason and collaboration with the Enemy, mirrors the circular movement of the narrative itself and subverts the notion of a plot built upon the horizontal line of a journey. (p. 27)

In addition to its frequent intersections with the sexual, the nutritional code is closely associated with the military. The first and most obvious meeting takes place at the semantic level of the plot. The Rouen bourgeois lodge and nourish the occupying army, affecting alienation and animosity in the street while displaying an obliging hospitality and even a certain affection for the soldiers in the privacy of their own homes. . . . The bourgeois' hypocrisy (represented by the interior-exterior opposition) stems both from their materialism (they would perhaps be given fewer soldiers to feed it they caused no trouble) and from their cowardice. . . . Such egotistical logic brought to the defence of what is in fact collaboration with the Enemy stands in direct contrast to the passionate patriotism of the lower classes, farmers, prostitutes, *petites gens* of all sorts whose silent nocturnal murders of Prussian soldiers endanger their lives without bringing them fame or glory. . . . It is not these fearless idealists, true heroes of the war, who are responsible for France's defeat, but rather the bourgeois whose economic clout has placed them in positions of military as well as social leadership. . . The exemplary value of Boule de suif's resistance is lost upon her bourgeois travelling companions who are incapable of any action which would jeopardize their own material welfare. In their betrayal of the prostitute, they are comparable to the bourgeois who quietly nourish the occupying soldiers: indeed, they "feed" Boule de suif to the Prussian in exchange for their own freedom. With their help, he realizes a sexual invasion of the unwilling prostitute which is but a metaphor for his army's military invasion of France. . . . Seen as a mirror-perfect image of France herself, *la belle, la douce France,* humiliated and betrayed by her very own people, those whom she had succoured and nourished, Boule de suif acquires a tragic grandeur. (pp. 28-9)

Boule de suif fails to overcome the egotism of her compatriots, inspires no one to patriotism. And yet she is, in a peculiar way, an *inspiratrice*. Among the many symbolic roles played by the fat prostitute, her extratextual role is no doubt the most important, for she is at once fictional creation and creator's muse, source of creation. The real-life harlot after whom Boule de suif is modeled, Adrienne Legay, is merely the first in a long series of women who awakened Maupasant's authorial being, provided it with the nourishment upon which it was to feed for ten years. Maupassant's unsuspected talent, revealed *du jour au lendemain* with the publication of **"Boule de suif",** may have caused some *mauvaises langues* to wag about collaboration with Flaubert (a rumour belied by the correspondence between the two men); a retrospective look reveals that Maupassant's true "collaborator", in this as in countless later stories and the novels as well, is *la Femme,* Woman, who becomes the inspiration and the meeting place for metaphors as widely divergent as those evoked here. Whether viewed as a nourishing mother, a symbol of the Empire, the desired Republic or a humiliated France, Boule de suif and her avatars throughout Maupassant's gynocentric fictional universe remain intimately linked to their creator's literary triumph. (pp. 33-4)

Mary Donaldson-Evans, "The Decline and Fall of Elisabeth Roussett: Text and Context in Maupassant's 'Boule de Suif'," in Australian Journal of French Studies, *Vol. XVIII, Part 1, January-April, 1981, pp. 16-34.*

ADDITIONAL BIBLIOGRAPHY

Artinian, Artine. *Maupassant Criticism in France: 1880-1940*. New York: King's Crown Press, 1941, 228 p.

A historical overview of Maupassant's critical reception in France. This work includes a bibliography of articles on Maupassant from European, English, and American books and periodicals covering the era 1880 to 1940.

Artinian, Robert Willard, and Artinian, Artine. *Maupassant Criticism: A Centennial Bibliography, 1880-1979*. Jefferson, N.C.: McFarland, 1982, 178 p.

Designed to expand and update the bibliography listed above.

Bourget, Paul. "Guy de Maupassant." In *Short Stories of the Tragedy and Comedy of Life,* Vol. I, by Guy de Maupassant, pp. xiii-xxv. Dingwall-Rock Ltd, 1903.

Praises the suppleness, variety, and freedom of Maupassant's art.

Donaldson-Evans, Mary. "The Matrical Marsh: A Symbol of Hope in Maupassant's Work." *French Forum* 2, No. 3 (September 1977): 255-262.

Discusses the importance of the marsh as a central, unifying symbol in Maupassant's work.

Fellows, Otis. "Maupassant's 'Apparition': A Source and a Creative Process." *Romanic Review* XXXIII, No. I (February 1942): 58-71.

Suggests that Maupassant made use of a story by Jules Lecomte as the source for his short story "Apparition." Fellows delineates Maupassant's reworking of the material to create a superb tale of horror.

Greaves, A. A. "Some Contradictions in the Work of Guy de Maupassant." *Nottingham French Studies* 7, No. 1 (May 1968): 80-9.

Discusses the influence of the works of the German philosopher Arthur Schopenhauer on Maupassant.

Hearn, Lafcadio. "A Great Prosateur." In his *Essays in European and Oriental Literature,* edited by Albert Mordell, pp. 80-6. New York: Dodd, Mead, 1923.

Faults the subject matter, pessimism, and repetition in Maupassant's work.

Ignotus, Paul. *The Paradox of Maupassant*. London: University of London Press, 1966, 288 p.

Biography and general critical survey of Maupassant.

Lavrin, Janko. "Chekhov and Maupassant." *Slavonic Review* 5, No. 13 (June 1926): 1-24.

Comparison of the short story techniques of Maupassant and Chekhov.

Lock, Peter W. "Pattern and Meaning in Maupassant's 'Amour'." *French Review* 41 (October 1967): 70-5.

Detailed analysis of structure and imagery in "Amour."

Lubbock, Percy. In his *The Craft of Fiction,* pp. 110-23. London: Jonathan Cape, 1921.

Comparison of William Thackeray and Maupassant in their exposition of the short story.

MacNamara, Matthew. "A Critical Stage in the Evolution of Maupassant's Story-Telling." *Modern Language Review* 71, No. 2 (April 1976): 294-303.

Explores the influence of Maupassant's periodical writing on his short story technique.

Matthews, J. H. "Oblique Narration in Maupassant's 'Pierrot'. *Modern Languages* XLII, No. 2 (June 1961): 48-54.

Discusses narrative stance in "Pierrot."

Maugham, Somerset W. "Preface to *Complete Short Stories,* Vol. I (American Edition)." In his *Selected Prefaces and Introductions of W. Somerset Maugham,* pp. 42-61. London: Heinemann, 1963.

Assesses Maupassant's current stature in literary history. While acknowledging Maupassant's influence on a generation of short story writers, Maugham faults what he sees as Maupassant's oversimplified characters.

Moger, Angela S. "Narrative Structure in Maupassant: Frames of Desire." *PMLA* 100, No. 3 (May 1985): 315-27.

Examines Maupassant's technique in utilizing the frame structure in his short stories.

Moore, Olin H. "The Romanticism of Guy de Maupassant." *PMLA* XXXIII, No. 1 (March 1918): 96-134.

Defines and analyzes the Romantic element in Maupassant's short stories.

Morris, D. Hampton. "Variations on a Theme: Five Tales of Horror by Maupassant." *Studies in Short Fiction* 17, No. 4 (Fall 1980): 475-81.

Discerns a similarity of structure in "Lui?," "La chevelure," "Le Horla," "La nuit," and "Qui sait?."

O'Connor, Frank. "Country Matters." *Kenyon Review* XXIX, No. 4 (Autumn 1962): 583-94.

Discusses Maupassant as an inferior writer, obsessed with sexual themes.

Pritchett, V. S. "Maupassant." In his *Books in General,* pp. 94-103. London: Chatto and Windus, 1953.

Claims that Maupassant is a genius, but one who was "selective" and "taught", as opposed to the broad, inclusive genius that characterizes the work of Tolstoy or Chekhov.

Sullivan, Edward D. "Maupassant and the Motif of the Mask." *Symposium* X, No. 1 (Spring 1956): 34-41.

Examines Maupassant's use of the mask and masking in his fiction.

Symons, Arthur. "Guy de Maupassant." In his *Studies in Prose and Verse,* pp. 97-107. New York: E. P. Dutton, 1904.

Finds Maupassant's realism superficial, lacking in depth, and concerned only with sensual pleasures.

Wallace, A. H. "Philogyny as an Element in Maupassant's Work." In *Studies in Honor of Alfred G. Engstrom,* edited by Robert T. Cargo and Emanuel J. Mickel, Jr., pp. 177-96. Chapel Hill: University of North Carolina Press, 1972.

In a break with the traditional view of Maupassant as a misogynist, depicts him as a great admirer and champion of women.

Wellek, René. "Guy de Maupassant." In his *A History of Modern Criticism,* pp. 12-14. New Haven: Yale University Press, 1965.

Brief discussion of Maupassant's literary theories and of his relationship with Flaubert.

Herman Melville

1819-1891

American novelist, short story and novella writer, and poet.

Melville is one of the major American literary figures of the nineteenth century. Although best known for his novel *Moby-Dick; or, The Whale*, which is considered a masterpiece, he is also recognized as an outstanding writer of short fiction. In his short stories and in the novella *Billy Budd, Sailor (An Inside Narrative),* he continued his exploration of the inscrutable ambiguity of the moral universe. A master of both the realistic and allegorical narrative, Melville is praised for his rich prose style and complex symbolism. The best of his short stories demonstrate that he was an incisive philosophical artist who strove to penetrate the ambiguities of life and to define the individual's relation to society and the universe.

Born and raised in New York, Melville lived comfortably until he was twelve, when his father died and he was forced to leave school to help support his family. After a succession of odd jobs, he sailed in 1839 as a cabin boy aboard a merchant ship bound for Liverpool, England. Upon his return to the United States he tried his fortune in the West, but with little success; what followed he described through the narrator of *Moby Dick:* "Having little or no money in my purse, and nothing in particular to interest me on shore, I thought I would sail about a little and see the watery part of the world." Aboard the whaler *Acushnet* he traveled widely, jumping ship in the Marquesas, living among a tribe of cannibals, landing in prison in Tahiti, and generally experiencing life as few Americans had experienced it before. Back in the United States and with no prospect of a career, he wrote about his remarkable journeys. *Typee: A Peep at Polynesian Life* and its sequel, *Omoo: A Narrative of Adventures in the South Seas*, were immediate successes, and other works in their vein followed. Melville became increasingly restless with the adventure narrative, however, and was eager to explore philosophical and metaphysical questions in his novels. He tried his hand at allegory, first in *Mardi: And a Voyage Thither* and later in ever more experimental works. Though now considered a classic work of American fiction, *Moby-Dick,* a highly symbolic and fully developed quest novel, did not achieve the critical or popular success of *Typee* or *Omoo,* nor did *Pierre; or, The Ambiguities*, a pessimistic, largely autobiographical romance.

By the early 1850s Melville was physically exhausted, emotionally distressed, and financially strapped by the failure of his recent efforts. He turned to short fiction, contributing tales and sketches through the mid-1850s to *Putnam's Monthly Magazine* and *Harper's New Monthly Magazine*. Collected in part as *The Piazza Tales,* the only short story collection published in Melville's lifetime, these short works were on the whole favorably received, and he welcomed the small income they provided. But soon Melville turned from the modest possibilities that magazine fiction offered, experimenting with satire in *The Confidence-Man: His Masquerade* and lecturing from time to time on such subjects as "Statues in Rome" and "Traveling," but with at best modest success. Around 1860 he began writing poetry, completing his first collection, *Battle-Pieces and Aspects of the War,* in 1866. That year he also became a customs official in New York, a post he held for twenty years.

The Bettmann Archive, Inc.

Melville continued to write poetry, but his writings were less and less known among the public. A brief revival of interest in his works spearheaded by two English writers in the late 1880s pleased and encouraged Melville, but he died, generally unknown and unappreciated, before making public any new writings of significance. *Billy Budd,* left in manuscript at the author's death, was not published until 1924. Its appearance, along with Raymond M. Weaver's 1921 biography *Herman Melville: Mariner and Mystic* and other critical attention, led to a revival of interest in the Melville canon.

Melville's short fiction divides neatly into two kinds: magazine stories and his one novella, *Billy Budd*. His best-known short stories are "Bartleby the Scrivener: A Story of Wall-Street," "Benito Cereno," the sketches of "The Encantadas; or, The Enchanted Isles," and "The Paradise of Bachelors and the Tartarus of Maids." "Bartleby" takes place mainly in a Wall Street law office. The story's lawyer-narrator recounts Bartleby's withdrawal from ordinary society, his imprisonment and death, and relates his own reactions to them. Variously seen as an alienated worker, a comic hero, a surrealistic artist who refuses to follow society's biddings, an incarnation of Christ, or the narrator's conscience, Bartleby is considered one of the most compelling characters of nineteenth-century American fiction. "Benito Cereno" is based on a factual account of a shipboard slave revolt taken from Amasa Delano's *Narrative of Voyages and Travels in the Northern and Southern Hemispheres,* published in 1817. The story unfolds through its narrator, who, happening upon the ship in peril, sees the evil before him but in his innocence, cannot comprehend it. Admired as a brilliant technical performance that illustrates Melville's belief in the ambiguity of good and evil, "Benito Cereno" has attracted much comment. Warner Berthoff found in the story "a seriousness of general implication and a closeness to common reality that reach beyond Poe's capacity as an artist," and Yvor Winters characterized the tale as "appalling in its completeness, in its subtle horror, and in its silky quiet." "The Encantadas," which comprise nine sketches, are set in the Galápagos Islands, which Melville visited as an *Acushnet* crewman. Although seven of the sketches are purely descriptive, three introduce human characters; critic Jay Leyda described their cumulative effect as "a single fiery glimpse of man's sins toward man." The intricate "Paradise of Bachelors and Tartarus of Maids" is commonly interpreted as Melville's comment on industrial society. Essentially a juxtaposition of bachelor life in London's Temple with working women's lives in a New England paper mill, the story has garnered less comment than the works discussed above, but it has attracted commentary for its audacious physiological symbolism.

Melville's *Billy Budd* has been adapted into a celebrated play, a highly praised opera, a popular motion picture, and a television drama, and it has been touched by every important school of modern literary criticism. Beneath the surface of this pared, refined, and direct tale of a youthful sailor's impressment and execution lies a morally oblique study of the collision of good and evil. Critics note that the story unites simple action with complex meaning, fusing history and imagination with Melville's own shipboard experiences. Among the most prominent commentators, Albert Camus saw the tale as a "flawless story that can be ranked with certain Greek tragedies," W. H. Auden admired the "insoluble paradoxes" raised by the work, and E. M. Forster viewed it as "a remote unearthly episode, but . . . a song not without words." Numerous aesthetic and interpretive problems surround the story, ranging from early and current claims that the tale is Melville's testament to religious faith to detailed explications of the characters' motives, psychological states, and symbolic meanings. The story also presents textual challenges, as critics continue to debate whether the work is unfinished. *Billy Budd*'s critics applaud Melville's final achievement, even as they remain at odds about exactly what Melville achieved, or why, or how.

Once nearly forgotten, Melville's short stories are now widely admired, and the best of them are considered among the finest in the genre. Equally, the novella *Billy Budd* is recognized as a masterpiece. Long canonized as one of America's greatest writers, Melville is acclaimed for his short fiction—fiction which, in the words of Edward J. O'Brien, makes Melville "one of the greatest visionary artists the world has had since William Blake."

(See also *Nineteenth-Century Literature Criticism,* Vols. 3, 12, and *Dictionary of Literary Biography,* Vol. 3.)

PRINCIPAL WORKS

SHORT FICTION

The Piazza Tales 1856
The Apple-Tree Table, and Other Sketches 1922
**Billy Budd, and Other Prose Pieces* 1924
Complete Stories of Herman Melville 1949
***Billy Budd, Sailor (An Inside Narrative)* 1962

OTHER MAJOR WORKS

Typee: A Peep at Polynesian Life (novel) 1846
Omoo: A Narrative of Adventures in the South Seas (novel) 1847
Mardi: And a Voyage Thither (novel) 1849
Redburn: His First Voyage (novel) 1849
White-Jacket; or, The World in a Man-of-War (novel) 1850
Moby-Dick; or, The Whale (novel) 1851; also published as *The Whale,* 1851
Pierre; or, The Ambiguities (novel) 1852
The Confidence-Man: His Masquerade (novel) 1857
Battle-Pieces and Aspects of the War (poetry) 1866

**Billy Budd* was probably written between 1885 and 1891.

**This edition contains the first printing of a genetic text of this work.

RICHARD HENRY DANA, SR. (letter date 1854)

[*A nineteenth-century American editor, poet, and essayist, Dana helped found the* North American Review *in 1815 and is remembered for promoting a simple and direct writing style. In the following excerpt from a letter to Evert Duyckinck, he responds to Duyckinck's 1853 disclosure that the anonymously published "Bartleby the Scrivener" is by Melville.*]

I was glad to learn from your paper [*The Literary World,* 3 December 1853] that **"Bartleby"** was by Mr. Melville. It touches the nicer strings of our complicated nature, & finely blends the pathetic & ludicrous. The secret power of such an inefficient & harmless creature over his employer, who all the while has a misgiving of it, shows no common insight.—The two other clerks relieve the picture, at the same time that they are skilfully & humorously set off against each other.

Richard Henry Dana, Sr., in a letter to Evert Duyckinck on January 25, 1854, in Bartleby the Inscrutable: A Collection of Commentary on Herman Melville's Tale "Bartleby the Scrivener," *edited by M. Thomas Inge, Archon Books, Hamden, CT, 1979, p. 31.*

MICHAEL SADLEIR (essay date 1922)

[*An outstanding twentieth-century English bibliographer and critic, Sadleir wrote pioneering studies of the nineteenth-century English book trade and of the period's fiction, including* XIX Century Fiction: A Bibliographical Record *(1951). His* Excursions in Victorian Bibliography *contains one of the earliest notices of Melville's short fiction, which is excerpted below. Sadleir here extols Melville's technical achievement in "Benito Cereno" and "The Encantadas."*]

"Benito Cereno" and **"The Encantadas"** hold in the small compass of their beauty the essence of their author's supreme artistry. They are profound and lovely and tenderly robust, but they are never tedious and never wilful. Surely it were generous to admit that Melville sought to improve on *Moby Dick* and that, in the matter of technical control, he succeeded? These two stories cannot as literary achievement compare with their vast and teeming predecessor. That is natural. But they may not be ignored as the last glimmer of a dying lamp. They mark the highest technical level of their author's work, and, had not within a year or two of their appearance the darkness of self-distrust descended on him, might well have proved a revelation of something yet to come from the brain of Herman Melville, something destined—but for the treacherous inhibition of human frailty—to excel in power everything to which that brain had previously given birth. (p. 220)

Michael Sadleir, "Herman Melville: Essay and Bibliography," in his Excursions in Victorian Bibliography, *Chaundy & Cox, 1922, pp. 217-34.*

[JOHN MIDDLETON MURRY] (essay date 1924)

[Murry was a distinguished twentieth-century English literary critic and editor. In the following excerpt, he argues that Billy Budd *is Melville's last testament.]*

With the mere fact of the long silence in our minds we could not help regarding ***Billy Budd*** as the last will and spiritual testament of a man of genius. We could not help expecting this, if we have any imaginative understanding. Of course, if we are content to dismiss in our minds, if not in our words, the man of genius as mad, there is no need to trouble. Some one is sure to have told us that ***Billy Budd,*** like *Pierre,* is a tissue of naivety and extravagance: that will be enough. And, truly, ***Billy Budd is*** like *Pierre*—startlingly like. Once more Melville is telling the story of the inevitable and utter disaster of the good and trying to convey to us that this must be so and ought to be so—chronometrically and horologically. He is trying, as it were with his final breath, to reveal the knowledge that has been haunting him—that these things must be so and not otherwise.

Billy Budd is a foretopman, pressed out of the merchant service into the King's Navy in the year of the Nore mutiny. He is completely good, not with the sickly goodness of self-conscious morality, but as one born into earthly paradise—strong, young, manly, loyal, brave, unsuspecting, admired by his officers and adored by his shipmates. And he is hated by the master-at-arms, the policeman of the lower deck. Claggart hates him, simply because he is Billy Budd, with the instinctive hatred of the evil for the good. Melville is careful to explain that there is no reason whatever for his hatred; he puts it deliberately before us as naked and elemental—the clash of absolutes. Claggart is subtle and cool, he works quietly, and he is also a man of courage. He involves Billy Budd in the thin semblance of revolutionary mutiny. The master-at-arms deliberately risks his own life in order to destroy his enemy's. He risks it, and loses it, for in the privacy of his own cabin the captain confronts the accuser with his victim, and in a flash of anger Budd strikes the master-at-arms dead. This moment in the story is unearthly. But Billy Budd is doomed: he has killed his officer in time of war. The captain who understands and loves him presides over the court-martial, and Budd is condemned to be hanged at dawn. . . . [***Billy Budd***] was Melville's final word, worthy of him, indisputably a passing beyond the nihilism of *Moby Dick* to what may seem to some simple and childish, but will be to others wonderful and divine.

[John Middleton Murry], "Herman Melville's Silence," in The Times Literary Supplement, *No. 1173, July 10, 1924, p. 433.*

SIR EDMUND GOSSE (essay date 1925)

[A distinguished English literary historian, critic, and biographer, Gosse wrote extensively on seventeenth- and eighteenth-century English literature. He is noted for his Seventeenth-Century Studies *(1883),* A History of Eighteenth-Century Literature *(1889), and* Questions at Issue *(1893), and he is also credited with introducing the works of the Norwegian dramatist Henrik Ibsen and other Scandinavian writers to English readers. In the following excerpt, he considers the form and style of "The Apple-Tree Table" and "Cock-A-Doodle-Doo!", noting Edgar Allan Poe's influence on Melville.]*

[The] careful reader will not fail to observe how much Melville owed to Poe, who was ten years his senior. The "Tales of the Grotesque and Arabesque" were the obvious precursors of Melville's stories of mystery and bewilderment. The younger man has even adopted some of Poe's tricks of language, with the use of such words as "Plutonian." Yet, so far as I can discover, the name of the elder writer does not once occur in any of Melville's books or correspondence.

In the strictest sense **"The Apple-Tree Table"** is a "tale of the Grotesque." Like most that Melville wrote, fancy seems in it to be woven inextricably into the texture of experience. At the top of a very old house in one of the oldest towns of America, the author explores a staircase leading to a garret which has been closed for years. The rusty key is found, and the tenant enters. He finds it "festooned and carpeted and canopied with cobwebs," and, what is more singular, thousands of insects are clustered on the skylight, while "millions of butterfly moles" are swarming "in a rainbow-tunnel clear across the darkness of the garret." I know not what is a "butterfly mole," and I leave it to the entomologists to decide how such profuse insect-life could have been fed through so long a seclusion. The whole description of the garret is extremely characteristic of Melville's perfervid and rather tormented imagination, and of his eloquent verbosity. The long and short of it is that the author discovers in the garret an old-fashioned table made of apple-wood, which he dusts and drags downstairs into the cedar-parlour, where his wife and daughters take their breakfast. The ladies do not much relish the intrusion of so unfashionable a piece of furniture, which makes them, they know not why, feel nervous.

The author, however, is charmed with his apple-tree table; but one night as he sits at it, like the gentleman in "The Raven," reading "many a quaint and curious volume of forgotten lore," the table begins to tick. There follow amusing, if somewhat preposterous, scenes in which this sound, repeated day after day and night after night, successively freezes the blood of the author, of his wife, of his daughters, and of Biddy, the maid-of-all-work. We are strung up to suspect a supernatural energy concealed, but the noise proves to be strictly zoological. It arises from a century-old beetle, which the warmth of the room has awakened, and which is forcing its way out of the wood. At last, while the author is watching in the darkness of the night, it escapes from its prison. It is radiantly lovely, luminous, and coloured like a fiery opal, "a beautiful bug, a Jew jeweller's bug, a bug like a sparkle of a glorious sunset." (Again, I must call the entomologists to the support of my little faith!) And that is the end of the matter, since the beetle (or "bug") continues to flash in death from a box "on the apple-tree table in the pier of the cedar-parlour."

The tale is somewhat spun out, but told with great vivacity, and spirit, with that curious breathless air of being in a terrible hurry yet magically rooted to the spot, which is one of Melville's peculiarities as a narrator. It would, of course, be extremely unfair to pit a trifle like **"The Apple-Tree Table"** against such massive enterprises as *Moby Dick* and *Typee,* but the elements of style are the same in each.

Another instance, almost sought at random, may continue our impression of Herman Melville's cumulative vehemence, almost hysteria, of description. It is taken from a shorter story [**"Cock-a-Doodle-Doo!"**]. In a mountain-village of New England, against a background of pines and hemlocks, the author meets a hero of the poultry-yard and this is how he sees the gallant bird. (Note the rising excitement!):—

> A cock, more like a golden eagle than a cock. A cock, more like a field-marshal than a cock. A cock, more like Lord Nelson with all his glittering arms on, standing on the Vanguard's quarter-deck, going into battle, than a cock. A cock, more like the Emperor Charlemagne in his robes at Aix-la-Chapelle than a cock. Such a cock!

And then the ecstasy flags a little. Melville finds it necessary to justify his rapture, and this is how he does it:—

> He was of a haughty size, stood haughtily on his haughty legs. His colours were red, gold, and white. The red was on his crest along, which was a mighty and symmetric crest, like unto Hector's crest, as delineated on ancient shields. His plumage was snowy, traced with gold. He walked in front of the shanty, like a peer of the realm; his crest lifted, his chest heaved out, his embroidered trappings flashing in the light. His face was wonderful. He looked like some Oriental king in some magnificient Italian opera.

Some of this is very good (the sentence about the "peer of the realm"): some very bad (the sentence about the "crest along"); on the whole, it exemplifies the extreme difficulty of estimating the real value of Melville's style, with its vividness, its exultation, and its unfortunate tendency to repetition and overemphasis. One perfect sentence about the extravagantly heraldic bird would doubtless produce a more lasting effect than does this chain of vehement hyperboles. Nevertheless, the image, if too garrulously insisted upon, is fine, and remains in the memory. Here is all Melville, in his baffling inconsistency. (pp. 358-61)

Sir Edmund Gosse, "Herman Melville," in his Silhouettes, *Charles Scribner's Sons, 1925, pp. 353-62.*

JOHN FREEMAN (essay date 1926)

[*A prolific early-twentieth-century English poet and critic, Freeman wrote the earliest British biography of Melville, in 1926. In the following excerpt from this work, he outlines the psychology of* Billy Budd *and describes "Bartleby the Scrivener" and "Benito Cereno."*]

If it seems fantastic to compare *Moby Dick* with Milton's *Paradise Lost* and assert a parallel conception in each, it will seem fantastic to say that in a shorter story, ***Billy Budd,*** may be found another *Paradise Regained.*

Like *Moby Dick* this late and pure survival of Melville's genius has a double interest, the interest of story and the interest of psychology. ***Billy Budd*** is the narrative of one who, like Pierre, is unpractised in the ways of life and the hearts of other men; guilelessness is a kind of genius and the better part of innocence in this handsome young sailor. His offence is his innocence, and it is Claggart, a subtle, dark demon-haunted petty-officer, that his innocence offends. (p. 131)

[With unlabouring imagination, Melville imparts to the final scene of ***Billy Budd***] a strange serentiy and solemn ease.

> Billy stood facing aft. At the penultimate moment his words, his only ones, words wholly unobstructed in the utterance, were these—"God bless Captain Vere!" Syllables so unanticipated coming from one with the ignominious hemp about his neck—a conventional felon's benediction directed aft toward the quarters of honour; syllables, too, delivered in the clear melody of a singing-bird on the point of launching from the twig, had a phenomenal effect, not unenhanced by the rare personal beauty of the young sailor, spiritualized now through late experiences so poignantly profound.
>
> (p. 134)

Exaltation of spirit redeems such a scene from burdens which otherwise might appear too painful to be borne. And beyond this, it is innocence that is vindicated, more conspicuously in death than it could be in life. Melville's MS. contains a note in his own hand—"A story not unwarranted by what happens in this incongruous world of ours—innocence and infirmity, spiritual depravity and fair respite"; the ultimate opposition is shown clearly here in this public vindication of the law, and the superior assertion at the very moment of death of the nobility of a pure human spirit. *Moby-Dick* ends in darkness and desolation, for the challenge of Ahab's pride is rebuked by the physical power and the inhumanness of Nature; but ***Billy Budd*** ends in a brightness of escape, such as the apostle saw when he exclaimed, "O death, where is thy sting?"

Finished but a few months before the author's death and only lately published, ***Billy Budd*** shows the imaginative faculty still secure and powerful, after nearly forty years' supineness, and the not less striking security of Melville's inward peace. After what storms and secret spiritual turbulence we do not know, except by hints which it is easy to exaggerate, in his last days he re-enters an Eden-like sweetness and serenity, "with calm of mind, all passion spent", and sets his brief, appealing tragedy for witness that evil is defeat and natural goodness invincible in the affections of man. In this, the simplest of stories, told with but little of the old digressive vexatiousness, and based upon recorded incidents, Herman Melville uttered his everlasting yea, and died before a soul had been allowed to hear him. (pp. 135-36)

[***The Piazza Tales***] contains six stories, of which two are superb and the rest comparatively insignificant. . . . One of the stories, **"Bartleby"**, is an exercise in unrelieved pathos, the pathos of an exile in city life, faint counterpart of Melville's own isolation and gathering silence. Something unbearable peers out of this story, to wring the heart of the reader, as the simple episodes of the life of a mute forlorn innocent are unfolded—type of all the ineffectual, the wounded and unwanted. (pp. 144-45)

Pathos is absent from the greatest of these stories, **"Benito Cereno"**, or rather is shut out by a more urgent passion. (p. 145)

[The full significance of **"Benito Cereno"**] could not be discovered until the late Joseph Conrad had written certain stories which, by their subjects and method of narration, offer inevitable reminders of Melville's short masterpiece. The American Captain Delano is a Conradian figure in his simplicity and slightly exaggerated obtuseness, the Spanish Captain is Conradian in his rich figure and mystery-making phrases and silences; the servant is Conradian, and the crowding business of the ferocious blacks; and, above all, the method of broken and oblique narration is Conradian. Anticipating Conrad's abundant short stories by fifty years, Melville has anticipated their excellence and given us a measure to measure them by. It is improbable that Conrad had the opportunity of reading a book which disappeared from currency so completely as ***The Piazza Tales*** did, and the likeness is emphasized here simply as sign of some spiritual likeness between the American novelist and the Polish novelist, which others may more fully trace. (pp. 148-49)

John Freeman, in his Herman Melville, *Haskell House Publishers Ltd., 1974, 200 p.*

THE TIMES LITERARY SUPPLEMENT (essay date 1927)

[In the following excerpt, the anonymous critic outlines the aesthetic and technical shortcomings of "Benito Cereno."]

[**"Benito Cereno"** belongs to the period when Melville's] sombre (or darkened) genius was not yet absorbed in justifying the ways of God to men. He was still a teller of tales, and in the craft to be reckoned a good deal less than Hawthorne, and perhaps a little less than Wilkie Collins—a good solid workman, but distinctly clumsy. Wilkie Collins would have delighted in the sheer dramatic idea of **"Benito Cereno";** and, had he known anything of seafaring and been able to write with confidence of such things as mizzenchains, would have handled it more effectively than Melville. The cloud of mystery that hangs over the ship San Dominick would have grown heavier and more oppressive, even though the methods of thickening might have seemed a little crude; but Wilkie Collins would have achieved his necessary psychological effect. Melville did not. The Englishman's device of telling a story through different characters would have served Melville admirably. If the good-hearted, unsuspecting American skipper, Amasa Delano, could have told his story, and the Spanish captain his, quite separately, the effect would have been heightened.

Melville never became a master of the technique of fiction. Even after *Moby Dick* had been written, *Pierre* was still to show with what crudity of expression his profundity of thought could be allied. Of all the great story-tellers of the nineteenth century he was surely the clumsiest; and when, as in **"Benito Cereno",** no "momentous depth of speculation" is yet apparent in his work, we are acutely conscious of the opportunities he has missed. That is not to say **"Benito Cereno"** is not a good story; it is, but it is by no means, as some have held, a masterpiece. What would not a master of fiction—a master not in the rarefied sense in which we predicate mastery of Henry James, but in the straightforward sense in which it can be ascribed equally to Scott, Dickens and Balzac—have made of the sinister figure of the negro Babo, to the outward eye the devoted servant of the Spanish captain Don Benito, in reality his subtle tyrant and torturer? But no brooding sense of his concealed iniquity is conveyed by Melville. We are as completely deceived by his ostensible devotion as is the guileless Captain Delano; and the sudden revelation of Babo's true character comes with a shock not of illumination but of bewilderment.

Melville's failure might be described as having involuntarily made a puzzle of a mystery. Nothing could well be imagined more sinister than the great ship San Dominick as she drifts into our view; three-quarters of her crew murdered, her supercargo nailed a skeleton where the figure-head should be, her decks thronged with negroes with here and there a silent Spanish sailor among them, the hull barnacled, her rigging grey for lack of tar. And sinister we feel her to be for the first few pages of Melville's story; a ghost-ship gliding into the misty calm of the Pacific morning. . . .

A perfect prelude, it seems, to a sea mystery. But Melville, as though he could not keep in his head more than one thing at a time, forgets (or knows not how) to maintain the atmosphere. He lets it dissipate in his concentration upon the mere outward-seeming of the elaborate and grim deception contrived by the negro leader, Babo; and at moments he indulged in a luxuriance of detail so fantastic that it becomes bewildering, as in the regular appearance before Don Benito of the padlocked and fettered negro Atufal. Above all, Melville forgets that so gruesome a comedy, a ship's captain who is the terrified instrument of his apparent servants, could not have failed to arouse the suspicions of so experienced a sailor as Delano; he could not have spent hours on that ghastly ship without the deepening certainty that everything was wrong. Such a growing apprehension, indefinite yet inescapable, is what the story must create if it is to be reckoned a masterpiece. It does not create it. Melville missed his opportunity.

"'Benito Cereno'," in The Times Literary Supplement, *No. 1309, March 3, 1927, p. 140.*

E. M. FORSTER (essay date 1927)

[Forster was a prominent twentieth-century English novelist, critic, and essayist, whose works reflect his liberal humanism. His most celebrated novels include Howards End *(1910) and* A Passage to India *(1924), and his major critical work,* Aspects of the Novel, *is regarded as a minor classic of literary criticism. In the following excerpt from that work, he elucidates Melville's depiction of good and evil in* Billy Budd.]

For a real villain we must turn to a story of Melville's called ***Billy Budd***. . . The hero, a young sailor, has goodness—. . . [a] goodness of the glowing aggressive sort which cannot exist unless it has evil to consume. He is not aggressive himself. It is the light within him that irritates and explodes. On the surface he is a pleasant, merry, rather insensitive lad, whose perfect physique is marred by one slight defect, a stammer, which finally destroys him. . . . Claggart, one of the petty officers, at once sees in him the enemy—his own enemy, for Claggart is evil. It is again the contest between Ahab and Moby Dick, though the parts are more clearly assigned, and we are further from prophecy and nearer to morality and common sense. But not much nearer. Claggart is not like any other villain. (pp. 141-42)

Billy Budd is a remote unearthly episode, but it is a song not without words, and should be read both for its own beauty and as an introduction to more difficult works. Evil is labelled and personified instead of slipping over the ocean and round the world, and Melville's mind can be observed more easily. What one notices in him is that his apprehensions are free from personal worry, so that we become bigger not smaller after sharing them. He has not got that tiresome little receptacle, a conscience, which is often such a nuisance in serious writers and so contracts their effects—the conscience of Hawthorne or of Mark Rutherford. Melville—after the initial roughness of his realism—reaches straight back into the universal, to a blackness and sadness so transcending our own that they are undistinguishable from glory. He says, "in certain moods no man can weigh this world without throwing in a something somehow like Original Sin to strike the uneven balance." He threw it in, that undefinable something, the balance righted itself, and he gave us harmony and temporary salvation. (pp. 142-43)

E. M. Forster, "Prophecy," in his Aspects of the Novel, *Harcourt Brace Jovanovich, 1927, pp. 125-47.*

CARL VAN DOREN (essay date 1928)

[*Van Doren is considered one of the most perceptive American critics of the first half of the twentieth century. He wrote and edited several American literary histories and was an acclaimed biographer as well as an influential promoter of Melville's works. In the following excerpt, he praises three stories in* The Piazza Tales *and especially extols* Billy Budd.]

[**"Benito Cereno," "Bartleby the Scrivener,"** and **"The Encantadas"** from ***The Piazza Tales*** and the short novel ***Billy Budd*** belong] with the most original and distinguished fiction yet produced on this continent. Perhaps **"Bartleby the Scrivener"** is a little thinner than the others, a little touched with the dry pallor of the fifties. Perhaps **"The Encantadas"** drifts rather than marches in its construction, quickening in one episode and then settling back again to a different tempo. But **"Benito Cereno,"** to use a more or less unavoidable standard of measurement, equals the best of Conrad in the weight of its drama and the skill of its unfolding. And ***Billy Budd*** surpasses the best of Conrad in the music of its language, as in the profundity and serenity of its reflections.

Billy Budd is particularly important among the works of Melville because in it alone he rises above the dark problems which tormented the later years of his life. No longer asking himself, of course vainly, why evil should exist, he asks instead how it moves on its horrid errands and what is to be done about it. Or rather, he answers by telling the story of Billy Budd, a handsome sailor who is hated by a petty officer on the ship, is unjustly accused to the captain, in a burst of worthy indignation strikes the petty officer and unintentionally kills him, and has to be hanged for his offense though the captain believes the sailor to be essentially without guilt. Hardly anywhere in fiction is there a more penetrating representation of native malice than in Melville's account of how Claggart comes to hate Billy for his beauty and his innocence. The processes of Iago are superficial in comparison. Seldom in fiction has any character been so powerfully and lucidly exhibited in any such moral plight as that of Captain Vere, faced with a plain duty and a conscience plainly urging him not to do it. And neither of these parts of the story is so memorable as the scene, at once terrible and exalted, in which Billy, innocent of everything but innocence and manslaughter, is hanged, the victim of his own victim, who was evil as Billy was innocent. The innumerable implications of the plot are broodingly revealed. Wisdom surrounds it as the water surrounds the ship. But the narrative has none of the dispersion, as of light in a prism, which often goes with wisdom. In this last story Melville wrote he thought of all he had ever thought, and yet moved forward through it with the tense, straight line of art.

Carl Van Doren, "A Note of Confession," in The Nation, *New York, Vol. CXXVII, No. 3309, December 5, 1928, p. 622.*

RAYMOND WEAVER (essay date 1928)

[*Weaver was an American scholar and critic who is credited, along with Michael Sadleir, H. L. Tomlinson, and Carl Van Doren, with renewing critical appreciation for and understanding of Melville's writings. The author of the earliest major biography of Melville,* Herman Melville: Mariner and Mystic *(1921), Weaver was also the first editor of* Billy Budd. *In the following excerpt, he argues that* Billy Budd *expresses the "final great revelation" of Melville's life.*]

[Melville's] last word upon the strange mystery of himself and of human destiny is ***Billy Budd:*** "A story," so Melville said in a pencilled note at the end, "not unwarranted by what happens in this incongruous world of ours—innocence and infirmity, spiritual depravity and fair respite." It is a brief and appealing narrative, unmatched among Melville's works in lucidity and inward peace. (p. xlix)

To pass from a normal nature to one haunted as was Claggart one must cross, Melville says, "the deadly space between, and this is best done by indirection." In attempting this oblique passage, Melville tells how "long ago an honest scholar, my senior, said to me in reference to one who like himself is no more, a man so unimpeachably respectable that against him nothing was ever openly said, though among the few something was whispered, 'Yes, X—is a nut not to be cracked by the tap of a lady's fan.'" And Melville's comment is as guarded as the rest of the passage: "At the time my inexperience was such that I did not quite see the drift of all this. It may be that I see it now."

But there are other and less ambiguous glimpses given us into Claggart's dark soul. "When Claggart's unobserved glance happened to light on belted Billy rolling along the upper gundeck in the leisure of the second dog-watch, exchanging passing broadsides of fun with other promenaders in the crowd, that glance would follow the cheerful sea-Hyperion with a settled, meditative, and melancholoy expression, his eyes strangely suffused with incipient feverish tears. Then would Claggart look like the man of sorrows. Yes, and sometimes the melancholy expression would have in it a touch of soft yearning, as if Claggart could even have loved Billy but for fate and ban." Claggart would seem to be an American forerunner of the Charlus of Marcel Proust. And as a study in abnormal psychology, ***Billy Budd*** is remarkably detached, subtle, and profound. In the writing of it, however, Melville's exclusive interest was not to probe clinically into "the mystery of iniquity."

Just as some theologians have presented the fall of man as evidence of the great glory of God, in similar manner Melville studies the evil in Claggart in vindication of the innocence in Billy Budd. For, primarily, Melville wrote ***Billy Budd*** in witness to his ultimate faith that evil is defeat and natural goodness invincible in the affections of man. ***Billy Budd,*** as *Pierre,* ends in disaster and death; in each case inexperience and innocence and seraphic impulse are wrecked against the malign forces of darkness that seem to preside over external human destiny. In *Pierre,* Melville had hurled himself into a fury of vituperation against the world; with ***Billy Budd*** he would justify the ways of God to man. Among the many parallels of contrast between these two books, each is a tragedy (as was Melville's life), but in opposed sense of the term. For tragedy may be viewed not

Pittsfield Nov 24th 1853

Gentlemen: — In addition to the work which I took to New York last Spring, but which I was prevented from printing at that time; I have now in hand, and pretty well on towards completion, another book — 300 pages, say — partly of nautical adventure, and partly — or, rather, chiefly, of Tortoise Hunting adventure. It will be ready for press some time in the coming January. Meanwhile, it would be convenient, to have advanced to me upon it $300. — My acct: with you, at present, can not be very far from square. For the abovenamed advance — if remitted me now — you will have security in my former works, as well as security prospective, in the one to come, (The Tortoise-Hunters) because if you accede to the aforesaid request, this letter shall be your voucher, that I am willing your house should publish it, on the old basis — half-profits.

Reply immediately, if you please,
And Believe Me, Yours
Herman Melville

Melville's 1853 letter to his publisher, Harper & Brothers, requesting an advance payment on a work in progress. As a penciled note indicates, the request was denied.

as being essentially the representation of human misery, but rather as the representation of human goodness or nobility. All of the supremest art is tragic: but the tragedy is, in Aristotle's phrase, "The representation of Eudaimonia," or the highest kind of happiness. There is, of course, in this type of tragedy, with its essential quality of encouragement and triumph, no flinching of any horror of tragic life, no shirking of the truth by a feeble idealism, none of the compromises of the so-called "happy ending." The powers of evil and horror must be granted their fullest scope; it is only thus we can triumph over them. Even though in the end the tragic hero finds no friends among the living or dead, no help in God, only a deluge of calamity everywhere, yet in the very intensity of his affliction he may reveal the splendour undiscoverable in any gentler fate. Here he has reached, not the bottom, but the crowning peak of fortune—something which neither suffering nor misfortune can touch. Only when worldly disaster has worked its utmost can we realize that there remains something in man's soul which is for ever beyond the grasp of the accidents of existence, with power in its own right to make life beautiful. Only through tragedy of this type could Melville affirm his everlasting yea. The final great revelation—or great illusion—of his life, he uttered in ***Billy Budd.*** (pp. xlix-li)

Raymond Weaver, in an introduction to Shorter Novels of Herman Melville *by Herman Melville, Liveright Publishing Corp., 1928, pp. vii-li.*

LEWIS MUMFORD (essay date 1929)

[*Mumford is a widely known American sociologist, historian, philosopher, critic, and author. In the following excerpt from his highly acclaimed and influential biography of Melville, he surveys the style and substance of the major short fiction.*]

Melville was not at home in the narrow confines of the short story: he had scarcely time to get under way before he was back again in port. The result is that the best of his short stories are really short novels, while the lesser ones, like **"The Lightning Rod Man,"** are little more than mediocre anecdotes. **"I and My Chimney," "The Appletree Table," "The Paradise of Bachelors," "The Tartarus of Maids,"** are more in the nature of discursive essays, "in character," than they are of tales: Melville was at his weakest in deliberately symbolic tales, like **"Cock-a-Doodle-Do"** and **"The Bell-Tower"**; indeed, the latter might be slipped into one of Hawthorne's volumes, without apology, as a minor work of his youth. (p. 236)

"Bartleby the Scrivener" is one of Melville's longer stories; and it gains much by its juxtaposition of incongruous personalities. (pp. 236-37)

"Bartleby" is a good story in itself: it also affords us a glimpse of Melville's own drift of mind in . . . [1853, the year in which **"Bartleby"** was written]: the point of the story plainly indicates Melville's present dilemma. People would admit him to their circle and give him bread and employment only if he would abandon his inner purpose: to this his answer was—I would prefer not to. By his persistence in minding his own spiritual affairs, those who might have helped him on their own terms . . . inevitably became a little impatient; for in the end, they foresaw they would be obliged to throw him off, and he would find himself in prison, not in the visible prison for restraining criminals, but in the pervasive prison of dull routine and meaningless activity. When that happened there would be no use assuring him that he lived in a kindly world of blue sky and green grass. "I know where I am!" Whether or not Melville consciously projected his own intuition of his fate, there is no doubt in my mind that, as early as 1853, he was already formulating his answer. To those kind, pragmatic friends and relatives who suggested that he go into business and make a good living, or at least write the sort of books that the public would read—it amounts to pretty much the same thing—he kept on giving one stereotyped and monotonous answer: I would prefer not to. (p. 238)

[Melville's description in **"The Encantadas"** of the Enchanted Isles] is as fine as anything in his earlier pages; if anything, there is more studious mastery. The final sketch, the story of Hunilla, who had been left in solitude on one of these islands, when her brother and her husband died, is poignant and terrible, all the more so because of the dark bestiality of the visiting crew, that Melville hints at, and then forgoes telling about, so moved is he by its inhumanity. (p. 239)

[In **"The Encantadas"** Melville] returned to the ultimate moral of *Pierre;* and it holds good of the tales of the Enchanted Isles: out of its stark ugliness, he breathed beauty. With just as abhorrent an insight into the cruelties of life as he had in *Pierre,* Melville here had a firmer hand on himself: he ruefully confesses that "in nature, as in law, it may be libellous to speak some truths." Within the dark rim of the horizon, the words move, like swift white sails on grey waters. The style is again accurate, pliant, subtle, bold; but it is never hectic nor forced, nor does it smell from the mothballs of old costume chests. There is not the faintest sign that his literary powers were falling off, or his voice sinking to a whisper. (pp. 239-40)

[**"Benito Cereno"**] is such a tale as one might hear, with good luck, during a gam in the South Seas or at a bar in Callao; and

Melville himself took it boldly from a book of voyages by Captain Amasa Delano, published in 1816. (p. 224)

[In **"Benito Cereno"**] the interplay of character, the cross-motives, the suspense, the central mystery, are all admirably done: in contrast to some of Melville's more prosy sketches, there is not a feeble touch in the whole narrative. (p. 245)

As in **"The Encantadas,"** the writing itself was distinguished: it had a special office of its own to perform, and did not, as in *Typee* and *Redburn,* serve merely as carriage for the story. One can mark Melville's literary powers in the complete transformation of Delano's patent story: he adds a score of details to heighten the mystery and deepen the sinister aspect of the scene; and by sheer virtuosity he transfers the reader's sympathies to the Spanish captain, who in the original story is far more cruel, barbarous, and unprincipled than the forces he contends against. In order to effect this change, Melville deliberately omits the last half of the story, in which the Spanish captain ignobly turns upon his benefactor and seeks to deprive him of the rights of salvage. The moral of the original tale is that ingratitude, stirred by cupidity, may follow the most generous act, and that American captains had better beware of befriending too whole-heartedly a foreign vessel. In **"Benito Cereno"** the point is that noble conduct and good will, like that Don Benito felt when his whole inner impulse was to save Delano and his crew, may seem sheer guile; and, further, that there is an inscrutable evil that makes the passage of fine souls through the world an endless Calvary. "Even the best men err, in judging the conduct of one with the recesses of whose condition he is not acquainted." The world is mortified for Don Benito by the remembrance of the human treachery he has encountered: no later benefaction, no radiance of sun and sky, can make him forget it. (p. 246)

[***Billy Budd***] is not a full-bodied story: there is statement, commentary, illustration, just statement, wise commentary, apt illustration: what is lacking is an independent and living creation. The epithets themselves lack body and colour: ***Billy Budd*** has nothing to compare with the description of boiling whale-oil in *Moby-Dick*—"a wild Hindoo odour, like the left wing of the Day of Judgement." (p. 353)

[***Billy Budd***] lacks the fecundity and energy of *White-Jacket:* the story itself takes place on the sea, but the sea itself is missing, and even the principal characters are not primarily men: they are actors and symbols. The story gains something by this concentration, perhaps: it is stripped for action, and even Melville's deliberate digressions do not halt it. Each of the characters has a Platonic clarity of form. (pp. 353-54)

Billy Budd is the story of three men in the British Navy: it is also the story of the world, the spirit, and the devil. Melville left a note, crossed out in the original manuscript, "Here ends a story not unwarranted by what happens in this incongruous world of ours—innocence and infirmity, spiritual depravity and fair respite." The meaning is so obvious that one shrinks from underlining it. Good and evil exist in the nature of things, each forever itself, each doomed to war with the other. In the working out of human institutions, evil has a place as well as the good: Vere is contemptuous of Claggart, but cannot do without him: he loves Budd as a son and must condemn him to the noose: justice dictates an act abhorrent to his nature, and only his inner magnanimity keeps it from being revolting. These are the fundamental ambiguities of life: so long as evil exists, the agents that intercept it will also be evil, whilst we accept the world's conditions: the universal articles of war on which our civilization rest. Rascality may be punished; but beauty and innocence will suffer in that process far more. There is no comfort, in the perpetual Calvary of the spirit, to find a thief nailed on either side. Melville had been harried by these paradoxes in *Pierre*. At last he was reconciled. He accepted the situation as a tragic necessity; and to meet that tragedy bravely was to find peace, the ultimate peace of resignation, even in an incongruous world. (pp. 356-57)

Lewis Mumford, in his Herman Melville, *Harcourt, Brace & Company, 1929, 377 p.*

YVOR WINTERS (essay date 1938)

[Winters was a twentieth-century American poet and critic who was associated with New Criticism. His critical precepts, which emphasize order, dignity, restraint, and morality, are embodied in his In Defense of Reason, *his best-known collection of essays, from which the following is excerpted. Here, in an essay originally published in 1938, Winters analyzes the moral and ethical issues raised in "Benito Cereno," "The Encantadas," and* Billy Budd.]

The greatest works of Melville, aside from *Moby Dick,* and contrary to the popular view, are among those which follow, not among those which precede it. They are **"Benito Cereno,"** **"The Encantadas,"** and ***Billy Budd.*** These works, in the matter of style, are essentially prose; **"The Encantadas"** contains traces of the style of *Moby Dick,* along with traces of its subject-matter, but the rhetoric is subdued in structure and in feeling. In **"Benito Cereno,"** and in other later works, there is scarcely a trace of the style of *Moby Dick;* we have the style of a novelist, and in **"Benito Cereno"** especially this style occurs in a form both classical and austere. (pp. 221-22)

In **"Benito Cereno"** the Spanish sea-captain of that name takes insufficient precautions in the transporting of a ship-load of negro slaves belonging to a friend; the slaves mutiny, kill most of the crew, and enslave the remainder, including the captain. When Cereno is finally rescued by Captain Delano, he is broken in spirit, and says that he can return home but to die. When Captain Delano inquires what has cast such a shadow upon him, he answers: "The negro." His reply in Spanish would have signified not only the negro, or the black man, but by metaphorical extension the basic evil in human nature. The morality of slavery is not an issue in this story; the issue is this, that through a series of acts of performance and of negligence, the fundamental evil of a group of men, evil which normally should have been kept in abeyance, was freed to act. The story is a portrait of that evil in action, as shown in the negroes, and of the effect of the action, as shown in Cereno. It is appalling in its completeness, in its subtle horror, and in its silky quiet.

In **"The Encantadas,"** we have a series of ten sketches, descriptive of the Galápagos Islands. (p. 222)

Melville's descriptive power in this series is at its best; the islands in all their barren and archaic horror are realized unforgettably. The climax of the series is the account of Hunilla, the Chola, who went to the islands with her husband and her brother to gather turtle oil, much as the Nantucketers went to sea for the oil of the whale. Her husband and her brother were drowned while fishing. The ship that left them did not return. She was ravished by the boat-crews of two whalers and left behind by them, and was ultimately rescued and returned to Peru by the ship of which Melville was one of the seamen. She was thus a victim of the sea; that is, of brute chance and brutal malice, forces over which she had no control, and in the face of which the only supporting virtues were absolute humility and absolute fortitude: "The last seen of the lone Hunilla she was passing into Payta town, riding upon a small gray ass; and before her on the ass's shoulders, she eyed the joined workings of the beast's armorial cross." (p. 223)

In [Melville's] final masterpiece, ***Billy Budd,*** the most profound of the later works, if not the best written—the prose, unfortunately, shows a little structural awkwardness, the result of thirty years of disuse—the problem posed in *Pierre* and *The Confidence Man* received its answer. (p. 230)

Vere can see only one solution to the situation [created by Billy's killing of his false accuser, Claggart]: to act according to established principle, which supports public order, and, for the margin of difference between established principle and the facts of the particular situation, to accept it as private tragedy.

The solution, with certain modifications, is the solution of Mrs. Wharton for the same moral problem as it was later posed by Henry James; the moral principle, in the better works of Mrs. Wharton, however, is usually incarnate in a code of manners, and at times appears less defensible than in Billy Budd, because of the tendency observable in codes of manners to become externalized and superficial, to become insulated from the principles informing them with life. The solution, in terms as baid and absolute as the terms of Melville, was likewise the solution of Socrates. It is not every situation, of course, which admits of a solution by virtue of so certain a reference to the "known": there may be cases, as Henry James was later to demonstrate almost to his own undoing, and as Melville asserted in *Moby Dick,* in which the problem of moral navigation, though not insoluble, is a subtler one, in which the exact relevance of any single principle is harder to establish, and in which there may appear to be the claims of conflicting principles. The solution, however, in the case of this story, and as a matter of general principle, is at once unanswerable, dignified, and profound; the characterization of Vere and of Claggart represents an insight worthy to be the final achievement of so long and so great a life. (pp. 230-31)

Yvor Winters, "Herman Melville, and the Problems of Moral Navigation," in his In Defense of Reason, *The Swallow Press Inc., 1947, pp. 200-33.*

F. O. MATTHIESSEN (essay date 1941)

[*A twentieth-century American academic and literary critic, Matthiessen wrote major studies of American writers and intellectual movements, including* American Renaissance: Art and Expression in the Age of Emerson and Whitman *(1941) and* Henry James: The Major Phase *(1944). In the following excerpt from the former work, Matthiessen describes the biblical imagery in* Billy Budd.]

[Melville's conception of Billy Budd] is Blakean. He has not yet "been proffered the questionable apple of knowledge." He is illiterate, and ignorant even of who his father was, since he is a foundling, in whom, nevertheless, "noble descent" is as evident as "in a blood horse." He is unself-conscious about this, as about all else, an instinctively "upright barbarian," a handsome image "of young Adam before the Fall." How dominantly Melville is thinking in Biblical terms appears when he adds that a character of such unsullied freshness seems as though it had been "exceptionally transmitted from a period prior to Cain's city and citified man." He had made a similar contrast between the country and the city in *Pierre;* and he had thought of unspoiled barbarianism at every stage of his writing since *Typee*. Here he focuses his meaning more specifically and submits "that, apparently going to corroborate the doctrine of man's fall, a doctrine now popularly ignored, it is observable that where certain virtues pristine and unadulerate peculiarly characterise anybody in the external uniform of civilization, they will upon scrutiny seem not to be derived from custom or convention, but rather to be out of keeping with these." (p. 501)

[In ***Billy Budd*** innocence is] inevitably foredoomed by black malice. Billy does not have the spiritual "insight of Dostoevsky's Idiot. . . ." "With little or no sharpness of faculty or any trace of the wisdom of the serpent, nor yet quite a dove, he possessed that kind and degree of intelligence going along with the unconventional rectitude of a sound human creature." But his simplicity was completely baffled by anything equivocal; he had no knowledge of the bad, no understanding even of indirection. Honest and open hearted, he concluded everyone else to be likewise. In such an undeveloped nature the only overt flaw was a blemish in his physical perfection, a liability to a severe blockage in his speech under moments of emotional pressure. Melville deliberately recurred in this detail to his memory of "the beautiful woman in one of Hawthorne's minor tales," that is to say, to "The Birthmark," and thus resumed . . . [an] element from his past. He found his hero's defect to be "a striking instance that the arch-interpreter, the envious marplot of Eden still has more or less to do with every human consignment to this planet." (p. 503)

[In Claggart, Melville] does not portray a monster. For when the master-at-arms'

> unobserved glance happened to light on belted Billy rolling along the upper gun-deck in the leisure of the second dog-watch, exchanging passing broadsides of fun with other young promenaders in the crowd, that glance would follow the cheerful sea-Hyperion with a settled meditative and melancholy expression, his eyes strangely suffused with incipient feverish tears. Then would Claggart look like the man of sorrows. Yes, and sometimes the melancholy expression would have in it a touch of soft yearning, as if Claggart could even have loved Billy but for fate and ban.

Evanescent as that tenderness was, it shows that Claggart is not wholly diabolic, and that the felt recognition of its miserable isolation by even the warped mind partakes in the suffering of the Christ.

Thus Melville's vision tended always to be more complex than the posing of a white innocence against a very black evil. In *Moby Dick,* and drastically in *Pierre,* the symbolical values of this contrast began so to interchange that they could not always be followed. In **"Benito Cereno"** they became distinct again, but the embodiment of good in the pale Spanish captain and of evil in the mutinied African crew, though pictorially and theatrically effective, was unfortunate in raising unanswered questions. Although the Negroes were savagely vindictive and drove a terror of blackness into Cereno's heart, the fact remains that they were slaves and that evil had thus originally been done to them. Melville's failure to reckon with this fact within the limits of his narrative makes its tragedy, for all its prolonged suspense, comparatively superficial. In ***Billy Budd*** he has progressed far from any such aribitrary manipulation of his symbols. Furthermore, he has added another dimension through the character of Captain Vere, whose experienced and just mind puts him in contrast with both Billy and Claggart. Melville indicates how this captain, though not brilliant, is set apart from his fellow officers by "a marked leaning toward everything intellectual," especially for "writers who, free from cant and convention, like Montaigne, honestly, and in the spirit of common sense, philosophise upon realities." It reinforces our knowledge of what Melville meant by "realities" to observe that this last phrase orginally read "upon those greatest of all mysteries, facts." (pp. 507-08)

[The struggle] between Claggart and Billy is re-enacted on a wholly different plane within the nature of Vere himself. He has the strength of mind and the earnestness of will to dominate his instincts. He believes that in man's government, "forms, measured forms, are everything." But his decision to fulfil the letter of his duty is not won without anguish. He holds to it, however, and thereby Billy, who had been defenseless before the evil mind of Claggart, goes to defeat before the just mind as well. It does not occur to him to make any case at his trial. He is incapable of piecing things together, and though certain odd details that other sailors had told him about the master-at-arms now flash back into his mind, his "erring sense of uninstructed honor" keeps him from acting what he thinks would be the part of an informer against his shipmates. So he remains silent, and puts himself entirely in his captain's hands. (p. 509)

Vere obeys the law, yet understands the deeper reality of the spirit. Billy instinctively accepts the captain's duty, and forgives him. Melville affirms the rareness of such forgiveness by means of the double image in which the sudden raising of Billy on the halter becomes also his ascension into heaven. . . . How carefully Melville is holding the scales, how conscious he is of the delicacy of the equilibrium he has created, is shown by the fact that the crew, swept in the moment of high tension into echoing Billy's words, reacts in the next with a murmur that implies a sullen revocation of their involuntary blessing, a murmur that is cut short by the command, "Pipe down the starboard watch, boatswain, and see that they go." (pp. 511-12)

[Throughout ***Billy Budd*** Melville showed] what he had meant by calling his age shallow. He knew, as he had known in *The Confidence Man,* that something more than mere worldly shrewdness was necessary for understanding such characters as those of his villain and hero. We have observed how often in his final story he reinforced himself at critical instances by Biblical allusions. His concern with both Testaments, pervasive throughout his work, now gave rise to his laconic statement that the great masters of legal policy, Coke and Blackstone, "hardly shed so much light into obscure spiritual places as the Hebrew prophets." Melville believed that he could probe Claggart's depravity only by means of the illumination gained in meditating on the Scriptural phrase, "mysteries of iniquity." And only by profound acceptance of the Gospels was he able to make his warmest affirmation of good through a common sailor's act of holy forgiveness. (p. 513)

F. O. Matthiessen, "Reassertion of the Heart," in his American Renaissance: Art and Expression in the Age of Emerson and Whitman, *Oxford University Press, 1941, pp. 488-516.*

F. BARRON FREEMAN (essay date 1948)

[In the following excerpt, Freeman analyzes the character Captain Vere in Billy Budd.*]*

Captain the Honorable Edward Fairfax Vere is the least human yet the most suffering of the characters in the tale [***Billy Budd***]. His associates consider him a martinet—a superior, highly intellectual, and "bookish" man. He sees clearly all the issues of the tragedy in which he is involved. Superficially, he is the author's mouthpiece who resolves the plot and points the moral. He is the severe disciplinarian who has the strength to do "right" according to earthly standards of justice when, on a heavenly plane of reasoning, to do "wrong" would have been more difficult and much wiser. Symbolically, he has been likened to a "wise father" in the Biblical sense. It has also been suggested that he is really Billy's "lost" father, although Melville states explicitly that he is writing a "realistic" tale and not one that deals with the hidden, anterior mysteries of a romance. Readers who consider Billy a modern counterpart of Christ compare Captain Vere to Pontius Pilate because he knowingly condemns an "innocent" man to death. But, unlike Pilate, he accepts the responsibility for the execution. All these analogies and speculations are concerned more with the allegorical significance of Captain Vere than with his validity as a human being. They overlook his physical, emotional, social, and intellectual characteristics and, thereby, fail to consider the terrible and painful dilemma in which his worldly wisdom and heavenly understanding place him. His character is "singular" because his make-up is contradictory. He loves Billy as a son yet he cannot overcome his rigid adherence to what he considers his earthly responsibility and duty. (pp. 92-3)

The marked ambivalence of Captain Vere's character shows clearly Melville's concept of the eternal conflict between the heart—or the "soul's recesses" as Melville once called it—and the head. Intellectually, Vere is a cold, highborn, almost clairvoyant disciplinarian who, recognizing the incompatibility of the laws of heaven with the ways of the world, speaks his piece and condemns Billy to be hanged. Melville felt that a true understanding of life comes not through reason alone but also through emotion. In the brief scenes which describe Billy and Vere together, Melville allows the reader to infer a little of Vere's understanding heart. When, for example, Captain Vere momentarily relaxes the rigor of his rank just after Billy has killed Claggart, when he physically betrays his emotional agony after telling Billy he must die, and finally, . . . when he dies with the name of Billy Budd upon his lips, the reader comes to understand, along with the Captain, that all the clear and cold intellectual truths of this world are not enough to achieve a realization of true goodness and true heavenly justice.

Vere's dying words, "Billy Budd, Billy Budd," reveal how much longer and how much deeper was Captain Vere's suffering than either Claggart's isolating, innate depravity or Billy's tragic, innate innocence. Claggart's suffering was cut off abruptly by sudden death. Billy's trusting and uncomprehending innocence precluded any deep suffering on his part. Melville forcefully points this in his description of Billy's hanging when he writes: "In the pinioned figure arrived at the yard-end, to the wonder of all no motion was apparent. . ." But Captain Vere, controlled and "erectly rigid" when on the point of death Billy cries, "God bless Captain Vere," exemplifies the tremendous, grievous burden and responsibility which comes to those who know well that the ways of the world cannot be the ways of heaven and that the wisdom of the mind must ultimately bow to the wisdom of the heart. (pp. 95-6)

F. Barron Freeman, in an introduction to Melville's "Billy Budd" *by Herman Melville, edited by F. Barron Freeman, Cambridge, Mass.: Harvard University Press, 1948, pp. 3-124.*

W. H. AUDEN (lecture date 1949)

[*An English-born American poet, Auden was also an essayist, playwright, critic, editor, and translator, and he is considered a major figure in twentieth-century literature. Among his best-known critical works are* The Dyer's Hand and Other Essays *(1962), and* Forewords and Afterwords *(1973). In the following excerpt, from the text of a lecture delivered in 1949, Auden discusses Melville's treatment of sinlessness and innocence in* Billy Budd, *studies Billy as Christ figure, and considers Claggart's motive in bearing false witness against him.*]

If, when we finish reading ***Billy Budd,*** we are left with questions which we feel have been raised but not answered, if so to speak the equation has not come out to a finite number, as in a work of art it should, this is not due to any lack of talent on Melville's part, but to the insolubility of the religious paradox in aesthetic terms.

For any writer who attempts a portrait of the Christ-like is faced with the following problems. His central figure

(a) must be innocent of sin, yet a man like us in all things tempted as we are. If he is given any aesthetic advantages, he at once ceases to be the God-Man and becomes the Man-God, the Aesthetic Hero, Hercules, who must be admired, but cannot be imitated. His sinlessness must be the result of faith, not of fortune.

(b) He must be shown as failing in a worldly sense, i.e., as coming into collision with the law of this world, otherwise there is no proof that his sinlessness is due, not to faith, but to mere worldly prudence.

(c) Failure and suffering, however, are in themselves no proof of faith, because the collision with the law may equally well be the result of pride and sin. The crucified Christ is flanked by two crucified thieves.

(d) The suffering must at one and the same time be willed and not-willed. If it seems entirely against the will of the sufferer, he becomes pathetic, if it seems entirely brought about by his own actions, he becomes tragic, and it is impossible to distinguish between pride and faith as the cause of his suffering. (pp. 119-20)

[Melville] solves this problem. The Passion of Billy Budd is convincing, but fails in respects where Cervantes succeeds, and the ways in which he fails are interesting for the light they throw on the romantic conception of life. Like many other romantics Melville seems to hold:

(1) That innocence and sinlessness are identical, or rather perhaps that only the innocent, i.e., those who have never known the law, can be sinless. Once a man becomes conscious, he becomes a sinner. As long as he is not conscious of guilt, what he does is not sin. This is to push St. Paul's remark "Except I had known the Law, I had not known sin" still further to mean that "Except I had known sin, I would not have sinned." Thus when Billy Budd first appears he is the Prelapsarian Adam:

> Billy Budd in many respects was little more than a sort of upright barbarian, much such perhaps as Adam presumably might have been ere the urbane Serpent wriggled himself into his company.

He may have done things which in a conscious person would be sin—there appears to have been a certain Bristol Molly—but he feels no guilt.

(2) That the unconscious and innocent are marked by great physical beauty, and therefore that the beautiful are sinless. This is true for Billy Budd as it was for Bulkington and Queequeg.

If the story were to be simply the story of the Fall, i.e., the story of how the Devil (Claggart) tempted Adam (Budd) into the knowledge of good and evil, this would not matter, but Melville wants Budd also to be the Second Adam, the sinless victim who suffers voluntarily for the sins of the whole world. But in order to be that he must know what sin is, or else his suffering is not redemptive, but only one more sin on our part. Further, as long as Billy Budd is only the Prelapsarian Adam, our nostalgic image of what we would still be if we had not fallen, his beauty is a perfectly adequate symbol but the moment he becomes the Second Adam, the saving example whom we all should follow, this beauty becomes an illegitimate aesthetic advantage. The flaw of the stammer will not quite do, for this is only an aesthetic weakness, not a deliberate abandonment of advantages. It succeeds in making Billy Budd the innocent who "as a sheep before the shearer is dumb so openeth he not his mouth," but it makes his dumbness against his will not with it. We can never look like that, any more than, once we have become conscious, we can go back to unconsciousness, so how can we imitate his example? He becomes an aesthetic hero to admire from a distance. Melville seems to have been aware that something must happen to Billy to change him from the unconscious Adam into the conscious Christ but, in terms of his fable, he cannot make this explicit and the decisive transition has to take place off-stage in the final interview between Billy and Captain Vere.

Similar insoluble paradoxes are raised by the demonic, the religious passion in reverse. For the demonic must be moved solely by pride, just as the religious must be moved solely by faith and love. Absolute pride cannot be manifested aesthetically because it tolerates no weakness except itself which thinks of itself as absolute strength.

Absolute pride denies that the six other deadly sins are its children and despises them as weakness, being incapable of seeing that it is the source of all weakness. The Devil, therefore, cannot himself be lustful, gluttonous, avaricious, envious, slothful, or angry, for his pride will not allow him to be anything less than proud. He can only pretend in disguise to be any of these without actually feeling them; he can only "act" them. His acts must appear to be arbitrary and quite motiveless. No accurate aesthetic portrayal, therefore, is possible; Iago has to be given some motive, yet if the motive is convincing, he ceases to be demonic.

So with Claggart. Just as the bias in Melville's treatment of Billy Budd is a tendency to identify consciousness and sin, so he makes Claggart identify innocence with love; "To be nothing more than innocent," he sneers on seeing Billy Budd. This is no doubt what the serpent says to Adam, but it is not what he says to himself, which is rather "To be nothing more than loving." For the difference between God and the Devil is not that God does not know the meaning of good and evil and that the Devil does, but that God loves and the Devil will not love. That is why the motive for Claggart's behaviour, half-stated only to be withdrawn because no motive will really do, is homosexual desire.

In *Moby Dick,* where Ahab's pride revolts against lack of absolute strength, against being finite and dependent, the sexual symbolism centres round incest and the Oedipus situation, because incest is the magic act of self-derivation, self-autonomy, with the annihilation of all rival power.

In ***Billy Budd,*** the opposition is not strength/weakness, but innocence/guilt-consciousness, i.e., Claggart wishes to annihilate the difference either by becoming innocent himself or by acquiring an accomplice in guilt. If this is expressed sexually, the magic act must necessarily be homosexual, for the wish is for identity in innocence or in guilt, and identity demands the same sex.

Claggart, as the Devil, cannot, of course, admit a sexual desire, for that would be an admission of loneliness which pride cannot admit. Either he must corrupt innocence through an underling or if that is not possible he must annihilate it, which he does. (pp. 120-23)

W. H. Auden, "Ishmael—Don Quixote," in his The Enchafèd Flood; or, The Romantic Iconography of the Sea, *1950. Reprint by Faber and Faber Limited, 1951, pp. 81-126.*

JAY LEYDA (essay date 1949)

[Leyda is a distinguished American critic, author, and editor who has written on Emily Dickinson and Melville. In the following excerpt, he comments on Melville's use of imagery and symbolism in his major short stories.]

[Melville's expression of his philosophy and art in his short stories] is as intense as in any novel or poem of Melville's—sometimes so intense as to require the mask of laughter or remoteness. Beneath Cereno's exterior are the worms in the flowering creeper of **"The Piazza"** and the apples of Sodom in **"The Encantadas"**—these are images of a tragedy that can be traced throughout Melville's art. The whole smouldering penal image of the clinkered Galápagos, once conjured up, remained a permanent symbol in his imagination. (p. xx)

The striking pictorial quality of all Melville's writing found a precise reflection within the medium of the short story in the form of the diptych. At least three times he displayed pairs of contrasting images (*Look here, upon this picture, and on this*), to make the light one brighter, and the dark one blacker; the coldness of orthodoxy and the warmth of humanity in **"The Two Temples"**; the determined meek have-nots in **"Poor Man's Pudding"** and the desperate revolting have-nots in **"Rich Man's Crumbs"**; lighthearted irresponsibility in **"The Paradise of Bachelors"** and burdensome responsibility in **"The Tartarus of Maids."** In another way the ten pictures of **"The Encantadas"** . . . are added up accumulatively to a single fiery glimpse of man's sins toward man; this "archipelago of aridities" presents images of isolation, desperation, punishment, deceit, misused authority, endurance, lonely struggle, and all the odds against life, hope, decency. Plucking all he needed from the history of the islands, he sharpened his pieces and turned them into the dry wind. (pp. xx-xxi)

It has been said, on various occasions, that Bartleby is Melville, that Helmstone is Melville, that Benito Cereno is Melville, but it cannot really surprise us that Melville should be writing of his own thoughts and fears. It is his attitude to these thoughts and fears, and his artistic expression of them that are at least as vital as the central identification. The variety of narrators employed has an interest of its own: a sixty-year-old lawyer; Melville (frankly, in **"The Encantadas"**); a country gentleman; a poor young doctor; a gentleman of 1814; Melville (half-frankly in the last diptych and **"The Lightning-Rod Man"**); an adolescent nephew; a poet, Helmstone; an old New Yorker, William Ford; the eyes but not the tongue of Captain Amasa Delano; Melville (frankly, in **"The Bell-Tower"**); an old country gentleman; an old town gentleman; a country gentleman. His concern to find so large and various a group of "I" narrators, against so few frankly third-person narratives, is . . . [a] disclosure of his policy of concealment. (p. xxi)

[As in so many of Melville's] stories, **"The Piazza"** contains a doubly hidden significance. The brighter region that the narrator struggles toward may also be the artist's ideal, made to gleam only in "the hottest, weariest hour" of creation. A similar ambiguity of symbol is to be found in **"Cock-a-Doodle-Doo!"** where it is difficult to distinguish between the indications of religious ideals and artistic ideals. The "career" group of stories is less obviously, but just as certainly, attached to Melville's own career: **"The Happy Failure"** with its symbol of a queerly involuted craft (does its climax tell neglect of the craftsman, or destruction by the craftsman—the destroyed novel of Agatha?); the Dead Sea fruits of fame in **"Jimmy Rose,"** and of ambition in **"The Bell Tower."** Who will say absolutely that **"Bartleby"** and **"Benito Cereno"** are allegories of the insurmountable barriers between man and man—or of the barriers that man sets up within himself? (pp. xxv-xxvi)

Taking the liberties of a poet whose special, perhaps unconscious mission is concealment, Melville's symbols slip away and elude one's keys. His most effective camouflage was also always his greatest artistic necessity—reality, the palpability with which all the greatest symbols continue to breathe beyond their year of publication. For him, as for Montaigne, "the Magazin of Memorie is per-adventure more stored with matter, than is the store-house of Invention." As the Melville symbol is usually embedded in situation, the most tangible elements are elsewhere, in character and atmosphere: the reality and poverty of the Merrymusks and the Coulters, the pathos of the uncle in **"The Happy Failure,"** and of Jimmy Rose. The intricate construction of **"The Tartarus of Maids"** had to be compounded of substance and the materiality of outer observation—and the machines and employees of the paper-mill he describes for his purposes were seen by him on his paper-buying excursions to Carson's "Old Red Mill" in Dalton, a sleigh-trip from Pittsfield.

Was this materiality employed as an aid or as a hindrance to the real meaning of these stories? Though some degree of communication is present in each artistic work (else the work would not have been brought into existence) much of these stories' materiality seems a minutely painted and deceptive screen erected across what is *really* taking place behind it—in Melville's mind. We are compelled to regard these stories as an artist's resolution of that constant contradiction—between the desperate need to communicate and the fear of revealing too much. In these stories the contradiction is expressed on various levels of tension—the fiercer the pull, the higher the accomplishment. There is also a level, closer to the surface, of *game,* for in **"The Tartarus of Maids"** Melville gives one the impression of seeing how close he can dance to the edge of nineteenth-century sanctities without being caught. In this story the very audacity of the physiological symbolism was the author's best protection against discovery; the keenest of contemporary readers (with the possibly sole exception of his friend, Dr. Augustus Kinsley Gardner, the gynecologist) would not have dared admit to himself that anyone had been so bold in *Harper's* pages; the perceptive reader must have blamed his own imagination for what he found in **"Tartarus"**—which may have been part of Melville's intent. (pp. xxvii-xxviii)

Jay Leyda, in an introduction to The Complete Stories of Herman Melville *by Herman Melville, edited by Jay Leyda, Random House, 1949, pp. ix-xxxiv.*

RICHARD CHASE (essay date 1949)

[*A distinguished American literary critic, Chase is the author of* The American Novel and Its Tradition *(1957), an influential study that examines the ''romance'' tradition in American fiction. In the following excerpt from his* Herman Melville: A Critical Study, *Chase studies the tone, style, and meaning of Melville's major short stories, focusing especially on the imagery, symbolism, and allegory of* Billy Budd.]

[It] is misleading to assume that after 1852 Melville was plunged into impotent despair, blind cynicism, and ''morbidity.'' It has too often and too easily been assumed that since Melville himself was poor, unhappy, and unhealthy after 1852, and especially during the 1853-1856 period, everything he wrote was injured by excessive introspection and pessimism. On the contrary, a look at such writings as **''The Lightning-Rod Man,'' ''The Tartarus of Maids,'' ''Bartleby the Scrivener,'' ''Benito Cereno,'' ''The Fiddler,'' ''Jimmy Rose,'' ''I and My Chimney,''** *Israel Potter, The Confidence Man,* and **''The Encantadas''** gives us the impression of a man carefully probing new areas of experience and seeking out new styles. Most of the short stories have faults of taste and conception, but **''Benito Cereno''** is surely one of the best of short stories. . . . (pp. 142-43)

''Bartleby'' is a starkly simple tale told with great economy of metaphor and symbol, for Melville is preeminently interested in simplicity—a kind of simplicity at once nakedly tragic and wistfully comic. The story is relieved of the clashing commotion and weight of *Moby-Dick* and *Pierre* largely because the central figure has no will. *Moby-Dick* and *Pierre* take their inner dynamism from compulsively violent assertions of will, building up slowly to an apocalyptic crescendo; **''Bartleby''** proceeds in reverse, toward a gradually encroaching silence. The mood and even the method of Melville's story remind one of Kafka's *The Trial,* the haunted inwardness of Kafka's Joseph K. *vis à vis* the bank where he works and the elusive but all-powerful bureaucracy which condemns him to death corresponding with the situation of Bartleby *vis à vis* the lawyer's office and the authorities who finally jail him. But the comparison cannot be pressed too far, for though Melville shares Kafka's interest in guilt and the weird futility of reason, he attempts, unlike Kafka, to beatify his hero. (p. 144)

On the aesthetic principles of unity, coherence, and style **''Benito Cereno''** is one of the best single pieces Melville wrote. The mood of the story is fully achieved and maintained to perfection. Melville's characteristic contrasts of light and dark are resolved into a gray monotone occasionally illumined by flashes of fire. . . . Heroic actions, such as those in *Moby Dick,* are absent; in **''Benito Cereno''** all is muted and somnambulant. . . . (pp. 150-51)

The whole action of the story takes place almost silently. Collisions of objects do not produce the normal volume of noise. The hatchets which certain old negroes are polishing and which they clash together in an occasional ritualistic rhythm sound dull and leaden; the forecastle bell rings ''with a dreary graveyard toll, betokening a flaw.'' The central figure remains in a twilit stage of consciousness. Benito Cereno is ''withdrawn.'' His spiritless passivity is stirred into action only in the form of sudden vague attempts at communicating with Captain Delano, attempts which are not always distinguishable from nervous starts and twitches. (p. 151)

[The mood of withdrawal] is a literary style in which Melville wrote some of his best prose. It is perhaps a peculiarly American style. In Melville, it is a twofold mood, varying from the infinitely moving lyricism of certain passages in *Moby-Dick* and **''Benito Cereno''** to a kind of closely knit textural style reproducing the complexity of subdued psychic experience. The lyrical mood carries us away from living experience toward the condition of sleep or death; the textural mood carries us back toward the sense of life. (p. 152)

Those who think Melville's sensibility is merely imprecise and his language mere vague rhetoric will do well to ponder how wonderfully poised is the universe evoked by [**''Benito Cereno''**]. It is a universe poised upon a present that continually merges with the opulent debris of a dying past and reaches into a vacant and terrifying future. It is a universe in which consciousness is poised between the rich texture of concrete fact existing in time (evoked by the images of decay and the historical references) and a void (evoked by the symbols of space: the dead-lights, the prairie at noon, the deserted chateau, the vague roads). It is a phantasmal world wonderfully conditioned by circumstance and yet trembling with the possibility of entirely unmotivated and irresponsible events, which may happen, as the cats-paw comes, ''unheralded, unfollowed''—a world poised between necessity and chance, between reason and madness. Consciousness, furthermore, is poised between the essential experience of different cultures, between the labyrinthine history of Europe and the timeless emptiness of America, between Man in ''the recesses of the hempen forest'' and Man alone at noon on the prairie. And it is a universe poised between speech and silence, communication and isolation, a universe almost intolerably rich in associable human experience but a universe, nevertheless, in which men must try to communicate with each other with half-formed, half-intended gestures—a universe in which consciousness is completely involved and yet completely alienated. To present a universe thus delicately at rest within the tensions of its own disequilibrium is an *intellectual* feat which disarms all talk of Melville's being merely a ''natural'' genius. (p. 156)

Like **''Bartleby,''** which presents the parallel relationship of Bartleby and his employer, **''Benito Cereno''** shows the limited grasp on life of the successful American gentleman. . . . Captain Delano is that familiar fictional American—the man of energy and good will bewildered by the European scene. For though Captain Delano eventually comes through to an equivocal happy ending, he is nearly lost in the miasma of ancient sin, chaos, and decay, an enigmatic world of ruined summer-houses in desolate gardens, of deserted chateaux and rotting balustrades—a savage forest of equivocations, treacheries, and uncommunicated talk among doomed men. The suffering of Don Benito, a son of the old culture, has given him spiritual light, but the ordeal has been fatal. Captain Delano, unacquainted with the further ranges of human experience, lives on. But plainly Melville is guessing that the accomplishment of the New World will be abortive if the American remains ignorant of the Old World's spiritual depths. . . . The American, in so far as he is like Captain Delano, remains spiritually unfulfilled because he cannot decisively ''withdraw.'' In Captain Delano we have . . . [a] false Prometheus, though his failure is spiritual obtuseness rather than a neurotic compulsion to violent ''escalade.''

"The Paradise of Bachelors and the Tartarus of Maids" is remarkable for its sexual symbolism. (pp. 158-59)

[The] second section of the story is one of the most uncompromising allegorizations of biological processes on record. Occasionally, it is *too* uncompromising, for Melville does not always find symbols which adequately transmute the brute facts into viable material, so that some of the symbols are monstrous, that is, half symbol, half fact. This is, of course, reprehensible in any work of art, though the half-symbols in this story have at least the psychological validity that they are like the half-symbols of dreams. (pp. 159-60)

The remarkable story called **"Cock-a-Doodle-Doo"** deals with the artist's need for the sense of power and the guilt-feelings which accompany it. (p. 163)

This story presents us with two pictures of Melville: the dejected and sickly man with certain neurasthenic symptoms who becomes joyful and strong after listening to the cock; and, on the other hand, Merrymusk, who is also buoyed up by the spiritual joy of the cock's song but over whom the cock gains a frightening ascendancy which somehow brings about his death. (p. 165)

[The] upshot of the story is an acceptance of "gladness" at the lower level of ecstasy: the narrator will sing "COCK-A-DOODLE-DOO!" This new resolution and new independence we cannot suppose a poor compromise or a superficiality in a writer who has faced so terrible a collaboration as that between the cock and Merrymusk. The artist who has had this vision is justified in indicating, through the death of Merrymusk, that the Merrymusk aspect of his personality does not point the direction which that personality will take; that, in fact, the creative artist's personality will be continually reborn out of the continual dying away of Merrymusk. (pp. 166-67)

The real theme of ***Billy Budd*** is castration and cannibalism, the ritual murder and eating of the Host. During his trial Billy proclaims his faithfulness to the king and to Captain Vere by saying, "I have eaten the King's bread, and I am true to the King." When, "without remorse," the dying Captain Vere murmurs, "Billy Budd, Billy Budd," he expresses faithfulness, dependence, and longing. He had eaten of the Host, and he was true to the Host. After forty years Melville had returned to the theme of *Typee*. In that book the young hero had extricated himself from the valley by a sudden exchange of passivity for action. Billy Budd is fatally passive, his acts of violence being unconsciously calculated to ensure his final submission. All of Billy's conscious acts are toward passivity, the first one being his quick acquiescence in his impressment, an act which causes the hero-worshiping sailors to regard him with "surprise" and "silent reproach." In symbolic language, Billy Budd is seeking his own castration—seeking to yield up his vitality to an authoritative but kindly father, whom he finds in Captain Vere. When anyone else stirs the depths of Billy's longing, threatening to bring his unconscious thoughts to consciousness, he flies into a sudden rage. When Red-Whiskers, a sailor who had once been a butcher, maliciously digs Billy in the ribs to show him "just whence a sirloin steak was cut," Billy gives him a "terrible drubbing." And when the minion of Claggart approaches Billy on the moonlit deck and, holding out two shining guineas, says, "See, they are yours, Bill," Billy Budd stammeringly theatens to toss him over the rail. The persistent feminine imagery Melville associates with Billy and his statement that "above all" there was "something in the mobile expression, and every chance attitude and movement suggestive of a mother eminently favored by Love and the Graces," indicate that Billy has identified himself with the mother at a pre-Oedipean level and has adopted the attitude of harmlessness and placation toward the father in order to avoid the hard struggle of the Oedipus conflict. The Oedipus conflict entails, of course, the idea of one's incestuous guilt and one's desire to kill one's father. The psychoanalyst might say that Billy Budd has avoided the Oedipus struggle by forming an attachment to the mother at the prephallic level of "oral eroticism" and has allayed his fears of castration by symbolically castrating himself (by being consciously submissive) and by repressing his rage and hostility against the father in order to placate him. That all Billy's rage and hostility against the father are unconscious is symbolized by the fact that whenever it is aroused it cannot find expression in spoken language. Billy can only stutter and use his fists. This is a mechanism for keeping himself from admitting his own guilt and his own destructiveness. For indeed Billy destroys not only Claggart but himself—and even Captain Vere. For a cloud seems to pass over Vere in his last days, and he dies without achieving the rewards his character had seemed to predestine him to achieve; he dies longing for a "child-man" he had once known.

The food symbolism need not be labored. It recurs frequently, and it is the symbolism which takes us down most swiftly into the coherent lower strata of the story, where there is "a subterranean fire . . . eating its way deeper and deeper." Melville even symbolizes moral qualities by their taste, the innocent character having an "untampered-with flavor like that of berries" as against the guilty character, which has the "questionable smack of a compounded wine." Frequently Billy Budd is compared with animals—a heifer, a horse, a dog, a nightingale, a goldfinch. When he is hanged, he ascends to the yardarm like a "singing-bird," watched from below by a "wedged mass of upturned faces"—as if the sailors were birds expecting to be fed. It is said of Billy Budd (the Lamb of God) that the serpent has never bitten him, but after the accusation Claggart is described as a snake.

The idea of Billy as Host is established early in the story. When the lieutenant of the *Indomitable* goes aboard the *Rights-of-Man* in search of new hands and immediately selects Billy Budd, he drinks some of the captain's grog almost as if conscious of performing a ritual. "Lieutenant," says the captain, "you are going to take my best man from me, the jewel of 'em." "'Yes, I know,' rejoined the other, immediately drawing back the tumbler preliminary to a replenishing; 'yes, I know. Sorry.'" The captain, referring to the pacifying effect Billy has had on his troublesome sailors, then says, "A virtue went out of him, sugaring the sour ones. They took to him like hornets to treacle." Metaphors such as these evoke the primitive rite of slaughtering the young hero in order to eat his flesh and thus obtain his "virtue," his strength, or his heroic quality.

Later in the story Billy Budd spills his soup at mess, and Claggart, happening to pass by at the moment, is inwardly enraged, though outwardly he is only suavely and ambiguously satirical. Melville seems to feel that the enormous eruption of hostile emotion in Claggart may strike the reader as excessive and hence unbelievable. He therefore prefaces one of his comments on the spilled soup with a paragraph which says in effect that the most ordinary event may be a symbolic act which can arouse momentous passions:

> Passion, and passion in its profoundest, is not
> a thing demanding a palatial stage whereupon

> to play its part. Down among the groundlings, among the beggars and rakers of the garbage, profound passion is enacted. And the circumstances that provoke it, however trivial or mean, are no measure of its power.

The palatial stage is surely the conscious mind or the realm of conscious art, and the abode of beggars and rakers of the garbage is the unconscious mind. There are "beggars" in the unconscious mind, calling the ego back among the rakers of garbage, as Billy Budd calls his own ego back. And is not this whole passage intended as a statement that ***Billy Budd*** does not present the reader with a "palatial stage" where profoundest passions are enacted but that, instead, these passions are being enacted "down among the groundlings"? This comes close to telling us not only what is wrong with the story—simply that its profound passions do not find adequate objective representation—but also what is wrong with Billy Budd as tragic hero—that there is no "palatial stage" in his personality, no conscious structure, no mind whose disintegration we should watch with pity and terror rather than merely with bewilderment and an obscure sense of loss.

When Claggart spies the spilled soup, it seemed to him "the sly escape of a spontaneous feeling on Billy's part more or less answering to the antipathy on his own." He feels that Billy has insulted him. But what is the nature of the insult? Presumably that, in spilling the soup, Billy has symbolically exposed himself to Claggart as the Host, the vessel from which issues "virtue." ("Handsomely done, my lad!" cries Claggart. "And handsome is as handsome did it, too!") The spilled soup has also exposed Claggart's guilt as an eater of the Host and, furthermore, Claggart's fear of his own unconscious desire to be like Billy; for the psychological content of Claggart's desire to share Billy's innocence is his desire to be the passive Host.

Melville tells us that Claggart's jaw is heavy out of proportion with his otherwise delicately shaped face—Claggart's unconscious motives center upon orality. This occurs to us when, for example, he smiles at Billy Budd with an ambiguously "glittering dental satire." One of Claggart's "cunning corporals" is called Squeak, "so nicknamed by the sailors on account of his squeaky voice and sharp visage ferreting about the dark corners of the lower decks after interlopers, satirically suggesting to them the idea of a rat in a cellar." Squeak spies on Billy Budd and in this capacity is described as the "purveyor" who "feeds Claggart's passions."

I am sure that much of the sacramental symbolism in ***Billy Budd*** is conscious and intended. But some of it may be less conscious. One cannot be sure how much Melville means by pointing out that two other partisans of Claggart in compromising Billy Budd (two of Claggart's "messmates," they are called) are the Armourer and the Captain of the Hold; but it is a haunting idea that the Armourer represents Teeth and the Captain of the Hold represents Belly. Nor can one say what Thyestean implications there may be in the use of parts of the body in referring to Claggart, whose nickname is Jimmy Legs and whose official title is Master-at-Arms.

As the story concludes, the grim symbolism occurs more frequently and with more intensity. In the captain's cabin Claggart's "mesmeric glance," which Melville compares with "the hungry lurch of the torpedo fish," quickly determines Billy's fate. It is the overt threat of castration which always sets off the explosion of Billy's unconscious fears and resentments. There is a terrible upwelling of his passive emotions, as if in a last attempt to control their aggressive counterparts. Briefly. Billy has the expression of "a condemned vestal priestess at the moment of her being buried alive, and in the first struggle against suffocation"—images which convey both the desire for, and the fear of, castration. But such emotions as these Billy cannot express consciously. He stutters, and strikes Claggart.

Describing the scene in which Vere informs Billy Budd of the sentence, Melville says, "there is no telling the sacrament." There is no telling; but the sacrament can be symbolized. Lying manacled on the deck during the night, Billy is like "a patch of discolored snow . . . lingering at some upland cave's black mouth." His terrible experiences are of the order that "devour our human tissues." The skeleton begins to show under Billy's cheek for the first time; he lies between two cannon as if "nipped in the vise of fate." After the hanging of this Lamb of God, after the chaplain has knelt down "on his marrow bones" to pray (as the ballad of "Billy in the Darbies" says), after the night has passed and it is full day, "the fleece of low-hanging vapor had vanished, licked up by the sun that late had so glorified it." The very patriarch of the universe feeds on Billy Budd.

The passage Melville calls a "Digression" is difficult and obscure; but I venture the following account. The purser and the surgeon discuss the absence of spasm in Billy's body. (They are at mess during this discussion: we are continually reminded in ***Billy Budd*** of the verbal kinship of "mess" with the ritual word "mass.") The purser is "a rather ruddy, rotound person, more accurate as an accountant than profound as a philosopher." The surgeon is "spare and tall" (the same words used to describe Claggart): he is caustic, austere, and something of an intellectual. The two men are opposite types. The purser is the unthinking human animal who kills vicariously, in order to eat. He is the simple cannibal, as is indicated by his placid rotundity (his being like a purse) and by his crude belief that Billy controlled his spasm by "will power." The surgeon is, like Claggart, a lean, emotionally complex and ambivalent sadist: he is more interested in murder than in food, as may be symbolized by his hastily leaving the mess table to get back to a patient in the sick bay. Thus, this very horrifying passage is not really a digression: it is a brief scene which universalizes the theme of the story by presenting two opposite mythical types of man lingering, as it were, over the body.

As the body of Billy Budd, wrapped in canvas and weighted with cannon balls, slides over the rail, the sailors "who had just beheld the prodigy of repose in the form suspended in air" think of the same form "foundering in the deeps"—an image of the act of eating. Over the spot where Billy has sunk, gaunt sea birds wheel and scream; and though the birds are predictably moved by "mere animal greed for prey," the sight has a surprising effect on the sailors. "An uncertain movement began among them, in which some encroachment was made." It is a brief moment of potentially mutinous commotion, which we can understand by noticing that the captain and his officers are symbolically connected with the birds, a connection the sailors unconsciously make. Immediately after the hanging, there had been a similar murmurous impulse to mutiny among the sailors. But the ship's officers had acted quickly. Their authoritative voice was heard in the whistle of the boatswain and his mates, which was "shrill as the shriek of the sea-hawk," which "pierced the low ominous sound" and "dissipated" it, so that in a moment or two "the throng was thinned by one half."

The hanging of Billy Budd, from the movie starring Terence Stamp. Culver Pictures, Inc.

In a man-of-war world, Melville is saying, law feeds on man, being only a translation into social forms of that "horrible vulturism of earth" of which he had spoken in *Moby-Dick.* And with a complex human vulturism Captain Vere feeds on Billy Budd. Notice the sexual-sacramental character of Vere's reaction to Billy's spontaneous "God bless Captain Vere." At these words, "Captain Vere, either through stoic self-control or a sort of momentary paralysis induced by emotional shock, stood erectly rigid as a musket in the ship-armor's rack." The sexual spasm does not occur in Billy Budd because Billy's vitality or "virtue" has been symbolically transferred to Vere. And yet the tranference is ambiguous; paralysis and rigidity suggest death just as surely as erection and the potentiality of the musket suggest life. New vitality has been given to Vere as captain and exponent of martial law (Vere as "musket"), but as man and father he has been stricken.

The intimation of Melville's passages about Lord Nelson is that had Nelson been aboard the *Indomitable* instead of Vere (the two are inferentially compared on several occasions), all this might not have happened, or—and perhaps this is the central point—if it had happened, no subsequent cloud would have passed over Nelson, as it does over Vere. Nelson is the invulnerable and fully mature father, a mythical hero standing behind Captain Vere, a less majestic figure. Nelson already has the qualities of Billy Budd, so that the ritual transference of vitality need not ruin him with its cruel ambiguities. Nelson has the heroic vitality of Billy Budd and the brilliance and audacity of the "jewel" among sailors; it is Nelson's fatherhood which allows him to make "ornate publication" of the very qualities, in sublimated form, which Billy Budd, in the form of infantile rage and hostility, represses. As Melville presents him, Nelson, the "Great Sailor," is the ultimate heroic possibility of the man-of-war world. (pp. 269-75)

The imposing structure of personality Melville attributes to Nelson is beyond the reach of Captain Vere because Vere's moral stability is not proof against the uprising of the sons. In Claggart he sees his own hostility toward Billy Budd. (The relation of Vere to Claggart and Billy is the relation of a father to his sons, one of whom assumes the aggressive and hostile role of the father and the other of whom assumes the passive role of the mother.) In Billy Budd, Captain Vere sees his own imperfectly redeemed childhood. Vere, imposing and even heroic as he is, must repeatedly return to his own childhood to feed on it and to murder it. For him there is no other way of supporting, of nourishing, the structure of consciousness, order, authority, and legality which constitutes the man-of-war world. The man-of-war world destroys itself by feeding on its own vitality, as the vulture feeds upon Prometheus.

This is in itself a moving idea; and so is the implied identification of Billy Budd with Christ. But is there not still another source of the massive emotion which rests uneasily beneath the imperfect surface of ***Billy Budd?*** Consider the connections Melville makes between the captains and literature. Nelson's ship is "poetic"; it has "symmetry" and "grand lines." Of Nelson at Trafalgar, Melville writes:

> If under the presentiment of the most magnificent of all victories, to be crowned by his own glorious death, a sort of priestly motive led him to dress his person in the jewelled vouchers of his own shining deeds; if thus to have adorned himself for the altar and the sacrifice were indeed vainglory, then affectation and fustian is each truly heroic line in the great epics and dramas, since in such lines the poet embodies in verse those exaltations of sentiment that a

> nature like Nelson, the opportunity being given, vitalizes into acts.

Homer is a kind of Nelson. They are the same mythical hero—great captains of the mind, the sea, and the man-of-war world. The author of *Moby Dick* was such a captain.

Captain Vere "loved books." His name, "Vere," signifies (besides "man") "truth"; he is a speaker of the truth. Both his mien and his interests connect him with different kinds of literature than that associated with Nelson. He likes books "treating of actual men and events, no matter of what era." Such a man of truth is Herman Melville, who writes concerning ***Billy Budd:*** "The symmetry of form attainable in pure fiction cannot so readily be achieved in a narration essentially having less to do with fable than with fact. Truth uncompromisingly told will always have its ragged edges."

In *Typee,* Melville had already pictured himself as Billy Budd, the youth with the nameless malady who shrank with such inexplicable fear from the tattooing instrument, tipped with a shark's tooth, and who discovered that his elders—the fathers and the warriors of the tribe—were cannibals.

Lord Nelson is not on "the main road"; he is on "a bypath." The central autobiographical figure in ***Billy Budd*** is Captain Vere. The dark and moving image of the book is Melville as the devourer of his own childhood. An old man with sons of his own, Melville is overwhelmingly moved with pity for the passive, hermaphrodite youth, an image of himself, who must continuously be killed in the rite of the sacrament if books are to be written or the man-of-war world sustained—or indeed if life is to go on at all. (pp. 275-77)

Richard Chase, in his Herman Melville: A Critical Study, *The Macmillan Company, 1949, 305 p.*

NATHALIA WRIGHT (essay date 1949)

[*Wright is an American academic and critic who has published widely on Herman Melville's works and nineteenth-century American letters. In the following excerpt, she discusses the theme of the crucifixion in* Billy Budd.]

By the time of *White Jacket* a criminal suspended above the deck of a ship seems to have been fixed in Melville's mind as an image of the Crucifixion. Bland, the smuggling master-at-arms on the *Neversink,* and a spiritual duplicate of Claggart, deserves to be so hanged, but White Jacket continues to defend him: ". . . I will stand by even a man-of-war thief, and defend him from being seized up at the gangway, if I can—remembering that my Saviour once hung between two thieves, promising one life eternal. . . ."

This passivity of Jesus's resistance, once the clash with evil has occurred, is also foreshadowed in Melville's depiction of character before ***Billy Budd.*** His nonresistance is at least as much naturalistic as religious in such characters as Pip, Bartleby, and Benito Cereno, but often it bears the seal of the New Testament. Jarl, Daniel Orme, and Agath are tattooed with the image of the Crucifixion; and Israel Potter becomes "the bescarred bearer of a cross" when the cut he received at Bunker Hill is traversed by a cutlass wound in the encounter of the *Bon Homme Richard* and the *Serapis*. The figure is repeated in the eighth sketch of **"The Encantadas,"** when Hunilla, the stoical Chola widow, is pictured "passing into Payta town, riding upon a small gray ass; and before her on the ass's shoulders, she eyed the jointed workings of the beast's armorial cross."

When the theme of the Crucifixion is taken up finally in ***Billy Budd,*** the New Testament story is clearly visible. Fundamentally, of course, the two main characters in the novel are embodiments of two abstractions. In one sense Budd is simple nature, a barbarian, "Adam . . . ere the urbane Serpent wriggled himself into his company." Yet his innocence is more than that of a natural man, completely unarmed in the world. It is a divine innocence, incorruptible by society or the forces of darkness. It is a communicable quality, too, to such an extent that Billy's captain on the *Rights of Man* says of him, as Jesus said of himself: "'Not that he preached to them or said or did anything in particular; but a virtue went out of him, sugaring the sour ones.'"

The spiritual antithesis of Billy is Claggart, the master-at-arms, who represents "depravity according to nature." It is a quality not consisting of petty vices nor engendered by experience, but innately residing in his inmost being. He is not so much an evil principle, described by such words as those in Proverbs 21:10, which Melville marked: "The soul of the wicked desireth evil. . . ." Admittedly Melville had some Biblical parallel in mind, for when he came to analyze Claggart he indulged in an illuminating digression. Recording a youthful conversation with a friend on the subject of penetrating character, he quoted the friend as saying:

> "Coke and Blackstone hardly shed so much light into obscure spiritual places as the Hebrew prophets. And who were they? Mostly recluses."
>
> At the time my inexperience was such that I did not quite see the drift of all this. It may be that I see it now. And, indeed, if that lexicon which is based on Holy Writ were any longer popular, one might with less difficulty define and denominate certain phenomenal men. As it is, one must turn to some authority not liable to the charge of being tinctured with the Biblical element.

Yet while Billy and Claggart are essentially abstractions, arrayed against each other by their very natures, for the purposes of the plot they play the roles of Jesus and Judas. Though he is not a creature of the secondary or auxiliary nature of Judas, Claggart is as effective a betrayer of an innocent man to authority. His first attempt is by bribery: he has a seaman offer Billy two guineas to join a proposed mutiny group. When that temptation is withstood, Claggart falsely charges that Billy is disloyal to the king. Only in this way, by treachery, can evil reach good. So Jesus was betrayed by Judas after he had resisted the temptations of Satan in the wilderness, and above him on the cross was hung the same charge: treason.

Both these indictments, moreover, go unanswered. When Budd is brought into the cabin and hears Claggart's accusation he does not utter a word in self-defense, just as Jesus remained silent before the priests and elders. The experience has brought out his defect of speech and he is momentarily paralyzed, though making agonized efforts to speak and defend himself. Perceiving the situation, Vere offers him more time in which to reply, but he is not successful in soothing the sailor:

> Contrary to the effect intended, these words, so fatherly in tone, doubtless touching Billy's heart to the quick, prompted yet more violent

> efforts at utterance—efforts soon ending for the time in confirming the paralysis, and bringing to the face an expression which was as a crucifixion to behold.

Then comes Budd's response to Claggart's accusation, not consciously but instinctively. There can be no compromise between the two forces which they represent, and Claggart falls fatally under Budd's blow. Nor can there be compromise between what remains: between Budd and the king's statute, under which he is now subject to trial. It does not matter that in nature he is free; it does not matter that in breaking an immediate law he thereby kept one higher. Nor does his intent enter into the case; he is judged solely by his deed. The purity of his conscience is reserved for consideration until the Last Assizes, where, as Vere remarks, it will surely acquit him. Here he is the double victim of malignity and of custom.

Thus poignantly and dramatically did Melville distinguish between the false and the true charge against Budd. The distinction is the same in the trial of Jesus. The charge of treason which the members of the Sanhedrin proffered, though necessary for his official execution, was not only false, it was superficial in their own minds. Their true grievance against him was the fact that in obeying the spirit of the law, even more faithfully than they, Jesus violated its letter. Under a similar primitive code both he and the Handsome Sailor are condemned: the Mosaic law and the Mutiny Act. The similarity between the two codes is not insignificant. For the Mutiny Act, demanding a life for a life, is in effect the same penalizing legalism as the Old Testament ethic—the same, in fact, which finally drove Pierre from Saddle Meadows.

Throughout these scenes Captain Vere stands in two relationships to Budd. Primarily he is the military superior and disciplinarian. He sacrifices everything to the end of having Billy convicted, calling a drumhead court together lest in the delay he be swayed by the essential right and wrong of the case from the execution of his duty as administrator of the drastic law. Like Pilate, he condemns to death a man whom he knows to be innocent, though unlike Pilate he accepts the full responsibility of his act. Melville may have known, too, that apocryphal story that Pilate was haunted by the memory of Jesus during his last years as praetor of Hispania Tarraconensis. Not far from this locality Vere murmurs Budd's name as he lies dying on Gibraltar.

Yet Vere also appears in the role of Billy's father; as Abraham to Isaac, as God to Jesus—or rather, not as Abraham to Isaac. Among numerous figures of speech emphasizing the general father-son relationship of the two men this one, brief as it is, provides a revealing contrast with the particular relationship which Melville was also at pains to establish between them. In the private interview between the foretopman and his captain before the execution Melville imagines:

> The austere devotee of military duty, letting himself melt back into what remains primeval in our formalised humanity, may in the end have caught Billy to his heart, even as Abraham may have caught young Isaac on the brink of resolutely offering him up in obedience to the exacting behest.

The figure is moving, but the parallel can be carried no further. For Isaac did not die. Even waiving the fact that his near sacrifice is a deliberate scheme of the Old Testament Jehovah, the obedience of Isaac and of Billy Budd are two different things. Isaac was not taken into Abraham's confidence any more than Abraham was taken into Jehovah's. All is blind obedience, dependent on a jealous and capricious deity.

Not so is the sympathy between Budd and Vere. The sailor and the officer meet as equals; neither conceals anything from the other. When confused at the trial Budd turns to Vere, his accuser, for counsel. His only concern is to have himself cleared in the mind of his captain, to be understood if not to understand; when that is accomplished he has no fear of the future. Their interview alone in Vere's cabin is not unlike the episode in Gethsemane. Afterward the foretopman possesses a peace marvelous and ineffable, which even the chaplain cannot fathom. As he goes to his death his last words are, "'God bless Captain Vere!'"

It is from this understanding which exists between Budd and Vere that the tone of acceptance in ***Billy Budd*** derives its peculiar quality. It is not stoicism, nor the exhaustion following such intense but vain resistance as that of Ahab and of Pierre. It is not even the negation of Jesus's injunction to "resist not evil," which Melville marked in his New Testament. It is a singular mystic communion with the heart of the creation. These two meet on a plane which their companions do not touch or comprehend. They are in a peculiar sense one being. Each shares "in the rarer qualities of one nature—so rare, indeed, as to be all but incredible to average minds, however much cultivated. . . ."

This role of Vere is, in fact, the chief addition Melville made in ***Billy Budd*** to his previous brief dramatizations of the great conflict of good and evil. In them there is no one corresponding to him, an administrator of the law who both knows and loves the law's victim, and in return is known and loved himself. Oro is inaccessible to Mardians, Ahab's fire spirit is disembodied, even Alma and the founder of Pierre's religion are but the instigators of a system, and the chaplain of the *Indomitable* is only a cog in that system. These characters cannot perceive the personality behind the mask, and therefore fear, defy, and blindly obey it. But Billy Budd sees Captain Vere face to face, and finds at the heart of creation the warmth of personality.

This is, of course, easily recognizable as a New Testament idea of the nature of the universe, presided over by a fatherly god. But Melville read something more than this into the Crucifixion story. There he found one more illustration for his notion that beyond the farthest known truth there is yet an untrodden realm, an undisclosed mystery. Unlike Jehovah in the Old Testament, God the Father seems to practice as well as to command obedience; hence his enigmatical willingness for Jesus to die. And so in ***Billy Budd*** even he who administers the law is bound by it. It is the fact that Vere did not formulate the Mutiny Act which makes possible the community of spirit between him and Billy Budd. Both are subject to a power beyond themselves.

What his power is, what this realm is in which, as in Hebrew wisdom, God himself does not reign, Melville never concluded. But it is clearly not simply evil. It is beyond good or evil; it is beyond conflict. The realm in which Budd meets Vere is not the same as that in which he meets Claggart, and beyond them all is an utterly amoral, mysteriously influential *terra incognita*. The last of all Melville's symbols, the death of Captain Vere in the encounter with the *Athéiste,* is a fitting one. Religion, even in its noblest aspect, remained for him penultimate.

The mystery in ***Billy Budd*** is thus not altogether one of iniquity. It is the mystery of a boundless creation, an infinite number of superficially exclusive, deeply related spheres. Symbolic of their existence and of their interdependence is the fact that all nature is affected at Budd's death, as it was at the death of Jesus; it is an episode comparable to Nehemiah's burial in *Clarel,* when a rainbow appears in the sky. The moral conflict is not confined to its own world but reaches beyond it, even to the unyiedling elements. When Budd's body is hoisted aloft the violent motion usually noticeable at hangings is absent; it is suspended quietly above the heads of his comrades. At the same moment the appearance of the sea and sky becomes phenomenal:

> . . . the vapoury fleece hanging low in the east, was shot through with a soft glory as of the fleece of the Lamb of God seen in mystical vision, and simultaneously therewith, watched by the wedged mass of upturned faces, Billy ascended; and ascending, took the full rose of the dawn.

It is not accidental that the description contains a suggestion of the Ascension and of the doctrine of the Atonement. For in the manuscript of ***Billy Budd*** the word ''shekinah'' is crossed out in favor of ''rose,'' and at the beginning of the next chapter Melville first referred to Billy's ''ascension'' but changed it to his ''execution.''

Finally, when Billy's remains are lowered into the sea, throngs of birds fly screaming to the spot and circle it as the ship passes out of sight. And at last it is related that for several years the sailors of the *Indomitable* knew the whereabouts of the spar from which Billy was suspended, following it from ship to dockyard to ship again. ''To them a chip of it was as a piece of the Cross.''

This subtle yet inescapable connection between the natural and supernatural worlds was always part of Melville's vision. If they could not be fitted into one system of thought and action, they were as impossible to separate as the past and the present. The mystery of their relationship never ceased to fascinate him. And though he found it impossible to resolve, he constantly made one distinction between these two parts of the universe. The invisible sphere is absolute, as the themes of Old Testament prophecy and of New Testament ethics and theology insist. But the vast scene which meets the eye, as the Hebrew sages also knew, is ambiguous, equivocal, disguised, relative, masked, multiple. (pp. 127-35)

Nathalia Wright, in her Melville's Use of the Bible, *Duke University Press, 1949, 203 p.*

NEWTON ARVIN (essay date 1950)

[Arvin is an American biographer and critic who has written lives of Nathaniel Hawthorne, Walt Whitman, and Henry Wadsworth Longfellow. In the following excerpt from his acclaimed biography of Melville, he considers the merits and faults of ''Benito Cereno,'' ''The Encantadas,'' and ''Bartleby the Scrivener.'']

Much praise has been lavished on the art with which an atmosphere of sinister foreboding and malign uncertainty is evoked and maintained through all the earlier parts of [**''Benito Cereno''**]. It is hard to see why. There are a few fine touches in the very first paragraphs—the ''flights of troubled gray fowl,'' for example, skimming fitfully over the smooth waters like swallows over a meadow before a storm—but even in these first pages the rhythms of the prose are slow, torpid, and stiff-limbed; and they remain so, with a few moments of relief, throughout. Nor is the famous ''atmosphere'' of **''Benito''** created swiftly, boldly, and hypnotically, as Melville at his highest pitch might have created it; on the contrary, it is ''built up'' tediously and wastefully through the accumulation of incident upon incident, detail upon detail, as if to overwhelm the dullest-witted and most resistant reader. Many of the details, too, are of poor imaginative quality: the hatchet-polishers on the poop are rather comic than genuinely sinister; the symbolism of the key hanging round Don Benito's neck is painfully crude; and it needed only a very commonplace and magazinish inventiveness to conceive the scene in which Benito is shaved by the wily Babo. The traces of contrivance, and fatigued contrivance too, are visible everywhere in the story, and the sprinkling of clichés on every page—''a joyless mien,'' ''the leaden calm,'' ''fiends in human form,'' ''a dark deed''—is only a verbal clue to the absence of strong conviction with which Melville is here writing.

In all the intangible senses, moreover, the substance of **''Benito Cereno''** is weak and disappointing. A greater portentousness of moral meaning is constantly suggested than is ever actually present. Of moral meaning, indeed, there is singularly little. This is partly because the two or three leading personages are too simply conceived to be the bearers of any greatly significant burden. Captain Delano is moral simplicity in a form that borders upon weak-wittedness, as his perversely misdirected suspicions end by indicating; Babo is a monster out of Gothic fiction at its worst, not at its best; and as for Don Benito, with his husky whisper, his tottering step, and his constant attacks of faintness, he is not only hopelessly unheroic, as an image of persecuted goodness, but he is not even deeply pathetic: in his state of nerveless moral collapse he can only be the object of a half-reluctant compassion. The result would be an undermining of the moral structure of **''Benito Cereno''** even if the action itself were not so wanting in large significance as it is. It is certainly very credible that a shipload of African slaves should break out into mutiny, and massacre most of the white officers and crew; it is equally credible that the surviving captain should be intimidated and even persecuted by the mutineers, and that their ringleader should be cunning enough to impose upon a simple-minded ship-captain visiting the bedeviled vessel. As a parable of innocence in the toils of pure evil, however, all this is singularly unremarkable, and we are forced to feel that Don Benito has gone very little beyond the rudiments when, at the end, he enforces the lesson his terrible experiences have taught him: ''To such degree may malign machinations and deceptions impose. So far may even the best man err, in judging the conduct of one with the recesses of whose condition he is not acquainted.'' To be sure!

Neither the story nor the images in the real Captain Delano's book had succeeded in rousing Melville from the lethargy into which he was falling: a year or two earlier, when he wrote the long piece called **''The Encantadas,''** he had worked in a much happier and more characteristic vein. It is true that **''The Encantadas''** is only a loosely organized series of sketches, with no very intense unity among them, rather than a completely fused whole; that one or two of these sketches, the fourth and fifth, are hardly more than pedestrian; and that the eighth sketch, the story of the Chola widow, Hunilla, touching though its subject is, is written in a manner so forcedly and self-consciously pathetic that not even its substance redeems it from the lachrymose. It remains true that nowhere in Melville are there grander images of utter desolation than those evoked, in the first three sketches, of the uninhabited and uninhabitable islands, the Galápagos, solitary, rainless, strewn with volcanic ashes, and overhung by a swirl of gray, haggard mist. ''Apples of Sodom, after touching, seem these isles''; and in these first three wonderful sketches Melville's deepest, most despairing sense of abandonment and sterility is expressed. There is a powerful and intended incongruity, later, in the rather wild humor of the seventh sketch, the story of the Dog-King of Charles's Isle, with its Mark Twainish note of the mock heroic; and the ninth sketch, **''Hood's Isle and the Hermit Oberlus,''** is as dismally convincing, in its dramatization of pure deviltry, the delight in degradation for its own sake, as **''Benito Cereno''** is unconvincing. One touch in this sketch—the spectacle of the hermit Oberlus planting his potatoes, with gestures so malevolent that he seems rather to be dropping poison into wells than potatoes into soil—is worth all the heaped-up horrors of **''Benito.''**

There is an extraordinary harmony of image and feeling, of matter and meaning, in the best passages of **''The Encantadas'':** it is only because the piece as a whole is so loosely and unequally formed that it falls short, as it does, of the highest effect. A few months earlier Melville had written the solitary tale of this period in which the substance seems wholly adequate to the mold, the embodiment wholly adequate to the meaning. This is **''Bartleby''**—or, to use the fuller title it originally bore in *Putnam's,* **''Bartleby, the Scrivener: A Story of Wall-Street.''** Very little that Melville elsewhere wrote succeeds in suggesting quite so much, with means so simple and even stark, as **''Bartleby''** does. In nothing else that he wrote did he achieve, by the accumulation of details in themselves commonplace, prosaic, and humdrum, a total effect of such strangeness and even madness as this. It reminds one of no other American story, certainly no other of Melville's time; if it reminds one of anything, it is of some tale by Gogol or Dostoevsky, ''A Madman's Diary'' perhaps or ''The Double''; some tale of life in a Petersburg government bureau, with a pathetic understrapper in the leading role, that creates, in the midst of dinginess, an effect of wildness and terror. Is the setting of **''Bartleby''** a Wall Street law office or the cosmic madhouse?

It is of course both, and **''Bartleby''** has the quality, small though its scale is, of suggesting a whole group of meanings, no one of which exhausts its connotativeness. On one level doubtless it is a parable of the frustrated relations between the man of letters and the man of affairs, between the artist's world and the world of practice. Bartleby, who is rumored to have been a clerk in the Dead Letter Office, has already learned that communication between man and man is mostly impossible; and now, like a thwarted writer, he is reduced to the mechanical and uninspired drudgery of a scrivener, a mere copyist of dull documents that have no creative meaning whatever. Something of Melville's own plight is obviously reflected here, and when one remembers that Melville's brother Allan, for whom he entertained no strong affection, was a Wall Street lawyer, one can hardly miss the personal bearing of Bartleby's behavior: he very soon discovers that he would ''prefer not to'' engage in copying or indeed in any useful activity at all, and thus succeeds admirably in frustrating his employer. The sound practical solution to the embarrassment thus created would seem to be simple enough: let Bartleby take a month's wages in advance and clear out. But, alas, fruitless as the relation between Bartleby and his employer is bound to be, it is one that, like all human relations, cannot be dissolved. They are both, despite their lack of mutual understanding, ''sons of Adam,'' and the practical man soon learns, with a terrified sense that the world of ordinary sanity is beginning to reel about him, that he is irrevocably responsible for a madman.

Is he himself, meanwhile, as sane as he has always supposed? He begins to doubt it; and as for his other clerks, Turkey and Nippers, competent though they both are, they too are only half sane, sane each of them during only half the day. There is a core of the irreducibly irrational in human existence itself, and poor meek Bartleby is being a kind of philosopher, though a wrongheaded one, when he answers his employer's plea (''Say now, that in a day or two you will begin to be a little reasonable'') by responding mildly: ''At present I would prefer not to be a little reasonable.'' What he would prefer is quietly to withdraw from the business of living and retreat farther and farther into his own gentle indifference and apathy: there is a level on which **''Bartleby''** can be described as a wonderfully intuitive study in what would now be called schizophrenia, and in Melville himself there were certainly the germs of schizophrenic detachment. This is far, however, from being the deepest meaning of the tale. What Bartleby essentially dramatizes is not the pathos of dementia praecox but the bitter metaphysical pathos of the human situation itself; the cosmic irony of the truth that men are at once immitigably interdependent and immitigably forlorn. ''Immediately then,'' says the narrator, alluding to Bartleby, ''the thought came sweeping across me, what miserable friendlessness and loneliness are here revealed! His poverty is great; but his solitude, how horrible!'' If poor Bartleby is a lunatic, it is not because other men are somehow merely sane; it is because he has accepted his forlornness as a final fact and forgotten the fact of dependence. To forget it is an act of suicide, and Bartleby very fittingly expires of physical and moral inanition, in the shadow of his prison wall. (pp. 239-44)

Newton Arvin, in his Herman Melville, *William Sloane Associates, 1950, 316 p.*

ALBERT CAMUS (essay date 1952)

[An Algerian-born French novelist, essayist, dramatist, and short story writer, Camus is celebrated for his multifaceted contribution to world literature. Throughout his writings, he consistently, often passionately, explored his major theme: the belief that happiness is possible in a world without meaning. Although his world view has led some observers to link Camus with existentialism, he himself rejected this classification. In the following excerpt from an essay originally published in 1952, he describes the tone of Billy Budd *and comments on the artistry and intent of ''Benito Cereno.'']*

[Melville's] unwearying peregrination in the archipelago of dreams and bodies, on an ocean ''whose every wave is a soul,'' this Odyssey beneath an empty sky, makes [him] the Homer of the Pacific. But we must add immediately that his Ulysses never returns to Ithaca. The country in which Melville approaches death, that he immortalizes in ***Billy Budd,*** is a desert island. In allowing the young sailor, a figure of beauty and innocence whom he dearly loves, to be condemned to death, Captain Vere submits his heart to the law. And at the same time, with his flawless story that can be ranked with certain Greek tragedies, the aging Melville tells us of his acceptance for the first time of the sacrifice of beauty and innocence so that order may be maintained and the ship of men may continue to move forward toward an unknown horizon. Has he truly found the peace and final resting place that earlier he had said could not be found in the Mardi archipelago? Or are we, on the contrary, faced with a final shipwreck that Melville in his despair asked of the gods? ''One cannot blaspheme and live,'' he had cried out. At the height of consent, isn't ***Billy Budd*** the worst blasphemy? This we can never know, any more than we can know whether Melville did finally accept a terrible order, or whether, in quest of the spirit, he allowed himself to be led, as he had asked, ''beyond the reefs, in sunless seas, into night and death.'' But no one, in any case, measuring the long anguish that runs through his life and work, will fail to acknowledge the greatness, all the more anguished in being the fruit of self-conquest, of his reply.

But this, although it had to be said, should not mislead anyone as to Melville's real genius and the sovereignty of his art. It bursts with health, strength, explosions of humor, and human laughter. It is not he who opened the storehouse of sombre allegories that today hold sad Europe spellbound. As a creator, Melville is, for example, at the furthest possible remove from Kafka, and he makes us aware of this writer's artistic limitations. However irreplaceable it may be, the spiritual experience in Kafka's work exceeds the modes of expression and invention, which remain monotonous. In Melville, spiritual experience is balanced by expression and invention, and constantly finds flesh and blood in them. Like the greatest artists, Melville constructed his symbols out of concrete things, not from the material of dreams. The creator of myths partakes of genius only insofar as he inscribes these myths in the denseness of reality and not in the fleeting clouds of the imagination. In Kafka, the reality that he describes is created by the symbol, the fact stems from the image, whereas in Melville the symbol emerges from reality, the image is born of what is seen. This is why Melville never cut himself off from flesh or nature, which are barely perceptible in Kafka's work. On the contrary, Melville's lyricism, which reminds us of Shakespeare's, makes use of the four elements. He mingles the Bible with the sea, the music of the waves with that of the spheres, the poetry of the days with the grandeur of the Atlantic. He is inexhaustible, like the winds that blow for thousands of miles across empty oceans and that, when they reach the coast, still have strength enough to flatten whole villages. He rages, like Lear's madness, over the wild seas where Moby Dick and the spirit of evil crouch among the waves. When the storm and total destruction have passed, a strange calm rises from the primitive waters, the silent pity that transfigures tragedies. Above the speechless crew, the perfect body of Billy Budd turns gently at the end of its rope in the pink and grey light of the approaching day.

T. E. Lawrence ranked *Moby Dick* alongside *The Possessed* or *War and Peace*. Without hesitation, one can add to these ***Billy Budd***. *Mardi*, **''Benito Cereno,''** and a few others. These anguished books in which man is overwhelmed, but in which life is exalted on each page, are inexhaustible sources of strength and pity. We find in them revolt and acceptance, unconquerable and endless love, the passion for beauty, language of the highest order—in short, genius. ''To perpetuate one's name,'' Melville said, ''one must carve it on a heavy stone and sink it to the bottom of the sea; depths last longer than heights.'' Depths do indeed have their painful virtue, as did the unjust silence in which Melville lived and died, and the ancient ocean he unceasingly ploughed. From their endless darkness he brought forth his works, those visages of foam and night, carved by the waters, whose mysterious royalty has scarcely begun to shine upon us, though already they help us to emerge effortlessly from our continent of shadows to go down at last toward the sea, the light, and its secret. (pp. 291-94)

Albert Camus, ''Critical Essays: Herman Melville,'' in his Lyrical and Critical Essays, *edited by Philip Thody, translated by Ellen Conroy Kennedy, Alfred A. Knopf, 1968, pp. 288-94.*

LAWRANCE THOMPSON (essay date 1952)

[*A distinguished American critic and Pulitzer Prize-winning biographer, Thompson was an acknowledged authority on Robert Frost's life and works and the author of important studies of Edwin Arlington Robinson, William Faulkner, and Henry Wadsworth Longfellow. In the following excerpt from his study of Melville, he interprets the meaning and function of Claggart's ''Natural Depravity'' in* Billy Budd.]

[As ***Billy Budd*** progresses, the] mysteriousness of Claggart's character becomes a subject over which Melville cunningly causes his stupid narrator to puzzle. Quite unintentionally, of course, the narrator establishes some analogies which are of value on the deeper level of meaning; that deeper level which the narrator, as such, never perceives. The narrator opines that the Bible, and even Biblical Commentaries, might be of value here, but that unfortunately and regrettably these are not ''any longer popular.'' Consequently the narrator feels the necessity of referring to ''some authority not liable to the charge of being tinctured with Biblical element.'' His goal here is complete detachment. So he chooses Plato as his authority, and extracts from a list of definitions *attributed* to Plato this seemingly trivial definition of Natural Depravity:

> ''Natural Depravity: a depravity according to nature.'' The fun, here, begins as soon as we notice that this is no definition at all! While the narrator blandly expounds the significance of the definition, however, the alert reader makes his own computation in terms of Melville's sinister frame of reference: a depravity according to nature has its source in nature, or in the source of the source: in God. Natural Depravity is thus an emblem of Divine Depravity. The narrator brightly comments on the definition thus: ''A definition which though savouring of Calvinism, by no means involves Calvin's dogma as to total mankind.'' Indeed not, when construed in a sinister sense. After the narrator completes his elegant exegesis, Melville puts this into his mouth: ''Now something such was Claggart, in whom was the mania of an evil nature, not engendered by vicious training or corrupting books or licentious living, but born with him and innate, in short 'a depravity according to nature.'''

Now the cogged meanings of Melville's darker thoughts begin to turn, and the reader is obliged to reckon with the wheels within wheels. Although Claggart is an emblem of Satan, and Billy is an emblem of Adam, it would seem from this exegesis on ''Natural Depravity'' that there is a striking parallelism between Claggart and Billy, between Satan and Adam: each has his God-given birthmark; each has some kind of imperfection which controls his destiny and yet for which each is not responsible. (''Responsibility'' is a major motif in ***Billy Budd***.) Such a concept is a precise inversion of that parallelism between Satan and Adam which occurs in another artistic illumination of meaning in the Genesis story: the major parallelism which Milton develops, in *Paradise Lost,* between the story of Satan's fall and the story of Adam's fall. It will be recalled that Milton uses this technical device of parallelism to underline the concept that each character has brought on himself his own fate: "Whose fault? Whose but his own!" By contrast, Melville proceeds to invert Milton's central concept, here, in order to illuminate his own bitter conclusion: "Whose fault? Whose but God's!"

The narrator's little treatise on "Natural Depravity" and what he refers to as "those intricacies involved in the question of moral responsibility" is brought to a conclusion in a final paragraph that points one way, in terms of the narrator's purpose, and another way in terms of Melville's allegorical purpose:

> Dark sayings are these, some will say. But why? Is it because they somewhat savour of Holy Writ in its phrase 'mysteries of iniquity'? If they do, such savour was foreign from my intention for little will it commend these pages to many a reader of today. The point of the present story turning on the hidden nature of the master-at-arms has necessitated this chapter.

Captain Vere subsequently becomes interested in Paul's phrase, "mystery of iniquity," and quotes it. The narrator rounds off his discussion by returning to his starting point: he has been puzzling over the mysterious "hidden nature" of Claggart, and this is all he has in mind when he speaks about the "mysteries of iniquity." So much, then, for the narrator. Melville's witty equivocation, for the enjoyment of the careful reader, affords an entirely different construction. The narrator has been right when he has said that the point of the present story turns on the hidden nature of the Master-at-Arms; but the point turns on an aspect which the narrator does not see or mention. In a sinister sense, or an allegorical sense, Melville implies, Satan's fall and Adam's fall were predestined; caused by forces beyond their control; caused by certain birthmark attributes. Even as Billy's fateful impediment is God's birthright gift to Billy, so Claggart's "natural depravity" is God's birthright gift to Claggart. Darkly, then, the point of the present story turns on the hidden nature of the Master-at-Arms because this leads us directly to the hidden nature of God: the malice of God, the "Original Sin" of God. As the narrator very precisely puts it, if such a concept seems somewhat to savour of *Holy* Writ, such was quite foreign to Melville's intention! (pp. 377-79)

Lawrance Thompson, in his Melville's Quarrel with God, *Princeton University Press, 1952, 475 p.*

WILLIAM YORK TINDALL (lecture date 1954-55)

[*An American authority on the works of James Joyce, Wallace Stevens, and others, Tindall wrote numerous studies of modern literature. In the following excerpt, originally delivered as a lecture in 1954-55, he describes the form and structure of* Billy Budd *and explores the moral basis of the contrast between good and evil in the story.*]

Billy Budd seems to make something almost too tidy out of what remains uncertain in *Moby Dick*. Melville's story of the captain, the villain, and the tar, apparently less a story than a commentary on one, may strike the hasty reader as a product of reason rather than imagination, as something reduced to discourse for ready apprehension by basic Englishmen. What had to be said has been said by Captain Vere or Melville himself. As critics, therefore, we may feel frustrated, as Romantics we may prefer a little teasing mystery around, and as esthetes, confronted with discourse, we are sure that talking about a thing is less admirable than embodying it in image or action. Of Kierkegaard's three categories, the esthetic, the moral, and the divine, Melville seems to have chose the second—to the applause of some and the departure of others, for *Don Giovanni* maybe.

That the matter of ***Billy Budd*** gratifies what Melville calls "the moral palate" is plain. . . . (p. 73)

The subject is a quandary or what Melville calls "the intricacies involved in the question of moral responsibility." As the captain ponders "the moral phenomenon presented in Billy Budd" and the "elemental evil" of Claggart, he fathoms the "mystery of iniquity." The case of Billy seems, as the captain says, a matter for "psychologic theologians."

Although, as T. S. Eliot observes in *After Strange Gods,* "It is . . . during moments of moral and spiritual struggle . . . that men [in fiction] . . . come nearest being real," Billy and Claggart, who represent almost pure good and pure evil, are too simple and too extreme to satisfy the demands of realism; for character demands admixture. Their all but allegorical blackness and whiteness, however, are functional in the service of Vere's problem, and Vere, goodness knows, is real enough. Claggart is black because, as Philipp G. Frank once observed, a sinner is necessary for the realization of a moral code; and an innocent is almost equally instructive. These abstractions, a sacrifice of verisimilitude to tactical necessity, reveal the "moral quality" of the captain's mind, which becomes a theater for contending opposites and eventual choice. Such dramatic crises are not only the favorite stuff of novelists but of philosophers and poets as well: Kierkegaard wrote *Either/Or* and Yeats "The Choice."

Not only rational, Vere's choice involves his whole sensitive, adult being. Agony shows on his face as he emerges from his interview with Billy, and a final exclamation shows how deeply he is stirred. Involving more than black and white, the captain's choice is between two moral codes, military and natural. The first is evident; the second is either that of the noble savage, in whom Melville was interested, or what Western culture takes for granted. In other words, the captain's conflict is between the balanced claims of justice and equity, order and confusion, law and grace, reason and feeling, or, as Melville puts it, "military duty" and "moral scruple." Vere's eloquent and moving speech to the drumhead court, the climax of such drama as there is, leaves little to add about these issues and his dilemma.

The conflict of military with natural may occupy the stage, but Melville recognizes other codes, that of custom or respectability, for example. Claggart's "natural depravity" appears in respectable guise. Melville also recognizes the cultural, psychological, and absolute bases for morality, and hints in a very modern way at their operation.

"Moral," Melville's favorite word—in this book at least—is one which, though commonly taken for granted, is slippery. . . . As I shall use it and as I think Melville did, morality implies not only action but motive, attitude, and being. It involves a sense of obligation to self, community, and the absolute, which provide a frame by conscience, law, tradition, or revelation. If we demand a single equivalent, Melville's "responsibility" will do.

Vere's action, however sudden and whether we approve of it or not, is plainly responsible. Billy and Claggart act, to be sure: one bears false witness and the other delivers a blow, but neither actor follows reason and each is more important for

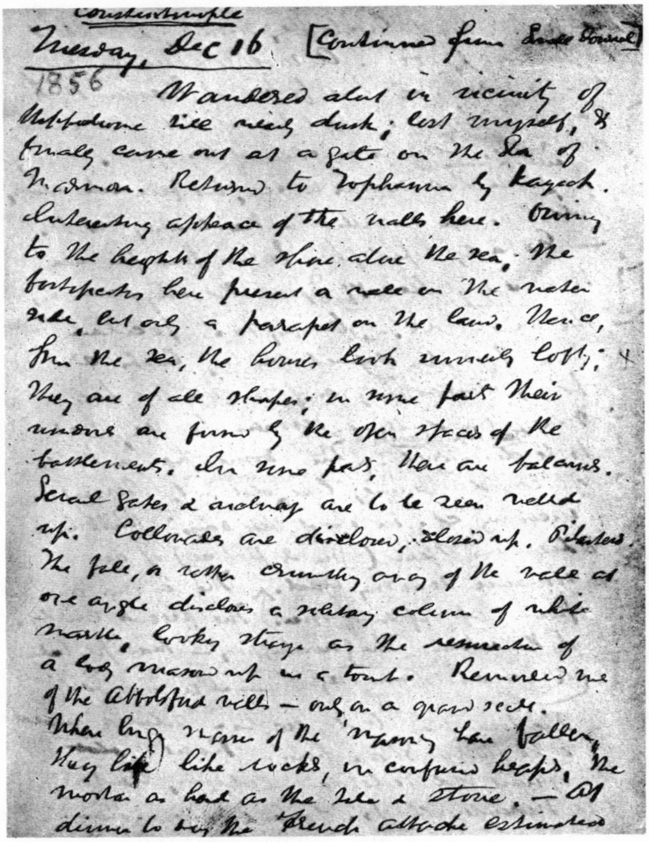

A page from Melville's journal, written in Constantinople (Istanbul) in 1856. The Granger Collection, New York.

what he is than what he does. If being as well as action can be moral, however, they are moral figures, too, existing like cherubs or fiends in a moral atmosphere. Good and bad, they occupy the region of good and evil. (pp. 74-5)

[The question we must consider in reading ***Billy Budd***] is not how much morality is there but how much is under control, how fully insight and moral intelligence have submitted to esthetic discipline. Our problem, then, is not morality itself but moral art or morally significant form.

Captain Vere's speech to the court adequately embodies the idea of "moral responsibility" in dramatic form; but we must find if Billy's history has found fitting embodiment. At first reading, that history seems a curious and eccentric structure of essays on ethics, digressions or "bypaths," character sketches, and chronicles of the navy, an arrangement that after uncertain progress tails inconclusively off. Such image and action as we find, failing to halt the lamentable decline, seem occasions for an analysis or digression, like biblical texts in a pulpit. Since the crucial interview between Vere and Billy is disappointingly offstage, Melville seems to have avoided the dramatic possibilities of his theme. That the book calls for the dramatization he failed to give it, is proved by attempts at play and opera, which, while affirming excellence of theme, imply that action or image are better ways of presenting it. But something that continues to fascinate us in its present form and calls forth responses beyond the capacity of discourse, suggests art of another kind. Maybe Melville avoided drama in the interests of a less obvious medium. (p. 76)

That Melville was aware of form is clear from passages in ***Billy Budd.*** When Captain Vere says, "With mankind forms, measured forms, are everything," he probably means usage and custom; but Melville himself, applying Vere's remark to esthetics, says that the symmetry of form desirable in pure fiction cannot be achieved in factual narrative like this. The story is not factual in fact. But Melville, wanting it to seem so, excuses apparent formlessness as a form for giving the illusion of a bare report; for truth, he continues, will always have its ragged edges and matters of fact must lack the finish of an "architectural finial." (pp. 76-7)

What seems at first to be factual is presented, we find, in part by images and allusions that are incompatible with a pretense of factuality. Though unapparent, those images are livelier than we thought. Consider the coloring of the scene between decks before the execution as Billy lies in white amid profound blackness. Catching up the abstract whiteness and blackness of Billy and Claggart, this image of black and white embodies them. At the execution the rosy dawn that seems "the fleece of the Lamb of God seen in mystical vision" promises a kind of renewal while implying much else. Circling birds after the burial at sea offer by the aid of tradition some spiritual import. And that spilt soup, perhaps more action than image, carries suggestions beyond the demands of plot, suggestions so indefinite, what is more, that they confound its rational progress. Even the names of ships, though serving a more comprehensible purpose, are as significant as those in *Moby Dick.* Billy is removed from the *Rights of Man,* for instance, and Vere is mortally wounded by a shot from the *Athéiste.*

The words of ***Billy Budd*** carry more than denotation. "Sinister dexterity," at once witty and desolating, sounds like something from *Finnegans Wake,* where, indeed, it reappears. Vere's last words, "Billy Budd," are equivocal. Do they imply feeling, regret, self-realization, understanding? Are they a form for something incompletely realized? However "factual" the words of this pseudoreport, they function like the words of poetry.

Not only last words and indeterminate images but a number of hints about Billy's "all but feminine" nature plague our assumptions. Roses and lilies dye his cheeks. He comports himself like a "rustic beauty" at times and like a vestal virgin at others. These qualities and appearances, astonishing in an able seaman, calling forth an "ambiguous smile" from one or another of his shipmates, suggest psychological depths and motives below the level of the plain report. By virtue of such intimations Billy seems at once more and less bottomless than we had supposed, and so do the motives of Claggart, if not those of the captain himself. Among such suggestions, avoidance of the obviously dramatic becomes implicit embodiment that escapes the limits of drama.

What pleases me most, however, is the accompaniment of biblical allusions which, however unobtrusive and irregular, recurs like Wagnerian *leitmotiv.* Time and again Billy is compared to Adam and Jesus. Billy's innocence is as much that of Adam before the Fall as that of the more secular noble savage. As a "peacemaker," a term implying beatitude, Billy seems destined for "crucifixion"; and his hanging, condensing events, becomes an ascension. Vere is compared to Abraham about to sacrifice Isaac, obeying God's will with fear and trembling. Becoming a shadow of God, Vere weighs the claims of Adam and Satan. Claggart, whose denunciation is reported in Mosaic terms as "false witness," is compared not only to the Serpent of Eden but to Ananias and to one struck dead by an angel of God, "yet," as the captain says, "the angel must hang!'' Man's fall and redemption and all troubles between seem suggested by this large though not fully elaborated analogy, which, bringing to mind the mythical parallels in *Ulysses* and *The Waste Land,* removes Billy a little farther from the abstraction to which, for all his stutter and those rosy cheeks, he seems committed. However incapable of supporting this mythical burden, he becomes by its aid almost as portentous as choosing Vere. The sailors, whose testimony cannot be ignored, are more impressed by Billy than by Vere, reason and all. Not only being and secular victim, Billy becomes saint and martyr and his hanging an omen. Pieces of the spar to which he quietly ascends are venerated like pieces of the true cross, suitable for reliquaries or the holiest of duffle bags. By the aid of myth and military ritual the story of Billy, transformed from an essay on good, evil, and choice, approaches what Yeats called ''the ceremony of innocence.''

We must conclude that Melville avoided the attractions of the obvious in the interests of indefinite suggestiveness and myth. His work, whatever its air of the factual and the discursive, is symbolist and richer for scarcity of drama and image. Such drama and images as are there function more intensely in their abstract context than profusion could. That the structure as a whole also serves esthetic purpose is likely. As we have seen, the book is a queer arrangement of discourse, action, image, and allusion, with discourse predominanting. We have seen how image and action work in this mixture; but we must examine the function of discourse. In such context, discourse, increasing tension, makes allusion and image dramatic or enlarges them, and, working with allusion, image, and action may produce a third something by juxtaposition as in Eliot's *Four Quartets* or Wallace Stevens' *Notes Toward a Supreme Fiction*. Seeming now a structure of conflicts, not only of men and codes but of methods, which become a technical echo of the theme, the book emerges as a structural drama or a drama of structure. An ending that seemed weak afterthought (and was not there in the first version) now unifies all. Vere's exclamation, the saint's legend, and inconclusiveness, working together, comprise a form, which may tail off but tails suggestively off, leaving endless reverberations in our minds. There is more mystery around than we had thought, and we may agree with dying Gertrude Stein that answers are less important than questions. What at a superficial reading had the appearance of exhaustive discourse becomes inexhaustible. The shapeless thing becomes suggestive shape. Neither as loose nor as tight as it once seemed, the strange sequence of precise discourse and indefinite suggestiveness corresponds to our experience of life itself. That the form Melville made fascinates while it eludes and teases is shown no less by popular favor than by the abundance of critical comment.

However different it looks, ***Billy Budd*** is not altogether different in kind from *Moby Dick,* another structure of digression, discourse, action, and image. The proportions and impact may be different, the images of *Moby Dick* may be more compelling, but both serve symbolic suggestion and both are forms for offering a vision of reality. Not the tidy discourse of our first impression, the work is almost as inexplicable as *Moby Dick*.

What exactly does this form present? It is impossible to answer this question for any symbolist work; for works of this kind escape discursive accounting. We may say that ***Billy Budd*** is a vision of man in society, vision of man's moral quandary or his responsibility; but its meaning is more general than these, and that is why it haunts us. So haunted, I find the work not an essay on a moral issue but a form for embodying the feeling and idea of thinking about a moral issue, the experience of facing, of choosing, of being uneasy about one's choice, of trying to know. Not a conclusion like a sermon, ***Billy Budd*** is a vision of confronting what confronts us, of man thinking things out with all the attendant confusions and uncertainties. Disorder is a form for this and the apparently formless book a formal triumph. To do what it does it has to be a fusion of tight-loose, shapeless-shaped, irrelevant-precise, suggestive-discursive—a mixture of myth, fact, and allusion that has values beyond reference. The discursive parts represent our attempts at thinking, while the action, images, and allusions represent what we cannot think but must approximate. Arrangement of these discordant elements forms a picture of a process.

From my guess at meaning it follows that the center of this form is neither Vere nor Billy but rather the teller of the story or Melville himself. Though ghostlier, he is not unlike the Marlow of Conrad's *Lord Jim* and *Heart of Darkness* or the Quentin of Faulkner's *Absalom, Absalom!* Using Vere and Billy as materials, Melville's thought-process, like those of Marlow and Quentin, is the heart of this darkness and its shape the objective correlative, a form for something at once imperfectly understood and demanding understanding. Morality, the substance of this form, becomes an element that limits and directs the feelings and ideas created by the whole. Moral substance, what is more, may be what engages our minds while the form does its work. Value, not from morality alone, issues from the form that includes it and in which it serves. If the form concerned less, I repeat, it would be trivial, but without its formal presentation the morality would remain in Sunday school.

United now, the beautiful and the good create a vision larger than either, a vision transcending the case of Billy Budd or the quandary of Captain Vere. The teller, now any man, presents man's feeling in the face of any great dilemma. Thought and feeling, outdistancing themselves, become objects of contemplation, remote yet immediate. The effect of this form is moral in the sense of enlarging our awareness of human conditions of relationships and of improving our sensitivity. In such a form Kierkegaard's esthetic, moral, and divine become a single thing. (pp. 77-81)

William York Tindall, ''The Ceremony of Innocence (Herman Melville: 'Billy Budd'),'' in Great Moral Dilemmas in Literature, Past and Present, *edited by R. M. MacIver, The Institute for Religious and Social Studies, 1956, pp. 73-81.*

MILTON R. STERN (essay date 1957)

[Stern is an American authority on nineteenth- and twentieth-century American literature, especially the works of Nathaniel Hawthorne, F. Scott Fitzgerald, and Melville. In the following excerpt from his full-length study of Melville, he probes Captain Vere's purpose and function in Billy Budd.]

What would happen if there were a man who did manage to understand the proper relationship between heart and mind, a man who was not blind to history, a man who had a political or social position—say a ship's captaincy—which would allow him to translate his realizations into action? What if this man were exposed to a choice between pure ideal and ''fallen'' human history, with its present actuality of a crime-filled man-of-war world? Wanted: a hero.

Captain Vere [in ***Billy Budd***] is the man created to fill this position. (p. 26)

[Billy Budd] is pictured as the childlike barbarian, the pure creature whose only experience really is just the experience of his own inner purity and ideality. His spontaneous responses preclude control by mind. This Christ figure also deceives by silence, albeit unwittingly, and finally becomes a murderer and a causer of his own death. Billy himself is the lure which Vere painfully rejects with all the insight created by an understanding of human history. Vere is educated, with the reader, to see Claggart as Satan and Baby Budd as Christ. But Vere's one overriding fact is the fact of the temporal world, the reality of his human community to which he owes his primary allegiance. He cannot choose the ideal which, by itself, is beautiful. And Claggart becomes the other facet of Budd. Budd is the ideal, Claggart is the consequence. He is the completely mad and satanized quester who has withdrawn from quest. He is Ahab, retired in his New Bedford home, staring silently and crazily out at the sea. He is Ahab who has given up the chase, but who still watches. . . . This demonized isolation seeks out and hates and yearns to believe in ideal Billy in exactly the same monomaniacal relationship which Ahab has to the white whale. Just as the reader sees that for Ahab the whale is only what Ahab thinks he is, and the whale, in a sense, becomes Ahab, so for Melville, Christ and Satan are ultimately one entity with a dual face. Like all Melvillean dualities, absolute identities are man-made products which unite in the flow of historical consequence in the Great God Time. The bright and the dark are the *same*.

Vere rejects both lure and quester. His heartbroken rejection of Budd as a beautiful impossibility in favor of an ugly reality, his decision to force his position of command to operate according to what his head dictates and his heart detests, is his acceptance of this world as the only possible one. It is not, as many critics have attempted to demonstrate, an acceptance of God and a submission to Fate. It is quite the opposite. It is Melville's reluctant, modified, but final acceptance of historical necessity in a naturalistic universe. It is a consequent call for man to control his fate by controlling his actions in the historical world—and it is also Melville's statement of inability to find the way to do so. Vere decides to remain unwithdrawn, to accept the responsibility of the human community by accepting the responsibility of command. His decision to maintain order because of man's blindness is his sacrifice of self to the necessities of moral responsibility historically defined. Moreover, it is in his sacrifice of individual self to his social self that Vere finds his greatest identity, in the book as well as in the reader's mind. Vere is the polar opposite and instinctive antagonist to the quester. He offers the alternative behavior which had to be created once the quester's behavior was anatomized and rejected.

In ***Billy Budd*** the cast of characters changes. The quester as such drops out and the hero takes his place. And here the limitations (or perhaps the accuracy) of Melville's nineteenth-century naturalism become most apparent. For even the hero does not create a purged world. The lesson of Vere's sacrifice is lost. The lesson of Billy Budd's final realization is lost. The world gains not social insight but myth, and the cycle continues. Various studies have tried to identify Melville with his questers. But if he is to be identified with any of his characters, it must be with Captain Vere rather than with anyone else except Ishmael. (The two combined offer a very fair approximation of Melville's political, social, and metaphysical perceptions.) He is the man who turns to history for direction, yet who, when faced with the mystery of *human* nature, calls "Billy Budd! Billy Budd!" He calls for the perfection-aspiring human heart, and not in accents of remorse. (pp. 26-7)

[Vere] is a man whose experience had not been lost in innocence nor yet sterilized in [cynicism]. . . . Vere is totally active. He will not delay in making decisions, even when the decision is totally painful and when just a three-day wait would allow him to dump the entire problem in the lap of a superior officer. Yet, like Nelson, he is not the enthusiast or the gloryhog. Totally aware of the fact of consequences, he does not subordinate reflection to physical courage, which, Melville said, is the one characteristic that man shares with the beasts of the field. Vere's is the communal prudence; he is "thoroughly versed in the science of his profession, and intrepid to the verge of temerity, though never injudiciously so." (p. 220)

Vere is neither innocently mirthful like Billy, nor cynical like the Dansker. He is prominently and predominantly serious. His seriousness comes from history, and not from idealism. Hard-headedly realistic, Vere rejects the pretentious Titanism of the quester. Whether he realizes that there is nothing in the blankness to strike, like whether he realizes the fact of a naturalistic universe, is not anchored in direct evidence within the story. One can assume the affirmative in both cases, for in his non-idealistic actions, Vere subordinates self to community and desire to history; thus his wisdom that is woe does not slip over into the woe that is madness. He becomes the one man who sees and who is not the confidence man or the zero or the quester. (p. 221)

In Vere, Melville has the unopportunistic character through whom he can morally pronounce the necessity for pragmatic judgment. Moreover, unlike the bureaucrats who wrote the official version of Budd's deed, Vere sees through official, conventional appearances and does not save the officer caste for its own sake at all—indeed he condemns that caste to the necessities and responsibilities for the public judgments which slay the private judge. He realizes that one must defend the forms and appearances in order to use them in the struggle to reform the actualities which makes the "frontage" necessary. For Vere the historical must always take precedence over the ideal: first things first. (p. 223)

Vere is Melville's complete man of action, mind, and heart. His experience demands that his acts proceed from an understanding of history, and, empirically, "his bias was toward those books to which every serious mind of superior order occupying any active post of authority in the world, naturally inclines; books treating of actual men and events no matter of what era—history, biography and unconventional writers, who, free from cant and convention, like Montaigne, honestly, and *in the spirit of common sense* philosophize upon *realities*" [italics mine]. And coupled with heartful and mindful empiricism is an eclectic time sense which sees all history as the unfolding of a pattern, all aspects of man's life equatable in different eras in the blank and inevitable passage of time. "In illustrating of any point touching the stirring personages and events of the time he would be as apt to cite some historic character or incident of antiquity as that he would cite from the moderns." Thus, though set off from the rest of mankind as a man of superior insight and power, Vere never passes from the way of understanding. He can effect the kind of border-crossing eclecticism which the quester, who tried to cross borders, needed so desperately. Nonidealistic eclecticism gives men like Vere direct insight into the heart of the matter, and their "honesty prescribes to them directness, sometimes far-reaching like that of a migratory fowl that in its flight never heeds when it crosses a frontier." His entire rationale for being is based upon the final characteristic necessary for the complete man: his goal is the betterment of the race and the communal attainment of the earthly felicities. (p. 225)

Milton R. Stern, in his The Fine Hammered Steel of Herman Melville, *University of Illinois Press, 1957, 297 p.*

MARVIN FELHEIM (essay date 1962)

[Felheim was an American academic, editor, critic, essayist, and translator. In the following excerpt, he discusses the meaning and structure of "Bartleby the Scrivener."]

[**"Bartleby the Scrivener"**] is a first-person narrative and, although the story is *about* Bartleby, we know him and come to understand his situation through the eyes and words of the lawyer who employs him. The story appropriately begins with "I . . . a rather elderly man"; it concludes with a comment, set off by itself, a kind of universal sigh, uttered by no one, addressed not even to "the reader":

> Ah, Bartleby! Ah, humanity!

The story, I submit, is not Bartleby's, but, on the first level, the lawyer's; secondly, it is the reader's, for as the lawyer learns so must the reader. The fact that both the lawyer and the reader do learn is, then, communicated by means of this final chorus, appropriately a paragraph to itself, unadorned except for the exclamation marks which emphasize the awful awareness contained in the expression itself. (pp. 370, 375)

The opening section of the story does not center about Bartleby, except indirectly. It introduces, first of all, the lawyer, who makes it clear that his procedure throughout will be absolutely in character, for even "the late John Jacob Astor . . . had no hesitation in pronouncing my first grand point to be prudence; my next, method." The story, then, will be unfolded cautiously and methodically. Almost immediately we meet "first, Turkey; second, Nippers; third, Ginger Nut." And we notice at once that the lawyer is nameless; the employees have nicknames; for Bartleby alone is a true name reserved. Only after the eccentricities of the lawyer and the employees have been fully revealed is Bartleby introduced:

> In answer to my advertisement, a motionless young man one morning stood upon my office threshold, the door being open, for it was summer. I can see that figure now—pallidly neat, pitiably respectable, incurably forlorn! It was Bartleby.

The middle third of the story deals with subsequent happenings in the law office, in particular with the lawyer-scrivener relationship. This longest section of the narrative can in turn be divided into three segments. It begins "on the third day" of Bartleby's employment. Called upon "to examine a small paper," Bartleby, "in a singularly mild, firm voice, replied, 'I would prefer not to.'" Thus Bartleby poses the first problem. (We must note that he is not being whimsical; his behavior is eccentric but, as is the case with the other characters, it is absolute; he acts on the basis of "some paramount consideration.") Bartleby's actions provoke the lawyer's first response: selfish acceptance. "Here I can cheaply purchase a delicious self-approval," he writes; after all, Bartleby's "steadiness, his freedom from all dissipation, his incessant industry . . . his great stillness, his unalterableness of demeanor under all circumstances, made him a valuable acquisition." He was, in truth, no more difficult than Turkey or Nippers.

But now Bartleby poses a second problem: the lawyer discovers that his scrivener has been living at the office. (Here, again, we must note that Bartleby's eccentricity is a matter of degree: the others eat gingernut cakes whereas Bartleby consumes only these spicy tid-bits and some cheese; the others spend their days in the office, but here Bartleby "makes his home" never even going out for a walk.) "What miserable friendliness and loneliness are here revealed! His poverty is great; but his solitude, how horrible!" Bartleby's state forces a new response from the lawyer: pity. It is significant that the lawyer does not simply feel sorry for his clerk; he can as well pity himself: "A fraternal melancholy! For both I and Bartleby were sons of Adam." The upshot of his discovery and the violence of his reactions prevent him from going to church. (There is no answer in formal religion?)

The third problem which Bartleby poses now emerges: he gives up copying. He has become "a millstone." And the lawyer's response? The perfect Christian reaction: charity. The lawyer, after a variety of excuses and plans, simply recalls "the divine injunction: 'A new commandment give I unto you, that ye love one another.'" Thus the middle section of the tale is brought to a close. The lawyer concludes with Job-like resignation that "these troubles . . . had been all predestined from eternity, and Bartleby was billeted upon me for some mysterious purpose of an allwise Providence, which it was not for a mere mortal like me to fathom."

In 1853, in the [original] publication of **"Bartleby"** in two parts in *Putnam's Magazine,* the break between the two installments occurred after Bartleby's announcement that he had given up copying and after the employer's decision to try to cope with this situation. The actual stopping place was the moment when the lawyer, having left Bartleby a generous amount of money, having requested him to leave the key under the mat, departs his office, "charmed" with the "beauty" of his handling of the matter. This is a dramatic high point in the narrative, of a kind to excite readers' curiosity: will Bartleby leave the premises? But it is not the philosophic and structural climax of the story, which takes place a bit later, after the lawyer's acceptance of the situation.

But now we must move to the concluding section of the story: society enters, in the persons of the lawyer's "professional friends" and other visitors. They are the first; they force the lawyer to desert his chambers, his principles, and Bartleby. New "tenants" now add their complaints. Finally, the landlord sends for the police, who remove Bartleby to the Tombs. Here there are more social beings: "murderers and thieves," the "grub-man," several "turnkeys." The final section of the narrative truly enlarges the implications. As long as relationships were on a personal, one-to-one basis (as was true also of the employer's attitude toward Turkey and Nippers) the lawyer could, and did, behave as a Christian. But once the situation was allowed to go further, was invaded by others, new considerations arose. In this third section, the role of the lawyer subtly changes: he is no longer an involved character; he has become simply the narrator. Society has become involved; it has taken over the lawyer's role. But society has no method, no way of coping with the issues Bartleby raises. It can resort only to its one effective institution, the jail, ironically named the Tombs. There, Bartleby dies, to join others like

Wall Street, New York City, the setting of "Bartleby the Scrivener," as it appeared shortly before the story's publication in 1853.

himself, "kings and counselors." At last, he can absolutely be identified with a society.

It is significant that Melville added a kind of postscript to this story: the lawyer's divulgence of "one little item of rumor." The information, "that Bartleby had been a subordinate clerk in the Dead Letter Office at Washington, from which he had been suddenly removed by a change in the administration," . . . adds a specific political dimension to the social one, but it in no way diminishes the central point, that society must be responsible. The "charity" or "pardon," the "hope" or "good tidings" which those dead letters contained are all useless, too late. Indeed, only a choral comment could end this story. Any personal remark would be inadequate and artistically out of key. (pp. 375-76)

Marvin Felheim, "Meaning and Structure in 'Bartleby'," in College English, *Vol. 23, No. 5, February, 1962, pp. 369-70, 375-76.*

C. B. IVES (essay date 1962)

[Ives here considers why Captain Vere argued to condemn Billy Budd.]

[Did Melville make Captain Vere's case so strong that the problem of whether or not Billy should be condemned] disappeared?—so strong that every reasonable captain would have acted as he did? If so, [***Billy Budd***] has lost some of its realistic appeal. Vere's position was exactly that; he said that he had no choice and that, in fact, he was faced with no problem at all. I believe that the reader is mistaken if he accepts Vere's position at face value. Let us analyze it somewhat.

Vere's argument was founded mainly on the Articles of War, a combination of enactments by Parliament and regulations by the Admiralty. He appealed also to the Mutiny Act, but the body of laws falling under that title applied only to the army and were without significance to his situation.

Examine, then, that section of the Articles of War that applied to Billy's act:

> If any Officer, Mariner, Soldier or other Person in the Fleet, shall strike any of his Superior Officers . . . on any Pretense whatsoever, every such Person being convicted of any such Offense, by the Sentence of a Court Martial, shall suffer Death. . . .

This provision makes it clear that Billy Budd's offense was punishable by death under the Articles, but it is equally clear that Vere was wrong in asserting that the Articles required him to hang Billy forthwith. They required no such thing. On the contrary, they provided the punishment of death only upon conviction by a "Court Martial," by which term was meant a general court-martial, called by the commander of a detachment, a squadron, or a fleet. The Articles of War provided nowhere for such summary court-martial as was held by Captain Vere.

In an emergency, however, and in the event of a mutiny, a captain might hang the mutineers as a matter of necessity, in disregard of the Articles of War. In such cases it was normal to secure the advice and judgment of his officers in a summary court. (pp. 32-3)

But Billy Budd was not a mutineer and was not hanged for mutiny. Mutiny required a "combination of two or more persons," and, besides, Vere declared emphatically, "I believe you, my man," when Billy protested his loyalty. Nor was he hanged for murder, since Vere agreed that intent was lacking. Vere's stated reasons for the hanging were that Billy had struck his superior and that there was *danger* of mutiny by some other members of the crew.

For his decision, Vere could undoubtedly find support in the British naval customs that allowed latitude to a captain's authority even in defiance of statute, the attitude of naval officers being, as one might expect, that politicians knew nothing about discipline at sea and that even the Admiralty was too much of an ivory tower for its members to make consistently sensible regulations. Thus, for example, although printed instructions of the Admiralty limited captains of ships to imposing punishments of not more than a dozen lashes, in practice these autocrats seldom gave less than the allowance and frequently gave several dozen more.

Discretion was customarily allowed in the direction of leniency also. The faults of sailors sometimes passed without punishment at all, and sometimes received lighter punishments than the Articles called for. Thus, a captain might impose a minor punishment for desertion although the Articles demanded that a court-martial try the offender for his life; and not only was sleeping on watch regularly overlooked. . ., but, according to at least one experienced officer of those days, it was actually encouraged. Billy's offense, striking a superior officer, for which the Articles allowed no alternative to death, did not always receive that punishment.

In short, a captain of a man-of-war was godlike and might exercise his disciplinary discretion or even his disciplinary whims freely with little expectation of reproof.

Was not Captain Vere aware of his broad powers? The considerable argument that he made to the officers of his drumhead court-martial implies that he was; and when he said, "one of two things we must do—condemn or let go," he explicitly recognized the power to let go that he—advised, though not bound, by his court—possessed by naval custom. His appeals at one moment to the Articles of War and at the next to the "practical consequences" demonstrate his own confidence that the Articles did not control him.

In addition to the alternatives of hanging and acquittal, his officers also recognized the availability of two other lines of action: conviction with a penalty less than hanging or reference of the case to the Admiral as provided by the Articles. The first of these was called to Vere's attention by the junior lieutenant; and Vere was aware of the second, though he did not discuss it at the trial.

We must, then, conclude that Captain Vere, contrary to some of his statements to his officers, had, as a matter of fact, the broadest powers in dealing with Billy. He could let him off, he could impose a minor punishment, he could refer the case to a general court-martial, or he could hang him. He chose to hang him.

Consider now some of the irregularities in the so-called trial ordered by Captain Vere. When Vere told the surgeon of his determination to call a drumhead court-martial immediately, the surgeon thought Vere was "suddenly affected in his mind." He recalled Vere's "excited exclamations so at variance with his normal manner." The lieutenants and the captain of marines "fully shared" the surgeon's "surprise and concern." The misgivings of these men were undoubtedly roused in part by the precipitancy of the "trial," the best procedure even in cases of minor crimes being to delay the decision as to punishment for at least twenty-four hours; but mainly their anxiety seems to have come from Vere's decison to try Billy at all, since they saw no reason not to comply with the provisions of the Articles of War. The "sense of the urgency of the case" that "overruled in Captain Vere every other consideration" did not possess his officers.

They also saw, no doubt, a violation of at least the spirit of the law in the secrecy with which Vere hurried on to his conviction of Billy. General courts-martial were required by the Articles of War to be held in the greatest possible publicity. Since drumhead courts were not provided for by statute, only by custom, nothing explicitly required Vere to give publicity to his trial; yet the general policy was made clear by the Articles, and, after news of the hanging got abroad in the fleet, Vere was criticized for his secrecy "in the confidential talk of more than one or two gun-rooms and cabins."

Finally, Vere's officers must have recognized that a basic element of judicial inquiry and trial was defied by Vere's pre-

Melville around 1868. The Bettmann Archive, Inc.

determination to hang Billy. It is true that they did not hear him address Billy as "Fated boy" the moment after Claggart gave his last gasp; but the surgeon had hardly confirmed Claggart's death when he heard the Captain exclaim that Billy must hang. The members of the court could not help seeing that the proceedings were sham, dominated and directed by Vere, who required them only for the sake of form—" 'With mankind' he would say 'forms, measured forms are everything. . . .' " (pp. 33-6)

What was there in the character of Vere that brought him to adopt his extraordinary course? Why, though appealing to the Articles of War, did he disregard them? And why did he disregard the advice of his officers, the suggestions of common sense, and the strong inclination of his own heart?

Melville gives the Captain many virtues, which need not be denied in putting emphasis on that side of his nature that seems to have been the chief cause of Billy's summary hanging.

Vere was a bachelor of "forty or thereabouts," who had "ruled out" the feminine in his personal life just as he demanded of the members of his court that they rule it out in deciding Billy's fate. He was not given to colorful talk or gestures, for when ashore "he never garnished unprofessional talk with nautical terms," and when afloat he might have been mistaken by any landsman for a civilian rather than the captain of the ship. He was undemonstrative and humorless. His bookishness was marked—"dry and bookish" some called him—and it was biased towards "actual men and events" rather than fiction or poetry. In his reading he "found confirmation" or certain "positive convictions" that he was determined never to change. So pedantic was his interest in historical fact and so stubborn his lack of interest in human nature that even with those of his fellow officers whose intellectual inclinations were thoroughly alien to his he freely alluded to his bookish research. In short, although the life he led was vigorous and dramatic, Vere turned from the enjoyment of it to books; and, although his reading might have been even more impressed with color and vitality than his adventurous life, he turned away from literary art or imagination or feeling to the dryness of recorded fact.

At Billy's trial, Vere's arguments were aimed primarily at making the decision that would be most difficult for human sympathy, most difficult for man as a living being having a natural love of life. He cited the Articles of War (which did not, in fact, support him), the Mutiny Act (which did not apply), the practicalities of the situation (which to every other judgment called for delay at least), and the necessity, as he said, of doing what no one wanted to do, of suppressing Nature, of injuring the heart—"the feminine in man"—even of violating the conscience. When he announced the court's decision to his sailors, they received his statement "like belivers in hell listening to the clergyman's announcement of his Calvinistic text."

In all this, Vere was guided not by the mind, as he professed, but by the heart turning against itself. Note well that in spite of his devotion to the facts of books, to a colorless simplicity of personal speech and appearance, to the coldest duties of his profession and rank, emotion was not always entirely concealed; for a "certain dreaminess of mood" revealed itself at times, signifying that, even before his surprising emotional outburts in the case of Billy Budd, Vere had never been entirely as dry as dust.

Give full weight also to Melville's chapter on Nelson, inserted with no casual intent. At Trafalgar, says Melville, Nelson dressed himself out in all his decorations, advertising his identity to the enemy and suffering death in consequence. His was "a sort of priestly motive," says Melville, and the admiral "adorned himself for the altar and the sacrifice." A similar priestly motive and and a similar sacrifice is declared in Melville's comparison of Vere to Abraham preparing to offer up Isaac. Although Abraham's sacrifice was not literally of himself, like Nelson's, it was of his son, whom he loved and who was, in no remote sense, a part of himself. Similarly, Vere loved Billy Budd and spoke to him in "fatherly" tone.

A review of these aspects of Vere's nature justifies the conclusion that the Captain's sudden decision to hang Billy was a sacrificial gesture, born of a kind of self-punishment that had become habitual in Vere's life, the sacrifice and denial that are involved in man's search for the comprehension of fact that destroys fancy, in man's search for the experience that gives him truth but robs him of innocence. All of his life Vere had devoted himself abnormally to this emphasis, killing repeatedly the affections that manifested themselves only in moments of dreaminess, moments that embarrassed and irritated him when they were discovered. Billy represented all of this nearly-destroyed side of him—the affectionate side, the heart, the feminine—and stirred him to such a pitch that when the innocent sailor delivered the death blow to Claggart, Vere's suppressed love for Billy and for all that Billy stood for rose suddenly to the surface. However, Vere's self-disciplinary passion for the harshness of fact-searching and heart-denial rose equally fast and dominated his will as it always had done.

A more normal captain would never have been so eager to hang Billy Budd, and a more practical one might not have hanged him at all, in view of his great value to the morale and efficiency of the crew. Billy's destruction was doomed not only by the abnormal malevolence of Claggart but also by the abnormal "inside narrative" of Vere's personality. The customs of the sea did not require it; and the Articles of War provided only a deceptive excuse for the exercise of Vere's extraordinary "priestly motive," which, as Melville suggests at the beginning of Chapter XXII, may well have contained the elements of true insanity. (pp. 37-9)

C. B. Ives, " 'Billy Budd' and the Articles of War," in American Literature, *Vol. XXXIV, No. 1, March, 1962, pp. 31-9.*

WARNER BERTHOFF (essay date 1962)

[An authority on American literature, Berthoff has written important studies of nineteenth- and twentieth-century literary culture, including Emerson's Nature *(1968) and* A Literature without Qualities: American Writing Since 1945 *(1979). In the following excerpt from his* The Example of Melville, *he examines the narrative structure of "Benito Cereno."]*

[If we take **"Benito Cereno"**] as a fable—of innocence and evil, or of spiritual obtuseness and spiritual suffering—we might indeed have to say that the narrative is awkward and negligent in composition, and that it really does not make its point. Surely a competent allegorist could have managed the display more efficiently, and a clear-headed moralist would have devised a less eccentric balance of forces. But is it not reasonably apparent that what caught Melville's practical interest as a writer was just the intense chiaroscuro strangeness of the situation and of its material facts, with their—literally—double meaning? Why else should he stick so closely to the data of his source, and set the additional incidents of his own invention in so nearly the same mold? Melville's leading impulse in working out the sequence of his retelling was to capitalize on just this material ambiguity, and on the delayed double-exposure it results in. That impulse was not greatly different from the conjuror's impulse behind those stories of Poe's (also written for magazines) which are exercises in the fine art of mystification. The appearances put before us in **"Benito Cereno"** constitute a riddle, and the business of two thirds of the narrative is the elaboration of this riddle and then its sudden clarification (thus the climax is no more a dramatic one than the climax of Poe's "The Gold-Bug").

Of course there is "more" to the story than this—a moral gravity, a psychological intensity, an appropriately shadowy atmosphere, an ironic realization of the stain of human slavery. All these things Melville drew out of his materials, and they have not gone unnoticed. But one way of appreciating his achievement in **"Benito Cereno"** is to see how all this "more" is built directly upon the central ambiguity, the mechanism of mystification. What we are shown comes largely by way of Captain Delano, through what he notices about the strange Spanish ship and its stranger captain and through what he progressively thinks—or gets almost to the point of thinking. At the end, it is true, the contrast between Captain Delano's awareness and Don Benito's rather displaces the riddle through which we have come to know it. Yet there is no real effort to harden this contrast into a generalized moral figure. It is presented simply as the consistent outcome of the harrowingly different circumstances through which these two lives have come to their strange meeting. **"Benito Cereno"** does have, I am sure, a seriousness of general implication and a closeness to common reality that reach beyond Poe's capacity as an artist. By its strict narrative fidelity to its particular core of truth, certain features of it are indeed powerfully suggestive of some general order of existence. The states of mind Captain Delano passes through are not, after all, essentially different from the ordinary ways by which we move, more or less blindly, through our works and days. So the story can fairly be seen as composing a paradigm of the secret ambiguity of appearances—an old theme with Melville—and, more particularly, a paradigm of the inward life of ordinary consciousness, with all its mysterious shifts, penetrations, and side-slippings, in a world in which this ambiguity of appearances is the baffling norm. But to say this of **"Benito Cereno"** is precisely not to lose sight of its form as a story, and of the curious way in which the exposition is actually carried out.

There remains the problem of the ending. The event clearing up the stretched-out riddle—Don Benito's leap, and then Babo's after him, into Captain Delano's whaleboat—takes barely a page and a half to describe; a few more pages quickly close out the main action of the story. But then everything that has happened so far is put before us a second time, and more besides—in the cumbersome style of a judicial exposition (modeled on documents given in the source narrative). Other than that it fills pages, is there anything to be said for this contrivance? Or do we concur in the judgment of the story's first reader, the knowledgeable G. W. Curtis, who told the editor of *Putnam's;* "It is a great pity he did not work it up as a connected tale instead of putting in the dreary documents at the end.—They should have been made part of the substance of the story."

No doubt an argument on the point of form which is involved can be made either way. My own judgment of the matter begins simply with my finding this part of the narrative exactly as interesting as the mystifying incidents which it follows and which it serves to review and explain. If we take **"Benito Cereno"** as allegory or fable, these court documents must seem a mistake, and a nearly inexplicable mistake. If our measure is dramatic organization, they are scarcely less troublesome. But if we accept it as, in form, an extended narrative riddle, then they are legitimate, or make themselves so. We are not finished with a serious riddle when we hear it solved. It remains to go back over all the significant detail of it from the point of view of the revealed solution. For both the riddler and (if he has been played with fairly) the beriddled, this orderly itemization of data which was first mystifying but now falls into place rounds out the pleasure given by the whole performance. And in this respect the riddle may be seen as a particular, highly stylized variety of the general form of the told story. (pp. 151-54)

Actually, in **"Benito Cereno,"** the introduction of explanatory documents is only the most abrupt of a series of shifts and starts in the presentation, roughly corresponding to the developing import of this curious story. The ambiguities of the riddle are acted out by a rapid alternation of moods, at once in the general atmosphere and in Captain Delano's mind. The compositional device that particularly sustains this pattern of alternation is the fragmenting of much of the narrative into very short paragraphs, a great many of which are just a sentence long and barely consecutive. (pp. 154-55)

[The brokenness and spareness of **"Benito Cereno"**] are central to the story's massed effect—the sense of tension increasing and diminishing, the irregular measuring out of time, the nervous succession of antithetical feelings and intuitions. But once the riddle is broken open and fairly explained, once our concern can go out at last to the passional outcome of the whole affair, a different tactic is in order. So on the last page of the story we find Melville spinning out the same kind of spare, rapid, matter-of-fact statement into longer paragraphs and a more sustained and concentrated emphasis. . . . (p. 155)

Especially after the teasing oscillations of mood in the long first part and the dry repetitions of the court records that follow, [the story's] fine last paragraphs, terse, rapid, taut with detail, seem a particularly impressive instance of Melville's ordinary boldness in fitting his performance to the whole developing occasion. There is no worked-up climax; what is said is shaped strictly to the job of making an end. (p. 156)

Once gained, this sensitivity in handling narrative became for Melville—especially after the drawing-in of his ambition as a declarer of prophetic truths—perhaps the steadiest of his working motives, and the surest source of his unflagging originality. In the closing chapters of ***Billy Budd*** we find the same deliberate use as in **"Benito Cereno"** of an interrupted, anti-climactic descent from the main line of action, for the sake of a further climax and consolidation of feeling. At another point in ***Billy Budd*** a curtain of silence and secrecy is abruptly brought down, in the middle of the thickly circumstantial narration, as a means of setting off the pivotal episode of Vere's last interview with Billy. A similar interruption figures at the center of the eighth **"Encantadas"** sketch, in the story of the Chola widow ("Against my own purposes a pause descends upon me here"); again, what lies deepest in the story is as if handed back to the imagination of the reader—for whom of course, the teller's abrupt gesture of reticence is as effective as any dramatic image.

In each case, we see, the effect is managed with a perfect simplicity of means. And it is in this free control of narrative succession, this precise formal response to his story's advancing power of implication, that we find the central compositional tact of Melville's art. It seems to me a creative tact of the very highest order. At his level best he will not force his tales out of their advancing line of truth—not for the sake of a moral argument, nor for dramatic sensation, nor for any preconceived formality of design. He is indeed, in managing his materials, the least arbitrary of the great American writers—which is one reason, I think, why his work as a writer of stories seems to move the most insistently and yet naturally toward the free suggestiveness, the profounder creativity, of myth. (pp. 157-58)

Warner Berthoff, in his The Example of Melville, *Princeton University Press, 1962, 218 p.*

A. R. HUMPHREYS (essay date 1962)

[*Humphreys is an English scholar and critic. In the following excerpt, he discusses the aesthetic merits of Melville's major short stories and comments on their form and features.*]

[The best of Melville's tales] are very good writing indeed, and Michael Sadleir was not far wrong in asserting that, supreme though *Moby Dick* is, Melville's genius is here "more perfectly and skilfully revealed," and that **"The Encantadas"** and **"Benito Cereno"** "hold in the small compass of their beauty the essence of their author's supreme artistry" [see excerpt dated 1922]. (p. 93)

The best of the tales do come home upon the imagination. The Duyckincks' *Cyclopædia* took **"Bartleby"** to be "a quaint and fanciful portrait," but it is far more than that. Its virtue lies in its memorable subject and its wonderful control. The rhapsodies of *Moby Dick* and *Pierre* are wholly absent, though the theme of temperamental withdrawal (Bartleby is the supreme *isolato*) is one which only the year before *Pierre* had handled with signs of hysteria. Comedy is present in the fully-flavoured humour, but the presiding impression is of the simple intensity of Bartleby's courteous, dignified, uncommunicating withdrawal, which obtains a moral ascendency over the reader as over the narrator. The story has its rhythm of increasing disquiet, from the quotidian comedy of the lawyer's office to the stark crudity of the prison and the physical death which succeeds the psychological. Bartleby's loneliness and dignity are expressed with a spare, unforced concentration; he remains inviolable with the untouchability of the psychotic, movingly rendered in his unexpressed despair.

"Cock-a-Doodle-Doo," almost contemporaneous in composition, shows how various Melville's successes can be. Lewis Mumford has called it one of his weakest tales, and one is up against the vagaries of Melville criticism, for Melville rarely exceeded the grip he shows here. The ability to create an expectation and keep it on the alert is as striking as in **"Bartleby"**; the commitment to the subject, the individuality and appreciativeness of the writing, are admirable. What the story says, in general, is that there is nothing good or bad but thinking makes it so. The early pages display, comically, two contrasting impressions of identical circumstances; nature's alphabet is being read in two different moods. Not much writing in English is more effectively hyperbolic than the successive renderings of the cock's crow; these have a valid fullness of effect. The crowing symbolises faith, glorifying daily life and easing misery. First heard to the east, the cock is not to be sold or given away, though its message can be shared. Not everybody hears it. The cock has been raised from the egg by Merrymusk, the woodman, himself; his ailing family find courage in it; it gives "stuff against despair"; it sounds like an angel in the Apocalypse; it "crows at the darkest; Glory to God in the highest!", "crowing the souls of the children out of their wasted bodies," dispelling the sting of death, the victory of the grave. But a moment after its last owner dies it dies too, and the narrator is left to crow on his own. Faith, one deduces, is a confidence-man whose counsels are effective as long as they are believed in; or perhaps Christianity, which once heartened men because taken as real, can now hearten only as a simulacrum. Belief works if one believes, and this tautology expresses the irony of the situation, since no reality need lie behind; faith can be solipsistic. **"Cock-A-Doodle-Doo"** is successfully ambiguous, cheerful in appearance, making a rueful grimace between the lines. Not bitter, though, as it has been thought—the feeling is richer than that, a glory in the subject, and a kind of glee in counterattacking a metaphysical puzzle. Behind the tale is the great dilemma: is faith (supposing it to be delusive) better than unfaith (supposing it to be true)?—the dilemma of Arnold's "Dover Beach," or Hardy's "Darkling Thrush," or *Clarel* itself. "Heartily wish Niebuhr & Strauss to the dogs," Melville was to comment in the 1856-7 *Journal*, "The deuce take their penetration & acumen. They have robbed us of the bloom. If they have undeceived any one—no thanks to them."

"The Encantadas" stories amount to a Nature-poem, but not of a Wordsworthian kind. . . . Melville drew on authorities, including Darwin (whose comparison of the islands to Wolverhampton iron-furnaces seems echoed in Melville's "dross of an iron-furnace"), but, far beyond anything he found, he treats the subject with his own realisation and a memorable energy. Such symbolism as there is does not work to the detriment of reality; **"Two Sides to a Tortoise"** earns its symbolical interpretation by the truth with which it conveys the animals' archaic and cumbersome endurance. The other best-known episode, that of the Chola Widow, is less concentrated and more touched with the South-Sea-sentimental, but it ends with a moving reticence which justifies the crucifixion theme.

As for **"I and my Chimney,"** some readers have and others have not discovered in it figures-in-the-carpet. Melville's brother Allan, in annotating his copy, took it to be about nothing but Melville and his chimney, and Raymond Weaver quotes Colonel Lathers, a Pittsfield neighbour of Melville's, in praise of Melville's library, conversation, home-made cider, and capacious fireplace with the inscription, verified on windy days, "I and my Chimney smoke together" [see Additional Bibliography]. This, of course, has not ended the problem. The agitation, in the story, over the chimney, interpreters inform us, is the Melville family's concern for his sanity, or neurasthenia, or physique, or backbone (the bricks being vertebrae; one is virtually told what the particular breadth at its base refers to). Or it is Melville's struggle to preserve [what Newton Arvin calls in his *Herman Melville* (1950)] "his essential and deepest self," or [according to E. H. Rosenberry in *Melville and the Comic Spirit* (1955)] "to live with his enormous and tantalising ego." Something of this has to be recognised. There are overtones of a private gesture, a personal pun; the story has a resonance as a manifesto of Melville's sense of autonomy. Newton Arvin interprets its tone as "deep resentment." But such things are deducible only by an intent process of reading between the lines, and if **"I and my Chimney"** is not a cross between Lamb-like exuberance and a Yankee gift for exaggeration its real tone and manner must be more deeply disguised than is at all reasonable.

Some of the other tales are less interesting, though Melville sometimes gets an accentuation by antithetical pairing, as with **"The Two Temples," "Poor Man's Pudding and Rich Man's Crumbs," "The Paradise of Bachelors,"** and **"The Tartarus of Maids." "The Tartarus of Maids,"** though one critic has thought it to be a symbolisation of gestation so daring that Melville's readers would refrain from recognising it, seems to be what it purports to be, Melville's reaction to industrial misery, with the natural reflexion that the girls thus enslaved to the machine have lost the fertility of their lives. (pp. 95-8)

But the story best worth attention is **"Benito Cereno."** The narrative is from Captain Amasa Delano's *Voyages and Travels* (1817). Delano provides the facts, Melville the imagination. The images of forlornness and sinister lethargy, the dream-like equivocal inconsequence which foils the sensible Delano, the isolation, the leaden day, the current's drift, the ship's slow roll, are the perfect accompaniment, like Conrad's descriptions of the Golfo Placido in *Nostromo*. Detail is used realistically, but with a poetic imagination. . . . Melville invents the oakum-pickers and axe-grinders as an ominous voiceless chorus, and also such details as the ship's forlorn picturesqueness, the skeleton, and Babo's murderous leap. These are natural embellishments. One other change, however, makes a radical difference. In Delano's account, Don Benito proves a monster of ingratitude and intrigue. In Melville's, he is a haunted, moody figure, spiritually destroyed by his experience of blackness, of "the negro" who has "cast such a shadow." In the imposition of its spell, in subtlety of detail, and in presentation of moral crisis, **"Benito Cereno"** can claim equivalence with Conrad's *Shadow Line*. (pp. 98-9)

A. R. Humphreys, in his Melville, *Barnes & Noble, Inc., 1962, 120 p.*

LOUISE K. BARNETT (essay date 1974)

[Barnett argues that the title character of "Bartleby the Scrivener" is Melville's depiction of an alienated worker.]

A decade after Karl Marx first described the worker's alienation in a capitalistic society, his contemporary, Herman Melville, independently created the perfect exemplum of this condition in his tale of **"Bartleby the Scrivener."** Although critics have seen Bartleby in a number of interesting and even heroic guises, I believe that he is a figure of another sort: the alienated worker who, realizing that his work is meaningless and without a future, can only protest his humanity by a negative assertion. Defined only by his job, and becoming increasingly dissociated from it, Bartleby sums up the worker's plight. Given a system committed to profits, the only alternative to working under such demeaning conditions is death. (p. 379)

That the conditions of labor in the law office are undesirable, likely to produce a feeling of misery rather than well being, is amply confirmed by the narrator. Describing the general surroundings—which, as he rightly notes, have some bearing on the story of Bartleby—he reveals satisfaction in the dehumanized but functional environment. The windows, for example, let in light but present no distracting vistas, only varieties of wall. Placing Bartleby's desk close to one of these viewless openings is part of the narrator's "satisfactory arrangement" for the new employee. Another detail is the use of a folding screen to remove Bartleby from sight while keeping him "within easy call, in case any trifling thing was to be done." The narrator is pleased with this way of achieving privacy and society at the same time, but what for him is the best of both these worlds is clearly the worst for Bartleby. Conveniently placed to answer his employer's summons with alacrity, he must inhabit a circumscribed and isolated cell whose lack of outlook mirrors the lack of prospects of his menial occupation.

In his solitary confinement Bartleby works *mechanically,* an adjective well suited to the tedious copying which comprises the chief part of his job. The other duty of a scrivener, verification, is "very dull, wearisome, and lethargic." According to the lawyer such labor would be intolerable to anyone of sanguine temperament or mettle—to almost any human being, we might assume.

Although the narrator has described himself as an easy-going man in a traditionally hard-driving profession, his description of himself and of office business undercuts this self-characterization. John Jacob Astor is referred to with approval three times in as many sentences; indeed, the narrator confesses that he loves to repeat the name because "it rings like unto bullion." The making of money is the only discernible motive in the lawyer's account of his practice, from his usual traffic in rich men's documents to the remunerative office of Master in Chancery. If a certain indolence is suggested by the lawyer's report of his efforts, it is not characteristic of what he demands from his employees, who are often expected to work at top speed. . . . The course of office events is punctuated by words like *speedily, quick, hurriedly, fast*.

In his attitude toward his employees, the narrator is a typically enlightened master who realizes that self-interest will be served by a charitable indulgence. When his scriveners assert their individuality and unconsciously rebel against their dehumanized labors, he tolerates the resulting eccentric behavior because it is still profitable to his business to do so. For all their idiosyncrasies, the other scriveners are an easily managed lot who neither challenge the employer's authority as Bartleby does nor support Bartleby in his disobedience. When Turkey offends the lawyer by sealing a mortgage with a ginger nut, he avoids dismissal by the exaggerated obeisance of "an oriental bow" and a speech beginning with his usual placatory formula: "With submission, sir."

As seen through the lawyer's eyes from an amused, paternalistic height, Turkey and Nippers are only caricatures—ludicrously nicknamed bundles of eccentricities. A keener observer might perceive that the montonous work itself engenders their antics, but the narrator makes only a superficial connection between the conditions of employment and the various foibles of his scriveners. All have hopes of more prestigious and less menial work: Turkey describes himself as the lawyer's right hand man; Nippers is guilty of "an unwarrantable usurpation of strictly professional affairs"; and the office boy, Ginger Nut, has been placed in the law office because of his working class father's desire that he rise in life. In the narrator's view these aspirations are only delusions of grandeur. He notices Nippers' endless adjusting of his table, but interprets this as simply a manifestation of indigestion—an affliction vaguely coupled in the narrator's mind with "diseased ambition." The response of Turkey to the gift of his employer's hand-me-down coat is similarly regarded as an example of that scrivener's failure to know his inferior place in the scheme of things. . . . Even Ginger Nut, whose youthful apprenticeship might auger possibility, seems little likely to escape his humble origin and present job. As the lawyer comments: "He had a little desk to himself, but he did not use it much. Upon inspection, the drawer exhibited a great array of the shells of various sorts of nuts.''

Physically as well as mentally, the scriveners illustrate Marx's diagnosis of malaise. Turkey's inflamed face witnesses his over-indulgence; Nippers is given to teeth grinding and nervous attacks; Bartleby is pale and thin. Nursing their vain expectations, Turkey and Nippers take what solace they can in cakes and ale and fits of temper. Bartleby chooses not to continue working.

The lawyer's possessive attitude towards the entire world of his law office exemplifies still another Marxian contention: that a factor contributing to the alienated character of work is its belonging not to the worker, but to another person. Giving Turkey a coat, the lawyer thinks to control his behavior completely; disobeyed by Bartleby, he feels the shameful anomaly of being stymied by a man who should be his creature. . . . Later, he justifies his unlocking of Bartleby's desk, and consequent infringement of his privacy, by his own proprietary right: ''The desk is mine, and its contents, too, so I will make bold to look within.'' Bartleby's family and past, however, are locked within a place that the narrator cannot violate. The scrivener absolutely refuses to respond to any of the narrator's overtures, and thus provokes his employer's exasperation. In the latter's opinion the lowly copyist's life ought to be accessible for his employer's convenience.

The narrator's belief in the sanctity of his property is further demonstrated when Bartleby maintains his intransigence. Finding the scrivener still on the premises after receiving an ultimatum to leave, the narrator, in an appropriate simile, compares himself to a man killed by lightning ''at his own warm open window''—where presumably he should enjoy security. A similar sense of injured property rights informs the series of questions that he puts to Bartleby: ''What earthly right have you to stay here? Do you pay any rent? Do you pay my taxes? Or is this property yours?'' Unable to free himself from the exigencies of ownership, the narrator temporarily reconciles himself to Bartleby's continued presence by transforming the scrivener into a piece of his property: ''I shall persecute you no more; you are harmless and noiseless as any of these old chairs.'' Finally, the thought that Bartleby might out-live him and establish the right of occupancy to the office is one of the ''dark anticipations'' that decide the lawyer to take action against the scrivener.

When Bartleby comes to the narrator's office, he appears to be a model employee—quiet, neat, and devoted to copying. Significantly, his first resistance to the lawyer's will is a refusal to perform the most tedious of the scrivener's duties, examination of copy. The astounded employer, too hurried to go into the matter fully, eventually decides that the business ethic of buying cheap and selling dear will apply to this peculiar case: ''Here I can cheaply purchase a delicious self-approval. To befriend Bartleby; to humour him in his strange wilfulness, will cost me little or nothing, while I lay up in my soul what will eventually prove a sweet morsel for my conscience.'' Moreover, Bartleby is still useful: while the other malleable scriveners examine copy, he can continue to write and thus earn the narrator's indulgence.

Later, when Bartleby refuses to do any work at all, he exhibits the mental and physical exhaustion characteristic of Marx's alienated worker. ''His eyes looked dull and glazed,'' which the narrator interprets as temporary eyestrain rather than an enduring physical and spiritual anguish. Now the employer's charity is truly tested, for there is no longer any material profit to be made from the recalcitrant scrivener.

Bartleby as neither profit nor loss can be tolerated, but when business begins to suffer, the narrator acts—radically, if not decisively. Rather than confront his inhumanity by taking violent measures, he moves his office, denies responsibility for Bartleby to the new tenant—even when implored ''in mercy's name''—and only reassumes the problem under threat of adverse publicity. Then, in their most extensive conversation of the story, Bartleby cryptically explains himself to the narrator. In preferring not to follow any of the unskilled occupations which the lawyer suggests, but at the same time affirming that he is not particular, Bartleby articulates the worker's dilemma. He is willling to do any meaningful work, but none of the jobs enumerated would be any improvement over the body- and mind-destroying labor he has just given up. Uncomprehending, and desperate to rid himself of a nuisance, the narrator now offers to install Bartleby temporarily in his own home, so that the process of money-making can continue without interruption. Whether or not genuine humanity could now rehabilitate the alienated worker is a useless conjecture: the profit system cannot accommodate it, and Bartleby must necessarily reject an offer so redolent of self-interest.

After this failure to move Bartleby, the lawyer, true to his commercial values, experiences relief *first* at the thought of having done all he could vis-à-vis the other parties of his class: the landlord and lawyer tenants who had been insisting on his responsibility for Bartleby. Concern for the scrivener takes second place. The narrator's next action is similarly prompted not by the proddings of conscience over Bartleby's now certain eviction but by fear of further bother: ''So fearful was I of being again hunted out by the incensed landlord and his exasperated tenants, that, surrendering my business to Nippers, for a few days, I drove about the upper part of the town and through the suburbs. . . .'' When Bartleby is safely behind bars, continuing the dead-wall revery he pursued in the law office, the narrator can patronize him once more and encourage him to make the best of it: '''And see, it is not so sad a place as one might think. Look, there is the sky, and here is the grass.''' Bartleby will not be deluded into seeing his situation falsely, however. He knows that the natural world is equally constrained in the Tombs and on Wall Street; the man-made wall is omnipresent. Knowing as he does their respective positions, and the lawyer's real unwillingness to blur the distinction between their roles, Bartleby repudiates the narrator firmly: '''I know you,' he said, without looking round—'and I want nothing to say to you'.'' When, on his last visit, the narrator reaches out to touch Bartleby—his first attempt at physical contact—the effort is once more too little and too late. His benediction over the dead scrivener, that he sleeps ''with kings and counsellors,'' is an ironic acknowledgment of the common humanity of all men, an idea subordinated to considerations of class and position in his treatment of the enigmatic Bartleby.

The narrator's epilogue is of a piece with his imperceptive evaluation of Bartleby throughout—a failure to see which is unconsciously motivated by self-protection. Wishing to view Bartleby as a man doomed ''by nature and misfortune'' rather than by the commercial values that have given himself a comfortable existence, the narrator finds Bartleby's past occupation symbolically fitting. The final exclamation, linking Bartleby and humanity, is a way of merging the individual into the vast human tide for which he need take no responsibility. (pp. 379-84)

Louise K. Barnett, "Bartleby as Alienated Worker," in Studies in Short Fiction, *Vol. XI, No. 4, Fall, 1974, pp. 379-85.*

R. BRUCE BICKLEY, JR. (essay date 1975)

[*Bickley is an American academic and scholar. In the following excerpt from his study of Melville's short fiction, he comments on irony and sentiment in "Jimmy Rose" and "I and My Chimney."*]

[**"Jimmy Rose"**] bears a certain structural resemblance to **"Bartleby."** It, too, is a character sketch in the form of a familiar essay; the narrator, William Ford, spends several pages describing his own surroundings and chatting about his likes and dislikes before he introduces his announced subject, the "gentle Jimmy Rose." Melville's point is, again, that Ford, like the lawyer in **"Bartleby,"** is in many ways the real subject of his own sketch. Philosophically, **"Jimmy Rose"** is a minor work, but rhetorically the story is a carefully rendered satire on the limits of human perception and self-knowledge.

As a piece of sentiment, **"Jimmy Rose"** owes a good deal to Irving's "Little Britain," in *The Sketch Book*. Both works, first of all, are gently ironic self-portraits of narrators who are nostalgic for the "good old days." Each is reluctant to accept the values of competition and the work ethic, and each is slow to adjust to the ever accelerating changes taking place in the modern world. The two sketches are essentially lamentations that the "antiquated folks and fashions" and "good old . . . manners" (Irving's phrases) have fallen by the way because of the debilitating effects of economic and social change.

Crayon [of "Little Britain"] had for many years lived in a small district of "very venerable" but now deteriorating houses in the center of London, where once the Dukes of Brittany resided. Unhappily, as London grew, "rank and fashion rolled off to the west, and trade creeping on at their heels took possession of their deserted abodes." Melville's character sketch begins as Irving's does: the narrator for several years had been making his home in an old ward of New York City, in a quaintly but richly furnished house formerly owned by a onetime millionaire, Jimmy Rose. Both Rose and this part of the city had, however, fallen into social decline as a result of economic change: "once the haunt of style and fashion, full of gay parlors and bridal chambers," the old district was now "transformed into counting-rooms and warehouses. These bales and boxes usurp the place of sofas; day-books and ledgers are spread where once the delicious breakfast toast was buttered." (pp. 45-6)

Despite the effects of time and change, both writers note, the process of transformation is fortunately not complete, for "Little Britain still bears traces of its former splendor," and in old New York "some monument[s] of departed days survived." Then follows a catalog of the still-elegant interiors of the mansions where the two narrators reside; in both works the reader is asked to look indulgently, if not reverently, at the grotesquely carved doorways and mantels, fretted ceilings, ornate cornices, panelled wainscots, and other furnishings typical of the previous century. Having created a sense of place and a feeling for the old styles, both narrators also sketch in profiles of the folk who still live in the two districts, meanwhile pointing out the similarities between themselves and these older inhabitants and affirming the values and traditions of the old times.

As a character sketch of a wealthy man whom fortune turned against, Melville's story is a particularized study of the economic perils of modern times, whereas Irving's is a more panoramic commentary on the rise and fall of a whole district. Despite the difference in scope, Irving's sketch apparently suggested a narrative design for Melville, while it gave him a rich thematic pattern to work with. Irving may even have planted the seed in Melville's imagination which would yield the central imagery, if not the central figure, in his sketch. A few lines of poetry scratched on Crayon's window-glass by a former inhabitant extolled the "charms" of "many a beauty of Little Britain, who has long, long since bloomed, faded, and passed away." And so the blooming roses in the cheek of charming Jimmy Rose faded, at last, in death, although Melville's narrator hopes that "[t]ransplanted to another soil" Jimmy's roses "may immortally survive!"

Paralleling his technique in "Agatha," Melville uses imagery in his story to help develop character and meaning. Jimmy's introduction comes at the end of a page-long rhapsody on the faded rose- and peacock-patterned Louis XVI wallpaper in the Fords' parlor—a room which the sentimental and old-fashioned narrator refuses to let his wife and daughters remodel. He loves to dwell upon the "real elegance," albeit rather dimmed, and the "sweet engaging pensiveness" of the peacocks in the room, but chiefly he associates the parlor with Jimmy Rose. From this point on the tale has a twofold development: as Ford entrenches himself in memories of Jimmy's social success and abrupt decline and reminds the reader that through it all Jimmy's carmine cheeks never lost their glow, he not only succeeds in evoking Jimmy himself but also reveals his own attraction for the gilt-edged showiness and social artificialities of the past.

Over the years the narrator has come to identify himself with Jimmy Rose. He is envious of Jimmy's flair for saying fine things finely, still loves to repeat the millionaire's stylized banquet toasts (even though acknowledging that Rose plagiarized them), and recalls Jimmy's charming sway over the female sex. Along with the social graces, Ford also celebrates the material trappings of Jimmy's domain, as in the following passage in which he fondly balances Jimmy's charm and effervescence with his physical furnishings: "His uncommon cheeriness; the splendor of his dress; his sparkling wit; radiant chandeliers; infinite fund of small-talk; French furniture; glowing welcomes to his guests; his bounteous heart and board; his noble graces and his glorious wine; what wonder if all these drew crowds to Jimmy's hospitable abode?" And what wonder that the narrator was among these crowds, for he liked grandeur and show as much as Jimmy did.

The narrator's repeated apostrophe to Jimmy, "Ah, poor, poor Jimmy—God guard us all—poor Jimmy Rose!" pulses like a sentimental heartthrob throughout the story, and by the end of the piece the narrator, as he speaks of his own tears, seems to pity himself almost as much as he does Jimmy. Yet Ford's departed hero was, after all, a shallow figure who turned not to work but to charity when his finances collapsed. In another passage, the narrator comes as close as he ever will to admitting the truth about his over-elegant friend:

> Neither did Jimmy give up his courtly ways [as he trudged about town for charitable tea and cakes]. Whenever there were ladies at the table, sure were they of some fine word; though, indeed, toward the close of Jimmy's life, the young ladies rather thought his compliments somewhat musty, smacking of cocked hats and small-clothes—nay, of old pawnbrokers' shoulder-lace and sword belts. For there still lingered in Jimmy's address a subdued sort of

> martial air; he having in his palmy days been. . .a general of the State militia. . . . Is it that this military leaning in a man of unmilitary heart—that is, a gentle, peaceable heart—is an indication of some weak love of vain display? But ten to one it is not so.

Jimmy *was* vain and artificial, but Ford could not let himself admit it. To do so would mean to acknowledge the shallowness in his own character and his reluctance, if not inability, to adjust to the modern world. (pp. 46-8)

The chatty, informal narrator of **"I and My Chimney"** is another of Melville's genial sentimentalists. Like Ford in **"Jimmy Rose,"** he is restless in a marriage to a youthful wife who is impatient with his idiosyncrasies, he worships the past, and he defends his old age and old-fashioned tastes with a stubborn, if not at times a blind, tenacity. As a contemporary of Melville's observed, **"I and My Chimney"** is "thoroughly magazinish." The humorous interplay between husband and wife is appealing in its own right, yet Melville's ribald punning, as well as the suggestive symbolic and psychological overtones of the story, have made the tale something of a cause célèbre among Melville readers.

"I and My Chimney" owes its vitality and charm, and much of its symbolic import, to Melville's success in synthesizing ideas and patterns from at least three different sources: his own experiences, some motifs in Irving, and Hawthorne's sketch "Fire Worship." Merton Sealts has discussed at some length the ways in which Melville's personal history informs his story, and only a brief recapitulation is needed here [see Additional Bibliography]. There are strong parallels between the narrator's concern for the health of his chimney and Melville's anxiety about his own condition in 1852-53. Both the author and his family were apprehensive about the possibility of mental derangement, and Oliver Wendell Holmes was called in—ostensibly for consultation about Melville's troubles with sciatica. The architect summoned to consider removing the chimney, Scribe ("writer"), may represent Holmes himself, and the assertive, enterprising, and unsympathetic wife in the tale is said to be modeled on Melville's mother, who was known to be energetic, industrious, and occasionally critical.

Irving's "Rip Van Winkle" seems also to have had an effect on **"I and My Chimney."** Both works develop the conflict between the old and the new, as had "Little Britain" and **"Jimmy Rose."** In "Rip Van Winkle" and **"I and My Chimney,"** however, Irving and Melville give psychological vitality to the conflict by pitting, archetypally, a youthful, energetic, and shrewish wife against her older, indolent, but likable husband, one who would have been far happier as a bachelor and who, therefore, seeks solace in bachelor pursuits. The patterns synthesize with neat irony in "Rip Van Winkle." Rip retreats to the Catskills and is finally freed from his termagant wife, although he must pay a price for his escape: the nervousness and bustle of post-Revolutionary America disconcert him, and

A fireplace at Arrowhead, Melville's home in the Berkshires where he wrote "I and My Chimney." Gansevoort-Lansing Collection, Rare Book and Manuscript Division, The New York Public Library, Astor Lenox and Tilden Foundations.

for a while he thinks he would have been better off in the old days, after all.

The stodgy old narrator of **"I and My Chimney"** is in a similar retreat before a predatory wife, but, unlike Rip, he barricades himself for the siege rather than seeking an escape. His young wife subscribes to the ladies' magazines for the latest fashions, keeps up with Swedenborgianism and spirit-rapping, and "always buys her new almanac a month before the new year." Furthermore she is a "natural projector. The maxim, 'Whatever is, is right,' is not hers. Her maxim is, Whatever is, is wrong; and what is more, must be altered; and what is still more, must be altered right away. Dreadful maxim for the wife of a dozy old dreamer like me, who. . .will. . .go out of my road a quarter of a mile, to avoid the sight of a man at work." Contrary to his wife, who "doesn't believe in old age," the narrator prefers oldness: "For that cause mainly loving old Montaigne, and old cheese, and old wine; and eschewing young people. . .new books, and early potatoes, and very fond of my old claw-footed chair, and. . .my betwisted old grape-vine. . .and. . .high above all, am fond of my high-mantled old chimney."

In developing the conflict between the old and the new, there is no doubt that Irving and Melville identified considerably with their protagonists' respect for the past. Both authors stressed the permanence of the past, hoping that the values of the old times could prove a buffer to the fragmenting, if not emasculating, forces of the present. Furthermore, Irving's images of eternally beautiful mountains and glens and Melville's emphasis on old cheese, an old grape-vine, and especially on the vitality of the old chimney, underscore the organic qualities of the past sadly lacking in the hurried mechanical motions of modern times—and in the impatient activities of aggressive wives. In his late unpublished essay, "Rip Van Winkle's Lilac," Melville finds another image of the past: an ever-youthful lilac tree appropriately symbolizes the presence of the past and Rip's refusal to sacrifice his identity to new world changes.

Irving may have helped Melville focus thematic ideas in **"I and My Chimney,"** but Hawthorne seems to have inspired his central symbol. [In his 1970 article "Melville and His *Mosses*"] Edward Rosenberry traces the motif of the hearth as sacred and the general theme of defending it from attack to Hawthorne's sentimental essay "Fire Worship" (which Melville had praised in his review of *Mosses from an Old Manse*). A closer analysis of the two works turns up additional parallels in rhetorical structure (schemes to replace the faithful hearth are recounted in detail) and in imagery associated with the hearth (both authors, for example, praise the fireplace as "sociable," as having a "warm heart," and as promoting brotherhood). Hawthorne's essay, however, remains a nostalgic apostrophe to the hearth, slight in comparison to the complexities of Melville's tale. The "elemental spirit" typifying "the picturesque, the poetic, and the beautiful" only flickers abstractly in Hawthorne's hearth, whereas Melville's solidly real chimney stands assertively for the narrator's ego and Job-like integrity. For Hawthorne the fireplace is a vaguely metaphoric "beacon light of humanity"; for Melville the chimney *is* humanity, in its eternal struggle for self-preservation. Yet at the same time the chimney is a great source of humor and good fun.

Melville's digressive and improvisatory mode keeps **"I and My Chimney"** in constant motion, and as a stylistic and verbal performance it is equal to anything in the Melville canon. In punning on the chimney's shape and size, the surgical operations it has undergone, and its position relative to the narrator, to say nothing of its power to hatch the wife's eggs, Melville toys with his nineteenth-century audience even more boldly than he had in describing Carlo's "hand-organ" in *Redburn,* or the whale's "grandissimus" in *Moby-Dick*. However, Melville's puns operate on a serious level, too. The wife's repeated endeavors to replace the grotesquely phallic chimney with a yonic entrance hall of "generous amplitude" threaten both the "foundation" of the house, and the old narrator's fundamental self, both physical and spiritual. So far as he is concerned, the narrator calmly explains to his wife, the chimney remains a "sober, substantial fact," incapable of replacement. But to the reader he reveals that the chimney is also his only "masculine prerogative" that has not yet fallen to his aggressive, indeed almost voracious, wife.

The chimney, like the whale, is a seemingly endless source of anecdote, as well as meaning. Following up his instincts in narrative portraiture, Melville develops in his tale the comic possibilities of human reflexes and involuntary gesture, as characters react to the chimney or are affected by it. For example, the narrator often finds himself in his cellar, pondering the fabulous dimensions of his chimney and wondering about its age and origins. One day he is so "penetrated with wonder" by the chimney's "druidical look" and its seeming connection with primeval nature that he unconsciously gets a spade from the garden and begins to dig around its base: "I was a little out of my mind, I now think . . . [and] obscurely prompted by dreams of striking upon some old, earthen-worn memorial of that by-gone day when, into all this gloom, the light of heaven entered, as the masons laid the foundation-stones." The scene turns, comically and dramatically, upon the narrator's embarrassment at being discovered at his work by a neighbor, who had entered unobserved:

> "Gold digging, sir?"
>
> "Nay, sir," answered I, starting, "I was merely—ahem!—merely—I say I was merely digging—round my chimney."
>
> "Ah, loosening the soil, to make it grow. Your chimney, sir, you regard as too small, I suppose. . . ."

(pp. 49-53)

Another episode involves "a certain stylish young gentleman, a great exquisite," who had come to call on one of the narrator's daughters. He passed the evening with Anna in the dining room, which was a chamber peculiarly affected by the chimney's location at the center of the house. The rooms downstairs were connected to each other, since there could be no central hallway, and the dining room had no less than nine doors, "opening in all directions, and into all sorts of places." The elegant young man stayed late, and

> after abundance of superfine discourse, all the while retaining his hat and cane, made his profuse adieus, and with repeated graceful bows proceeded to depart, after the fashion of courtiers from the Queen, and by so doing, opening a door at random, with one hand placed behind, very effectually succeeded in backing himself into a dark pantry, where he carefully shut himself up, wondering [sic] there was no light in the entry.

"After several strange noises as of a cat among the crockery," the narrator continues, "he reappeared through the same door looking uncommonly crest-fallen'' and, ''with a deeply embarrassed air,'' asked Anna for directions. The young man was gratifyingly matter-of-fact and unaffected thereafter. Indeed, he was ''more candid than ever,'' Melville quips, ''having inadvertently thrust his white kids into an open drawer of Havana sugar, under the impression, probably, that being what they call 'a sweet fellow,' his route might possibly lie in that direction.''

Amidst the punning and the comic anecdotes, the narrator's chimney assumes important philosophical dimensions in the story. In making proud claims for his chimney's impressiveness as the ''grand seignior'' and ''king'' in the house, and for its massiveness and majesty, as well as its mystery, the narrator is romantically celebrating himself. By worshipping the chimney, serving it, sentimentally communing with it, and defending it from harassment and possible destruction, he is simultaneously preserving his own identity. And yet the chimney represents more than the protagonist's own personality. It becomes a complex symbol for humanity as a whole—man's spirit, his inviolable soul, his masculinity, as well as his stubborn egotism and whimsical idiosyncrasies.

Melville's choice as narrator of a likable old hearty who has a penchant for sentiment and for philosophy also helps to expand the implications of the story. The protagonist's ''indolent'' habit of meditation, as he and his chimney ''smoke and philosophize together,'' makes the expository form of the story appear natural. Finally, the narrator's digressions on old age, integrity, and man's quest for identity and fulfillment convey the tragicomic nature of life itself. (pp. 53-4)

R. Bruce Bickley, Jr., in his The Method of Melville's Short Fiction, *Duke University Press, 1975, 142 p.*

HERSHEL PARKER (essay date 1979)

[Parker, a distinguished American Melville scholar, is best known for his critical editions of Melville's works. In the following excerpt, he discusses the limited perspective of the narrator in the final section of ''Bartleby the Scrivener.'']

[To understand the sequel in **"Bartleby the Scrivener,"** the] reader must distinguish between two kinds of melancholy, one all but annihilating and one somewhat pleasurable. Alone in his office on the Sunday morning on which he has discovered that Bartleby has been ''keeping bachelor's hall all by himself'' there, the lawyer is seized by ''a feeling of overpowering stinging melancholy.'' As he explains, he had never before experienced ''aught but a not-unpleasing sadness.'' Now he feels the ''bond of a common humanity'' drawing him ''irresistibly to gloom,'' to a ''fraternal melancholy.'' In this mood he has an insight into the way the world ignores suffering: ''Ah, happiness courts the light, so we deem the world is gay; but misery hides aloof, so we deem that misery there is none.'' Given the narrator's limitations, this comes apparently as a major perception, late in life though it is, but he instantly rejects all such thoughts as ''sad fancyings—chimeras, doubtless, of a sick and silly brain.'' So much for insight into the bond of common humanity: a moment later he is rifling the contents of Bartleby's desk under the well-rationalized theory that the desk is his own property. There is no place in his life for a dark view of human nature or the universe, no chance that he will come to anything like Ishmael's balanced perceptions in ''The Try-Works.'' Earlier he had chosen a course toward Bartleby which combined utility and charity, cheaply purchasing ''a delicious self-approval''; it is as if the good Samaritan helped the man who fell among thieves merely so he could later receive a reward, whether temporal or celestial. Now as a prudent feeling steals over him, the lawyer concludes that ''up to a certain point the thought or sight of misery enlists our best affections; but, in certain special cases, beyond that point it does not.'' This psychological law he attributes not to ''the inherent selfishness of the human heart'' but to ''a certain hopelessness of remedying excessive and organic ill.'' Before his solitary broodings in the office are finished, he has banished pity with the same rationality which damned Plinlimmon in *Pierre:* when pity ''cannot lead to effectual succor, common sense bids the soul be rid of it.'' The lawyer will continue on occasion to feel ''a not-unpleasing sadness,'' but he will never again subject himself to ''a feeling of overpowering stinging melancholy.''

When this easy-conscienced narrator murmurs ''With kings and counsellors'' over the body of Bartleby, he is experiencing not what he called ''pure melancholy'' or ''overpowering stinging melancholy'' but a comfortable, self-indulgent variety of melancholy. In reciting the words from Job 3 with prideful aptness, he characteristically perverts them from profound lament to sonorous urbanity. In the same way, the ''vague report'' about the Dead Letter Office has such a ''strange suggestive interest'' for him because it allows him to feel a gentle, superior sadness, a delicious melancholy. With the stubborn Bartleby no longer disturbing his carefully nurtured states of mind, he can indulge safely in such sentimentality. When he sighs, ''Ah Bartleby! Ah humanity!'' he is not consciously evoking the sense of ''common humanity'' which once plunged him briefly into something very near a tragic sense of life. Instead, the concluding words reduce his experience with the strange scrivener to manageable, not-unpleasing terms: they show that he is at last in control. The eagle-eyed reader (to use Melville's phrase from his essay on Hawthorne's *Mosses*) can never be satisfied by the evocative melancholy of the rumor about the Dead Letter Office, any more than he can satisfy himself that the depositions provide the key to unlock all the previous complexities in **"Benito Cereno."** In the later story only someone as imperceptive toward evil as Amasa Delano can assume the legal testimony removes all the mystery from the events; Benito Cereno's unlifting gloom is not so soothingly explained. Similarly, only someone like the narrator of **"Bartleby"** can ultimately find consolation in the rumor which is so tentatively introduced but is elaborated with such urgent eloquence.

While the scrivener's precise motivations are impenetrable, the narrator's frustration with him has become analogous to any nominal Christian's confrontation with someone behaving in Christlike absoluteness, not according to the commonsense values of this world. Bartleby is not necessarily a religious figure, much less an embodiment of Jesus, but by his refusal to compromise he impels the narrator to expose his own terrestrial, not celestial, values. The narrator never suspects that his readers will analyze more deeply than he does and interpret his prudence, his utilitarianism, and even his final sentimental solemnity in ways quite different from what he intends. Yet our ultimate opinion of him, the product less of what he means to tell than what he unknowingly divulges, is not contempt so much as bleak astonishment at his secure blindness. With a bitterer irony than the narrator is capable of, we murmur something like ''Ah narrator! Ah humanity!'' In his self-consciously eloquent sequel, after all, the lawyer has merely made his last cheap purchase of a ''delicious self-approval.'' (pp. 162-64)

Hershel Parker, "The 'Sequel' in 'Bartleby'," in Bartleby the Inscrutable: A Collection of Commentary on Herman Melville's Tale "Bartleby the Scrivener," *edited by M. Thomas Inge, Archon Books, Hamden, CT, 1979, pp. 159-65.*

ALLAN SMITH (essay date 1983)

[*Smith explores Melville's intention in calling* Billy Budd *an "inside narrative."*]

In calling ***Billy Budd, Foretopman*** an inside narrative Melville implied an intention to discriminate the "secret facts of the tragedy" both from the official version's misapprehension of Billy as a knife-murderer and from the common sailors' ignorance of the truth despite their "instinctive feeling that Billy was a sort of man as incapable of mutiny as of wilful murder." An inside narrative is, we expect, a narrative told by one who is in the know, and it deals with the intimate details of events and the psychology of participants as opposed to the versions offered in evidence to courts or accounts in naval gazettes which deal in externals of behaviour and are edited after the fact. (p. 16)

Billy Budd is not such a text: it evades the issues it raises and takes refuge in elaborate exterior views by which it indicates the position and form of what it will not specify. The narrator is not, as might have been supposed, privy to the dramatic action and is never identified as one of the participants; his apparently conservative views are subverted by his own comments on the injustices of naval discipline and war profiteering, and he perpetually falls back from the task of describing the truth of the characters and events of his story. Nor is his narrative an account of any honesty and simplicity: unlike Billy he is of a satirical turn and wants neither "sinister dexterity" nor the "will to it." To deal in "double meaning and insinuations of any sort" is by no means foreign to *his* nature. If he is an insider, his intention seems to be to keep the reader outside, as when he remarks that "This is to be wondered at. Yet not so much to be wondered at," or opines that if his words seem to be "dark sayings" and savor of the Holy Writ "such savor was foreign from my intention, for little will it commend these pages to many a reader of today." Among many other examples of this narrative sinistrality (to develop his own term, "sinister dexterity") we find: "At the time my inexperience was such that I did not quite see the drift of all this. It may be that I see it now"; and "as the late chance encounter may indicate to the discerning"; or, "something more, or rather, something else than mere shrewdness is perhaps needful for the due understanding of such a character as Billy Budd." (pp. 17-18)

These are more or less straightforward assaults on the sagacity of the reader, frequently indicative of a despair over discovering a suitable reader and an unwillingness to trail his coat for less. But another category of asides unpicks the form itself: "In this matter of writing, resolve as one may to keep to the main road, some bypaths have an enticement not readily to be withstood. I am going to err into such a bypath. If the reader will keep me company I shall be glad. At the least we can promise ourselves that pleasure which is wickedly said to be in sinning, for a literary sin the divergence will be." This chapter (4) is headed: "Concerning 'The greatest sailor since the world began'—Tennyson?"; it is one of four which break the form by their curious ironic headings, the others being chapter 12, "Lawyers, Experts, Clergy: an Episode"; 13, "Pale ire, envy and despair," and 27, "A Digression," all of which are reminiscent of the sly sketches in **"The Encantadas."** Other equivocal interpositions have to do with the credibility of the narrative: "The symmetry of form attainable in pure fiction" contrasted to the "ragged edges" of truth uncompromisingly told, or "the resumed narrative must be left to vindicate as it may, its own credibility." In situating his narrative in the area of realism, Melville's narrator takes up an ironic distance from the romance first of Hawthorne and then of Mrs Radcliffe. Billy is compared to the heroine of [Hawthorne's] "The Birthmark" in his trifling imperfection, the visiting card of "the envious marplot of Eden," which immediately becomes evidence "not alone that he is not presented as a conventional hero, but also that the story in which he is the main figure is no romance." In other words, Billy's similarity to a romance figure is proof that his tale is not a romance. The reference to Ann Radcliffe in describing Claggart's antipathy to Billy is no less disingenuous: "the cause, necessarily to be assumed as the sole one assignable, is in its very realism as much charged with that prime element of Radcliffian romance, the *mysterious* as any that the ingenuity of the author of the *Mysteries of Udolpho* could devise." Far from including the reader in his confidence in an inside narrative, the narrator appears to be promoting confusion as to what kind of text is being read.

But the "sinistrality" of narration is most apparent in the deception whereby the reader is led to expect a privilege that is not forthcoming. The scene in which Billy strikes Claggart is presented to us: that is, we are present in the cabin and are told what is said, but it is presented externally; we do not really discover what goes on in the minds of any of the three participants. We are shown Claggart and Billy from Vere's point of view, and Vere from Billy's, as when Claggart's eyes "gelidly protrude" like some creature's from the deep, or when Vere slowly uncovers his face "and the effect was as if the moon emerging from eclipse should reappear with quite another aspect than that which had gone into hiding." In the drumhead court we are left to infer Vere's state of mind from the formal advice he gives to his officers, and the crucial interview with Billy is not described: "what took place at the interview was never known" the narrator claims. The most that is hazarded is a guess that Vere would have concealed nothing from Billy, and that Billy not improbably would have received such a confession in the same spirit. Vere may have embraced Billy, developing "the passion sometimes latent under an exterior stoical or indifferent." "But there is no telling the sacrament. . . . There is privacy at the time, inviolable to the survivor. . . ." Finally, although we are told that Vere died with Billy Budd's name on his lips, some further and perhaps significant items are alluded to only to be concealed: "That these were not the accents of remorse, would seem clear from what the attendant said to the Indomitable's senior office of marines. . . ." What did he say? (pp. 18-19)

[In] ***Billy Budd,*** the significant defect of the handsome sailor is precisely his absence of voice at crucial moments or, to develop that more fully, an impediment in his speech, his use of language. This seems to me extremely suggestive considered from the perspective of the inside and the outside. The voice, as Walter Ong has pointed out [in *The Presence of the Word* (1967)], is both expressive and penetrative: it mediates between the inside and the outside and communicates from one innerness to another. In the absence of voice, Billy is forced to express his inner condition through violence, a blow being required to break through the exterior falseness. One might discriminate further here, between voice conceived as expression, individual utterance, and language, which is culturally acquired, the possession of the other. Billy's stammer interposes at the moment when his individual being attempts to find expression in the language of the other, but is unable to find accomodation within that language.

Melville's reference to "The Birthmark" obscures a more striking parallel in this area of language: one of the sources for the story of Billy Budd is Hawthorne's *The Marble Faun,* which he had read, and extensively marked, shortly before. The similarities between Billy and Donatello are remarkable: they both display Adamic innocence, great physical beauty and simplicity, they commit murder without premeditation, and both suffer punishment for this. Claggart has some similarity to Miriam's haunting Model; Keyon, like Vere, finds himself implicated in a very complex moral case, and the hint of homosexuality in one story parallels the hint of incest in the other. But further similarity exists in the attention paid to language in both works. In *The Marble Faun* Donatello is said to have had—and to have lost by his crime—the power of speaking to the animals and birds. Hawthorne does not attempt to offer this lost language of the natural man, but he does undertake to describe its failure, when Donatello tries to recapture the original tongue. It is a language previous to words, and therefore previous to the perversions, distortions and crimes of society. Donatello cannot remember how it was taught him, and it is suggested that the sound resembles what a boy might make, singing to himself, and "setting his wordless song to no other or more definite tune than the play of his own pulses." Billy, of course, was illiterate, "he could not read, but he could sing, and like the illiterate nightingale was sometimes the composer of his own song." He also has a singularly musical voice. His stammer is not so much the fatal flaw slipped in by the devil, as it is a token of his prelinguistic purity, his inability to become involved in the sinister dexterities of language. Compare Claggart, who found in the other petty officers "ears convenient to his confidential tongue," or the afterguardsman, the "too fair-spoken man." When Billy does speak he compels belief, as in Vere's "I believe you, my man," or a magnetic compulsion, when the crew repeat "God Bless Captain Vere" on hearing his words delivered "in the clear melody of a singing-bird on the point of launching from the twig." (pp. 21-3)

It is curious to note that Billy's stutter also has a sort of echo in the crew; they produce an inarticulate murmur on hearing of Billy's crime and sentence, which is immediately "pierced and suppressed" by the whistles piping down the watch. This recurs after Billy's execution when "the emphasised silence was gradually disturbed by a sound not easily to be here verbally rendered. Whoever has heard the freshet-wave of a torrent suddenly swelled by pouring showers in the tropical mountains, showers not shared by the plain; whoever has heard the first muffled murmur of its sloping advance through precipitate woods, may form some conception of the sound now heard." Again this is pierced by the whistles, and yet again the sound returns when Billy's body is consigned to the waves, blended this time with the "cracked requiem" of the sea fowl. This last murmur is overcome by the drum beating the order to quarters, which produces an effect akin to instinct in those long accustomed to martial discipline. The whistles and drums are to this inarticulate human expression what language is to prelinguistic song or Billy's innocent silence; they oppose exterior forms to interior truths, they suppress the inside.

Vere, on the other hand, displays a linguistic competence which goes beyond that of his fellow captains, who said that a pedantic cast ran through him like a strand of the King's yarn in a coil of navy-rope. He is apt to make remote allusions in his discourse, quite beyond the reach of his fellows, who read mostly the journals. It is this streak in him that makes him so quick to see the consequences of Billy's action and able to impose it on the members of his drumhead court, as though eager to take on himself the duty of sacrifice which only he is able fully to appreciate. In instructing the court, Vere points to the buttons worn by the officers as signs that their allegiance is not to Nature and the heart but to the King. That is, the outside must overrule the inside, martial law overcome natural justice.

In stressing that the martial law is the child of its parent, war, and that their allegiance is to the king, not to nature, Vere stresses that "war looks but to the frontage, the appearance." Much in that spirit, he instructs them not to look at Billy's intent or non-intent as "nothing to the purpose." . . . What went on inside Billy is immaterial, as is the question why the Master at Arms should have "so maliciously lied"; all that matters is the consequence of the blow. While pursuing strict interpretation of the law here, Vere then acts on a basis of policy in overruling clemency as liable to be mistaken for softness by his crew. Yet we see in the event how the execution of Budd comes near to provoking the feared rebellion itself. It is as though Vere's insistence that the court has to do with the deed alone seals off Billy's interior motives from the common gaze, as death has sealed off Claggart's. Nor is this Vere's impulse alone, since the narrative similarly stays on the outside of events, abjuring the interview, describing Billy's appearance in irons when the Chaplain visits him, but not his inner state, reporting the death but not Vere's emotions (the nearest we come to these is when the senior lieutenant encounters him leaving the compartment after the interview when the "face he beheld, for the moment one expressive of the agony of the strong, was . . . a startling revelation." In fact it is the ballad sung about Billy by the sailors that attempts to probe his feelings, and these have only to do with his immediate situation as condemned to be hung: "O, 'tis me, not the sentence they'll suspend."

The deliberate externality of this latter part of the narrative, like the ending of **"Benito Cereno,"** forces the reader back over the trail to discover what may occupy the implied interiority. On first reading the character of Claggart may seem to be quite thoroughly explicated, but reconsideration shows that his psychology is no more thrown open than the hull of the *San Dominick*. There are suggestions of homosexual desire, of envy based on sexual jealousy, or admiration of Billy's free and easy manner, but the narrator prefers to describe Claggart as a case of natural depravity, or "depravity according to nature," a definition that stays stubbornly on the outside of what it offers to elucidate. The portrayal of Claggart's psychology is mostly an account of the impossibility of knowing what goes on inside him: "an uncommon prudence is habitual with the subtler depravity, for it has everything to hide." His nature is described as labyrinthine (another indication of the ancestry of this figure, harking back to Mrs Radcliffe's Schedoni, or Hawthorne's Model; he even has skin of a marble pallor, discoloured and ancient looking), battening on deceit and controlling the men by "underground wires"; he is a creature of the inside of the ship cut off from enlightenment or disillusion by his own secrecy, his conscience merely the "lawyer to his will" justifying animosity into "retributive righteousness." "The Pharisee is the Guy Fawkes prowling in the hid chambers underlying the Claggarts," says the narrator, developing a theme of inner possession, of subterranean fire eating its way deeper and deeper in him. This contrasts with the "bonfire" within Billy, that lights his ruddy cheeks, and later becomes a self-devouring blaze: "In fervid hearts self-contained some brief experiences devour our human tissue as secret fire in a ship's hold consumes cotton in the bale." The chapters on Claggart thus posit a buried and secret innerness, which is despaired of as inexplicable and confirms the narrator's conviction that a "deadly space" exists between normal natures and Claggart and that "this portrait I essay, but shall never hit it." One might see this as conventional discounting of the possibility of fully describing the inner being of a romantic villain, and see in the same measure how Billy Budd's inner purity corresponds to a series of displaced "essences" like say, Beatrice in Hawthorne's "Rappaccini's Daughter." As that narrative progresses the "essence" of Beatrice is located at further and further removes: as an inhabitant of the garden—a beautiful girl—a gorgeous shrub—a broken fountain—the Beatrice of Dante—a departed spirit. Vere also occupies a familiar role: in much romantic fiction we find an intercessory figure, supposedly rational, whose function is to mediate between the extraordinary persons or events and the audience; like Giovanni in "Rappaccini's Daughter" or the narrator in **"Bartleby."** The vacant space of the "inside" can be a measure of the loss of romantic conviction, as in Henry James's figures, or a measure of skepticism as to any possibility of full integration, which seems to me the case in Melville's use of this pattern. (pp. 23-5)

Allan Smith, "Inside and Outside Narratives: Melville's 'Billy Budd' and 'Benito Cereno'," in Dutch Quarterly Review of Anglo-American Letters, *Vol. 13, 1983, pp. 16-27.*

ADDITIONAL BIBLIOGRAPHY

Abcarian, Richard. "The World of Love and the Spheres of Fright: Melville's 'Bartleby the Scrivener'." *Studies in Short Fiction* I, No. 3 (Spring 1964): 207-15.

Sees "Bartleby the Scrivener" as Melville's "most artistically successful and thematically enigmatic tale." The critic maintains that the story's narrator considers Bartleby a representative of the human condition.

Abrams, Robert E. "'Bartleby' and the Fragile Pageantry of the Ego." *ELH* 45, No. 3 (Fall 1978): 488-500.

Probes the concept of insincerity-in-sincerity in "Bartleby the Scrivener."

Adams, Timothy Dow. "Architectural Imagery in Melville's Short Fiction." *The American Transcendental Quarterly,* No. 44 (Fall 1979): 265-77.

Explores Melville's use of architectural theory and imagery in his short stories.

Review of *The Piazza Tales,* by Herman Melville. *The Athenæum,* No. 1500 (26 July 1856): 929.

Early review of *The Piazza Tales,* faulting the work as "sometimes barely intelligible" but conceding that the "legends themselves have a certain wild and ghostly power. . . ."

Avallone, C. Sherman. "Melville's 'Piazza'." *ESQ: A Journal of the American Renaissance* 22, No. 4 (1976): 221-33.

Argues that "The Piazza" is a parable of the mystery of faith.

Boswell, Jeanetta. *Herman Melville and the Critics: A Checklist of Criticism, 1900-1978.* The Scarecrow Author Bibliographies, No. 53. Metuchen, N. J.: The Scarecrow Press, 1981, 247 p.

Comprehensive bibliography of 3,215 items of Melville criticism written or published between 1900 and 1978. A subject index allows easy access to this period's short story criticism.

Boynton, Percy H. "Herman Melville." In his *More Contemporary Americans,* pp. 29-50. 1939. Reprint. Freeport, N. Y.: Books for Libraries Press, 1967.

Overview of Melville's literary career, describing *The Piazza Tales* stories as "pallid lotos-island reveries."

Casper, Leonard. "The Case against Captain Vere." *Perspective* 5, No. 3 (Summer 1952): 146-52.

Discusses the role of free will in *Billy Budd.*

Dillingham, William B. *Melville's Short Fiction, 1853-1856.* Athens, Ga.: The University of Georgia Press, 1977, 390 p.

General estimation of Melville's magazine stories, focusing on their forms and themes.

Fiene, Donald M. "A Bibliography of Criticism of 'Bartleby the Scrivener'." In *Melville Annual 1965—A Symposium: "Bartleby the Scrivener",* edited by Howard P. Vincent, pp. 140-90. Kent Studies in English, edited by Howard P. Vincent, No. III. Kent, Ohio: Kent State University Press, 1966.

Comprehensive annotated bibliography of "Bartleby the Scrivener" criticism published through 1966.

Fisher, Marvin. *Going Under: Melville's Short Fiction and the American 1850s.* Baton Rouge: Louisiana State University Press, 1977, 216 p.

Thematic study of Melville's short stories, seeing them as linked by a common interest in the American experience.

Foley, Mary. "The Digressions in *Billy Budd.*" In *Melville's Billy Budd and the Critics,* 2d ed., edited by William T. Stafford, pp. 220-23. Belmont, Calif.: Wadsworth Publishing Company, 1968.

Sees the digressions in *Billy Budd* as Melville's illustration of a conflict between organic form and externally imposed form.

Gargano, James W. "Melville's 'Jimmy Rose'." *Western Humanities Review* XVI, No. 3 (Summer 1962): 276-80.

Maintains that, far from being the story of one man's triumph over adversity, "Jimmy Rose" is an unsentimental account of its title character's failure to grow morally.

Gross, Seymour L., ed. *A "Benito Cereno" Handbook.* Belmont, Calif.: Wadsworth Publishing Company, 1965, 200 p.

Provides, along with a critical text of the story and of its source, selected new and previously published criticism of "Benito Cereno."

Hetherington, Hugh W. "After *Moby Dick*" and "Dead Letters." In his *Melville's Reviewers: British and American, 1846-1891,* pp. 227-64, 265-91. Chapel Hill: University of North Carolina Press, 1961.

Summarizes the critical reception of *The Piazza Tales* during the nineteenth century.

Inge, M. Thomas, ed. *Bartleby the Inscrutable: A Collection of Commentary on Herman Melville's Tale "Bartleby the Scrivener."* Hamden, Conn.: Archon Books, 1979, 238 p.

Collection of new and previously published "Bartleby the Scrivener" criticism, including annotated checklists of "Bartleby" notices published between 1863 and 1978.

Johnson, Arthur. "A Comparison of Manners." *The New Republic* XX, No. 251 (27 August 1919): 113-15.

Compares Henry James's and Melville's short stories.

Leavis, Q. D. "Melville: The 1853-6 Phase." In *New Perspectives on Melville,* edited by Faith Pullin, pp. 197-228. Kent, Ohio: The Kent State University Press, 1978.

Comments on the attitude, imagery, tone, and style of *The Piazza Tales.*

Magowan, Robin. "Masque and Symbol in Melville's 'Benito Cereno'." *College English* 23, No. 5 (February 1962): 346-51.

Considers "Benito Cereno" as an examination of the moral problem posed by slavery.

McWilliams, John P., Jr. "Confidence in Distrust: The Failings of Charity." In his *Hawthorne, Melville, and the American Character: A Looking-Glass Business,* pp. 176-83. Cambridge: Cambridge University Press, 1984.

Approaches Melville's magazine stories as evidence of his interest in particularly American concerns. McWilliams focuses on passages which subvert the idea of America as a land of plenty and opportunity.

Melville Society Extracts I— (1945—).
Quarterly review published by the Melville Society. Each issue carries critical essays on Melville's work, as well as updates of recently published secondary material.

"The Piazza Tales." In *Melville: The Critical Heritage*, edited by Watson G. Branch, pp. 354-60. The Critical Heritage Series, edited by B. C. Southam. London: Routledge & Kegan Paul, 1974.
Reprints ten unsigned 1856 notices of *The Piazza Tales*.

Miller, James E., Jr. "Tales and Sketches: Withdrawals and Reconciliations" and "*Billy Budd:* The Catastrophe of Innocence." In his *A Reader's Guide to Herman Melville*, pp. 152-69, 218-28. 1962. Reprint. New York: Octagon Books, 1973.
Provides plot summaries of Melville's major short stories, with some discussion of their meaning, form, and technique.

Oates, Joyce Carol. "Melville and the Tragedy of Nihilism." In her *The Edge of Impossibility: Tragic Forms in Literature*, pp. 61-83. London: Victor Gollancz, 1976.
Explore's Melville's idea of God as it is expressed in *Billy Budd*.

O'Brien, Edward J. "Hawthorne and Melville." In his *The Advance of the American Short Story*, pp. 42-64. New York: Dodd, Mead and Company, 1923.
Cursory review of Melville's major short stories, maintaining that, as the author of *The Piazza Tales*, Melville is "one of the greatest visionary artists the world has had since William Blake."

Oliver, Egbert S. "A Second Look at 'Bartleby'." *College English* 6, No. 8 (May 1945): 431-39.
Suggests that Bartleby's actions are based on Henry David Thoreau's withdrawal from society.

———. Introduction to *Piazza Tales*, by Herman Melville, edited by Egbert S. Oliver, pp. ix-xii. New York: Hendricks House, Farrar Straus, 1948.
Brief summary of *The Piazza Tales* centering on their early critical reception.

Pattee, Fred Lewis. "The Decade After Poe." In his *The Development of the American Short Story: An Historical Survey*, pp. 145-65. New York: Harper & Brothers, 1923.
Maintains that *The Piazza Tales* are "peculiarly typical" of the 1850s.

Riddle, Mary-Madeleine Gina. *Herman Melville's "Piazza Tales": A Prophetic Vision*. Gothenburg Studies in English, No. 55. Gothenburg, Sweden: Acta Universitatis Gothoburgensis, 1985, 250 p.
Discusses the stories in *The Piazza Tales* both individually and as part of a unified, larger whole. Riddle asserts that Melville arranged the stories in the 1856 collection to complement his apocalyptic vision.

Roundy, Nancy. "Fancies, Reflections and Things: The Imagination as Perception in 'The Piazza'." *CLA Journal* XX, No. 4 (1977): 539-46.
Philosophical reading of "The Piazza," centering on the story's epistemology and aesthetics.

Sandberg, A. "Erotic Patterns in 'The Paradise of Bachelors and the Tartarus of Maids'." *Literature and Psychology* XVIII, No. 1 (1968): 2-8.
Contends that "The Paradise of Bachelors and the Tartarus of Maids" is an exploration of impotency in which the narrator examines homosexuality, phallus worship, autoerotism, sexual initiation, violent coitus, and other psychosexual issues.

Scorza, Thomas J. *In the Time before Steamships: "Billy Budd," the Limits of Politics, and Modernity*. DeKalb, Ill.: Northern Illinois University Press, 1979, 210 p.
Evaluation of *Billy Budd*.

Scudder, Harold H. "Melville's *Benito Cereno* and Captain Delano's Voyages." *PMLA* XLIII, No. 2 (June 1928): 502-32.
Compares "Benito Cereno" with its 1817 source, Amasa Delano's *Narrative of Voyages and Travels in the Northern and Southern Hemispheres*.

Sealts, Merton M. "Herman Melville's 'I and My Chimney'." *American Literature* 13, No. 2 (May 1941): 142-54.
Close reading of "I and My Chimney," focusing on historical and autobiographical elements in the story.

Sedgwick, William Ellery. "Billy Budd." In his *Herman Melville: The Tragedy of Mind*, pp. 231-49. 1944. Reprint. New York: Russell & Russell, 1962.
Maintains that *Billy Budd* is Melville's "testament of acceptance."

Review of *The Piazza Tales*, by Herman Melville. *The Southern Literary Messenger* XXII, No. 6 (June 1856): 480.
Contemporary review of *The Piazza Tales*, noting that in this work Melville " 'turns up' once more . . . with much of his former freshness and vivacity."

Spiller, Robert E. "Romantic Crisis: Melville, Whitman." In his *The Cycle of American Literature: An Essay in Historical Criticism*, pp. 89-110. New York: The Macmillan Company, 1955.
Suggests that in such works as "Bartleby the Scrivener" and "Benito Cereno" Melville's skepticism prevented him from ever stating his case clearly.

Stafford, William T., ed. *Melville's "Billy Budd" and the Critics*. 2d ed. Belmont, Calif.: Wadsworth Publishing Company, 1968, 272 p.
Presents selected new and previously published criticism of *Billy Budd*. The book also includes a genetic text and an edition of Louis O. Coxe and Robert Chapman's stage play based on the novella.

Stern, Milton R. "Towards 'Bartleby the Scrivener'." In *The Stoic Strain in American Literature: Essays in Honour of Marston LaFrance*, edited by Duane J. MacMillan, pp. 19-41. Toronto: University of Toronto Press, 1970.
Reviews criticism of "Bartleby the Scrivener," stressing evaluations of the story's tone, humor, epilogue, and point of view.

Thomas, Russell. "Melville's Use of Some Sources in 'The Encantadas'." *American Literature* 3, No. 4 (January 1932): 432-56.
Careful elucidation of the major sources of "The Encantadas," focusing on Melville's prior reading and experiences.

"Herman Melville's Silence." *The Times Literary Supplement*, No. 1173 (10 July 1924): 433.
Praises *Billy Budd*'s "strange combination of naïve and majestic serenity," characterizing the work as Melville's "final word" on the question of nihilism.

Updike, John. "Three Talks on American Masters: Melville's Withdrawal." In his *Hugging the Shore: Essays and Criticism*, pp. 80-106. New York: Alfred A. Knopf, 1983.
Briefly considers the aesthetic merits of Melville's major short stories.

Verdier, Douglas L. "Who Is the Lightning-Rod Man?" *Studies in Short Fiction* 18, No. 3 (Summer 1981): 273-79.
Proposes that the title character of "The Lightning-Rod Man" is the Devil, who, in a triumph of good over evil, is thwarted at the end of the story.

Weaver, Raymond M. *Herman Melville: Mariner and Mystic*. New York: George H. Doran Company, 1921, 399 p.
Copiously illustrated critical biography, describing "The Bell Tower," "Benito Cereno," and "The Encantadas" as "the last glow of Melville's literary glamour, the final momentary brightening of the embers before they sank into blackness and ash."

Widmer, Kingsley. *The Ways of Nihilism: A Study of Herman Melville's Short Novels*. Los Angeles: Ward Ritchie Press for California State Colleges, 1970, 149 p.
Discusses the oppositional problems surrounding *Billy Budd*, "Benito Cereno," and "Bartleby the Scrivener."

(Mary) Flannery O'Connor

1925-1964

American short story writer, novelist, and essayist.

Joseph De Casseres/Photo Researchers

O'Connor has won a prominent place in modern American literature. She was an anomaly among post-World War II writers—a Roman Catholic from the Bible-belt South whose stated purpose was to reveal the mystery of God's grace in everyday life. Aware that few readers shared her faith, O'Connor chose to depict salvation through shocking, often violent action upon characters who are spiritually or physically grotesque. "To the hard of hearing you shout," she once said, commenting on her tendency toward bizarre action and caricature, "and for the almost blind you draw large and startling figures." While O'Connor used exaggeration to express her ideas, her prose style is considered compressed and brilliantly polished. Moreover, her stories are related with such ironic detachment and mordant humor that some consider them to be existentialist or even nihilistic in outlook. O'Connor also infused her fiction with the local color and rich comic detail of her Southern milieu, particularly through Southern dialect, which she recorded with a keen ear. Finally, a complex system of symbolism and allegory adds further resonance to her body of work. While her two novels are highly respected, commentators generally consider her gifts best suited to short fiction. Her posthumous volume, *The Complete Stories of Flannery O'Connor*, won the National Book Award in 1971, and many concur with A. L. Rowse's view that O'Connor is "probably the greatest short story writer of our time."

O'Connor was the only child of devout Roman Catholics from prominent Georgia families. She attended parochial schools in Savannah and the public high school in Milledgeville, where the family moved after her father developed disseminated lupus, the degenerative disease that Flannery was to inherit. Soon after her father's death when she was nearly sixteen, O'Connor entered the nearby Georgia State College for Women, where she majored in social sciences. In her spare time she edited and wrote for school publications and also contributed linoleum block and woodcut cartoons that embody key characteristics of her fiction: caricature, dry irony, and a strong sense of the absurd. O'Connor enrolled in the graduate writing program at Iowa State University, where she earned her Master's degree in 1947 with six stories, including "The Geranium," which had appeared the previous year in *Accent*. Throughout her career, O'Connor's stories were readily published, occasionally by popular magazines such as *Mademoiselle,* but more often by prestigious literary journals including *Sewanee Review, Shenandoah,* and *Kenyon Review*.

The young author spent the next few years working on her first novel, *Wise Blood,* while living in 1947-48 at Yaddo writers' colony in upstate New York, then briefly in New York City, and then in Connecticut, where she boarded with her friends Sally and Robert Fitzgerald, a young married couple who shared her Catholic faith and literary interests. But her independent writer's life ended abruptly at age twenty-five when she suffered her first attack of lupus. From that point onward, O'Connor lived with her mother at Andalusia, a small dairy farm outside Milledgeville. While her mother ran the farm, O'Connor maintained a steady if slow writing pace, publishing *Wise Blood* in 1952, followed by the story collection *A Good Man Is Hard to Find* in 1955, and a second novel, *The Violent Bear It Away,* in 1960. Each volume attracted significant critical attention, and she was awarded three O. Henry prizes for her short stories, in addition to several grants and two honorary degrees. As her reputation grew, her circle of correspondents widened, and she traveled when her health permitted to give readings and lectures. O'Connor also enjoyed her pastimes: oil-painting and raising exotic fowl—a lifelong fascination said to reflect her interest in the grotesque. Peacocks, her particular favorites, feature in some of O'Connor's stories and bear significant symbolic weight. Even during her final illness, a bout with lupus triggered by abdominal surgery, O'Connor wrote devotedly, and she finished her final story, "Parker's Back," just weeks before she died.

The recurrent theme in O'Connor's thirty-one short stories is that of God's grace descending in an often bizarre or violent way upon a spiritually deficient character or characters. These protagonists are most often afflicted with the sin of pride, whether the intellectual pride of the blasé, rational-thinking atheist, or the materialistic pride of the smug farmer. As critics have noted, O'Connor typically depicts a rural domestic situation featuring a parent and child who are suddenly invaded by an often criminal or perverse outsider, a distorted Christ figure who serves as the agent of grace. In one of O'Connor's best-known stories, "A Good Man Is Hard to Find," what begins as a comic portrayal of a family vacation ends with the smugly self-complacent grandmother being shocked into spiritual awareness by a murderer who kills first her family and then her. The story exemplifies O'Connor's remark about her work: "The look of this fiction is going to be wild . . . it is almost of necessity going to be violent and comic, because of the discrepancies it seeks to combine." Critics note that O'Connor's tales, while expressing intense action, are related in concise, almost epigrammatic prose, which is vividly expressive. Critics cite O'Connor's symbols, particularly those of nature, as richly complex, so that in her fictional world, the Georgia landscape not only embodies God's grandeur, but also reflects the spiritual tone: sunsets resemble blood-drenched Eucharistic hosts, preening peacocks represent Christ's transfiguration, and the trees themselves writhe in spiritual agony. Finally, critics praise O'Connor's skillful construction and pacing and her mastery of the traditional short story structure featuring a pronounced climax and denouement.

Critics agree that O'Connor's artistic style and vision were shaped by a variety of influences. In her stark imagery, caustic satire, and use of the grotesque, she clearly follows the black humor tradition exemplified by Nathanael West, whose novel *Miss Lonelyhearts* (1933) was among the twentieth-century works O'Connor most admired. O'Connor, also held in high regard the nineteenth-century American romance tales of Nathaniel Hawthorne. Critics often trace in O'Connor's work the influence of his intricate symbolism, use of allegory, and ascetic concern with salvation. While some commentators were eager to align O'Connor with her southern contemporaries, such as Eudora Welty, Carson McCullers, and Erskine Caldwell, she resisted being confined to regional status, and critics now generally recognize that her aims were wholly different from those of her colleagues. Nevertheless, many critics note William Faulkner's influence in his vision of the Southern gothic and his masterful prose rhythms and cadences. Most crucial, however, and underlying all O'Connor's fiction, is her deep grounding in biblical tradition and Catholic theology, which she nurtured all her life with intense reading in not only early Catholic literature, but also works by twentieth-century Catholic apologists. Particularly significant among modern influences were the French Catholic authors Georges Bernanos, François Mauriac, and Pierre Teilhard de Chardin, whose philosophical writings inspired the title of O'Connor's posthumous short story collection, *Everything That Rises Must Converge*.

The predominant feature of O'Connor criticism is its abundance. From her first collection, O'Connor garnered serious and widespread critical attention, and since her death the outpouring has been remarkable, including hundreds of essays and numerous full-length studies. While her work has occasioned some hostile reviews, including those which labeled her an atheist or accused her of using the grotesque gratuitously, she is almost universally admired, if not fully understood. Apart from wide-ranging studies of her style, structure, symbolism, tone, themes, and influences, critical discussion centers most often on theological aspects of O'Connor's work. In inquiries into the depth of her religious intent, critics usually find O'Connor to be the Orthodox Christian that she adamantly declared herself, although some, notably John Hawkes, trace the violence and sense of evil in her work to what Hawkes termed an "essential diabolicism."

Robert Fitzgerald wrote that O'Connor "was a girl who started with a gift for cartooning and satire, and found in herself a far greater gift, unique in her time and place, a marvel. She kept going deeper (this is the phrase she used) until making up stories became, for her, a way of testing and defining and conveying that superior knowledge that must be called religious." Because O'Connor expressed her religious beliefs with passion, humor, and supreme literary artistry, she holds a distinguished place among American fiction writers.

(See also *Contemporary Literary Criticism,* Vols. 1, 2, 3, 6, 10, 13, 15, 21; *Contemporary Authors,* Vols. 1-4R; *Contemporary Authors New Revision Series,* Vol. 3; *Dictionary of Literary Biography,* Vol. 2, *American Novelists Since World War II; Dictionary of Literary Biography Yearbook,* 1980; and *Concise Dictionary of Literary Biography,* Vol. 1, *The New Consciousness, 1941-1968.*)

PRINCIPAL WORKS

SHORT FICTION

A Good Man Is Hard to Find, and Other Stories 1955
Everything That Rises Must Converge 1965
**Three by Flannery O'Connor* 1969
Flannery O'Connor: The Complete Stories 1971

OTHER MAJOR WORKS

Wise Blood (novel) 1952
The Violent Bear It Away (novel) 1960
Mystery and Manners: Occasional Prose (prose) 1969
The Habit of Being (letters) 1979

*This volume includes *Everything That Rises Must Converge* and the novels *Wise Blood* and *The Violent Bear It Away*.

CAROLINE GORDON (essay date 1955)

[A novelist, short story writer, and critic, Gordon is considered a distinguished representative of the Southern Literary Renaissance in contemporary American letters. Gordon was an older and established writer when O'Connor made her acquaintance in the early 1950s, and she became O'Connor's lifelong mentor, offering advice, encouragement, and detailed commentary on her work. In the following excerpt from her review of A Good Man Is Hard to Find, *Gordon pinpoints O'Connor's essential attributes, including moral concerns, her precision, and inventive use of symbolism.]*

[***A Good Man Is Hard to Find***] exhibits what Henry James, in "a partial portrait" of Guy de Maupassant, called "the artful brevity of a master." . . . Miss O'Connor's works, like Maupassant's, are characterized by precision, density and an almost alarming circumscription. There are few landscapes in her stories. Her characters seem to move in the hard, white glare of a searchlight—or perhaps it is more as if the author viewed her subjects through the knot-hole in a fence or wall. . . . Miss O'Connor, for all her apparent preoccupation with the visible scene, is also fiercely concerned with moral, even theological, problems. In these stories the rural South is, for the first time, viewed by a writer whose orthodoxy matches her talent. The results are revolutionary.

Miss O'Connor has an unerring eye in the selection of detail and the most exquisite ear I know of for the cadences of everyday speech. The longer, statelier sentence which has come down to us from the great masters of English prose and which, in the hands of a writer like Joyce, throws into such dramatic relief his mastery of the vernacular, is not as yet in her repertory. She is, like Maupassant, very much of her time; and her stories, like his, have a certain glitter, as it were, of evil, which pervades them and astonishingly contributes to their lifelikeness. . . .

Miss O'Connor is as realistic and down to earth a writer as one can find. Yet many people profess to find her work hard to understand. This may be because she uses symbolism in a way in which it has not been used by any of her younger contemporaries. Mrs. Hopewell in **"Good Country People"** is thrifty, kind-hearted and optimistic, abounding in aphorisms such as "A smile never hurt anyone." "It takes all kinds to make a world." She cannot understand why her daughter Joy is not happy. Joy, who had her leg blown off in a shotgun explosion when she was 10 years old, has a doctor's degree in philosophy, a bad complexion and poor eyesight and at 32 is so joyless that she has changed her name to "Hulga" because she thinks that is an ugly name. It is not hard to find in the two women figures of the "Old" and the "New" South.

Perhaps a profounder symbolism underlies **"The Displaced Person."** The judge, a "dirty, snuff-dipping courthouse figure," may also—for the orthodox—symbolize the "Old" South, his study, "a dark, closet-like space as dark and quiet as a chapel," the scanty provision which the "Old" South was able to make for the spiritual needs of her children.

Caroline Gordon, "With a Glitter of Evil," in The New York Times Book Review, *June 12, 1955, p. 5.*

LOUIS D. RUBIN, JR. (essay date 1955)

[Rubin, an American critic, has written and edited numerous studies of Southern American literature. In the following excerpt from his review of A Good Man Is Hard to Find, *he compares O'Connor with her two Southern contemporaries, Erskine Caldwell and Carson McCullers, stressing that O'Connor differs from them in her spiritual, moral outlook and her avoidance of sentimentality. This essay originally appeared in the* Sewanee Review *in 1955.]*

Miss O'Connor's approach [in ***A Good Man Is Hard to Find***] is direct, precise, bounded. Evelyn Waugh is quoted as saying of Miss O'Connor's novel *Wise Blood* that "if this is the unaided work of a young lady it is a remarkable product." An odd way to put a compliment, and yet the stories of ***A Good Man Is Hard to Find*** represents a much greater success in conception and execution than her novel did. . . . In the short story form, . . . Miss O'Connor seems to have found the vehicle in which her literary attack would be at its surest and most congenial.

Something about Miss O'Connor's work is reminiscent of the best work of another Georgia writer, Erskine Caldwell. Perhaps it is subject matter most of all. Though in no sense concerned with the pornography and lasciviousness to which Caldwell often resorts, she too goes in for the miseries of the poor whites—faith healers, a one-armed vagrant who weds a deaf-and-dumb girl to steal her mother's old car and then abandons her on their wedding trip, hermaphrodites at the fair, country cousins mystified by the city's ways, a Bible salesman and a girl with a wooden leg, displaced tenant farmers. Perhaps the similarities are enhanced, too, by the style of Miss O'Connor's stories—realistic, plain, literal:

> The ugly words settled in Mr. Shiftlet's head like a group of buzzards in the top of a tree. He didn't answer at once. He rolled himself a cigarette and lit it and then he said in an even voice, "Lady, a man is divided into two parts, body and spirit."
>
> The old woman clapped her gums together.
>
> "A body and a spirit," he repeated. "The body, lady, is like a house; it don't go anywhere; but the spirit, lady, is like a automobile; always on the move, always. . . ."

There is much dialogue; Miss O'Connor has an outrageously keen ear for country talk. There is also considerable humor. The incongruous, the hilarious, the absurdly comic (the man doing the preaching above is the one who marries the deaf-mute in order to steal the family car) are grist to Miss O'Connor's mill. She relishes the ridiculous. . . . (pp. 25-6)

Where Miss O'Connor's art differs—profoundly—from Caldwell's is not in language or subject matter so much as in the attitude of the author. Caldwell is the naturalist, out to make a social point, preoccupied with the poor farmer's oppressed economic condition. Flannery O'Connor has no such intention, no such simple approach to people. More kin to the Bundrens of *As I Lay Dying,* her people confront spiritual and moral problems, not economics. There is in her characters a dignity, a human worthiness, that shows the real respect Miss O'Connor has for them. All of them are, in their own times and situations, responsible agents, not trapped automatons.

Miss O'Connor is in essence a religious writer. Knowledge of good and evil is at the heart of her stories. A most powerful, ironic tale is that called **"Good Country People,"** in which the central figure is a young woman with a wooden leg and a Ph.D. in philosophy, who lives on a farm with her mother. Along comes a seemingly starry-eyed Bible salesman, and the girl, who is avowedly an atheist who believes in "nothing," decides to seduce him. They retire to a barn, climbing the ladder to the hayloft. As a proof of her love, the Bible salesman persuades her to remove her wooden leg. He quickly seizes it, and takes from his satchel a bottle of whiskey, a pack of pornographic cards, and a tin of contraceptives. She repulses his advances then, whereupon as she watches in horror he places the wooden leg in the satchel:

> "I've gotten a lot of interesting things," he said. "One time I got a woman's glass eye this way. And you needn't to think you'll catch me because Pointer ain't really my name. I use a different name at every house I call at and don't stay nowhere long. And I'll tell another thing, Hulga," he said, using the name as if he didn't think much of it, "you ain't so smart. I been believing in nothing ever since I was born!"

The Bible salesman disappears down the ladder, leaving the helpless girl atheist sitting on the straw. She has learned a little more, now, about what it means to believe in "nothing."

Still another useful comparison for these stories is with the work of another Georgia lady, Miss Carson McCullers. For one thing, both Miss O'Connor and Miss McCullers seem to share a strong artistic sympathy for the wretched, the deformed, the physical and mental misfits. Some of the people in ***A Good Man is Hard to Find*** remind one forcibly of those unhappy folk who are described in *The Heart is a Lonely Hunter*. The significant difference has to do with the matter of pathos. Through all of Carson McCullers' writings run the strain of the sentimental, of a vague, undefined yearning. As a novel, *The Heart is a Lonely Hunter* is marred by the unresolved attitude on the part of the author. She is not sure whether to be ironic over the lonely plight of her misfits and adolescents, or to yearn with them for better things. At different times she does both. Flannery O'Connor, on the other hand, knows exactly where she stands, and so does the reader. Never once is she sentimental about a character: this is the situation, this is the person, this is what happens. There is a great deal of compassion in her work, but it is always compassion for characters because they are human beings with human limitations, not because they have limbs missing or have lost their jobs or are otherwise discomfited. The moral consciousness that runs throughout the stories of ***A Good Man is Hard to Find*** can accept evil, but not try to find excuses for it. (pp. 26-7)

> *Louis D. Rubin, Jr., "Two Ladies of the South," in* Critical Essays on Flannery O'Connor, *edited by Melvin J. Friedman and Beverly Lyon Clark, G. K. Hall & Co., 1985, pp. 25-8.*

ROBERT FITZGERALD (essay date 1962)

[An American poet and scholar, Fitzgerald was highly regarded for his verse translations of several classical Greek plays and particularly for his adaptations of Homer's The Odyssey *(1961) and* The Iliad *(1974). He and his wife, Sally Fitzgerald, were among O'Connor's closest friends, and she chose them to be the executors of her literary estate. Here Fitzgerald gives a detailed reading of "The Displaced Person," tracing the Christian themes that lie beneath the story's local color and comedy.]*

In this article I will be doing, or trying to do, something very limited. A full critical study of Flannery O'Connor's work remains to be done, and it will still remain to be done when I have finished. All I propose is to give a reading of one short story. One reason for my choice is that I believe it to be an important story and well achieved. Another reason is that a contrary opinion in a book review has been lodged for a long time in my copy of the book, and I'd like to dislodge it, so to speak. The review, of Miss O'Connor's collection called ***A Good Man is Hard to Find,*** appeared in *Time* for June 6, 1955 [see Additional Bibliography]. The impact of Miss O'Connor's writing had not been entirely lost on the reviewer. But this is what he had to say of the story in question:

> Only in her longest story, **"The Displaced Person,"** does Ferocious Flannery weaken her wallop by groping about for a symbolic second-story meaning—in this case, something about salvation. But despite such arty fumbling, which also marred Author O'Connor's novel *Wise Blood* . . . , this is still a powerful and moving tale of an innocent Pole who stumbles against the South's color bar.
>
> (p. 380)

There is difficulty for me right away in the notion of "groping." I can imagine a story itself seeming to grope; there are good stories that sometimes do. But the reviewer does not say this of Miss O'Connor's story. He says it of the writer, and there is something about the story which makes him say it. What it is about the story, I think, is that its meaning is unclear to the reviewer. He is aware of a meaning that eludes him, and perhaps because it eludes him he has hard words for it: it is "symbolic" and "second-story" and "something about salvation." Apparently he has done some groping of his own, as we might properly expect him to do, without being able to lay his hand on what he wanted. He blames this failure on the writer. He speaks as though the groping were all hers. My sympathy for the reviewer undergoes a strain when I see that all he has to show for his own groping, all he can offer as a hint of the meaning he cannot grasp, is the phrase "something about salvation." This comes from the blurb, which declares that **"The Displaced Person"** is "about the problem of salvation." A book reviewer should improve on blurbs or leave them alone. (pp. 380-81)

As nearly as I can make it out now, our reviewer's reservation goes like this: **"The Displaced Person"** would be all right, or first rate, if one were not aware in reading it that its personages and action bear a meaning that one does not understand. If one has tried in vain to comprehend this meaning, that indicates that the writer has tried in vain to foist it on her story, being in this a slave to literary fashion. Too bad, because even though weakened by wasted motion and the *trop voulu* it is still a powerful and moving tale.

The judgment, if I am right and that is it, would impress me more, or depress me less, if there were evidence that the reviewer had really gone to much trouble in making it. But I have already remarked how he resorted to the blurb for his shot at the intended meaning of the story. And that is not all. He also gives us a brief account of the subject and action: "an innocent Pole who stumbles against the South's color bar." You never can tell, of course, whose hand is responsible for any given sentence in *Time*. This one could have been written by an editor impatient to condense his book reviewer's painstaking distinctions. In any case, the brevity was a great mistake. Let me look at the story.

It begins:

> The peacock was following Mrs. Shortley up the road to the hill where she meant to stand. Moving one behind the other, they looked like a complete procession. Her arms were folded and as she mounted the prominence she might have been the giant wife of the countryside, come out at some sign of danger to see what the trouble was. She stood on two tremendous legs, with the grand self-confidence of a mountain, and rose, up narrowing bulges of granite, to two icy blue points of light that pierced forward, surveying everything. . . . The peacock stopped just behind her, his tail—glittering green-gold and blue in the sunlight—lifted just enough so that it would not touch the ground. It flowed out on either side like a floating train and his head on the long blue reed-like neck was drawn back as if his attention were fixed in the distance on something no one else could see.

Now, I can easily conceive a reader thinking the peacock just incidental decoration, though the peacock is mentioned first, and a vanishing point for the story's perspective is suggested by his gaze. An inattentive reader might overlook this, but even an inattentive reader would assume from the beginning that the protagonist of the story is going to be Mrs. Shortley, and in this he would be right. The protagonist will be that giant wife of the countryside first personified by Mrs. Shortley and later by her successor in the role. In the opening sentence the reader is informed of the giant wife's purpose: she meant to stand.

The danger to be measured is the arrival of a Polish D.P., Mr. Guizac, with his family, on the farm of Mrs. McIntyre, for whom Mrs. Shortley's husband works as a dairyman. The countryside is Deep South, and just to make the intrusion thorough-going it is an old Catholic priest who has arranged to place the Guizacs with Mrs. McIntyre. We are given several pages in which to relish this situation through Mrs. Shortley's view of it. . . .

> Mrs. Shortley recalled a newsreel she had seen once of a small room piled high with bodies of dead naked people all in a heap, their arms and legs tangled together, a head thrust in here, a head there, a foot, a knee, a part that should have been covered sticking out, a hand raised clutching nothing. Before you could realize that it was real and take it into your head, the picture changed and a hollow-sounding voice was saying, "Time marches on!" This was the kind of thing that was happening every day in Europe where they had not advanced as in this country. . . . If the Guizacs had come from where that kind of thing was done to them, who was to say they were not the kind that would also do it to others?

It is cool work, this writing, in which not one but several human abysses are skated over with an ironic flick, and all in Mrs. Shortley's mind. We need not be deceived by the bare idiom, the parsimony of rhetoric. Here is Yeats' "uncontrollable mystery on the bestial floor." And these intimations of the abysmal, like the previous hint of a horizon beyond the actors' vision, should warn us that the story is religious. Other indications are soon to follow. By allusion and figure the religious background grows, and the foreground is ever more explicit. Going forward to be introduced,

> Mrs. Shortley looked at the priest and was reminded that these people did not have an advanced religion. There was no telling what all they believed since none of the foolishness had been reformed out of it.

The priest is admiring the peacock behind her.

> "So beauti-ful," the priest said. "A tail full of suns," and he crept forward on tiptoe and looked down on the bird's back where the polished gold and green design began. The peacock stood still as if he had just come down from some sun-drenched height to be a vision for them all.

Peacock and priest may seem equally exotic on the scene, but the Negroes, Astor and Sulk, are as much a part of it as the mulberry tree behind which Mrs. Shortley finds them. There are several distinct kinds of pleasure in reading Flannery O'Connor, and I find one kind in her dialogues between Negroes and whites.

> The old man, Astor, raised himself. "We been watching," he said, as if this would be news to her. "Who they now?"
>
> "They come from over the water," Mrs. Shortley said with a wave of her arm. "They're what is called Displaced Persons."
>
> "Displaced Persons," he said. "Well now. I declare. What do that mean?"
>
> "It means they ain't where they were born at and there's nowhere for them to go—like if you was run out of here and wouldn't nobody have you."
>
> "It seem like they here, though," the old man said in a reflective voice. "If they here, they somewhere."
>
> "Sho is," the other agreed. "They here."
>
> The illogic of Negro-thinking always irked Mrs. Shortley. "They ain't where they belong to be at," she said.

I have quoted this not only for itself but to show how deliberately the story goes and how close to the skin it is in local detail. It will continue to be leisured and joyously exact as the wife of the countryside, standing embattled, becomes an exponent of the countryside's religion. The intrusion of the D. P.s kindles Mrs. Shortley's inner life to great intensity. (p. 382-85)

In three weeks the Pole, who is expert, industrious and clean, has made such an impression on Mrs. McIntyre that she remarks to Mrs. Shortley, "That man is my salvation."

> Mrs. Shortley looked straight ahead as if her vision penetrated the cane and the hill and pierced through to the other side. "I would suspicion salvation got from the devil," she said in a slow detached way.
>
> "Now what do you mean by that?" Mrs. McIntyre asked, looking at her sharply.
>
> Mrs. Shortley wagged her head but would not say anything else. The fact was she had nothing else to say, for this intuition had only at that instant come to her. She had never given much thought to the devil for she felt that religion was essentially for those people who didn't have the brains to avoid evil without it. For people like herself, for people of gumption, it was a social occasion providing the opportunity to sing; but if she had ever given it much thought, she would have considered the devil the head of it and God the hanger-on. With the coming of these displaced people, she was obliged to give new thought to a good many things.

Several further revelations come to Mrs. Shortley before the last and most enlightening. She perceives that the Negroes are not the only ones who may have to find another place. Her husband's job is also in danger, especially if the vigilant Pole should discover that he is running a still on the side. It occurs to her that the priest, who is trying to convert Mrs. McIntyre, hopes to bring still another Polish family to the place. Then she finds out something about the Pole that would floor Mrs. McIntyre, but before she can use it two things happen. The first is a vision.

> Suddenly while she watched the sky folded back in two pieces like the curtain to a stage and a gigantic figure stood facing her. It was the color of the sun in the early afternoon, white-gold. It was of no definite shape but there were fiery wheels with fierce dark eyes in them, spinning rapidly all around it. She was not able to tell if the figure was going forward or backward because its magnificence was so great. She shut her eyes in order to look at it and it turned blood-red and the wheels turned white. A voice, very resonant, said the one word, "Prophesy!"

(pp. 386-87)

Just after this she overhears Mrs. McIntyre telling the priest that she is going to give Mr. Shortley notice. Mrs. Shortley has not been described as a giantess for nothing. Flaming with pride, she makes her husband help her to pack with fury all night, and loading their old car they decamp with their two girls before milking time in the morning. Only when they are on the dark road does he ask for the first time where they are going. At this, Mrs. Shortley's final revelation begins, coinciding with the heart attack that kills her. (p. 387)

That is Part I of **"The Displaced Person."** What is potential in the situation has been realized only in part: the ironic displacement of Mrs. Shortley, in a physical and then in a metaphysical sense. Along with a lot of comedy (most of it I have reluctantly skipped) we have had frequent intimations that the action is to be understood in religious terms: Mrs. Shortley herself so understands it. Her religious terms, as they become explicit under stress, are those of the countryside. I see no groping or fumbling in the way they are rendered but rather a widening of focus, at high velocity, from simple fear of the wicked nations to an Apocalyptic inner light. Miss O'Connor's insight into what is left of Christianity in backcountry Bible-reading sections is profoundly empathic and satiric at the same time. Mrs. Shortley belongs to a great company of O'Connor revivalists and visionaries who are funny but by no means figures of fun. A page of prophecy in the Old Testament is hardly more eloquent than some of them, and I can think of nothing in literature that teaches better than they do why the Old Testament had to be completed by the New. Or, rather, why the whole Scripture overbrims all interpreters but one, the most capacious.

The mystery I have just mentioned certainly lies at the heart of this particular story. In most O'Connor stories we are aware of the Roman or universal Church mainly by its absence. Here it is present from the start. I wonder if the handling of the peacock can justly be called arty. An unpredictable splendor, a map of the universe, doted upon by the priest, barely seen by everyone else: this is a metaphor, surely, for God's order and God's grace. Is it arbitrary and imposed? Can the reader be expected to see it? The *Time* reviewer did not, but then there is much that he did not see. What induced me to look at the story in detail was above all his brief account of protagonist and action: "an innocent Pole who stumbles against the South's color bar." Throughout Part I there is no doubt as to the chief actor; it is Mrs. Shortley. The Pole scarcely appears, his innocence or lack of it is neither here nor there, and the barrier he is up against has many bars besides the color bar. All this will be apparent to any fairly attentive reader. But it may be that few readers are prepared to understand the metaphor of the peacock, fewer still to approve. If our reviewer had understood it, he might still have called it arty, as a critic of another generation would have called it *recherché*. I can imagine him objecting that a peacock is a rare adornment on a Southern farm. To this I could only reply that that, in a way, is the point.

After Mrs. Shortley's death, her role as the giant wife of the countryside devolves upon Mrs. McIntyre, who being still more formidable will engage in a harder struggle. I have noted more than once how Mrs. Shortley became an exponent of the countryside's religion. Mrs. McIntyre does not know it, but she holds a later form of the same religion, so far reformed that no nonsense at all remains. It is a managerial religion, the one by which daily business in a realm gets done. This makes it still a little old-fashioned. If it were citified here, or professional or academic, Miss O'Connor on her record would parody it to put life into it, for her talent is Pauline in abiding not the lukewarm. But Mrs. McIntyre has savor and is played straight. She is rendered in fact with as much economy and energy as Mrs. Shortley, for whom she properly feels a kinship; she, too, undoubtedly feels that religion is for people without enough gumption to avoid evil without it. (pp. 388-89)

The industrious D. P. had imperilled the Shortleys' position; for Mrs. McIntyre he soon appears to imperil the social order that she must govern, and on which she depends. Mrs. Shortley's discovery, now repeated by Mrs. McIntyre, is that the Pole has promised his sixteen-year-old cousin to the colored boy, Sulk, if Sulk will pay half the expense of bringing her from a refugee camp to America. As Sulk explains, "She don't care who she mah she so glad to get away from there." For Mrs. McIntyre, in her complacency over having found at last a really efficient hired man, the discovery is a terrible blow. Nothing the Pole could have done would have been more hopelessly wrong. Let me be a little insistent about this. It is not merely that he has stumbled against the color bar. It is the classic situation of tragedy in which each party to the conflict is both right and wrong and almost incomprehensible to the other. (p. 390)

When the priest comes to see her again, Mrs. McIntyre cannot listen to his talk about Purgatory. She interrupts to tell him that if she can find a white man who understands her Negroes, Mr. Guizac will have to go. (pp. 390-91)

Mrs. McIntyre does not in fact try to find another hired man. She doesn't have to; after a few weeks Mr. Shortley turns up again. In her relief she tells him she will give the Pole notice on the first of the month, but the day arrives and she does not do so. Before firing the Pole she wants to persuade the priest—who has been staying away—that she has no moral obligation to keep him. Meanwhile the sight of the D. P. moving quickly about the place becomes more and more irritating to her. When the priest returns, she is so wrought up that in the course of giving him all her arguments she tells him fiercely that as far as she is concerned, Christ was just another D. P. Mrs. McIntyre's inner life, like Mrs. Shortley's before her, has now become intense, and her expression of the countryside's religion more pointed. Still she delays. The first of the month comes again, and again she cannot act on the choice that she has made. There are sleepless nights, debates in dream. But now Mr. Shortley turns the town against her, and when this comes home to her she realizes that she has a moral obligation to get rid of the Pole.

As she approaches the toolshed for this purpose, Mr. Guizac is getting under the small tractor to repair it and Mr. Shortley is backing the large tractor out of the shed.

> He had headed it toward the small tractor but he braked it on a slight incline and jumped off and turned back toward the shed. Mrs. McIntyre was looking fixedly at Mr. Guizac's legs lying flat on the ground now. She heard the brake on the large tractor slip and, looking up, she saw it move forward, calculating its own path. Later she remembered that she had seen the Negro jump silently out of the way as if a spring in the earth had released him and that she had seen Mr. Shortley turn his head with incredible slowness and stare silently over his shoulder and that she had started to shout to

> the Displaced Person but that she had not. She had felt her eyes and Mr. Shortley's eyes and the Negro's eyes come together in one look that froze them in collusion forever, and she had heard the little noise the Pole made as the tractor wheel broke his backbone. The two men ran forward to help and she fainted.

The catastrophe is of course Mrs. McIntyre's. Her hired helpers leave her, she must sell her cows, and she lives on, bed-ridden with "a nervous ailment." It is a powerful and moving tale, but it is not the tale of an innocent Pole nor except incidentally of the South's color bar. It is a tale of the displacement of persons, or, better, of the human Person displaced. (When Mrs. McIntyre came to, she "felt she was in some foreign country where the people bent over the body were natives, and she watched like a stranger while the dead man was carried away in the ambulance").

I should say that this has been Flannery O'Connor's essential subject. Her satire and irony, exuberance of ear and invention, are inseparable from the cental knowledge that in varying degrees they serve. "Religious" is a poor word for this knowledge if it does not mean "knowledge of the world." She sees the South, it seems to me (who am no Southerner but no Northerner, either), as populated by displaced persons. Almost all her people are displaced and some are either aware of it or become so. But it is not a sectional or regional condition; it is a religious condition, common to North and South alike, common indeed to the world we live in.

The stories not only imply, they as good as state again and again, that estrangement from Christian plenitude is estrangement from the true country of man. Peacock and priest in this story are not really exotic; the fantasies of Mrs. Shortley are, and so is the self-sufficient pragmatism of Mrs. McIntyre. The story goes beyond most in exploring the reformed religion. Clearheaded and hard beset, Mrs. McIntyre embodies the giant wife of our countryside more effectively than Mrs. Shortley, and is the worthy protagonist of a tragic action. For, as I have said, her situation is tragic in the classic sense, and tragic in the commitment of will. Being what she is, she must reject not only the salvation offered, in terms of farm work, by the Pole, but that other salvation that she finds so exasperating to hear of from the priest. It is an ambitious and responsible work of fiction, and there is no fumbling about it. (pp. 392-94)

Robert Fitzgerald, "The Countryside and the True Country," in The Sewanee Review, *Vol. LXX, No. 3, Summer, 1962, pp. 380-94.*

FLANNERY O'CONNOR (essay date 1963)

[*O'Connor delivered the following remarks at a reading she gave at Hollins College, Virginia on 14 October 1963. In introducing her "A Good Man Is Hard to Find," O'Connor touches upon the function of violence and the grotesque in her fiction, especially in relation to the characters of the Grandmother and the Misfit in the story.*]

Much of my fiction takes its character from a reasonable use of the unreasonable, though the reasonableness of my use of it may not always be apparent. The assumptions that underlie this use of it, however, are those of the central Christian mysteries. These are assumptions to which a large part of the modern audience takes exception. About this I can only say that there are perhaps other ways than my own in which [**"A Good Man Is Hard to Find"**] could be read, but none other by which it could have been written. Belief, in my own case anyway, is the engine that makes perception operate.

The heroine of this story, the Grandmother, is in the most significant position life offers the Christian. She is facing death. And to all appearances she, like the rest of us, is not too well prepared for it. She would like to see the event postponed. Indefinitely.

I've talked to a number of teachers who use this story in class and who tell their students that the Grandmother is evil, that in fact, she's a witch, even down to the cat. One of these teachers told me that his students and particularly his Southern students, resisted this interpretation with a certain bemused vigor, and he didn't understand why. I had to tell him that they resisted it because they all had grandmothers or great-aunts just like her at home, and they knew, from personal experience, that the old lady lacked comprehension, but that she had a good heart. The Southerner is usually tolerant of those weaknesses that proceed from innocence, and he knows that a taste for self-preservation can be readily combined with the missionary spirit.

This same teacher was telling his students that morally the Misfit was several cuts above the Grandmother. He had a really sentimental attachment to the Misfit. But then a prophet gone wrong is almost always more interesting than your grandmother, and you have to let people take their pleasures where they find them.

It is true that the old lady is a hypocritical old soul; her wits are no match for the Misfit's, nor is her capacity for grace equal to his; yet I think the unprejudiced reader will feel that the Grandmother has a special kind of triumph in this story which instinctively we do not allow to someone altogether bad.

I often ask myself what makes a story work, and what makes it hold up as a story, and I have decided that it is probably some action, some gesture of a character that is unlike any other in the story, one which indicates where the real heart of the story lies. This would have to be an action or a gesture which was both totally right and totally unexpected; it would have to be one that was both in character and beyond character; it would have to suggest both the world and eternity. The action or gesture I'm talking about would have to be on the anagogical level, that is, the level which has to do with the Divine life and our participation in it. It would be a gesture that transcended any neat allegory that might have been intended or any pat moral categories a reader could make. It would be a gesture which somehow made contact with mystery.

There is a point in this story where such a gesture occurs. The Grandmother is at last alone, facing the Misfit. Her head clears for an instant and she realizes, even in her limited way, that she is responsible for the man before her and joined to him by ties of kinship which have their roots deep in the mystery she has been merely prattling about so far. And at this point, she does the right thing, she makes the right gesture.

I find that students are often puzzled by what she says and does here, but I think myself that if I took out this gesture and what she says with it, I would have no story. What was left would not be worth your attention. Our age not only does not have a very sharp eye for the almost imperceptible intrusions of grace, it no longer has much feeling for the nature of the violences which precede and follow them. The devil's greatest wile, Baudelaire has said, is to convince us that he does not exist.

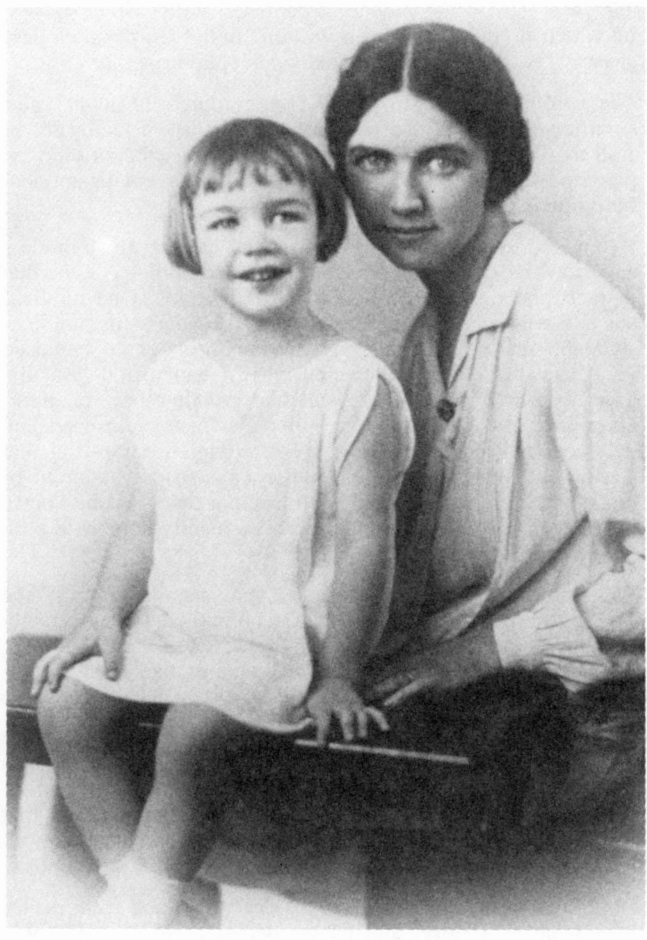

O'Connor, age two, with her mother, Regina Cline O'Connor. The Flannery O'Connor Collection, Ina Dillard Russell Library, Georgia College.

I suppose the reasons for the use of so much violence in modern fiction will differ with each writer who uses it, but in my own stories I have found that violence is strangely capable of returning my characters to reality and preparing them to accept their moment of grace. Their heads are so hard that almost nothing else will do the work. This idea, that reality is something to which we must be returned at considerable cost, is one which is seldom understood by the casual reader, but it is one which is implicit in the Christian view of the world.

I don't want to equate the Misfit with the devil. I prefer to think that, however unlikely this may seem, the old lady's gesture, like the mustard-seed, will grow to be a great crow-filled tree in the Misfit's heart, and will be enough of a pain to him there to turn him into the prophet he was meant to become. But that's another story.

This story has been called grotesque, but I prefer to call it literal. A good story is literal in the same sense that a child's drawing is literal. When a child draws, he doesn't intend to distort but to set down exactly what he sees, and as his gaze is direct, he sees the lines that create motion. Now the lines of motion that interest the writer are usually invisible. They are lines of spiritual motion. And in this story you should be on the lookout for such things as the action of grace in the Grandmother's soul, and not for the dead bodies.

We hear many complaints about the prevalence of violence in modern fiction, and it is always assumed that this violence is a bad thing and meant to be an end in itself. With the serious writer, violence is never an end in itself. It is the extreme situation that best reveals what we are essentially, and I believe these are times when writers are more interested in what we are essentially than in the tenor of our daily lives. Violence is a force which can be used for good or evil, and among other things taken by it is the kingdom of heaven. But regardless of what can be taken by it, the man in the violent situation reveals those qualities least dispensable in his personality, those qualities which are all he will have to take into eternity with him; and since the characters in this story are all on the verge of eternity, it is appropriate to think of what they take with them. In any case, I hope that if you consider these points in connection with the story, you will come to see it as something more than an account of a family murdered on the way to Florida. (pp. 109-14)

Flannery O'Connor, "On Her Own Work," in her Mystery and Manners: Occasional Prose, *edited by Sally Fitzgerald and Robert Fitzgerald, Farrar, Straus and Giroux, 1969, pp. 107-18.*

THOMAS MERTON (essay date 1964)

[*Merton, a French-born American writer, was strongly interested in both Zen and Catholicism, and he eventually became a Trappist monk. A poet, philosopher, essayist, playwright, and translator, he is best known for his autobiography,* The Seven-Story Mountain, *which became a best-seller and brought him wide acclaim. Merton and O'Connor were friends and correspondents. In the following memorial tribute, originally published in* Jubilee *in 1964, he offers an admiring analysis of O'Connor's clearsightedness—a quality of ironic respect for her subject that permeates her stories.*]

Now Flannery is dead and I will write her name with honor, with love for the great slashing innocence of that dry-eyed irony that could keep looking the South in the face without bleeding or even sobbing. Her South was deeper than mine, crazier than Kentucky, but wild with no other madness than the crafty paranoia that is all over the place, including the North! Only madder, craftier, hung up in wilder and more absurd legends, more inventive of more outrageous lies! And solemn! Taking seriously the need to be respectable when one is an obsolescent and very agile fury.

The key word to Flannery's stories probably is "respect." She never gave up examining its ambiguities and its decay. In this bitter dialectic of half-truths that have become endemic to our system, she probed our very life—its conflicts, its falsities, its obsessions, its vanities. Have we become an enormous complex organization of spurious reverences? Respect is continually advertised, and we are still convinced that we respect "everything good"—when we know too well that we have lost the most elementary respect even for ourselves. Flannery saw this and saw, better than others, what it implied.

She wrote in and out of the anatomy of a word that became genteel, then self-conscious, then obsessive, finally dying of contempt, but kept calling itself "respect." Contempt for the child, for the stranger, for the woman, for the Negro, for the animal, for the white man, for the farmer, for the country, for the preacher, for the city, for the world, for reality itself. Contempt, contempt, so that in the end the gestures of respect they kept making to themselves and to each other and to God became desperately obscene.

But respect had to be maintained. Flannery maintained it ironically and relentlessly with a kind of innocent passion long after it had died of contempt—as if she were the only one left who took this thing seriously. One would think (if one put a Catholic chip on his shoulder and decided to make a problem of her) that she could not look so steadily, so drily and so long at so much false respect without herself dying of despair. She never made any funny faces. She never said: "Here is a terrible thing!" She just looked and said what they said and how they said it. It was not she that invented their despair, and perhaps her only way out of despair herself was to respect the way they announced the gospel of contempt. She patiently recorded all they had got themselves into. Their world was a big, fantastic, crawling, exploding junk pile of despair. I will write her name with honor for seeing it so clearly and looking straight at it without remorse. Perhaps her way of irony was the only possible catharsis for a madness so cruel and so endemic. Perhaps a dry honesty like hers can save the South more simply than the North can ever be saved.

Flannery's people were two kinds of very advanced primitives: the city kind, exhausted, disillusioned, tired of imagining, perhaps still given to a grim willfulness in the service of doubt, still driving on in fury and ill will, or scientifically expert in nastiness; and the rural kind: furious, slow, cunning, inexhaustible, living sweetly on the verge of the unbelievable, more inclined to prefer the abyss to solid ground, but keeping contact with the world of contempt by raw insensate poetry and religious mirth: the mirth of a god who himself, they suspected, was the craftiest and most powerful deceiver of all. Flannery saw the contempt of primitives who admitted that they would hate to be saved, and the greater contempt of those other primitives whose salvation was an elaborately contrived possibility, always being brought back into question. (pp. 68-9)

Flannery's people were two kinds of trash, able to mix inanity with poetry, with exuberant nonsense, and with the most profound and systematic contempt for reality. Her people knew how to be trash to the limit, unabashed, on purpose, out of self-contempt that has finally won out over every other feeling and turned into a parody of freedom in the spirit. What spirit? A spirit of ungodly stateliness and parody—the pomp and glee of arbitrary sports, freaks not of nature but of blighted and social willfulness, rich in the creation of respectable and three-eyed monsters. Her beings are always raising the question of *worth*. Who is a good man? Where is he? He is "hard to find." Meanwhile you will have to make out with a bad one who is so respectable that he is horrible, so horrible that he is funny, so funny that he is pathetic, but so pathetic that it would be gruesome to pity him. So funny that you do not dare to laugh too loud for fear of demons.

And that is how Flannery finally solved the problem of respect: having peeled the whole onion of respect layer by layer, having taken it all apart with admirable patience, showing clearly that each layer was only another kind of contempt, she ended up by seeing clearly that it was funny, but not merely funny in a way that you could laugh at. Humorous, yes, but also uncanny, inexplicable, demonic, so you could never laugh at it as if you understood. Because if you pretended to understand, you, too, would find yourself among her demons practicing contempt. She respected all her people by searching for some sense in them, searching for truth, searching to the end and then suspending judgment. To have condemned them on moral grounds would have been to connive with their own crafty arts and their own demonic imagination. It would have meant getting tangled up with them in the same machinery of unreality and of contempt. The only way to be saved was to stay out of it, not to think, not to speak, just to record the slow, sweet, ridiculous verbalizing of Southern furies, working their way through their charming lazy hell.

That is why when I read Flannery I don't think of Hemingway, or Katherine Anne Porter, or Sartre, but rather of someone like Sophocles. What more can be said of a writer? I write her name with honor, for all the truth and all the craft with which she shows man's fall and his dishonor. (pp. 70-1)

Thomas Merton, "Flannery O'Connor: A Prose Elegy," in Critical Essays on Flannery O'Connor, *edited by Melvin J. Friedman and Beverly Lyon Clark, G. K. Hall & Co., 1985, pp. 68-71.*

RICHARD POIRIER (essay date 1965)

[*In the following excerpt from his review of* Everything That Rises Must Converge, *Poirier discusses pride and religious faith in O'Connor's stories. This essay originally appeared in the* New York Times Book Review *on 30 May 1965.*]

"To know oneself," [Flannery O'Connor] remarked in 1957, "is, above all, to know what one lacks. It is to measure oneself against Truth, and not the other way around. The first product of self-knowledge is humility." (p. 45)

Humility in the claims made for oneself, for what one knows and values, is in fact the operative standard within the stories [in ***Everything That Rises Must Converge***]. Pride makes a fool at some time or other of nearly all of her characters. It gets expressed not grandly but within the grotesqueries of daily, mostly Southern life, and within simple people who are aware of no alternatives to that life, once pride is destroyed, except death or a strange God.

Everything that rises must indeed converge, joining the anonymity either of oblivion or the blessed. The pride of her characters may be for a new hat, a bit of money, a college degree or clean hogs; it is her particular genius to make us believe that there are Christian mysteries in things irreduceably banal. (pp. 45-6)

Her characters seem damned precisely to the degree that they lack Miss O'Connor's own "measure" of their trivialities. They have no measure for them *but* pride, and they can therefore appeal for authority only to mundane standards that never threaten it, to platitudes and to prejudices, very often racial ones. Necessarily, she is a mordantly comic writer. She offers us the very sounds of platitude ("If you know who you are you can go anywhere," remarks the mother to her intellectualist son in **"Everything that Rises Must Converge"**), or of prejudice (as in the imagined dialogue with God of the pretentious lady in **"Revelation,"** who would have asked Him to make her anything but white trash: "'All right make me a nigger, then—but that don't mean a trashy one.' And he would have made her a neat clean respectable Negro woman, herself but black.")

Except for sloth, pride is of all human failings the one that can be most difficult for a writer to translate into actions. Most often it expresses itself in a smugness of *in*action, the hostilities it creates in others being the result merely of the tones of voice, the gestures, the placidities which are its evidence. Miss O'Connor can produce as much violence from a quiet conversation as can other writers from the confrontations of gangsters or fanatics, though she can manage that, too.

The action in the best of these stories, **"Revelation,"** is to a large extent dialogue, in which the veritable sounds of people talking gently in a doctor's office about everything from the heat to the ingratitude of children leads to a sudden but somehow expected flare-up of violence and disaster. With very little room for maneuver—most of her stories are about 20 pages long—she achieves transitions and even reversals of tone with remarkable speed, and she can show in people who have been almost preposterously flat a sudden visionary capacity. This absolute sureness of timing is, I think, what makes the reader assent to the religious direction which her stories take: from involvement in the most common stuff they move toward the Heaven and the Hell weirdly apprehended by her characters.

Miss O'Connor's major limitation is that the direction of her stories tends to be nearly always the same. Caring almost nothing for secular destinies, which are altogether more various than religious ones, she propels her characters toward the cataclysms where alone they can have a tortured glimpse of the need and chance of redemption. The repetitiousness inherent in her vision of things is more bothersomely apparent in this collection than anyone would have guessed who read the various pieces over the interval of their periodical publication. (pp. 46-7)

In one sense, Miss O'Connor's repetitiousness is an indication of how serious a writer she is. As against what might be called writers by occupation (who can of course always "pick" their subjects) she was obsessed by arrangements of life and language in which she saw some almost eschatological possibilities. And her religious commitment is the more powerful in determining the shape of her stories precisely because it is never made overt merely in rhetoric. It exists, as strong commitments often do, in a form unspoken, inseparable from the very processes of her sight and feeling. She may be the only writer of English or American fiction in this century whose style, down to the very placing of a comma, is derived from a religious feeling for the simplest actualities. Obviously, being a religious writer in this way is different from anything in, say, Graham Greene, who merely lugs theological rhetoric into stories that were by nature best left as mildly entertaining adventures.

I cannot describe her very rare distinctions in this vein more clearly than she did in an essay called "The Fiction Writer and His Country": "I see," she wrote, "from the standpoint of Christian orthodoxy. This means that for me the meaning of life is centered in our Redemption by Christ and that what I see in the world I see in relation to that." To see the world from such a standpoint means caring about the possibilities of Redemption literally in what ones sees, in the grossest things, and it is no wonder, therefore, that she has such a sharp eye for the grotesqueness and the pathos of the most ordinary vanities. But the test is in the reading and for that nothing better illustrates her intensely applied power than the story **"Revelation."** It belongs with the few masterpieces of the form in English. (pp. 47-8)

Richard Poirier, "If You Know Who You Are You Can Go Anywhere," in Critical Essays on Flannery O'Connor, *edited by Melvin J. Friedman and Beverly Lyon Clark, G. K. Hall & Co., 1985, pp. 45-8.*

NAOMI BLIVEN (essay date 1965)

[*In her review of* Everything That Rises Must Converge, *excerpted below, Bliven praises O'Connor's prose style and suggests that the greatest limitation of the collection is the repetition of theme.*]

Being a Southern Catholic is not Miss O'Connor's most striking literary asset [in ***Everything That Rises Must Converge***]. Her language is: her prose is powerful, economical, and elegant. Her stories begin easily, and the elements she will mix in a tale—the characters, landscape, and conflicts—appear immediately, but the reader is not at first aware how briskly Miss O'Connor's language moves her narrative, because her style is an unmannered and exact translation of things into words. Her prose seems to accelerate as she propels her sinners toward destruction, and the reader has time only to respond as she wishes. (p. 220)

[Robert Fitzgerald's introduction] mentions objections a few people have raised to Miss O'Connor's work [see Additional Bibliography]. Somebody told him that Miss O'Connor lacked a sense of beauty, and several readers have claimed that her sticking to Southern people and places is a serious limitation. As for the beauty, it is hard to imagine what more the beauty lover wanted, unless it was descriptions of Tahitian sunsets. Miss O'Connor gives us beauty as it occurs: fleeting, as it proverbially is, or distractedly perceived, or, like the divine commands, rejected. In **"A View of the Woods"** she describes a greedy old man trying not to notice the beauty of a view because he has decided to sell the land from which he sees it. The second objection is nonsense. Miss O'Connor uses her native region as a concrete setting, but she is not a provincial writer. Or, if she is, her province is Christendom rather than the South.

The limitation I do find in these stories is that they seem more often than not the products of a very young imagination. Miss O'Connor's illness, which made her an invalid so early in life, undoubtedly prevented her from extending her observations and multiplying her experiences. In any case, the conflict between parent and child, the main theme of six of the nine stories, absorbs most of her attention. The struggle between generations is apt to engage people who still think of themselves as somebody's child. It is a topic most writers outgrow. Miss O'Connor's gallery of dependent children (some as old as thirty-five), each with his obtuse parent, lacks variety. Other kinds of people—lovers, say, or friends—are missing.

The severity of Miss O'Connor's judgments and the terrible punishments she awards her characters also seem to me marks of youthfulness, for the young are usually stern and disinclined to forgive such mediocre sins as hypocrisy and smugness. I find Miss O'Connor's exacting, uncompromising standards more youthful than doctrinal. The dooms she visits on her characters are frequently out of proportion to their offenses; unlike her prose, her catastrophes are forced. In two stories in this collection, **"The Enduring Chill"** and **"Revelation,"** the main characters are not destroyed but taught. They are the two funniest stories and the most clearly religious—**"Revelation"** is an illustration of "The last shall be first." These two are not only the most successful in this book, they are just about as good as short stories can be. I do not know what Miss O'Connor believed, but her collection shows God's mercies as more edifying than His punishments. (pp. 220-21)

Naomi Bliven, "Nothing But the Truth," in The New Yorker, *Vol. XLI, No. 30, September 11, 1965, pp. 220-21.*

STANLEY EDGAR HYMAN (essay date 1966)

[*As a longtime literary critic for the* New Yorker, *Hyman rose to prominence in American letters during the middle decades of the twentieth century. In the following excerpt from his* Flannery O'Connor, *one of the first detailed overviews of her work, Hyman describes the major themes and images of O'Connor's fiction. He also discusses her radical Christian dualism, her treatment of race, the limitations of her fiction, and her place in literary history.*]

In all her writing, Flannery O'Connor has certain preoccupations that seem almost obsessional. A few simple images recur so strikingly that every reader notices them: the flaming suns, the mutilated eyes, the "Jesus-seeing" hats, the colorful shirts. These images may be obsessive with the author, but they are used organically in the fiction. The sun in **"A Circle in the Fire"** is a symbol and specific foreshadowing of the boys' incendiary threat: "It was swollen and flame-colored and hung in a net of ragged cloud as if it might burn through any second and fall into the woods." The sunset in **"Greenleaf"** is another "swollen red ball," but as Mrs. May watches, "it began to narrow and pale until it looked like a bullet." It is narrow and pale to resemble the moon, since the bull first appeared to woo Mrs. May "silvered in the moonlight"; it looks like a bullet because the bull will soon come like a streak to penetrate her body, bull-bullet indeed.

A few recurrent symbols are more complex than these. One is the young preacher in bright blue suit and stern black hat. His principal embodiments are Hazel Motes and the False Prophet in *Wise Blood,* and the Bible salesman in **"Good Country People,"** but we see traces of him everywhere: the bright blue suit on the preacher who introduces the girl evangelist who tells Rayber that he is a damned soul in *The Violent;* the stern black hat on the old man in **"Judgement Day."** These are not simply a uniform, but emblems: the blue suit glares with raw Fundamentalist fervor, the black hat represents what the old man's daughter dismisses as "a lot of hardshell Baptist hooey." (p. 29)

The peacock is another complex symbol. It is central in **"The Displaced Person,"** but it appears in many places: the innocent deaf girl in **"The Life You Save May Be Your Own"** has "eyes as blue as a peacock's neck," and learns to say only one word, "bird"; Joy-Hulga is "as sensitive about the artificial leg as a peacock about his tail." . . . As the peacock was a personal image of the Second Coming for the old priest and of wealth for the old Judge in **"The Displaced Person,"** so it seems to have been a personal image of freedom and beauty (that is, of *art*) for Miss O'Connor. (pp. 29-30)

Another complex symbol can only be called, in acknowledgment of Miss O'Connor's debt, Georgia Snopesism. It is principally embodied in two families, the Shortleys in **"The Displaced Person"** and the Greenleafs in **"Greenleaf,"** but there is more than a touch of it in the Pritchards in **"A Circle in the Fire"** and the Freemans who are the "good country people" of the story of that title. These families of tenant farmers usually include a man who is stupid, incompetent, and malevolent; a wife with "a special fondness for the details of secret infections, hidden deformities, assaults upon children"; and two or more mindless and voracious children. More than any other figures in Miss O'Connor's work, these Snopes families are social, even class, symbols (as are their Mississippi counterparts in Faulkner). They represent the southern poor white class seen as intrinsically vicious. In the stories, they murder Mr. Guizac and let the bull gore Mrs. May; in our newspapers, they have other victims.

As this suggests, not only do images and symbols recur, but fixed groupings of people recur, and certain figures in these fixed groups are consistently travestied. Fitzgerald's introduction to ***Everything That Rises Must Converge*** [see Additional Bibliography] refers to what he calls the "family resemblance" shown by many of the characters in the stories and novels, but this is less a matter of recurrent figures than of recurrent relationships. One is the duo of practical mother and dreamy child on a dairy farm. In **"A Circle in the Fire"** they are a "very small and trim" woman and a "pale fat girl of twelve"; in **"Good Country People"** they are a mother who "had no bad qualities of her own but she was able to use other people's in such a constructive way that she never felt the lack," and Joy-Hulga; and so on. This mother and daughter are complementary in a curious fashion: each is caricatured as seen by the other, the resourceful widow as smug and empty, the arty child as useless and affected. In the later stories of ***Everything That Rises Must Converge,*** this pairing is varied. Mrs. May in **"Greenleaf"** has two sons, of whom only the younger is an intellectual, although the older manages to be equally unsatisfactory: he sells insurance, but it is "the kind that only Negroes buy." Mrs. Fox in **"The Enduring Chill"** similarly has two children, who between them compose the familiar character: Asbury has the artistic pretensions, his sister Mary George the scathing tongue. (pp. 30-1)

A relationship that does not involve mutual travesty is one between a boy and his mother's brother or father. . . . In **"The Artificial Nigger"** this pair becomes Mr. Head and his daughter's son Nelson. . . . In **"A View of the Woods,"** the pairing becomes mother's father and *girl.* In **"The Lame Shall Enter First,"** Rufus Johnson lives with his crazy grandfather (presumably his mother's father), until the old man goes off "with a remnant to the hills," to prepare against the destruction of the world by fiery flood. The point of this relationship is that the grandfather or uncle is the true father, and the grandson or nephew (however he resists it) is the true heir. This replacement of the father as authority by the mother's brother or father would be natural enough in the writing of an author whose father died in her childhood, but before settling for an autobiographical cause here we should notice that the mother's brother rather than the father as family authority is an important feature of primitive matriliny, and thus of much of our most resonant myth and legend.

The third set of characters is the trio of parent, child, and wolf cub. . . . We see it . . . in **"The Lame Shall Enter First,"** with Sheppard, Norton, and Rufus Johnson, and less satisfactorily in **"The Comforts of Home,"** with Thomas' mother, Thomas, and Star, the nymphomaniac girl the mother brings home. Travesty consistently accompanies this grouping, too, but here parent and child do not judge each other, but are both judged harshly by the outsider. . . . [Through] Rufus' eyes we see Sheppard as a blasphemous do-gooder and Norton as a spiritless nonentity. This is not so neat in **"The Comforts of Home,"** since "Star Drake" is too preposterous a character to judge anyone; essentially, there we see the absurd gullibility of Thomas' mother's absolute faith in human goodness through his eyes, and we similarly reject Thomas' absolute lack of charity as evidenced by his behavior.

Half a dozen important themes run through all Miss O'Connor's work. One is a profound equation of the mysteries of sex and religion. . . . As the title of **"A Temple of the Holy Ghost"** (a Christian metaphor for the body) makes clear, the story is centrally concerned with this equation. The twelve-year-old girl protagonist is initiated into sexual mystery by her older cousins, who tell her of the hermaphrodite they saw at the carnival; at the same time she imagines herself a Christian martyr in a Roman arena; when the sun goes down "like an elevated Host drenched in blood" to end the story, it is the blood of menstruation and childbirth as well as of martyrdom and Christ's Passion. The neatest of these sex-religion equations is Mrs. McIntyre's reaction, in **"The Displaced Person,"** to the priest's own equation of Christ and the peacock's tail: "Mrs. McIntyre's face assumed a set puritanical expression and she reddened. Christ in the conversation embarrassed her the way sex had her mother."

Another recurrent theme is change of identity, transformation, death-and-rebirth. Parker in **"Parker's Back"** is transformed by the tattoo, but most often in the fiction transformation occurs by renaming. Harry Ashfield becomes Bevel, who counts, in **"The River"**; Joy chooses a way of life by becoming Hulga in **"Good Country People"**; . . . even Parker needs a baptismal name change from O. E. to Obadiah Elihue to be fully transformed. (pp. 31-3)

Miss O'Connor's principal theme is what Walter Allen in *Esprit* [see *Esprit* entry in Additional Bibliography] excellently calls "a world of the God-intoxicated." . . . Miss O'Connor's male characters are God-intoxicated in a variety of ways. Those who have found their calling as preachers articulate the author's radical dualism. The preacher in **"The River"** challenges: "Believe Jesus or the devil! . . . Testify to one or the other!" Old Tarwater [in *The Violent Bear It Away*] similarly rejects everything not Christ as anti-Christ. We see a youthful version of this figure in Rufus Johnson. Rejecting salvation from Sheppard, Rufus hisses: "Nobody can save me but Jesus." "If I do repent, I'll be a preacher," he says. "If you're going to do it, it's no sense in doing it half way." Sheppard sees him as "a small black figure on the threshold of some dark apocalypse." Rufus may continue to choose the devil, . . . or he may yet accept the call. . . . (p. 34)

One way that intoxication with God expresses itself . . . is Satanism. The Misfit in **"A Good Man Is Hard to Find"** is a ruthless killer because "Jesus thown everything off balance." The Misfit preaches the same radical Christian dualism from a different pulpit: "If He did what He said, then it's nothing for you to do but thow away everything and follow Him, and if He didn't, then it's nothing for you to do but enjoy the few minutes you got left the best way you can—by killing somebody or burning down his house or doing some other meanness to him. No pleasure but meanness." The Misfit has chosen the second alternative, but he admits at the end of the story, after wiping out the harmless family, "It's no real pleasure in life." (pp. 34-5)

Another form God-intoxication paradoxically takes is Rationalism. The first of these antagonists in Miss O'Connor's work is the enigmatic figure of Mr. Paradise in **"The River,"** who comes to the healings to mock and to display his unhealed cancerous ear, but who always comes. He is a curious ritual figure, the ceremonial scoffer, the Bishop of Misrule, and his shepherd's crook as mock-pastor is the giant peppermint stick with which he tries to save Harry from his death. (p. 35)

If the male characters are all God-intoxicated, the female characters in Flannery O'Connor's fiction are mainly self-intoxicated. Smugness and self-satisfaction, often represented by women, is another important theme. Here is Mrs. Cope in **"A Circle in the Fire"** talking to Mrs. Pritchard: "'Every day I say a prayer of thanksgiving,' Mrs. Cope said. 'Think of all we have. Lord,' she said and sighed, 'we have everything.'" The hoodlum boys who bring her to judgment state the truth she has forgotten: "Man, Gawd owns them woods and her too." Mrs. Cope, reciting all they have to be thankful for, "a litany of her blessings," becomes the monstrous comic figure of Mrs. Turpin in **"Revelation."** When she proclaims in the doctor's waiting room, "Thank you, Jesus, for making everything the way it is!" the Wellesley girl springs at her throat with a howl. . . .

[Miss O'Connor's] dualism relates to another theme, the transvaluation of values in which progress in the world is retrogression in the spirit. When Mr. Shiftlet in **"The Life You Save May Be Your Own"** tells the old woman, "the monks of old slept in their coffins!" she replies, "They wasn't as advanced as we are." This is Miss O'Connor's standard joke. (p. 36)

It is thus necessary to imitate the monks of old, to deny the world, and Naysaying is another of Flannery O'Connor's major themes. . . . Mary Fortune [in **"A View of the Woods"**] denies that anyone has ever whipped her or ever could, although her grandfather has just seen her whipped; "I don't need no new shoe," Rufus Johnson insists to Sheppard, with his clubfoot barely covered by the old torn shoe. These lying denials are a higher truth, the truth of the spirit that contradicts the weakness of the flesh. (p. 37)

Miss O'Connor is said to have been pleased when the London *Times* identified her as a "theological" writer. As a fiction-writing theologian, she seems the most radical Christian dualist since Dostoevski. There are two of everything in her work, one Christ's and one anti-Christ's. . . . There are two rivers in **"The River,"** one "the rich red river of Jesus' Blood," the other the mundane river in which Mr. Paradise appears "like some ancient water monster." There are two fires in **"A Circle in the Fire,"** one the fiery furnace in which the prophets dance, "in the circle the angel had cleared for them," the other set in the woods by the boys. (pp. 37-8)

Two more thematic consequences of Flannery O'Connor's radical Christian dualism remain to be noticed. One is the False Christ. . . . The car Mr. Shiftlet acquires by marrying and deserting the deaf girl is . . . a substitute Christ; when he finally gets it running "He had an expression of serious modesty on his face as if he had just raised the dead." Mr. Shiftlet explains his philosophy to the old woman: "The body, lady, is like a house: it don't go anywhere; but the spirit, lady, is like a automobile: always on the move." Thomas in **"The Comforts of Home"** and Sheppard in **"The Lame Shall Enter First"** do not have false Christs, they *are* false Christs.

The remaining Christian theme is best put by St. Paul in I Corinthians 1: 25, "Because the foolishness of God is wiser than men," and 3: 19, "For the wisdom of this world is foolishness with God." The way to wisdom is through folly as the way to sanctity is through sin. Old Tarwater, taken to the insane asylum in a straitjacket for his wild prophesying, is God's Fool, and young Tarwater's vision of following "the bleeding stinking mad shadow of Jesus" hinges on the same paradox: Jesus' way is mad only by "the wisdom of this world."

Protestant Fundamentalism is thus Miss O'Connor's metaphor, in literary terms, for Roman Catholic truth (in theological terms, this reflects ecumenicism). (pp. 38-9)

As a Catholic born and brought up in Georgia, Miss O'Connor always insisted, not only on her right to the imagery of southern Protestantism, but on its peculiar fitness for her as a Catholic. In a letter, she wrote: "Now the South is a good place for a

Catholic literature in my sense for a number of reasons. 1) In the South belief can still be made believable and in relation to a large part of the society. We're not the Bible Belt for nothing. 2) The Bible being generally known and revered in the section, gives the novelist that broad mythical base to refer to that he needs to extend his meaning in depth. 3) The South has a sacramental view of life. . . . 4) The aspect of Protestantism that is most prominent (at least to the Catholic) in the South is that of man dealing with God directly, not through the mediation of the church, and this is great for the Catholic novelist like myself who wants to get close to his character and watch him wrestle with the Lord.'' (pp. 40-1)

[On the race question,] Miss O'Connor maintained a consistent public silence. There are, however, curious symbolic statements in her work. ''Her fiction does not reflect the social issues, particularly the racial problems, which beset the South during her lifetime,'' says John J. Clarke in *Esprit* [see *Esprit* entry in Additional Bibliography]. I think that it does, and more powerfully and truly than that of anyone else, but the expression is always implicit, covert, cryptic. As her mad prophets are metaphoric for Roman Catholic truth, so in a sense all the fierce violence in her work is metaphoric for violence done the Negro. (p. 41)

The Negroes in the stories are seen externally, as a conventional white southern lady would see them, with no access to their concealed sensibility, but occasionally one of them will say something (there are several such remarks in **''The Displaced Person''**) that shows how much the author knows about that sensibility. Negroes in the fiction sometimes carry profound spiritual meaning, as in **''The Artificial Nigger.''** . . . In several stories, and in the fragment of the unfinished novel [''Why the Heathens Rage''], Negroes are images of fraternity. In the deepest sense, Harry in **''The River,''** who goes to his death because he wants to *count,* or Norton in **''The Lame Shall Enter First,''** who hangs himself because he wants to be *some*-where, are symbols for Negro aspirations and frustrations; they are symbolic Negroes or ''artificial niggers,'' in fact, and the author knew it. (pp. 41-2)

It is not easy to place Flannery O'Connor in a literary tradition. The writer to whom she is most indebted stylistically, Mark Twain, is never mentioned in discussions of her work, nor did she ever identify him as an influence, so far as I know. Yet if *The Violent Bear It Away* has any single progenitor, it is *Adventures of Huckleberry Finn.* Miss O'Connor's mature writing has very little to do with Faulkner or any of what is called ''southern'' literature. The writer who most influenced her, at least in her first books, is Nathanael West. . . . The European writer Flannery O'Connor most profoundly resembles (in method, not in scale) is Dostoevski. Like him she created a deeply understood Enemy out of her own liberal and enlightened dreams. ''Ivan Karamazov cannot believe,'' she wrote in her introduction to *A Memoir of Mary Ann,* ''as long as one child is in torment''—no more can Rayber or Sheppard, she might have added. (p. 43)

The strengths of Flannery O'Connor's writing are those qualities in it that have been most disliked and attacked: the apocalyptic violence, the grotesque vision, the vulgarity. ''Her novels suffer, I believe, from an excessive violence of conception,'' Warren Coffey wrote in *Esprit* [see *Esprit* entry in Additional Bibliography], contrasting them with her stories. But it is precisely this violence in the novels—these murders and burnings, blindings and rapes—that is the heart of their imaginative power, as is murder in Dostoevski's novels. It is the violence of desperate Christianity, of the desperate and verbally inarticulate South, of a nation no longer quiet about its desperation. William Esty wrote scornfully, in *Commonweal,* of Flannery O'Connor's ''cult of the Gratuitous Grotesque'' [see Additional Bibliography]. Her fiction is grotesque, certainly, but never gratuitously so. For example, in the opening scene of **''The Lame Shall Enter First,''** Norton eats a piece of chocolate cake spread with peanut butter and ketchup; when his father gets him upset, he vomits it all up in ''a limp sweet batter.'' This is not only grotesque but thoroughly repulsive, and no less repulsive to the author, but it is entirely functional and necessary in the story: it perfectly symbolizes the indigestible mess of Sheppard's ''enlightened'' views, which Norton will similarly be unable to keep down. (p. 44)

We must not ignore the weaknesses of Flannery O'Connor's fiction. Her stories came to rely too often and too mechanically on death to end them. The deaths are ruinous to **''A View of the Woods,''** and unnecessary in other stories. Her best stories—**''The Artificial Nigger,'' ''Good Country People,'' ''Parker's Back''**—neither end in death nor need to. One reason for her melodramatic endings seems to be theological. ''I'm a born Catholic and death has always been brother to my imagination,'' Miss O'Connor told an interviewer in *Jubilee,* ''I can't imagine a story that doesn't properly end in it or in its foreshadowings.'' It was one of her rare confusions of theology with aesthetics.

These endings result from a misjudgment in craft, as do those occasions—in **''Good Country People''** and **''A View of the Woods''**—in which she runs on past a story's natural finish. Other than these, the only fault in her fiction is a tendency to travesty. Caricature is a legitimate resource of art, and a magnificently effective one in her hands, but her caricature sometimes fell into over-caricature and lost its truth, so that we cannot believe in the existence of certain of her secular intellectuals or Negroes. If they are not people, they cannot function as symbols, since, as she says in the lecture on the grotesque, ''It is the nature of fiction not to be good for much else unless it is good in itself.'' (p. 45)

Few of Flannery O'Connor's readers, few even of her Roman Catholic readers, can share her desperate and radical Christian dualism, as she was fully aware. But it constituted a natural dramatism for fiction, as did Dostoevski's religion, and a fiction in no sense parochial. As a writer she had the additional advantage, as West did, of multiple alienation from the dominant assumptions of our culture: he was an outsider as a Jew, and doubly an outsider as a Jew alienated from other Jews; she was comparably an outsider as a woman, a southerner, and a Roman Catholic in the South. This is not to say that her views, or her alienation, produced the fiction; many have held more radical views, and been far more alienated, while producing nothing. Her gifts produced the fiction, but her situation gave them opportunities, and enabled her to exercise her intelligence, imagination, and craft most effectively. (p. 46)

Stanley Edgar Hyman, in his Flannery O'Connor, *University of Minnesota Press, Minneapolis, 1966, 48 p.*

ROBERT DRAKE (essay date 1966)

[In his Flannery O'Connor, *Drake, an American critic, views O'Connor's fiction specifically in light of her religious faith. In the following excerpt, the critic considers O'Connor's Christian orthodoxy and its implications for her as a modern artist. He*

discusses her depiction of God's grace through the grotesque and touches upon her limitations as a writer, including a discussion of the problem of the non-believer confronting O'Connor's work.]

In the essay "The Fiction Writer and His Country" . . . , Flannery O'Connor made her Christian commitment as an artist absolutely plain:

> I see from the standpoint of Christian orthodoxy. This means that for me the meaning of life is centered in our Redemption by Christ and that what I see in the world I see in its relation to that. I don't think that this is a position that can be taken halfway or one that is particularly easy in these times to make transparent in fiction.

In the same essay she also observed:

> I have heard it said that belief in Christian dogma is a hindrance to the writer, but I myself have found nothing further from the truth. Actually, it forces the storyteller to observe. It is not a set of rules which fixes what he sees in the world. It affects his writing primarily by guaranteeing his respect for mystery.

And, again in the same essay, she concluded:

> The novelist with Christian concerns will find in modern life distortions which are repugnant to him, and his problem will be to make these appear as distortions to an audience which is used to seeing them as natural; and he may well be forced to take ever more violent means to get his vision across to this hostile audience. When you can assume that your audience holds the same beliefs you do, you can relax a little and use more normal ways of talking to it; when you have to assume that it does not, then you have to make your vision apparent by shock—to the hard of hearing you shout, and for the almost blind you draw large and startling figures.

These three statements categorically define Miss O'Connor's conception of her role as a writer with "Christian concerns." Indeed, one might conclude that she throws them down almost like a gauntlet: if this be treason, make the most of it. And treason or heresy it is to many contemporary writers and critics, who, commendably shying away from the concept of literature-as-ideology, assume that the further any writer can get from any kind of dogmatic commitment (unless perhaps to some kind of vague humanitarianism), the better an artist he is apt to be. But these three statements go a long way—in so far as *any* writer can be taken as speaking definitively about his own work—toward explaining Miss O'Connor's "concerns" as an artist, both thematically and structurally. For her these opinions were fundamental and in no way "negotiable," and any serious consideration of her work must start there. (pp. 13-14)

[Miss O'Connor] has no truck with fashionable existentialist *Angst*—Christian or otherwise. She apprehends man's predicament in terms of classical Christian theology; and she uses the traditional terms without flinching: *sin, grace, redemption, Heaven, Hell,* and all the rest. Furthermore, she often seems to regard her function as prophetic or evangelistic and no bones about it: she *has,* in a sense, come to call the wicked to repentance—and none more so than the modern intellectuals who have no use for Christianity, the Church, or its traditional

O'Connor at twelve. She once wrote: "I was a very ancient twelve . . . I am much younger now than I was at twelve, or anyway, less burdened. The weight of the centuries lies on children, I'm sure of it." The Flannery O'Connor Collection, Ina Dillard Russell Library, Georgia College.

doctrines. And this may be what does limit her audience: she makes a crucial problem of *belief*. And the fact that she was writing in what has been called the post-Christian world (as Dante or even Milton were not) may have forced her, as she herself intimated, to adopt the violent methods of shock tactics, to draw bolder and bolder *cartoons* rather than representational or realistic sketches.

But by no means is this to say that Miss O'Connor was writing programmatic or propagandistic fiction: if she had been, she would not have written nearly so well. She does not oversimplify either her characters or the dilemmas which confront them, or the conflicts in which they are involved. And she certainly does not offer Christianity as the simple solution or the pat answer to their anguish: if anything, it's quite the reverse—as indeed it is in the Gospels themselves. Miss O'Connor was not writing just tracts for the times, though, in the broadest sense, her fiction is that too. But her vision of man in this world *was* uncompromisingly Christian; she saw all of life in Christian terms; she thought the Gospels were really *true;* and she accepted the historic teachings of the Church. And this intellectual and philosophical position informed everything she wrote. She was not trying to "sell" Christianity; she was—as indeed any writer is—trying to "sell" her particular perception of life in this world as valid. (pp. 15-16)

Certainly, it does not seem true, as has been once or twice suggested, that Miss O'Connor was a sophisticated Roman

[Catholic] making sport with the eccentricities and grotesqueries of her good Southern Baptist brethren. Such a charge is quite wide of the mark. If anything, she seems to take a grim ironic pleasure in siding *with* the Southern fundamentalists against the modern, will-ful intellectuals and the genteel, self-sufficient schemers who are her greatest villains. The Southern Baptists, the Holy Rollers may be violent or grotesque or at times even ridiculous; but, she implies, they are a whole lot nearer the truth than the more "enlightened" but godless intellectuals or even the respectable do-gooders and church-goers who look on the Church as some sort of glorified social service institution while preferring to ignore its pricklier doctrines. Occasionally, her misguided characters take a more muddled view, falling between these two extremes, like Mrs. Shortley of **"The Displaced Person"**:

> She had never given much thought to the devil for she felt that religion was essentially for those people who didn't have the brains to avoid evil without it. For people like herself, for people of gumption, it was a social occasion providing the opportunity to sing; but if she had ever given it much thought, she would have considered the devil the head of it and God the hanger-on.

Significantly, Mrs. Shortley's son, H. C., "was going to Bible school now and when he finished he was going to start him a church. He had a strong sweet voice for hymns and could sell anything."

In the light of these observations, then, Miss O'Connor's major theme should come as no surprise to us. It is that the Christian religion is a very shocking, indeed a scandalous business ("bidness" some of her characters would say) and that its Savior is an offense and a stumbling block, even a "bleeding stinking mad" grotesque to many. He "upsets the balance around here"; He "puts the bottom rail on top"; He makes the first last and the last first. In short, He revolutionizes the whole Creation and turns the whole world upside down, to the scandal of those who believe that two plus two always equals four (and, with craft, possibly five) or those who believe that they don't need any outside help (a savior) because they're doing all right by themselves. And this Christ comes not lamb-like and meek, as a rule, but in terrifying glory, riding the whirlwind: He is more like Eliot's "Christ the tiger" than gentle Jesus meek and mild. There is nothing sweet or sentimental about Him, and He terrifies before He can bless. Jesus Christ is finally the principal character in all Miss O'Connor's fiction, whether offstage or, in the words and actions of her characters, very much on. And their encounter with Him is the one story she keeps telling over and over again.

This theme, along with several related sub-themes, constitutes the principal burden of Miss O'Connor's work; and, even when it is not obvious, it is usually lurking in the background (like her Christ), ready to spring out to confront her rationalists and do-gooders (and the reader) with its grisly imperative: "Choose you this day whom ye will serve." And it is impossible, implies Miss O'Connor, to blink the issue: there is no place for Laodiceans in her world. For this reason, her fiction, though carefully ordered, even sedate and regular in its narrative progressions, has often the urgent intensity, the ordered ferocity, even, of a dramatic but sober evangelistic sermon. And one feels that, in her continuing insistence on the immediacy and importance of the Four Last Things, she recaptures (as indeed the fundamentalist sects try to do) something of the pentecostal atmosphere of the Primitive Church.

Indeed, the world of Miss O'Connor's fiction seems to wait hourly for Judgment Day—or some new revelation or perhaps a transfiguration, in any case, some sign that the Almighty is still "in charge here." Exactly *what* the event will be is not so important as that her world is subject to the continuous supervision of the Management, who makes itself known sometimes quietly and sedately but, more often here, in a "purifying terror." (pp 16-18)

But what about the imagery and the forms in which [Miss O'Connor's] unsettling visions are embodied?

The discerning reader notices again and again in her works what seems to be almost a predilection for the grotesque as manifested in physical or mental *deformity*. Characters sometimes have one leg or one arm missing, sometimes a club foot or a cast in one eye. Sometimes they are deaf-mutes, lunatics, mental defectives, even hermaphrodites. Frequently, also, Miss O'Connor even manages to suggest physical or mental deformity in her seemingly undeformed characters by comparing them or their appurtenances to that which is inanimate or non-human—for example, the wife in **"A Good Man Is Hard to Find,"** "whose face was as broad and innocent as a cabbage," with her "green head-kerchief that had two points on the top like rabbit's ears." (p. 38)

In [Miss O'Connor's] view, physical or mental deformity of the outward and visible sort always suggests inner, spiritual deformity. And when she compares man to the non-human, she is suggesting that his efforts to assert his own will, to provide his own "savior," make him into just that—*non-human,* sometimes even *inhuman*. Human beings are most *human* and their personalities as individuals are most nearly fulfilled, she implies, when they remember the Source of all Humanity, the Fountain of all Life and Light Whose creatures they are. And, for Christians, at least one aspect of the Incarnation is God's revelation in Christ of what true *humanity,* true *personality* can be for all of us. (p. 39)

[An] aspersion against Miss O'Connor, often made along with the charge of her insistence on deformity, is that her stories have little that is beautiful in them. True it is that Miss O'Connor's characters often have little of physical beauty about them. And often the natural world itself seems ugly, if not downright sinister or hostile, with ominous turnip-shaped clouds lowering overhead and the sun "like a furious white blister in the sky." But more often it is not nature itself which is ugly here but, rather, what man *has made of nature*. . . . [At] least one critic has noted that the sordid winding streets of Atlanta in **"The Artificial Nigger"** suggest the labyrinthine circles of Dante's Hell. (pp. 39-40)

Some of Miss O'Connor's more villainous characters . . . are apt to look on nature as something which can be controlled and mastered, finally perhaps even exploited. To them, it may be just one more *commodity;* it certainly holds no particular *mystery* for them. In **"A Circle in the Fire,"** to the strong-willed Mrs. Cope (surely the name is significant here), "her Negroes were as destructive and impersonal as the nut grass." And this same impiety toward nature may, as the foregoing quotation implies, carry with it an impiety towards others of God's creatures.

A quite different view is represented in the old priest of **"The Displaced Person,"** who marvels at the transfigured beauty of a peacock's raised tail. . . . (p. 40)

The natural world is mysterious and strange, Miss O'Connor implies, sometimes baffling, ugly, even disgusting. In any case, it's surely a "fallen" one. And it is for her very much as it was for Hopkins: bleared and seared by man, wearing his smudge and sharing his smell. But always over this brown bent world there broods the Holy Ghost, with His warm breast and bright wings, blessing and sanctifying our smudged world and lightening our darkness, whether in rest and quietness or in the blinding revelation of the Damascus Road.

Perhaps, to sum it all up, no sentence Miss O'Connor ever wrote better embodies her attitude toward the Creation than one Robert Fitzgerald has pointed out [in his introduction to ***A Good Man Is Hard to Find;*** see Additional Bibliography] in **"A Good Man Is Hard To Find":** "The trees were full of silver-white sunlight and the meanest of them sparkled." Surely, surely the operative word here is *meanest*. Miss O'Connor's view then of both man and nature is thoroughly sacramental. If man's body, no matter how warped or deformed, is a temple of the Holy Ghost, the earth also is the Lord's and the fullness thereof. And man violates neither with impunity.

Miss O'Connor's awareness of the ugly, the perverse, and the grotesque is further reflected in her prose style, which at times seems deliberately plain and graceless, sometimes even cacophonous. One might almost say that she had a healthy respect for the ugly—for all that had not been lightened, brightened, and de-odorized by secularism and by de-humanizing "efficiency" and "progress." For her, the Old Adam is *still* a pretty hairy creature. But ugliness, like vulgarity, for which she once observed that she had a "natural talent," is often a sign of vitality, even if it's vitality gone wrong. And, for Miss O'Connor, ugliness was usually preferable to the desiccated decorum of death—and damnation. (Her lady-villains insist particularly, as a rule, on decorum.) But such "decorum" represents not so much a clean, well-lighted soul as it does a whited sepulchre.

Occasionally, also, Miss O'Connor's deliberate awkwardness and cacophony of style remind one of Donne or Hopkins—a stylistic comparison which may suggest a further, thematic resemblance to those two poets of the warped and the skew. They, also, knew a freak when they saw it; and they, also, knew something of the terrible speed of mercy.

Perhaps, finally, it is with such major-minor figures in our literature that Miss O'Connor will be ranked. Her range was narrow, and perhaps she had only one story to tell. (But then didn't Hemingway?) But each time she told it, she told it with renewed imagination and cogency. From some of her remarks in conversation a year before her death, one might have gathered that she had grown tired of her one story, was even perhaps desperately trying to find another one—or perhaps some new way of re-telling the old one. Speculation about what the result of this search might have been is, of course, profitless. But one feels almost certain that, whatever form her possible "new" story might have taken, her fundamental assumptions—and perhaps her methods—would have remained substantially unchanged.

What *is* important is that she remains absolutely unique in American fiction, more skilled perhaps as a short story writer than as a novelist. (She does seem to lose some depth or density of texture in the longer fictional form.) But her vision and her methods were distinctively her own; and her rage for the *holy*—and the *whole*—has left its indelible mark on our literature and our literary consciousness.

What then about those readers who do not—or can not—share Miss O'Connor's "Christian concerns"? How far can they enter into both the substance and the shadow of her work? There *does* seem a point beyond which such readers, even with the best will in the world, finally cannot go: they cannot honestly share the theological assumptions which *are* part of her *donnée*. Some tension in that quarter does seem inevitable, and perhaps finally does deny her the complete acceptance of some very discriminating readers.

And yet, as she herself once indicated, no really good story can be ultimately "accounted for" in terms of a right theology—even for the deeply committed Christian writer or reader. (Such a view as this would certainly set her apart from the programmatic writer with "Christian concerns.") If it's a good story, it's not the theology as such which makes it so, even for the reader who is a professing Christian. Presumably, then, what makes Miss O'Connor's stories good and at times brilliant is that, in her own way, she does seem to have man's number—and the world's. People *are* often as she says; and they *do* often express themselves, in violent words and actions, as she represents them, and not just in darkest Georgia either.

Many non-Christian readers would have finally to agree that Miss O'Connor's diagnosis of the human condition—or predicament—is substantially valid: man does seem "warped" away from *something*, and he does seem to need reconciling with that *something* somehow, perhaps even by violent force. Furthermore, it often does appear in this world that those who are furthest on the way to some sort of reconciliation, nearest to some sort of ruling principle which, after darkness and terror, makes for light and order and peace, seem like extremely unlikely or even unappetizing customers; they truly often seem the least of us all. For such readers, of course, the Good News that this reconciliation is impossible for man to achieve on his own but that it has already been made for him in Christ is literally too good (or illogical? or absurd?) to be true. There they must finally part company with Miss O'Connor. But though they cannot choose here the one thing needful, they find nevertheless that she speaks dark home truths to their hearts, though often in a language which is foreign to them and difficult for them to understand. But Miss O'Connor's Georgia, though often terrible and dark, is no foreign country, finally, for any of us; none of us, finally, is a stranger there. If it *is* foreign, it is foreign only as this world itself is foreign to those of us who feel that our "true country" lies elsewhere. (pp. 41-4)

Robert Drake, in his Flannery O'Connor: A Critical Essay, *William B. Eerdmans/Publisher, 1966, 48 p.*

JOSEPHINE HENDIN (essay date 1970)

[Hendin wrote a controversial study of O'Connor's work based partially on biographical-psychological speculation and interpretation. In the following excerpt, from a chapter that does not adhere to the psychological-biographical approach, Hendin examines duality in "The Life You Save May Be Your Own."]

Conflict appears in [***A Good Man Is Hard to Find***] as the duality of matter and spirit, the body and the mind. Although many an American writer before her has been preoccupied with this peculiar, almost Manichean, duality, O'Connor's conception and resolution of the problem are unique. (p. 62)

[**"The Life You Save May Be Your Own"**] describes the gap between physical and spiritual life or, in other words, the incommensurability of facts and essences. . . . O'Connor consistently opposes the spiritual and physical, keeping them so separate and dual that no one seems to have both a mind and body at the same time. Never mingling or reaching equilibrium, they seem . . . locked in an endless struggle for supremacy. The alternation appears in style as an uneasy wavering between symbolism, allegory, and literal description. (pp. 62-3)

[**"The Life You Save May Be Your Own"**] is a good example of the tendency of O'Connor's real portraits to overpower her allegorical ones. That she obviously hoped to give symbolic overtones to the story is suggested by Shiftlet's figure forming a crooked cross against the sky, his occupation as an itinerant carpenter, his assertion that the spirit is more important than the body, his teaching Lucynell what might be a Holy Ghost reference, the word "bird," and his association with sun and light imagery. What emerges most powerfully in the story is more literal: a landscape of a withered universe reduced to the size of a small farm, bounded by three mountains and a chicken coop. Everyone in it is in some way warped or deformed; its air is thick and so dusty that clouds grow in it like turnips.

The owner of the world is Mrs. Crater, whose name suggests the abyss in a dwarfed universe. The abyss is sheer mortality, the inescapable crater of the grave. Mrs. Crater is associated with time and decay, with the whole of the organic world in decline. She is not a cedar, symbol of wealth and prosperity, but is "the size of a cedar fence post," a durable bit of weathered wood. When she reminds Shiftlet of his physical being, calling him a homeless, disabled drifter, "the ugly words settled in Mr. Shiftlet's head like a group of buzzards on top of a tree." These are the vultures of Shiftlet's mind, birds that remind him of his mortality.

Denying the relevance of the body, Shiftlet greets Lucynell as though she were not afflicted, offers Mrs. Crater chewing gum although she has no teeth, and ignores his own problem. His own body emerges slowly from the road through bright sunlight that first screens it and then turns it into a silhouette of a crooked cross until he comes near, when he looks like "a bird that had come up very close." After Lucynell thinks of him as a bird, he spots the old automobile. The bird and car are images for Shiftlet, who is always associated with motion, speed, and detachment. When he learns the car stopped running when Mr. Crater died, he comments on the mystery of life, the enigma of the heart and, perhaps, of love. He tells about an Atlanta doctor who cut out a human heart and held it in his hand "and studied it like it was a day-old chicken, and lady, . . . he don't know more about it than you or me."

The dissection of the heart in Atlanta is the first of four dissections in the story. Shiftlet tries to probe the mystery of flame, lighting a match and staring at it until it seems about to burn his fingers and nose. Unable to solve the enigma of flame, he begins to anatomize himself into the possible selves he contains. He demands of Mrs. Crater

> "How you know my name ain't Aaron Sparks, lady, and I come from Singleberry, Georgia, or how you know it's not George Speeds and I come from Lucy, Alabama, or how you know I ain't Thompson Bright from Toolafalls, Mississippi?"

Shiftlet may be all of these. Like Aaron, his embodiment of spirit, his god, is an object—not a golden calf but an automobile. Sparks and Bright suggest fire and light, with which he is associated in imagery. Speeds, like his association with birds, drifting, and motion defines what he thinks of as spirit: constant motion. All of these names suit him as well as Shiftlet.

For Mrs. Crater, a man is what he does—what tools he carries in his box. When she tells him she cannot pay for his carpentry, he says that some things mean more to him than money. Yet, in imagery, when he says this he suggests the opposite. Lucynell watches the "trigger that moved up and down in his neck" hearing words spoken like bullets, denials of the material world. Yet his life is remarkably literal. He has been in the "Arm Service" and lost a serviceable arm. While he insists the world seems whole only in desolate country where he can see the sunset, his eyes keep returning to the automobile gleaming in the dark. When Mrs. Crater offers it to him as a house, Shiftlet likens it to the coffins monks sleep in. As death is to the monks, so the car is to him, a way of life. . . . [He] likes living in a car. It gives him a place to "be" while he thinks of moving around.

On Mrs. Crater's farm, O'Connor's microcosmic universe, Shiftlet repairs the fence and steps, and works up to his most spectacular feat, the resurrection of the car. Like the Atlanta doctor, he cuts up its insides after he "raised the hood and studied its mechanism." He repairs it by a kind of inspiration, a mechanical afflatus: a fan belt. As the car begins to move, Mrs. Crater begins pushing Lucynell, who yells "burrddttt!" over and over. The life Shiftlet saves is not his own but is the life of his ideal self-image, the car.

When Mrs. Crater explicitly tells him to marry Lucynell, and reminds him she is offering a home to a lone, disabled man, he answers

> "Lady, a man is divided into two parts, body and spirit. . . . The body, lady, is like a house: it don't go anywhere; but the spirit, lady, is like a automobile, always on the move, always."

When Mrs. Crater reminds him of the comforts of her home, agrees to let him paint the car, and gives him money for his honeymoon, she figuratively gilds his calf, his idol. The similitude between the car and spirit disappears into metaphor: the car *is* spirit or motion.

Nothing but paper work and blood tests, Shiftlet's marriage is too physical for him. Leaving Mrs. Crater at her farm, he drives as fast as he can toward Mobile. He abandons Lucynell without malice or pleasure, leaving her in the Hot Spot at a time when things are getting hot for him, when his fantasy of himself as a good man is about to be threatened as his detachment is threatened by the presence of a woman for the night. Perhaps he fears that "sly isolated little thought like a shoot of green in the desert" that changes Lucynell's placid expression.

After he abandons Lucynell, the feelings he cannot demonstrate are objectified in a real encounter and in the description O'Connor provides of the real world. The story becomes a projection of his emotional state. His perception of the world gradually changes, becoming more childlike. He sees that "deep in the sky a storm was preparing very slowly and without thunder as if it meant to drain every drop of air from the earth before it broke." The storm suggests Shiftlet's quiet, affectless cruelty as much as it prepares for the rainfall to come. The sun, first appearing in the story as shapeless light, then as a sphere balanced on a mountain, then as a visitor of the chicken coop, is now a ball, a child's toy. It rolls toward him "directly in front of the automobile. It was a reddening ball that through his windshield was slightly flat on the bottom and top." After seeing the sun as a ball, he sees a boy who he knows intuitively is a hitch-hiker and whose "hat was set on his head in a way to indicate that he had left somewhere for good."

His encounter with the boy offers an objective recapitulation of his own abandonment of the security of Mrs. Crater's farm and, as we learn, of his own abandonment of his mother. Like Lucynell, his mother was an "angel of Gawd" whom he deserted. He has persistently denied the significance of the heart (love) and the blood (kinship). Yet he was deeply hurt by the word "milk" when Mrs. Crater told him not to try to milk her any more. While denying the value of what she gives, he cannot stop himself from taking it. Perhaps he is so pained by Mrs. Crater's unwillingness to be milked because he needs as much mother's milk as he can get. While running away from his wife and mother-in-law Shiftlet meets himself running away from home as a child.

His loathing of his own body is so great that he can love only a machine, a car that can carry a woman who is an "angel of Gawd" but permits him to run away before she becomes a sexual being. By seeing his wife and mother as angels who cannot and should not be touched, he evades his own sexual fear, justifying it as a sign of his moral sense and spiritual bias.

Instead of escaping from his body, from a sense of organic decay, he is literally drowning in mud. Through thick and suffocating air lit dimly by a sun like a child's toy, the boy calls his own mother a stinking polecat and Shiftlet's a fleabag. Shiftlet feels the rottenness of the world lies in its physicality—in both its vegetable and animal life. He resents that even clouds can be the color of a boy's hat, that some human element can put the lid on him and the world, and that he is cosmically confined in his own mortality. As the turnip-cloud descends he appeals to God to help him, to "break forth and wash the slime from this earth!" He is answered not by a human God but by a kind of eternal machine that guffaws, explodes in thunder, and lets a shower of metal fall. "Fantastic raindrops, like tin-can tops, crashed over the rear of Mr. Shiftlet's car." Shiftlet is restored. He sticks his stump out the window of the car, touching the only substance he can touch: rain like tin, rain like part of the metallic world. Racing toward Mobile, the only city in the state looking out on the open sea, he drives toward motion unlimited by clay. (pp. 63-9)

Josephine Hendin, in her The World of Flannery O'Connor, *Indiana University Press, 1970, 177 p.*

KATHLEEN FEELEY (essay date 1972)

[In the following excerpt from her noted theological study of O'Connor, Feeley considers comic perversion in "Good Country People" and explores O'Connor's perception of the "numinous quality of reality" in "The Artificial Nigger."]

Perhaps it was [Flannery O'Connor's] utter truthfulness which, paradoxically, allowed her to imagine and create characters who have destroyed their own integrity to pursue a false good. In a catalog of her freaks, characters who re-create themselves according to a chosen image would mark an extreme position. They are farthest away from grace because they lack the truthful appraisal of reality which grace demands. They have set up a false god—education, or art, or economic security, or comfort—and they falsify their very being in order to pay it homage. A number of Flannery O'Connor's short stories show her imagination working on the idea of falseness in a character. Some of the protagonists in these stories look perfectly normal; others have a physical deformity which is symbolic of a spiritual one. In the course of the action, all are given an opportunity to recognize their self-deception. In the author's vision, this recognition is the first step toward truth, which is, in turn, the necessary condition of Redemption. Conversion—a change of direction—is possible only after one recognizes his perversion.

Comic perversion is a key concept in **"Good Country People."** Both the girl Joy-Hulga and the Bible salesman have perverted their true selves, and each is revealed in his falsity after the word of God is perverted during a seduction scene—itself a perversion of love. Even the structure of the story appears to be a perversion of a traditional short-story form. Two-thirds of the story elapse before the initial meeting of Joy-Hulga and Manley Pointer, the Bible salesman, occurs. In the first section, Flannery O'Connor sets up a relationship between Mrs. Freeman, the hired man's wife, and Mrs. Hopewell, her employer, and between each of these women and the one-legged protagonist, Joy-Hulga. These relationships structure the story. . . . From Manley Pointer's opening question ("You ever ate a chicken that was two days old?") to his final assertion ("I been believing in nothing since I was born") the story moves "like the advance of a heavy truck" to its moment of truth.

That the salesman is peddling Bibles is the central perversion of the story. Flannery O'Connor believed in the power of the word of God. The Bible was for her, as it is for Jews and for Scripture-oriented Christians, the power of God and the wisdom of God. God's scriptural word is not a dead letter; it is a living presence. Reading it does more than enlighten the intellect; it unleashes power that moves the spirit. As a perversion of Christianity has driven Joy to become Hulga, so a perversion of the meaning of Scripture jolts her into self-recognition. In her raging accusation of the deceitful salesman—"You're a fine Christian! You're just like them all—say one thing and do another"—Hulga identifies Christianity with hypocrisy. She adds another indication of the emptiness of the Christianity she sees when, earlier in the story, she cries out to her mother: "Woman, do you ever look inside and see what you are not?" The obvious disparity between what Christians should be and what marks the Christians she knows moves Hulga to embrace Heidegger's emphasis on "being" and his consequent agnosticism. The Bible salesman quoted one verse of Scripture—"He who losest his life shall find it"—to emphasize his desire to be a missionary (one sent). In the climactic scene, this verse is rephrased when Hulga assents to showing Manley Pointer (almost too suggestive a name) her wooden leg. ". . . It was like surrendering to him completely. It was like losing her own life and finding it again, miraculously, in his." This perverse application of Scripture holds an ironic truth: Hulga does lose her life—her self-created being, symbolized by her wooden leg and her new name—by the salesman's deception. Given the structure of the story, there emerges the strong possibility that, having lost her false life, she will see herself (as her cliché-prone mother would say) "without a leg to stand on" and she will hobble toward "home." (pp. 22-4)

[Her] physical deformity is the fulcrum of the plot and the motivating force of Joy-Hulga's character. Evidently her life took a new direction after the accident [that destroyed her leg] in her tenth year, and the change was epitomized in her twenty-first year when she changed her name from Joy to Hulga—"the name of her highest creative act. One of her major triumphs was that her mother had not been able to turn her dust into Joy, but the greater one was that she had been able to turn it herself into Hulga.'' Philosophically, to name a thing is to encompass it, to know it, to control it. To bestow a name indicates power, and to rename shows—biblically—the special call of God. Abram became Abraham to begin the dynasty of God's chosen people; Jacob became Israel to form the Israelite nation; Simon became Peter to head the Church of Christ. God summoned his prophets; Hulga summoned herself to a new life. Her renaming is a comic perversion of God's practice, a self-call to a life of sterile intellectualism.

The residue of ''Joy'' which remains in Hulga becomes a wry humor, perhaps her saving grace. None of the characters respond to it, but it shows that Hulga has a certain respect for truth. ''Get rid of the salt of the earth and let's eat,'' she advises her mother after overhearing the salesman's line. But her mother responds stolidly, ''I can't be rude to anybody.'' Hulga's humor is also lost on Mrs. Freeman. When the hired woman boasts that her son-in-law is so convinced of the sacredness of marriage that ''he wouldn't take five hundred dollars for being married by a preacher,'' Hulga asks, ''How much would he take?'' but the quip falls flat. These humorous remarks suggest that Hulga would realize the ridiculousness of her situation at the story's end—deserted in a barn loft far from the house, with her wooden leg stolen—and that she would renew her claim to Joy.

A foil for the self-deluded protagonist is the hired woman, Mrs. Freeman, who is absolutely true to her own myopic vision of the world. Her interaction with Mrs. Hopewell opens and closes the story, framing the encounter between Hulga and Manley Pointer. This interaction shows that Mrs. Hopewell takes refuge in clichés to cloak her inability to deal with Mrs. Freeman and that Mrs. Freeman can cope with anything that crosses her path. The opening description of her ''forward'' and ''reverse'' expressions might lead one to suspect that Mrs. Freeman will be the center of the story, especially when she and her husband are designated as ''good country people.'' But once the relationship between Mrs. Freeman and the Hopewells is established, the hired man's wife drops out of the story until the last two paragraphs. Stanley Edgar Hyman calls these two paragraphs ''superfluous irony,'' but actually they are essential to the structure of the story. For Mrs. Freeman exhibits a quality similar to Joy-Hulga's: she is an all-or-nothing person. She has two expressions which she uses for all human dealings: forward and reverse, and she seldom needs the latter. She admits that ''I've always been quick.'' Hulga's deformity attracts her (Mrs. Freeman and the Bible salesman show an interesting kinship there), and she knows Hulga better than the girl's own mother does. This is evident when she begins to call the girl ''Hulga,'' which Hulga regards as an invasion of her privacy. Mrs. Freeman's statement that ''some people are more alike than others'' obviously refers to Hulga and the Bible salesman; she senses an affinity between them. Perhaps she suspects that they are both role-playing. One can see that she tends to analyze people and situations; she admits this at the end when she says, answering Mrs. Hopewell's comment about the ''simple'' (naive, guileless) Bible salesman: ''Some can't be that simple; I know I never could.'' Neither could Hulga be that ''simple''; if she could not be Joy, then she had to be Hulga. It was either forward or reverse; there was no in-between. On a more mundane level, Mrs. Freeman reflects Hulga's characteristic mental orientation. And because Hulga has been going in ''reverse'' of her intrinsic potential for many years, one accepts the possibility that her traumatic experience will thrust her ''forward'' to the positive pole of her personality. (pp. 25-6)

Something within her induces Hulga to make possible her encounter with the salesman. Only this is told: ''Joy had been standing in the road, apparently looking at something in the distance, when he came down the steps towards her.'' Many O'Connor characters gaze at something in the distance, and one feels the presence of mystery. The mystery of grace comes close to the surface of the story in Hulga's expression of her slight hope that there *is* goodness in the world, even though she wants to pervert it. When the salesman presents his unholy trinity of offerings—liquor to dull the mind, pornography to excite the senses, and contraceptives to lock the body—the girl is immobile, mesmerized. Then she speaks in an ''almost pleading'' voice:

> ''Aren't you,'' she murmured, ''aren't you just good country people?''

It is the voice of faint hope, evidence of an interior struggle against despair. Near the end of the story, after Manley Pointer has removed Hulga's glasses, the narrator enters her consciousness and she views the world with her eyes: the sky is ''hollow''; the trees are ''a black ridge''; and the fields are ''two green swelling lakes.'' The whole landscape is ''shifty.'' Her firm world—to which she had formerly paid very little attention—has become as shifting sand to her now, with her sight and mobility impaired. ''He who losest his life will find it.'' And the story closes with ''Mrs. Freeman's gaze drove forward.'' (p. 27)

''The Comforts of Home'' [is] a story which explores two modes of falseness: sterile rationality and sticky sentimentality. Both Thomas, a middle-aged bachelor and local historian, and his mother, a mindlessly benevolent woman, are overdrawn figures of comedy in a story which ends in melodrama. Cartooning was O'Connor's hobby as a child, and she became expert in it as she grew older. Her sharp, satiric cartoons in her high school and college newspaper achieved local renown. Her college linoleum block cuts show the deft strokes which exaggerate one feature of a character to suggest an identity. O'Connor stopped cartooning when she began writing fiction, but one can see the mind of the cartoonist working in some of her fiction, notably this story. Thomas is large, overbearing, and indecisive; his mother is small, round, and resembles a sibyl. Thomas's procrastination is caught aptly by the narrator's comment: ''His plan for all practical action was to wait and see what developed.'' His mother's righteous benevolence echoes in her statement, ''We are not the kind of people who hate,'' delivered as positively ''as if this were an imperfection that had been bred out of them generations ago.'' Throughout his thirty-five years, Thomas's plan of action has accomplished his goals; through her lifetime his mother's ''box of candy'' benevolence has nourished her sense of being good to the world. But the advent of Sarah Ham, a nymphomaniac, into their lives precipitates Thomas into action to curb his mother's sentimentality, which was destroying ''the comforts of home'' for him. Their encounter with Sarah, alias Star Drake, illumines the false premises on which they have based their lives, and the story's pervading horror is that they do not recognize that falseness. (p. 32)

Under the temptation to rehabilitate Star Drake, the mother lets her ''hazy charity'' degenerate into sentimentality. Obeying the diabolical promptings of his dead father, Thomas tries to preserve the peace of his home by framing the young girl and, that having failed, by shooting her. That he kills his mother instead is, some critics believe, her salvation and his awakening, but the story does not effectively compel the reader to accept the notion of grace offered and accepted. The whole story points, instead, to a shallowness of character which would, in the absence of any signs to the contrary, preclude an openness to grace.

Thomas's mother—nameless, perhaps to suggest her ubiquity—exhibits a certain tendency in all her actions. She seems "with the best intentions in the world, to make a mockery of virtue, to pursue it with such a mindless intensity that everyone involved was made a fool of and virtue itself became ridiculous." This perversion of virtue is exemplified when she uses her son as the touchstone of all her actions. "It might be you," she tremulously repeats to Thomas as her motive for helping Star beyond the limits of reason. Clearly Thomas's mother is a victim of sentimentality.

Flannery O'Connor despised sentimentality, a quality which has been defined as "giving to any creature more love than God gives it." She saw sentimentality as an attempted short cut to the grace of Redemption which overlooks its price. She saw its enervating effect in every aspect of life. . . . [O'Connor] equated sentimentality with false compassion. In a lecture entitled "The Grotesque in Southern Fiction," she speaks of compassion in a writer:

> Compassion is a word that sounds good in anybody's mouth, and which no book jacket can do without. It is a quality which no one can put his finger on in any exact critical sense, so it is always safe for anybody to use. Usually I think what is meant by it is that the writer excuses all human weakness because human weakness is human.

Thomas's mother has evidently made such excuses for Thomas all his life; by no other means could he have become so grounded in his selfishness. . . . Thomas tells his mother that the power of good stimulates the devil to act, so he opts for the truce of mediocrity. The story negates this specious reasoning by demonstrating that it is rather a corruption of good (his mother's sentimentality masquerading as charity) which creates an evil counteraction. The mother's "out of hand" virtue really threatens the comfort of her son for the first time; this threat causes his father's unconscious influence, dormant until now, to come alive in his mind. His father's spirit does not rattle a pot; he squats in the historian's mind to suggest devious and finally criminal ways to remove Star Drake from the once-peaceful home.

Thomas sees Star as the devil, unrecognized by his mother, with whom she is enmeshed in a "most foolhardly engagement." But he finds the nymphomaniac, at the same time, "blameless corruption" and "the most unendurable form of innocence" because she is not morally responsible. Because he really does not believe in the devil, he fails to recognize his responsibility for the real devil of the story, the devil in his mind, speaking to him in his father's characteristic position and tone. An unseen power in the story, the father is introduced into Thomas's thoughts gradually, almost casually; at the story's end, his influence is so strong that his commands to Thomas receive instant response. Thomas believes that he has inherited his father's reason without his ruthlessness, and his mother believes that her son has "no bad inclinations, nothing bad you were born with." This unthinking denial that Thomas had inherited what theologians term original sin, together with her using her love for her son to measure all her dealings with others, shows that the mother's "virtue" is mere sentimentality. The final evidence lies in her reaction to Star's suicide hoax:

> Some new weight of sorrow seemed to have been thrown across her shoulders, and not only Thomas, but Sarah Ham was infuriated by this, for it appeared to be a general sorrow that would have found another object no matter what good fortune came to either of them. The experience of Sarah Ham had plunged the old lady into mourning for the world.

Such sentimentality as this is a perversion of love. On the other hand, Thomas's ruthless measures to regain the comforts of home show how selfish reasonableness can quickly degenerate into crime. Both characters fall into the dragon's jaws.

Yet Thomas's fall is greater, because initially he has the greater respect for truth. Although selfish and indecisive, he is not dishonest. He evidently hated his unscrupulous father and firmly rejects his evil suggestions until his father's influence becomes too strong for him to resist. To make the sketch of the diabolical old man convincing, O'Connor uses a caricaturist's device: she describes a characteristic view of him, and lets it suggest the lie that was his life.

> . . . His father took up a squatting position in his [Thomas's] mind. The old man had the countryman's ability to converse squatting, though he was no countryman but had been born and brought up in the city and only moved to a smaller place later to exploit his talents. With steady skill he had made them think him one of them. In the midst of a conversation on the courthouse lawn, he would squat and his two or three companions would squat with him with no break in the surface of the talk. By gesture he had lived his lie; he had never deigned to tell one.

The squatting father, whose voice sometimes hisses in Thomas's ear, is, by his dwarfed position, reminiscent of small-Southerntown officials who still carry on business on the courthouse lawn. Behind him is the dim figure of Milton's Satan, who squatted beside Eve to whisper his temptation. The father "lived his lie" by adopting Southern customs for his own ends; for Flannery O'Connor, this was high treason. The squatting position both expresses the father's cold duplicity and suggests his diabolical influence on his son. The son recognizes the evil inspirations, abhors them, and then knowingly succumbs to them.

In accord with the author's expressed philosophy of fiction, there should be a moment of grace in the story. In speaking of the "tired reader," who needs to be "lifted up," Flannery O'Connor said, "There is something in us, as storytellers and as listeners to stories, that demands the redemptive act, that demands that what falls at least be offered the chance to be restored." In this story there is only the suggestion of the possibility of grace. (pp. 32-6)

The story ends in "failure" (although the grotesque sheriff would count the accidental murder a success), but in the biblical framework such failure contains the possibility of reversing itself. That the mother's attempt to protect the girl was an act of pure selflessness and counteracted her lifelong sentimentality is a distinct possibility. That Thomas will become as aware of his own shortcomings as he has been of his mother's is another possibility. With these intimations of the power of Redemption in the lives of unbelievers, the story is content to rest.

"The Comforts of Home" is an anomaly in Flannery O'Connor's imaginative excursions into the theme of truth. Its charcters seem to be consciously overdrawn, and the story does not have in it the strong sense of "place" which characterizes the author's best work. . . . [Because] the characters seem detached from their surroundings, the story veers into melodrama. In Richard Chase's *The American Novel and Its Tradition,* O'Connor marked his definition of melodrama: "tragedy in a vacuum." Unwittingly, she seems to have illustrated this concept. The only scene in the story which anchors it firmly in a small Southern town (a placement which is Flannery O'Connor's strength) is the scene between Thomas and Farebrother, the sheriff which takes place on the courthouse lawn. Infused with Southern scenery and mores, this brief scene is strong enough to create the character of Farebrother, which substantiates the references Thomas has made to him. . . . More of the "local universe" would have rendered this conflict between sentimentality and rationality more persuasive, but the story does succeed in illuminating a perversion of truth by excess—too much "love": too much "reason." (pp. 37-8)

O'Connor says in her lecture "Novelist and Believer" that "the artist penetrates the concrete world in order to find at its depths the image of its source, the image of ultimate reality." It is this penetration of the visible world and consequent revelation of ultimate reality which is the strength of her fiction.

In certain of Flannery O'Connor's stories in which a child is the central figure this penetration of reality is especially poignant because it involves an initial apprehension of the presence of evil in the heart of man. O'Connor never underestimated the awareness of a child. In one of her lectures, speaking of the writer's need to experience life, she said dryly that "anybody who has survived his childhood has enough information about life to last him the rest of his days." The children in her stories undergo an initiation bound up with the sacredness of matter. In some, an older person is part of the initiation scene, ostensibly as teacher, but actually as one whose eyes are opened to reality through the child. These stories show a child in a world of both sacred and secular dimensions. (p. 120)

In **"The Artificial Nigger,"** the grandfather, Mr. Head, has decided to bring his grandson, Nelson, face to face with the real world. For ten years the boy has lived in the isolation of the country, and, knowing that he will soon yearn for a larger world, Mr. Head intends to give him his fill in one visit to the city. He has planned carefully for this day, with a "moral mission" in mind. He will show him "everything there is to see in a city so that he would be content to stay at home for the rest of his life." But there is an unseen reality of which Mr. Head knows nothing. The opening of the story suggests this spiritual reality by its description of the "miraculous moonlight" which charges the old man's rustic bedroom with grandeur. It transforms the wooden floor boards into silver, the pillow ticking into brocade, the straight chair into an attentive servant, and the slop jar near Nelson's bed into "a small personal angel." The day will unfold to Mr. Head the spiritual reality which silvers all of life: the mercy of God. That same reality will also be grasped—in a measure suited to his capacity—by the boy. But each must be readied; each must be purged of his pride.

Mr. Head has the pride of Adam. He is "entirely confident that he could carry out the moral mission of the coming day." He knows himself to be "a suitable guide for the young." Even when he fails to awaken before his grandson as he had planned, his self-confidence is unshaken. During the train ride to the city, he lords it over Nelson, even to demonstrating the ice water cooler "as if he had invented it." Only after he is in the city for a while and he realizes that he has lost both their lunch sack and the direction back to the station does his confidence weaken. But, gathering his pride, he decides to increase Nelson's dependence on him. He hides while the boy sleeps and then watches Nelson waken alone, terrified, and dash madly down the street and into an old woman carrying groceries. Fear of reprisal for the boy's misdeed grips him—the same fear which forced the apostle Peter to say, "I do not know the man." With his grandson panting against him, he repeats the great denial: "This is not my boy; I never seen him before." An instant later, when he feels "Nelson's fingers fall out of his flesh," he knows for the first time that he is a sinner. He is ready for a revelation of God's mercy.

Nelson has only one cause for pride: he was born in the city. His insistence that this will be his second visit infuriates his grandfather. The old man plans to test the validity of Nelson's claim by seeing whether he will recognize a "nigger." Nelson fails the test, and his experiences on the train make him cling to his grandfather with uncharacteristic dependence. "For the first time in his life, he understood that his grandfather was indispensable to him." But during the day's journey, as he becomes aware of his grandfather's insecurity in the city, his independence reasserts itself. His grandfather's explanation of the "endless pitchblack tunnels" which make up the city sewer system (the boy immediately connects them with hell) shakes him momentarily, but moving away from the dangerous openings at the curb, he still insists, "This [the city] is where I come from." The scene in which he sees—really sees for the first time—a woman (the fact that she is a Negro is essential to the design of the story but not to Nelson's initiation) teaches him more than his grandfather had anticipated.

> He stood drinking in every detail of her. His eyes traveled up from her great knees to her forehead and then made a triangular path from the glistening sweat on her neck down and across her tremendous bosom and over her bare arm back to where her fingers lay hidden in her hair. He suddenly wanted her to reach down and pick him up and draw him against her and then he wanted to feel her breath on his face. He wanted to look down and down into her eyes while she held him tighter and tighter. He had never had such a feeling before. He felt as if he were reeling down through a pitchblack tunnel.

This encounter drains all pride from Nelson; in some obscure way, he realizes what Mr. Head has not learned in sixty years: that one's moral reactions cannot always be "guided by his will and strong character," as Mr. Head asserts. His face "burning with shame," Nelson takes the old man's hand. His trembling mouth could have told his grandfather that he had seen enough, even before he voiced his capitulation: "I only said I was born here and I never had nothing to do with that. I want to go home." But unaware of the reality called "feelings," the grandfather subjects the boy to one last test, which leads to his denial of the boy and to Nelson's experience of being betrayed. Then the boy's humility moves into hatred. He is unable to deal with this new reality; "this was the first time he had ever had anything to forgive." He, too, is ready for a revelation of what forgiveness means.

The agent of revelation is an "artificial nigger" on a front lawn, which catches Mr. Head's attention "like a cry out of the gathering dusk." The plaster figure of an ageless Negro sitting unsteadily on a wall, "a wild look of misery" in his eyes, draws Mr. Head and Nelson together, and each says in wonder, "An artificial nigger." Then the statue becomes more than it is; reality becomes the bearer of grace. Both the offender and the offended "could feel it dissolving their differences like an action of mercy." Words fail Mr. Head, who all during the day has definitely explained the urban world to Nelson. When he tries "to explain once and for all the mystery of existence," he hears himself saying, "They ain't got enough real ones here. They got to have an artificial one." In some distorted way, this statement attributes value to the Negro race, which, through the day, Mr. Head has been demeaning to Nelson. Earlier, he had showed the boy how "they rope them off" in the train diner; he had pointed out the store "where you walked in and sat on a chair with your feet on two rests and let a Negro polish your shoes"; he had identified the evil of the city with its Negroes, growling from time to time, "Anybody wants to be from this nigger heaven can be from it." But the close of the story indicates that the world is charged with grandeur, even where one least expects to find it—in the statue of a "nigger."

When the travelers return home, the moonlight reappears, silvering the grass, glittering on the clinkers, and turning clouds into lanterns as Mr. Head and Nelson step off the train at the junction. But it falls upon a different grandfather and grandson: each has become aware of a new reality. Mr. Head, "an ancient child," understands the mercy of God; Nelson, "a miniature old man," has experienced a lifetime of emotions—carnal desire and treachery and hate and mercy. Each has led the other to wisdom. Although the opening suggests that this will be Mr. Head's story—his stature and name suggest universal man—as the story proceeds it becomes equally Nelson's story. Both teacher and pupil are initiated into the mystery of spiritual reality. (pp. 120-23)

Kathleen Feeley, in her Flannery O'Connor: Voice of the Peacock, *1972. Reprint by Fordham University Press, 1982, 198 p.*

GILBERT H. MULLER (essay date 1972)

[Muller places O'Connor within the tradition of grotesque art, emphasizing that her approach is remarkable because it involves "invoking religion as a way of confronting the absurd." He also discusses characters from various short stories in order to describe and define O'Connor's typical grotesque creation.]

Flannery O'Connor once remarked that the most memorable event in her life prior to the publication of *Wise Blood* was the featuring of a bantam chicken which she had trained to walk backwards by Pathé newsreels. Mary Flannery was six years old at the time, attending parochial school in Savannah, Georgia. Later, while enrolled at Peabody High School in Milledgeville, where the family had moved in 1938, she confounded her home economics teacher by outfitting another bantam hen in a white piqué coat and striped trousers which she had designed and sewn to specification. Up to the time of her death . . . , Miss O'Connor retained this fondness for domestic fowl, especially those varieties which were eccentric rather than normative. She even confessed to favoring barnyard birds "with one green eye and one orange or with overlong necks and crooked combs. I wanted one with three legs or three wings but nothing in that line turned up."

Unable to locate her ideal grotesque among God's humbler creatures, Miss O'Connor turned to her fellow human beings. And here she discovered a Goyaesque assortment of deformed individuals which she made as unique and imperishable as her bantam hens. In dealing with these human grotesques, the author was writing from personal and drastic experience; she lived in a region where Bible Belt values strongly affected both culture and the human will. Moreover, Miss O'Connor's own affliction, which she carried with her during the major part of her literary career, forced a certain austerity upon her fiction; inevitably she transferred personal agony and suffering to her work. Yet in dealing with her characters' agonies, and in sustaining her own, Flannery O'Connor was sardonic rather than sentimental. She wielded a literary hatchet rather than a handkerchief; she realized that only a stern intellect, an adamant faith, and an accretion of humor which usually shaded into the grotesque could confront suffering, violence, and evil in this world.

In the fictive landscape which she created, Flannery O'Connor's grotesques—deformed in body and soul alike—wrangle with ultimate problems which also must have beset their creator. Her use of the grotesque to establish the moral and aesthetic climate of a work is pronounced. . . . (pp. 1-2)

[The vision of grotesque art] presents existence as deprived of meaning. All traces of natural order are willfully subverted so as to produce an alienated world, a world in which man, sensing the radical discontinuity of things, is estranged from his environment. This division between man and his environment is what actually produces the grotesque, or the absurd, wherein man discovers that in a universe which is disjointed and senseless, which is contradictory in every aspect, he is something less than what he should be. (p. 5)

To the extent that both words refer to the alienated world, we can say that the grotesque and the absurd are synonymous. . . . [Wolfgang Kayser] suggests that the grotesque is a literature of extreme situation, and indeed mayhem, chaos, and violence seem to predominate in the genre, causing characters to be projected in curious ways. As the world disintegrates and categories merge, these characters frequently become burlesque figures whose actions mime the grotesque world which they inhabit.

The grotesque character therefore is one who either exerts himself against the absurd or who is a part of the absurd. This character frequently assumes recognizable postures: guilt, obsession, and madness are among his peculiarities, and at his best he is simultaneously a rebel, rogue, and victim. He can also be prankster, saint, demonist, fanatic, clown, moron, or any combination of these; or at the more mundane level the grotesque can be reflected in an absurd family group. All these types appear in Flannery O'Connor's gallery of grotesques. . . . (pp. 5-7)

The grotesque character is a comic figure. It is impossible to sympathize with him, despite his agonies, because we view him from a detached perspective, and when we are not emotionally involved in his suffering, we are amused. . . .

As with the grotesque character the entire technique of the grotesque is also essentially comic, for we always view the grotesque from a vantage point. To be certain, the subject matter of the grotesque—the raw material which creates the

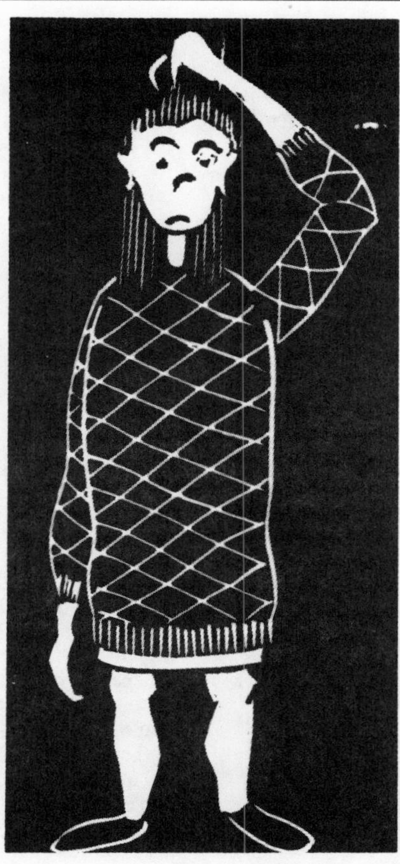

Untitled linoleum block cartoons by O'Connor for the yearbook at Georgia State College. Spectrum *photo taken from the 1944 edition, Georgia College, Milledgeville, GA.*

vision—is always potentially horrible, but the treatment of this material is comic: this explains the peculiar complexity of tone, combining both horror and the ludicrous, which characterizes the grotesque as an art form. Pure horror, of course, cannot produce a grotesque effect: as subject matter it is unrelieved horror and nothing more. But the grotesque, through the interjection of humor, releases the terror and makes it understandable. (p. 7)

[Miss O'Connor] goes beyond many writers of what we might term the secular grotesque by invoking religion as a way of confronting the absurd. As Kayser remarks, a true art of the grotesque not only reveals but also subdues the demonic. If O'Connor utilizes Catholic values to arrive at certain truths about the grotesque, it is because she wants to provide a corrective to man's desperate and meaningless condition by emphasizing the theological foundations of nature and grace.

In promulgating an antidote to the absurd, Flannery O'Connor creates what properly should be termed an art of the Catholic grotesque. She maneuvers her characters through dark and inpenetrable mazes which seemingly lead nowhere, but which unexpectedly reveal an exit into Christianity's back yard. While she affirms the contradictory aspects of the universe, her fiction nevertheless embodies a transcending principle of order. For Miss O'Connor spiritual vitality lies precisely in the strength of the antithesis between the negative aspects of the grotesque and the affirmation of religion: it is between these extremes that she paints her Catholic landscape of the grotesque. (p. 18)

Flannery O'Connor was pre-eminently successful in character depiction because she realized that the grotesque was the ideal vehicle for objectifying fears, obsessions, and compulsions. Within her southern landscape (only two of her stories are set outside the South, and they involve southern characters), it is the common everyday confrontations, such as a family trip or a visit to the doctor's office, that are filled with horror, and it is the sudden irrationality of the familiar world that induces distortions in character. Thus the grotesque suggests that the visible world is incomprehensible and unregenerate, and that the individual is floundering in a sea of contradictions and incongruities.

The typical grotesque character in Miss O'Connor's fiction is an individual who projects certain extreme mental states which, while psychologically valid, are not investigations in the tradition of psychological realism. To be certain, the reality of the unconscious life—incorporating dream, fantasy, and hallucination—is expressed, but grotesque characterization is not interested in the subtleties of emotion and feeling, but rather in their larger outlines. This method actually tends toward the symbolic, where distillation of character into a basic set of preoccupations serves to crystallize attitudes toward the ethical circumstances being erected. Here a basic point to emphasize is that grotesque characterization does not necessarily make the characters in a story remote or improbable, since the sacrifice in psychological realism is more counterbalanced by the impact of the grotesque. For instance, it is clearly evident in O'Connor's fiction that boldly outlined inner compulsions are reinforced dramatically by a mutilated exterior self, as with Tom T. Shiftlet in **"A Good Man is Hard to Find,"** Hulga in **"Good Country People,"** and Rufus in **"The Lame Shall Enter First."** Moreover, these compulsions are frequently projected into the surrounding environment: in **"A Circle in the Fire,"** for example, Mrs. Cope ironically conceives of the farm as an image of her own indomitable nature, as an extension of her own creation; and in **"A View of the Woods"** there is a deliberate effort to link the obsessions of the main character, Mr. Fortune, with the landscape, which is frequently rendered through terse, unpleasant, and decidedly violent imagery. (pp. 21-2)

[An] impulse toward the secular is a characteristic affliction of Flannery O'Connor's grotesques, for she sees the modern world divided between those who would eliminate mystery and those who are trying to rediscover it. The secular world which seduces her characters typically divorces eternity from temporality in order to negate the precise area of mystery which Miss O'Connor insists upon. It is a world which values discrete data and the appurtenances of technology, which fragments experience and transforms people into prophets of a new objectivity. (p. 25)

[In **"The Lame Shall Enter First,"**] Sheppard, the welfare worker, an extreme projection of the militant atheist and scientific objectivist, is forced to admit defeat when confronted with the inexplicable evil of the boy Rufus. Sheppard, who relies on scientific inquiry instead of compassion, is emblematic of the failure of science to satisfy man's basic emotional, psychological, and spiritual needs. He purchases a telescope for the edification of Rufus; but the boy, who is totally alienated from a scientific universe and who adheres to a more traditional world picture, medieval in origin, in which the universe exists between the extremes of heaven and hell, begins to use the telescope for demonic ends. Finally he induces Sheppard's emotionally crippled son to hang himself and thereby launch a trip into space in quest of his deceased mother.

Norton's flight into space, like Rufus Johnson's demonic and violent actions, is not really senseless; in fact it fixes the precise meaning of the story—that the familiar world, illuminated by science, still remains alien and mysterious, even as the source of hope within man's grotesque condition has been known for two thousand years, although that too remains unverifiable. This story, like many others by O'Connor, is a ruthless study of the vulgarity of the secular spirit, a spirit which while assuming such guises as psychology in **"The Partridge Festival,"** art in **"The Enduring Chill,"** and popular culture in **"A Late Encounter With the Enemy,"** more often than not focuses on those manifestations of atheism that are witnessed in . . . Sheppard.

When Miss O'Connor treats this petrification of spirit, this refusal to believe, she creates a startling malignancy beneath the comic texture of her stories, because atheism never enables grotesque characters to get by in the world that they live in. People are pitted against an overpowering spiritual reality which makes their absurd contortions even more poignant, since it creates an existence so oppressive that individuals literally fall apart. (pp. 26-7)

[O'Connor often employs a grotesque trickster, who] tends to explode surface pretensions in others in order to expose man's absurd condition. The supreme trickster, of course, is the devil, who frequently appears in Flannery O'Connor's fiction wearing a variety of disguises. The Bible salesman, for example, is one of Miss O'Connor's most startling demonic tricksters: his red hands and glittering eyes make him a curiously resonant satanic figure. The benevolent Mr. Paradise in **"The River,"** whose protrusions on his head are a good indication of his origins and his mission, is another incarnation of the devil. . . . These devils are not the sort of disembodied gothic demons associated with tales of the supernatural, but distinct and palpable aspects of existence. "I want to be certain," Miss O'Connor wrote in a letter to John Hawkes, "that the devil gets identified as the devil and not simply taken for this or that psychological tendency." Like Gogol, whom she read assiduously, Flannery O'Connor believed that the devil was a formative influence in life.

When the devil is not present himself in O'Connor's fiction, he nevertheless can exert considerable influence on character behavior. To the extent that her characters are criminal types, they are in the hands of the devil, whether willingly or reluctantly, and by surrendering themselves to infernal forces they commit themselves as well to a grotesque existence. For instance, in **"A Good Man is Hard to Find,"** Miss O'Connor's memorable antagonist is an astute madman who deliberately places himself in opposition to Christ. The Misfit is cast into a hopeless situation because of the demonic aspects of the world, and his sense of alienation is intensified by his belief that God has abandoned him. What we encounter at the beginning of the story—an absurdly comic narrative of a family trip that is almost a parody of Wilder's "The Happy Journey to Trenton and Camden"—gradually assumes the proportions of a wholesale revolt against the cultural distortions of Christianity.

Preoccupied with the myth of Christ, the Misfit becomes judge and executioner in order to do justice to a social situation in which punishment does not seem to fit the wrong. The Misfit, like it or not, is the religious consciousness of his age. For him the alternatives are simple—belief or disbelief. He chooses the latter course of action, but although he murders all six members of the Bailey family, he doesn't take any pleasure in killing. He murders people because he *wants* to be a sinner in the hands of the devil: he seemingly partakes of Rufus Johnson's premonition that sinners, especially if they repent, are capable of receiving curious dispensations from God. Both Rufus and the Misfit conceive of their criminality in strict theological terms. Both perform their criminal acts for the sake of evil and both consider themselves damned because of them. Yet these criminals do not regard themselves as complete losses because they realize that salvation is a simple matter of repentance, that Jesus is the only one who can save them.

These "criminals" are therefore grotesques of a very special sort. Deliberately cutting themselves off from transcendent values, they lapse into what is essentially an attitude of despair. And with the recession of belief which they experience comes the isolation, alienation, and sense of abandonment that most grotesque protagonists and antagonists feel. This point is strikingly illustrated in one of Miss O'Connor's earlier stories, **"The Life You Save May Be Your Own,"** where we encounter the black outrageous figure of Tom T. Shiftlet, an individual much more than a criminal—actually a grotesque Christ figure who is decadent and evil. Shiftlet, the one-armed carpenter whose figure forms a crooked cross, marries and abandons a retarded girl in exchange for a dilapidated Ford. What is significant here is that there is an appalling logic and certitude in his actions. Perplexity about his own identity and the mysteries of the human heart drives him to desperate extremities and forces him to investigate demonically the possibilities of evil which arise from his key question—what is man? Shiftlet's self-styled "moral intelligence" tells him that man really isn't benevolent, a point which he fully realizes; yet in the inherent potentialities of Shiftlet's moral intelligence for cruelty and evil a statement of the human condition is made which contains the bleak pessimism concerning the moral sense that Mark Twain revealed in *The Mysterious Stranger*.

Tom T. Shiftlet—the trickster who at the end of the story is also tricked—is a grotesque parody of Christ. He cannot save others or even himself. After his abandonment of Lucynell, which constitutes a deliberate act of deception and evil, he encounters road signs which read: "Drive carefully. The life you save may be your own." Yet Shiftlet is unable to comprehend the portent of this message, since any kind of solution to man's infernal condition is beyond his control. By effectively removing himself from grace, he encounters despair and alienation. However, his condition, like that of Rufus and the Misfit, is not entirely hopeless. Miss O'Connor hinted at this when she remarked: "I did have some trouble with the end of that story. I got it up to his taking the girl away and leaving her. I knew I wanted to do that much, and I did it. But the story wasn't complete. I needed that little boy on the side of the road, and that little boy is what makes the story work." . . . Many critics . . . overlook that little boy. It is he who perceives Shiftlet's hypocrisy, and is he who makes Shiftlet cognizant of his own evil. Shiftlet, after being abandoned by the boy just as he had deserted Lucynell, suddenly turns inward upon himself and, in a moment of agony, an infinitely small prayer is the only thing he possesses in order to redeem himself. But the astonishing conclusion suggests that salvation first requires a ritualistic purification: "After a few minutes there was a guffawing peal of thunder from behind and fantastic raindrops, like tin-can tops, crashed over the rear of Mr. Shiftlet's car. Very quickly he stepped on the gas and with his stump sticking out of the window he raced the galloping shower into Mobile." Shiftlet in his flight from God's wrath recognizes his own complicity in the face of total estrangement and an impersonal universe which is actively hostile to him. His world is chaotic, and the reader is merely given a glimpse of the antidote to it. A Christ-like life, despite the degradation and perversity that Shiftlet brings to it, somehow remains a mysterious possibility. The anarachy of the finite human situation—and its reconciliation in the religious absolute—finds its grotesque expression in Shiftlet, who affirms negatively the body and symbol of the Catholic tradition.

The distance of Shiftlet from the true Christ represents the dominant experience of our time as interpreted from the viewpoint of the grotesque, insisting as it does upon a fragmentation of man from the world and from common bodies of belief. This fragmentation not only transforms men into cultural and spiritual grotesques, but it also forces new attitudes toward Christ upon the imagination, as Tom T. Shiftlet demonstrates. (pp. 30-5)

[The] Christ figure, O. E. Parker, the protagonist in the superlative story **"Parker's Back,"** is the most engaging of Flannery O'Connor's grotesques, perhaps because he is one of the few who are not harmful or seriously harmed. When Parker has a Byzantine Christ tattooed on his back, he undergoes a remarkable transformation in which he literally becomes identified with the numerous bearers of religious mystery who serve to rejuvenate society and to form its consciousness. The Christ on Parker's back is a genuine presence: Parker himself is altered by its mystical power—a power which loses its force only when there is a shift to a rational point of view, where the mystic symbol becomes a mere sign, quite conventional and ridiculous, as it is to Parker's wife.

The reaction of Parker's wife to his tattoo is a carefully executed stroke of irony. This reception by Sarah Ruth is delightfully comic, but on a more serious level it is a prefiguration of the Crucifixion: as Parker stands before the barred door, he is shocked by the revelation of a tree of fire, and he falls backward against the door "as if he had been pinned there by a lance." It is at this moment that Parker's transformation is complete: previously possessed by Christ, he now becomes identified with Him. The story then ends in an absurd imitation of the death of Christ. Parker's "death" comes at the hands of his incensed wife, who is outraged by his latest tattoo. Any picture of God is merely an indication of idolatry to her, and she thus subjects her husband to yet another purgation, this time with a broom. She beats him until large welts appear on the face of the tattooed Christ. Parker comically emulates the passion of Christ. He does not die, however, as did his predecessors Haze Motes and Guizac, and he remains in the world. He becomes a child of Christ and, we may assume, attains a higher reality and a higher consciousness, for by taking up the Cross, he finally loses his ego.

O. E. Parker might well be the author's greatest comic grotesque. The story itself certainly is a masterpiece, tightly organized and remarkable in its pictorial quality. Miss O'Connor's regard for figure and perspective creates a memorable figure and an extraordinary situation. The story's insistence upon the ambiguities of existence, and upon the pain and suffering of life are skillfully evoked. And in its imaginative use of materials, the story is as picaresque as anything Flannery O'Connor wrote.

Parker's complaint arises not only from his own obsessions, but also from a dialectical opposition to the religious groundings of his culture. In a sense all the author's misbelievers, who range from the falsely pious to the thoroughly damned, are cultural grotesques: the enduring values of their society throw their miscreant behavior into stark focus. In her fictive world common existence is seemingly limited and provincial; but a single religion, the old backwoods Fundamentalism, still dominates, and this makes for piety and awe, as well as for madness and violence. The squalid cities and towns, the piedmont farms, the sinister topography of pine tree and sand flat, of shabby movie marquees and Jesus Saves signs, impress themselves upon the protagonists' sensibilities until the very physical and spiritual qualities of the landscape are linked with their destinies. The result of this amalgamation is almost always disorder, a chaotic mental state in the characters which is balanced only by the ordering power of Miss O'Connor's fiction. (pp. 37-9)

Gilbert H. Muller, in his Nightmares and Visions: Flannery O'Connor and the Catholic Grotesque, *University of Georgia Press, 1972, 125 p.*

MARTHA STEPHENS (essay date 1973)

[Stephens here describes a flaw in what she terms the "tonal dimension" of O'Connor's fiction. According to Stephens, the problem arises from a jarring difference in tone between O'Connor's comic, folksy portrayal of characters and the horrifying disasters that befall them. Stephens also raises the issue of the

reader's problem with accepting O'Connor's view of life, which the critic describes as bleak, austere, and rigid, opposed to both secular humanism and Christian humanism.]

That [Flannery O'Connor] was a gifted writer—astonishingly good at times—certainly no one wishes to dispute; but the fact is that she was possessed of so eccentric, at times so—we must face this to begin with—repugnant a view of human life that the strain of trying to enter emotionally into her work is often very great indeed. No one was more conscious of this problem than she herself; she was very much aware of facing an audience essentially hostile to her assumptions about human life, and she did not expect—nor, one sometimes thinks, did she even desire—easy acceptance from it. She said that what she wanted to do was to restore the reader's "sense of evil," and she obviously did not expect that he would wholly enjoy it.

The problem, then, in trying to make a balanced judgment about this writer is simple enough to state. O'Connor clearly had a great natural gift for the story-telling art—the better one knows her work, the more one comes to respect her ability. But she was also a highly doctrinal writer with a marked evangelical strain, and like all such writers—like D. H. Lawrence, for instance, and in France her fellow Catholics François Mauriac and Georges Bernanos—she poses so personal, so goading a challenge to a reader's perceptions of life that coming to terms with her as an artist is difficult.

To say that Miss O'Connor was a devout Catholic hardly begins to suggest how formidable the distance is between her view of life and the prevailing view of modern readers. To find so bleak, so austere and rigid, so other-worldly a Christian view of life as hers, one is forced back into the distant past of English religious literature—into the dark side of medieval Christian thought with its constant injunction to renunciation of the world. "All Christen people, biholde and see / This world is but a vanytee"—her stories, like the twelfth-century verse, seem to enjoin us. (pp. 3-4)

One must, of course, say *seem*—the stories *seem* to enjoin, to ask, to urge, for one does not wish to imply that the O'Connor stories and novels are not wholly dramatic. On the contrary, there is not a word of authorial argument as such. And yet the message and the warning are there; in story after story O'Connor sets up her Sodom and brings it down, sets it up and brings it down. Here the wretched Mrs. Mays, the Mrs. Copes, the Raybers and Julians and Asburys suffer their terrible Christian comeuppance—foolish, deluded creatures who think they possess something, know something, can achieve something, who (as if, like brute animals, they have never discovered the fact of their own mortality) take some dumb pride in having reached a position of material or emotional security. "I've seen them come, and I've seen them go," says Mrs. McIntyre of her hired help, and we know she's thinking, "But I'm here, I stay, I'm safe." But of course no one is safe; eventually the fire and brimstone is rained down—O'Connor brings on, to wreak their destruction, her mad bulls, her demonic children, her escaped convicts. See, these stories seem to say, devastation, annihilation always around the corner, and yet the godless go on acting as if they held their fates in their own hands.

Of course the disasters that overtake these people, in their blind struggle toward some foolish worldly end, are not meant to seem gratuitous. They are presented, typically, as blessings in disguise, really as acts of grace; for even if they are not fatal, they provide such violent shocks to the characters' egos, to their sense of well-being, that they are forced to see themselves (we are given to understand) as they really are. And often enough, the descent of grace, as it were, *is* fatal, as in the case of Mrs. May in **"Greenleaf."** A veteran O'Connor reader prepares himself for the worst when, midway through this story, the smug Mrs. May, reacting to the taunts of her sons, mutters, "They needn't think I'm going to die any time soon . . . I'll die when I get good and ready." We know that she is never going to get by with that, and . . . a biblical line as it is echoed in *Everyman* springs to mind: "O Death, thou camest when I had thee least in mind!" And indeed when Mrs. May sees the bull racing toward her, she cannot grasp, she cannot believe, what is happening to her: she stands quite still, in a state not of fright, but of "freezing unbelief":

> She stared at the violent black streak bounding toward her as if she had no sense of distance, as if she could not decide at once what his intention was, and the bull had buried his head in her lap, like a wild tormented lover, before her expression changed. One of his horns sank until it pierced her heart and the other curved around her side and held her in an unbreakable grip. She continued to stare straight ahead but the entire scene in front of her had changed—the tree line was a dark wound in a world that was nothing but sky—and she had the look of a person whose sight had been suddenly restored but who finds the light unbearable.

More than this—of Mrs. May's death epiphany—we do not know, except that as she sinks down over the bull's head, she seems to be "whispering some last discovery into the animal's ear." And yet the reader feels that he must regard her as being radically changed, perhaps "saved," by her violent death—as if for some people, so set in their prideful, ungodly ways, it is only the ultimate trauma of being separated from their bodies that can induce them to see. Some such thing as this happens, apparently, to the grandmother in **"A Good Man Is Hard to Find,"** for when the Misfit shoots her he says, "She would have been a good woman if there had been somebody there to shoot her every minute of her life."

The idea of death as a manifestation of grace, which is central to a number of O'Connor works, is fully explained in a book by the Jesuit priest to whose writings Miss O'Connor often paid her respects, Teilhard de Chardin. Describing, in *The Divine Milieu,* the soul's progress toward the final leap out of itself which delivers it from its own bondage into full union with the divine, Teilhard writes that near the end of the "progressive breaking down of our self-regard" we may still have the impression of "possessing ourselves in a supreme degree," for we will not yet have "crossed the critical point of our excentration, of our reversion to God."

> There is a further step to take: the one that makes us lose all foothold within ourselves. . . .
>
> In itself, death is an incurable weakness of corporeal beings, complicated, in our world, by the influence of an original fall. It is the sum and type of all the forces that diminish us, and against which we must fight without being able to hope for a personal, direct and immediate victory. Now the great victory of the Creator and Redeemer, in the Christian vision, is to have transformed what is in itself a universal power of diminishment and extinction into an essentially life-giving factor. God must, in some

> way or other, make room for himself, hollowing us out and emptying us, if he is finally to penetrate into us. . . . The function of death is to provide the necessary entrance into our inmost selves. It will make us undergo the required dissociation. It will put us into the state organically needed if the divine fire is to descend upon us.

Thus Teilhard on the transforming power of death. In O'Connor we see it again in **"The Displaced Person,"** where the hired man's wife, Mrs. Shortley, dies of a sudden convulsive seizure, trying desperately to clutch to her everything within her reach, including "her own moon-like knee." Suddenly, with a look of astonishment on her face, she collapses, "displaced . . . from all that belonged to her" and seeming to contemplate for the first time "the frontiers of her true country." (pp. 4-7)

But we have said that the O'Connor doctrine was, even in comparison with that of other Catholics, eccentric, that it could even be repugnant; and perhaps there is nothing in the idea of the redemptive power of death, of death as rebirth, to bear this out. But having broached the work of Teilhard, we need only look at certain radical differences between his thought and O'Connor's to see how forbidding O'Connor is, even in the context of modern Catholic theology. She differs, that is, from Teilhard in one quite crucial area: in her attitude toward human life on earth, on the value and significance of worldly endeavor and experience. (p. 8)

[Teilhard] himself often gives lyrical, almost Whitmanesque, expression to his adoration of the created universe; and of course he was by scholarly profession a geologist, occupied with the physical history of the earth, with mere matter. He believed that one ought wholeheartedly to participate in the life of this "holy place," the earth; to do so is to prepare oneself for life in Christ, for though in the end one surrenders self, one must have, after all, a self to surrender. (p. 9)

How contrary all of this is to the doctrine of the O'Connor fiction. For what is oppressive about the O'Connor work as a whole, what is sometimes intolerable, is her stubborn refusal to see any good, any beauty or dignity or meaning, in ordinary human life on earth. A good indication of what must be called O'Connor's contempt for ordinary human life is the loathing with which she apparently contemplated the human body. She liked to describe faces—she hardly ever passed up an opportunity—and nearly all her faces are ugly. In the first novel, *Wise Blood,* this seems to be true without exception; human faces remind her of rodents, cats, hogs, mandrills, and vegetables; they are frog-like, hawk-like, gap-toothed, mildewed, shale-textured, red-skinned, stupid, demented, and simply "evil." Each part of the physiognomy comes in for its share of abuse; hair is likened to dirty mops and rings of sausages—it is said to stream down the face like ham gravy. One could continue the catalog—but the point, I think, is clear. Human beings are ugly in every way; the human form itself is distinctly unpleasant to behold; human life is a sordid, almost unrelievedly hideous affair. The only human act that is worthy of respect is the act of renouncing all worldly involvement, pleasure, and achievement.

Now, about the short stories, it is quite true that if we take the O'Connor stories individually they seem in this respect much less oppressive; but reading them back to back by volume—one of the ways, surely, that we expect to be able to read short stories—one may find his resistance mounting to the view of life that together they present. We may well grant that here is Mrs. May, comically self-adoring and self-righteous in spite of the fact that, as all can plainly see, she is a narrow-minded, deluded, ridiculous old fool; here is Asbury, a failed artist—contemptibly convinced of his total superiority over everyone else and yet childishly blaming his failures on his mother; here are poor old Mrs. Cope, Mrs. Turpin (who thanks God for good disposition), the appalling Ruby Hill. The images of these people rise up so graphically before us as we read—their manners, their speech are so cunningly done—that we freely respond to their reality within the story. Yet at the same time, one is dimly aware that the author is trying to make their stories say something, prove something about life, to which one cannot respond. For the revelation that O'Connor wanted to push us to—the truth about life that she wanted to force us to grant—was that these people represent, even at their comic worst, the norm of modern society.

And one's own experience simply will not support such a view. With all one's admiration for the high technical brilliance of O'Connor's work, for her cunning selection of detail and delicate sense for nuance in speech and manners, and for the wonderfully controlled momentum with which her stories move—even with all this, one's pleasure is at least diminished by the fact that what the stories are moving *to* is a truth or hypothesis about life that sometimes seems hardly worth our consideration. We may feel that the stories would appear, seen from a certain point of view, nearly perfectly executed, but that that point of view is not ours, that—to restate the dilemma in Boothian terms—we cannot be the readers the stories require us to be. (pp. 9-11)

Critics have been fond of indirectly reminding readers that they must not be prejudiced against O'Connor because she is a Catholic; they say, in effect: "It's her art that matters, not what she believed." But of course what she believed—the view of the world that her stories offer us—does matter very much. (pp. 12-13)

[One] does not wish to say, flatly, that the O'Connor view is "not convincing." Her reading, for instance, of the delusions, the weaknesses, the hypocrisy—in short, the bad—in human nature is, in itself, highly persuasive. But what is false in her work springs from her failure to see that though man is all the things herein implied, he is not only these things—and the total picture of human society that emerges from her work as a whole is one that is difficult to accept.

But the argument I have been making about the O'Connor work had better be bent now in another direction. Thus far I have deliberately left out of account, as much as possible, the celebrated O'Connor comedy. . . . [We] have our ways, in American criticism today, of evading doctrinal problems in the writers we admire, and it seems that one of our ways of averting the religious fundamentalism in O'Connor has been to overemphasize her comedy. The reader who sums O'Connor up as "a fine comic writer"—*a comic writer,* that is, and just that—cannot finally be taken very seriously. . . . One may even grant that O'Connor's real forte was for comic writing, or that what one most enjoys in her stories is their comedy—but that does not make her "a comic writer." (p. 14)

[There] are indeed a few stories that can safely be termed comedies and it is true that they are among her very best. Probably the three finest of this type are **"The Life You Save May Be Your Own," "Good Country People,"** and **"Parker's Back,"** a wonderfully funny story written during the last painful months of Miss O'Connor's life. One does not mean to say that these stories constitute a special set, clearly different from the other work—like all O'Connor works they are concerned with the problem of Christian belief; but the comically absurd aspects of the search for belief, which in O'Connor are seldom lost sight of completely, are continually in the foreground; the comic tone prevails, and the stories end, not—like most of the others—in sudden violent death or devastation for the protagonist, but as comic stories rightly do: in a much less painful ironic comeuppance. Hulga, for instance, in **"Good Country People,"** has her wooden leg stolen by the phony Bible salesman she has been intending tenderly to convert to atheism. All three of these tautly controlled stories are full of exuberant comedy (one hardly knows anything funnier than the first meeting of Mr. Shiftlet and the old woman in the opening scene of **"The Life You Save May Be Your Own"**), and they are all "stretchers," parable-like tall tales in the tradition of frontier and southern country humor of which Faulkner's "Was" is perhaps the modern classic.

In most of the other short stories the comedy is much more caustic and more tense, and something sinister is at work all along, preparing the reader to have the grin wiped off his face at the end. Having quoted the final scene of **"Greenleaf,"** we can use it again here as an example. This story contains one of the funniest O'Connor episodes: the fastidious Mrs. May discovering, on her walk through her precious woods, her farmhand's wife on her knees moaning over some newspaper clippings in some kind of primitive religious rite; but the story ends, as we have seen, with Mrs. May being gored to death by a bull—one of his horns piercing her heart, making the tree line look like a "dark wound in a world that was nothing but sky." Certainly the emotions elicited here are those of horror, surprise, and pain; we may feel that in a sense what happened to the prideful Mrs. May "served her right," but surely the dominant feeling here is not a satisfied sense of comic comeuppance. (pp. 15-16)

One raises this issue of the pervasiveness of the comedy in O'Connor not at all to prepare the reader for a tired struggle with this generic term, but because the tonal dimension in O'Connor is an important critical issue and because it is directly related to the central fact about this writer with which we have been dealing—the fact that she is a highly doctrinal writer whose view of human life often seems to modern readers strange and eccentric in the extreme. Such terms as comedy, farce, tragedy are, of course, loaded words in more ways than one. Those who see O'Connor as "a comic writer" can certainly find plenty of O'Connor's own statements to quote to their advantage. There is her famous statement about *Wise Blood,* that it was to her a "comic novel" but—and surely this is to beg the question—"like all comic novels" about "matters of life and death." There is an even stranger statement which describes as "comic" the bizarre and, surely for most readers, ultimately painful story **"A Good Man Is Hard to Find."** It is this latter story that I wish to pause here to examine in detail.

"A Good Man Is Hard to Find" is a story that contains some of the best O'Connor comedy but which ends in a highly unsatisfactory way; and the failure of the final scene—and hence of the story—seems to result from the fact that a tonal shift that occurs midway through the story finally runs out of control. The story is interesting for our purposes in that we get a clearer view here than anywhere else of the tonal problem that exists in one degree or another in nearly all of O'Connor's fiction—the problem, that is, of how to "take," how to react to, the disasters that befall her characters. (pp. 17-18)

"A Good Man Is Hard to Find" divides, in terms of the time it encompasses, into two parts. The opening page of the story describes the grandmother's attempt to get the family to go to Tennessee instead of Florida on their vacation; this serves as a kind of brief prologue to the rest of the tale, all of which takes place the following day as the family begins its fatal trip to Florida. (pp. 18-19)

Plainly it is a comic view of the family that we get in the first half of the story—and it is rich comedy indeed. The comedy issues, as it often does in O'Connor, from the author's dry, deadpan, seemingly unamused reporting of the characters' hilarious actions and appearance. Like many good modern comedies, the story is, in other words, all the funnier for not appearing to be told in a funny way. The grandmother, of course, is the largest and funniest figure, and she is the character from whose point of view the tale unfolds. (p. 20)

[We] relish the comical side of the grandmother's character: her busy-body backseat driving—which so infuriates her ill-natured son Bailey ("He didn't have a naturally sunny disposition like she did."); her awful humor ("'Where's the plantation?' John Wesley asked. 'Gone with the Wind,' said the grandmother."); the inevitable childlike recounting of her early courting days ("She would have done well to marry Mr. Teagarden because he was a gentleman and had bought Coca-Cola stock when it first came out."). (p. 21)

But for all the grandmother's innocence and absurdity, one's feelings about her are by no means totally negative. If she is not endowed with insight into the eternal scheme of things—well, what of that? It is certainly possible to feel affection for the grandmother—though one may not be sure, as he reads, whether against the grain of the story or not. And yet surely there are lines and passages where the story is designedly setting our sympathies astir. The grandmother has a liveliness, curiosity, and responsiveness that the others seem to lack. Her true delight in telling stories ("she rolled her eyes and waved her head and was very dramatic") and in watching June Star dance ("the grandmother's eyes were very bright . . . she swayed her head from side to side") does not cast her in an ugly light. And the tone of such a passage as this, for instance, where she plays with the baby, is hardly ambiguous: "The grandmother offered to hold the baby and the children's mother passed him over the front seat to her. She set him on her knee and bounced him and told him about the things they were passing. She rolled her eyes and screwed up her mouth and stuck her leathery thin face into his smooth bland one. Occasionally he gave her a faraway smile." It is the grandmother, moreover, who sees the beauties of the Georgia landscape—the "blue granite," for instance, "that in some places came up to both sides of the highway; the brilliant red clay banks slightly streaked with purple; and the various crops that made rows of green lacework on the ground." (pp. 23-4)

[All] in all, the comedy of the grandmother's portrait is not wholly without warmth, is not totally abusive and satiric. Certainly one cannot view the grandmother as one whose malignity of soul is such that one can welcome—be amused by, or, let us say, accept in a comic spirit—her fatal comeuppance at the hands of the Misfit. There is not, in other words, such heavy stylization, such gross distortion, in the characterization of the old lady that one's distance from her is great enough to preclude any pain that her tortured death might bring. Indeed, there is everywhere in the first part of this story the most scrupulous comic realism. It is the averageness, the typicality of this old grandmother that is so nicely caught by the story. (p. 24)

[What we have in the story until the family's car wreck] is a skillful and richly entertaining domestic comedy of a not very lighthearted if not totally abusive kind. . . . [If] it crosses our minds, as we read, to wonder at all where the story is heading (and because O'Connor always *seems* to have her tales so well in hand, usually it doesn't cross our minds), the actual appearance of a death-dealing Misfit does not seem a very likely possibility. Some final sumptuous comic irony—harmlessly or indirectly involving, perhaps, the real or an imagined Misfit—is probably what one half-consciously expects.

Then the story breaks in two. Behind the [car] wrecked family, sitting paralyzed with fear and shock in the ditch, the woods, which seen a few hours ago from the highway were full of silver-white sunlight, are now described as "tall and dark and deep." After the arrival of the convicts, the line of woods behind them will be said in fact to *gape* "like a wide open mouth"; and when the first member of the family is taken off to the woods and shot, the wind will seem to the grandmother "to move through the tree tops like a long satisfied insuck of breath." A very different story indeed! (pp. 26-7)

What *is* the reader to think or feel about anything in the massacre scene? There is pain and shock but much that mocks that pain and shock—the heavy comedy, for instance, indeed one might say the almost burlesque treatment, of the three killers. There is the feeling that though we cannot help but pity the tormented family, the story continues to demand our contempt for them. One feels that somehow the central experience of the story—in spite of the affecting, the chilling details surrounding these deaths, in spite even of the not altogether abusive treatment of the grandmother in Part One—will elude anyone who gives way to these feelings of pain and pity. If the writer's task is, as Conrad said, to make us "see," what is here to be seen? Surely not that life is wholly senseless and contemptible and that our fitting end is in senseless pain.

Looking at the narrative skeleton of the story again, having corrected our original notion of it after reading the final half, what now do we have? An ordinary and undistinguished family, a family even comical in its dullness, ill-naturedness, and triviality, sets out on a trip to Florida and on an ordinary summer day meets with a terrible fate. In what would the interest of such a story normally lie? Perhaps, one might think, in something that is revealed about the family in the way it meets its death, in some ironical or interesting truth about the nature of those people or those relationships—something we had been prepared unbeknownst to see, at the end plainly dramatized by their final common travail and death. But obviously, as regards the family as a whole, no such thing happens. The family is shown to be in death just as ordinary and ridiculous as before. With the possible exception of the grandmother, we know them no better; nothing about them of particular significance is brought forth.

The grandmother, being . . . the last to die, suffers the deaths of all her family while carrying on the intermittent conversation with the Misfit, and any reader will have some dim sense that it is through this encounter that the story is trying to transform and justify itself. One senses that this conversation—even though our attention is in reality fastened upon the horrible acts that are taking place in the background (and apparently against the thrust of the story)—is meant to be the real center of the story and the part in which the "point," as it were, of the whole tale lies.

But what is the burden of that queer conversation between the Misfit and the grandmother; what power does it have, even when we retrospectively sift and weigh it line by line, to transform our attitude towards the seemingly gratuitous—in terms of the art of the tale—horror of the massacre? The uninitiated reader will not, most likely, be able to unravel the strange complaint of the killer without some difficulty, but when we see the convict's peculiar dilemma in the context of O'Connor's whole work and what is known of her religious thought, it is not difficult to explain.

The Misfit's most intriguing statement—the line that seemingly the reader must ponder, set as it is as the final pronouncement on the grandmother after her death—is from the final passage . . . : "She would of been a good woman if it had been somebody there to shoot her every minute of her life." Certainly we know from the first half of the story that the grandmother has seen herself as a good woman—and a good woman in a day when good men and women are hard to find, when people are disrespectful and dishonest, when they are not nice like they used to be. The grandmother is not common but a lady. . . . (pp. 29-31)

A good woman, perhaps we are given to believe, is one who understands the worthlessness and emptiness of being or not being a "lady," of having or not having Coca-Cola stock, of "being broad" and seeing the world, of good manners and genteel attire. "Woe to them," said Isaiah, "that are wise in their own eyes, and prudent in their own sight," The futility of all the grandmother's values, the story strives to encapsulate in this image of her disarray after the car has overturned and she has recognized the Misfit: "The grandmother reached up to adjust her hat brim as if she were going to the woods with him but it came off in her hand. She stood staring at it and after a second she let it fall on the ground."

The Misfit is a figure that seems, one must say to the story's credit, to have fascinated more readers than any other single O'Connor character, and it is by contrast with the tormented spiritual state of this seeming monster that the nature of the grandmother's futile values becomes evident. We learn that the center of the Misfit's thought has always been Jesus Christ, and what becomes clear as we study over the final scene is that the Misfit has, in the eyes of the author, the enormous distinction of having at least faced up to the problem of Christian belief. And everything he has done—everything he so monstrously does here—proceeds from his inability to accept Christ, to truly believe. . . . The crucial modern text for the authorial view here, which belongs to a tradition in religio-literary thought sometimes referred to as the sanctification of the sinner, is T. S. Eliot's essay on Baudelaire, in which he states: "So far as we are human, what we do must be either evil or good; so far as we do evil or good, we are human; and it is better, in a paradoxical way, to do evil than to do nothing; at least, we exist. It is true that the glory of man is his capacity for salvation; it is also true to say that his glory is his capacity for damnation."

Thus observe how, in the context of these statements, **"A Good Man Is Hard to Find"** begins to yield its meaning. What O'Connor has done is to take, in effect, Eliot's maxim—"It is better, in a paradoxical way, to do evil than to do nothing"—and to stretch our tolerance of this idea to its limits. The conclusion that one cannot avoid is that the story depends, for its final effect, on our being able to appreciate—even to be startled by, to be pleasurably struck with—the notion of the essential moral superiority of the Misfit over his victims, who have lived without choice or commitment of any kind, who have in effect not "lived" at all.

But again, in what sense is the grandmother a "good woman" in her death, as the Misfit claims? Here even exegesis falters. Because in her terror she calls on the name of Jesus, because she exhorts the Misfit to pray? Is she "good" because as the old lady sinks fainting into the ditch, after the Misfit's Jesus speech . . . , she mumbles, "Maybe he didn't raise the dead"? Are we to see her as at last beginning to face the central question of human existence: did God send his son to save the world? Perhaps there is a clue in the dead grandmother's final image: she is said to half lie and half sit "in a puddle of blood with her legs crossed under her like a child's and her face smiling up at the cloudless sky." For Christ said, after all, that "whosoever shall not receive the kingdom of God as a little child shall in no wise enter herein."

To see that the Misfit is really the one courageous and admirable figure in the story; that the grandmother was perhaps—even as he said—a better woman in her death than she had ever been; to see that the pain of the other members of the family, that any godless pain or pleasure that human beings may experience is, beside the one great question of existence, *unimportant*—to see all these things is to enter fully into the experience of the story. Not to see them is to find oneself pitted not only against the forces that torture and destroy the wretched subjects of the story, but against the story itself and its attitude of indifference to and contempt for human pain.

Now as it happens, **"A Good Man Is Hard to Find"** was a favorite story of O'Connor's. . . . The intrusion of grace in **"A Good Man Is Hard to Find"** comes, Miss O'Connor said [see excerpt dated 1963], in that much-discussed passage in which the grandmother, her head suddenly clearing for a moment, murmurs to the Misfit, "Why, you're one of my babies. You're one of my own children!" and is shot just as she reaches out to touch him. The grandmother's gesture here is what, according to O'Connor, makes the story work; it shows that the grandmother realizes that "she is responsible for the man before her and joined to him by ties of kinship which have their roots deep in the mystery she has been merely prattling about so far," and it affords the grandmother "a special kind of triumph . . . which we instinctively do not allow to someone altogether bad."

This explanation does solve, in a sense, one of the riddles of this odd story—although, of course, one must say that while it is interesting to know the intent of the author, speaking outside the story and after the fact, such knowledge does not change the fact that the intent of the narrator manifested strictly within the story is damagingly unclear on this important point. And what is even more important here is that O'Connor's statement about the story, taken as a whole, only further confirms the fact that the tonal problem in this tale is really a function of our difficulty with O'Connor's formidable doctrine. About the Misfit, O'Connor says that while he is not to be seen as the hero of the story, yet his capacity for grace is far greater than the grandmother's and that the author herself prefers to think "that the old lady's gesture, like the mustard-seed, will grow to be a great crow-filled tree in The Misfit's heart, and will be enough of a pain to him there to turn him into the prophet he was meant to become" [see excerpt dated 1963]. The capacity for grace of the other members of the family is apparently zero, and hence—Christian grace in O'Connor, one cannot help noting, is rather an expensive pro-

Editor O'Connor surrounded by the staff of The Corinthian, *the literary quarterly of Georgia State College.* Spectrum *photo taken from the 1945 edition, Georgia College, Milledgeville, GA.*

cess—it is proper that their deaths should have no spiritual context whatever. (pp. 31-5)

[In O'Connor], to shock, confuse, and frighten the reader seems to be part of the authorial strategy. No one, I think, can now doubt that Flannery O'Connor saw herself as a writer with a gift of prophecy. In one of the last speeches Miss O'Connor made before her death, she said: "The Lord doesn't speak to the novelist as He did to his servant Moses, mouth to mouth. He speaks to him as He did to those two complainers, Aaron and Aaron's sister Mary: through dreams and visions, in fits and starts, and by all the lesser ways of the imagination." The Lord may not speak this way or that—but he speaks! Her work must certainly be seen as, whatever else it is, a message and a warning, in the same way that the work of Bunyan is—and of Bernanos, Wright, and Lawrence—and in the way that the work of, say, Joyce, Faulkner, Warren, and Hemingway, is not.

O'Connor was continually deploring, in her public statements, the absence of common assumptions between herself and her secular readers; one sees over and over again a writer brooding on the radical differences in the Catholic (or, let us say, the religious-intuitive) and the secular views of the world and on what these differences imply for her art. "The Catholic novelist believes," she said, "that you destroy your freedom by sin; the modern reader believes, I think, that you gain it that way." (p. 38)

[Most] of the O'Connor short stories can be viewed as admonitory parables. "There was once a proud woman of great estate," some of them seem to go, "and this woman believed that the name of her saviour should only be said in church." The reader must learn to see himself in the absurd and deluded O'Connor characters—in the family of **"A Good Man Is Hard to Find,"** for instance, in Julian and Mrs. May. As the radio evangelists continue to tell their "lest-nin' audiences" every day: "You got to know you're lost before you can be saved—you got to see your condition for what it is." And if a writer must use harsh and violent means to wrench the unbeliever from his sweet bed of illusions, then he must.

Be all this as it may, what has been particularly troublesome about much of the O'Connor criticism of the past decade has been the assumption that merely by virtue of their power to pain and shock and disturb, the O'Connor stories are somehow good stories. But surely it takes only a moment's reflection to remind us that a story that appalls and shocks may or may not be a good story; the crudest, most fragmented accounts of human events—accounts that depict, for instance, however artlessly, terrifying scenes of pain and death—have the power to stun and frighten. The excesses of the modern film in this regard have taught many of us to regard the aesthetically meaningless use of pain and shock with particular disgust. One does not mean to say that O'Connor's depiction of human suffering is—in terms of the author's peculiar point of view—gratuitous; the reader's frustration comes from not being able to share, from being, indeed, sometimes repelled by, the authorial attitude towards the events described.

There is a sense in which, as I have suggested, the O'Connor stories are designed as calculated affronts to humanistic thought. One often has the feeling, in reading an O'Connor story, of being initially quite in harmony with the authorial viewpoint, of enjoying the story exactly in the way it seemed meant to be enjoyed, and then of being—often almost without warning—shaken violently off the track, so that one feels almost deliberately shut out from the final, and thus the overall, experiences of the story. This state of affairs is disconcerting indeed; for one assumes that the power that the narrative artist has generally strived to acquire has been the power finally to accomplish the full seduction of the reader, to bring him finally into full and exciting union with the teller of the tale.

And yet of course, even with O'Connor, the aim really *was* to make the reader *see,* above all the futility of his life and the saving power of Christ; but many of us are simply too far gone in anthropocentric irreligiosity to make very good pupils for such a course of study. Much of the Christian art of the past still has, of course, the power to make us feel, if not the truth, at least the beauty and appeal of a certain side of Christian thought, of its doctrine, for instance, of a loving savior in whom all one's pain and failure can be laid; one thinks, for instance, of the gentle Christian lyricism of the poet Hopkins, and of the shattering drunken monologue of the wretched Marmeladov in *Crime and Punishment.* Christian art is not dead for us, and there would still seem to be a great deal of common ground between humanistic Christian thought and secular humanism for the Christian artist to occupy if he can. But perhaps the crucial word here is "humanistic." For certainly O'Connor's Christian faith was as grim and literalistic, as joyless and loveless a faith, at least as we confront it in her fiction, as we have ever seen in American letters—even, perhaps, in American theology. (pp. 39-41)

And yet with all that one has now said about the philosophical and tonal dilemma in O'Connor, there is also a great deal to say positively about her art. . . . One can be sure that O'Connor felt, along with the temptation simply to punish and outrage her rationalist readers, a deep desire to communicate a vision of life the oddness of which no one was more aware of than she herself. A strategy for finding some common ground between herself and her readers did certainly exist in her work and was often highly successful. (p. 42)

Martha Stephens, in her The Question of Flannery O'Connor, *Louisiana State University Press, 1973, 205 p.*

ALICE WALKER (essay date 1975)

[*A black American novelist, short story writer, and poet, Walker is noted for works that powerfully express her concern with racial, sexual, and political issues, particularly the black woman's struggle for spiritual and political survival. She is best known for her novel* The Color Purple *(1982), which was awarded both the American Book Award and the Pulitzer Prize. Raised in poverty in a large sharecropping family, Walker lived during 1952 "within minutes" of the O'Connor farm, Andalusia. In the essay excerpted below, Walker recounts a 1974 visit with her own mother to their former home and to Andalusia. Walker here describes "Everything That Rises Must Converge" to her mother, and then she reflects on O'Connor's artistic achievement, praising her unsentimental portrayal of white Southern women and her depiction of blacks which, according to Walker, became more accurate as O'Connor matured as a writer.*]

"O'Connor wrote a story once called **'Everything That Rises Must Converge.'"**

"What?"

"Everything that goes up, comes together, meets, becomes one thing. Briefly, the story is this: an old white woman in her fifties—"

"That's not old! I'm older than that, and I'm not old!"

"Sorry. This middle-aged woman gets on a bus with her son, who likes to think he is a Southern liberal . . . he looks for a black person to sit next to. This horrifies his mother who, though not old, has old ways. She is wearing a very hideous, very expensive hat, which is purple and green."

"Purple and *green*?"

"Very expensive. *Smart*. Bought at the best store in town. She says, 'With a hat like this, I won't meet myself coming and going.' But in fact, soon a large black woman, whom O'Connor describes as looking something like a gorilla, gets on the bus with a little boy, and she is wearing this same green and purple hat. Well, our not-so-young white lady is horrified, out*done*."

"I *bet* she was. Black folks have money to buy foolish things with too, now."

"O'Connor's point exactly! Everything that rises, must converge."

"Well, the green-and-purple-hats people will have to converge without me."

"O'Connor thought that the South, as it became more 'progressive,' would become just like the North. Culturally bland, physically ravished, and, where the people are concerned, well, you wouldn't be able to tell one racial group from another. Everybody would want the same things, like the same things, and everybody would be reduced to wearing, symbolically, the same green and purple hats."

"And do you think this is happening?"

"I do. But that is not the whole point of the story. The white woman, in an attempt to save her pride, chooses to treat the incidence of the identical hats as a case of monkey-see, monkey-do. She assumes she is not the monkey, of course. She ignores the idiotic-looking black woman and begins instead to flirt with the woman's son, who is small and black and *cute*. She fails to notice that the black woman is glowering at her. When they all get off the bus she offers the little boy a 'bright new penny.' And the child's mother knocks the hell out of her with her pocketbook."

"I bet she carried a large one."

"Large, and full of hard objects."

"Then what happened? Didn't you say the white woman's son was with her?"

"He had tried to warn his mother. 'These new Negroes are not like the old,' he told her. But she never listened. He thought he hated his mother until he saw her on the ground, then he felt sorry for her. But when he tried to help her, she didn't know him. She'd retreated in her mind to a historical time more congenial to her desires. 'Tell Grandpapa to come get me,' she says. Then she totters off, alone, into the night."

"Poor *thing*," my mother says sympathetically of this horrid woman, in a total identification that is *so* Southern and *so* black.

"That's what her son felt, too, and *that* is how you know it is a Flannery O'Connor story. The son has been changed by his mother's experience. He understands that, though she is a silly woman who has tried to live in the past, she is also a pathetic creature and so is he. But it is too late to tell her about this because she is stone crazy."

"What did the black woman do after she knocked the white woman down and walked away?"

"O'Connor chose not to say, and that is why, although this is a good story, it is, to me, only half a story. *You* might know the other half. . . ."

"Well, I'm not a writer, but there *was* an old white woman I once wanted to strike . . ." she began.

"Exactly," I said.

I discovered O'Connor when I was in college in the North and took a course in Southern Writers and the South. The perfection of her writing was so dazzling I never noticed that no black Southern writers were taught. The other writers we studied—Faulkner, McCullers, Welty—seemed obsessed with a racial past that would not let them go. They seemed to beg the question of their characters' humanity on every page. O'Connor's characters—whose humanity if not their sanity is taken for granted, and who are miserable, ugly, narrow-mined, atheistic, and of intense racial smugness and arrogance, with not a graceful, pretty one anywhere that is not at the same time, a joke—shocked and delighted me.

It was for her description of Southern white women that I appreciated her work at first, because when she set her pen to them not a whiff of magnolia hovered in the air (and the tree itself might never have been planted), and yes, I could say, yes, these white folks without the magnolia (who are indifferent to the tree's existence), and these black folks without melons and superior racial patience, these are like Southerners that I know.

She was for me the first great modern writer from the South, and was, in any case, the only one I had read who wrote such sly, demythifying sentences about white women as: "The woman would be more or less pretty—yellow hair, fat ankles, muddy-colored eyes."

Her white male characters do not fare any better—all of them misfits, thieves, deformed madmen, idiot children, illiterates, and murderers, and her black characters, male and female, appear equally shallow, demented, and absurd. That she retained a certain distance (only, however, in her later, mature work) from the inner workings of her black characters seems to me all to her credit, since, by deliberately limiting her treatment of them to cover their observable demeanor and actions, she leaves them free, in the reader's imagination, to inhabit another landscape, another life, than the one she creates for them. This is a kind of grace many writers do not have when dealing with representatives of an oppressed people within a story, and their insistence on knowing everything, on being God, in fact, has burdened us with more stereotypes than we can ever hope to shed. (pp. 102, 104)

But *essential* O'Connor is not about race at all, which is why it is so refreshing, coming, as it does, out of such a *racial* culture. If it can be said to be "about" anything, then it is "about" prophets and prophesy, "about" revelation, and "about" the impact of supernatural grace on human beings who don't have a chance of spiritual growth without it.

An indication that *she* believed in justice for the individual (if only in the corrected portrayal of a character she invented) is shown by her endless reworking of **"The Geranium,"** the first story she published, when she was 21. She revised the story several times, renamed it at least twice, until, nearly 20 years after she'd originally published it (and significantly, I think, after the beginning of the Civil Rights Movement), it became a different tale. Her two main black characters, a man and a woman, underwent complete metamorphosis.

In the original story, "Old Dudley," a senile racist from the South, lives with his daughter in a New York City building that has "niggers" living in it too. The black characters are described as being passive, self-effacing people. The black woman sits quietly, hands folded, in her apartment; the man, her husband, helps Old Dudley up the stairs when the old man is out of breath, and chats with him kindly, if condescendingly, about guns and hunting. But in the final version of the story, the woman walks around Old Dudley (now called Tanner) as if he's an open bag of garbage, scowls whenever she sees him, and "didn't look like any kind of woman, black or white, he had ever seen." Her husband, whom Old Dudley persists in calling "Preacher" (under the misguided assumption that to all black men it is a courtesy title), twice knocks the old man down. At the end of the story he stuffs Old Dudley's head, arms, and legs through the banisters of the stairway "as if in a stockade," and leaves him to die. The story's final title is **"Judgement Day."**

The quality added is rage, and in this instance, O'Connor waited until she saw it *exhibited* by black people before she recorded it. . . .

Her view of her characters pierces right through to the skull. Whatever her characters' color or social position she saw them as she saw herself, in the light of imminent mortality. Some of her stories, **"The Enduring Chill"** and **"The Comforts of Home"** especially, seem to be written out of the despair that must, on occasion, have come from this bleak vision, but it is for her humor that she is most enjoyed and remembered. . . .

It mattered to [Flannery O'Connor] that she was a Catholic. This comes as a surprise to those who first read her work as that of an atheist. She believed in all the mysteries of her faith. And yet, she was incapable of writing dogmatic or formulaic stories. No religious tracts, nothing haloed softly in celestial light, not even any happy endings. It has puzzled some of her readers and annoyed the Catholic church that in her stories not only does good not triumph, but it is not usually present. Seldom are there choices and God never intervenes to help anyone win. To O'Connor, in fact, Jesus was God, and he won only by losing. She perceived that not much has been learned by his death by crucifixion, and that it is only by his continual, repeated dying—touching one's own life in a direct, searing way—that the meaning of that original loss is pressed into the heart of the individual. (p. 104)

There is a resistance by some to read O'Connor because she is "too difficult," or because they do not share her religious "persuasion." A young man who studied O'Connor under the direction of Eudora Welty some years ago, amused me with the following story, which may or may not be true:

"I don't think Welty and O'Connor understood each *other*," he said, when I asked if he thought O'Connor would have liked or understood Welty's more conventional art. "For Welty's part, she wrung her hands a lot, and when we reached a particularly dense and symbolic section of one of O'Connor's stories she would sigh very loudly and ask desperately, 'Is there a Catholic in the class?'"

Whether one "understands" her stories or not, one knows her characters are new and wondrous creations in the world and that not one of her stories—not even the earliest ones in which her consciousness of racial matters had not evolved sufficiently to be interesting or to differ much from the insulting and ignorant racial stereotyping that preceded it—could have been written by anyone else. As one can tell a Bearden from a Keene or a Picasso from a Hallmark card, one can tell an O'Connor story from any story laid next to it. Her Catholicism did not in any way limit (by defining it) her art. After her great stories of sin, damnation, prophesy, and revelation, the stories one reads casually in the average magazine seem to be about love and roast beef. (pp. 105-06)

She destroyed the last vestiges of sentimentality in white Southern writing; she caused white women to look ridiculous on pedestals, and she approached her black characters—as a mature artist—with unusual humility and restraint. She also cast spells and worked magic with the written word. (p. 106)

Alice Walker, "Beyond the Peacock: The Reconstruction of Flannery O'Connor," in Ms., *Vol. IV, No. 6, December, 1975, pp. 77-9, 102-06.*

ROBERT COLES (essay date 1980)

[An American psychiatrist and scholar, Coles is a leading authority on poverty and racial discrimination in the United States. Eschewing traditional academic research methods, Coles involves himself with the people he is studying, whether they are sharecroppers, civil rights activists, or distressed children. Coles has also written studies of various authors, examining their works in a sociological context; his subjects include James Agee, Elizabeth Bowen, George Eliot, Walker Percy, and O'Connor. He explains in the introduction to his Flannery O'Connor's South, *a study of the Southern milieu in O'Connor's life and work, that he first read O'Connor's fiction, and eventually met the writer while he was involved in civil rights activities in Georgia. In the following excerpt from his study, Coles discusses "The Lame Shall Enter First" as a tale about pride in collision with pride, stressing the secular-rationalist pride of Sheppard, the child-psychologist protagonist.]*

[Each] time I read **"The Lame Shall Enter First,"** I am all too sadly reminded of all of us: the child psychiatrists of the twentieth century, evangelist heroes to others, and all too quickly, to ourselves. We believe we know so much. We are going to do so much, rescue so many people, prevail over all sorts of conditions and difficulties. This story of Miss O'Connor's is, in utter brevity, a concrete instance of a constant temptation this life presents: that in trying to gain the whole world we end up lost. . . .

For the author the story was about pride, the sin of sins. The pride of someone who wants to rescue someone else—"a therapeutic triumph," as we hear it called in clinics. (p. 124)

It is a contemporary kind of pride that Flannery O'Connor was interested in depicting—working into the grain of a few of her characters, among them, certainly, Sheppard. Perhaps Sheppard is drawn a bit implausibly. The author is writing a sardonic, tragic short story; she might have, even so, tried to explore the persistent, self-sacrificing idealism of this twentieth-century "shepherd." Instead, she takes a certain cast of mind for granted. In an authorial comment at the beginning of the story she observes that for Sheppard "almost any fault would have been preferable to selfishness—a violent temper, even a tendency to lie." We are given the irony that his own son, Norton, is behaving selfishly. We will soon enough learn that this boy, whose mother has died, is a terribly forlorn child, who needs desperately the kind of father his own father wants to be for a difficult, pugnacious delinquent. Norton commits suicide—the author's revenge, arguably, on "health care professionals" who go proselytizing everywhere (among people, often, who want no part of them) while neglecting to take care of their home fires. A not very original plot; a plot we all have conjured up in our minds at one time or another: the fire in the firehouse, the robbery in the police station, the unrecognized illness in the doctor's home.

But the author is after something more than an especially tasty irony. Her disinterest in the psychology of a psychologist is deliberate, and stubbornly maintained. She is stalking pride. She grabbed it from its everyday rural Georgia life and put it in story after story: collapsing southern pride; the pride of landowners, of preachers, of dirt-farmers, of mothers and sons and mothers and daughters and a grandfather and his grandson. Why not the pride of a "counselor," a reformer, "an agent of psychiatric change," as the dreary expression goes in what is called (speaking of ironies) "the literature?"

No doubt a different writer, with a different sensibility, and as Miss O'Connor once put it, with "different fish to fry," could have taken the same, essential plot and evoked a poignance in Sheppard's life: the contours of human kindness—connected, as is often the case, with personal failings, or with the occurrence of tragedy. But this particular storyteller had a Christian's interest in pride, and her story is, really, one of pride in collision with pride in collision with pride. (p. 127)

We are made uncomfortable, distressed, unnerved by the pious self-righteousness of a man who aims to be unstinting in his personal kindness to a stranger, a provocative, mean-spirited one, at that. Who is this Sheppard? What about him is so incredible? That he should compare his own son unfavorably, in certain respects, to a stranger—a troubled delinquent, no less? Is it so unlikely, really, that a certain kind of intensely humanitarian person could be so virtuously giving to the lowly, the base, even—and then turn on his own kin with annoyance or worse? We are given this comparison: "Johnson's sad thin hand rooted in garbage cans for food while his own child, selfish, unresponsive, greedy, had so much that he threw it up." Whereas the lame and belligerent Johnson "had a capacity for real response and had been deprived of everything from birth," the "counselor" Sheppard's son "was average or below and had had every advantage." Those words: *capacity, deprived, advantage:* they are the moral words of our time, the means by which all too many of us judge the worth of people. It is no longer a matter of each soul before God; it is no longer a matter of His inscrutable wisdom—or of the three Fates doing their mysterious work. The issues for us are psychological, sociological, but, as the author makes clear, the inclination toward moral judgment is not thereby diminished. As Sheppard put it: "Johnson's worth any amount of effort because he had potential." Another word: potential. Did Christ have it in mind, as He walked the roads of that outlying province of the Roman Empire and healed *His* lame, and promised *them* a boost toward a Heavenly rest? Did He go around evaluating "capacities" for this or that, and studying who was or was not psychologically capable of a "real response?" The author has such questions directly on her mind as she moves us right away from the above comparison a father makes between his son and his patient, to the following most interesting, and, I believe, utterly critical comparison, so far as the story goes, not to mention the teller's intentions: "Sheppard's office at the reformatory was a narrow closet with one window and a small table and two chairs in it. He had never been inside a confessional but he thought it must be the same kind of operation he had here, except that he explained, he did not absolve. His credentials were less dubious than a priest's; he had been trained for what he was doing."

Again, the words that go with professionalism: *credentials,* and *trained*—and the uses to which they are put. It is no matter-of-fact mental comparison this man has felt impelled to make. He is the smart one, the knowing one, and for us, in this culture, the chosen one. He is not here to forgive, but to "evaluate." And so he does, as precisely as he knows how. The next paragraph delivers a crushing reminder of what such a mentality relies upon—ideologically, rather than, sure enough, spiritually: "When Johnson came in for his interview, he had been reading over the boy's record—senseless destruction, windows smashed, city trash boxes set afire, tires slashed—the kind of thing he found where boys had been transplanted abruptly from the country to the city as this one had. He came to Johnson's I.Q. score. It was 140. He raised his eyes eagerly."

In one paragraph, and with no polemical gesture, the author has given us a glimpse of our unselfconscious sociological cast of mind: a move to the city as an "explanation" of crimes, if not sins. And then the pride: a bright patient! A mirror of himself, the therapist! And then the I.Q. score—the moral judgment of a number! A meritocratic version of Heaven and Hell. A Calvinism of quotients. And soon enough, the rally of interpretations, explanations, justifications. The boy had "a monstrous club foot." It was bound "in a heavy black battered shoe with a sole four or five inches thick." What to make of that? Everything: "The case was clear to Sheppard instantly." The boy's "mischief was compensation for the foot."

Is the author straining the plausible, the credible, the realistic with such a line of narration? The issue here is pride; and the other person's pride, Miss O'Connor knew, is always easier to accept, talk about, write about, than one's own. Arrogant businessmen are everywhere in evidence to liberal or radical academics, say—who easily dismiss any charge that they might have their own arrogant language or habits. And vice-versa. Miss O'Connor makes sure we know that the pride of the delinquent is as "monstrous" as that of his therapist. "The line of his thin mouth was set with pride," we are told—a youth standing fast against the attempted inroads of a man whose assumptions are regarded as altogether different. This is an "adolescent" who yells "Satan"; who insists that Satan has him "in his power." The author describes the "sociocultural background," as social scientists put it, from which such belief has emerged: "This boy's questions about life had been answered by signs nailed on the pines trees: DOES SATAN HAVE YOU IN HIS POWER? REPENT OR BURN IN HELL. JESUS SAVES. He would know the Bible with or without reading it." The counselor has recognized an adversary—southern, rural, religious life. So doing, he falls back on his own ideas and ideals: "Where there was intelligence anything was possible." The kind of rumination soon gets put into the preliminary foray of a battle between two minds, and by extension, two cultures: "I'm going to arrange for you to have a conference with me once a week," the counselor tells his about-to-be patient. And adds: "Maybe there's an explanation for your explanation. Maybe I can explain your devil to you."

Miss O'Connor carefully develops the tension between the psychological mind of one person and the crime-driven, religion-haunted mind of another. It is interesting that critics worry about the construction of the counselor's character—as if the plausibility of the delinquent, Johnson, is of no real matter: another one of those southern freaks for which an author had a penchant. Yet, the portrayal of this youth, at once tough and hurt, resourceful and perversely stiff-necked, is strangely successful. Miss O'Connor demonstrates a brilliant sense of the canniness a certain kind of troubled youth can muster—a match, rather often, for even the best "trained" of us, who think of ourselves as graced by radarlike intelligence, able to pick up every single message sent our way. And she is altogether successful with the mind of this "therapist." In her own fashion she has conjured up the temptations that all the time threaten intellectuals—the treacherous self-satisfaction that spells spiritual doom.

The delinquent himself begins to realize how vain this apparently altruistic rescuer is. But the author doesn't throw such a development at us; she moves slowly toward it, a remarkably keen and patient build-up. If Miss O'Connor had no use for the present-day resort to psychology and psychotherapy as pagan religions, she held her grudge tightly in check:

> He had talked to Johnson every Saturday for the rest of the year. He talked at random, the kind of talk the boy would never have heard before. He talked a little above him to give him something to reach for. He roamed from simple psychology and the dodges of the human mind to astronomy and the space capsules that were whirling around the earth faster than the speed of sound and would soon encircle the stars. Instinctively he concentrated on the stars. He wanted to give the boy something to reach for besides his neighbor's goods. He wanted to stretch his horizons. He wanted him to *see* the universe, to see that the darkest parts of it could be penetrated. He would have given anything to be able to put a telescope in Johnson's hands.

The youth's pride persists. He doesn't yield, but his therapist begins to believe that he is "hitting dead center." The boy uses his clubfoot as a weapon and a shield: stay away, or else. The therapist fights on—calmly, persistently, ingeniously, intelligently, or so he hopes. He wants to channel energies misspent into what we all would regard as "constructive" directions. He understands his patient. He knows him—the terrible past, the fearful present, the anxiety about tomorrow, never mind next week, next year. And he begins to love him: fantasies of taking him in, working things out with him "in the home setting"—another expression of the clinic that blends that mixture of distance and intimacy which Miss O'Connor, in fact, is struggling hard to maintain between these two, at least in the early moments of their "relationship." And that is what she is sketching out, knowingly and tactfully. If we begin to squirm, it is because one of the two parties refuses to go along—ever. It is because we are witnessing the failure of what those in the so-called "helping professions" call an "approach." The more disarmingly "supportive" the therapist tries to be, the more reassuring he is, the more contemptuous the youth becomes. He is, indeed, what he has declared himself to be, a devilishly conniving character. He insinuates himself into his therapist's mind, then life—and the proudly "aware" therapist doesn't realize what is going on. A helper is trying to help someone who wants no such thing, but the harder the older one tries, the more elusive the younger one turns out to be.

For a while there is a standstill. The therapist persists in wanting to take the youth into his home—an ultimate escalation of "treatment" not unheard of: special circumstances require heroic efforts at retrieval. Delinquents especially stimulate in ardent therapists a Rousseau-like dream: this victim of so much worldly evil can yet be saved from his developing and severe "problems." But the youth (whose nasty talk and brutish behavior are viewed, with as much neutrality and equanimity as the counselor can mobilize, as "defensive mechanisms") won't take the "appropriate" steps, won't turn "constructive." At one point, after a good long time of acquaintance, the counselor makes a short speech. He is telling his son and his patient (and himself) why this exceedingly antisocial youth is to come live in the Sheppard household. Among the observations he offers, this one stands out: "I'd simply be selfish if I let what Rufus thinks of me interfere with what I can do for Rufus. If I can help a person, all I want is to do it. I'm above and beyond simple pettiness."

This is no oracular nonsense, the stuff of a writer intent on parody. It is a comment that snaps with the everyday reality of countless psychiatric clinics. I recall only too well the struggle waged in one of them to capture the right vocabulary, the right facial expression, the right tone of voice, the right manner of self-presentation. The self-assurance that risks turning into a needling haughtiness, a provocative presumptuousness. When Rufus Johnson tells the counselor Sheppard's son, Norton, that his father thinks he's Jesus Christ, we are not in the midst of a badly overwrought story, with an implausibility of character definition. We are distressingly close to a significant segment of this century's professional life. (pp. 128-33)

Miss O'Connor splits her story in half, ends the first part with that sharp judgment, that brilliant insight: Sheppard as, in his own estimate, the Son of God. The rest of the story is a judgment of another kind: the traditional tragedy that befalls hubris. A man has shaken his fist at the heavens, shown he dares dismiss another's faith, however flawed its human vessel—and even shown a wish to turn someone else into a copy of himself. The response of the avenging heavens is swift, terrible. The Bible-talking delinquent comes into the home of the psychology-thinking counselor, whose motherless son becomes, in no time, a pawn of retribution. Deftly, shrewdly, the author moves her light from one to another shadowy element in the relationship of these three: the delinquent's wayward brilliance—a powerful, if malevolent defense against smug, opinionated knowledge; the counselor's self-centeredness, fanatically summoned in the apparent service of another's salvation, but increasingly revealed as its own unyielding master; and a child's lost, fragile, anxious soul—used by one person, ignored by another, claimed at last by (we are given to believe) a desperately sought God.

An intellectual storyteller is taking pains to separate God's kingdom from man's, the saved from the damned, the just from the unjust. But she shuns neat psychological categories. Finally, we are judged elsewhere than on earth. Her task as a novelist is to let each character shed light on how life is variously lived. The delinquent acts, sins, quotes from the Bible. The child reveals the pride that innocence only masks—the Original Sin that we who describe early childhood reject as an explanation for the assertiveness, the petulance, the spitefulness, the egoism to be found in boys and girls. (As for the "aggression," the "oedipal rivalry" and jealousy and hostility we feel more comfortable describing, they are treatable.) The counselor takes on the entire universe. He buys a telescope for his charge, then a microscope: "If he couldn't impress the boy with immensity, he would try the infinitesimal." He is unceasingly the reformer, the man who will turn around the seeming destiny of another. A troubled mind will be heard, rendered whole through patient understanding. A lame leg will also be attended—a new, right-fitting shoe.

But the boy refuses to talk about what any therapist would call his problems; he also refuses the orthopedic rehabilitation extended him. His counselor thinks him "not mature enough" to want to wear the new shoe. What to do but wait and hope? The author has Sheppard "glumly entrenched behind the Sunday New York *Times*." Maybe an unnecessary touch, but hardly an inappropriate symbol. Miss O'Connor knows that, in the clutch, we all fall back on what we have—in this case, a Sunday paper that for the Sheppards of this land stands for moderation, rationality, a cosmopolitan outlook. Language also serves to reassure us—words such as *insecurity,* the *self* and of course, *identity.*

The harder Sheppard clings to his particular faith, the nearer he brings himself and his young patient to the edge of things. The youth is full of outrage, won't yield an inch of his self. He regards Sheppard as, ironically, a fraud: a would-be Christ, therefore the greatest sinner of all. In contrast he, Johnson (or is it John the Baptist's Son?) believes in Christ, believes the Devil has claimed him from Christ, believes no one can save him "but Jesus." Another one of Miss O'Connor's, and our heretics—a Jansenist dressed up as a clubfooted delinquent? Yes or no, some will argue that this engagement or confrontation is staged, all too calculated. How "real" is Sheppard?

Sheppard is, if anything, a character whose moral flaws are understated. His vanity emerges gradually—is suggested discreetly. He is not blind to his shortcomings. He is caught in a cultural web he never thought to examine—so busy was he examining the heads of others. We are not asked, in the tradition of Nietzsche, to embrace this raging, animal-like young man as the repository of nature's (antiacademic) truth. There is nothing heroic about the delinquent youth, Johnson. This is one of Flannery O'Connor's harshest, most vexing stories, especially difficult for her readers to take, precisely because the soft psychological and moral belly of secular, agnostic liberalism is not exposed by a saint, or a marvelous religious polemicist in the Dostoievsky tradition. Filling in for Alyosha, and Ivan, too, is a dreary wise guy, a bully who deserves to be locked up for a good long time. But a bully with a working knowledge of the Bible. A bully who knows he's going to hell—and who has a sharp-eye out for others, who may well already be there! An irony of ironies in this story, is the eventual realization, too late, by the counselor of *his* mental dodges, the evasions he uses, which put others in their places, so to speak, but leave him homeless.

"Satan has you in his power," Johnson tells Sheppard; then the youth stresses, "Not only me. You too." No self-righteousness from a disciple of Satan; rather, a candid claim that there are a lot more fellow travelers than someone may realize. Meanwhile, the counselor plays his last card, scoffs at the Bible, pulls out one interpretation after another from the psychological canon he has mastered, and slides into the despair he has avoided only by concentrating with all his mind and heart upon another's condition. Miss O'Connor does not, of course, object to such a devotion; nor is she working up a propaganda tract for Satan. She isn't really "against" psychology or psychiatry in the conventional, ideological sense of that preposition, "against." She is trying to dramatize an incompatibility she has seen about her in this modern world: intellectuals who mock traditional religion, then take a certain religious way of getting along with others; and believers of the Word, of the Book, who are challenged these days in a new manner, and who must defend themselves, as has been the case over the centuries, with every bit of guile it is possible to summon.

The suicide of Norton is no mere melodramatic ending, by a writer unafraid of violence. The boy dies with his own willful faith intact. He has launched a flight into space. He told his father that through the telescope he saw his (dead) mother—up there, waving to him. The father had, once more, interpreted "reality," made his clarification, taken on an illusion, without coming to terms with his own illusion— that, thereby, he is addressing himself to the mysteries and confusions of this terrible life so many of us live, his son included. We are left in the end, ironically, with psychology: a father who has neglected his own son in favor of a troubled patient, ends up losing both, the one to the police and the other in consequence of a suicide. But another point of view would insist that we are left with something else. Many times on the side of rural Georgia roads such as those the delinquent youth in this harsh and sad story could well have traveled, I have seen a cautionary sign that may well serve as a summation of the author's implicit moral lesson: PRIDE KILLETH. (pp. 135-38)

Robert Coles, in his Flannery O'Connor's South, *Louisiana State University Press, 1980, 166 p.*

ANDRÉ BLEIKASTEN (essay date 1982)

[*Bleikasten asserts that a strictly religious approach to O'Connor's work is often limiting. Offering a secular reading of "Parker's Back," Bleikasten traces the pure strangeness and wonder that lie beneath the religious allegory in O'Connor's fiction.*]

Flannery O'Connor's novels and stories are not all of equal merit, yet each of them has its moments of eerie intensity, each of them at some point verges on what Freud, in one of his essays, termed "the uncanny," *das Un heimliche*—that disquieting strangeness apt to arise at every turn out of the most intimately familiar, and through which our everyday sense of reality is made to yield to the troubling awareness of the world's otherness. Much of the impact and lasting resonance of O'Connor's work proceeds from its ability to *bewilder* the reader, to take him out of his depths and jolt him into a fictional environment which is both homely (*heimisch, heimlich*) and uncannily estranged.

"Parker's Back" is a case in point: homely, indeed, in its rural setting and characters, homely too in its action—a domestic tragicomedy pitting wife against husband—yet at the same time wildly extravagant, throbbing with violence, ablaze with madness and terror, *unheimlich*. . . . As a short story, it is perhaps not to be counted among [O'Connor's] finest achievements. Yet, to me at least, it is one of her most enigmatic and most gripping texts, the more so as it was her last, written in a hospital, a few weeks before her death.

What is it that makes **"Parker's Back"** so uniquely intriguing? Not its manner, assuredly, nor its subject. In most respects it is a very typical O'Connor story. . . . What we have here is another narrative of *conversion,* and once again conversion is achieved most unexpectedly through the sudden and brutal action of grace. **"Parker's Back"** belongs with O'Connor's most explicitly religious stories. The Old Testament names of the two central characters, the harsh fundamentalism of Parker's wife, the "burning bush" experience undergone by Parker in the farming accident, and the Byzantine Christ tattooed on his back are as many signposts, clearly pointing to the religious issues at stake in the text, and fastidious readers might well wince at the bluntness of its symbolism and at the unambiguousness of its intended message. O'Connor obviously wanted the story to be read in religious terms. . . . (pp. 8-9)

Whether she succeeded is of course open to question. She has indeed succeeded insofar as she has persuaded most critics to follow up her clues: nearly all readings of **"Parker's Back"** are merely elaborations of the religious meaning intended by its author. . . . [We] cannot disregard the apologetic intentions encoded in her texts. They are unmistakably there, and no honest reading of her fiction can leave them out of account. Other avenues of inquiry and interpretation, however, are not only possible, but legitimate, and some of them are well worth exploring. (pp. 9-10)

[Let's] try to reread her strange fictions as if we read them for the first time, in full response to their strangeness and wonder. What is it that startles and shocks us in reading a story like **"Parker's Back"**? Obviously, its most arresting feature, the one most likely to disturb a modern reader, is Parker's *tattooing*. The more surprising it is that in most discussions of the story it should have been given so little consideration. To be sure, all commentators refer to it, vaguely puzzled and perhaps even a bit disgusted (tattooing, in our "civilized" countries, has come to be considered an "unnatural" practice, associated with either savagery or deviant behavior), yet, in their eagerness to convert it at once into a secular metaphor for Parker's supposed spiritual quest, they tend to overlook its complex and shifting implications in the story of his development.

Parker's obsession with tattoos, we are told, begins when he is fourteen (in many cultures the canonical age for initiation) and sees a circus performer tattooed from head to foot. . . .

> Parker had never before felt the least motion of wonder in himself. Until he saw the man at the fair, it did not enter his head that there was anything out of the ordinary about the fact that he existed. Even then it did not enter his head, but a peculiar unease settled in him. It was as if a blind boy had been turned so gently in a different direction that he did not know his destination had been changed.

O'Connor here emphasizes—rather heavily, as she is often prone to do—the turning-point the experience at the country fair represents in Parker's destiny, and the reader is clearly "programmed" to see it not only as the beginning of a new life of "unease" and unrest, but also as a prefiguration of Parker's later conversion. One might see it too, however, less spiritually and more psychologically, as the beginning of an "identity crisis," a period of psychic disturbance taking Parker to the verge of madness. And what seems to be at stake in this crisis is above all his *body*. (pp. 10-11)

What enthralls Parker [about the tattooed man] is a body or, more precisely, a body *image,* the seductive spectacle of a pattern engraved on a human skin. The word "pattern" could not be more apropos, referring as it does to either an ornamental design or a model worthy of imitation. To Parker it is clearly both. . . . The man, as Parker sees him, is "one intricate arabesque of colors"; he has managed, that is, to achieve unity, integrity, and harmony, by making his body into an artifact, a work of art, and so comes quite naturally to serve as paradigm to Parker's own imaginarily anticipated metamorphosis. A boy, up to then, "whose mouth habitually hung open," he could hardly be credited with a self of his own. The sight of the tattooed man startles him out of his drooling stupor into awareness of a body not yet totally his, a body, to be appropriated and made whole and beautiful. An "awakening" has indeed occurred, but not in any spiritual sense, as Parker's exclusive concern, once he has had his "revelation," is the individuation of his body through systematic adornment of his skin. His enthrallment with the tattooed man points to nothing else but his late awakening to the exorbitant demands of narcissism.

By tattooing his skin, Parker, one might argue, attempts to phallicize his body, to turn it into a living fetish. . . . [All his tattoos] illustrate his narcissistic fantasies and attest to his desire for sexual daring, sexual potency, and unrestrained sexual gratification. One might add that they even seem to make some of his secret wishes come true. After being tattooed, Parker sets out to assert his manhood according to established norms of manliness. He begins, that is, "to drink beer and get in fights," and, what is more, his self-fetishization transforms him into a successful seducer: "He found out that the tattoos were attractive to the kind of girls he liked but who had never liked him before." In his amorous career at least, the investment he has made in his body seems to pay off rather nicely.

Parker's tattooing, then, has most remarkable effects in his life, altering as it does his relationship to himself as well as to others. Yet, . . . far from dispelling what O'Connor calls his "dissatisfaction," each new tattoo only makes it more acute. The more tattoos on his skin, the deeper his internal disorder and distress. As might be expected, the narcissistic attempt to transfigure his body ends in a shambles. In looking at himself in the mirror, Parker realizes with dismay that the tattoos fail to cohere, and that their overall effect is "of something haphazard and botched." . . . [His] series of cheap sexual triumphs comes likewise to a sorry end when he meets his wife-to-be, Sarah Ruth Cates.

His encounter with her marks the second turning-point in his destiny, and what follows it is his daily confrontation with someone who, in all conceivable respects, is his very opposite. Daughter of a "Straight Gospel preacher," Sarah Ruth is a fanatical fundamentalist. . . . Sara Ruth destroys his dream of carefree philandering by insisting on lawful marriage. It is she, too, who coaxes him into owning his Christian name, Obadiah Elihue, which he had been concealing behind noncommittal initials, and so brings him to acknowledge his identity as shaped by language and lineage. True, there is much more at issue in his Old Testament name, but, before searching for scriptural parallels, one would perhaps do well to recognize that Sarah Ruth's immediate function in the story is to discipline the unruly male, to cure him of his extravagant fantasies and make him conform to the accepted standards of a cultural order, and that, in this role, she performs a socializing (or "civilizing") task often assigned to woman in American fiction. To point out these secular implications of **"Parker's Back"** is not to belittle its religious significance, but rather to emphasize the interrelatedness of the sacred and the profane in its densely woven texture. While **"Parker's Back"** is clearly another O'Connor story about the bizarre and brutal workings of divine grace, it is also a grimly humorous folk tale about a boy's blundering search for selfhood and about the taming of a husband by a shrew, and it is all the better for being both. (pp. 11-14)

If sin and salvation are indeed central issues in **"Parker's Back,"** there is at least one other theme just as worthy of consideration: the theme of the *image,* and more specifically the question of the legitimacy—or illegitimacy—of representing the sacred. Parker and Sarah Ruth disagree on practically everything, but it is precisely on this point that their antagonism appears to be the sharpest. Whereas Parker pays allegiance to the image from first to last, Sarah Ruth remains throughout a consistent and militant iconoclast. As such, she is true not only to her fundamentalist faith, but to a fundamental and millenary religious tradition. In sharp contrast to pagan polytheism, monotheistic religions, from Judaism to Islam, have always been prone to condemn representations of God and have always been suspicious about images and icons at large. . . . It was a common accusation brought against the Jews and early Christians alike that they had neither altars, nor temples, nor any visible aids to devotion, and this charge was never denied. True, Christianity was later to give rise to a luxuriant proliferation of sacred images, yet it is probably not fortuitous that two of the most critical periods in the history of Christendom have been marked by fierce controversies about the legitimacy of their use: the iconoclastic movement, the "quarrel over images," is the most dramatic episode in the history of the Byzantine Empire, and in 16th century Europe, during the Reformation, the issue was likewise a matter of hot dispute between Catholics and Protestants. These historical reminders are only meant to suggest that Sarah Ruth's position is by no means eccentric, and that it will not do to dismiss her offhandedly as the mouthpiece of benighted bigotry. A heartless fanatic she may well be, and, insofar as she implicitly denies the mystery of Incarnation, her Christianity itself becomes extremely questionable. Yet she also stands, albeit, as a caricature, for one of Christianity's essential dimensions, for what we might call its Judaic heritage. In objecting to the Christ figure tattooed on Parker's back and telling him that "He's a spirit. No man shall see his face," she voices not only the letter but also the spirit of the biblical tradition. (pp. 14-15)

When Parker returns home and whispers his full name through the keyhole to get admittance from Sarah Ruth, he experiences a short moment of radiant stillness and harmony, as he feels "the light pouring through him, turning his spider web soul into a perfect arabesque of colors, a garden of trees and birds and beasts." The intimation is that his desire for patterned wholeness has eventually fulfilled itself, not, as he first expected, through a transformation of his body, but through a transfiguration of his soul. Yet the story does not end in beatitude, and in the closing scene we see poor Parker thrown out of his own house and thrashed by Sarah Ruth: "There he was—who called himself Obadiah Elihue—leaning against the tree, crying like a baby." Reborn, perhaps, but rather than accession to a new and higher identity, the last glimpse we get of Parker evokes regression to the utter helplessness of the newborn child, and if we try to imagine his future, we can think of nothing but further confusion, further humiliation, further suffering, in a grotesque *imitatio Christi* most likely to end in another crucifixion.

The half-comic, half-pathetic ending of **"Parker's Back"** may well have the reader puzzling whether, after all, he has not been treated to a stark and savage travesty à la Nathanael West, rather than to an edifying religious fable. For all overt symbols and authorial intrusions, ambiguity doggedly persists to the story's very end, and the contradictions and tensions that give it life are not dissolved. Perhaps they also remained unresolved in the author, and it is indeed tempting to read O'Connor's text as well as an almost autobiographical parable, in which are raised in analogical fashion some of the questions she had herself to face as artist and believer. Was the image, the representation of the sacred not also *her* problem? The writer

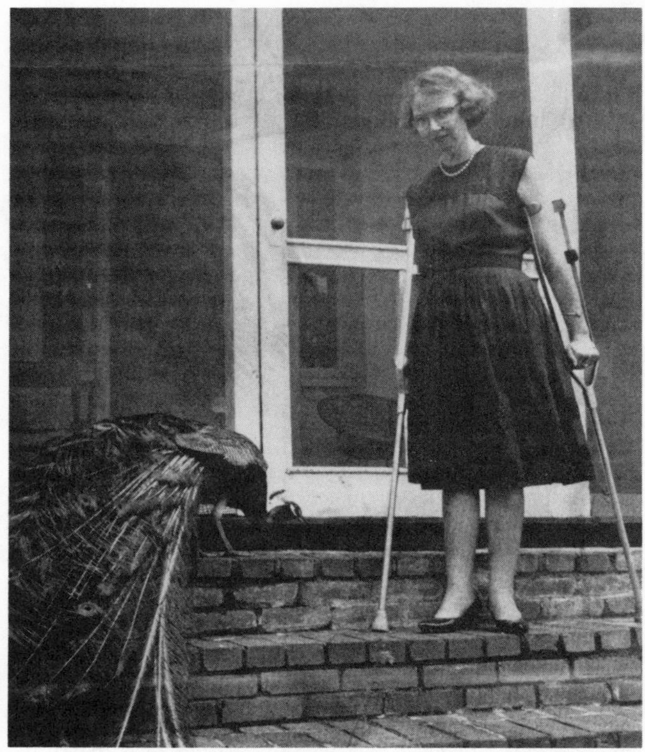

*O'Connor on the steps of her home, Andalusia, with one of her pet peacocks. Joe McTyre/*Atlanta Constitution.

deals in words, not in images, yet good writers have always been credited with "imagination," and whoever writes fiction attempts to make words into images, to move from the abstract mediacy of language to the vivid immediacy of the actual, and to render, as Joseph Conrad put it, "the highest kind of justice to the visible universe." [A footnote states: Flannery O'Connor quotes this statement from Conrad's preface to his *The Nigger of the Narcissus* in one of her letters.] As to O'Connor, she wanted moreover to render the highest kind of justice to the invisible universe, to reconcile, as the Byzantine artists had done, the aesthetic with the religious. Yet, alert as she was to all manifestations of evil, she must have sensed from the outset that artistic activity is never quite innocent, that it is always potentially guilty, especially when it takes over and turns into an exclusive passion. Art springs from a refusal of life *as given*. And so does tattooing, which is perhaps one of the most elementary and most archaic forms taken by the aesthetic impulse. The urge to adorn one's body reflects dissatisfaction with one's body in its natural state, as a mere given, a random and transient fragment of the world. As we have pointed out, Parker's tattooing rage, at least in its early phase, has no other source: he rejects his given body, even as he rejects his given name, because he wishes to become the sovereign shaper of his own gorgeous self. This wish is surely also the artist's, the writer's, and Parker, therefore, should be seen, not only as one of O'Connor's preacher figures, but also as an artist figure, and probably even as a comically distorted projection of the writer. Which is to say that tattooing in **"Parker's Back"** is as well a metaphor of writing, a metaphor the more relevant as its tenor and vehicle are indeed homologous: as tattooing is to the flesh, writing is to the blank page, to the ground of writing, and in both cases the move is from blankness to inscription, from undifferentiated and senseless matter to an "arabesque" of signs expanding into a unique individual blazon, a signature that cannot be mistaken for any other. Writing, in the last resort, is perhaps little more than an elaborate and displaced form of tattooing, a sublimation of the tattooed body into the *corpus,* tomb and temple of the written self. (pp. 16-17)

André Bleikasten, "Writing on the Flesh: Tattoos and Taboos in 'Parker's Back'," in The Southern Literary Journal, *Vol. 14, No. 2, Spring, 1982, pp. 8-18.*

RUSSELL KIRK (essay date 1987)

[*An American historian, political theorist, novelist, and journalist, Kirk is considered one of America's most eminent conservative intellectuals. His works, particularly* The Conservative Mind *(1953), have provided an impetus to a conservative revival in the United States since the 1950s. Kirk was acquainted with O'Connor, and in the following excerpt from a review of* Flannery O'Connor: Images of Grace, *by Harold Fickett and Douglas R. Gilbert (see Additional Bibliography), he summarizes her literary achievement, particularly in light of her radical Christian orthodoxy. Kirk also recounts remarks on O'Connor's fiction by the renowned American poet T. S. Eliot.*]

In our era of debased literary criticism and the fiction of nihilism, Flannery O'Connor's triumph is a phenomenon almost astounding. . . .

Her books appeared at a time when America's intellectual milieu—or at least the desiccated intellectuality of New York's reviewers and publishers, with few exceptions—clearly was hostile to Christian orthodoxy, the politics of prescription, the South, oldfangled rural life, and the mysteries of being. Yet today, no American novelist is more discussed than O'Connor. . . . In Harold Fickett's phrase [which he borrowed from O'Connor herself], she gives our decadent time an "incarnational art" that may wean us away from our present diet of literary Dead Sea fruit. (p. 429)

[Although] O'Connor was a talented comic writer, commonly she wrote of ugly actions here below. Innocent herself, so far as any of us can be, she perceived with high power of vision the boredom of most lives, the horror of fallen human nature, and the glory of grace and redemption. (p. 430)

Having acquainted myself with nearly everything that she had written by 1956, I wrote to T. S. Eliot—then my London publisher—that really he ought to read her, if he hadn't already. (There was precious little new fiction that I commended to Eliot.) He replied, in February 1957, that he had seen a book of her stories when he had visited New York, "and was quite horrified by those I read. She has certainly an uncanny talent of high order but my nerves are just not strong enough to take much of a disturbance."

Had Eliot penetrated below the surface of O'Connor's stories to the power of her moral imagination, he would have admired Flannery O'Connor as he admired Simone Weil, and for similar reasons; O'Connor's work, like Eliot's, rose out of faith in the Incarnation. But that acquaintance never came to pass. "Similarly with another book shown me in New York," Eliot went on in his same letter to me, "a novel by Nelson Algren; that is terrifying too and I do not like being terrified. Apart from the general aversion to prose fiction which I share with Paul Valery. I like pleasant, sunny comedies such as I write myself."

Eliot was unaware that a gulf was fixed between Nelson Algren (whose name he garbled in his letter) and Flannery O'Connor: the gulf between the diabolic imagination and the moral imagination, a subject discussed by Eliot himself in *After Strange Gods.* As for Eliot, so for O'Connor "the reverence and the gaiety" were not "forgotten in later experience"; no, not in "bored habituation," or fatigue, or tedium or "the awareness of death, the consciousness of failure."

Had Eliot summoned up courage sufficient to read O'Connor through, he would have discovered her similarities to Nathaniel Hawthorne, one of the few major American writers Eliot admired. For what fascinated O'Connor was sin—and redemption. As Pope John Paul I wrote not long before his death, without an understanding of the nature of sin it is not possible to form a conscience—or to become fully human. That is the teaching of *The Marble Faun, The Blithedale Romance. The Scarlet Letter;* it is the teaching of Flannery O'Connor through her tales ludicrous and violent. (pp. 431-32)

Many of O'Connor's readers, though fascinated by the oddity and misadventures of her characters, must wonder what her stories are all about. Her theological premises are unfamiliar to the common reader of our day—to put the deficiency mildly. (p. 432)

[Her] major stories have to do with what Max Picard called "the light from God." Modern man flees rebelliously from what Burke called "this world of reason, and order, and peace, and virtue, and fruitful penitence"; but God pursues.

A desperado is a being who has given up hope of salvation from the body of this death; who despairs of obtaining grace. (Our word is drawn from the Spanish, the language of Christian devotion.) The most forlorn and terrifying desperado in all Flannery's tales, to my mind, is The Misfit of **"A Good Man Is Hard to Find":** . . .

"Some fun!" squeals Bobby Lee the Misfit's piggish murdering accomplice, after he has shot the father, the mother, and the little girl.

"Shut up, Bobby Lee," The Misfit said. "It's no real pleasure in life."

Deprived of grace, the world ends with a whimper for some, with a bang for others. Multitudes of Misfits rise up, as if modernity had sown dragons' teeth. Resisting this antagonist world, Flannery O'Connor went out (in her own words) "to explore and penetrate a world in which the sacred is reflected." . . .

[You] may find it difficult to escape from the bright strangeness of O'Connor's fiction, which offers salvation through grace in death. Without preaching and without explaining her symbols, Flannery O'Connor became the great philosophical and theological novelist—better far than Graham Greene—of this dissolving twentieth century. (p. 433)

Russell Kirk, "Flannery O'Connor and the Grotesque Face of God," in The World and I, *Vol. 2, No. 1, January, 1987, pp. 429-33.*

ADDITIONAL BIBLIOGRAPHY

Abbot, Louise Hardeman. "Remembering Flannery O'Connor." *Southern Literary Journal* II, No. 2 (Spring 1970): 3-25.

Warm personal reminiscence by O'Connor's close friend. Abbot, who is probably the correspondent identified as "A" in *The Habit of Being*, was the recipient of some of O'Connor's most penetrating letters, and she here vividly evokes her friend.

Asals, Frederick. *Flannery O'Connor: The Imagination of Extremity*. Athens: University of Georgia Press, 1982, 268 p.
Asserts that the subject and form of O'Connor's fiction was shaped by the author's passion for extremes. Asals examines O'Connor's oeuvre within the framework of her "fascination with tensions and polarities."

Bertrande, Sister. "Four Stories of Flannery O'Connor." *Thought* 37, No. 146 (Autumn 1962): 410-26.
States that O'Connor's artistic purpose was to portray the "mystery of redemptive grace" acting upon spiritually deprived persons. According to Sister Bertrande, O'Connor employed scriptural parallels to convey this spiritual message.

Browning, Preston M., Jr. *Flannery O'Connor*. Carbondale: Southern Illinois University Press, 1974, 143 p.
Overview emphasizing dualism in O'Connor's fiction, particularly the opposition of the criminal and the holy.

Cheatham, George. "Jesus, O'Connor's Artificial Nigger." *Studies in Short Fiction* 22, No. 4 (Fall 1985): 475-79.
Brief discussion of the symbolism of the statue in "The Artificial Nigger."

Cheney, Brainard. "Miss O'Connor Creates Unusual Humor out of Ordinary Sin." *Sewanee Review* 71, No. 4 (Autumn 1963): 644-52.
Noted essay refuting John Hawkes's assertion that O'Connor's fiction is diabolical (see Hawkes's second annotation below dated 1962). Cheney, a friend of O'Connor, emphasizes her Christian viewpoint, stating that her humor lies in her ability to transform the everyday into the metaphysical.

———. "Flannery O'Connor's Campaign for Her Country." *Sewanee Review* 72, No. 4 (Autumn 1964): 555-58.
Obituary article describing O'Connor's vocation as a Christian writer.

Coffey, Warren. "Flannery O'Connor." *Commentary* 40, No. 5 (November 1965): 93-9.
Highly respectful review of *Everything That Rises Must Converge* stressing the effects—mostly negative, according to Coffey—of Irish Jansenism on O'Connor's work.

Driskell, Leon V., and Brittain, Joan T. *The Eternal Crossroads: The Art of Flannery O'Connor*. Lexington: University Press of Kentucky, 1971, 175 p.
Focuses on literary and theological influences on O'Connor's work and stresses its "essential unity and pervasive artistry." The authors establish the influences, especially those of François Mauriac and Pierre Teilhard de Chardin, and then chronologically examine O'Connor's published work.

Eggenschwiler, David. *The Christian Humanism of Flannery O'Connor*. Detroit: Wayne State University Press, 1972, 148 p.
Approaches O'Connor as a Christian humanist, aligning her with modern theologians, psychologists, and sociologists and placing her within the modern intellectual tradition. The critic defends O'Connor against charges of provincialism and demonstrates that humanist concerns were essential to the creation of her "complexly coherent literature."

Esprit 8 (Winter 1964).
A special memorial issue containing tributes to O'Connor by such critics as Saul Bellow, Cleanth Brooks, Granville Hicks, and Katherine Anne Porter.

Esty, William. "In America, Intellectual Bomb Shelters." *Commonweal* LXVII, No. 23 (7 March 1958): 586-88.
Brief judgment of O'Connor from an essay lamenting the political and social attitudes of America's younger writers. Esty identifies O'Connor as belonging to the "Cult of the Gratuitous Grotesque."

Farmer, David. *Flannery O'Connor: A Descriptive Bibliography*. New York: Garland, 1981, 132 p.
Catalogues and describes O'Connor's published writings from her student publications to the appearance of *The Habit of Being* in 1979. Farmer includes the cartoons O'Connor published in college as well as translations, adaptations, films, and parodies of her work.

Fickett, Harold, and Gilbert, Douglas R. *Flannery O'Connor: Images of Grace*. Grand Rapids, Mich.: William B. Eerdmans, 1986, 151 p.
Detailed biographical and critical essay by Fickett stressing O'Connor's Christian revolt against Modernist literary tradition. This volume includes a number of photos of O'Connor, her family, and friends, as well as a collection of photographs by Gilbert illustrating O'Connor's Southern milieu.

Fitzgerald, Robert. Introduction to *Everything That Rises Must Converge*, by Flannery O'Connor, pp. 5-30. New York: Farrar, Straus and Giroux, 1965.
Essay by O'Connor's close friend that is noted for its affectionate personal portrait and perceptive critical overview.

Flannery O'Connor Bulletin. I (1972-).
Quarterly bulletin devoted to biographical, bibliographical, and critical works on O'Connor.

Friedman, Melvin J., and Lawson, Lewis A., eds. *The Added Dimension: The Art and Mind of Flannery O'Connor*. New York: Fordham University Press, 1977, 263 p.
Collection of eleven original essays. The majority of essays concern general issues, including the grotesque, the influence of the fundamentalist South, and the role of prophecy in O'Connor's fiction. The book was first published in 1966, and many contributors do not consider *Everything That Rises Must Converge* in their discussions.

———, and Clark, Beverly Lyon, eds. *Critical Essays on Flannery O'Connor*. Boston: G. K. Hall, 1985, 227 p.
Anthology of original and reprinted material on O'Connor's fiction and nonfiction, as well as a selected, annotated secondary bibliography. Included are both reviews and more scholarly essays on O'Connor's work and a selection of tributes and reminiscences.

Gentry, Marshall Bruce. *Flannery O'Connor's Religion of the Grotesque*. Jackson: University Press of Mississippi, 1986, 177 p.
Attempts "fresh approaches to O'Connor's use of the grotesque and to her narration."

Getz, Lorine M. *Nature and Grace in Flannery O'Connor's Fiction*. Studies in Art and Religious Interpretation, Vol. 2. New York: Edwin Mellen Press, 1982, 182 p.
Investigates the theology of grace in O'Connor's fiction. Getz attempts to analyze the various actions of grace depicted in O'Connor's work and the literary devices used to convey them.

Golden, Robert E., and Sullivan, Mary C. *Flannery O'Connor and Caroline Gordon: A Reference Guide*. Boston: G. K. Hall, 1977, 333 p.
Detailed bibliography listing first editions of O'Connor's works, descriptive annotations of secondary sources published from 1952 to 1976, and Ph.D dissertations on O'Connor. Also included is an alphabetical index to titles by O'Connor, works about her, and their authors.

Gordon, Caroline. "Heresy in Dixie." *Sewanee Review* LXXVI, No. 2 (April-June 1968): 263-97.
Biographical essay including a detailed comparison of O'Connor's art, particularly the story "Parker's Back," with *Temptation of Saint Anthony* by Gustave Flaubert.

Grimshaw, James A., Jr. *The Flannery O'Connor Companion*. Westport, Conn.: Greenwood Press, 1981, 133 p.
Intended as an introduction to O'Connor's writings, both fiction and nonfiction. The study features an introductory overview, a chronological survey of O'Connor's work, a catalogue of her fictional characters, illustrations, and two appendices.

Hardwick, Elizabeth. "Flannery O'Connor, 1925-1964." *New York Review of Books* III, No. 4 (8 October 1964): 21, 23.

Memorial tribute and admiring retrospective of O'Connor's career.

Hawkes, John. "Notes on the Wild Goose Chase." *Massachusetts Review* 3, No. 4 (Summer 1962): 784-88.

Brief discussion grouping O'Connor, Djuna Barnes, and Nathanael West as experimental fiction writers who are outstanding in their detached and comic treatment of violence.

———. "Flannery O'Connor's Devil." *Sewanee Review* 70, No. 3 (Summer 1962): 395-407.

Controversial examination of evil in O'Connor's work. Hawkes suggests that because her fiction is based on knowledge of the devil, it is founded at least partially on "immoral impulse" and her authorial attitude is "in some measure diabolical." Brainard Cheney refuted Hawkes (see annotation above dated 1963).

Kahane, Claire. "The Artificial Niggers." *Massachusetts Review* XIX, No. 1 (Spring 1978): 183-98.

Examines the subtleties of relations between blacks and whites in several of O'Connor's short stories. Kahane asserts that black characters serve in some stories as a "metaphor of redemption and humility" and provide the basis for complex psychological and social commentary.

Martin, Carter W. *The True Country: Themes in the Fiction of Flannery O'Connor*. Nashville: Vanderbilt University Press, 1968, 253 p.

Explores the religious content of the stories and novels and identifies the thematic significance of various features of O'Connor's fictional technique.

May, John R. *The Pruning Word: The Parables of Flannery O'Connor*." Notre Dame, Ind.: University of Notre Dame Press, 1976, 178 p.

Places O'Connor's fiction in the Biblical parable tradition.

McDermott, John V. "Julian's Journey into Hell: Flannery O'Connor's Allegory of Pride." *Mississippi Quarterly* 28, No. 2 (Spring 1975): 171-79.

Pessimistic reading of "Everything That Rises Must Converge." In contrast with several critics who believe that the protagonist gains wisdom and grace through the action of the story, McDermott believes that Julian ultimately enters the "world of hell."

McFarland, Dorothy Tuck. *Flannery O'Connor*. New York: Frederick Ungar, 1976, 132 p.

Introduction to key aspects of O'Connor's fiction. McFarland devotes a chapter to each of the two story collections and the two novels and provides an illuminating introduction and conclusion.

Montgomery, Marion. *Why Flannery O'Connor Stayed Home*. La Salle, Ill.: Sherwood Sugden, 1981, 476 p.

First of a proposed three-volume study. Montgomery's chapters range in subject from general topics such as O'Connor's avoidance of sentimentality to more detailed analyses, but he emphasizes throughout the significance of the South and Roman Catholicism on O'Connor's fiction.

Orvell, Miles. *Invisible Parade: The Fiction of Flannery O'Connor*. Philadelphia: Temple University Press, 1972, 232 p.

Places O'Connor within the context of the South, Roman Catholicism, and particularly the romantic tradition in American letters, elucidating her connection with such writers as Hawthorne and Herman Melville. Orvell then analyzes and evaluates O'Connor's fiction in light of his findings.

Rose Alice, Sister. "Flannery O'Connor: Poet to the Outcast." *Renascence* 16, No. 3 (Spring 1964): 126-32.

Views the physical deformities of O'Connor's characters as representing her view of the human condition. The critic illustrates her point by examining the novel *Wise Blood* and several stories.

Shloss, Carol. *Flannery O'Connor's Dark Comedies: The Limits of Inference*. Baton Rouge: Louisiana State University Press, 1980, 158 p.

Explores O'Connor's artistic aims and her perception of her audience. Shloss examines *The Violent Bear It Away* and selected short stories.

Spivey, Ted R. "Flannery O'Connor's View of God and Man." *Studies in Short Fiction* 1, No. 3 (Spring 1964): 200-06.

Regards "The Lame Shall Enter First" as a work incorporating O'Connor's major themes, notably the struggle between empty humanism and religious fanaticism.

Smith, J. Oates. "Ritual and Violence in Flannery O'Connor." *Thought* 41, No. 163 (Winter 1966): 545-60.

Describes how O'Connor's characters often experience spiritual epiphanies violently, through religious rituals. Smith cites examples from the novels and several stories, and names Soren Kierkegaard and Franz Kafka O'Connor's most important artistic ancestors.

"Such Nice People." *Time* LXV, No. 23 (6 June 1955): 114.

Review of *A Good Man Is Hard to Find* including a brief discussion of "The Displaced Person," which Robert Fitzgerald disputed (see excerpt dated 1962).

Walters, Dorothy. *Flannery O'Connor*. Boston: Twayne, 1973, 172 p.

Biographical-critical study.

Westling, Louise. *Sacred Groves and Ravaged Gardens: The Fiction of Eudora Welty, Carson McCullers, and Flannery O'Connor*. Athens: University of Georgia Press, 1985, 217 p.

Feminist reading of O'Connor and two of her contemporaries, emphasizing their attitudes toward Southern heritage and female identity. The two chapters on O'Connor discuss her depiction of mother-daughter relationships and her use of the Southern landscape to convey sacramental power.

Wynne, Judith F. "The Sacramental Irony of Flannery O'Connor." *Southern Literary Journal* VII, No. 2 (Spring 1975): 33-49.

Study of irony in several of O'Connor's short stories. Wynne asserts that O'Connor's irony can be regarded as a vehicle of revelation in itself, separate from religious critical interpretation.

Zoller, Peter T. "The Irony of Preserving the Self: Flannery O'Connor's 'A Stroke of Good Fortune'." *Kansas Quarterly* 9, No. 2 (Spring 1977): 61-3.

Reads "A Stroke of Good Fortune" as a religious parable on the foibles of human pride. Zoller calls the story "the *Divine Comedy* in modern dress."

Edgar Allan Poe

1809-1849

American short story writer, novelist, poet, critic, and essayist.

Poe's stature as a major figure in world literature is primarily based on his ingenious and profound short stories and his critical theories, which established a highly influential rationale for the short form in both poetry and fiction. Regarded in literary histories and handbooks as the architect of the modern short story, Poe was also the principal forerunner of the "art for art's sake" movement in nineteenth-century European literature. Whereas earlier critics predominantly concerned themselves with moral or ideological generalities, Poe focused his criticism on the specifics of style and construction that contributed to a work's effectiveness or failure. In his own work, he demonstrated a brilliant command of technique as well as an inspired and original imagination.

The Bettmann Archive, Inc.

Poe's father and mother were professional actors who at the time of his birth were members of a repertory company in Boston. Before he was three years old both of his parents had died, and he was raised in the home of John Allan, a prosperous exporter from Richmond, Virginia. In 1915 Allan took his wife and foster son, whom he never formally adopted, to visit Scotland and England, where they lived for the next five years. While in England, Poe spent two years at the school he later described in the story "William Wilson." Returning with his foster parents to Richmond in 1820, Poe attended the best schools available, wrote his first poetry, and, when he was sixteen years old, became involved in a romance which ended when Allan sent him to the University of Virginia at Charlottesville. There Poe distinguished himself academically but, as a result of bad debts and inadequate financial support from Allan, he was forced to leave after less than a year. A now established discord with his foster father deepened on Poe's return to Richmond in 1827, and soon afterward Poe left for Boston, where he enlisted in the army for lack of other means of supporting himself and where he also published his first poetry collection, *Tamerlane, and Other Poems,* "By a Bostonian." The book went unnoticed by readers and reviewers, and a second collection was only slightly more conspicuous when it appeared in 1829. That same year Poe was honorably discharged from the army, having attained the rank of regimental sergeant major, and, after further conflict with Allan, he entered West Point. However, because Allan would neither provide his foster son with sufficient funds to maintain himself as a cadet nor give the consent necessary to resign from the academy, Poe gained a dismissal by ignoring his duties and violating regulations. He subsequently went to New York, where his book *Poems* was published in 1831, and then to Baltimore, where he lived at the home of his aunt, Mrs. Clemm.

Over the next few years Poe's first stories appeared in the Philadelphia *Saturday Courier,* and his "MS. Found in a Bottle" won a cash prize for best story in the Baltimore *Saturday Visitor*. Nevertheless, Poe was still not earning enough to live independently, nor did Allan's death in 1834 provide him with a legacy. The following year, however, his financial problems were temporarily alleviated when he went back to Richmond to become editor of the *Southern Literary Messenger,* bringing with him his aunt and his cousin Virginia, whom he married in 1836. The *Southern Literary Messenger* was the first of several magazines Poe would direct over the next ten years and through which he rose to prominence as one of the leading men of letters in America. Poe made himself known not only as a superlative author of fiction and poetry but also as a literary critic whose level of imagination and insight had been unapproached in American literature until this time. Nonetheless, while Poe's writings gained attention in the late 1830s and 1840s, the profits from his work remained meager, and he was forced to move several times in order to secure employment that he hoped would improve his situation, editing *Burton's Gentleman's Magazine* and *Graham's Magazine* in Philadelphia and the *Broadway Journal* in New York. In addition, the royalties for his *The Narrative of Arthur Gordon Pym, Tales of the Grotesque and Arabesque,* and other titles was always nominal or nonexistent. After his wife's death from tuberculosis in 1847, Poe became involved in a number of romances, including the one that had been interrupted in his youth with Elmira Royster, now the widowed Mrs. Shelton. It was during the time they were preparing for their marriage that Poe, for reasons unknown, arrived in Baltimore in late September of 1849. On October 3, he was discovered in a state of semiconsciousness; he died on October 7 without regaining the necessary lucidity to explain what had happened during the last days of his life.

Poe's most conspicuous contribution to world literature derives from the analytical method he practiced both as a creative author and as a critic of the works of his contemporaries. His self-declared intention was to formulate strictly artistic ideals in a milieu that he thought overly concerned with the utilitarian value of literature, a tendency he termed the "heresy of the Didactic." While Poe's position includes the chief requisites of pure aestheticism, his emphasis on literary formalism was directly linked to his philosophical ideals: through the calculated use of language one may express, though always imperfectly, a vision of truth and the essential condition of human existence. This doctrine had its greatest influence among the French Symbolists of the late nineteenth century, who in turn influenced the direction of modern literature, and it is this artistic and philosophical transaction that accounts for much of Poe's importance in literary history. Specifically, Poe's theory of literary creation is noted for two central points: first, a work must create a unity of effect on the reader to be considered successful; second, the production of this single effect should not be left to the hazards of accident or inspiration, but should to the minutest detail of style and subject be the result of rational deliberation on the part of the author. In poetry, this single effect must arouse the reader's sense of beauty, an ideal that Poe closely associated with sadness, strangeness, and loss; in prose, the effect should be one revelatory of some truth, as in "tales of ratiocination" or works evoking "terror, or passion, or horror."

Aside from a common theoretical basis, there is a psychological intensity that is characteristic of Poe's writings, especially the tales of horror that comprise his best and best-known works. These stories—which include "The Black Cat," "The Cask of Amontillado," and "The Tell-Tale Heart"—are often told by a first-person narrator, and through this voice Poe probes the workings of a character's psyche. This technique foreshadows the psychological explorations of Fedor Dostoevski and the school of psychological realism. In his Gothic tales, Poe also employed an essentially symbolic, almost allegorical method which gives such works as "The Fall of the House of Usher," "The Masque of the Red Death," and "Ligeia" an enigmatic quality that accounts for their enduring interest and also links them with the symbolical works of Nathaniel Hawthorne and Herman Melville. The influence of Poe's tales may be seen in the work of later writers, including Ambrose Bierce and H. P. Lovecraft, who belong to a distinct tradition of horror literature initiated by Poe. In addition to his achievement as creator of the modern horror tale, Poe is also credited with parenting two other popular genres: science fiction and the detective story. In such works as "The Unparalleled Adventure of Hans Pfaall" and "Von Kempelen and His Discovery," Poe took advantage of the fascination for science and technology that emerged in the early nineteenth century to produce speculative and fantastic narratives which anticipate a type of literature that did not become widely practiced until the twentieth century. Similarly, Poe's three tales of ratiocination—"The Murders in the Rue Morgue," "The Purloined Letter," and "The Mystery of Marie Rogêt"—are recognized as the models which established the major characters and literary conventions of detective fiction, specifically the amateur sleuth who solves a crime that has confounded the authorities and whose feats of deductive reasoning are documented by an admiring associate. Just as Poe influenced many succeeding authors and is regarded as an ancestor of such major literary movements as Symbolism and Surrealism, he was also influenced by earlier literary figures and movements. In his use of the demonic and the grotesque, Poe evidenced the impact of the stories of E. T. A. Hoffman and the Gothic novels of Ann Radcliffe, while the despair and melancholy in much of Poe's writing reflects an affinity with the Romantic movement of the early nineteenth century. It was Poe's particular genius that in his work he gave consummate artistic form both to his personal obsessions and those of previous literary generations, at the same time creating new forms which provided a means of expression for future artists.

While his works were not conspicuously acclaimed during his lifetime, Poe did earn due respect as a gifted fiction writer, poet, and man of letters, and occasionally he achieved a measure of popular success, especially following the appearance of "The Raven." After his death, however, the history of his critical reception becomes one of dramatically uneven judgments and interpretations. This state of affairs was initiated by Poe's one-time friend and literary executor R. W. Griswold, who, in a libelous obituary notice bearing the byline "Ludwig," attributed the depravity and psychological aberrations of many of the characters in Poe's fiction to Poe himself. In retrospect, Griswold's vilifications seem ultimately to have elicited as much sympathy as censure with respect to Poe and his work, leading subsequent biographers of the late nineteenth century to defend, sometimes too devotedly, Poe's name. It was not until the 1941 biography by A. H. Quinn that a balanced view was provided of Poe, his work, and the relationship between the author's life and his imagination. Nevertheless, the identification of Poe with the murderers and madmen of his works survived and flourished in the twentieth century, most prominently in the form of psychoanalytical studies such as those of Marie Bonaparte and Joseph Wood Krutch. Added to the controversy over the sanity, or at best the maturity of Poe (Paul Elmer More called him "the poet of unripe boys and unsound men"), was the question of the value of Poe's works as serious literature. At the forefront of Poe's detractors were such eminent figures as Henry James, Aldous Huxley, and T. S. Eliot, who dismissed Poe's works as juvenile, vulgar, and artistically debased; in contrast, these same works have been judged to be of the highest literary merit by such writers as Bernard Shaw and William Carlos Williams. Complementing Poe's erratic reputation among English and American critics is the more stable, and generally more elevated opinion of critics elsewhere in the world, particularly in France. Following the extensive translations and commentaries of Charles Baudelaire in the 1850s, Poe's works were received with a peculiar esteem by French writers, most profoundly those associated with the late nineteenth-century movement of Symbolism, who admired Poe's transcendent aspirations as a poet; the twentieth-century movement of Surrealism, which valued Poe's bizarre and apparently unruled imagination; and such figures as Paul Valéry, who found in Poe's theories and thought an ideal of supreme rationalism. In other countries, Poe's works have enjoyed a similar regard, and numerous studies have been written tracing the influence of the American author on the international literary scene, especially in Russia, Japan, Scandinavia, and Latin America.

Today, Poe is recognized as one of the foremost progenitors of modern literature, both in its popular forms, such as horror and detective fiction, and in its more complex and self-conscious forms, which represent the essential artistic manner of the twentieth century. In contrast to earlier critics who viewed the man and his works as one, criticism of the past twenty-five years has developed a view of Poe as a detached artist who was more concerned with displaying his virtuosity than with expressing his "soul," and who maintained an ironic rather than an autobiographical relationship to his writings. While at one time critics such as Yvor Winters wished to remove Poe from literary history, his works remain integral to any conception of modernism in world literature. Herbert Marshall McLuhan wrote in an essay entitled "Edgar Poe's Tradition": "While the New England dons primly turned the pages of Plato and Buddha beside a tea-cozy, and while Browning and Tennyson were creating a parochial fog for the English mind to relax in, Poe never lost contact with the terrible pathos of his time. Coevally with Baudelaire, and long before Conrad and Eliot, he explored the heart of darkness."

(See also *NCLC*, Vols. 1, 17; *Something About the Author*, Vol. 23; and *Dictionary of Literary Biography*, Vol. 3.)

PRINCIPAL WORKS

SHORT FICTION

Tales of the Grotesque and Arabesque 1840
Tales by Edgar A. Poe 1845

OTHER MAJOR WORKS

Tamerlane, and Other Poems (poetry) 1827
Al Aaraaf, Tamerlane, and Minor Poems (poetry) 1829
Poems (poetry) 1831
The Narrative of Arthur Gordon Pym (novel) 1838
The Raven, and Other Poems (poetry) 1845
Eureka: A Prose Poem (essay) 1848
The Literati: Some Honest Opinions about Authorial Merits and Demerits, with Occasional Words of Personality (criticism) 1850

EDGAR ALLAN POE (essay date 1842)

[*In the following excerpt from his review of Nathaniel Hawthorne's* Twice-Told Tales, *Poe expounds his theory of the short story. This essay was originally published in* Graham's Magazine *in May 1842.*]

The tale proper, in our opinion, affords unquestionably the fairest field for the exercise of the loftiest talent, which can be afforded by the wide domains of mere prose. Were we bidden to say how the highest genius could be most advantageously employed for the best display of its own powers, we should answer, without hesitation—in the composition of a rhymed poem, not to exceed in length what might be perused in an hour. Within this limit alone can the highest order of true poetry exist. We need only here say, upon this topic, that, in almost all classes of composition, the unity of effect or impression is a point of the greatest importance. It is clear, moreover, that this unity cannot be thoroughly preserved in productions whose perusal cannot be completed at one sitting. We may continue the reading of a prose composition, from the very nature of prose itself, much longer than we can persevere, to any good purpose, in the perusal of a poem. This latter, if truly fulfilling the demands of the poetic sentiment, induces an exaltation of the soul which cannot be long sustained. All high excitements are necessarily transient. Thus a long poem is a paradox. And, without unity of impression, the deepest effects cannot be brought about. Epics were the offspring of an imperfect sense of Art, and their reign is no more. A poem *too* brief may produce a vivid, but never an intense or enduring impression. Without a certain continuity of effort—without a certain duration or repetition of purpose—the soul is never deeply moved. There must be the dropping of the water upon the rock. De Béranger has wrought brilliant things—pungent and spirit-stirring—but, like all immassive bodies, they lack *momentum,* and thus fail to satisfy the Poetic Sentiment. They sparkle and excite, but, from want of continuity, fail deeply to impress. Extreme brevity will degenerate into epigrammatism; but the sin of extreme length is even more unpardonable. *In medio tutissimus ibis.*

Were we called upon however to designate that class of composition which, next to such a poem as we have suggested, should best fulfil the demands of high genius—should offer it the most advantageous field of exertion—we should unhesitatingly speak of the prose tale, as Mr. Hawthorne has here exemplified it. We allude to the short prose narrative, requiring from a half-hour to one or two hours in its perusal. The ordinary novel is objectionable, from its length, for reasons already stated in substance. As it cannot be read at one sitting, it deprives itself, of course, of the immense force derivable from *totality*. Worldly interests intervening during the pauses of perusal, modify, annul, or counteract, in a greater or less degree, the impressions of the book. But simple cessation in reading would, of itself, be sufficient to destroy the true unity. In the brief tale, however, the author is enabled to carry out the fulness of his intention, be it what it may. During the hour of perusal the soul of the reader is at the writer's control. There are no external or extrinsic influences—resulting from weariness or interruption.

A skilful literary artist has constructed a tale. If wise, he has not fashioned his thoughts to accommodate his incidents; but having conceived, with deliberate care, a certain unique or single *effect* to be wrought out, he then invents such incidents—he then combines such events as may best aid him in establishing this preconceived effect. If his very initial sentence tend not to the outbringing of this effect, then he has failed in his first step. In the whole composition there should be no word written, of which the tendency, direct or indirect, is not to the one pre-established design. And by such means, with such care and skill, a picture is at length painted which leaves in the mind of him who contemplates it with a kindred art, a sense of the fullest satisfaction. The idea of the tale has been presented unblemished, because undisturbed; and this is an end unattainable by the novel. Undue brevity is just as exceptionable here as in the poem; but undue length is yet more to be avoided.

We have said that the tale has a point of superiority even over the poem. In fact, while the *rhythm* of this latter is an essential aid in the development of the poem's highest idea—the idea of the Beautiful—the artificialities of this rhythm are an inseparable bar to the development of all points of thought or expression which have their basis in *Truth*. But Truth is often, and in very great degree, the aim of the tale. Some of the finest tales are tales of ratiocination. Thus the field of this species of composition, if not in so elevated a region on the mountain of Mind, is a table-land of far vaster extent than the domain of the mere poem. Its products are never so rich, but infinitely more numerous, and more appreciable by the mass of mankind. The writer of the prose tale, in short, may bring to his theme a vast variety of modes or inflections of thought and expression—(the ratiocinative, for example, the sarcastic or the humorous) which are not only antagonistical to the nature of the poem, but absolutely forbidden by one of its most peculiar and indispensable adjuncts; we allude of course, to rhythm. It may be added, here *par parenthèse,* that the author who aims at the purely beautiful in a prose tale is laboring at great disadvantage. For Beauty can be better treated in the poem. Not so with terror, or passion, or horror, or a multitude of such other points. And here it will be seen how full of prejudice are the usual animadversions against those *tales of effect* many fine examples of which were found in the earlier numbers of Blackwood. The impressions produced were wrought in a legitimate sphere of action, and constituted a legitimate although sometimes an exaggerated interest. They were relished by every man of genius: although there were found many men of genius who condemned them without just ground. The true critic will but demand that the design intended be accomplished, to the fullest extent, by the means most advantageously applicable. (pp. 571-73)

Edgar Allan Poe, in a review of "Twice-Told Tales," in his Essays and Reviews: Reviews of American Authors and American Literature, *The Library of America, 1984, pp. 569-77.*

D. H. LAWRENCE (essay date 1923)

[Lawrence was an English novelist, poet, and essayist who is noted for his introduction of the themes of modern psychology to English fiction. In his lifetime he was a controversial figure, both for the explicit sexuality he portrayed in his novels and for his unconventional personal life. In the following excerpt, Lawrence discusses love relationships in "Ligeia" and "The Fall of the House of Usher."]

Poe is rather a scientist than an artist. He is reducing his own self as a scientist reduces a salt in a crucible. It is an almost chemical analysis of the soul and consciousness. Whereas in true art there is always the double rhythm of creating and destroying.

This is why Poe calls his things 'tales'. They are a concatenation of cause and effect.

His best pieces, however, are not tales. They are more. They are ghastly stories of the human soul in its disruptive throes.

Moreover, they are 'love' stories.

"Ligeia" and **"The Fall of the House of Usher"** are really love stories.

Love is the mysterious vital attraction which draws things together, closer, closer together. For this reason sex is the actual crisis of love. For in sex the two blood-systems, in the male and female, concentrate and come into contact, the merest film intervening. Yet if the intervening film breaks down, it is death. (pp. 70-1)

"Ligeia" is the chief story. Ligeia! A mental-derived name. To him the woman, his wife, was not Lucy. She was Ligeia. No doubt she even preferred it thus.

"Ligeia" is Poe's love-story, and its very fantasy makes it more truly his own story.

It is a tale of love pushed over a verge. And love pushed to extremes in a battle of wills between the lovers.

Love is become a battle of wills.

Which shall first destroy the other, of the lovers? Which can hold out longest, against the other?

Ligeia is still the old-fashioned woman. Her will is still to submit. She wills to submit to the vampire of her husband's consciousness. Even death. (p. 74)

Poe has been so praised for his style. But it seems to me a meretricious affair. 'Her marble hand' and 'the elasticity of her footfall' seem more like chair-springs and mantel-pieces than a human creature. She never was quite a human creature to him. She was an instrument from which he got his extremes of sensation. His *machine à plaisir,* as somebody says.

All Poe's style, moreover, has this mechanical quality, as his poetry has a mechanical rhythm. He never sees anything in terms of life, almost always in terms of matter, jewels, marble, etc.,—or in terms of force, scientific. And his cadences are all managed mechanically. This is what is called 'having a style.'

What he wants to do with Ligeia is to analyse her, till he knows all her component parts, till he has got her all in his consciousness. She is some strange chemical salt which he must analyse out in the test-tubes of his brain, and then—when he's finished the analysis—*E finita la commedia!* (pp. 74-5)

Poe wanted to know—wanted to know what was the strangeness in the eyes of Ligeia. She might have told him it was horror at his probing, horror at being vamped by his consciousness.

But she wanted to be vamped. She wanted to be probed by his consciousness, to be KNOWN. She paid for wanting it, too.

Nowadays it is usually the man who wants to be vamped, to be KNOWN.

Edgar Allan probed and probed. So often he seemed on the verge. But she went over the verge of death before he came over the verge of knowledge. And it is always so.

He decided, therefore, that the clue to the strangeness lay in the mystery of will. 'And the will therein lieth, which dieth not . . .'. (p. 76)

But Ligeia wanted to go on and on with the craving, with the love, with the sensation, with the probing, with the knowing, on and on to the end.

There is no end. There is only the rupture of death. That's where men, and women are 'had'. Man is always sold, in his search for final KNOWLEDGE. (p. 77)

So Ligeia dies. And yields to death at least partly. *Anche troppo.* (p. 79)

The other great story . . . is **"The Fall of the House of Usher."** Here the love is between brother and sister. When the self is broken, and the mystery of the recognition of *otherness* fails, then the longing for identification with the beloved becomes a lust. (pp. 81-2)

[Roderick and Madeline Usher] are the last remnants of their incomparably ancient and decayed race. Roderick has the same large, luminous eye, the same slightly arched nose of delicate Hebrew model, as characterized Ligeia. He is ill with the nervous malady of his family. It is he whose nerves are so strung that they vibrate to the unknown quiverings of the ether. He, too, has lost his self, his living soul, and become a sensitized instrument of the external influences; his nerves are verily like an aeolian harp which must vibrate. He lives in 'some struggle with the grim phantasm, Fear,' for he is only the physical, post-mortem reality of a living being. (p. 83)

It is this mechanical consciousness which gives 'the fervid facility of his impromptus'. It is the same thing that gives Poe his extraordinary facility in versification. The absence of real central or impulsive being in himself leaves him inordinately, mechanically sensitive to sounds and effects, associations of sounds, associations of rhyme, for example—mechanical, facile, having no root in any passion. It is all a secondary, meretricious process. So we get Roderick Usher's poem. "The Haunted Palace," with its swift yet mechanical subtleties of rhyme and rhythm, its vulgarity of epithet. It is all a sort of dream-process, where the association between parts is mechanical, accidental as far as passional meaning goes.

Usher thought that all vegetable things had sentience. Surely all material things have a *form* of sentience, even the inorganic: surely they all exist in some subtle and complicated tension of vibration which makes them sensitive to external influence and causes them to have an influence on other external objects, irrespective of contact. It is of this vibration or inorganic consciousness that Poe is master: the sleep-consciousness. Thus Roderick Usher was convinced that his whole surroundings, the stones of the house, the fungi, the water in the tarn, the very reflected image of the whole, was woven into a physical oneness with the family, condensed, as it were, into one atmosphere—the special atmosphere in which alone the Ushers could live. And it was this atmosphere which had moulded the destinies of his family.

But while ever the soul remains alive, it is the moulder and not the moulded. It is the souls of living men that subtly impregnate stones, houses, mountains, continents, and give these their subtlest form. People only become subject to stones after having lost their integral souls.

In the human realm, Roderick had one connection: his sister Madeline. She, too, was dying of a mysterious disorder, nervous, cataleptic. The brother and sister loved each other passionately and exclusively. They were twins, almost identical in looks. It was the same absorbing love between them, this process of unison in nerve-vibration, resulting in more and more extreme exaltation and a sort of consciousness, and a gradual break-down into death. The exquisitely sensitive Roderick, vibrating without resistance with his sister Madeline, more and more exquisitely, and gradually devouring her, sucking her life like a vampire in his anguish of extreme love. (pp. 83-4)

It is the same old theme of 'each man kills the thing he loves'. He knew his love had killed her. He knew she died at last, like Ligeia, unwilling and unappeased. So, she rose again upon him. . . .

It is lurid and melodramatic, but it is true. It is a ghastly psychological truth of what happens in the last stages of this beloved love, which cannot be separate, cannot be isolate, cannot listen in isolation to the isolate Holy Ghost. (p. 85)

The Ushers, brother and sister, betrayed the Holy Ghost in themselves. They would love, love, without resistance. They would love, they would merge, they would be as one thing. So they dragged each other down into death. For the Holy Ghost says you must *not* be as one thing with another being. Each must abide by itself, and correspond only within certain limits.

The best tales all have the same burden. Hate is as inordinate as love, and as slowly consuming, as secret, as underground, as subtle. All this underground vault business in Poe only symbolizes that which takes place *beneath* the consciousness. On top, all is fair-spoken. Beneath, there is awful murderous extremity of burying alive. Fortunato, in **"The Cask of Amontillado,"** is buried alive out of perfect hatred, as the lady Madeline of Usher is buried alive out of love. The lust of hate is the inordinate desire to consume and unspeakably possess the soul of the hated one, just as the lust of love is the desire to possess, or to be possessed by, the beloved, utterly. But in either case the result is the dissolution of both souls, each losing itself in transgressing its own bounds. (pp. 85-6)

In **"William Wilson"** we are given a rather unsubtle account of the attempt of a man to kill his own soul. William Wilson the mechanical, lustful ego succeeds in killing William Wilson the living self. The lustful ego lives on, gradually reducing itself towards the dust of the infinite.

In the **"Murders in the Rue Morgue"** and **"The Gold Bug"** we have those mechanical tales where the interest lies in the following out of a subtle chain of cause and effect. The interest is scientific rather than artistic, a study in psychologic reactions. (p. 86)

Poe knew only love, love, love, intense vibrations and heightened consciousness. Drugs, women, self-destruction, but anyhow the prismatic ecstasy of heightened consciousness and sense of love, of flow. The human soul in him was beside itself. But it was not lost. He told us plainly how it was, so that we should know.

He was an adventurer into vaults and cellars and horrible underground passages of the human soul. He sounded the horror and the warning of his own doom.

Doomed he was. He died wanting more love, and love killed him. A ghastly disease, love. Poe telling us of his disease: trying even to make his disease fair and attractive. Even succeeding.

Which is the inevitable falseness, duplicity of art, American art in particular. (pp. 87-8)

D. H. Lawrence, "Edgar Allan Poe," in his Studies in Classic American Literature, 1923. *Reprint by The Viking Press, 1964, pp. 70-88.*

HOWARD PHILLIPS LOVECRAFT (essay date 1927)

[Lovecraft is considered one of the foremost modern authors of supernatural horror fiction. Strongly influenced by Poe, Lord Dunsany, and early science fiction writers, he developed a type of horror tale that combined occult motifs, modern science, and the regional folklore of his native New England to produce the personal mythology on which he based much of his work. His Supernatural Horror in Literature, *originally published in 1927, is one of the earliest and most comprehensive studies of this genre. In the following excerpt from that work, Lovecraft praises Poe's achievement as the creator of the modern horror story.]*

Poe's fame has been subject to curious undulations, and it is now a fashion amongst the "advanced intelligentsia" to minimize his importance both as an artist and as an influence; but it would be hard for any mature and reflective critic to deny the tremendous value of his work and the persuasive potency of his mind as an opener of artistic vistas. True, his type of outlook may have been anticipated; but it was he who first realized its possibilities and gave it supreme form and systematic expression. True also, that subsequent writers may have produced greater single tales than his; but again we must comprehend that it was only he who taught them by example and precept the art which they, having the way cleared for them and given an explicit guide, were perhaps able to carry to greater lengths. Whatever his limitations, Poe did that which no one else ever did or could have done; and to him we owe the modern horror-story in its final and perfected state.

Before Poe the bulk of weird writers had worked largely in the dark; without an understanding of the psychological basis of the horror appeal, and hampered by more or less of conformity to certain empty literary conventions such as the happy ending, virtue rewarded, and in general a hollow moral didacticism, acceptance of popular standards and values, and striving of the author to obtrude his own emotions into the story and take sides with the partisans of the majority's artificial ideas. Poe, on the other hand, perceived the essential impersonality of the real artist; and knew that the function of creative fiction is merely to express and interpret events and sensations as they are, regardless of how they tend or what they prove—good or evil, attractive or repulsive, stimulating or depressing, with the author always acting as a vivid and detached chronicler rather than as a teacher, sympathizer, or vendor of opinion. He saw clearly that all phases of life and thought are equally eligible as subject matter for the artist, and being inclined by temperament to strangeness and gloom, decided to be the interpreter of those powerful feelings and frequent happenings which attend pain rather than pleasure, decay rather than growth, terror rather than tranquility, and which are fundamentally either adverse or indifferent to the tastes and traditional outward sentiments of mankind, and to the health, sanity, and normal expansive welfare of the species.

Poe's spectres thus acquired a convincing malignity possessed by none of their predecessors, and established a new standard of realism in the annals of literary horror. The impersonal and artistic intent, moreover, was aided by a scientific attitude not often found before; whereby Poe studied the human mind rather than the usages of Gothic fiction, and worked with an analytical knowledge of terror's true sources which doubled the force of his narratives and emancipated him from all the absurdities inherent in merely conventional shudder-coining. This example having been set, later authors were naturally forced to conform to it in order to compete at all; so that in this way a definite change began to affect the main stream of macabre writing. Poe, too, set a fashion in consummate craftsmanship; and although today some of his own work seems slightly melodramatic and unsophisticated, we can constantly trace his influence in such things as the maintenance of a single mood and achievement of a single impression in a tale, and the rigorous paring down of incidents to such as have a direct bearing on the plot and will figure prominently in the climax. Truly may it be said that Poe invented the short story in its present form. His elevation of disease, perversity, and decay to the level of artistically expressible themes was likewise infinitely far-reaching in effect; for avidly seized, sponsored, and intensified by his eminent French admirer Charles Pierre Baudelaire, it became the nucleus of the principal aesthetic movements in France, thus making Poe in a sense the father of the Decadents and the Symbolists. (pp. 52-4)

Poe's tales, of course, fall into several classes; some of which contain a purer essence of spiritual horror than others. The tales of logic and ratiocination, forerunners of the modern detective story, are not to be included at all in weird literature; whilst certain others, probably influenced considerably by Hoffmann, possess an extravagance which relegates them to the borderline of the grotesque. Still a third group deal with abnormal psychology and monomania in such a way as to express terror but not weirdness. A substantial residuum, however, represent the literature of supernatural horror in its acutest form; and give their author a permanent and unassailable place as deity and fountain-head of all modern diabolic fiction. Who can forget the terrible swollen ship poised on the billow-chasm's edge in **"MS. Found in a Bottle"**—the dark intimations of her unhallowed age and monstrous growth, her sinister crew of unseeing greybeards, and her frightful southward rush under full sail through the ice of the Antarctic night, sucked onward by some resistless devil-current toward a vortex of eldritch enlightenment which must end in destruction?

Then there is the unutterable M. Valdemar [from **"The Facts in the Case of M. Valdemar"**], kept together by hypnotism for seven months after his death, and uttering frantic sounds but a moment before the breaking of the spell leaves him "a nearly liquid mass of loathsome, of detestable putrescence." In the *Narrative of Arthur Gordon Pym* the voyagers reach first a strange south polar land of murderous savages where nothing is white and where vast rocky ravines have the form of titanic Egyptian letters spelling terrible primal arcana of earth; and thereafter a still more mysterious realm where everything is white, and where shrouded giants and snowy-plumed birds guard a cryptic cataract of mist which empties from immeasurable celestial heights into a torrid milky sea. **"Metzengerstein"** horrifies with its malign hints of a monstrous metempsychosis—the mad nobleman who burns the stable of his hereditary foe; the colossal unknown horse that issues from the blazing building after the owner has perished therein; the vanishing bit of ancient tapestry where was shown the giant horse of the victim's ancestor in the Crusades; the madman's wild and constant riding on the great horse, and his fear and hatred of the steed; the meaningless prophecies that brood obscurely over the warring horses; and finally, the burning of the madman's palace and the death therein of the owner, borne helpless into the flames and up the vast staircase astride the beast he has ridden so strangely. Afterward the rising smoke of the ruins takes the form of a gigantic horse. **"The Man of the Crowd,"** telling of one who roams day and night to mingle with streams of people as if afraid to be alone, has quieter effects, but implies nothing less of cosmic fear. Poe's mind was never far from terror and decay, and we see in every tale, poem, and philosophical dialogue a tense eagerness to fathom unplumbed wells of night, to pierce the veil of death, and to reign in fancy as lord of the frightful mysteries of time and space.

Certain of Poe's tales possess an almost absolute perfection of artistic form which makes them veritable beacon-lights in the province of the short story. Poe could, when he wished, give to his prose a richly poetic cast; employing that archaic and Orientalised style with jeweled phrase, quasi-Biblical repetition, and recurrent burthen so successfully used by later writers like Oscar Wilde and Lord Dunsany; and in the cases where he has done this we have an effect of lyrical phantasy almost narcotic in essence—an opium pageant of dream in the language of dream, with every unnatural colour and grotesque image bodied forth in a symphony of corresponding sound. **"The Masque of the Red Death," "Silence, a Fable,"** and **"Shadow, a Parable,"** are assuredly poems in every sense of the word save the metrical one, and owe as much of their power to aural cadence as to visual imagery. But it is in two of the less openly poetic tales, **"Ligeia"** and **"The Fall of the House of Usher"**—especially the latter—that one finds those very summits of artistry whereby Poe takes his place at the head of fictional miniaturists. Simple and straightforward in plot, both of these tales owe their supreme magic to the cunning development which appears in the selection and collocation of every least incident. **"Ligeia"** tells of a first wife of lofty and mysterious origin, who after death returns through a preternatural force of will to take possession of the body of a second wife; imposing even her physical appearance on the temporary reanimated corpse of her victim at the last moment. Despite a suspicion of prolixity and topheaviness, the narrative reaches its terrific climax with relentless power. **"The Fall of the House of Usher,"** whose superiority in detail and proportion is very marked, hints shudderingly of obscure life in inorganic things, and displays an abnormally linked trinity of entities at the end of a long and isolated family history—a brother, his twin sister, and their incredibly ancient house all sharing a single soul and meeting one common dissolution at the same moment.

These bizarre conceptions, so awkward in unskilful hands, become under Poe's spell living and convincing terrors to haunt our nights; and all because the author understood so perfectly the very mechanics and physiology of fear and strangeness—the essential details to emphasise, the precise incongruities and conceits to select as preliminaries or concomitants to horror, the exact incidents and allusions to throw out innocently in advance as symbols or prefigurings of each major step toward the hideous denouement to come, the nice adjustments of cumulative force and the unerring accuracy in linkage of parts which make for faultless unity throughout and thunderous effectiveness at the climactic moment, the delicate nuances of scenic and landscape value to select in establishing and sustaining the desired mood and vitalising the desired illusion—principles of this kind, and dozens of obscurer ones too elusive to be described or even fully comprehended by any ordinary commentator. Melodrama and unsophistication there may be—we are told of one fastidious Frenchman who could not bear to read Poe except in Baudelaire's urbane and Gallically modulated translation—but all traces of such things are wholly overshadowed by a potent and inborn sense of the spectral, the morbid, and the horrible which gushed forth from every cell of the artist's creative mentality and stamped his macabre work with the ineffaceable mark of supreme genius. Poe's weird tales are *alive* in a manner that few other can ever hope to be. (pp. 55-9)

Howard Phillips Lovecraft, "Edgar Allan Poe," in his Supernatural Horror in Literature, *Dover Publications, Inc., 1973, pp. 52-9.*

DARREL ABEL (essay date 1949)

[In the following excerpt, Abel analyzes "The Fall of the House of Usher" with respect to Poe's chief criterion for a successful tale—unity of effect.]

By common consent, the most characteristic of Poe's "arabesque" tales is **"The Fall of the House of Usher."** It is usually admired for its "atmosphere" and for its exquisitely artificial manipulation of Gothic claptrap and décor, but careful reading reveals admirable method in the author's use of things generally regarded by his readers as mere decorative properties.

Poe insisted that the "calculating" and "ideal" faculties, far from being "at war" with each other, were complementary aspects of the creative imagination—a doctrine vigorously reasserted by critics in our own day. He further maintained that "it is an obvious rule of Art that effects should be made to spring as directly as possible from their causes." Such an emphasis on logical exactitude in the calculation of artistic effect invites inquiry into the question: How far is the unity of effect (which he called "that vital requisite of all works of Art") in one of Poe's most characteristic and successful works directly analysable into its causes? It will be seen that his effects are produced by deeper causes than has been supposed by those casual critics who believe that the horror of **"The Fall of the House of Usher"** is merely an adventitious product of "atmosphere."

Too much of the horror of the tale has usually been attributed to its setting superficially considered. But the setting does have a double importance, descriptive and symbolic. It first operates descriptively, as suggestively appropriate and picturesque background for the unfolding of events. It later operates symbolically: certain features of the setting assume an ominous animism and function; they become important active elements instead of mere static backdrop.

Descriptively the setting has two uses: to suggest a mood to the observer which makes him properly receptive to the horrible ideas which grow in his mind during the action; and to supply details which reinforce, but do not produce, those ideas.

The qualities of the setting are remoteness, decadence, horrible gloom. Remoteness (and loss of feature) is suggested by details of outline, dimension, and vista. Decadence is suggested by details of the death or decrepitude of normal human and vegetable existences and constructions, and by the growth of morbid and parasitic human and vegetable existences, as well as by the surging sentience of inorganism. Gloom and despair are suggested by sombre and listless details of colour and motion (at climactic points, lurid colour and violent action erupt with startling effect from this sombre listlessness). The narrator points out in the opening passage of the tale that the gloom which invested the domain of Usher was not sublime and pleasurable (which would have made it an expression of "supernal beauty" in Poe's opinion), but was sinister and vaguely terrible.

Five persons figure in the tale, but the interest centres exclusively in one—Roderick Usher. The narrator is uncharacterized, undescribed, even unnamed. (I shall call him Anthropos, for convenient reference.) In fact, he is a mere point of view for the reader to occupy, but he does lend the reader some acute, though not individualizing, faculties: five keen senses which shrewdly perceive actual physical circumstances; a sixth sense of vague and indescribable realities behind the physical and apparent; a clever faculty of rational interpretation of sensible phenomena; and finally, a sceptical and matter-of-fact propensity to mistrust intuitional apprehensions and to seek natural and rational explanations. In short, he is an habitual naturalist resisting urgent convictions of the preternatural.

The doctor and valet are not realized as characters; they are less impressive than the furniture; and Anthropos sees each only once and briefly. No duties requiring the attendance of other persons are mentioned, so our attention is never for a moment diverted from Roderick Usher. His sister Madeline's place in the story can best be explained in connection with comment on Usher himself.

The action of the story is comparatively slight; the energetic symbolism, to be discussed later, accomplishes more. Anthropos arrives at the House of Usher, and is conducted into the presence of his host. Usher has invited Anthropos, a friend of his school-days, in the hope that a renewal of their association will assist him to throw off a morbid depression of spirits which has affected his health. Anthropos is shocked at the ghastly infirmity of his friend. He learns that Madeline, Roderick's twin and the only other living Usher, is near death from a mysterious malady which baffles her physicians. Presently she dies and Roderick Usher, fearing that the doctors who had been so fascinated by the pathology of the case might steal her body from the grave, places it in a sealed coffin in a subterranean vault under the House of Usher. Anthropos assists in this labour.

Immediately there is an observable increase in the nervous apprehensiveness of Roderick Usher. He finds partial relief from his agitation in the painting of horribly vague abstract pictures and in the improvisation of wild tunes to the accompaniment of his "speaking guitar." For seven or eight days his apprehensiveness increases and steadily communicates itself to Anthropos as well, so that, at the end of that time, a night arrives when Anthropos' state of vague alarm prevents his going to sleep. Usher enters and shows him through the window that, although the night is heavily clouded, the House of Usher's environs are strangely illuminated. Anthropos endeavours, not very judiciously, to calm him by reading aloud from a romance that might have come from the library of Don Quixote. At points of suspense in this romance, marked by description of loud noises, Anthropos fancies that he hears similar sounds below him in the House of Usher. Roderick Usher's manner, during this reading, is inattentive and wildly preoccupied; at the noisy climax of the romance Usher melodramatically shrieks that the noises outside had actually been those of his sister breaking out of the coffin in which she had been sealed alive. The door bursts open; Madeline appears and, falling forward dead in her gory shroud, carries Roderick Usher likewise dead to the floor beneath her. Anthropos rushes from the House of Usher, turning in his flight to view its shattering collapse into the gloomy tarn beneath it. How these events become invested with horror can only be understood by discerning the meanings which the symbolism of the tale conveys into them.

Roderick Usher is himself a symbol—of isolation, and of a concentration of vitality so introverted that it utterly destroys itself. He is physically isolated. Anthropos reaches the House of Usher after a whole day's journey "through a singularly dreary tract of country" that is recognizably the same sort of domain-beyond-reality as that traversed by Childe Roland and his medieval prototypes. Arrived at the mansion, he is conducted to Usher's "studio" "through many dark and intricate passages." And there "the eye struggled in vain to reach the remoter angles of the chamber" in which his host received him.

Usher is psychologically isolated. Although he has invited his former "boon companion" to visit and support him in this moral crisis, clearly there has never been any conviviality in his nature. "His reserve had always been habitual and excessive," and he has now evidently become more singular, preoccupied, and aloof than before. "For many years, he had never ventured forth" from the gloomy House of Usher, wherein "he was enchained by certain superstitious impressions." ("Superstitious" is the sceptical judgment of Anthropos.) Thus, although his seclusion had probably once been voluntary, it is now inescapable. His sister Madeline does not relieve his isolation; paradoxically, she intensifies it, for they are twins whose "striking similitude" and "sympathies of a scarcely intelligible nature" eliminate that margin of difference which is necessary to social relationship between persons. They are not two persons, but one consciousness in two bodies, each mirroring the other, intensifying the introversion of the family character. Further, no collateral branches of the family survive; all the life of the Ushers is flickering to extinction in these feeble representatives. Therefore no wonder that Anthropos cannot connect his host's appearance "with any idea of a simple humanity."

The isolation and concentration of the vitalities of the Ushers had brought about the decay of the line. Formerly the family energies had found magnificently varied expression: "His very ancient family had been noted, time out of mind, for a peculiar sensibility of temperament; displaying itself, through long ages, in many works of exalted art, and manifested, of late, in repeated deeds of munificent yet unobtrusive charity, as well as in a passionate devotion to the intricacies perhaps even more than to the orthodox and easily recognizable beauties, of musical science." For all the splendid flowering of this "peculiar sensibility," its devotion to intricacies was a fatal weakness; in tending inward to more hidden channels of expression, the family sensibility had become in its current representative morbidity introverted from lack of proper object and exercise, and its only flowers were flowers of evil. It was fretting Roderick Usher to death: "He suffered much from a morbid acuteness of the senses; the most insipid food was alone endurable; he could wear only garments of a certain texture; the odors of all flowers were oppressive; his eyes were tortured by even a faint light; and there were but peculiar sounds, and these from stringed instruments, which did not inspire him with horror." These specifications detail the hyper-acuity but progressive desuetude of his five senses. The sum of things which these five senses convey to a man is the sum of physical life; the relinquishment of their use is the relinquishment of life itself. The hyper-acuity of Roderick Usher's senses was caused by the introverted concentration of the family energies; the inhibition of his senses was caused by the physical and psychological isolation of Usher. It is noteworthy that the only willing use he makes of his senses is a morbid one—not to sustain and positively experience life, but to project his "distempered ideality" on canvas and in music. This morbid use of faculties which ought to sustain and express life shows that, as Life progressively loses its hold on Roderick Usher, Death as steadily asserts its empery over him. The central action and symbolism of the tale dramatize this contest between Life and Death for the possession of Roderick Usher.

Some of the non-human symbols of the tale are, as has been mentioned, features of the physical setting which detach themselves from the merely picturesque ensemble of background particulars and assume symbolical meaning as the tale unfolds. They have what might be called an historical function; they symbolize what has been and is. The remaining symbols are created by the "distempered ideality" of Roderick Usher as the narrative progresses. These have prophetic significance; they symbolize what is becoming and what will be. The symbols which Usher creates, however, flow from the same dark source as the evil in symbols which exist independently of Usher: that evil is merely channelled through his artistic sensibility to find bold new expression.

All the symbols express the opposition of Life-Reason to Death-Madness. Most of them are mixed manifestations of those two existences; more precisely, they show ascendant evil encroaching upon decadent good. On the Life-Reason side are ranged the heavenly, natural, organic, harmonious, featured, active qualities of things. Against them are ranged the subterranean, subnatural, inorganic, inharmonious, vague or featureless, passive qualities of things. Although most of the symbols show the encroachment of Death-Madness on Life-Reason, two symbols show absolute evil triumphant, with no commixture of good even in decay. One of these is the tarn, a physically permanent feature of the setting; the other is Roderick Usher's ghastly abstract painting, an impromptu expression of the evil which has mastered his sensibility. There are no symbols of absolute good.

The House of Usher is the most conspicuous symbol in the tale. It displays all the qualities (listed above) of Life-Reason, corrupted and threatened by Death-Madness. It stands under the clouded heavens, but it is significantly related to the subterranean by the zigzag crack which extends from its roof (the most heavenward part of the house) to the tarn. The trees about it connect it with nature, but they are all dead, blasted by the preternatural evil of the place; the only living vegetation consists of "rank sedges" (no doubt nourished by the tarn), and fungi growing from the roof, the most heavenward part. The house is also a symbol of the organic and harmonious because it expresses human thought and design, but the structure is crazy, threatened not only by the ominous, zigzag, scarcely discernible fissure, but also by the perilous decrepitude of its constituent materials, which maintained their coherency in a way that looked almost miraculous to Anthropos: "No portion of the masonry had fallen; and there appeared to be a wild inconsistency between its still perfect adaptation of parts, and the crumbling condition of the individual stones." In the interior of the house, the furnishings seemed no longer to express the ordered living of human creatures: "The general furniture was profuse, comfortless, antique, and tattered. Many books and musical instruments lay scattered about, but failed to give any vitality to the scene." That is, the human life it expressed was not ordered and full, but scattered and tattered. The "eyelike windows," the most conspicuous feature of the house, looked vacant from without, and from within were seen to be "altogether inaccessible"; they admitted only "feeble gleams of encrimsoned light." Life and motion within the house were nearly extinct. "An air of stern, deep, and irredeemable gloom hung over and pervaded all."

Roderick Usher resembles his house. It is unnecessary to point out the ways in which a human being is normally an expression of Life-Reason—of heavenly, natural, organic, harmonious, featured, and active qualities. The Death-Madness opposites to these qualities are manifested in interesting correspondences between the physical appearance of Usher and that of his house. The zigzag crack in the house, and the "inconsistency" between its decayed materials and intact structure, are like the difficultly maintained composure of Usher. Anthropos declares: "In the manner of my friend I was at once struck with an incoherence—an *inconsistency* [my italics]; and I soon found this to arise from a series of feeble and futile struggles to overcome an habitual trepidancy—an excessive nervous agitation." The "minute fungi . . . hanging in a fine tangled webwork from the eaves" of the house have their curious counterpart, as a symbol of morbid vitality, in the hair of Usher, "of a more than web-like softness and tenuity rather than fell about the face, [so that] I could not, even with an effort, connect its Arabesque expression with any idea of simple humanity." (We are reminded of the hair reputed to grow so luxuriantly out of the heads of inhumed corpses.) Usher's organic existence and sanity seem threatened: his "cadaverousness of complexion"is conspicuous; and he not only attributes sentience to vegetable things, but also to "the kingdom of inorganization" which he evidently feels to be assuming domination over him. His most conspicuous feature was "an eye large, liquid, and luminous beyond comparison"; after Madeline Usher's death, Anthropos observes that "the luminousness of his eye had utterly gone out." It was thus assimilated to the "vacant eyelike windows" of his house. And the active qualities of Usher were also fading. We have noticed that his malady was a combined hyper-acuity and inhibition of function of the five senses which maintain life and mind. Altogether, the fabric of Usher, like that of his house, exhibited a "specious totality."

The only other important mixed symbol is Usher's song of the "Haunted Palace." It is largely a contrast of before and after. Before the palace was assailed by "evil things, in robes of sorrow," it had "reared its head" grandly under the heavens:

> Never seraph spread a pinion
> Over fabric half so fair!

It displayed several of the characteristics of Life-Reason. But after the assault of "evil things," the Death-Madness qualities are triumphant. Order is destroyed; instead of

> Spirits moving musically
> To a lute's well-tuned law,

within the palace are to be seen

> Vast forms that move fantastically
> To a discordant melody.

Instead of a "troop of Echoes" flowing and sparkling through the "fair palace door," "a hideous throng rush out for ever" through the "pale door" "like a rapid ghastly river." Reason has toppled from its throne, and this song intimated to Anthropos "a full consciousness on the part of Usher of the tottering of his lofty reason upon her throne." The perceptible fading of bright features in the palace is like the fading of the features and vitality of both Usher and his house.

The principal symbols of decrepit Life-Reason having been explicated, it remains to comment on the two symbols of ascendant Death-Madness—the tarn, and Roderick Usher's madly abstract painting. These show the same qualities that we have seen evilly encroaching upon the Life-Reason symbols, but these qualities are here unmitigated by any hint or reminiscence of Life-Reason. The juxtaposition of the tarn-house symbols is crucial: the zigzag fissure in the house is an index to the source of the evil which eventually overwhelms the Ushers. The tarn is an outlet of a subterranean realm; on the surface of the earth this realm disputes dominion with the powers of heaven and wins. This subnatural realm manifests itself in the miasma that rises from the tarn. "About the mansion and the whole domain there hung an atmosphere peculiar to themselves and their immediate vicinity—an atmosphere which had no affinity with the air of heaven, but which had reeked up from the decayed trees, and the gray wall, and the silent tarn—a pestilent and mystic vapor, dull, sluggish, faintly discernible, and leaden-hued." This upward-reeking effluvium has its counterpart in the "distempered ideality" of Usher while he is producing his mad compositions after the death of Madeline: they are products of "a mind from which darkness, as if an inherent positive quality, poured forth upon all objects of the moral and physical universe in one unceasing radiation of gloom."

"Radiation of gloom" is as interesting an idea as "darkness visible." It reminds us that another mark of this emanation of evil was lurid illumination. The feeble gleams of light that entered Usher's studio were encrimsoned. The "luminous win-

Woodcut illustration of "The Gold Bug" by Fritz Eichenberg, 1944. The Granger Collection, New York.

dows" of the "radiant palace" became the "red-litten windows" of the "haunted palace." Oddly, even Usher's mad music is described in a visual figure as having a "sulphureous lustre." On the catastrophic last night of the House of Usher, the environs are at first illuminated, not by any celestial luminaries, but by the "unnatural light of a faintly luminous and distinctly visible gaseous [so our matter-of-fact Anthropos] exhalation which hung about and enshrouded the mansion." And finally, the collapse of the house is melodramatically spotlighted by "the full, setting, and blood-red moon, which now shone vividly through that once barely perceptible fissure."

Roderick Usher's dread of the "kingdom of inorganization" as a really sentient order of existence reminds us of the animate inanimation of the tarn. Activity and harmony are really related qualities; harmony is an agreeable coincidence of motions. The tarn's absolute stillness is the negation of these qualities. Water is a universal and immemorial symbol of life; this dead water is thus a symbol of Death-in-Life. It lies "unruffled" from the first, and when at last the House of Usher topples thunderously into it, to the noisy accompaniment of Nature in tumult, its waters close "sullenly and silently over the fragments." This horrid inactivity is the condition toward which Usher is tending when he finds the exercise of his senses intolerable.

The tarn is as featureless as any visible thing can be; its blackness, "unruffled lustre," and silence are like the painted "vaguenesses" at which Anthropos shuddered "the more thrillingly" because he shuddered "not knowing why." Here are blank horrors, with only enough suggestion of feature to set the imagination fearfully to work.

This leads us to the only remaining symbol of importance, Usher's terrible painting. It is more horrible than the "Haunted Palace" because, whereas the song described the lost but regretted state of lovely Life and Reason, the painting depicts Death-Madness horribly regnant, with no reminiscence of Life and Reason. The scene pictured is subterranean (Madeline's coffin was deposited in a suggestively similar vault): "Certain accessory points of the design served well to convey the idea that this excavation lay at an exceeding depth below the surface of the earth." It is preternaturally lurid: "No torch or other artificial source of light was discernible; yet a flood of intense rays rolled throughout, and bathed the whole in a ghastly and inappropriate splendor." The picture shows a lifeless scene without features—"smooth, white, and without interruption or device."

Before these remarks on the symbolism of the tale are concluded, some notice should be taken of the part which musical symbols play in it. Poe uses his favorite heart-lute image, from Béranger, as a motto:

> Son coeur est un luth suspendu;
> Sîtot qu'on le touche il résonne.

The "lute's well-tuned law" symbolizes ideal order in the "radiant palace," and the whole of that song is an explicit musical metaphor for derangement of intellect. For Poe, music was the highest as well as the most rational expression of the intelligence, and string music was quintessential music (wherefore Usher's jangled intellect can endure only string music). Time out of mind, music has symbolized celestial order. His conception was not far from that expressed in Dryden's "Song for St. Cecilia's Day," with "The diapason closing full in Man." The derangement of human reason, then, "sweet bells jangled out of tune and harsh," cannot be better expressed than in a musical figure. (pp. 176-83)

"The Fall of the House of Usher" has that "vital requisite of all works of Art, Unity." It achieves unity by a concentration and remarkably subtle co-operation of carefully calculated, complex causes. Instead of the more familiar methods of realistic narrative specification and progressive logical explication, it operates through parallel symbolic suggestions. These build up to such a climax of intensity that the final shattering crash of all these piled-up effects affords a powerful release of psychological tension.

Throughout the tale, alternative explanations, natural and supernatural, of the phenomena are set forth; and we are induced, by the consistently maintained device of a common-sense witness gradually convinced in spite of his determined scepticism, to accept imaginatively the supernatural explanation.

The tale is a consummate psychological allegory which produces its intended totality of effect by perfectly unobtrusive means; there are no seams, bastings, or other interfering reminders of its being artificially put together. It is, indeed, too successful: readers take it to be all shell, and, although it irresistibly makes its intended impression, its method is so concealed that the too casual reader may take the impression to be meretricious. Those who admire Kafka only this side of idolatry for employing a method which they look upon as a brilliant innovation, will find his technique anticipated in Poe without the baffling obscurities and seeming irrelevancies of Kafka: Poe's is the art which conceals art. (p. 185)

Darrel Abel, "A Key to the House of Usher," in University of Toronto Quarterly, *Vol. XVIII, No. 2, January, 1949, pp. 176-85.*

ALLEN TATE (lecture date 1949)

[*Tate, an American poet and critic, is closely associated with two critical movements, the Agrarians and the New Critics. A conservative thinker and convert to Catholicism, Tate attacked the tradition of Western philosophy which he felt has alienated persons from themselves, one another, and from nature by divorcing intellectual functions from natural in human life. For Tate, literature is the principal form of knowledge and revelation which restores human beings to a proper relationship and nature and the spiritual realm. In the following excerpt from a lecture given in 1949, the centenary of Poe's death, Tate discusses symbol, theme, characterization, and style in Poe's stories. For a rebuttal of Tate's contention that "Ligeia" is superior in style to "William Wilson," see the essay by Donald Barlow Stauffer (1965).*]

[In] discussing any writer, or in coming to terms with him, we must avoid the trap of mere abstract evaluation, and try to reproduce the actual conditions of our relation to him. It would be difficult for me to take Poe up, "study" him, and proceed to a critical judgment. One may give these affairs the look of method, and thus deceive almost everybody but oneself. In reading Poe we are not brought up against a large, articulate scheme of experience, such as we see adumbrated in Hawthorne or Melville, which we may partly sever from personal association, both in the writer and in ourselves. Poe surrounds us with Eliot's "wilderness of mirrors," in which we see a subliminal self endlessly repeated, or, turning, a new posture of the same figure. It is not too harsh, I think, to say that it is stupid to suppose that by "evaluating" this forlorn demon in the glass, we dispose of him. For Americans, perhaps for most modern men, he is with us like a dejected cousin: we may "place" him but we may not exclude him from our board. This is the recognition of a relationship, almost of the blood, which we much in honor acknowledge: what destroyed him is potentially destructive of us. Not only this; we must acknowledge another obligation, if, like most men of my generation, we were brought up in houses where the works of Poe took their easy place on the shelf with the family Shakespeare and the early novels of Ellen Glasgow. This is the obligation of loyalty to one's experience: he was in our lives and we cannot pretend that he was not. Not even Poe's great power in Europe is quite so indicative of his peculiar "place" as his unquestioned, if unexamined, acceptance among ordinary gentle people whose literary culture was not highly developed. The horrors of Poe created not a tremor in the bosoms of young ladies or a moment's anxiety in the eyes of vigilant mothers. I suppose the gentlemen of the South did not read him much after his time; in his time, they could scarcely have got the full sweep and depth of the horror. Nothing that Mr. Poe wrote, it was said soon after his death, could bring a blush to the cheek of the purest maiden.

But I doubt that maidens read very far in the Tales. If they had they would have found nothing to disconcert the image that Miss Susan Ingram recorded from a visit of Poe to her family a few weeks before his death:

> Although I was only a slip of a girl and he what seemed to me then quite an old man, and a great literary one at that, we got on together beautifully. He was one of the most courteous gentlemen I have ever seen, and that gave great charm to his manner. None of his pictures that I have ever seen look like the picture of Poe that I keep in my memory . . . there was something in his face that is in none of them. Perhaps it was in the eyes.

If he was a madman he was also a gentleman. Whether or not we accept Mr. Krutch's theory [that Poe was sexually impotent], we know, as this sensible young lady knew, that she was quite safe with him. A gentleman? Well, his manners were exemplary (when he was not drinking) and to the casual eye at any rate his exalted idealization of Woman (even of some very foolish women) was only a little more humorless, because more intense, than the standard cult of Female Purity in the Old South.

What Mr. Poe on his own had done with the cult it was not possible then to know. A gentleman and a Southerner, he was not quite, perhaps, a Southern gentleman. The lofty intellect of Ligeia, of Madeline, of Berenice, or of Eleonora, had little utility in the social and economic structure of Virginia, which had to be perpetuated through the issue of the female body, while the intellect, which was public and political, remained under the supervision of the gentlemen. Although Morella had a child (Poe's only heroine, I believe, to be so compromised), she was scarcely better equipped than Virginia Clemm herself to sustain more than the immaculate half of the vocation of the Southern lady. "But the fires," writes Morella's narrator-husband, "were not of Eros." And we know, at the end of the story, that the daughter is no real daughter but, as Morella's empty "tomb" reveals, Morella herself come back as a vampire to wreak upon her "lover" the vengeance due him. Why is it due him? Because, quite plainly, the lover lacked, as he always lacked with his other heroines, the "fires of Eros." The soul of Morella's husband "burns with fires it had never before known . . . and bitter and tormenting to my spirit was the gradual conviction that I could in no manner define their unusual meaning, or regulate their vague intensity." Perhaps in the soul of John Randolph alone of Virginia gentlemen strange fires burned. The fires that were not of Eros were generally for the land and oratory, and the two fires were predictably regulated.

Poe's strange fire is his leading visual symbol, but there is not space in an essay to list all its appearances. You will see it in the eye of the Raven; in "an eye large, liquid, and luminous beyond comparison," of Roderick Usher; in the burning eye of the old man in **"The Tell-Tale Heart";** in "Those eyes! those large, those shining, those divine orbs," of the Lady Ligeia. Poe's heroes and heroines are always burning with a hard, gemlike flame—a bodyless exaltation of spirit that Poe himself seems to have carried into the drawing room, where its limited visibility was sufficient guarantee of gentlemanly behavior. But privately, and thus, for him, publicly, in his stories, he could not "regulate its vague intensity."

I cannot go into this mystery here as fully as I should like; yet I may, I think, ask a question: Why did not Poe use explicitly the universal legend of the vampire? Perhaps some instinct for aesthetic distance made him recoil from it; perhaps the literal, businesslike way the vampire went about making its living revolted the "ideality" of Poe. At any rate D. H. Lawrence was no doubt right in describing as vampires his women characters [see excerpt dated 1923], the men, soon to join them as "undead," have by some defect of the moral will, made them so.

The mysterious exaltation of spirit which is invariably the unique distinction of his heroes and heroines is not quite, as I have represented it, bodyless. *It inhabits a human body but that body is dead. The spirits prey upon one another with destructive fire which is at once pure of lust and infernal.* All Poe's characters represent one degree or another in a movement towards an archetypal condition: the survival of the soul in a dead body; but only in **"The Facts in the Case of M. Valdemar"** is the obsessive subject explicit.

In none of the nineteenth-century comment on **"The Fall of the House of Usher"** that I have read, and in none of our own period, is there a feeling of shock, or even of surprise, that Roderick Usher is in love with his sister: the relation not being physical, it is "pure." R. H. Stoddard, the least sympathetic of the serious early biographers, disliked Poe's morbidity, but admitted his purity. The American case against Poe, until the first World War, rested upon his moral indifference, or his limited moral range. The range is limited, but there is no indifference; there is rather a compulsive, even a profound, interest in a moral problem of universal concern. His contemporaries could see in the love stories neither the incestuous theme nor what it meant, because it was not represented literally. The theme and its meaning as I see them are unmistakable: the symbolic compulsion that drives through, and beyond, physical incest moves towards the extinction of the beloved's will in complete possession, not of her body, but of her being; there is the reciprocal force, returning upon the lover, of self-destruction. Lawrence shrewdly perceived the significance of Poe's obsession with incestuous love. Two persons of the least dissimilarity offer the least physical resistance to mutual participation in the *fire* of a common being. Poe's most casual reader perceives that his lovers never do anything but contemplate each other, or pore upon the rigmarole of preposterously erudite, ancient books, most of which never existed. They are living in each other's insides, in the hollows of which burns the fire of will and intellect.

The fire is a double symbol; it lights and it burns. It is overtly the "light" of reason but as action it becomes the consuming fire of the abstract intellect, without moral significance, which invades the being of the beloved. It is the fire that, having illuminated, next destroys. Lawrence is again right in singling out for the burden of his insight the epigraph to **"Ligeia,"** which Poe had quoted from Glanvill: "Man does not yield himself to the angels, nor unto death utterly, save through the weakness of his own feeble will." Why do these women of monstrous will and intellect turn into vampires? Because, according to Lawrence, the lovers have not subdued them through the body to the biological level, at which sanity alone is possible, and they retaliate by devouring their men. This view is perhaps only partly right. I suspect that the destruction works both ways, that the typical situation in Poe is more complex than Lawrence's version of it.

If we glance at **"The Fall of the House of Usher"** we shall be struck by a singular feature of the catastrophe. Bear in mind that Roderick and Madeline are brother and sister, and that the standard hyperaesthesia of the Poe hero acquires in Roderick a sharper reality than in any of the others, except perhaps William Wilson. His naked sensitivity to sound and light is not "regulated" to the forms of the human situation; it is a mechanism operating apart from the moral consciousness. We have here something like a capacity for mere sensation, as distinguished from sensibility, which in Usher is atrophied. In terms of the small distinction that I am offering here, sensibility keeps us in the world; sensation locks us into the self, feeding upon the disintegration of its objects and absorbing them into the void of the ego. The lover, circumventing the body into the secret being of the beloved, tries to convert the spiritual object into an object of sensation: the intellect which knows and the will which possesses are unnaturally turned upon that center of the beloved which should remain inviolate. (pp. 387-92)

[Poe's] characters are, in the words of William Wilson's double, "dead to the world"; they are machines of sensation and will, with correspondences, in the physical universe, to particles and energy. Poe's engrossing obsession in *Eureka* with the cosmic destiny of man issued in a quasi-cosmology, a more suitable extension of his vision than any mythology, homemade or traditional, could have offered him. The great mythologies are populous worlds, but a cosmology need have nobody in it. In Poe's, the hyperaesthetic egoist has put all other men into his void: he is alone in the world, and thus dead to it. If we place Poe against the complete Christian imagination of Dante, whom he resembles in his insistence upon a cosmic extension of the moral predicament, the limits of his range are apparent, and the extent of his insight within those limits. The quality of Poe's imagination can be located, as I see it, in only two places in Dante's entire scheme of the after-life: Cantos XIII and XXXII of the *Inferno*. In Canto XIII, the Harpies feed upon the living trees enclosing the shades of suicides—those "violent against themselves," who will not resume their bodies at the Resurrection, for "man may not have what he takes from himself." In XXXII, we are in Caïna, the ninth circle, where traitors to their kin lie half buried in ice, up to the pubic shadow—"where the doleful shades were . . . sounding with their teeth like storks." Unmotivated treachery, for the mere intent of injury, and self-violence are Poe's obsessive subjects. He has neither Purgatory nor Heaven; and only two stations in Hell.

Let me turn briefly to the question of Poe's style. He has several styles, and it is not possible to damn them all at once. The critical style, which I shall not be able to examine here, is on occasion the best; he is a lucid and dispassionate expositor, he is capable of clear and rigorous logic (even from mistaken premises, as in "The Rationale of Verse"), when he is not warped by envy or the desire to flatter. He is most judicial with his peers, least with his inferiors, whom he either overestimates or wipes out. As for the fictional style, it, too, varies; it is perhaps at its sustained best, in point of sobriety and restraint, in the tales of deduction. Exceptions to this observation are **"Descent into the Maelström,"** *The Narrative of Arthur Gordon Pym*, and perhaps one or two others in a genre which stems from the eighteenth-century "voyage." These fictions demanded a Defoe-like verisimilitude which was apparently beyond his reach when he dealt with his obsessive theme. Again I must make an exception: **"William Wilson,"** one of the serious stories (by serious, I mean an ample treatment of the obsession), is perspicuous in diction and on the whole credible in realistic detail. I quote a paragraph:

> The extensive enclosure was irregular in form, having many capacious recesses. Of these, three or four of the largest constituted the play-ground. It was level, and covered with a hard fine gravel. I well remember it had no trees, nor benches, nor anything similar within it. Of course it was in the rear of the house. In front lay a small

> parterre, planted with box and other shrubs, but through this sacred division we passed only upon rare occasions indeed—such as a first advent to school or a final departure hence, or perhaps, when a parent or a friend having called upon us, we joyfully took our way home for the Christmas or midsummer holidays.

It is scarcely great prose, but it has an eighteenth-century directness, and even elegance, of which Poe was seldom capable in his stories. I surmise that the playground at Dr. Bransby's school at Stoke-Newington, where, as a child, he was enrolled for five years, recalled one of the few periods of his life which he could detach from the disasters of manhood and face with equanimity. Now a part of the description of the lady Ligeia:

> . . . I examined the contour of the lofty and pale forehead—it was faultless—how cold indeed that word when applied to a majesty so divine!—the skin rivalling the purest ivory, the commanding extent and repose, the gentle prominence of the regions above the temples; and the raven-black, the glossy, the luxuriant, the naturally curling tresses, setting forth the full force of the Homeric epithet, "hyacinthine." I looked at the delicate outline of the nose. . . .

But I refrain. It is easy enough to agree with Aldous Huxley and Yvor Winters, and dismiss this sort of ungrammmatical rubbish as too vulgar, or even too idiotic, to reward the time it takes to point it out. But if Poe is worth understanding at all (I assume that he is), we might begin by asking why the writer of the lucid if not very distinguished passage from **"William Wilson"** repeatedly fell into the bathos of **"Ligeia."** I confess that Poe's serious style at its typical worst makes the reading of more than one story at a sitting an almost insuperable task. The Gothic glooms, the Venetian interiors, the ancient wine cellars (from which nobody ever enjoys a vintage but always drinks "deep")—all this, done up in a glutinous prose, so fatigues one's attention that with the best will in the world one gives up, unless one gets a clue to the power underlying the flummery.

I have tried in the course of these remarks to point in the direction in which the clue, as I see it, is to be found. I do not see it in the influence of the Gothic novel. This was no doubt there; but no man is going to use so much neo-Gothic, over and over again, unless he means business with it; I think that Poe meant business. If the Gothic influence had not been to hand, he would have invented it, or something equally "unreal" to serve his purpose. His purpose in laying on the thick décor was to simulate sensation. Poe's sensibility, for reasons that I cannot surmise here, was almost completely impoverished. He could feel little but the pressure of his predicament, and his perceptual powers remained undeveloped. Very rarely he gives us a real perception because he is not interested in anything that is alive. Everything in Poe is dead: the houses, the rooms, the furniture, to say nothing of nature and of human beings. He is like a child—all appetite without sensibility; but to be in manhood all appetite, all will, without sensibility, is to be a monster: to feed spiritually upon men without sharing with them a real world is spiritual vampirism. The description of Ligeia's head is that of a dead woman's.

Does it explain anything to say that this is necrophilism? I think not. Poe's prose style, as well as certain qualities of his verse, expresses the kind of "reality" to which he had access: I believe I have indicated that it is a reality sufficiently terrible. In spite of an early classical education and a Christian upbringing, he wrote as if the experience of these traditions had been lost: he was well ahead of his time. He could not relate his special reality to a wider context of insights—a discipline that might have disciplined his prose. From the literary point of view he combined the primitive and the decadent: primitive, because he had neither history nor the historical sense; decadent, because he was the conscious artist of an intensity which lacked moral perspective. (pp. 396-99)

Allen Tate, "Our Cousin, Mr. Poe," in his Essays of Four Decades, *The Swallow Press Inc., 1970, pp. 385-400.*

ROBERT DANIEL (essay date 1951)

[In the following excerpt, Daniel discusses the character C. Auguste Dupin in Poe's detective stories.]

The centenary of Poe's death in 1849 evoked new tributes to the keenness of his intelligence, in proof of which his detective stories were freely cited. Forty years earlier he had been called the inventor of the detective story, by no less an authority than Arthur Conan Doyle; but this claim has since been challenged. Dorothy L. Sayers' *Omnibus of Crime* begins with four "primitives," from pre-Christian times, though under "The Modern Detective Story" it includes none earlier than **"The Mystery of Marie Rogêt."** At any rate we may safely say that Poe invented the detective, so far as fiction is concerned, as well as his characteristic milieu. Much has been written about the influence of this character, C. Auguste Dupin, upon subsequent literary sleuths. Yet something can be added on Poe's creation of him, on the significance of his residing in Paris, and on the supernatural impressiveness of his exploits. If detectives work miracles, this fact will help to answer a question much debated lately: Why are detective stories popular?

One of Paul Elmer More's Shelburne Essays ["The Origin of Hawthorne and Poe"] contains a hint that may be applied to the analysis of Dupin. More discusses only such stories of Poe's as **"The Fall of the House of Usher"** which overtly employ supernatural events, as many of Hawthorne's do. He sees the origin of their supernaturalism in the Pre-Revolutionary imagination, which, largely Puritan, had been obsessed by phantasms of witches and devils. After the relaxation of religious belief at the end of the eighteenth century, so More believed, these terrors persisted in stories of the weird. The popularity of Hawthorne and Poe thus stemmed from the substitution of fearsome symbols for Christian myths that were no longer literally believed.

But are not the Dupin stories also stories of the supernatural? In one important respect More's idea is incomplete: it finds no deities among the characters with which it deals, although religions center on gods, demi-gods, or super-men at least. If Dupin is rightly understood as a worker of miracles, the empty niche in More's pantheon will then be filled. Dupin is a sort of secular god; and Poe's Romanticism, which led him to exalt the gifted individual while discrediting the institutions of society in the persons of the police, produced the most enduring religious substitute in the imagination of what has been called A Century of Hero-Worship. The detective story, which has marched into our century almost unaltered in the deepest respects, probably arouses the same feelings now as one hundred years ago.

When the publication of **"The Murders in the Rue Morgue"** in *Graham's Magazine* for April, 1841, introduced the modern detective, Poe was well known for other kinds of writing. In imagining Dupin, he had only to combine three elements that he had already developed in his earlier work: his fancied genius for solving puzzles, the love of paradox that characterizes his reviewing, and the decadent aristocrat (the prototype being Roderick Usher) who dominates the tales of horror and terror. These three characters—Dupin, the Usher-hero, and Edgar A. Poe the Critic—are essentially the same personage.

The kinship of Dupin and Usher is easily seen, but it is not generally recognized how profoundly Poe's criticism relies on paradox, in the sense of statements contrary to received opinions. Poe's view of society as organized stupidity is reflected in the French sentence with which he opened his review of Longfellow's *Ballads and Tales,* and which appealed to him so strongly that he used it again in **"The Purloined Letter."** It may be loosely translated as, "Whatever the majority believes is probably nonsense." Guided by this maxim, he centered most of his reviews on ridicule of a popular idea. In 1845 he denies that the drama has declined. Elsewhere he denies that the imagination is creative, that there is a difference between theory and practice, and that a critic should ever praise a book. His review of Macaulay's *Essays* perfectly exemplifies the habit, which virtually became Poe's trademark as a critic: "Macaulay," it begins, "has obtained a reputation which, although deservedly great, is yet in a remarkable measure undeserved."

Poe's longer essays are equally dissident. "The Rationale of Verse" starts with an assault upon all who have presumed to speak on the subject of prosody. In explaining how "a thousand profound scholars" can have been wrong, Poe maintains among other things that they have been misled by the simplicity of the subject—a paradox which reappears in **"The Murders in the Rue Morgue"** and is of course the foundation of **"The Purloined Letter."** ("Perhaps it is the very simplicity of the thing that puts you at fault," observes Dupin.) Passing to Poe's description of how he wrote "The Raven," we find him maintaining that the writing of a poem has "the precision and rigid consequence of a mathematical problem"—which contradicts not only the common notion but also the description of the poetic mood in Poe's best-known essay, "The Poetic Principle." The burden of the latter is the enforcement of two paradoxes: that long poems do not exist, and that the object of poetry is not truth. The public was expected to be startled by both these propositions, as is plain from Poe's remark that "by being generally condemned as falsities they will not be essentially damaged as truths."

So it is seen that Poe's criticism reflects his sense of alienation from society. For their lack of understanding he repaid his contemporaries with scorn. It remains to show how this cast of his mind influenced his later fiction. There are several ways in which the detective stories appear to be extensions of Poe's criticism. As a reviewer he is very much the sleuth-hound; he ferrets out plagiarism, and hunts down writers guilty of bad taste, confused thinking, or the murder of the language. Contrariwise, the detective stories may be regarded as essays in criticism—Dupin's adverse criticism of the bumbling policemen, whom he treats much as Poe treated most of the authors whom he reviewed. Above all, as the structure of **"The Murders in the Rue Morgue"** shows, when Poe turned to the detective story he was mainly concerned to dramatize a superior character, the detective, much as he had dramatized himself in his reviews. He would often try out particular paradoxes there and then rework them round the figure of Dupin; but the grand paradox is the transformation of a human character into a god.

> "The mass of the people regard as profound only him who suggests *pungent contradictions* of the general idea."
>
> C. Auguste Dupin

It required effrontery for Poe to have Dupin disparage contradictions of what the majority believes. The quoted sentence gives the correct account of Dupin's reputation for profundity, while at the same time suggesting that he follows only such views as are commonly held to be true. Itself a paradox, it affords no contrast to the paradoxes and contradictions out of which the figure of Dupin is woven. When we analyze the Dupin stories in the light of this dictum, we are led to make three observations: first, Poe is concerned above all to project a remarkable character, his own alter ego; second, the character is remarkable largely because of his supernatural exploits, most of which are made credible by trickery; and third, his function in society is one that allowed Poe to dominate society imaginatively, when in fact society pretty much rejected him.

The characterization of Dupin in **"The Murders in the Rue Morgue"** depends upon contradiction from the start. Like Usher he is an invalid. Nobly born but with his energy destroyed by the shipwreck of his fortunes, he inhabits a "time-eaten and grotesque mansion," ventures forth only at night, and passes his days in reading and dreaming. Yet though unable to cope with the ordinary exigencies of life, he solves crimes that have baffled the trained intelligence of the Paris police. His success seems intuitive, but really results from the methodical analysis of data. Poe has him refer to his peculiar faculty as that of "educated thought."

Poe's absorption in this character explains the odd form of the story, with its long opening essay which delays the plot. Poe is developing the character of "The Analyst," as he calls him; Dupin is the Analyst *par excellence;* the discovery that an orang-utan has committed the murders is but an illustration of his powers. The introductory section, which modern critics find intrusive and unaccountable, was in 1841 of paramount importance to the success of the idea that a debilitated amateur would triumph where the police had failed. At that time it was not known that the amateur can regularly beat the professional on his own ground.

The preliminary paradoxes, in other words, put the reader in a frame of mind where he will believe anything. He first encounters an extended and—it must be admitted—specious demonstration that checkers is a more profound game than chess; checkers more decidedly tasks "the higher powers of the reflective intellect." Whereas winning at chess is a mere matter of paying attention, games of checkers are won by "some strong exertion of the intellect," such as putting oneself in one's opponent's place. Before the reader can object that the successful chess-player must do the same, he is hurried into a discussion of the frivolity of chess as compared with whist. Here is found the slighting reference to common opinion: to remember the cards and follow the rules "are points commonly regarded as the sum total of good playing." But the Analyst, we are told, wins because of the inferences he can draw from the expressions and actions of the other players.

All is now in readiness for the introduction of Dupin. The first incident in the story shows his ability to read men's thoughts, as though they "wore windows in their bosoms": during a walk, the narrator is immersed in a reverie about an actor, and Dupin reads his mind.

The narrator's comment on this feat deserves attention:

> "Dupin," said I, gravely, "this is beyond my comprehension. I do not hesitate to say that I am amazed, and can scarcely credit my senses."

Such language is the language appropriate to miracle and, in fact, a miracle has just been wrought. Outbursts of this kind are from now on to accompany the fictional detective's discoveries; they are one of the hardiest devices that Poe gave to the form. Dr. Watson is particularly prone to them. Dupin's feat scarcely goes beyond the possible—though some strain may be felt in the transitions from "stereotomy" to atomies to the theories of Epicurus; but what makes the incident miraculous is that it is supposed to be representative. That is, we are led to feel that Dupin can read thoughts whenever he chooses, not only when the reverie has been specially arranged for discovery, but always.

The same applies to Dupin's discovery that the women in the Rue Morgue were slain by an orang-utan. What outrages probability is not the process of his reasoning but the phenomena that he reasons about. The police arrest a bank clerk named Le Bon. An oddity of the witnesses' testimony, however, shows Dupin that the crimes have not been done by a human being: though all agree that one of the suspects spoke French, all differ on the language of the other. Conceivably, Paris being the cosmopolitan place that it is, a murderer's voice could be overheard by four foreigners in addition to a normal quota of Frenchmen. But is it likely that the "fiendish jabberings of the brute" would be mistaken for Russian by the Italian, for German by the Englishman, for English by the Spaniard, for French by the Hollander, for Spanish by one Frenchman, and for Italian by another? We might expect at least one witness to exclaim: "It sounded precisely like the fiendish jabberings of a brute!"

At all events the police arrest Le Bon and, as foils to the sagacity of Dupin, overlook several other improbable clues. The windows of the bedroom not only fasten by secret springs but also appear to be nailed down. Dupin, however, noticing that one of the nails is broken in two, readily opens the window by manipulating its spring. The window stood open when the murderer arrived, afforded him a means of escape, and locked by the spring after he had departed. Presumably it shut of its own accord, since an orang-utan would not have bothered.

Though first on the premises, the police also ignore the gold coins that are scattered about, a greasy ribbon from which Dupin deduces the murderer's companion to have been a Maltese sailor, and, most astonishing of all, a tuft of coarse hair clenched in the fingers of the murdered Mme. L'Espanaye. Even the narrator can see that it is not the hair of a human being.

From the detecting standpoint Dupin's fancy reasoning about the languages and the window-fastening is made supererogatory by his possession of the tuft of hair. These passages lead not to the identification of the murderer but to the establishment of Dupin's omniscience. And such was Poe's main design in writing the story.

A year and a half later, in a magazine called *The Ladies' Companion,* Poe brought out **"The Mystery of Marie Rogêt."** Labeled a sequel to the first Dupin story, it resembles it in many ways. The narrator, though too stupid to follow Dupin's deductions except at a distance, discusses coincidence with the same easy mastery of paradox that he showed in his observations on chess and whist. Dupin has progressed from Monsieur to Chevalier, an archaic title of nobility that sets him still farther apart from the mass of men. His supercilious indolence is more marked than ever, yet the police have by this time come to regard his ability as "little less than miraculous."

The important difference between the stories is that Marie Rogêt was a thin disguise for Mary Rogers, the name of a real girl whose body had been found floating in the Hudson River on 28 July 1841. Dupin's powers were now to be displayed in the solution of an actual crime, the clues to which had not been arranged by his creator.

Dupin's solution . . . proves to have been a triumph of error. Living in Philadelphia at the time, Poe worked from newspaper accounts of the affair. His solution hinted at the guilt of the girl's lover (another sailor!). Though the case has never been cleared of mystery, the evidence of Poe's blunder is his revision of the story, which appeared in ***Tales by Edgar A. Poe*** in 1845. By then Poe had moved to New York and had probably heard discussions of the case that made him change his mind. Wimsatt's comparison of the two versions shows that the reasoning which had first brought the lover under suspicion, leads in the second edition to the conclusion that Mary died accidentally, as the result of an abortion.

One other story completes the saga of Dupin. In **"The Purloined Letter"** (1845) he is as supercilious as ever: "The Parisian police," he allows, "are exceedingly able in their way." Though most people suppose that the way to hide a document is to conceal it, Dupin shows that it is better to leave it in plain sight. The paradox of The Obvious Hiding-Place is hedged about by demonstrations that mathematicians cannot reason and that in climbing it is easier to get up than to come down. Dupin finds the letter by identifying himself with the intellect of the purloiner, and his feat is again accompanied by the language of miracle. At his success, the narrator tells us,

> I was astounded. The Prefect appeared absolutely thunder-stricken. For some minutes he remained speechless and motionless, looking incredulously at my friend with open mouth, and eyes that seemed starting from their sockets. . . .

Besides these likenesses, **"The Purloined Letter"** presents Dupin in a new relation. It is suggested towards the end of the story that he is a savior and, doubtless, had Poe continued his saga, this strain would have been developed. Only a hint of it actually occurs, but from this hint much may be concluded about Poe's attitude towards his detective, and hence towards himself. When Dupin retrieves the letter, he dares not do so openly, for, as he explains, the Minister's desperate character placed him in grave danger. "Had I made the wild attempt you suggest, I might never have left the Ministerial presence alive. The good people of Paris might have heard of me no more." Dupin is both far withdrawn from humanity and at its service. His talents expose him to the risk of being sacrificed for the welfare of the herd, whom he patronizes.

Since Poe wrote no more stories about Dupin, the development of the detective as sacrificial victim was left to Conan Doyle. It will be noted that Sherlock Holmes, whose "people" are the citizens of London, inherited from Dupin the milieu of the great metropolis. Does this likeness not serve to introduce one further paradox, of which Poe could not have been entirely aware? The city is the typical setting for realistic novels; and no fact about the detective story is odder than its emergence at a time when the public was demanding realism above all other qualities in its fiction. Though the trappings of the detective story—its dialogue and descriptions, its obsession with fingerprints and microscopes—are realistic to the point of literalness, in the characteristic example of the form two fantastic elements stand out against their commonplace surroundings: the bizarre nature of the crime, and the intuitive solution by an amateur. In reality, as the newspapers daily attest, most murders are committed by such humdrum means as stabbing or gunshot, and all but an isolated few of the solutions are effected by the methodical methods of the professional police. A solution by an amateur is rarer than an eclipse of the sun. (pp. 45-52)

Robert Daniel, ''Poe's Detective God,'' in Furioso, *Vol. VI, No. 3, Summer, 1951, pp. 45-54.*

WOLFGANG KAYSER (essay date 1957)

[*Kayser's 1957 study* The Grotesque in Art and Literature, *from which the following is drawn, was the earliest attempt at a critical history of the grotesque as a distinct category of aesthetics. Kayser traces the evolution of the term ''grotesque'' from its first application to an ornamental style in Roman architecture through its various manifestations in the works of nineteenth and twentieth-century authors and artists, among them Poe, Franz Kafka, and the Surrealist painters. Here Kayser focuses on the grotesque in Poe's fiction.*]

Edgar Allan Poe followed E.T.A. Hoffmann in developing a type of story that is suffused with grotesque elements and that just as strongly affected the fiction of subsequent ages. Poe called the first collection of twenty-five of his stories ***Tales of the Grotesque and Arabesque***. . . . (p. 76)

What first strikes one in the title of Poe's collection is the fact that, contrary to the then current usage, the word ''grotesque'' is no longer meant derogatorily, as was still true of Walter Scott. One further notes that the arabesque is also drawn into the realm of literature as a category. . . . Moreover, the word, as it appears in the title of Poe's book, seems to be more closely related to Hazlitt's impressionistic than to Scott's structural use of it. Poe's preface begins with the sentence, ''The epithets 'Grotesque' and 'Arabesque' will be found to indicate with sufficient precision the prevalent tenor of the tales here published.'' And Poe further underscored his intentions by using the words ''gloom'' and ''Germanism.''

But Poe employed the word ''grotesque'' in still another sense, which was more closely related to that which Scott preferred. . . . The novella ***The Masque of the Red Death*** . . . , for instance, contains an interpretive description of the phenomenon that goes much beyond Scott and is perhaps the most complete and authoritative definition any author has given of the grotesque. In trying to escape the plague, the Italian Prince Prospero and his guests have withdrawn into an abbey. The Prince has ordered the seven halls, which had been built according to his own eccentric taste, to be decorated for a splendid ball and given instructions as to the kind of masks to be worn by the participants. . . . (p. 78)

The distortion of all ingredients, the fusion of different realms, the coexistence of beautiful, bizarre, ghastly, and repulsive elements, the merger of the parts into a turbulent whole, the withdrawal into a phantasmagoric and nocturnal world (Poe used to speak of his ''daydreams'')—all these features have here entered into the concept of the grotesque. This world is

Aubrey Beardsley's illustration of ''The Murders in the Rue Morgue,'' 1895. The Granger Collection, New York.

well prepared for the intrusion of the deadly nocturnal powers personified by Death in his red mask.

In another tale, **''The Murders in the Rue Morgue,''** Poe characterizes the appearance of the room in which the double murder has taken place by calling it ''a *grotesquerie* in horror absolutely alien from humanity.'' Poe thus uses the word ''grotesque'' on two different levels of meaning: to describe a concrete situation in which chaos prevails, and to indicate the tenor of entire stories concerned with terrible, incomprehensible, inexplicable, bizarre, fantastic, and nocturnal happenings. In these stories Poe makes use of a considerable number of motifs made familiar by E.T.A. Hoffmann and the literature of horror in general: the double (which, in **''The Black Cat,''** is extended to a terrifying animal); artistry consummated in a work that causes the artist's death; the mysterious presence of past and distant things, which drives sensitive souls to their death, etc. Yet no one will confuse the author of the *Nachtgeschichten* with that of the ***Tales of the Grotesque and Arabesque.*** Poe's work, for one thing, shows a marked preference for repulsive, ghastly, and criminal phenomena. Written in 1841 or 1842 and published in 1843, **''The Black Cat''** somewhat resembles Hoffmann's *Sandmann,* which Poe must have known at least through Scott's summary of it. While in the latter story the world is estranged for the narrator by the mysterious figure of the sandman (Coppelius), the uncanny cat effects the estrangement in the former. Both characters offend against the apparition, and in both the estrangement is heightened by the baffling return of the hostile principle, which precipitates the catastrophe. But instead of the madness which causes Nathanael's death in Hoffmann's story, Poe uses the protagonist's cruel murder of his wife. The detailed description of the deed, burial of the corpse, and its discovery are so compelling that the grotesque seems to be quenched by the horror. In the grotesqueries of the Rue Morgue, too, the horror of the crime prevails; here Dupin's intelligence triumphantly solves the crime, which was so inhuman as to seem altogether inexplicable. Still another difference between Poe and Hoffmann comes to light in this connection. Hoffmann confronts the sinister elements with an average intelligence unable to cope with them, while Poe, in a number of his stories, counters them with an amazing talent for combination. The ominous has thus been transformed into a puzzle capable of being solved by a sharp-witted individual. (pp. 79-80)

As far as their size, their structure, and the narrative technique employed in them are concerned, Poe's ***Tales of the Grotesque and Arabesque*** are strikingly different from Hoffmann's *Nachtgeschichten*. The younger writer, no doubt, was inspired by the older one. But in assimilating these influences, Poe turned them into something new and unique that was to acquire its own historical sphere of influence. (p. 81)

Wolfgang Kayser, "The Grotesque in the Age of Romanticism: Narrative Prose," in his The Grotesque in Art and Literature, *translated by Ulrich Weisstein, Indiana University Press, 1963, pp. 59-81.*

PATRICK F. QUINN (essay date 1960)

[In the following excerpt, Quinn clarifies some of the problems confronting critics of Poe's stories.]

No simple statement will define the particular kind of experience we may have when reading Poe. It is not enough—certainly for literary criticism it is not enough—to call his stories, strange, extraordinary, fantastic. These words are useful only in a general or introductory way. They mainly serve to help set up the problem, the problem being: What is the content of Poe's strangeness? To be sure, his stories are extraordinary and fantastic; but in what special way are they so?

In trying to answer these questions we must keep several things in mind. First among them is a remark made by Poe himself. In his discussion of Hawthorne's stories, Poe says that the goal or aim of poetry is Beauty; whereas, in prose fiction, the goal or aim is Truth [see excerpt dated 1842]. Immediately we are puzzled. What did he mean by these terms Beauty and Truth? Consider the extreme but instructive instance of "The Conqueror Worm." In this poem we find a distinctively Poe-esque vision of mortality. The poem is a kind of allegorical scenario, with human beings as puppets or actors on the stage of life, enacting a drama that is meaningless to them, a drama made with "much of Madness, and more of Sin / And Horror the soul of the plot." The climax of the drama, and of the poem, occurs with the entrance on the stage of an enormous red and writhing worm, which with "vermin fangs" feeds on "human gore," and so brings the play, and life, to an end. For the play, writes Poe, is the tragedy "Man," and its hero the Conqueror Worm.

Whatever else can be said about this poem, it cannot be said to involve the contemplation of Beauty. And yet Poe repeatedly made it clear that, in his opinion such contemplation—or the aspiration towards it—was the sole province and justification of poetry. Between this opinion and the poem I have cited there is a sharp contradiction.

Similarly, we wonder what Poe had in mind when he said, in the second half of the remark alluded to, that "Truth is often, and in very great degree, the aim of the tale." His own tales, beyond argument, are strange, fantastic, and the like. What have they to do with Truth? What meaning did this word have for him?

The answer seems to be that he saw two different meanings in this word: the truth of logic and fact, on the one hand, and the truth of insight and imagination, on the other. Almost everyone who has written about Poe has emphasized or at least referred to some kind of *dualism* as characteristic of his mind and his writing. Thus, for example, among the characters he created, he seems to resemble most the doomed dreamer Roderick Usher. But he also resembles Legrand, the successful empiricist who is the hero of **"The Gold Bug."** We find something of Poe in the obsessed criminal whose story of defeat is **"The Black Cat."** But Poe is also recognizable in the analytical criminologist, the detective-hero Dupin. If we say that Poe's world is a nightmare world, we must add that his world is also one of facts and figures and logical inferences. The "people" we encounter in his stories are dream-figures, phantoms; yet at the same time they are firmly sketched and carefully studied. Or, as a final instance, *The Narrative of Arthur Gordon Pym* is the story of an imaginary voyage. Only if read in this way can it become intelligible. However, in spite of its inwardness, *Gordon Pym* is crammed with data about the actual and outward world. How, then, should we understand Poe's remark that Truth is the aim of the tale when the tale is that of Gordon Pym?

Another difficulty we should be aware of, also in relation to the same remark, is that Poe seldom if ever identifies the nature of the truth conveyed in his stories. We know that he disliked didactic poetry. Apparently this distaste for didacticism was carried over from his poetic theory into his practice as a writer of fiction, for it is hard to recall any important story of his which is clearly, self-evidently, didactic. And this is probably why the objection is sometimes made that Poe's stories are empty of significance because they have no themes. For Poe almost never states his theme. He only dramatizes it. In the final lines of "The Conqueror Worm" he does clarify his gruesome allegory, as we saw. In a story that somewhat resembles that poem, in **"The Masque of the Red Death,"** we find no such clarification of meaning. No key to interpretation is presented. Instead, the meaning of the story is left latent within the details of the story itself. This is Poe's usual procedure.

The curious fact to take note of here is that he does provide a key to the interpretation of his poem "The Conqueror Worm," but he does not normally do this in his stories. And yet Poe's doctrine was that stories, and not poems, have Truth for their province or goal. It would be consistent with this principle if the stories stated their thematic point. But this rarely happens. If the stories "aim at Truth," they do so indirectly, by suggestion rather than by statement.

Poe, then, is a symbolist writer, and a symbolist writer of a certain kind. He belonged to no school or tradition, nor did he devise for himself a theory and method of literary symbolism. This is one way in which Poe differs from another great symbolist writer, James Joyce. Poe's stories, many of them, are symbolical, but not in the way Joyce's are. If we accept the thorough *explications de texte* that have been made of the stories in *Dubliners,* we must conclude that Joyce was able to invest multiple significance in almost every detail he used, no matter how trivial the detail might at first appear. The details chosen are graphically real; they convey a sense of actuality almost painful in its acuteness. And yet almost every time these details are there, for the reader who will study them, to bring in associations and reverberations that could never be summoned by merely realistic exactitude. Poe's stories cannot be successfully read, or rather studied, in this fashion. Details in his writing sometimes have a symbolic overtone, and sometimes they do not. For example, the narrator of **"MS. Found in a Bottle"** mentions that at one stage in his adventures he and a Swedish sailor were the only survivors of a tempest at sea. To ask the question: Why a *Swedish* sailor?—this is to assume, in effect, that Joyce rather than Poe wrote the story. Even in the final pages, when the narrator describes his experiences aboard an ancient and enormous ship, manned by a silent, aged, and infirm crew, even here, although we know how far behind us have been left the assumptions and criteria of realism, it is still hazardous to attempt particular symbolic identifications, to say that this detail represents one thing, and that other detail another. Usually in a story by Poe the details, the individual parts, resist what is called "symbol-hunting." Nevertheless, these parts do cohere in a totality—a *gestalt* or configuration—that does impress us as having symbolic force. It is as if the whole proves to be more than the sum of its parts. For this reason Poe's stories are difficult to analyze. In an effort to account for what is *felt* as their overall symbolic significance, we turn back, in analysis, to individual details. And these, we usually find, are lacking in symbolic resonance.

In other words, Poe's stories resist a direct gaze. The literal-minded reader will find them empty of meaning. The opposite kind of reader, who expects Poe to speak always in a consistently symbolic language, is also disappointed. The stories should be read obliquely, in accordance with the method, to call it that, used by Gordon Pym. After many days of confinement in the dark hold of the ship on which he had secretly taken passage, Pym came upon a message from the only other person on board who knew of his presence. In describing his attempt to read this message, Pym says: "The white slip of paper could barely be discerned, and not even that when I looked at it directly; by turning the exterior portions of the retina towards it,—that is to say, by surveying it slightly askance, I found that it became in some measure perceptible." By analogy, Poe's stories, too, become perceptible and intelligible if they are surveyed "slightly askance", if they are read, that is, indirectly and obliquely. So much for a *theory* as to how Poe should be read.

Practically, one can find no better introduction to Poe, no more effective way of getting to know the nature of his writing, than the story of Gordon Pym in its entirety. For in this, the longest of his stories, we find Poe's imagination at work on a large scale, and so we are given a larger opportunity than usual to study it and respond to it. *Arthur Gordon Pym* is a romance of the sea, a narrative of storm, shipwreck and other disasters on the oceans between Massachusetts and the South Pole. Some of the pages in this work are among the very best to be found in Poe. But if it is read only as an adventure story it is found to be unsatisfactory. A reader who expects to find a recital of adventures undergone by "real" people in realistic settings soon finds himself bored and puzzled by *Gordon Pym*. Although the prose is conventional, straightforward, and clear, and although the story begins on a solidly realistic basis, most of the experiences in Pym's narrative are inward rather than outward. Interior, imaginary, emotional disasters are translated, or projected outward, into the form of adventures at sea. To be aware only of this form, to notice only the dramatic events of the story, is to miss their interior meaning, where the essence of their life is.

To the question, therefore, What is *Gordon Pym* about? or What is Poe trying to say? one valid answer is probably this: The story is a graphic and dramatic representation of what it feels like to have the temperament of Gordon Pym. And what kind of temperament is that? Pym is the kind of person for whom the values of stability and security are meaningless, for whom everything that exists is deceptive and finally hostile. He is the kind of person who wants to sustain no firm link with the real world, the natural and the human environment, and who instead converts his life into a frenzied pursuit of death. For him, death is not to be feared but rather to be sought. *It* is the goal. But there are no goals worth finding in the course of normal life. In Poe's extended metaphor of the sea-voyage, life is represented as a long and agonizing journey to nowhere. This is one meaning, and the major one, of the whole story.

The most important lesson to be learned through a study of *Gordon Pym* is the one indicated earlier: Poe's true subject matter is not made of the incidents he writes about. These incidents, forming the action or plot, are his ways of getting at the subject. If we confine our attention only to the external details—to what is in effect the scaffolding—of the story, we can hardly claim to have read it.

For another example, **"The Fall of the House of Usher"** has been interpreted in various ways, even as a kind of political allegory of the relationship between England and Ireland. Such an interpretation is absurd, of course. Yet whoever thought of it was more responsive to the idiom of Poe than is someone who can find only the plot, and for whom **"The Fall of the House of Usher"** is only the story of a murder, the story of how Roderick killed his sister Madeline. To assume that the Ushers are meant to serve as representations of real people and that the events of the story might actually have happened, this is to set the story in an altogether misleading perspective.

"The Fall of the House of Usher" is not the story of a murder case. It is rather a representation of the experience of dread. As Poe understood this feeling, it was not equivalent to anxiety or fear. To some extent, dread contains both those feelings. But, in addition, as its distinctive characteristic, it also involves their opposite: the feeling of desire. Thus there results an explosive combination of antipathy and sympathy. Thus, what Usher feared was the death of his sister, and yet he killed her precisely because he at the same time longed for what he feared.

It is possible to say that the story of Usher dramatizes this insight into the complexity of the feeling of dread, that this insight is the basic subject and significant content of the story. But there is more to it than that. Roderick Usher is related to Gordon Pym in that for both of them the term *reality* in its commonsense, everyday meaning is meaningless. The reality they want is a dreamed reality, beyond the dimensions of time and space, and hence a nirvana attainable only through death. Pym's story concerns a quest for this nirvana, and so too, though less obviously, the story of Usher. Both stories are further alike in a still more fundamental way. They are written out of Poe's conviction that reality, consciousness, the "human condition", is false and limited. He refuses to accept it. Ultimately, what is conveyed in both stories is Poe's hatred of reality.

Hatred may seem an extravagant word, perhaps a wrong word. But I think it can be justified. It is true that in many of his stories Poe begins with the world of reality, the public world we all can recognize, and he writes about the specific actualities of this world with precision and care. Indeed, he seems at times almost too much interested in concrete particulars, as every reader of *Gordon Pym* can testify, and as is illustrated nicely in an early paragraph from **"MS. Found in a Bottle"**:

> Our vessel was a beautiful ship of about four hundred tons, copper fastened, and built at Bombay of Malabar teak. She was freighted with cotton-wool and oil, from the Lachadive islands. We had also on board coir, jaggeree, ghee, cocoa-nuts, and a few cases of opium. The stowage was clumsily done, and the vessel consequently crank.

However, as we go on reading we find that Poe's care and precision remain, but the real world does not. It has been dissolved into a dream or nightmare world. What we experience when we read is this process of transformation, dissolution, dislocation. Natural facts are alluded to, but they no longer retain their factual quality. Thus the streams of water in the final section of *Gordon Pym* are recognizable as streams of water, but in Poe's description they more resemble colorless streams of blood. This is typical of what he does; as is also, in **"The Oval Portrait"**, the way in which the creative power of art is made over into its opposite, the power to destroy. Poe himself, in his own art, works in a similar way.

If we return now to the remark quoted a while ago—Poe's remark that poetry has Beauty as its aim, whereas prose fiction aims at Truth—we find it less puzzling than we did before. Beauty, for Poe, was a transcendental, present in a realm above and beyond the realm of the real, the realm of Truth. While on earth and living in time, we can attain "to but brief and indeterminate glimpses" of the "divine and rapturous joys" that belong to the realm of Beauty. Such glimpses are afforded by poetry and music. But [it] is only when we are "beyond the grave" that Beauty can be apprehended in its fullness. Meantime we are living in the realm of actuality, of reality, of Truth. For Poe this was a kind of prison in which he felt himself trapped. His fear of and abhorrence for this prison are the recurrent sensations conveyed by his stories, which, in this way, and in Poe's own terms, *are* concerned with the realm of Truth. Accordingly, a major theme of the stories is that to know this realm for what it is is to loathe and reject it. In one of the most perceptive studies ever written about Poe, a study based on the pervasive presence in Poe's writing of images of imprisonment, encirclement, and circumscribed space, Georges Poulet reaches this conclusion, among others: "L'homme est pour lui un enterré vivant qui a pour mission d'explorer les surfaces intérieures de sa chambre." This one sentence of Poulet's is the best statement that can be made to define Poe's view of reality and actual human life. (pp. 140-44)

For him, to advance in the direction of one's dreams is to leave real life behind. No foundations on earth can be put under Poe's castles, for these castles—like the ones in "The City in the Sea" and the House of Usher—are destined to fade from sight in the water that reflects them. . . . And for him the perfect future existed somewhere "out of this world." . . . (p. 145)

Poe's few attempts—in some of his poems and in the prose poem "The Domain of Arnheim"—to go somewhere out of this world and reconnoitre the supernal realm of Essence are interesting attempts. But they failed. His imaginative powers in this respect fell far short of the task he set them. For that task was nothing less than to equal or surpass the achievement of Dante in the *Paradiso*. This he could not possibly do; and that Poe was aware of his inability is evidenced by the very limited number of poems he wrote.

Where Poe's imagination was successfully employed was along what may be referred to as the negative line of his argument, his hatred for and repudiation of the real, existential world. In the year before his death he gave this attitude its maximum expression in the most ambitious of all his writings, his treatise on the cosmos, *Eureka*. What we find as the conclusion of all the guesses and demonstrations in *Eureka* is that all of creation, all of reality, is unstable; that the entire universe is in a state of progressive collapse; and that this drive towards collapse is the one meaningful fact in the constitution of reality. In greater or less degree almost all of Poe's important writings may be read as individual variations on this, his paramount theme. (p. 146)

Patrick F. Quinn, "Four Views of Edgar Poe," in Jahrbuch für Amerikastudien, *Vol. 5, 1960, pp. 128-46.*

JAMES W. GARGANO (essay date 1963)

[*Gargano is an American critic who has written extensively on the works of Poe. In the following essay, he argues against the common critical assumption that the personality traits and prose style of the narrators of Poe's tales can be attributed to Poe himself.*]

Part of the widespread critical condescension toward Edgar Allan Poe's short stories undoubtedly stems from impatience with what is taken to be his "cheap" or embarrassing Gothic style. Finding turgidity, hysteria, and crudely poetic overemphasis in Poe's works, many critics refuse to accept him as a really serious writer. Lowell's flashy indictment of Poe as "two-fifths sheer fudge" agrees essentially with Henry James's magisterial declaration that an "enthusiasm for Poe is the mark of a decidedly primitive stage of reflection." T. S. Eliot seems to be echoing James when he attributes to Poe "the intellect of a highly gifted young person before puberty." Discovering in Poe one of the fountainheads of American obscurantism, Ivor Winters condemns the incoherence, puerility, and histrionics of his style. Moreover, Huxley's charge that Poe's poetry suffers from "vulgarity" of spirit, has colored the views of critics of Poe's prose style.

Certainly, Poe has always had his defenders. One of the most brilliant of modern critics, Allen Tate finds a variety of styles in Poe's works; although Tate makes no high claims for Poe as stylist, he nevertheless points out that Poe could, and often did, write with lucidity and without Gothic mannerisms [see excerpt dated 1949]. Floyd Stovall, a long-time and more enthusiastic admirer of Poe, has recently paid his critical respects to "the conscious art of Edgar Allan Poe." Though he says little about Poe's style, he seems to me to suggest that the elements of Poe's stories, style for example, should be analyzed in terms of Poe's larger, artistic intentions. Of course, other writers, notably Edward H. Davidson, have done much to demonstrate that an intelligible reationale informs Poe's best work.

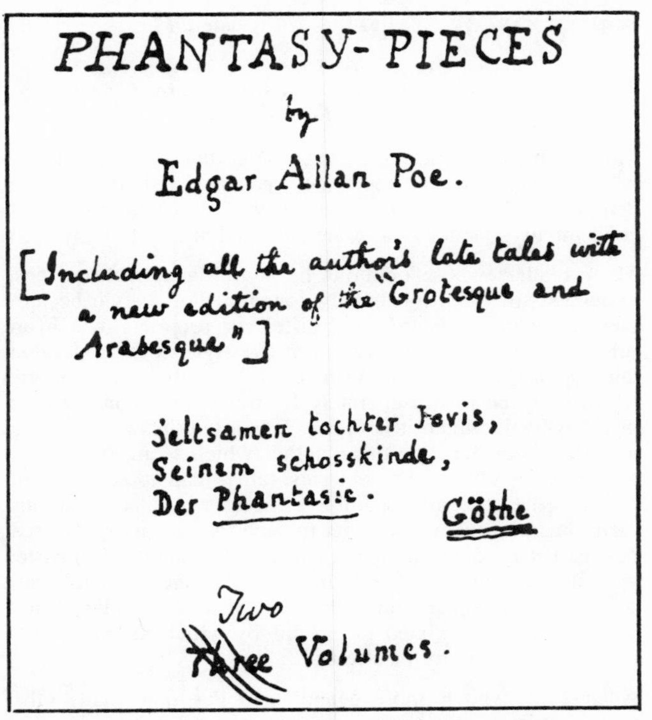

PHANTASY-PIECES

by

Edgar Allan Poe.

[Including all the author's late tales with a new edition of the "Grotesque and Arabesque"]

Seltsamen tochter Jovis,
Seinem schosskinde,
Der Phantasie. Göthe

Two
~~Three~~ Volumes.

Poe's holograph title page for Phantasy-Pieces.

It goes without saying that Poe, like other creative men, is sometimes at the mercy of his own worst qualities. Yet the contention that he is fundamentally a bad or tawdry stylist appears to me to be rather facile and sophistical. It is based, ultimately, on the untenable and often unanalyzed assumption that Poe and his narrators are identical literary twins and that he must be held responsible for all their wild or perfervid utterances; their shrieks and groans are too often conceived as emanating from Poe himself. I believe, on the contrary, that Poe's narrators possess a character and consciousness distinct from those of their creator. These protagonists, I am convinced, speak their own thoughts and are the dupes of their own passions. In short, Poe understands them far better than they can possibly understand themselves. Indeed, he often so designs his tales as to show his narrators' limited comprehension of their own problems and states of mind; the structure of many of Poe's stories clearly reveals an ironical and comprehensive intelligence critically and artistically ordering events so as to establish a vision of life and character which the narrator's very inadequacies help to "prove."

What I am saying is simply that the total organization or completed form of a work of art tells more about the author's sensibility than does the report or confession of one of its characters. Only the most naive reader, for example, will credit as the "whole truth" what the narrators of *Barry Lyndon, Huckleberry Finn,* and *The Aspern Papers* will divulge about themselves and their experiences. In other words, the "meaning" of a literary work (even when it has no narrator) is to be found in its fully realized form; for only the entire work achieves the resolution of the tensions, heterogeneities, and individual visions which make up the parts. The Romantic apologists for Milton's Satan afford a notorious example of the fallacy of interpreting a brilliantly integrated poem from the point of view of its most brilliant character.

The structure of Poe's stories compels realization that they are more than the effusions of their narrators' often disordered mentalities. Through the irony of his characters' self-betrayal and through the development and arrangement of his dramatic actions, Poe suggests to his readers ideas never entertained by the narrators. Poe intends his readers to keep their powers of analysis and judgment ever alert; he does not require or desire complete surrender to the experience of the sensations being felt by his characters. The point of Poe's technique, then, is not to enable us to lose ourselves in strange or outrageous emotions, but to see these emotions and those obsessed by them from a rich and thoughtful perspective. I do not mean to advocate that, while reading Poe, we should cease to feel; but feeling should be "simultaneous" with an analysis carried on with the composure and logic of Poe's great detective, Dupin. For Poe is not merely a Romanticist; he is also a chronicler of the consequences of the Romantic excesses which lead to psychic disorder, pain, and disintegration.

Once Poe's narrative method is understood, the question of Poe's style and serious artistry returns in a new guise. Clearly, there is often an aesthetic compatibility between his narrators' hypertrophic language and their psychic derangement; surely, the narrator in **"Ligeia,"** whose life is consumed in a blind rage against his human limitations, cannot be expected to consider his dilemma in cooly rational prose. The language of men reaching futilely towards the ineffable always runs the risk of appearing more flatulent than inspired. Indeed, in the very breakdown of their visions into lurid and purple rhetoric, Poe's characters enforce the message of failure that permeates their aspirations and actions. The narrator in **"Ligeia"** blurts out, in attempting to explain his wife's beauty in terms of its "expression": "Ah, words of no meaning!" He rants about "incomprehensible anomalies," "words that are impotent to convey," and his inability to capture the "inexpressible." He raves because he cannot explain. His feverish futility of expression, however, cannot be attributed to Poe, who with an artistic "control," documents the stages of frustration and fantastic desire which end in the narrator's madness. The completed action of **"Ligeia,"** then, comments on the narrator's career of self-delusion and exonerates Poe from the charge of lapsing into self-indulgent, sentimental rodomontade.

In **"The Tell-Tale Heart"** the cleavage between author and narrator is perfectly apparent. The sharp exclamations, nervous questions, and broken sentences almost too blatantly advertise Poe's conscious intention; the protagonist's painful insistence in "proving" himself sane only serves to intensify the idea of his madness. Once again Poe presides with precision of perception at the psychological drama he describes. He makes us understand that the voluble murderer has been tortured by the nightmarish terrors he attributes to his victim: "He was sitting up in bed listening;—just as I have done, night after night, harkening to the death watches in the wall"; further the narrator interprets the old man's groan in terms of his own persistent anguish: "Many a night, just at midnight, when all the world slept, it has welled up from my own bosom, deepening, with its dreadful echo, the terrors that distracted me." Thus, Poe, in allowing his narrator to disburden himself of his tale, skillfully contrives to show also that he lives in a haunted and eerie world of his own demented making.

Poe assuredly knows what the narrator never suspects and what, by the controlled conditions of the tale, he is not meant to suspect—that the narrator is a victim of his own self-torturing obsessions. Poe so manipulates the action that the murder, instead of freeing the narrator, is shown to heighten his agony and intensify his delusions. The watches in the wall become the ominously beating heart of the old man, and the narrator's vaunted self-control explodes into a frenzy that leads to self-betrayal. I find it almost impossible to believe that Poe has no serious artistic motive in **"The Tell-Tale Heart,"** that he merely revels in horror and only inadvertently illuminates the depths of the human soul. I find it equally difficult to accept the view that Poe's style should be assailed because of the ejaculatory and crazy confession of his narrator. (pp. 177-79)

Evidence of Poe's "seriousness" seems to me indisputable in **"The Cask of Amontillado,"** a tale which W. H. Auden has belittled. Far from being his author's mouthpiece, the narrator, Montresor, is one of the supreme examples in fiction of a deluded rationalist who cannot glimpse the moral implications of his planned folly. Poe's fine ironic sense makes clear that Montresor, the stalker of Fortunato, is both a compulsive and pursued man; for in committing a flawless crime against another human being, he really (like . . . the protagonist in **"The Tell-Tale Heart"**) commits the worst of crimes against himself. His reasoned, "cool" intelligence weaves an intricate plot which, while ostensibly satisfying his revenge, despoils him of humanity. His impeccably contrived murder, his weird mask of goodness in an enterprise of evil, and his abandonment of all his life-energies in one pet project of hate convict him of a madness which he mistakes for the inspiration of genius. The brilliant masquerade setting of Poe's tale intensifies the theme of Montresor's apparently successful duplicity; Montresor's ironic appreciation of his own deviousness seems further to justify his arrogance of intellect. But the greatest irony of all, to which Montresor is never sensitive, is that the "injuries" supposedly perpetrated by Fortunato are illusory and that the vengeance meant for the victim recoils upon Montresor himself. In immolating Fortunato, the narrator unconsciously calls him the "noble" Fortunato and confesses that his own "heart grew sick." Though Montresor attributes this sickness to "the dampness of the catacombs," it is clear that his crime has begun to "possess" him. We see that, after fifty years, it remains the obsession of his life; the meaning of his existence resides in the tomb in which he has, symbolically, buried himself. In other words, Poe leaves little doubt that the narrator has violated his own mind and humanity, that the external act has had its destructive inner consequences. (p. 180)

Poe, I maintain, is a serious artist who explores the neuroses of his characters with probing intelligence. He permits his narrator to revel and flounder into torment, but he sees beyond the torment to its causes. . . .

If my thesis is correct, Poe's narrators should not be construed as his mouthpieces; instead they should be regarded as expressing, in "charged" language indicative of their internal disturbances, their own peculiarly nightmarish visions. Poe, I contend, is conscious of the abnormalities of his narrators and does not condone the intellectual ruses through which they strive, only too earnestly, to justify themselves. In short, though his narrators are often febrile or demented, Poe is conspicuously "sane." They may be "decidedly primitive" or "wildly incoherent," but Poe, in his stories at least, is mature and lucid. (p. 181)

James W. Gargano, "The Question of Poe's Narrators," in College English, *Vol. 25, No. 3, December, 1963, pp. 177-81.*

DONALD BARLOW STAUFFER (essay date 1965)

[In the following excerpt, Stauffer challenges Allen Tate's contention that "Ligeia" *and* "William Wilson" *exhibit significant stylistic differences (see excerpt dated 1949).]*

From his own lifetime to the present, controversy has flourished between those holding the widely accepted but inadequately demonstrated view that Poe was a master stylist and those who condemn his style for its awkwardness and lack of taste. (p. 316)

Many readers whose opinions lie somewhere between these extremes still often too hastily condemn Poe's style because they are using standards of "taste" or propriety which are seldom related to consideration of the style in the individual tales themselves. No judgment of the quality of a style can legitimately be made separately from a critical consideration of the work in which it is found. It is often disturbing to find remarks about the style of an author which seem to be based on the reader's own personal tastes, rather than upon his awareness that the style is inseparable from the work itself and must therefore, like its symbols, its metaphors, and its paradoxes, be organically related to it. Such an assumption must be insisted upon in the instance of Poe, who was not a careless, haphazard writer, but a conscious and skilled craftsman—technician even—who carefully calculated the means by which to bring about his celebrated "unity of effect."

Allen Tate, who is more generous to Poe than many other modern critics, still has reservations about his style in some of his tales [see excerpt dated 1949]. Setting two passages together, one from **"William Wilson"** and one from **"Ligeia,"** Tate concludes that he finds it difficult to admire what he calls the "ungrammatical rubbish" of the **"Ligeia"** passage. But, he says,

> . . . if Poe is worth understanding at all (I assume that he is), we might begin by asking why the writer of the lucid if not very distinguished passage from **"William Wilson"** repeatedly fell into the bathos of **"Ligeia."** I confess that Poe's serious style at its typical worst makes the reading of more than one story at a sitting an almost insuperable task.

Poe's subjects, he writes, are done up in a "glutinous prose" that "so fatigues one's attention that with the best will in the world one gives up, unless one gets a clue to the power underlying the flummery."

There is the strong suggestion in these and other remarks by Tate that, stylistically, **"William Wilson"** and **"Ligeia"** are poles apart, and that the former, which is "perspicuous in diction and on the whole credible in realistic detail," is therefore to be preferred to the latter. But is the matter this simple? Closer inspection shows us that some of what looks very much like the "ungrammatical rubbish" of **"Ligeia"** can be found in **"William Wilson."** And much of **"Ligeia,"** on the other hand, is written in a style not so different from that in many passages of **"William Wilson."** Actually, as I shall attempt to show, the same stylistic elements appear in both stories. The difference in the total effect produced by stylistic means derives from the difference in order and proportion of various stylistic ingredients rather than from the kind of polarity which Tate's remarks suggest. (pp. 316-17)

Looking first at **"Ligeia,"** we notice that the style is in many ways extravagant, lying somewhere between the youthful exuberance and heterogeneity of **"The Assignation,"** and the ratiocinative and expository prose of **"The Murders in the Rue Morgue."** One of the first things we notice about the style of **"Ligeia"** is its incantatory quality, which makes us feel that the narrator is intoning his story. Rhythm and sound effects, especially in the opening paragraphs, are extremely important in establishing the tone of the tale. (p. 318)

Other stylistic traits which occur to a noticeable extent . . . in **"Ligeia"** are repetition, inversions, and parenthetical expressions. Repetition, like the use of certain rhythmic patterns, gives his style an incantatory quality: "her wild desire for life—for life—*but* for life." Ligeia's voice "grew more gentle—grew more low." And emphasis is achieved by such expressions as "far more, very far more" and "a too-too glorious effulgence." The irrational quality of this kind of writing becomes even more evident when we pull from context the phrases of which it is composed. Such is the case also with inversions of normal word order, a device which gives the style a distant, archaic, otherworldly tone: "In the classical tongues was she deeply proficient." (Note the choice of *tongues* instead of *languages,* and note also how different in tone is a more nearly normally ordered phrase: "In the classical languages she was deeply proficient," or "She was deeply proficient in the classical languages.") Other inversions occur throughout the story: ". . . not until the last instance . . . was shaken the external placidity of her demeanor"; ". . . in death only was I fully impressed"; "For long hours . . . would she pour out . . . the overflowing of a heart."

Poe consistently uses parenthetical expressions in **"Ligeia"** to emphasize or heighten the mood. Frequently they are in the form of interjections or exclamations: "a love, alas! all unmerited, all unworthily bestowed"; "And (strange, oh, strangest mystery of all!)"; "I could restore her to the pathways she had abandoned—ah, *could* it be forever?—upon the earth." All of these heighten the emotional tone, or in some way emphasize the disturbed psychological state of the narrator. Another smacks of Poe's particular brand of hokum, but it, too, is consistent with the mood of the passage, "And there are one or two stars in heaven (one especially, a star of the sixth magnitude, double and changeable, to be found near the large star in Lyra) in a telescopic scrutiny of which I have been made aware of the feeling."

The use of what W. M. Forrest, in a discussion of the biblical qualities of Poe's style, [*Biblical Allusions in Poe*], has described as the "genitive of possession" is another syntactical feature giving an archaic or exotic texture to the style. "The learning of Ligeia"; "the eyes of Ligeia"; "the person of Ligeia"; "the fetters of Death"; "the acquisition of Ligeia" are more frequent than "Ligeia's eyes" or "Ligeia's beauty." The effect of this construction, and others in which *of* appears, such as "The hue of the orbs was the most brilliant of black, and, far over them, hung jetty lashes of great length," is, like the effect of inversion, repetition, and the use of exclamatory parentheses, a heightening, an emotionality, a sense of the mysterious, the irrational and the unreal.

Much, but by no means all, of **"Ligeia"** is written in this half-hysterical, highly emotional style, since Poe varies the style in this tale as he does in almost all his serious tales. Later in the tale we discover a much more measured, rational tone, as the narrator describes the fantastic interiors of the English abbey to which he retires after the death of Ligeia. The center portion is marked by complex, compound, and compound-complex sentences quite different from the simpler syntax of sentences in the early part of the tale. In his recollections of Ligeia he has been rhapsodic, conveying to the reader the frame of mind into which the memory of her puts him; now, in the second half of the tale, as he recalls the sequence of events leading up to the reappearance of Ligeia, he attempts to get a grip on himself and his emotions as he recounts the early history of Rowena dispassionately and with apparent detachment. He tries to view his actions and his taste for arabesque interiors with some objectivity—and even asks how the bride's family permitted her "to pass the threshold of an apartment *so* bedecked." But as he again recalls the evidence of his own senses, the narrator dwells on details of the appearance of the dying woman in a "naturalistic" description as he endeavors by this means to explain the inexplicable. He reports the "facts" as nearly as he can remember them. But as he draws nearer in memory to the appearance of Ligeia, he becomes more and irrationally affected by that memory, and the last paragraph differs markedly in style from those preceding it. Inversions, repetitions, questions, exclamations, dashes, italics, capitals are all there, ending with the wild speech of the narrator himself with Poe's calculated use of repetition and parallelism for a maximum of emotional effect: "can I never—can I never be mistaken—these are the full, and the black, and the wild eyes—of my lost love—of the lady—of the LADY LIGEIA." (pp. 321-22)

But many passages in the second half indicate quite clearly that Poe was in control of his material and knew what he was about in his treatment of it. Balanced sentence structure and a painstaking building-up of circumstantial detail surrounding the reappearance of Ligeia demonstrate that he was carefully and patiently combining—denying as usual the office of inspiration in the act of creation. The emotion of the narrator of **"Ligeia"** should not, of course, be confused with the emotion of the author, and such obvious devices as the narrator's parenthetical "(what marvel that I shudder while I write?)" should be read as part of Poe's deliberate effort to give the narrator's emotions an air of verisimilitude. In dismissing the style of **"Ligeia"** as ungrammatical rubbish, then, Tate most certainly exaggerates, for most of it *is* grammatical and indeed much of it is highly ordered, highly formal prose. The predominantly emotional quality of its style may be defended by its appropriateness to both the agitated mental state of the narrator and to the supernatural events he relates. (p. 323)

Analysis of the style of **"William Wilson"** shows it to be a carefully written story. Although it is interspersed with passages reminiscent of the style of **"Ligeia,"** it is dominated by the eighteenth-century *ordonnance* mentioned by Tate. The style, for the most part, is highly ordered, marked by connectives and transitional elements, balanced and periodic sentences, a relatively high level of abstraction, little concrete imagery (outside of the descriptions of the school of Wilson's boyhood), few vivid adjectives, and a precision of diction. Certain key passages deviate from this pattern, notably the first and last paragraphs.

In this tale Poe seems to be concentrating not on creating a poetic effect but rather on telling a tale rationally and logically. Mood is therefore secondary to the orderly development of a series of causally related events. Certain qualities which were latent in the style of his early tales, and which are more evident in his critical writing, are highly developed and fully exploited here: parallelism; a measured rhythm (the rhythm of good prose, not "rhythmic prose," as in **"Ligeia"**); and abstract diction, which is sometimes latinate, sometimes cumbersome and even ludicrous. This diction combines with the orderliness of his sentence structure to give his prose a particularly eighteenth-century quality. The pace of the story, which is dictated by the formal style resulting from longer sentences, is leisurely but not halting, measured rather than uneven. (p. 324)

The dominant stylistic note of the tale is not struck until the third paragraph, in which the narrator begins to relate the sequence of events in a dispassionate, rational, analytical style. Analysis is the keynote of Wilson's remarks; in fact, we may say that Poe wrote **"William Wilson"** in the language of *analysis,* as contrasted to the language of emotion in which he wrote most of **"Ligeia."** The narrator of **"William Wilson"** constantly subjects himself and the motives for his actions to a careful scrutiny, evidently in an effort to answer the questions he has so passionately posed in the opening paragraph. The narrative intention of this scrutiny is clear enough. Wilson, at a loss to account satisfactorily for the state of spiritual death and moral depravity in which he finds himself at the opening of the tale, attempts to exercise his faculties of reason and analysis over the sequence of events which led to its disastrous conclusion. He therefore begins by carefully noting his inherited characteristics: he is descended from a race of "imaginative and easily excitable temperament"—and he develops into a child who is "self-willed, addicted to the wildest caprices, and a prey to the most ungovernable passions." Driven by his impulse to recall and analyze his extraordinary behavior, Wilson then turns to "minute recollections" of his first school days. Like Egaeus in **"Berenice,"** he seeks relief in "the weakness of a few rambling details." But he also attributes meaning to these details: ". . . the first ambiguous monitions of the destiny which afterward so fully overshadowed me." These school-day recollections take up fully a third of the story, recollections which he finds "stamped upon memory in lines as vivid, as deep, and as durable as the *exergues* of the Carthaginian medals." Most of them relate to the character of the schoolmate with the remarkable resemblance to himself. Only a great many quotations would demonstrate the analytic quality of the style of this section of the tale: the number of times which Wilson speculates on the possible causes for having understood or misunderstood the conduct of his double, and the descriptions of his relationship with him. I shall quote two:

> I could only conceive this singular behavior to arise from a consummate self-conceit assuming the vulgar airs of patronage and protection. Perhaps it was this latter trait in Wilson's conduct, conjoined with our identity of name, and the mere accident of our having entered the school upon the same day, which set afloat the notion that we were brothers, among the senior classes in the academy.
>
> . . . . .
>
> Wilson's retaliations in kind were many; and there was one form of his practical wit that disturbed me beyond measure. How his sagacity first discovered at all that so petty a thing would vex me, is a question I never could solve; but having discovered, he habitually practised the annoyance. I had always felt aversion to my uncourtly patronymic, and its very common, if not plebeian praenomen.

Both of these passages are typical of the dominant style of the tale: highly abstract, rather stilted—even mannered. Because it is not heavily latinate, the latinate expressions themselves seem actually to be affectations: *sagacity, consummate;* and sometimes even absurd: *patronymic, plebeian praenomen*. These words give a weightiness to certain sentences which the subject hardly demands. But more to the immediate point is the language of speculation and conjecture: *perhaps, conceive, solve*. These words suggest that the narrator is constantly attempting to analyze and explain rationally the motives for his actions; something which the narrator of **"Ligeia"** does not do.

Formality and order, then, are the chief characteristics of the dominant style of **"William Wilson,"** and parallelism is one of the syntactical devices through which Poe achieves these. Note, for example, the eighteenth-century quality of this passage: ". . . a profligacy which set at defiance the laws, while it eluded the vigilance of the institution." Or this: "He appeared to be destitute alike of the ambition which urged, and of the passionate energy of mind which enabled me to excel." These parallelisms are different in their logical clarity from the predominantly emotional quality of similar constructions in **"Ligeia."**

Formality of sentence structure is achieved in other ways as well. In this sentence are three successive phrases, each composed of three elements, and in the final coupling of two phrases modifying *affectionateness,* each phrase contains three modifiers:

> In his rivalry he might have been supposed actuated solely by a whimsical desire to thwart, astonish, or mortify myself; although there were times when I could not help observing, with a feeling made of wonder, abasement, and pique, that he mingled with his injuries, his insults, or his contradictions, a certain most inappropriate, and assuredly most unwelcome *affectionateness* of manner.

Such formal groupings of three elements are often found in Poe's periodic sentences (periods also occur more frequently in **"William Wilson"** than they do in **"Ligeia"**): "That the school, indeed, did not feel his design, perceive its accomplishment, and participate in his sneer. . . ." Less formal groupings of threes occur not only in the formal rational style, but also in Poe's emotional style, as in the first paragraph of **"William Wilson,"** suggesting, therefore, that such groupings are a characteristic trait of all of Poe's styles.

But the stylistic trait which at the same time links these two tales and indicates their essential difference is the parenthetical expression. **"Ligeia,"** we have observed, is full of parentheses. **"William Wilson"** has many, if not more. But while in the former they are used to heighten or emphasize the mood or atmosphere by their exclamatory or interjectional character, in this tale they slow down the pace by qualifying and amplifying ideas. The parentheses in **"William Wilson"** are halting, hesitant, fussy, over-precise, reflecting the deliberations of a mind committed to discovering the truth. They contain additional, sometimes gratuitous, information that seems to satisfy the narrator's overwhelming need for facts and details. They also reflect the complexity of his mind, a complexity already more than once suggested by the references to the "many little nooks and recesses" of which the school mansion is composed. If the tale is symbolically a mental journey, this "wilderness of narrow passages" suggests the labyrinthine quality of the mind itself. Thus the style, which is itself full of similar nooks and recesses, becomes organically related to Wilson's own psychological state. The following passage illustrates the kinds of parentheses (indicated by brackets)—and parentheses within parentheses—typical of the style of **"William Wilson"**:

> . . . but, [in the latter months of my residence at the academy,] [although the intrusion of his ordinary manner had, [beyond doubt,] [in some measure,] abated,] my sentiments, [in nearly similar proportion,] partook very much of positive hatred. Upon one occasion he saw this, [I think;] and afterward avoided, [or made a show of avoiding] me.
>
> It was about the same period, [if I remember aright,] that, [in an altercation of violence with him,] [in which he was more than usually thrown off his guard, and spoke and acted with an openness of demeanor rather foreign to his nature,] I discovered, [or fancied I discovered,] in his accent, in his air, and general appearance, a something which first startled, and then deeply interested me, by bringing to mind dim visions of my earliest infancy—wild, confused and thronging memories of a time when memory herself was yet unborn.

The general character and function of these parentheses in **"William Wilson,"** then, differ radically from those of the intensifying parentheses of **"Ligeia."** Here they are authorial comments written not in an emotional frenzy but in the coolness of recollection. They often have not only an analytic but a strongly moralistic tone as well. For example: "It was no doubt the anomalous state of affairs existing between us, which turned all my attacks upon him (and there were many, either open or covert) into the channel of banter or practical joke (giving pain while assuming the aspect of mere fun). . . ." Or even more overtly moral in tone : "I was anxiously seeking (let me not say with what unworthy motive) the young, the gay, the beautiful wife of the aged and doting Di Broglio." Syntax in this tale, then, is actually a means of characterization, since the narrator's use of parentheses gives the impression of a man extremely interested in being both accurate and honest. (pp. 325-28)

At first reading, **"Ligeia"** and **"William Wilson"** seem entirely dissimilar in style, yet the more closely we examine them, the more similarities we find. The reason for these similarities—as well as the differences—lies partly in the similarity of structure and theme. In **"Ligeia"** the narrator is attempting to reproduce the state of mind he was in when he was in contact with Ligeia. This state of mind is evoked in the beginning and vanishes with the death of Ligeia. With the narrator's move to England and the return of his rational faculties, the style resembles the rational style of **"William Wilson."** But as the symptoms of Rowena's disease become more and more evident, the narrator gradually discards the rational style, in which he has attempted clinically to recall every detail of the circumstances of Ligeia's return, and returns to the state of mind he was in on that memorable night. His final outburst recalls the style, and even echoes some of the words, of the opening passages of the tale, thereby relating the beginning of the tale to the end. The mood and attitude of the speaker are primarily nostalgic, or evocative, as he attempts to reproduce in his own mind, as well as in the mind of the reader, an idea of what he experienced. This attempt to relate the barely perceived world, of which only the poet may achieve momentary glimpses, to the things of this world which bear only an imperfect relation to them, is the attempt Poe makes in all his poetry. But language fails him, as he himself is aware, and only by calling up an atmosphere roughly analogous to what he has perceived can the narrator-hero-poet hope to put what is intranslatable into words.

We may similarly read **"William Wilson"** as a parable of the war between the external world and the world of the spirit. Whereas in **"Ligeia"** the hero has renounced the physical world and achieved a momentary union with the absolute, in this tale Wilson has succumbed to the corrupting material world and has thereby lost his soul. Both tales begin in recollection and end in hysteria, but **"William Wilson"** is not so much an attempt to reproduce the quality of his experience, which he finds almost unendurably painful, as an attempt to trace the *causes* leading up to it. The experience itself, therefore, although it comes at a climactic moment in both tales, is not as important in **"William Wilson"** as are the causally related events leading up to it. One indication of the difference in emphasis in the two tales is that in **"Ligeia"** we know from the outset that she is dead, but we do not learn of the death of Wilson's double until the end; we know only that Wilson has committed an "unpardonable crime." The direction of **"William Wilson"** is towards rediscovery—not of the moment of confrontation, which nevertheless is inevitable, but of the sequence of events leading up to it. In short, the narrator of **"William Wilson"** finds himself in a fallen state and seeks a rational explanation for it; the narrator of **"Ligeia"** finds himself in a state of lost happiness and seeks to reproduce that happiness—hence the difference in stylistic organization and emphasis. (pp. 329-30)

Donald Barlow Stauffer, "Style and Meaning in 'Ligeia' and ' William Wilson'," in Studies in Short Fiction, *Vol. II, No. 4, Summer, 1965, pp. 316-30.*

CLARK GRIFFITH (essay date 1972)

[In the following excerpt, Griffith discusses the influence on Poe's work of earlier Gothic fiction and explains the way in which Poe employed the conventions of Gothicism for his own purposes.]

Despite the emphasis in his criticism upon a need for novelty, Poe's tales of terror are clearly indebted to some literary forebears. From Gothic fiction of the English eighteenth century, Poe took the *imagery* of terror: the blighted, oppressive countryside; the machinery of the Inquisition; in particular, the haunted castle, swaddled in its own atmosphere of morbidity and decay. From the nineteenth-century Gothicized tales in *Blackwood's Magazine,* which he both ridiculed and admired, he took the *form* of terror: a first-person narrator, lingering typically over a single, frightening episode, and bringing matters to a climax in which he has grown deaf to every sound except the noise of his unique sensations. So close are the resemblances that one passes from Anne Radcliffe's architecture to the effusions of a *Blackwood's* speaker, convinced that Poe's effects often result from his combining the murky details of the one with the inveterate, uninterrupted talkativeness of the other. Yet I wish to argue that even as Poe borrowed, he also made a significant contribution. Imperfectly at first, but then with greater assurance, he was concerned with shifting what I shall call the locus of the terrifying. This change in stance is one measure of his originality as a practitioner in the Gothic mode. And to watch him make it is to find special meaning in his famous declaration that the terror of which he wrote came not from Germany but from the soul.

As the basis for contrast, let us glance briefly at Emily St. Aubert, before the Castle of Udolpho. Confronting it for the first time, she can only see the castle as a real and utterly objective fact. For Emily is a true child of the *Essay Concerning the Human Understanding*. It would please her to suppose that she has somehow been transported into "one of those frightful fictions in which the wild genius of the poet delights." But aware that there is nothing in the mind not first in the senses, she recognizes that she has no grounds for distrusting her perceptions; hence she must scorn as "delusion" and "superstition" the notion that the source of her agitation is anywhere except in the world around her. In Emily's case, therefore (as throughout Mrs. Radcliffe and the eighteenth-century Gothic generally), the direction of the horrifying is from without to within: from setting to self. Terror comes in consequence of what no less an authority than Horace Walpole had called the "extraordinary position," as it impinges upon "mere men and women" to alarm and dismay them.

The situation seems identical in the early portions of **"MS. Found in a Bottle."** The storm at sea, which overtakes Poe's narrator, or the engulfing waves that "surpass . . . anything [he] had imagined possible": both appear to be examples of the received, physical ordeal, such as Walpole and Mrs. Radcliffe had devised. Halfway through **"MS. Found in a Bottle,"** however, a change in emphasis occurs. Now, for the first time, the narrator speaks of strange "conceptions" which are arising from inside his mind. They consist of "feelings" and "sensations" to which no name can be given; nevertheless, they cause him to spell out the word "Discovery" as he beholds—in any case, apparently beholds—an entire new order of experience. At this point, I suggest, Poe has commenced to modify the traditional Gothic relationship. If terror is to be the effect of inner conceptions, it is no longer necessary to regard his narrator as a "mere man," beset and beleaguered by appalling circumstances. Instead, one can as readily think of him as Creative Man, and of the circumstances themselves as the products of his terrible creativity. At least potentially, the locus of the terrifying has passed from the spectacle into the spectator.

Admittedly, though, the change remains no more than implied and potential in **"MS. Found in a Bottle."** It breaks down ultimately, because the scenery in the tale still seems too much founded upon the eighteenth-century convention of the "outer wonder." What Poe needed, if he intended to psychologize the Gothic, was nothing so spacious or openly exotic as the South Indian Ocean. He required the smaller, less public *mise-en-scène,* one which could more plausibly be transfigured by his narrators, and, above all, one which would dramatize the processes of transfiguration in action. He is best off, in short, when he returns to the dark, secluded interiors of eighteenth-century fiction, but portrays them in such a way that the interiors are made suggestive of the human mind itself. And this of course is the technique he has perfected two years later, with the publication in 1835 of **"Berenice,"** his first example of a genuinely new Gothic.

Sitting within his ancestral mansion, Poe's Egaeus turns out to be both projector and voice, the source of a strange predicament as well as its spokesman. He has spent a lifetime gazing for "long unwearied hours" at objects which he half-suspects are trivial and without purpose—and watching while, gradually and inexplicably, they acquire some momentous significance. The story makes it clear, however, that the details present this heightened aspect only to Egaeus's "mind's eye"; whatever the meaning they come to possess, it is due solely to his fierce concentration upon them. Obviously, then, there has ceased to be any distance, or difference, between the terror and the terrified. Egaeus's realities are the realities of his own making; his world resembles a mirror in a madhouse, wherein distortions and phantasms appear, but only as the reflections of a particular sort of observer. And nowhere is this fact more evident than in his obsession with the teeth of Berenice:

> The teeth!—the teeth! they were here, and there, and everywhere, and visibly and palpably before me; long, narrow, and excessively white, with the pale lips writhing about them. . . .

At first glance, we are likely to be struck by the sheer, intense *physicalness* of these dreadful molars. Superficially, in fact, they may well seem of a kind with the highly tangible horrors which *The Monk* presents. Yet they function in quite another way. M. G. Lewis's ghoulish occurrences were rooted in a thoroughly Lockean landscape. The putrefying head, in the convent vaults at St. Clare, had to exist independently of Agnes de Medina, first to accost Agnes's senses and then to register on her appalled sensibility. By contrast, the teeth in Poe have no meaningful existence outside a sensibility; as Egaeus acknowledges, *"tous ses dients étaient des idées."* What the teeth might be like apart from Egaeus, or whether, for that matter, they even have an identity except in his vision of them: these are issues of no real moment. So successfully has Poe internalized the Gothic that the old "outer wonders" of the eighteenth century now disappear into the stream of consciousness. They have become the conditions and consequences (if one likes, the "objective correlatives") of a psychic state.

The strategy of **"Berenice"** is one that with the slightest variations Poe would continue to utilize for the rest of his life. Barring the allegorical **"The Masque of the Red Death"** and the fact-bound *Pym* (with its return to a glamorous out-of-doors), I know of none of the horror tales in which the perceiving mind does not seem much more nearly the originator of the terrifying than it is a mere passive witness. Moreover, I am convinced that to read them as though they were notes composed from within is often to clarify and enrich the stories. For example, the real key to the somewhat baffling **"Fall of the House of Usher"** appears to me to lie in the way it opens by re-enacting an episode out of Mrs. Radcliffe, but repeats the event for a totally different purpose.

Like Emily St. Aubert, Poe's speaker also rides up, at the end of a long day's journey, before an apparently haunted castle. He too feels it to be a massive and brooding presence in the foreground. And then, in an effort to dispel the alarm with which it quickly envelopes him, he decides to examine the place from a different perspective. But when he reins in his horse and proceeds to the new location, nothing happens. Where Emily could always look forward to being physically delivered from peril, the physical change in Poe only means that his narrator seems menaced anew. The "ghastly tree stems" and "vacant eyelike windows" continue to glare back at him with the same old ominousness.

Of course nothing happens. The truth about the speaker in **"The Fall of the House of Usher"** is that he has all along been engaged in a kind of symbolic homecoming. When at length he crosses the causeway and goes indoors, he finds himself among rooms and furnishings that are oddly familiar, because he has arrived at nothing less than the depths of his own being. Thereafter, it is not his talkativeness—his descriptive abilities, in the usual sense—that summon up Roderick and Madeline.

The Ushers are products of the narrator's psyche; for they and their behavior become the embodiments of his trance, or they appear as the *personae* in his dream vision, or perhaps their incestuous relationship is a working out of his own, dark, tabooed, and otherwise inexpressible desires. Thus every subsequent event in **"The Fall of the House of Usher"** is prepared for by an opening tableau in which the power to terrorize could not be blotted from the landscape, because it had actually been brought into the landscape by the mind of the narrator. The organic unity, of which Poe makes so much, is a unity between the single creating self at the center of the story, and those shapes and forms which radiate outward as the marks of his continuous creative act. To me at least, no other interpretation of the tale can justify the amount of attention paid its narrator, or is so true to the form and manner of his narration.

Poe's tinkerings with tradition are probably less eccentric and ultra-personal than, at first look, they appear to be. Behind them, after all, one discerns nothing more remarkable than a particular manifestation of the Romantic Movement. If the terrors of the eighteenth century were accountable in terms of Locke's *Essay,* then what is terror for Poe except an adjunct to the thirteenth chapter of the *Biographia Literaria?* That is, the horrifying now looms up out of a world in which the imagination "dissolves, diffuses, dissipates, in order to re-create" and wherein imaginative tendencies are "essentially *vital,* even as all objects (*as* objects) are essentially fixed and dead."

Granted that they represent extreme cases, Poe's narrators have to be understood as figures who are deeply involved in just the activity that Coleridge describes. Until their inner lives impinge upon the outer, the outer, if it is consequential at all, remains a dull and prosaic affair. It gains its extraordinary qualities, as we have seen, through the transforming and the transfiguring capacities of an imaginative self. To cite a last example, we are told by the speaker in **"Ligeia"** of how the *décor* in Lady Rowena's bedchamber "partook of the true character of the Arabesque only when regarded from a single point of view." As we read, however, it is to find that the single point of view has nothing to do with physical positioning. Rather, it seems expressive of the narrator's personality, an extension of his inward state. One concludes therefore that it is akin to Coleridge's "secondary imagination." In Poe's hands this faculty has become more nearly an instrument of the appalling than it is a strictly aesthetic principle. Nevertheless, it still operates as the means of discovering relevance, pattern, even a certain sort of beauty and ideality in objects which, left to themselves, would be "essentially fixed and dead."

Small wonder, consequently, that Poe's fiction is better unified but, at the same time, darker and much gloomier than the eighteenth-century Gothic had been. With their stress upon horror as an objective phenomenon, the earlier Gothic writers could introduce a whole range of tones and effects. As they evoked terror from the outside, so they were likewise free to suspend and withdraw it from without. Having opened what amounted to a trapdoor onto the world of menace, they found it possible to snap the door shut again, and so to conduct their characters back into a world of happy endings: of order, security and (typically) the celebration of marriage vows. The waking nightmare succeeded by the nuptials! It is the regular drift of events from *The Castle of Otranto* to *The Monk* and on into *Blackwood's.*

But Poe possessed no such latitude. Since the stimulus for terror comes from within, there can, in the tale he tells, be no real survivors, no remissions of the terrible, no protagonists who, by pluck or by luck, either earn or are at least vouchsafed the right to turn backward through the trapdoor. Self-afflicted and self-victimized (so to speak, their own executioners), Poe's characters must perform a persistently downward journey, sinking further and further into voluble wonderment at themselves, until they arrive at one of those shattering silences with which their narratives customarily end. And yet, even as they descend, they are granted a kind of glory which no hero of the earlier Gothic could ever have matched. We may feel that the next step for Poe's narrators will be the tomb or the lunatic asylum. During a single, transcendent moment, however, they have had the privilege of calling up out of their very beings a totally new order of reality. They are Romantic heroes without peer, for they have been the masters, because the creators, of all that they survey.

And small wonder, finally, that *their* creator was fascinated by what he called "the power of words." Once he had got hold of his true theme, it was never enough for Poe simply to set a scene, describe an action, use words to provoke a shudder or two; that was the business of those attuned to the terrors of Germany. The test of language in his work lay in its ability to delve deeply within and bring to light the most hidden crannies of a suffering, yet oddly prolific self. Thus the descriptive devices of his Gothic predecessors re-emerge as Poe's metaphors of mind; their rhetorical flourishes are turned by him into a rhetoric of revelation. Out of the magic of words, Poe brings forth the symbolic countryside, self-contained and self-sustaining, utterly devoid of connections with the world as it is, yet recognizable still in the terms of its own special topography. And behind the countryside, he shows us the figure of the owner. This is the soul of man, cloaked in the works which it has made, and rendered thereby into a visible and articulate entity. (pp. 21-7)

Clark Griffith, "Poe and the Gothic," in Papers on Poe: Essays in Honor of John Ward Ostrom, *edited by Richard P. Veler, Chantry Music Press, Inc., 1972, pp. 21-7.*

HAROLD BEAVER (essay date 1976)

[*Beaver examines Poe's science fiction stories and their relationship to scientific discoveries of the early nineteenth century.*]

Electro-chemistry dominated the early nineteenth century. Galvani and Watt, Volta and Ohm, Ampère, Bunsen, Morse—its pioneers embedded their very names into the language. (p. vii)

American newspapers of the 1830s and 1840s were agog with strange reports: of ballooning, exotic voyages, premature burials, automata, trances, plagues. In February 1838, while Poe was working in Greenwich Village, the new electric telegraph was demonstrated at the White House. (p. viii)

It was an age for amateurs. De Quincey and Coleridge, Emerson and Poe, could still speak as 'philosophers', as literary gentlemen. they linger on the very edge between the old Newtonian order and the new, between Sir William Herschel and Clerk Maxwell, between Munchausen and H. G. Wells. Professionalism and the gathering complexity of research had not yet overwhelmed all but committed 'scientists'. After mid-century such confidence became less and less attainable. Between science and literature no neutral ground now remained. So no room for 'natural philosophy' remained—except in that new, eccentric and bastard form, their communal offspring, 'science fiction'.

The main line of descent is usually reckoned from Verne and H. G. Wells. But Jules Verne himself acknowledged his debt to Poe; so it was the French who first saluted the American as master: *'le créateur du roman merveilleux-scientifique'*. Hubert Matthey presented **"The Facts in the Case of M. Valdemar"**, **"A Tale of the Ragged Mountains"**, and **"A Descent into the Maelström"** as *'les types d'un genre qui devait se développer après lui'*; the genre itself he defined as *'ce mélange de la logique et de la narration'*. And the emphasis ever since (following Poe's lead) had been on logic, on reason, on coherent forecast and calculation. As the master himself observed in praise of *Eureka:* 'these conditions themselves have been imposed upon me, as necessities, in a train of ratiocination as rigorously logical as that which establishes any demonstration in Euclid'.

Facts and figures, as scholars have demonstrated, were commonly adapted—plagiarized verbatim even—from published sources. That was inevitable, no doubt. It is also irrelevant. Poe is celebrated as 'Science Fiction Pioneer' (in Clarke Olney's phrase) for being the first 'to base his stories firmly on a rational kind of extrapolation, avoiding the supernatural'. Extrapolation! The very concept, borrowed from statistical projection, is his. Even in the gush of a passionate love letter, in mid-flight, he could declare:

> Think, too, of the rare agreement of name . . . think of all these coincidences, and you will no longer wonder that, to one accustomed as I am to the Calculus of Probabilities, they wore an air of positive miracle.

For the Calculus of Probabilities had been long familiar to Poe from the work of Condorcet and Laplace, Cournot and Quetelet.

'All that is necessary,' taught the Marquis de Condorcet, 'to reduce the whole of nature to laws similar to those which Newton discovered with the aid of the calculus, is to have a sufficient number of observations and a mathematics that is complex enough. From a mathematical theory of probability he turned to a social mathematics, or calculus of history, to tame the future: 'a science to foresee the progressions of the human species'. Even future moral data were to be mathematicized. In the *Esquisse d'un tableau historique des progrès de l'esprit humain,* he charted human development through nine epochs to the French Revolution, predicting in a tenth the ultimate perfection of man. The Marquis de Laplace, in *Théorie analytique des probabilités* (1812) continued his rigorous approach to formulaic, mathematical prediction.

Poe has nothing but scorn for 'human-perfectibility' spokesmen like Condorcet. But his 'C. Auguste Dupin', master detective, is heir to the great French tradition. He is Poe's spokesman in praise of 'the theory of probabilities—that theory to which the most glorious objects of human research are indebted for the most glorious of illustration'. In **"The Mystery of Marie Rogêt"** he expounds, and refines on, its technique:

> It is through the spirit of this principle, if not precisely through its letter, that modern science has resolved to *calculate upon the unforeseen*. But perhaps you do not comprehend me. The history of human knowledge has so uninterruptedly shown that to collateral, or incidental, or accidental events we are indebted for the most numerous and most valuable discoveries, that it has at length become necessary, in any prospective view of improvement, to make not only large, but the largest allowances for inventions that shall arise by chance, and quite out of the range of ordinary expectation. It is no longer philosophical to base, upon what has been, a vision of what is to be. *Accident* is admitted as a portion of the substructure. We make chance a matter of absolute calculation. We subject the unlooked for and unimagined, to the mathematical *formulae* of the schools.

With 'the Calculus of Probabilities' it is but a short step from Poe's Detective to his Science Fiction. For 'this Calculus', he explains, 'is, in its essence, purely mathematical; and thus we have the anomaly of the most rigidly exact in science applied to the shadow and spirituality of the most intangible in speculation'.

What was once stuff for ritual or religious myths, or tall tales for entertainment, was thus transformed by Poe to a new speculative fiction. Utopian voyages had long presented all kinds of rational laboratories; but Sir Thomas More and his successors were concerned with the permutation of mainly moral and political hypotheses. The hypotheses of science fiction were wholly material, whether psychological or technological. Their pragmatic claim was the inevitable change (for better or for worse) of both man's outer and his inner or spiritual environment. Yet, cast as fantasy, the pressure persisted towards the journal-entry, in the present tense; not to recollection, but lived intensity; not as theoretical exercises, but adventures (in the tradition of Lucian, Swift, Defoe) by sea, land or air, foraging into the unknown.

In 1785 an Oxford printer had published an anonymous shilling pamphlet, entitled *Singular Travels, Campaigns and Adventures of Baron Munchausen*. Rudolph Erich Raspe, its author, seems oddly to prefigure Poe. An amateur scientist and antiquarian, who had earlier written on volcanic geology and the Ossianic poems, he even became a fellow of the Royal Society (until a German scandal caught up with him). Equally fascinated by Lucian, the *Arabian Nights,* Captain Cook's voyages in the South Seas and the ballooning exploits of Blanchard or the Montgolfier brothers, he became an avid reader of Swift and Defoe. An anonymous and penniless hoaxer, he foisted his fantastical tall tales upon the world. Poe's **"The Unparalleled Adventure of One Hans Pfaall"**, however, starting from the same grotesquely exaggerated note, soars, once aloft, into a new and mathematically exacting realm. In that shift, in that unbridgeable gap between the poetic quips of Raspe and the scientific imagination of Poe lay the seeds of the new genre. Both insist on their total veracity; both delight in the elusive antics of the absurd. But while the one dallies solely with metaphoric suggestions, the other explicates, rationalizes, presses inexorably on to hoodwink his bourgeois, materialistic audience. The German concludes his baronial descent of Mount Etna with a plunge through the centre of the earth to the South Seas, adding:

> This was a much shorter cut than going round and one which no man has ever before accomplished, or even attempted. However, the next time I do it, I shall endeavour to make proper scientific observations.

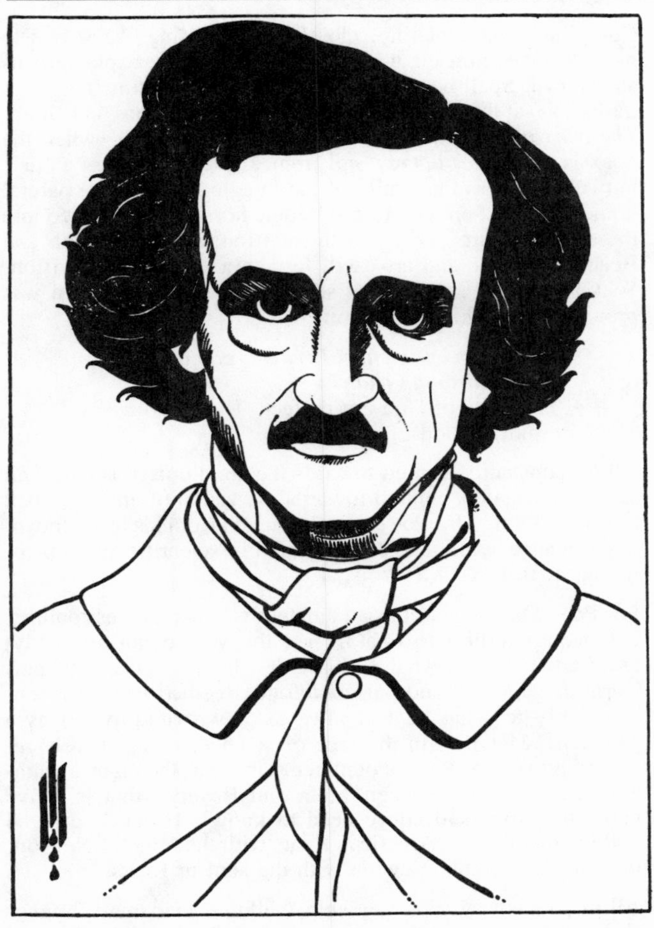

Aubrey Beardsley's portrait of Poe. The Granger Collection, New York.

The American—as balloonist, sailor or mesmerist—from the start played the experimental, philosophical role: making 'proper scientific observations'.

But Poe has never been without his detractors. When his originality has not been ignored, it has been undermined. H. Bruce Franklin is the most recent to launch a two-pronged attack. The first concerned his themes:

> Rarely in Poe's science fiction does one find science itself as a subject and nowhere does one find any kind of true scientist as a consequential figure.

But precisely this respect for the 'true scientist' and his 'science' is what Poe himself, again and again, rejected: '*merely* scientific men' he called them, to be trusted with nothing but 'scientific *details*':

> Of all persons in the world, they are at the same time the most bigoted and the least capable of using, generalizing, or deciding upon the facts which they bring to light in the course of their experiments.

Which makes nonsense of Franklin's second objection—the matter of treatment:

> But if science fiction is merely a popularizer of science rather than the literature which, growing with science, evaluates it, and relates it meaningfully to the rest of existence, it is hardly worth serious attention.

Very little science fiction, of course, could pass that exacting test. But who would claim that **"Mesmeric Revelation",** *Eureka,* or **"Mellonta Tauta",** for example, are 'popularizers'? Their very role, successful or not, is the exact opposite: to evaluate scientific method and technological achievement, by confronting both with a vision of life ('Out of Space—out of Time') in its widest spiritual dimensions.

Poe's *"Sonnet—To Science"*, written [when he was] only twenty, begins:

> Science! true daughter of Old Time thou art!
> Who alterest all things with thy peering eyes.
> Why preyest thou thus upon the poet's heart,
> Vulture, whose wings are dull realities?

But it was not science he abhorred so much as the triumph of mechanical reason, confirmed by technical progress. In **"The Colloquy of Monos and Una"** Monos denounces 'the harsh mathematical reason of the schools', sweeping aside the 'rectangular obscenities' with which technology has littered our globe. Poe used speculative theory from the start to frustrate technological methods and aims. Each 'advance in practical science' meant 'a retro-gradation in the true utility'. Industrialization led only to regimentation; regimentation to that ultimate disease of the 'poetic intellect', the expropriation of the imagination. A pure mathematics—blending calculation with the ideal—of the circle, the sphere, the oval, of the curving arabesques that spiral through dreams and the screwed form of a helix (as on a watchspring or electromagnetic coil of wire), controlled his visionary quests.

One critical fight he was intent on waging:

> The mistake . . . of the old dogma, that the calculating faculties are at war with the ideal; while, in fact, it may be demonstrated that the two divisions of mental power are never to be found in perfection apart. The *highest* order of the imaginative intellect is always preeminently mathematical; and the converse.

His fascination with lunar investigation, sound and colour, the cosmology of Newton, von Humboldt, and Laplace, was a cult of homage to pure science. 'Poe was opening up a way,' wrote Paul Valéry, 'teaching a very strict and deeply alluring doctrine, in which a kind of mathematics and a kind of mysticism became one. . . .' The beauty of number was that point, that configuration, where mathematics and mysticism met.

Something of this ambivalence, ever since, has haunted science fiction. Itself an offshoot of gothicism, the new genre was to evoke a horror both of the future and of the science which could bring that future about. By identifying with the collapse of technology, it was already critically undermining that technology. Yet its only appeal was to science. It had nowhere to turn but to science for its salvation. The fiction, then, was that somehow science must learn to control its own disastrous career. Poe too—quite self-consciously, of course— was working in this gothic vein. Within his husk of mathematics, as often as not, lurks an old-fashioned kernel of magic. In a sense, he recreated all the traditional feats of magic in pseudo-scientific terms (of galvanism and mesmerism). Alchemy became the synthetic manufacture of **"Von Kempelen and His Discovery"**; resurrection of the dead, the time travel of **"Some Words with a Mummy"**; demonic possession, the hypnotic or 'magnetic relation' of **"A Tale of the Ragged Mountains"**; apocalyptic vision, the cataclysmic fire of **"The Conversation of Eiros and Charmion"**. Just as the pseudo-scholarship (in antiquarian statutes and genealogies) of Scott, or gothic elaboration of Hawthorne, was part of an attempt to make the imaginative spell more potent, more binding, so Poe's detailed and mathematical science intensifies his imaginative fusion with the occult.

There is far more of literary burlesque, of outright parody, in all this than . . . H. Bruce Franklin, appeared to realize. Yet clues abound. Those zany, zestful surfaces are all deceitful. The reckless playfulness invades even the august vision of *Eureka*. For his science ultimately is admitted to be a kind of hoax; his fiction openly and ironically conceived as a lie. Like Lucian, in his *True History,* he might have declared:

> The motive and purpose of my journey lay in my intellectual restlessness and passion for adventure, and in my wish to find out what the end of the ocean was, and who the people were that lived on the other side.

But what he contrived was the inversion of romantic fiction from the antiquarian hoax (of a Chatterton or Macpherson) into a futuristic hoax. It proved a brilliant reversal of time-scale, made possible by the wide-spread willingness of an ever-proliferating, journal-reading, stock investing, news addicted, male and female public to be duped.

'His purpose in the hoaxes,' Constance Rourke astutely remarked, 'was to make his readers absurd, to reduce them to an involuntary imbecility. His objective was triumph. . . .' Or in Poe's own caustic words:

> Twenty years ago credulity was the characteristic trait of the mob, incredulity the distinctive feature of the philosophic; now the case is exactly conversed.

"The Unparalleled Adventure of One Hans Pfaall" stands in a direct line of descent from the pseudo-scientific 'Memoirs of Martinus Scriblerus': the literary hoax from the start was bound up with literary burlesque. Compared to Queen Anne's England, however, Jacksonian America presented even more fertile ground:

> As the tall tale came into its great prime in the early '30s a sudden contagion was created. A series of newspaper hoaxes sprang into life in the East. The scale was western, the tone that of calm, scientific exposition of wonders such as often belonged to western comic legend.

Americans 'who like so much to be fooled', Baudelaire commented in a note to **"The Unparalleled Adventure of One Hans Pfaall"** adding that fooling people was Poe's main 'dada', or hobbyhorse. The American hoax, or tall story, was indeed a kind of pioneer *dada*—a violent, endlessly protracted game with the absurd. What Poe, the Southerner, initiated, Mark Twain (the very name is a hoax) from the South-West was lovingly to perfect, and William Faulkner with reckless rhetoric to explore for a twentieth-century topology of the South.

But by detaching himself from the prosaic present, in imaginatively identifying with the future, Poe himself was duped. Compiling, extrapolating, closely paraphrasing, he seems to have deceived himself at last into claiming his very plagiarisms as his own. Spell-bound, he became his own victim. There are moments—at the climax of **"The Colloquy of Monos and Una"**, *The Narrative of Arthur Gordon Pym,* or *Eureka*—when the hoax is no longer openly and ironically confessed as a 'lie', but celebrated as the 'truth' of the imagination, whose natural home is located on remote geographic horizons or pursued into the distant future. There, with intuition as guide, Truth and Beauty—science and art—will fuse in a single poetic vision. Why not fiction as a kind of science, when science itself was proving to be a kind of fiction?

> *A perfect consistency, I repeat, can be nothing but an absolute truth.*
> The plots of God are perfect. The Universe is a plot of God.

All art constantly aspired towards the condition of science: all science constantly aspired towards the vision of art. The spell of science fiction for Poe derived as much from his long-drawn-out romance with science as from his scientific concept of romance. (pp. ix-xviii)

For Poe, what he learnt as an amateur scientist and astronomer led incontrovertibly to what he had always known (intuitively) as an artist. Just as what Teilhard de Chardin, a century later, learnt as geologist and palaeontologist seemed to lead incontrovertibly to what he had always known (intuitively) as a Christian. Melville, in the face of science, imaginatively retreated into myth. Poe encountered science as the precise mathematical equation between Truth and Beauty; 'that is all ye know on earth, and all ye need to know'. He aspired to be nothing less than an American Keats with the mind of Newton, or rather a sublimer Newton with the soul of Keats.

All his imaginary trips—by ship, balloon, laudanum, hypnosis—were aimed at setting the soul free from the demands of the body and so from the restraints of normal perception; simultaneously releasing the mind from its own tomb, the prison of its endlessly inturned and ramifying nervous complexes (where Madeline Usher or Fortunato were buried). For, above all, they express 'the thirst *to know* which is forever unquenchable'—reaching out for knowledge, beyond waking, in sleep; beyond sleep, in death; beyond death, pushed to further and further extremes of consciousness on voyages as dreams, or dreams as voyages ('Out of Space—out of Time'), to a confrontation with the abyss, the whirlpool, the void which is eternity. There are voices of those who have plunged into the ultimate abyss, but survived (like the Norse fisherman [in **"Descent into the Maelstrom"**]); voices that seem to rebound from the fatal impact (like that of Arthur Gordon Pym); voices that hover suspended at the point of transition (like M. Valdemar); voices retrieved from beyond the point of no return (via bottles or Moon-men); voices that continue the quest on the far side of the grave in angelic dialogues among the stars.

Baudelaire, long ago, had mourned Poe's 'eccentric and meteoric literary destiny'. Mallarmé enshrined that image in a passionate tribute, *Le Tombeau d'Edgar Poe,* recited at the unveiling over Poe's grave in 1875 of a block of basalt. Walt Whitman attended the ceremony in Baltimore but declined to speak. Tennyson and Swinburne sent letters from England. But Mallarmé alone transfigured that tomb:

> *Calme bloc ici-bas chu d'un désastre obscur*
> *Que ce granit du moins montre à jamais sa borne*
> *Aux noirs vols du Blasphème épars dans le futur.*

[[A] Stern block here fallen from a mysterious disaster,
Let this granite at least show forever their bound
To the old flights of Blasphemy [still] spread in the
future
(translation by Stéphane Mallarmé)]

That meteorite, plunged down from some cosmic disaster, still survives. Far off it seems to loom—as dim, eternal witness of this interloper among 'the tribe of Stars', apocalyptic prophet and pioneer victim of science fiction. (pp. xix-xxi)

Harold Beaver, in an introduction to The Science Fiction of Edgar Allan Poe *by Edgar Allan Poe, edited by Harold Beaver, Penguin Books, 1976, pp. vii-xxi.*

WALTER EVANS (essay date 1977)

[*In the following excerpt, Evans contends that there are significant discrepancies between Poe's theory of the tale and his literary practice as exemplified by "The Fall of the House of Usher."*]

Virtually every standard study, reference work, or anthology which includes his fiction recognizes Poe's vast influence on the formal development of the short story. Some scholars may ascribe the form's dubious paternity to such figures as Irving or Hawthorne, but, whether or not he fathered the form, Poe's seminal anatomy of the tale in his *Twice Told Tales* reviews [see excerpt dated 1842] did supply a sheltering theoretical home for the genre soon after its birth.

Ironically, however, despite the supposedly monolithic influence of Poe's fiction and criticism in establishing the old fashioned "traditional" short story described by such scholars as Brander Matthews, Frederick Lewis Pattee, Arnold Bader, and Whit and Hallie Burnett: (I) The formal principles outlined in Poe's reviews are dramatically divorced from the practice in what may be his best, most popular, and most influential story, **"The Fall of the House of Usher"**; (II) the structural principles and techniques of that story seem to be those characteristically identified, in English language fiction, only with the formally revolutionary work of James Joyce, Sherwood Anderson, and their heirs; (III) in initiating his reader to this new form by explaining how to read his story in the text of the story itself Poe implicitly outlines these twentieth-century principles so antithetical to his own explicit theories.

Though Poe revised his 1842 anatomy of the tale for his 1847 review of Hawthorne's short fiction certain essential principles remain unchanged. The paramount importance of effect remains the unimpeachable foundation for Poe's theory of the tale, an importance clearly evident in **"The Fall of the House of Usher."** Also essentially unchanged in the second review is Poe's emphasis on incident as the principal tool with which to create effect in the tale. In the 1842 *Graham's* Poe notes that after the skillful artist has conceived a unique "*effect* to be wrought out, he then invents such incidents—he then combines such events as may best aid him in establishing this preconceived effect." Incident and combination of incident, the core of the "traditional" short story, thus play the crucial role in creation of effect. The 1847 *Godey's* review differs to some extent; when the writer has conceived "a certain *single effect* to be wrought, he then invents such incidents, he then combines such events, and discusses them in such tone as may best serve him in establishing this preconceived effect."

Tone functions as a crucial if critically ambiguous term in more than one theory of the short story, and precisely what Poe may have meant by the word is unclear. John Conron states that by tone Poe "means the implicit auctorial attitude towards both the subject and the audience." Walter Blair feels there is "some ambiguity" in Poe's use of the term "since at times Poe uses it merely to denote style. When he is using it most carefully, however, he seems to have in mind that it means the connotations of words." Blair also remarks that "from the beginning to the end of the tale, then, tone is seen as an adjunct to the incidents." In any event, Poe's ranking clearly and consistently establishes the priority of effect, which is to be created by incident, arrangement of incident, and (in 1847) tone.

Emphasis on effect undeniably forms **"The Fall of the House of Usher"** and Poe's attitudes toward his subject and audience clearly contribute to that effect, but a student who closely analyzes the story may find a surprising and paradoxical shortage of incident on the one hand, and on the other a radical deemphasis of certain incidents which do appear. In fact, the bulk of the work consists of images rather than incidents, of description rather than narration. Only if we force Poe to parallel James' celebrated blending of incident and character by assuming that Poe recognized no essential distinction between image and incident (and I know of no authority for such a radical assumption) can we conclude that the effect of the story derives principally from incident and arrangement of incident. (pp. 137-39)

In fact, the incidents Poe does employ seem practically lost in the descriptive passages. For instance, he barely mentions one event which, in a story based on incident and arrangement of incident, should logically deserve a great deal more emphasis: the supposed death of Madeline prior to her interment. The whole episode receives only thirteen words ("one evening, having informed me abruptly that the lady Madeline was no more), far, far fewer even than the narrator's description of Roderick's room, of the underground vault, or of the house and its reflection in the tarn.

I do not conclude, or invite anyone else to conclude, that the story is without incident or arrangement of incident. It does seem, however, that incident and arrangement of incident, the foundation of innumerable "traditional" stories and the preeminent elements in creation of effect as outlined in Poe's theory of the tale, are remarkably deemphasized, almost perfunctorily developed, in **"The Fall of the House of Usher."**

If Poe has not structured incident and arrangement of incident to carry the burden of effect, the need arises to explain what strategies he does employ, for the story's powerful impact on several generations of widely different sorts of readers has certainly been created by something.

Fortunately, as demonstrated above, several critics have described Poe's power in terms of "atmosphere" or "mood" and in their explications have demonstrated that these qualities result largely from Poe's genius for imagery. An analysis of the story's elements clearly supports such critics' focus on thematically patterned images.

The story proper begins (after the vivid introductory paragraph which is discussed below) with the narrator describing the situation accounting for his visit to Usher. This background information on Usher and his family Poe follows with a second description of the house: first an impression, compared to a "dream," emphasizing a peculiar hazy atmosphere surrounding the scene; the narrator then comments on the sense of disintegration and "instability" among the individual stones and notes a ragged fissure extending from roof to ground.

He finally enters the house and then Usher's private room, only partly illuminated through distorting windows and filled with scattered "books and musical instruments." Usher's personal appearance is described in the same highly figured language employed before to describe the landscape and house; later his peculiar infirmity, "a constitutional and family evil," is described in terms suggestive of a particularly "lyrical" malady, in terms of "unnatural sensations" and "a morbid acuteness of the senses."

The tale is then developed in a series of vivid and superficially disjointed images: the lady Madeline passing silently through the hall as Usher and the narrator discuss her; Usher's wild musical improvisations and awesome paintings, notably that of the endless tunnel; Usher's poem, "The Haunted Palace"; the esoteric books of mystic knowledge; the dungeon in which Madeline is elaborately entombed after her death; the wild storm; the tale of Ethelred; the vivid climactic image of Usher and Madeline in a horrible deathly embrace; the final image of the decayed house sinking into the tarn.

Poe demonstrably composed the body of the story of elements central to the lyric method but largely irrelevant to plotted narrative progression; he clearly subordinates combined incidents to patterned images. As noted above, the incidents necessary for narrative development, the lady Madeline's presumed death, for example, which would logically require detailed development and significant emphasis, are treated perfunctorily; even Ethelred and "The Haunted Palace" are given much more emphasis than the rationalization for the entombment so crucial to the narrative movement.

In fact, narrative elements and patterns are subordinate to lyric elements and patterns throughout the piece, not only in the concentrated opening paragraph and in the succession of awesome and terrible images which make up the bulk of the tale, but perhaps most significantly in the image of the siblings' deaths succeeded by the disintegration of the house. Here the elements Poe scattered before he concentrates and integrates in a final sensual image of desolate destruction incorporating the romance of Ethelred, the "blood-red moon," the fissured house, and "a long tumultuous shouting sound like the voice of a thousand waters—" as all sinks into the "deep and dank tarn."

In **"The Fall of the House of Usher"** then, Poe has borrowed heavily from techniques ordinarily associated with lyric poetry, the form he identified as the highest literary genre. Fortunately, a few fine critics seem to appreciate the story's essentially lyric structure. Thomas Woodson states that all Poe's fiction "tends toward the conditions of lyric poetry." Caroline Gordon and Allen Tate point to the deemphasis of plot characteristic of Poe's better tales and to a "poetical" unity in **"The Fall of the House of Usher"** which they relate to the influence of the Romantic poets; they conclude that the "active structure of the story is mechanical and thus negligible; but its lyric structure is impressive"; indeed, they feel the story, like many of Poe's best, is "based upon scenic reality." Darrel Abel concludes of **"The Fall of the House of Usher"**: "It achieves unity by a concentration and remarkably subtle co-operation of carefully calculated, complex causes. Instead of the more familiar methods of realistic narrative specification and progressive logical explication, it operates through parallel symbolic suggestions" [see excerpt dated 1949].

These critics do not, however, seem finally to recognize the significance of such lyric structural principles for either Poe's theory of the tale or for the formal development of the short story. Recent theorists and historians of the short story characteristically identify Sherwood Anderson as the first American to discover a "lyric" mode in the short story. This "new" mode, which relies heavily on the techniques of lyric poetry, such critics as Sister M. Joselyn strongly oppose to the incident and plot-oriented tradition of short fiction supposedly established by Poe:

> All stories, of course, have a "mimetic" base, and many, perhaps the majority, achieve their entire effect by presenting in ordinary prose a chronologically straightforward series of events whose significance is contained in and completed by the resolution of events. Other stories, however, by means of the amalgamation of additional elements into the mimetic base, elements characteristically expected in verse, constitute what I have called a class of "lyric" stories. . . . The "poetic" elements which, in my view, sometimes appear in the prose narrative, include (1) marked deviation from chronological sequence, (2) exploitation of purely verbal resources such as tone and imagery, (3) a concentration upon increased awareness rather than upon a completed action, and (4) a high degree of suggestiveness, emotional intensity, achieved with a minimum of means.
>
> (pp. 139-42)

Among the elements Sister Joselyn lists only the first fails to characterize **"The Fall of the House of Usher"**; countless critics have discussed the relevance to the story of such "purely verbal resources . . . as tone and imagery"; as many readers realize, and as Thomas Woodson notes: "the protagonist (here the narrator and both Ushers combined) ends teetering on the verge of a supreme revelation that is also his destruction"; even Poe's detractors would be hard pressed to deny the story's "suggestiveness, emotional intensity" and economy "of means."

The structural principles of **"The Fall of the House of Usher"** then seem to violate Poe's formal theory and to conform to patterns in America identified with the short story only in the twentieth century.

Poe's awareness that **"The Fall of the House of Usher"** represented serious experimentation with a new mode (a mode so new that it wasn't supposed to exist in America for eighty years) seems to be signalled by the care he took to orient his readers at the beginning of the story. Poe demonstrably recognized a compelling need to guide reader expectations in a way which would not have been necessary in a story formally closer to works such as Irving's "Rip Van Winkle" or "The Legend of Sleepy Hollow" or Hawthorne's "The Gray Champion" or "The Wedding Knell" or "Legends of the Province House" or, a little later, Melville's "The Town-Ho's Story" or Fitz-James O'Brien's "The Diamond Lens" or "What Was It? A Mystery." Such works conform admirably both to Poe's anatomy of the tale in his Hawthorne reviews and to more recent critics' descriptions of the "traditional" short story.

Long before Anderson, Poe seems to have implicitly realized himself to be one of the very first writers to create short prose fiction in which elements and patterns commonly associated with lyric poetry were employed with genius, that he was one of the first to create a story in which atmosphere and mood derived from imagery were the most effective elements and in which the most meaningful structural principle was not the logical organization of incidents into a plot, but the thematic organization of images to form an impression or effect. Images are far from the only generative elements in the story, but certainly the most effective, as a glance at the opening pages should indicate; indeed, Poe establishes the rich lyrical dimension of **"The Fall of the House of Usher"** by the end of the initial paragraph.

The opening quotation from De Béranger ("Son coeur est un luth suspendu;/Sitôt qu'on le touche il résonne.") presents a vivid image of the lyric protagonist (who might be either Usher or the narrator, or even both) as a perceiving consciousness inextricably involved with and unusually affected by sensation. Perhaps even more important, the lines must also refer to the ideal reader, for such a consciousness must also be developed by the reader who would properly approach and appreciate Poe's story.

Poe next turns attention to the oft-remarked symbolic metaphor of the "house" of Usher: a presentation of the house and surrounding landscape in terms which many have interpreted as a portrait of Usher himself, or even of Poe, whose own face, at least in popular imagination, is dominated by "bleak" cheeks, huge eyes, a "rank" and slightly bushy mustache, and perhaps even "white trunks of decayed" teeth. This highly effective, elaborately wrought image is then duplicated and inverted (as it is possible to see the narrator somehow duplicated and inverted in Usher) in the tarn, a projection, duplication, and inversion quite meaningful in terms of the story's form and content.

Finally, the narrtor expresses his horrified reaction to the house in terms which outline the fundamental principle underlying lyric technique: "beyond doubt, there *are* combinations of very simple natural objects which have the power of thus affecting us," and goes on to speculate that "a mere different arrangement of the particulars of the scene, of the details of the picture, would be sufficient to modify, or perhaps to annihilate its capacity for sorrowful impression." Here Poe simply and effectively goes beyond his reviews' emphasis on incident to indicate how the all-important effect actually is created in his story.

In the dense first paragraph of this intensely concentrated story Poe has then indicated the critical significance of a heightened sensibility, provided a highly wrought example of his method in the elaborate symbol-metaphor-image of the house, and finally linked the two in narrative exposition detailing the essence of lyric technique whereby a pattern of disparate images creates a whole greater than its parts.

In summary, the evidence indicates that: (I) the formal principles of **"The Fall of the House of Usher"** clearly contradict fundamental elements of Poe's theory of the tale as outlined in his *Twice-Told Tales* reviews; (II) the formal principles of the story are essentially those of the twentieth-century "lyric" short story; (III) in the story itself Poe implicitly outlines these principles so antagonistic to his later explicit theory. (pp. 142-44)

Walter Evans, "'The Fall of the House of Usher' and Poe's Theory of the Tale," in Studies in Short Fiction, *Vol. 14, No. 2, Spring, 1977, pp. 137-44.*

DAVID GALLOWAY (essay date 1983)

[In the following excerpt, Galloway offers a reevaluation of Poe's satirical and comic stories, emphasizing their importance for gaining a full appreciation of his major fiction.]

Poe came to speak of his early comedies as 'grotesques', thereby stressing the exaggerations of Gothic convention and elevated Yankee language on which most depended—though he once, somewhat confusingly, described them as 'arabesques'. Despite the author's persistent efforts to find a publisher, the tales never appeared in the single volume Poe had begun planning as early as 1833. His letters give the total number variously as eleven, sixteen, and seventeen, but the proposed frame narrative describes only eleven charter members of the Folio Club. Like Chaucer's pilgrims, each is to present a tale which reflects his own character, and presumably a prize would have been awarded for the most entertaining. The descriptions of the 'remarkable men' who compose this 'Junto of *Dunderheadism* 'are worth quoting for what they reveal of the concept of this unpublished work:

> There was, first of all, Mr Snap, the President, who is a very lank man with a hawk nose, and was formerly in the service of the *Down-East Review*.
> Then there was Mr Convolvulus Gondola, a young gentleman who had travelled a good deal.
> Then there was De Rerum Naturâ, Esqr., who wore a very singular pair of green spectacles.
> Then there was a very little man in a black coat with very black eyes.
> Then there was Mr Solomon Seadrift who had every appearance of a fish.
> Then there was Mr Horribile Dictu, with white eyelashes, who had graduated at Göttingen.
> Then there was Mr Blackwood who had written certain articles for foreign magazines.
> Then there was the host, Mr Rouge-et-Noir, who admired Lady Morgan.
> Then there was a stout gentleman who admired Sir Walter Scott.
> Then there was Chronologos Chronology who admired Horace Smith, and had a very big nose which had been in Asia Minor . . .

Had a publisher been willing to sponsor the project, Poe might have modified somewhat the prankishness of this brief outline; certainly, the concept of a club of windy literary gentlemen belaboring the literary fashions of the day was not without promise, and the frame narrative might have provided *Tales of the Folio Club* with a substance that is lacking in many of the individual narrations.

Even where we have lost all direct awareness of Poe's allusions, his sheer exuberance of language and bizarre inventiveness can sometimes pull an old chestnut entertainingly from the fire—as in **"How to Write a *Blackwood* Article"** and its accompanying cautionary tale, **"A Predicament"**. Here Poe drew literally on "The Man in the Bell", published by *Blackwood's* in 1830, which relates how a man climbs the belfry of a cathedral and is caught with his head in a narrow window of the clockface, until the minute hand decapitates him. **"A Predicament"** gains its comic force, however, not from any specific knowledge of the original, and not even from the ludicrous poetics spelled out in the preceding essay, but from the bewitchingly addle-brained voice of the literary lady who narrates it. Accompanied by her faithful companions, Diana the poodle and Pompey the slave, she embarks on a quest for

> the *very* disturbing influence of the serene, and godlike, and heavenly, and exalting, and elevated, and purifying effect of what may be rightly

> termed the most enviable, the most *truly* enviable—nay! the most benignly beautiful, the most deliciously ethereal, and, as it were, the most *pretty* (if I may use so bold an expression) *thing* (pardon me, gentle reader!) in the world . . .

At the end of her outing in Edinburgh, where *Blackwood's* was published, Senora Psyche Zenobia finds herself 'Dogless, niggerless, headless'. The poetic heroine refers to the clock hand relentlessly pressing against her neck as the *Scythe of Time* (a phrase which provided the title for the story's first publication in 1838), who despite the absurdity of her predicament, Poe's fans will recognize an immediate parallel to a tale published four years later—namely, **"The Pit and the Pendulum".** As the clock hand descends, Zenobia notes, 'I threw up my hands and endeavored, with all my strength, to force upward the ponderous iron bar.' The nameless narrator of **"The Pit and the Pendulum"** relates, 'I grew frantically mad, and struggled to force myself upward against the sweep of the fearful scimitar.' The parallels in language, the repetitions which build toward hysterical effect, underscore the cousinage of the two tales. 'Down, down, down it came,' Zenobia thrills, 'closer and yet closer . . . Down and still down it came.' The victim of the fiendish tortures of the Inquisition borrows her breathless tone: 'Down—steadily down it crept . . . Down—certainly, relentlessly down . . . Down—still unceasingly—still inevitably down.' And when these improbably parallel narrators realize the hopelessness of their positions, both experience brief but transcendent moments of euphoria in the face of death.

"A Predicament" and **"The Pit and the Pendulum"** offer an important clue to Poe's method: starting with a pre-existent pattern borrowed from a contemporary periodical, he first makes it his own through the inversions of comedy, calculatedly exaggerating the superficial elements of narrative; later, when his own mastery of the pattern is established, the transformation is achieved by concentrating on the interior, psychological implications of plot. In **"King Pest",** for example, Poe composed a grotesque farce based on an episode entitled "The Palace of Wines" from Benjamin Disraeli's *Vivian Grey*. In Poe's version, a pair of sailors carouse through the waterfront pubs of fourteenth-century London; unwittingly, they cross a barrier that cordons off the diseased area of the city and there, in an undertaker's establishment, encounter King Pest and the royal family drinking wine from human skulls. Though the seamen eventually best their murderous host and escape with two ladies of the court, the story's darker elements cannot be overlooked. The vivid descriptions of pestilence certainly owed a debt to the observations Poe made during the cholera epidemic that ravaged Baltimore in 1831, and they anticipate his later treatment of physical disease and mortal decay as an indication of man's spiritual condition. Crossing the barrier between the known and the unknown, between sanity and madness, the waking life and the dream, would also become a powerful physical symbol in the serious writings, as it is in the apocalyptic vision of *The Narrative of Arthur Gordon Pym*. The closest and most telling parallel to **"King Pest",** however, is **"The Masque of the Red Death",** which Poe published eight years later; here a nobleman barricades himself and his friends in a magnificent, castellated abbey to escape the plague, only to find the sinister figure of the Red Death awaiting them there.

Such transformations and re-transformations of narrative premises are typical of Poe; individual stories, too, were reworked for subsequent publication, occasionally retitled, and some were fundamentally altered in tone. Collections (and proposed collections) of both verse and prose were continuously reshuffled, recycled and revised. As his own confidence and his reputation grew, he would even mock his own most cherished fictional devices. In **"The Unparalleled Adventure of One Hans Pfall"** (1835) Poe had spoofed the sensationalist, pseudo-scientific accounts of space travel then so much in vogue, but his imaginative descriptions of a bankrupt's voyage to the moon were so plausible that they inevitably gave the vogue new impetus. In 1844 Poe trumped his competitors with **"The Balloon Hoax",** whose appearance in New York's first penny newspaper as an historic 'Extra' caused the offices of the *Sun* to be mobbed by curiosity-seekers. Having established his own mastery of the form, he once more inverted it in the punning parody of **"Mellonta Tauta"** (1849).

Similarly, with **"The Murders in the Rue Morgue"** (1841) Edgar Allan Poe staked his claim as originator of the modern detective story; numerous authors, including Voltaire, had written crime-solving stories, but it was Poe who created the figure of the eccentric, ratiocinative private detective who perceives the pattern in a series of apparently unrelated facts and events. Poe borrowed the name of his master detective, C. Auguste Dupin, from the heroine, Marie Dupin, of an episode in the "Unpublished Passages in the Life of Vidocq, the French Minister of Police". In this fictionalized memoir of a real detective (who is casually referred to in **"The Murders in the Rue Morgue"**), the narrator remains outside the main events, and his solution of a crime is likely to be a matter of *felix culpa*. After ingeniously transforming the suggestions he found in Vidocq, Poe applied Dupin's skills to the solution of an actual murder in **"The Mystery of Marie Rogêt"** (1842), then burlesqued his own creation in **"Thou Art the Man"** (1844). The latter is not only a detective story without a detective, but one in which both the crime and its solution are treated farcically. For aficionados of detective fiction, to be sure, another classic device emerges here: the prime suspect, saved from the gallows at the last minute, is a scoundrel, while the true murderer is a man of seemingly unimpeachable probity. The total effect, however, remains one of broad and rather vulgar burlesque.

Though the numerous tales dealing with that subject have led some critics to label Poe as morbid, the fear of being buried alive was commonplace in his time; charnel houses were equipped with alarm systems so that the 'dead' could signal for help, and luxury coffins were fitted with ventilators and speaking tubes. Both factual and fictional accounts of premature burial were a journalistic staple of the nineteenth century, and Poe incorporated the motif in numerous short stories, of which **"The Fall of the House of Usher"** (1839) proved the most celebrated and influential. He had, however, first used the motif in one of the projected *Tales of the Folio Club*. Under the original title of **"A Decided Loss"**, the story related the misadventures of a man who, soon after his wedding, literally loses his breath while vilifying his wife (the sort of perverse quarrel that leads to murder in **"The Black Cat"**). Searching for his lost breath, the narrator, Mr Lackobreath, discovers love-letters to his wife from their neighbor, Mr Windenough; this, together with his 'pulmonary incapacity', persuades him to seek the refuge of a 'foreign climate'. After being crushed by a fat fellow-traveler, he is taken for dead and flung from the coach, breaking his arms and his skull; the surgeon and the apothecary who attend him pronounce him dead in spite of his guttural protests, rob him and remove various parts of his body for their experiments. Trussed and gagged and stored in an attic, the narrator is so alarmed when two cats begin eating his nose that he springs from the window and into a hangman's cart on its way to the gallows. The convicted man escapes, and Mr Lackobreath is hanged in his stead, but later leaves his coffin and retrieves his breath from the neighbor who had accidentally caught it. Poe subtitled his caprice "A Tale Neither In Nor Out of *Blackwood*", and the Scottish publication had, indeed, specified the requisite pattern: 'the record of a gentleman's sensations when entombed before the *breath* was out of his body'. Poe subsequently revised the story, adding a long description of the sensations of a man being hanged, and generously peppering the whole with obscure literary allusions; he also changed the title to **"Loss of Breath"**.

Five years after the publication of **"The Fall of the House of Usher"**, Poe once more spoofed the motif of **"The Premature Burial"**, in a story of that title which appeared in the *Philadelphia Dollar Newspaper* in 1844. Beginning with a series of allegedly factual accounts intended to establish the credibility of his own experience, the cataleptic narrator describes awakening in a coffin, his jaws bound shut, feeling the wooden lid a few inches above his head and smelling freshly turned earth. His screams bring to his bedside the gruff crew of the sloop on which he is sailing: the coffin is a wooden berth, the cerements binding his jaws a silk scarf, the smell of moist earth comes from the ship's cargo. What begins as a tale of terror ends as a comedy of errors, and both elements will figure prominently in Poe's next treatment of the theme— **"The Cask of Amontillado"**.

The problem of identity is another motif which threads through Poe's classic tales, in which dead wives take possession of their husbands' brides, brothers and sisters share a single spirit, and sinister *Doppelgänger* warn of the consequences of dividing moral and physical existence. We know that the concept of the multiple nature of self was one of intense personal concern to Poe: he endowed the tormented hero of **"William Wilson"** (1840) not only with his own birthdate, but with numerous details of his own childhood and youth. A comic equivalent to the crisis of identity is the story of mistaken identity, which provided the central mechanism for **"The Spectacles"** (1843), where a nearsighted young man falls hopelessly in love with his own great-great-grandmother. In a fragment of song ('Ninon, Ninon, Ninon, à bas . . .'), Poe alludes to his source in the remarkable life of Ninon de l'Enclos (1615-1705); celebrated for her extraordinary beauty, intelligence and wit, even at the age of seventy she was said to have a numerous entourage of lovers. Her son by the Marquis de Gersai was never told of his mother's identity, and she was over sixty when he was presented to her salon and instantly fell in love with his brilliant hostess. Intrigued and no doubt flattered by the remarkable coincidence, Ninon delayed telling the young man about his origin, but her rejection of his amorous advances drove him to suicide. To exaggerate the comic effect, and perhaps to distance somewhat the problem of incestuous love touching his own life, Poe made his heroine the narrator's great-great-grandmother. Eugénie Lalande is a bald, wrinkled, toothless woman of eighty-two who retains her brilliant air through the 'art' of make-up and pretends to accept her suitor's proposal of marriage in order to punish him for his refusal to wear spectacles. Vanity is thus the central target of Poe's story; the fashionable ruses of wigs and make-up, false teeth and flounces are another; the romantic fantasy of 'love at first sight' sets the plot in motion, and it climaxes in a burlesque of the complex interrelationships of Europe's noble families. Nonetheless, the familiar problem of identity is central to the tale—as it is to **"The Man that was Used Up"**, in which wigs and prosthetic devices also play a crucial role in establishing a 'counterfeit' identity. (pp. 9-16)

Poe's acute sense for the grotesque and the perverse, which informed some of his most chilling narratives, suggested a virtually limitless range of comic themes: the sentimental rituals of courtship in **"Why the Little Frenchman Wears his Arm in a Sling"** and **"The Spectacles"**; the free-wheeling, self-made entrepreneur in **"The Business Man"** and **"Diddling Considered as One of the Exact Sciences"**; biblical history and religious bigotry in **"A Tale of Jerusalem"**; supernatural visitations in **"The Devil in the Belfry"**, **"Never Bet the Devil Your Head"**, and **"The Angel of the Odd"**. But his most recurrent themes were politics and philosophy, literary fashions and foibles, science and pseudo-science. All were drawn together in **"The System of Doctor Tarr and Professor Fether"**, where the inmates of a French asylum take advantage of the liberties permitted by the new 'soothing system' to overpower and confine their keepers. When the narrator, intrigued by the humanistic advances of modern medicine, visits the establishment, the roles of the director and his family are played by the inmates. They have, they claim, found the soothing method impracticable, and have once more caused their patients to be locked away. During a drunken, tumultuous dinner, their descriptions of the patients' maladies grow increasingly animated, until it becomes clear the eccentricities they describe are their own. Allusions to the excesses of the French Revolution are frequent, as are those to the slavocracy of the Southern states. The new, permissive 'system of soothing', which provides the dramatic impulse for the story, was personally familiar to Poe: he had met Dr Pliny Earle, who served as resident physician for institutions in Frankford, Pennsylvania, and Bloomington, New York, that promoted a so-called 'Moral Treatment' of the insane. The results had so favorably impressed Charles Dickens on his American tour of 1842 that it may well have provided a topic of conversation when he met with Poe in Philadelphia. In that case, even if Poe was unfamiliar with the euphoric description of such treatments in Dickens's *American Notes*, he may well have been parodying Dickensian heartiness. At the core of the tale, however, rest sober and sobering reflections on the fine line dividing madness and sanity, and the speed with which the roles can be interchanged in a world governed by appearances. It is a lunatic who delivers the story's most disturbing moral:

> There is no accounting for the caprices of madmen; and, in my opinion, as well as in that of Doctor Tarr and Professor Fether, it is *never* safe to permit them to run at large unattended. A lunatic may be 'soothed', as it is called, for a time, but, in the end, he is very apt to become obstreperous. His cunning, too, is proverbial, and great. If he has a project in view, he conceals his design with a marvellous wisdom; and the dexterity with which he counterfeits sanity presents, to the metaphysician, one of the most singular problems in the study of mind. When a madman appears *thoroughly* sane, indeed, it is high time to put him in a strait-jacket.

Even if we radically discount (as we must) the sensationalist legends of Poe's own mental instability, it is clear that the subject treated in **"The System of Doctor Tarr and Professor Fether"** was of intense personal concern to its author. In a remarkably candid letter written to an admirer in 1848, he sought to analyze the sources of his own instability, citing as a primary cause the recurrent illnesses preceding the death of his young wife Virginia Clemm. With each of her painful collapses, he wrote.

> I felt all the agonies of her death—and at each accession of the disorder I loved her more dearly and clung to the life with desperate pertinacity. But I am constitutionally sensitive—nervous in a very unusual degree. I became insane, with long intervals of horrible sanity. During these fits of absolute unconsciousness, I drank—God only knows how often or how much. As a matter of course, my enemies referred the insanity to the drink, rather than the drink to the insanity.

Even a man of hardier temperament might well have been plunged into depressions by the illnesses and deaths, frustrations and reversals that punctuated Edgar Allan Poe's brief life. Numerous commentators have suggested that art itself was the therapy with which Poe held absolute insanity at bay; some claim he invented the detective story in order to keep from going mad. Such arguments often seem inspired by the glamorous and tragic image of Poe given such lustrous patina by the Decadents, though it is unimpeachably true that many of the recurrent themes of Poe's art sprang directly from his own private agonies. Yet it is not merely in his tales of doomed brides, sinister chambers and obsessive geniuses that he struggled to come to terms with subjective griefs and fears; the cleansing, distancing power of laughter also frequently came to his aid. Alcoholism and insanity, the subjects of the letter quoted above, are frequent elements in the comedies, and the raucous fantasies of **"The Angel of the Odd"** deal with delirium tremens. Incest, too, is a theme of the grotesques: the hero of **"The Spectacles"** is deflected from marrying his great-great-grandmother, but does marry his own distant, youthful cousin. (pp. 18-20)

[Even] the author's greatest devotees have frequently ignored these accomplishments. Arthur Hobson Quinn's definitive critical biography disposes of most of the comic works with a single phrase; of the revisions to **"The Man That Was Used Up"** he notes, 'It has fifteen corrections of the 1840 text, but the trivial nature of the story makes any comparison superfluous.' The reader who ignores these works, comprising more than half of Poe's fictional efforts, not only risks a distorted view of the author's achievements; he loses important insights into some of Poe's most 'classic' tales. Sometimes with venom, sometimes with burlesque, and sometimes with libel actions, Edgar Allan Poe dueled with contemporary critics, and the celebrated revenge thriller, **"The Cask of Amontillado"**, is often thought to encapsulate his sense of literary injury. Wearing jester's motley and bells, the foolish victim is lured to his death by his lust for wine, then walled up alive by the vengeful Fortunato; the figure of the clown, alcoholism and premature burial had all been extensively examined in the comic tales that precede **"The Cask of Amontillado"**, and it too is a kind of savage comedy in which the victim dies laughing at the 'excellent jest' his host has played, and the host is never apprehended for his crime. The story was a turning-point for Poe, a reversal of the murder-will-out premise of **"The Tell-Tale Heart"** and **"The Black Cat"**. The triumph of revenge is also the theme of Poe's last published story. **"Hop-Frog"**, in which a dwarf in motley and bells repays a monarch's cruelty with a joke that costs the king and his ministers their lives. In such stories the comic is established as an integral part of Poe's fictional achievement; it is one too long neglected as a major aspect of his remarkable, multi-valenced talent. (p. 22)

David Galloway, in an introduction to The Other Poe: Comedies and Satires *by Edgar Allan Poe, edited by David Galloway, Penguin Books, 1983, pp. 7-22.*

ADDITIONAL BIBLIOGRAPHY

Alexander, Jean. *Affidavits of Genius: Edgar Allan Poe and the French Critics, 1847-1924.* Port Washington, N.Y.: Kennikat Press, 1971, 246 p.

Lengthy introduction discussing the reception of Poe's works among French writers of the late nineteenth and early twentieth centuries. A selection of translated studies and statements includes criticism by Baudelaire, J. Barbey d'Aurevilly, Joris Karl Huysmans, Stéphane Mallarmé, Remy de Gourmont, and Paul Valéry.

Baudelaire, Charles Pierre. *Baudelaire on Poe.* Translated and edited by Lois Hyslop and Francis E. Hyslop, Jr. State College, Pa.: Bald Eagle Press, 1952, 175 p.

Incorporates biographical and critical studies by Baudelaire written at various times, including *Edgar Poe: His Life and Works* (1852 and 1856) and *New Notes on Edgar Poe.*

Beebe, Maurice. "The Universe of Roderick Usher." *Personalist* 17, No. 2 (Spring 1956): 147-60.

Maintains that "The Fall of the House of Usher" illustrates in its artistic structure Poe's cosmological theories outlined in his essay *Eureka.*

Blair, Walter. "Poe's Conception of Incident and Tone in the Tale." *Modern Philology* 41, No. 4 (May 1944): 228-40.

Analysis of Poe's theory and practice of the short story, examining how he manipulated narrative elements for various artistic and emotional effects.

Bloom, Harold, ed. *Edgar Allan Poe: Modern Critical Views.* New York: Chelsea House Publishers, 1985, 155 p.

Collects major critical essays, including studies by Valéry, Lawrence, Allen Tate, and Richard Wilbur.

Bonaparte, Marie. *The Life and Works of Edgar Allan Poe: A Psycho-Analytic Interpretation.* London: The Hogarth Press, 1949, 749 p.

Story-by-story analysis of psychosexual symbolism and motifs in Poe's tales.

Brooks, Cleanth, Jr., and Warren, Robert Penn. "The Fall of the House of Usher." In their *Understanding Fiction,* pp. 202-5. New York: F. S. Crofts & Co., 1943.

Reduces "The Fall of the House of Usher" to a "relatively meaningless" horror story which serves principally as a case study in morbid psychology and lacks any quality of pathos or tragedy.

Carlson, Eric W., ed. *The Recognition of Edgar Allan Poe: Selected Criticism Since 1829.* Ann Arbor: The University of Michigan Press, 1970, 316 p.

Selected criticism organized into three periods: 1829-99, 1900-48, and 1949 to present. These seminal writings on Poe include commentary by Fyodor Dostoevski, A. C. Swinburne, James, Shaw, Valéry, Winters, Eliot, Auden, and Wilbur.

Cohen, Hennig. "Roderick Usher's Tragic Struggle." *Nineteenth-Century Fiction* 14, No. 3 (December 1959): 270-72.

Argues against the contention by Cleanth Brooks and Robert Penn Warren (see entry in Additional Bibliography) that "The Fall of the House of Usher" "lacks tragic quality" because Roderick Usher does not struggle against his psychological aberrations.

Davidson, Edward. *Poe: A Critical Study.* Cambridge, Mass.: The Belknap Press, 1957, 296 p.

Assumes the viewpoint that "Poe was a 'crisis' in the Romantic and the symbolic imagination. He came near the end . . . of the idealist or Romantic expression and mind. Occupying such a place in the history of art, Poe dramatized the whole problem of what the creative imagination does when it is seeking ways of communicating those ideas lying beyond the common denotative discourse of men."

Defalco, Joseph M. "The Source of Terror in Poe's 'Shadow—A Parable'." *Studies in Short Fiction* VI, No. 5 (Fall 1969): 643-48.
Discusses "Shadow—A Parable" as an allegorical work in which the source of terror resides not in the apprehension of physical death but in the realization of the metaphysical loss of personal identity at death.

Eddings, Dennis W., ed. *The Naiad Voice: Essays on Poe's Satiric Hoaxing*. Port Washington, N.Y.: Associated Faculty Press, 1983, 175 p.
Reprints essays viewing Poe's serious and comic stories alike as essentially ironic. Contributors include James W. Gargano, James M. Cox, G. R. Thompson, and Benjamin Franklin Fisher IV.

Franklin, H. Bruce. "Edgar Allan Poe and Science Fiction." In his *Future Perfect: American Science Fiction of the Nineteenth Century*, pp. 93-103. London: Oxford University Press, 1966.
Refutes the long-standing recognition of Poe as the "father of science fiction" and concludes that Poe "may be the father not of science fiction but rather of what is so often associated with the term science fiction—fiction which popularizes science for boys and girls of all ages while giving them the creeps."

Gargano, James W. "'The Black Cat': Perverseness Reconsidered." *Texas Studies in Language and Literature* 2, No. 2 (Summer 1960): 172-78.
Argues that the "spirit of perverseness," which the narrator of "The Black Cat" names as the motive of his cruel behavior, is a psychological defense invented to avoid moral responsibility for evil actions.

Haycraft, Howard. "Time: 1841—Place: America." In his *Murder for Pleasure: The Life and Times of the Detective Story*, pp. 1-27. New York: D. Appleton-Century Co., 1941.
Details the conventions of detective fiction that Poe established in "The Murders in the Rue Morgue," "The Mystery of Marie Rogêt," and "The Purloined Letter."

Hoffman, Daniel. "I Have Been Faithful to You in My Fashion: The Remarriage of Ligeia's Husband." *The Southern Review* 8, No. 1 (January 1972): 89-105.
A meditation on the relations between death and sexuality in "Ligeia," concluding that for Poe, "death is a metaphor of sexuality—and of something more. It is the multiple associations of death in Poe's work which lend his tales their particular fascination, their concatenation of terror and sublimity inextricably intermingled."

Howarth, William L., ed. *Poe's Tales: A Collection of Critical Essays*. Englewood Cliffs, N.J.: Prentice-Hall, 1971, 116 p.
Includes essays by Clark Griffith, Donald Barlow Stauffer, James Gargano, Robert Daniel, and William Carlos Williams.

Hudson, Ruth. "Poe Recognizes 'Ligeia' as His Masterpiece." In *English Studies in Honor of James Southall Wilson*, edited by Fredson Bowers, pp. 35-44. Charlottesville, Va.: n.p., 1951.
Adduces various statements from Poe's letters to establish that he considered "Ligeia" his best story. Hudson then compares revisions made in "Ligeia" and several other tales to illustrate that "in writing "Ligeia" Poe gathered up the threads of his dreams—the figures of speech, the phrases, the ideals of characters and interiors, the poetic overtones—which had been taking shape in earlier stories and wove them unconsciously into its fabric. It is the essence of Poe in phraseology, in subject-matter, in emotional effect. In all likelihood, it marked the peak of his creative vigor as a tale-writer."

James, Henry. "Charles Baudelaire." In his *French Poets and Novelists*, edited by Leon Edel, pp. 57-66. New York: Grosset & Dunlap, 1964.
Comments that to take Poe "with more than a certain degree of seriousness is to lack seriousness one's self. An enthusiasm for Poe is the mark of a decidedly primitive stage of reflection."

Kesterton, David B., ed. *Critics on Poe*. Coral Gables, Fla.: University of Miami Press, 1973, 128 p.
Divided into four sections of selected excerpts and essays: (1) Critics on Poe: 1845-1940 (2) Critics on Poe since 1940 (3) General Critical Evaluations (4) Critics on Specific Works.

Ketterer, David. *The Rationale of Deception in Poe*. Baton Rouge: Louisiana State University Press, 1979, 285 p.
Sees the conflict between reality and illusion, along with the struggle to transcend this duality, as the major theme in Poe's work. The critic explores in depth Poe's concept of the "arabesque."

Krutch, Joseph Wood. *Edgar Allan Poe: A Study in Genius*. New York: Alfred A. Knopf, 1926, 244 p.
Traces "Poe's art to an abnormal condition of the nerves and his critical ideas to a rationalized defense of the limitations of his taste," considering the legend of the author's tormented life his "supreme artistic achievement."

Ljungquist, Kent. *The Grand and the Fair: Poe's Landscape Aesthetics and Pictorial Techniques*. Potomac, Md.: Scripta Humanistica, 1984, 216 p.
Studies the thematic significance of landscape and other types of imagery in Poe's work, relating Poe's techniques and theories of pictorialism to aesthetic schools of the eighteenth and nineteenth centuries.

Quinn, Arthur Hobson. *Edgar Allan Poe: A Critical Biography*. New York: D. Appleton-Century Co., 1941, 804 p.
Complete and authoritative biography.

Regan, Robert. *Poe: A Collection of Critical Essays*. Englewood Cliffs, N.J.: Prentice-Hall, 1967, 183 p.
Includes essays by Huxley, Tate, Quinn, Wilbur, and Gargano.

Robinson, E. Arthur. "Poe's 'The Tell-Tale Heart'." *Nineteenth Century Fiction* 19, No. 4 (March 1965): 369-78.
Studies psychology of the narrator of "The Tell-Tale Heart."

Roppolo, Joseph Patrick. "Meaning and 'The Masque of the Red Death'." *Tulane Studies in English*, Vol. XIII (1963): 59-69.
Survey of representative critical statements on "The Masque of the Red Death" and an interpretation which argues that "life itself . . . is the Red Death, the one 'affliction' shared by all mankind."

Rourke, Constance, "I Hear America Singing." In her *American Humor*, pp. 163-203. New York: Harcourt, Brace and Co., 1931.
Considers the relationship of Poe's stories to conventions of oral storytelling in nineteenth-century America. Rourke concludes that "Poe seems near those story-tellers of the West who described wild and perverse actions with blank undisturbed countenances, and whose insistent use of the first person brought them to the brink of inner revelation."

Symons, Julian. *The Tell-Tale Heart: The Life and Works of Edgar Allan Poe*. New York: Harper & Row, 1978, 259 p.
Critical biography designed to isolate discussion of Poe's life from interpretation of his works.

Thompson, G. R. *Poe's Fiction: Romantic Irony in the Gothic Tales*. Madison: The University of Wisconsin Press, 1973, 254 p.
Contends that in both his Gothic and his comic stories Poe employed a conscious irony derived from writers of the German Romantic movement. Thompson argues that "critics have underestimated [Poe's] complexity and subtlety in the short story, misconstrued ironic techniques as flaws, and ignored an important aspect of Romanticism that provides a historical context for reading Poe as an ironist instead of a completely serious Gothicist."

Thompson, G. R., and Lokke, Virgil L. *Ruined Eden of the Present: Hawthorne, Melville, and Poe*. West Lafayette, Ind.: Purdue University Press, 1981, 383 p.

Essays on Poe by Barton Levi St. Armand, Quinn, G. R. Thompson, and Benjamin Franklin Fisher IV.

Woodberry, George E. *Edgar Allan Poe*. 1885. Reprint. New York: AMS Press, 1968, 354 p.
One of the earliest full-length examinations of Poe and his work.

Woodson, Thomas, ed. *The Fall of the House of Usher: A Collection of Critical Essays*. Englewood Cliffs, N.J.: Prentice-Hall, 1969, 122 p.
Important interpretations by Caroline Gordon and Allen Tate, Darrel Abel, Harry Levin, and Edward H. Davidson.

Zayed, Georges. *The Genius of Edgar Allan Poe*. Cambridge, Mass.: Schenkman Publishing Co., 1985, 223 p.
Critical study divided into two parts, the first tracing the development of Poe's reputation in France and the second examining his achievements as a critic, short story writer, poet, and philosopher.

James (Grover) Thurber

1894-1961

American essayist, short story, fable, and fairy tale writer, and dramatist.

Critics acknowledge Thurber as one of the foremost humorists in American literature. As a staff writer for the *New Yorker* magazine during the late 1920s and early 1930s, Thurber established his reputation with stories and essays that combine an eccentric comic sensibility with a clear, sophisticated literary style. He also won acclaim as a cartoonist, often illustrating his writings with line drawings of men, women, and dogs that his fellow humorist Dorothy Parker described as looking like ''unbaked cookies.'' Many of his stories are wry vignettes about upper-middle-class intellectual New York society. *My Life and Hard Times,* in contrast, focuses on Thurber's youth in Columbus, Ohio, while other works, such as the mock-Aesopian allegories in *Fables for Our Time and Famous Poems Illustrated* and *Further Fables for Our Time,* display his gifts for social satire, wordplay, and fantasy. What most intrigues critics about his work, however, is the dark, unsettling view of the modern world that underlies his comedy. In short fictional works such as ''The Catbird Seat,'' ''The Unicorn in the Garden,'' and his most famous story, ''The Secret Life of Walter Mitty,'' Thurber used humor to explore the conflicts and neurotic tensions that he believed characterize twentieth-century life, particularly the phenomenon he termed ''the war between men and women.'' ''The central concern of Thurber's best stories,'' according to critic Robert H. Elias, ''is nothing less than the predicament of the individual in our gadget-cluttered, career-woman-minded, theory-burdened time.''

Thurber began his career as a newspaper reporter in Ohio and New York; he also spent time in France as a correspondent for the Paris *Tribune*. Harold Ross, founder of the *New Yorker,* hired Thurber as managing editor in 1927, but Thurber soon joined the magazine's distinguished list of writers, which included Robert Benchley, Clarence Day, and Thurber's close friend and mentor, E. B. White. White's simple, concise prose style had a tremendous influence on Thurber's work. ''Until I learned discipline from studying Andy White's stuff,'' Thurber commented, ''I was a careless, nervous, headlong writer, trailing the phrases and rhythms of Henry James, Hergesheimer, Henly, and my favorite English teacher at Ohio State, Joe Taylor.'' Thurber remained a lifelong admirer of James, whose influence is evident in Thurber's work, particularly such stories as ''The Interview'' and ''A Final Note on Chanda Bell.''

As editor of the *New Yorker,* Ross steered his contributors away from the type of conventional, plot-centered short stories featured in other magazines of the era. Thurber and White helped to develop the *New Yorker*-style ''sketch,'' a casual, loosely structured essay or short fictional work. Thurber did not distinguish between his stories and nonfiction essays; he referred to all his short works as ''pieces.'' This approach is evident in the collection of autobiographical sketches that many critics consider his finest work, *My Life and Hard Times*. Thurber added outrageous exaggerations and often outright inventions to factual incidents, producing such examples of semi-fictional *tour-de-force* as ''The Night the Bed Fell'' and ''The Day the Dam Broke.'' These pieces also evidence Thurber's approach to humor: he related wild or strange incidents in a deadpan manner and delighted in the absurd, as in the antics of the Get-Ready Man in ''The Car We Had to Push.'' Mordant irony underlies much of his work, exemplified by the sardonic mottoes that conclude his fables, such as ''Early to rise and early to bed makes a male healthy and wealthy and dead.''

The Granger Collection, New York

Commentators identify a recurring figure in Thurber's pieces whom they refer to as ''the little man'' or ''the Thurber male'': a timid, neurotic middle-aged man typified by the daydreaming protagonist of ''The Secret Life of Walter Mitty.'' With quiet irony, the narrative focus of the piece shifts between Mitty's meek, ineffectual behavior as he follows his wife on a shopping trip and the wildly heroic fantasies which constantly interrupt his thoughts. Mitty, like Erwin Martin in ''The Catbird Seat,'' Mr. Monroe in *The Owl in the Attic, and Other Perplexities,* and many other Thurber heroes, is an eccentric individual struggling to maintain his integrity, as well as his sanity, against the oppressive forces of modern society. Society's main oppressors in Thurber's universe are women, who represent the stifling effect of civilization on the male's natural biological and creative instincts. In his fables, the Mr. and Mrs. Monroe tales in *The Owl in the Attic,* and a number of stories including ''The Breaking Up of the Winships'' and ''The Private Life of Mr. Bidwell,'' Thurber depicts marriage as an unpleasant series of power struggles between husbands and wives. The typical Thurber woman, such as Mrs. Mitty or Ulgine Barrows in ''The Catbird Seat,'' is portrayed as an obnoxious, domineering bully, and for this reason Thurber has often been accused of misogyny. When interviewed late in life, however, he declared himself a feminist. ''If I have sometimes seemed to make fun of Woman,'' he remarked, ''I assure you it has only been for the purpose of egging her on.''

A conscientious craftsman, Thurber often reworked his material through several versions before he considered it worthy of publication. ''The Secret Life of Walter Mitty,'' for instance, a story of about 4,000 words, was written in fifteen drafts and took several weeks to complete. Thurber reported that in an early version of the story, Mitty becomes involved in a nightclub brawl with Hemingway, but Thurber's wife, Helen, objected that the scene was not appropriate to the tone of the story. ''Well, you know how it is when your wife is right,'' Thurber recalled. ''You grouse around the house for a week and then you follow her advice.''

Critics often distinguish between earlier and later phases of Thurber's career. In the period between the late twenties and early 1940s, Thurber achieved international fame with such collections as *My Life and Hard Times* and *The Middle-Aged Man on the Flying Trapeze: A Collection of Short Pieces,* as well as with his cartoons and a successful play, *The Male Animal,* which he coauthored with Elliot Nugent. While the dark themes of alienation and gender warfare are evident in his early pieces, including ''A Box to Hide In'' and ''A Couple of Hamburgers,'' Thurber softens his baleful view of contemporary life with glimpses of romantic optimism. This changed in the 1940s, when Thurber, whose left eye had been destroyed in a childhood accident, began to suffer a series of illnesses that would leave him permanently blind. His unsettling story ''The Whip-Poor-Will'' reflects the severe emotional stress he experienced at this time. By developing new work methods, writing with crayon on yellow paper, using magnifying glasses, and finally dictating to secretaries after his vision failed completely, Thurber found he could continue drawing and writing. In this later period, critics observe, Thurber's literary style reflects his new methods of conceptualizing his stories. Rather than visualizing dramatic scenes, for example, he relies on dialogue to establish character and suggest action, as in ''The Interview'' and ''The Cane in the Corridor.'' Also, he indulges in extravagant wordplay and literary allusion to an extent that some critics deem excessive. Troubled by failing health and disgusted by events such as the anticommunist purges of the 1950s, Thurber in his last years expressed a new sense of pessimism and misanthropy in his work. The change in his temperament is evident in the contrast between the relatively good-natured irony of *Fables for Our Time,* published in 1940, and the *Further Fables for Our Times* of 1956, with its bitter political and social commentary.

Although he took great pride in his literary accomplishments, Thurber made no attempt to write a ''serious'' work; he was content with his reputation as an author of diverting light sketches. As a result, most critics have regarded him as a typical *New Yorker* writer, a composer of slick entertainment according to the magazine's set formula. Reviewers during the 1930s and 1940s wrote of his work with affection and delight, but offered little significant commentary. Some later critics attempt a more sober and scholarly approach, usually choosing to examine the darker thematic aspects of his work. Thurber has been compared with modernist writers such as James Joyce and T. S. Eliot for his wordplay and his recognition of the absurdity of the human condition—Peter DeVries called him a ''comic Prufrock''—and other critics have likened him to the surrealists and Dadaists for his sometimes wild distortions of speech and reality.

Thurber's reputation, however, rests on his ability to express the humor of a neurotic and anxious time, particularly in his most notable works, including *My Life and Hard Times,* his fables and drawings, and a few short stories, all represented in his collection *The Thurber Carnival*. Perhaps his most popular creation is Walter Mitty the daydreamer, who from his introduction in 1943 has remained an American cultural archetype. Although critics celebrate Thurber for his wit and eccentric humor, it is his latent seriousness that is perhaps most valued by critics. ''Thurber's genius,'' concluded John Updike, ''was to make of our despair a humorous fable.''

(See also *Contemporary Literary Criticism,* Vols. 5, 11, 25; *Contemporary Authors,* Vols. 73-76; *Contemporary Authors New Revision Series,* Vol. 17; *Something about the Author,* Vol. 13; and *Dictionary of Literary Biography,* Vols. 4, 11, 22.)

PRINCIPAL WORKS

SHORT FICTION AND SKETCHES

The Owl in the Attic, and Other Perplexities 1931
My Life and Hard Times 1933
The Middle-Aged Man on the Flying Trapeze: A Collection of Short Pieces 1935
Let Your Mind Alone! And Other More or Less Inspirational Pieces 1937
Cream of Thurber 1939
Fables for Our Time and Famous Poems Illustrated 1940
My World—And Welcome to It 1942
The Thurber Carnival **1945**
The Beast in Me, and Other Animals: A New Collection of Pieces and Drawings about Human Beings and Less Alarming Creatures 1948
Thurber Country: A New Collection of Pieces about Males and Females, Mainly of Our Own Species 1953
Further Fables for Our Time 1956
Alarms and Diversions 1957
Lanterns and Lances 1961
Credos and Curios 1962
Vintage Thurber: A Collection of the Best Writings and Drawings. 2 vols. 1963

OTHER MAJOR WORKS

Is Sex Necessary? Or Why You Feel the Way You Do [with E. B. White] (satire) 1929
The Seal in the Bedroom, and Other Predicaments (drawings) 1932
The Last Flower (fable) 1939
The Male Animal [with Elliot Nugent] (drama) 1940
Many Moons (fairy tale) 1943
The Great Quillow (fairy tale) 1944
The 13 Clocks (fairy tale) 1950
The Thurber Album (memoirs) 1952

The Wonderful O (fairy tale) 1957
The Years with Ross (memoirs) 1959
A Thurber Carnival (drama) 1960

ROBERT M. COATES (essay date 1933)

[*Coates was an American novelist, nonfiction writer, and critic. Thurber's friendship with Coates began when they met in Paris during the 1920s and continued when they later became colleagues at the* New Yorker, *where Coates was an art critic and staff writer. The following excerpt is from Coates's appreciative review of* My Life and Hard Times.]

Isn't it about time, people have been demanding lately—with, it must be confessed, occasionally a hint of grimness in their tones—that we discovered just what this man Thurber is up to? Those stories of ladies who supervise their own axe-murders, and of men looking for little boxes to hide in: what do they mean? Those drawings, of crowds running as if the wind harried them, of people collapsing in slow involutions over obscure problems of their own: what do they signify?

Whither is he leading us? Or, to put it another way, is he leading us anywhere? We have only to open [***My Life and Hard Times***] to come upon a clue. There we find him, in one of its opening pages, describing as if inadvertently a curious hallucination that often overcomes him—a fear that he is being followed " . . . by little men padding along in single file, about a foot and a half high, large-eyed, and whiskered." In the next breath, of course, he is speaking of Ford Madox Ford and Walter Lippmann, in the next of his (Thurber's) digestion, and in the next after that (though by then he's getting a little bit breathless himself) of the shrinkage of the earth's crust. But the reader will not be misled by such tergiversations. We have seen generals who were at times hard put to it to determine whether they were leading an army or being pursued by a mob, and to the serious student of psychoanalysis (there must still be some serious students of psychoanalysis left, mustn't there?) it will be obvious that Mr. Thurber is in something of the same predicament. He isn't really trying to lead anybody anywhere. Mostly, he is trying to escape.

But then, one may find many clues to an understanding of this strange personality, in a reading of this chronicle of the author's younger, more settled years. For, unlike most of us, it wasn't till he was nearing middle age that he took to wandering—with what results his epilogue sets forth. His youth he spent in Columbus, Ohio (in itself a feat to tax the strongest), and had nobody but his grandfather to worry about. To be sure, his grandfather was the victim of a slight obsession: namely, that the Civil War was still being fought, usually just outside the front door—and to the sensitive artist, particularly in the formative period of his life, this would be upsetting. But when you have added to this an uncle who suffered from chestnut blight and an aunt who whanged shoes up and down the hall at night to scare away burglars; a succession of hired girls, some of whom saw ghosts and others who did their dusting at three in the morning—well, you get some idea of what the boy Thurber was up against. . . . Mr. Thurber came through it all, unscathed or nearly so—through the night the bed fell on father, and the night the ghost got in, through wild escapades with electric runabouts and still wilder ones with roller coasters, through even that historic day when the whole town of Columbus went momentarily cuckoo, and ran madly en masse from a dam that hadn't burst—came through it to write about these youthful adventures, in the pleasantest possible mixture of fantasy and understanding, one of the funniest books of recent times.

. . . Oh, what the hell! Let's say *the* funniest. (pp. 137-38)

Robert M. Coates, "James G. Thurber, the Man," in The New Republic, *Vol. LXXVII, No. 993, December 13, 1933, pp. 137-38.*

DAVID GARNETT (essay date 1937)

[*Garnett was a British novelist and nonfiction writer whose works are noted for their distinctively clear, compressed style. Garnett, according to Thurber's biographer Charles S. Holmes, was one of the earliest commentators to engage in serious discussion of Thurber's style. In the following excerpt from a review of* Let Your Mind Alone!, *Garnett surveys the progress of Thurber's career.*]

"The learned Doctor James Thurber," as his publishers call him, is at present, I think, the most original and humorous writer living, so it is interesting to see what will become of him. Great humorists start as solitary men, their laughter is first thought to be a sign of insanity; presently everyone begins to see their jokes, or laughs with them, and they become pneumatic cushions for humanity. How will Thurber support the massive weight with which we threaten him? . . . ***My Life and Hard Times*** was, as its title indicates, an autobiographical sketch of early years in Columbus, Ohio, and is one of the funniest and most lovable books I know; the humour is intensely original and individual; every man, woman and dog in it has an overpowering personality. ***The Middle-aged Man on the Flying Trapeze*** is a collection of stories of varying quality. Some of them have an extremely penetrating savage humour of the kind which

Thurber, age twelve.

scares the ordinary person. Women are roughly handled, and, in **"A Box to Hide In,"** Thurber shows what he feels of the attractions of the world. That story is, incidentally, one of the most alarming things in literature. But since we all long for a chance to laugh, the crowd has been growing and Thurber has now a very large audience. He himself is feeling more comfortable, and he naturally has become less savage and more serious. . . .

I really enjoy Thurber most (and feel he is on safest ground) when he doesn't deal with ideas or institutions, but with personal experiences, and when he's not trying to be funny at all. Three such chapters in [***Let Your Mind Alone! And Other More or Less Inspirational Pieces***] have for me an inexplicable charm. The **"Wood Duck"** is simply a piece of realism—describing a wild duck which left the woods, preferring to live near a roadside apple-stand on a concrete highway, black in the centre with the dropped oil of a million cars. It is a perfect short dramatic story. **"Memories of D. H. Lawrence"** and **"Doc Marlowe"** and **"The Wood Duck"** make me believe that Thurber will have sufficient strength of character and is enough of an artist to refuse to be forcibly made a Twain of, and that he will develop along his own lines as a first-rate writer and not as a funny man or a prophet.

David Garnett, "Books in General," in The New Statesman & Nation, *n.s. Vol. XIV, No. 345, October 2, 1937, p. 490.*

WALTER BLAIR (essay date 1942)

[Blair, an American critic, has written several works on American humorists. In the following excerpt, he contrasts Thurber's ineffectual, beleaguered heroes with the cocky, tall-tale-telling characters common to nineteenth-century American humor.]

During most of his career, in spite of the fact that Mr. Thurber has expressed himself in several mediums, he has kept on saying practically the same thing. In a preface to his comic autobiography [***My Life and Hard Times***], he has written some keen things about humorists in general which apply very well to him in particular when he writes in the first person. Of humorists, he says:

> They lead . . . an existence of jumpiness and apprehension. . . . In the house of Life they have the feeling that they have never taken off their overcoats. . . . Authors of such pieces have . . . a genius for getting into minor difficulties: they walk into the wrong apartments, they drink furniture polish for stomach bitters, they drive their cars into the prize tulip beds of haughty neighbors. . . .
>
> Such a writer moves restlessly wherever he goes, ready to get the hell out at the drop of a pie-pan or the lift of a skirt. His gestures are the ludicrous reflexes of the maladjusted; his repose is the momentary inertia of the nonplussed. . . . He talks largely about small matters and smally about great affairs.

The point is that . . . the character in this humorist's skits has insomnia in a bed of neuroses. . . . Furthermore, as his analysis of a humorist shows, Mr. Thurber . . . is victimized by inanimate things; he lives a life which is ruined by tremendous trifles. (pp. 284-85)

[The] pitiable fellow suffered because he was victimized not only by chairs and clocks but also by women. In the battle of the sexes, he saw, males were doomed to helpless and ignoble defeat. In an essay, "Women Go On Forever," noting the way females outlived males, he bravely pushed on to the inescapable conclusion that "Man's day is indeed done; the epoch of Woman is upon us." Look at a man, he says, and you will see signs of a crack-up—"an air of uncertainty, an expression of futility, a general absence of 'hold.'" Look at a woman, though, and you will see that she is strong exactly where he is weak.

It seems clear, too, that Mr. Thurber has a good deal of trouble with machines. "No man," he says, "who has wrestled with a self-adjusting card table can ever be quite the man he once was." He shows fear of all the mechanical devices he meets "because he recognizes the menace of the machine as such." (pp. 286-87)

When Mr. Thurber writes not in the first person but in the third, he is likely to take as his hero—in the broad sense of the term—a pestered little man much like the "I" who appears in his essays. In a whole series of stories about one Mr. Monroe, that gentleman proves that in him—to quote his creator—

> we have . . . the makings of a character study—or would have except for the fact that Mr. Monroe didn't really have any character. He had a certain charm, yes; but no character. He avoided difficult situations; he had no talent for firm resolution; he immolated badly; and he wasn't even very good at renunciation, except when he was tired and a little sick.

Time after time, one sees Mr. Monroe forming a high opinion of himself, only to have it flop down when he fails to justify it. When, for example, he took charge of some moving-men at work in his apartment, he started with confidence to issue orders. But shortly he had so much trouble making up his mind how they should be directed that "the 'chief' and 'mister' with which they had first addressed him changed to 'buddy' and 'pardner'" and finally, as Mr. Monroe strove desperately for an air of dignity and authority, to "sonny." Or, just when he had managed to make himself believe that he was a great one to get along in a summer cottage, he was driven into a panic by his fear that there was a bat in his room. Always, insignificant little things made a shambles of his dignity and self-respect. (pp. 287-88)

In typical pieces of writing, then, Mr. Thurber has not been likely to espouse common sense. Since, according to the way he has been looking at it, no man is wise except in his own foolish daydreams, the humorist usually has found it impossible to picture a character who, with plain horse sense, finds the answers to the questions life puts to him. A Davy Crockett or a Hosea Biglow, if he happened to stray into one of Mr. Thurber's typical pieces, might think he knew the answers—probably would be cocksure about knowing them, but the whole point of a story about either of them, as Mr. Thurber told it, would be to show that the character had too high a notion of himself. Thus he would write humor of a pattern very different from that in [works of earlier humorists].

His "I," his Mr. Monroe, and his Tommy Turner, in other words, are related not to the horse-sense characters but to the fool characters of the old homespun tradition. However, they contrast even with these—contrast sharply. It is obvious, of course, that they have nothing like the same rural background. Moreover, as Mr. Bernard De Voto has said, "The literary comedians . . . after the Civil War presented themselves as Perfect Fools, whereas our comedians present themselves as Perfect Neurotics.'' In other words, these humorous figures are more than stupid: they are close to insanity.

The difference goes even deeper. When Mark Twain sentimentalized over the tomb of Adam, the joke was that Mark the fool was set off against the canny horse-sense character (Clemens) who knew all the time that Mark was making a dunce of himself. The fool was funny largely because the reader realized that his creator was a wise man who amusingly contrasted with the fool because he knew the answers. But Mr. Thurber is superior to his creation only in one thing—that he knows that his hero is foolish in the belief that there are any answers. This gives Mr. Thurber a chance to stand back somewhat from the poor suffering fool and laugh at him. ''Humor,'' this comic writer has said, ''is a kind of emotional chaos, told about calmly and quietly in retrospect.'' The chaos comes about because the character struggles against inevitable frustration. The calmness, possibly, is the result of the knowledge that the struggle naught availeth.

What students of Mr. Thurber's life and writings stress is that the humorist writes of sufferers who are like him. . . . Instead, then, of developing a chump character unlike himself, Mr. Thurber develops one like himself and, what is more, like all mankind. (pp. 290-92)

[In Thurber and Robert Benchley] satire has been expanded so far that it has lost a great deal of its sting. Old-timers made fun of only a small group of men—the ones who did not use their gumption to arrive at sound opinions. These modern humorists make fun of all mankind, and of all its opinions except one—the opinion that no ideas are very sound. Mankind is made up, they hint, of Benchleys and Thurbers who lack their skill to record its follies in tranquillity. (p. 293)

[Thurber's] recent collection called ***Fables for Our Time*** has as its burden that common-sense truisms in a large number of instances just do not work out.

Such futilitarians as these two humorists, in short, take little stock in Josh Billings' old-fashioned claim that ''you hav got to be wize before you can be witty.'' Their point seems to be that nobody is wise, and nobody can be. (p. 294)

Walter Blair, ''Crazy Men,'' in his Horse Sense in American Humor from Benjamin Franklin to Ogden Nash, *The University of Chicago Press, 1942, pp. 274-94.*

PETER DE VRIES (essay date 1943)

[*In his highly acclaimed comic novels, including* The Mackerel Plaza *(1958),* The Cat's Pajamas *(1968), and* The Prick of Noon *(1985), De Vries comments on contemporary moral values with **satirical portraits of upper-middle-class life in urban northeastern** America. De Vries was Thurber's colleague on the* New Yorker *editorial staff. In the following excerpt from an essay originally published in* Poetry *magazine in 1943, he compares Thurber's style of humor with the poetic vision of T. S. Eliot.*]

I am not sure what poetic sensitivity is, but I am practically certain Thurber has got it. Though artists work in different forms there is a contemporary tissue which connects them, and the things they have in common spiritually are greater than the differences among them technically. Thurber has more in common with modern poets than, for instance, he has with any other present-day humorist you might mention.

I do not know whether the critical landlords of Axel's Castle—our customary symbol for Symbolism—list him among the occupants or not, or whether they are aware he is on the premises. . . . If fancy and the imagination and ''subjective'' as opposed to ''objective'' reality is the emphasis we are talking about, then Thurber can certainly be included. The filaments of individual sensibility are seldom more sharply wrought, or more constantly manifest, than in his work. The psychological nuance is rarely more intricately drawn, even in those tidy sketches in which he is reducing it to absurdity. His inner states and private convolutions are, if not as profound, as skillfully projected as any. He may be least of the family—indeed perhaps just a quizzical lodger cutting up in some remote corner of the premises—but this is the address all right.

It is hard to think of anyone who more closely resembles the Prufrock of Eliot than the middle-aged man on the flying trapeze. This preoccupied figure is Prufrock's comic counterpart, not in intensity of course, but in detail. There is, for instance, the same dominating sense of Predicament. The same painful and fastidious self-inventory, the same detailed anxiety; the same immersion in weary minutiae, the same self-disparagement, the same wariness of the evening's company. And the same fear, in summary, that someone—in Thurber's case a brash halfback or maybe even a woman—will ''drop a question on his plate.'' (pp. 37-8)

If Eliot symbolizes his spiritual intricacies in terms of mythological beings . . . , Thurber can personify his own modest nemeses in figures as concrete, always afraid he is ''being softly followed by little men padding along in single file, about a foot and a half high, large-eyed and whiskered.'' This ability to project the fanciful enables him to get pretty much the effect of poetry itself. . . . Poetry is where you find it, and I find it in **''The Black Magic of Barney Haller,''** one of the best of those exquisite little sketches which see more drafts than many poems. You will remember it as the account of the caretaker whom storms follow home, whom Thurber suspects of trafficking with the devil and exorcises by incantations of Frost and Lewis Carroll.

The title of Eliot's poem is ironic—it is a ''love song.'' It is certain that Prufrock never got around to asking his lady the question: the masculinity of this parched sophisticate seems specifically inoperative. In that other landmark of Eliot's early period, *The Portrait of a Lady,* the female is roundly satirized, but the narrator is singularly unable to cope with her; there is a ''sensation of being ill at ease.'' Is there a sensation of which Thurber has given more repeated illustration? . . . The woman satirized in *The Portrait of a Lady* was trite, but she was alive and certainly operating conversationally, and the women lampooned in Thurber are alive and operating too, at their worst when they are a little too much like the preoccupied men (like the woman who came up and announced to the man shrinking in the chair: ''I have a neurosis''), at their best possessing a certain virility lacking in the male. They perch confidently on the arms of sofas, drag their men to bridge parties, drive cars well, are in the embalming game. The male is on the wane, corroded with introspection, deflated by all his own inefficient efficiency, without ''strength to force the moment to its crisis,'' his love lyric in desuetude. There is a sketch in which Thurber does not want to go some place—out some place, perhaps a bridge party or something like that—and he says he would rather stay home. ''That's the place for a man to be anyhow—home.'' It is not a long step from there to: ''A man's place is in the home,'' a generalization the feminists of the hour might like to adopt as a battle cry. (pp. 39-40)

"The poet of *The Waste Land,*" writes Edmund Wilson, "is living half the time in the real world of contemporary London and half the time in the haunted wilderness of medieval legend." Thurber too is half the time God knows where. . . . Reality in Thurber undergoes filterings and transmutations as curious and as abrupt. . . . Confronted by details, moments, of that dull environment with which he is long weary of coping, he contrives his own little substitutions, and his transformer is always at work altering, to suit his fancy, the currents of experience. With characteristic self-deploration he admits to the inanity of many of the oddments that "slip by the guardian at the portal of his thoughts," but vouches for their tenacity. Thus

A message for Captain Bligh
And a greeting to Franchot Tone!

sung to a certain part of *For He's a Jolly Good Fellow,* occupied him for some time. A connoisseur of mispronunciation, he was happy when a malapropping domestic called the icebox "doom shaped," thus investing it with a quality which fascinated him for days, and by a similar alchemy exercised by Barney Haller, the caretaker already mentioned, there are warbs in the garrick, grotches in the wood and fletchers on the lawn—all details possessing a charm with which their real-life counterparts cannot compete. To make the transformation complete, the maid has only to step on his glasses. Then do the flags of South American republics fly over the roofs of Manhattan banks, cats cross the street in striped barrels, old women with parasols walk through the sides of trucks, bridges rise "lazily into the air like balloons." (pp. 41-2)

I referred, with rather loose whimsicality I suppose, to Thurber as jester in Axel's Castle, and his work may be a rivulet running "individual sensibility" off into a kind of *reductio ad absurdum*—not that some of the serious exponents of Symbolism haven't already done so. But whatever the excesses of Symbolism may have been, it has not only made a notable contribution to modern literature but by its emphasis on subjective experience has helped us to a richer idea of what "reality" is. Just as poetry and profit are where you find them, reality is what you make it. The angle of refraction according to the perceiving psyche is *always* there, and the individual's extracting from the world around him constitutes an experience that is itself a reality; a point which modern artists have been trying to make for over a generation. (p. 42)

Peter De Vries, "James Thurber: The Comic Prufrock," in Thurber: A Collection of Critical Essays, *edited by Charles S. Holmes, Prentice-Hall, Inc., 1974, pp. 37-43.*

MALCOLM COWLEY (essay date 1945)

[*Cowley has made valuable contributions to contemporary letters with his editions of important American authors, his writings as a literary critic for the* New Republic, *and above all, with his chronicles and criticism of modern American literature. A close friend of Thurber, Cowley was also his editor at the* New Republic. *In the following excerpt, he praises Thurber's literary style in* A Thurber Carnival.]

Most of [the pieces in ***The Thurber Carnival***] might have been written to illustrate the difference between wit and humor. Wit, says the *Shorter Oxford,* is "that quality of speech or writing which consists in the apt association of thought and expression, calculated to surprise by its unexpectedness; later always with ref. to the utterance of brilliant or sparkling things in an amusing way." Humor, says *Webster's Collegiate,* "implies, commonly, broader human sympathies than wit, and a more kindly sense of the incongruous, often blended with pathos." There is not much wit in Thurber's writing, although there is plenty of it in his conversation. Occasionally in a story he permits himself a relatively brilliant or sparkling metaphor—he says, for example, "This midsummer Saturday had got off to a sulky start, and now, at three in the afternoon, it sat, sticky and restive, on our laps"; but for the most part he confines himself to the almost businesslike description of incongruous situations that are often blended with pathos.

He doesn't always bother to be funny. Eight of the pieces, by my count, are quite serious in effect and intention, and several of the others balance on the edge between farce and disaster, like a clown on a very high trapeze. Four of them—all funny ones—end with the murder of the hero, and two—both serious—end with his natural death (one of these last heroes is a dog). Four others end with dreams of killing or being killed, and two with the hero of one and the villainess of the other reduced to raving madness. There are fifteen pieces—almost half the selections in the book—that are largely based on nightmares, hallucinations or elaborate and cruel practical jokes. Entering Thurber's middle-class world is like wandering into a psychiatric ward and not being quite sure whether you are a visitor or an inmate. The author himself bustles around in a white jacket, but sometimes he stops to say in a pleasant, matter-of-fact voice, "You know, they don't suspect. They think I'm a doctor."

He writes so naturally and conversationally that it is hard to realize how much work goes into his stories. His art is in fact extremely conscious, and it is based on a wide knowledge of contemporary writing. In a letter to Fred B. Millett, written in 1939, Thurber listed some of his favorite authors: Henry James first of all, then Conrad Aiken, Hemingway, Fitzgerald, Edmund Wilson and Willa Cather, among others. The list would indicate, he said, "that I like the perfectly done, the well ordered, as against the sprawling chunk of life. . . . I also owe a debt to E. B. White . . . whose perfect clarity of expression is it seems to me equaled by very few and surpassed by simply nobody. . . . I came to the *New Yorker* a writer of journalese and it was my study of White's writing, I think, that helped me to straighten out my prose so that people could see what it meant." Besides learning to write with an easy flow and coherence that very few authors achieve, he also learned to omit everything inessential, including the winks, the rib-nudgings and the philosophical remarks of older American humorists. He achieves a sort of costly simplicity, like that of well tailored clothes or good conversation.

Within his fixed limits of length and sympathy and subject, one feels almost nothing but admiration for Thurber's work; one's only regret is that he hasn't made the limits broader. Other things being equal, a good long story is better than a good short one; and most of Thurber's begin and end within 3,000 words, a convenient length for the *New Yorker.* Most of his characters are upper-middle-class couples from the upper Middle West, who have moved to New York, prospered financially and bought or rented houses in Connecticut. His favorite subject is their domestic quarrels. . . . (p. 362)

The women in [Thurber's] stories are hard, logical, aggressive. . . . The husbands, on the other hand, are widely read, dreamy, introspective; they are helpless without their wives, but at the same time they try to escape into an imagined world of men. Thus Walter Mitty, driving the family car, pictures himself as the commander of a huge, hurtling eight-engined navy hydroplane. He imagines the crew looking up and grinning as a storm beats against the wings. "The Old Man'll get us through," they say to one another. "The Old Man ain't afraid of Hell!" . . . "Not so fast! You're driving too fast," says Mrs. Mitty; and the hydroplane of Walter Mitty's dream comes hurtling down.

Almost all of Thurber's heroes are dreamers and escapists, even when they are happily married. The author defends them in his illustrated ***Fables for Our Time.*** The moral of one fable is, "Who flies afar from the sphere of our sorrow is here today and here tomorrow"; of another, "Run, don't walk, to the nearest desert island." In his autobiographical sketches, Thurber describes two easy methods for escaping into a fantastic world: by sound and by sight. The first method consists in misunderstanding or misinterpreting words and phrases. Thus, he hears a station agent repeating time and again over the telephone, "Conductor Reagan on the 142 has the lady the office was asking about"; and soon, brooding over the sentence, he imagines himself among silky, desperate spies. On another occasion his maid, who always mispronounces words, comes to his study and says, "They are here with the reeves." His hired man, who has the same bad habit, tells him, "I go hunt grotches in de voods," and again, "We go to the garrick now and become warbs." The servants are referring to wreaths and crotches and wasps in the garret; but before Thurber succeeds in unraveling their remarks, they have sent him wandering off into surrealist landscapes that he compares, at one point, to the secret world of Salvador Dali.

His other means of escape is simply by taking off his glasses. Because his vision is defective, the whole world thereupon assumes a different shape for him. . . .

There is in fact a curious similarity between one type of fantastic American humor and the current in European poetry that is represented in various phases by Rimbaud and Lautréamont, by expressionism, dadaism and surrealism. None of these schools has flourished here (although surrealism now has more disciples than the others possessed), and I think the reason may be that our sense of rightness is offended when we hear a young man proclaiming that he has a wild, satanic imagination whose disorder he finds sacred, and then describing his dreams. But the truth is that we enjoy fantasy much more than the French; and we gladly listen to the same type of dreams when they are described by Thurber in a matter-of-fact voice and with a self-deprecatory air. (p. 363)

Malcolm Cowley, "James Thurber's Dream Book," in The New Republic, *Vol. 112, No. 11, March 12, 1945, pp. 362-63.*

OTTO FRIEDRICH (essay date 1955)

[*Friedrich, an American journalist, critic, and nonfiction writer, has been an editor and staff writer at* Time, The Saturday Evening Post, *and other periodicals. In the following excerpt, he identifies characteristics of Thurber's style, such as his penchant for trivial subject matter. Thurber offered a witty response to Friedrich's essay in his sketch "The Tyranny of Trivia" (see excerpt below dated 1955).*]

One morning in 1939, an anonymous "little old gentleman" woke up and opened the window to let in the sun. The black widow spider that slashed at him from the window ledge represented only the first of a series of misfortunes. His grandson pulled the chair out from under him, and he sprained his hip. Out in the street, he was tripped by a hoop "sent rolling at him with a kind of disinterested deliberation by a grim little girl." A robber held up the old man, but the victim continued on his way toward "a little park with many trees, which was to him a green isle in the sea."

"When at last the old gentleman staggered into the little park, which had been to him a fountain and a shrine, he saw that half the trees had been killed by a blight, and the other half by a bug. Their leaves were gone and they no longer afforded any protection from the skies, so that the hundred planes which appeared suddenly overhead had an excellent view of the little old gentleman through their bombing-sights."

There ends the story of **"The Green Isle in the Sea,"** one of James Thurber's ***Fables for Our Time*** and a dismal reflection of our time. "The world is so full of a number of things, I am sure we should all be as happy as kings," says the moral, "and you know how happy kings are."

"There is no safety in numbers," goes another moral to another fable for our time, "or in anything else."

"You can fool too many of the people too much of the time," goes a third.

"Run, don't walk, to the nearest desert island."

The old gentleman, the morning sunlight and the trees that once grew provide evidence that our world and our times are not totally evil, but the manifest preponderance of evil, the painfulness and ugliness of life, make it doubtful not only whether life can continue but whether it is worth continuing. (pp. 159-60)

The scientist [in **"Interview with a Lemming"**], who has made a study of lemmings, says he understands everything about them except their curious practice of rushing down to the sea and drowning themselves.

"How curious," replies the lemming. "The one thing I don't understand is why you humans don't." (p. 161)

Thurber often appears limited to a world of suburban homes and cocktail parties, a world of upper-middle-class New York. Like any major artist, however, Thurber can imply the general in describing the specific. In portraying a limited area, he can show a whole era of confusion and misery. Kirk [in **"One Is a Wanderer"**], like anyone else, is miserable because he is confused and lonely, he doesn't know what he wants and he has nowhere to go. He doesn't want to see the people whom he knows, and he doesn't want to do the work that he has to do. Instead, he wanders from a movie that he doesn't want to see to a hotel lobby that he doesn't want to get drunk in, through the slush of February in the streets.

Being alone is a terrible state. Almost anything, one tells oneself, would be better than this. One can, then, turn again towards death, like the lemming, or take instead the milder anesthesia of hiding in a large box. "I still have this overpowering urge to hide in a box," says the narrator of **"A Box to Hide In."** "Maybe it will all go away, maybe I'll be all right. Maybe it will get worse. It's hard to say."

Since most people are as reluctant to stay hidden in a box as they are to jump into the sea, however, the escape from loneliness leads more often into the jungle of courtship. . . . Mr. Monroe plans to telephone a girl who aroused him at a party the night before, but "to fortify himself for this adventure . . . he got out a volume of Henry James. . . . He lighted a cigar and began reading *The Golden Bowl.*" In **"The Evening's at**

Thurber and friend, by Thurber. The Bettmann Archive, Inc.

Seven," the hero visits a former love, but an intrusion by the woman's sister cuts off the brief and rather emotional episode. The man goes back to his wife, arriving promptly at seven-thirty, the time that supper is served every evening in the hotel. "The waitress said clam chowder tonight and consomme: you always take the clam chowder, ain't I right? No, he said, I'll have the consomme."

The mood is one of quiet melancholy, a sorrowful nostalgia over happiness that never existed, a consideration of past decisions that remained untaken. The reference to *The Golden Bowl* was not accidental, and Thurber's mood, like his prose, often recalls the resignation of Henry James, whose genius Thurber has admired and assimilated. Even when James' all-pervading influence is least directly evident, one understands much more of Thurber's best work by recalling the complexities of the defeat of Lambert Strether, the renunciation of Fleda Vetch and most of all the anticipation of the beast in the jungle that "lay in wait for him, amid the twists and the turns of the months and the years."

Differing from most of James, however, Thurber continues to watch as his heroes flounder through married life. Despite the conventions of literature, the wedding bells do not end the book but only the volume. The next volume finds the once-lonely man, like Charlie Deshler in **"The Curb in the Sky,"** "coming out of the anesthetic of her charms and beginning to feel the first pains of reality." Everything before this has been reconnoitering; only after the man and woman are married does the real battle begin.

This battle of men and women has often been considered as Thurber's attack on women, or as a description of the persecution of idealistic men by grimly practical women, but the persectuion is really a series of patrol skirmishes, of attacks and counter-attacks, and Thurber is less a propagandist than a war correspondent. . . . In **"A Couple of Hamburgers"** . . . the wife insists on the refinements of not eating in a diner in a factory town, a diner with a nickname, or a diner set at an angle from the road; the husband insists on being coarse because he knows it annoys his wife. So they drive on through the rain, the husband loudly singing songs his wife hates, the wife gloating over a suspicious noise in the car's engine. . . . This war of attrition is less a war than a mutual state of uneasiness, a kind of befuddled hostility. Even when it threatens to erupt into violence, the threat is usually nothing more than a distant rumble. In **"Mr. Preble Gets Rid of His Wife,"** the husband plans to bury his wife in the cellar and run away with his secretary, but instead he finds himself stalemated.

> "Let's go down in the cellar," Mr. Preble said to his wife.
>
> "What for?" she said, not looking up from her book.

''Oh, I don't know,'' he said. ''We never go down in the cellar any more. The way we used to.''

''We never did go down in the cellar that I remember,'' said Mrs. Preble. ''I could rest easy the balance of my life if I never went down in the cellar.'' Mr. Preble was silent for several minutes.

''Supposing I said it meant a whole lot to me,'' began Mr. Preble.

''What's come over you?'' his wife demanded. ''It's cold down there and there is absolutely nothing to do.''

''We could pick up pieces of coal,'' said Mr. Preble. ''We might get up some kind of a game with pieces of coal.''

''I don't want to,'' said his wife. ''Anyway, I'm reading.''

''Listen,'' said Mr. Preble, rising and walking up and down. ''Why won't you come down in the cellar? You can read down there as far as that goes.''

''There isn't a good enough light down there,'' she said, ''and anyway, I'm not going to go down in the cellar. You may as well make up your mind to that.''

''Gee Whiz!'' said Mr. Preble, kicking at the edge of a rug. ''Other people's wives go down in the cellar. . . . ''

Mr. Preble does get his wife down in the cellar, and she is fully aware of why he wants her there, but we are never told whether he kills her with the ''piece of iron or something'' that she sends him out into the street to find. It is implied that after he has failed to find a piece of iron he will stop in at the cigar store on the way home.

The war between man and wife, however, is only a miniature of the war between the man and the world. The one who was a wanderer has found a home, but instead of being a box to hide in it has become a prison cell within a prison. He is trapped, as Thurber put it in **''The Vengeance of 3902090,''** ''like a mouse in a trap in Sing Sing.''

> This type of badgered human being is given to the short nervous essay rather than the 972-page novel or autobiography. He is more likely to fret about the discomforts of his particular cell than to concern himself with prison problems as a whole. . . . This frailty, this preoccupation with, and affinity for, the smaller enormities of life, permits him to be overwhelmed by minor tyrannies and persecutions to the extent that, for days on end, he forgets his part in the struggle for that larger Freedom which now engages the attention of all right-minded prisoners of the world.

This concentration on details is reflected not only in the episodic brevity of Thurber's work, but in the lives of his characters. Each one, trapped in his mousetrap in Sing Sing, is overwhelmed by the ''minor tyrannies and persecutions'' that make Thurber's portrait of our times so genuine. The tensions and pressures in the private lives of Thurber's characters, concentrating similar tensions and pressures from the outside world, slowly build up until the strain becomes unbearable and something breaks. Thurber's victims, like the people who daily run away with their neighbors' wives, murder their mothers-in-law, wander into amnesia or jump off buildings, are rarely overwhelmed by a major crisis, for their lives are too uneventful for such crises to arise. Instead, they crack up under the weight of the last straw; in their imaginations, the straw itself becomes an unbearable weight simply because any more weight is unbearable.

Just as the war between the man and wife in **''A Couple of Hamburgers''** consisted of such minute attacks and counter-attacks as the man singing ''Harrigan'' and the woman anticipating disaster, so the marriage of Gordon and Marcia Winship broke up over the comparative merits of Greta Garbo and Donald Duck. Both the victims of **''The Breaking Up of the Winships''** realized that the quarrel itself was ridiculous, ''but behind their contrition lay sleeping the ugly words each had used and the cold glances and the bitter gestures.'' Mr. Bidwell, in **''The Private Life of Mr. Bidwell,''** started holding his breath, and the opposition of Mrs. Bidwell swelled his momentary whim into a major crisis, just as each of the Winships had turned the respective abilities of Greta Garbo and Donald Duck into a high moral issue. As soon as the Bidwells had decided to break up over Mr. Bidwell's habit of holding his breath, ''he oddly enough, and quite without effort, lost interest in holding his breath.'' Instead, when he found himself bored at the parties his wife enjoyed, he started multiplying numbers in his head. ''George Bidwell lives alone now (his wife remarried). He never goes to parties any more, and his old circle of friends rarely sees him. The last time that any of them did see him, he was walking along a country road with the halting, uncertain gait of a blind man: he was trying to see how many steps he could take without opening his eyes.''

Thurber's heroes of our world and our time spend their lives wandering along the edge of a cliff, only half aware of what lies below, for what lies below is all imaginary until the moment of the actual fall. Unwilling to jump in the sea like lemmings, they stumble on a pebble instead. (pp. 162-66)

Thurber's ''humorous sketches'' represented a magazine development of his newspaper reporting, but it was a road that led down a blind alley. At best, this kind of writing has a very limited interest and value; at worst, the author's unsuccessful efforts to sustain an attitude of pleasantry toward what is usually a trivial subject makes the ''humorous sketch'' forced, artificial and tiresome.

Despite his reputation, based largely on his cartoons, Thurber is not at his best as a humorist. He lacks the virtuosity of S. J. Perelman on the one hand and the unerring manner of Robert Benchley on the other. Thurber's best work, like that of Ring Lardner, makes important use of humor, because both writers have a wonderful sense of humor, in the most literal meaning of the phrase, a wonderful feeling and perception of what is humorous. But Thurber, like Lardner, is a fundamentally serious writer. ''To call such persons humorists,'' he wrote in the preface to ***My Life and Hard Times,*** ''a loose-fitting and ugly word, is to miss the nature of their dilemma and the dilemma of their nature. The little wheels of their invention are set in motion by the damp hand of melancholy.''

The ''humorous sketch,'' apparently worked out with White for ''The Talk of the Town,'' thus became in Thurber simply a bad habit, and it is the kind of habit that only grows worse as long as it remains uncorrected. The sketches fulfill a constant need for money, and probably also a need to write about trivia, for Thurber is as much obsessed with trivia as are his characters. The image of the ''mouse in a trap in Sing Sing'' was originally applied to himself, ''a badgered human being . . . given to the short nervous essay.'' ''This type of writing,'' he remarked elsewhere, ''is not a joyous form of self-expression but the manifestation of a twitchiness.'' As Thurber continues to turn out these ''humorous sketches'' with little humor and less content, each new book contains minor masterpieces surrounded by work that is scarcely distinguishable from the productions of a syndicated columnist. ***My World—and Welcome to It*** and ***The Middle Aged Man on the Flying Trapeze*** include such treasures as **''The Secret Life of Walter Mitty''** and **''The Greatest Man in the World''** but they also include no less than three pieces devoted entirely to Thurber's misunderstandings of phrases and sentences addressed to him by various cooks, maids and hired men. (pp. 170-71)

Thurber's lifelong eye trouble, which finally became so severe that he was forced to give up drawing for a number of years, goes virtually unmentioned in his writing. . . .

[In] 1949 Thurber told an interviewer, ''All the apparatus by which a man sees I don't have. Out of 30,000 cases such as mine there are three that see. I'm one of the three. When I write now I am not handicapped by vision. I am undisturbed by distraction—by the grass outside my window, or by flying birds. . . . I used to be a writer who thought on the typewriter. . . . I have shifted from being an eye-writer to being an ear-writer.''

This ear-writing has often led Thurber off into a kind of dream-style. . . . (p. 183)

[Thurber's] development of ear-writing has played [an] . . . important part in perfecting the style of his later short stories. **''The Cane in the Corridor,''** for instance, pits a married couple against a man who has just come out of the hospital and resents the fact that they didn't visit him. The ex-patient suggests that if the sensitive husband were hospitalized, he would not get lonely, and Thurber moves rapidly through the wonderfully realistic dialogue of three people talking at cross purposes:

> ''It just so happens that it might take the form of me calling on George every day, from the time he goes in until he gets out.''
>
> ''You can't do that,'' said George. ''There's such a thing as the law.''
>
> ''Of course, he can't,'' said Mrs. Minturn. ''Besides, George is not going to the hospital.''
>
> ''I'm not going to the hospital,'' said Minturn.
>
> ''Everybody goes to the hospital sooner or later,'' said Fletcher. His voice was rising.
>
> ''Nine hundred million people don't,'' said Mrs. Minturn, ''all the time.''
>
> ''I'm stating a pathological case!'' shouted Fletcher. ''Hypothetical. George has been lying there in that bed for six weeks!''
>
> ''No,'' said Minturn.
>
> ''. . .He's convalescing, but he can't get up.''
>
> ''Why can't I get up?'' asked Minturn.
>
> ''Because you're too weak. You have no more strength than a house mouse. You feel as if you were coming apart like a cheap croquet mallet. If you tried to stand, your knees would bend the wrong way, like a flamingo's.''
>
> ''I want to go home,'' mumbled Minturn.
>
> ''You *are* home,'' said his wife.

Fletcher tells Minturn that Minturn now hears a perpetual tap-tap-tap of the approaching cane of his visitor. Mrs. Minturn tells her husband that they will take him away to the Mayo Clinic, where Fletcher can't find him, but Minturn says he doesn't want to go to the Mayo Clinic. Fletcher now starts bringing presents, ''puzzles that won't work, linked nails that won't come apart, pigs in clover in which the little balls are glued to the bottom of the box. I bring you mystery novels in Yiddish and artificial flowers made out of wires and beads, and horehound candy.''

''Terrible, terrible rat,'' says Mrs. Minturn, and the story plunges on into its bizzare ending.

> ''I see,'' said Fletcher. ''You don't even feel sorry for poor old tap-tap. Tap, tap, tap, tap, tap.''
>
> ''What's that?'' said Minturn.
>
> ''That's my cane in the corridor,'' said Fletcher. ''You are lying there, trying to unwrassle something I have brought you, when tap, tap, tap, here I come again.''
>
> ''Terrible rat, go home,'' said Mrs. Minturn. . . .
>
> ''Don't throw anybody out,'' said Minturn. ''Tap, tap, tap,'' he added.
>
> Halfway to the hall door, Fletcher turned. ''That's right, laugh,'' he said. ''Tap, tap, tap, tap, tap, then.''
>
> ''Tap, tap, tap,'' said Minturn from far down near the floor. . . .

The closing again recalls Eliot's ''Sweeney Agonistes,'' with its sinister ending, ''And you wait for a knock and the turning of a lock for you know the hangman's waiting for you / And perhaps you're alive / And perhaps you're dead / Hoo ha ha / Hoo ha ha / Hoo / Hoo / Hoo / KNOCK KNOCK KNOCK / KNOCK KNOCK KNOCK / KNOCK / KNOCK / KNOCK.'' Ear-writing again leads Thurber toward the poets, but the preceding section provides a more representative example of Thurber's style, a style so neat and spare and unobtrusive that it enables him to project his characters almost entirely through dialogue. Even the best of Thurber's earlier stories leaned on either an external narrator, as in **''The Greatest Man in the World,''** or on the crutch of interior monologue, as in **''One Is a Wanderer.''** Thurber's short stories have become increasingly rare in his later work, but the few have been increasingly careful and excellent. In such triumphs as **''The Cane in the Corridor,'' ''The Interview''** and **''Am I Not Your Rosalind?''** the tightened structure and sure workmanship bring the narration so close to the action, and the action so close to the characters, that one feels no alien presence in the scene. The author's perceptive eye has become one's own.

One cannot, of course, attribute this steady growth entirely to the Mandarin influence, for Thurber, after all, does not write like Henry James, any more than he writes like T. S. Eliot. Although he has become increasingly aware of literary criteria, he has never abandoned the basic rules of simplicity and clarity that he ascribes to E. B. White. Thurber's mockery of Chanda Bell and her admirers [in **"A Final Note on Chanda Bell"**] provides good evidence, corroborated by the consistent directness of his style, that Thurber is aware of the defects and excesses of the Mandarins. At the same time, his appreciation of the value of such a Mandarin as Henry James has taught him that writing is more than a job, and that the simple declarative sentence also has its limitations. Thurber's style has developed out of the conflict between these two extremes, White and James, tending first toward the one and then toward the other, assimilating and rejecting parts of each. The conflict in style, in turn, comes from a similar conflict in Thurber's ideas and attitude, a conflict between the remembered world of Columbus, Ohio, the real contemporary world of fears and confusions, and the imagined world of *The Ambassadors*. Out of these conflicts has come some of the finest writing in contemporary literature. (pp. 184-87)

Thurber ended one of his fables with the moral, "If you do as the humans do, it will be the end of you." When someone wrote that Thurber thought animals were superior to humans, however, he rejected the idea by commenting that the critic was just trying to annoy him. "Man is born to the belief that he is superior to the lower animals," he was quoted by Harvey Breit in an interview in *The New York Times,* "and . . . critical intelligence comes when he realizes that he is more similar than dissimilar. Extending this theory, it has occurred to me that Man's arrogance and aggression arise from a false feeling of transcendency, and that he will not get anywhere until he realizes, in all humility, that he is just another of God's creatures, less kindly than the dog, possessed of less dignity than the swan, and incapable of being as magnificent an angel as the black panther. I have become a little tired of the capitalization of man, his easy assumption of a dignity more apparent than real, and his faith in a high destiny for which he is not fitted by his long and bloody history."

This attitude, that man "is just another of God's creatures," has provided Thurber's work, especially his later writing, with an overall tone of resignation and tranquility. This tone appears contradictory to the struggles of Thurber's characters, and even to the fears and confusions of his own life, but actually it lends perspective to the tortures of the Prebles, the Winships and the Deshlers. . . . The harried "prisoner of the world" may be a mouse in a mousetrap in Sing Sing, but both the trap and the prison acquire their significance by contrast with a larger world outside the world of Sing Sing. Even the cliff can broaden out into a plain when one realizes that it is a man-made cliff. "I shall go on in the same way," says Levin at the end of *Anna Karenina,* and at the end of *Moby Dick* the sea rolls on as it did five thousand years ago.

Thurber's tranquility has grown through the years—"Now I have got over my middle age," he told Breit, "I have gone past it into something better"—but the growth was not an abrupt change. . . . [Even] in the tragedies and defeats of the early stories there is a kind of peaceful resignation, even if it is only the peace of insanity. Mr. Bidwell was last seen staggering contentedly along a country road, and Mr. Bruhl died with a satisfied smile on his lips. Even here, Thurber realized, although he was not fully able to accept it, that his characters and he himself were just some more of God's creatures. Thus by not equating human folly with human viciousness, and by not equating human viciousness with universal evil, Thurber avoided the artistic trap of hating his own creations, the intellectual trap of misanthropy. (pp. 189-91)

The growth of this tranquility is reflected in his two autobiographical books. ***My Life and Hard Times,*** one of his first books, is made up almost entirely of humorous confusions: the night the bed fell, the day the dam broke, the night the ghost got in. It contains little of Thurber's life and less of his times, and one is surprised in reading *The Thurber Album* twenty years later to see how much more clearly he has portrayed the same parents who dominated the earlier book. Charles and Mary Thurber, who wandered through ***My Life and Hard Times*** like a pair of half-crazy buffoons, have completely changed as Thurber brought them into focus in the affectionate portraits of *The Thurber Album*. The later book about "people of whom I am especially fond" may not be the first creation of the "something better" that Thurber mentioned to Breit, but it is the first extensive example of how the "something better" that struggled against the uncertainty and despair in Thurber's early work has become dominant in his later writing. (pp. 191-92)

Otto Friedrich, "James Thurber: A Critical Study," in Discovery, *Vol. 5, 1955, pp. 158-92.*

JAMES THURBER (essay date 1955)

[In the following excerpt from his essay "The Tyranny of Trivia," originally published in the New Yorker *in 1955, Thurber offers a witty response to Otto Friedrich's allegations (see excerpt above dated 1955) that his writings reflect his obsession with trivial matters.]*

An intrepid young literary explorer named Otto Friedrich recently stumbled upon the body of my work lying sprawled and unburied on the plain, and was distressed to discover that it had been ravaged by trivia. Mr. Friedrich thinks that preoccupation with trivia is unbecoming in a writer who belongs to the Solemn if not, indeed, the Sombre tradition of American letters. (How do you like it now, gentlemen?) The critic . . . detected what he called my need to write trivia, and shrewdly coupled it with "a constant need to make money." By trivia, the author meant the minor and the unimportant (unless I misread him, he included sex in this category), and not grammar, logic, and rhetoric, the big trivia of the dictionary definitions of the word.

I could begin by insisting that Mr. Friedrich has confused my armor with its chink, but this might lead to an intricate and turgid flow of metaphor. It is simpler to say, in another figure, that Trivia Mundi has always been as dear and as necessary to me as her bigger and more glamorous sister, Gloria. They have both long and amicably inhabited a phrase of Coleridge's, "All things both great and small," and I like to think of them taking turns at shooting albatrosses and playing the bassoon.

Some notable trivia, such as the last straw, the lost horseshoe nail, and a piece of string, became involved with larger issues, but my own, I am afraid, never rise to such heights. They consist mainly of a preoccupation, compulsive perhaps, but not obsessive, with words and the alphabet, and most of them never get into print. Their purpose is the side-tracking of worrisome trains of thought. The modern mind has many shuttles and shuntings, the principal one being, I suppose, the reading of mystery novels in bed, to shut out the terrors of the night and the world. Profound thought or plain positive thinking does not conduce to repose. Every man, laying his book aside, still has the night and the world to bypass. The late Bert Leston Taylor used to find comfort in contemplating Canopus, "a star that has no parallax to speak of." I happen to get cold up there in the inmeasurable spaces of the outer constellations, and my own system of mental sedation is more mundane. (pp. 75-6)

James Thurber, "The Tyranny of Trivia," in his Lanterns & Lances, *Harper & Brothers, Publishers, 1961, pp. 75-89.*

ROBERT H. ELIAS (essay date 1958)

[*Elias, an American scholarly critic, specializes in modern American authors such as Thurber and Theodore Dreiser. In the following excerpt, Elias stresses the quality of affirmation in Thurber's work, particularly in the pieces after 1939.*]

For more than a generation James Thurber has been writing stories, an impressive number of them as well shaped as the most finely wrought pieces of Henry James, James Joyce and Ernest Hemingway, as sensitively worded as the most discriminatingly written prose of H. L. Mencken, Westbrook Pegler and J. D. Salinger, and as penetrating—especially during what we can call his "major phase"—as the most pointed insights of those two larger poets of our century, E. A. Robinson and Robert Frost. Yet, slightly older than Hemingway and Faulkner, he has been the subject of no full-length studies, nor has he been prominently mentioned, as he long ago should have been, for the Nobel Prize. In fact, it is only within the past four years that he has been treated to any adequately extended critical consideration at all. For the most part, when he has not been dismissed as simply a cartoonist, he has been condemned by a conglomeration of whimsical reviews, human interest features full of newsworthy legends and pictures, and that extinguisher of merit, the label, to the minor category of humorist—a kind of latter-day Mark Twain saved from the lamented excesses by *New Yorker* sophistication. The truth, however, is that among our living writers he is virtually our only creator of serious comedy and one of the few humanists who can make an affirmation without either a chip or a Christ symbol on his shoulder. (pp. 355-56)

Thurber . . . is clearly no misanthrope. One always feels that something worth recovering has been defeated; hence that recovery of this something is still a good. Man is not necessarily *all* destruction, but he is so *unless*—. This *unless*—is what distinguishes Thurber's preoccupation from 1939 onward; and a wonderful little story, **"The Wood Duck,"** in ***Let Your Mind Alone,*** provides an unmistakable indication of the realm in which hope is to lie. In its opposition of inescapably symbolic details—especially between the graceful fowl and the speeding car that hits him—it celebrates all that can be contrasted to a mechanized life. On the other hand, the farmer, the men in the truck, the narrator and his wife, all feel that the duck confers a distinction on the farm he has adopted; on the other, the driver is unaware of, or at least indifferent to, the unspoiled beauty the machine has violated. When the duck flutters into the woods, something precious is lost; when he returns, he brings value into the institutional world. In the words of the narrator's wife near the end there is evidence of human gratitude for experiencing something close to nature. "I am glad he is [back] . . . ," she says. "I hated to think of him all alone out there in the woods." Even more important than the gratitude, though, there is here an understated awareness of the needs of men.

These needs clearly require a sense of what Thoreau called "the infinite state of our relations." The human being is lost when he loses his sense of his limitation, his mortality; when he equates the private with the absolute. Emerson could preach self-reliance because he had the oversoul in the offing; but Thurber's society has ignored the relationship and thereby denied both the self and the context for its being. Our only morality is embodied in our clichés. Heed their purveyors and be saved. *The Last Flower, a Parable in Pictures* and ***Fables for Our Time and Famous Poems Illustrated*** remind us how suicidal unself-critical man can be. The acceptance of empty forms is not only frustrating; it is utterly catastrophic. *The Last Flower* exhibits the disastrous course of human habits, the way men and women forget that their source and inspiration lie in what we may term nature—and the way that this forgetting allows mankind to become pretentious, arrogant and, finally, fatally warlike. The last, the best, the only hope is of earth itself: it is lodged in the natural cycle, the regenerative power of nature whose lone flower will seek invincibly to bloom again. The ***Fables*** makes this point in another way. Thurber simply turns Aesop about to examine the empty forms of words, platitudes, in the light of the life they are meant to describe. The animal world and the human world are compared to reveal the superiority of the animal. "If you do as humans do, it will be the end of you." The hen that shouts "The heavens are falling down" is not so foolish as everyone laughingly thinks. The heavens *do* fall; everyone *is* killed. And the narrator is not a bit surprised. (pp. 356-60)

The sense of relation that humanity needs is, thus, a sense of a saving connection with a primary spirit, something elemental that civilization disclaims at its peril. To disclaim this something is ultimately to deny the whole self. (p. 360)

"The Secret Life of Walter Mitty" may be said to usher in the major period. As ever, Thurber is trying to find a realm where the individual can maintain his self; and as ever, too, there seems to be no answer without qualifications—an appropriate enough way of assaulting rigid forms. Yet there is ultimately what has already been suggested, a humanistic affirmation. Of course, at no time does Thurber forsake one kind of writing and immerse himself exclusively in another. Although there may be no ***My Life and Hard Times,*** there are still instances of great humor, more fairy tales and fables. But most of them are marked by the increasing complexity and depth that are best embodied in such important and challenging masterpieces as **"The Secret Life of Walter Mitty," "The Whip-Poor-Will," "The Catbird Seat," "The Cane in the Corridor," "A Friend of the Earth," "Teacher's Pet"** and *The Thirteen Clocks* (1950).

Among the most successful protagonists in these stories are Walter Mitty and Erwin Martin (of **"The Catbird Seat"**), both of whom win not too dissimilar victories over the commonplace, the dead level of practicality, the enemies of the imagination. A definition of the character of these victories suggests their meaning. When Mitty faces the firing squad, "erect and motionless, proud and disdainful, Walter Mitty the Undefeated, inscrutable to the last," the victory has its limits. It is not only private—one that cannot give him a place in society; it is ridden by the clichés of pulp romances and Grade C movies. Nonetheless, it is a victory, even if qualified, that contributes to self-preservation. Mr. Martin, whose stature is greater insofar as he does bear real arms against his sea of troubles, likewise wins substantially and privately. By perceiving the thin line between humor and pathos, absurdity and terror, that is reflected in the details, point of view and very tone of the story, he is able to make his usual ineffectualness unusually effectual; Ulgine Barrows, the threat to his sensibilities and his status, is ironically defeated. But even as he, by actual act, gives genuine dignity to those sensibilities and that status, it is clear that both the cause and the reward of his success must be isolation. His employer does not truly understand either Mrs. Barrows or Mr. Martin, and Mr. Martin can never enjoy his accomplishment except in private. Although he can never be again what he once was, he has to appear to others unchanged. Irony and cross-purposes must be the order of the day. This, though, is in part Mr. Martin's insight. He exploits the relationships of strangers and, like Walter Mitty, saves something worth saving: he saves, indeed, the inner life itself, the life that is not to be harnassed like the atom, streamlined like a spaceship, manipulated, calculated, fed to Univac; he saves the very seat of the self that is the universe—the realm that makes it possible to say, as was said some centuries ago, that the unexamined life is not worth living.

Mitty and Martin, and especially Martin, who after all *does* more than Mitty, are then an impressive distance from the eccentrics of ***My Life and Hard Times*** and the lonely wanderers and frustrates of ***The Middle-Aged Man*** and ***Let Your Mind Alone.*** They bear, generally speaking, the marks of solider affirmations. (pp. 361-62)

A respect for nature, for action, for the inner life, for mind—it is a single complex, inseparable from what we mean by the sense of proportion that is to help the individual know his predicament. **"Teacher's Pet,"** one of Thurber's most intense stories, provides, perhaps, a succinct concluding insight into the individual's essential situation. When the reflective, brooding Kelby, in a fury of self-accusation, hits the little boy who, bullied and afraid, reminds him of his own boyhood predicament and cowardice, he is ironically taken for a bully by the boy's father. And when the father tells a mutual friend, "I've seen some bullies in my time, but I never saw anything to match that," the friend puffs thoughtfully on a cigarette and says: "You never know about a man, Reynolds. You just never know."

This is the nub of it. And because it is, there are a variety of social implications. Not the least is the necessity for a structure in which the human mystery is secure, in which action can be more than bare reaction, in which individuals are respected as ends and not exploited as means, whether by political dictators or social relations experts. Or slogan writers. For the very use of language is related to the argument in behalf of individuality and the sense of relation. Insofar as perceptions are verbalized, words must be precise, sharp, telling. Whether employing an arresting metaphor or playfully juxtaposing the trite and the fresh, or simply inveighing against jargon, "polysyllabic monstrosities," Thurber is warring for meaning—and for the only mind for whom that objective can make sense. (p. 362)

To attribute to man the ability both . . . to learn and then to act in consequence is almost to pay him the tribute that painters represent with the halo—almost but not quite—and yet better—because ordinary men are more complex than the saints. (p. 363)

Robert H. Elias, "Reappraisals: James Thurber, the Primitive, the Innocent, and the Individual," in The American Scholar, *Vol. 27, No. 3, Summer, 1958, pp. 355-63.*

E. B. WHITE (essay date 1961)

[White was an American essayist, poet, humorist, and children's author. His essays are characterized by their wit and directness, and he is considered an outstanding prose stylist. Thurber often acknowledged White's influence on his writing style, and as Thurber's close friend and mentor at the New Yorker, *White was instrumental in promoting Thurber's career as both a writer and cartoonist. He also coauthored* Is Sex Necessary? *with Thurber and wrote the introduction to his first collection,* The Owl in the Attic. *The following is excerpted from White's memorial tribute to Thurber.]*

I am one of the lucky ones; I knew [Thurber] before blindness hit him, before fame hit him, and I tend always to think of him as a young artist in a small office in a big city, with all the world still ahead. It was a fine thing to be young and at work in New York for a new magazine when Thurber was young and at work, and I will always be glad that this happened to me.

It was fortunate that we got on well; the office we shared was the size of a hall bedroom. There was just room enough for two men, two typewriters, and a stack of copy paper. The copy paper disappeared at a scandalous rate—not because our production was high (although it was) but because Thurber used

Early photo of Thurber (right) and E. B. White, his friend and New Yorker *colleague. Reproduced by permission of Cornell University Library and Joel White.*

copy paper as the natural receptacle for discarded sorrows, immediate joys, stale dreams, golden prophecies, and messages of good cheer to the outside world and to fellow-workers. His mind was never at rest, and his pencil was connected to his mind by the best conductive tissue I have ever seen in action. The whole world knows what a funny man he was, but you had to sit next to him day after day to understand the extravagance of his clowning, the wildness and subtlety of his thinking, and the intensity of his interest in others and his sympathy for their dilemmas—dilemmas that he instantly enlarged, put in focus, and made immortal, just as he enlarged and made immortal the strange goings on in the Ohio home of his boyhood. His waking dreams and his sleeping dreams commingled shamelessly and uproariously. Ohio was never far from his thoughts, and when he received a medal from his home state in 1953, he wrote, "The clocks that strike in my dreams are often the clocks of Columbus." It is a beautiful sentence and a revealing one.

He was both a practitioner of humor and a defender of it. The day he died, I came on a letter from him, dictated to a secretary and signed in pencil with his sightless and enormous "Jim." "Every time is a time for humor," he wrote. "I write humor the way a surgeon operates, because it is a livelihood, because I have a great urge to do it, because many interesting challenges are set up, and because I have the hope it may do some good." Once, I remember, he heard someone say that humor is a shield, not a sword, and it made him mad. He wasn't going to have anyone beating his sword into a shield. That "surgeon," incidentally, is pure Mitty. During his happiest years, Thurber did not write the way a surgeon operates, he wrote the way a child skips rope, the way a mouse waltzes.

Although he is best known for **"Walter Mitty"** and *The Male Animal,* the book of his I like best is *The Last Flower*. In it you will find his faith in the renewal of life, his feeling for the beauty and fragility of life on earth. Like all good writers, he fashioned his own best obituary notice. Nobody else can add to the record, much as he might like to. And of all the flowers, real and figurative, that will find their way to Thurber's last resting place, the one that will remain fresh and wiltproof is the little flower he himself drew, on the last page of that lovely book.

E. B. White, "James Thurber," in The New Yorker, *Vol. XXXVII, No. 39, November 11, 1961, p. 247.*

JOHN UPDIKE (essay date 1962)

[*Considered a perceptive observer of the human condition and an extraordinary stylist, Updike is one of America's most distinguished men of letters. Best known for such novels as* Rabbit Run *(1960),* Rabbit Redux *(1971), and* Rabbit Is Rich *(1981), he is also a short story writer, poet, essayist, and noted critic, and, like Thurber, he is closely affiliated with the* New Yorker. *In the following excerpt, Updike describes the stories and essays in Thurber's posthumous collection* Credos and Curios *as evidence of Thurber's declining skills in his last years.*]

[The bulk of the pieces in ***Credos and Curios*** are from Thurber's] last years and as such tend to be cranky, formless and lame. "The claw of the sea-puss," Thurber once wrote (quoting F. Hopkinson Smith), "gets us all in the end"; and toward the end Thurber's humor was overwhelmed by puns and dismay.

The puns are understandable. Blindness, in severing langauge from the seen world of designated things, gives words a tyrannical independence. Milton and Joyce wrung from verbal obsession a special magnificence, and Thurber's late pieces, at their best—for example, "The Tyranny of Trivia," collected in *Lanterns and Lances*—do lead the reader deep into the wonderland of the alphabet and the dictionary. But in such weak rambles as, in [***Credos and Curios***], **"The Lady From the Land"** and **"Carpe Noctem, If You Can,"** logomachic tricks are asked to pass for wit and implausible pun-swapping for human conversation.

As to the dismay: Mrs. Thurber, in her gracious and understated introduction to this posthumous collection, defends her husband against the charge of "bitterness and disillusion." But stories like **"The Future, If Any, of Comedy Or, Where Do We Not-Go from Here?"** and **"Afternoon of a Playwright"** do display, by way of monologue in the ungainly disguise of dialogue, an irritation with the present state of things so inclusive as to be pointless.

Television, psychoanalysis, the Bomb, the deterioration of grammar, the morbidity of contemporary literature—these were just a few of Thurber's terminal pet peeves. The writer who had produced ***Fables for Our Time*** and *The Last Flower* out of the thirties had become, by the end of the fifties, one more indignant senior citizen penning complaints about the universal decay of virtue.

The only oasis, in the dreadful world of post-midnight forebodings into which he had been plunged, is the Columbus, Ohio, of his boyhood, which he continued to remember "as fondly and sharply as a man on a sinking ship might remember his prairie home." In ***Credos and Curios,*** for a few pages entitled **"Return of the Native,"** his prose regains the crisp lucidity and glistening bias of *The Thurber Album*. Then the dark tangled curtain falls again. . . .

[If] Thurber, whose international celebrity made him seem to loom unduly over the other American humorists of his vintage, is to be measured against his peers, the first name we strike is Benchley's. The surprising thing about Benchley is that he remains rereadable. His writings were so ephemeral they seem to defy being outdated; their utterly casual and innocent surface airily resists corrosion. I wonder how much of Thurber will weather so well. . . .

Of the humorists of this century, he and Don Marquis were the most complex, the most pessimistic and the most ambitious. Thurber, in comparison to Marquis and Benchley, was not especially sensitive to the surface currents of American life, and as a journalist, uncomfortable, and, as a writer of straight fiction, unconvincing.

His great subject, springing from his physical disability, was what might be called the enchantment of misapprehension. His masterpieces, I think, are ***My Life and Hard Times*** and *The White Deer*—two dissimilar books alike in their beautiful evocation of a fluid chaos where communication is limited to wild, flitting gestures and where humans revolve and collide like glowing planets, lit solely from within, against a cosmic backdrop of gathering dark. Thurber's genius was to make of our despair a humorous fable. It is not surprising that such a gallant feat of equilibrium was not maintained to the end of his life.

John Updike, "Indignations of a Senior Citizen," in The New York Times Book Review, *November 25, 1962, p. 5.*

NORRIS W. YATES (essay date 1964)

[*Yates is an American critic who specializes in American humorists. In the following excerpt, Yates discusses the personae of "the little man" and the "liberal citizen" in Thurber's writings.*]

Thurber has acknowledged the influence on his humor of both Robert Benchley and Clarence Day, Jr., as well as of White. All four writers frequently wear the mask of a bewildered, more or less meek Little Man of the white-collar class. In Thurber's case, the Little Man is bothered most of all by Sex, with its marital concomitant, but also by all disciplines whose names begin with "psych"; by mechanical devices; by the upper-middle-class ceremonials of suburbia; by the bureaucratic organization of modern society, and by the deterioration of communications between man and man and between man and woman. (p. 278)

The chief difference between Benchley's man and Thurber's male is that Thurber much more often gives the female a direct and central part in the male's humiliation by his world. Benchley wrote a number of pieces about children (whom Thurber largely ignored, despite his many portrayals of household life), but the humiliation of Benchley's man rarely comes from his spouse, and marital difficulties, including sexual tension, are almost never a major factor in Benchley's writing. His Little Man is almost sexless, and the wife is a shadowy figure. Benchley's wildest fantasies are underlaid by a certain placidity when compared to the sexuality that charges Thurber's males and their environment.

Not only is Thurber's man a captive of his wife and of his own inadequacies, he is also enslaved by time. Thurber usually depicts his males as middle-aged or verging thereon, and their aging is often related directly to their sexual and marital problems. . . . Thus the age of Thurber's males is another of their handicaps in the marital scheme of things as well as in the world at large.

As do Benchley's characters, Thurber's Little Men sometimes become aggressive, and their aggressions tend likewise to be futile or disastrous to one or both parties. . . . In a short story, **"The Indian Sign,"** Mr. Bentley accomplishes nothing except a momentary release of what Freud called psychic energy. To express his disgust with his wife's interest in a sturdy ancestress who had killed nineteen Indians (male), Mr. Bentley cuts loose with a Pequot war whoop, "Ah-wah-wah-wah-wah!" Even in his rebellion he thus reveals his unconscious identification with the victims of the pioneer matron. In another story, when Mrs. Brush and her female friends try to play poker with all sorts of wild cards, Mr. Brush, exercising dealer's choice, invents an absurd variation in which "The red queens, the fours, fives, sixes and eights are wild." Mr. Brush defeats his wife for the moment, but the reader feels that her revenge will come somehow.

Sometimes the husband's "aggression" manifests itself as withdrawal (if that statement is not a descent into psychoanalytic jargon). Mr. Bidwell takes to holding his breath, even at parties; the result is extreme connubial tension—"They knifed each other, from head to stomach, with their eyes"—and finally, divorce. In **"The Curb in the Sky,"** the male's aggression takes the form of telling an outlandish dream he has had. When his wife begins "correcting" his dream, he withdraws into insanity. . . . Thurber has been called a "comic Prufrock" [see excerpt by Peter DeVries dated 1943], and he shares Prufrock's inner futility, but he is more like James Joyce's Leopold Bloom in his position as a harassed and ineffective husband. . . . (pp. 282-86)

On the rare occasions when the male's rebellion improves his situation with respect to the female, there are always circumstances that have mitigated his original plight. In **"The Catbird Seat,"** Erwin Martin, an office worker, foils a dominating woman who has wholly captured his boss with her notions of efficiency. Mr. Martin eliminates this threat to his routine and to his job—but Mr. Martin is not married to Mrs. Barrows; they are merely colleagues. In **"Am Not I Your Rosalind?"** the husband tempts his wife and the wife of a guest into trying to read Shakespeare aloud while high on cocktails. The two wives make fools of themselves, but afterwards the tempter and his wife forget their differences in criticizing their guests. . . . (p. 286)

Some of Thurber's wives all but smother their husbands with too merciless an understanding coupled with a sympathy that is half contempt ("My great big wonderful husband," Mrs. Monroe says with gentle irony). Madge Kinstrey, however, has contempt without sympathy or understanding; she calls her husband "a spoiled brat" who is "fussing about nothing at all, like an invalid in a wheel chair." Kinstrey finally begins to show signs of schizophrenia: ". . . he had the oddly disturbing feeling that it wasn't he who had spoken but somebody else. . . ." The next morning he suddenly kills his wife, the two servants, and himself. He goes far beyond Lardner's husband in "Ex Parte" who merely smashed up the furniture, but the principle is the same: the male who is misunderstood and feels oppressed may revolt in blind, destructive violence. (pp. 286-87)

Mary McCarthy, another frequent contributor to the *New Yorker*, refers in one of her works to "the thrifty bourgeois love-insurance, with its daily payments of patience, forbearance, and resignation." Thurber deplores marriages without these qualities, but he is not attacking marriage as an institution in his tales about the Prebles, the Winships, and the Kinstreys any more than he and White did in *Is Sex Necessary?* If there are any males worse off than his subdued husbands, they are the forlorn bachelors of **"Evening's at Seven"** and **"One Is a Wanderer."** The plight of the male in the latter story is especially pathetic; he drinks and thinks, "One's life is made up of twos, and of fours. The Graysons understood the nice little arrangements of living, the twos and fours. Two is company, four is a party, three is a crowd. One is a wanderer." Man can live neither with woman nor without her. (pp. 287-88)

Thurber's attitude has some of the blackness of Don Marquis, and shows affinity also with writers outside the sphere of humor who disparage reason and stress the maladjustment of man when he moves beyond his animal origins. Sherwood Anderson envied the lot of children and illiterate Negroes; the crew in O'Neill's *The Hairy Ape* advise Yank to "Drink, don't think!" Hemingway's Nick Adams and Frederick Henry are better off when they are fishing, swimming, drinking, or fornicating than when the wheels of their reflection are spinning. Being more cerebral than Yank and more inhibited than Hemingway's males, Thurber's characters find little solace in drink—though not from lack of trying—and their sexual ventures seldom get beyond wishful thinking. But they too are specimens of nature; the introductory quotation for ***The Beast in Me*** concerns "the beast inside, the beast that haunts the moonlit marges of the mind."

Charles Child Walcutt has emphasized the intimate relationship between naturalism and Freudianism, and an orthodox Freudian would see Thurber's Little Man as tormented by the conflict between the unconscious "beast" of sex and the repression of it by the superego, which is shaped and dominated by this man's "civilized" environment. The repressed animal finds its outlet in anxieties, fixations, and obsessions. Basically, society is at fault for repressing rather than channeling the primary urge. (pp. 288-89)

[Some] of Thurber's ideas about sex and personality are not necessarily in conflict with those of Freud. Thurber feels that the male animal is unduly repressed by his environment, an environment which includes another animal, his wife, who both abets and conceals her ruthlessness by means of more resolution, solicitude for her mate, and competence in the small matters of everyday living than he shows. Part of his environment is also a society going mad through a misapplication of technology; so-called neurosis is often merely "a natural caution in a world made up of gadgets that whir and whine and whiz and shriek and sometimes explode." Thurber differs from Freud in ignoring the Oedipus complex, whereas Freud regarded this as the major component of sex. He also differs in feeling that it is futile for man to expect to throw off his repressions or even to sublimate them satisfactorily. The civilized (or repressing and repressed) elements in the Little Man's character and environment often have the same cosmic finality as the natural traits. Thurber's people rarely succeed in changing any aspect of either their surroundings or themselves, and such "adjustment" as the male achieves usually comes only through complete withdrawal, as in the cases of Mitty, and of Grandfather in ***My Life and Hard Times.***

One can hardly blame them, so full of terror is their world. The naturalistic portrait of man as the helpless creature of chance, heredity, and environment was conducive to the view that he was the frequent prey of violence and disaster, as Malcolm Cowley and others have pointed out. The violence and terror in Thurber's work is also part of a tradition in American humor that stretches back into the frontier of pre-Civil War days, with its tales of backwoods bullies in crude, dangerous circumstances. (p. 289)

To be impressed by the proportion of violence in Thurber's narratives, one need only look at ***The Thurber Carnival,*** a cross section of his writing and drawing up to 1945. The first four sections of this book contain thirty-three pieces. Fifteen—or nearly half of these—deal with terror, violence, and disaster, including a nightmare in which gangsters are about to bump off the dreamer and his wife; a woman who goes violently insane; a man who does likewise; several other people who are on the verge; a man who dies by accident; and two who are murdered (three if one counts **"The Macbeth Murder Mystery"**). The fifth section is ***My Life and Hard Times,*** complete, a fictionalized autobiography of certain episodes in the life of Thurber and his family. This section includes three chapters about panic in the home, one about mass panic in the streets (**"The Day the Dam Broke"**), one about various family servants—most of whom go berserk—and one about a vicious dog.

The sixth section consists of pieces from ***Fables for Our Time.*** The brief allegories in the book of that title and in ***Further Fables for Our Time*** are, as a group, the most violent and bitter in Thurber's satires. Like Bierce and Ade, Thurber often gives an old adage a new and ironic twist, but Ade's fables are spiritual milk for babes by comparison with those of Thurber. In one, for example, a chipmunk is safe from the shrikes so long as he loiters in his cave, but when his energetic wife—a typical Thurber female—persuades him to go out, they are both killed. The moral is, "Early to rise and early to bed make a male healthy and wealthy and dead." (p. 290)

Several of the fables carry a message also found in *Is Sex Necessary?* and ***Let Your Mind Alone:*** namely, the naturalistic theme that man, in trying to act as if he were above his place in nature's order, has muddled himself into disaster. A "seal" leaves his natural habitat to join a circus; when he returns home to impress the stay-at-homes he tries to swim, but

> . . . he was so hampered by his smart city clothes, including a pair of seventeen-dollar shoes, that he began to founder at once. Since he hadn't been in swimming for three years, he had forgot what to do with his flippers and tail, and he went down for the third time before the other seals could reach him. They gave him a simple but dignified funeral.
>
> *Moral:* Whom God has equipped with flippers should not monkey around with zippers.
>
> (pp. 290-91)

A pessimistic naturalism has thus permeated Thurber's depiction of the Little Man, but in the late nineteen-thirties, as the economic depression persisted and war began to threaten, he began to say things about public affairs that call for classifying his literary double also with the heirs of the Progressive "New Citizen," that is, with the liberals of the thirties and forties and with the active opponents of McCarthyism in the frightened fifties. In the anger of *The Last Flower* itself one senses—. . . in Auden's words—"an affirming flame" of zeal and hope which is scarcely consistent with despair, and for over a quarter of a century Thurber was outspoken in his attacks on authoritarianism of both left and right. (pp. 291-92)

Some of the ***Fables for Our Time*** also suggest a citizen-writer for whom all is not lost, practicing the eternal vigilance cited by the forefathers as the price of liberty. In **"The Birds and the Foxes,"** the latter animals "civilize" the geese and ducks, and "liberate" the orioles by killing and eating them. "Moral: Government of the orioles, by the foxes, and for the foxes, must perish from the earth." (p. 293)

Thurber's humor in his last decade shows the same inconsistent mixture of despair and of militancy with its concomitant of hope. In ***Further Fables for Our Time,*** one finds some of the older, skeptical pessimism about the human race—see **"The Human Being and the Dinosaur"**—but one also finds that at least ten out of the forty-seven fables in this book are disguised tracts in defense of free expression. In **"The Peacelike Mongoose,"** an animal of that species is persecuted for his use of "reason and intelligence" by those who cry "Reason is six-sevenths of treason." Two more fables are likewise thrusts at McCarthyism: **"The Trial of the Old Watchdog"** and **"Ivory, Apes and People,"** but at least two of these ***Further Fables*** are satires of Soviet communism, which Thurber hated as much as he disliked professional Americanism ("The nature of humor is anti-communistic," he declared in his Ohio lecture). (pp. 294-95)

Thurber's liberalism resembles that of Day and Benchley in being sharply limited by his middle-class angle of vision. Most of his neurotic males and females are suburbanites with hired "help" and summer cottages; people who earn their living with their hands are among the threats to this white-collar cocktail crowd. Mr. Monroe shrinks before the furniture movers; Walter Mitty is buffaloed by the parking-lot attendant; Mr. Pendly by garage mechanics, and several of Thurber's protagonists by waiters, maids, or butlers. In 1934 Thurber served on a committee for the welfare of waiters during a strike by these workers, but he admitted that he didn't have the slightest idea of what waiters do when they go home. In his essays,

Thurber or rather his *persona,* has difficulty with waiters, office help, street-gang laborers, house-servants, and hired yardmen. Oftener than any humorist of note since Bangs, Thurber makes comedy out of "difficult" servants. . . . If their employers are neurotic, Emma Inch, Barney Haller, and several Negro maids are "odd," cross-grained, stupid, or downright psychotic. The servants of the Thurber family in ***My Life and Hard Times*** usually seem even more unbalanced than their employers, and in a revealing piece called **"A Friend of the Earth,"** Thurber's *alter ego* psychologically grapples with Zeph Leggins, a village roustabout, philosopher, and joker who can also be taken as a symbol of the author's rejection of crackerbarrel humor.

Only occasionally are the manual workers shown as mentally healthy, in contrast to the neurotic persons with more money and book-learning. One such worker is the cabdriver who tells Kirk in **"One Is a Wanderer"** that "I got a home over in Brooklyn and a wife and a couple kids, and, boy, I'm tellin' you that's the best place . . ." The point is not that Thurber makes a principle of relating neurosis to social class, but that nearly all manual workers in his writings are seen only from the viewpoint of their employers, and the author does not seem interested in any other viewpoint. When not butts of satire, they are mere foils for his educated, middle-class neurotics.

Thus, one of Thurber's masks has been that of a Little Man helpless in the grip of nature, his wife, and his own nature; the other, used somewhat less often, has been that of a militant of the Progressive-New Deal stamp. (One recalls that many Progressive-New Dealers were conservative in their values and liberal in their advocation of reforms to conserve those values.) The two attitudes existed simultaneously throughout Thurber's career, although most of his pessimistic pieces appeared in the earlier part of his career and most of his more optimistic pieces were written since about 1939. . . . Thurber's pessimistic determinism appears chiefly in his writings about personal and domestic matters, whereas his belief in free will and freedom crops out mainly in his pieces dealing with social and political topics. Rarely, as in *The Male Animal,* does he try to fuse the two realms of subject matter and the two philosophies, and when he does try, the result is not convincing either as ideology or as art.

In the work of Benchley one sees a family man and citizen who is seldom victorious and often defeated but who rarely gives up his theoretical hold on certain hard and fast values. In Thurber's writing, this figure is more often driven over the brink to psychosis and separated from any sense of values. The *persona* who fights the liberal fight for a freedom he refuses to consider dead in theory or in practice is separate and distinct from the beaten-down Little Man. Faced with the dilemma of naturalism—the belief that man is an animal whose character and fate are predetermined by his heredity and his environment—and the contradictory need for some form of belief in free will and morality if one is to live harmoniously among one's fellows or to write humor, Thurber solved the problem no better than did Mencken. Mencken blithely ignored the dilemma; Thurber divided his conception of man and embodied each conception in a separate image inconsistent with the other. (pp. 295-98)

Norris W. Yates, "James Thurber's Little Man and Liberal Citizen," in his The American Humorist: Conscience of the Twentieth Century, *Iowa State University Press, 1964, pp. 275-98.*

CHARLES S. HOLMES (essay date 1965)

[*Holmes, an American critic, wrote* The Clocks of Columbus: The Literary Career of James Thurber *and edited* Thurber: A Collection of Critical Essays [*see Additional Bibliography*]. *In the following excerpt, Holmes examines the role of fantasy in Thurber's writings.*]

James Thurber is the outstanding American humorist of the twentieth century. It would be hard to find anywhere an image of modern life at once more perceptive, more amusing, and more unsettling than we are given in his work. Literary recognition is sometimes rather grudgingly accorded the humorous writer, but Thurber's importance as an interpreter of the American scene was recognized early, and it is a safe guess that his life and work will receive increasing attention from critics and historians of American culture as time goes on. The best of his work is already, in Charles Brady's phrase, part of "the living folklore of the present": Walter Mitty is a more significant culture figure to twentieth-century Americans than Rip Van Winkle, and in the predicaments pictured in Thurber's tales and drawings, we recognize ourselves. (p. 17)

Like all genuine artists, Thurber looks at life in a highly original way. What he sees is a curious blend of reality and fantasy. He was a journalist by profession, and he placed a high value on the accurate observation of the real: the best comedy, he maintained, should represent "the recognizable American Scene." On the other hand, he was unusually responsive to the world of dream and fantasy, and it is no coincidence that he was a lifelong admirer of Lewis Carroll, the great master of purposeful nonsense. What he said of his friend John McNulty, that "his world bordered on Oz and Wonderland," is even more true of Thurber himself. Fantasy is the distinguishing quality of his imagination, which at its best transmutes the familiar into the strange and the real into the sur-real. (pp. 17-18)

The strong bias of Thurber's imagination toward fantasy is . . . evident in his fables. The fable form, in which truth is refracted through the glass of fantasy, was particularly congenial to him, and the Aesopian ***Fables for Our Time*** and ***Further Fables for Our Time*** . . . are among the best things he ever wrote. Taken as a group, the fables are probably Thurber's most representative body of writing; and certain individual pieces stand out with particular authority as quintessential expressions of his themes and values. **"The Unicorn in the Garden,"** for example, could well serve as an introduction to Thurber's work as a whole. It tells the tale of man who looks out one morning to see a unicorn in his garden, eating roses. Happy at the sight, he tells his wife, who says only, "The unicorn is a mythical beast," and turns her back on him. When he returns with the news that the unicorn has eaten a lily, his wife looks at him coldly and says, "'You are a booby, and I am going to have you put in the booby-hatch.'" When her husband leaves the house, she has "a gloat in her eye," and she telephones the police and a psychiatrist, telling them to bring a straitjacket. The police and the psychiatrist arrive, and when she tells them that her husband has seen a unicorn, they seize her and put her in the straitjacket. They ask the husband if he told his wife that he saw a unicorn. He says, "'Of course not. The unicorn is a mythical beast.'" They take the wife away to an institution, and the husband lives happily ever after. Here, the battle of the sexes is presented as a part of the larger conflict between fantasy and reality; and—significantly—the fantasy-principle (male, loving, peaceable) triumphs over the reality-principle (female, cold, hostile).

This conflict between the world of fantasy and the world of reality (and the worlds of husband and wife) is the theme of Thurber's most famous story, **"The Secret Life of Walter Mitty."** Inadequate to the demands of the real world, Walter Mitty finds both refuge and strength in fantasy and daydream. His wife bullies him, the parking lot attendant sneers at his awkward efforts to park the car, he cannot remember the shopping list. But in his secret world of fantasy, derived largely from bad movies, he triumphs over the humiliating forces of the actual. . . . Mitty's daydreams are the veriest claptrap, and their triteness serves to underline the pathos as well as the comedy of his situation, but at the same time they are a source of strength, the means by which he makes his life significant. The issue is not as clear-cut here as in **"The Unicorn in the Garden,"** because Mitty is so obviously, by the standards of the world, a pathetic and inadequate figure; but as the closing image of the story suggests, he is in a deeper sense triumphant, and thus the point of the two tales is essentially the same. . . . (pp. 18-20)

Fantasy is at the center of Thurber's work as a whole. It is not only the esthetic hallmark of his drawings and his prose, but it is also a principle, a standard of value, a quality of experience richer than that offered by everyday life. (p. 20)

The fantasy principle is, in fact, the keystone of a set of closely related values which, until his later years, Thurber habitually champions in opposition to the dominant values of contemporary society. In a world committed to logic, organization, conformity, and efficiency, Thurber stands for fantasy, spontaneity, idiosyncrasy, and confusion. "Confusion" is a bad word in the world's dictionary, but it is an honorific in Thurber's lexicon. It represents the forces of the irrational and the unpredictable which are always upsetting the world of convention, order, and system. Hence Thurber's fondness for situations involving eccentric behavior, elaborate practical jokes, breakdowns of communication, and the disruption of bureaucratic machinery. (pp. 20-1)

The whole of ***My Life and Hard Times,*** Thurber's wonderful account of his youthful days in Columbus, Ohio, is a celebration of oddity, eccentricity, chaos, and confusion. The titles of the separate pieces are indicative: **"The Night the Bed Fell," "The Day the Dam Broke," "The Night the Ghost Got In," "More Alarms at Night,"** and so on. All of these episodes show the disruption of the orderly pattern of everyday life by the idiosyncratic, the bizarre, the irrational. (p. 21)

One of Thurber's major subjects is the use and abuse of language, and here, too, his treatment of the real leads out toward the sur-real. Because as a writer he valued langauge as a necessary principle of order, and as an instrument of precision and beauty in its own right, he was acutely aware of its possibilities for muddle, chaos, and confusion. The precarious nature of language, where the thinnest line separates sense from nonsense, is one of his central concerns. . . . The likelihood that people will misunderstand more often than they will understand each other is the theme of one of the grim little parables in ***Further Fables for Our Time,*** **"The Weaver and the Worm."** The weaver, admiring the silkworm spinning its cocoon, asks, "'Where do you get that stuff?'" The silkworm answers, "'Do you want to make something out of it?'" Both think they have been insulted. "We live, man and worm, in a time when almost everything can mean almost anything, for this is the age of gobbledygook, doubletalk, and gudda."

Thurber took language seriously, because he saw it as an instrument of order, clarity, and good sense, but at the same time he was fascinated by its capacity to create an Alice-in-Wonderland world where ordinary rational communication is transcended, and the real gives way to the sur-real. In the sounds of words and in the chains of association set in motion by unexpected combinations of familiar words, he found a special avenue to the world of fantasy. Lewis Carroll is the presiding genius here, as he is in so much of Thurber's work. His classic nonsense poem "The Jabberwock" ["Jabberwocky"] is a kind of imaginative touchstone for Thurber, the definitive creation of a fantasy-world through language. A relatively early piece, **"What Do You Mean It *Was* Brillig?,"** explores the comic possibilities of the nonsense associations set off by the distortions of ordinary English words in speech. To talk with Della, the colored cook, is to enter a strange and mysterious world. She has a brother who "works into an incinerator where they burn the refuge," and a sister who "got tuberculosis from her teeth, and it went all through her symptom." . . . Thurber sums up these exchanges with Della as "the most satisfying flight from actuality I have ever known." (pp. 23-4)

Thurber's sight began to fail in the late 1940's (during the last ten years of his life he was almost totally blind), and as he became progressively isolated from the world of the eye, his imagination grew more and more responsive to verbal experience. The sound of words, the meaning of words, words as the medium through which we know reality become a major subject in his work after 1950. His comic method undergoes a significant change: whereas his earlier work depends chiefly on character and anecdote, his later pieces make their points through conversational repartee, intricate puns, elaborately garbled quotations, anagrams, and other kinds of complicated verbal games. The word-game piece, a bravura display of dictionary learning, wit, and verbal acrobatics, becomes one of Thurber's most characteristic forms. The setting is usually a half-drunken conversation late at night, where the inhibitions of logic and custom have been melted away, or the lonely hours waiting for sleep, during which the insomniac's mind plays fast and loose with whatever it contemplates.

The prototype of these word-game pieces is **"Do You Want to Make Something Out of It?,"** a lively exercise in word-making which shows Thurber's linguistic originality and inventiveness at their best. The first part of the essay describes a highly sophisticated spelling game in which the players are required to start in the middle of a word and spell backwards and forwards. Asked to spell something with *sgra,* Thurber exhausts the possibilities sanctioned by the dictionary with *disgrace, grosgrain, cross-grained,* and *misgraff,* and then, leaving the realm of the actual behind, he begins to invent, offering a list of what he calls "bedwords," make-believe *sgra* words which have come to him in the small hours of the night. All of them are combinations of familiar everyday words into fanciful compounds, and Thurber presents them in mock-dictionary style:

> BLESSGRAVY. A minister or cleric; the head of a family; one who says grace. Not to be confused with praisegravy, one who extolls a woman's cooking, especially the cooking of a friend's wife; a gay fellow, a flirt, a seducer. *Colloq.,* a breakvow, a shrugholy.
>
> FUSSGRAPE. 1. One who diets or toys with his food, a light eater, a person without appetite, a scornmuffin, a shuncabbage. 2. A man, usually American, who boasts of his knowledge of wines, a smugbottle.

And there are such other expressive coinages as *Kissgranny, Pussgrapple, Cussgravy, Bassgrave,* and *Hossgrace.* All of these comic compounds show Thurber's interest in remaking language, playing with the relationship between sound and meaning, pushing back the limits of the familiar, and transforming the terrain into something strange and new.

In **"Here Come the Tigers"** two tipsy friends descend upon Thurber late at night announcing that they have discovered a new dimension of meaning in the old word-game of anagrams. The key to the game is in the haunting quatrain:

There are lips in pistol
And mist in times
Cats in crystal
And mice in chimes.

Developing the theme that there are animals hidden in a wide variety of common words, the guests identify the wolf in "flower," the gander in "danger," and the frog in "forget." Moving on, they discover a startling constellation of entities in the single word "crystal": salt, slat, cyst, and cart, as well as star, cry, and satyr. At the end, Thurber is tossing restlessly in bed, hunting for the tiger in three six-letter words. The game of anagrams (or complicated versions of it) becomes an obsessive activity in Thurber's later work. There is a kind of desperation in the restless energy with which he takes words apart, spells them backwards, and rearranges them into new patterns, as though he were looking for the key to reality in the structure of a word. . . . Here, as in most of Thurber's explorations of the hidden world of language, the effect is to transform the familiar into the strange, to move from the everyday into the world of fantasy. The sheer abundance, brilliance, and virtuosity of Thurber's verbal antics is dizzying, and after reading two or three of these word-game pieces in succession, one feels lost in a strange country where everything always seems to be turning into something else.

Thurber's later work is darker in tone, harsher in judgment, and more penetrating in moral wisdom than the work of his early and middle years. . . . He saw the postwar world as a time of intellectual and moral confusion. "I think there's been a fall-out of powdered fruitcake—everyone's going nuts," he remarked in an interview. Yet the vein of fantasy and the antic humor run as strongly as ever through his work. The comedy of these later years is a wild, dark comedy, often playing on the brink of hysteria, and in its bizarre anecdotes and extravagant verbal effects suggesting a world collapsing into chaos.

The most characteristic form of his later period is the conversation piece, an invention of Thurber's own in which all sorts of fantastic variations are played upon a central theme. The setting is usually a party or other convivial occasion, and the talkers are expansive and uninhibited, creating out of the play of wild generalization, false example, garbled quotation, and outrageous pun a strange and dream-like world.

"Midnight at Tim's Place" is typical of the surreal quality of many of these later pieces. The line between reality and fantasy blurs and shifts as the conversationalists assume false names, get off complex and subtle puns, and engage one another in contests of fanciful invention. The man across the table pretends to take Thurber for Bing Crosby. "How are you, Bing?" he asks. "*Non sum qualis eram sub regno bony Sinatra,*" replies Thurber, mixing ancient and modern cultures in an impressive display of linguistic virtuosity. The central anecdote, an unsettling parody of modern man's search for guidance and reassurance, deals with the experience of the man across the table when, on the edge of a nervous breakdown, he went to see his old philosophy professor, "the greatest symbol of security in my life." The professor, who specialized in such inspiring mottoes as "You can keep a stiff upper lip and smile too!" seemed totally unchanged after twenty years as he sat in his study, except that he was wearing two hats. "They were both gray felt hats, one on top of the other. The terrifying thing was that he didn't say anything about them. He just sat there with two hats on, trying to cheer me up." At the close of the sketch the worlds of fantasy and reality collide. Moved by the story of the mad professor, Thurber leaves the party wearing two hats, and hails a cab. The driver looks at him and says, "Not in this cab, Jack." (pp. 25-9)

The most striking formal characteristic of the conversation pieces is the ceaseless play of pun, twisted quotation, and literary allusion, in which familiar patterns of sound and meaning are constantly shifting and changing. There are the concise, classic puns which are woven into the very texture of Thurber's prose—"We battle for the word while the very Oedipus of reason crumbles beneath us," and so on. Thurber's most elaborate and original puns, however, depend upon famous quotations and titles, or familiar adages. Most often the quotations are garbled or twisted to fit an incongruous situation, and the effectiveness of the device depends upon the unexpected and ludicrous significance given to a familiar line or saying. In **"Get Thee To A Monastery,"** Thurber and the pedantic Dr. Bach conclude an involved discussion of the fate of Shakespeare in the woman-dominated theater of today: "The rest is silex," intones Dr. Bach as he goes off to make himself a cup of coffee; "Good night, sweet Prince," says Thurber, picking up the cue from *Hamlet,* "and flights of angels sing thee to thy rest." Here, the effect is that of burlesque. The famous lines from Shakespeare are twisted out of shape and made to bear an incongruous meaning. In Bergsonian terms what takes place is a sudden transposition of key, from a higher to a lower level of discourse. In a more subtle variation of the method, the quotation is given intact, but a preposterous meaning is assigned it, as in **"The Danger in the House,"** where Thurber describes a curious dream about a woman in a long white dress who appears to be holding some sort of mechanism in her right hand, and Dr. Prell, the heavy-footed Freudian psychologist, asks whether the mechanism might not have *been* her hand, quoting T. S. Eliot's famous lines in evidence:

When lovely woman stoops to folly
And finds herself again alone,
She combs her hair with automatic hand
And puts a record on the gramophone

Titles of well-known books, songs, and plays undergo the same sort of antic transformation: the anxieties of the Cold War bring on dreams in which familiar titles become strange and unsettling—*Alias in Wonderland, Traitor-Island, Look Homeward, Agent,* and so on. Television's tendency to make the classics into Westerns raises some distressing possibilities—*Trelawney of the Wells Fargo . . . She Shoots to Conquer . . . The Sheriff Misses Tanqueray*. The obsession of the modern theater with neurotic and morbid themes suggests such revisions of popular titles as *Abie's Irish Neurosis* and *Oklahomasexual*.

The puns, quotations, and literary allusions of these later pieces are not isolated jokes or simply decorative flourishes, but a central part of Thurber's literary method. His mind was a storehouse of quotations from the standard authors, particularly Shakespeare and the nineteenth-century writers. A rough count of the literary references in his work puts Henry James, his favorite author, in first place, followed by Lewis Carroll, Shakespeare, Tennyson, Browning, Longfellow, Henley,

Wordsworth, Shelley, Poe, and Landor. (There are scattered references to such twentieth-century figures as Joyce, T. S. Eliot, Fitzgerald, and Hemingway.) Authors, titles, and familiar quotations were an important part of Thurber's imagination, and so, when he wished to make a point, comic or otherwise, it is entirely natural that he would set it in the context of famous literary treatments of the subject.

If one were to look for the quintessence of Thurber's later world-view, it would most likely be found in one of the apocalyptic fables—**"The Human Being and the Dinosaur,"** for example, or **"The Shore and the Sea."** (pp. 29-31)

Although it will not do to claim Thurber for the cult of the Absurd in modern literature (Thurber having formed his view of life independently and long before the Absurd became a literary movement), the world of his later work is nonetheless close to the world as we find it in Ionesco—the apocalyptic vision, the fascination with the breakdown of communication as the primary symptom of a cosmic sickness, and the comic virtuosity are present in both.

But such parallels should not be pushed too far. The sense of modern life as too bizarre and outrageous to be presented as anything other than a grotesque comedy is, in fact, a striking characteristic of much postwar writing, and Thurber's brilliant expression of this sense is not a matter of literary fasion, but an independent response to a common cultural and philosophical situation. In any case, the world of Thurber is larger than that of Ionesco. The dark fantasies and the melancholy strain in his work are balanced by a basic sanity and a positive relish of the whole human scene. The essential quality of Thurber's imagination is the tension between a strong sense of fact (throughout his life he considered himself primarily a journalist) and a strong bias toward fantasy. In his earlier career he searched out and celebrated disorder, illogic, and confusion, feeling that these qualities were desirable counterbalances in a society over-committed to logic and organization. Later, as history changed the world he knew, and as illogic and disorder on an international scale threatened to engulf mankind, he began to champion those things which hold a society together, and his fantasies and his brilliant images of disorder became warnings and distress-signals rather than signs of revelry.

But he never lost his compensating faith in the saving power of humor and intelligence. "Let us not forget the uses of laughter or store them away in the attic," he wrote in **"The Duchess and the Bugs."** Comedy, humor, and laughter he saw as essential to the health of any society, because they demolish humbug and reveal the truth. The title of his last collection, *Lanterns and Lances* (1960), with its suggestion of attack and illumination, defines the role he thought comedy should play; and his basic faith in comedy, in intelligence, and in life is finely expressed in the advice he gives to the reader in the Foreword of that volume: "In this light, let's not look back in anger, or forward in fear, but around in awareness." (pp. 32-3)

Charles S. Holmes, "James Thurber and the Art of Fantasy," in The Yale Review, *Vol. LV, No. 1, October, 1965, pp. 17-33.*

"All right, have it your way—you heard a seal bark"

One of Thurber's best-known cartoons. From The Seal in the Bedroom, *by James Thurber. Harper & Row. Copyright © 1932, 1960 James Thurber. Reproduced by permission of Rosemary A. Thurber.*

LOUIS HASLEY (essay date 1974)

[Hasley is an American critic, poet, and humorist. In the following excerpt, Hasley discusses recurring themes in Thurber's stories and sketches.]

Beyond question the foremost humorist of the twentieth century, James Thurber was a divided man. With minor exceptions he did not explore the century's large social and political problems. War, religion, crime, poverty, civil rights—these were not his subjects. Instead he struck at the immemorial stupidities, cruelties, and perversities of men that lie at the root of our ills. A disillusioned idealist, he satirized mean behavior to sound the clearest note of his discontent. Yet he considered himself an optimist or near kin to one. He insisted that the perceptive reader would detect in his work "a basic and indestructible thread of hope."

How valid, the reader may ask, are Thurber's strictures against our civilization when one finds scarcely a momentary glimpse of childhood, romantic love, the businessman, the scientist, the engineer, the clergyman, the factory worker, the lawyer, the physician? If none of these, who then are his subjects, his characters?

Aside from relatives and family servants, he gives us artists and intellectuals like himself, isolatoes in our time, self-exiled by a temperament alien to the world and at the same time treated contemptuously by that world. Validity might then be dismissed as an irrelevance because we are faced with two conflicting sets of ideas. It was the study of man, however, that absorbed Thurber, and the proof of his right to the title of artist lies in his ability to universalize his subjects.

The world of James Thurber is conjugal, social, artistic, and psychological, as it is in his favorite author, Henry James. It is, of course, less genteel, less sinister, less subtle, less refined, less elaborate than in James, but it fits the pace of life in today's journalistic offices and studios, as well as its upper-middle-class social gatherings that are viable only with plentiful alcoholic stimulation. Here the artist-intellectuals and their long-suffering spouses communicate among themselves, having only tangential contact with this or that "outsider" from the practical world of affairs. James Thurber found man a frightening subject, although a large part of his best work was in perceptive, affectionate, admiring tribute to [friends and family]. (pp. 504-05)

Of [Thurber's] pieces that appear to be clearly fiction in the more or less currently realistic sense of the term, only a handful are outstanding. Triumphant among these is the incomparable story, **"The Secret Life of Walter Mitty."** In a civilization in which women were winning the battle of the sexes, Mitty the non-hero is among the defaulters by virtue of allowing his wife to dominate him. He achieves secretly a kind of compensatory victory by indulging in interludes of stream-of-consciousness fantasy, triggered whenever the immediate outside event threatens to run him down—fantasy in which he vividly and heroically figures as a man among men. The story is a masterpiece of associational psychology in its shuttling between the petty, humiliating details of his outer life and the flaming heroism of his self-glorifying reveries. (pp. 505-06)

"The Catbird Seat" presents a vigorous, blustery woman, Mrs. Ulgine Barrows (note that "Ulgine" suggests "ugly" and that "barrow" can mean a pig) and a mousy Erwin Martin, head file clerk, whose department is threatened by the efficiency ax of Mrs. Barrows. Martin first plans a quiet murder of his enemy, then changes to an extremely ingenious plan by which she is routed, and by which Martin becomes, so to speak, the canary that swallowed the cat.

If Mitty has only an escapist's psychological victory, Martin's triumph is complete and unalloyed; but both are widely considered exceptions in the female-dominated world of James Thurber. Still a third "exception" occurs in the fable, **"The Unicorn in the Garden,"** wherein the man, whom the wife tries to have put in the booby-hatch, manages to have her put away instead. . . . Perhaps the number of such "exceptions" is sufficient to puncture the legend of the monolithic triumph of women over men in Thurber's world.

"The Catbird Seat" is a short story of traditional structure. So too is **"The Greatest Man in the World,"** told in deadly earnest and with devastating effect. It presents a thoroughly detestable minor criminal, Jack "Pal" Smurch, who flies a flimsy airplane solo, nonstop, around the world. While the millions, including the President and other dignitaries, having been treated by the press to rose-tinted descriptions of Smurch's past life, make plans to honor him, Smurch arrogantly demands money and the parties which he expects as his due. His behavior is so egregious that the nation's leaders adopt a drastic expedient to dispose of him. In its contempt and grotesquerie, it is equaled only by Ring Lardner's story "Champion" (with its anti-hero, Midge Kelly), in depicting a blind and indiscriminate hero worship by the American public, with a secondary indictment of the press in pandering to the debased tastes of its masses of readers. The nation's political leaders likewise share guilt with the press for their time-serving part in the ignoble dispatch of Smurch.

In the realm of slangy satire, **"The White Rabbit Caper"** is a hilarious take-off on radio mystery stories as written for children. An animal story with clever dialogue that teems with puns and is touched with rare fantasy, it is one of the funniest pieces Thurber ever wrote. At another extreme is **"A Call on Mrs. Forrester,"** a beautifully imagined and sensitive account of a visit by the narrator to the charming Marian Forrester, the central character in the novelette, *A Lost Lady,* done in the manner of its author, Willa Cather. (pp. 506-07)

This century has seen the fable genre used distinctively by George Ade, Ambrose Bierce, Don Marquis, and James Thurber. The best of Ade's and of Thurber's vie for first honors, though they are very different. Ade's fables are realistic, the characters are people, and the application is principally to the life of the day. Thurber's fables are more nearly Aesopian, most of the characters are animals, and their extension is more widely philosophical.

Given Thurber's passion for brevity, clarity, and conciseness, and his satirist's desire to teach, it was reasonable that the fable as a form should exert a magnetic attraction upon him. That his didacticism was intentional many of the morals readily show:

> "Where most of us end up there is no knowing,
> but the hell-bent get where they are going."
>
> "It is wiser to be hendubious than cocksure."
>
> "A word to the wise is not sufficient if it doesn't
> make sense."
>
> "He who dies of a surfeit is as dead as he who
> starves."

Though most of the fables are universal in their cast, several are geared to political relevance in our day. The moral of **"The Birds and the Foxes"** is readily seen to have contemporary application: "Government of orioles, by the foxes, and for the foxes, must perish from the earth." The moral of **"The Very Proper Gander"** is ironic: "Anybody who you or your wife thinks is going to overthrow the government by violence must be driven out of the country." The most fully worked out and best realized symbolically is **"The Rabbits Who Caused All the Trouble,"** an allegory of the operation of the Big Lie among nations and a satire of imperialistic, protective invasion. Ultimately the most charming and probably the most enduring of the fables is **"The Unicorn in the Garden,"** a parable justifying the imagination and its sense for beauty, telling us that only those who can see a unicorn can truly see reality. (p. 508)

The border warfare which Thurber so persistently waged with our machine civilization seems to have been a natural inheritance both from parents and from grandparents, including a grandfather who scolded and handled his electric runabout as he would a colt that had to be broken. Excellent incidents illustrative of Thurber's encounters with machines, along with suitable psychological, even Freudian, analysis, are found in **"Sex Ex Machina," "The Car We Had to Push," "Recollections of the Gas Buggy,"** and **"A Ride with Olympy."** . . . A sense of mystery emerges as mechanical objects seem to try to speak. Thurber can tell of tires that "booped and whooshed" and fenders that "queeled and graked," while the machine in the operating room of Walter Mitty's mind goes on immortally with its "pocketa-pocketa-pocketa."

One of the passions of James Thurber was his devotion to language. He battled often and zealously against obfuscation, against "the carcinomenclature" of "an agglomerative phenomenon of accumulated concretations." What he insisted on was clarity, accuracy, and sense. He blamed the merchandisers and the "political terminologists of all parties" for the continuing debasement of our language, asking instead that it be used with dignity and grace. Some of this advocacy is straight, but much of it is woven lightly and wittily into a great variety of situations and contexts, including word games, of which he was inordinately fond and which cost him many night hours of sleepless tossing. (pp. 509-10)

During the last ten years of his life, Thurber turned more and more to serious treatments of literary subjects and people. His spirit followed a less creative, more critical turn, and while he never yielded wholly to despair, the note of gloom is unmistakable. Art, he declared, was "the one achievement of Man which has made the long trip up from all fours seem well advised." But the present time, he said, meaning around 1960, "is one of formlessness in literature, in drama, and in comedy as well as in speech." (p. 511)

Thurber's style is an enviable model of twentieth-century American—supple, witty, unmannered, sensitive to words, marked by humor that ranges from the quiet to the explosive, and by inspired metaphor. One of his women "whisked a cork out of a wine bottle as if it had been a maidenhair fern." In **"The Day the Dam Broke"** we were all "as safe as kittens under a cookstove." As a quarrel develops with her husband, Marcia Winship's "sentences were becoming long and wavy." In **"The Catbird Seat,"** "the door to the office blew open with the suddenness of a gas-main explosion and Mrs. Barrows catapulted through it." About the only device of humor that crops up with regularity is some form of paronomasia—elaborate punning or word play, often done with song lyrics, as in "I want a ghoul just like the ghoul that buried dear dead Dad." Confusion is sometimes served by a snowballing technique or by exaggeration, as in **"The Night the Ghost Got In."** That night the police answered a burglar alarm from the Thurber residence by "a Ford sedan full of them, two on motorcycles, and a patrol wagon with about eight in it and a few reporters."

Thurber once declared in a letter to this writer, "I almost never plan the use of a literary device, but just take it when it comes along." Of course a number of them occasionally came along, several of which are the incongruous catalogue, the *reductio ad absurdum,* the comic neologism, understatement, altered clichés, nonsense, alliteration, slang, parody, literary allusion, and invective.

Thurber was, it must be conceded, a fastidious stylist with psychological depth, subtlety and complexity; with a keen sense of pace, tone, ease, and climax; and with imagination that often wandered into surrealism. He handled minor tragedy with unparalleled expertness. Revisions were frequent and painstaking, a given piece often being revised ten or (as with **"Mitty"**) fifteen times. . . . The positive delight that the reader takes in his style, along with his often greater intellectual range and understanding, tells why he outdoes his contemporaries in his chosen métier. (pp. 512-13)

Louis Hasley, "James Thurber: Artist in Humor," in South Atlantic Quarterly, *Vol. 73, No. 4, Autumn, 1974, pp. 504-15.*

ANN FERGUSON MANN (essay date 1982)

[In a departure from previous interpretations of "The Secret Life of Walter Mitty," Mann offers a sympathetic view of Mitty's wife.]

James Thurber's **"The Secret Life of Walter Mitty"** was an immediate success with the American reading public when it was first published in 1939, and it continues to be widely anthologized and read today. The fact that "Mitty's name, like Babbit's, is now part of our language," attests to the broad appeal of the story. [The quote is attributed in a footnote to Charles S. Holmes in his *The Clocks of Columbus: The Literary Career of James Thurber;* see Additional Bibliography.] Critics and readers do not always agree about the correct response to Mitty: should he be considered a kind of hero or a pathetic, even suicidal, figure? But there is almost universal agreement about Mrs. Mitty. She is a nag, an extremely overbearing woman, who is perhaps the ultimate cause of Walter's secret life. While readers' reactions to Mitty are always expected to be sympathetic, Mrs. Mitty has been greeted with almost universal scorn. (p. 351)

Despite this . . . , a reexamination of Mrs. Mitty's function in the story seems in order, and a clearer understanding of her role in her husband's life can clarify the appropriate response of the reader toward Walter Mitty. Relevant to this discussion are the tightly controlled structure of the story, which has been closely examined by critics, and Thurber's final comment about his character, "Walter Mitty, the Undefeated, inscrutable to the last." Such an analysis of the story will show that Mrs. Mitty's behavior can just as easily be understood as a response to, and not a cause of, Mitty's fantasy life. In fact, Mrs. Mitty can be considered the ideal wife for Walter Mitty. Furthermore, the paradoxical enabler-scapegoat role of Mrs. Mitty is one that recurs for female characters throughout American literature.

Why does Walter Mitty fantasize? In particular, can we determine whether Mitty lapses into fantasies because he is married to a nagging wife and is physically and emotionally inept, or do his wife's complaints and his own blunders stem from his proclivity toward fantasizing? Most critics have assumed the former conclusion to account for the structure of Mitty's life. As Charles Holmes writes, "In reality, Walter Mitty is inadequate to the demands of the real world: his wife bullies him, the parking lot attendant sneers at his awkward efforts to park the car, he cannot remember the shopping list. But in his secret world of fantasy, derived largely from bad movies, he triumphs over the humiliating forces of the actual" [see excerpt dated 1965]. This at first seems to be a logical assumption. Nevertheless, a close examination of the structure of the story suggests that Mitty's problems with his wife and with the rest of the outside world could just as easily be the result and not the cause of his fantasies. But this explanation is generally overlooked by readers and critics.

The story begins in the middle of Walter Mitty's Naval Commander fantasy. Although the immediate cause of this fantasy is not apparent, we soon learn that driving his wife to town through bad weather triggered the daydream. In the same way throughout the story, Mitty's fantasies stem directly from some detail of his environment that he transforms imaginatively, not directly from reactions to his wife or to other people. He imagines being the famous physician after he drives past the hospital, the defendant after the newspaper boy yells out the headline about the Waterbury trial, the bombardier after reading the magazine headline, "Can Germany Conquer the World Through the Air?" and the hero facing the firing squad after lighting a cigarette and leaning against a stone wall. This is not to suggest that Mrs. Mitty has had no part in influencing Walter's imaginative life: she is the reason he is driving to town in the first place; she instructs him to wear his gloves and to purchase overshoes and puppy biscuits; he has to wait in the hotel lobby and outside the drugstore for her. At the same time, the fact that Mitty uses such physical details as the starting points for his reveries would suggest how easily he lapses into an imaginary world. As Carl Sundell has noted, "**'The Secret Life'** begins with him dreaming and ends with him dreaming. He is, in fact, a chronic daydreamer" [see Additional Bibliography]. (pp. 351-52)

A second observation that can be made about Mitty's fantasy life is that Mrs. Mitty's nagging and the derision expressed by others toward Mitty often occur during or after one of Mitty's fantasies. It is only when Mitty, totally absorbed in his Naval Commander fantasy, begins driving too fast that Mrs. Mitty interrupts him. Only after Mitty, while he is imagining himself to be a great surgeon, drives into the Exit Only lane does the attendant yell at him. And the woman on the street laughs at him after he mumbles "puppy biscuit" to himself, thinking of the "miserable cur" of his third fantasy. While Mitty might fantasize to overcome low self-esteem, it is important not to overlook the fact that at least on some occasions Mitty's daydreaming is responsible for the negative reaction of other people toward him. Neither Mrs. Mitty nor Walter Mitty's feelings of inadequacy, therefore, are necessarily the only or the primary causes of Mitty's fantasy life.

Clearly, living with Mrs. Mitty poses certain problems and creates frustrations for her husband. What is interesting is that no critics and few readers of the story have tried to imagine the difficulties resulting from living with Walter Mitty. Is Mrs. Mitty's behavior that reprehensible if we try to imagine ourselves in the role of caring for a "chronic daydreamer"? If Mrs. Mitty is bossy, her husband rarely complains. He drives her to town each week although "in a way he hated these weekly trips to town"; he does her errands for her; he gets to the hotel first; he waits for her repeatedly, all without protest. Mrs. Mitty has little opportunity to realize the extent to which her commands are a burden to this man who so dutifully and uncomplainingly follows them. The only signs of rebellion from Mitty are when he tells his wife, "I don't need overshoes" and when he races "the engine a little" and removes his gloves after letting her off at the hairdresser's. The only direct confrontation between the Mittys, furthermore, occurs after Mrs. Mitty fusses at Walter for "hiding" from her in the hotel lobby and for not wearing his overshoes. Mitty's most overt complaint is to say to her, "Does it ever occur to you that I am sometimes thinking?" When Mrs. Mitty here and earlier in the story suggests that Mitty visit the doctor, her reaction hardly seems insensitive in light of Mitty's bizarre behavior and absentmindedness. If we think seriously about what life with a man like Mitty would be like, Mrs. Mitty seems responsible and concerned. While some critics have acknowledged Mrs. Mitty's strengths of character, they still view her antagonistically. Morsberger acknowledges that "many of Thurber's own stories and drawings show a weak man dependent upon a strong woman; but such a situation appears deplorable rather than to be desired." As Norris Yates states, "Thurber feels that the male animal is unduly repressed by his environment, an environment which includes his wife, who both abets and conceals her ruthlessness by means of more resolution, solicitude for her mate, and competence in the small matters of everyday living than he shows" [see excerpt dated 1964]. Furthermore, any attempt by Mrs. Mitty to understand her husband's behavior is sure to fail since he guards his "secret life" in "the remote, intimate airways of his mind." All intimacy for Mitty, possibly all feeling, is relegated to the remote airways of his mind. Not only is Mitty extremely uncommunicative, but he also so completely blocks his wife out of his consciousness that, returning from one of his fantasies, he views her as "grossly unfamiliar, like a strange woman who had yelled at him in a crowd."

Why doesn't Walter Mitty rebel or complain about his wife? Does his lack of rebellion or complaint indicate that he is finally defeated by life, or does he manage to triumph over his circumstances? Either Walter Mitty is so weak a character that he cannot stand up to Mrs. Mitty and the only appropriate response to him is pity, or he finds a way to defeat her through his current lifestyle and therefore prefers his own situation as it is. The most important clue to judging Walter Mitty is Thurber's final comment about his character, "Walter Mitty, the Undefeated, inscrutable to the last." This statement suggests that Mitty is finally triumphant over his wife and the forces within the real world. But what is the nature of Walter Mitty's triumph?

Here it is crucial to understand what Mitty is "battling" for and against. Critics have identified Mitty's major enemy as his wife and all that she stands for. Some critics, like Brooks and Warren, view Mrs. Mitty as the individual who has effectively limited her husband's potential, that "overbearing and unimaginative wife who evidently long ago suppressed Mr. Mitty's yearnings for the heroic and venturesome." Similarly, Tobias labels her "the oppressive element . . . that kind of mind which prevents the hero from living the rich, full and deliberate life." Morsberger goes on to suggest that not only the nagging wife but the institution of marriage as well are what hamper "would-be explorers and adventurers" like Walter Mitty. But can we honestly view Walter Mitty as a man with stifled or untapped heroic potential? Is it possible to imagine Walter Mitty behaving self-confidently, let alone heroically, with or without his overbearing wife? The details of his character in the story fail to confirm this view. What Mitty yearns for is not the "heroic and venturesome," "rich, full and deliberate life" or "would-be explorers and adventurers," but the opportunity to fantasize about this kind of life. What Walter Mitty most wants and is most successful in obtaining is freedom—not from his wife—but from the petty details of living so that he can spend time in the world of his imagination.

If we view Walter Mitty's true ambition or desire as the preservation of his fantasy life, he is clearly triumphant. At the same time, we will begin to view Mrs. Mitty's role quite differently. After all, how is Mitty able to devote most of his time to his imaginary life? How else, but through the efforts of the often-accused cause of his fantasies—Mrs. Mitty. The best argument against Carl Sundell's interpretation of Mitty as a potential suicide or victim of a nervous breakdown is Mrs. Mitty, Walter's constant companion. Walter Mitty, the daydreamer, who is "not a young man anymore," has survived for some time in the real world because of his wife. She is there to keep him from driving too fast, to get him to wear gloves and overshoes, to take him to the doctor, but, most importantly, to free him from all the practical responsibilities of living so that he can pursue his real career—his fantasy life. It is not inconceivable that Mitty, the architect of so many intricate fantasies, unconsciously chose for himself a wife like Mrs. Mitty.

What sense, then, can we make of Mrs. Mitty, who is at once the enabler of Mitty's career and his ultimate enemy? To explain the paradoxical character of Mrs. Mitty, we have to examine the mind set not only of a Walter Mitty but also of the critics who have laid the blame for Mitty's problems on his wife. Richard Tobias hints at the way to unravel this paradox when he identifies Mitty with the "mind" and Mrs. Mitty with the "body." The greatest enemy of the fantasizer is his existence in the real world, the fact of his physical being. . . . What Walter Mitty would ultimately reject is his physical being, half of what it means to be human. Such an attempt is one way of trying to deny mortality. Unable to do this, Mitty looks

Home

Thurber cartoon. From Men, Women and Dogs, *by James Thurber. Harcourt Brace Jovanovich, Inc. Copyright © 1943 James Thurber. Copyright © 1971 Helen Thurber and Rosemary A. Thurber. Reproduced by permission of Rosemary A. Thurber.*

for an explanation for the uncomfortable situation in which he finds himself. The explanation that satisfies him is an old one. Mrs. Mitty, another Eve, relegated to the realm of the physical, having less of a mind than her mate, is viewed as the ultimate cause of his predicament when she attempts to secure a more powerful role for herself. Both Eve and Mrs. Mitty can and do serve the paradoxical role of helpmate-scapegoat, and both are attempts by the male to account for the problem of mortality.

If Mrs. Mitty is like Eve, Walter Mitty is less like Adam than he is like the first popular American folk hero, Rip Van Winkle. While Rip sleeps, Mitty daydreams, but the impetus for both kinds of escape is the same. Rip Van Winkle and Walter Mitty are both trying to evade adult responsibility and to avoid a shrewish wife. . . . Mrs. Mitty, as stereotyped by Thurber as was Dame Van Winkle by Irving, is simply one of a long list of female characters particularly in American literature who have been emasculated by their male creators. At once enablers and scapegoats, they do not make sense as real women but only as male fantasies of women.

Finally, Thurber's last line contains an interesting allusion that further clarifies his attitudes and can help account for the different responses of readers toward Walter Mitty. Critics frequently mention the allusion to Conrad's Lord Jim in Thurber's description of Mitty as "inscrutable to the last." A more significant allusion in this same line, however, is "the Undefeated," which was the title of a Hemingway short story, published in 1927 in the collection *Men Without Women*. Morsberger has argued that Thurber was interested in portraying a different kind of heroism from that of Hemingway.

> Despite Walter Mitty's dreams of derring-do, Thurber challenged the workshop of the bellicose heroics. He wrote that none of his memoirs "is stained with blood or bright with danger, in the active or Hemingway sense of the word. My experiences . . . have been distinguished by an average unremarkableness, toughed with grotesquerie, discomfort, and humiliation, but definitely lacking in genuine .50 caliber peril." . . . [A] more geniune heroism is the quiet, modest confrontation of day by day problems. . . . [O]ne of his favorite heroes in modern belles-lettres is the man who accepts a situation with calm and resignation.

The "calm and resignation" of the Thurber hero is not unlike the stoicism of Hemingway's heroes, but this is only one of many similarities between the attitudes of the two writers. In fact, Thurber was interested in portraying heroics that were different in degree but not in kind from Hemingway's.

Mitty, like Hemingway's heroes, confronts a hostile world. He envisions escape into a world of "men without women." (Most of Mitty's daydreams are all-male; the "pretty nurse" of his second fantasy and the "lovely, dark-haired girl" of his third fantasy are minor romantic interests without any character development.) Walter Mitty's dreams place their hero in progressively more dangerous situations not, as Sundell believes, because Mitty is dangerously existing on the edge of insanity and/or suicide, but to test the hero's mettle and because of Thurber's, like Hemingway's, pessimistic world view. There is an "enemy" out there that will destroy but not defeat the Thurber hero of the mind, just as it would destroy but not defeat Hemingway's heroes. For both Thurber and Hemingway that enemy is, in its least avoidable form, the biological fact of existence. (Mitty would surely agree with Frederick Henry's statement, "You always feel trapped biologically.") In its most pernicious form, the enemy is that aggressive female—Mrs. Mitty/Margot Macomber—that is out to destroy its prey, the male. Both Thurber's Mitty and Hemingway's heroes are a continuation of the male-female relationship first depicted in Rip Van Winkle's and Dame Van Winkle's marriage. . . . (pp. 353-57)

Understanding the role of Mrs. Mitty clarifies the heroic-pathetic nature of Walter Mitty. Walter is a hero, triumphant in terms of the rules of the game plan he has designed for his life. As critics have rightly pointed out, however, his is a limited victory: "it is a victory only in the frame of his own experience and values." It is not only private—one that cannot give him a place in society; it is ridden by the cliches of pulp romances and Grade C movies. . . ." The triteness of Walter Mitty's victory is not as significant as its limitation. Walter Mitty is one of those people whose lifestyle and self-image depend on the presence of the OTHER, on whom all life's problems can be blamed. Such an outlook produces its own kind of oppression and naturally stifles the development of such individuals who shun responsibility for their own failings and often for their own lives. What Thurber's story can show us, while it delights us with its clever humor, is that what traps the Walter Mittys of this world and insures that they will remain "little men" is their own limited view of themselves and others. (p. 357)

Ann Ferguson Mann, "Taking Care of Walter Mitty," in Studies in Short Fiction, *Vol. 19, No. 4, Fall, 1982, pp. 351-57.*

MELVIN MADDOCKS (essay date 1985)

[*Maddocks asserts that critics who extol Thurber as a great writer exaggerate his modest talent.*]

While he was still alive, James Thurber was judged to be the best humorist since Mark Twain—if not something more. After calling him his "favourite humorist," T. S. Eliot weightily pronounced Thurber's writing and illustrations to be "a document of the age they belong to." Ernest Hemingway appeared on Thurber dustjackets, declaring that here was the "best writing coming out of America."

Nothing kills a soufflé like praising it in terms of a roast-beef dinner. The pleasures of Thurber are still there for the rereading, but one savors them moderately. The superlatives applied by Thurber's colleagues and contemporaries seem excessive to the point of embarrassment today, especially when applied to his essays. In retrospect the essays of *New Yorker* humorists—those famous "casuals"—come across as group representatives of a journalistic genre. Frank Sullivan, Russell Maloney, E. B. White, Thurber—there is something institutional and anonymous, something interchangeable, about the way these writers and others domesticated madness into mere whimsy and clothed it in the finest English-tweed prose native Americans could produce. (p. 597)

When an ambitious case is being made for Thurber, ***My Life and Hard Times*** almost invariably gets nominated as his masterpiece. The comparison with Mark Twain is a little too glibly justified by this fanciful autobiography, pitting a boyhood in Columbus, Ohio, against a boyhood in Hannibal, Missouri. "I suppose that the high-water mark of my youth in Columbus, Ohio, was the night the bed fell on my father," Thurber began, and the hyperbole flowed freely from there.

Thurber was not a subtle inventor. When he set out to invent confusion, he invented chaos. When he set out to invent a character, he invented an eccentric. The chaos verged on slapstick humor; the eccentric verged on a comic-strip cartoon. Take first-cousin Briggs Beall, apparently a total fabrication. Beall kept a glass of camphor by his bed from fear that he might suffocate in his sleep one night without the aid of this pungent reviver. Instead he almost suffocated from the camphor.

The "night the bed fell" is neatly bracketed with the "time I fell out of the gun room in Mr. James Stanley's house," an anecdote Thurber introduces in the last chapter and then coyly evades. But the general pattern remains constant. Our raconteur is a man to whom the oddest people, the most personable dogs, and the orneriest automobiles are attached. There is a charm to Thurber's manner—offhand and meandering, setting up one tall tale after another by making a virtue of the non sequitur. In effect he is a snob of the comic disaster, taking every mishap as "one of those bewildering involvements for which my family had, I am afraid, a kind of unhappy genius." The more fantastic, the more grandly muddled, he makes his Columbus and his people, the more he is able to love them.

Thurber's short stories share the same simple if not simplistic outline of his essays and autobiography. His most famous short story, **"The Secret Life of Walter Mitty,"** is a single joke ingeniously sustained. The Caspar Milquetoast, dreaming of heroic deeds as a navy commander or a surgeon while waiting meekly for his wife to finish shopping, is the raw material of a *New Yorker* cartoon. Thurber stories provide few second insights. A rereading of **"Walter Mitty"** only makes Thurber seem excessively tender and indulgent toward the Small Boy he treasured in men—and found threatened by Thurber women.

"The Breaking Up of the Winships" explicitly treats the war between the sexes as an absurd escalating argument over the merits of Greta Garbo and Donald Duck as cinematic geniuses. Thurber maintains an evenhanded position through most of the story, before tipping the balance against the wife at the end.

"The Catbird Seat" measures, even more starkly than his cartoons, Thurber's animosity and fear toward women. The discrediting of poor Ulgine Barrows, the office efficiency-expert, is savage revenge beyond any reasonable provocation within the story. . . . (pp. 598-99)

"Jim had it in for women," E. B. White, perhaps his closest friend, conceded.

Whatever emotion Thurber's short stories possess derives from two chief plots: men harassed by women; and men abandoned by women, like the protagonist of **"One Is a Wanderer,"** drinking himself into a fit state to retire to sleep in his lonely hotel room. (p. 599)

Toward the end of his life Thurber wrote more and more pieces with titles like "A Farewell to Speech" and "The Decline and Fall of the King's English." His preoccupation with language became fastidious to the point of being cranky. An insomniac, he counted words the way other men counted sheep, winding up with lists of words beginning with "P, the purloining letter, the stealer of sleep." He struck the posture of a Minister of Culture in a very small republic.

The social critic Otto Friedrich accused Thurber of becoming obsessed with trivia [see excerpt dated 1955]. Thurber did not deny it, but huffily defended himself with his latter-day loftiness: "Trivia Mundi has always been as dear and as necessary to me as her bigger and more glamorous sister, Gloria" [see excerpt dated 1955].

He called anger "one of the necessary virtues," but he seemed to get angry about less and less. His life became a litany of gripes. A reader found Thurber besieged and beleaguered by rock music, radio news broadcasts, junk mail, and unwanted phone calls. Everything shoddy flourished, while worthy institutions, like the railroad, went to hell.

Thurber constantly complained about the decline of humor, even in the *New Yorker* ("the magazine is turning grim and long"). But while criticizing glumness in others, he wrote, "I cannot confine myself to lightness in a period of human life that demands light."

The allusions to Henry James went up and up. Within a few pages he used the same tag from Horace twice. "He was pompous and unbelievably humorless when he decided that he was a man of letters," his longtime friend Ann Honeycutt complained. (p. 600)

When Thurber cultists who admired his art threatened to turn his head by overblown comparisons, mostly to Matisse, E. B. White sensibly told him: "If you ever got good you'd be mediocre." A reconsiderer of Thurber almost a quarter of a century after his death might extend White's clever observation to argue that Thurber "got good" as a writer, and became as other writers. (p. 601)

Melvin Maddocks, "James Thurber and the Hazards of Humor," in The Sewanee Review, *Vol. XCIII, No. 4, Fall, 1985, pp. 597-601.*

ADDITIONAL BIBLIOGRAPHY

Attebery, Brian. "The Baum Tradition." In his *The Fantasy Tradition in American Literature: From Irving to LeGuin*, pp. 134-53. Bloomington: Indiana University Press, 1980.

Discusses Thurber's gift for fantasy and how his work relates to that of L. Frank Baum, creator of the "Oz" books.

Bernstein, Burton. *Thurber: A Biography*. New York: Dodd, Mead, 1975, 532 p.

Authorized biography by one of Thurber's former *New Yorker* colleagues.

Black, Stephen A. *James Thurber: His Masquerades*. The Hague: Mouton, 1970, 126 p.

Critical study presenting Thurber as a grim, iconoclastic humorist.

Coates, Robert M. "Thurber, Inc." *The Saturday Review* XXI, No. 6 (2 December 1939): 10-11, 28.

Biographical essay by a friend and colleague.

Cowley, Malcolm. "Lions and Lemmings, Toads and Tigers." *The Reporter* 15, No. 9 (3 December 1956): 42-4.

Discussion of Thurber's style in an appreciative review of *Further Fables for Our Times*.

Hackett, Francis. "Odd Man Out." In his *On Judging Books: In General and in Particular*, pp. 29-40. New York: John Day, 1947.

General appreciation of Thurber's comic sense.

Holmes, Charles S. *The Clocks of Columbus: The Literary Career of James Thurber*. New York: Atheneum, 1972, 360 p.

Critical biography by a major Thurber scholar.

———, ed. *Thurber: A Collection of Critical Essays*. Englewood Cliffs, N.J.: Prentice-Hall, 1974, 180 p.

Reprints many significant reviews and essays about Thurber, including pieces by Holmes, Malcolm Cowley, Peter De Vries, and Dorothy Parker.

Lindner, Carl M. "Thurber's Walter Mitty: The Underground Hero." *The Georgia Review* XXXVIII, No. 2 (Summer 1974): 283-89.

Places Walter Mitty in the tradition of other heroes of American literature, such as Rip Van Winkle and Huckleberry Finn, who escape the pressures of ordinary life through fantastic adventures.

Morsberger, Robert E. *James Thurber*. New York: Twayne, 1964, 224 p.

Critical survey that discusses Thurber's role as a satirist and social critic.

Plimpton, George, and Steele, Max. "The Art of Fiction X: James Thurber." *The Paris Review* 3, No. 10 (Fall 1955): 34-49.

An interview in which Thurber discusses his blindness, his techniques of composition, and other matters relating to his work.

Satterfield, Leon. "Thurber's 'The Secret Life of Walter Mitty'." *The Explicator* XXVII, No. 8 (April 1969): 57.

Parallels Mrs. Mitty and the villainous District Attorney of Walter's fantasy.

Sheed, Wilfred. "The Thurber Carnival." *Horizon* XIII, No. 4 (Autumn 1971): 16-17.

Appreciative personal essay.

Sundell, Carl. "The Architecture of Walter Mitty's Secret Life." *English Journal* 56, No. 9 (December 1967): 1284-87.

A guide to teaching "The Secret Life of Walter Mitty." A high school English instructor relates his method of delineating the themes and stylistic elements of the story to his students.

Tobias, Richard C. *The Art of James Thurber*. Athens, Ohio: Ohio University Press, 1970, 196 p.

A critical study identifying the major themes in Thurber's work.

———. "Thurber in Paris: 'Clocks' Kept Different Time." *Lost Generation Journal* III, No. 1 (Winter 1975): 2-6.

Considers Thurber's writings about Americans in Paris.

Tracy, Honor. "The Claw of the Sea-Puss." *Listener* XLV, No. 1158 (10 May 1951): 760-61.

Descriptive appreciation of Thurber's fictional world.

Triesch, Manfred. "Men and Animals: James Thurber and the Conversion of a Literary Genre." *Studies in Short Fiction* III, No. 3 (Spring 1966): 307-13.

Examines Thurber's fables in relation to the traditional allegorical tales of Aesop and La Fontaine.

Underwood, Marylyn. "Thurber's 'The Catbird Seat.'" *The Explicator* 40, No. 4 (Summer 1982): 49-50.

Analyzes bird imagery in "The Catbird Seat."

Weales, Gerald. "The World in Thurber's Fables." *Commonweal* 65, No. 16 (18 January 1957): 409-11.

Identifies a growing pessimism in Thurber's later works, illustrated by the contrast between his early fable collection and the gloomier *Further Fables for Our Time*.

Jean Toomer

1894-1967

(Born Nathan Eugene Toomer) American short story writer, poet, and essayist.

Courtesy of Fisk University

Cane is one of the most admired and frequently studied literary creations of the Harlem Renaissance, a period in the 1920s which saw a flowering of Afro-American culture. Described by Hugh M. Gloster as "a potpourri of stories, sketches, poetry, and drama," *Cane* is an intimate portrait of Afro-American life, depicting such themes as slavery, sexuality, and, most importantly, self-identity. It is this latter theme, so often highlighted by critics, that forms the quest in *Cane*. Toomer envisioned the book as a "swan song" for the dying black folk spirit, and in it he suggests that in order to understand the present and to maintain hope for the future, one must understand the past. Toomer's work is highly praised both for its rich use of symbol and myth and for its experiments with language and form and is often cited as an extremely influential work in the canon of black literature. Despite the encouragement of Sherwood Anderson, Hart Crane, and particularly Waldo Frank, who called Toomer "a literary force of whose incalculable future I believe no reader of [*Cane*] will be in doubt," Toomer never equaled the success of his initial work. Although he published several essays, poems, and stories in small-press periodicals during the more than thirty years of his subsequent writing, he never sold another book to a commercial publisher.

Born in Washington, D.C., Toomer claimed his ancestry to be "Scotch, Welsh, German, English, French, Dutch, Spanish, with some dark blood"; his grandfather was black, his mother of mixed blood, and his father a white Georgia farmer. Toomer spent much of his childhood in an affluent white section of Washington, relatively free of racial prejudice, in the home of his maternal grandfather, P.B.S. Pinchback, a prominent Louisiana politician of the Reconstruction era. It was after the death of Toomer's mother in 1909 that the Pinchbacks experienced extreme financial losses, requiring the family to move to a modest black neighborhood. Toomer's position in both black and white society offered him an unusual perspective on racial identity. Early in his life he concluded that he was a member of the American race, neither black nor white, a conviction that deeply affected both his literary career and the course of his life.

As a young man, Toomer lived a transient existence, studying various subjects at several universities and working a number of jobs. Toomer enjoyed a literary apprenticeship for several months in 1919 and 1920 in Greenwich Village, where he met some prominent New York intellectuals, including Edwin Arlington Robinson and Frank. In the fall of 1921, Toomer accepted a temporary teaching position in Sparta, Georgia, a rural southern town of poor black folk that gave Toomer the opportunity to discover his black roots, which he further explored on a tour of the South with Waldo Frank in 1922. This exposure to the South inspired much of Toomer's writing in *Cane*.

Cane includes many pieces that originally appeared in the avant garde literary magazines *Broom, The Crisis,* and *S 4 N*. The work is divided into three sections and reflects Toomer's impressions of Afro-American life in both the rural South and in the black neighborhoods of Washington, D.C. and Chicago. Employing a structure often compared to musical composition, particularly elements of gospel and blues, Toomer unifies *Cane*'s various pieces with recurring themes and motifs and with parallel and contrapuntal relationships between the urban and rural black experience. In the first section of *Cane*, Toomer interweaves six stories with twelve poems, using imagery drawn from nature to create the lyrical, impressionistic, and often mystical portraits of six Southern women. Images of sunset, dusk, ripening fruit, and canefields in the stories "Karintha," "Becky," "Carma," and "Fern" suggest the richness of a passing way of life, while ghosts, full moons, and fire in "Esther" and "Blood-Burning Moon" announce its dissolution. By turns strong and vulnerable, exotic and ordinary, innocent and misunderstood, Toomer's women, commentators note, convey the essence of this Southern life, which was soon to be altered by encroaching cultural change. In "Song of the Son," a poem in section one deemed central to *Cane*'s thematic development, Toomer sings, "for though the sun is setting on / A song-lit race of slaves, it has not set; / Though late, O soil, it is not too late yet." Critics conclude that in section one Toomer successfully captures the beauty and dignity as well as the pain and suffering of these people and their lives.

Cane's second section, which comprises seven prose sketches and five poems, shifts in setting from the rural South to the urban North. In "Seventh Street," the opening piece, Toomer establishes the frantic tone and urban landscape that characterize this section. His rhythms, ragged and jazz-influenced, contrast with the flowing, lush texture of section one. Houses, alleys, asphalt streets, machines, theaters, and nightclubs function as symbols of confinement that limit growth and thwart self-understanding. In his examinations of sexual and emotional relationships between men and women in such stories as "Avey," "Theater," "Box Seat," and "Bona and Paul," Toomer challenges the conventions of modern industrialized society and illustrates how a pseudo-culture robs one of life-giving, creative instincts and uproots one from the nurturing provided by the soil. "Rhobert" serves as a distillation of Toomer's views on the inescapable corruption of bourgeois values and ambitions, for here the protagonist is unable to sacrifice the status of owning a home, even though he is victimized by the burden it creates. Section two is a skillful portrayal, commentators note, of characters spiritually bankrupt and devoid of vitality because they have abandoned their natural heritage and adopted society's stifling values.

Cane's third section consists of "Kabnis," Toomer's longest, most sustained piece, which incorporates the themes of both sections one and two. Variously described by critics as a play, novella, and short story, "Kabnis" is a thinly-veiled autobiographical portrait of an educated but spiritually confused northern black who travels to the South to teach school in a small, rural town in the hope of discovering his ancestry. Much as the stories in section one feature women, "Kabnis" focuses on various men who each embody some part of the black experience: among its leading figures critics point to Kabnis, the northern black idealist inflated by bourgeois white values and disillusioned with his race; Lewis, the northern black of intelligence and stature who accepts his history; Hanby, the black school principal who plays the aristocrat among his people; and Father John, the old black man made wise by the experience of slavery and by intimacy with his black heritage. Critics see in these and other figures the dilemma of the black American caught between conflicting and alienating life styles and values. There is little agreement among critics, however, whether Toomer effectively resolves in "Kabnis" the conflicts he has so skillfully evoked. Some believe that Toomer has achieved his goal by suggesting that blacks can help themselves and the stifled, dying nation by returning to their spiritual roots from which a new birth is possible. Other reviewers argue that Toomer ends *Cane* inconclusively at best, with each of the characters of "Kabnis" despairing of their future or resigned to it.

Cane drew early critical interest because of its engaging approach to subject and its experimental form. Critics were quick to point out that *Cane* was not a diatribe on racial relations, nor a strident reformist doctrine, as were many works by other Harlem Renaissance writers, but was instead a lyrical, passionate, and artistic creation. The influence of Anderson and Frank, acknowledged by Toomer, is evidenced in the centrality of folk life; Toomer also attributed his work to the influence of the Imagist poets whose economy of line and image he praised and emulated. But critical reaction to *Cane* as a masterpiece of Afro-American literature angered Toomer, who declared his work to be a depiction of American experience written by an American author, not a black one. Although he wrote voluminously after the publication of *Cane*, Toomer found his works were uniformly rejected, a fact he attributed to his refusal to write another *Cane*. Toomer felt that *Cane* had voiced his essential message about the dying black folk spirit. He wrote: "*Cane* was a song of an end. And why no one has seen and felt that, why people have expected me to write a second and a third and a fourth book like *Cane* is one of the queer misunderstandings of my life."

Toomer's private writings, which are housed at Fisk University, contain novels, plays, short stories, poems, and several autobiographical volumes. None of these—with the exception of a privately printed collection of aphorisms entitled *Essentials* and the posthumously published *The Wayward and the Seeking: A Collection of Writings by Jean Toomer*—has appeared in book form. Toomer's encounter in 1924 with the teachings of George Gurdjieff, a Greek and Armenian spiritual leader who taught a complex program of philosophy, psychology, and dance movements designed to achieve spiritual wholeness, led Toomer to eschew the literary world he cultivated during the early 1920s. Toomer joined Gurdjieff's movement, attended the Gurdjieff Institute at Fontainebleau, France, and taught Gurdjieff philosophy from 1926 until 1933. As a result, many of Toomer's subsequent writings reflect his dedication to Gurdjieffian philosophy and methods and display little of *Cane*'s poignant lyricism, beauty, or sorrow. Toomer married in 1931, but lost his wife in childbirth. When Toomer remarried in 1934, he moved with his second wife to Pennsylvania, where he became a Quaker.

Darwin T. Turner concludes his introduction to the 1975 edition of *Cane* with this observation: "*Cane* was not Jean Toomer's total life; it was perhaps merely an interlude in his search for understanding. No matter what it may have been for him, *Cane* still sings to readers, not the swan song of an era that was dying, but the morning hymn of a Renaissance that was beginning."

(See also *CLC*, Vols. 1, 4, 13, 22; *Contemporary Authors*, Vols. 85-88; and *Dictionary of Literary Biography*, Vols. 45, 51.)

PRINCIPAL WORKS

SHORT FICTION AND MULTI-GENRE

Cane 1923
The Wayward and the Seeking: A Collection of Writings by Jean Toomer 1980

OTHER MAJOR WORKS

Essentials (aphorisms) 1931
The Flavor of Man (lecture) 1949

WALDO FRANK (essay date 1923)

[Frank, an American novelist and critic, is best known as an interpreter of contemporary civilization. A socialist and supporter of various radical groups in the United States, he was a founding editor of the Seven Arts *(1916-17), a distinguished leftist, avant-garde magazine of literature and opinion. One of Frank's most significant works of criticism,* Our America *(1919), derides the "genteel tradition" in American letters and calls for a spiritual revolution in the nation's life and literature. Along with such writers as Van Wyck Brooks, Paul Rosenfeld, Sherwood Anderson, and Gorham Munson, Frank helped to create a social, philosophical, and literary atmosphere that deeply influenced Toomer's developing sensibilities. Frank met Toomer around 1920,*

and he quickly became Toomer's mentor, proving instrumental in launching the young author's career. In the following excerpt from his foreword to the first edition of Cane, *Frank cites* Cane *as a new development in Southern literature because of its movement away from racial problems and polemics toward a celebration of life and art.*]

Reading [***Cane***], I had the vision of a land, heretofore sunk in the mists of muteness, suddenly rising up into the eminence of song. Innumerable books have been written about the South; some good books have been written in the South. This book *is* the South. I do not mean that ***Cane*** covers the South or is the South's full voice. Merely this: a poet has arisen among our American youth who has known how to turn the essences and materials of his Southland into the essences and materials of literature. A poet has arisen in that land who writes, not as a Southerner, not as a rebel against Southerners, not as a Negro, not as apologist or priest or critic: who writes as a *poet*. The fashioning of beauty is ever foremost in his inspiration: not forcedly but simply, and because these ultimate aspects of his world are to him more real than all its specific problems. He has made songs and lovely stories of his land . . . not of its yesterday, but of its immediate life. And that has been enough.

How rare this is will be clear to those who have followed with concern the struggle of the South toward literary expression, and the particular trial of that portion of its folk whose skin is dark. The gifted Negro has been too often thwarted from becoming a poet because his world was forever forcing him to recollect that he was a Negro. The artist must lose such lesser identities in the great well of life. . . . The French novelist is not forever noting: "This is French." It is so atmospheric for him to be French, that he can devote himself to saying: "This is human." This is an imperative condition for the creating of deep art. The whole will and mind of the creator must go below the surfaces of race. And this has been an almost impossible condition for the American Negro to achieve, forced every moment of his life into a specific and superficial plane of consciousness.

The first negative significance of ***Cane*** is that this so natural and restrictive state of mind is completely lacking. For Toomer, the Southland is not a problem to be solved; it is a field of loveliness to be sung: the Georgia Negro is not a downtrodden soul to be uplifted; he is material for gorgeous painting: the segregated self-conscious brown belt of Washington is not a topic to be discussed and exposed; it is a subject of beauty and of drama, worthy of creation in literary form.

It seems to me, therefore, that this is a first book in more ways than one. It is a harbinger of the South's literary maturity: of its emergence from the obsession put upon its minds by the unending racial crisis—an obsession from which writers have made their indirect escape through sentimentalism, exoticism, polemic, "problem" fiction, and moral melodrama. It marks the dawn of direct and unafraid creation. And, as the initial work of a man of twenty-seven, it is the harbinger of a literary force of whose incalculable future I believe no reader of this book will be in doubt.

How typical is ***Cane*** of the South's still virgin soil and of its pressing seeds! and the book's chaos of verse, tale, drama, its rhythmic rolling shift from lyrism to narrative, from mystery to intimate pathos! But read the book through and you will see a complex and significant form take substance from its chaos. Part One is the primitive and evanescent black world of Georgia. Part Two is the threshing and suffering brown world of Washington, lifted by opportunity and contact into the anguish of self-conscious struggle. Part Three is Georgia again . . . the invasion into this black womb of the ferment seed: the neurotic, educated, spiritually stirring Negro. As a broad form this is superb, and the very looseness and unexpected waves of the book's parts make ***Cane*** still more *South,* still more of an aesthetic equivalent of the land.

What a land it is! What an Aeschylean beauty to its fateful problem! Those of you who love our South will find here some of your love. Those of you who know it not will perhaps begin to understand what a warm splendor is at last at dawn.

> A feast of moon and men and barking hounds,
> An orgy for some genius of the South
> With bloodshot eyes and cane-lipped scented mouth
> Surprised in making folk-songs. . . .

So, in his still sometimes clumsy stride (for Toomer is finally a poet in prose) the author gives you an inkling of his revelation. An individual force, wise enough to drink humbly at this great spring of his land . . . such is the first impression of Jean Toomer. But beyond this wisdom and this power (which shows itself perhaps most splendidly in his complete freedom from the sense of persecution), there rises a figure more significant: the artist, hard, self-immolating, the artist who is not interested in races, whose domain is Life. The book's final Part is no longer "promise"; it is achievement. It is no mere dawn: it is a bit of the full morning. These materials . . . the ancient black man, mute, inaccessible, and yet so mystically close to the new tumultuous members of his race, the simple slave Past, the shredding Negro Present, the iridescent passionate dream of the To-morrow . . . are made and measured by a craftsman into an unforgettable music. The notes of his counterpoint are particular, themes are of intimate connection with us Americans. But the result is that abstract and absolute thing called Art. (pp. vii-xi)

Waldo Frank, in a foreword to Cane *by Jean Toomer, 1923. Reprint by University Place Press, 1967, pp. vii-xi.*

ROBERT LITTELL (essay date 1923)

[*Littell was an American critic and editor who served as associate editor of the* New Republic *from 1922-27. In the following excerpt, Littell briefly compares* Cane *with the work of Waldo Frank and discusses the contrast between the narrative and poetic sections of Toomer's book.*]

"Reading this book," says Mr. Waldo Frank in his introduction, "I had the vision of a land, heretofore sunk in the mists of muteness, suddenly rising up into the eminence of song. . . . This book *is* the South" [see excerpt dated 1923]. Not the South of the chivalrous gentleman, the fair lady, the friendly, decaying mansion, of mammies, cotton and pickaninnies. Nor yet the South of lynchings and hatreds, of the bitter, rebellious young Negro, and of his emigration to the North. ***Cane*** does not remotely resemble any of the familiar, superficial views of the South on which we have been brought up. On the contrary, Mr. Toomer's view is unfamiliar and bafflingly subterranean, the vision of a poet far more than the account of things seen by a novelist—lyric, symbolic, oblique, seldom actual.

In many respects Mr. Toomer recalls Waldo Frank. They seem curiously to coincide at their weakest points. Such sentences as these might have been written by either of them: "Dark swaying forms of Negroes are street-songs that woo virginal houses . . . Dan Moore walks southward on Thirteenth Street . . .

girl eyes within him widen upward to promised faces . . . Negroes open gates and go indoors, perfectly." Such phrases mean either almost nothing, or a great deal too much. In the case of Mr. Frank they seem to contain, bottled up within them, the very essence of what he wants to say; in the case of Mr. Toomer, they are occasional, accidental, and could be brushed off without damage to the whole. While Mr. Toomer often tries for puzzling and profound effects, he accomplishes fairly well what he sets out to do, and ***Cane*** is not seething, like nearly all Mr. Frank's books, with great inexpressible things bursting to be said, and only occasionally arriving, like little bubbles to the surface of a sea of molten tar.

Cane is sharply divided into two parts. The first is a series of sketches, almost poetic in form and feeling, revolving about a character which emerges with very different degrees of clarity. The second half is a longish short story, **"Kabnis,"** quite distinct from the sketches, and peculiarly interesting. In this Mr. Toomer shows a genuine gift for character portrayal and dialogue. In the sketches, the poet is uppermost. Many of them begin with three or four lines of verse, and end with the same lines, slightly changed. The construction here is musical, too often a little artificially so. The body of the sketch tends to poetry, and to a pattern which begins to lose its effectiveness as soon as one guesses how it is coming out. . . .[Once] we begin to regard Mr. Toomer's shorter sketches as poetry, many objections to the obscurer symbolism and obliqueness of them disappear. There remains, however, a strong objection to their staccato beat. The sentences fall like small shot from a high tower. They pass from poetry into prose, and from there into Western Union.

"Kabnis," the longest piece in the book, is far the most direct and most living, perhaps because it seems to have grown so much more than been consciously made. There is no pattern in it, and very little effort at poetry. And Mr. Toomer makes his Negroes talk like very real people, almost, in spots, as if he had taken down their words as they came. A strange contrast to the lyric expressionism of the shorter pieces. A real peek into the mind of the South, which, like nearly all such genuinely intimate glimpses, leaves one puzzled, and—fortunately—unable to generalize.

Cane is an interesting, occasionally beautiful and often queer book of exploration into old country and new ways of writing.

Robert Littell, in a review of "Cane," in The New Republic, *Vol. XXXVII, No. 473, December 26, 1923, p. 128.*

W.E.B. Du BOIS (essay date 1924)

[*Du Bois is regarded as a leading figure in Afro-American thought. He wrote extensively on the sociology and history of black Americans, was a founding member of the National Association for the Advancement of Colored People, and edited two highly respected periodicals, the* Crisis *and* Phylon, *both dedicated to the exploration and advancement of black culture and society. Rejecting the conciliatory policies of Booker T. Washington, who supported gradual assimilation of Afro-Americans into American society, Du Bois advocated immediate equality and full citizenship. His early collection of sketches concerning Afro-American life,* The Souls of Black Folk *(1903), is considered a landmark in the quest for black identity in America. In the following excerpt, Du Bois comments on the sexual themes present in* Cane, *puzzles over the obliqueness of many sketches, and finally praises Toomer as an artist whose best work is yet to come.*]

The world of black folk will some day arise and point to Jean Toomer as a writer who first dared to emancipate the colored world from the conventions of sex. It is quite impossible for most Americans to realize how straightlaced and conventional thought is within the Negro World, despite the very unconventional acts of the group. Yet this contradiction is true. And Jean Toomer is the first of our writers to hurl his pen across the very face of our sex conventionality. In ***Cane,*** one has only to take his women characters *seriatim* to realize this: Here is Karintha, an innocent prostitute; Becky, a fallen white woman; Carma, a tender Amazon of unbridled desire; Fern, an unconscious wanton; Esther, a woman who looks age and bastardy in the face and flees in despair; Louise, with a white and a black lover; Avey, unfeeling and unmoral; and Doris, the cheap chorus girl. These are his women, painted with a frankness that is going to make his black readers shrink and criticize; and yet they are done with a certain splendid, careless truth.

Toomer does not impress me as one who knows his Georgia but he does know human beings; and, from the background which he has seen slightly and heard of all his life through the lips of others, he paints things that are true, not with Dutch exactness, but rather with an impressionist's sweep of color. He is an artist with words but a conscious artist who offends often by his apparently undue striving for effect. On the other hand his powerful book is filled with felicitous phrases. . . . (pp. 161-62)

His emotion is for the most part entirely objective. One does not feel that he feels much and yet the fervor of his descriptions shows that he has felt or knows what feeling is. His art carries much that is difficult or even impossible to understand. The artist, of course, has a right deliberately to make his art a puzzle to the interpreter (the whole world is a puzzle) but on the other hand I am myself unduly irritated by this sort of thing. I cannot, for the life of me, for instance see why Toomer could not have made the tragedy of Carma something that I could understand instead of vaguely guess at; **"Box Seat"** muddles me to the last degree and I am not sure that I know what **"Kabnis"** is about. All of these essays and stories, even when I do not understand them, have their strange flashes of power, their numerous messages and numberless reasons for being. But still for me they are partially spoiled. Toomer strikes me as a man who has written a powerful book but who is still watching for the fullness of his strength and for that calm certainty of his art which will undoubtedly come with years. (p. 162)

W.E.B. Du Bois, in an excerpt from "The Younger Literary Movement," in The Crisis, *Vol. 27, No. 4, February, 1924, pp. 161-63.*

WILLIAM STANLEY BRAITHWAITE (essay date 1924)

[*Braithwaite was an American poet and anthologist who founded and edited for seventeen years the* Anthology of Magazine Verse and Yearbook of American Poetry *(1913-29). In the following excerpt from his survey of Afro-American literature, Braithwaite praises Toomer's artistry in* Cane.]

I believe that of all the writers I have mentioned [in these remarks on the Negro in literature], the one who is most surely touched with genius is Jean Toomer the author of ***Cane.*** I believe this, not only on account of what he has actually accomplished in ***Cane,*** but for something which is partly in the accomplishment and partly in the half articulate sense and impression of his powers. This young man is an artist; the very first artist in his Race who, with all an artist's passion and sympathy for life, its hurts, its sympathies, its desires, its joys, its defeats, and strange yearnings, can write about the Negro without the surrender or compromise of the artist's vision. It's a mere accident that birth or association has thrown him into contact with the life that he has written about. He would write just as well, just as poignantly, just as transmutingly, about the peasants of Russia, or the peasants of Ireland, had experience but given him the knowledge of their existence. ***Cane*** is a book of gold and bronze, of dusk and flame, of ecstacy and pain, and Jean Toomer is a bright morning star of a new day of the Race in literature! (p. 210)

William Stanley Braithwaite, "The Negro in Literature," in The Crisis, *Vol. 28, No. 5, September, 1924, pp. 204-10.*

GORHAM B. MUNSON (essay date 1925)

[Munson was an American social and literary critic perhaps best known as the founder and editor of Secession *(1922-24), an avant-garde magazine whose contributors included E. E. Cummings, Tristan Tzara, Hart Crane, Marianne Moore, and many other experimental writers of the 1920s. Munson's relationship with Toomer was initiated by Waldo Frank, who suggested that Toomer submit a story to* Secession. *Munson rejected the piece, but began an ongoing correspondence with Toomer. In the following excerpt from an essay originally published in* Opportunity *in 1925, Munson explores Toomer's purposes for writing* Cane *and discusses the author's subsequent search for personal meaning.]*

There can be no question of Jean Toomer's skill as a literary craftsman. A writer who can combine vowels and liquids to form a cadence like "she was as innocently lovely as a November cotton flower" has a subtle command of word-music. And a writer who can break the boundaries of the sentence, interrupt the placement of a fact with a lyrical cry, and yet hold both his fact and his exclamation to a single welded meaning as in the expression: "A single room held down to earth . . . O fly away to Jesus . . . by a leaning chimney . . ." is assuredly at home in the language and therefore is assuredly free to experiment and invent. Toomer has found his own speech, now swift and clipped for violent narrative action, now languorous and dragging for specific characterizing purposes, and now lean and sinuous for the exposition of ideas, but always cadenced to accord with an unusually sensitive ear.

It is interesting to know that Toomer, before he began to write, thought of becoming a composer. One might have guessed it from the fact that the early sketches in ***Cane*** depend fully as much upon a musical unity as upon a literary unity. **"Karintha,"** for example, opens with a song, presents a theme, breaks into song, develops the theme, sings again, drops back into prose, and dies away in a song. But in it certain narrative functions—one might mention that lying back of the bald statement, "This interest of the male, who wishes to ripen a growing thing too soon, could mean no good to her"—are left undeveloped. Were it not for the songs, the piece could scarcely exist.

But electing to write Toomer was too canny to try to carry literature further into music than this. ***Cane*** is, from one point of view, the record of his search for suitable literary forms. We can see him seeking guidance and in several of the stories, notably **"Fern"** and **"Avey,"** it is the hand of Sherwood Anderson that he takes hold. But Anderson leads toward formlessness and Toomer shakes him off for Waldo Frank in such pieces as **"Theater"** where the design becomes clear and the parts are held in a vital esthetic union. (pp. 178-79)

Cane is the projection of a vivid personality. What the fundamental motives were that impelled this projection we cannot say, but we can pick out a few probably subsidiary motives that will perhaps indicate Toomer's status at the moment he completed ***Cane***. Clearly, he desired to make contact with his hereditary roots in the Southland. (p. 181)

What can we add to this purpose? We can say that Toomer makes a very full response to life, a response that is both robust and sensitive, and we can say, to use the conventional phrase, that he "accepts life." It is plain that he has strong instincts, welling and deep and delicate emotions, and a discriminating and analytical intellect (more fully revealed in his critical work); and these are all keenly aware of life. This life that floods in upon his psychology Toomer finds to be potent and sweet, colorful and singing, interesting and puzzling, pathetic and worthy of respect; he is able to accept it,—perhaps because his survey of it shows it to be beautiful and mysterious. At any rate, the only fully adumbrated attitude in ***Cane*** is that of the spectatorial artist. But that raises the question: Under what circumstances can the artist be a spectator?

To be a spectator one must have a firm and fixed point of vantage. Where can such a point be found to-day? Our social framework is admittedly unsettled, but it is less generally perceived that culturally we are being blown into chaos. . . . The great movement of the last few centuries has been romanticism which has glorified personal uniqueness and universal flux and has driven us all away from any possible center of human experience. Born into such circumstances, what is the artist to do? He must choose to work either toward integration or toward disintegration.

Nietzsche, it should be recalled, looked upon artists as casters of glamour over progression and retrogression alike. That is, by virtue of their magic they could glorify either, they could be either saviors or betrayers. An artist who does not care where the lure and grace that he sheds over objects lead his entranced followers naturally will not inquire very deeply into the purpose for creation. He creates beauty and lets truth and goodness go hang. But an artist who feels that his gifts entail a grave responsibility, who wishes to fight on the side of life abundant rather than for life deficient, must pause and seek the answers to certain questions. What is the function of man? What are the potentials of man and what may he become? What is experience and what is knowledge? What is the world?

The significance of Jean Toomer lies in his strenuous attempt to answer these questions. Shortly after writing ***Cane***, he formed two convictions. One was that the modern world is a veritable chaos and the other was that in a disrupted age the first duty of the artist is to unify himself. Having achieved personal wholeness, then perhaps he would possess an attitude that would not be merely a reaction to the circumstances of modernity, merely a reflection of the life about him, but would be an attitude that could act upon modernity, dissolve away the remainder of an old slope of consciousness, and plant the seeds for a new slope. (pp. 182-85)

He is a dynamic symbol of what all artists of our time should be doing, if they are to command our trust. He has mastered his craft. Now he seeks a purpose that will convince him that his craft is nobly employed. Obviously, to his search there is no end, but in his search there is bound to occur a fusion of his experience, and it is this fused experience that will give profundity to his later work. His way is not the way of the minor art master, but the way of the major master of art. (pp. 185-86)

Gorham B. Munson, "The Significance of Jean Toomer," in his Destinations: A Canvass of American Literature Since 1900, *J. H. Sears & Company, Inc., 1928, pp. 178-86.*

PAUL ROSENFELD (essay date 1925)

[*Rosenfeld was a respected music and literary critic whose work is noted for its sensitivity and discernment. He coedited the* Seven Arts *with Waldo Frank and James Oppenheim, and served for seven years as music critic for the* Dial. *An acquaintance of Toomer's through the literary circle surrounding* Seven Arts *magazine, Rosenfeld was a model for a major character in Toomer's short story "York Beach," which was published in* The New American Caravan, *a five-volume series of contemporary writing edited by Alfred Kreymborg, Lewis Mumford, and Rosenfeld. In the following excerpt, Rosenfeld expounds on the innovative style of* Cane *and Toomer's literary influences.*]

Momentarily the prose of ***Cane*** is artificially exalted, hooked to the Frankian pitch as to a nail high up in the wall. And night is the soft belly of a pregnant negress, and "her mind" a pink mesh bag filled with baby toes. But quickly the inflations subside. The happy normal swing resumes, the easy rhythm of a strainless human frame.

Not all the narratives intend the quality of legendary song. Certain give the fragmentated moods of the contemporary psychic conflict, and throb with hysterical starts and tearing dissonance. Yet saving the few derailing exaltations, the swing and balance of the limber body walking a road is ever-present. The musical state of soul seems primary in Jean Toomer. The pattern generates the tale. He tunes his fiddle like a tavern minstrel, and out of the little rocking or running design there rises the protagonist, solidifying from rhythm as heroes once solidified from mist: crouched whitewoman Becky who had two negro sons; Carma in overalls and strong as any man; Kabnis with his jangling nerves and flooding nostalgic lyricism. The rhythm forms the figures most. The words are but flecks of light gleaming on the surface of bronze.

He has his hand lightly, relaxedly, upon substances. The words transmit the easy sensations. They come warm and fuzzy and rich not with the heat and density of bodies crowded in tenements, but with the level beat of a blood promenaded in resinous forests amid blotches of June sun on needles and cones. . . . [Toomer] assembles words as a painter negligently rubbing pastels; leaving where he touches warm singing blobs of brown and red.

There are no rings laming this imagination, most the time: and binding it in on his proper person. Toomer's protagonists, symbols and situations are not of the nature of prearrangements: objects glued together on a mental plane and revealing through wooden joints and inner dislocation the artificial synthesis. His creative power offers to bring this young poet-novelist high in the ranks of living American letters. Characters and narratives move, and move in unpremeditated, unpredictable curves. Yet in their sudden tangential departures and radical developments they remain logical with a logic profounder than the intellect's. Not all the personages and situations of the stories, it is true, are submitted to extended composition and developed. The majority remain exposed in a single scene and through a single view. Yet in the nouvelle **"Kabnis"** Toomer has produced an extended composition. The focal character is moved through several episodes, and with each episode the scope of the story deepens. Characters and situations are satisfying both as symbol and as fact; and toward the conclusion both are transposed without violence to a level of reality deeper than that upon which they were launched. (pp. 227-29)

Toomer's free gift has given him the vision of a parting soul, and lifted his voice in salutation to the folk-spirit of the negro South. He comes like a son returned in bare time to take a living full farewell of a dying parent; and all of him loves and wants to commemorate that perishing naïveté, only beautiful one America has had, before universal ugly sophistication cover it also. Those simple singing people who have joy and have pain, and voice them frankly, largely, utterly have come to hold for him a great earthly beauty and tragedy. Their sheer animal litheness and pathos has become savage and satisfying to his breast. . . . He follows the elasticity, resiliency of young rubber, into the brown belt of Washington: feels it in its conflict with the sophistication and mechanization of white America; watches it weakened and threatened and torn in the bodies of self-conscious, half-educated people, girls become self-centered and men playing the piano in vaudeville theatres and going dreaming of Walt Whitman under the lamps of Seventh Street. And here he perceives, like new strange harmonies sounding through the subtle dissonances of life, promises of an inner healing for these splintered souls, a new strength, swiftness and singleness of motive. A new soul calls. The negroid poet of the story pulled from his base by the wilfulness of a passionate white girl, half lets his amorous opportunity pass in a proud gesture of balladry. Through the woof of **"Kabnis"** there go the figures of Lewis and Carrie; and Lewis is a man who has become fearless and self-confident and fine; and Carrie is a girl in whom has persisted flowerlike a beauty of instinct.

But these figures are prophetic not only for men of negro blood. They throw forward much in America; for they are symbols of some future America of which Jean Toomer by virtue of the music in him is a portion. He looks two ways. Through this recognition of the beauty of a doomed simplicity some simplicity, sensuosity, passionateness not of the South or of the past asserts, cries out, comes conscious of itself: some America beyond the newspapers, regimented feelings, edgeless language—timid, uncertain, young—in streaming music nevertheless drawing more imminent.

Both Anderson and Frank have helped rouse the impulse of Toomer. Yet it was the imagists with their perfect precision of feeling that fevered him most for work. Some clarity in himself must have responded to the clearness of these poets. That his definiteness remains as yet less intense than theirs is plain. Perhaps because his gift is warmer and more turbulent, it is also less white and clear. Whatever the cause, the Frankian inflations, and the wobbling of the focus between Kabnis and Lewis in the finale of the novelette, leave the indecision a little plainer than we would have it. Large as is the heralding which comes through him, Toomer remains as yet much of the artist trying out his colors, the writer experimenting with a style. And still, these movements of prose are genuine and new. Again a creative power has arrived for American literature: for fiction, perhaps for criticism; in any case, for prose. Other writers have tried, with less happiness, to handle the material of the South. They have had axes to grind; sadisms to exhaust in whipping up passion for the whites; masochisms to release in waking resentment for the blacks. But Toomer comes to unlimber a soul, and give of its dance and music. (pp. 230-33)

Paul Rosenfeld, "Jean Toomer," in his Men Seen: Twenty-Four Modern Authors, *The Dial Press, 1925, pp. 227-33.*

STERLING BROWN (essay date 1937)

[*Brown is an American poet best known for his collection* Southern Road *(1932) in which he weaves elements of the black folk tradition into narrative poems whose subject and source is the ordinary person. In the following excerpt from his* Negro Poetry and Drama and the Negro in American Fiction, *originally published in 1937, Brown discusses various aspects of* Cane *and regards Toomer's "failure to write a novel about Negro life one of the undoubted losses of contemporary literature."*]

Deriving in part from Anderson and Waldo Frank, Jean Toomer's ***Cane*** has much greater intimacy with Negro life, dealing equally well with the black belt of Georgia and bourgeois Washington. Toomer is master of fluid, evocative prose; some of his stories are prose-poems. . . . His faithfully portrayed Georgia landscape Toomer has peopled with faithfully drawn characters, such as Fern, the shiftless, ignorant beauty of the Georgia Pike, and Becky, a white outcast, who bears two Negro children. **"Blood-Burning Moon"** tells of the rivalry between a Negro and a white man for a Negro girl, that ends in a murder and a lynching. Not propaganda in the manner of the apologists, it is tragic realism at its best.

Toomer at about thirteen.

Neither debunking Negro society nor glorifying it, Toomer pictures Washington with the thoroughness of one who knew it from the inside. The futile, and in the story of **"Avey,"** the drably tragic revolt against the smugness of a rising middle-class, are brilliantly set before us. Toomer was sharply criticized by Negroes for his "betrayal"; his insight and tenderness seemed to escape them. **"Kabnis"** is a long, occasionally obscure story of a northern Negro teaching school in Georgia. No one has done so well as Toomer the hypocritical school principal, a petty, puritanical tyrant who truckles to the whites. Laymon, a preacher-teacher who "knows more than would be good for anyone other than a silent man"; Halsey, a self-assured, courageous artisan; and Kabnis, a weakling idealist driven to cynicism and dissipation until he discovers, mystically, the strength of his people, are similarly well drawn. Toomer reveals in **"Kabnis"** an insight that makes his failure to write a novel about Negro life one of the undoubted losses of contemporary literature. (pp. 153-54)

Sterling Brown, "Southern Realism," in his Negro Poetry and Drama and The Negro in American Fiction, *Atheneum, 1969, pp. 151-68.*

HUGH M. GLOSTER (essay date 1948)

[*In the following excerpt, Gloster discusses* Cane *in three sections: folk life in Georgia, bourgeois blacks in Washington, D.C., and Northern blacks in the rural South.*]

Toomer's ***Cane***—a potpourri of stories, sketches, poetry, and drama—is one of the more significant productions of the Negro Renascence. In this book a colored writer, for possibly the first time in American Negro fiction, handles inflammatory interracial themes without abandonment of the artist's point of view. (p. 128)

Cane is divided into three parts. The first, with rural Georgia as a background, sets forth the tragic lives of women of that section. Karintha inevitably becomes a prostitute. Becky, a wanton white woman, bears two colored sons who, after their mother's lonely death, leave their home town bitterly hated by whites and Negroes. Carma is discovered in marital unfaithfulness. Fern unresponsively submits to lustful men who are baffled and ashamed after selfishly satiating their passions. Esther, near-white daughter of a colored merchant, is strangely attracted to a black religious fanatic. Louisa's Negro admirer slashes her white paramour to death and is subsequently lynched. The chief importance of these stories lies in their departure from the traditional treatment of sex by Negro authors. The candor, shamelessness, and objectivity manifested by Toomer in the presentation of these women caused Du Bois to designate him as the "writer who first dared to emancipate the colored world from the conventions of sex" [see excerpt dated 1924].

The second part of ***Cane*** shifts from the folk life of Georgia to the bourgeois Negro society of Washington. Here again Toomer neither debunks nor glorifies but, as Sterling Brown observes, "pictures Washington with the thoroughness of one who knew it from the inside" [see excerpt dated 1937]. **"Seventh Street,"** called "a bastard of Prohibition and the War," is a description of a Washington background. **"Avey"** reflects the trend away from middle-class conventions by revealing the affection of a young man for an orphan woman who is "no better than a whore." **"Theater,"** a study of class-consciousness within the Negro group, unfolds the mutual attraction between a chorus girl and the "dictie, educated, stuck-up" brother of the manager of the show. **"Box Seat"** recounts an ill-fated middle-class romance. **"Bona and Paul,"** having Chicago as a setting, describes the failure of a white girl and a passing mulatto youth to become lovers because of the boy's own race-consciousness and his associates' suspicion of his swarthy complexion. In the stories of the second part of ***Cane,*** therefore, Toomer shows the Negro facing the problems of caste, respectability, and prejudice in Washington and Chicago.

The third section, returning to rural Georgia, contains one long and occasionally obscure story, **"Kabnis,"** a character study of a learned but excessively emotional Northern Negro teaching in a small town. Sensitive to white oppression and disgusted by Negro inertia, Kabnis resorts to dissipation and is fired by Hanby, the principal of the school. In his characterization of Hanby, Toomer satirizes the dissimulating Negro administrator who poses as a haughty aristocrat among his own people, as an Uncle Tom among Southern whites, and as a staunch Yankee supporter among Bostonians. Another interesting character is Layman, a soft-pedaling teacher-preacher "who has traveled in almost every nook and corner of the state and hence knows more than would be good for anyone other than a silent man." Layman does not believe in disturbing Southern whites:

> "An Mr. Kabnis, kindly remember youre in the land of cotton—hell of a land. Th white folks get th boll; the niggers get th stalk. An dont you dare touch th boll, or even look at it. They'll swing y sho."

Lewis, a purposeful and clear-headed young man, "is what Kabnis might have been," if he had not succumbed to debauchery and despair. Analyzing the character of Kabnis, Lewis says:

> "Life has already told him more than he is capable of knowing. It has given him in excess of what he can receive. I have been offered. Stuff in his stomach curdled, and he vomited me."

Evidently Toomer's implication, as Montgomery Gregory suggests, "is that there must be a welding into one great personality of Kabnis and Lewis: the great emotionalism of the race guided and directed by a great purpose and super-intelligence."

Cane, being an experimental work in its quest for appropriate literary forms and diction, is debilitated by occasional incoherence, which may have been inspired by Waldo Frank, and undue striving for effect. Munson has noted the architectonic influence of Sherwood Anderson in **"Fern"** and **"Avey"** as well as that of Frank in **"Theater"** [see excerpt dated 1925]. All these considerations notwithstanding, ***Cane*** is noteworthy because of its departure from argumentation and apologetics in the treatment of interracial subject matter as well as because of its prefiguration of Southern realism and Negro self-revelation. (pp. 128-30)

Hugh M. Gloster, "Fiction of the Negro Renascence: Southern Realism," in his Negro Voices in American Fiction, *1948. Reprint by Russell & Russell, Inc., 1965, pp. 127-30.*

ROBERT BONE (essay date 1965)

[*Bone, critic and educator, is the author of the critical histories* The Negro Novel in America *(1958) and* Down Home: The Pastoral Impulse in Afro-American Short Fiction *(1975). A student of Afro-American, English, and American literature, with a special interest in William Shakespeare, Bone has said of himself: "A white man and critic of black literature, I try to demonstrate by the quality of my work that scholarship is not the same thing as identity." In the following excerpt from his* The Negro Novel in America *(1965), Bone concentrates on* Cane *as a document of Toomer's search for identity.*]

The writers of the Lost Generation, as John Aldridge has observed, "were engaged in a revolution designed to purge language of the old restraints of the previous century and to fit it to the demands of a younger, more realistic time." Stein and Hemingway in prose, Pound and Eliot in poetry, were threshing and winnowing, testing and experimenting with words, stretching them and refocusing them, until they became the pliant instruments of a new idiom. The only Negro writer of the 1920's who participated on equal terms in the creation of the modern idiom was a young poet-novelist named Jean Toomer.

Jean Toomer's ***Cane*** is an important American novel. By far the most impressive product of the Negro Renaissance, it ranks with Richard Wright's *Native Son* and Ralph Ellison's *Invisible Man* as a measure of the Negro novelist's highest achievement. Jean Toomer belongs to that first rank of writers who use words almost as a plastic medium, shaping new meanings from an original and highly personal style. Since stylistic innovation requires great technical dexterity, Toomer displays a concern for technique which is fully two decades in advance of the period. While his contemporaries of the Harlem School were still experimenting with a crude literary realism, Toomer had progressed beyond the naturalistic novel to "the higher realism of the emotions," to symbol, and to myth. (pp. 80-1)

In spite of his wide and perhaps primary association with white intellectuals, as an artist Toomer never underestimated the importance of his Negro identity. He attained a universal vision not by ignoring race as a local truth, but by coming face to face with his particular tradition. His pilgrimage to Georgia was a conscious attempt to make contact with his hereditary roots in the Southland. Of Georgia, Toomer wrote: "There one finds soil in the sense that the Russians know it—the soil every art and literature that is to live must be embedded in." This sense of soil is central to ***Cane*** and to Toomer's artistic vision. "When one is on the soil of one's ancestors," his narrator remarks, "most anything can come to one."

What comes to Toomer, in the first section of ***Cane,*** is a vision of the parting soul of slavery:

> . . . for though the sun is setting on
> A song-lit race of slaves, it has not set;
> Though late, O soil, it is not too late yet
> To catch thy plaintive soul, leaving, soon gone.

The soul of slavery persists in the "supper-getting-ready songs" of the black women who live on the Dixie Pike—a road which "has grown from a goat path in Africa." It persists in "the soft, listless cadence of Georgia's South," in the hovering spirit of a comforting Jesus, and in the sudden violence of the Georgia moon. It persists above all in the people, white and black, who have become Andersonian "grotesques" by virtue of their slave inheritance. Part I of ***Cane*** is in fact a kind of Southern *Winesburg, Ohio*. It consists of the portraits of six women—all primitives—in which an Andersonian narrator mediates between the reader and the author's vision of life on the Dixie Pike.

There is Karintha, "she who carries beauty" like a pregnancy, until her pefect beauty and the impatience of young men beget a fatherless child. Burying her child in a sawdust pile, she takes her revenge by becoming a prostitute; "the soul of her was a growing thing ripened too soon."

In **"Becky"** Toomer dramatizes the South's conspiracy to ignore miscegenation. Becky is a white woman with two Negro sons. After the birth of the first, she symbolically disappears from sight into a cabin constructed by community guilt. After the birth of the second, she is simply regarded as dead, and no one is surprised when the chimney of her cabin falls in and buries her. Toward Becky there is no charity from white or black, but only furtive attempts to conceal her existence.

Carma's tale, "which is the crudest melodrama," hinges not so much on marital infidelity as on a childish deception. Accused by her husband of having other men ("No one blames her for that") she becomes hysterical, and running into a canebrake, pretends to shoot herself. "Twice deceived, and the one deception proved the other." Her husband goes berserk, slashes a neighbor, and is sent to the chain gang. The tone of the episode is set by the ironic contrast between Carma's apparent strength ("strong as any man") and her childish behavior.

Fern, whose full name is Fernie May Rosen, combines the suffering of her Jewish father and her Negro mother: "at first sight of her I felt as if I heard a Jewish cantor sing. . . . As if his singing rose above the unheard chorus of a folksong." Unable to find fulfillment, left vacant by the bestowal of men's bodies, Fern sits listlessly on her porch near the Dixie Pike. Her eyes desire nothing that man can give her; the Georgia countryside flows into them, along with something that Toomer's narrator calls God.

"Esther" is a study in sexual repression. The protagonist is a near-white girl whose father is the richest colored man in town. Deprived of normal outlets by her social position, she develops a neurotic life of fantasy which centers upon a virile, black-skinned, itinerant preacher named King Barlo. At sixteen she imagines herself the mother of his immaculately conceived child. At twenty-seven she tries to translate fantasy into reality by offering herself to Barlo. Rebuffed and humiliated, she retreats into lassitude and frigidity.

Louisa, of **"Blood-Burning Moon,"** has two lovers, one white and the other colored. Inflamed by a sexual rivalry deeper than race, they quarrel. One is slashed and the other is lynched. Unlike most Negro writers who have grappled with the subject of lynching, Toomer achieves both form and perspective. He is not primarily concerned with antilynching propaganda, but in capturing a certain atavistic quality in Southern life which defies the restraints of civilized society.

Part II of ***Cane*** is counterpoint. The scene shifts to Washington, where Seventh Street thrusts a wedge of vitality, brilliance, and movement into the stale, soggy, whitewashed wood of the city. This contrast is an aspect of Toomer's primitivism. The blacks, in his color scheme, represent a full life; the whites, a denial of it. Washington's Negroes have preserved their vitality because of their roots in the rural South, yet whiteness presses in on them from all sides. The "dickty" Negro, and especially the near-white, who are most nearly assimilated to white civilization, bear the brunt of repression and denial, vacillating constantly between two identities. Out of this general frame of reference grow the central symbols of the novel.

Toomer's symbols reflect the profound humanism which forms the base of his philosophical position. Man's essential goodness, he would contend, his sense of brotherhood, and his creative instincts have been crushed and buried by modern industrial society. Toomer's positive values, therefore, are associated with the soil, the cane, and the harvest; with Christian charity, and with giving oneself in love. On the other side of the equation is a series of burial or confinement symbols (houses, alleys, machines, theaters, nightclubs, newspapers) which limit man's growth and act as barriers to his soul. Words are useless in piercing this barrier; Toomer's intellectualizing males are tragic figures because they value talking above feeling. Songs, dreams, dancing, and love itself (being instinctive in nature) may afford access to "the simple beauty of another's soul." The eyes, in particular, are avenues through which we can discover "the truth that people bury in their hearts."

In the second section of ***Cane,*** Toomer weaves these symbols into a magnificent design, so that his meaning, elusive in any particular episode, emerges with great impact from the whole. **"Rhobert"** is an attack on the crucial bourgeois value of home ownership: "Rhobert wears a house, like a monstrous diver's helmet, on his head." Like Thoreau's farmer, who traveled through life pushing a barn and a hundred acres before him, Rhobert is a victim of his own property instinct. As he struggles with the weight of the house, he sinks deeper and deeper into the mud. . . . (pp. 81-5)

The basic metaphor in **"Avey"** compares a young girl to the trees planted in boxes along V Street, "the young trees that whinnied like colts impatient to be free." Avey's family wants her to become a school teacher, but her bovine nature causes her to prefer a somewhat older profession. Yet, ironically, it is not she but the narrator who is a failure, who is utterly inadequate in the face of Avey's womanhood.

In **"Theater"** Toomer develops his "dickty" theme, through an incident involving a chorus girl and a theater-manager's brother. As John watches a rehearsal, he is impressed by Dorris' spontaneity, in contrast to the contrived movements of the other girls. He momentarily contemplates an affair, but reservations born of social distance prevent him from consummating his desire, except in a dream. Dorris, who hopes fleetingly for home and children from such a man, is left at the end of the episode with only the sordid reality of the theater.

"Calling Jesus" plays a more important role than its length would indicate in unifying the symbolism of the novel. It concerns a woman, urbanized and spiritually intimidated, whose "soul is like a little thrust-tailed dog that follows her, whimpering." At night, when she goes to sleep in her big house, the little dog is left to shiver in the vestibule. "Some one . . . eoho Jesus . . . soft as the bare feet of Christ moving across bales of Southern cotton, will steal in and cover it that it need not shiver, and carry it to her where she sleeps, cradled in dream-fluted cane."

In **"Box Seat"** Toomer comes closest to realizing his central theme. The episode opens with an invocation: "Houses are shy girls whose eyes shine reticently upon the dusk body of the street. Upon the gleaming limbs and asphalt torso of a dreaming nigger. Shake your curled wool-blossoms, nigger. Open your liver-lips to the lean white spring. Stir the root-life of a withered people. Call them from their houses and teach them to dream." (p. 85)

The thought is that of a young man, whose symbolic role is developed at once: "I am Dan Moore. I was born in a canefield. The hands of Jesus touched me. I am come to a sick world to heal it." Dan, moreover, comes as a representative of "powerful underground races": "The next world-savior is coming up that way. Coming up. A continent sinks down. The new-world Christ will need consummate skill to walk upon the waters where huge bubbles burst." (p. 86)

The feminine lead is played by Muriel, a school teacher inclined toward conventionality. Her landlady, Mrs. Pribby, is constantly with her, being in essence a projection of Muriel's social fears. The box seat which she occupies at the theater, where her every movement is under observation, renders her relationship to society perfectly. Her values are revealed in her query to Dan, "Why don't you get a good job and settle down?" On these terms only can she love him; meanwhile she avoids his company by going to a vaudeville performance with a girl friend.

Dan, a slave to "her still unconquered animalism," follows and watches her from the audience. The main attraction consists of a prize fight between two dwarfs for the "heavy-weight championship"; it symbolizes the ultimate degradation of which a false and shoddy culture is capable. Sparring grotesquely, pounding and bruising each other, the dwarfs suggest the traditional clown symbol of modern art. At the climax of the episode the winner presents a blood-spattered rose to Muriel, who recoils, hesitates, and finally submits. The dwarf's eyes are pleading: "Do not shrink. Do not be afraid of me." Overcome with disgust for Muriel's hypocrisy, Dan completes the dwarf's thought from the audience, rising to shout: "JESUS WAS ONCE A LEPER!" Rushing from the theater, he is free at last of his love for Muriel—free, but at the same time sterile: "He is as cool as a green stem that has just shed its flower."

Coming as an anticlimax after **"Box Seat," "Bona and Paul"** describes an abortive love affair between two Southern students at the University of Chicago—a white girl and a mulatto boy who is "passing." The main tension, reminiscent of Gertrude Stein's *Melanctha,* is between knowing and loving, set in the framework of Paul's double identity. It is not his race consciousness which terminates the relationship, as one critic has suggested, but precisely his "whiteness," his desire for knowledge, his philosophical bent. If he had been able to assert his Negro self—that which attracted Bona to him in the first place—he might have held her love.

In **"Kabnis"** rural Georgia once more provides a setting. This is the long episode which comprises the concluding section of ***Cane.*** By now the symbolic values of Toomer's main characters can be readily assessed. Ralph Kabnis, the protagonist, is a school teacher from the North who cringes in the face of his tradition. A spiritual coward, he cannot contain "the pain and beauty of the South"; cannot embrace the suffering of the past, symbolized by slavery; cannot come to terms with his own bastardy; cannot master his pathological fear of being lynched. Consumed with self-hatred and cut off from any organic connection with the past, he resembles nothing so much as a scarecrow: "Kabnis, a promise of soil-soaked beauty; uprooted, thinning out. Suspended a few feet above the soil whose touch would resurrect him."

Lewis, by way of contrast, is a Christ figure, an extension of Dan Moore. Almost a T. S. Eliot creation ("I'm on a sort of contract with myself"), his function is to shock others into moral awareness. It is Lewis who confronts Kabnis with his moral cowardice. (pp. 86-7)

Halsey, unlike Kabnis, has not been crushed by Southern life, but absorbed into it. Nevertheless, his spiritual degradation is equally thorough. An artisan and small shopkeeper like his father before him, he "belongs" in a sense that Kabnis does not. Yet in order to maintain his place in the community, he must submit to the indignities of Negro life in the South. Like Booker T. Washington, whose point of view he represents, Halsey has settled for something less than manhood. Restless, groping tentatively toward Lewis, he escapes from himself through his craft, and through an occasional debauch with the town prostitute, whom he loved as a youth.

Father John, the old man who lives beneath Halsey's shop, represents a link with the Negro's ancestral past. Concealed by the present generation as an unpleasant memory, the old man is thrust into a cellar which resembles the hold of a slave ship. There he sits, "A mute John the Baptist of a new religion, or a tongue-tied shadow of an old." When he finally speaks, it is to rebuke the white folks for the sin of slavery. The contrast between Lewis and Kabnis is sharpened by their respective reactions to Father John. Through the old slave, Lewis is able to "merge with his source," but Kabnis can only deny: "An' besides, he aint my past. My ancestors were Southern bluebloods."

In terms of its dramatic movement **"Kabnis"** is a steep slope downward, approximating the progressive deterioration of the protagonist. Early in the episode Kabnis is reduced to a scarecrow replica of himself by his irrational fears. His failure to stand up to Hanby, an authoritarian school principal, marks a decisive loss in his power of self-direction. Gradually he slips into a childlike dependence, first on Halsey, than on the two prostitutes, and finally on Halsey's little sister, Carrie Kate. In the course of the drunken debauch with which the novel ends, Kabnis becomes a clown, without dignity or manhood, wallowing in the mire of his own self-hatred. The stark tragedy of **"Kabnis"** is relieved only by the figure of Carrie Kate, the unspoiled child of a new generation, who may yet be redeemed through her ties with Father John.

A critical analysis of ***Cane*** is a frustrating task, for Toomer's art, in which "outlines are reduced to essences," is largely destroyed in the process of restoration. No paraphrase can properly convey the aesthetic pleasure derived from a sensitive reading of ***Cane.*** Yet in spite of Toomer's successful experiment with the modern idiom—or perhaps because of it—***Cane*** met with a cold reception from the public, hardly selling 500 copies during its first year. This poor showing must have been a great disappointment to Toomer, and undoubtedly it was a chief cause of his virtual retirement from literature. Perhaps in his heart of hearts Jean Toomer found it singularly appropriate that the modern world should bury ***Cane.*** Let us in any event delay the exhumation no loner. (pp. 87-9)

Robert Bone, "The Harlem School," in his The Negro Novel in America, *revised edition, Yale University Press, 1965, pp. 65-94.*

TODD LIEBER (essay date 1969)

[*In the following excerpt, Lieber discusses* Cane *in relation to some of the literary movements of the 1920s and examines key aspects of the work's style and form.*]

Although [***Cane***] undeniably has its roots deep in Toomer's subjective experience, it is also highly representative of certain movements of the period in which it was written and can profitably be read in connection with two of the prevailing patterns of thought of the nineteen twenties: first, of course, the affirmation of race that formed the heart of the Harlem Renaissance, and second, the experimentation with form and language that dominated the work of the literary coterie of which Toomer was a part. Viewed from this perspective, the various fragments of ***Cane*** reveal more than merely the "thematic" unity that

Margolies observes [in his *Native Sons;* see Additional Bibliography], and it becomes clear that the book has a comprehensive design that transcends and encompasses its separate bits and a progressive movement that is sustained from beginning to end.

The writers of the twenties with whom Toomer was intimate were, as Bone writes, "threshing and winnowing, testing and experimenting with words, stretching them and refocusing them, until they became the pliant instruments of a new idiom" [see excerpt dated 1965]. The function of this "new idiom" of which Bone speaks was to recreate a sense of fundamental relatedness between art and experience, to make language once more a viable and powerful means of approaching reality. Many of Toomer's closest friends, notably Hart Crane, felt keenly the gap between man's spiritual life and the materiality of a machine culture, and they were exploring the symbolic and mythical qualities of language, searching for a "usable past" out of which to create a new myth to replace the ones that had failed, a myth that would reestablish man's connection with his environment and his roots and give him a vital sense of his own identity and being.

For Toomer, a light-skinned racial hybrid who had lived in both white and black worlds without an integral sense of belonging to either, the need for such relatedness and identity had become crucial. . . . In the lives of Southern Negroes and the heritage of slavery, Toomer found a reality to which his spirit could respond, a "usable past" from whose roots his art could grow and flower. It was in this mood that ***Cane*** was written, not only as a celebration of blackness, but as a record of Toomer's own search for blackness and a portrayal of the possibility of communion with the racial heritage that exists for every "lost" black man in America. (pp. 36-7)

Cane is designed to function in both objective and subjective terms. In an objective sense, it is a chronicle of what the "souls of slavery" were. In a personal sense, it is a description of "what they are to me" and, by inference, what they can be to any man who accepts them and the heritage they represent: the substance of spiritual life and survival.

Such an acceptance, however, is not an easy task, for it must include the pain and suffering of the past along with its beauty, and the beauty that remains is rapidly being buried beneath the dominant, material culture of white America. As Margolies suggests . . . the basic structural principle of ***Cane*** is the conflict between two life styles and systems of value, that of the South, which Toomer associates with the "soul of slavery" and to which his being responds, and that of the North, the industrial, white culture that threatens to create an unbreachable gap between the black man and his world as it destroys the inherent value of his racial heritage. The two are juxtaposed at virtually every point: the North is cold and passive, the South warm and full of emotion; sexual sterility and perversion are opposed to sexual consummation, cynicism to faith, transience to endurance, and spiritual death to the possibility of spiritual resurrection through an acceptance of self and race.

The efforts of the black man to break away from the engulfing white culture to an acceptance of his own racial heritage gives to ***Cane*** a unity and a continuous movement that progresses through its three major divisions. (p. 38)

Part I takes place in the atmosphere of a setting sun, with a strong sense of the diminishing vitality of the "soul of slavery." Most of the stories and poems are set either at dusk or at night, and the dominant motif throughout is of beauty and value that have somehow been distorted and dissipated. The prevailing metaphor, running through and unifying all the stories, is that of the frustration or perversion of the sexual act. The valuable, passionate instincts and desires of men and women are in each case warped, and as a result, Part I appears, as Bone holds, much like an Andersonian gallery of grotesques. . . .

Despite these distortions and perversions, however, there remains in each story a strong image of a potential value and beauty that remains vibrant and vital, although it has become intimately mixed with pain and suffering. (p. 39)

Part II of ***Cane*** is counterpoint. Set in the North, the stories and poems of this section reflect the spiritual sterility of black men and women cut off from their roots, lacking a sense of their heritage, trying to live with their minds the kind of life ordained by the dominant group, while their souls, divorced, lie buried. . . . Part II is dominated by two controlling themes: the divorce of mind from body and body from soul in the spiritually stifling environment of the North; and the result of this divorce, which is conveyed through images of burial and spiritual death. (pp. 41-2)

The spiritual corruption and fragmentation of the figures of Part II deprives them of all the vitality that typifies the characters of the first section. The dominant tone of Part II is not one of frustration, but simply one of hopelessness. The perversions and distortions of Part I, of Karintha, Becky, Carma, Fern, Esther, Louisa, and of the narrator himself, are imbued with passion and an almost tragic sense of having almost grasped some essential value. The failures of Part II, on the other hand, are little more than pathetic. Rhobert, John, the unnamed woman of **"Calling Jesus,"** and Muriel of **"Box Seat,"** are people so overburdened by northern culture that almost all sense of life and passion has been squeezed out of them; their vitality has, indeed, "rusted in the white and whitewashed wood of Washington." (pp. 43-4)

Part III of ***Cane*** contains [a] return to the South. That Toomer dedicated this particular section to Waldo Frank is, I think, no accident, for, as Toomer wrote to the editors of the *Liberator,* his journey South with Frank "was the starting point of almost everything of worth that I have done." In the total experience of ***Cane,*** Part III performs the same function as Toomer felt the 1922 trip had performed in his own life, a reestablishment of contact and communion with his roots, the achievement of a new sense of life and creativity, and a resurrection from the death that overwhelms the spirit in Part II. The focal point of Part III, in fact the central symbol of the entire book, is Father John, the ancient patriarch who lives in the hole of Halsey's cellar and, as Bone says, "represents a link with the Negro's ancestral past" [see excerpt dated 1965]. Each of the main characters in the drama of **"Kabnis"** reacts to Father John in his own way, and the various reactions suggest several alternative attitudes which black men may adopt toward their own past. The main characters can be divided into two groups: Halsey, Hanby, and Lewis are members of an older generation whose attitudes are set and will not change; they represent the alternatives from which a younger generation, Carrie Kate and Kabnis, must choose. The decision that faces Carrie Kate and Kabnis forms the dramatic core of the play, and their choices bring the movement of ***Cane*** to its culmination. (pp. 46-7)

In writing ***Cane,*** Toomer set out to make his art "an everlasting song, a singing tree," which, by "caroling softly souls of slavery, / what they were, and what they are to me," might become a new myth for the black man to live by, a myth that would reinforce his sense of relatedness to his roots and save him from the isolation and impotency imposed upon him by life in a white dominated society and culture to which he had little fundamental connection. With this final scene of communion, Toomer's goal has been achieved, and the achievement is symbolized by Carrie Kate's humble but loving acceptance of the old man, the pain and anguish and sin that he represents along with his intrinsic beauty and vitality. Toomer's "Song of the Son," which began in the atmosphere of a setting sun and moved through the spiritual death of northern exile, ends with the rising of a new sun, symbolizing the rebirth and resurrection of the Negro spirit, the new life-giving force that Toomer had attempted to create in ***Cane***. . . . (pp. 49-50)

Todd Lieber, "Design and Movement in 'Cane'," in CLA Journal, *Vol. XIII, No. 1, September, 1969, pp. 35-50.*

S. P. FULLINWIDER (essay date 1969)

[*In the following excerpt from his study on black American thought, Fullinwider explores the central themes in* Cane *and relates them to the ideas that dominated Harlem Renaissance literature, particularly the concept of black identity.*]

Perhaps the most beautifully written book of the Renaissance, Jean Toomer's ***Cane,*** is an expression of the pain involved in casting out the old faiths. In it there is Kabnis, a weak young Negro from the North, a product of the Negro's faith in Christ. The face of Kabnis is round, broad-browed, but weak-chinned, and it gets smashed by fists belonging to square faces. Kabnis is literally afraid of his own shadow. He recognizes his weakness, and hates himself for it. He is a product of the Christian religion, a religion, he believes, that has made his race weak. He hates the religion as he hates himself. Hatred is the dominant motive in his life. Not that he does not sometimes struggle to see beauty in the world—he does, but its ugliness overcomes him. He feels utterly crushed by a malignant world—a world that is the creation of a cruel, unjust God: ". . . look at me now. Earth's child. The earth my mother. God is a profligate red-nosed man about town. Bastardy; me. A bastard son has got a right to curse his maker." The special object of Kabnis' hatred turns out to be an ex-slave, blind and deaf from years of toil. To Kabnis, the old man represents the generations gone before—generations made docile and servile by white man's religion. In the old man he sees himself. He turns his self-hatred outward against the old man, the old man's God and the white Christ. Apparently the old man has guessed something of all this, for, though he can speak only with the greatest difficulty, he forces himself to mutter, "Th sin whats fixed . . . upon th white folks—f tellin Jesus—lies. O th sin th white folks 'mitted when they made the Bible lie."

"Kabnis," the final story in the book ***Cane,*** is the most devastating attack upon "Uncle Tomism" penned by a Renaissance writer. Like the book as a whole, it is full of despair and self-doubt. But what helps to lift ***Cane*** above the level of the ordinary is that in it quest struggles with despair, and hope does battle with resignation.

Toomer was struck with what seemed to him the debilitating effects of Christianity as a slave religion. In consequence (in ***Cane***) he rejected the religion and the type of personality he supposed it developed—the Christ-like Negro, or "Uncle Tom." But what he pushed away with one hand he drew back with the other; if his despair was expressed by the servile Kabnis, his hope lay in Dan, a Negro with a redemptive mission. Dan appears in a short story named **"Box Seat."** The setting of **"Box Seat"** is Washington, D.C., or, in other words, the large city. There one is crushed, shorn of spirit by crowding civilization. "Houses are shy girls whose eyes shine reticently upon the dusk body of the street. Upon the gleaming limbs and asphalt torso of a dreaming nigger. Shake your curled wool-blossoms nigger. Open your liver lips to the lean white spring. Stir the root-life of a withered people." Dan, hot-blooded and virile, is up from the primitive regions of the South to restore vigor and passion to a jaded, overcivilized people—people conquered by "zoo-restrictions and keeper-taboos." "I am Dan More," he says, "I was born in an canefield. The hands of Jesus touched me. I am come to a sick world to heal it."

In ***Cane,*** Toomer fully participated in the general revolt of the Renaissance writers—the revolt against the Christ-like mythology. But the redemptive myth—the idea of Negro mission—held him fast. In searching for a new concept of the Negro he succeeded merely in altering the imagery somewhat. For the patient and long-suffering Christ-like Negro he substituted a primitive man of passion. But Dan, like the earlier concept, was to be redemptive because more human than the white man.

One point that ***Cane*** makes over and over is the pain and misery out of which will be born a new creativity. The Southland is, to Toomer, a land of agony as well as a land of beauty. It is from the marriage of these two opposites that a new Negro will arise. Dan, at one point, is made to admonish his girl, "Life bends joy and pain, beauty and ugliness, in such a way that no one may isolate them. No one should want to. Perfect joy, or perfect pain, with no contrasting element to define them, would mean a monotony of consciousness, would mean death."

Through Dan the author was giving voice to what would be a constant, though not always dominant, theme (or, perhaps better, mood) of the Renaissance. Accept the reality of pain, it said, and rise above it. Yet more: pain is in its way a blessing—those who have not experienced it miss a vital insight into life. Those who have known only comfort will lapse into contented somnolence. Pain and anguish can be the springboard to the creative life—only those who have known them are motivated to overcome. With this a new note of realism begins to be heard in Negro thought. Its source goes back to the suffering Christ-like Negro, but it has cast off the utopian and idealized elements of the old mythology. If the Negro Renaissance had a message, perhaps this theme, or mood, was it.

With this concept (the social utility of pain?) Toomer was enabled to evince a timid and halting step into reality—an optimism that is not necessarily bound up with the myth of redemption that colors much of ***Cane.*** The new mood is embodied in the character Lewis, who appears in **"Kabnis."** The self-despising Kabnis saw in the ancient ex-slave the father of the race's degradation. Lewis, a much stronger figure than Kabnis, saw in the old man something different: "That forehead. Great woolly beard. Those eyes. A mute John the Baptist of a new religion—or a tongue-tied shadow of an old." Lewis is strong and wise, and he too is a legacy of the slave. Toomer seemed to see in Lewis a new force, but his vision was blurred. Unlike his portrait of Kabnis, which is well-defined, his portrait of Lewis is shadowy and ill-defined. Moreover, in the end Lewis was defeated. He appeared in the small southern town of the story as a possible emancipator, but he ultimately fled from the overwhelming pain he found there. Obviously, Toomer was overcome with doubt at the end. He was unable to predict victory over the misery that held the southern Negro in bondage. Toomer was unable to give meaning to Lewis' life.

In the end Toomer had been unable to find meaning in being Negro, and in this his experience was the crucial experience of the Renaissance. This was the fundamental break the Renaissance made with the old synthesis as epitomized by Du Bois's thought. This was the break which made it impossible for the older leaders to grasp the meaning of the Renaissance. A man like Du Bois drew his sense of identity and meaning of life from race. A man like Toomer did not. Toomer was forced to seek a new identity, and it was this very search that the older leaders could neither understand nor sympathize with. This was the break that isolated the Renaissance writer from the race leader as militant agitator—from the racial betterment movements of the NAACP stamp. At this point Negro art ceases to be narrow propaganda and strives to become universal. It strives, in other words, to cease being Negro expression and to become art.

Jean Toomer carried the tendency to disassociate himself from identity with the black race further than did any of his contemporaries within the Renaissance. While never refusing to admit his direct blood relationship with his Negro grandfather, he did refuse to consider himself in any sense Negro. Once, in 1930, James Weldon Johnson wrote to Toomer with the request that some of the poems from ***Cane*** be included in the revised edition of Johnson's *The Book of American Negro Poetry*. Toomer replied in the negative ". . . My poems are not Negro poems, nor are they Anglo-Saxon or white or English poems. My prose likewise. They are, first, mine. And, second, in so far as general race or stock is concerned, they spring from the result of racial blendings here in America which has produced a new race or stock. We may call this stock the American stock or race. My main energies are devoted and directed towards the building of a life which will include all creative people or corresponding type."

Jean Toomer's is a story of success—at age 31 his search for an identity-giving absolute culminated in success. It is also a story of tragedy; as long as he was searching he was a fine creative artist; when the search ended so did his creative powers. So long as he was searching, his work was the cry of one caught in the modern human condition; it expressed modern man's lostness, his isolation. Once Toomer found an identity-giving absolute, his voice ceased to be the cry of modern man and became the voice of the schoolmaster complacently pointing out the way—his way. (pp. 133-37)

Meanwhile the Negro Renaissance passed him by, continuing the course Johnson and Locke had laid down for it—the coming to grips with painful reality. The sadness of it all was that in losing Toomer the Renaissance lost the one man who had come to terms with modern art and who had the talent to symbolize so beautifully the inner experience of that reality. (p. 144)

S. P. Fullinwider, "The Renaissance in Literature," in his The Mind and Mood of Black America: 20th Century Thought, *The Dorsey Press, 1969, pp. 123-71.*

DONALD G. ACKLEY (essay date 1970)

[*In the following excerpt, Ackley examines the images, symbols, and themes that pervade* Cane.]

Cane presents a number of special critical problems. In terms of *genre,* it can hardly be considered as a novel, for it is made up of a number of seemingly independent short stories, verse and prose poems, and a free-form play. These parts do not share common characters; the narrator's identity, degree of involvement, and point of view are seldom made clear or constant. Time and place are seldom detailed, and always shifting. But while there appear to be no convenient links between its parts, ***Cane*** can be approached as a whole. A diligent reading will show ***Cane*** to be bound together by recurrent images, symbols, and themes, which contribute to a progressively growing vision of life. (p. 47)

The first section of ***Cane*** is primarily an effort to catch the parting soul of slavery and pour it into song. To Toomer, that soul is the essence of the American Negro, the spiritual experience that corresponds to the physical captivity, degradation, and exploitation of a people; it is the sum total of the life that has encompassed the Negro in America and it is made up of all the individual experiences of life. It is clear then, why ***Cane*** does not focus on one event, or on one character, and it is clear how the many events and many characters that make up the book are linked: the common factor is an emotional response—one which is intense or weak, blind or clear-sighted, a success or a failure—a coming to terms with the life that surrounds the Negro. And it is also clear why ***Cane*** is not directed toward the racial or social issues that dominate so much Negro literature: ***Cane*** is focused on another level, where the social and historical context is accepted as given, and where the most intense and meaningful manifestations of American society are found—in the soul of a people.

"Song of the Son" contains the dominant symbolism and imagery of the first section of ***Cane***: the pines which line and guard the horizons, traditionally protecting the cradle of Negro identity; the smoldering sawdust piles which testify to the presence of machine dominated, white dominated, sawmills, and which symbolize the destruction of the natural barrier which is the Negro's hope for continuity; the song itself, which is the Negro's expression of his soul and his avenue of retreat and release; and above all the soil. Soil in ***Cane*** is first and foremost the stuff into which the Negro's roots are thrust—it is saturated with the blood and sweat of the Negro's history, and nurtures the soul of a race of slaves. It is to this soil that Toomer has returned to anchor himself, for "when one is on the soil of one's ancestors, most anything can come to one. . . ." Herein lies the significance of all the plant and growth imagery of the book, and of the title, for the roots of pines, sweet-gum, and sugar cane grow down and mingle with the Negro's in the land of Toomer's ancestors.

In the first section of ***Cane,*** Toomer has poured "that parting soul" into song, into the poem and stories of Negro life in Georgia. But that soul is indeed parting, and Toomer has no doubt about that which is driving it out; a new soul, a white soul, a "futile" and "dead" soul. (pp. 48-50)

Although ***Cane*** rests on the tension created as the dying black soul gives way to the dead white soul, that is, as the Negro loses contact with his soil, Toomer can't be classed as a member of the primitivist movement with its similar opposition of black and white. Toomer doesn't fall into the appealing trap which temporarily caught poets like Langston Hughes, for Toomer realizes that the American Negro is just that—American, the product of his experience in this country—and he doesn't make the convenient but meaningless identification of the Negro soul with the racial past as symbolized by Africa. The "Dixie Pike," the road which the Negro soul travels, may have "grown from a goat path in Africa", but it doesn't lead back there; it goes on to become Seventh Street in Washington. Thus ***Cane*** does not display primitivism, or exist as a literary manifestation of the "back to Africa" movement of the twenties. It is not a relationship to Africa or a racial trait which distinguishes the black soul from the white soul in Toomer's vision of America. Toomer realizes that visible racial characteristics and long-broken racial ties with Africa, while easily exploitable symbols, are superficial and meaningless. For Toomer, the white soul is not distinguished by whiteness as much as by a life style which has left modern Western man materialistic, mechanistic, and emotionally impotent; the black soul, by contrast, as a result of the slave experience in America, is still free, natural, untrammeled, and ultimately human. The nature of the life the two groups lead, not the nature of their race, determines the nature of their souls. Thus it is that the black man can and does take on an increasingly "white" soul. (pp. 50-1)

By and large, the first section of ***Cane*** seeks the few remaining "seeds" of the departing soul, and finds them in conflict. The second clarifies the vague specter which haunted the early stories and thus makes the conflicts meaningful, and goes on to bring Toomer's vision of the Negro life in America to a state of near completeness. The first section of ***Cane*** finds its theme compressed in "Song of the Son": that which the second section adds to the growing vision is largely captured in **"Seventh Street"** and **"Rhobert"** the two prose poems with which the section begins.

P.B.S. Pinchback, Toomer's maternal grandfather, in the early 1900s.

We have already seen Seventh Street, "the wedge of nigger life" driven into the "stale and soggy wood of Washington." Seventh Street is the Dixie Pike extended, and it is the road down which the soul of slavery continues to move—toward its death. In symbolic opposition to the street, is the house, as set out in **"Rhobert."** . . . Houses and buildings are the recurrent symbols for the business-oriented and possession-oriented life, the life whose "inner content . . . is decreasing," as Toomer put it in [his essay] "Race Problems and Modern Society," a life tantamount to suicide. The symbol of the house appeared earlier in ***Cane,*** in **"Esther"** and in **"Blood-Burning Moon,"** but it dominates the stories of section two: the Howard Theater whose walls are dead until Negro jazz and dance "sets them throbbing" in **"Theater;"** the house in **"Calling Jesus"** that won't let the soul in past the vestibule; the boarding house and theater in **"Box Seat;"** and the dormitories, houses, and night club in **"Bona and Paul."** Throughout, the houses are contrasted with the street. (pp. 54-6)

[In] **"Box Seat,"** the central story of sections one and two, . . . the street and house symbols combine with those of the soil. **"Box Seat"** adds another element to Toomer's vision of America, for here the theme of the redemptive qualities which the black soul offers the white soul is clearly set out. The qualities

Emily Hethorne, Toomer's maternal grandmother, in the mid-to-late 1800s.

which comprise the parting soul of slavery are being replaced by the white world and the result is a spiritual death for both. But the black soul, if recognized and assimilated, is the potential savior. The suicide foreseen by Toomer can be avoided if the murder of the black soul is prevented. In **"Box Seat,"** Dan Moore takes on the role of a black Christ capable of redeeming the white soul and bringing it new life. . . . Moore's power comes, significantly, from that same "red soil" of which Toomer sings. The roots which Toomer wants to re-establish are the source of Moore's power and the society's hope for rejuvenation. . . . Urban blacks and whites lack any such roots; they are like the trees standing in wooden boxes on "V" Street in **"Avey."** Held in boxes—houses—the trees can't send down roots, and must eventually die. But in **"Avey,"** the Christ-like role of the Negro is present too: young Negro boys stand around the boxes and whittle away at the wood, eventually to set the trees free. In **"Box Seat"** this role is made explicit. (pp. 56-7)

In a sense, then, the image of the Negro presented in the first two sections of ***Cane*** is archetypal. . . . Toomer doesn't view the Negro as a symbol of the American existential dilemma—he sees the Negro as the potential spiritual savior for a dying nation. But the vision is not necessarily a hopeful one: Dan Moore doesn't succeed. Like the vision proclaimed by Barlo in **"Esther,"** Moore's shout in the Theater is not understood.

Nina Pinchback, Toomer's mother, in the late 1880s or early 1900s.

And he is left as impotent as the world he would redeem. (pp. 57-8)

Thus far I have not mentioned **"Kabnis,"** the play which makes up the third section of ***Cane.*** In terms of the vision of life Toomer portrays, **"Kabnis"** is not just a further development. It goes back and incorporates much of sections one and two in a new form, through the use of one major character and one sustained story. **"Kabnis"** takes the major thematic content of sections one and two and puts them into a dramatic presentation. (p. 58)

Ralph Kabnis, the central character in the play (and perhaps the only real person) is a type we have met before in ***Cane,*** although never seen in full detail: a Negro raised and educated in the North and filled with frustration and cynicism because he has been cut off from his roots. Kabnis returns to Georgia as a school teacher, and there feels the desperate need for the life-giving nourishment of his racial past. But he is unable to satisfy that need. . . . Kabnis is "suspended" by a skepticism which we see as the product of his conversion to the white modern world. The prime force in that skepticism is the shame he feels toward the Negro slave heritage. When confronted with Father John, the ancient, blind, deaf Negro who lives in the prison- or slave-ship-like cellar and symbolizes the slave past, Kabnis cries, "he ain't my past!" Kabnis clings to the belief that his true ancestors were the "blue-blood" Negroes of the Reconstruction who came North (like Toomer's own ancestors, one of whom was Reconstruction Governor of Louisiana). . . . Kabnis adopts a false past, and that past is expressed in terms which illustrate why and how the soul of the Negro is parting: it is repudiated, and the rootless Negro is crushed or absorbed by the dominant white soul.

Kabnis is surrounded by a number of other Negroes, most of whom have the appearance of stereotypes, but who in fact represent isolated traits of Negro life: Layman, the "teacher and preacher," whose name as well as behavior show him to be neither; Hanby, the school headmaster, an extreme Kabnis in his affectation of white behavior and his repudiation of the Negro as he really is; Halsey, the worker of wood and metal, happy only in his laboring for whites, well-adjusted, but unaware of his identity; Carrie K., Halsey's sister, whose Sunday School virtues are so complete that she lives in isolation from the present; Cora and Stella, amateur whores because they have nothing to care for; Father John who can only mutter "sin;" and Lewis, who "is what a stronger Kabnis might have been." Next to Kabnis, Lewis is the most important character, for he is the counterpart of Dan Moore, but here an alterego to Kabnis rather than a black Christ to the white world. Lewis represents the sum of the characteristics represented by the other characters around Kabnis, for he can "take in the pain and beauty of South," can hold the opposites that make up life: "Master; slave. Soil; and the overreaching heavens. Dusk; dawn." In this he is like Moore to whom "a monotony of consciousness, would mean death." But like Moore, Lewis is rejected even by the Negroes to whom he offers salvation. (pp. 59-60)

"Kabnis" goes one step further toward completing the vision developed in the first two sections of ***Cane:*** the force which keeps Kabnis from accepting the salvation offered by Lewis is delineated. Kabnis is able to give expression to the "savage, cynical twisting about" that causes him to reject Lewis. . . . The key to understanding the form burned into Kabnis' soul is its source: a dream. It is the dream that led his "blue-blood" ancestors North, that in fact turned the blood blue, not red-black. It is the dream of being white, and it is a nightmare because it can never be. ***Cane*** has made it clear that the Negro soul can never be white, because its roots are in slavery. But words, meaningless because they don't acknowledge this basic truth, feed the dream and keep it alive. The white man's looks, his whiteness, feed it by leading the Negro on, by existing as the always-visible but never attainable goal. The black man's looks feed it too, because in the dream the Negro is taught that his blackfaced past is evil. And the dream can only be killed by a spiritual lynching, some violent expression of the underlying reality that the black man is not and cannot be white. Toomer's apocalypse must evidently take the violent form of Moore's vision. . . . Evidently Toomer feels that only such violence can force the recognition that the two races are different, and only with that recognition can one be the savior of the other: the "monotony of consciousness" that means death can be relieved by the encompassing of the discordant qualities of joy and pain, love and hate, slave and master.

The stress Toomer places on words in section three relates to the other sections of ***Cane*** in another sense as well. Words are the inadequate means of communication so often used without result in the earlier stories: words which Paul wanted to tell Bona but which weren't really capable of expressing his thoughts; words which put Avey to sleep; words which filled Mrs. Pribby's newspaper. Words are not only the food on which the nightmare feeds—they are substitutes for feeling. And in both these senses, it is the Negro more than the white who is at fault, for it is the Negro who claims equality and creates the dream of words.

In evaluating Toomer's artistry, we must note briefly in closing that on the subject of words, the form and content of ***Cane*** are inseparable. In ***Cane,*** Toomer shows his participation in the revolution in literary expression that surged through American prose in the early years of this century. Toomer's experimentation with words is evidently designed to invest them with a meaning they lack for his characters, and to make them capable of expression. (pp. 61-3)

Toomer's idiom need not be given a name, although his affinities with the imagists can be seen in his prose poems. Toomer, like so many modern writers, sought to free himself from restrictions of form and let his words work to their utmost potential. He rejected abstraction, seeking always to be concrete, to objectify his views and ideas. Thus, while his position may well find sympathy among present-day Black social thinkers, ***Cane*** remains a piece of art rather than a piece of propaganda. (pp. 63-4)

Donald G. Ackley, "Theme and Vision in Jean Toomer's 'Cane'," in Studies in Black Literature, *Vol. 1, No. 1, Spring, 1970, pp. 45-65.*

DARWIN T. TURNER (essay date 1969)

[*A noted literary historian and critic, Turner has written and edited numerous studies on Afro-American literature, including* Images of the Negro in America *(1965) and* In a Minor Chord: Three Afro-American Writers and Their Search for Identity (1971). *Widely recognized as a leading authority on Toomer's life and writings, having worked extensively with Toomer's unpublished papers, Turner is the author of the introduction to the 1975 edition of* Cane *and the editor of* The Wayward and the Seeking: A Collection of Writings by Jean Toomer *(1980). Here Turner discusses* Cane's *lyric qualities and examines its limitations.*]

Cane inspires critical rhapsodies rather than analysis. As Robert Bone wrote [see excerpt dated 1965], "A critical analysis of ***Cane*** is a frustrating task, for Toomer's art, in which 'outlines are reduced to essences,' is largely destroyed in the process of restoration. No paraphrase can properly convey the aesthetic pleasure derived from a sensitive reading of ***Cane.***"

It is not a novel, not even the experimental novel for which Bone pled to justify including it in his study of novels by Negroes. It is, instead, a collection of character sketches, short stories, poems, and a play, which form one of the distinguished achievements in the writings of Negro Americans.

Six women are the focus of the first section, the most appealing part of ***Cane.*** One is Karintha, who personifies the physical beauty for which men yearn:

> Men had always wanted her, this Karintha, even
> as a child, Karintha carrying beauty, perfect as
> dusk when the sun goes down. . . .

As **"Karintha"** typifies Toomer's style, so the protagonist typifies his women. After reading ***Cane***, a woman complained to Toomer that his female characters are unreal. They all love, she protested, as Toomer thought women should. Perhaps this judgment is accurate. Each in her own way is an elusive beauty, who charitably or indifferently or inquisitively offers her body to men who will never understand her soul. Each portrait haunts the reader as the woman haunted the narrator. (pp. 54-5)

The most fully developed story of the first section is **"Blood-Burning Moon."** It is the tale of Louisa, "color of oak leaves on young trees in fall; . . . breast, firm and up-pointed like ripe acorns"; Louisa, apex of a triangle whose other angles are her two lovers—white Bob Stone, son of her employers, and black Tom Burwell. Lyrically and perceptively Toomer explores the minds of Louisa and, particularly of Bob, who, reared to believe in white supremacy, cannot understand why he loves a black woman and cannot share her with a black man.

These portraits are the work of an artist who skillfully and vividly relates human beings to non-human objects: Karintha, a November cotton flower, against the pine-needles and pine smoke; Becky, visible only through her dark children, against the blue-sheen locomotive God; white-skinned Esther against flames and tobacco juice. These sketches are the work of a lyric poet, deceptively simple in style, careful with words.

When reading the sketches and stories set in the North, one perceives the intended contrast between a natural response to sexual drives and a self-conscious, frustrating inability to realize oneself. The women of Section One respond naturally and instinctively to their urges. Only near-white Esther experiences frustrating conflicts. In Washington and Chicago, however, sexual realization becomes impossible. In two of the four stories, conflict develops between a primitive being—instinctively, shamelessly, seeking gratification and realization and a society-sophisticated being—repressed, frustrated, unable to forget the image which society has ordered for him. In the other two, "Bona and Paul" and "Theater," protagonists are frustrated by their fears of social disapproval. (p. 57)

Longer than the earlier stories of ***Cane***, **"Theater," "Box Seat,"** and **"Bona and Paul"** reveal the weaknesses that restricted Toomer as a short-story writer and, later, as a novelist. They end vaguely and inconclusively. The material remains amorphous—a disappointment to a reader persuaded to expect more than a sketch.

"Kabnis" is the longest work in ***Cane.*** Although Toomer tried to have it produced as a play, Kenneth Macgowan rejected it because it lacked a plot. A producer might be more charitable in these days of the Theater of the Absurd. Like Samuel Beckett's *Waiting for Godot,* it is a spectacle of futility; like Ionesco's *The Chairs,* it substitutes a meaningless whimper for the anticipated climactic explosion. **"Kabnis,"** however, is not developed as artistically as either of these. Toomer failed to focus the multitudinous rays of light into one clear beam. (p. 58)

The play ends inconclusively but with obvious pessimism. After a night of debauchery and disappointment, Kabnis, carrying a bucket of dead coals, climbs the stairs to begin his labor as apprentice blacksmith. Behind him, in the cellar, Father John lies dying in the arms of Carrie K.

The only ray of optimism in the allegory of impotence and nonrealization is Lewis, a Christ-figure, who is what a stronger Kabnis might have been. Northern, educated, capable of acting according to emotional impulse or of controlling his emotion by will power, Lewis has come South for a month to observe and to communicate with his people. Compassionately he wishes to assist them, but he is driven away when they swallow the anodynes of drink and sex. (pp. 59-60)

From a vantage point 40 years later it is possible to discern limitations and unevenness in ***Cane***. First, Toomer's canvas is limited. Except in **"Kabnis,"** Toomer did not interpret the Southern Negro. Instead, he wrote lyrically about Southern women isolated or destroyed because they have ignored society's restrictions on sexual behavior.

An additional weakness appears in the stories located in Washington and Chicago. Toomer shifted from the stance of sympathetic observer or recorder of the tale of folk; he joined in the dance. Lewis replaced Kabnis. The change of point of view was unfortunate. Whereas Toomer could sing of women, he could not write effectively about Jean Toomer. Toomer, the character, is a neurotic, vanity-driven figure, like Paul in **"Bona and Paul."** Or he is a somewhat pompous, ineffectual reformer of souls, like the nameless narrator of **"Avey."**

John McClure, an editor, analyzed Toomer's talent and weakness perceptively when he wrote,

> The moment he attempts to make characters talk in the accents of life he falls from his highest level. He can divine what they think and what they feel but the only way he can express it is in his own language by stepping into their shoes and their uttering his own words in quotation marks, or else by avoiding quotation marks altogether and simply telling in his own words, by indirect discourse, what is going on in the other fellow's mind. The lyrical genius is not restricted to poetry. A novel can be lyrical.

But once Toomer imprisoned himself within the story, he surrendered part of his freedom to speak from within the minds of his other characters. He then needed to distinguish their phrasings and their thought patterns from his own.

A third weakness in later sections of ***Cane*** is Toomer's substitution of satire for sympathy. Part of the reason can be traced to Toomer's contrasting attitudes about his relationship to the characters in the tales. He had identified himself temperamentally with the Southern Negroes. When he wrote of Washington and Chicago, however, he lost his detachment. He wanted to reform the people, to rid them of their indolence or their anxieties or their inhibitions. Consequently, his tone becomes sharper, sardonic, satirical. For instance, he lamented that Avey is too much like a cow because she lives by instinct, with few drives and fewer goals. Yet Toomer had not sat in judgment upon Karintha and Fern, who were also creatures of instinct. One suspects that Jean Toomer expected such behavior from them because they were Southern Negroes, the children of nature. But Avey had been reared in Washington. She had been educated and had had opportunities to improve her economic position. She should have been able to rise above the animal.

In ***Cane,*** then, although Toomer said that he wrote about a waning way of life, he also wrote unconsciously of the death of an artist. Jean Toomer the lyricist was dying; Jean Toomer the philosopher, reformer was coming into being. (pp. 60-1)

Darwin T. Turner, "Jean Toomer's 'Cane," in Negro Digest, *Vol. XVII, No. 3, January, 1969, pp. 54-61.*

FRANK DURHAM (essay date 1972)

[Durham was a respected critic and editor of Southern literature; his Studies in "Cane" *(1971) reprints a variety of significant essays and reviews. In the following excerpt, Durham asserts that critics often overlook in* Cane *Toomer's subtle but powerful protest against racism.]*

When Jean Toomer's strange book ***Cane*** appeared in 1923, the few who read it were treated to a vision of the Southern Negro, a vision seen, I believe, through bifocals, or even trifocals. But most of the critics then and since have peered at this vision through only one or at most two of Toomer's lenses. The result has been that Toomer's picture of the Southern Negro has been only partially understood and partially interpreted. (p. 13)

[The facet of Toomer's vision] most generally ignored or denied entirely is his subtly presented protest at, not only the diminution of the Negro soul by its contacts with white society, but, more relevant to today, the oppression and brutality which the Negro must endure as a result of white fear, bigotry, injustice, and violence. (p. 18)

Eugene Holmes, a black critic, in 1932 praised Toomer by saying: "At first, critics could not understand that a Negro could write poetry that did not reek with rebellion and propaganda. Toomer wrote as a poet, never as an apologist." Comparing ***Cane*** to "the turbulent and rebellious poetry of the [Claude] McKay of that time," he found Toomer's work "a breath of sweet, cool air." Robert Littell maintained that here was not "the South of lynchings and hatreds, of the bitter, rebellious young Negro, and of his emigration to the North" [see excerpt dated 1923]. . . .

It is undeniable that first and foremost Jean Toomer was the artist, the poet. But there is no law prohibiting the artist and poet from holding and expressing through his work pronounced opinions. Often the most effective persuasive writing is that which, on the surface at any rate, seems least intended to persuade. It is my belief that, consciously or unconsciously, Jean Toomer presented as a constant element in his picture of the Negro an anger at the injustice, bigotry, and cruelty to which the Negro was subjected. Again and again he portrays examples of this oppression and of its effects on the Negro soul. (p. 19)

In **Blood-Burning Moon,"** Louisa, the black girl, is loved by a white boy and a black boy. When her black lover knifes the white boy, Toomer gives a vivid, moving description of the lynching—artistically done, yes, but with an impact that goes beyond art or rather extends art into a violent protest against injustice and violence:

> Shotguns, revolvers, rope, kerosene, torches. Two high-powered cars with glaring searchlights. They came together. . . . The moving body of their silence preceded them over the crest of the hill into factory town. It flattened the Negroes beneath it. . . . Tom knew that they were coming. He couldn't move. . . . That humming. No words. . . . Kerosene poured on the rotting floor boards. Tom bound to the stake. . . . Now Tom could be seen within the flames. Only his head, erect, lean, like a blackened stone. Stench of burning flesh soaked the air. Tom's eyes popped. His head settled down. The mob yelled. Its yell echoed against the skeleton stone walls and sounded like a hundred yells. Like a hundred mobs yelling.

Though individualized, this is not an isolated case, Toomer is saying. The echo of the mob's yell "sounded like a hundred yells. Like a hundred mobs yelling."

His treatment of the educated, sensitive, poetic observer in the book is also an example of the Negro's plight. He is Jean Toomer, whether he is named Kabnis or remains nameless or appears in other fictional guises. In one sense ***Cane*** is a protest against the destruction and degradation, almost the spiritual castration, of the educated Negro in the America of the 1920's. Making a pilgrimage from the North to find his ancestral roots, he finds them, but also finds that he can no longer establish a sense of their belonging to him. His white man's culture has, if one may mix a metaphor, severed the umbilical cord. Furthermore, the Negroes who still share in this heritage reject him too, for he is no longer of them, he now has acquired the aura of whiteness. (pp. 19-20)

But in the white world, both South and North, he is also an alien, a stranger. Even as Paul's Negritude attracts the white Bona [in **"Bona and Paul"**], she fears it, and Paul, aware that the discovery of his blackness may blast his romance and his social ties in white circles, is left solitary in the empty street, as he is solitary in an empty world. Rejected by both races, Kabnis ends dissipated and degraded. . . . (p. 20)

Two characters in **"Kabnis"** carry in them a suggestion, but only a suggestion, of Toomer's tentative solution to the problems of the Negro. These are Carrie Kate and Lewis. The girl seems to represent the pure, untouched Negro soul, throbbing with the promise of life and love, a kind of fertility symbol—the ideal lover and the potential earth mother. She is a food-bringer, nurturing Father John, the Negro's ancestral past. Lewis is the educated Negro from the North. "His mouth and eyes suggest purpose guided by an adequate intelligence. He is what a stronger Kabnis might have been. . . ." . . . Toomer possibly offers a solution to the Negro's subjection by the white—the union of "purpose guided by an adequate intelligence" and strength with the Negro's ancient spirit, his life force drawn from the soil and the sun and the primal past. Of course, he does hint that the solution will be delayed until the Negro can cast aside the restrictive, bourgeois moral-religious taboos of the white man's code. But he does, at least, hint at a way of battle.

In conclusion, then, Toomer's vision of the rural Southern Negro is indeed characterized, as many critics agree, by a pioneering glimpse of the vitality of the Negro soul, its beauty, its freedom, its uninhibited expression of the inheritance of two worlds—the paganism of Africa and the vibrant, fertile soul of the South. It is true, too, that he shows the corroding effects of white culture on this soul. But, equally true, though rarely if ever noted, is the fact that Toomer could not write of the Negro soul without an awareness of more than just the gradual diminution of its exuberance and power; he could not write of it without portraying the violence and oppression by the white man and without, consciously or unconsciously, raising his voice in protest, a voice subtler than those of Walter White, T. S. Stribling, Claude McKay, Langston Hughes, and others of his own time; a voice certainly subtler than those of Richard Wright, James Baldwin, LeRoi Jones, Ralph Ellison, and Eldridge Cleaver. His very subtlety is deceptive, for without shrillness, without overt propaganda, he made his readers share his sorrow and his burning anger. (pp. 21-2)

Frank Durham, "Jean Toomer's Vision of the Southern Negro," in The Southern Humanities Review, *Vol. VI, No. 1, Winter, 1972, pp. 13-22.*

W. EDWARD FARRISON (essay date 1972)

[In the following excerpt, Farrison questions the literary influence that critics have claimed for Cane *and disputes the common belief that parts one and two of the book are meant to contrast the North and South.]*

[***Cane***] was from the beginning and still is a uniquely interesting work. Its uniqueness consists primarily in the fact that it portrays phases of Negro life in places whence those phases had not previously received authentic, extensive literary treatment. (p. 295)

Although Frank's predictions concerning ***Cane*** [see excerpt dated 1923] can hardly be said to have come true, many have written about the book as if they did. . . . "In ***Cane,***" said Eugene Holmes somewhat ecstatically in 1932, "raving critics and poetasters recognized a naturalism of such a distinctive kind that the applause was deafening," and "It [***Cane***] has also given the necessary influence and impetus to those younger Negro poets who did not know about what to write." In 1966 and again in his introduction of 1969, Bontemps said that the reaction to ***Cane*** of "practically an entire generation of young Negro writers then just beginning to emerge" marked the awakening of what came to be called "a Negro Renaissance." Also in 1966 Bontemps had remarked that "Subsequent writing by Negroes in the United States as well as in the West Indies and Africa has continued to reflect its mood and often its method, and, one feels, it also has influenced the writing about Negroes by others" [see excerpt dated 1966]. In Durham's opinion the influence which ***Cane*** has had upon Negro writers is the product of Toomer's having learned his craft of writing from such white writers and artists as Sherwood Anderson, Hart Crane, Waldo Frank, and others of their kind. . . .

Interestingly enough it is easier to maximize than to minimize literary influence, and still easier to generalize than to be specific about it. Herein lies the probable reason why the influences by which ***Cane*** has been said to have been affected and the influence attributed to it have been generally left unexplained as well as overemphasized. Some clarification concerning both of these kinds of influence now seems well in order—in fact overdue.

As to the craft of writing, it is indeed probable that Toomer learned something especially from Anderson and Frank about the effective portrayal of folk life, but it is not improbable that he also learned something about this directly from Edgar Lee Masters' *Spoon River Anthology* (1915). From that work Anderson himself might have learned something about the art of portraying what a reviewer of his *Winesburg, Ohio* (1919) called "the inner individual life of a typical American small town." Also, since Frank and Toomer were closely associated while Frank was writing *Holiday* and Toomer was writing ***Cane,*** they might have influenced each other's writing. Moreover, Toomer, like many other writers, might have learned a great deal independently about writing by constant practice—by trial and error, by studious rewriting.

If Toomer was influenced by Masters, Anderson, Frank, and similar writers, it is at least probable that other Negro writers of his time, like non-Negro writers, were directly influenced by them rather than only indirectly through ***Cane.*** This probability is strengthened by the fact that ***Cane*** was never an easily available book until the paperback edition of it was published in 1969.

There seems to be no good reason to believe that ***Cane,*** which until recently was not widely circulated, could have had the extensive influence which some seem to think it has had. Nor is there any good reason for considering Toomer the father of the Harlem Renaissance, or a pioneering delver into and portrayer of "the soul of the Negro," "the Negro's psyche," "the Negro's spirit," "the race-soul," or "the great emotionalism of the race"—whatever these jargonistic phrases mean. It should be noted, by the way, that in ***Cane*** Toomer neither philosophized about Negroes nor made any of his characters do so. The Harlem Renaissance evolved from what became known at least as early as 1916 as "The Renaissance of the Negro Race" and also as the "New Negro" movement—long before Toomer's ***Cane*** or Alain Locke's *The New Negro* (1925) was published. Like other writers, Toomer the writer was as much the creation as the creator of the literary milieu in which he flourished. Doubtless the Harlem Renaissance helped to make him the writer that he became, and with other writers, probably he in turn helped to some extent, whether great or small, to make some of the writing of his time and afterwards what it became. (pp. 296-98)

The subject matter of ***Cane*** is the imaginatively treated product of Toomer's actual experiences and observations in Washington, D.C., where he was born and where he made his home until late in the 1920's, in Chicago, where he studied briefly in a school of physical education, and in Sparta, Georgia, where he spent three months as a schoolteacher in the fall of 1921. (p. 299)

Recently Toomer has been credited with contrasting Washington as the North in the second part of ***Cane*** with the South in the first part. It is difficult to believe that Toomer would have been naive enough to attempt such a thing, for he certainly knew that Washington in the 1920's was not a part of the North vis-à-vis the South, but was in fact a part of the South. He knew that as far as matters racial were concerned, Washington then had much less in common with New York than with Atlanta, and that Colonel James Crow was as much an habitué of Pennsylvania Avenue as of Peachtree Street. Moreover none of the parts of ***Cane*** contain anything that suggests such a contrast. (p. 300)

W. Edward Farrison, "Jean Toomer's 'Cane' Again," in CLA Journal, *Vol. XV, No. 2, March, 1972, pp. 295-302.*

HOUSTON A. BAKER, JR. (essay date 1974)

[In the following excerpt, Baker considers the significance of Cane *in the development of Afro-American art and provides a detailed thematic study of the work.]*

William Stanley Braithwaite's "The Negro in American Literature," concludes with the rhapsodic assertion that "***Cane*** is a book of gold and bronze, of dusk and flame, of ecstasy and pain, and Jean Toomer is a bright morning star of a new day of the race in literature" [see excerpt dated 1924]. . . . Braithwaite's statement reflects the energy and excess, the vibrancy and hope of a generation of young black authors who set out in the 1920s to express their "individual dark-skinned selves without fear or shame." . . . Ironically, it was ***Cane,*** a book written by a very light-complexioned mulatto, that portrayed—without fear or shame—a dark-skinned self that transcended the concerns of a single period and heralded much of value that has followed its publication. (pp. 53-4)

The 1920s presented a problem for the writer who wished to give a full and honest representation of black American life; for him the traditional images, drawn from the authors of the Plantation Tradition and the works of Paul Laurence Dunbar, were passé. The contemporary images, captured in Carl Van Vechten's *Nigger Heaven* (1926) and Claude McKay's *Home to Harlem* (1928), were not designed to elucidate a complex human existence, for they were reflections of that search for the bizarre and the exotic that was destined to flourish in an age of raccoon coats, bathtub gin, and "wine-flushed, bold-eyed" whites who caught the A-train to Harlem and spent an evening slumming, or seeking some *élan vital* for a decadent but prosperous age. That only two small printings of ***Cane*** appeared during the 1920s is not striking: the miracle is that it was published at all. Toomer did not choose the approbation that a scintillating (if untrue) portrayal of the black man could bring in the twenties, nor did he speak *sotto voce* about the amazing progress the black man had made in American society and his imminent acceptance by a fond white world. ***Cane*** is a symbolically complex work that employs lyrical intensity and stream-of-consciousness narration to portray the journey of an artistic soul toward creative fulfillment; it is unsparing in its criticism of the inimical aspects of the black American heritage and resonant in its praise of the spiritual beauty to be discovered there. An examination of the journey toward genuine, liberating black art presented in ***Cane*** reveals Toomer as a writer of genius and the book itself as a protest novel, a portrait of the artist, and a thorough delineation of the black situation. These aspects of the work explain its signal place among the achievements of the Harlem Renaissance, and they help to clarify the reactions of a white reading public—a public nurtured on the minstrel tradition, the tracts of the New Negro, and the sensational antics of Carl Van Vechten's blacks—which allowed it to go out of print without a fair hearing. (pp. 54-5)

The essential theme of **"Karintha"** [the opening story of the first section of ***Cane***] is the debasement of innocence. Men are attracted to the heroine but fail to appreciate what is of value—the spirituality inherent in her dusky beauty. They are awed by the pure yet wish to destroy it; evil becomes their good, and they think only in terms of progressive time and capitalistic abundance—"The young fellows counted the time to pass before she would be old enough to mate with them" and ran stills to make her money. These conditions result, in part, from a southern Manichaeanism; for the land whose heritage appears in **"Karintha"** stated its superiority and condoned an inhumane slavery, spoke of its aristocracy and traded in human flesh, lauded its natural resources and wantonly destroyed them to acquire wealth. Good and evil waged an equal contest in a South that contained its own natural harmonies but considered blacks as chattels personal, bound by no rights that a white man need respect. In such an instance, love could only be an anomaly, and the narrator of Part One seems fully aware of this. When black women are considered property (the materialism surrounding Karintha and Fern) and white women goddesses (the recrimination that accompanies Becky's sacrilegious acts), deep relationships are impossible; the evil of the encompassing universe and the natural compulsion of man to corrupt the beautiful inform the frustrating encounters of Part One. (pp. 56-7)

While exploring the nature of Karintha's existence, the author has been constructing the setting that is to appear throughout Part One. The first story's effect is heightened by the presence of the religious, the suggestive, and the feminine, and certain aspects of the landscape linger in the reader's mind: a sawmill, pine trees, red dust, a pyramidal sawdust pile, and rusty cotton stalks. The folk songs convey a feeling of cultural homogeneity; they are all of a religious character, rising spontaneously and pervading the landscape. The finishing details of this setting—the Dixie Pike and the railroad—are added in **"Becky,"** which deals with a mode of interaction characteristic of primitive, homogeneous societies.

"Becky" is the story of a white woman who gives birth to two mulatto sons, thus violating one of the most rigid taboos of southern society. As a consequence, she is ostracized by the community. . . . Unlike Karintha, Becky is seldom portrayed in physical terms. The narrator has never seen her, and the community as a whole merely speculates on her actions and her changing appearance. She is primarily a psychological presence to whom the community pays an ironical homage: a spectral representation of the southern miscegenatory impulse that was so alive during the days of American slavery and was responsible for countless lynchings even in Toomer's own day. As early as the seventeenth century, southern legislatures were enacting laws to prevent sexual alliances between blacks and whites; hence, the community in **"Becky"** reacts in a manner sanctioned by law and custom.

"Becky" presents a further exploration of the duality theme encountered in **"Karintha,"** and here the psychological element seems to predominate. The heroine's exile first calls to mind repression; she is set apart and finally buried. A more accurate description of Becky, however, is that she is a shaman. Among certain Asian groups and American Indian tribes, a person who engages in unsanctioned behavior (homosexuality, for example) is thought to have received a divine summons; he becomes a public figure and devises and leads ritualistic ceremonies that project his abnormal behavior. The function of the shaman is twofold; he enables the community to act out, by proxy, its latent abnormalities, and he reinforces its capacity to resist such tendencies. He is tolerated and revered because of his supernatural power, yet hated as a symbol of moral culpability and as a demanding priest who exacts a penitential toll. The most significant trait of the shaman, however, is that—despite his ascribed powers—he is unable to effect a genuine cure. (pp. 58-9)

Becky has engaged in a pattern of behavior that the surrounding community considers taboo, and she is relegated to a physical position outside the group but essentially public. Her house is built (by the townspeople) in a highly visible location, an "eye-shaped piece of sandy ground. . . . Islandized between the road and railroad track." The citizens scorn her and consider her deranged ("poor-white crazy woman, said the black folks' mouths"), but at the same time they pray for her, bring her food, and keep her alive. Becky, in turn, continues her activities; she has another mulatto son and remains in the tottering house until it eventually crumbles beneath the weight of its chimney. In essence, we witness the same dichotomy presented in **"Karintha"**; the South professes racial purity and abhorrence of miscegenation, but the fundamental conditions of the region nourish a subconscious desire for interracial relationships and make a penitential ritual necessary. It seems significant, moreover, that Becky—who is a Catholic and in that respect also one of the South's traditional aversions—assumes a divine role for the community. Attraction toward and repulsion by the spiritually ordained are as much a part of the landscape in **"Becky"** as in **"Karintha."** (pp. 59-60)

The narrator [of Part One] speaks in a tone that combines awe and reverence with effective irony and subtle criticism. There are always deeper levels of meaning beneath his highly descriptive surface, and this is not surprising when one considers Toomer's statement that in the South "one finds soil in the sense that the Russians know it—the soil every art and literature that is to live must be embedded in."

The emblematic nature of the soil is reflected in the tone and technique of the narrator and particularly in the book's title. Throughout Part One there is an evocation of a land of sugar cane whose ecstasy and pain are rooted in a communal soil. But the title conveys more than this. Justifications of slavery on scriptural grounds frequently traced the black man's ancestry to the race of Cain, the slayer of Abel, in the book of Genesis. Toomer is concerned not only with the Southern soil but also with the sons of Cain who populate it. In a colloquial sense, "to raise Cain" is to create disorder and cacophony, and in a strictly denotative sense, a cane is an instrument of support. Toomer's narrator is attempting to create an ordered framework that will contain the black American's complex existence, offer supportive values, and act as a guide for the perceptive soul's journey from amorphous experience to a finished work of art.

The third story of Part One, **"Carma,"** is called by the narrator "the crudest melodrama," and so it is—on one level. When Carma's husband, Bane (surely an ironical name to set against *karma*), discovers that she has been unfaithful, he slashes the man who has told him, and is sentenced to the chain gang. This is melodramatic to be sure, but only (to quote the narrator) "as I have told it." Beneath the sensational surface is a tragedy of black American life. Bane, like Jimboy in Langston Hughes's *Not Without Laughter,* is forced by economic pressures to seek work away from home; thus, his wife is left alone in an environment where (again, according to the narrator) promiscuity is a norm. But Carma is also a woman who flaunts her sensuality, and can hardly be said to possess a strong sense of responsibility.

As in the previous stories, there are positive and redeeming elements in **"Carma."** The heroine herself is "strong as any man," and, given her name, this at least implies that her spirituality—that which is best and most ineffable in her—is capable of enduring the inimical aspects of her surroundings. This is particularly important when one considers that **"Carma"** introduces a legendary African background to the first section: "Torches flare . . . juju men, greegree, witch-doctors . . . torches go out. . . . The Dixie Pike has grown from a goat path in Africa." . . . (pp. 61-2)

"Carma" is also the first story in which the narrator clearly identifies himself as a conscious recounter ("whose tale as I have told it"), and the poems that follow read like invocations to the heritage that he is exploring. "Song of the Son" states his desire to sing the "souls of slavery," and "Georgia Dusk," which makes further use of the legendary background encountered in **"Carma,"** evokes the spirits of the "unknown bards" of the past. It is not surprising, then, that the story [**"Fern"**] should follow. (p. 62)

"If you have heard a Jewish cantor sing, if he has touched you and made your own sorrow seem trivial when compared with his, you will know my [the narrator's] feeling when I follow the curves of her profile, like mobile rivers, to their common delta," and Fern's full name is Fernie May Rosen. The narrator is thus making use of the seminal comparison between the history of the Israelites and that of black America, which frequently appears in the religious lore of black American culture. In effect, the slaves appropriated the myth of the Egyptian captivity and considered themselves favored by God and destined in time to be liberated by His powers; this provided unity for a people who found themselves uprooted and defined by whites—historians and others—as descendants of wild savages on the "dark continent" of Africa. Despite the fact that she dislikes the petty people of the South and apparently needs to express an underlying spirituality, Fern seems to act as a symbolic representation of the black man's adoption of this myth. When the narrator has brought about a hysterical release from her, however, he fails to comprehend what he has evoked. The story ends with an injunction to the reader to seek out Fern when he travels South. The narrator feels that his ideal holds significance, but that his aspirations toward it are unfulfilled. There is some naivety in this assumption; for the teller of Fern's story has explored the ironies inherent in the merger of white religion and black servitude. The religion of the Israelites is out of place in the life of Fern. While she captures—in her mysterious song like that of a Jewish cantor—the beauty of its spirit (and, in this sense, stands outside the narrow-minded community), she is imprisoned by the mores it occasions. Like Becky and Karintha, Fern is a victim, and the narrator skillfully captures her essence. The apparent naivety at the story's conclusion is in reality an act of modesty; for the art the narrator implies is humble actually holds greater significance (in its subtle didactic elements) for the culture he is attempting to delineate.

"Esther" is a story of alienation and brings an inquietude that grows into the concluding terror of the book's first section. Apocalyptic images abound as the heroine dreams of King Barlo (a figure who first appeared in **"Becky"**) overcoming her pale frigidity with a flaming passion that will result in a "black, singed, woolly, tobacco-juice baby—ugly as sin." . . . [One] can make excessive claims for King Barlo. While it is true that he falls into a religious trance and sketches, in symbolic oratory, the fate of Africans at the hands of slave traders, it is also true that he is a vagrant preacher, a figure whom Toomer sketches fully (and with less than enthusiasm) in Layman of **"Kabnis."** And though Barlo is the prophet of a new dawn for the black American, he is also a businessman who makes money during the war, and a lecherous frequenter of the demimonde. It thus seems an overstatement to make a one-to-one correlation between Barlo and Africa, or Afro-America. (pp. 63-4)

Barlo does contain within himself the unifying myth of black American culture, and he delivers it to the community in the manner of the most accomplished black folk preachers. In this character, however, he paradoxically contributes to Esther's stifled sensibility, which continually projects visions of sin. As a feat hero (the best cotton picker) and a skillful craftsman of words (his moving performance on the public street), he contains positive aspects, but the impression that remains—when one has noted his terrified and hypocritical response in **"Becky"** and his conspicuous materialism and insensitive treatment of Esther—is not as favorable as some critics would tempt us to believe. (p. 65)

Part One is a combination of awe-inspiring physical beauty, human hypocrisy, restrictive religious codes, and psychological trauma. In **"Fern"** the narrator says: "That the sexes were made to mate is the practice of the South." But sexual consummation in the first section often results in dissatisfaction or in a type of perverse motherhood. . . . The women of Part One are symbolic figures, but the lyrical terms in which they are described can be misleading. With the exception of their misdirected sexuality, they are little different from the entrapped and stifled women of the city seen in Part Two. In short, something greater than the pressure of urban life accounts for the black man's frustrated ambitions, violent outbursts, and tragic deaths at the hands of white America. The black American's failure to fully comprehend the beautiful in his own heritage—the Georgia landscape, folk songs, and women of deep loveliness—is part of it. But the narrator places even greater emphasis on the black man's ironical acceptance of the "strange cassava" and "weak palabra" of a white religion. Throughout Part One, he directs pointed thrusts—in the best

Toomer and his Uncle Bismarck in the 1920s. Courtesy of Susan Loeb Sandberg.

tradition of David Walker, Frederick Douglass, and William Wells Brown—at Christianity. Although he appreciates the rich beauty of black folk songs that employ Protestant religious imagery ("Georgia Dusk"), he also sees that the religion as it is practiced in the South is often hypocritical and stifling. . . . [The narrator] clearly realizes that the psychological mimicry that led to the adoption of a white religion often directed black Americans away from their own spiritual beauties and resulted in destruction.

But the importance of white America's role cannot be minimized. King Barlo views the prime movers behind the black situation as "little white-ant biddies" who tied the feet of the African, uprooted him from his traditional culture, and made him prey to alien gods. The essential Manichaeanism of a South that thrived on slavery, segregation, the chattel principle, and violence is consummately displayed in the first section of ***Cane,*** and Barlo realizes that a new day must come before the black man will be free. The brutality directed against the black American has slowed the approach of such a dawn, but the narrator of Part One has discovered positive elements in the black Southern heritage that may lead to a new day: a sense of song and soil, and the spirit of a people who have their severe limitations but cannot be denied.

Part Two of ***Cane*** is set in the city and constitutes a male cycle. The creative soul that was characterized by a type of "negative capability" in Part One becomes an active agency of dreams and knowledge, and the narrator recedes to a more objective plane, where he can view even himself somewhat impartially. **"Avey"** has a first-person point of view, but the remainder of the stories come from the hand of an omniscient narrator who seems aware that as a creator he needs "consummate skill to walk upon the waters where huge bubbles burst." The urban environment demands more careful analysis, and thus the lyrical impulse is diminished in the second section—there are only half as many connecting poems here as in Part One.

"Seventh Street" and **"Rhobert,"** the opening sketches of Part Two, capture the positive and negative aspects of a new environment. The driving, cutting, inexorable energy seen in "Reapers" and "Cotton Song" has become "A crude-boned, soft-skinned wedge of nigger life" thrusting its way "into the white and white-washed wood of Washington." And the epigraph of the first sketch evokes a lower-echelon black urban environment—with its easy spending, bootleggers, silken shirts, and Cadillacs—not a dusky, natural beauty like Karintha's. . . . After reading **"Rhobert"** and **"Seventh Street,"** one is aware that one is in the presence of a narrator who has learned to look intelligently beneath the surface of life. His irony is more subtle, and the near-Swiftian satire of the second sketch demonstrates his ability to make accurate, undisguised value judgments. Moreover, he has moved toward greater self-knowledge; if Rhobert is portrayed as a man engaged in a somewhat fruitless contest, so, too, is the first-person narrator of **"Avey."** (pp. 66-9)

At the outset of **"Avey,"** the narrator comments:

> I like to think now that there was a hidden purpose in the way we [he and his childhood friends] hacked them [boxes on V Street containing saplings] with our knives. I like to feel that something deep in me responded to the trees, the young trees that whinnied like colts impatient to be let free. . . .

As the story progresses, the manner in which he hopes to bestow freedom becomes less violent, and in his last encounter with Avey, he (as in **"Fern"**) conceives of talk as artistic expression, as an agency of liberation. . . . But while the narrator evoked, at least, a hysterical response from Fern, he finds Avey asleep when he has finished talking. He realizes finally that Avey's is not the type of loveliness that characterizes a new day: "She did not have the gray crimson-splashed beauty of the dawn."

Bone ventures the idea that "Toomer's intellectualizing males are tragic because they value talking above feeling" [see excerpt dated 1965], but such a formulation implies that beautiful talk and profound feelings are mutually exclusive in ***Cane,*** which is not the case. The narrator derides himself for having "dallied dreaming" instead of making advances to Avey during a youthful holiday, and he realizes the absurdity of his situation when he finds her asleep. However, he also depicts himself as a man with his mind "set on freedom" and knows that art can play a role in achieving this end. Moreover, he is the character who evokes that sense of song and soil that received such positive valuations in Part One. . . . The feeling of frustration that concludes the story, therefore, does not result totally from a flaw in the narrator's character, but also from the intractability of his artistic materials. Avey, who is one of the more languorous and promiscuous members of the new urban black bourgeoisie, is hopelessly insensible to the artist's rendering of "a larger life," and one would scarcely expect her to respond to a beautiful heritage. She is, indeed, an "orphan-woman." (pp. 69-71)

With the exception of **"Bona and Paul,"** the stories and poems that follow "Storm Ending" in Part Two are restatements of concerns that have been treated earlier. The protagonists of **"Theater"** and **"Box Seat"** are both dreamers who envision passionate affairs with women bound by convention. Dorris in **"Theater,"** like Muriel in **Box Seat,"** dances with energy, but neither could conceive of saying, in Imamu Baraka's words,

> I want to be sung. I want
> all my bones and meat hummed
> against the thick floating
> winter sky. I want myself
> as dance. As what I am
> given love, or time, or space
> to feel myself.
>
> (pp. 71-2)

The whole of Part Two might justifiably be called a portrait of the artist who has been removed from a primitive and participatory culture to suffer the alienation of modern life. One means of overcoming this estrangement is the dream, which calls forth positive images from the past; but when the artist's reveries become—for any reason—simply acts of self-indulgence (a word that might describe John's imaginings), he must move beyond the dream in a search for greater self-knowledge and a broader definition of the artist's role. The theme of **"Bona and Paul,"** the concluding story of the second section, involves such a quest. When the story opens, Paul has become so introspective that his associates are baffled; even Bona, who is white (reviving the miscegenation theme of **"Becky"** and **"Blood-Burning Moon"**), though attracted to Paul, fails to comprehend him. . . . The essence of the black southern heritage is in Paul's dream, but what is more important is that the dreamer incorporates the sun of this heritage into himself: "He is at Bona's window. With his own eyes he looks through a dark pane." Bona contains no light, and Art, Paul's roommate, "is like the electric light which he snaps on.'' At Crimson Gardens the illumination is artificial. Paul, whom Bona designates ''a poet—or a gym instructor,'' becomes a source of natural light, and he is neither a lyric poet like the speaker of ''Reapers,'' nor a regimented victim of ''mental concepts'' like the drillers seen at the beinning of the story. He has transcended a narrowly personal stage of art and moves toward a stance as the knowing, philosophical creator. His epiphany occurs at Crimson Gardens. . . . Paul turns first to a brief exploration of the white world, which he finds lovely in its artificial light. He dances with Bona, and passion flares for an instant. The couple leaves the garden. But night is alien to Bona. . . . When Paul is suddenly possessed by the night and the face of the black doorman (the man outside the garden), Bona realizes that she cannot contain, or comprehend, his desires. The fact that Bona has left when Paul returns does not mean the story's conclusion is pessimistic. Paul has come to greater self-knowledge. . . . It is Bona who is cold, imprisoned by the white mental restraints her companion has rejected. Paul is like a nascent black sun and has taken the first step toward sharing his vision with his people.

Part Two, therefore, moves beyond the dream to knowledge. . . . From the lyrical, awed, contemplative narrator of **''Karintha,''** ***Cane*** has progressed to a self-conscious, philosophical creator who contains ''his own glow'' and rejects the artificial garden of white life. **''Kabnis,''** the concluding section of ***Cane,*** deals with the actions of such an artist vis-à-vis black southern life. It brings the action of the book full circle and completes the portrait of the artist.

The narrator of **''Avey''** seeks ''the simple beauty of another's soul'' and ''the truth that people bury in their hearts.'' . . . The artist in **''Kabnis,''** however, searches for knowledge of his own soul and an artistic design that will express it. From the simple observation of the physical beauty of women, the narrator has moved to a fuller exploration of the complexities that beset the black soul. Most of the symbolic figures in the drama are men, and the process of making undisguised value judgments, at work in **''Rhobert,''** is fundamental to **''Kabnis.''** The work is not only a return to the South, but also an open protest (as opposed to the subtle, lyrical criticism dominant in Part One) against its stifling morality and brutal violence. (pp. 73-5)

Ralph Kabnis is a Northerner who has come South to teach. He is fired by Hanby, the school superintendant (and an unctuous counterpart to Mrs. Pribby), and taken in by the wagonsmith, Halsey. Kabnis meets Layman, a southern preacher, and Lewis, a Northerner who has made a contract with himself—presumably to investigate the South for a month. The introspective Kabnis proves a hopeless failure as a manual worker and spends much of his time in the cellar of the wagon shop, which is reached by stairs located behind ''a junk heap.'' ''Besides being the home of a very old man, . . . [the cellar] is used by Halsey on those occasions when he spices up the life of the small town.'' The old man is attended by Carrie K., Halsey's sister, and when first encountered he has been mumbling and fasting for two weeks. Halsey arranges a night of debauchery for himself, Kabnis, Lewis, and the play concludes on the morning afterward, when the old man speaks. As in **''Bona and Paul,''** however, action plays a minor role in **''Kabnis''**; description, dialogue, and reflection provide the points of focus. The message they render is that the old ethic of the southern black man—composed of Protestantism, vocational education, shopkeeping, and accommodation—will not suffice in a violent white society. Moreover, the new scientific approach to the complexities of black American life, represented by Lewis . . . is unsatisfactory. (pp. 75-6)

A similarly critical attitude surrounds all those activities of the black American's southern existence which the narrator and the author consider ineffective or inimical. Negative images abound, for example, wherever religion is mentioned. . . . God is seen as the creator of shopkeepers and moralizers; Layman is portrayed as a reticent vagabond too frightened to speak against the evils of lynching, and the singing and shouting of a black church service are the backdrop for a chilling story of mob violence. Negative images also surround Halsey, a descendant of seven generations of shopkeepers and a man for whom time has stopped—''an old-fashioned mantelpiece supports a family clock (not running).'' Finally, Lewis—who at different points in **''Kabnis''** appears as a Christ figure, a race man, and an alter ego for the protagonist—becomes ''a dead chill'' when confronted with the depths of the black southern experience. . . . (pp. 76-7)

The laudable characters in the play are Kabnis and Carrie K. The protagonist is the knowing artist who confronts the desert places in himself, and Carrie K. is the young, chaste ideal of a new art. Both characters, however, have their limitations. Carrie is constrained by conventional ethics. . . . Kabnis is often self-indulgent, overly ceremonious, and terrified at the violence of the South. He is a Kurtzian vision, and his mulatto status (as with Paul and several of the other characters in ***Cane***) comes to represent the gray world of alienation confronting modern man.

Carrie K. and Kabnis, however, are the individuals who function most effectively in the cellar, or ''the hole,'' which represents the collective unconscious of Black America. The hole is presided over by an enthroned figure whom Halsey and Carrie K. call ''Father,'' but upon whom the awestruck Lewis bestows a religious title, ''Father John.'' It is finally Kabnis who elicits from the black father his wisdom; the old man denounces: ''Th sin whats fixed . . . upon th white folks . . . f tellin Jesus—lies. O th sin th white folks 'mitted when they made the Bible lie.'' Carrie K.'s reaction is one of tears and tolerance, but Kabnis—as well he might be—is incensed. For though the old man has condemned the hypocrisy of whites, his vocabulary is one of sin and the Bible. . . . The protagonist is aware that a new vocabulary, one that will ''fit m soul'' and capture that ''twisted awful thing that crept in [to my soul] from a dream, a godam nightmare,'' is needed; the black man must have a new vision of life crafted by the sensitive artist. Black art can function as a new and liberating religion. (pp. 77-8)

The tone of the last two acts reflects solemnity, hope, and a new birth. . . . The concluding scene witnesses Kabnis, a new-world creator, ascending from the cellar as the herald and agent of the dawn prophesied by Barlo in **''Esther.''** In his hands are the dead coals of a past ritual, and the expectations generated by the opening of Act Five are fulfilled:

> Outside, the sun arises from its cradle in the tree-tops of the forest. Shadows of pines are dreams the sun shakes from its eyes. The sun arises. Gold-glowing child, it steps into the sky and sends a birth-song slanting down gray dust streets and sleepy windows of the southern town.
>
> (pp. 78-9)

Kabnis beseeches that he not be tortured with beauty and goes on to say, ''Dear Jesus, do not chain me to myself and set these hills and valleys, heaving with folk-songs, so close to me that I cannot reach them." The deeper meanings of the songs have touched him, and in an early soliloquy that combines the narrator's goals in Parts One and Two, he says: "If I, the dream (not what is weak and afraid in me) could become the face of the South. How my lips would sing for it, my songs being the lips of its soul." He realizes, however, that there are also inimical aspects of the past and describes them in scathing, oftentimes bitter terms. What distinguishes him from others (like Layman and Halsey, who have seen the darker side of the South) is his self-awareness; he realizes that the paranoia, aggressiveness, ambivalence, and hypocrisy of the South find counterparts in his own personality. One expects, therefore, that a portion of his new art will be devoted to serious introspection. . . . Kabnis is the fully emergent artist—a singer of a displaced "soil-soaked beauty" and an agent of liberation for his people.

Cane led the way in a return to the black folk spirit, which Eugenia Collier has seen as one of the most vital developments of the Harlem Renaissance, and it did so in a form and style that have scarcely been surpassed by subsequent American authors. Toomer knew—and did not attempt to sublimate—the pains and restrictions of a black Southern heritage. This angst is astutely criticized in ***Cane*** and magnificently portrayed as the somber result of white America's exploitation and oppression, black America's too willing acceptance, and the inherent duality in the nature of man—the Manichaeanism of the universe, emblemized by the southern past—which both marvels at and seeks to destroy beauty. Opposed to "the burden of southern history"—indeed, to the darker side of human history, with its inhibitions, omnipresent violence, and moral ineptitude—however, are the pristine loveliness and indomitable spirit of the folk, to be discovered and extolled by the sensitive observer. A folk culture containing its own resonant harmonies, communal values and assumptions, and fruitful proximity to the ancestral soil offers a starting point for the journey toward black art. The artist, however, cannot simply observe the surface beauties of this culture; he must comprehend the self-knowledge and nobility of spirit that made its creation possible in the midst of an inhuman servitude. Toomer repeatedly asserts this in ***Cane,*** and at times the book reads like a tragic allegory, posing good against evil, suffering against redemption, hope against despair. As the reader struggles to fit the details together, he becomes increasingly involved in the complexities of the black situation. He moves, in short, toward that freedom that always accompanies deeper self-knowledge and a genuine understanding of one's condition in the universe. In this sense, ***Cane*** is not only a journey toward liberating black American art but also what philosophy calls the *Ding-an-Sich*—the thing in itself. (pp. 79-80)

Houston A. Baker, Jr., "Journey Toward Black Art: Jean Toomer's 'Cane'," in his Singers of Daybreak: Studies in Black American Literature, *1974. Reprint by Howard University Press, 1983, pp. 53-80.*

ROBERT BONE (essay date 1975)

[Bone provides biographical information about Toomer related to his literary career and examines three representative stories from Cane.*]*

When Toomer writes of "a song-lit race of slaves," whose plaintive soul is "leaving, soon gone," he employs the language and the form of pastoral elegy. For ***Cane*** is in essence a pastoral interlude, like Thoreau's trip to the woods, through which the author seeks to achieve a consolidation of the self, in order to move forward to the fundamental task of prophecy.

Cane was Jean Toomer's hail-and-farewell to his blackness. Springing from a sojourn of several months in Sparta, Georgia, the impulse that gave birth to ***Cane*** was soon exhausted. Toomer was never to touch on these materials again. "The folk-spirit," as he explains in the *Outline of an Autobiography,* "was walking in to die on the modern desert. That spirit was so beautiful. Its death was so tragic. Just this seemed to sum up life for me. And this was the feeling I put into ***Cane. Cane*** was a swan song. It was a song of an end. And why no one has seen and felt that, why people have expected me to write a second and a third and a fourth book like ***Cane*** is one of the queer misunderstandings of my life." (pp. 207-08)

Toomer's intellectual gropings began in 1916, during his first sojourn in Chicago. Under the influence of Clarence Darrow and Carl Sandburg, he became an agnostic and a socialist. On moving to New York in 1917, he read intensively in Shaw and Ibsen, Santayana and Goethe. Brief employment in a Jersey shipyard cured him of his socialism, while a reading of Goethe's *Wilhelm Meister* made him an esthete. His esthetic tendencies were reinforced by a meeting with Waldo Frank in 1919. Back in Washington in the summer of 1920, he read "all of Waldo Frank, most of Dostoievsky, much of Tolstoi, Flaubert, Baudelaire, Sinclair Lewis, Dreiser, most all of the American poets, Coleridge, Blake, Pater—in fine, a good portion of the modern writers of all western countries."

From 1920 to 1923 Toomer lived in Washington, caring for his aging grandparents and serving his literary apprenticeship. Setting the most exacting standards, he accumulated a trunkful of manuscripts before he was satisfied with their quality: "I wrote and wrote and put each thing aside, regarding it as simply one of the exercises of my apprenticeship." For three months in the fall of 1921 he served as Acting Principal of a Negro school in Sparta, Georgia. This pilgrimage to his sources inspired Toomer's first book. ***Cane*** was written in approximately thirteen months, from November 1921 to December 1922. (pp. 209-10)

Of the twenty-nine units of which ***Cane*** is composed, fifteen are plainly poems, written for the most part in free verse. **"Kabnis"** is a free-form play, complete with stage directions. Six of the less substantial pieces are sketches, or vignettes, or prose poems, too slender to afford much narrative development. The seven that remain may reasonably be regarded as short stories. Of these seven stories, we have chosen to discuss three: **"Fern," "Theater,"** and **"Bona and Paul."** They will serve to illustrate the tendency of Toomer's art to move beyond mere surfaces to a realm of transcendent reality.

"Fern," which first appeared in the *Little Review* of Autumn 1922, has been as widely anthologized as it has been misconstrued. Restricting their vision to the psychological plane, critics have variously regarded Fern as a victim of sexual repression, a promiscuous, castrating female, and an emblem of the mystery of Negro womanhood. The bafflement of the young narrator, in short, has been shared by most commentators, who have failed to perceive that the story functions primarily on a philosophical or religious plane. The heroine's sexual passivity is evoked merely to accentuate her otherworldly qualities. The story's theme, which may be traced to Vachel Lindsay's poem, "The Congo," is the spirituality of the Negro race.

Fern spiritualizes everything and everyone with whom she comes in contact. The story opens with the sentence: ''Face flowed into her eyes.'' The eyes, in Toomer, are windows to the soul, and in Fern's countenance they dominate, and even obliterate, the surrounding flesh. They seem to focus on some vague spot above the horizon, seeking always to transcend, or rise above, the Georgia landscape. The movement of the imagery is upward, and it defines Fern's relation to the world. Her domain is the unseen and intangible: the noumenal world that exists beyond the senses. The men that she encounters, including the narrator, are uplifted and ennobled by the contact, and struggle subsequently to transcend their selfishness.

Fern's spiritual force is redoubled by virtue of her mixed ancestry. The daughter of a Jewish father and a Negro mother, she is the inheritor of two sets of sorrow songs. At his first sight of her, the narrator recalls, ''I felt as if I heard a Jewish cantor sing. As if his singing rose above the unheard chorus of a folk-song.'' Fernie May Rosen possesses the Jewish genius for suffering. She takes upon herself the agony of others, including the sexual torment of her lovers. She is the eternal scapegoat who must suffer in order that others (specifically the narrator) may be born. That is why, in the minds of the townspeople, she remains a virgin, and why she is associated, in Toomer's iconography, with the Virgin Mary.

Fern embodies not only the Negro of the folksongs, but also of the revival meeting and the emotional church. That is the point of the climactic episode in which the narrator—half curious concerning Fern, and half in love with her—escorts her through a canebrake. Vaguely conscious of her spiritual power, but acting from force of habit, he takes her in his arms. She responds by running off, sinking to her knees, swaying back and forth, and uttering convulsive sounds, ''mingled with calls to Christ Jesus.'' She thus performs a priestly, if not a sexual office. Her body, although he doesn't recognize the gift, has been offered as the instrument of his salvation.

Fern is a symbol, in short, of the Negro folk-spirit. As such, she is the repository of a doomed spirituality. The quality of soul that she embodies, and whose cultural expression is folksong and revivalist religion, is about to disappear. It will not survive the Great Migration: ''Besides, picture if you can, this cream-colored solitary girl sitting at a tenement window and looking down on the indifferent throngs of Harlem.'' Fern could not exist apart from her pastoral milieu, and yet this rural folk-culture is fading into memory. The elegiac note is unmistakable. It is in the Georgia dusk that Fern weaves her most potent spell. Images of evening suffuse the story, producing that peculiar blend of sadness and tranquillity which is the hallmark of pastoral elegy.

"Theater" was inspired by a two-week stint that Toomer served as assistant manager of the Howard Theater in Washington, D.C. It was long enough to absorb the atmosphere of a Negro vaudeville house and to fashion out of this milieu a complex symbol. In the opening paragraph, the walls of the theater are described as a kind of semipermeable membrane through which a complicated process of osmosis takes place. The ''nigger life'' of alleys, poolrooms, restaurants, and cabarets nourishes the shows that are presented within these walls, and conversely, the shows exert a shaping influence on the life-style that gave them birth. The theater thus emerges as an emblem of the two-way, reciprocal relationship of life and art.

The walls of the theater press in upon the human world until they become symbolic of the prison of the flesh, from which imagination alone can offer an escape. In the translucent glow of the lighted theater, human flesh seems to dissolve: ''Stage lights, soft, as if they shine through clear pink fingers.'' The theater is a place of shadowy forms, of artificial contrivances, of elaborate mirrorings of life. Throughout the story, Toomer never lets us forget the paraphernalia of illusion: the scenery and costumes and lighting effects that function to transform reality. His theme is precisely the relationship between the image and the life it represents, or, in Ralph Ellison's illuminating phrase, between the shadow and the act.

Toomer's theater is a place where magical transformations occur. The throbbing life of Washington's black belt is translated by the black musicians into jazz forms. The raw sexuality of brown and beige chorus girls is converted before our very eyes into dance forms. Dorris, the most talented among them, is transfigured into a woman of surpassing loveliness by the writer-hero's dream. The instrument of all these metamorphoses is the human imagination, symbolized by the shaft of light that streaks down from a window to illuminate the afternoon rehearsal.

On this symbolic stage the plot unfolds. John, the manager's brother, and a writer, watches Dorris dance. He entertains erotic fantasies, but finally dismisses them, not because of the obvious barrier of background and education, but rather on complicated philosophic grounds. While he is dedicated, in a priestly vein, to contemplation of the noumenal, she represents precisely the attractions of the phenomenal world. Putting it another way, John is torn between the higher and lower functions of his being. Dorris, on her part, does her best to win him through the only art at her command: the dance. Failing to ignite his passion, she mistakenly concludes that he has rejected her on the grounds of social class.

Momentarily the philosophic gulf between them is bridged in the imagery of John's dream. This climactic episode, where daydream shades off into fiction, is emblematic of the transforming power of imagination. In it the raw materials of John's experience are transfigured by the writer's art. Dorris becomes a woman of surpassing beauty; their imagined union, disembodied and ideal: ''But his feet feel as though they step on autumn leaves whose rustle has been pressed out of them by the passing of a million satin slippers.'' In this image of nature *dematerialized* by art, Toomer reveals the heart of his esthetic. John's dream is a vision of the union of flesh and spirit, of the phenomenal and noumenal worlds.

Art-as-transfiguration is Toomer's theme. He is concerned in **"Theater"** with the death of experience and its rebirth as art. Thus John's renunciation of a love affair with Dorris, and his distillation of their encounter into poetry. John is to Dorris as an artist to his material: she represents *untransformed* experience. But the artist, by definition, is a man who cannot tolerate the untransformed world. Through his imagination, he must remove the rustle from the autumn leaves. Paradoxically, the artist must renounce the phenomenal world, even as he celebrates it. The result is a tragic alienation, whose subjective mood is melancholy.

"Bona and Paul" derives from Toomer's undergraduate experience at the American College of Physical Training in Chicago. (pp. 222-26)

The kernel of the story is contained in the opening tableau. On the floor of a gymnasium, students are engaged in precision drilling. Paul, out of step with the rest, is dressed in nonregulation blue trousers. It is precisely this nonconformity that Bona finds appealing. The precision drilling is symbolic of a regimented society that not only marches, but thinks in rigid line formation. Paul's white companions, as the story unfolds, are alternately fascinated and repelled by his ambiguous exoticism. Tormented by uncertainty, and desirous of reassuring absolutes, they press him to declare his race. They remain, in short, *unawakened* to the possibilities of life, to the individual reality that lies beyond the social category.

The theme of the story is epistemological. Verbs of cognition predominate, as Paul and Bona grope across the color line for a deeper knowledge of each other. Toomer's central metaphor, which compares the lovers to opaque windows, is drawn from St. Paul's first epistle to the Corinthians: "For now we see through a glass darkly; but then face to face: now I know in part; but then shall I know even as I am known." The color line, symbolized by the South-Side L track that divides the city, constitutes an artificial barrier to human understanding. Based on *a priori* rather than *a posteriori* knowledge, it serves to blind rather than illuminate.

The story moves to a climax in the episode of the Crimson Gardens. As he enters the nightclub with Bona, Paul feels inclined to cheer, for the Crimson Gardens represents a yea-saying, an affirmation of life. With its white patrons and Negro music, the club is a symbol of cultural amalgamation. It is also the Garden of Eden, where Paul loses Bona by eating of the Tree of Knowledge. As the young couple whirl around the floor, "The dance takes blood from their minds and packs it, tingling, in the torsos of their swaying bodies." Intoxicated with passion, they head for the exit, but their progress is interrupted by a leering Negro doorman. Paul steps back to assure the man that something beautiful is about to happen, but when he returns for his companion, Bona has disappeared.

The resolution of the story is conveyed entirely through the imagery. The style becomes intensely lyrical, as it attempts to shape the moment of epiphany: "I came back to tell you, brother, that white faces are petals of roses. That dark faces are petals of dusk. That I am going out and gather petals. That I am going out and know her whom I brought here with me to these Gardens which are purple like a bed of roses would be at dusk." Reality, in other words, is not categorical, but contingent. A flower that is red in daylight is purple in the dusk. And dusk is the point in time when day and night mingle and become one.

What Paul has mastered, in short, is a new epistemology, a new way of knowing. He has discovered the imagination as a mode of knowledge. He has learned that while thought divides (categorizes), imagination synthesizes. Through metaphor, the language of poetry, the imagination transcends categories and frees the human mind for a genuine encounter with reality. At the same time, Toomer's hero pays an awesome price for his new knowledge. Intent on philosophic clarity, he loses the girl. It is Toomer's characteristic gesture of renunciation: the eternal paradox of earthly values lost, even as transcendent aims are realized.

"Bona and Paul" is a model of artistic economy and symbolic compression. In its density of texture and profundity of theme, it is one of Toomer's richest stories. On the face of it, the story seems to undermine the central thrust of ***Cane.*** Once we take account of its strategic position at the end of Part II, however, this difficulty is resolved. The urbanization of the Negro, Toomer feels, will lead inexorably to his assimilation. In the process, America will be transformed. Like Toomer's hero, we will one day discover within ourselves the courage to transcend our racial categories. Then we will see not through a glass darkly, but face to face at last. (pp. 226-28)

Robert Bone, "Jean Toomer," in his Down Home: A History of Afro-American Short Fiction from Its Beginnings to the End of the Harlem Renaissance, *G. P. Putnam's Sons, 1975, pp. 204-38.*

ADDITIONAL BIBLIOGRAPHY

Bell, Bernard W. "Jean Toomer's 'Cane'." *Black World* 23, No. 11 (September 1974): 4-19, 92-7.
Commentary on the pastoral and religious elements in *Cane*.

Bontemps, Arna. "The Negro Renaissance: Jean Toomer and the Harlem Writers of the 1920s." In *Anger and Beyond: The Negro Writer in the United States,* edited by Herbert Hill, pp. 20-36. New York: Harper & Row, 1966.
Explores the influence of *Cane* on black American literature.

Chase, Patricia. "The Women in *Cane*." *College Language Association Journal* 14, No. 3 (March 1971): 259-73.
A study of the links among female characters in *Cane*.

Christ, Jack M. "Jean Toomer's 'Bona and Paul': The Innocence and Artifice of Words." *Negro American Literature Forum* 9, No. 2 (Summer 1975): 44-6.
Explores the function and significance of language in "Bona and Paul."

Duncan, Bowie. "Jean Toomer's *Cane:* A Modern Black Oracle." *College Language Association Journal* 15, No. 2 (March 1972): 323-33.
A study of the "unity or organic quality" of *Cane*. The critic associates Toomer's use of word groups with Cubist art.

Durham, Frank. "The Poetry Society of South Carolina's Turbulent Year: Self-Interest, Atheism, and Jean Toomer." *Southern Humanities Review* 5, No. 1 (Winter 1971): 76-80.
An account of the crisis that ensued when the Poetry Society of South Carolina discovered in 1923 that one of its members, Jean Toomer, was black. The critic emphasizes that the incident "reflects both the parochial nature and outmoded racial attitudes of a good many of the literary groups of the Southern Renascence."

Durham, Frank, ed. *Studies in "Cane."* Columbus, Ohio: Charles E. Merrill, 1971, 113 p.
Reprints, in whole or in part, significant reviews of *Cane* by such critics as Robert Bone, Arna Bontemps, Alain Locke, and Gorham Munson.

Fischer, William C. "The Aggregate Man in Jean Toomer's *Cane*." *Studies in the Novel* 3, No. 2 (Summer 1971): 190-215.
Explores *Cane* as a "representative Afro-American work" whose central theme is the black man's loss of identity through assimilation into American culture.

Fullinwider, S. P. "Jean Toomer: Lost Generation, or Negro Renaissance?" *Phylon* 27, No. 4 (Winter 1966): 396-403.
First study based largely upon Toomer's unpublished papers at Fisk University. The critic outlines Toomer's intellectual development from his school years through his later years of searching for social and political values.

Goede, William J. "Jean Toomer's Ralph Kabnis: Portrait of the Negro Artist as a Young Man." *Phylon* 30, No. 1 (Spring 1969): 73-85.
A brief examination of the themes and techniques in *Cane,* focusing on the story "Kabnis." In response to S. P. Fullinwider (see Additional Bibliography), the critic asserts Toomer's concern with the role of art in the black experience.

Grant, Mary Kathryn. "Images of Celebration in *Cane*." *Negro American Literature Forum* 5, No. 1 (Spring 1971): 32-4, 36.
A discussion of the themes of celebration evident in *Cane*.

Helbling, Mark. "Sherwood Anderson and Jean Toomer." *Negro American Literature Forum* 9, No. 2 (Summer 1975): 35-9.
An account of Toomer's friendship with Sherwood Anderson based largely upon the study of Toomer's unpublished papers, including correspondence between the two writers.

Huggins, Nathan Irvin. "Art: The Black Identity." In his *Harlem Renaissance,* pp. 137-89. New York: Oxford University Press, 1971.
Contains a brief discussion of Toomer in the context of such contemporaries as Claude McKay and Countee Cullen. The critic focuses on Toomer's "conscious exploration of Negro identity" in *Cane*, particularly as expressed in slavery and the history of the South.

Hughes, Langston. "Gurdjieff in Harlem." In his *The Big Sea,* pp. 241-43. New York: Alfred A. Knopf, 1945.
A brief insight by this prominent poet and literary figure into the nature of Toomer's experience spreading the teachings of Gurdjieff in New York City.

Innes, Catherine L. "The Unity of Jean Toomer's *Cane*." *College Language Association Journal* 15, No. 2 (March 1972): 306-22.
An examination of the imagery in *Cane* in which the critic finds the influence of P. D. Ospensky's *Tertium Organum,* a work that expresses the "logic of intuition."

Jackson, Blyden. "Jean Toomer's *Cane:* An Issue of Genre." In his *The Waiting Years,* pp. 189-202. Baton Rouge: Louisiana State University Press, 1976.
An essay concerning the genre of *Cane*.

Jung, Udo O. H. "Jean Toomer: 'Fern' (1922)." In *The Black American Short Story in the Twentieth Century: A Collection of Critical Essays,* edited by Peter Bruck, pp. 53-69. Amsterdam: B. R. Grüner Publishing Co., 1977.
A close textual analysis of "Fern."

Kerman, Cynthia Earl, and Eldridge, Richard. *The Lives of Jean Toomer: A Hunger for Wholeness.* Baton Rouge: Louisiana State University Press, 1987, 411 p.
Detailed biography emphasizing Toomer's quest for spiritual fulfillment.

Kopf, George. "The Tensions in Jean Toomer's 'Theater'." *College Language Association Journal* 17, No. 4 (June 1974): 498-503.
A brief analysis of "Theater," which the critic describes as the "product of its author's perception of tensions and countertensions in the reality of black experience in the United States."

Kraft, James. "Jean Toomer's *Cane*." *The Markham Review* 2, No. 4 (October 1970): 61-3.
An exploration of the symbolic dimensions of *Cane*.

Margolies, Edward. "The First Forty Years: 1900-1940." In his *Native Sons,* pp. 21-46. Philadelphia: J. B. Lippincott, 1968.
Contains a brief biographical-critical discussion of Toomer and *Cane*.

McKay, Nellie Y. *Jean Toomer, Artist: A Study of His Literary Life and Work, 1894-1936*. Chapel Hill: University of North Carolina Press, 1984, 262 p.
An analysis centered around *Cane* of the "growth, development, and decline of Jean Toomer as a literary artist." The book connects Toomer's writing and personal life in order to achieve insight into the unifying elements of his work.

McKeever, Benjamin F. "*Cane* as Blues." *Negro American Literature Forum* 4, No. 2 (July 1970): 61-3.
A mixture of quotations, comments, and allusions used to emphasize the influence of blues music on the style of *Cane*.

Parsons, Alice Beal. "Toomer and Frank." *The World Tomorrow* VII, No. 3 (March 1924): 96.
Describes the "disastrous effect" of Waldo Frank upon Toomer's writing and notes differences in their literary styles.

Redding, J. Saunders. "Emergence of the New Negro." In his *To Make a Poet Black,* pp. 93-125. 1939. Reprint. College Park, Md.: McGrath Publishing, 1968.
A brief overview of Toomer's contribution to black American literature to 1939. The critic considers *Cane* "significant because of the influence it had on the course of Negro fiction."

Reilly, John M. "The Search for Black Redemption: Jean Toomer's *Cane*." *Studies in the Novel* 2, No. 3 (Fall 1970): 312-24.
Places *Cane* in the line of Afro-American literary tradition derived from W.E.B. DuBois's *The Souls of Black Folk* and explores Toomer's thematic emphasis on the search for identity as a liberating force in an oppressive environment.

Scruggs, Charles W. "The Mark of Cain and the Redemption of Art: A Study in Theme and Structure of Jean Toomer's *Cane*." *American Literature* 44, No. 2 (May 1972): 276-91.
Discusses *Cane* in terms of biblical themes and imagery and describes the book's structure as "circular." The critic makes reference to Toomer's unpublished papers at Fisk University.

Scruggs, Charles [W.]. "Jean Toomer: Fugitive." *American Literature* 47, No. 1 (March 1975): 84-96.
A biographical-critical portrait that emphasizes the influence of French writer Romain Rolland's ten-volume novel *Jean-Christophe* on Toomer's personal values and artistic vision.

Stein, Marian L. "The Poet-Observer and 'Fern' in Jean Toomer's *Cane*." *The Markham Review* 2, No. 4 (October 1970): 64-5.
An analysis of Toomer's use of language in "Fern."

Thompson, Larry E. "Jean Toomer: As Modern Man." In *The Harlem Renaissance Remembered,* edited by Arna Bontemps, pp. 51-62. New York: Dodd, Mead, 1972.
An examination of Toomer's quest for identity in his life and work.

[Turner, Darwin T.]. "Obituary." *Negro American Literature Forum* 1, No. 1 (Fall 1967): 3-4.
Memorial tribute to Toomer.

Turpin, Waters E. "Four Short Fiction Writers of the Harlem Renaissance: Their Legacy of Achievement." *College Language Association Journal* 11, No. 1 (September 1967): 59-62.
Brief essay concerning "Blood-Burning Moon" in which the critic praises Toomer's style, effective characterizations, and evocation of the South.

Waldron, Edward E. "The Search for Identity in Jean Toomer's 'Esther'." *College Language Association Journal* 14, No. 3 (March 1971): 277-80.
Examines the thematic layers of the story "Esther."

Watkins, Patricia. "Is There a Unifying Theme in *Cane*?" *CLA Journal* XV, No. 3 (March 1972): 303-05.
Interprets *Cane* as a study in alienation.

Westerfield, Hargis. "Jean Toomer's 'Fern': A Mythical Dimension." *College Language Association Journal* 14, No. 3 (March 1971): 274-76.
Study of the Judeo-Christian allusions in the story "Fern."

Eudora Welty

1909-

American novelist, short story writer, and essayist.

Photograph © 1987 Jill Krementz

Welty is considered one of the most important contemporary authors of short fiction. Although the majority of her stories are set in the American South and reflect the region's language and culture, critics agree that Welty's treatment of universal themes and her wide-ranging artistic influences clearly transcend regional boundaries. Welty is frequently linked with modernist authors such as James Joyce and Virginia Woolf, and some of her works, including the stories in her *The Golden Apples,* are similar to theirs in the creation of a complex fictional world that is made comprehensible through a network of symbols and allusions, drawn primarily from classical mythology. The outstanding features of some of Welty's best-known work are her authentic replication of the Southern dialect, as in the story "Why I Live at the P.O.," and her skillful manipulation of realistic detail and elements of fantasy to create vivid character portrayals.

Born in Jackson, Mississippi at a time when that city had not yet lost its rural atmosphere, Welty grew up in the bucolic South she so often evokes in her stories. She attended the Mississippi State College for Women and the University of Wisconsin, where she majored in English Literature, then studied advertising at Columbia University; however, graduating at the height of the depression, she was unable to find work in her chosen field. Returning to Jackson in 1931, Welty worked as a part-time journalist and copywriter and as a WPA photographer. The latter job took her on assignments throughout Mississippi, and she began using these experiences as material for short stories. In June, 1936, her story "Death of a Traveling Salesman" was accepted for publication in the journal *Manuscript,* and within two years her work had appeared in such prestigious publications as the *Atlantic* and the *Southern Review.* Critical response to Welty's first collection of stories, *A Curtain of Green,* was highly favorable, with many commentators predicting that a first performance so impressive would no doubt lead to even greater achievements. Yet when *The Wide Net, and Other Stories* was published two years later, several critics, most notably Diana Trilling, deplored Welty's marked shift away from the colorful realism of her earlier stories toward a more impressionistic style, objecting in particular to her increased use of symbol and metaphor to convey themes. Other critics responded favorably, including Robert Penn Warren, who wrote that in Welty's work, "the items of fiction (scene, action, character, etc.) are presented not as document but as comment, not as a report but as a thing made, not as history but as idea."

As Welty continued to refine her vision her fictional techniques gained wider acceptance. Indeed, her most complex and highly symbolic collection of stories, *The Golden Apples,* won critical acclaim, and she received a number of prizes and awards throughout the following decade, including the William Dean Howells Medal of the Academy of Arts and Letters for her novella *The Ponder Heart.* Occupied primarily with teaching, traveling, and lecturing between 1955 and 1970, Welty produced little fiction. Then, in the early 1970s, she published two novels, *Losing Battles,* which received mixed reviews, and the more critically successful *The Optimist's Daughter,* which won a Pultizer Prize. Although Welty has published no new volumes of short stories since *The Bride of the Innisfallen* in 1955, the release of her *Collected Stories* in 1980 renewed interest in her short fiction and brought unanimous praise. In addition, the 1984 publication of Welty's *One Writer's Beginnings,* an autobiographical work chronicling her own artistic development, further illuminated her work and inspired critics to reinterpret many of her stories.

In his seminal 1944 essay on *The Wide Net, and Other Stories,* Robert Penn Warren located the essence of Welty's fictional technique in a phrase from her story "First Love": "Whatever happened, it happened in extraordinary times, in a season of dreams." It is, states Warren, "as though the author cannot be quite sure what did happen, cannot quite undertake to resolve the meaning of the recorded event, cannot, in fact, be too sure of recording all of the event." This tentative approach to narrative exposition points to Welty's primary goal in creating fiction, which is not simply to relate a series of events, but to convey a strong sense of her character's experience of that specific moment in time, always acknowledging the ambiguous nature of reality. In order to do so, she selects those details which can best vivify the narrative, frequently using metaphors and similes to communicate sensory impressions, while revealing only those events which enter her characters' experience. The resulting stories are highly impressionistic. Welty typically uses traditional symbols and mythical allusions in her work and, in the opinion of many, it is through linking the particular with the general and the mundane with the metaphysical that she attains her transcendent vision of human existence.

Welty's stories display a marked diversity in content, form, and mood. Many of her stories are light and humorous, while others deal with the tragic and the grotesque. Her humorous stories frequently rely upon the comic possibilities of language, as in both "Why I Live at the P.O." and *The Ponder Heart,* which exploit the humor in the speech patterns and colorful idiom of their southern narrators. In addition, Welty employs irony to comic effect, and many critics consider this aspect of her work one of its chief strengths. Opinions are divided, however, on the effectiveness of Welty's use of the grotesque. While Trilling and others find Welty's inclusion of such elements as the carnival exhibits in "Petrified Man" exploitative and superfluous, Eunice Glenn maintains that Welty created "scenes of horror" in order to "make everyday life appear as it often does, without the use of a magnifying glass, to the person with extraordinary acuteness of feeling."

Critics of Welty's work agree that these same literary techniques which produced her finest stories have also been the cause of her most outstanding failures, noting that she is at her best when objective observation and subjective revelation are kept in balance and that where the former is neglected, she is ineffective. They remark further, however, that such instances are comparatively rare in Welty's work. Many contemporary critics consider Welty's skillful use of language her single greatest achievement, citing in particular the poetic richness of her narratives and her acute sensitivity to the subtleties and peculiarities of human speech. Yet the majority of commentators concur with Glenn's assertion that "it is her profound search of human consciousness and her illumination of the underlying causes of the compulsions and fears of modern man that would seem to comprise the principal value of Miss Welty's work."

While critics do not concur on all aspects of Welty's fiction, the preeminence of her work remains unquestioned. Despite some early resistance to her style, Welty has garnered much critical and popular respect for both her humorous colloquial stories and her more experimental works. Although she is known chiefly as a southern writer, the transcendent humanity conveyed in her stories places her beyond regional classification, and she is widely regarded as one of the foremost fiction writers in America.

(See also *CLC,* Vols. 1, 2, 5, 14, 22, 33; *Contemporary Authors,* rev. ed., Vols. 9-11; Bibliographical Series, Vol. 1; *Dictionary of Literary Biography,* Vol. 2; and *Concise Dictionary of American Literary Biography,* Vol. 1.)

PRINCIPAL WORKS

SHORT FICTION

A Curtain of Green 1941
The Robber Bridegroom 1942
The Wide Net, and Other Stories 1943
The Golden Apples 1949
The Ponder Heart 1954
Selected Stories 1954
The Bride of the Innisfallen 1955
Thirteen Stories 1965
The Collected Stories of Eudora Welty 1980

OTHER MAJOR WORKS

Delta Wedding (novel) 1946
Losing Battles (novel) 1970
The Optimist's Daughter (novel) 1972
One Writer's Beginnings (autobiography) 1984

KATHERINE ANNE PORTER (essay date 1941)

[Porter was an American short story writer, novelist, and critic who is widely acknowledged as a major twentieth-century short fiction writer. The novellas Noon Wine *(1937) and* Pale Horse, Pale Rider *(1939) are generally regarded as her best work and are viewed as near-perfect examples of the genre. Porter met and befriended Welty in 1938 and provided an introduction for* A Curtain of Green, *Welty's first short story collection. In the following excerpt from that essay, which is acknowledged as a critical touchstone of Welty's work, Porter briefly assesses Welty's talents.]*

[The stories in ***A Curtain of Green***] offer an extraordinary range of mood, pace, tone, and variety of material. The scene is limited to a town the author knows well; the farthest reaches of that scene never go beyond the boundaries of her own state, and many of the characters are of the sort that caused a Bostonian to remark that he would not care to meet them socially. Lily Daw is a half-witted girl in the grip of social forces represented by a group of earnest ladies bent on doing the best thing for her, no matter what the consequences. Keela, the Outcast Indian Maid, is a crippled little Negro who represents a type of man considered most unfortunate by W. B. Yeats: one whose experience was more important than he, and completely beyond his powers of absorption. But the really unfortunate man in this story is the ignorant young white boy, who had innocently assisted at a wrong done the little Negro, and for a most complex reason, finds that no reparation is possible, or even desirable to the victim. . . . The heroine of **"Why I Live at the P.O."** is a terrifying case of dementia praecox. In this first group—for the stories may be loosely classified on three separate levels—the spirit is satire and the key grim comedy. Of these, **"The Petrified Man"** offers a fine clinical study of vulgarity—vulgarity absolute, chemically pure, exposed mercilessly to its final subhuman depths. Dullness, bitterness, rancor, self-pity, baseness of all kinds, can be most interesting material for a story provided these are not also the main elements in the mind of the author. There is nothing in the least vulgar or frustrated in Miss Welty's mind. She has simply an eye and an ear sharp, shrewd, and true as a tuning fork. She has given to this little story all her wit and observation, her blistering humor and her just cruelty; for she has none of that slack tolerance or sentimental tenderness toward symptomatic evils that amounts to criminal collusion between author and character. Her use of this material raises the quite awfully sordid little tale to a level above its natural habitat, and its realism seems almost to have the quality of caricature, as complete realism so often does. Yet, as painters of the grotesque make only detailed reports of actual living types observed more keenly than the average eye is capable of observing, so Miss Welty's little human monsters are not really caricatures at all, but individuals exactly and clearly presented: which is perhaps a case against realism, if we cared to go into it. She does better on another level—for the important reason that the themes are richer—in such beautiful stories as **"Death of a Traveling Salesman," "A Memory," "A Worn Path."** Let me admit a deeply personal preference for this particular kind of story, where external act and the internal voiceless life of the human imagination almost meet and mingle on the mysterious threshold between dream and waking, one reality refusing to admit or confirm the existence of the other, yet both conspiring toward the same end. This is not easy to accomplish, but it is always worth trying, and Miss Welty is so successful at it, it would seem her most familiar territory. There is no blurring at the edges, but evidences of an active and disciplined imagination working firmly in a strong line of continuity, the waking faculty of daylight reason recollecting and recording the crazy logic of the dream. There is in none of these stories any trace of autobiography in the prime sense, except as the author is omnipresent, and knows each character she writes about as only the artist knows the thing he has made, by first experiencing it in imagination. But perhaps in **"A Memory,"** one of the best stories, there might be something of early personal history in the story of the child on the beach, alienated from the world of adult knowledge by her state of childhood, who hoped to learn the secrets of life by looking at everything, squaring her hands before her eyes to bring the observed thing into a frame—the gesture of one born to select, to arrange, to bring apparently disparate elements into harmony within deliberately fixed boundaries. But the author is freed already in her youth from self-love, self-pity, self-preoccupation, that triple damnation of too many of the young and gifted, and has reached an admirable objectivity. In such stories as **"Old Mr. Marblehall," "Powerhouse," "The Hitch-Hikers,"** she combines an objective reporting with great perception of mental or emotional states, and in **"Clytie"** the very shape of madness takes place before your eyes in a straight account of actions and speech, the personal appearance and habits of dress of the main character and her family.

In all of these stories, varying as they do in excellence, I find nothing false or labored, no diffusion of interest, no wavering of mood—the approach is direct and simple in method, though the themes and moods are anything but simple, and there is even in the smallest story a sense of power in reserve which makes me believe firmly that, splendid beginning that this is, it is only the beginning. (pp. xix-xxiii)

Katherine Anne Porter, in an introduction to A Curtain of Green and Other Stories *by Eudora Welty, Harcourt Brace Jovanovich, 1941, pp. xi-xxiii.*

LOUISE BOGAN (essay date 1941)

[Bogan was a distinguished American poet who served for many years as the poetry critic at the New Yorker; *her* Achievement in American Poetry: 1900-1950 *(1951) is a respected volume of criticism. In the following discussion of style in* A Curtain of Green, *Bogan likens Welty to Nikolai Gogol in her use of humor and detail.]*

The definite Gothic quality which characterizes so much of the work of writers from the American South has puzzled critics. Is it the atmosphere of the *roman noir,* so skilfully transferred to America by Poe? Or is it a true and indigenous atmosphere of decaying feudalism? Faulkner treats the horrifying and ambiguous situations thrown up by a background which has much in common with nineteenth-century Russia in a style darkened and convoluted by, it would seem, the very character of his material. Eudora Welty, who is a native and resident of Mississippi, in the stories ***[A Curtain of Green]*** has instinctively chosen another method which opens and widens the field and makes it more amenable to detached observation. She proceeds with the utmost simplicity and observes with the most delicate terseness. She does not try mystically to transform or anonymously to interpret. The parallel forced upon us, particularly by those of Miss Welty's stories which are based on an oblique humor, is her likeness to Gogol.

The tramp musicians, the inhabitants of a big house (either mad, drunk, or senile), the idiots and ageless peasant women, the eccentric families tyrannized over by an arch-eccentric, the pathetic and ridiculous livers of double lives, even the Negro band leader with his sadism and delusion of grandeur—all these could come out of some broken-down medieval scene, and all could be treated completely successfully—with humorous detachment, combined with moments of tenderness and roaring farce—by the author of *The Inspector General* and *Dead Souls.* Like Gogol, Miss Welty opens the doors and describes the setting, almost inch by inch. She adds small detail to small detail: the fillings in people's teeth, the bright mail-order shirts of little boys, the bottles of Ne-Hi, the pictures of Nelson Eddy hung up like icons. We see what happens to representatives of an alien commercial world—here, traveling salesmen: how they become entangled against their will in this scene, which goes on under its own obscure decomposing laws; or dissolve back into it, symbolically enough, in delirium and death. Even the women in the beauty parlor have a basic place in the composition; they are not so much modernly vulgar as timelessly female—calculating, shrewd, and sharp. Miss Welty's method can get everything in; nothing need be scamped, because of romantic exigencies, or passed over, because of rules of taste. Temperamentally and by training she has become mistress of her material by her choice of one exactly suitable kind of treatment, and—a final test of a writer's power—as we read her, we are made to believe that she has hit upon the only possible kind. But it is a method, in Miss Welty's hands, only suitable for her Southern characters on their own ground. The one story dealing with the North, **"Flowers for Marjorie",** goes completely askew.

Louise Bogan, "The Gothic South," in The Nation, *New York, Vol. 153, No. 23, December 6, 1941, p. 572.*

DIANA TRILLING (essay date 1943)

[Trilling is a respected and influential American critic and author. Her writing often concerns what she considers the deterioration of American society and its effects upon the individual. Thus, in her critical assessments, Trilling often focuses on the social or political statements inherent in a work of literature, considering purely aesthetic factors insufficient justification for art. In the following excerpt from an essay originally published in The Nation *in 1943, Trilling objects to the apparent predominance of style and lack of content in* The Wide Net, and Other Stories. *For a response to Trilling's comments, see the excerpt by Robert Penn Warren dated 1944.]*

[In] ***The Wide Net*** Eudora Welty has developed her technical virtuosity to the point where it outweighs the uses to which it is put, and her vision of horror to the point of nightmare. Of course even in her earlier work Miss Welty had a strong tendency toward stylism and "fine" writing. She liked to move toward the mythical. She had a heart for decay and an eye for Gothic detail. But she also had a reliable and healthy wit, her dialogue could be as normally reportorial as Ring Lardner's, and for the most part she knew how to keep performance subservient to communication; she told her story instead of dancing it, and when she saw horror it could be the clear horror of day-to-day life, not only the horror of dreams. There was surrealist paraphernalia, if you will, in a story like **"The Petrified Man"**: the falling hair of the customer, the presence of the three-year-old boy amid the bobbie-pins and sexual confidences of the beauty parlor, the twins in a bottle at the freak show, even the petrified man himself. But compare to **"The Petrified Man"** the story **"Asphodel"** from Miss Welty's current volume, with its Doric columns and floating muslins, its pomegranate stains and blackberry cordial and its "old goats and young," and you will recognize the fancy road up which Miss Welty has turned her great talents.

The title story of Miss Welty's new volume is its best but not typical. An account of a river-dragging party which starts out to recover the body of a supposed suicide but forgets its mission in the joys of the occasion, **"The Wide Net"** has elements of a tour de force, but it has more communicated meaning than the rest of the stories in the book, and best fuses content and method. Of the six other stories **"Livvie"** is the only one which I like at all, and the only story, in addition to **"The Wide Net,"** which I feel I understood. Yet despite its obscurity the volume has tremendous emotional impact. But this seems to me to be beside the point. The fear that a story or a picture engenders is often in inverse proportion to its communicated content: witness the drawings of children or psychotics, or most of surrealist art. Miss Welty employs to good effect the whole manual of ghostliness: wind and storm, ruined buildings, cloaks, horses' hooves on a lonely highway, fire and moonlight and people who live and ride alone. But her evocation of the mood of horror or dream has become an end in itself, and if, for each story, there is a point of departure in narrative, so that I can report, for instance, that **"First Love"** is about a deaf-and-dumb boy who falls in love with Aaron Burr, or that **"Asphodel"** is about a tyrannical half-mad Southern gentlewoman, or that **"A Still Moment"** is a legend of Audubon, the stories themselves stay with their narrative no more than a dance stays with its argument. This, indeed, is the nature of **"The Wide Net":** it is a book of ballets. Even the title piece is a *pastorale macabre*.

And it is my belief that to make a ballet out of words is a misuse of their function. I dislike, because it breeds exhibitionism and insincerity, the attitude toward narrative which allows an author to sacrifice the meaning of language to its rhythms and patterns. The word "sincerity" has lost caste in the criticism of serious writing, which is unfortunate. We live in a crafty literary period in which what aims to be art but is only artful is regularly mistaken for the real thing. If, describing something which exists outside himself, an author says "Look at me" instead of "Look at it," there, in my opinion, is insincerity. The test of sincerity is wasted, however, in the sphere of popular art where criticism has sent it; most popular art is nothing if not sincere, and where it is not, it is usually because it is aping the manners of its betters. In these new stories Miss Welty's prose constantly calls attention to its author, away from her object. When she writes, ". . . Jenny sat there . . . in the posture of a child who is appalled at the stillness and unsurrender of the still and unsurrendering world," or "He walked alone, slowly through the silence, with the sturdy and yet dreamlike walk of the orphan," she is being falsely poetic, also untrue. How does the walk of an orphan differ in its sturdiness and in its dreamlike quality from the walk of a child with two parents? How would one explain "unsurrender" to a child, and wouldn't a child be appalled precisely by the *surrender* of the world, if the concept could reach him? This is the sin of pride, this self-conscious contriving, and it is endemic to a whole generation of writers since Katherine Mansfield, especially women writers.

Diana Trilling, in a review of "The Wide Net," in Reviewing the Forties, *Harcourt Brace Jovanovich, 1978, pp. 56-60.*

ROBERT PENN WARREN (essay date 1944)

[Warren is considered one of the most distinguished contemporary American authors. Acclaimed as a poet, novelist, and short story writer, he is also a respected critic who is closely associated with two major critical movements, the Agrarians and the New Critics. A native of Kentucky, Warren was strongly influenced by the South, often drawing inspiration from the land, the people, and the history of that region. In the following excerpt from an essay written in 1944, Warren refutes Diana Trilling's charges against The Wide Net, and Other Stories *(see excerpt dated 1943) by affirming the validity of Welty's literary techniques and defending her use of symbol and allegory to convey themes.]*

If we put ***The Wide Net,*** Eudora Welty's second collection of stories, up against her first collection, ***A Curtain of Green,*** we can immediately observe a difference: the stories of ***The Wide Net*** represent a specializing, an intensifying, of one of the many strains which were present in ***A Curtain of Green.*** All of the stories in ***A Curtain of Green*** bear the impress of Miss Welty's individual talent, but there is a great variety among them in subject matter and method and, more particularly, mood. It is almost as if the author had gone at each story as a fresh start in the business of writing fiction, as if she had had to take a new angle each time out of a joy in the pure novelty of the perspective. (p. 156)

Behind the innocent delight of the craftsman, and of the admirer of the world, there was also a seriousness, a philosophical cast of mind, which gave coherence to the book, but on the surface there was the variety, the succession of surprises. In ***The Wide Net*** we do not find the surprises. The stories are more nearly cut to one pattern.

We do not find the surprises. Instead, on the first page, with the first sentence of the first story, **"First Love,"** we enter a special world: "Whatever happened, it happened in extraordinary times, in a season of dreams . . .". And that is the world in which we are going to live until we reach the last sentence of the last story. "Whatever happened," the first sentence begins, as though the author cannot be quite sure what did happen, cannot quite undertake to resolve the meaning of the recorded event, cannot, in fact, be too sure of recording all of the event. This is coyness, of course; or a way of warning the reader that he cannot expect quite the ordinary direct light on the event. For it is "a season of dreams"—and the faces and gestures and events often have something of the grave retardation, the gnomic intensity, the portentous suggestiveness of dreams. The logic of things here is not quite the logic by which we live, or think we live, our ordinary daylight lives. In **"The Wide Net,"** for example, the young husband, who thinks his wife has jumped into the river, goes out with a party of friends to dredge for the body, but the sad occasion turns into a saturnalian fish-fry which is interrupted when the great King of the Snakes raises his hoary head from the surface of the river. But usually, in ***The Wide Net,*** the wrenching of logic is not in terms of events themselves, though **"The Purple Hat"** is a fantasy, and **"Asphodel"** moves in the direction of fantasy. Usually the events as events might be given a perfectly realistic treatment (Dreiser could take the events of **"The Landing"** for a story). But in these cases where the events and their ordering are "natural" and not supernatural or fantastic, the stories themselves finally belong to the "season of dreams" because of the special tone and mood, the special perspective, the special sensibility with which they are rendered.

Some readers, in fact, who are quite aware of Miss Welty's gifts, have recently reported that they are disturbed by the recent development of her work. Diana Trilling, in her valuable and sobering comments on current fiction [see excerpt dated 1943] . . . , says that the author "has developed her technical virtuosity to the point where it outweighs the uses to which it is put, and her vision of horror to the point of nightmare." There are two ideas in this indictment, and let us take the first one first and come to the second much later. The indictment of the technique is developed along these lines: Miss Welty has made her style too fancy—decorative, "falsely poetic" and "untrue," "insincere." ("When an author says 'look at me' instead of 'look at it,' there is insincerity. . . .") This insincerity springs from "the extreme infusion of subjectivism and private sensibility." But the subjectivism, Mrs. Trilling goes on to say, leads not only to insincerity and fine writing but to a betrayal of the story's obligation to narrative and rationality. Miss Welty's stories take off from a situation, but "the stories themselves stay with their narrative no more than a dance, say, stays with its argument." That is the summary of the indictment.

The indictment is, no doubt, well worth the close attention of Miss Welty's admirers. There is, in fact, a good deal of the falsely poetic in Miss Welty's present style, metaphors that simply pretend to an underlying logic, and metaphors (and descriptions) that, though good themselves, are irrelevant to the business in hand. And sometimes Miss Welty's refusal to play up the objective action—her attempt to define and refine the response rather than to present the stimulus—does result in a blurred effect. But the indictment treats primarily not of such failures to fulfill the object the artist has set herself but of the nature of that object. The critic denies, in effect, that Miss Welty's present kind of fiction is fiction at all: "It is a book of ballets, not of stories."

Now is it possible that the critic is arguing from some abstract definition of "story," some formalistic conception which does not accommodate the present exhibit, and is not concerning herself with the question of whether or not the present exhibit is doing the special job which it proposes for itself, and, finally, the job which we demand of all literature? Perhaps we should look at a new work first in terms of its effect and not in terms of a definition of type, because every new work is in some degree, however modest, wrenching our definition, straining its seams, driving us back from the formalistic definition to the principles on which the definition was based. Can we say this, therefore, of our expectation concerning a piece of literature, new or old: That it should intensify our awareness of the world (and of ourselves in relation to the world) in terms of an idea, a "view." This leads us to what is perhaps the key statement by Diana Trilling concerning ***The Wide Net:*** she grants that the volume "has tremendous emotional impact, despite its obscurity." In other words, she says, unless I misinterpret her, that the book does intensify the reader's awareness—but *not* in terms of a presiding idea.

This has led me to reread Miss Welty's two volumes of stories in the attempt to discover the issues which are involved in the "season of dreams." To begin with, almost all of the stories deal with people who, in one way or another, are cut off, alienated, isolated from the world. There is the girl in **"Why I Live at the P.O."**—isolated from her family by her arrogance, meanness, and sense of persecution; the half-witted Lily Daw, who, despite the efforts of "good" ladies, wants to live like other people; the deaf-mutes of **"The Key,"** and the deaf-mute of **"First Love"**; the people of **"The Whistle"** and **"A Piece of News,"** who are physically isolated from the world and who make their pathetic efforts to re-establish something lost. . . . In some of the cases, the matter is more indirectly presented. For instance, in **"Keela, the Outcast Indian Maiden,"** we find, as in *The Ancient Mariner,* the story of a man who, having committed a crime, must try to re-establish his connection with humanity; or in the title story of ***The Wide Net,*** William Wallace, because he thinks his wife has drowned herself, is at the start of the story cut off from the world of natural joy in which he had lived.

We can observe that the nature of the isolation may be different from case to case, but the fact of isolation, whatever its nature, provides the basic situation of Miss Welty's fiction. The drama which develops from this basic situation is of either of two kinds: first, the attempt of the isolated person to escape into the world; or second, the discovery by the isolated person, or by the reader, of the nature of the predicament.

As an example of the first type, we can remember Clytie's obsessed inspection of faces [in **"Clytie"**] ("Was it possible to comprehend the eyes and the mouth of other people, which concealed she knew not what, and secretly asked for still another unknown thing?") and her attempt to escape, and to solve the mystery, when she lays her finger on the face of the terrified barber who has come to the ruinous old house to shave her father. Or there is Jennie, of **"At the Landing,"** or Livvie, or the man of **"Keela, the Outcast Indian Maiden."** As an example of the second type, there is the new awareness on the part of the salesman in **"The Hitch-Hikers,"** or the new awareness on the part of the other salesman in the back-country cabin.

Even in **"A Still Moment"** we have this pattern, though in triplicate. The evangelist Lorenzo, the outlaw Murrell, and the naturalist and artist Audubon stand for a still moment and watch a white heron feeding. Lorenzo sees a beauty greater than he can account for (he had earlier "accounted for" the beauty by thinking, "Praise God, His love has come visible"), and with the sweat of rapture pouring down from his forehead, shouts into the marshes, "Tempter!" He has not been able to escape from his own obsession, or in other words, to make his definition of the world accommodate the white heron and the "natural" rapture which takes him. Murrell, looking at the bird, sees "only whiteness ensconced in darkness," and thinks that "if it would look at him a dream penetration would fill and gratify his heart"—the heart which Audubon has already defined as belonging to the flinty darkness of a cave. Neither Lorenzo nor Murrell can "love" the bird, and so escape from their own curse as did, again, the Ancient Mariner. But there remains the case of Audubon himself, who does "love" the bird, who can innocently accept nature. There is, however, an irony here. To paint the bird he must "know" the bird as well as "love" it, he must know it feather by feather, he must have it in his hand. And so he must kill it. But having killed the bird, he knows that the best he can make of it now in a painting would be a dead thing, "never the essence, only a sum of parts,'' and that ''it would always meet with a stranger's sight, and never be one with beauty in any other man's head in the world.'' Here, too, the fact of the isolation is realized: as artist and lover of nature he had aspired to a communication, a communion, with other men in terms of the bird, but now ''he saw his long labor most revealingly at the point where it met its limit'' and he is forced back upon himself.

''A Still Moment,'' however, may lead us beyond the discussion of the characteristic situation, drama, and realization in Miss Welty's stories. It may lead us to a theme which seems to underlie the stories. For convenience, though at the risk of incompleteness, or even distortion, we may call it Innocence and Experience. Let us take Audubon in relation to the heron. He loves the bird, innocently, in its fullness of being. But he must subject this love to knowledge; he must kill the bird if he is to commemorate its beauty, if he is to establish his communion with other men in terms of the bird's beauty. There is in the situation an irony of limit and contamination.

Let us look at this theme in relation to other stories. **''A Memory,''** in ***A Curtain of Green,*** gives a simple example. Here we have a young girl lying on a beach and looking out at the scene through a frame made by her fingers, for the girl can say of herself, ''To watch everything about me I regarded grimly and possessively as a need.'' (As does Audubon, in **''A Still Moment.''**) And further: ''It did not matter to me what I looked at; from any observation I would conclude that a secret of life had been nearly revealed to me. . . .'' Now the girl is cherishing a secret love, a love for a boy at school about whom she knows nothing, to whom she has never even spoken, but whose wrist her hand had once accidentally brushed. The secret love had made her watching of the world more austere, had sharpened her demand that the world conform to her own ideas, and had created a sense of fear. This fear had seemed to be realized one day when, in the middle of a class, the boy had a fit of nosebleed. But that is in the past. This morning she suddenly sees between the frame of her fingers a group of coarse, fat, stupid, and brutal people disporting themselves on the sand with a maniacal, aimless vigor which comes to climax when the fat woman, into the front of whose bathing suit the man had poured sand, bends over and pulls down the cloth so that the lumps of mashed and folded sand empty out. ''I felt a peak of horror, as though her breasts themselves had turned to sand, as though they were of no importance at all and she did not care.'' Over against this defilement (a defilement which implies that the body, the breasts which turn to sand, has no meaning), there is the refuge of the dream, ''the undefined austerity of my love.''

''A Memory'' presents the moment of the discovery of the two poles—the dream and the world; the idea and nature; innocence and experience; individuality and the anonymous, devouring life-flux; meaning and force; love and knowledge. It presents the contrast in terms of horror (as do **''Petrified Man''** and **''Why I Live at the P.O.''** when taken in the context of Miss Welty's work) and with the issue left in suspension, but other stories present it with different emphases and tonalities. (pp. 157-63)

If this general line of interpretation is correct, we find that the stories represent variations on the same basic theme, on the contrasts already enumerated. It is not that there is a standard resolution for the contrasts which is repeated from story to story; rather, the contrasts, being basic, are not susceptible of a single standard resolution, and there is an implicit irony in Miss Welty's work. But if we once realize this, we can recognize that the contrasts are understood not in mechanical but in vital terms: the contrasts provide the terms of human effort, for the dream must be carried to, submitted to, the world, innocence to experience, love to knowledge, knowledge to fact, individuality to communion. What resolution is possible is, if I read the stories with understanding, in terms of the vital effort. The effort is a ''mystery,'' because it is in terms of the effort, doomed to failure but essential, that the human manifests itself as human. Again and again, in different forms, we find what we find in Joel of **''First Love'':** ''Joel would never know now the true course, or the true outcome of any dream: this was all he felt. But he walked on, in the frozen path into the wilderness, on and on. He did not see how he could ever go back and still be the boot-boy at the Inn.''

It is possible that, in trying to define the basic issue and theme of Miss Welty's stories, I have made them appear too systematic, too mechanical. I do not mean to imply that her stories should be read as allegories, with a neat point-to-point equating of image and idea. It is true that a few of her stories, such as **''The Wide Net,''** do approach the limit of allegory, but even in such cases we find rather than the system of allegory a tissue of symbols which emerge from, and disappear into, a world of scene and action which, once we discount the author's special perspective, is recognizable in realistic terms. The method is similar to the method of much modern poetry, and to that of much modern fiction and drama, but at the same time it is a method as old as fable, myth, and parable. It is a method by which the items of fiction (scene, action, character, etc.) are presented not as document but as comment, not as a report but as a thing made, not as history but as idea. Even in the most realistic and reportorial fiction, the social picture, the psychological analysis, and the pattern of action do not rest at the level of mere report; they finally operate as expressive symbols as well.

Fiction may be said to have two poles, history and idea, and the emphasis may be shifted very far in either direction. In the present collection the emphasis has been shifted very far in the direction of idea, but at the same time there remains a sense of the vividness of the actual world: the picnic of **''The Wide Net''** is a real picnic as well as a ''journey,'' Cash of **''Livvie''** is a real field hand in his Easter clothes as well as a field god. In fact, it may be said that when the vividness of the actual world is best maintained, when we get the sense of one picture superimposed upon another, different and yet somehow the same, the stories are most successful.

The stories which fail are stories like **''The Purple Hat''** and **''Asphodel,''** in which the material seems to be manipulated in terms of an idea, in which the relation between the image and the vision has become mechanical, in which there is a strain, in which we do find the kind of hocus-pocus deplored by Diana Trilling.

And this brings us back to the criticism that the volume ''has tremendous emotional impact, despite its obscurity,'' that the ''fear'' it engenders is ''in inverse ratio to its rational content.'' Now it seems to me that this description does violence to my own experience of literature, that we do not get any considerable emotional impact unless we sense, at the same time, some principle of organization, some view, some meaning. This does not go to say that we have to give an abstract formulation to that principle or view or meaning before we can experience the impact of the work, but it does go to say that it is implicit in the work and is having its effect upon us in immediate aesthetic terms. Furthermore, in regard to the particular work in question, I do not feel that it is obscure. If anything, the dreamlike effect in many of the stories seems to result from the author's undertaking to squeeze meaning from the item which, in ordinary realistic fiction, would be passed over with a casual glance. Hence the portentousness, the retardation, the otherworldliness. For Miss Welty is like the girl in **"A Memory"**:

> . . . from any observation I would conclude that a secret of life had been nearly revealed to me, and from the smallest gesture of a stranger I would wrest what was to me a communication or a presentiment.

In many cases, as a matter of fact, Miss Welty has heavily editorialized her fiction. She wants us to get that smallest gesture, to participate in her vision of things as intensely meaningful. And so there is almost always a gloss to the fable.

One more word: It is quite possible that Miss Welty has pushed her method to its most extreme limit. It is also possible that the method, if pursued much farther, would lead to monotony and self-imitation and merely decorative elaboration. Perhaps we shall get a fuller drama when her vision is submitted more daringly to fact, when the definition is plunged into the devouring river. But meanwhile Miss Welty has given us stories of brilliance and intensity; and as for the future, Miss Welty is a writer of great resourcefulness, sensitivity, and intelligence, and can probably fend for herself. (pp. 166-69)

Robert Penn Warren, "Love and Separateness in Eudora Welty," in his Selected Essays, *Random House, 1958, pp. 156-69.*

EUNICE GLENN (essay date 1947)

[In the following excerpt from a highly regarded essay, Glenn discusses the mingling of fantasy and reality in A Curtain of Green, The Wide Net, and Other Stories, *and* The Robber Bridegroom, *comparing Welty's technique with that of such authors as Nathaniel Hawthorne, Edgar Allan Poe, and Franz Kafka. This essay originally appeared in the collection* A Southern Vanguard *(1947).]*

Somewhere between the prose fiction regarded as "realism" and that, on the other hand, which purports to deal only with the inner life of the mind, is the fiction of Eudora Welty; in its method implicating both tendencies and yet, somehow, transcending each. The kind of reality which is not immediately apparent to the senses is described by the late Virginia Woolf as "what remains over when the skin of the day has been cast into the hedge." Miss Welty takes full account of the "skin of the day," even withholding it from the hedge; it is a vital element in her work, for she is not afraid to face and report the harsh, even the brutal reality of everyday life. But at the same time she is fully sensitive to "what remains over." The kernel, with all its richness and germinative power, is there, well preserved; but it is covered by the husk, coarse and substantial.

It is in the inter-relationship of the external and the internal—reality and the imagination—that the particular significance of Miss Welty's method would seem to be. Logic is her background, the logic in the relationship of ideas. The dream, reflecting the irrational world in which we live, goes out to meet it. Sometimes near the beginning of a story, sometimes at intervals throughout it, and again perhaps only at the end, these two worlds become fused; and usually a reconciliation is produced, for both are concurring toward the same end. Instead of serving as an escape from ordinary experience, fantasy brings it into a fuller light and contributes to its interpretation. It is as though the author brought actual events up under a microscopic lens and threw the force of an illuminating mirror upon them. What she shows us could not be seen with the naked human eye; therefore, it appears as improbable. Reality, thus magnified, becomes fantasy.

A microscopic vision such as this, naturally, involves careful focusing; and within the limits of the short story, which is Miss Welty's chief medium, it is understandable that much exclusion is necessary. Her characters, representing ideas as they do, cannot be fully realized as individuals *per se*. She leaves that to the novelist, whose scope is larger, and to the writer of short stories who is concerned primarily with the portrayal of character. She is not interested, in her short pieces, in telling us everything about a character; instead, she selects only such material as will suit her needs. Deliberately fixing her boundaries, like those of a picture frame, she arranges the elements within a particular area of experience that will fit into the frame and produce a harmonious result.

In her concern with theme, however, Miss Welty does not succumb to a mere manipulation of her characters, like puppets, for the representation of ideas. Her people are real individuals, even when they may seem to be only caricatures. They are never oversimplified, though, from the standpoint of art, they may exist in the smallest sphere. This remarkable achievement is undoubtedly due to the author's power of discrimination; her keen psychological insight—her understanding of the subtleties of human behavior.

Miss Welty is very much interested in abnormal behavior and treats it with deep discernment. But her mentally deficient and particularly her mentally ill individuals consistently show traits that are commonly regarded as normal. Thus they symbolize insane persons living in an insane modern world. Out of their crazed brains, however, there always emerges some rationality, some sanity: the backfire of the inner life against prevailing disorder. Many other types of "unfortunates," as well, in Miss Welty's stories exemplify this tendency to assume individual dignity, from an inner direction. There are members of racial minorities, the economically oppressed, shut-ins, and various individuals in the grip of social forces. Little Lee Roy, a Negro man in the story, **"Keela, the Outcast Indian Maiden,"** does not wish or need the reparation offered him for a terrible wrong. Partly because of their utter lack of comprehension of the intricate reason for this, those who have done him the wrong are the ones who suffer; they are their own victims. In the beautiful story, **"A Worn Path,"** the nurse at the clinic becomes aware of a barrier, the nature of which she is unable to explain, between herself and Grandma, an old Negro woman. Similarly, **"A Visit of Charity"** reveals a Campfire Girl's helplessness on the occasion of a dutiful visit to an Old Ladies' Home. Then there is the half-witted girl, in **"Lily Daw and the Three Ladies,"** who is superior to misdirected efforts to help her. The well-meaning but patronizing ladies are pathetically unable to cross the imponderable distance between themselves and the girl; to grasp her real needs.

In all of these and in many other stories of Miss Welty the conventional pattern is rearranged and the people appear in new positions. Those who are seemingly defenseless become superior; while those who are tangibly superior become the really unfortunate, because of a more important deficiency within themselves. They are inevitably turned back upon their feelings of guilt.

Thus, Miss Welty shows us the individual pitted against modern society—a diseased society, which finds its reflection in distorted minds and lives. But the individual's conscious, or perhaps more often unconscious reaction to a mad world is one of defiance. At the most unexpected moments those who would seem to be in total despair manage somehow to rise out of it. The pathos of the heroine in **"Why I Live at the P.O.,"** who is a victim of painful self-consciousness and the will to be imposed upon, is balanced by something in her that exults; she strikes back. So does Little Lee Roy, and Lily Daw, and Grandma; the frustrated old maid in **"Clytie,"** who walks upon the street looking at faces and for beauty, and finds it in the face of a child; and the heroine in the story, **"Livvie,"** who has her own way of ascendancy.

The neuroses that result from the individual's inability to reconcile himself with society are thoroughly realized in Miss Welty's characters. She writes of those whose lives are circumscribed by corruption, many forms of it—triviality, malignity, vulgarity, snobbery, self-pity, bitterness, power mania, and human cruelty that cuts deep. But her superior technique relieves her work from many of the faults common to fiction which attempts to deal with bare reality. She escapes the mere spreading of grossness and evil before your eyes, and asking you to weep, or approve, or to conclude that human nature is hopeless. Nor is there in her work the slightest hint of collusion with characters who exemplify symptomatic wrongs; an impression which is so often obtained from realistic fiction, in spite of the intentions of the author. Miss Welty is, indeed, far removed from any trace of such slackness or negativism; or tender indulgence, so easily resolving into soft sentimentality. Her tolerance is one that is more magnanimous, superseding that which is remiss. For it is apparent that Miss Welty believes that there is such a thing as individual responsibility; and also that conscious volition is a quality to be taken into account, if not the core of human existence—a sane human existence.

Miss Welty's knowledge and attitudes can only be realized, however, in terms of her art. Her transcendence of bold sensationalism and of slackness, on the one hand, and hardness and restricted moral teaching, on the other, is inherent in the structure of her stories. Tone is controlled with sureness and delicacy. Her diverse shadings in tone, the shifts, the blending of two or more tones together, and the complexity—all do wonders with the material. It would be simplifying the matter to say only that she has a qualifying irony; but that lies over it all: toughness continuously controls, where otherwise pathos would get out of hand, and bring ruin. Her blade of satire cuts through human evil with unfailing sharpness; and she adds her scalding humor; as well as an enviable compound of compassion and just condemnation. The result is a totality, that refuses to be restricted to any one conventional attitude.

Miss Welty often employs the grotesque for evoking a sense of the horror of evil. Intensified, magnified into unreasonable proportions, the baseness of the everyday world confronts the reader, whose first impulse is to revolt: at the humiliation of Little Lee Roy when he is forced to eat live chickens and drink their blood, for the amusement of spectators; at the highly symbolical jeweled hat pin as it enters the ribs and pierces the heart of its victim, in **"The Purple Hat"**; at the spectacle of the old maid drowning herself in a barrel of rain water, her feet sticking up ludicrously, in **"Clytie"**; at the morbid river-dragging party in **"The Wide Net"**; and at the stone man, pygmies and twins in a bottle, of the traveling freak show, in **"Petrified Man."** Unlike Poe, Miss Welty is far removed from conjuring scenes of horror for its own sake. She uses it for a specific purpose: to make everyday life appear as it often does, without the use of a magnifying glass, to the person with extraordinary acuteness of feeling. Her fantastical characters become actual persons; her incongruous events those that are taking place every day. As in Thomas Mann's novel of the grotesque, *The Transposed Heads,* gruesomeness sharpens the sense of social and individual distortion.

Symbols achieve much of the meaning in such stories. In **"Petrified Man"** the little stone man symbolizes the pettiness, hypocrisy, all the shallowness in the lives of the beauty parlor women in the story. Formidable and hard, the stone is their obdurateness, their death-in-life. The jeweled hat pin is the flashing, steely substance that represents lurking, criminal passions. Symbols like these are strongly reminiscent of some of those used by Nathaniel Hawthorne: in "Ethan Brand," for example, where the leaping flames of the lime-kiln, the fiend-like facial expression, the fearful peals of laughter, and the snow white skeleton crumbling into fragments, characterize Ethan's "Unpardonable Sin."

The story, **"Old Mr. Marblehall,"** is one of the best examples of Miss Welty's unique device in interweaving fantasy and surface reality. Each world, the real and the imagined, impinges upon the other, without obtruding in the actual sense. Both are so real to Mr. Marblehall that he has lost the power to distinguish them, one from the other. And in terms of the story, they are not to be distinguished: at certain points they become one and the same thing, even while maintaining their separate identities, because their end is the same. This coalescence takes place in Mr. Marblehall's mind, particularly when he catches on, ". . . he thinks, to what people are supposed to do. That is it: they endure something inwardly—for a time secretly; they establish a past, a memory; thus they store up life. . . ." His is a soul obsessed with terror (he even reads *Terror Tales*), to be treated with the ironical indulgence, or pity that one might bestow upon a crazy world. But out of his chaotic mind streams some logic that gives him hope. He speculates upon the future, ". . . upon some glorious finish, a great explosion of revelations." Roderick Usher, in Poe's story, is without such an outlook; he is *completely* enveloped in fear; he realizes his terror, but, unlike Mr. Marblehall, lacks the vision that would give him relief. Mr. Marblehall's "castle in the air," like that of Dickens's character in "The Poor Relation's Story," is his *only secure* "castle." (pp. 506-10)

All of the stories that have been referred to, with the exception of **"The Wide Net"** and **"The Purple Hat,"** are to be found in the volume entitled ***A Curtain of Green.*** In a later volume, ***The Wide Net,*** Miss Welty moves, for the most part, in a slightly different realm. The imagination has fuller play; there is less of the actual world, except by implication; more of the dream. In no sense are these stories farther from life; on the contrary, they seem to be closer to the very heart of life. But in almost all of them the setting is strange and unearthly. (p. 510)

It is in ***The Robber Bridegroom*** that Miss Welty's fantasy has its fullest reach. Whereas many of her short stories are in the nature of parables, some partaking of the nature of allegory, this longer tale is more purely allegory, in its greater consistency in the representation of ideas by characters. Yet it goes beyond an allegory like *Pilgrim's Progress,* where the pattern is more obvious, the meaning cut in straighter, sharper and simpler lines. Structure in ***The Robber Bridegroom*** is infinitely more complicated: ideas and characters are interwoven in a system that ingeniously reveals meaning. In its satire, as well as its subtlety and complexity, it is much closer to *Gulliver's Travels*.

Yet the characters in ***The Robber Bridegroom,*** as in Miss Welty's short stories, could never be said to exist *only* for the conveyance of ideas. Indeed, they are thoroughly realized as individuals; for in the larger expanse that is here, there is more room for a complete presentation of characters. In fact, the story may be said to possess three distinct levels. First, the mere surface, which itself comprises an entertaining and interesting tale that could be read (and probably has been by many) as a story of horror and mystery. There is the strange and exciting wilderness setting, and the romantic and gruesome happenings, in the medieval manner. Bandits capture young maidens and whisk them away on their horses to huts in the woods, where they engage in idyllic and sometimes strange lovemaking. People wrestle with ghosts, who suddenly appear on pathways in the forest, and sometimes turn out to be willow trees! Someone is hidden in a trunk for days, and cries to be let out. And they slice off one another's heads at the slightest provocation. A second level is the story of the characters as such, and much value could be obtained by the reader who never got beyond that level.

The real significance of the work would be lost, however, by the reader who failed to get to what we shall call the third level; for that is where the richest meaning lies, and where the power of Miss Welty's artistry shows to greatest advantage. Each of the characters, some to a larger extent than others, tends to embody certain general traits of humanity at large. Jamie Lockhart, the chief protagonist, has a double role in life—one as a bad, ruthless bandit, the other as a respectable, prosperous merchant. His purposes are many and complex; as are his deeds. He has the "power to look both ways and to see a thing from all sides." The mixture of good and evil in him—the cunning, the treachery, brutality counterbalancing the kindliness, the wisdom, the humaneness—is, without saying, universal. But, more particularly, the dualistic nature of his character symbolizes the conflict between idealism and realism, the neuroses that result from modern man's inability to attain his ideals. Interestingly enough, Jamie manages to free himself, by refusing to feel any guilt: he will not discriminate between right and wrong. He permits no one to ask of him *what* he is; *who* he is becomes all that is important to him. He determines not to recognize evil as a part of himself; it is, to him, merely something that he has been caught up into, and over which he has no control. In his imagination he keeps his personal *self* inviolable, and in that manner comes to terms with reality. Clement, one of his victims, is a sort of Don Quixote, caught in his own trap. Clement's wife, Salome, a catlike creature, having suffered great loss and cruelty, has nothing left in her destroyed heart but ambition, which she exerts in her domineering treatment of Clement and Rosamond (whom she hates but also seems to love). She even commands the sun to stand still and dances in order to make it obey her. The convincing force of the story is in the juxtaposition of the rough-and-tumble and grotesque life in the wilderness with the conventional, the real; and the harmonizing of the two. The beginning is in the realm of the actual; there is reversion to it at intervals: and at the end the sense of reality is restored, when Jamie and Rosamond settle in New Orleans, and there is a shift of scene to the streets of that city. Yet the magic and dreamlike quality of those surroundings, where "beauty and vice and every delight" are hospitable to one another, repeats the nature of the wilderness, and ties the actual world with the dream world.

Miss Welty's exploration of the adult mind is closely allied to her extraordinary penetration of the mind of childhood. Like Franz Kafka, she seems to regard the relationship of childhood and the dream as very near; since the dream has childlike qualities. Her reproduction of the sensibilities of childhood has a decidedly Proustian quality. In the little but exceedingly dimensional story, **"A Memory,"** she brings the whole world of impressionable childhood up against the adult world, with all of its sordidness. The child, estranged from adults, can look upon them only as observer and dreamer. Out of the wisdom she possesses, intensified by love, she constructs her own vision of it. A story entitled **"The Winds"** also is an illustration of the author's acute insight into the perceptions of children, with all of the implications. Nothing seems omitted that would illuminate their inner minds.

This skill in getting inside the minds of her characters, in establishing motivation from within, is a very essential part of Miss Welty's technique. In this connection, she is a master in implying inner states of mind by physical description. In **"Death of a Traveling Salesman"** there are such subtle strokes as these, which transfer the intangible to the tangible: "People standing in the fields now and then, or on top of the haystacks, had been too far away, looking like leaning sticks or weeds . . . the stares of these distant people had followed him solidly like a wall, impenetrable, behind which they turned back after he had passed." And, ". . . When that was done she lit the lamp. It showed its dark and light. The whole room turned golden-yellow like some sort of flower, and the walls smelled of it and seemed to tremble with the quiet rushing of the fire and the waving of the burning lampwick in its funnel of light." In such a way as this the portrait of the salesman's mind comes through; description has a definite function, and is not just tacked on for purposes of decoration. And in the same story one comes across such arresting similes as this: "He could not hear his heart—it was as quiet as ashes falling." Or a metaphysical figure like this one: "In docility he held his eyes stiffly wide; they fixed themselves on the woman's clasped hands as though she held the cord they were strung on." Miss Welty's work is liberally sprinkled with such striking poetry; and the poetizing in each instance is identified with the characters; it assists in revealing the state of their thoughts and feelings.

Miss Welty's primary interest in theme is easily confused with moral intention; and there an important distinction should be made. Only by a consideration of her method does it become apparent that she is not interested in enforcing any moral "truth"; or in exhortation—far from it—to any particular line of conduct. True enough, her characters are clear symbols for basic ideas. But by means of the attitudes that are taken toward the characters any moral purpose is subdued. The reader is required to take full stock of the context; in this way the resolution cannot appear as simple. The moral conviction, when and if it comes, does so through the process of the story; which is to say that it is realized in the experiences of the characters, and the reader draws his own conclusions, without direct assistance from the author. In the story, **"Asphodel,"** for example, the reader, while he is horrified at Miss Sabine's domineering cruelty to innocent people, feels also the tragedy of her life and the necessity within her for wreaking vengeance upon others. In Salome, as well, is a demonstration of the same psychologically basic truth. This—and, as we have seen, it is representative of the ideas in Miss Welty's stories—is not really a moral, but a truth upon which there is no necessity for the reader to agree or disagree. It is generally recognized among mature and thoughtful readers that any inflicting of wrong is due to an inadequacy within the wrongdoer, and that he is likely to suffer more than his victims; so, without disputing it, the reader will concede that it is a question that is worthy of serious reflection. He may judge that his own reflection, or someone else's, is more fruitful than the author's; but in this case the author would have no objection; Miss Welty, like any other of like caliber, would be ready to admit that she is only a fellow explorer.

But the fiction writer has more opportunity than those using other writing mediums, to make his idea convincing and alive. Tension, a necessary device for this accomplishment, in Miss Welty's fiction takes the form of conflict between the real and the imagined. Fantasy, therefore, serves as an agent in making the conflict more dramatic, in *rendering* the idea. The same device is recognizable in much of the work of Hawthorne, who works out his ideas in terms of structure, although not with the craftsmanship that in every instance comes up to Miss Welty's. "The Birthmark," among others of his stories, comes to mind as an illustration of his method of presenting a basic truth, not a moral. For, though Hawthorne is closer to Puritanism as an institution, and perhaps in spirit, almost the same could be said of him in answer to a charge of moral intention as can be said of Miss Welty. Both are sensitive to a distinction between right and wrong—not, of course, the conventional or puritanical standards, even though Hawthorne in some instances does come nearer the latter. Although we are more concerned with their similarity in method, a conclusion of Henry James seems applicable to a clarification of the moral purpose of both: "There is, I think, no more nutritive or suggestive truth than that of the perfect dependence of the 'moral' sense of a work of art on the amount of felt life concerned in producing it." The reader of Eudora Welty can entertain no doubt concerning the amount of "felt life" that is in her work.

It is her profound search of human consciousness and her illumination of the underlying causes of the compulsions and fears of modern man that would seem to comprise the principal value of Miss Welty's work. She, like other best writers of this century, implies that the confusion of our age tends to force individuals back upon conscience, as they have not been since the seventeenth century; for in the intervening centuries, values were more clearly defined, behavior was more outwardly controlled. Miss Welty's prose fiction, like much of the poetry and fiction of this era that seeks to explore the possibilities of the imagination, is comparable to the rich prose of Sir Thomas Browne; and reminiscent of the poetry of the seventeenth century.

Franz Kafka precedes Miss Welty in an analysis of the backgrounds of abnormal human behavior and an understanding of the psychology of the feeling of guilt. He, too, was concerned with modern man's ambivalence, with the potentialities that are within him of dispensing with the rationalizations, the impotence of will, and the laxness that grow out of a diseased society. And a general impression gained from his work, as from that of Miss Welty, is that it is the world that we regard as actual that is irrational; that the positions are reversed—the actual world becoming a dream and the one created by the imagination the only reality.

Miss Welty's distinction, then, is rather in her method: one that, as we have observed, effects a reconciliation of the inner and outer worlds in a particular way. Kafka, too, uses fantasy, but not in detail as does Miss Welty. The contrast in the style of the two is another matter; suffice it to say here that Miss Welty relies more upon fantasy, by it implying much of the factual; while Kafka, at least in his short stories, does the opposite. Miss Welty employs fantasy to reveal the heightened consciousness of man, and relates it to surface reality. The individual, even in his irrational state, becomes rational and capable of choice. The effect is one that is compelling, and rare in modern literature.

For all her strange and dreamlike settings, Miss Welty never strays far from the Natchez Trace, in Mississippi, her home state. This in itself is evidence of the sense of reality that she conveys. She observes a Bird Festival in a Negro church in her home town, Jackson, and describes it in [her essay "Pageant of Birds"]. Yet the piece is as steeped in fantasy as some of her fiction. She has caught the tendency of man to dream, to build a world of his own, and, without violating reality greatly, used it as a device in fiction. Actuality is placed on the plane of the dream; and thereby a more perfect realism is attained.

Her characters are thoroughly Southern—in temperament, customs and speech. Yet they transcend any geographical limitation. She is concerned with Southern traditionalism only in respect to the values which it seeks to conserve; and only, apparently, as those values relate to people anywhere, in any society. (pp. 512-17)

Eunice Glenn, "Fantasy in the Fiction of Eudora Welty," in Critiques and Essays on Modern Fiction: Representing the Achievement of Modern American and British Critics, 1920-1951, *edited by John W. Aldridge, The Ronald Press Company, 1952, pp. 506-17.*

FRANCIS STEEGMULLER (essay date 1949)

[*Steegmuller is a prominent American critic, biographer, novelist, and translator. The following excerpt is from his positive appraisal of* The Golden Apples.]

[***The Golden Apples***] is made up of seven short stories, or cantos; these are of varying length, and each, although more or less complete in itself (several have been published separately), is greatly strengthened and enriched by the presence of the others. This very form of the book is shared by its characters: every (white) person in Morgana is a delineated human entity; but all are closely bound together by the remorseless ties of small-town life, and they take their importance from these relationships. The single section dealing with a character who has moved away shows him a "little man," an utter nonentity, lost among strangers. (Symbolically, he has left an identical twin behind in Morgana, who becomes Mayor.)

The rare artistic power displayed by the author in this fusion of characters and form is also visible elsewhere: in the delineation of each member of Morgana's families, in the enchanting passages of description of gardens, swamps and indeed anything, however humble; in the jewel-like metaphors and similes; and not the least in the humor. The narrative flow of the book is, with rare exceptions, outstanding: the whole thing is a "good story" made up of countless "good stories."

Miss Welty is a happy writer: happy in being utterly familiar with her material, in having great quantities of it at her disposal, and especially happy, even triumphant, in her mastery of selection and presentation.

Before the best of her fiction, before, for example, the sections of this book called **"June Recital"** and **"Moon Lake,"** one is all admiration. It is like (and one makes an analogy with painting advisedly, so extraordinary a sense does this writer have of human beings and other objects in space) standing before a canvas by one of the great, though not one of the most monumental, masters of space, color and light, before a masterpiece by Pissarro, Seurat or Villon. Everything glows in a personal, private light created by the artist; human beings, objects, background, atmosphere—all are parts of the unique form; and the attuned spectator is moved by the art to feelings of joy, or sorrow, or both together.

So marvelously successful are the best sections of this anatomy of one aspect of American life (likenesses could be pointed out to *Huckleberry Finn,* to certain American poets, to *Winesburg, Ohio,* and to the best work of William Maxwell) that it would be a fascinating, though intricate, task to explore the reasons that lie behind the author's failures. Not *all* the obscurities of the language, for example, are due to local habits of speech, local usages and local rhythms. These, indeed, clear themselves easily away in the very fascination of rereading phrases and sentences. There is over-indulgence, or, rather, partially inappropriate indulgence, in the currently fashionable deliberate use of myth, and in the equally fashionable immersion of fictional fact in mystery.

In so beautifully balanced and interrelated a book as this such defects show up all too clearly in characterization and narrative.

Virgie Rainey, an otherwise powerful creation, wanders weakly and foolishly away from herself in the Perseus myth, and the suicide of a ruined country girl, which one has long assumed to have taken place within the sordid cabin in which ends the melodramatic, sentimental section called **"The Whole World Knows,"** is in the end capriciously revealed to have happened later and elsewhere. Except for its making of the point mentioned above, the value of the one section not laid in Morgana, **"Music From Spain,"** eludes this reviewer. And another, **"Sir Rabbit,"** seems strained and murky.

But in so generally fine an achievement as ***The Golden Apples,*** one lingers on faults only when one has time to extract the interest that is in them.

Thanks to the unity of its parts, this book passes beyond any need of being evaluated on the crowded, dreary judging stand of the contemporary short story. It is a work of art at once eloquent and entertaining, whose very form is in a lovely, nonspectacular way the original creation of an invaluable artist.

Francis Steegmuller, "Small-Town Life," in The New York Times Book Review, *August 21, 1949, p. 5.*

V. S. PRITCHETT (essay date 1954)

[Pritchett, a contemporary English writer, is respected for his mastery of the short story and for what critics describe as his judicious, reliable, and insightful literary criticism. In the following excerpt, Pritchett praises The Ponder Heart.*]*

Sometimes the regional writer becomes the professional topographer of local oddity. With one sophisticated foot outside his territory, he sets out to make his folk quaint or freakish (the abnormal becomes a matter of local pride), and he can be said to condescend to and even exploit them. He may even go so far as to suggest that people are not real until they are eccentric and decorative and then we have the disastrous impression that the author is philandering with his characters. . . . Of course isolated provincial societies *do* live a sort of family life, all rough and tumble but fundamentally close-knit, where mild lunatics, simples, notorious public nuisances, gossips and embarrassing relations have a great importance as personalities.

Indeed it is an awkward fact that there is more personality in the small worlds than in the big ones. All the critic can do is to warn against accepting the more endearing clichés of this expanded family reminiscence.

As Eudora Welty's [***The Ponder Heart***] shows, it all depends on depth and technical skill; and in Miss Welty's case on a sardonic comic brio. She has written some excellent short stories in the last ten years and an especially brilliant first volume, so that she comes to her subject with a good deal of experience. She has had the art to place her Uncle Dan in a complex position in the narrative. He is embedded in the mind of a bustling, hoydenish, bossy niece, a girl of fierce practical capacity, snooty manners and possessive temperament, who will scornfully defend the old idiot partly because she passionately loves him, partly to keep her head up among the neighbors. She is the soul of small-town pugnacity and self-conceit and has an endless tongue.

It is part of the beauty of the telling that this young limb, Edna Earle, runs a small hotel (the setting is unmistakably Miss Welty's native Mississippi) and is forcing a traveling salesman to listen to her. She is really a more considerable character than Uncle Dan and it is her apparent normality which sets off his idiocy perfectly. The underlying suggestion that she may be as dotty as he is adds to the pleasure.

Uncle Dan is an amiable freak with a low I.Q. He has one dominant passion: he loves everybody with childish ingenuity. His love takes the delicate form of an irresistible desire to give everything away. He sheds property as a tree sheds leaves. He is a saint of the compulsion to distribute, and in the course of the tale even distributes himself twice in marriage. Edna Earle keeps a prim, head-tossing silence about what went on in these marriages—one of them he described as a "trial"; certainly his wives left him in time, though without rancor. The bother about people who are not all there is that one can never be quite sure of the nature of what *is* there: it is likely to be unnerving. Once or twice it was thought that Uncle Dan ought to be put away, but uncle had a sort of somnambulistic instinct for last-minute success. When his father took him to the asylum, it was father, not the son, who found himself consigned.

Edna Earle's narrative is remarkable for its headlong garrulity and also for its preposterous silences and changes of subject at the crises of the tale. She is a respectable young scold with a long tradition in English sentimental comedy. If it was a shade tricky and arch of Miss Welty to make her tell the tale, she has the advantage of being able to bring a whole town to life in her throwaway lines and she has the scolds of Scott, Stevenson and Katherine Mansfield behind her in the world of feminine tongue rattling. Her breathless, backhanded, first person singular has been caught, word by awful word, in all its affectionate self-importance, by a writer with a wonderful ear. ***The Ponder Heart*** is one of Miss Welty's lighter works, but there is not a mistake in it.

V. S. Pritchett, "Bossy Edna Earle Had a Word for Everything," in The New York Times Book Review, *January 10, 1954, p. 5.*

THEODORE HOFFMAN (essay date 1955)

[*In the following negative assessment of* The Bride of the Innisfallen, *Hoffman characterizes Welty's work as unfocused and marred by trite situations and overused themes.*]

The stories in Eudora Welty's ***The Bride of the Innisfallen*** are about as good as her others. The subject range is wider, but they are still hazy and humid, life seen in a disconnected dream which focuses and fades, and behind it all arrives a vision of horror, or a spontaneous but unresolved decision, or else people grope for each other only to pass like ships in the night. There is the same sociological data, embellished beautifully when nature, interiors, or the life of the past are described; distilled and quaintly bottled when human motivations are involved. It is, of course, so artfully attenuated and so skillfully softened that it bears little resemblance to formal sociology and comes across as a kind of arcane wit, as if she could tell all she chose if only the pulse of life were not so feeble.

Her themes are familiar by now. A Northern lady and gentleman take an automobile ride into the Bayou country and encounter an isolated Negro roadhouse where things are popping. No harm comes to them, and they leave, somehow shamed by it, and don't have an affair. Instead they discover the insufficiency of each other, and themselves. Character portrayal is intended, but then again Miss Welty is always delineating the character of the empty, or the insane. In another story, two Southern ladies, made for nothing but ante-bellum life, hang themselves grotesquely when Sherman burns their home, but this one is that old Faulkner tale with the hot-house atmosphere, the compulsive but agonizingly deliberate action that is supposed to take on the significance of eternity, and was very good the first eight times Southern writers did it. The title story concerns an American girl who has left her husband and rides the night train and boat to Ireland with an assortment of talkative passengers whose chatter influences her personal problems, I think by making her recognize her need for the bright life and solace of strangers. There are others: a bunch of ebullient Italians going to Naples, a rather jejune monologue by Circe retailing her finely spun grief, several having to do with the somnolent luxuriousness and wonder of Southern life.

I don't much enjoy Miss Welty's work. She keeps evoking things as if I had experienced them and relish them. I tire of her endless descriptions of clothing and furniture. I enjoy the talky dialogue only to a point. I don't find passionate people as incomprehensible as she does, nor do I go for the unshakeable quiet frustration her characters are inflicted with. In short, life doesn't seem as difficult to get at as all *that*. (pp. 562, 564)

Theodore Hoffman, "Two Southerners," in Partisan Review, *Vol. XXII, No. 4, Fall, 1955, pp. 561-62, 564.*

LOUIS D. RUBIN, JR. (essay date 1955)

[*Rubin is an American critic who has written and edited numerous studies of southern literature. In the following excerpt, he discusses the treatment of time in the stories of* The Bride of the Innisfallen, *focusing on the story "Kin."*]

The adjective "elusive" is one of the more overworked words used to describe Miss Welty's work. "Elusive" is just the word, however, because though she seldom lacks for praise, what Miss Welty is really doing in her fiction often eludes even the most perceptive of critics. In all her work, a great deal goes on, much of it humorous, piquant, graceful; and beneath the surface there is another and deeper dimension entirely. We see it in the story **"Kin"** of [***The Bride of the Innisfallen***], if we read carefully, and since it is a dimension that is necessary to the proper appreciation of Miss Welty's extraordinary art, I should like to devote particular attention to the one story. (p. 671)

"Kin" has to do with a young woman, Miss Dicey Hastings, who was born in Mississippi but who now lives in the North. It describes Dicey's reactions to a visit home. She and her cousin Kate ride out into the country to visit their ailing great Uncle Felix at Mingo, the family homestead. An old maid relative, Sister Anne, is presiding over the home, and when they arrive it is to find Mingo filled with visitors. Their immediate thought is that Uncle Felix has died, but quickly they learn that Sister Anne has merely loaned out the parlor of Mingo to an itinerant photographer to use as a studio for the day. (p. 672)

[In Uncle Felix's room,] Dicey sees lying on a barrel nearby an old stereopticon, which long ago had reposed in the parlor. "It belonged to Sunday and to summertime . . . My held hand pained me through the wish to use it and lift that old, beloved, once mysterious contraption to my eyes, and dissolve my sight, all our sights, in that. In that delaying, blinding pain, I remembered Uncle Felix. That is, I remembered the real Uncle Felix, and could hear his voice, respectful again, asking the blessing at the table."

The sight of the stereopticon momentarily recalls to Dicey the image of her childhood, of family dinners at Mingo on Sunday with her dead parents and all the others present. Afterwards she would run to the front porch steps, and sit with Uncle Felix to look through the stereopticon, handing him the cards as he signaled for them, while he peered intently through the lens and she watched him at it. (pp. 672-73)

The three-dimensional image of the stereopticon used to transport the child Dicey to fabulous, faraway lands; now the vision of the old device there (actually a sterescope rather than a true stereopticon) on the barrel serves to take the adult Dicey back into the past, to the "real Uncle Felix"—to the real world of her childhood, as it was, "cypressy and sweet, cool, reflecting, dustless." For the moment Mingo, just as the house in St. Louis does in Thomas Wolfe's "The Lost Boy," has ceased to be a curio, an old museum of a homestead where an old man is dying and strangers are being photographed, and has become a moment of Dicey's life. She has, swiftly, momentarily, reached back through decades of time to what she was as a child. (p. 673)

[When Dicey drives away from Mingo, she knows she] is leaving a moment of her childhood, of herself, never again to be recaptured. Nor does the old homestead remain, either, because Mingo has gone, too. Mingo is the sound and smell and feel and weather of that long ago Sunday of childhood, gone forever. . . . The real Uncle Felix has gone forever, too. The old man who is in the house, gradually dying, has traveled far from that past day, though not the way Dicey has. Rather, he has gone backward toward his own youth, talking confusedly of joining the Confederate army (Miss Welty is careful to point out that there is a Civil War musket in the corner of his room), arranging a tryst with a long-forgotten girl—Dicey, Daisy—at midnight by the river. From the moment in time and space that was Mingo, with the cool cypressy smell, the old, kitchen-like soft airs, the fragrances winding through the fields, the stereopticon with its views of sand-pink cities, fountains, waterfalls—childhood—from that moment time and mortality have sent the participants spinning far away like an exploding galaxy. It is this knowledge of time, of loss, of the weather of a childhood remembered and gone again that assails Dicey's consciousness then. (pp. 674-75)

[We] see that, beneath the humor of Sister Anne's rendezvous with the photographer, beneath the assiduous and delightful description of place and the acute delineation of personality, Miss Welty has all along been exploring, with penetrating insight, the nature of memory, the meaning of time and the past. **"Kin"** is the story of a moment recaptured from past time: "when I had left for ever, I wondered at the moment." Achieved, it liberated as well the place where it occurred, and the child who had experienced it.

In a sense, each of the stories in ***The Bride of the Innisfallen*** is about time—a moment, an afternoon, a day. The search for the meaning of the moment of time provides the structure of the story, and each has this for its progression. Each is a development toward inactivity, to the reality of self freed of the distractions of elapsing events. In **"No Place for You, My Love,"** two strangers, a man and a woman, go for a long drive southward from New Orleans, only to return eventually to the city. It is a silent, passive, inactive liaison. They say little; they do not even discuss their lives and families back home, for that is in time. Time seems to have stopped, while they have been suspended outside of it for a day. When they leave each other, the man "remembered for the first time in years when he was young and brash, a student in New York, and the shriek and horror and unholy smother of the subway has its original meaning for him as the lilt and expectation of love."

In a bizarre story, **"The Burning,"** an idiotic Negro slave girl undergoes a harrowing day during the Civil War in Mississippi. Here the reverse of the usual situation occurs: the idiocy of the girl can permit no meaning, no knowledge to become real. Events are not "lost" for her; they do not even exist. She cannot understand that her two mistresses are dead; nothing but the most trivial can make any impression on her consciousness. She wades into a river: "she had forgotten how or when she knew, and she did not know what day this was, but she knew—it would not rain, the river would not rise, until Saturday."

The title story of Miss Welty's collection, **"The Bride of the Innisfallen,"** concerns an American girl in England who leaves her husband to board a train that will travel to a seaport, where she will journey by boat to Cork. Beautifully written, it records the delightfully inane conversations of her fellow travelers, with all Miss Welty's gift for that sort of thing. Through it all, the American girl is inactive, impersonal; merely a listener to talk. Finally, in Cork, she hears the speech of the Irish, sees the trees and sights, drinks in the weather of spring in Ireland. This is all, and this is everything: "it was the window herself that could tell her all she had come here to know—or all she could bear this evening to know, and that was light and rain, light and rain, dark, light and rain." She tries to write out a telegraph message to her husband. But she pauses. To do it, to do anything, she realizes, would interfere with the sudden access of life, of complete stasis. Nothing else matters but the moment; she is by herself, among strangers in a strange land, and in the very anonymity of her status she finds herself closer to her real self, furthest removed from the conditionings of her life in time, than for many months. Upon the precious moment of now, the "evening of extraordinary splendour and beauty," nothing else must be allowed to impinge: "The girl let her message go into the stream of the street, and opening the door walked into the lovely room full of strangers."

So with each of her stories, the moment, the realized experience, is the goal, the key. In a fine story of a Southern youngster who plays hookey to join his father at fishing, it will be years before the true significance of the day's events are to be understood, until the youngster will realize that his father had intended a liaison with a girl that day when he had interrupted. One of Miss Welty's funniest stories is **"Going To Naples,"** in which she describes the activities aboard ship of a group of Italian-Americans going home again. A half-dozen characters are delightfully realized, and at the end it is to the awkward, good-natured, reluctant Gabriella that it all "happens":

> all seemed caught up and held in something: the golden moment of touch, just given, just taken, in saying good-by. The moment—bright and effortless of making, in the end, as a bubble—seemed to go ahead of them as they walked, to tap without sound across the dust of the emptying courtyard, and alight in the grandmother's homely buggy, filling it.

That is the "meaning" of the long and pleasant sea voyage, the discovery: it was a time, a sequence, and now it is over. For each of the tales in ***The Bride of the Innisfallen,*** the plot is the character's discovery of himself, and events all occur for that final purpose. The progress of Miss Welty's art is in time, directed toward the movement outside of it, the matchlessly revealed moment of knowledge and feeling in a perfect inutility of place. (pp. 675-77)

Louis D. Rubin, Jr., "Two Ladies of the South," in The Sewanee Review, *Vol. LXIII, No. 4, Autumn, 1955, pp. 671-81.*

ROBERT Y. DRAKE, JR. (essay date 1960)

[*Drake is an American critic and short story writer. In the following excerpt, he analyzes "Why I Live at the P.O.," focusing on the juxtaposition of ordinary and epic elements.*]

In her introduction to Eudora Welty's first volume of stories, ***A Curtain of Green*** [see excerpt dated 1941], Katherine Anne Porter observes that Sister, the postmistress-narrator of **"Why I Live at the P.O.,"** is "a terrifying case of dementia praecox." I interpret this remark as meaning that Miss Porter believes that Sister, who has quarrelled with her family and left home to live in the post office, is suffering from the delusions of persecution which constitute paranoia. Now nothing could be further from the truth—except that we are all surely paranoid, to some extent.

The whole point of Miss Welty's delicious (that is the only word for it) story is its exalting of the everyday and familiar to the level of the heroic and epic. In this case, the tone is apparently mock-heroic because it is the absurd which has been exalted to the sublime. For the narrator, China Grove, Mississippi, is the whole world; and her family are the royal figures in that world. ("My family are naturally the main people in China Grove," she remarks.) And the quarrel which takes place "on the Fourth of July, or the day after" is an epic struggle. Indeed, one is even tempted to compare Sister's retreat to the post office to Achilles' sulking in his tent. This assumption—that the family, with all its rich and complex giving and taking, constitutes the ultimate reality—is fundamental in much of

Miss Welty's work; and, consequently, I can view such an observation as Miss Porter's only as indicative of an inexplicable failure to apprehend an important part of Miss Welty's world. But Miss Porter, whose condescension in her introduction now seems ludicrous in the light of Miss Welty's achievement, is not the only reader who has come to grief on **"Why I Live at the P.O."** Many less distinguished readers, while granting Miss Welty's stylistic virtuosity in the story, are apt to dismiss it as only a *tour de force*. A careful examination, though, reveals that it is more than that.

The situation is this. Stella-Rondo, the narrator's "baby sister" (she is "exactly twelve months to the day younger"), comes home to China Grove with "a completely unexpected child of two," after having separated from her husband, Mr. Whitaker, up in Illinois. The child, Shirley-T., is "adopted," according to Stella-Rondo; and Mama, Papa-Daddy, who is "Mama's papa," and Uncle Rondo, who is Mama's brother, all proceed to accept Stella-Rondo and Shirley-T. on the terms laid down by Stella-Rondo. Sister, of course, is sceptical. She believes that Mr. Whitaker left Stella-Rondo rather than the other way around and that Shirley-T. is not adopted. "Stella-Rondo had her just as sure as anything in this world and just too stuck up to admit it." Before the day is over Stella-Rondo succeeds in alienating the whole family's affection from Sister and making them "side" with her. It is then that Sister decides the time has come for her to make a strategic retreat in good order.

> There I was with the whole entire house on Stella-Rondo's side and turned against me. If I have anything at all I have pride.
>
> So I just decided I'd go straight down to the P.O. There's plenty of room there in the back, I says to myself.

Exactly what Stella-Rondo's "side" is would be difficult to explain to someone, who, like Miss Porter, attempts to demythologize the story. Most southerners, especially those from big families, are perfectly familiar with the guerilla warfare which exists within that secular Communion of Saints which is the family. They know that such warfare can never, in the minds of the participants, be dismissed simply as "inter-family tensions" or "personality stresses." To simplify it thus is to violate the complexity of family life and to blaspheme its sanctity. (Indeed, I am at a loss to understand how Miss Porter, whose roots are essentially southern, could fall into the pit digged for this particular form of modern impiety.) But it is not so much Stella-Rondo's "side" as it is Stella-Rondo herself that the "whole entire" family are accepting.

Perhaps Sister feels something like this. Here, she has stayed at home, right there in China Grove, "getting along fine" with the family; and Stella-Rondo, having taken Mr. Whitaker, "this photographer with the popeyes," away from her, comes back from the big wide world of married life and Illinois, bring her "adopted" child and expecting to find China Grove ready to accept her as though she has never been away. Mama, Papa-Daddy, and Uncle Rondo seem ready to acquiesce; but Sister has not forgotten a thing. Speaking of Stella-Rondo right at the beginning of the story, she gives us a clue to her attitude toward her baby sister.

> She's always had anything in the world she wanted and then she'd throw it away. Papa-Daddy gave her this gorgeous Add-a-Pearl necklace when she was eight years old and she threw it away playing baseball when she was nine, with only two pearls.

Stella-Rondo is in some sense the prodigal daughter come home again, and perhaps Sister is the righteously indignant elder brother, turned sister. But perhaps what really keeps Stella-Rondo from being the returned prodigal is her lack of penitence, and this Sister finds particularly vexing. She resents also the family's willingness to be dazzled by Stella-Rondo's glamor as a separated woman. Indeed, we suspect that Sister has gone through life with Stella-Rondo's praises ringing in her ears. We are particularly aware of this when Sister tells us she overheard Papa-Daddy trying to turn Uncle Rondo against her.

> Oh, he told Uncle Rondo I didn't learn to read till I was eight years old and he didn't see how in the world I ever got the mail put up at the P.O., much less read it all, and he said if Uncle Rondo could only fathom the lengths he had gone to to get me that job! And he said on the other hand he thought Stella-Rondo had a brilliant mind and deserved credit for getting out of town.

It is, then, not so much the fickleness of the rest of the family (Sister has come to expect that) as it is Stella-Rondo's lack of penitence (her "flesh-colored kimonos, all cut on the bias" and her insistence that Shirley-T. is "adopted") that is the real thorn in Sister's flesh.

Sister's vocation seems clear enough, and it is one with which southerners are apt to be familiar. Sister *serves*—like Edna Earle Ponder in Miss Welty's ***The Ponder Heart*** and like many another old-maid in a large southern family. And if this *service* is apt to make her careful and troubled about many things, we must remember that saints have never been easy to live with—from St. Paul all the way down to "St." John Milton, who had some pertinent things to say about the people who also serve, though they can only stand and wait. Surely, this interpretation of Sister's vocation is implicit in such passages as the one where she expresses scepticism about Stella-Rondo's assertion that she can prove that Shirley-T. is adopted.

> "How?" says Mama, but all I says was, "H'm!" There I was over the hot stove, trying to stretch two chickens over five people and a completely unexpected child into the bargain, without one moment's notice.

Again, after Sister defends Uncle Rondo, who has "drunk another bottle of that prescription" and dashed out into the front yard in one of Stella-Rondo's kimonos, in the face of Stella-Rondo's snide observations, she reverts once more to her vocation of service.

> So I merely slammed the door behind me and went down and made some green-tomato pickle. Somebody had to do it. Of course Mama had turned both the niggers loose; she always said no earthly power could hold one anyway on the Fourth of July, so she wouldn't even try. It turned out that Jaypan fell in the lake and came within a very narrow limit of drowning.

But they are her family, her vocation, her cross; and she can never really let them go. Even after Stella-Rondo tells Uncle Rondo that Sister has been sneering at the way he looks in her flesh-colored kimono and he retaliates by throwing a whole package of fire-crackers into her room at 6:30 A.M., even after she decides to move to the post office, the bond is by no means broken. Ostensibly, Sister tries to sever every connection between the family and herself. She "marches in" and unplugs her electric fan and radio and takes down all the jars of food she has canned. But the family ties are ultimately indissoluble, as we learn indirectly in her final lines. "And that's the last I've laid eyes on any of my family or my family laid eyes on me for five solid days and nights," she says, implying that the family bond is so powerful that even a few days' absence seems momentous.

And this brings me to my final point, on which I have already touched briefly. It is this: that **"Why I Live at the P.O."** is an epic, but a cater-corned one, an epic cut on the bias. The obvious thing to say is that the story is mock-heroic in its exalting of the ridiculous to the sublime. But I will go further and comment that here the treatment is more complex and many-sided than in the conventional satire.

In her concluding remarks Sister says, of her new quarters, ". . . I like it here. It's ideal, as I've been saying. You see, I've got everything cater-cornered, the way I like it." And Sister tells us a great deal in these lines. For what she is saying, without knowing it, is that she likes the multiple view and is, on a fairly elementary level, aware of the ironic possibilities of any situation. We have seen this irony at work before in the necklace Stella-Rondo lost "with only two pearls" and in the coupling of Jaypan's near-drowning with the necessity of making green-tomato pickle. Another good example of this ironic vision may be noted in the exchange between her and Mama about Stella-Rondo.

> "Why, Sister," says Mama. "Here I thought we were going to have a pleasant Fourth of July, and you start right out not believing a word your own baby sister tells you!"
>
> "Just like Cousin Annie Flo. Went to her grave denying the facts of life," I remind Mama.
>
> "I told you if you ever mentioned Annie Flo's name I'd slap your face," says Mama, and slaps my face.
>
> "All right, you wait and see," I says.
>
> "I," says Mama, "*I* prefer to take my children's word for anything when it's humanly possible." You ought to see Mama, she weighs two hundred pounds and has real tiny feet.

These relevant irrelevancies, this complexity of vision is, as a rule, not possible in the epic, which by its very definition, must be one-sided; but it is possible in the mock-epic and in the cater-cornered epic. But perhaps the cater-cornered epic is even more complex than the mock-epic. For the mock-epic defines its *rationale* by the very things it ridicules; we certainly know, by negation if by no other way, some of the things Pope is *for* in *The Rape of the Lock*.

But in **"Why I Live at the P.O."** we are hard put to define the *rationale* so directly. Perhaps, by indirection, Miss Welty is saying that the sanctity of the family circle, based as it is on a complex give and take and a service of love, is paramount. And when this sanctity is violated, as it is when the rest of the family reject or are indifferent to Sister's "service," the most far-reaching consequences result. In this case, the consequences are ludicrous because they are made, so self-consciously, to exceed the provocation. It is almost as though Sister is inwardly aware of the absurdity of her self-imposed exile but is determined, once and for all, to show the family that they cannot abuse their claim on her. Perhaps, also, like Ruby Fisher in Miss Welty's **"A Piece of News,"** she begins to feel an "eye in the world . . . looking in on her"; and this dawning awareness of the world outside China Grove makes for a conscious determination, on her part, to assert the importance and dignity of China Grove to the rest of the world. Indeed, perhaps it is this conscious effort to bear witness, to justify one's position which constitutes the *raison d'etre* of the cater-cornered epic. Certainly, the epic and the mock-epic do not find apologetics necessary. But Sister does not repudiate the family's claim on her, only their abuse of it. And lest we be tempted to dismiss the story—and Sister's "exile"—as diverting but ridiculous, we should remember that Sister might well have taken after Stella-Rondo with the butcher knife—and doubtless would, had some more "realistic" and less reverent hand than Miss Welty's held the pen.

But Miss Welty is never presumptuous, and she is never condescending. She displays nothing but compassion and love in her quiet and long look at life—life which is, at every moment, fraught with the possibility of harmony and dissociation, the possibility of Heaven and Hell. And her "vision" is, in large measure, embodied here in Sister's seemingly ridiculous epic flights. For if Sister can speak of *suing* Stella-Rondo to get her radio back and can attribute *manners* to the man in the moon (Shirley-T. "has no more manners than the man in the moon"), she knows, in her own China Grove way, that you really can hold infinity in the palm of your hand. Indeed, that is where it is most likely to be found. (pp. 126-31)

Robert Y. Drake, Jr., "Comments on Two Eudora Welty Stories," in The Mississippi Quarterly, *Vol. 13, No. 3, Summer, 1960, pp. 123-31.*

RUTH M. VANDE KIEFT (essay date 1962)

[Vande Kieft, an American critic, is the author of the first full-length study of Welty, which is excerpted below. The critic, who is currently preparing an updated edition of her study, here discusses the prominent strengths and weaknesses of Welty's fiction.]

There is no valid reason for setting arbitrary limits to the form of the short story, especially at this stage of its development, when the "rules" for the genre have so often been broken—and often with happy results. A short story can become anything the writer chooses to make of it: there is no *a priori* reason why it should not be as close to a poem, or a piece of music, or choreography, or an Impressionist painting (or a series of such paintings) as words can make it, and achieve a comparable effect of interest and beauty. But I believe Miss Welty's greatest contribution to the genre has so far been made in those stories in which the traditional elements of fiction—plot, character, setting, theme—are most freely and spontaneously blended, in which no single element appears to be manipulated, radically out-balancing the others. She seems to be able to achieve this balance most effectively when she is, in every sense, closest to home. "Home" refers not only to the Mississippi setting (though perhaps mostly to that), but also to the kinds of characters with whom she is "at home" in her fiction, whether from the inside or the outside, and to the kinds of social custom and environment she has observed closely enough to have understood. "At home," she has both her distance and involvement: more than enough knowledge of her material to make the story convincing; the objectivity to shape it; and the feeling and sensibility to give it the unmistakable lyric impulse which identifies it as her own unique product.

It seems true of Miss Welty, as of many original artists, that a peculiar artistic virtue may, if slightly misplaced, overemphasized, or reduced from its highest uses, turn into a particular flaw or weakness. Miss Welty has a great power to reveal the atmosphere of place, and a great power to reveal mystery, when the *reality itself* is mystery. But with a slight shift in emphasis, mystery may become either ambiguity or obscurity—a fact not faced, a secret kept, a mystery (in the popular sense) never cleared up. There are times when Miss Welty does not mediate clearly enough between the reader and the actuality of persons and events presented.

"The Purple Hat" is a story in which Miss Welty pushes to a dangerous point both her fascination with place (in this case the New Orleans "Palace of Pleasure") and her cultivation of fantasy. One reviewer found the story "so confused that a reader tires finally of wondering where the fantastic leaves off and reality begins," but he adds that this confusion "seems to represent merely the unsuccessful application of the very methods by which Miss Welty achieves her finest stories." The reader is asked to "give over" to the mood of strange fascination, but the abundance of sharply drawn realistic details makes it impossible to accept the story as pure fantasy. Its meaning remains a puzzle.

Another of Miss Welty's powers is her intuitive knowledge of the mysteries of the inner life. And yet her knowledge about her own characters very often resembles our knowledge of people in real life: it is filled with mysterious gaps. The paradox is that as creator of her characters she has every right to full knowledge of the facts of their lives, their relationships and motives; but often she chooses not to know—or at least not to be forthright—as though a writer's pressing for or even assuming knowledge were as much a violation of human privacy as it would be in real life. In **"No Place for You, My Love,"** the "exposed" young woman reflects, "How did it leave us—the old, safe, slow way people used to know of learning how one another feels, and the privilege that went with it of shying away if it seemed best?" There is a good deal of "shying away" from both fact and motivation in ***The Bride of the Innisfallen.***

Lack of factual explicitness may be seen in **"The Burning."** What do the soldiers actually do to Miss Myra and Miss Theo? What is implied by Delilah's being "dragged down on the grass" outside the house? Who is Phinney? This kind of obscurity about facts can become a source of annoyance to the reader who hunts for "clues"—and we are taught by Miss Welty's fiction to read closely because so much of the meaning is conveyed by subtle intimations and hints. This is the kind of mystery that does not reveal, but rather obfuscates. In ***The Golden Apples,*** however, obscurity is often put to better use. We do not know how many of the children of Morgana have been fathered by King MacLain, but the mystery here is enhancing because it adds to the heroic or legendary dimension of these altogether human characters.

Sometimes Miss Welty shies away from the clear presentation of a character's motivation. An example of this is to be found in **"The Whole World Knows."** Because Randall MacLain soliloquizes, we should be able to perceive the reasons for his behavior—just as we know the motivations of the self-revealing heroine of **"Why I Live at the P.O."** But as Snowdie says, "Son, you're walking in a dream." Randall is totally confused. It takes a good deal of intuitive "sleuthing" to determine what "ails" Randall, or what ails the American wife in **"The Bride of the Innisfallen,"** or to determine what kind of relationship has come into existence by the chance encounter and journey of the couple in **"No Place for You, My Love."**

And these demands made on the reader's sensibility apply not only to the understanding of motivations and relationships, but often to the smallest gestures, words, and metaphors. As early as 1944, Robert Penn Warren observed in the first two volumes of her stories Miss Welty's tendency to "squeeze meaning from the item which, in ordinary realistic fiction, would be passed over with a casual glance. . . . She wants us to get that smallest gesture, to participate in her vision of things as intensely meaningful" [see excerpt dated 1944]. By now readers have seen stories in which that sensibility has been enormously compounded; they have seen her attempt to convey virtually ineffable psychic glimmerings in the smallest gestures and by the use of the most dazzling and elusive metaphors.

As an artist, in her most sensitive area Miss Welty is, naturally, most vulnerable: that is, most susceptible to attack. In real life, there is sometimes a hair's-breadth—dizzying to contemplate because of the importance of giving things their right value—between what is deeply portentous, though ever so slight and small, and what is simply trivial, inconsequential. And so it is with some of the fleeting, elusive feelings, motives, gestures, relationships presented in Miss Welty's fiction. They are presented to us with the strong suggestion that they are meaningful; usually, as in life, it is only our impatience, blindness, and insensitivity which make them appear meaningless. Sometimes, however, Miss Welty has not convinced us of the importance of each small impression; she has not shown that either individually, or taken together, these impressions may reveal to us a genuine, or significant, human mystery. The reader's reaction will depend on the kind and quality of his attention. Miss Welty does not rely greatly on her own or her reader's logical and rational powers. She uses, and must be met with, an active creative imagination, the free exercise of intuition, rapid shifts in mood, the ability to perceive by way of metaphor and symbol, and the power to feel with interest, concern, and love.

It will by now be clear that Miss Welty's creative imagination is wholly, and in the best sense, feminine. To use Robert Heilman's terms . . . , this is an "endowment," and endowments "are not possessed in entire freedom, without price." From the woman's or child's point of view she sees beautifully and convincingly. But she has not often entered into a male consciousness with assurance, though she has done so, I think, in the two salesman stories (possibly because she had learned from observation and experience how it feels to be heartsick and tired on the road). The portraits of George and Battle Fairchild and Troy Flavin in *Delta Wedding* are all the more convincing for being done from the outside. **"The Whole World Knows"** seems to me the least effective story in ***The Golden Apples*** not, finally, because of its obscurity, but because it is unconvincing as the soliloquy of Randall MacLain. It is a piece of narrative patchwork, the only authentic parts of which are straight dialogue, the passages given over to Miss Perdita Mayo's rambling advice, and snatches of the town gossip. Even granting the weakened and confused state of Randall, he never sounds like a man speaking or thinking: he begins to *look* like one, however, in **"The Wanderers,"** where he is observed by a character whose consciousness Miss Welty knew thoroughly, Virgie Rainey. One suspects that in telling Randall's story Miss

Welty was "going out on a limb"—and was lured to do so by an untried point of view, a new technical device. This may well have been the case also with **"June Recital,"** but the narrative technique of that story seems to me a triumph and that of **"The Whole World Knows"** a failure.

In her use of myth and symbolism, however, Miss Welty has been consistently effective. Symbols and myths are always *inherent in* the materials of her stories: characters, names, and actions are not manipulated or denatured to underscore their deeper meanings, but all are subtly extended, infused with something greater than their surface values. In a symbol, as Carlyle said, "there is concealment and yet revelation"; the use of the symbol is therefore natural to Miss Welty's kind of vision, because it serves to deepen and enhance the mysteries she seeks to convey. By her use of myth she suggests what is permanent in the human race—in character types, rituals, and heroic action. In her fiction the less obvious uses of myth and symbol seem to have the greatest power to provide depth and beauty. King MacLain as Zeus, particularly in **"Sir Rabbit,"** is less convincing as a mythical type of person than is Old Phoenix, whose bright coloring, fabulous old age, and ritual act of sacrifice, quietly suggest the self-immolation and resurrection of the ancient bird whose name she bears so naturally.

A summary of Miss Welty's achievement would be incomplete without . . . mention of how her two initial artistic interests—that of painting and photography—have shaped her writing. The eye of the painter is especially evident in her descriptive writing, which indicates a close scrutiny of the details of the natural world—chinaberry, fig, plum, mimosa trees, roses and four-o'clocks, butterflies, humming birds, mourning doves, June bugs, slow deep rivers with their watersnakes and twisted roots, and the "curtain of green" with its thickly interlaced, impenetrable patterns of leaves—all this detail, together with a rapturous feeling for light, color, texture, atmosphere. In **"A Sketching Trip"** Miss Welty presents a young painter who had always, from childhood, loved the textures of the natural world and rejoiced in putting out her hands to touch this world. But she had never been able to show her joy in painting, nor render the "pulse of life," that "tender surface underneath which flowed and trembled and pressed life itself. It was as if this pulse became the green of leaves, the roundness of fruit, the rise and fall of a hill, when she began to paint, and could have become—anything." Miss Welty turned that pulse of life into words—nor did she stop with the natural world. She applied the same close and loving scrutiny to human faces, forms, gestures. Atmosphere in the outside world was translated directly into human feeling, and her characters retain something of the mystery of nature's voiceless beauty.

In an article on "Literature and the Lens," Miss Welty made some interesting observations about the parallels between the "lowly" art of photography and the higher arts of painting and literature. She described how, after she had taken a snapshot of Royal Street one day in New Orleans, three old ladies had started to mutter in vague protest. Why, she asked, is the act of taking a picture always suspect?

> Perhaps it goes back to atavistic beliefs that to carry off an image of something, or its picture, means you want to steal its soul. In Mexico a woman forbade me to photograph her baby because he had not yet been christened, and an eccentric old lady in Louisiana threatened to shoot me with her gun if I dared photograph a beautiful statue in her garden. It is clear that the fascination of a photograph of anything is that it imprisons a moment in time—and is that really different from stealing its spirit, its soul? Perhaps one does right to protest.
>
> Yet this must be, in a sense, the purpose of nearly everything we do—certainly in the arts, painting and writing, we steal spirits and souls if we can, and in love and devotion, what do we do but pray: Keep this as it is, hold this moment safe? So in the lowly photograph we can do this to anything—a little boy walking fast in a shuttered street—with a little machine and the slightest motion of the finger. Photography is crude in itself, but the act of photography is kin to something better. . . .

The moment crystallized in time and forever removed out of time, the still moment, the quiet center, the instant of revelation, the elusive gesture captured—these are all moments in Miss Welty's fiction when a picture is taken, and she has caught for permanent safe-keeping a precious scene or person, an act, a thought, a feeling.

The power of the painter—and of the eyes behind the lens—is the power to focus, to bring the gaze that looks outward to a steady point where the subject is. In *Place in Fiction* Miss Welty defines the attributes of focus as "awareness, discernment, order, clarity, insight—they are like the attributes of love. The act of focusing itself has beauty and meaning; it is the act that, continued in, turns into meditation, into poetry." Miss Welty herself has this power of focusing, and to this fundamental artistic act she brings a pure and benevolent mind, a loving temper, an open sensibility, an impressive gift with language.

She has also the kind of love for her characters which John Bagley has described as "a delight in their independent existence as *other people,* an attitude toward them which is analogous to our feelings towards those we love in life; and an intense interest in their personalities combined with a sort of detached solicitude, a respect for their freedom. The logical consequence of the artist's love, his feeling for the freedom and independence of his creation, is the sense of "joy in Nature," "lightness of touch," buoyancy and humor. Because her stories are celebrations, springing from the lyrical impulse to praise or wonder, it is not difficult to see why Miss Welty has always enjoyed writing, and hopes for readers who will come to any story fresh, prepared for pleasure, "with a storehouse of hope and interest." (pp. 183-89)

Ruth M. Vande Kieft, in her Eudora Welty, *Twayne Publishers, Inc., 1962, 203 p.*

ALUN R. JONES (essay date 1963)

[*Jones presents an appreciative overview of Welty's writing.*]

Naturally, in her work Miss Welty draws for her material largely on the world of the South, familiar and immediately to hand, but it is human nature and the human dilemma that are explored, and her art is distinctive. Only the most provincial reader confuses the writer with the raw material of his art. Certainly the South seems to lend her an assured sense of personal identity—because you know where you are, you know who you are—and this assurance has, in a sense, enabled her to pursue her art with a freedom and single-mindedness rare among those writers with apparently more fluid, less stable social backgrounds. But indeed, even among the writers of the South, she is the only one to have acknowledged the autonomy of the imagination. Behind her work there lies a fragile, profound and essentially lyrical imagination strengthened by characteristic wit and shrewdness. Thus her art brings together the delicate, introspective refinement of Chekhov, Katherine Mansfield, and Virginia Woolf and the tough, American know-how of Mark Twain, Stephen Crane and Ring Lardner.

The sheer variety of ***A Curtain of Green*** is immediately impressive. The stories vary in tone from broad and sometimes grotesque farce to delicate melancholy; there are stories of fairy-tale simplicity and fantasies of nightmare complexity, stories of greed, and pride, and horror, and of innocence and love. Yet above all else they portray a wide variety of attitudes and peoples living in a recognizably human world of beauty and corruption, tenderness and hate, wonder and boredom. The stories are concerned largely with single moments of personal crisis and move towards and explore the nature of conflict as the characters struggle to clarify their choices, to come to terms with themselves and the world around them. Although a strong sense of an ordered community binds the settings of the stories together, it is the dark, inner lives of the characters that interest her more than their public faces. She is more concerned with individual self-deception than with social hypocrisy.

She has, too, the storyteller's gift of compelling attention, of capturing her reader's interest in what happens and, more particularly, in what happens next. Moreover, although her subject is often fabulous, bizarre and in itself improbable, she has the unfailing ability to maintain what she has called "believability"—to establish that imaginative confidence between reader and writer which constitutes a mutual act of poetic faith.

Stories such as **"Death of a Traveling Salesman"** and **"The Hitchhikers"** contrast the settled life of traditional values and the restless commercial world, a contrast between love and loneliness. In **"Death of a Traveling Salesman,"** R. J. Bowman, forced by illness to recognize the restlessness and futility of his life is brought by accident into contact with a couple whose life is slow, intimate and secure. It is the meeting of two worlds, the past and the present, the simple and the complex, the loved and the loveless. . . . The couple receive Bowman with kindness, hospitality and warmth and without ceremony. He knows he has nothing to offer in return, except money, and in desperation he tries to escape back to the emptiness of his life. His need for love—the struggle his heart puts up inside him—betrays him:

> Just as he reached the road, where his car seemed to sit in the moonlight like a boat, his heart began to give off tremendous explosions like a rifle, bang, bang, bang.
>
> He sank in fright on to the road, his bags falling about him. He felt as if all this had happened before. He covered his heart with both hands to keep anyone from hearing the noise it made.
>
> But nobody heard it.

The symbolism in this story (the first to be published) is more direct than in her later stories, but it states the theme that is in so many ways fundamental to an understanding of her fiction: man's loneliness and his search for a world of love.

"The Hitchhikers," for instance, is a more complex and more oblique treatment of a similar theme. A commercial traveler and the two hitchhikers to whom he gives a lift form a community of drifters. Because they exist on the surface of life they are trivial and superficial, unable to give or receive love, unable to realize themselves except as travelers to whom movement from one town to another has become an escape from life. The gratuitousness with which one hitchhiker kills the other, brings home to the commercial traveler an awareness of the rootlessness of his own life. The commercial traveler's ambition is to be "somewhere on a good gravelled road, driving his car past things that happened to people, quicker than their happening." He wants life to be ordered and straightforward and without ties, but life, Miss Welty insists, is a matter of strong roots and slow growth.

Miss Welty reserves her deepest compassion for those who recognize their need for love but are refused—as in the pathetic story [**"Clytie"**] in ***A Curtain of Green,*** trapped in a house of lonely and demanding selfishness, who finds release from the sufferings of her absurd, unlovely and unloved life in the companionship of death. Clytie lives in a mysterious world of her own. Aware of the potentiality of wonder and beauty in the world around her, she meets at every turn only horror and brutality. Her spirit is wild and demented with half-understood longings. She is the pathetic victim of her family's selfishness, of a bullying sister, her drunken brother and invalid father. The house is a prison in which the family has interned itself so as to prevent any contact between the Farr family and the villagers of Farr's Gin. Only Clytie goes out, pathetically wandering in the rain and searching for a world of love which she associates faintly with her youth. Later, when the barber is summoned from the village to attend her father, she reaches out "with breath-taking gentleness" towards him only to be rejected in fear. Automatically she obeys her sister's command:

> "Clytie! Clytie! The water! The water!" came Octavia's monumental voice.
>
> Clytie did the only thing she could think of to do. She bent her angular body further, and thrust her head into the barrel, under the water, through its glittering surface into the kind, featureless depth, and held it there.
>
> When Old Lethy found her, she had fallen forward into the barrel, with her poor ladylike black-stockinged legs upended and hung apart like a pair of tongs.

Clytie, a curious kind of Narcissus, has been horrified by the reflection of her own ugly, suffering face. She is shocked into an awareness of how life has perverted and deformed her vision. She is found, significantly, by her father's devoted nurse whom her sister would not allow into the house. Old Lethy represents childhood and affection trying to re-enter the family but her name suggests death and oblivion. (Frequently in her stories Miss Welty uses classical references. In this particular story the sister is called Octavia, which suggests the cold, Roman matron; and the barber is seen, for a moment, standing "like the statue of Hermes," which wonderfully conveys both his physical attitude and the fact that Clytie mistakenly took him to be a messenger from the better world outside.)

Miss Welty moves with assurance through those worlds of feeling where comedy and pathos meet and become inseparable. **"Clytie"** is both grimly comic and profoundly moving. There is in the character of Clytie herself a tragic incongruity between the wonder of what we know to be her inner life and the pathetic figure she cuts in her public actions. In the final line when she describes Clytie's legs upended, she shocks us into an awareness of the casual way that life has picked up Miss Clytie and put her down again as if she were quite trivial and dispensable. By reconciling incongruities in this way, Miss Welty shows how tragic feeling can be expressed in laughter, and laughter in her work is often the release of otherwise unbearable pathos.

The stories are often concerned with those who are in some way deprived and living on the very edge of life but they see deprivation not as a social question but as a human one, a matter not of income and status but of love and loneliness. They cover the social range from faded gentry to sharecroppers and Negroes, yet their concern is always with the human dilemma, with man's failure or success in dealing with his own nature, with the realities of the life within him and the needs of those around him.

Each of the stories in ***A Curtain of Green*** is very different, yet in all of them incident and speech are observed and reported with dispassionate fidelity and patterned with unobtrusive artistry. In **"Lily Daw and the Three Ladies,"** three old spinsters cluck and fuss over their irresponsible charge, desperately trying to reduce her wayward life to some semblance of ordered dignity. The world of Lily Daw is hugely comic and contrasts violently with that of **"Petrified Man"** which is fraught with hypocrisy, petty spite, greed and shallow ambitions. The world of the hairdresser and her client in **"Petrified Man"** is exposed relentlessly in the course of two conversations between the women. The story has a biting satiric edge that cuts deeply into the vulgar triviality of commercial, small-town life. It is a world both cheap and sinister, in which human relationships have been grotesquely perverted, a world ruthlessly dominated by women who are themselves dominated by spite, cheap sensation and material possessions. The beauty salon is seen as a cave of primeval tortures producing a succession of Medusa-like creatures who turn their men to stone at a glance. The men are impotent before this monstrous regiment of women. The petrified man of the title is an exhibit at a freak show. The discovery that he is "not really petrified at all," but was, in fact, wanted by the police for raping four women provides the story with its climax and with its central symbol. It is a kind of poetic justice to learn that subjugated man has reasserted himself even if in a violent way against this monstrous regiment. The conversation of the women is recorded with amazing fidelity as relentlessly they expose the shallowness and perversity of their own attitudes. The story, emerging casually out of the conversation, is a shrewd and incisive comment on the social scene and shows a complete mastery of the comedy of manners.

"Why I Live at the P.O." is the indignant and gushing monologue—Katherine Anne Porter describes it as a "terrifying case of dementia praecox" [see excerpt dated 1941]—in which the heroine describes how her sister, separated from her husband, comes back home and turns the family against her, forcing her out of the house. The sheer technical skill involved would seem to mark each of these stories as a tour de force, and yet more significant than this is the way in which each, while maintaining a convincing illusion of reality, creates its own world, with its own distinct logic, language and being. Each creates an immediate sense of actuality, of people talking and things happening before the reader's eyes, and this powerful, almost tactual illusion of reality is strongest when the stories themselves are closest to pure fantasy.

Indeed, one of Miss Welty's outstanding characteristics as a writer is her Tennysonian ability to sustain an atmospheric mood. The world of the imagination is so fully realized in terms of the sensuous and ordinary that it is accepted without question. Although these stories are clearly informed by compassionate intelligence and shaped by an acute feeling for artistic form, we are aware that for the author life continually moves towards the fabulous, sometimes—as in **"Petrified Man"**—towards the perverse, just as magic shades off into witchcraft. She is conscious of mythical and imaginative reality impinging on and informing the trivial and the banal.

As her stories become longer, her texture richer and more complex in effect, she increasingly explores in depth the world in which the significant and the mythical lie thinly disguised beneath the everyday world around us. In her next collection, ***The Wide Net,*** she begins to build with gathering assurance on the territory already cleared and charted in her early stories. For, like all great writers, she is continually in competition with herself. In a story such as **"First Love"** the myth is embodied in the past and is associated particularly with the way in which the past impresses itself on and enriches the present. There is a strong feeling of the organic unity of life, of tradition as a creative, positive force shaping the present and lending individual lives a general validity.

Her imagination is essentially poetic; her fiction is clearly centripetal, structured like poetry with an intuited center and everything subdued to the demands of this central insight. As her art develops, so her fiction accumulates a more profound sense of human suffering and dignity and it covers a wider area of human activity without losing any of its original power. She continues to affirm the beauties and terrors inherent in the human situation while asserting the right to love and the need to dream. Through dream, as through art, man can express and realize his secret self: through love, as through art, he can communicate that secret self to others; for art, she believes, is the power to convey love. In **"A Still Moment"** she brings together the themes of loneliness, love and time, "God's giving Separateness first and then giving Love to follow and heal in its wonder." The tragedy of man is to be separate and lonely, his glory is to be capable of dissolving his loneliness in love.

Legend, a more specific land of mythology, plays a larger part in her later work. In **"First Love"** and in **"A Still Moment"** she incorporates legendary figures into the story. **"First Love,"** for instance, is concerned with Joel Mayes, a deaf and dumb boy who is caught up in the romantic and mysterious conspiracy of Aaron Burr. Painfully, through love, the boy achieves self-awareness. The love is, of necessity, unspoken and unacknowledged. His life is touched by the historical past being enacted around him and he achieves self-consciousness, shame, love and adulthood. The unthinking innocence of childhood is lost to him and his life to that point takes on an entirely different meaning. Even the world of nature, to which he was formerly drawn as by a bond of sympathy, now seems completely changed:

> He held the bud, and studied the burned edges of its folds by the pale half-light of the East. The buds came apart in his hand, its layers like small velvet shells, still iridescent, the shrivelled flower inside. He held it tenderly and yet timidly, in a kind of shame, as though all disaster lay pitifully disclosed now to the eyes.

In a way the story re-enacts the Fall of Man, the child moving out of the world of innocence into the world of experience. It is the kind of romantic dynamic associated with Blake who also regarded love as the great regenerative force by virtue of which man could regain a vision of that Eden from which self-conscious knowledge had exiled him. There is a general feeling in Miss Welty's work that man, driven forward by dreams of the future has, with dignity and humor, created a precarious present out of the wilderness and chaos of the past.

Her novel ***The Robber Bridegroom*** is a direct tribute to the legendary past. Set in Mississippi in 1798 when it was still Spanish, the action is mostly centered on the Old Natchez Trace which ran for two hundred miles through the wilderness between Natchez and Nashville. The story opens in Rodney's Landing—now a ghost town—with a mock-heroic encounter between the two legendary figures, Mike Fink and Jamie Lockhart, and ends in New Orleans with the happy reunion of Jamie Lockhart, the Robber Bridegroom, and Rosamond, his bride. In this brilliant, loving parody of fairy-tale, the legends of the past are recreated with magical simplicity and directness. All the elements of the fairy tale, including its traditional style, are accommodated; the heroes are suitably romantic and heroic; the heroine is virtuous and trusting, with a proper sense of curiosity; the wicked stepmother is, of course, in league with the forces of evil and plotting against the heroine; the father is kind and doting and everyone—at least every one of the virtuous characters—lives happily ever after. Miss Welty's attitude towards her material is detached, even ironic, though she leaves no doubt that it is a parody written without sentimentality but with profound admiration and respect. (pp. 176-84)

Undoubtedly the seven separate stories [of ***The Golden Apples***] create a unity of a sort, linked as they are by their locale, a small town, Morgana, and by the reappearance of many of the same characters throughout. The stories vary in tone from the broad comedy of **"Shower of Gold"** to the desperate melancholy of **"The Whole World Knows." "Shower of Gold"** tells of the disappearance and reappearance of Snowdie MacLain's husband. Like so many of [Miss Welty's] stories, this one is characterized by a strong feeling for the casual—the mark of the consummate craftsman. The more extraordinary the event, the more the style tends toward the throw-away. The opening of **"Shower of Gold"** is a fine example:

> That was Miss Snowdie MacLain.
>
> She comes after her butter, won't let me run over with it from just across the road. Her husband walked out of the house one day and left his hat on the banks of the Big Black River.—That could have started something, too.
>
> We might have had a little run on doing that in Morgana, if it had been so willed. What King did, the copy-cats always might do. Well, King MacLain left a new straw hat on the banks of the Big Black and there are people that consider he headed West.

Her use of the garrulous narrator not only enables her to exploit her uncanny gift for reproducing the authentic accents of colloquial speech but provides her with another source of interest in the character of the narrator as well as another perspective.

In **"June Recital,"** the most complex of these stories, she uses two quite different narrators to define two quite separate attitudes toward the same incident. The young boy, Loch, and his older sister, Cassie, are both spectators of the sinister happening in the deserted house next door. Loch sees a sailor making love to a girl in an upstairs room and an old woman scattering paper around the living room downstairs who then sits down to play the piano. Loch in his innocence accepts these events with wonder but without serious questioning; Cassie, a little more experienced than her brother, questions these events and tries to make sense of them, but her mind is on the hayride for which she is making herself ready. Thus three lives and three points of view are brought together, each working at a different level of consciousness, but each in its separate way affected by the others. One is without experience or anticipation, one with a little experience is filling her life with the excitement of anticipation, the third, old, deranged and embittered, has had her ambitions and expectations cruelly frustrated. Yet the story as a whole affirms the mystery and wonder of life rather than its disappointments.

Similarly, in **"The Whole World Knows,"** which tells the story of Randall MacLain's desertion by Jinny Love and his affair with Maideen Sumrall, the tone is pervasively melancholic, but it is life itself that is affirmed—in spite of the treachery of time and transience. Indeed, the town of Morgana suggests the claustrophobic, painful and distracting landscape in which all of us, in a sense, came to terms with the adult world for the first time. It is a different place for each character as they emerge from their private worlds to face the larger world outside. It is essentially a secure landscape, still to some extent dominated by parents.

What the characters in ***The Golden Apples*** all learn is that to live in harmony demands a strenuous act of creation; it entails reshaping one's inner world to meet the needs of others. In fact, ***The Golden Apples*** maps that whole area of consciousness that we vaguely call "growing up." It is in many ways Miss Welty's most complex and satisfying achievement, for she seems to be drawing on all her considerable resources, both technical and thematic, and bringing them together to make a statement about life that is rich and profound in all its fabulous, banal, comic, tragic and human variety.

Morgana becomes finally as complete a map of Eudora Welty's imaginative world as she has given us. The act of creative imagination is seen now to be the act of life itself. The effort of living is an act of imagination, and like the regeneration of the Ancient Mariner (which has often been interpreted as a poem about the workings of the creative imagination) must begin with an act of love.

Allen Tate once observed that "the typical Southern conversation is not going anywhere, it is not about anything. It is about the people who are talking—conversation is only an expression of manners, the purpose of which is to make everybody happy." Miss Welty's hugely comic book, ***The Ponder Heart,*** is clearly written in this tradition. Breathlessly, Edna Earle describes the life of her Uncle Daniel—a life devoted to making everybody happy. Uncle Daniel is the richest man in the small town of Clay although money means nothing to him, for the world in which he lives is the golden world of the heart where wealth is counted in love, generosity, kindness and happiness. (pp. 185-88)

Uncle Daniel is impregnable and incorruptible for, as Edna Earle explains, "he's been brought up in a world of love." ***The Ponder Heart*** is a glorious comic invention, a masterpiece of contrived lunacy that affirms love as the source of human activity and Uncle Daniel a fabulous representative of human virtue.

In her latest collection of stories, ***The Bride of the Innisfallen,*** Miss Welty has broadened the scope, as well as enriched the texture of her writing still further. Her eye and her ear are as sharp as ever, but her compassion leads her to a more subdued consideration of personal suffering. Her work takes on a sculptured, timeless solidity. At the same time, her thematic material becomes denser and more complex, and an increased artistic assurance enables her to treat her narrative more obliquely than in her previous work. She no longer draws her material exclusively from the South and she explores new areas of experience with more somber restraint and from a viewpoint withdrawn from the center of the stories' interest. Taken as a whole the stories are an exciting departure. They are experiments in a kind of impressionistic writing that depends hardly at all on traditional narrative techniques but relies largely on *montage,* an approach to writing that has its parallel in the cinema of the *Nouvelle Vague.* Three of the stories in the volume—**"No Place for You, My Love," "The Bride of the Innisfallen,"** and **"Going to Naples"**—are concerned with journeys and with strangers briefly and loosely thrown together because of their common destination. The climax of each story is arrived at obliquely as imperceptibly the consciousness of each character leaves its impression on his fellow travelers.

For example, **"No Place for You, My Love"** is deliberately vague on the conventional level of plot and characterization. A man and a woman, not themselves southerners, meet accidentally in a New Orleans restaurant and take a car ride over the Mississippi toward the South. They drive compulsively onwards through the intense and merciless heat into a country which becomes more unreal the further they travel. They are exposed finally to a wasteland of light without shadows and without purpose—except that they follow the road, until the road just ends. The journey has many of the features of a bad dream as the couple unknown to each other move deeper and deeper into a country which is also unknown. (pp. 189-90)

The story is completely unified at a symbolic, impressionist level and the mood is sustained with great subtlety. Although at the end of the story we know little more about the characters than we did at the beginning, there is a sense also in which we know all there is to know about them. The story is a complete and satisfying "objective correlative" for a certain kind of shock experienced by those with courage enough to face life unprotected by the buffers of habit or custom. Similarly, **"The Burning"** is a pitiless exposure of a deranged world set at the time of the Civil War when Sherman was marching and burning his way through the South. The tone of these stories is meditative and compassionate and depicts a strange modern Odyssey into disturbing areas of human consciousness.

Each of Miss Welty's works seems to present her with a different challenge and in each she has extended herself in a new direction. For her, writing is a means of exploration and in the stories of ***The Bride of the Innisfallen*** she reaches deep into a new and darker side of experience. (p. 191)

Between ***A Curtain of Green*** and ***The Bride of the Innisfallen*** Miss Welty has developed a vision of life that is matched by her consummate skill. Writing with love, she restores our illusions about the world of love. Her fiction is exuberant with life, rich in comedy, pathos and color, quick with movement and firmly disciplined. Each of her stories creates its own level of reality and succeeds in the business of fiction which is to make reality real. Replete with sensuous and meaningful detail, the meaning itself is often suspended in that private world somewhere between dreaming and waking. Indeed, it is the particular, personal moment that her imagination seizes with concrete and urgent immediacy.

Her writing as a whole is characterized by an elegant and correct compassion that interpenetrates life's disordered vitality in such a way that, in her own words, "life on earth is intensified in its personal meaning and so restored to human terms." Her art shapes the experience, lending it style and direction; life informs her art at every turn, giving it variety and intensity. The most immediate and most lasting impression created by reading her work is an admiration for the sheer abundance of human life. Her achievement has won her comparison with the best writers of the century and the prospect of her future work assures readers of fresh and exciting excellence. (p. 192)

Alun R. Jones, "The World of Love: The Fiction of Eudora Welty," in The Creative Present: Notes on Contemporary American Fiction, *edited by Nona Balakian and Charles Simmons, Doubleday & Company, Inc., 1963, pp. 173-92.*

WILLIAM M. JONES (essay date 1967)

[*Jones, an American critic and author, discusses the significance of mythic imagery in* The Golden Apples.]

[There] is much to be said for an artist such as Welty, who refuses to be restricted by current fashions in literature. She is neither the faddishly obscure nor the faddishly direct. Her own works are the works of an experimenter conversant with, but liberated from, the bonds of her own age. She does, perhaps, favor the Faulknerian view that her work ought not to be immediately comprehensible. She demands of her readers a complete cooperation that the superficial reader will not offer. In Welty's mature writing, the challenged reader has plentiful opportunity to exert all his critical efforts of comprehension.

A key to Welty's experimental method can be found in her own critical writing. In commenting on the method of writing that she advocates, she said that "In any group of stories we might name as they might occur to us, the plot is search. It is the ancient Odyssey and the thing that was ancient when first the Odyssey was sung." The search to which she refers is twofold. First, it is the admission on the part of an author that when he begins the plot he is not sure where this plot will take him. For the creative artist with the open mind there can be no contrived outline. From the beginning of the story to the end there is always the potential for infinite change within the creative process. From the reader's point of view also, the plot is search. The author puts into the plot the multiplicity and ambiguity of his own experience and assumes that the reader will, as he pursues the sometimes wispy strand of the plot line, also permit the multiplicity of his experience to function freely.

In a successful Welty story the author and the reader are collaborators in a search for some nameless end that continues to elude both author and reader. No story ever follows the same path. Each looks in a different direction, and the reader who feels that he has the Welty pattern carefully worked out is likely to be shocked into new doubt by the next story. (pp. 37-8)

In her most successful collection of stories, ***The Golden Apples,*** she tries a much more ambitious task. While continuing to take her reader with her on the plot search, she also seems to regard the entire collection of stories as a psychotherapeutic exercise. This work is not so much a collection of stories as it is a progress through an exceedingly unorthodox ritual. Each story,

Eudora Welty. © *Rollie McKenna.*

though apparently independent, performs a function similar to that of religious celebrations in the holy calendar. An analysis of these stories demonstrates the successful intricacy of a very subtle literary shaping at work. Almost any artistic choice that Welty makes in ***The Golden Apples*** has meaning in terms of the total work, but the doubtful reader is never sure, critically, whether it is his own imagination at work on an artistic fact or whether it is the consciousness of the author shaping his literary interpretation. For example, ***The Golden Apples*** contains seven stories. Are these seven stories the seven candles of the sacred Hebraic candelabra? Are they seven because of Pythagoras' number symbolism? Are Virtues and the deadly sins behind this numerical choice? Or is it accidental after all?

Such questions hover on the edge of the reader's consciousness, but are rarely verbalized. The mythic and the real are so integrated that they seem to be, as Welty probably believes them to be, a single unified world. The careful realism of her characters' actions and speech makes them true representatives of the finest regional literary tradition. But over this regional realism hovers the universality of a world that contains eternal truths that inform the actions of the people in the stories, and in the audience. Vicarious experience for Miss Welty's readers is of a multifoliate variety. The temporary is always reaching around to the mythic, the symbolic, the philosophic, the religious, the eternal. Readers often feel this depth before they know it.

The reader's uncertainty about the numerical choice extends also to Miss Welty's naming pattern. The cast of characters, which is listed separately at the beginning of the book, clearly indicates that she is thinking of one cast of characters. Each name is fraught with significance. The man who stands behind all the stories, the initiator of the action, is King MacLain. A fairly obvious Zeus figure, his comings and goings lead to the various plots of the individual stories. It is his sons that move to fulfillment or sterility. The names of the other characters are equally significant, but not nearly so immediately evident.

The name of the town is as important, however, as the name of the central character. The action, with one outstanding exception, takes place in Morgana, Mississippi. The name Morgana suggests the world of Morgan la fée, Arthur's half-sister. What we have in this collection of stories is the enchanted world of the Arthurian legend translated to contemporary Mississippi. What we discover in this enchanted world of the romantic legend is a world of truth revealed by a progression through a year of rituals.

In the first story, **"Shower of Gold,"** Mrs. Kate Raney tells the story of the conception of Ran and Eugene MacLain, sons to King MacLain. The realism of a first-person narrator, who was herself pregnant at the time, gives a realistic tone to a modernizing of the story of Zeus' visit to Danaë in the shower of gold. In this first-person narration, a disciple of the fertility cult reveals the mystery of the conception and birth of heroic twins in terms of contemporary rural Mississippi. The reader sees here the strange juxtaposing in the narrator's thought and in his own of the pagan and Christian. The conception is at Easter and the birth is at Halloween. Throughout this story the masque and the antimasque of Christian and pagan are thoroughly fused in the reader's thinking.

The movement from this ritualistic reporting of the heroic births to the next ritual is a movement from simple and direct narration to multiple complexity. In the story **"June Recital"** we move through the calendar year from spring to June. An adolescent boy, Loch Morrison, watches the vacant house next door with the telescopic eyes of Argus. What he sees is a fantastic processional that moves along the walk in the present, but also reminds him and the narrator of other moments in the past. The center of the story, however, is the account of the German piano teacher, Miss Eckhart, who returns to make a burnt offering of the home that she formerly inhabited with King MacLain. The sacrifice is observed and understood only by the boy, Loch. Miss Eckhart places her metronome on the piano, strings papers around the scene of her former successes, and sets fire to the room. Two old men who have been fishing in Moon Lake return in time to go through a mock-epic race to thwart the sacrifice. They throw the metronome out the window under the impression that it is some sort of explosive device. Miss Eckhart escapes while King MacLain walks along the sidewalk in the company of ladies returning from an afternoon tea. Here again we see the imposing of mythic significance upon the trivial. The metronome takes on a central symbolic significance in terms of fertility ritual. Loch Morrison, who retrieves the metronome, sees it for what it is, the active phallic power that guides the universe to which Miss Eckhart, unlike so many of the townspeople, gives her faithful service.

> Then he turned a little key in the side of the box and that controlled it. The stick stopped and he poked it into place within the box, and shut the door of the thing.
>
> It might not be dynamite: especially since Mr. Fatty thought it was.
>
> What was it?

> He opened his shirt and buttoned it in. He thought he might take it up to his room. It was this; not a bird that knew how to talk. The sandpile was before him now. He planed away the hot layer and sat down. He held still for awhile, while nothing was ticking. Nothing but the crickets. Nothing but the train going through, ticking its two cars over the Big Black Bridge.

After Loch's retrieval of the intended sacrifice, a recessional is sounded, and the characters return to their normal everyday lives; but for a minute there has been the possibility of a sacrifice of the active center of the universe, and Loch Morrison has been the one who has taken the blessed sacrificial object into his own breast. This story, like those preceding it, has the smooth surface of the quotidian, but the ritual is that of the burnt offering. As the reader moves through the apparently casual detail, he begins to respond to a ritualistic order that Miss Welty imposes on Loch Morrison's observation of life. He is the audience to a ceremony that brings the assurance of an ordered universe to the agonized Miss Eckhart, and through her burnt offering to Loch and the reader.

The third story in the collection, **"Sir Rabbit,"** is a light-hearted, ritualistic mid-summer revel. In a very irreverent story Mattie-Will Sojourner romps in the woods with the twins Ran and Eugene, then with their father, while her future husband, Junior, sleeps in the woods. The effect on Mattie-Will is a massive broadening of her vision, on the reader the involvement in a positive affirmation of the physical life of summer abundance.

The next story, however, also occurring in July, is a more serious one. **"Moon Lake,"** probably the central story of the seven, deals with the ceremony of baptism. But the baptism is far from the thin ritual of many contemporary Protestant churches. An orphan girl, Easter, goes through a number of experiences at a summer camp where other girls from Morgana are in residence. She is the one who is carefully pampered, catechized, anointed, so that she may be committed to the depths as a sacrificial victim. Those involved in the sacrifice-baptism are unaware toward what they are proceeding, even as the unsuspecting reader who moves through the detailed ritual preparatory to the immersion. But the efficacy of the ritual is heightened by this unconscious progress toward a cleansing.

Loch Morrison, the boy-scout life-saver, fulfills his role of savior, too, not knowing what he has done; but at the conclusion of the story he stands in a position reminiscent of Cellini's statue of Perseus holding the Medusa's head. There is no doubt at the conclusion of the story that Easter and Loch have both been reborn through a descent into Moon Lake. Their submission to the destructive element has led to their final salvation.

After this story of baptism come a pair of stories that deal with the two MacLain sons, one with Ran and one with Eugene. Both of these are in the form of confessions made in August. Ran's confession is that of a man who has had the possibility of becoming a hero, but in his denial of the meaning of life he has missed his chance. Eugene, on the other hand, makes a confession to a Spanish guitarist who does not understand a word of English, but his confession is nevertheless an efficacious one. As a result, at the conclusion of his confession, he struggles in a physical way on the edge of an archetypal cliff with the high priest who has heard his confession and returns to the everyday world that he has left with a renewed love and tenderness, ready to receive the sacramental supper his wife has prepared for him.

The final story, occurring in October, deals with another conception of a hero. Virgie Raney has returned home from her wandering because of the death of her mother, Kate Raney, who told the first story in the collection. What we see demonstrated here is what Welty has said about plot, that the search is more important than the discovery. Those who remain safely blind in Morgana are now dying, tired and empty; but Virgie and Eugene and King, the people who have wandered through the physical universe seeking, have prepared themselves for a meaning that is mystically poured upon them by the natural world to which they have been receptive. At the conclusion of the story, Virgie, responsive to the death of her mother, has immersed herself in the Big Black River and felt the slimy things from below the surface crawl over her sensitive skin. She is now ready to sit in the autumnal rain and feel its fertilizing power. She is, in short, worthy to be the mother of the next culture hero. In spite of her fleshly involvement, she has maintained a spiritual virginity that is really a receptivity to life worthy of a blessed virgin. She sits on a stile in the October rain beside an old Negro woman, and the two of them are liberated from the temporal bonds of the culture which surrounds them:

> She smiled once, seeing before her, screenlike, the hideous and delectable face Mr. King MacLain made at the funeral, and when they all knew that he was next—even he. Then she and the old beggar woman, the old black thief, were there alone and together in the shelter of a big public tree, listening to the magical percussion, the world beating in their ears. They heard through falling rain the running of the horse and bear, the stroke of the leopard, the dragon's crusty slither, and the glimmer and the trumpet of the swan.

What we have here is what Miss Welty and her audience both hope for, an opportunity to suspend temporarily allegiance to the temporary world and listen to the mythic power of the natural world, the mythic power symbolized in the last sentence by characters from Germanic, classical, and English mythic systems. With the intricacy of an arabesque, Miss Welty weaves the mundane and the mythic. The trivial detail takes on significance because of its place in a cosmic whole. The ornate prose and the ornate symbol grace the summer camping experiences and lead the readers to awareness of the deep ritualistic possibilities in every life.

But the mundane-mythic system is not the total answer. This search takes no single direction to salvation or truth. What Welty has rehearsed in these stories is a glorious anti-orthodox religious celebration, a celebration of the validity of the natural life as opposed to the culturally limited life. By taking a culture and looking deeply into it, Miss Welty has, with her readers, dived beneath the depths of the Big Black; and, when she has arisen, she has taken upon herself the possibility of being the Blessed Virgin, the transmitter of the God that is in us all. (pp. 38-43)

William M. Jones, "The Plot as Search," in Studies in Short Fiction, *Vol. V, No. 1, Fall, 1967, pp. 37-43.*

JOHN EDWARD HARDY (essay date 1968)

[*Hardy is an American poet and critic. In the following excerpt, he explores Welty's unsentimental depiction of the absurd and her treatment of racial issues.*]

Welty's mind not only visits, but takes up residence with, goes adventuring with, in total unselfconsciousness, people of an astonishing social variety. Mississippi alone, to be sure, offers her a wide enough range—from the houses of the Jackson bourgeoisie to Greenwood or Greenville and plantation environs, by way of the beauty parlors and hotels of the highway towns, and the cabins of the river-rats and the sharecroppers, white and black. I, for one, am not as unhappy as some critics have claimed to be even about the "tourist" stories of ***The Bride of the Innisfallen.*** She has, of course, an extraordinarily fine "ear," one of the most sensitive in modern literature. But it is more than idiom; the ear leads to the mind. Miss Welty's frequent stand-ins are readily enough recognizable. She has made no effort to conceal them—Laura of *Delta Wedding,* Dicey of **"Kin,"** etc. But let us think only of the stories in which no such character appears. It would be extremely difficult to demonstrate that her treatment of Ruby Fisher in **"A Piece of News"** is either more or less essentially sympathetic, or, on the other hand, more or less objective, detached, than her rendering of Mrs. Larkin in **"A Curtain of Green."** In short, Miss Welty has fully recognized, and come fully to terms with, the reality of people other than her "own sort." For whom, I would ask, is that likely to be a more difficult realization than for a well-bred, upper-middle class Mississippian, male or female?

She has faced, too, and unflinchingly, the reality of the absurd. No modern writer has accepted with greater calmness than hers the diminished stature of man in the universe, and, having accepted it, more "thoughtfully" set about, in Mlle de Beauvoir's phrases, "reconsidering," "re-creating," the "ambiguity," the "abyss," the "mystery" which is the truth of human experience. . . . Let us consider two stories in which murder actually occurs.

Traditionally—I mean, from any point of view which supposes man's belonging to a community of moral purpose and responsibility—murder is the most absurd of actions. And, at least in the emotional responses demanded by the stories, Miss Welty fully recognizes that traditional view in **"Flowers for Marjorie"** and **"The Hitch-Hikers."** The descriptive details are not especially grisly; she understates, as always. But the blood-terror is unmistakably evoked. And the terror of the inexplicable.

Yet, however strongly one wants to protest that it is Marjorie's death that is "not possible," rather than, as her husband has been thinking a few minutes before, her pregnant life—". . . while he drew deep breaths of the cloverlike smell of her tightening skin and her swollen thighs. . . . Why, this is not possible! he was thinking."—Howard is vindicated at the end. A false clue has been deliberately provided at the beginning. Before stabbing his wife with the butcher-knife, Howard momentarily entertains a lively fantasy of snatching a daisy from the buttonhole of her coat and throwing it on the floor to stamp it to pieces. The discovery that this violence has been an hallucination leaves the reader, and, presumably, Howard, to wonder throughout the subsequent action whether the murder too hasn't been a fantasy. But, no, the corpse and the smashed clock are still there when Howard returns from his day of terrifying, "lucky" adventures—hitting the jackpot on the slot-machine, as the ten-millionth person through the turnstile of Radio City receiving the bouquet of roses and the key to the city. Finally, in a world of experience that consists entirely of *seem,* of dreams seemingly come true, the fact of the murder is the only dependable truth, the only dream really brought whole and irrevocable into the clear light of day. Insupportable, perhaps, emotionally; morally inexplicable; but undeniable.

"Flowers for Marjorie" suffers somewhat from contrivance—the series of coincidences and a clutter of object symbols—the result of an intrusive satiric purpose. **"The Hitch-Hikers"** is not so encumbered, and leaves us with a purer sense of the absurd in its conclusion. The enigma in the killing itself is identical with the lack of detective-story "mystery." The quiet one of the pair of hitch-hikers, the man called Sobby, readily admits having killed his loquacious companion and sarcastically points out the irrelevance of his being questioned on the matter, since there were a number of eye-witnesses. The "motive," too, is clear enough. The victim, Sobby says, "was uppity. . . . He bragged. He carried a gittar around." There remains some question as to which of the two had the idea of running off with Harris's car. Sobby "whimpers," in self-defensive afterthought, that it was the guitar-player. But there is no way of proving the point, one way or the other; and, indeed, it is never clear whether there really was a proposal, by either or both, to steal the car in the first place. The intention of theft might well have been invented by one of the by-standers—the woman in the crowd who is "explaining it all," probably to her husband, as Harris comes on the scene—and then adopted by Sobby for obvious reasons. One question cancels out the other. And with everything so neatly and quickly "explained" for police purposes, there is absolutely no way of getting at the human truth of the incident.

But the killing is only accessory, of course, to our central interest in Harris, the traveling salesman. It is Harris's story. And the effect of the episode for him is simply to focus his awareness of his lifelong inability to become involved. Everybody knows Harris. He is much in demand. He is, as one of the guests at the party puts it, "the famous 'he' that everybody talks about all the time." It would seem even that the girl named Carol, who comes to see him after the party, is in love with him—or thinks she is. But it is as if all of his experience, climaxed now by the murder of the hitch-hiker in his car, were somehow accidental—never the consequence of any clearly definable intention on his part, and never affecting his life thereafter. He does not witness the murder, which occurs while he is inside the hotel trying to find a place for the two hitch-hikers to stay. And it is clear that he is not to be held in any way responsible. It is not, in effect, really Harris who is involved in the episode of the murder, but only his car, which all the townspeople immediately recognize, with "the out-of-town license and . . . all the stuff he all time carries around with him, all bloody." But Harris might seem to feel at times that he has no identity apart from the car. He is as anonymous as the two hitch-hikers themselves, murderer and victim. He is, in fine, [Albert Camus's] Stranger.

And yet, if there is no blinking the facts of deprivation, no sentimental reassurance, a further measure precisely of Miss Welty's realism, it seems to me, is the dignity with which she endows her heroes of the absurd. If, indeed, the whole world of **"Flowers for Marjorie"** is a world of dreams, and always more or less bad dreams, at least Howard has, in Charles Marlow's words, "a choice of nightmares." In the vulgar imagination, hitting the jackpot and being the ten-millionth person to go through the turnstile of Radio City are the ultimate "dreams come true." But Howard instinctively flees these meretricious and dehumanizing satisfactions. It is only when he has returned to the apartment and found the body of his wife that the cliché phrase occurs, ironically, *because* it is cliché, underlining the verity of the awe and wonder he then feels. "It was just as he had feared, just as he had dreamed. He had had a dream to come true."

Finally, in both these stories Miss Welty recognizes—again, not sentimentally, but merely realistically—a dimension of the absurd that is beyond most writers in the mode. I mean, the absurd persistence of hope beyond the individual disaster, a hope that attaches to, or is inherent in, the capacity of physical objects to survive the death or despair of their users. At the end of **"Flowers for Marjorie,"** as Howard starts back for the last time to the apartment, accompanied by the policeman he has summoned, the bouquet of roses he was given at Radio City begins to fall apart. But he has earlier noticed a crowd of children playing on the street, and now—"When the roses slid from Howard's fingers and fell on their heads all along the sidewalk the little girls ran stealthily up and put them in their hair." In **"The Hitch-Hikers"** the statement of the motif is identical with the assertion of Harris's final dignity. Harris recognizes, and accepts, the fact of his incapacity for involvement, of his anonymity and radical irresponsibility. But he accepts it without bitterness, with a kindly commonsense. For the absurdity of his encounter with the hitch-hikers has, after all, left something in his custody—the dead man's guitar. And if that is of no value to him, if he does not want it, by the same token he is in no position to dispute the claim of anyone who does want it. Thus, when at the end of the story the little Negro boy asks him—"Does you want the box?. . . the po' kilt man's gittar. Even the policemans didn't want it"—Harris answers simply "No," and hands it over. In so doing, he avows, on behalf of Miss Welty, a responsibility that does not defy recognition of the absurd in human experience, but which has that recognition, rather, as its sole justification.

In conclusion, we may consider Miss Welty's confrontation of the racial problem. There is no other modern American writer, not even Faulkner, who has been so intensely and responsibly alert to the significance of the Negro's presence in our society as Eudora Welty has been. (pp. 272-76)

[What] I want principally to emphasize now is Miss Welty's intellectual independence in continuing to see the Negro as a very special *kind* of human being, at the same time that she has, from the beginning, insisted upon his humanity. . . . [Seymour L.] Gross used the phrase "from stereotype to archetype" to describe the evolution of the Negro's image in our national literature from Colonial times to the present. In general, the description is accurate enough. But I suspected from the outset that some Negro readers of the book might see little to cheer about in the indicated "enlightenment" of our new generation of white writers. . . . In brief, what a great many Negro intellectuals seem to feel is that "archetype" may well be but a more highfalutin kind of "stereotype"—that "type" is still the most significant part of the word, and that what the white authors are still doing, though in ever more refined and subtle ways, is using the Negro as a bearer of spiritual burdens that are essentially products of the white man's cultural history. (p. 276)

Miss Welty [saw] as early as **"Powerhouse,"** how dangerous a presumption it is for the white to reach too eagerly for the man in the black, for the common human denominator—at least as dangerous as the more familiar folly of assuming there is no man there. A very recent story, in *The New Yorker* for November, 1966, ironically entitled **"The Demonstrators,"** explores further the painful mystery of the division of the races.

A white doctor in a small Mississippi town winds up a wearisome evening attending a Negro woman and her estranged common-law husband, who have fatally stabbed each other with the same ice-pick. Although the next day's account of the incident in the local newspaper asserts, with supporting statements from the mayor and the sheriff, that there was "No Racial Content Espied," the doctor's experience at the house of the dying woman has made him agonizingly aware of the new difficulties of communication that the Civil Rights movement has created. The doctor, it is made plain, is a decent and right-thinking, moderately "liberal" man—who has even suffered a mild ostracism on account of having entertained a bearded Eastern student who had come down on one of the freedom trains. But he is also tired, "so increasingly tired, so sick and even bored with the bitterness, the intractability that divided everybody and everything." And in a moment of near-hysterical exhaustion, on the way home, he suffers an excruciating nostalgia for the old order, "an assault of hope . . . merciless" that there might be "still allowed to everybody on earth *a self*—savage, death-defying, private." But it is clear from the conclusion of the story that if the nostalgia is to be turned into a true and responsible hope, creatively energizing, then the "self" must be radically re-defined.

I think Miss Welty suggests that it cannot be, if the Negroes are going to be let in on the search for it, quite the same old self that most modern thinkers have been after in the celebrated "quest for identity"—what is, essentially, the *lost* identity of Western man, i.e., the white man. For, of course, the Negro never had that identity to lose, because he hadn't the cultural history that produced it, and therefore cannot know what he is looking for if sent out to find it. Earlier in the evening of the fatal stabbings, the doctor has attended an old patient, a long-retired white schoolteacher, Miss Marcia Pope, who in her recurrent delirium is wont to repeat lines from literature—Shakespeare and the classics. The one passage specifically mentioned is the famous first line of the *Aeneid*. The story ends with the doctor's thinking once more of Miss Pope, early the next morning after he has read the newspaper account of the night's happenings. "He thought that in all Holden, as of now, only Miss Marcia Pope was able to take care of herself—or such was her own opinion." And we might remember that favorite quotation of the self-assured old schoolteacher—"arma virumque cano"—as an ironically appropriate motto for the story. Arms, indeed, and the man. But what arms, for the battle facing us, and who or what the man in question? Will the classical definitions, Miss Pope's opinions notwithstanding, hold?

I submit that it is a remarkable, and a remarkably courageous, creative intelligence which can raise such questions in response to the demands of our age upon the writer to "take a stand" on the racial issue. And I submit, further, that Miss Welty has that intelligence, and exercises it. . . . (pp. 277-78)

John Edward Hardy, "The Achievement of Eudora Welty," in The Southern Humanities Review, *Vol. 2, No. 3, Summer, 1968, pp. 269-78.*

ASHLEY BROWN (essay date 1969)

[Brown is a southern American critic. In the following excerpt, he places The Robber Bridegroom *within the tradition of the romance legend and traces the novella's major themes.]*

Miss Welty, who is of German Swiss descent on her father's side, has more feeling for European legends and *märchen* than other American writers of our time. She sometimes seems closer to Isak Dinesen than she does to her contemporaries in Mississippi. Recently a friend of mine in Connecticut, who has loved her stories for many years, told me that he never thinks of her as a Southern writer. Perhaps this chance remark points to an important feature of her work: as it moves toward romance, the less Southern it becomes. Her marvelous sense of the vernacular and her response to the local community (in such stories as **"Why I Live at the P.O."**) are unmistakably Southern. We know where we are as soon as her characters start talking. When she works in romance this is not altogether the case. So it is with Flaubert: his St. Julian, a typical romance hero, does not talk like Charles Bovary or Félicité, but Flaubert makes him as convincing as any resident of 19th Century Normandy. As Albert Thibaudet pointed out long ago, Flaubert has a particular *clef* (tonality) for each novel, and one can make a similar observation about Miss Welty's stories. Her stylistic range is considerable.

All the same, it is not easy to rewrite a European fairy tale like ***The Robber Bridegroom*** in an American setting. Having taken the story and set it along the Natchez Trace in the first years of the 19th Century, Miss Welty would hardly be content to tell it in a simple predictable fashion. She has drawn on some of the lore of this American frontier rather freely, and in fact the original story is transformed even in its outlines. In Grimm's version the miller's daughter goes into the woods in search of her suitor. As she approaches his solitary house she is warned, first by a bird, then an old woman, that she is in a murderers' den: ". . . death will be thy marriage." She hides behind a great cask and watches another victim brought in. After this second girl falls down dead, one of the murderers chops off her finger to get at a gold ring; it falls into the lap of the miller's daughter. She escapes to her father's house, where her suitor presents himself for the wedding. And that is the occasion when she tells her ghastly story and produces the finger with the gold ring. The bridegroom tries to escape, but he and his band are captured and executed.

This story even as it stands could be treated in more than one way. The girl's motives, for instance, could be complicated. . . . In general we like more subtle states of mind than those we get in the heroes of ballads and *märchen*. Readers of Dostoevsky and Proust and James, we are very much aware of the duplicities of human behavior. We accept the simplistic manner of the *märchen* only if it invites us to speculate on the terrors that haunt us as they once did anonymous peasants in an age of superstition. Grimm's stories (the best of them) have this permanent fascination.

Miss Welty, of course, is anything but simplistic here. She has, to begin with, established a kind of central intelligence in the girl's father. He is not a miller at all, but a rich "innocent" planter, Clement Musgrove, and much of the action is conveyed to us through his meditations. His second wife, Salome, is the wicked stepmother (Miss Welty works her in from Grimm's "Snow-White"). Her malice, however, cannot be altogether explained by envy. She is very ugly (the Indians are afraid of her looks), but at an important moment her hatred for the beautiful Rosamond turns to love. This would never happen in the *märchen*. And near the end, when Clement and his family are captured again by Indians and threatened with torture, Salome dances till she drops dead; for the second time Clement and Rosamond are saved. Clement's attitude towards her "destroyed heart" is clearly ambiguous.

The hero is a river bandit, Jamie Lockhart. He is wonderfully brave and adept, like all romance heroes, and he seems to come out of a springtime world of eternal youth. When we first meet him, he outfoxes the legendary giant, Mike Fink the flatboatman, and saves Clement. Mike Fink has a raven who sings, like the bird in Grimm, *"Turn back, my bonny, Turn away home."* But Fink deserts the raven, which then becomes Jamie's. (Romance heroes are frequently accompanied by animals or birds.) Clement, out of gratitude, invites Jamie to his house with the further intention of securing a husband for Rosamond. Jamie, however approaches Rosamond in disguise (his face stained by blackberry juice), kidnaps and seduces her. Later she finds him in his house with the robbers and lives with him. He never removes the berry stain and she is sad only because she doesn't see his face. "But then," says Miss Welty, "the heart cannot live without something to sorrow and be curious over."

Nothing goes according to expectation in this story. Clement rides through the forest (the typical setting for romance) in search of his daughter's abductor—he doesn't yet realize that it is the dashing Jamie. He wrestles all night with a "monster," which turns out by daylight to be a willow tree. When Rosamond returns to him he relents, and the speech he makes at this moment is central to the meaning of the book:

> "If being a bandit were his breadth and scope, I should find him and kill him for sure," said he. "But since in addition he loves my daughter, he must be not one man, but two, and I should be afraid of killing the second. For all things are double, and this should keep us from taking liberties with the outside world, and acting too quickly to finish things off. All things are divided in half—night and day, the soul and body, and sorrow and joy and youth and age, and sometimes I wonder if even my own wife has not been the one person all the time, and I loved her beauty so well at the beginning that it is only now that the ugliness has struck through to beset me like a madness. And perhaps after the riding and robbing and burning and assault is over with this man you love, he will step out of it all like a beastly skin, and surprise you with his gentleness. . . ."

Some readers will observe a resemblance between the situation here and the one in that consummate romance, *The Tempest*. Clement is momentarily bent on revenge, like Prospero, but his gentle nature prevails and his main purpose is to "educate" his daughter in the ways of humanity. Unlike Prospero, his powers are limited. (Since he is the central intelligence in a novel, he must earn his sad wisdom through experience; in this respect he is closer to Adam Verver in *The Golden Bowl* than he is to Prospero.)

Rosamond is not as innocent as Miranda, either. Like Miranda she has to contend with a spirit of earth, in this case the ruttish white-trash boy named Goat. Nobody can control him. But Goat is not really important to the action. The relationship between Rosamond and Jamie is Miss Welty's primary subject. When Rosamond returns to the house of the robbers Jamie is absent. His place is taken momentarily by the cruel bandit Little Harp, "the ugliest man she had ever seen." She hides behind a barrel, like the miller's daughter, and witnesses the sacrifice of an Indian girl (the story re-creates Grimm precisely here). Jamie appears. In the night as he sleeps she secretly removes the blackberry stain with a formula given her by Salome and thus identifies him. This he cannot stand: "For you did not trust me, and did not love me, for you wanted only to know who I am. Now I cannot stay in the house with you." At this point Miss Welty shifts her perspective, as it were, and moves us out of Grimm into the Hellenistic myth of Cupid and Psyche. Like the solitary Psyche, who is abandoned by the lover after she has made the mistake of looking on his beauty, she wanders the earth in search of him. (Perhaps Miss Welty read the story in *The Golden Ass* of Apuleius, Books IV-VI; there it is told by an old woman to amuse a girl held by robbers.) Eventually, like Psyche, she finds and marries the young god, but only after overcoming certain obstacles.

In the great climactic scene, which brings together all the characters in the forest, everyone is put to the test. Each in turn, Clement, Salome, Little Harp, Rosamond, then Jamie, is captured by the Indians, who intend to put them to death in retribution for the murdered girl. Most of them are guilty of self-pity, and each one except Jamie cries out to the wilderness in his solitary anguish. (Mr. Warren's "Love and Separateness in Eudora Welty" [see excerpt dated 1944] is very relevant here.) Clement, as usual, transcends the situation:

> . . . And even the appearance of a hero is no longer a single and majestic event like that of a star in the heavens, but a wandering fire soon lost. A journey is forever lonely and parallel to death, but the two watch each other, the traveler and the bandit, through the trees. Like will-o'-the-wisps the little blazes burn on the rafts all night, unsteady beside the shore. Where are they even so soon as tomorrow? Massacre is hard to tell from the performances of other rites, in the great silence where the wanderer is coming. Murder is soundless as a spout of blood, as regular and rhythmic as sleep. Many find a skull and a little branching of bones between the two floors of leaves. In the sky is the perpetual wheel of buzzards. A circle of bandits counts out the gold, with bending shoulders more slaves mount the block and go down, a planter makes a gesture of abundance with his riding whip, a flatboatman falls back from the tavern door to the river below with scarcely time for a splash, a rope descends from a tree and curls into a noose. And all around again are the Indians.

This superb passage has something of the quality of a choral ode. It properly generalizes the action and is no more external to it than, say, Addie Bundren's speech in *As I Lay Dying*. It accompanies the movement of summer into autumn, which is proper to romance, and prepares for the conclusion.

The characters are now confronted with the grossest kind of reality. The amoral Goat offers to release all the prisoners. Rosamond lies to him (compromising her dedication to Jamie) and is thus saved. Jamie is rescued and kills Little Harp. Salome shrieks her defiance of nature, dares to stop the sun, even as she dances to her death. And again the Indians pity Clement, a widower for the second time.

As Little Harp and probably Salome have known for some time, Jamie's other self is a New Orleans gentleman. Clement's speech on doubleness midway in the book of course prepares for this possibility. As for Rosamond, she makes her way to New Orleans, where she sees Jamie just about to embark on a ship going to Zanzibar. He takes her home and marries her on the way. "And indeed it was in time's nick." So she comes to her happy reward. And nobody is happier than Clement as he sees her the following spring with her beautiful twins in her great house on the shores of Lake Ponchartrain. As for Jamie,

> . . . the outward transfer from bandit to merchant had been almost too easy to count it a change at all, and he was enjoying all the same success he had ever had. But now, in his heart Jamie knew that he was a hero and had always been one, only with the power to look both ways and to see a thing from all sides.

The Robber Bridegroom, then, turns on questions of identity, as several commentators have noted. The romantic mode allows. Miss Welty to deal with the doubleness of human nature as cogently as tragedy or comedy would have. This is ironic, because traditionally the romance celebrates the hero with scarcely any qualifications. But Miss Welty is post-Jamesian and cannot accept the simplicities of behavior that would have satisfied, say, Spenser. Her Clement (again like Adam Verver) *feels* more deeply the vicissitudes of other people's lives than Merlin or Prospero (the "old wise men" so often found in romance). This little novel fulfills the mode almost pefectly, and probably readers today . . . will be able to approach it more easily than they did a generation ago. (pp. 31-5)

Ashley Brown, "Eudora Welty and the Mythos of Summer," in Shenandoah, *Vol. XX, No. 3, Spring, 1969, pp. 29-35.*

LEE J. RICHMOND (essay date 1971)

[Richmond, an American critic, examines values and symbolism in Welty's "Petrified Man."]

One of the most pitiless indictments of the venal spirit of modern civilization is constructed by Eudora Welty in **"Petrified Man."** The corruption of love is at the core of the story. This theme is developed primarily by a spate of soil-flavored dialog which, ironically, allows the two principal characters, Leota, a beautician, and Mrs. Fletcher, her customer, to damn themselves unavoidably. With the objective ear of a tape recorder, Welty collects starkly the self-defeating speeches of two women whose vanity, deceit, betrayal, envy, jealousy, and material obsession are inflexible. Not a single line is uttered by either which would redeem them of their relentless exercise of self-love.

The beauty shop setting lends itself ideally to a lively exchange of gossip and perjury. Moreover, it is one of the three pivotal symbols which vivify the story's theme. From a place which women visit to beautify themselves, the beauty shop is transformed by Welty into a place where the ugliest features of these women's inner selves are revealed. Mrs. Fletcher's vanity is taken to task early by Leota's half-spiteful admonition: "Hair fallin'." Later, Mrs. Fletcher's rejection of true beauty through having a baby is linked again with this vanity of her external appearance when Leota suggests that falling hair is problematic to some women who are pregnant. That she is pregnant is a bane to Mrs. Fletcher's existence: "Well! I don't like children that much. . . . I'm almost tempted not to have this one." Obviously, her reason is related to a fear of losing her looks. She implies that Mr. Fletcher—who, like the other males in the story, comes through indirectly as a milquetoast—is as unfeeling as she is about this matter. Further, Mrs. Fletcher had even considered getting an abortion with or without her husband's consent:

> "I said you sure can tell it when I'm sitting straight on and coming at you this way," Mrs. Fletcher said.
>
> "Why, honey, naw you can't," said Leota gloomily. "Why, I'd never know. If somebody was to come up to me on the street and say, 'Mrs. Fletcher is pregnant!' I'd say, 'Heck, she don't look it to me'."
>
> "If a certain party hadn't found it out and spread it around, it wouldn't be too late even now," said Mrs. Fletcher frostily.

Her self-indulgence has made a parody of modern marriage:

> Mrs. Fletcher sat up straight. "Mr. Fletcher can't do a thing with me. . . . If he so much as raises his voice against me, he knows good and well I'll have one of my sick headaches, and then I'm not fit to live with. . . ."

Marital tyranny, then, is added to her catalog of failings. And in a denial of Mrs. Pike's youthfulness (Mrs. Pike is the initiator of the rumor of the pregnancy), she affirms her jealous, mean-spirited nature.

All of these details about Mrs. Fletcher are presented as she insistently watches herself in the mirror. This second key symbol correlates precisely with the pervasive egoism which informs her dialog and, accordingly, Welty's oblique characterization of her. She is interested only in external beauty. The beautiful miracle of childbearing is an odious sacrifice.

Leota, too, is emotionally malformed. Her envy and betrayal of friends, her idle gossiping, and her materialism make her function as a creator of beauty grossly ironic. One of her speeches, concerning a fortune-teller, discloses covertly her spite towards a former beau and her self-deception about her true mercenary nature:

> "So I ast Lady Evangeline for one of my questions, was he happily married, and she says, just like she was glad I ask her, 'Honey,' she says, 'naw, he isn't. You write down this day, March 8, 1941,' she says, 'and mock it down: three years from today him and her won't be occupyin' the same bed.' There it is, up on the wall with them other dates—see, Mrs. Fletcher? And she says, 'Child, you ought to be glad you didn't git him, because he's so mercenary.' So I'm glad I married Fred. He sure ain't mercenary, money don't mean a thing to him. But I sure would like to go back and have my other palm read."

Fred, like Mr. Fletcher, is a foil. He is literally supported by his wife: another travesty of the inversion of meaningful human relationships in Welty's vision.

It is through Leota that the third, and most potent, symbol of the fiction is elaborated. With great gusto, she tells Mrs. Fletcher about the travelling freak show in town. The Siamese twins and pygmies delight her. But it is the petrified man that gratifies most her sadistic energies: "But they got this man, this petrified man, that ever'thing ever since he was nine years old, when it goes to his joints has been turning to stone." It is this "freak" that discloses her resentment towards and rejection of her "friends," the Pikes. Quite by accident her boarder, Mrs. Pike, identifies in *Startling G-Man Tales* the petrified man as a wanted man, the rapist Mr. Petrie. Leota is glum in her ill-fortune:

> "So Mr. Pike says, 'Well whatta you know about that,' an' he looks real hard at the photo and whistles. And she starts dancin' and singin' about their good luck. She meant our bad luck! I made a point of tellin' that fortune-teller the next time I saw her. I said, 'Listen, that magazine was layin' around the house for a month, and there was the freak show runnin' night an' day, not two steps away from my own beauty parlor, with Mr. Petrie just settin' there waitin'. An' it had to be Mr. and Mrs. Pike, almost perfect strangers'."

To her, the four women Mr. Petrie raped were "worth a hundred an' twenty-five bucks a piece." Leota's mortification at losing the five-hundred dollars supersedes either her friendship with the Pikes (who themselves are unyielding in their cynicism) or her imaginative sympathy towards the mentally-disturbed Mr. Petrie.

The image of the petrified man is Welty's most ambitious symbolic projection. By the story's end, the perceptive reader is aware that the title, with its purposeful omission of the article "the," relates to Leota and Mrs. Fletcher. Their hearts are stony, rigid, impenetrable. They are the "freaks" outside the traveling show. By extension, of course, Welty's indictment of them is expressive of a culture which bets on appearances, on callousness, and on material values. The last paragraphs show the women frantically in pursuit of Mrs. Pike's son, Billy Boy. His speech ends the dark comedy and reveals the terrible legacy which an adult world leaves to its young: "If you're so smart, why ain't you rich?" The theme of spiritual pertification is embodied devastatingly in a child's ingenuous, yet prophetic, words. (pp. 1201-03)

Lee J. Richmond, "Symbol and Theme in Eudora Welty's 'Petrified Man'," in English Journal, *Vol. 60, No. 9, December, 1971, pp. 1201-03.*

EUDORA WELTY (essay date 1974)

[In the following essay, originally published in 1974, Welty explains the significance of her story "The Worn Path."]

A story writer is more than happy to be read by students; the fact that these serious readers think and feel something in response to his work he finds life-giving. At the same time he may not always be able to reply to their specific questions in kind. I wondered if it might clarify something, for both the questioners and myself, if I set down a general reply to the question that comes to me most often in the mail, from both students and their teachers, after some classroom discussion. The unrivaled favorite is this: "Is Phoenix Jackson's grandson really *dead*?"

It refers to a short story I wrote years ago called **"A Worn Path,"** which tells of a day's journey an old woman makes on foot from deep in the country into town and into a doctor's office on behalf of her little grandson; he is at home, periodically ill, and periodically she comes for his medicine; they give it to her as usual, she receives it and starts the journey back.

I had not meant to mystify readers by withholding any fact; it is not a writer's business to tease. The story is told through Phoenix's mind as she undertakes her errand. As the author at one with the character as I tell it, I must assume that the boy is alive. As the reader, you are free to think as you like, of course: the story invites you to believe that no matter what happens, Phoenix for as long as she is able to walk and can hold to her purpose will make her journey. The *possibility* that she would keep on even if he were dead is there in her devotion and its single-minded, single-track errand. Certainly the *artistic* truth, which should be good enough for the fact, lies in Phoenix's own answer to that question. When the nurse asks, "He isn't dead, is he?" she speaks for herself: "He still the same. He going to last."

The grandchild is the incentive. But it is the journey, the going of the errand, that is the story, and the question is not whether the grandchild is in reality alive or dead. It doesn't affect the outcome of the story or its meaning from start to finish. But it is not the question itself that has struck me as much as the idea, almost without exception implied in the asking, that for Phoenix's grandson to be dead would somehow make the story "better."

It's *all right,* I want to say to the students who write to me, for things to be what they appear to be, and for words to mean what they say. It's all right, too, for words and appearances to mean more than one thing—ambiguity is a fact of life. A fiction writer's responsibility covers not only what he presents as the facts of a given story but what he chooses to stir up as their implications; in the end, these implications, too, become facts, in the larger, fictional sense. But it is not all right, not in good faith, for things *not* to mean what they say.

The grandson's plight was real and it made the truth of the story, which is the story of an errand of love carried out. If the child no longer lived, the truth would persist in the "wornness" of the path. But his being dead can't increase the truth of the story, can't affect it one way or the other. I think I signal this, because the end of the story has been reached before old Phoenix gets home again: she simply starts back. To the question "Is the grandson really dead?" I could reply that it doesn't make any difference. I could also say that I did not make him up in order to let him play a trick on Phoenix. But my best answer would be: "*Phoenix* is alive."

The origin of a story is sometimes a trustworthy clue to the author—or can provide him with the clue—to its key image; maybe in this case it will do the same for the reader. One day I saw a solitary old woman like Phoenix. She was walking; I saw her, at middle distance, in a winter country landscape, and watched her slowly make her way across my line of vision. That sight of her made me write the story. I invented an errand for her, but that only seemed a living part of the figure she was herself: what errand other than for someone else could be making her go? And her going was the first thing, her persisting in her landscape was the real thing, and the first and the real were what I wanted and worked to keep. I brought her up close enough, by imagination, to describe her face, make her present to the eyes, but the full-length figure moving across the winter fields was the indelible one and the image to keep, and the perspective extending into the vanishing distance the true one to hold in mind.

I invented for my character, as I wrote, some passing adventures—some dreams and harassments and a small triumph or two, some jolts to her pride, some flights of fancy to console her, one or two encounters to scare her, a moment that gave her cause to feel ashamed, a moment to dance and preen—for it had to be a *journey,* and all these things belonged to that, parts of life's uncertainty.

A narrative line is in its deeper sense, of course, the tracing out of a meaning, and the real continuity of a story lies in this probing forward. The real dramatic force of a story depends on the strength of the emotion that has set it going. The emotional value is the measure of the reach of the story. What gives any such content to **"A Worn Path"** is not its circumstances but its *subject:* the deep-grained habit of love.

What I hoped would come clear was that in the whole surround of this story, the world it threads through, the only certain thing at all is the worn path. The habit of love cuts through confusion and stumbles or contrives its way out of difficulty, it remembers the way even when it forgets, for a dumbfounded moment, its reason for being. The path is the thing that matters.

Her victory—old Phoenix's—is when she sees the diploma in the doctor's office, when she finds "nailed up on the wall the document that had been stamped with the gold seal and framed in the gold frame, which matched the dream that was hung up in her head." The return with the medicine is just a matter of retracing her own footsteps. It is the part of the journey, and of the story, that can now go without saying.

In the matter of function, old Phoenix's way might even do as a sort of parallel to your way of work if you are a writer of stories. The way to get there is the all-important, all-absorbing problem, and this problem is your reason for undertaking the story. Your only guide, too, is your sureness about your subject, about what this subject is. Like Phoenix, you work all your life to find your way, through all the obstructions and the false appearances and the upsets you may have brought on yourself, to reach a meaning—using inventions of your imagination, perhaps helped out by your dreams and bits of good luck. And finally too, like Phoenix, you have to assume that what you are working in aid of is life, not death.

But you would make the trip anyway—wouldn't you?—just on hope. (pp. 159-62)

Eudora Welty, "Is Phoenix Jackson's Grandson Really Dead?" in her The Eye of the Story: Selected Essays and Reviews, *Vintage Books, 1979, pp. 159-62.*

REYNOLDS PRICE (essay date 1980)

[*Price is a renowned southern American novelist and critic. In the following excerpt from a review of Welty's* Collected Stories, *he praises the vitality and diversity of her short fiction.*]

[Eudora Welty's has been] a long performance . . . and one which, though it has never lacked praise and devoted readers, has presented critics with the kind of fearless emotional intensity, the fixed attention to daily life, and the technical audacity that have mercilessly revealed the poverty of scholastic critical methods. In the 1940s the lucid early stories and *Delta Wedding* were automatically accused of gothicism and indifference to the plight of southern blacks. The connected stories of ***The Golden Apples*** set off a dismal and apparently endless hunt for mythological underpinning (a curse that the stories innocently brought on themselves). The internalized experiments of the long stories of the 1950s met with general bafflement. Though prizes descended and though a handful of stories were rushed into most anthologies while Welty fans around the land stood ready to burst into recitations from **"Petrified Man"** or **"A Shower of Gold,"** it was only with Ruth Vande Kieft's discerning *Eudora Welty* in 1962 [see excerpt dated 1962] that the size of the achievement began to be acknowledged and mapped—the size and the peculiar pitfalls of the stories as objects for contemplation, guides to action.

The difficulties are big, both of matter and of manner. As the center of critical power shifted in the 1950s from the south to the northeast, a vestigial resistance to southern fiction quickly enlarged and hardened. The south had had too long an inning as Literary Central; its writers were obsessed with the ruling classes of a society rotten with greed and racist inhumanity (as though Tolstoy, Flaubert, or Bellow had more exemplary subjects). Thus Welty's Christian white ladies and their ineffectual mates, her resigned fieldhands and maids, her garrulous white trash, were obstacles for a high proportion of trained readers. And no native southern critics of distinction rose in succession to Ransom, Tate, and Warren to mediate such work to the nation. But even more daunting than the unabashed southern grounding of the work was the statement at its center, a quiet reiterated statement that declared two polar yet indissoluble things. Most disturbing of all, the statement proved itself by locating characters and actions of recognizable solidity and pursuing them with a gaze that occasionally seemed serpentine in its steadiness—or angelic (as in angel of judgment). On first acquaintance one might be tempted to link the Welty of the stories with an apparent progenitor and paraphrase the statement by quoting D. H. Lawrence's essay on Poe—"A ghastly disease love. Poe telling us of his disease: trying to make his disease fair and attractive. Even succeeding."

If we substitute *Homo sapiens* for Poe we do have a crucial beam for the scaffolding of any of Welty's stories. The fact was realized in other terms in Robert Penn Warren's important early essay ["Love and Separateness in Miss Welty"; see excerpt dated 1944]. For the stories from first to last do say this clearly: "Human creatures are compelled to seek one another in the hope of forming permanent bonds of mutual service, not primarily from an instinct to continue the species" (children are only minor players in her cast), "but from a profound hunger, mysterious in cause, for individual gift and receipt of mutual care." ("Tenderness" is Welty's most sacred word.) "So intense is the hunger however that, more often than not, it achieves no more than its own frustration—the consumption and obliteration of one or both of the mates." (The words "bitter" and "shriek" occur as frequently, and weightily, as "tenderness.")

To that extent, Poe or even Strindberg is a truer ancestor to the stories than Virginia Woolf or E. M. Forster, who have often been mentioned. But such whimsical genealogies are of interest only to literary historians. They give little help to a reader whose aim is the enjoyment of and kinetic response to fiction that is so obviously the report of a particular pair of eyes on a particular place. For the dense matrix of observed life—mineral, bestial, human—which surrounds Welty's statement of the doomed circularity of love is the source of her originality, the flavor which quickly distinguishes a stretch of her prose from any other writer's.

> She knew that now at the river, where she had been before on moonlit nights in autumn, drunken and sleepless, mist lay on the water and filled the trees, and from the eyes to the moon would be a cone, a long silent horn, of white light. It was a connection visible as the hair is in air, between the self and the moon, to make the self feel the child, a daughter far, far back. Then the water, warmer than the night air or the self that might be suddenly cold, like any other arms, took the body under too, running without visibility into the mouth. As she would drift in the river, too alert, too insolent in her heart in those days, the mist might thin momentarily and brilliant jewel eyes would look out from the water-line and the bank. Sometimes in the weeds a lightning bug would lighten, on and off, on and off, for as long in the night as she was there to see.
>
> Out in the yard, in the coupe, in the frayed velour pocket next to the pistol was her cache of cigarettes. She climbed inside and shielding the matchlight, from habit, began to smoke cigarettes. All around her the dogs were barking. [**"The Wanderers"**]

Her monitoring senses record two main strands of data—the self-sufficient splendor of the natural world (in a number of American and European places) and the enciphered poetry of human thought and speech which rises, sometimes through fits of laughter, to moments of eloquently plain truth-telling. The first-written of the stories provides a pure example. In **"Death of a Traveling Salesman,"** the lost itinerant shoe-salesman comes suddenly to understand the fertile union of a couple in whose home he has harbored after an automobile accident.

> Bowman could not speak. He was shocked with knowing what was really in this house. A marriage, a fruitful marriage. That simple thing. Anyone could have had that.
>
> Somehow he felt unable to be indignant or protest, although some sort of joke had certainly been played upon him. There was nothing remote or mysterious here—only something private.

Such yearning for love is found in numerous other mouths in the stories, as character after character (male and female indifferently) reaches the boundary of illusion. But the second half of their repeated discovery is almost never spoken, by character or author. Only at the solitary ends of fated action do the characters perceive an inexorably closing circle. Having earned his vision, the salesman flees the scene of care and continuance and dies of heart failure, literally felled by his knowledge. Virgie Rainey at the end of **"The Wanderers"** is driven from her home and all she has known by the collapse of her dream of transcending love; and her first stopping place—perhaps her final destination—is a heightened awareness of the gorgeous nonhuman world that coils round our species (the only species, so far as we know, capable of contemplating that world). The casual pair who nearly connect in **"No Place for You, My Love"** are actually prevented by a watchful and judging world, the sunstruck land below New Orleans.

> At length he stopped the car again, and this time he put his arm under her shoulders and kissed her—not knowing ever whether gently or harshly. It was the loss of that distinction that told him this was now. Then their faces touched unkissing, unmoving, dark, for a length of time. The heat came inside the car and

> wrapped them still, and the mosquitoes had begun to coat their arms and even their eyelids.
>
> Later, crossing a large open distance, he saw at the same time two fires. He had the feeling that they had been riding for a long time across a face—great, wide, and upturned. In its eyes and open mouth were those fires they had had glimpses of, where the cattle had drawn together: a face, a head, far down here in the South—south of South, below it. A whole giant body sprawled downward then, on and on, always, constant as a constellation or an angel. Flaming and perhaps falling, he thought.

Similar ambush awaits the characters of her novels, though the greater length of a novel generally results in a more ambiguous, if not truer, statement. The stories preserve the naked cry—as sane, inevitable, and unanswerable as the evening call of a solitary beast from the edge of a wood.

No wonder that admirers of Welty's fiction have concentrated most of their scrutiny and affection on comic stories like **"Why I Live at the P.O."** or the numerous others that richly summon atmospheres of serene nature and the warm conglomerations of family life—weddings, funerals, reunions. The choice has been instinctive, a normal reflex of narrative hunger (which craves consolation, with small side-orders of fright or sadistic witness).

The favorites are certainly worthy. In previous American fiction, only Mark Twain displays as skillfully poised a comic gift, poised on the razor that divides compassion and savagery (Faulkner's comedy is oddly gentler). Welty's power over loving and tussling groups of kin gathered on magnetizeed family ground is matched only by the 19th-century Russians, as is her courage for the plain declaration of loyalty and duty. A story like **"A Worn Path"** is unimaginable in any hands but hers or Chekhov's (and it is only illustrative of my point that this uncomplicated tale of duty has evoked a blizzard of nutty mytho-symbolist explications). And her effortless entry into masculine minds as various as the traveling salesman, the younger salesman in **"The Hitch-Hikers,"** the young husband of **"The Wide Net,"** the black jazz-pianist of **"Powerhouse,"** and the majestically thoughtless King McClain of ***The Golden Apples*** is a sustaining assurance (in the presently gory gender wars) that the sexes can occasionally comprehend and serve one another if they choose to.

But such selective attention—and the popular anthologies have been as monotonous as her admirers—has resulted in a partial, even distorted, sense of Welty as the mild, sonorous, "affirmative" kind of artist whom America loves to clasp to its bosom and crush with belated honors (Robert Frost endured a similar reputation, but he had handmade it assiduously). It is one of the qualities of genius to provide wares for almost any brand of shopper—it has taken ages to wrestle Jane Austen from the chaste grip of the Janeites or Dickens from the port-and-Stilton set—and Welty's stories have, without calculation, stocked most departments. But such an embarrassment of choice endangers understanding. (pp. 31-4)

The breadth of Welty's offering is finally most visible not in the variety of types—farce, satire, horror, lyric, pastoral, mystery—but in the clarity and solidity and absolute honesty of a lifetime's vision. That it's a Janus-faced or Argus-eyed vision, I've also suggested—even at times a Gorgon stare. Yet its findings are not dealt out as one more of the decks of contradictory and generally appalling polaroids so prevalent in our fiction and verse. A slow perusal here—say a story a night for six weeks—will not fail to confirm a granite core in every tale: as complete and unassailable an image of human relations as any in our art, tragic of necessity but also comic (even the latest story, a chilling impersonation of the white assassin of a black civil rights leader, jokes to its end). As real a gift in our legacy as any broad river or all our lost battles. (p. 34)

Reynolds Price, in a review of "The Collected Stories of Eudora Welty," in The New Republic, *Vol. 183, No. 18, November 1, 1980, pp. 31-4.*

ELIZABETH EVANS (essay date 1981)

[Evans analyzes humor in Welty's work, placing it within the tradition of American humor and examining Welty's various comic techniques.]

The range of Miss Welty's comic devices includes many that are traditional in American humor. Disingenuous characters like Huckleberry Finn provide humor that stems from the disparity between the character's and the reader's understanding and judgment. Unaware of the humor she creates, Leota (in **"Petrified Man"**) sees nothing amiss in announcing to her ten o'clock shampoo-and-set customer, "Honey, them goobers has been in my purse a week if they's been in it a day." Utterly puzzled by his wife's suicide note, William Wallace Jamison (in **"The Wide Net"**) labors the point to his matter-of-fact friend Virgil. Since Hazel was in mortal fear of water, William Wallace cannot understand how she could kill herself by jumping into the river to drown. Virgil's explanation is deadpan: "Jumped backward. Didn't look."

Walter Blair and Hamlin Hill in *American Humor: From Poor Richard to Doonesbury,* note that "stretchers" were the essence of early American humor; and many of Miss Welty's comic characters fall with ease into stretching or exaggerating, especially Edna Earle, that indefatigable narrator of ***The Ponder Heart.*** Having described herself as "a great reader that never has time to read," she contradicts herself, claiming to have read *The House of a Thousand Candles* for the thousandth time. With Narciss at the wheel of the Studebaker, Uncle Daniel and Bonnie Dee Peacock, a clerk from Woolworth's, end up in Silver City to be married. Disgruntled over this unexpected turn of events, Edna Earle laments that Silver City "was the only spot in Creation they could have gone to without finding somebody that knew enough to call Clay 123 and I'd answer." From the details Edna Earle presents about the Peacock family's eating, the reader expects plump rather than pencil-slim characters, but she stretches things when she says Mrs. Peacock "was big and fat as a row of pigs." Leota exaggerates about recounting her love life to Mrs. Pike in **"Petrified Man"**—"I tole her ever'thing about ever'thing, from now on back to I don't know when—to when I first started goin' out." (pp. 23-4)

Like such Ring Lardner characters as the barber in "Haircut," Gullible in *Gullible's Travels, Etc.,* Jack Keefe in *You Know Me, Al,* and Fred Gross in *Own Your Own Home,* many of Miss Welty's comic narrators expose their warped natures as they disingenuously relate their deeds. While pathos and tragedy often follow close behind the comedy, her characters seldom are callous toward the feelings of others or indifferent to the well-being of family and friends (as Lardner's can be), although characters in **"Petrified Man"** and **"Why I Live at the P.O."** come close to viciousness. Her fiction never approaches the bitterness Mark Twain and many contemporary writers share—frustration over the damned human race. Intent on celebration, Eudora Welty's comic characters perpetuate family history by telling its stories and by participating in weddings, reunions, and funerals. Through these words and actions, they keep the past part of the present.

Homely figures of speech are staples throughout Miss Welty's fiction, and often the comparisons are amusing. Uncle Daniel cannot handle money and "giving it to him would be like giving matches to a child." The strange Spanish guitarist in **"Music from Spain"** flexed his long fingers along his thighs "like a cat testing her claws on a cushion." . . . In **"The Bride of Innisfallen,"** a schoolgirl joins others in the train compartment and her hat "hid her bent head like a candle snuffer." The somewhat mysterious lady in this group smoothed down her raincoat "with a rattle like the reckless slamming of bureau drawers." The sometime exhibitionist in **"June Recital,"** Mr. Voight, "ran up the steps with a sound like a green stick along a fence." King MacLain, that Zeus-Casanova, appears in **"Sir Rabbit"** standing "on top of the gully, wearing a yellowy Panama hat and a white linen suit with the sleeves as ridgy as two washboards." (pp. 25-6)

Comic migrations, the mixing of different social levels by moving characters from one region to another, occur as a major device in ***The Ponder Heart***. . . . The murder trail of Daniel Ponder has often been described as splendid comedy and as a jolt to the entire judicial system. Part of the comedy comes from the victim's family, the Peacocks, who have traveled from Polk to Clay for the trial. Edna Earle is sure that more of the family has showed up for Uncle Daniel's trial than showed up for Bonnie Dee's funeral; their mode of transportation, a pick-up truck. Amusing details of their dress and behavior quickly show the reader that the Peacocks are socially unacceptable to Clay residents. Mrs. Peacock wears new bedroom slippers with pompoms on the toes, and Mr. Peacock (face as red as a Tom turkey and not a tooth in his head) has on a new pair of pants—the tag still sticks out of one seam. Johnnie Rae Peacock is decked out in her dead sister's "telephone-putting-in costume—very warm for June." Taking up two rows in the courtroom, the Peacocks are all sizes and ages; they sit with gaping mouths and constantly go to the water fountain, which stopped working years ago. When court is interrupted while Miss Edna Earle's girl takes count for dinner at the Beulah Hotel, the Peacocks do not raise their hands, since they have brought theirs—and all the dogs as well. Rather than listening to the testimony, Mrs. Peacock talks through the trial, asking about churches in Clay and seeking remedies for her swollen finger joints. Sporadically, Old Man Peacock rises to ask if anyone has a timepiece. The daughters sit in a row, the eight-year-old brother walks up and down the aisle with a harmonica in his breathing mouth, and babies slide to the floor making straightway for the door. Treva chews gum. It is true that all the residents of Clay at the trial perform antics of their own, but the Peacock clan, away from home and out of place, sparks exceptional humor. (pp. 26-7)

Although Miss Welty views comedy as sociable, positive, and exacting, some of her characters engage in deeds and conversations that are not light-hearted and arouse laughter only with an accompanying shock. Some episodes can be described as black humor, which "discovers cause for laughter in what has generally been regarded as too serious for frivolity: the death of man, the disintegration of social institutions, mental and physical disease, deformity, suffering, anguish, privation, and terror." Although more prevalent since World War I, black humor has surfaced briefly whenever time provides distance. In **"Clytie,"** varying degrees of mental distress plague Clytie Farr, her sister Octavia, and her brother Gerald—remnants of the once prominent family for whom the town Farr's Gin was named. Clytie in her wanderings about takes no account of a driving rain, and ladies in town watch the drenched figure as her straw hat from the furnishing store sags on each side until it looks "like an old bonnet on a horse." Clytie herself makes no move to seek shelter until someone tells her to. She then turns and runs up the street, creating a ridiculous picture as she goes, "sticking out her elbows like chicken wings." Octavia, the tyrannical sister above stairs, has thick hair (grown back after an illness) dyed almost purple, and Gerald lives in a barricaded room with his whiskey. Their isolation is almost total except for Mr. Bobo, who comes regularly, but reluctantly, to shave the paralyzed father. Clytie's longings for acceptance and love lead to her death, an event at once pathetic and ludicrous. "When Old Lethy found her, she had fallen forward into the [rain] barrel, with her poor ladylike black-stockinged legs upended and hung apart like a pair of tongs." (pp. 32-3)

When *Delta Wedding* appeared in 1946, several critics, including Diana Trilling, expressed their disappointment. Mrs. Trilling regretted that this apparent shift to the narcissistic southern fantasy drew Miss Welty "away from the lower middle-class milieu of, say, The [sic] Petrified Man." That milieu, of course, was not abandoned, but has been prominent in much Welty fiction since 1946, including *Losing Battles* and *The Optimist's Daughter*. Within it, Miss Welty shows how well she knows the southern poor—their faults, their deficiencies, their virtues, their cadence of speech. Yet "she never degrades or dehumanizes them by reducing them to a stereotype." The lower middle-class characters ring true, from Leota (**"Petrified Man"**) to Wanda Fay Chisom McKelva (*The Optimist's Daughter*). Although differences exist among these characters, they nevertheless share many recognizable traits. Neither Sister and her family, Mrs. Katie Rainey or her relatives the Mayhews, the Dalzells, the Chisoms, the Beechams, the Renfros, Homer Champion, Ora Stovall, or Pet Hanks assume privacy, and thus "life for them is a matter of public display; they can only blunder forward from moment to moment, unaware of any continuity to experience."

Lack of manners, sophistication, and experience make these characters ready vehicles of humor. Eating scenes, for example, amply illustrate their natural behavior. Over the hot kitchen stove, Sister tries "to stretch two chickens over five people and a completely unexpected child into the bargain, without one moment's notice." After Uncle Rondo has consumed enough of his Fourth of July prescription to disport himself in Stella Rondo's flesh-colored kimono, his stomach can only tolerate cold biscuit and catsup. At Katie Rainey's funeral, her relatives appear from Stockstill and Lastingwell, communities near the Tennessee line, having traveled in pick-up trucks now drawn up to the porch. Along with the adults "was a string of tow-headed children . . . finishing some bananas," and they all came upon Virgie at once, "kissed her in greedy turn and begged before they got through the door for ice water or iced tea or both." When court takes a noon recess in ***The Ponder Heart,*** the Peacock family perch on the court-house stile to consume a meal Edna Earle can describe without seeing: "jelly sandwiches and sweet milk and biscuit and molasses in a tin bucket—poked wells in the biscuits to hold the molasses—and sweet potatoes wrapped in newspapers." They finish up with three or four watermelons "that couldn't have been any too ripe, to judge by what they left lying on the Courthouse grass for the world to see and pick up.'' The contents of the supper the Dalzells eat in the hospital waiting room are not named except for chicken legs, but since the meal was transported in shoe boxes and paper sacks, the reader, like Edna Earle, can make a pretty good guess at the entire menu. (pp. 39-41)

Clothing images frequently add to the humor. While Laurel McKelva Hand ''wore clothes of an interesting cut and texture'' and donned her Sibyl Connolly suit for the return trip to Chicago, Wanda Fay delights in wearing long green ear drops and matching green shoes with stiletto heels; Bubba's windbreaker, Mrs. Chisom's tennis shoes, and Wendell's cowboy suit identify their taste in clothes. Leota urges Mrs. Fletcher to disguise her pregnancy by wearing a Stork-a-Lure dress, and Bonnie Dee Ponder was buried in ''a Sunday-go-to-meeting dress, old-timey looking and too big for her—never washed or worn, just saved: white.'' Like clothing, keepsakes and possessions also indicate the unsophisticated taste of many characters. Sister treasures a picture of Nelson Eddy, bluebird wall vases, and an Add-a-Pearl necklace; Wanda Fay fancies peach-colored satin sheets. Ruby Fisher (**''A Piece of News''**) considers a sack of coffee marked in red letters ''SAMPLE,'' sufficient payment for her afternoon with the traveling salesman. Bonnie Dee Peacock buys a washing machine and installs it on the front porch. Reading material in Leota's beauty shop includes a drugstore rental book, *Life Is Like That,* and *Screen Secrets* magazine, and Mrs. Pike identifies Mr. Petrie through a picture story in *Startling G-Man Tales*. Furthermore, these characters' occupations seldom involve professional training or extensive education: they work in beauty shops, millinery shops, and country stores; they farm, repair appliances, and operate wrecking concerns. (pp. 41-2)

From the ironic to the farcical, Eudora Welty's humor enriches her work; overall, the humor is not relegated to mere entertainment, but rather it is established as a staple of life and of fiction. (pp. 49-50)

Comedy sports with the frivolous, the ironic, and the satiric; it is quite able, Miss Welty has said, ''to tackle the most serious matters that there are.'' When Charles Bunting quoted a *New York Times* critic who had written that ''Eudora Welty possesses the surest comic sense of any American writer alive,'' Miss Welty's response made it clear that comedy is a sure foundation of her fiction. ''I'm delighted that the critic thinks I have a good comic spirit. And I think that's taking me seriously.'' (p. 50)

Elizabeth Evans, in her Eudora Welty, *Frederick Ungar Publishing Co., 1981, 172 p.*

CAROL S. MANNING (essay date 1985)

[In the following excerpt, Manning discusses the importance of the southern oral tradition in the evolution of Welty's narrative voice.]

In ''The Corner Store'' (1975), an essay about her childhood, Eudora Welty remembers people she saw and adventures she had as she ran to and from the corner grocery on errands for her mother. Generalizing about this experience, she writes, ''Setting out in this world, a child feels so indelible. He only comes to find out later that it's all the others along his way who are making themselves indelible to him.'' A sensitive comment on the forming of a child's consciousness, the remark also seems suggestive about the making of an artist. Surely Welty's own art has been influenced by all that she has met along her way. A keen observer and listener with a prodigious memory, she has a vast store of things seen and things heard on which she draws. She said as much in an interview when asked the source of the dialogue of her characters: ''Once you have heard certain expressions, sentences, you almost never forget them. It's like sending a bucket down the well and it always comes up full. . . . And you listen for the right word, in the present. . . . [W]hat you overhear on a city bus is exactly what your character would say on the page you're writing.'' (p. 3)

But obviously ordinary life alone does not define her fiction, or the author would not have been called a romantic as well as a realist or have been said to write such varied fiction that it defies generalization. There is a second crucial influence on her fiction, one that might seem to run counter to the first. It is a love of stories and storytelling. (p. 4)

In the South that Welty knows, storytelling is a part of everyday life, and its subjects arise from the life of the community. Storytelling is not, however, mere imitation of life. Indeed, its major attraction might be the divergence of the story told *from* everyday life. Oral or written, storytelling appeals to and draws on the imagination. Whereas everyday life may seem dull and shapeless, storytelling brings structure to happenings (''you're following a story''), prunes away some things and emphasizes or exaggerates others to provide drama (''of a narrative and dramatic structure''), creates suspense and promises resolution (''[y]ou're listening for how something is going to come out''). In *One Writer's Beginnings,* Welty describes her childhood fascination with a neighbor's tale-telling: ''What I loved about her stories was that everything happened in *scenes*. I might not catch on to the root of the trouble in all that happened, but my ear told me it was dramatic. Often she said, 'The crisis had come!' '' (pp. 5-6)

Welty's early writing, represented in three books published in rapid succession—***A Curtain of Green, The Robber Bridegroom,*** and ***The Wide Net***—served her, it seems, as an apprenticeship: an apprenticeship in the art of storytelling. In these works the young author introduced themes and tried out methods that she would expand, contract, refine, remold, or dispense with in the subsequent fiction. She seems to have been energetically learning her craft, stretching herself, experimenting. She varied technique and context in the seventeen stories of ***A Curtain of Green,*** so much so that, despite their Southern settings and their implications about place, no unifying vision emerges from the whole. The variety is such that, for Robert Penn Warren, ''It is almost as if the author had gone at each story as a fresh start in the business of writing fiction'' [see excerpt dated 1944], and for Robert Van Gelder, ''[I]t is as though there were no brand of one mind upon the stories.'' Her next collection, ***The Wide Net,*** containing stories written within roughly a year's time, does give evidence of the ''brand of one mind,'' but though seven of the eight stories are set along the Old Natchez Trace, the volume's unity does not derive from a shared image or theme related to a culture but, as critics regularly note, from a shared dreamlike quality. The legend and romance associated with the Natchez Trace and reflected in several of these stories seem to have inspired the author to experiment with various ways of evoking the suggestiveness of dreams. ***The Robber Bridegroom,*** also set along the Old Natchez Trace, was a different experiment. Several times longer than any of the early stories, it is recognized as an exuberant mixture of motifs from fairy tales and American folklore, uniquely adapted to a Southern frontier setting. (pp. 6-7)

Evidently, in these early works Welty did not set out to mimic life—though that might be included, and certainly, as she has said, the story had to be "true to life"—but to tell a good story. In fact, some of the stories were inspired by stories she had heard others tell. Her very first published story, **"Death of a Traveling Salesman,"** had such an origin. A neighbor in Jackson, Mr. Johnson, told a tale about going to a farmer's house on business and being informed by the farmer's wife that her husband had "'gone to borry some fire.'" That remark stuck with Welty: "I could not have made up 'He's gone to borry some fire,' but, beginner though I was as a writer, I think now I began truly, for *I knew that for a story when I heard it*" (emphasis added). Similarly, **"Keela, the Outcast Indian Maiden"** was inspired by a tale about a bizarre incident that someone told her. (p. 8)

Whereas early in her career the love of storytelling had led [Welty] to delight in the act itself of telling a story, eventually it would lead her to the oral culture of her region for subject and theme. For from *Delta Wedding* to *The Optimist's Daughter* (1972), Welty's portrayal of the family and community is, in large measure, a portrayal of a talkative, storytelling people. This development had been anticipated by a handful of early stories, stories such as **"Why I Live at the P. O.," "Petrified Man,"** and **"Lilly Daw and the Three Ladies."** Welty has said that **"P. O.,"** a dramatic monologue narrated by a gregarious post mistress, "grew out of . . . a lifelong listening to talk on my block where I grew up as a child," and clearly **"Petrified Man," "Lily Daw,"** *Delta Wedding,* and most of the subsequent fiction are also dependent on the author's lifelong interest in the South's oral tradition. (p. 18)

Given Welty's long fascination with family storytelling and Southern talk, it is not surprising that the oral culture should come to be represented prominently in her fiction. What may be surprising is not the frequency of her portrayal of the oral culture but the complexity and incisiveness of the resulting portrait. Despite her immersion in the oral culture, she is able to see it with objectivity. She exploits the realism and inherent comedy of ordinary speech, but not merely for the picturesqueness of such speech. She exposes the roles the oral tradition plays for the Southerner and hence its importance to the culture. She shows it to be ritual and mask, diversion, and sustainer of the past. It is at one and the same time a social art, entertaining the family and community, and a social menace, boring strangers and serving to villainize and to exclude persons deemed outsiders. Perhaps most crucially, through it the society makes heroes of ordinary men. In *Delta Wedding,* ***The Golden Apples, The Ponder Heart,*** *Losing Battles, The Optimist's Daughter,* and several separate stories, Welty characterizes, and undercuts, the Southerner's propensity for romanticizing. (pp. 19-20)

The oral tradition has shaped Welty's narrative voice extensively and deliciously. In the attitude she sometimes takes toward her characters, the way she describes their actions, the insight she brings to such descriptions, we can recognize a local tale-teller amusingly narrating a tale about a local event or a town character. In **"June Recital,"** the author smoothly and convincingly falls into the tone and style of oral narration when Old Man Moody and Mr. Fatty Bowles appear on the scene. In this story, which combines tragedy with comedy, the portrayal of Moody and Bowles provides a moment of bold comedy that relieves the tension created by the subtle portrayal of Miss Eckhart's unhappiness and isolation and that contrasts with the ironic but sympathetic portrayals of little Loch Morrison and his sister Cassie, through whose eyes much of the action is seen. As Miss Eckhart, now senile and more alone than ever, begins a fire in her former piano studio, town marshal Old Man Moody and Mr. Fatty Bowles arrive at the house on an errand. Peering through a porch window and discovering Miss Eckhart's arson, they turn brave crime-stoppers.

> They lifted the screen out, and Mr. Fatty accidentally stepped through it. They inched the sash up with a sound that made them draw high their muck-coated heels. They could go in now: they opened their mouths and guffawed silently. They were so used to showing off, they almost called up Morgana then and there.
>
> Mr. Fatty Bowles started to squeeze himself over the sill into the room, but Old Man Moody was ready for that, pulled him back by the suspenders, and went first. He leap-frogged it. Inside, they both let go a holler.
>
> "Look out! You're caught in the act!"

This portrayal of Old Man Moody and Mr. Fatty Bowles reveals Welty the storyteller at work—and play. The passage has all the marks of oral tale-telling. Its direct focus is actions; its sentence structure is simple; its language concrete, largely monosyllabic, and frequently colloquial; and its verbs in particular strong and colorful. Like many folk humor tales, it makes a recent happening seem absurd by reducing the people involved to stick figures or buffoons.

But the men look foolish not only because of their actions but especially because of the attitudes giving rise to the actions, which are the real point of the tale. Although young Loch Morrison observes the two men from his perch in a tree nearby, it is clearly not his view but Welty's—or a raconteur's—ironic view that is given, for it is an amused storyteller, not little Loch, who would be able to recognize, and likely to exaggerate, the men's feelings of self-importance: "They were so used to showing off, they almost called up Morgana then and there." Neither man wants the other to be more of a hero than is he, as is effectively intimated in the second paragraph quoted. Moreover, their yell "'Look out! You're caught in the act!'" is a bit of swaggering, an excessive display of authority and courage, given that the villain is obviously weak and disoriented and the danger only the struggling flickerings of an unprofessionally set fire. And in the paragraph which follows those quoted, the storytelling voice is heard in simple diction and images which implicitly ridicule the men's grasping at the heroic and their attempt to prolong and intensify their little adventure. Rather than reporting flatly that the men ran around the table and into the parlor, Welty, the raconteur, adopts language appropriate to a description of the football players they might like to be: they "made a preliminary run around the table to warm up" and then "charged the parlor." Like explorers making their way through a dense jungle, they "trod down the barrier of sparky matting and stomped in"; heavyweights that they imagine themselves, "they boxed at the smoke" but only succeeded in hitting each other. Thus does the storyteller depict, and mock, the men's bravado. Yet while she reduces the men to buffoons for the sake of amusing her audience, they seem real nonetheless. They are local folk known to the tale-teller and to everyone else as "Old Man Moody" and "Mr. Fatty," and their desire to be heroic, to shine for a moment, is very human indeed.

The tone of delight which seems inherent in Welty's fiction and which we have observed previously has, then, still another chord. The characters' "tireless relish of life" is frequently enhanced by a tone suggesting the delight a small-town raconteur takes in regaling an audience with tales about local folk whom she expects the audience to recognize. This storyteller may embroider or color the facts and paint characters with irony, but she nonetheless views the characters with a mixture of love, penetrating insight, and tolerant amusement.

To return for a moment to the contrast between the early stories and the mature fiction, the elements of love and tolerant amusement are what are often missing in Welty's treatment of the early characters. Typically, the narrative voice of the early stories invites the reader to delight in the characters *as characters,* not as breathing, feeling, ordinary human beings. Does Old Mr. Marblehall of [**"Old Mr. Marblehall"**] really lead a secret double life with nearly identical wives and sons at opposite ends of the same town? Or does he only imagine that he does? But does the reader care whether he does or not, except as the ambiguity creates a literary puzzle to solve? In this story, in fact, Welty increases the reader's detachment from the main character by unsubtly employing an omniscient narrator or storyteller who, directly addressing her audience as "you," in effect invites the audience to join her in viewing Mr. Marblehall as a figure in a tale. Unlike the implicit raconteur of the Old Man Moody-Mr. Fatty Bowles passage, who gives the impression of reporting (and making understandable) the actions of a couple of local fellows who are very much a part of a community, this omniscient storyteller seems to be pulling the strings of a puppet:

> Old Mr. Marblehall never did anything, never got married until he was sixty. You can see him out taking a walk. Watch and you'll see how preciously old people come to think they are made. . . . They stand long on the corners but more impatiently than anyone, as if they expect traffic to take notice of them, rear up the horses and throw on the brakes, so they can get where they want to go. That's Mr. Marblehall. He has short white bangs, and a bit of snapdragon in his lapel. He walks with a big polished stick, a present. . . . He has on his thick, beautiful, glowing coat—tweed, but he looks as gratified as an animal in its own tingling fur. You see, even in summer he wears it, because he is cold all the time.
>
> (pp. 23-5)

But though her stance as storyteller grows more subtle and tolerant as her vision matures, Welty is, early and late, a storyteller. She is also—but late more consistently than early—the poet and historian of a storytelling people . . . [She] has progressively painted a revealing picture of the Southern oral tradition ("a treasure I helped myself to") and the families and communities who share it. Writing in a conversational style born itself of the region's active oral tradition, Welty proves herself the oral culture's most discriminating admirer and its most incisive critic. (p. 25)

Caròl S. Manning, in her With Ears Opening Like Morning Glories: Eudora Welty and the Love of Storytelling, *Greenwood Press, 1985, 221 p.*

ADDITIONAL BIBLIOGRAPHY

Allen, John A. "Eudora Welty: The Three Moments." *Virginia Quarterly Review* 51, No. 4 (Autumn 1975): 605-27.
Allen discusses Welty's essentially benevolent attitude toward her characters.

Appel, Alfred A. *A Season of Dreams.* Baton Rouge: Louisiana State University Press, 1965, 274 p.
Comprehensive study of Welty's fiction

Bornhauser, Fred. "Book Reviews." *Shenandoah* VII, No. 1 (Autumn 1955): 71-81.
Review of *The Bride of the Innisfallen.* Bornhauser states that "Miss Welty stabilizes a tragic world, resolves it with vivid imagination, clean control of language, and her comic gift. It emerges a world of sensibility, [and] subtle psychological play."

Bowen, Elizabeth. "*The Golden Apples.*" In her *Seven Winters and Afterthoughts,* pp. 215-18. New York: Alfred A. Knopf, 1962.
Discusses *The Golden Apples,* noting that in that work "Welty would seem to have found, for her art, the ideal form."

Boyle, Kay. "Full-Length Portrait." *The New Republic* 105, No. 21 (24 November 1941): 707-08.
Laudatory review of *A Curtain of Green* predicting further accomplishments by Welty.

Bradbury, John M. "The Awakening." In his *Renaissance in the South,* pp. 7-21. Chapel Hill: University of North Carolina Press, 1963.
Discusses Welty's principal works.

Bryant, J. A., Jr. *Eudora Welty.* Minneapolis: University of Minnesota Press, 1968, 48 p.
Pamphlet intended as a brief survey of and introduction to Welty's work.

———. "Seeing Double in *The Golden Apples.*" *Sewanee Review* LXXXII, No. 2 (Spring 1974): 300-15.
Discusses the transcendent nature of *The Golden Apples,* concluding that Welty restores life to "all its richness and undeniable immediacy."

Daniel, Robert W. "Eudora Welty: The Sense of Place." In *South: Modern Literature in Its Cultural Setting,* edited by Louis D. Rubin Jr. and Robert D. Jacobs, pp. 276-86. Garden City, N. Y.: Doubleday, 1961.
Discusses the importance of setting in Welty's work.

Desmond, John F., ed. *A Still Moment: Essays on the Art of Eudora Welty.* Metuchen, N. J.: The Scarecrow Press, 1978, 142 p.
Collection of essays which explore the diversity of Welty's fiction.

Dollarhide, Louis, and Abadie, Ann, eds. *Eudora Welty: A Form of Thanks.* Jackson: University of Mississippi Press, 1979, 138 p.
Collection of speeches delivered at a 1977 symposium held in Welty's honor.

Donlan, Dan. "'A Worn Path': Immortality of Stereotype." *English Journal* 62, No. 4 (April 1973): 549-50.
Examines the significance of the Phoenix symbol in "A Worn Path."

Fritz-Piggott, Jill. "The Sword and the Song: Moments of Intensity in *The Golden Apples.*" *Southern Literary Journal* 18, No. 2 (Spring 1986): 27-39.
Discusses Joycean epiphanies in *The Golden Apples.*

Givner, Joan. "Katherine Anne Porter, Eudora Welty and 'Ethan Brand'." *The International Fiction Review* (January 1974): 32-7.
Dismisses the characterizations in "Petrified Man" as superficial and clumsy.

Griffith, Benjamin W. "'Powerhouse' as a Showcase of Eudora Welty's Methods and Themes." *Mississippi Quarterly* 19, No. 1 (Winter 1965-66): 79-84.
Analysis of "Powerhouse" emphasizing the importance of setting, characterization, and symbol in the story.

Hauser, Marianne. "*A Curtain of Green* and Other New Works of Fiction." *The New York Times Book Review* (16 November 1941): 6.
Laudatory review of *A Curtain of Green*.

Hicks, Granville. "Eudora Welty." *College English* 14, No. 2 (November 1952): 69-76.
Considers the evolution of Welty's works.

Hoffman, Frederick J. "Eudora Welty and Carson McCullers." In his *The Art of Southern Fiction*, pp. 51-73. Carbondale: Southern Illinois University Press, 1967.
Discusses the way in which Welty's work imposes order upon a seemingly chaotic mass of information.

Howard, Maureen. "A Collection of Discoveries." *The New York Times Book Review* (2 November 1980): 1, 31-2.
Review of the *Collected Stories*, which Howard judges "magnificent."

Howell, Elmo. "Eudora Welty and the City of Man." *The Georgia Review* XXXIII, No. 4 (Winter 1979): 770-82.
Provides an overview of Welty's work, focusing on the social relationships of her characters.

Isaac, Neil D. *Eudora Welty*. Austin, Tex.: Steck-Vaughn, 1969, 43 p.
Brief critical survey of Welty's works.

Kennebeck, Edwin. "People of Clay." *Commonweal* 59, No. 16 (22 January 1954): 410-11.
Review finding *The Ponder Heart* entertaining, though lacking in substance.

Kirkpatrick, Smith. "The Anointed Powerhouse." *Sewanee Review* 77, No. 1 (Winter 1969): 94-108.
Examines mythical and religious allusions in the story "Powerhouse."

Kloss, Robert J. "The Symbolic Structure of Eudora Welty's 'Livvie'." *Notes on Mississippi Writers* 7, No. 3 (Winter 1975): 70-82.
Discusses sexual symbols and imagery in "Livvie."

Kreyling, Michael. *Eudora Welty's Achievement of Order*. Baton Rouge: Louisiana State University Press, 1980, 188 p.
Comprehensive critical study of Welty's works.

Liscio, Lorraine. "The Female Voice of Poetry in 'The Bride of the Innisfallen'." *Studies in Short Fiction* 21, No. 4 (Fall 1984): 357-62.
Analyzes "The Bride of the Innisfallen." Liscio concludes: "As is often the case in Welty's fiction, it is difficult to draw any neat conclusions about the meaning" of the story.

McHaney, Thomas L. "Eudora Welty and the Multitudinous Golden Apples." *Mississippi Quarterly* 26, No. 4 (Fall 1973): 589-624.
Explicates mythical allusions in *The Golden Apples*.

Mortimer, Gail L. "'The Way to Get There': Journeys and Destinations in the Stories of Eudora Welty." *Southern Literary Journal* XIX, No. 2 (Spring 1987): 62-9.
Analysis of "Death of a Traveling Salesman" and "The Key," considering the significance of Welty's approach to the classic theme of human journeys.

Pawloski, Robert S. "The Process of Observation: *Winesburg, Ohio* and *The Golden Apples*." *University Review* 37, No. 4 (June 1971): 292-98.
Parallels in *The Golden Apples* and Sherwood Anderson's *Winesburg, Ohio*.

Prenshaw, Peggy Whitman, ed. *Eudora Welty: Critical Essays*. Jackson: University of Mississippi Press, 1979, 444 p.
Collection of essays by such prominent Welty scholars as Ruth Vande Kieft and Michael Kreyling.

Rosenfeld, Isaac. "Consolations of Poetry." *The New Republic* 109, No. 16 (18 October 1943): 525-26.
Negative review of *The Wide Net*. Rosenfeld agrees with Diana Trilling's assessment (see excerpt dated 1943), stating that Welty has "forced poetry" into her prose.

Shenandoah: Special Eudora Welty Issue XX, No. 2 (Spring 1969).
Presents a number of essays and shorter commentaries by such noted critics as Robert Penn Warren, Allen Tate, and Joyce Carol Oates.

Stafford, Jean. "Empty Net." *Partisan Review* XI, No. 1 (Winter 1944): 114-15.
Derogatory review of *The Wide Net* asserting that Welty, "warily picking her way through meanings and the amorphous produce of the soul, or rocketing out of sight in a burst of fantasy, loses her humor, leaves fissures in her masonry, forgets her breeding, and writes eight stories in a language so vague that not only actual words but syntax itself [has] the improbable inexactitude of verbal dreams."

Swearingen, Bethany C. *Eudora Welty: A Critical Bibliography, 1936-1958*. Jackson: University Press of Mississippi, 1984, 82 p.
Bibliography of secondary sources including extensive annotations.

Thompson, Victor. *Eudora Welty: A Reference Guide*. Boston: G. K. Hall, 1976, 175 p.
Comprehensive annotated bibliography of primary and secondary sources.

Trilling, Lionel. "American Fairy Tale." *The Nation* 155, No. 25 (19 December 1942): 687-88.
Negative review of *The Robber Bridegroom*. Trilling states that Welty "has used the manner of a secret archly shared but (ah!) even more archly not shared, for although she seems to have attached no specific meanings to her fantastic episodes, the whole work has the facetious air of having a profound meaning for herself."

Weiner, Rachel V. "Eudora Welty's *The Ponder Heart:* The Judgement of Art." *Southern Studies* XIX, No. 3 (Fall 1980): 261-73.
Describes the characters and action of *The Ponder Heart*.

Yardley, Jonathan. "The Last Good One." *The New Republic* 162, No. 19 (9 May 1970): 33-6.
Discusses the universality of Welty's work.

Appendix

The following is a listing of all sources used in Volume 1 of *Short Story Criticism*. Included in this list are all copyright and reprint rights and acknowledgments for those essays for which permission was obtained. Every effort has been made to trace copyright, but if omissions have been made, please let us know.

THE EXCERPTS IN SSC, VOLUME 1, WERE REPRINTED FROM THE FOLLOWING PERIODICALS:

Accent, v. XVI, Summer, 1956.

American Literature, v. XXXIV, March, 1962. Copyright © 1962 Duke University Press, Durham, NC. Reprinted by permission of the publisher.

American Mercury, v. 14, May, 1928.

The American Scholar, v. 27, Summer, 1958 for "Reappraisals: James Thurber, the Primitive, the Innocent, and the Individual" by Robert H. Elias. Copyright © 1958, renewed 1986 by the author. Reprinted by permission of the publisher.

Arizona Quarterly, v. 26, Winter, 1970 for "William Faulkner's Chickasaw Legacy: A Note on 'Red Leaves'" by Elmo Howell. Copyright © 1970 by *Arizona Quarterly*. Reprinted by permission of the publisher and the author.

The Atlantic Monthly, v. 67, June, 1891./ v. 231, June, 1973 for "Cheever to Roth to Malamud" by John Leonard. Copyright 1973 by The Atlantic Monthly Company, Boston, MA. Reprinted by permission of Curtis Brown Ltd.

Australian Journal of French Studies, v. XVIII, January-April, 1981. Copyright © 1981 by *Australian Journal of French Studies*. Reprinted by permission of the publisher.

The Bookman, New York, v. LXIII, May, 1926; v. LXIX, April, 1929.

Books and Bookmen, v. 22, March, 1977 for "Ballard in Bondage" by Duncan Fallowell. © copyright the author 1977. Reprinted with permission of the author.

Books on Trial, v. XIV, August-September, 1955.

The CEA Critic, v. XXVIII, June, 1966; v. 45, March & May, 1983. Copyright © 1966, 1983 by the College English Association, Inc. Both reprinted by permission of the publisher.

The Chesterton Review, v. 12, November, 1986; v. 13, February, 1987. © 1986, 1987 *The Chesterton Review*. Both reprinted by permission of the publisher.

Chicago Daily News, September 3, 1919.

The Chicago Daily Tribune, June 7, 1919.

CLA Journal, v. XIII, September, 1969; v. XV, March, 1972. Copyright, 1969, 1972 by The College Language Association. Both used by permission of The College Language Association.

Claremont Quarterly, v. 11, Winter, 1964 for "John Cheever: A Vision of the World" by Frederick Bracher. Copyright, Claremont Graduate School and University Center, 1964. Reprinted by permission of the author.

College English, v. 23, February, 1962 for "Meaning and Structure in 'Bartleby'" by Marvin Felheim; v. 25, December, 1963 for "The Question of Poe's Narrators" by James W. Gargano. Copyright © 1962, 1963 by the National Council of Teachers of English. Both reprinted by permission of the publisher and the respective authors.

Commentary, v. 10, October, 1950 for "William Faulkner: An American Dickens" by Leslie A. Fiedler; v. 16, October, 1953 for "New England and Hollywood" by Morris Freedman. Copyright 1950, 1953 by American Jewish Committee. All rights reserved. Both reprinted. by permission of the publisher and the respective authors.

Commonweal, v. XCIX, November 30, 1973. Copyright © 1973 Commonweal Publishing Co., Inc. Reprinted by permission of Commonweal Foundation./ v. LXIX, December 19, 1958. Copyright © 1958, renewed 1986, Commonweal Publishing Co., Inc. Reprinted by permission of Commonweal Foundation.

The Crisis, v. 27, February, 1924; v. 28, September, 1924.

The Dallas Morning News, April 26, 1925.

The Dial, v. LXXII, January, 1922; v. LXXXII, October, 1924.

Discovery, v. 5, 1955.

Dutch Quarterly Review of Anglo-American Letters, v. 13, 1983. Reprinted by permission of the publisher.

English Journal, v. 60, December, 1971 for "Symbol and Theme in Eudora Welty's 'Petrified Man'" by Lee J. Richmond. Copyright © 1971 by the National Council of Teachers of English. Reprinted by permission of the publisher and the author.

Essays in Literature, v. X, Fall, 1983. Copyright 1983 by Western Illinois University. Reprinted by permission of the publisher.

The Evening Sun, Baltimore, December 8, 1923.

Folio, v. XX, Spring, 1955.

The Fortnightly Review, n.s. v. XLIII, March, 1888.

French Studies, v. V, January, 1951.

Furioso, v. VI, Summer, 1951.

Graham's Magazine, v. XXI, May, 1842.

Harper's, v. 268, March, 1984. Copyright © 1984 by *Harper's Magazine*. All rights reserved. Reprinted by special permission.

Harper's New Monthly Magazine, v. 75, September, 1887.

Jahrbuch für Amerikastudien, v. 5, 1960 for "Four Views of Edgar Poe" by Patrick F. Quinn. Reprinted by permission of the author.

The Literary Review (New York Evening Post), October 25, 1924.

Lively Arts and Book Review, April 30, 1961. © 1961 I.H.T. Corporation. Reprinted by permission of the publisher.

Manchester Guardian Weekly, 1911.

MidAmerica, v. I, 1974. Copyright 1974 by The Society for the Study of Midwestern Literature. Reprinted by permission of the publisher.

The Mississippi Quarterly, v. 13, Summer, 1960. Reprinted by permission of the publisher./ v. XXXVII, Summer, 1984. Copyright 1984 Mississippi State University. Reprinted by permission of the publisher.

Modern Fiction Studies, v. 32, Summer, 1986. Copyright © 1986 by Purdue Research Foundation, West Lafayette, IN 47907. All rights reserved. Reprinted with permission.

Modern Languages, v. XLIII, December, 1962. Reprinted by permission of the publisher.

Ms., v. IV, December, 1975 for "Beyond the Peacock: The Reconstruction of Flannery O'Connor" by Alice Walker. Copyright © 1975 by Alice Walker. Reprinted by permission of The Wendy Weil Agency, Inc.

The Nation, New York, v. CXXV, November 16, 1927; v. CXXVII, December 5, 1928; v. CXXXVI, May 3, 1933; v. 153, December 6, 1941./ v. CXXXIII, November 4, 1931 for "Mr. Faulkner's World" by Lionel Trilling. Reprinted by permission of the Estate of Lionel Trilling.

Negro Digest, v. XVII, January, 1969 for "Jean Toomer's Cane" by Darwin T. Turner. © 1969 Johnson Publishing Company, Inc. Reprinted by permission of *Negro Digest* and the author.

The New Leader, v. LXI, September 11, 1978. © 1978 by The American Labor Conference on International Affairs, Inc. Reprinted by permission of the publisher.

The New Republic, v. XXXVII, December 19, 1923; v. XXXVII, December 26, 1923; v. LXXVII, December 13, 1933; v. 128, May 25, 1953./ v. 106, June 29, 1942 for "Go Down to Faulkner's Land" by Malcolm Cowley; v. 112, March 12, 1945 for "James Thurber's Dream Book" by Malcolm Cowley. Copyright 1942, 1945 The New Republic, Inc. Renewed 1969, 1972 by Malcolm Cowley. Both reprinted by permission of the author./ v. 127, October 6, 1952 for "With Grace under Pressure" by Mark Schorer. Copyright 1952 The New Republic, Inc. Renewed 1980 by Ruth Schorer, Suzanne Macotsis and Page Schorer. Reprinted by permission of *The New Republic.*/ v. 183, November 1, 1980. © 1980 The New Republic, Inc. Reprinted by permission of *The New Republic.*

New Statesman, v. 30, November 26, 1927./ v. 80, July 10, 1970; v. 92, December 3, 1976. © 1970, 1976 The Statesman & Nation Publishing Co. Ltd. Both reprinted by permission of the publisher.

The New Statesman & Nation, n.s. v. XIV, October 2, 1937.

New York Herald Tribune Books, v. 9, October 9, 1927. Copyright 1927 I.H.T. Corporation. Reprinted by permission of the publisher.

The New York Review of Books, v. XXV, November 9, 1978. Copyright © 1978 Nyrev, Inc. Reprinted with permission from *The New York Review of Books.*

The New York Times Book Review, May 30, 1965 for "If You Know Who You Are You Can Go Anywhere" by Richard Poirier. Copyright © 1965 by The New York Times Company. Reprinted by permission of the publisher and Richard Poirier./ December 10, 1922; March 28, 1943; August 21, 1949; January 10, 1954. Copyright 1922, 1943, 1949, 1954 by The New York Times Company. All reprinted by permission of the publisher./ June 12, 1955; November 25, 1962; October 22, 1972. Copyright © 1955, 1962, 1972 by The New York Times Company. All reprinted by permission of the publisher.

The New Yorker, v. III, October 28, 1933 for "A Letter to Mr. Hemingway" by Clifton Fadiman. Copyright 1933, renewed 1961, by The New Yorker Magazine, Inc. Reprinted by permission of the author./ v. XXXVII, November 11, 1961; v. XLI, September 11, 1965. © 1961, 1965 by The New Yorker Magazine, Inc. Both reprinted by permission of the publisher.

The Paris Review, v. 26, Winter, 1984. © 1984 The Paris Review, Inc. Reprinted by permission of the publisher.

Partisan Review, v. XXVI, Winter, 1959 for a review of "The Housebreaker of Shady Hill" by Irving Howe. Copyright © 1959 by *Partisan Review.* Reprinted by permission of the publisher and the author./ v. XXII, Fall, 1955. Copyright © 1955 by *Partisan Review.* Reprinted by permission of the publisher.

Perspective, v. 2, Summer, 1949; v. 7, June, 1954.

PMLA, v. XLII, March, 1927./ v. 81, March, 1986. Copyright © 1986 by the Modern Language Association of America. Reprinted by permission of the Modern Language Association of America.

Poetry, v. LXIII, December, 1943.

The Saturday Evening Post, v. 190, December 8, 1917. Copyright 1917, renewed 1945, The Curtis Publishing Company. Reprinted from *The Saturday Evening Post* by permission.

The Saturday Review, New York, v. XLI, September 13, 1958.

The Saturday Review of Literature, v. II, February 13, 1926; v. IX, April 29, 1933./ v. XXVI, April 24, 1943. Copyright 1943 *Saturday Review* magazine. Reprinted by permission of the publisher.

Science Fiction & Fantasy Book Review, n. 15, June, 1983. Copyright © 1983 by Science Fiction Research Association. Reprinted by permission of the publisher.

Science-Fiction Studies, v. 12, November, 1985. Copyright © 1985 by SFS Publications. Reprinted by permission of the publisher.

The Sewanee Review, v. LXIII, Autumn, 1955 for "Two Ladies of the South" by Louis D. Rubin, Jr. © 1955, renewed 1983, by the author. Both reprinted by permission of the author./ v. XCIII, Fall, 1985 for "James Thurber and the Hazards of Humor" by Melvin Maddocks. © 1985 by the author. Reprinted by permission of the editor of *The Sewanee Review.*/ v. LXX, Summer, 1962; v. LXXXV, Winter, 1977. © 1962, 1977 by The University of the South. Both reprinted by permission of the editor of *The Sewanee Review.*/ v. LV, Winter, 1952. Copyright 1952, renewed 1980, by The University of the South. Reprinted by permission of the editor of *The Sewanee Review.*

SF Horizons, 1965 for "The Wounded Land: J. G. Ballard" by Brian Aldiss. Copyright, ©, 1965 by SF Horizons, Ltd. Reprinted by permission of the Robin Straus Agency, Inc. as agents for Brian Aldiss.

Shenandoah, v. 13, Spring, 1962 for "The Simplicity of 'Winesburg, Ohio'" by Walter B. Rideout; v. XX, Spring, 1969 for "Eudora Welty and the Mythos of Summer" by Ashley Brown. Copyright 1962, 1969 by Washington and Lee University. Both reprinted from *Shenandoah* with the permission of the Editor and the respective authors.

The Smart Set, v. LIX, August, 1919.

South Atlantic Quarterly, v. 73, Autumn, 1974. Copyright © 1974 by Duke University Press, Durham, NC. Reprinted by permission of the publisher.

The Southern Humanities Review, v. 2, Summer, 1968; v. VI, Winter, 1972; v. VIII, Winter, 1974. Copyright 1968, 1972, 1974 by Auburn University. All reprinted by permission of the publisher.

The Southern Literary Journal, v. 14, Spring, 1982. Copyright 1982 by the Department of English, University of North Carolina at Chapel Hill. Reprinted by permission of the publisher.

The Southern Review (Louisiana State University), v. V, Summer, 1969 for "G. K. Chesterton's 'Father Brown' Stories" by W. W. Robson. Copyright, 1969, by the author. Reprinted by permission of the author./ v. III, Winter, 1938. Copyright, 1938, renewed 1965, by Louisiana State University. Reprinted by permission of the publisher.

Studies in Black Literature, v. 1, Spring, 1970. Copyright 1970 by the editor. Reprinted by permission of the publisher.

Studies in Short Fiction, v. II, Summer, 1965; v. V, Fall, 1967; v. XI, Fall, 1974; v. XII, Summer, 1975; v. 14, Spring, 1977; v. 19, Fall, 1982; v. 22, Summer, 1985. Copyright 1965, 1967, 1974, 1975, 1977, 1982, 1985 by Newberry College. All reprinted by permission of the publisher.

This Quarter, v. 1, Autumn-Winter, 1925.

The Times Literary Supplement, n. 1173, July 10, 1924; n. 1309, March 3, 1927./ n. 3567, July 9, 1970; n. 3905, January 14, 1977; n. 4147, September 24, 1982. © Times Newspapers Ltd. (London) 1970, 1977, 1982. All reproduced from *The Times Literary Supplement* by permission.

University of Toronto Quarterly, v. XVIII, January, 1949.

Twentieth Century Literature, v. 14, January, 1969. Copyright 1969, Hofstra University Press. Reprinted by permission of the publisher.

The World, New York, December 6, 1921.

The World and I, v. 2, January, 1987 for "Flannery O'Connor and the Grotesque Face of God" by Russell Kirk. Copyright © 1986 by News World Communications, Inc. Reprinted by permission of the author.

The Yale Literary Magazine, v. XCIII, July, 1928.

The Yale Review, v. LV, October, 1965. Copyright 1965, by Yale University. Reprinted by permission of the editors.

THE EXCERPTS IN SSC, VOLUME 1, WERE REPRINTED FROM THE FOLLOWING BOOKS:

Aldridge, John W. From *Time to Murder and Create: The Contemporary Novel in Crisis*. David McKay Company, Inc., 1966. Copyright © 1966 by John W. Aldridge. All rights reserved. Reprinted by permission of the author.

Amis, Kingsley. From an introduction to *G. K. Chesterton: Selected Stories*. By G. K. Chesterton, edited by Kingsley Amis. Faber & Faber, 1972. Introduction © 1972 by Kingsley Amis. All rights reserved. Reprinted by permission of Faber & Faber Ltd.

Anderson, David D. From *Sherwood Anderson: An Introduction and Interpretation*. Holt, Rinehart and Winston, 1967. Copyright © 1967 by Holt, Rinehart and Winston, Inc. All rights reserved. Reprinted by permission of Holt, Rinehart and Winston, Inc.

Anderson, Sherwood and others. From "'Inquiry' into the Present Fame of Maupassant in Europe and the United States," in *Maupassant Criticism in France: 1880-1940*. By Artine Artinian. King's Crown Press, 1941. Copyright, 1941, renewed 1969, by Artine Artinian. Reprinted by permission of Artine Artinian.

Arvin, Newton. From *Herman Melville*. William Sloane Associates, 1950. Copyright 1950 by William Sloane Associates, Inc. Renewed 1978 by John A. Zeigler and Jean E. Fischer. Abridged by permission of William Morrow & Company, Inc.

Ash, Brian. From *Faces of the Future: The Lessons of Science Fiction*. Taplinger Publishing Co., Inc, 1975. Copyright © 1975 by Brian Ash. All rights reserved. Reprinted by permission of the publisher.

Auden, W. H. From *The Enchafed Flood; or, The Romantic Iconography of the Sea*. Random House, 1950. Copyright 1950 by The Rector and Visitors of the University of Virginia. Renewed 1977 by Monroe K. Spears and William Meredith. All rights reserved. Reprinted by permission of Random House, Inc.

Baker, Carlos. From *Hemingway: The Writer as Artist*. Third edition. Princeton University Press, 1963. Copyright © 1952, 1956, 1963, renewed 1980 by Carlos Baker. Reprinted with permission of Princeton University Press.

Baker, Houston A. From *Singers of Daybreak: Studies in Black American Literature*. Howard University Press, 1974. Copyright © 1974 by Houston A. Baker, Jr. All rights reserved. Reprinted by permission of the publisher.

Beaver, Harold. From an introduction to *The Science Fiction of Edgar Allan Poe*. By Edgar Allan Poe, edited by Harold Beaver. Penguin Books, 1976. Introduction copyright © Harold Beaver, 1976. All rights reserved. Reproduced by permission of Penguin Books Ltd.

Benson, Jackson J. From *Hemingway: The Writer's Art of Self-Defense*. University of Minnesota Press, 1969. © copyright 1969 by the University of Minnesota. All rights reserved. Reprinted by permission of the publisher.

Berthoff, Warner. From *The Example of Melville*. Princeton University Press, 1962. Copyright © 1962 by Princeton University Press. All rights reserved. Reprinted with permission of the publisher.

Bickley, R. Bruce, Jr. From *The Method of Melville's Short Fiction*. Duke University Press, 1975. Copyright © 1969, 1975 by Duke University Press, Durham, NC. Reprinted by permission of the publisher.

Blair, Walter. From *Horse Sense in American Humor from Benjamin Franklin to Ogden Nash*. The University of Chicago Press, 1942. Copyright 1942 by The University of Chicago. Renewed 1969 by Walter Blair. All rights reserved. Reprinted by permission of the author.

Bone, Robert. From *Down Home: A History of Afro-American Short Fiction from Its Beginnings to the End of the Harlem Renaissance*. G. P. Putnam's Sons, 1975. Copyright © 1975 by Robert Bone. All rights reserved. Reprinted by permission of the author.

Bone, Robert. From *The Negro Novel in America*. Revised edition. Yale University Press, 1965. Copyright © 1965 by Yale University. All rights reserved. Reprinted by permission of the author.

Borges, Jorge Luis. From *Other Inquisitions: 1937-1952*. Translated by Ruth L. C. Simms. University of Texas Press, 1964. Copyright © 1964 by the University of Texas Press. All rights reserved. Reprinted by permission of the publisher.

Brooks, Cleanth and Robert Penn Warren. From *Understanding Fiction*. Edited by Cleanth Brooks and Robert Penn Warren. Second edition. Appleton-Century-Crofts, 1959. Copyright © 1959, renewed 1987, by Appleton-Century-Crofts, Inc. All rights reserved. Excerpted by permission of Prentice-Hall, Inc., Englewood Cliffs, NJ.

Brown, Sterling. From *The Negro in American Fiction*. The Associates in Negro Folk Education, 1937.

Burbank, Rex. From *Sherwood Anderson*. Twayne, 1964. Copyright 1964 by Twayne Publishers. All rights reserved. Reprinted with the permission of Twayne Publishers, a division of G. K. Hall & Co., Boston.

Burgess, Anthony. From an introduction to *The Best Short Stories of J. G. Ballard*. By J. G. Ballard. Holt, Rinehart and Winston, 1978. Copyright © 1978 by J. G. Ballard. Introduction Copyright © 1978 by Anthony Burgess. All rights reserved. Reprinted by permission of the author.

Camus, Albert. From *Lyrical and Critical*. Edited and translated by Philip Thody. Hamilton, 1967. © copyright 1967 by Hamish Hamilton, Ltd. Reprinted by permission of the publisher.

Carothers, James B. From "Faulkner's Short Stories: 'And Now What's to Do'," in *New Directions in Faulkner Studies: Faulkner and Yoknapatawpha, 1983*. Edited by Doreen Fowler and Ann J. Abadie. University Press of Mississippi, 1984. Copyright © 1984 by the University Press of Mississippi. All rights reserved. Reprinted by permission of the publisher.

Chase, Cleveland B. From *Sherwood Anderson*. R. M. McBride & Company, 1927.

Chase, Richard. From *Herman Melville: A Critical Study*. The Macmillan Company, 1949. Copyright, 1949, by Richard Chase. Renewed 1976 by Frances W. Chase. All rights reserved. Reprinted with permission of Macmillan Publishing Company.

Cheever, John. From *The Stories of John Cheever*. Knopf, 1978. Copyright © 1978 by John Cheever. All rights reserved. Reprinted by permission of Alfred A. Knopf, Inc.

Chesterton, G. K. From *Autobiography*. Hutchinson & Co., Ltd., 1936. Copyright Gilbert Keith Chesterton 1936. Renewed 1964 by Dorothy Edith Collins. Reprinted by permission of A. P. Watt Ltd. on behalf of Miss D. E. Collins.

Coale, Samuel. From *John Cheever*. Ungar, 1977. Copyright © 1977 by The Ungar Publishing Company. Reprinted by permission of the publisher.

Coles, Robert. From *Flannery O'Connor's South*. Louisiana State University Press, 1980. Copyright © 1980 by Louisiana State University Press. All rights reserved. Reprinted by permission of the publisher.

Conrad, Joseph. From a preface to *Yvette and Other Stories*. By Guy de Maupassant. Duckworth & Co., 1904.

Cowley, Malcolm. From an introduction to *The Portable Faulkner*. By William Faulkner, edited by Malcolm Cowley. Viking Press, 1946. Copyright 1946, copyright © renewed 1974 by The Viking Press, Inc. All rights reserved. Reprinted by permission of Viking Penguin Inc.

Cowley, Malcolm. From an introduction to *The Portable Hemingway*. Edited by Malcolm Cowley. Viking Penguin, 1944.

Cowley, Malcolm. From an introduction to *Winesburg, Ohio*. By Sherwood Anderson. Revised edition. Viking Press, 1960. Copyright © 1960 by The Viking Press, Inc. All rights reserved. Reprinted by permission of Viking Penguin Inc.

Croce, Benedetto. From *European Literature in the Nineteenth Century*. Translated by Douglas Ainslie. Alfred A. Knopf, 1924.

Dana, Richard Henry, Sr. From a letter in *Bartleby the Inscrutable: A Collection of Commentary on Herman Melville's Tale "Bartleby the Scrivener."* Edited by M. Thomas Inge. Archon Books, Hamden, CT, 1979. © M. Thomas Inge 1979. All rights reserved. Reprinted by permission of Archon Books, an imprint of The Shoe String Press, Inc.

DeFalco, Joseph. From *The Hero in Hemingway's Short Stories*. University of Pittsburgh Press, 1963. Copyright © 1963 by University of Pittsburgh Press. Reprinted by permission of the author.

Drake, Robert. From *Flannery O'Connor: A Critical Essay*. Eerdmans, 1966. Copyright © 1966 by Wm. B. Eerdmans Publishing Co. All rights reserved. Reprinted by permission of the publisher.

Dreiser, Theodore. From "Sherwood Anderson," in *Homage to Sherwood Anderson: 1876-1941*. Edited by Paul P. Appel. Paul P. Appel, Publisher, 1970. Reprinted by permission of the publisher.

Dugan, John Raymond. From *Illusion and Reality: A Study of Descriptive Techniques in the Works of Guy de Maupassant*. Mouton, 1973. © copyright 1973 Mouton & Co., Publishers. Reprinted by permission of Mouton de Gruyter, a Division of Walter de Gruyter & Co.

Evans, Elizabeth. From *Eudora Welty*. Frederick Ungar, Inc., 1981. Copyright © 1981 by The Ungar Publishing Company. Reprinted by permission of the publisher.

Evans, Maurice. From *G. K. Chesterton*. Cambridge at the University Press, 1939.

Faulkner, William. From a review of "The Old Man and the Sea," in *Essays, Speeches & Public Letters*. By William Faulkner, edited by James B. Meriwether. Random House, 1965. Copyright © 1965 by Random House, Inc. All rights reserved. Reprinted by permission of the publisher.

Faulkner, William and Robert A. Jellife. From an interview in *Faulkner at Nagano*. By William Faulkner, edited by Robert A. Jellife. Kenkyusha, 1956.

Feeley, Kathleen. From *Flannery O'Connor: Voice of the Peacock*. Rutgers University Press, 1972. Copyright © 1972 by Rutgers University, The State University of New Jersey. Copyright © 1982 by Fordham University Press. All rights reserved. Reprinted by permission of the publisher.

Flaubert, Gustave. From *Letters*. Translated by J. M. Cohen. George Weidenfeld & Nicolson Ltd., 1950.

Forster, E. M. From *Aspects of the Novel*. Harcourt Brace Jovanovich, 1927, Edward Arnold & Co., 1927. Copyright, 1927, by Harcourt Brace Jovanovich. Renewed, 1955, by E. M. Forster. Reprinted by permission of Harcourt Brace Jovanovich, Inc. In Canada by Edward Arnold (Publishers) Ltd.

France, Anatole. *On Life and Letters, first series*. Translated by A. W. Evans. Dodd, Mead and Company, 1924.

Frank, Waldo. From a foreword to *Cane*. By Jean Toomer. Boni and Liveright, 1923. Copyright 1923 by Boni & Liveright. Copyright renewed 1951 by Jean Toomer. Reprinted by permission of Liveright Publishing Corporation.

Frank, Waldo. From "'Winesburg, Ohio'," in *Homage to Sherwood Anderson: 1876-1941*. Edited by Paul P. Appel. Paul P. Appel, Publisher, 1970. Reprinted by permission of the publisher.

Franklin, H. Bruce. From "What Are We to Make of J. G. Ballard's Apocalypse?" in *Voices for the Future: Essays on Major Science Fiction Writers, Vol. II*. Edited by Thomas D. Clareson. Bowling Green University Popular Press, 1979. Copyright © 1979 by the Bowling Green University Popular Press. Reprinted by permission of the publisher.

Freeman, F. Barron. From an introduction to *Melville's "Billy Budd."* By Herman Melville, edited by F. Barron Freeman. Cambridge, Mass.: Harvard University Press, 1948. Copyright 1948, renewed 1975, by the President and Fellows of Harvard College.

Freeman, John. From *Herman Melville*. Macmillan & Co., 1926.

Fullinwider, S. P. From *The Mind and Mood of Black America: 20th Century Thought*. Dorsey Press, 1969. © The Dorsey Press, 1969. All rights reserved. Reprinted by permission of the publisher.

Galloway, David. From an introduction to *The Other Poe: Comedies and Satires*. By Edgar Allen Poe, edited by David Galloway. Penguin Books, 1983. Copyright © David Galloway, 1983. Reproduced by permission of Penguin Books Ltd.

Garland, Hamlin. From *Afternoon Neighbors: Further Excerpts from a Literary Log*. The Macmillan Company, 1934. Copyright, 1934, by Hamlin Garland. Renewed 1962 by Constance G. Doyle and Isabel Garland Lord. All rights reserved. Reprinted by permission of the Literary Estate of Hamlin Garland.

Glenn, Eunice. From "Fantasy in the Fiction of Eudora Welty," in *A Southern Vanguard: The John Peale Bishop Memorial Volume*. Edited by Allen Tate. Prentice-Hall, Inc., 1947.

Gloster, Hugh M. From *Negro Voices in American Fiction*. University of North Carolina Press, 1948. Copyright, 1948, by The University of North Carolina Press. Renewed 1975 by Hugh Morris Gloster. Reprinted by permission of the publisher and the author.

Gosse, Edmund, Sir. From *Silhouettes*. Charles Scribner's Sons, 1925.

Griffith, Clark. From "Poe and the Gothic," in *Papers on Poe: Essays in Honor of John Ward Ostrom*. Edited by Richard P. Veler. Chantry Music Press, Inc., 1972. Copyright 1972 by Chantry Music Press, Inc. at Wittenberg University. Reprinted by permission of the publisher.

Gurko, Leo. From *Ernest Hemingway and the Pursuit of Heroism*. Thomas Y. Crowell Company, 1968. © Leo Gurko, 1968. All rights reserved. Reprinted by permission of Harper & Row, Publishers, Inc.

Hamblen, Abigail Ann. From *The New England Art of Mary E. Wilkins Freeman*. The Green Knight Press, 1966. © 1966. Reprinted by permission of the author.

Hendin, Josephine. From *The World of Flannery O'Connor*. Indiana University Press, 1970. Copyright © 1970 by Indiana University Press. All rights reserved. Reprinted by permission of the publisher.

Hicks, Granville. From *The Great Tradition: An Interpretation of American Literature Since the Civil War*. Revised edition. Macmillan Publishing Company, 1935.

Howe, Irving. From *Sherwood Anderson*. William Sloane Associates, Inc., 1951. Copyright 1951 by William Sloane Associates, Inc. Renewed 1979 by Irving Howe. Abridged by permission of William Morrow & Company, Inc.

Howe, Irving. From *A World More Attractive: A View of Modern Literature and Politics*. Horizon Press, 1963. © 1963 by Irving Howe. Reprinted by permission of the author.

Humphreys, A. R. From *Melville*. Barnes & Noble, Inc., Totowa, NJ, 1962. © 1962 A. R. Humphreys. Reprinted by permission of the publisher.

Hyman, Stanley Edgar. From *Flannery O'Connor*. American Writers Pamphlet No. 54. University of Minnesota Press, 1966. © 1966, University of Minnesota. All rights reserved. Reprinted by permission of the publisher.

Ingram, Forrest L. From *Representative Short Story Cycles of the Twentieth Century: Studies in Literary Genre*. Mouton, 1971. © copyright 1971 Mouton & Co., Publishers. Reprinted by permission of Mouton de Gruyter, a Division of Walter de Gruyter & Co.

Jones, Alun R. From "The World of Love: The Fiction of Eudora Welty," in *The Creative Present: Notes on Contemporary American Fiction*. Edited by Nona Balakian and Charles Simmons. Doubleday, 1963. Copyright © 1963 by Nona Balakian and Charles Simmons. All rights reserved. Reprinted by permission of Doubleday, a division of Bantam, Doubleday, Dell Publishing Group, Inc.

Kayser, Wolfgang. From *The Grotesque in Art and Literature*. Translated by Ulrich Weisstein. Indiana University Press, 1963. Translation copyright © 1963 by Indiana University Press. Reprinted by permission of the publisher.

Kazin, Alfred. From *Bright Book of Life: American Novelists & Storytellers from Hemingway to Mailer*. Atlantic-Little, Brown, 1973. Copyright © 1971, 1973 by Alfred Kazin. All rights reserved. Reprinted by permission of Little, Brown and Company in association with The Atlantic Monthly Press.

Kazin, Alfred. From "Old Boys, Mostly American: William Faulkner, the Short Stories," in *Contemporaries*. Little, Brown and Company, 1962. Copyright © 1961 by Alfred Kazin. Reprinted by permission of the author.

Kirk, Russell. From "Chesterton, Madmen, and Madhouses," in *Myth, Allegory and Gospel: An Interpretation of J. R. R. Tolkien, C. S. Lewis, G. K. Chesterton, Charles Williams*. Edited by John Warwick Montgomery. Bethany Fellowship, 1974. Copyright © 1974 Bethany Fellowship, Inc. All rights reserved. Reprinted by permission of the publisher.

Knox, R. A. From *Literary Distractions*. Sheed and Ward, 1958. © Evelyn Waugh, 1958. Reprinted by permission of A. P. Watt Ltd. on behalf of The Earl of Oxford and Asquith.

Lawrence, D. H. From *Studies in Classic American Literature*. Thomas Seltzer, 1923, The Viking Press, 1964. Copyright 1923 by Thomas Seltzer, Inc. Renewed 1950 by Frieda Lawrence. Copyright © 1961 by The Estate of the late Mrs. Frieda Lawrence. All rights reserved. Reprinted by permission of Viking Penguin Inc.

Lemaître, Jules. From *Literary Impressions*. Translated by A. W. Evans. Daniel O'Connor, 1921.

Lewis, R. W. B. From *The Picaresque Saint: Representative Figures in Contemporary Fiction*. Lippincott, 1959. Copyright © 1956, 1958 by R. W. B. Lewis. Reprinted by permission of the author.

Lewis, Wyndham. From *Men without Art*. Cassell & Company, Limited, 1934.

Leyda, Jay. From an introduction to *The Complete Stories of Herman Melville*. By Herman Melville, edited by Jay Leyda. Random House, 1949. Copyright 1949 by Random House, Inc. Renewed 1976 by Jay Leyda. Reprinted by permission of the publisher.

Lovecraft, Howard Phillips. From *Supernatural Horror in Literature*. Ben Abramson, Publisher, 1945.

Manning, Carol S. From *With Ears Opening Like Morning Glories: Eudora Welty and the Love of Storytelling*. Contributions in Women's Studies, No. 58. Greenwood Press, 1985. Copyright © 1985 by Carol S. Manning. All rights reserved. Reprinted by permission of Greenwood Press, Inc., Westport, CT.

Martin, Jay. From *Harvests of Change: American Literature, 1865-1914*. Prentice-Hall, 1967. Copyright © 1967 by Prentice-Hall, Inc. All rights reserved. Reprinted by permission of the author.

Matthiessen, F. O. From *American Renaissance: Art and Expression in the Age of Emerson and Whitman*. Oxford University Press, 1941.

Merton, Thomas. From *Raids on the Unspeakable*. New Directions, 1966. © 1964 by The Abbey of Gethsemani, Inc. Reprinted by permission of New Directions Publishing Corporation.

Miller, Henry. From "The Storyteller," in *Homage to Sherwood Anderson: 1876-1941*. Edited by Paul P. Appel. Paul P. Appel, Publisher, 1970. Reprinted by permission of the publisher.

Moldenhauer, Joseph J. From "The Edge of Yoknapatawpha: Unity of Theme and Structure in 'The Wild Palms'," in *William Faulkner: Three Decades of Criticism*. Edited by Frederick J. Hoffman and Olga W. Vickery. Michigan State University Press, 1960. Copyright © 1960 by Michigan State University Press. All rights reserved. Reprinted by permission of the publisher.

Muller, Gilbert H. From *Nightmares and Visions: Flannery O'Connor and the Catholic Grotesque*. University of Georgia Press, 1972. Copyright © 1972 by the University of Georgia Press. All rights reserved. Reprinted by permission of the publisher.

Mumford, Lewis. From *Herman Melville*. Harcourt, Brace, 1929. Copyright 1929, renewed 1956 by Lewis Mumford. Reprinted by permission of Gina Maccoby Literary Agency.

Munson, Gorham B. From *Destinations: A Canvass of American Literature Since 1900*. J. H. Sears & Company, Inc., 1928.

O'Connor, Flannery. From *Mystery and Manners: Occasional Prose*. Edited by Sally Fitzgerald and Robert Fitzgerald. Farrar, Straus and Giroux, 1969. Copyright © 1957, 1961, 1963, 1964, 1966, 1967, 1969 by the Estate of Mary Flannery O'Connor. Copyright © 1962 by Flannery O'Connor. Copyright © 1961 by Farrar, Straus and Cudahy. All rights reserved. Reprinted by permission of Farrar, Straus and Giroux, Inc.

O'Connor, Frank. From *The Lonely Voice: A Study of the Short Story*. The World Publishing Company, 1963. Copyright © 1962, 1963 by Frank O'Connor. All rights reserved. Reprinted by permission of Joan Daves, as agents for the author.

O'Faolain, Sean. From *The Short Story*. Collins, 1948.

O'Faolain, Sean. From *The Vanishing Hero: Studies in Novelists of the Twenties*. Eyre & Spottiswoode, 1956. Copyright © 1956, 1957, 1984, 1985 by Sean O'Faolain. All rights reserved. Reprinted by permission of Sean O'Faolain and Curtis Brown Associates, Ltd. In Canada by A. P. Watt Ltd. on behalf of Sean O'Faolain.

Parker, Hershel. From "The 'Sequel' in 'Bartleby'," in *Bartleby the Inscrutable: A Collection of Commentary on Herman Melville's Tale "Bartleby the Scrivener."* Edited by M. Thomas Inge. Archon Books, Hamden, CT, 1979. © M. Thomas Inge 1979. All rights reserved. Reprinted by permission of Archon Books, an imprint of The Shoe String Press, Inc.

Peden, William. From *The American Short Story: Continuity and Change, 1940-1975*. Revised edition. Houghton Mifflin, 1975. Copyright © 1964, 1975 by William Peden. All rights reserved. Reprinted by permission of Houghton Mifflin Company.

Perluck, Herbert A. From "'The Bear': An Unromantic Reading," in *Religious Perspectives in Faulkner's Fiction: Yoknapatawpha and Beyond*. Edited by J. Robert Barth, S. J. University of Notre Dame Press, 1972. Copyright © 1972 by University of Notre Dame Press; Notre Dame, IN 46556. Reprinted by permission of the publisher.

Porter, Katherine Anne. From an introduction to *A Curtain of Green and Other Stories*. By Eudora Welty. Harcourt Brace Jovanovich, 1941. Copyright, 1941, renewed 1968, by Eudora Welty. All rights reserved. Reprinted by permission of William Morris Agency, Inc. on behalf of author.

Porter, Thomas E. From "Gilbert Keith Chesterton," in *Twelve Englishmen of Mystery*. Edited by Earl F. Bargainnier. Bowling Green University Popular Press, 1984. Copyright © 1984 by Bowling Green University Popular Press. Reprinted by permission of the publisher.

Pryse, Marjorie. From an afterword to *Selected Stories of Mary E. Wilkins Freeman*. By Mary E. Wilkins Freeman, edited by Marjorie Pryse. Norton, 1983. Copyright © 1983 by Marjorie Pryse. All rights reserved. Reprinted by permission of W. W. Norton & Company, Inc.

Rosenfeld, Paul. From *Men Seen: Twenty-Four Modern Authors*. The Dial Press, 1925.

Routley, Erik. From *The Puritan Pleasures of the Detective Story: A Personal Monograph*. Victor Gollancz Ltd., 1972. © Erik Routley, 1972. Reprinted by permission of The Literary Estate of Erik Routley.

Rupp, Richard H. From "Of That Time, of Those Places: The Short Stories of John Cheever," in *Critical Essays on John Cheever*. Edited by R. G. Collins. Hall, 1982. © 1982 by R. G. Collins. Reprinted with the permission of the author.

Sadleir, Michael. From *Excursions in Victorian Bibliography*. Chaundy & Cox, 1922.

Steegmuller, Francis. From *Maupassant: A Lion in the Path*. Random House, 1949.

Stein, Gertrude. From a letter in *Sherwood Anderson/Gertrude Stein: Correspondence and Personal Essays*. Edited by Ray Lewis White. University of North Carolina Press, 1972. Copyright © 1972 by The University of North Carolina Press. All rights reserved. Reprinted by permission of the Literary Estate of Gertrude Stein.

Stephens, Martha. From *The Question of Flannery O'Connor*. Louisiana State University Press, 1973. Copyright © 1973 by Louisiana State University Press. All rights reserved. Reprinted by permission of the publisher.

Stern, Milton R. From *The Fine Hammered Steel of Herman Melville*. University of Illinois Press, 1957. © 1957 by the Board of Trustees of the University of Illinois. Renewed 1985 by Milton R. Stern. Reprinted by permission of the publisher and the author.

Sullivan, Edward D. From *Maupassant: The Short Stories*. Barron's Educational Series, 1962. © E. D. Sullivan 1962. Reprinted by permission of Barron's Educational Series, Inc., Hauppauge, NY 11797.

Tate, Allen. From *Essays of Four Decades*. The Swallow Press Inc., 1970. © 1968, 1965, 1963, 1959 by Allen Tate. All rights reserved. Reprinted by permission of Ohio University Press, Athens.

Taylor, Welford Dunaway. From *Sherwood Anderson*. Frederick Ungar Publishing Co., 1977. Copyright © 1977 by The Ungar Publishing Company. Reprinted by permission of the publisher.

Thompson, Lawrance. From *Melville's Quarrel with God*. Princeton University Press, 1952. Copyright 1952, © renewed 1980 by Princeton University Press. Reprinted with permission of the publisher.

Thurber, James. From *Lanterns & Lances*. Harper & Brothers, Publishers, 1961. Copyright © 1961 James Thurber. Reprinted by special permission of the Estate of Helen Thurber.

Tindall, William York. From "The Ceremony of Innocence (Herman Melville: 'Billy Budd')," in *Great Moral Dilemmas in Literature, Past and Present*. Edited by R. M. MacIver. The Institute for Religious and Social Studies, 1956.

Tolstoy, Leo. From *Guy de Maupassant*. Translated by V. Tcherkoff. Brotherhood Publishers, 1898.

Trilling, Diana. From *Reviewing the Forties*. Harcourt Brace Jovanovich, 1978. Copyright © 1978 by Diana Trilling. Reprinted by permission of the author.

Trilling, Lionel. From *The Liberal Imagination: Essays on Literature and Society*. The Viking Press, 1950. Copyright 1950 Lionel Trilling. Copyright renewed © 1978 Diana Trilling and James Trilling. Reprinted by permission of the Estate of Lionel Trilling.

Turnell, Martin. From *The Art of French Fiction: Prévost, Stendhal, Zola, Maupassant, Gide, Mauriac, Proust*. New Directions, 1959. Copyright © 1959 by Martin Turnell. Reprinted by permission of New Directions Publishing Corporation.

Updike, John. From "On Such a Beautiful Green Little Planet," in *Hugging the Shore: Essays and Criticism*. Knopf, 1983. Copyright © 1983 by John Updike. All rights reserved. Reprinted by permission of Alfred A. Knopf, Inc.

Van Doren, Carl. From *Contemporary American Novelists: 1900-1920*. The Macmillan Company, 1922. Copyright 1922 by Macmillan Publishing Company. Renewed 1949 by Carl Van Doren. All rights reserved. Reprinted by permission of the Literary Estate of Carl Van Doren.

Vande Kieft, Ruth M. From *Eudora Welty*. Twayne, 1962. Copyright 1962 by Twayne Publishers. Reprinted with the permission of Twayne Publishers, a division of G. K. Hall & Co., Boston.

Volpe, Edmond L. From *A Reader's Guide to William Faulkner*. Farrar, Straus and Giroux, 1964. Copyright © 1964 by Edmond L. Volpe. Reprinted by permission of Farrar, Straus and Giroux, Inc.

Waldeland, Lynne. From *John Cheever*. Twayne, 1979. Copyright 1979 by Twayne Publishers. All rights reserved. Reprinted with the permission of Twayne Publishers, a division of G. K. Hall & Co., Boston.

Waldhorn, Arthur. From *A Reader's Guide to Ernest Hemingway*. Farrar, Straus and Giroux, 1972. Copyright © 1972 by Arthur Waldhorn. All rights reserved. Reprinted by permission of Farrar, Straus and Giroux, Inc.

Warren, Robert Penn. From *Selected Essays*. Random House, 1958. Copyright © 1958, renewed 1986, by Robert Penn Warren. All rights reserved. Reprinted by permission of Random House, Inc.

Watson, James G. From "The American Short Story: 1930-1945," in *The American Short Story: 1900-1945, A Critical History*. Edited by Philip Stevick. Twayne, 1984. Copyright 1984 by Twayne Publishers. All rights reserved. Reprinted with the permission of Twayne Publishers, a division of G. K. Hall & Co., Boston.

Weaver, Raymond. From an introduction to *Shorter Novels of Herman Melville*. By Herman Melville. Liveright, 1928. Copyright 1928, renewed 1955, by Liveright Publishing Corporation. All rights reserved. Reprinted by permission of W. W. Norton & Company, Inc.

Weeks, Robert P. From an introduction to *Hemingway: A Collection of Critical Essays*. Edited by Robert P. Weeks. Prentice-Hall, 1962. Copyright © 1962 by Prentice-Hall, Inc. Reprinted by permission of Prentice-Hall, Inc., Englewood Cliffs, NJ 07632.

Welty, Eudora. From *The Eye of the Story: Selected Essays and Reviews*. Vintage Books, 1979. Copyright © 1978 by Eudora Welty. All rights reserved. Reprinted by permission of Random House, Inc.

West, Julius. From *G. K. Chesterton: A Critical Study*. Martin Secker, 1915.

Westbrook, Perry D. From *Acres of Flint: Sarah Orne Jewett and Her Contemporaries*. Revised edition. The Scarecrow Press, Inc., 1981. Copyright © 1981 by Perry D. Westbrook. Reprinted by permission of the publisher.

Wilson, Edmund. From *The Wound and the Bow: Seven Studies in Literature*. Houghton Mifflin Company, 1941. Copyright 1929, 1932, 1938, 1939, 1940, 1941 by Edmund Wilson, copyright renewed © 1966, 1968, 1970 by Edmund Wilson. All rights reserved. Reprinted by permission of Farrar, Straus and Giroux, Inc.

Winters, Yvor. From *In Defense of Reason*. The Swallow Press Inc., 1947. Copyright 1937 by Yvor Winters. Copyright 1938, 1943 by New Directions. Copyright renewed © 1965 by Yvor Winters. Reprinted by permission of Ohio University Press/Swallow Press.

Woolf, Virginia. From *The Moment and Other Essays*. Hogarth Press, 1947, Harcourt Brace Jovanovich, 1948. Copyright 1948, renewed 1976 by Harcourt Brace Jovanovich and Marjorie T. Parsons. Reprinted by permission of Harcourt Brace Jovanovich, Inc. In Canada by the Literary Estate of Virginia Woolf and The Hogarth Press.

Wright, Nathalia. From *Melville's Use of the Bible*. Duke University Press, 1949. Copyright, 1949, by Duke University Press, Durham, NC. Renewed 1976 by Nathalia Wright. Reprinted by permission of the author.

Yates, Norris W. From *The American Humorist: Conscience of the Twentieth Century*. Iowa State University Press, 1964. All rights reserved. © 1964 by the Iowa State University Press, Ames, Iowa 50010. Reprinted by permission of the publisher.

Young, Philip. From a preface to *The Nick Adams Stories*. By Ernest Hemingway. Charles Scribner's Sons, 1972. Copyright © 1972 Charles Scribner's Sons. All rights reserved. Reprinted with the permission of Charles Scribner's Sons, a division of Macmillan, Inc.

Ziff, Larzer. From *American 1890s: Life and Times of a Lost Generation*. The Viking Press, 1966. Copyright © 1966 by Larzer Ziff. All rights reserved. Reprinted by permission of Viking Penguin Inc.

Literary Criticism Series
Cumulative Author Index

This index lists all author entries in the Gale Literary Criticism Series and includes cross-references to other Gale sources. For the convenience of the reader, references to the *Yearbook* in the *Contemporary Literary Criticism* series include the page number (in parentheses) after the volume number. References in the index are identified as follows:

AITN: *Authors in the News,* Volumes 1-2
CAAS: *Contemporary Authors Autobiography Series,* Volumes 1-5
CA: *Contemporary Authors* (original series), Volumes 1-121
CABS: *Contemporary Authors Bibliographical Series,* Volumes 1-2
CANR: *Contemporary Authors New Revision Series,* Volumes 1-21
CAP: *Contemporary Authors Permanent Series,* Volumes 1-2
CA-R: *Contemporary Authors* (revised editions), Volumes 1-44
CDALB: *Concise Dictionary of American Literary Biography*
CLC: *Contemporary Literary Criticism,* Volumes 1-45
CLR: *Children's Literature Review,* Volumes 1-14
CMLC: *Classical and Medieval Literature Criticism,* Volume 1
DLB: *Dictionary of Literary Biography,* Volumes 1-59
DLB-DS: *Dictionary of Literary Biography Documentary Series,* Volumes 1-4
DLB-Y: *Dictionary of Literary Biography Yearbook,* Volumes 1980-1986
LC: *Literature Criticism from 1400 to 1800,* Volumes 1-6
NCLC: *Nineteenth-Century Literature Criticism,* Volumes 1-16
SAAS: *Something about the Author Autobiography Series,* Volumes 1-4
SATA: *Something about the Author,* Volumes 1-48
SSC: *Short Story Criticism,* Volume 1
TCLC: *Twentieth-Century Literary Criticism,* Volumes 1-26
YABC: *Yesterday's Authors of Books for Children,* Volumes 1-2

Author Index

Author Index

Author Index

Author Index

Author Index

Author Index

Author Index

Author Index

Author Index

Author Index

Author Index

SSC Cumulative Title Index